AF572473

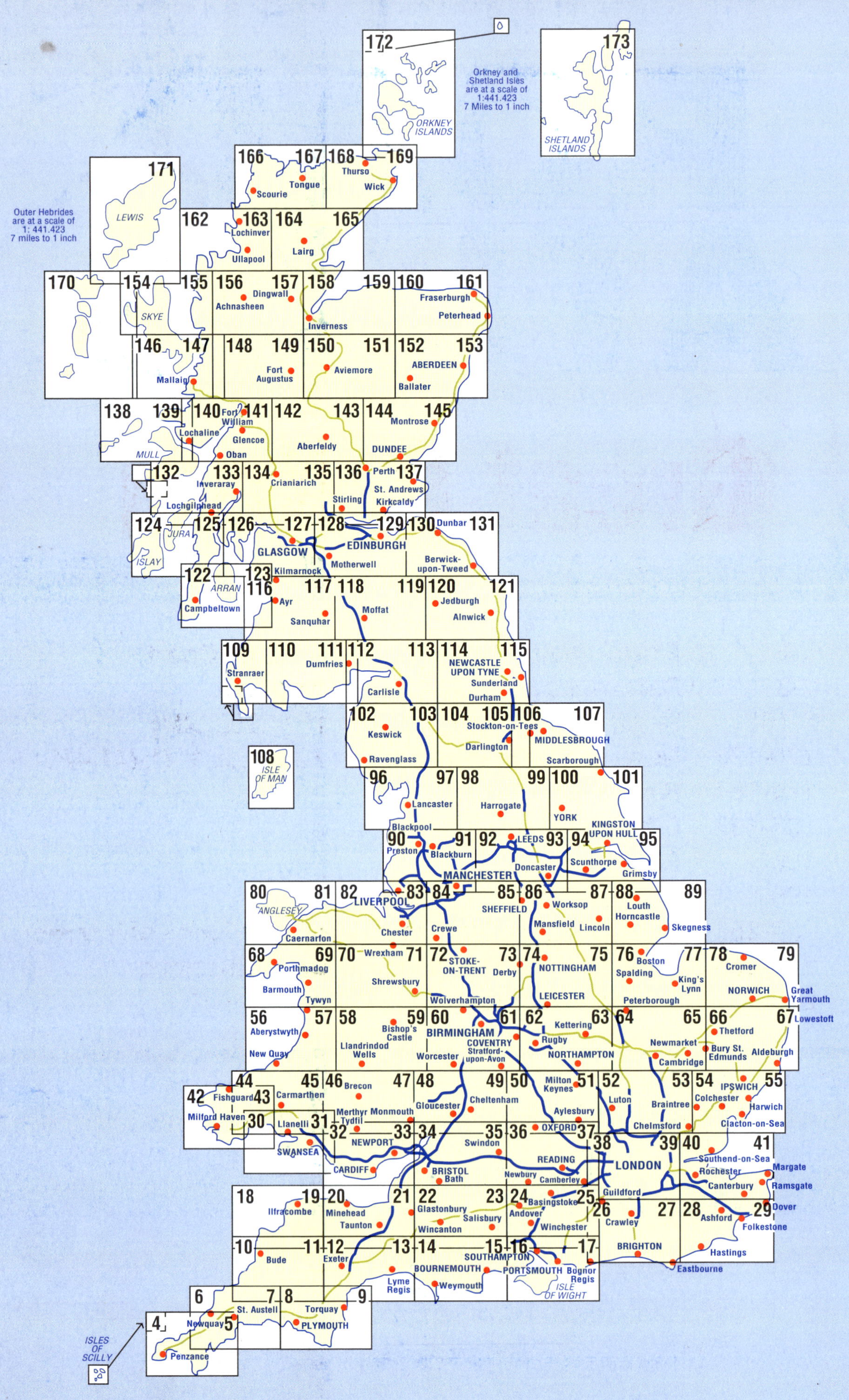

Orkney and Shetland Isles are at a scale of 1:441.423 7 Miles to 1 inch
ORKNEY ISLANDS
SHETLAND ISLANDS
Outer Hebrides are at a scale of 1: 441.423 7 miles to 1 inch
LEWIS
SKYE
MULL
JURA
ISLAY
ARRAN
ISLE OF MAN
ANGLESEY
ISLE OF WIGHT
ISLES OF SCILLY
Thurso
Wick
Tongue
Scourie
Lochinver
Ullapool
Lairg
Dingwall
Achnasheen
Inverness
Fraserburgh
Peterhead
Mallaig
Fort Augustus
Aviemore
ABERDEEN
Ballater
Fort William
Glencoe
Oban
Lochaline
Aberfeldy
Montrose
DUNDEE
Perth
St. Andrews
Kirkcaldy
Stirling
Crianlarich
Inveraray
Lochgilphead
GLASGOW
EDINBURGH
Dunbar
Motherwell
Kilmarnock
Berwick-upon-Tweed
Campbeltown
Ayr
Sanquhar
Moffat
Jedburgh
Alnwick
Stranraer
Dumfries
Carlisle
NEWCASTLE UPON TYNE
Sunderland
Durham
Keswick
Ravenglass
Stockton-on-Tees
Darlington
MIDDLESBROUGH
Scarborough
Lancaster
Harrogate
YORK
KINGSTON UPON HULL
Blackpool
Preston
Blackburn
LEEDS
Doncaster
Scunthorpe
Grimsby
MANCHESTER
LIVERPOOL
SHEFFIELD
Worksop
Louth
Horncastle
Skegness
Caernarfon
Chester
Crewe
Mansfield
Lincoln
Porthmadog
Barmouth
Tywyn
Wrexham
Shrewsbury
STOKE-ON-TRENT
Derby
NOTTINGHAM
Boston
Spalding
King's Lynn
Cromer
NORWICH
Great Yarmouth
Lowestoft
Wolverhampton
LEICESTER
Peterborough
Aberystwyth
New Quay
Llandrindod Wells
Bishop's Castle
BIRMINGHAM
COVENTRY
Stratford-upon-Avon
Worcester
Rugby
Kettering
NORTHAMPTON
Newmarket
Cambridge
Thetford
Bury St. Edmunds
Aldeburgh
Fishguard
Milford Haven
Carmarthen
Brecon
Merthyr Tydfil
Monmouth
Gloucester
Cheltenham
Milton Keynes
Aylesbury
Luton
Braintree
Colchester
IPSWICH
Harwich
Clacton-on-Sea
Chelmsford
Llanelli
SWANSEA
NEWPORT
CARDIFF
Swindon
OXFORD
READING
LONDON
Southend-on-Sea
Margate
Rochester
Canterbury
Ramsgate
BRISTOL
Bath
Newbury
Camberley
Guildford
Dover
Ilfracombe
Minehead
Taunton
Glastonbury
Salisbury
Wincanton
Basingstoke
Andover
Winchester
Crawley
Ashford
Folkestone
Bude
Exeter
BOURNEMOUTH
SOUTHAMPTON
PORTSMOUTH
Bognor Regis
BRIGHTON
Hastings
Eastbourne
Lyme Regis
Weymouth
St. Austell
Torquay
Newquay
PLYMOUTH
Penzance

ROAD ATLAS *of* Great Britain

CONTENTS

II-V	Route Planning Maps and Mileage Chart
2-3	Reference and Tourist Information
4-169	Road Maps at 3.5 miles to 1" (1:220,594)
170-173	Northern & Western Isles at 7 miles to 1" (1:441,423)
174-184	Main Route Maps
185-197	City and Town Centre Plans
198	Port Plans
199	Airport Plans
200-253	Index to Place Names & Selected Places of Interest
254-255	Limited Interchange Motorway Junctions
256	Channel Tunnel

Edition 12 2005
An AtoZ Publication

Geographers' A-Z Map Company Ltd.
Head Office : Fairfield Road, Borough Green, Sevenoaks, Kent TN15 8PP
Enquiries & Trade Sales: 01732 781000 Retail Sales: 01732 783422
www.a-zmaps.co.uk

II
ISLE OF MAN
Peel
Douglas
Castletown
IRISH SEA
EIRE
Cavan
Carrickmacross
Newry
Warrenpoint
Newcastle
Dundalk
Kells
Drogheda
Navan
Mullingar
DUBLIN
Dun Laoghaire
Bray
Kildare
Naas
Portlaoise
Wicklow
Carlow
Arklow
Kilkenny
Gorey
Enniscorthy
New Ross
Wexford
Rosslare Harbour
Waterford
Kendal
Kirkby Lonsdale
Ulverston
Barrow-in-Furness
Morecambe
Heysham
Lancaster
Settle
Fleetwood
Blackpool
Clitheroe
Blackburn
Nelson
Burnley
Lytham St.Anne's
Preston
Southport
Chorley
Darwen
Rochdale
Bolton
Bury
Ormskirk
Formby
Wigan
St. Helens
LIVERPOOL
Wallasey
Birkenhead
Warrington
Sale
Runcorn
Ellesmere Port
Northwich
Macclesfield
Chester
Crewe
Nantwich
Newcastle-under-Lyme
Wrexham
(Wrecsam)
Whitchurch
STOKE-ON-TRENT
Ellesmere
Wem
Market Drayton
Oswestry
Shrewsbury
Newport
Oakengates
Telford
Wolverhampton
Dudley
Bridgnorth
Stourbridge
Kidderminster
Bromsgrove
Worcester
Amlwch
Holyhead
(Caergybi)
Llangefni
Beaumaris
Llandudno
Rhyl
Conwy
Colwyn Bay
(Bae Colwyn)
Denbigh
(Dinbych)
Flint
(Y Fflint)
Mold
(Yr Wyddgrug)
Bangor
Llanrwst
Caernarfon
Ruthin
(Rhuthun)
Betws-y-Coed
Llan Ffestiniog
Llangollen
Bala
Porthmadog
Pwllheli
Dolgellau
Barmouth
(Abermaw)
Llanfyllin
Welshpool
(Trallwng)
Tywyn
Machynlleth
Montgomery
(Trefaldwyn)
Church Stretton
CARDIGAN BAY
Aberystwyth
Llanidloes
Newtown
(Y Drenewydd)
Bishop's Castle
Ludlow
Llangurig
Knighton
(Tref-Y-Clawdd)
Rhayader
(Rhaeadr Gwy)
Presteigne
(Llanandras)
Leominster
Llandrindod Wells
Aberaeron
New Quay
(Ceinewydd)
WALES
(CYMRU)
Lampeter
(Llanbedr Pont Steffan)
Builth Wells
(Llanfair-ym-Muallt)
Kington
Hereford
Great Malvern
Fishguard
(Abergwaun)
Cardigan
(Aberteifi)
Llandovery
(Llanymddyfri)
Brecon
(Aberhonddu)
Tewkesbury
Ross-on-Wye
St. David's
(Tyddewi)
Carmarthen
(Caerfyrddin)
Llandeilo
Abergavenny
(Y Fenni)
Monmouth
(Trefynwy)
Gloucester
Haverfordwest
(Hwlffordd)
St. Clears
Ammanford
(Rhydaman)
Merthyr Tydfil
(Merthyr Tudful)
Ebbw Vale
Milford Haven
(Aberdaugleddau)
Tenby
(Dinbych-Y-Pysgod)
Pembroke
Llanelli
Aberdare
(Aberdar)
Tredegar
Abertillery
Chepstow
(Cas-gwent)
Nailsworth
Neath
(Castell-nedd)
Pontypool
(Pontypwl)
Cwmbran
SWANSEA
(Abertawe)
Pontypridd
Caerphilly
(Caerffili)
Newport
(Casnewydd)
Malmesbury
Port Talbot
Cork
Porthcawl
Bridgend
(Pen-y-Bont-Ar-Ogwr)
Penarth
CARDIFF
(Caerdydd)
BRISTOL
Chippenham
Barry
(Barri)
Weston-Super-Mare
Bath
Trowbridge
BRISTOL CHANNEL
Radstock
Frome
Ilfracombe
Lynton
LUNDY
Watchet
Minehead
Burnham-on-Sea
Wells
Glastonbury
Shepton Mallet
Warminster
Barnstaple
Williton
Bridgwater
Bideford
Taunton
Wincanton
Great Torrington
South Molton
Wellington
Sherborne
Shaftesbury
Tiverton
Yeovil
Bude
Holsworthy
Honiton
Chard
Crewkerne
Blandford Forum
Okehampton
Exeter
Sidmouth
Bridport
Launceston
Exmouth
Lyme Regis
Dorchester
Wareham
Padstow
Wadebridge
Tavistock
Ashburton
Dawlish
Teignmouth
Weymouth
Bodmin
Liskeard
Newton Abbot
Torquay
Fortuneswell
Newquay
Saltash
Buckfastleigh
Paignton
Lostwithiel
Devonport
Totnes
Brixham
Guernsey
Jersey
St. Malo
Redruth
St. Austell
Looe
PLYMOUTH
Dartmouth
Truro
Kingsbridge
St. Ives
Camborne
Salcombe
Roscoff
Santander
St. Just
Falmouth
Penzance
Helston
LAND'S END
ISLES OF SCILLY
ENGLISH

ROUTE PLANNING
III
REFERENCE
MOTORWAY WITH NUMBER
M4
Service Area
MOTORWAY (Under Construction/Proposed)
MOTORWAY JUNCTIONS
PRIMARY ROUTE
A5
A ROAD
A272
NATIONAL BOUNDARY
TOWNS SHOWN IN THE MILEAGE CHART
NORWICH
SCALE
0 10 20 30 40 Miles
0 10 20 30 40 50 60 Kilometres
NORTH SEA
THE WASH
Humber
Rotterdam Zeebrugge
Esbjerg Hamburg Hook of Holland
Bilbao Caen Cherbourg Guernsey Jersey Le Havre St. Malo
Cherbourg Guernsey Jersey St. Malo
ISLE OF WIGHT
CHANNEL
Channel Tunnel
ENGLAND
FRANCE
Scarborough
Filey
Bridlington
Hornsea
Withernsea
Leyburn
Thirsk
Ripon
Malton
Driffield
Knaresborough
Harrogate
Skipton
Ilkley
Keighley
Wetherby
YORK
Beverley
KINGSTON UPON HULL
LEEDS
BRADFORD
Selby
Goole
Castleford
Pontefract
Wakefield
Halifax
Huddersfield
Hedon
Immingham
Grimsby
Cleethorpes
Scunthorpe
Barnsley
Doncaster
Oldham
Rotherham
Gainsborough
Market Rasen
Louth
Mablethorpe
SHEFFIELD
Worksop
Chesterfield
Buxton
Lincoln
Horncastle
Skegness
Bakewell
Matlock
Mansfield
Alfreton
Leek
Ashbourne
Hucknall
Newark-on-Trent
Boston
NOTTINGHAM
Sleaford
Ilkeston
DERBY
Beeston
Grantham
Hunstanton
Wells-next-the-sea
Cromer
North Walsham
Uttoxeter
Stafford
Burton upon Trent
Loughborough
Melton Mowbray
Bourne
Spalding
King's Lynn
Fakenham
Cannock
Lichfield
Coalville
Oakham
Wisbech
Swaffham
Wymondham
NORWICH
Great Yarmouth
Tamworth
LEICESTER
Stamford
Peterborough
Downham Market
Walsall
Hinckley
Nuneaton
Market Harborough
Oundle
March
Bungay
Lowestoft
BIRMINGHAM
Solihull
COVENTRY
Rugby
Corby
Kettering
Ramsey
Ely
Thetford
Diss
Halesworth
Southwold
Redditch
Warwick
Royal Leamington Spa
Daventry
Wellingborough
Northampton
Huntingdon
St. Ives
Newmarket
Bury St. Edmunds
Stratford-upon-Avon
St. Neots
Cambridge
Stowmarket
Aldeburgh
Evesham
Bedford
Haverhill
Hadleigh
Ipswich
Banbury
Newport Pagnell
Milton Keynes
Royston
Sudbury
Chipping Norton
Letchworth
Saffron Walden
Felixstowe
Cheltenham
Stow-on-the-Wold
Buckingham
Stevenage
Bishop's Stortford
Halstead
Harwich
Bicester
Dunstable
Luton
Braintree
Colchester
Woodstock
Aylesbury
Welwyn Garden City
Clacton-on-Sea
Witney
OXFORD
Thame
Hemel Hempstead
St. Albans
Hertford
Harlow
Chelmsford
Cirencester
Abingdon
High Wycombe
Chesham
Amersham
Epping
Wallingford
Watford
Enfield
Swindon
Wantage
Henley-on-Thames
Maidenhead
Slough
Harrow
LONDON
Romford
Basildon
Southend-on-Sea
READING
Windsor
Staines
Dartford
Tilbury
Gravesend
Sheerness
Herne Bay
Margate
Broadstairs
Ramsgate
Marlborough
Newbury
Bracknell
Wokingham
Wimbledon
Rochester
Devizes
Camberley
Croydon
Sandwich
Woking
Leatherhead
Sevenoaks
Maidstone
Canterbury
Deal
Andover
Basingstoke
Aldershot
Guildford
Reigate
Tonbridge
Dover
Alton
Farnham
Dorking
East Grinstead
Godalming
Crawley
Royal Tunbridge Wells
Tenterden
Ashford
Folkestone
Hythe
Winchester
Horsham
New Romney
Salisbury
Romsey
Eastleigh
Midhurst
Haywards Heath
Uckfield
Rye
Petersfield
Lewes
Chichester
Worthing
Hastings
Bexhill
SOUTHAMPTON
Ringwood
Gosport
Havant
Newhaven
Wimborne Minster
Lymington
Cowes
PORTSMOUTH
Bognor Regis
BRIGHTON
Eastbourne
Christchurch
Bournemouth
Yarmouth
Ryde
Newport
Sandown
Swanage
Dunkerque
Calais
St. Omer
Boulogne
Béthune
Le Touquet-Paris-Plage
Montreuil
St. Pol
Abbeville
Dieppe
Amiens

MILEAGE CHART

Places featured in this mileage chart are highlighted in YELLOW on the routeplanning maps.

PRIMARY ROUTES, Shown in green throughout this atlas, are a national network of recommended through routes which compliment the motorway system. Selected places of major traffic importance are known as Primary Route Destinations and on road signs have a green background.

The distances for the mileage chart have been compiled by using a combination of Primary Routes and Motorways between any two towns shown.

To find the distance between any two towns shown, follow the horizontal line of one town and the vertical line of the other; at the intersection read off the mileage.

ie : Horizontal - LONDON
Vertical - LIVERPOOL
Intersection 216 miles

ABERDEEN
449 ABERYSTWYTH
181 324 AYR
400 114 272 BIRMINGHAM
330 159 196 124 BRADFORD
562 258 441 169 263 BRIGHTON
503 122 375 88 215 129 BRISTOL
447 198 366 102 156 117 167 CAMBRIDGE
505 106 377 106 233 168 42 201 CARDIFF
217 232 89 183 107 345 286 256 288 CARLISLE
437 134 297 18 124 157 102 84 129 200 COVENTRY
397 137 269 41 88 188 134 99 159 180 43 DERBY
340 192 239 95 40 232 184 117 210 150 94 57 DONCASTER
558 315 477 195 284 81 194 118 233 393 180 208 244 DOVER
125 340 75 284 198 466 377 326 379 91 303 266 212 444 EDINBURGH
553 199 425 161 282 170 75 232 107 336 166 213 257 244 439 EXETER
148 430 136 391 305 568 478 456 486 198 415 387 345 591 131 549 FORT WILLIAM
148 322 36 291 203 468 378 355 384 96 313 282 245 491 46 449 100 GLASGOW
445 109 317 53 171 152 35 132 53 228 59 93 149 189 331 107 435 324 GLOUCESTER
520 258 411 170 224 130 203 64 234 323 152 167 185 129 397 262 524 419 171 HARWICH
443 96 315 151 158 330 204 252 209 226 167 156 169 358 316 279 423 323 189 331 HOLYHEAD
107 492 198 449 353 620 536 490 558 260 458 421 369 601 157 607 63 162 496 554 481 INVERNESS
505 268 420 156 210 125 206 54 240 311 138 155 171 127 381 264 510 409 177 21 307 538 IPSWICH
269 182 139 151 62 324 235 215 232 50 170 136 99 344 141 307 248 146 200 279 180 310 268 KENDAL
357 235 255 139 68 243 228 134 239 165 123 94 37 254 230 290 367 255 195 204 218 387 189 127 KINGSTON UPON HULL
316 171 198 119 9 256 209 144 226 111 117 74 32 275 190 279 309 208 167 217 162 345 197 72 60 LEEDS
407 155 294 43 99 163 118 70 140 214 24 30 73 183 282 189 412 312 83 146 182 431 125 166 98 97 LEICESTER
376 208 249 87 80 207 170 88 192 178 76 53 41 206 247 241 376 274 135 152 204 402 124 140 46 72 52 LINCOLN
327 120 199 99 67 267 180 179 169 110 113 90 89 294 201 240 308 213 142 265 95 370 236 75 126 73 110 118 LIVERPOOL
321 128 204 87 37 252 167 159 188 117 99 58 51 273 208 239 315 215 132 230 120 363 211 72 96 42 95 87 34 MANCHESTER
273 233 181 174 69 316 265 196 287 92 175 130 84 316 147 337 279 192 230 266 226 306 253 77 88 64 154 127 134 106 MIDDLESBROUGH
230 266 146 209 98 345 300 232 312 58 209 165 115 350 104 369 237 153 263 297 257 263 287 88 130 96 188 153 167 136 40 NEWCASTLE UPON TYNE
476 270 348 163 185 174 234 62 256 280 142 146 142 169 351 284 478 378 193 72 289 505 44 249 145 178 112 103 222 177 221 252 NORWICH
381 155 267 54 78 191 140 84 165 188 52 15 48 210 256 218 386 286 108 165 177 410 140 141 92 72 27 37 107 68 128 159 118 NOTTINGHAM
485 151 335 68 167 106 73 92 106 267 57 101 138 142 358 151 465 365 47 134 208 515 128 223 175 162 76 123 168 157 218 253 159 104 OXFORD
680 301 552 269 394 279 184 343 218 463 278 316 369 355 551 109 663 561 217 374 388 715 375 419 412 391 310 359 353 344 449 481 393 323 261 PENZANCE
87 366 85 336 245 509 412 370 422 134 346 309 254 485 43 487 103 59 362 439 360 113 424 184 273 233 326 290 244 254 191 148 394 299 404 598 PERTH
589 232 461 203 325 206 111 274 159 372 209 254 300 286 485 43 592 490 150 305 322 648 305 348 326 323 231 284 299 281 379 412 327 255 193 75 529 PLYMOUTH
575 231 440 147 274 50 95 132 138 357 132 184 231 137 448 127 555 455 114 161 303 603 158 308 268 245 166 209 254 237 315 360 200 191 83 235 486 170 PORTSMOUTH
526 180 399 103 213 79 77 90 112 309 90 138 184 115 402 141 506 406 75 129 264 554 126 263 209 207 113 168 193 197 264 295 152 129 25 251 445 184 60 READING
529 178 383 121 245 82 53 140 101 312 113 159 207 158 400 91 510 408 73 177 262 569 177 265 251 230 132 187 213 208 287 318 200 162 65 201 443 132 43 57 SALISBURY
355 173 235 79 40 225 163 121 193 154 75 35 21 268 230 245 352 250 139 185 164 387 176 102 66 33 68 46 74 40 102 133 144 37 137 361 273 293 228 160 203 SHEFFIELD
388 73 260 47 100 216 116 140 107 171 64 67 114 249 262 175 369 267 77 215 104 424 195 125 163 102 79 123 59 67 166 203 196 86 105 286 309 218 195 147 150 85 SHREWSBURY
547 213 401 128 235 64 75 129 122 330 114 167 201 150 433 106 528 426 98 157 287 590 162 276 249 230 136 189 235 215 288 320 190 162 66 217 476 149 20 47 23 206 175 SOUTHAMPTON
520 258 431 152 220 85 177 64 211 342 129 168 185 89 395 226 548 438 152 57 303 549 57 283 200 213 139 156 255 225 262 299 99 160 105 337 439 269 117 98 132 197 173 126 SOUTHEND-ON-SEA
374 108 243 47 75 217 127 137 140 150 64 36 74 236 241 202 348 248 95 201 122 410 179 121 117 78 55 87 56 36 142 173 171 55 118 311 287 241 201 147 168 50 35 183 199 STOKE-ON-TRENT
496 76 368 124 220 209 80 236 41 279 150 184 244 264 370 154 477 375 91 279 172 578 279 249 262 229 174 226 168 187 293 323 286 178 144 266 446 196 175 147 136 202 124 159 245 159 SWANSEA
213 584 304 557 461 728 644 589 640 352 552 529 475 706 262 715 169 268 604 657 589 108 654 402 492 453 544 510 463 471 410 367 613 519 621 823 220 758 709 662 664 506 523 682 659 502 631 THURSO
437 96 309 29 135 162 62 119 73 220 46 68 124 197 306 136 418 311 28 168 151 480 174 169 166 146 72 118 108 101 203 229 180 85 57 244 350 177 146 95 101 103 49 124 150 65 97 572 WORCESTER
312 193 201 129 34 269 227 151 237 116 129 84 33 269 187 289 314 214 181 232 185 344 200 81 38 24 108 76 96 65 48 83 176 84 174 400 230 331 257 217 244 54 132 244 214 114 268 450 164 YORK
501 206 390 118 203 53 118 58 150 305 97 128 165 76 373 171 503 403 101 79 264 527 76 264 188 196 102 143 216 200 246 278 114 130 55 282 416 214 74 39 84 161 160 78 43 160 187 636 110 203 LONDON

V

NORTH SEA

SCOTLAND

John o'Groats
Scrabster
Thurso
Tongue
Wick
Scourie
Lochinver
Helmsdale
LEWIS
(EODHAIS)
Lairg
Brora
Golspie
Ullapool
Bonar Bridge
Dornoch
Poolewe
Tain
Gairloch
Alness
Invergordon
Moray Firth
Cromarty
Lossiemouth
Kinlochewe
Dingwall
Fortrose
Nairn
Forres
Elgin
Portsoy
Banff
Fraserburgh
Achnasheen
Keith
Aberchirder
Turriff
Shieldaig
Inverness
Rothes
Huntly
Peterhead
RAASAY
Strathcarron
Dufftown
Kyle of Lochalsh
Grantown-on-Spey
Oldmeldrum
Ellon
Loch Ness
Inverurie
Invermoriston
Fort Augustus
Aviemore
ABERDEEN
Invergarry
Kingussie
Mallaig
Newtonmore
Peterculter
Arisaig
Braemar
Ballater
Banchory
Spean Bridge
Stonehaven
Fort William
Inverbervie
Acharacle
Brechin
Glencoe
Pitlochry
Kirriemuir
Montrose
Lochaline
Aberfeldy
Blairgowrie
Forfar
Dunkeld
Arbroath
Dundee
Oban
Carnoustie
Perth
Crieff
Crianlarich
St. Andrews
Auchterarder
Cupar
Inveraray
Callander
Kinross
Dunblane
Glenrothes
Loch Lomond
Doune
Methil
Pittenweem
Stirling
Alloa
Dunfermline
Kirkcaldy
Lochgilphead
Cowdenbeath
Firth of Forth
Zeebrugge
North Berwick
Helensburgh
Kilsyth
Forth Bridge
Falkirk
Dumbarton
GLASGOW
EDINBURGH
Dunbar
Dunoon
Greenock
Clydebank
Bathgate
Haddington
Musselburgh
Dalkeith
Wemyss Bay
Airdrie
Livingston
Eyemouth
Rothesay
Paisley
Kennacraig
Largs
BUTE
Hamilton
Motherwell
Penicuik
Duns
Berwick-upon-Tweed
East Kilbride
Lauder
Tayinloan
Ardrossan
Lanark
Galashiels
Coldstream
GIGHA
Kilmarnock
Irvine
Biggar
Peebles
Kelso
Wooler
Troon
Brodick
Selkirk
Prestwick
ISLAND OF ARRAN
Ayr
Cumnock
Jedburgh
Alnwick
Campbeltown
Hawick
Sanquhar
Maybole
Moffat
Amble
Girvan
A74(M)
Langholm
Ashington
Morpeth
New Galloway
Lockerbie
Bedlington
Blyth
Amsterdam
Bergen
Gothenburg
Haugesund
Kristiansand
Stavanger
Whitley Bay
Dumfries
Cairnryan
Castle Douglas
Annan
NEWCASTLE UPON TYNE
Tynemouth
South Shields
Newton Stewart
Gatehouse of Fleet
Hexham
Gateshead
Washington
Stranraer
Dalbeattie
Carlisle
Brampton
Sunderland
Wigtown
Kirkcudbright
Solway Firth
Stanley
Consett
Seaham
Whithorn
Alston
Tow Law
Durham
Maryport
Peterlee
Penrith
Hartlepool
Workington
Cockermouth
Appleby-in-Westmorland
Bishop Auckland
Newton Aycliffe
Stockton-on-Tees
Redcar
Keswick
Whitehaven
MIDDLESBROUGH
Brough
Barnard Castle
Egremont
Darlington
Whitby
Ambleside
Richmond
Scotch Corner
Windermere
Catterick
Ramsey
Ravenglass
Coniston
Northallerton
Kendal
Leyburn
Peel
ISLE OF MAN
Kirkby
Thirsk
BELFAST
Strangford Lough
Newcastle

REFERENCE | Légende | Zeichenerklärung

REFERENCE	Légende	Zeichenerklärung	Symbol
MOTORWAY	Autoroute	Autobahn	M1
MOTORWAY UNDER CONSTRUCTION	Autoroute en construction	Autobahn im Bau	
MOTORWAY PROPOSED	Autoroute prévue	Geplante Autobahn	
MOTORWAY JUNCTIONS WITH NUMBERS Unlimited interchange 4 Limited interchange 5	Echangeur numéroté Echangeur non limité 4 Echangeur limité 5	Autobahnanschlußstelle mit Nummer Unbeschränkter Fahrtrichtungswechsel 4 Beschränkter Fahrtrichtungswechsel 5	4 5
MOTORWAY SERVICE AREA with access from one carriageway only	Aire de services d'autoroute à sens unique	Rastplatz oder Raststätte Einbahn	HESTON S S
MAJOR ROAD SERVICE AREAS with 24 hour Facilities Primary Route Class A Road	Aire de services de route prioritaire Ouverte 24h sur 24 Route à grande circulation Route de type A	Raststätte Durchgehend geöffnet Hauptverkehrsstraße A-Straße	LEEMING S OLDBURY S
PRIMARY ROUTE	Route à grande circulation	Hauptverkehrsstraße	A41
PRIMARY ROUTE JUNCTION WITH NUMBER	Echangeur numéroté	Hauptverkehrsstraßenkreuzung mit Nummer	5
PRIMARY ROUTE DESTINATION	Route prioritaire, direction	Hauptverkehrsstraße Richtung	DOVER
DUAL CARRIAGEWAYS (A & B Roads)	Route à deux chaussées séparées (route A & B)	Zweispurige Schnellstraße (A- und B-Straßen)	
CLASS A ROAD	Route de type A	A-Straße	A129
CLASS B ROAD	Route de type B	B-Straße	B177
NARROW MAJOR ROAD (Passing Places)	Route prioritaire étroite (possibilité de dépassement)	Schmale Hauptverkehrsstaße (mit Überholmöglichkeit)	
MAJOR ROADS UNDER CONSTRUCTION	Route prioritaire en construction	Hauptverkehrsstaße im Bau	
MAJOR ROADS PROPOSED	Route prioritaire prévue	Geplante Hauptverkehrsstaße	
GRADIENT 1:5(20%) & STEEPER (Ascent in direction of arrow)	Pente égale et supérieure à 20% (dans le sens de la montée)	20% Steigung und steiler (in Pfeilrichtung)	«
TOLL	Péage	Gebührenpflichtig	TOLL
MILEAGE BETWEEN MARKERS	Distance en milles entre les flèches	Strecke zwischen Markierungen in Meilen	8
RAILWAY AND STATION	Voie ferrée et gare	Eisenbahnlinie und Bahnhof	
LEVEL CROSSING AND TUNNEL	Passage à niveau et tunnel	Bahnübergang und Tunnel	
RIVER OR CANAL	Rivière ou canal	Fluß oder Kanal	
COUNTY OR UNITARY AUTHORITY BOUNDARY	Limite des comté ou de division administrative	Grafschafts- oder Verwaltungsbezirksgrenze	
NATIONAL BOUNDARY	Frontière nationale	Landesgrenze	
BUILT-UP AREA	Agglomération	Geschlossene Ortschaft	
VILLAGE OR HAMLET	Village ou hameau	Dorf oder Weiler	
WOODED AREA	Zone boisée	Waldgebiet	
SPOT HEIGHT IN FEET	Altitude (en pieds)	Höhe in Fuß	• 813
HEIGHT ABOVE SEA LEVEL 400' - 1,000' 122m - 305m 1,000' - 1,400' 305m - 427m 1,400' - 2,000' 427m - 610m 2,000'+ 610m +	Altitude par rapport au niveau de la mer 400' - 1,000' 122m - 305m 1,000' - 1,400' 305m - 427m 1,400' - 2,000' 427m - 610m 2,000'+ 610m +	Höhe über Meeresspiegel 400' - 1,000' 122m - 305m 1,000' - 1,400' 305m - 427m 1,400' - 2,000' 427m - 610m 2,000'+ 610m +	
NATIONAL GRID REFERENCE (Kilometres)	Coordonnées géographiques nationales (Kilometres)	Nationale geographische Koordinaten (Kilometer)	100
PAGE CONTINUATION	Suite à la page indiquée	Seitenfortsetzung	48
AREA COVERED BY MAIN ROUTE MAP	Répartition des cartes des principaux axes routiers	Von Karten mit Hauptverkehrsstrecken	
AREA COVERED BY TOWN PLAN	Répartition des cartes des plans des villes	Von Karten mit Stadtplänen erfaßter Bereich	SEE PAGE 188

1:220,594

SCALE

3.5 Miles to 1 inch (2.54 cm) / 2.2 Km to 1 cm

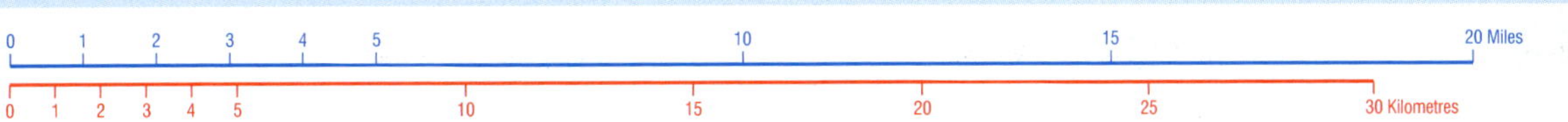

Tourist Information	Information	Touristeninformationen
AIRPORT	Aéroport	Flughafen
AIRFIELD	Terrain d' aviation	Flugplatz
HELIPORT	Héliport	Hubschrauberlandeplatz
BATTLE SITE AND DATE 1066	Champ de bataille avec date 1066	Schlachtfeld mit Datum 1066
CASTLE (Open to Public)	Château (ouvert au public)	Schloss / Burg (für die Öffentlichkeit zugänglich)
CASTLE WITH GARDEN (Open to Public)	Château et parc (ouvert au public)	Schloß mit Garten (für die Öffentlichkeit zugänglich)
CATHEDRAL, ABBEY, CHURCH, FRIARY, PRIORY	Cathédrale, abbaye, église, monastère, prieuré	Kathedrale, Abtei, Kirche, Mönchskloster, Kloster
COUNTRY PARK	Parc régonal	Landschaftspark
FERRY (Vehicular, sea) (Vehicular, river) (Foot only)	Bac (véhicules, mer) (véhicules, rivière) (Piétons)	Fähre (Autos, meer) (Autos, fluß) (nur für Personen)
GARDEN (Open to Public)	Jardin ouvert au public	Garten (für die Öffentlichkeit zugänglich)
GOLF COURSE (9 Hole) (18 Hole)	Terrain de golf (9 trous) (18 trous)	Golfplatz (9 Löcher) (18 Löcher)
HISTORIC BUILDING (Open to Public)	Monument historique (ouvert au public)	Historisches Gebäude (für die Öffentlichkeit zugänglich)
HISTORIC BUILDING WITH GARDEN (Open to Public)	Monument historique avec jardin (ouvert au public)	Historisches Gebäude mit Garten (für die Öffentlichkeit zugänglich)
HORSE RACECOURSE	Hippodrome	Pferderennbahn
INFORMATION CENTRE	Syndicat d'initiative	Information
LIGHTHOUSE	Phare	Leuchtturm
MOTOR RACING CIRCUIT	Circuit automobile	Automobilrennbahn
MUSEUM, ART GALLERY	Musée	Museum, Galerie
NATIONAL PARK OR FOREST PARK	Parc national ou forêt domaniale	National- oder Waldpark
NATIONAL TRUST PROPERTY (Open) NT (Restricted Opening) NT (National Trust of Scotland) NTS NTS	National Trust Property (ouvert) NT (heures d'ouverture) NT (National Trust of Scotland) NTS NTS	National Trust-Eigentum (geöffnet) NT (beschränkte Öffnungszeit) NT (National Trust of Scotland) NTS NTS
NATURE RESERVE OR BIRD SANCTUARY	Réserve naturelle botanique ou ornithologique	Natur- oder Vogelschutzgebiet
NATURE TRAIL OR FOREST WALK	Chemin forestier, piste verte	Naturpfad oder Waldweg
PLACE OF INTEREST Monument	Site, curiosité Monument	Sehenswürdigkeit Monument
PICNIC SITE	Lieu pour pique-nique	Picknickplatz
RAILWAY, STEAM OR NARROW GAUGE	Chemin de fer, à vapeur ou à voie étroite	Eisenbahn, Dampf- oder Schmalspurbahn
THEME PARK	Centre de loisir	Vergnügungspark
VIEWPOINT (360 degrees) (180 degrees)	Vue panoramique (360 degré) (180 degré)	Aussichtspunkt (360 grade) (180 grade)
WILDLIFE PARK	Réserve de faune	Wildpark
WINDMILL	Moulin à vent	Windmühle
ZOO OR SAFARI PARK	Parc ou réserve zoologique	Zoo oder Safari-Park

ISLES OF SCILLY
Round Island
St. Helen's
White Island
Tean
ST. MARTIN'S
BRYHER
TRESCO
EASTERN ISLES
ST. MARY'S
Hugh Town
Samson
Annet
Gugh
ST. AGNES
Western Rocks
Bishop Rock
Crim Rocks
Hugh Town to Penzance 2hrs. 40mins.
The Isles of Scilly lie 28 miles S.W. of Land's End
Godrevy Island
Navax Point
Crane Islands
Portreath
St. Ives Bay
St. Ives
The Carracks
Gurnard's Head
Pendeen Watch
Pendeen
Cape Cornwall
The Brisons
St. Just
Whitesand Bay
Longships
LAND'S END
Sennen
St. Buryan
Gwennap Head
Runnel Stone
Cribba Head
PENZANCE
Newlyn
Mousehole
St. Clement's Isle
MOUNT'S BAY
Marazion
St. Michael's Mount
Cudden Point
Trewavas Head
Porthleven
Helston
Hayle
CAMBORNE
Penzance to Hugh Town 2hrs. 40mins.
Poldhu Point
Mullion Island
Vellan Head
Wolf Rock
C O R N W A

NEWQUAY
Newquay Bay
Towan Head
Fistral Bay
Kelsey Head
Pentire
Crantock
Holywell Bay
Penhale Point
Ligger or Perran Bay
Cubert
Bawden Rocks
Perranporth
St. Agnes Head
St. Agnes
Goonhavern
St. Newlyn East
Mitchell
St. Columb Major
St. Columb Road
Indian Queens
Roche
Bugle
Lanivet
Luxulyan
St. Dennis
Nanpean
Stenalees
Foxhole
ST. AUSTELL
St. Blazey
Par
Charlestown
Polgooth
St. Austell Bay
Black Head
Mevagissey
Mevagissey Bay
Chapel Point
Gorran Haven
Dodman Point
Veryan Bay
Veryan
Portloe
Gerrans Bay
Nare Head
Gull Rock
Portscatho
Gerrans
Greeb Point
St. Mawes
St. Anthony Head
Zone Point
Grampound
Probus
Tresillian
Ladock
TRURO
Chacewater
REDRUTH
St. Day
Carharrack
Perranarworthal
Devoran
Stithians
Penryn
FALMOUTH
Pendennis Point
Falmouth Bay
Carrick Roads
Constantine
Mawnan
Rosemullion Head
Nare Point
Manaccan
St. Keverne
Manacle Point
The Manacles
Coverack
Black Head
Mullion
Ruan Minor
Lizard
Hot Point
LIZARD POINT
A30
A39
A390
A391
A392
A394
A3058
A3059
A3078
A3083
E
F
G
H
1
2
3
4
5
7

6
Newland
Pentire Point
Padstow Bay
Gulland Rock
Gunver Head
TREVOSE HEAD
Quies
Constantine Bay
Park Head
Padstow
Wadebridge
Berryl's Point
Watergate Bay
Towan Head
NEWQUAY
Fistral Bay
Kelsey Head
Holywell Bay
Penhale Point
Ligger or Perran Bay
Bawden Rocks
Perranporth
St. Agnes Head
St. Agnes
St. Columb Major
Indian Queens
St. Newlyn East
ST. AUSTELL
Mevagissey
TRURO
REDRUTH
CAMBORNE
Crane Islands
Portreath
FALMOUTH
Penryn
St. Mawes
Gerrans Bay
Nare Head
Gull Rock
Veryan Bay
Dodman Point
Zone Point
Rosemullion Head
Helston
Falmouth Bay

Treligga
Delabole
Camelford
Tregoodwell
Crowdy Resr.
Bowithick
St. Clether
Laneast
Pool
Launceston
Lifton
Westdowns
Pengelly
Trevia
Valley
Trewalder
Trekne
Pencarrow
Helstone
Tresinney
St. Teath
Rough Tor
Altarnun
Wesleys Cottage
Treween
Polyphant
Tredaule
Fivelanes
Trewen
Tregadillet
South Petherwin
Daw's House
Lewannick
Lawhitton
Tregada
Trewarlett
Kelly
Bradstone
Meadwell
Dunterton
Abbot
Pendoggett
Treveighan
Michaelstow
Fentonadle
St. Breward
Row
Trelill
St. Tudy
Lank
Wenfordbridge
Penpont
Blisland
Waterloo
St. Kew Highway
St. Mabyn
Croanford
Hellandbridge
Helland
Washaway
Brown Willy
Garrow Tor
King Arthur's Hall
Codda
Bolventor
Smugglers at Jamaica Inn
Jamaica Inn
BODMIN MOOR
Temple
Dozmary Pool
Colliford Lake
Maidenwell
Millpool
DANGER AREA
Trevadlock
Congdon's Shop
Trebartha
North Hill
Middlewood
Kilmar Tor
Henwood
The Cheesewring
Hurlers Stone Circles
Minions
Upton Cross
Siblyback Lake
Caradon Hill
Caradon Town
Downgate
Darite
Illand
Newtown
Trebullett
Coad's Green
Lezant
Trekenner
Trebullett
Treburley
Rezare
Bealsmill
Tutwell
Sydenham Damerel
Venterdon
Stoke Climsland
Bray Shop
Bathpool
Rilla Mill
Linkinhorne
Plushabridge
South Hill
Luckett
Kelly Bray
Kit Hill
Golberdon
Latchley
Chilsworthy
St. Ann's Chapel
Gunnislake
Albaston
Metherell
Callington
Harrowbarrow
Bodmin
Cardinham
Cardinham Castle
Warleggan
Fawton
St. Neot
Common Moor
Redgate
St. Cleer
Tremar
Pensilva
Gang
St. Ive
Keason
Trevigro
Frogwell
Dupath Well Ho.
Bere Alston
Lanivet
Tregullon
Mount
Tredinnick
Ley
Carnglaze Slate Caverns
Dobwalls
Dobwalls Family Adventure Park
Liskeard
Merrymeet
Parkfield
Cadson Bury
St. Mellion
Pengover Green
Quethiock
Pillaton
Cutmadoc
Lanhydrock
West Taphouse
East Taphouse
Middle Taphouse
Doublebois
Trevelmond
St. Pinnock
Lamellion
Menheniot
Trehunist
Blunts
Cuttivett
Ellbridge
Botusfleming
Hatt
Cargreen
Trebyan
Maudlin
Bokiddick
Sweetshouse
Lockengate
Red Moors
Restormel
Polscoe
Lostwithiel
Bodrane
Deerpark Wood
Herodsfoot
St. Keyne
Trewidland
Tideford Cross
Landrake
Budge's Shop
Tideford
St. Erney
Trematon
Saltash
Burraton
Lanlivery
Couch's Mill
Luxulyan
Rosevean
Rescorla
Penwithick
Trethurgy
Milltown
St. Winnow
Lerryn
Bocaddon
Lanreath
Duloe
Tredinnick
Sandplace
Widegates
Trerulefoot
Hessenford
St. Germans
Markwell
Trehan
St. Stephens
Pelynt
Muchlarnick
Morval
Polbathic
Narkurs
St. Winnolls
Sheviock
Maryfield
Antony
St. Blazey
St. Blazey Gate
Tywardreath Highway
Tywardreath
Golant
St. Veep
Penpoll
Lanteglos Highway
Trenewan
St. Martin
Plaidy
Seaton
Downderry
Portwrinkle
Crafthole
Torpoint
St. John
Millbrook
Par
Tregrehan Mills
Holmbush
Carlyon Bay
Charlestown
Polkerris
Fowey
Bodinnick
Readymoney
Menabilly
Polruan
Lansallos
Polperro
Porthallow
West Looe
East Looe
Looe
Looe Bay
Talland Bay
St. George's or Looe Island
Freathy
Tregonhawke
Whitsand Bay
Rame
Rame Head
Higher Porthpean
St. Austell Bay
Gribbin Head
Pencarrow Head
Ropehaven Cliffs
Trenarren
Black Head
Mevagissey Bay
Chapel Point
Eddystone Rocks
A30
A39
A38
A390
A388
A391
A3082
A387
A374
B3314
B3267
B3266
B3268
B3269
B3257
B3254
B3362
B3359
B3252
B3253
B3247
B3249
B3251
10
E
F
G
H
1
2
3
4
5
7
8

8
A
B
C
D
1
2
3
4
5
7
11
DARTMOOR
DARTMOOR NATIONAL FOREST PARK
DANGER AREA
Lifton
Dippertown
Coryton
Marystow
Liddaton
Lawhitton
Kelly
Meadwell
Chillaton
North Brentor
Milton Abbot
Dunterton
Mary Tavy
Chaddlehanger
Lamerton
Sydenham Damerel
Rushford
Tutwell
Bealsmill
Rezare
Horsebridge
Stoke Climsland
Luckett
Latchley
Chilsworthy
Downgate
Kit Hall
Gunnislake
St. Ann's Chapel
Albaston
Drakewalls
Harrowbarrow
Metherell
Calstock
St. Dominick
Bere Alston
St. Mellion
Cotts
Bere Ferrers
Ellbridge
Cargreen
Botusfleming
Hatt
Cuttivett
Landulph
Carkeel
SALTASH
Saltash
Trematon
Landrake
St. Germans
Markwell
Sheviock
Crafthole
Antony
Torpoint
St. John
Millbrook
Cremyll
Freathy
Tregonhawke
Kingsand
Cawsand
Rame
Rame Head
Penlee Point
Whitsand Bay
Drake's Island
The Sound
Plymouth Breakwater
Eddystone Rocks
Great Mew Stone
Plymouth to:
Roscoff 6hrs.
Santander 18hrs. (Seasonal)
TAVISTOCK
Brook
Whitchurch
Grenofen
Horrabridge
Buckland Monachorum
Crapstone
Milton Combe
Tamerton Foliot
Roborough
Whitleigh
Ernesettle
Estover
PLYMOUTH
SEE PAGE 195
Eggbuckland
Leigham
Woodford
Plympton
Compton
Devonport
Wilcove
Maryfield
Ford
Ham
Pennycross
Budeaux
St. Budeaux
The Hoe
Turnchapel
Plymstock
Elburton
Underwood
Saltram
Hooe
Goosewell
Staddiscombe
Down Thomas
Knighton
Wembury
Heybrook Bay
Newton Ferrers
Noss Mayo
Bridgend
Netton
Stoke Point
Brixton
Yealmpton
Torr
Dunstone
Kitley Caves
National Shire Horse Centre
Luson
Battisborough Cross
Mothecombe
Holbeton
Ford
Flete
Willsworthy
Horndon
Cudlipptown
Peter Tavy
Merrivale
Rundlestone
Princetown
Two Bridges
Sampford Spiney
Walkhampton
Yelverton
Dousland
Sheepstor
Meavy
Clearbrook
Burrator Resr.
Shaugh Prior
Wotter
Bickleigh
Woolwell
Lee Moor
Cornwood
Lutton
Sparkwell
Hemerdon
Lee Mill
Ivybridge
Harford
Moor Cross
Bittaford
Godwell
Ugborough
Cut Hill
Sittaford Tor
Fernworthy Resr.
Postbridge
Bellever
Tor Royal
Whiteworks
Cater's Beam
Ryder's Hill
Shell Top
Ugborough Moor
Hexworthy
Huccaby
Dartmeet
Poundsgate
Ponsworthy
Leusdon
Buckland in the Moor
Lower Town
Widecombe in the Moor
Dunstone
Bonehill
Haytor Vale
Hameldown Tor
Grimspound
Manaton
North Bovey
Lettaford
Venford Resr.
Holne
Michelcombe
Scorriton
Combe
Ashburton
Buckfast
Buckfastleigh
Avon Dam Resr.
Didworthy
Harbourneford
Lower Dean
Dean Prior
Rattery
Aish
South Brent
Cheston
Avonwick
Diptford
Harberton
Tigley
North Huish
Curtisknowle
Lupridge
Brownston
Moreleigh
Boreston
Penquit
Westlake
Ermington
Modbury
East Leigh
Woodleigh
Ashford
Aveton Gifford
Loddiswell
East Allington
Churchstow
Ledstone
Goveton
Buckland-tout-Saints
Kingsbridge
Dodbrooke
Great Torr
Kingston
Ringmore
St. Ann's Chapel
Bigbury
Challaborough
Bigbury-on-Sea
Burgh Island
Bantham
Thurlestone
Buckland
Upton
West Alvington
South Milton
Woolston
West Charleton
East Charleton
Bigbury Bay
South Huish
Outer Hope
Inner Hope
Bolt Tail
Galmpton
Bolberry
Malborough
Collaton
Batson
Salcombe
Rew
East Portlemouth
Rickham
Bolt Head
Prawle Point
South Pool
A386
A388
A38
A390
A374
A379
A3121
A385
A381
A384
B3362
B3257
B3357
B3212
B3387
B3413
B3373
B3417
B3432
B3416
B3186
B3392
B3196
B3194
B3247
30
40
250
60
70

9
EXMOUTH
Budleigh Salterton
Lympstone
Starcross
Cockwood
Dawlish Warren
Dawlish
Holcombe
Teignmouth
Shaldon
Bishopsteignton
Kingsteignton
NEWTON ABBOT
Bovey Tracey
Chudleigh
Chudleigh Knighton
Stokeinteignhead
Babbacombe Bay
Maidencombe
Kingskerswell
Abbotskerswell
Ipplepen
Marldon
TORQUAY
Hope's Nose
TORBAY
PAIGNTON
Tor Bay
Brixham
Berry Head
Sharkham Point
Totnes
Dartmouth
Kingswear
Mew Stone
Stoke Fleming
Start Bay
Slapton
Chillington
Stokenham
Torcross
Beesands
Hallsands
Start Point
A38
A380
A376
A385
A379
12
E
F
G
H
1
2
3
4
5
80
70
60
50
40
30
90
300
10

10
18
A
B
C
D
1
2
3
4
5
6
7
Hartland Quay
Stoke
Hartland
Velly
B3248
Natcott
B3237
Higher Clovelly
Buck's Mills
Buck's & Keivell's Woods
Milford
Elmscott
Philham
Edistone
Welsford
A39
Woolfardisworthy or Woolsery
Buck's Cross
South Hole
Alminstone Cross
Parkham Ash
Knaps Longpeak
Welcombe
Welcombe & Marsland Valleys
Mead
Gooseham
Woolley
Meddon
R. Torridge
Ashmansworthy
East Putford
West Putford
Morwenstow
Shop
Eastcott
West Youlstone
East Youlstone
Dinworthy
Higher Sharpnose Point
Lower Sharpnose Point
Woodford
Bradworthy
Coombe Valley
Coombe
Kilkhampton
Pixieland Funpark
Stibb
Alfardisworthy
Upper Tamar Lake
Lower Tamar Lake
Thurdon
Sutcombe
Soldon Cross
Waldon
B3254
Dexbeer
A388
Holsworthy Beacon
Bude Bay
Poughill
Flexbury
Bush
Hersham
Stratton
Grimscott
Lana
Chilsworthy
Bude
Lynstone
Launcells
Pancrasweek
Holsworthy
A3072
Red Post
Upton
Phillip's Point Cliffs
Marhamchurch
Bridgerule
Derril
Derriton
Staddon
Whimble
Pyworthy
Martyn's Wood
Chasty
Holsworthy Woods
Widemouth Bay
Titson
Box's Shop
Coppathorne
Leworthy
Clawford Vineyard
Dizzard Point
Dizzard
Poundstock
Bangors
Treskinnick Cross
Whitstone
R. Deer
River Tamar
Clawton
Tregole
Trewint
Penhallam
Week St. Mary
Week Green
Street
R. Claw
Crackington Haven
St. Gennys
Moortown
Cambeak
Wainhouse Corner
Jacobstow
North Tamerton
Tetcott
Lana
CORNWALL
Sweets
Luffincott
Higher Whiteleigh
West Curry
Chapmans Well
Tresparrett Posts
Trengune
South Wheatley
Fire Beacon Point
Beeny
B3263
Tresparrett
Langdon
Maxworthy
Northcott
Boyton
Peter's Wood
Marshgate
Canworthy Water
River Ottery
Bennacott
Hele
West Panson
Boscastle
Trelash
Brazacott
Lesnewth
Otterham
Warbstow
North Petherwin
Otter Park
Langdon Cross
St. Giles on the Heath
Trevalga
Tintagel Head
Bossiney
Tremaine
Petherwin Gate
Tintagel
Halgabron
B3262
Hallworthy
Splatt
Treneglos
Ladycross
Werrington
Old Post Office
Tresmeer
Yeolmbridge
Trewarmett
Davidstow
Tregeare
Egloskerry
Langore
Gull Rock
Trebarwith
Trewassa
Tremail
Trevivian
Cold Northcott
A395
Badgall
Steam Railway
St. Stephens
Dutson
Littondown
Rockhead
B3266
New Mills
Newport
Treligga
Delabole
Treffrew
Pipers Pool
North Cornwall
Slate Quarry
Treveia
Tregoodwell
Crowdy Resr.
St. Clether
Laneast
Tregadillett
Launceston
Leisure Farm
Westdowns
Camelford
Pengelly
Valley Truckle
Trewalder
Bowithick
R. Inny
Trewen
South Petherwin
Daw's House
Lawhitton
Port Isaac Bay
Delabole Wind Farm
Pencarrow
Helstone
Town Hall
Tresinney
Rough Tor
Treween
Altarnun
Polyphant
Wesleys Cottage
Tredaule
Five Lanes
A30
Lewannick
Tregada
Port Quin
Port Isaac
Port Gaverne
St. Teath
Trewetha
Trewarlett
Greystone Bridge
B3267
Long Cross
Trelights
Pendoggett
Treveighan
1377 Brown Willy
1209
B3257
Trevadlock
Illand
Trepawell Manor
Lezant
Trekenner
Howard's Wood
B3314
St. Endellion
Trelill
Michaelstow
Fentonadle
Codda
Congdon's Shop
Newtown
Trebullett
Treburley
Lakeside Gallery
St. Minver
King Arthur's Hall
Garrow Tor
BODMIN MOOR
Smugglers at Jamaica Inn
Bolventor
1082
Trebartha
Coad's Green
Rezare
Bealsmill
Lower Amble
Chapel Amble
St. Kew
R. Allen
St. Tudy
St. Breward
Row
De Lank R.
North Hill
Middlewood
A388
Venterdon
St. Kew Highway
Lank
Wenfordbridge
River Fowey
1280 Kilmar Tor
Bathpool
Bray Shop
Stoke
Camel Estuary
Trevanson
Bodieve
Penpont
Blisland
Dozmary Pool
Henwood
Oldmill
Wadebridge
A39
St. Mabyn
Egloshayle
Croanford
Lavathan Wood
Waterloo
Temple
Colliford Lake
The Cheesewring
Hurlers Stone Circles
Upton Cross
Minions
Rilla Mill
Linkinhorne
Plushabridge
South Hill
Kelly Bray
St. Breock
Sladesbridge
Hawke's Wood
Pencarrow
Hellandbridge
Helland
A389
Maidenwell
Danger Area
Millpool
Siblyback Lake
1216 Caradon Hill
Caradon Town
Downgate
Golberdon
Burlawn
Washaway
Polbrock
Darite
Pensilva
Trevigro
Callington
Hayes
St. Breock Downs Monolith
Bodmin
Berry Tower
Cardinham
Warleggan
Fawton
St. Neot
Redgate
Common Moor
Trethevy Quoit
Tremar
Golitha Falls
King Doniert's Stone
St. Cleer
Gang
Keason
Frogwell
Dupath Well Ho.
Ruthernbridge
Nanstallon
Forest Trails
Cardinham Castle
Mount
Carnglaze Slate Caverns
Dobwalls Family Adventure Park
Thorburn Gallery
St. Ive
Parkfield
Cadson Bury
Withiel
Tremore
St. Lawrence
Beacon Hill
Tredinnick
Ley
Dobwalls
Liskeard
A390
Merrymeet

Great Torrington
Littleham
Buckland Brewer
Weare Giffard
High Bickington
Umberleigh
George Nympton
Bishop's Nympton
King's Nympton
Roborough
St. Giles in the Wood
Langtree
Little Torrington
Burrington
Chulmleigh
Chawleigh
Beaford
Ashreigney
Dolton
Merton
Bulkworthy
Milton Damerel
Shebbear
Petrockstowe
Meeth
Winkleigh
Wembworthy
Eggesford
Lapford
Morchard Bishop
Cookbury
Black Torrington
Sheepwash
Highampton
Hatherleigh
Monkokehampton
Bondleigh
Zeal Monachorum
Copplestone
North Tawton
Sampford Courtenay
Exbourne
Jacobstowe
Bow
Halwill Junction
Northlew
Folly Gate
Okehampton
Belstone
South Zeal
Bratton Clovelly
Sourton
Drewsteignton
Throwleigh
Chagford
Moretonhampstead
North Bovey
Stowford
Lydford
Lifton
Mary Tavy
Peter Tavy
Milton Abbot
Lamerton
Sydenham Damerel
TAVISTOCK
Princetown
Two Bridges
Postbridge
Lustleigh
Haytor Vale
Widecombe in the Moor
Buckland in the Moor
Ashburton
Buckfast
Buckfastleigh
Gunnislake
Chilsworthy
Calstock
Bere Alston
Buckland Monachorum
Yelverton
Dousland
Horrabridge
Walkhampton
Whiteworks
DARTMOOR
DARTMOOR NATIONAL PARK
FOREST
Meldon Resr.
Roadford Lake (Reservoir)
Burrator Resr.
Venford Resr.
Avon Dam Resr.
Fernworthy Resr.
A30
A386
A377
A3072
A3079
A3124
A382
A38
B3227
B3217
B3216
B3215
B3220
B3212
B3357
B3362
B3260
B3257
B3042
B3096
11
12
19
8

12
A
B
C
D
20
9
11
1
2
3
4
5
Bish Mill
Newtown
Bishop's Nympton
Mariansleigh
Alswear
Cross Side
East Knowstone
Knowstone
Roachill
Ash Mill
Rose Ash
Oldways End
Exebridge
Bampton
Shillingford
Petton
Clayhanger
Bathealton
Chipley
Langford Budville
Stawley
Kittisford
Kyrle
Appley
Runnington
Thorne St. Margaret
Tonedale
Ashbrittle
Greenham
Holywell Lake
Oakfordbridge
Oakford
Cove
Huntsham
Staple Cross
Hockworthy
Holcombe Rogus
Sampford Arundel
Creacombe
Meshaw
Venhay
Rackenford
Stoodleigh Beacon
Stoodleigh
Ford Barton
Fair Oak
Westleigh
Burlescombe
Nicholashayne
Bradford Barton
Queen Dart
Mogworthy
North Coombe
Loxbeare
Washfield
Chevithorne
Whitnage
Uplowman
Ayshford
Week
Lutworthy
Witheridge
Yeo Copse
Templeton
Bolham
Knightshayes Ct.
Chettiscombe
Appledore
Whitehall
East Worlington
West Worlington
Drayford
Nomansland
Calverleigh
Cowley moor
Halberton
Sampford Peverell
Prescott
Cheldon
Chawleigh
Thelbridge Barton
Withleigh
Cotteylands
TIVERTON
Manley
Uffculme
Culmstock
Craddock
Hackpen Hill
Washford Pyne
Pennymoor
Cruwys Morchard
Ash Thomas
Smithincott
Ashill
Filleigh
Littleborough
Puddington
Way Village
East Butterleigh
Willand
Stenhill
Eastington
Black Dog
Poughill
Blackborough
Lapford
Brownstone
Woolfardisworthy
Upham
Butterleigh
CULLOMPTON
Kentisbeare
Sheldon
Nymet Rowland
Morchard Bishop
Kennerleigh
Hayne
Cadeleigh
Bickleigh
Stoneyford
Saint Hill
Oldborough
Stockleigh English
Cheriton Fitzpaine
Cadbury Castle (Hill Fort)
Cullompton
Colebrook
Kerswell
Weeke
Ford Park Wood
East Village
Fursdon
Bickleigh
Dulford
Broadhembury
Down St. Mary
Zeal Monachorum
Chilton
Cadbury
Chitterley
Mutterton
Westcott
Colliton
Newbuildings
West Sandford
Upton Hellions
Stockleigh Pomeroy
Up Exe
Silverton
Bradninch
Norman's Green
Copplestone
Coleford
Elston
Uppincott
Hele
Langford
Plymtree
Lower Tale
Luton
Upton
Bow
Knowle
Sandford
Thorverton
Ellerhayes
Payhembury
Nymet Tracey
Penstone
Colebrooke
Crediton
Shobrooke
Efford
Shute
Nether Exe
Clyst Hydon
Higher Tale
Colestocks
Cheriton
Wyke
Brampford Speke
Rewe
Budlake
Clyst St. Lawrence
Talaton
Feniton
Hillerton
Fordton
Hookway
Sweetham
Killerton House
Westwood
Fenny Bridges
Uton
Smallbrook
Yeoford
Venny Tedburn
Newton St. Cyres
Upton Pyne
Stoke Canon
Huxham
Broadclyst
Whimple
Escot
Fairmile
Alfington
Woodland Head
Oldridge
Poltimore
Dog Village
Hand and Pen
Hittisleigh Barton
Hittisleigh
Cowley
Taleford
Tedburn St. Mary
Pennsylvania
Pinhoe
Rockbeare
West Hill
Ottery St. Mary
Whitestone
Exwick
Whipton
Allercombe
Cheriton Bishop
Cheriton Cross
Crockernwell
SEE PAGE 189
EXETER
Heavitree
Clyst Honiton
Marsh Green
Broad Oak
Fluxton
Wiggaton
Halstow
Wheatley
Sowton
Aylesbeare
Metcombe
Coombe
Drewsteignton
Prestonbury Castle (Fort)
Longdown
St. Thomas
Bowhill
Clyst St. Mary
Farringdon
Venn Ottery
Southerton
Tipton St. John
Harpford
Bowd
Sandypark
Easton
Cranbrook Castle (fort)
Dunsford
Culver
Ide
Alphington
Woodbury Salterton
Burrow
Newton Poppleford
Drewston
Shillingford St. George
Lower Wear
Topsham
Clyst St. George
Hawkerland
Woodbury
Woodbury Castle Fort
Stowford
Colaton Raleigh
Sloncombe
Doccombe
Bridford
Bridfordmills
Clapham
Exminster
Ebford
Exton
Moretonhampstead
Doddiscombsleigh
Scanniclift Copse
Kennford
Kenn
Bicton Park
Otterton
North Bovey
Christow
Bennah
Higher Ashton
Woodmanton
Yettington
East Budleigh
Mill Centre
Kennick Resr.
Tottiford Resr.
Lower Ashton
Powderham
Lympstone
A La Ronde
Hulham
Withycombe Raleigh
Knowle
Kersbrook
Otter Estuary
Canonteign Falls
Trenchford Resr.
Devon & Exeter
Kenton
South Town
Miniature Pony Centre
Lustleigh
Lustleigh Cleave
Manaton
Trusham
Starcross
Littleham
Budleigh Salterton
Hennock
Waddon
Cockwood
EXMOUTH
World of Country Life
Water
Becky Falls
Bovey Valley Woodlands
Chudleigh
Ashcombe
Dartmoor Nature Trail & Woodland Walk
Shaptor Woods
Yarner Wood
Bovey Tracey
Ugbrooke Ho.
Milton Hill
Dawlish Warren
Hound Tor Deserted Village
Bonehill
Brimley
Teign Valley Glass
Chudleigh Knighton
Gappah
Ideford
Luton
Little Haldon
Dawlish
Haytor Rocks
Haytor Vale
Ilsington
Heathfield
Lewthorn Cross
Liverton
Halford
Goldeast
Preston
Stover Ctry Pk.
Sandygate
Humber
Holcombe
Buckland in the Moor
Sigford
Teigngrace
Bishopsteignton
Rural Life
Coombe
Teignmouth
Lower Town
Kingsteignton
Highweek
Shaldon
Ringmore
Bickington
Caton
Goodstone
NEWTON ABBOT
Netherton
Combeinteignhead
Stokeinteignhead
Ashburton
Hele
River Dart
West Ogwell
East Ogwell
Wolborough
Decoy Ctry Pk.
Lower Gabwell
Higher Gabwell
Collinswell
Woodland
Denbury
Abbotskerswell
Kingskerswell
Maidencombe
Babbacombe Bay
Buckfast
Abbey
Forder Green
Two Mile Oak Cross
Torbryan
Ipplepen
Watcombe Barton
Kfastleigh
Landscove
Woolston Green
Broadhempston
North Whilborough
Compton
Shiphay
Model Village
St. Marychurch
Cliff Railway
Babbacombe
DEVON
A361
A396
A377
A30
A38
A380
A376
A373
A3072
A3124
A3052
A3015
A382
A383
A381
A379
A3022
A38
B3137
B3227
B3222
B3042
B3181
B3440
B3391
B3181
B3185
B3212
B3193
B3344
B3184
B3180
B3179
B3178
B3174
B3177
B3176
B3206
B3387
B3192
M5
27
28
29
30
31
Grand Western Canal
R. Exe
R. Dart
R. Culm
R. Clyst
R. Kenn
R. Teign
R. Bovey
R. Otter
R. Tale
R. Yeo
Little Dart R.

TAUNTON
SEE PAGE 197
M5
Wellington
Bradford on-Tone
Rockwell Green
TAUNTON DEANE
SOMERSET
BLACK DOWN HILLS
Hemyock
Churchstanton
Dunkeswell
Upottery
Yarcombe
Stockland
Chard
Ilminster
Crewkerne
Martock
South Petherton
Shepton Beauchamp
Barrington
Isle Abbotts
Curry Mallet
Fivehead
Ruishton
Corfe
Pitminster
Combe St. Nicholas
Broadway
Horton
Chardstock
South Chard
Tytherleigh
Winsham
Thorncombe
Misterton
Merriott
Hinton St. George
North Perrott
South Perrott
Haselbury Plucknett
Norton sub Hamdon
Stoke sub Hamdon
Montacute
Odcombe
West Coker
East Chinnock
Hardington Mandeville
Tintinhull
Chilthorne Domer
Kingsbury Episcopi
Corscombe
Broadwindsor
Stoke Abbott
Beaminster
Netherbury
Hawkchurch
Axminster
Kilmington
Honiton
Awliscombe
Wilmington
Colyton
Colyford
Seaton
Axmouth
Beer
Branscombe
Sidmouth
Sidford
Musbury
Uplyme
Lyme Regis
Charmouth
Chideock
Morcombelake
Bridport
Bothenhampton
Bradpole
Shipton Gorge
Burton Bradstock
LYME BAY
Seaton Bay
Beer Head
DORSET
A30
A303
A358
A35
A375
A3052
A356
A3066
A3088
A378
B3170
B3167
B3165
B3162
B3163
B3157
B3261
B3168
B3165
13
14
E
F
G
H
1
2
3
4
5
20
30
40
350
80
70

14
13
A
B
C
D
1
2
3
4
5
350
60
70
80
YEOVIL
Sherborne
DORCHESTER
WEYMOUTH
Ilchester
Limington
Mudford
Tintinhull
Chilthorne Domer
Stoke sub Hamdon
Montacute
Norton sub Hamdon
Odcombe
Brympton
Chiselborough
West Chinnock
West Coker
East Chinnock
North Coker
East Coker
Hardington Mandeville
Haselbury Plucknett
North Perrott
South Perrott
Corscombe
Chedington
Halstock
Melbury Osmond
Melbury Sampford
Evershot
Chetnole
Leigh
Yetminster
Bradford Abbas
Thornford
Nether Compton
Trent
Marston Magna
Rimpton
Corton Denham
Charlton Horethorne
Milborne Port
Abbas Combe
Henstridge
Stalbridge
Kington Magna
Marnhull
Hinton St. Mary
Sturminster Newton
Okeford Fitzpaine
Child Okeford
Iwerne Minster
Iwerne Courtney or Shroton
Shillingstone
Durweston
Bishop's Caundle
Longburton
BLACKMOOR VALE
Glanvilles Wootton
Buckland Newton
Minterne Magna
Up Cerne
Cerne Abbas
Sydling St. Nicholas
Piddletrenthide
Piddlehinton
Cattistock
Maiden Newton
Frome St. Quintin
Toller Porcorum
Powerstock
Beaminster
Bridport
Bothenhampton
Burton Bradstock
Shipton Gorge
Litton Cheney
Askerswell
Puncknowle
Abbotsbury
Portesham
Martinstown or Winterborne St. Martin
Frampton
Charminster
Stratton
Puddletown
Tolpuddle
Bere Regis
Milborne St. Andrew
Winterborne Kingston
Winterborne Whitechurch
Milton Abbas
Winterborne Stickland
West Stafford
West Knighton
Broadmayne
Moreton
Bovington Camp
Wool
Winfrith Newburgh
East Lulworth
West Lulworth
Osmington
Overcombe
Preston
Melcombe Regis
Weymouth Bay
Chickerell
Broadwey
Upwey
Langton Herring
Portland Harbour
Fortuneswell
Castletown
Chesil
West Bay
Easton
Weston
Southwell
ISLE OF PORTLAND
BILL OF PORTLAND
Chesil Beach
Ringstead Bay
Worbarrow Bay
Durdle Door
Lulworth Cove
DANGER AREA
D O R S E T
E N
A30
A37
A35
A352
A354
A356
A303
A3088
A3066
A357
A3030
A350
A31
B3157
B3159
B3143
B3146
B3142
B3390
B3163
B3070
Weymouth to:
Guernsey 2hrs. (Fast Ferry)
Jersey 3hrs. 30mins.
(Fast Ferry)
St. Malo 5hrs. 30mins.
(Fast Ferry, Seasonal)

Donhead St. Mary
Shaftesbury
A30
Melbury Abbas
Compton Abbas
Ashmore
Cann Common
Charlton
Ludwell
Milkwell
White Sheet Hill
Alvediston
West End
Ebbesbourne Wake
Broad Chalke
Bowerchalke
Woodminton
Farthing
A354
Berwick St. John
Winklebury Camp Hill Fort
B3081
Win Green
CRANBORNE CHASE
Tollard Royal
New Town
Deanland
Sixpenny Handley
Woodyates
Woodcutts
Tollard Farnham
Farnham
Minchington
Dean
Gussage St. Andrew
Cashmoor
Chettle
Chettle House
Stubhampton
Tarrant Gunville
Tarrant Hinton
Gussage St. Michael
Gussage All Saints
Long Crichel
Tarrant Launceston
A354
Pimperne
Blandford Camp
Tarrant Monkton
Blandford Forum
Royal Signals
Manswood
Moor Crichel
Hogstock
Witchampton
Tarrant Rawston
Tarrant Rushton
Hemsworth
Langton Long Blandford
Charlton Marshall
Charlton on the Hill
Tarrant Keyneston
Tarrant Crawford
Spetisbury
Badbury Rings
Shapwick
Kingston Lacy
Sturminster Marshall
Pamphill
Wimborne Minster
B3082
Stanbridge
Hillbutts
Colehill
Almer
Mapperton
Anderson
Winterborne Zelston
West Morden
East Morden
East Bloxworth
Bloxworth
Whitefield
A31
A350
Combe Atmer
East End
Lambs Green
Corfe Mullen
Merley
Lytchett Matravers
Post Green
Lytchett Minster
A35
Sherford
Slepe
Wareham Forest
Organford
Holton Heath
Turlin Moor
Upton
Hamworthy
Trigon Hill
Cold Harbour
Sandford
Northport
Wareham
Binnegar
A352
Holmebridge
Stoborough
Ridge
Middlebere Heath
Furzebrook
Creech
East Creech
Grange
Steeple
Tyneham
Church Knowle
Corfe Castle
Kingston
Kimmeridge
Kimmeridge Bay
Worth Matravers
Harman's Cross
Langton Matravers
Acton
Dancing Ledge
ST. ALDHELM'S OR ST. ALBAN'S HEAD
ISLE OF PURBECK
Woolgarston
B3351
Studland
Studland Bay
The Foreland or Handfast Point
Ulwell
New Swanage
Swanage Bay
Swanage
Herston
Durlston
Durlston Bay
DURLSTON HEAD
Brownsea Island
Arne
Poole Harbour
POOLE
Parkstone
Sandbanks
Canford Cliffs
Compton Acres
POOLE BAY
Poole to:
Cherbourg 4hrs. 30mins.
Cherbourg 2hrs. 30mins.
(Fast Ferry, Seasonal)
Guernsey 2hrs. 30mins.
(Fast Ferry, Seasonal)
Jersey 3hrs.
(Fast Ferry, Seasonal)
St. Malo 4hrs. 30mins.
(Fast Ferry, Seasonal)
Branksome
Newtown
Oakdale
Creekmoor
Broadstone
Hillbourne
Waterloo
A3049
Wallisdown
Bearwood
Canford Magna
Little Canford
Hampreston
Longham
West Howe
Kinson
East Howe
Moordown
Winton
BOURNEMOUTH
SEE PAGE 186
Boscombe
Southbourne
Westbourne
Tuckton
Pokesdown
CHRISTCHURCH
Mudeford
Christchurch Bay
HENGISTBURY HEAD
Highcliffe
Barton on Sea
Milford on Sea
New Milton
Ashley
Hordle
Everton
Downton
Walkford
Hinton
Waterditch
Burton
Somerford
Jumpers Common
Winkton
Sopley
Bransgore
Neacroft
Bashley
Beckley
Wootton
Sway
North Bockhampton
Ripley
Avon
Thorney Hill
Bisterne
Sandford
Burley
Bisterne Close
Burley Street
Crow
Picket Post
A31
Poulner
Hangersley Hill
Linford
Rockford
Ringwood
Ashley Heath
Moortown
St. Ives
St. Leonards
Kingston
Tricket's Cross
Ferndown
A338
Parley Cross
West Parley
Hurn
BOURNEMOUTH (International)
Dudsbury
Ensbury
West Moors
Three Legged Cross
Holt
Holt Heath
Broom Hill
Pilford
Clapgate
Hinton Martell
Gaunt's Common
Chalbury
Chalbury Common
Horton
Mannington
Woodlands
Whitmore
Romford
Wigbeth
Crab Orchard
Verwood
Ebblake
Blashford
Ellingham
Moyles Court
Mockbeggar
Linwood
Ibsley
Harbridge
Bickton
Hungerford
North Gorley
South Gorley
HAMPSHIRE
NEW FOREST
Frogham
Blissford
Stuckton
Godshill
Fordingbridge
Ashford
Sandleheath
Alderholt
Daggons
Cripplestyle
Crendell
Cranborne
Edmondsham
Boveridge
Pentridge
Martin
Martin Down
Tidpit
Rockbourne
Rockbourne Roman Villa
Damerham
Whitsbury
Upper Street
Outwick
Lower Burgate
Upper Burgate
Breamore
Woodgreen
Hale
North Charford
Woodfalls
Redlynch
Lover
Hamptworth
Landford
Nomansland
Downton
Wick
Morgan's Vale
Newton
Whiteparish
Pepperbox Hill
Charlton
Fritham
Bramshaw
Brook
Upper Canterton
Stoney Cross
Minstead
Newtown
Emery Down
Bolderwood
Brockenhurst
South Weirs
A35
A36
A27
A338
B3078
B3081
B3072
B3073
B3074
B3347
B3058
B3055
B3068
B3065
B3369
B3070
B3069
A351
A348
A349
A341
A3040
A3060
E
F
G
H
15
16
23
1
2
3
4
5
ENGLISH CHANNEL

16
A
B
C
D
1
2
3
4
5
15
Whiteparish
Newton
Romsey
Ampfield
Chandler's Ford
North Baddesley
Otterbourne
Colden Common
Owslebury
Upham
Lower Upham
Bishopstoke
EASTLEIGH
Fair Oak
Durley
Bishop's Waltham
Swanmore
Droxford
Corhampton
Exton
Plaitford
Landford
Nomansland
West Wellow
East Wellow
Chilworth
Rownhams
Nursling
Bassett
Totton
Testwood
Cadnam
Copythorne
Winsor
Bartley
Netley Marsh
Woodlands
Minstead
Stoney Cross
SOUTHAMPTON
SEE PAGE 196
Marchwood
West End
Hedge End
Botley
Curdridge
Shedfield
Wickham
Waltham Chase
Shirrell Heath
Soberton
Soberton Heath
Newtown
Burridge
Swanwick
Bursledon
Lower Swanwick
Sarisbury
Park Gate
Locks Heath
Warsash
Titchfield
Stubbington
FAREHAM
Portchester
Bridgemary
Hill Head
Lee-on-the-Solent
GOSPORT
Stokes Bay
Gilkicker Point
NEW FOREST
Lyndhurst
Emery Down
Ashurst
Bank
Brockenhurst
Boldre
Pilley
Sway
Lymington
LYMINGTON
Beaulieu
Hythe
HYTHE
Dibden Purlieu
Fawley
Blackfield
Calshot
Netley
Hamble-le-Rice
Hardley
Holbury
Langley
Exbury
Lepe
East Boldre
Bucklers Hard
New Milton
Barton on Sea
Highcliffe
Milford on Sea
Keyhaven
Everton
Hordle
Ashley
Walhampton
THE SOLENT
Cowes Roads
COWES
East Cowes
Gurnard
Gurnard Bay
Thorness Bay
Osborne Bay
Whippingham
Wootton
Wootton Bridge
Fishbourne
Ryde Roads
RYDE
Binstead
Haylands
Havenstreet
Nettlestone
St. Helens
Brading
SANDOWN
Lake
SHANKLIN
Luccombe Village
DUNNOSE
Bonchurch
VENTNOR
St. Lawrence
Wroxall
Whitwell
Niton
Godshill
Rookley
Chillerton
Gatcombe
Arreton
NEWPORT
Carisbrooke
Northwood
Parkhurst
Shalfleet
Newtown
Yarmouth
Freshwater
Totland
Colwell Bay
Totland Bay
Alum Bay
THE NEEDLES
Compton Bay
Brook
Brighstone
Shorwell
Calbourne
Thorley Street
Wellow
Mottistone
Chale
Chale Bay
Atherfield Point
Brighstone Bay
ST. CATHERINE'S POINT
ISLE OF WIGHT
ENGLISH
Sconce Point
Needs Ore Point
Hurst
M27
M271
M3
A36
A31
A35
A33
A27
A326
A337
A3054
A3055
A3020
A3021
A3056
A3054
B3399
B3401
B3058
B3054
B3055
B3056
80
90
70
30
40
450
60

PETERSFIELD
MIDHURST
Petworth
17
Rogate
Trotton
Dumpford
Stedham
Easebourne
Lodsworth
Tillington
Byworth
Fittleworth
Stopham
Pulborough
West Meon
East Meon
Clanfield
Buriton
South Harting
Cocking
West Lavington
Graffham
Duncton
Sutton
Bignor
Hambledon
HORNDEAN
Cowplain
WATERLOOVILLE
Purbrook
HAVANT
Cosham
Emsworth
Westbourne
Southbourne
Hermitage
Nutbourne
Chidham
Bosham
Broadbridge
Fishbourne
CHICHESTER
Westhampnett
Tangmere
Boxgrove
Halnaker
East Lavant
Mid Lavant
West Dean
Singleton
Charlton
Chilgrove
Compton
East Marden
North Marden
Up Marden
West Marden
Forestside
Rowland's Castle
Stoughton
Walderton
Funtington
West Ashling
East Ashling
Hambrook
Woodmancote
Slindon
Fontwell
Walberton
Eastergate
Westergate
Woodgate
Barnham
Yapton
Ford
Arundel
LITTLEHAMPTON
Wick
Clymping
Middleton-on-Sea
Felpham
BOGNOR REGIS
Aldwick
Pagham
Nyetimber
North Mundham
Runcton
Merston
Hunston
Donnington
Apuldram
Birdham
West Itchenor
West Wittering
East Wittering
Bracklesham
Earnley
Almodington
Highleigh
Sidlesham
Church Norton
Selsey
SELSEY BILL
Thorney Island
West Thorney
North Hayling
SOUTH HAYLING
HAYLING ISLAND
Hayling Bay
PORTSEA ISLAND
PORTSMOUTH
SEE PAGE 195
Southsea
Eastney
Langstone
Farlington
Drayton
Bedhampton
Leigh Park
Denmead
Lovedean
Catherington
Southwick
Nab Tower
Bembridge
FORELAND
Whitecliff Bay
Culver Cliff
Seaview
SPITHEAD
S O U T H   D O W N S
W E S T   S U S S E X
C H A N N E L
Portsmouth to:
Bilbao 35hrs.
Caen 6hrs.
Caen 3hrs. 25mins.
(Fast Ferry, Seasonal)
Cherbourg 5hrs.
Cherbourg 2hrs. 45mins.
(Fast Ferry, Seasonal)
Guernsey 6hrs. 30mins.
Jersey 10hrs.
Le Havre 5hrs. 30mins.
(Fast Ferry)
St. Malo 9hrs.
(Seasonal)
A27
A272
A3(M)
M275
A259
A286
A285
A29
E
F
G
H
1
2
3
4
5

BRISTOL
LUNDY
North West Point
NT
Bird Observatory
Marisco
South West Point
Rat Island
Lundy to:
Bideford 1hr. 45mins.
Ilfracombe 1hr. 45mins.
(Seasonal)
BARNSTAPLE
OR
BIDEFORD BAY
HARTLAND POINT
Windbury Point
Titchberry
Hartland Quay
Hartland Abbey
Stoke
Hartland
Clovelly
Higher Clovelly
Velly
Natcott
Brownsham
Lifeboat, Fishermans Cottage & Kingsley
Buck's & Keivell's Woods
Buck's Mills
Buck's Cross
Milford
Elmscott
Edistone
Philham
Welsford
Bird of Prey Centre
Lynbarn Railway
A39
B3248
Woolfardisworthy or Woolsery
South Hole
Alminstone Cross
Parkham Ash
Knaps Longpeak
Welcombe
Mead
R. Torridge
Meddon
Ashmansworthy
Welcombe & Marsland Valleys
Gooseham
Woolley
East Youlstone
Morwenstow
Eastcott
West Youlstone
Dinworthy
West Putford
East Putford
Shop
Higher Sharpnose Point
CORNWALL
Bradworthy
Woodford
Lower Sharpnose Point
Coombe Valley
Coombe
Kilkhampton
Pixieland Funpark
Upper Tamar Lake
Alfardisworthy
Sutcombe
Thurdon
Lower Tamar Lake
Stibb
Soldon Cross
B3254
Dexbeer
A388
Holsworthy Beacon
Poughill
Bush
Bude Bay
Flexbury
Bude
Stratton
Hersham
Grimscott
Lana
Chilsworthy
Pancrasweek
Lynstone
Launcells
10

19
CHANNEL
E
F
G
H
1
2
3
4
5
Foreland Point
Woody Bay
Lynton
Lynmouth
Countisbury
Lynbridge
Brendon
Malmsmead
Tippacott
Doone Valley
Brendon Common
Trentishoe
Martinhoe
Heale
Barbrook
Cheriton
Dean
Martinhoe Cross
Furzehill
Shallowford
Churchtown
EXMOOR NATIONAL PARK
EXMOOR FOREST
Parracombe
Blackmoor Gate
Pinkworthy Pond
Challacombe
West Lyn
B3358
Simonsbath
Shoulsbarrow Common
Barton Town
Lewsborough
Exmoor Steam Railway
Lydcott
Brayford
High Bray
North Heasley
Heasley Mill
North Radworthy
South Radworthy
Charles
East Buckland
West Buckland
Stoodleigh
Accott
Gunn
Northleigh
Goodleigh
Landkey Newland
Landkey
Swimbridge Newland
Swimbridge
Hannaford
A361
Heddon
North Molton
South Molton
Castle Hill
Filleigh
Stag's Head
Chittlehampton
Cobbaton
East Stowford
Combat Collection
Hemer
Umberleigh
Eastacott
Warkleigh
Satterleigh
Clapworthy
George Nympton
Bish Mill
Bishop's Nympton
Mariansleigh
Alswear
Ash Mill
Romansleigh
Meshaw
King's Nympton
Chittlehamholt
High Bickington
Atherington
Langridgeford
Yarnscombe
Sherwood Green
High Bullen
St. Giles in the Wood
Roborough
Owlacombe Wood
Kingscott
Burrington
Elstone
Aylescott
Riddlecombe
Ashreigney
Chulmleigh
Cheldon
Chawleigh
East Worlington
West Worlington
Thelbridge Barton
Bridge Reeve
Eggesford
Eggesford Forest
Heywood Wood
East Ashley
Hollocombe
Wembworthy
Lapford
Coldridge
Nymet Rowland
Morchard Bishop
Eastington
Filleigh
Brushford
West Leigh
Oldborough
Weeke
Winkleigh
Iddesleigh
Ingleigh Green
Broadwoodkelly
Bondleigh
Monkokehampton
Meeth
Upcott
Dowland
Stears Copse
Dolton
Halsdon
Beaford
Merton
Little Potheridge
Great Potheridge
Winswell
Berry Cross
Peters Marland
Petrockstowe
North Town
Little Torrington
Taddiport
Great Torrington
Dartington Crystal
Rosemoor
Frithelstock
Frithelstock Stone
Priory
Southcott
Langtree
Stibb Cross
Tythecott
Thornehillhead
Haytown
Bulkworthy
Eastbridge
Abbots Bickington
Newton St. Petrock
Gratton
Caute
Milton Damerel
Shebbear
Buckland Filleigh
Folly Cross
Bradford
Thornbury
Cookbury
Cookbury Wick
Holemoor
Black
Sheepwash
R. Torridge
Weare Giffard
Huntshaw
Monkleigh
Saltrens
Littleham
Buckland Brewer
Landcross
Hallspill
Woodtown
Horns Cross
Fairy Cross
Ford
Goldworthy
Parkham
DEVON
BIDEFORD
Orchard Hill
Abbotsham
The Big Sheep
East-the-Water
Woodtown
Stony Cross
Alverdiscott
Hiscott
Harracott
Newton Tracey
Horwood
Holmacott
Eastleigh
Westleigh
Tapeley Park
Instow
Bickleton
Northam
Westward Ho!
Buckleigh
Appledore
Northam Burrows
Maritime
St. John's Chapel
Eastacombe
Tawstock
Bishop's Tawton
Week
Ensis
Chapelton
Church Gatehouse
Lake
Newport
BARNSTAPLE
Bickington
Fremington
Yelland
Isley Marshes
Brannam Pottery
Jungleland
Woodside
Bradiford
Ashford
Heanton Punchardon
Chivenor
Wrafton
Braunton
Braunton Burrows
DANGER AREA
Saunton
Croyde
Croyde Bay
Baggy Point
Putsborough
Georgeham
Darracott
Lobb
Pickwell
North Buckland
Nethercott
Knowle
Winsham
Halsinger
Middle Marwood
Milltown
Marwood
Guineaford
Marwood Hill
Pippacott
Prixford
Muddiford
Shirwell
Lower Loxhore
Loxhore
Stoke Rivers
Bratton Fleming
Knightacott
Arlington
Arlington Court
Kentisbury Ford
Beccott
Wistlandpound Res.
Exmoor Bird Gardens
Churchill
Clifton
East Down
Patchole
Kentisbury
Berry Down Cross
Bittadon
West Down
Cheglinch
Trimstone
Dean
Once Upon a Time
Chapel Wood
Woolacombe
Morte Bay
Mortehoe
Morte Point
Rockham Bay
Bull Point
Lee
Slade
Mullacott
House of Marbles
ILFRACOMBE
Hele
Watermouth Castle
Berrynarbor
Combe Martin Bay
Combe Martin
Motorcycle
Dean
Ilfracombe to Lundy 1hr. 45mins. (Seasonal)
Bideford to Lundy 1hr. 45mins.
A39
A399
A361
A3123
A377
A386
A388
A3124
B3230
B3231
B3233
B3232
B3227
B3226
B3217
B3220
B3343
B3236
B3229
B3234
B3223
B3137
B3042
B3096
A377
11
40
250
60
70

20
BRISTOL CHANNEL
Foreland Point
Lynmouth
Countisbury
Brendon
Malmsmead
Porlock Bay
Porlock Weir
Porlock
West Porlock
Oare
Oareford
Culbone Hill
Doone Valley
Barbrook
Tippacott
Cheriton
Furzehill
Brendon Common
Bossington
Lynch
Selworthy Beacon
Allerford
Selworthy
Woodcombe
North Hill
Higher Town
MINEHEAD
Brandish Street
Horner
Tivington
Luccombe
Stoke Pero
Cloutsham
Huntscott
Wootton Courtenay
Dunkery Beacon
Dunkery Hill
Burrow
Alcombe
Dunster
Marsh Street
Carhampton
Timberscombe
Withycombe
Blue Anchor
Blue Anchor Bay
Watchet
Doniford
Williton
Washford
Old Cleeve
Five Bells
EXMOOR FOREST
EXMOOR NATIONAL PARK
Pinkworthy Pond
Dure Down
Simonsbath
Edgcott
Exford
Newland
Luckwell Bridge
Cutcombe
Wheddon Cross
BRENDON HILLS
Luxborough
Kingsbridge
Croydon Hill
Rodhuish
Golsoncott
Roadwater
Treborough
Leighland Chapel
Chidgley
Monksilver
Stogumber
Sampford Brett
Capton
Yarde
Huish
Elworthy
Combe Sydenham
Withypool
Withypool Common
Winsford Hill
Winsford
Exton
Bridgetown
Week
Gupworthy
Brompton Regis
Withiel Florey
Clatworthy Reservoir
Brompton Ralph
Rooks Nest
Tolland
Clatworthy
North Heasley
Heasley Mill
North Radworthy
South Radworthy
Twitchen
Molland Common
Dane's Brook
Liscombe
Tarr Steps
Hawkridge
Caratacus Stone
Wimbleball Lake
Woolcotts
Haddon Hill
Upton
Huish Champflower
Langley Marsh
Langley
Wiveliscombe
North Molton
Molland
West Anstey
East Anstey
Dulverton
Battleton
Nightcott
Brushford
Lee
Yeo Mill
Oldways End
Exebridge
Bury
Skilgate
Morebath
Chipstable
Hartswell
Waterrow
Milverton
South Molton
Newtown
Cross Side
East Knowstone
Knowstone
Roachill
Ash Mill
Bishop's Nympton
Mariansleigh
Rose Ash
Alswear
Meshaw
Creacombe
Oakfordbridge
Oakford
Bampton
Shillingford
Petton
Clayhanger
Stawley
Kittisford
Kyrle
Appley
Ashbrittle
Thorne St. Margaret
Langford Budville
Runnington
Tonedale
Greenham
Huntsham
Staple Cross
Hockworthy
Stoodleigh Beacon
Stoodleigh
Cove
Ford Barton
Vennaw
Rackenford
DEVON
Holcombe Court
Holcombe Rogus
Fair Oak
Westleigh
Burlescombe
Sampford Arundel
Nicholashayne
Bradford Barton
Queen Dart
Mogworthy
North Coombe
Loxbeare
Washfield
Chevithorne
Uplowman
Whitnage
Ayshford
Week
Lutworthy
Witheridge
Nomansland
East Worlington
West Worlington
Drayford
Cheldon
Chawleigh
Thelbridge Barton
Templeton
Calverleigh
Withleigh
Bolham
Knightshayes Ct.
Chettiscombe
Cowley Moor
Halberton
Sampford Peverell
Appledore
Prescott
Whitehall
Uffculme
Culmstock
TIVERTON
Cotteylands
Manley
Ash Thomas
Craddock
Smithincott
Ashill
Washford Pyne
Pennymoor
Cruwys Morchard
Way Village
Filleigh
Eastington
Littleborough
Puddington
Black Dog
Poughill
East Butterleigh
Willand
Stenhill
Kentisbeare
Blackborough
Sheldon
Lapford
Brownstone
Woolfardisworthy
Upham
Cadeleigh
Bickleigh
Butterleigh
CULLOMPTON
Cullompton
Colebrook
Stoneyford
Saint Hill
Nymet Rowland
Morchard Bishop
Kennerleigh
Oldborough
Stockleigh English
Weeke
Ford Park Wood
East Village
Cheriton Fitzpaine
Cadbury Castle (Hill Fort)
Hayne
Dulford
Kerswell
Broadhembury
A39 A396 A361 A377 A373 A38 M5 B3223 B3224 B3190 B3191 B3227 B3222 B3137 B3042 B3181 B3440 B3391

22
34
21
14
A
B
C
D
1
2
3
4
5
BATH & N.E. SOMERSET
SOMERSET
MENDIP HILLS
BLACKMOOR VALE
BATH
Bradford-on-Avon
TROWBRIDGE
FROME
Wells
Glastonbury
Street
Shepton Mallet
Midsomer Norton
Radstock
Paulton
Wincanton
Sherborne
YEOVIL
Castle Cary
Bruton
Somerton
Ilchester
Mere
Chew Magna
Chew Stoke
Pensford
Keynsham
Blagdon
Bishop Sutton
Clutton
High Littleton
Timsbury
Farmborough
Peasedown St. John
Compton Martin
West Harptree
East Harptree
Litton
Chewton Mendip
Chilcompton
Stratton-on-the-Fosse
Holcombe
Coleford
Mells
Beckington
Buckland Dinham
Rode
Southwick
North Bradley
Dilton Marsh
Westbury-sub-Mendip
Wookey Hole
Wookey
Draycott
Rodney Stoke
Cheddar
Priddy
Croscombe
Gurney Slade
Binegar
Stoke St. Michael
Nunney
Corsley Heath
Horningsham
Maiden Bradley
Kingston Deverill
Witham Friary
Evercreech
Batcombe
Pilton
West Pennard
Baltonsbury
Butleigh
Barton St. David
Keinton Mandeville
Ansford
Pitcombe
Ditcheat
North Cadbury
Sparkford
Queen Camel
West Camel
Marston Magna
Charlton Horethorne
North Cheriton
Abbas Combe
Holton
Cucklington
Buckhorn Weston
Kington Magna
Gillingham
Milton on Stour
Bourton
Zeals
Stourton
East Stour
Stour Provost
Henstridge
Milborne Port
Marnhull
Stalbridge
Hinton St. Mary
Sturminster Newton
Child Okeford
Iwerne Minster
Shillingstone
Okeford Fitzpaine
Durweston
Kingsdon
Charlton Mackrell
Charlton Adam
Babcary
Long Sutton
Tintinhull
Chilthorne Domer
Stoke sub Hamdon
Montacute
Norton sub Hamdon
Odcombe
West Coker
East Coker
North Coker
Chiselborough
West Chinnock
East Chinnock
Haselbury Plucknett
Hardington Mandeville
North Perrott
South Perrott
Corscombe
Yetminster
Chetnole
Melbury Osmond
Leigh
Glanvilles Wootton
Bradford Abbas
Thornford
Nether Compton
Longburton
Bishop's Caundle
Rimpton
Corton Denham
Mudford
Trent
Stoford
Barwick
A4
A36
A37
A38
A39
A30
A303
A350
A357
A359
A361
A362
A363
A366
A367
A368
A371
A372
A3088
A3098

23
24
MELKSHAM
Bromham
St. Edith's Marsh
Roundway Hill Covert Countryside Trust
Bishops Cannings
Allington
Stanton St. Bernard
Pewsey Downs
White Horse
Huish
Oare
Wootton Rivers
Great Bedwyn
Durley
Bowerhill
Sells Green
Rowde
Dunkirk
Roundway
Horton
Alton Priors
West Stowell
New Mill
Ram Alley
Burbage
Crofton
Stibb Green
Semington
Seend Cleeve
DEVIZES
Coate
All Cannings
Alton Barnes
Honey Street
Wilcot
Pewsey
Milton Lilbourne
Easton Royal
Eastcourt
West Grafton
Grafton
Wilton
A361
A365
A342
A346
A338
A345
A350
A360
A303
A36
A30
A354
A3094
A31
A27
A343
A3028
A3026
B3098
B390
B3086
B3083
B3089
B3081
B3078
B3079
B3080
B3084
Poulshot
Stert
Nurstead
Beechingstoke
Woodborough
Sharcott
Southcott
Great Hinton
Hilperton
Ashton Common
Keevil
Bulkington
Potterne
Worton
Urchfont
Patney
Wedhampton
Marden
Chirton
Gores
Bottlesford
Hilcott
Manningford Bruce
Manningford Bohune
Wilsford
North Newton
Rushall
Charlton
Conock
Pewsey Down
Pewsey Hill
Easton Hill
White Horse
Tidcombe
Wexcombe
Steeple Ashton
Marston
Potterne Wick
Eastcott
Easterton
West Ashton
Dunge
Heywood
Edington
Bratton
East Coulston
Great Cheverell
Erlestoke
Little Cheverell
Littleton Pannell
Market Lavington
West Lavington
DANGER AREA
Upavon
Lower Everleigh
Everleigh
East Everleigh
Collingbourne Kingston
Aughton
Brunton
Sunton
Cadley
Collingbourne Ducis
Ludgershall
West Chisenbury
East Chisenbury
Compton
Enford
Littlecott
Longstreet
Compton Down
Black Heath
Littleton Down
Bratton Camp
White Horse
Westbury
W I L T S H I R E
Stradbrook
Haxton Down
Coombe
Fifield
Fittleton
Netheravon
North Tidworth
Tidworth
South Tidworth
Tidworth Camp
Shoddesden
Great Shoddesden
Little Shoddesden
Perham Down
Summer Down
Imber
West Lavington Down
West Down
Tilshead
Orcheston Down
Enford Down
Figheldean
Ablington
Brigmerston
Milston
Durrington
Bulford
Bulford Camp
Kimpton
Thruxton
Shipton Bellinger
Beacon Hill
S A L I S B U R Y
P L A I N
WARMINSTER
Weapons Museum
Dewey
Boreham
Norton Bavant
Heytesbury
Bishopstrow
Chitterne
White Barrow
Orcheston
Elston
Maddington
Shrewton
Knighton Down
Larkhill
Woodhenge
Stonehenge
Countess
Amesbury
West Amesbury
Rare Breeds Farm
Cholderton
Quarley
Grateley
Sutton Veny
Tytherington
Knook
Longbridge Deverill
Upton Lovell
Corton
Codford St. Peter
Codford St. Mary
Boyton
Sherrington
Fisherton de la Mere
Bapton
Stockton
Deptford
Wylye
Wylye Down
Hanging Langford
Steeple Langford
Berwick St. James
Winterbourne Stoke
Parsonage Down
Over Street
Stapleford
Wilsford
Lake
Great Durnford
Boscombe Down
Boscombe
Newton Toney
Allington
Palestine
Over Wallop
Idmiston
Porton
Great Ridge
Pertwood
Chicklade
Little Langford
Great Wishford
Stoford
South Newton
Upper Woodford
Middle Woodford
Lower Woodford
Heale
Netton
Salterton
Winterbourne Dauntsey
Winterbourne Gunner
Winterbourne Earls
Gomeldon
Lopcombe Corner
East Winterslow
Middle Winterslow
The Common
Firsdown
West Winterslow
Grovely Wood
Hindon
Berwick St. Leonard
Fonthill Bishop
Fonthill Gifford
Chilmark
Ridge
Teffont Magna
Teffont Evias
Dinton
Philipps House
Little Clarendon
Baverstock
Barford St. Martin
Chilhampton
Ditchampton
Ugford
Fugglestone St. Peter
Stratford sub Castle
Old Sarum
Hurdcott
Ford
Bishopdown
Laverstock
SALISBURY
SEE PAGE 195
Petersfinger
Pitton
Farley
West Tytherley
Tisbury
Lower Chicksgrove
Upper Chicksgrove
Place Tithe Barn
Compton Chamberlayne
Burcombe
Wilton
Quidhampton
Bemerton
Wilton House
Netherhampton
West Harnham
East Harnham
Britford
Farley Hospital
East Grimstead
West Dean
Newtown
East Hatch
Pythouse
Sutton Mandeville
Fovant
Regimental Badges (Chalk)
Chiselbury Hill Fort
Swallowcliffe
Ansty
Wardour Castle
Old Wardour Castle
Semley
St. Bartholomew's Hill
Donhead St. Andrew
Donhead St. Mary
Shaftesbury
Regimental Badges
Fifield Bavant
Broad Chalke
Bishopstone
Stoke Farthing
Croucheston
Stratford Tony
Coombe Bissett
Homington
Odstock
Nunton
Iron Age Farm
Alderbury
Bodenham
Whaddon
West Grimstead
Dean Hill
East Dean
Pepperbox Hill
Whiteparish
Odstock Down
Clearbury Ring
Charlton
Newton
Milkwell
White Sheet Hill
Alvediston
West End
Ebbesbourne Wake
Bowerchalke
Woodminton
Ludwell
Charlton
Berwick St. John
Winklebury Camp Hill Fort
Cann Common
Melbury Abbas
Win Green
Rockbourne Down
Wick Down
Downton
Wick
Morgan's Vale
Newhouse
Redlynch
Hamptworth
Woodfalls
Martin Drove End
Martin Down
Martin
Woodyates
Tidpit
Whitsbury
Breamore House
Countryside Museum
Upper Street
North Charford
Hale
Hamptworth Lodge
Lover
Landford
Plaitford
Nomansland
Compton Abbas
Ashmore
Fontmell Down
Fontmell Magna
CHASE
CRANBOURNE
Tollard Royal
Larmer Tree
Tollard Farnham
New Town
Deanland
Sixpenny Handley
Woodcutts
Pentridge
Pentridge Hill
Rockbourne
Outwick
Breamore
Woodgreen
Well Bottom
Farnham
Dean
Gussage St. Andrew
Minchington
Monkton Up Wimborne
Boveridge
Damerham
Rockbourne Roman Villa
Lower Burgate
Upper Burgate
Sandleheath
Fordingbridge
Godshill
N E W
F O R E S T
Fritham
Furzley
Bramshaw
Newbridge
Brook
Stubhampton
Chettle
Chettle House
Tarrant Gunville
Tarrant Hinton
Cashmoor
Gussage St. Michael
Gussage All Saints
Wimborne St. Giles
Cranborne
Cranborne Manor
Crendell
Cripplestyle
Alderholt Mill
Ashford
Alderholt
Daggons
Bickton
Stuckton
Blissford
Frogham
Hungerford
North Gorley
NEW FOREST
HAMPSHIRE
Rufus Stone
Upper Canterton
Stoney Cross
Minstead
Newtown
Furzey Gardens
Edmondsham
Dorset Heavy Horse Centre
Harbridge
South Gorley
Linwood
Canadian Monument
Ibsley
Moyles Court
Mockbeggar
Deer Fields
Bolderwood Arboretum
Emery Down
Pikeshill
Fireplace Reptiliary
Pimperne
Tarrant Launceston
Long Crichel
Sovell Down
Knowlton Circles & Church
Woodlands
Whitmore
Verwood
Ringwood Forest
Ebblake
Ellingham
Rockford
Hangersley Hill
Linford
Bolderwood Ornamental Drive
Knightwood Oak
Bank
Rhinefield Ornamental Drive
Royal Signals Museum
Blandford Camp
Blandford Forum
Tarrant Monkton
Manswood
Moor Crichel
Hogstock
Witchampton
Tarrant Rawston
Langton Long Blandford
Tarrant Rushton
Hemsworth
Hinton Martell
Horton
Chalbury
Chalbury Common
Gaunt's Common
Wigbeth
Crab Orchard
Mannington
Moors Valley
Three Legged Cross
Ringwood
Blashford
Poulner
Picket Post
Claylake

24
WILTSHIRE
HAMPSHIRE
NEW FOREST
Great Bedwyn
Shalbourne
Burbage
East Grafton
Wilton
Marten
Oxenwood
Tidcombe
Fosbury
Linkenholt
Faccombe
Ashmansworth
Highclere
Burghclere
Kingsclere
Newtown
Woolton Hill
Tadley
Baughurst
Hannington
Monk Sherborne
Wootton St. Lawrence
BASINGSTOKE
Oakley
Overton
Whitchurch
Laverstoke
North Waltham
Dummer
Popham
Preston Candover
Litchfield
Collingbourne Ducis
Collingbourne Kingston
Ludgershall
Tidworth
North Tidworth
South Tidworth
Vernham Dean
Upper Chute
Hurstbourne Tarrant
St. Mary Bourne
Hurstbourne Priors
Enham-Alamein
Penton Mewsey
Appleshaw
Fyfield
Thruxton
Monxton
Shipton Bellinger
ANDOVER
Middleton
Longparish
Abbots Ann
Upper Clatford
Goodworth Clatford
Wherwell
Chilbolton
Barton Stacey
Sutton Scotney
South Wonston
Micheldever
Over Wallop
Nether Wallop
Middle Wallop
Longstock
Stockbridge
Crawley
Kings Worthy
Headbourne Worthy
Itchen Abbas
New Alresford
Bishops Sutton
Old Alresford
Littleton
Sparsholt
Up Somborne
King's Somborne
Houghton
Broughton
West Tytherley
Lockerley
Mottisfont
Michelmersh
Braishfield
Hursley
WINCHESTER
SEE PAGE 197
Oliver's Battery
Twyford
Owslebury
Cheriton
Tichborne
Romsey
Ampfield
Chandler's Ford
North Baddesley
Otterbourne
Colden Common
Upham
Lower Upham
Corhampton
Bishop's Waltham
Droxford
Swanmore
Waltham Chase
Shirrell Heath
EASTLEIGH
Fair Oak
Durley
Horton Heath
West End
Hedge End
Botley
Curdridge
Wickham
TOTTON
SOUTHAMPTON
SEE PAGE 196
Marchwood
HYTHE
Netley
Hamble-le-Rice
Bursledon
Swanwick
Park Gate
Locks Heath
Titchfield
FAREHAM
Whiteparish
Landford
Nomansland
Plaitford
West Wellow
Copythorne
Cadnam
Minstead
Lyndhurst
Ashurst
Woodlands
Netley Marsh
Emery Down
Rownhams
M3
M27
M271
A34
A303
A338
A36
A31
A30
A33
A27
A343
A35

25
SEE PAGE 189
NORTH DOWNS
SURREY
WEST SUSSEX
SOUTH DOWNS
Crowthorne
Bagshot
Windlesham
Addlestone
Ottershaw
Sandhurst
CAMBERLEY
Yateley
Frimley
WOKING
Blackwater
Farnborough
FARNBOROUGH
Fleet
Hook
Old Basing
Hartley Wintney
ALDERSHOT
Ash
Tongham
GUILDFORD
Shalford
Chilworth
Compton
Godalming
GODALMING
Milford
Witley
FARNHAM
Crondall
Long Sutton
Upton Grey
Cliddesden
Bentworth
Alton
Chawton
Medstead
Four Marks
Ropley
East Worldham
Kingsley
Selborne
Bordon
Lindford
Headley
Grayshott
Hindhead
Haslemere
Liphook
Liss
Greatham
Petersfield
PETERSFIELD
Steep
Sheet
Rogate
Midhurst
MIDHURST
Fernhurst
Chiddingfold
Dunsfold
Plaistow
Kirdford
Petworth
Fittleworth
Duncton
Sutton
Bury
Houghton
Arundel
Fontwell
Slindon
Boxgrove
Westhampnett
Tangmere
CHICHESTER
West Dean
Singleton
Chilgrove
Horndean
Cowplain
Waterlooville
Havant
HAVANT
Emsworth
Southbourne
Hermitage
Westbourne
Rowland's Castle
Buriton
East Meon
Clanfield
Hambledon
Purbrook
Cosham
A3
A3(M)
A31
A27
A272
A286
A283
A29
A33
A339
A325
A287
A331
A323
A320
A322
A324
A3100
B3004
B3006
B2070
B2146
B2141
M3

CATERHAM
SEVENOAKS
Westerham
Oxted
Limpsfield
Godstone
REDHILL
Bletchingley
Nutfield
M23
South Nutfield
South Godstone
Crockham Hill
Sevenoaks Weald
Hildenborough
TONBRIDGE
Tandridge
Edenbridge
Four Elms
Marlpit Hill
Chiddingstone
Hever
Penshurst
Bidborough
Southborough
Paddock
Pembury
Matfield
Golden Green
East Peckham
Hadlow
Five Oak Green
HORLEY
Outwood
Smallfield
Burstow
Copthorne
Felbridge
Lingfield
Dormansland
Dormans Park
Blindley Heath
Felcourt
Markbeech
Speldhurst
Langton Green
Rusthall
Fordcombe
KENT
EAST GRINSTEAD
ROYAL TUNBRIDGE WELLS
Crawley Down
Turners Hill
Ashurstwood
Forest Row
Hartfield
Groombridge
Frant
Lamberhurst
Wadhurst
Durgates
Cousley Wood
Sparrow's Green
Ticehurst
CROWBOROUGH
Poundfield
Rotherfield
Mark Cross
Town Row
Mayfield
Stonegate
HIGH WEALD
ASHDOWN FOREST
Wych Cross
Coleman's Hatch
Chuck Hatch
Sharpthorne
West Hoathly
Balcombe
Ardingly
HAYWARDS HEATH
Horsted Keynes
Danehill
Chelwood Gate
Chelwood Common
Nutley
Heron's Ghyll
Fairwarp
Cuckfield
Lindfield
Whitemans Green
Five Ash Down
Maresfield
Buxted
Uckfield
Hadlow Down
Heathfield
Broad Oak
Punnett's Town
Burwash
Burwash Weald
Fletching
Piltdown
Newick
Scayne's Hill
North Chailey
Framfield
Blackboys
Cross in Hand
Ridgewood
BURGESS HILL
Wivelsfield
Wivelsfield Green
Hurstpierpoint
Hassocks
Keymer
Ditchling
Plumpton Green
Plumpton
Westmeston
Isfield
Barcombe Cross
Halland
East Hoathly
Horam
Chiddingly
Laughton
Ringmer
Broyle Side
Herstmonceux
Windmill Hill
Lower Dicker
Upper Dicker
HAILSHAM
Magham Down
Hellingly
Ripe
Chalvington
Glynde
Glyndebourne
LEWES
Falmer
Kingston near Lewes
Woodingdean
Iford
Rodmell
Beddingham
West Firle
Selmeston
Arlington
Wilmington
Polegate
Folkington
Wannock
Willingdon
Alfriston
Stone Cross
Westham
Pevensey
Pevensey Bay
Hankham
BRIGHTON
Rottingdean
Saltdean
Ovingdean
Telscombe
Telscombe Cliffs
Peacehaven
NEWHAVEN
South Heighton
Denton
Bishopstone
SEAFORD
East Dean
Friston
Exceat
Westdean
Litlington
Jevington
Ratton Village
EASTBOURNE
BEACHY HEAD
Birling Gap
Langney Point
SOUTH DOWNS
EAST SUSSEX
CHANNEL
Newhaven to: Dieppe 4hrs. Dieppe 2hrs. (Fast Ferry, Seasonal)
SEE PAGE 186
SEE PAGE 188
A21
A22
A23
A26
A27
A228
A259
A264
A267
A272
A275
M23
27
28

Mereworth
Wateringbury
Barming Heath
East Barming
Teston
West Farleigh
East Farleigh
Loose
Nettlestead
Nettlestead Green
West Peckham
A228
28
Peckham Bush
Hadlow
Hadlow Castle
Hale Street
Barnes Street
East Peckham
Hop Farm
Yalding
Laddingford
Beltring
Benover
Coxheath
Linton
Boughton Monchelsea
Boughton Green
Chart Sutton
Chart Corner
Langley
Bearsted
Thurnham
Otham
Leeds
Leeds Castle
Broomfield
Dog Collar
Kingswood
40
Sutton Valence
Ulcombe
Harrietsham
Lenham
Lenham Heath
M20
Platt's Heath
Fairbourne Heath
Grafty Green
Boughton Malherbe
Leadingcross Green
Sandway
NORTH
Warren Street
Stalisfield Green
Throwley Forstal
Leaveland
Badlesmere
Charing
Charing Heath
Charing Hill
Stocker's Head
Challock
Westwell
Westwell Leacon
Egerton
Egerton Forstal
Southernden
Pluckley
Little Chart
Ram Lane
Hothfield
Godinton House
ASHFORD
Great Chart
Boughton Lees
Goat Lees
Bybrook
Willesborough
Sevington
Singleton
Chilmington Green
Kingsnorth
Stubb's Cross
Shadoxhurst
Bromley Green
A2070
Orlestone
Hamstreet
Golden Green
TONBRIDGE
Tudeley
Five Oak Green
Whetsted
Queen Street
Collier Street
Paddock Wood
Colt's Hill
Matfield
Pembury
Brenchley
Castle Hill
Horsmonden
Marden
Marden Beech
Marden Thorn
Claygate
Chainhurst
Milebush
Wanshurst Green
Cross-at-Hand
Hawkenbury
Staplehurst
Brattle Farm
LOW WEALD
Headcorn
Smarden Bell
Smarden
Sinkhurst Green
Frittenden
Lashenden
Biddenden Green
Maltman's Hill
Haffenden Quarter
Wissenden
Bethersden
Daniel's Water
Brissenden Green
Standen
Hareplain
Three Chimneys
Biddenden
Curtisden Green
Winchet Hill
Kipping's Cross
Lamberhurst Quarter
Hazel Street
ROYAL TUNBRIDGE WELLS
Goudhurst
Flishinghurst
Cranbrook Common
Sissinghurst
Iden Green
Glassenbury
Wilsley Green
Goddard's Green
Cranbrook
Hemsted Forest
East End
Durrant Green
High Halden
Shirkoak
Woodchurch
South of England Rare Breeds Farm
St. Michaels
Tenterden
Bells Yew Green
Hook Green
Lamberhurst
Bayham Abbey
Scotney Castle
Kilndown
Riseden
Bedgebury Forest
Bedgebury National Pinetum
Hartley
WEALD
Benenden
Goddard's Green
Strood
Rolvenden
Rolvenden Layne
Brook Street
Leigh Green
Reading Street
Kenardington
Warehorne
Appledore
Appledore Heath
Snave
HIGH
Wood's Green
Cousley Wood
Sparrow's Green
Wadhurst
Durgates
Bewl Water
Three Leg Cross
Union Street
Flimwell
Hawkhurst
Gill's Green
Iden Green
Gun Green
Standen Street
Dingleden
Great Maytham Hall
Small Hythe
Smallhythe Place
Peening Quarter
Isle of Oxney
Wittersham
Stone in Oxney
Snargate
Brenzett
Ticehurst
Wallcrouch
Stonegate
Tidebrook
Horns Corner
The Moor
Four Throws
Sandhurst
Sandhurst Cross
Swiftsden
Hurst Green
Newenden
Kent & East Sussex Railway
Moon's Green
The Stocks
Stock Rother
Fairfield
Brookland
Etchingham
Witherenden Hill
Bodiam
Bodiam Castle
Great Dixter
Northiam
A268
Beckley
Four Oaks
Peasmarsh
Rye Foreign
Iden
Houghton Green
Playden
WALLAND MARSH
East Guldeford
Burwash
Bateman's
Burwash Common
Burwash Weald
Salehurst
Robertsbridge
Ewhurst Green
Mill Corner
Staplecross
Clayhill
Flatropers Wood
Broad Oak
Punnett's Town
Three Cups Corner
Brightling
Oxley's Green
Hollingrove
John's Cross
Vinehall Street
Cripp's Corner
Chitcombe
Broad Oak
Udimore
Rye
Camber
Jury's Gap
Dallington
Rushlake Green
Mountfield
Netherfield
Darwell Resr
Powdermill Resr
Brede
Winchelsea
Icklesham
Rye Harbour
Rye Bay
Winchelsea Beach
Canada
Whatlington
Sedlescombe
Penhurst
Pont's Green
Brownbread Street
Battle
Kent Street
Westfield
Three Oaks
Guestling Thorn
Pett
Guestling Green
Cliff End
Fairlight
Fairlight Cove
Bodle Street Green
Cowbeech
Herstmonceux
Windmill Hill
Ninfield
Catsfield
Henley's Down
Crowhurst
Telham
Baldslow
Hollington
St. Helen's
Ore
Boreham Street
Lunsford's Cross
Hooe Common
Hooe
Little Common
Sidley
Bulverhythe
HASTINGS
St. Leonards
Cooden
BEXHILL
Norman's Bay
Pevensey
Pevensey Bay
Westham
Langney
Langney Point
EASTBOURNE
SEE PAGE 188
Pevensey Levels
A259
A27
A21
A22
ENGLISH
A
B
C
D
1
2
3
4
5
70
80
90
600
BEACHY HEAD

29
E
F
G
H
1
2
3
4
5
Shottenden
Bagham
Shalmsford Street
Chartham
Nackington
Patrixbourne
Bridge
A2
Adisham
Goodnestone
Eastry
Ham
Sandown
The Small Downs
Chilham
Chilham Castle
Park Wood
Watermill
Lower Hardres
Bishopsbourne
Aylesham
Nonington
Chillenden
Heronden
Knowlton
Finglesham
Betteshanger
Northbourne
Northbourne Ct.
Sholden
Local History
Victoriana
Time-Ball Twr.
DEAL
Deal
The Downs
Molash
Godmersham
Chainge Green
Denge Wood
Petham
B2068
Kingston
B2046
Frogham
Tilmanstone
A256
Great Mongeham
Ripple
Walmer
Wye (Crundale Downs)
Earley Wood
41
Womenswold
Elvington
Barfrestone
East Kent Light Rly.
Eythorne
East Studdal
Sutton
Bilting
Crundale
Boughton Aluph
Sole Street
Waltham
Yockletts Bank
Bossingham
Derringstone
Woolage Green
Shepherdswell or Sibertswold
Coldred
Ashley
Ringwould
Kingsdown
DANGER AREA
A28
Wye Crown Memorial
Hassell Street
North Leigh
Stelling Minnis
Elham Valley Vineyard
Denton
West Langdon
Martin
Martin Mill
Wye
Great Stour
Bodsham Green
Park Gate Down
Wingmore
Wootton
Lydden
East Langdon
A258
Dover Patrol Monument
St.Margaret's at Cliffe
Hastingleigh
Parsonage Farm
Whitfield
Guston
Kennington
Brook
Agricultural
Elmsted
West Wood
Elham
Selsted
St. John's Commandery
Temple Ewell
Kearsney
A2
West Cliffe
The Bay
St. Margaret's Bay
The Pines
SOUTH FORELAND
Willesborough Lees
West Brabourne
Lymbridge Green
Rhodes Minnis
Swingfield Minnis
Acrise
Butterfly Centre
Swingfield Street
Ewell Minnis
River
Crabble Corn Mill
Buckland
Hinxhill
Stowting
Ottinge
Alkham
St. Radigund's Abbey
SEE PAGE 188
DOVER
Mersham-le-Hatch
Brabourne Lees
Brabourne
Broad Street
Lyminge
Densole
Drellingore
Maxton
B2011
Smeeth
Paddlesworth
Hawkinge
West Hougham
Church Hougham
Mersham
The Forstal
A20
Stone Hill
Priory
Postling Farm Trails
Etchinghill
CHANNEL TUNNEL
Battle of Britain
Capel-le-Ferne
Western Docks
A20
Dover to:
Boulogne 50mins. (Fast Ferry)
Calais 1hr. 10mins.
Calais 1hr. (Fast Ferry)
Dunkirk 2hrs.
Cheeseman's Green
Sellindge
Postling
Elham Rly
Stanford
Newington
Samphire Hoe
CHANNEL TUNNEL
Folkestone to
Calais 35mins.
M20
Clap Hill
Evegate Farm
Aldington
Westenhanger
Pedlinge
Saltwood Castle
Cheriton
East Wear Bay
Martello Towers
Bonnington
Folkestone
B2067
Lympne
A261
Saltwood
Court-at-Street
Port Lympne
West Hythe
Seabrook
Sandgate
Castle
FOLKESTONE
SEE PAGE 189
Bilsington
Monument
Ruckinge
Royal Military Canal
Towers
HYTHE
Palmarsh
DANGER AREA
Martello Tower
Lathe Barn
Burmarsh
Newchurch
A259
Martello Tower
STRAIT OF DOVER
ROMNEY MARSH
No. 24
Dymchurch
St. Mary in the Marsh
Martello Towers
Ivychurch
St. Mary's Bay
Romney, Hythe & Dymchurch Railway
Old Romney
Littlestone-on-Sea
Toy & Model
New Romney
B2071
Town Hall
East Road
Greatstone-on-Sea
Dunrobin Stud
B2075
Lydd
LYDD (LONDON ASHFORD)
Denge Marsh
Lydd-on-Sea
Dungeness Nuclear Power Station
Dungeness
Old Dungeness
DUNGENESS
CHANNEL

30
43
A
B
C
D
1
2
3
4
5
PEMBROKESHIRE
CARMARTHEN BAY
BRISTOL
CARMARTHEN
(Caerfyrddin)
Llanycefn
Llandissilio
Login
Cwm-miles
Crosshands
Llanboidy
Gellywen
Meidrim
Abernant
Bwlchnewydd
Newchurch
Bronwydd Arms
Merthyr
Tre-vaughan
Penfford
Hiraeth
Henllan Amgoed
Llanfallteg
Llanfallteg West
Cwmfelin Boeth
Llangynin
Caerlleon
Esgair
Drefach
Dyffryn
Clunderwen
Gelli
Bethesda
Llanddewi Velfrey
Whitland
Pwlltrap
St. Clears
Bancyfelin
Llangynog
Llangain
Llanllwch
Johnstown
Pensarn
Llangunnor
Cwmffrwd
Robeston Wathen
Narberth
(Arberth)
Trevaughan
Llwyn-y-brain
Llanddowror
Backe
Robeston Back
Narberth Bridge
Crinow
Lampeter Velfrey
Llan-mill
Princes Gate
Cold Blow
Tavernspite
Red Roses
Halfpenny Furze
Llanybri
Llansteffan
Morfa Bach
Idole
Bancycapel
Pontantwn
Llandyfaelog
Templeton
Ludchurch
Llanteg
Llandawke
Laugharne
Broadway
Ferryside
Canaston Woods
Reynalton
Thomas Chapel
Lovesto
Begelly
Jeffreyston
Cresselly
Kilgetty
(Cilgeti)
Stepaside
Colby
Summerhill
Sardis
Amroth
Marros
Pendine
(Pentywyn)
Llansadurnen
Brook
Llanmiloe
DANGER AREA
Ginst Point
St. Ishmael
Broadlay
Llansaint
Kidwelly
(Cydweli)
Llangadog
Mynyddygarreg
Pontyates
(Pont-iets)
Four Roads
Meinciau
Broadmoor
Pentlepoir
Saundersfoot
East Williamston
Redberth
Broadfield
Monkstone Point
New Hedges
Tenby
(Dinbych-y-Pysgod)
Gumfreston
St. Florence
Penally
(Penalun)
Tudor Merchant's House NT
Giltar Point
Caldey Sound
Lydstep
Manorbier
St. Margaret's Island
Caldey Island
Chapel Point
Old Castle Head
Pembrey Forest
Pembrey
Pinged
Trimsaran
Waun-y-Clyn
Cwm Capel
Graig
Carway
Whiteford Point
Whiteford
Llanmadoc
Cheriton
Burry Holms
Llangennith
Hillend
Rhossili Bay
Burry Green
Llanddewi
Rhossili
Middleton
Pitton
Pitton Green
WORMS HEAD
(Penrhyn-gwyr)
Mewslade Bay
Overton
The Salt House
A40
A477
A478
A48
A4066
B4313
B4314
B4315
B4316
B4318
B4328
B4298
B4299
B4312
B4308
B4317
B4585
B4586
B4247
A4118
A4139
A4115
A484
A485
B4300
B4306
B4309
90
80
70
10
20
30
40

31
32
BLACK MOUNTAIN
POWYS
FFOREST FAWR
BRECON BEACONS NATIONAL PARK
CARMARTHENSHIRE
NEATH
PORT TALBOT
AFAN FOREST PARK
SWANSEA
GOWER
Swansea Bay
(Bae Abertawe)
Swansea to Cork 10hrs.
CHANNEL
Llandeilo
Ammanford
(Rhydaman)
Glanaman
Garnant
Gwaun-Cae Gurwen
Brynamman
Upper Brynamman
Lower Brynamman
Cwmllynfell
Ystradgynlais
Abercraf
Coelbren
Seven Sisters
(Blaendulais)
Glyn-neath
Ystalyfera
Godre'r-graig
Cilmaengwyn
Pontardawe
Trebanos
Clydach
Pontardulais
Llanelli
Gorseinon
Penllergaer
Llangyfelach
Morriston
Skewen
Neath
(Castell-nedd)
Tonna
(Tonnau)
Briton Ferry
(Llansawel)
Baglan
Cwmafan
Aberavon
(Aberafan)
Port Talbot
Margam
Maesteg
Nantyffyllon
Pyle
North Cornelly
Porthcawl
Swansea
(Abertawe)
SEE PAGE 197
Swansea West
Mumbles Head
The Mumbles
(Mwmbwls)
Pwlldu Head
Oystermouth
Bishopston
Southgate
Port-Eynon Point
Kenfig Pool & Dunes
Sker Point
Tusker Rock
Pont Abraham
M4
A40
A48
A483
A465
A4138
A474
A4067
A4109
A4107
E
F
G
H
1
2
3
4
5
250
60
70
80

32
46
20
31
POWYS
NEATH
PORT TALBOT
AFAN FOREST PARK
RHONDDA
CYNON
TAFF
MERTHYR TYDFIL
THE VALE OF GLAMORGAN
BRISTOL CHAN
Lower Brynamman
Cwmllynfell
Abercraf
Ystradgynlais
Ystalyfera
Coelbren
Onllwyn
Seven Sisters (Blaendulais)
Glyn-neath
Penderyn
Hirwaun
Pontneddfechan
Crynant
Resolven
Clyne
Blaengwrach
Cwmgwrach
Glyncorrwg
Rhos
Cilfrew
Tonna (Tonnau)
NEATH (Castell-nedd)
Cimla
Briton Ferry (Llansawel)
Baglan
Cwmafan
Aberavon (Aberafan)
PORT TALBOT
Margam
Goytre
Taibach
Pyle
Kenfig Hill
Cefn Cribwr
North Cornelly
Kenfig
South Cornelly
Sker Point
Nottage
PORTHCAWL
Newton
Tusker Rock
Ogmore-by-Sea
Southerndown
Merthyr Mawr
Tythegston
Laleston (Trelales)
Newcastle
BRIDGEND (Pen-y-Bont Ar Ogwr)
Pen-y-fai
Sarn
SARN PARK
Tondu
Aberkenfig
Coytrahen
Bryncethin
Heol-y-Cyw
Pencoed
Coity
Brackla
Coychurch
Ewenny
Ogmore
St. Bride's Major
Wick
Broughton
Monknash
Marcross
St. Donat's (Sain Dunwyd)
Nash Point
Llantwit Major (Llanilltud Fawr)
Boverton
St. Athan (Sain Tathan)
Gileston
West Aberthaw
East Aberthaw
Fonmon
Rhoose (Y Rhws)
Breaksea Point
Penmark
Llancarfan
Llanblethian (Llanfleiddan)
Cowbridge (Y Bont-Faen)
Colwinston (Tregolwyn)
Llandow (Llandw)
Llysworney
St. Hilary (Sain Hilari)
Bonvilston (Tresimwn)
Peterston-super-Ely
St. Nicholas
Wenvoe
Dyffryn
St. Fagans
Creigiau
Pentyrch
CARDIFF WEST
Radyr
Llantrisant
Talbot Green
Pontyclun
Miskin
Llanharry
Llanharan
Brynna
Beddau
Church Village
Llantwit Fardre
Efail Isaf
Pontypridd
Treforest
Tonyrefail
Porth
Ynyshir
Ynysybwl
Abercynon
Tonypandy
Penygraig
Llwynypia
Ystrad
Pentre
Treorchy
Treherbert
Tynewydd
Blaenrhondda
Ferndale
Maerdy
Mountain Ash (Aberpennar)
Aberaman
Cwmaman
ABERDARE (Aberdâr)
Llwydcoed
Cefn-coed-y-cymmer
Merthyr Vale
Aberfan
Treharris
Troedyrhiw
Bedlinog
Dowlais
Rhymney (Rhymni)
Pontlottyn
Maesteg
Caerau
Nantyffyllon
Blaengarw
Pontycymer
Nant-y-moel
Ogmore Vale
Price Town
Llangeinor
Blackmill
Bettws
Cymmer
Croeserw
Abergwynfi
Blaengwynfi
Cynonville
Cwmfelin
Llangynwyd
Garth
M4
A465
A470
A4060
A4232
A48
A473
A4119
A4061
A4063
A4107
A4093
Bristol Channel
Margam Park
Kenfig Pool & Dunes
Dunraven Park
Heritage Coast
St. Donat's Castle
St. Donat's Art Centre
Old Beaupre Castle
Welsh Hawking Centre
Lliswerry
Lluest-wen Resrvoir
80
90
300
10
70
60
A
B
C
D
1
2
3
4
5

MONMOUTH
(Trefynwy)
MONMOUTHSHIRE
BLAENAU
GWENT
TORFAEN
EBBW VALE
(Glyn Ebwy)
Beaufort
Bryn-mawr
Nantyglo
Blaenavon
Blaina
Abersychan
ABERTILLERY
(Abertyleri)
New Tredegar
Bargoed
Oakdale
Blackwood
(Coed Duon)
Crumlin
Newbridge
(Cefn Bychan)
CWMBRAN
PONTYPOOL
(Pontypwl)
Usk
(Brynbuga)
Raglan
Llangovan
Trellech
Tintern Parva
Devauden
St. Arvans
Chepstow
Llantrisant
Llangybi
Caerleon
Shirenewton
Llanvaches
Caerwent
Caldicot
Portskewett
Rogiet
Magor
(Magwyr)
Undy
Bishton
Llanmartin
NEWPORT
(Casnewydd)
Risca
Malpas
Bettws
Rogerstone
Bassaleg
Machen
Bedwas
CAERPHILLY
(Caerffili)
Abercarn
Crosskeys
Cwmfelinfach
Hengoed
Tongwynlais
Marshfield
St. Mellons
Rumney
Castleton
CARDIFF
(Caerdydd)
Penarth
Dinas Powys
BARRY
(Barri)
Sully
Lavernock Point
Sully Island
Flat Holm
Steep Holm
SEVERN
THE
MOUTH
OF
Portland Grounds
Portishead Point
Portishead
Avonmouth
Easton-in-Gordano
Portbury
CLEVEDON
Nailsea
Backwell
NORTH
SOMERSET
Yatton
Congresbury
Wrington
Lower Langford
Kingston Seymour
Sand Point
Sand Bay
Kewstoke
St. George's
WESTON-SUPER-MARE
Weston Bay
Banwell
Sandford
Churchill
Winscombe
Shipham
Blagdon
Bleadon
Uphill
Brean
Christon
Loxton
SEE PAGE 194
SEE PAGE 187
M4
M48
M5
A40
A449
A4042
A48
A470
A465
A370
A371
A368
A38
A403
33
34
47
E
F
G
H
N
E
L

34
MONMOUTH
(Trefynwy)
FOREST OF DEAN
Coleford
Staunton
Berry Hill
Cinderford
Littledean
Ruspidge
Soudley
Yorkley
Parkend
Bream
Lydney
Aylburton
Alvington
Blakeney
Awre
Newnham
Arlingham
Frampton on Severn
Saul
Whitminster
Hardwicke
Quedgeley
Brookthorpe
Harescombe
Whiteshill
Randwick
Stonehouse
STROUD
Brimscombe
Woodchester
Nailsworth
Horsley
Kingscote
Eastington
King's Stanley
Leonard Stanley
Cam
Dursley
Uley
Berkeley
Sharpness
Purton
Slimbridge
Cambridge
Stinchcombe
North Nibley
Wotton-under-Edge
Charfield
Kingswood
Tortworth
Cromhall
Thornbury
Oldbury-on-Severn
Alveston
Olveston
Tockington
Almondsbury
Patchway
Bradley Stoke
Frampton Cotterell
Winterbourne
Yate
Chipping Sodbury
Hawkesbury Upton
Badminton
Acton Turville
Tormarton
Marshfield
Pucklechurch
MANGOTSFIELD
Kingswood
Hanham
Oldland
Bitton
KEYNSHAM
Saltford
Kelston
Weston
Batheaston
Bathford
BATH
Bathampton
Claverton
Monkton Combe
Bradford-on-Avon
Corsham
Box
Colerne
Atworth
Melksham
TROWBRIDGE
Westwood
Freshford
Hinton Charterhouse
Peasedown St. John
Radstock
Paulton
Midsomer Norton
Timsbury
High Littleton
Clutton
Farmborough
Marksbury
Pensford
Whitchurch
Chew Magna
Chew Stoke
Winford
Felton
Blagdon
Ubley
Compton Martin
West Harptree
Wrington
Congresbury
Backwell
Nailsea
Flax Bourton
Long Ashton
Failand
BRISTOL
SEE PAGE 187
Portishead
Portbury
Easton-in-Gordano
Pill
Avonmouth
Shirehampton
Sea Mills
Henbury
Filton
Horfield
Stoke Gifford
Hambrook
Frenchay
Downend
Staple Hill
Fishponds
Stapleton
Redland
Clifton
Bedminster
Knowle
Brislington
Bishopsworth
Hengrove
Whitchurch
Keynsham
Severn Beach
Pilning
Redwick
Easter Compton
Caldicot
Portskewett
Rogiet
Crick
CHEPSTOW
(Cas-gwent)
Tutshill
Sedbury
Woodcroft
St. Arvans
Devauden
Tintern Parva
Llandogo
St. Briavels
Whitebrook
Trellech
Itton Common
Mathern
Severn Road Bridge
Second Severn Crossing
SEVERN VIEW
MICHAELWOOD
GORDANO
SOUTH GLOUCESTERSHIRE
BATH & N.E. SOMERSET
RIVER SEVERN
VALE OF BERKELEY
BRISTOL INTERNATIONAL
SEE PAGE 186
M4
M5
M48
M49
M32
A4
A36
A37
A38
A46
A48
A403
A420
A432
A433
48
33
22

35
36
SEE PAGE 197
Burford
Sherborne
Northleach
Great Barrington
Little Barrington
Windrush
Eastington
Yanworth
Chedworth
Chedworth Roman Villa
Coberley
Colesbourne
Cowley
Birdlip
Great Witcombe
Cranham
Brimpsfield
Elkstone
Syde
Caudle Green
Sheepscombe
Whiteway
Winstone
The Camp
Miserden
Througham
Duntisbourne Abbots
Duntisbourne Leer
Middle Duntisbourne
Duntisbourne Rouse
Sudgrove
Edgeworth
Bisley
Waterlane
Eastcombe
Bournes Green
Bussage
Chalford
Oakridge
Far Oakridge
Sapperton
Frampton Mansell
Daglingworth
Woodmancote
Rendcomb
North Cerney
Calmsden
Bagendon
Perrott's Brook
Baunton
Stratton
CIRENCESTER
Coates
Minchinhampton
Hyde
Aston Down
Chesterton
Preston
Ampney Crucis
Ampney St. Mary
Ampney St. Peter
Harnhill
Barnsley
Barnsley House
Pancakehill
Fossebridge
Coln St. Dennis
Calcot
Coln Rogers
Winson
Ablington
Arlington
Bibury
Coln St. Aldwyns
Hatherop
Quenington
Eastleach Turville
Eastleach Martin
Fyfield
Southrop
Little Faringdon
Langford
Broughton Poggs
Filkins
Kencot
Broadwell
Alvescot
Little Clanfield
Grafton
Westwell
Holwell
Shilton
Signet
Asthall
Fulbrook
Taynton
Aldsworth
Fairford
Horcott
Poulton
Milton End
Meysey Hampton
Marston Hill
Whelford
Lechlade on Thames
Kelmscott
Buscot
Eaton Hastings
Faringdon
Great Coxwell
Little Coxwell
Coleshill
Highworth
Hampton
Hannington
Hannington Wick
Kempsford
Upper Inglesham
Marston Meysey
Castle Eaton
Fairford
Siddington
Driffield
South Cerney
Down Ampney
Latton
Cerney Wick
Cricklade
Chelworth Upper Green
Chelworth Lower Green
Ashton Keynes
North End
Shorncote
Somerford Keynes
Poole Keynes
Ewen
Kemble
Tarlton
Rodmarton
Cherington
Avening
Hampton Fields
Culkerton
Tetbury Upton
Tetbury
Ashley
Chelworth
Oaksey
Eastcourt
Crudwell
Chedglow
Long Newton
Hankerton
Minety
Upper Minety
Charlton
Perry Green
Garsdon
Shipton Moyne
Brokenborough
Easton Grey
Malmesbury
Milbourne
Lea
Foxley
Norton
Corston
Rodbourne
Little Somerford
Great Somerford
Startley
Dauntsey
Dauntsey Green
Dauntsey Lock
Lower Stanton St. Quintin
Stanton St. Quintin
Hullavington
Lower Seagry
Upper Seagry
Sutton Benger
Kington St. Michael
Kington Langley
Christian Malford
Bradenstoke
Lyneham
Foxham
East Tytherton
West Tytherton
Langley Burrell
Charlcutt
Hilmarton
CHIPPENHAM
Bremhill
Studley
Derry Hill
Rowden Hill
Calne
Quemerford
Blackland
Calstone Wellington
Cherhill
Compton Bassett
Yatesbury
Lacock
Notton
Reybridge
Gastard
Bowden Hill
Sandy Lane
Stockley
Chittoe
Heddington
Netherstreet
St. Edith's Marsh
Bromham
Sandridge
Beanacre
Westbrook
MELKSHAM
Bowerhill
Sells Green
Rowde
Dunkirk
DEVIZES
Seend
Seend Cleeve
Semington
Poulshot
Potterne
Potterne Wick
Worton
Marston
Bulkington
Keevil
Steeple Ashton
Great Hinton
Ashton Common
Hilperton
West Ashton
Nursteed
Roundway
Bishops Cannings
Horton
Coate
Bourton
All Cannings
Allington
Etchilhampton
Stert
Urchfont
Wedhampton
Patney
Chirton
Conock
Marden
Beechingstoke
Stanton St. Bernard
Alton Priors
Alton Barnes
Honey Street
Woodborough
Wilcot
West Stowell
Huish
Oare
Pewsey
Milton Lilbourne
Easton Royal
Manningford Bruce
Manningford Bohune
Wilsford
North Newnton
Bottlesford
Hilcott
Gores
Charlton
Rushall
Upavon
Southcott
Easton Hill
Pewsey Down
West Grafton
East Grafton
Wexcombe
Tidcombe
Collingbourne Kingston
Aughton
Brunton
Burbage
Eastcott
Wootton Rivers
New Mill
Ram Alley
Stibb Green
Durley
Great Bedwyn
Crofton
Wilton
Cadley
Clench Common
Marlborough
Mildenhall
Stitchcombe
Preshute
Manton
Lockeridge
West Overton
East Kennett
West Kennett
Fyfield
Avebury
Avebury Trusloe
Beckhampton
Winterbourne Monkton
Berwick Bassett
Winterbourne Bassett
Ogbourne Maizey
Ogbourne St. Andrew
Ogbourne St. George
Rockley
Axford
Ramsbury
Knighton
Preston
Aldbourne
Baydon
Upper Upham
Woodsend
Chiseldon
Draycot Foliat
Hodson
Badbury
Overtown
Wroughton
Elcombe
Uffcott
Broad Town
Broad Hinton
Clevancy
Clyffe Pypard
Bushton
Goatacre
Preston
Church End
Tockenham
Tockenham Wick
Grittenham
Woodshaw
Wootton Bassett
Callow Hill
Brinkworth
The Common
Cleverton
Hook
Lydiard Millicent
Lydiard Plain
Restrop
Purton
Purton Stoke
Widham
Common Platt
Nine Elms
Haydon Wick
Penhill
Even Swindon
Walcot
SWINDON
Okus
North Wroughton
Coate
Covingham
Stratton St. Margaret
Kingsdown
South Marston
Stanton Fitzwarren
Blunsdon St. Andrew
Broad Blunsdon
Sevenhampton
Shrivenham
Watchfield
Longcot
Bourton
Compton Beauchamp
Woolstone
Ashbury
Idstone
Bishopstone
Hinton Parva
Wanborough
Liddington
Horpit
M4
A4
A40
A361
A417
A419
A420
A429
A433
A435
A346
A350
A3102
A342
A345
A338
A365
A4361
B4425
B4019
B4040
B4042
B4696
B4553
B4005
B4192
B4000
B4508
B4069
B4006
LEIGH DELAMERE
WILTSHIRE
COTSWOLDS
GLOUCESTERSHIRE
VALE OF PEWSEY

36
Burford
Witney
Eynsham
Oxford
See page 194
Oxford Pear Tree
Carterton
Brize Norton
Ducklington
Stanton Harcourt
Cumnor
Kennington
Littlemore
Wheatley
Bampton
Clanfield
Langford
Faringdon
Buckland
Kingston Bagpuize
Marcham
Abingdon
Stadhampton
Dorchester
Warborough
Shillingford
Wallingford
Didcot
Harwell
Steventon
Drayton
Sutton Courtenay
Wantage
Grove
East Hanney
West Hanney
Stanford in the Vale
Uffington
Shrivenham
Highworth
Watchfield
Ashbury
Bishopstone
Lambourn
Upper Lambourn
Chaddleworth
Chieveley
Hermitage
Cold Ash
Thatcham
Newbury
Hungerford
Kintbury
Great Bedwyn
Shalbourne
Highclere
Kingsclere
Burghclere
Aldermaston
Tadley
Baughurst
Compton
Aldworth
Goring
Streatley
Cholsey
Moulsford
Blewbury
Chilton
East Ilsley
West Ilsley
Aldbourne
Ramsbury
Froxfield
Faccombe
Linkenholt
Vernham Dean
Collingbourne Kingston
Oxfordshire
Vale of White Horse
West Berkshire
Membury
Chieveley
Ot Moor
M4
A34
A40
A420
A338
A4
A339
A4130
A415
A417

37
AYLESBURY
Stone
Aston Clinton
Weston Turville
Tring
Aldbury
Little Gaddesden
Haddenham
Long Crendon
Thame
Chearsley
Cuddington
Stoke Mandeville
Halton
Wendover
Wigginton
Berkhamsted
Northchurch
Bourne End
Ellesborough
Great Kimble
Askett
Monks Risborough
Princes Risborough
Longwick
Towersey
Kingsey
Tetsworth
Sydenham
Chinnor
Bledlow
Great Missenden
Prestwood
Little Missenden
Chesham
Bovingdon
Chipperfield
Amersham
Chorleywood
Chalfont St. Giles
Chalfont St. Peter
Gerrards Cross
Beaconsfield
High Wycombe
West Wycombe
Stokenchurch
Watlington
Lewknor
Ibstone
Cadmore End
Lane End
Frieth
Hambleden
Marlow
Bourne End
Cookham
Maidenhead
Taplow
Burnham
Slough
Eton
Windsor
Datchet
Colnbrook
Staines
Egham
Virginia Water
Sunningdale
Ascot
Sunninghill
Bracknell
Wokingham
Twyford
Henley-on-Thames
Sonning Common
Nettlebed
Nuffield
Pangbourne
Reading
Caversham
Shinfield
Finchampstead
Crowthorne
Sandhurst
Camberley
Yateley
Blackwater
Frimley
Bagshot
Lightwater
Woking
Knaphill
Bisley
Chobham
Addlestone
Ottershaw
Woodham
Sheerwater
Horsell
Mayford
Pirbright
Brookwood
Fleet
Hartley Wintney
Mattingley
Sherfield on Loddon
Bramley
Silchester
Mortimer
Swallowfield
Burghfield Common
Sulhamstead
Theale
Tilehurst
Purley on Thames
Whitchurch-on-Thames
Goring Heath
Woodcote
Ipsden
Stoke Row
Checkendon
Kidmore End
Harpsden
Binfield Heath
Shiplake
Wargrave
Hurley
Knowl Hill
Waltham St. Lawrence
White Waltham
Holyport
Bray
Oakley Green
Winkfield
Warfield
Binfield
Winnersh
Arborfield Cross
Barkham
Eversley
BUCKINGHAMSHIRE
THE CHILTERNS
AYLESBURY VALE
CHILTERN HUNDREDS
WINDSOR GREAT PARK
SEE PAGE 195
SEE PAGE 197
M40
M4
M25
M3
A404(M)
A41
A413
A4010
A355
A404
A329
A322
A33
A331
25
38
51

38
AYLESBURY
CHESHAM
Bovingdon
Kings Langley
Abbots Langley
Chiswell Green
Bricket Wood
London Colney
POTTERS BAR
SOUTH MIMMS
RADLETT
BOREHAMWOOD
AMERSHAM
WATFORD
BUSHEY
Elstree
BARNET
CHORLEYWOOD
RICKMANSWORTH
LONDON GATEWAY
Chalfont St. Giles
Maple Cross
NORTHWOOD
STANMORE
EDGWARE
FINCHLEY
BEACONSFIELD
Chalfont St. Peter
HARROW
KENTON
PINNER
Gerrards Cross
RUISLIP
HENDON
Denham
Ickenham
NORTHOLT
WEMBLEY
HAMPSTEAD
Cookham
UXBRIDGE
WILLESDEN
Burnham
SLOUGH
GREENFORD
HAYES
EALING
ACTON
PADDINGTON
DENHEAD
West Drayton
Yiewsley
SOUTHALL
KENSINGTON
Eton
HEATHROW
HESTON
Brentford
CHISWICK
HAMMERSMITH
WINDSOR
SEE PAGE 197
Colnbrook
ISLEWORTH
FULHAM
PUTNEY
HOUNSLOW
RICHMOND
WANDSWORTH
WINDSOR GREAT PARK
Stanwell
ASHFORD
FELTHAM
TWICKENHAM
WIMBLEDON
EGHAM
STAINES
TEDDINGTON
SUNBURY
KINGSTON UPON THAMES
MERTON
MORDEN
NEW MALDEN
BRACKNELL
Ascot
Virginia Water
Shepperton
CHERTSEY
WEYBRIDGE
WALTON-ON-THAMES
SURBITON
CARSHALTON
Bagshot
Addlestone
ESHER
SUTTON
CAMBERLEY
Woodham
EWELL
Byfleet
Cobham
EPSOM
Frimley
WOKING
Ashtead
BANSTEAD
LEATHERHEAD
Fetcham
Tadworth
East Horsley
Great Bookham
GUILDFORD
SEE PAGE 189
DORKING
REIGATE
FARNHAM
Shere
Gomshall
M25
M4
M40
M3
M1
A1(M)

39
Cuffley
CHESHUNT
Waltham Cross
WALTHAM ABBEY
EPPING
Theydon Bois
Chipping Ongar
North Weald Bassett
Toot Hill
ENFIELD
SOUTHGATE
EDMONTON
CHINGFORD
LOUGHTON
CHIGWELL
Abridge
Stapleford Abbotts
Kelvedon Hatch
Doddinghurst
Mountnessing
Ingatestone
BRENTWOOD
Ingrave
Herongate
Laindon
WALTHAMSTOW
WOODFORD
TOTTENHAM
HORNSEY
ROMFORD
UPMINSTER
HORNCHURCH
STOKE NEWINGTON
SEE PAGE 192
LONDON
LEYTON
WANSTEAD
ILFORD
BARKING
DAGENHAM
STRATFORD
HACKNEY
ISLINGTON
FINSBURY
SHOREDITCH
BETHNAL GREEN
STEPNEY
POPLAR
CITY
WEST END
WESTMINSTER
EAST HAM
WEST HAM
Rainham
Aveley
South Ockendon
North Stifford
THURROCK
Chadwell St. Mary
Tilbury
Horndon on the Hill
BERMONDSEY
LAMBETH
CAMBERWELL
DEPTFORD
GREENWICH
WOOLWICH
Blackwall Tunnel
Thamesmead
Abbey Wood
ERITH
Belvedere
Purfleet
Dartford Crossing
West Thurrock
GRAYS
TILBURY
BATTERSEA
BRIXTON
CLAPHAM
LEWISHAM
ELTHAM
Welling
Bexleyheath
Crayford
DARTFORD
Stone
Greenhithe
Swanscombe
NORTHFLEET
GRAVESEND
CATFORD
Blackfen
BEXLEY
SIDCUP
Wilmington
Hawley
Bean
Betsham
Southfleet
Shorne
STREATHAM
Dulwich
Sydenham
Penge
BECKENHAM
CHISLEHURST
Foots Cray
Hextable
Swanley
Sutton at Hone
South Darenth
Horton Kirby
Longfield
New Barn
Hartley
Meopham
MITCHAM
Norwood
BROMLEY
Hayes
ORPINGTON
St. Paul's Cray
Crockenhill
Farningham
Eynsford
CROYDON
Addiscombe
West Wickham
Keston
Farnborough
Chelsfield
Badgers Mount
Halstead
Shoreham
Otford
Kemsing
West Kingsdown
Wrotham
Vigo Village
Culverstone Green
Snodland
WALLINGTON
PURLEY
New Addington
Downe
Knockholt
Sevenoaks
SEVENOAKS
Seal
Ightham
Borough Green
Platt
West Malling
Offham
Kings Hill
Mereworth
Wateringbury
COULSDON
Chaldon
WARLINGHAM
CATERHAM
Woldingham
Biggin Hill
Tatsfield
Westerham
Brasted
Sundridge
Chipstead
Riverhead
Dunton Green
Ivy Hatch
Plaxtol
Shipbourne
Oxted
Limpsfield
Godstone
REDHILL
Merstham
Bletchingley
Nutfield
Tandridge
Crockham Hill
Toy's Hill
Ide Hill
Sevenoaks Weald
Hildenborough
Hadlow
East Peckham
TONBRIDGE
Four Elms
Marlpit Hill
Edenbridge
Chiddingstone
Leigh
Golden Green
Five Oak Green
South Nutfield
Outwood
Blindley Heath
E S S E X
K E N T
N O R T H   D O W N S
M11
M25
M26
M20
M23
A10
A12
A13
A127
A2
A20
A21
A22
A23
A25
A26
A228

40
A414
A12
A130
A127
A13
A129
A132
A1245
A1015
A1159
A1014
A1089
A126
A128
A226
A228
A229
A249
A250
A2
A20
A26
A274
A252
A251
A21
M2
M20
M25
B1012
B1010
B1018
B1021
B1013
B1017
B1016
B1014
B1007
B1002
B1036
B1464
B148
B1420
B2000
B2004
B2005
B2006
B2008
B2010
B2015
B2163
B2231
B2246
53
54
28
39
A
B
C
D
1
2
3
4
5
Danbury
Sandon
Galleywood
Margaretting
Ingatestone
Stock
Billericay
Brentwood
Ingrave
Herongate
Laindon
Basildon
Pitsea
Vange
Wickford
Runwell
Shotgate
Nevendon
Rawreth
Battlesbridge
Hullbridge
South Woodham Ferrers
Woodham Ferrers
Bicknacre
Cold Norton
Purleigh
Maylandsea
Mayland
Mundon
Latchingdon
Steeple
Tillingham
St. Lawrence
Dengie
Asheldham
Southminster
Althorne
North Fambridge
South Fambridge
Burnham-on-Crouch
Canewdon
Paglesham Churchend
Paglesham Eastend
Wallasea Island
Potton Island
Foulness Island
Churchend
DANGER AREA
River Crouch
Ashingdon
Hockley
Hawkwell
Rayleigh
Rochford
Stambridge
Great Stambridge
Barling
Little Wakering
Great Wakering
Thundersley
Hadleigh
Benfleet
South Benfleet
Leigh-on-Sea
Westcliff-on-Sea
Southend-on-Sea
Shoeburyness
Shoebury Ness
Southchurch
Thorpe Bay
Canvey Island
Corringham
Stanford-le-Hope
Fobbing
Coryton
Horndon on the Hill
Orsett
Bulphan
Chadwell St. Mary
Tilbury
East Tilbury
West Tilbury
Linford
Mucking
River Thames
Thames Haven
Blythe Sands
Cliffe
Cooling
High Halstow
Allhallows
Allhallows-on-Sea
Lower Stoke
Grain
Isle of Grain
Thamesport
Hoo St. Werburgh
Stoke
Sheerness
Minster
Eastchurch
Warden
Queenborough
Rushenden
Isle of Sheppey
Elmley Island
The Swale
Gravesend
Northfleet
Shorne
Higham
Strood
Rochester
Chatham
Gillingham
Rainham
Walderslade
Upchurch
Lower Halstow
Newington
Iwade
Kemsley
Sittingbourne
Milton Regis
Bapchild
Teynham
Conyer
Faversham
Ospringe
River Medway
Medway Towns
See Page 191
Maidstone
Aylesford
Larkfield
West Malling
Snodland
Borstal
Bearsted
Hollingbourne
Harrietsham
Lenham
Charing
Charing Heath
Challock
Sutton Valence
Headcorn
Marden
Yalding
Coxheath
Linton
Langley
Leeds
Detling
Boxley
North Downs
Kent Downs
Eccles
Wouldham
Halling
Cuxton
Culverstone Green
Vigo Village
Meopham
Istead Rise
Southfleet
Longfield
New Ash Green
Hartlip
Stockbury
Bredgar
Doddington
Newnham
Sheldwich
Throwley
Eastling
Lynsted
Rodmersham
Borden
Tonbridge
East Peckham
Hadlow
Mereworth
Wateringbury
Offham
Kings Hill
Teston
East Farleigh
Loose
Boughton Monchelsea
Chart Sutton
Ulcombe
Egerton
Pluckley
Westwell
Boughton Lees

41
Dengie Marshes
Holliwell Point
Foulness Point
Foulness Sands
Courtsend
Maplin Sands
N O R T H
S E A
Warden Point
Leysdown-on-Sea
Leysdown Coastal Park
Shell Ness
The Swale
South Swale
Whitstable Bay
WHITSTABLE
Seasalter
Tankerton
Swalecliffe
Chestfield
Greenhill
Herne Bay
HERNE BAY
Hampton
Eddington
Beltinge
Reculver
Reculver Towers
Regulbium Roman Fort
Hillborough
Broomfield
Hunters Forstal
Herne
Herne Common
Brambles Wildlife Park
West End
Radfall
South Street
Yorkletts
Denstroude
Clowes Wood
Calcott
Broad Oak
Honey Hill
Bird Garden
Blean
Blean Wood
Tyler Hill
University of Kent
Sturry
Hersden
Westbere
Fordwich
Fordwich Town Hall
Stodmarsh
Grove
Preston
Marshside
Boyden Gate
Maypole
Chislet
Hoath
Upstreet
St. Nicholas at Wade
Sarre
West Stourmouth
East Stourmouth
Minnis Bay
Birchington
Westgate on Sea
MARGATE
Westbrook
Lifeboat House
Cliftonville
Kingsgate
Foreness Point
NORTH FORELAND
Bleak House
Dickens' House
ISLE OF THANET
Quex House
Westwood
Lydden
R.A.F.
Manston
London Manston
Northwood
St. Peter's
BROADSTAIRS
RAMSGATE
Acol
Monkton
Minster
Cliffs End
Pegwell Bay
Ebbsfleet
Richborough Port
Richborough Castle
Goldstone
Paramour Street
Westmarsh
Ware
Elmstone
Hoaden
Nash
Wickhambreaux
Cooper Street
Great Stonar
Sandwich
Sandwich Bay
Ash
Marshborough
Woodnesborough
Wingham
Staple
Ickham
Littlebourne
Howletts Zoo Park
Bramling
Bekesbourne
Patrixbourne
Adisham
Goodnestone
Goodnestone Park
Hammill
Eastry
Heronden
Knowlton
Chillenden
Nonington
Aylesham
Worth
Ham
Finglesham
Betteshanger
Northbourne
Sholden
Great Mongeham
DEAL
Walmer
Ripple
The Small Downs
Sandown
Victoriana
Local History
Time-Ball Tower
The Downs
Tilmanstone
Elvington
Frogham
Barfrestone
Eythorne
East Studdal
Sutton
Ashley
West Langdon
East Langdon
Ringwould
Kingsdown
Martin
Martin Mill
DANGER AREA
Dover Patrol Monument
St.Margaret's
Shepherdswell or Sibertswold
Coldred
Whitfield
Womenswold
Woolage Green
Barham
Derringstone
Kingston
Bishopsbourne
Bridge
Lower Hardres
Nackington
CANTERBURY
SEE PAGE 187
Harbledown
Thanington Without
Rough Common
Chartham
Chartham Hatch
Shalmsford Street
Petham
Garlinge Green
Denge Wood
Lees
Old Wives Lees
Chilham
Chilham Castle
Godmersham
Molash
Wye
Wye (Crundale Downs)
Wye Crown Memorial
Hassell Street
Crundale
Sole Street
Waltham
North Leigh
Bossingham
Stelling Minnis
Elham Valley Vineyard
Denton
Wingmore
Wootton
Lydden
Bodsham Green
Boughton Aluph
Graveney
Goodnestone
Hernhill
Dargate
Mount Ephraim
Boughton under Blean
Dunkirk
South Street
Oversland
Selling
Shottenden
Perry Wood
Badgam
Hogben's Hill
A299
A28
A2
A253
A256
A257
A258
A290
A291
A2050
A252
A260
A251
A255
A254
B2205
B2050
B2190
B2052
B2068
B2046
55
29
R. Stour
Great Stour
Little Stour
South Channel
E
F
G
H
1
2
3
4
5

Fishguard to:
Rosslare 3hrs. 30mins.
Rosslare 1hr. 50mins.
(Fast Ferry)
STRUMBLE HEAD
Carregwastad Point
Pen Brush
Llanwnda
Goodwick
(Wdig)
Trefasser
Dyffryn
Penbwchdy
Manorowen
Fishguard
(Abergwaun)
St. Nicholas
Granston
Scleddau
A40
Abercastle
Penclegyr
Porthgain
Trefin
Mathry
Jordanston
Llangloffan
Blue Lagoon
Abereiddy
Llanrian
Castlemorris
Newbridge
Carreg-gwylan-fach
Penclegyr
Croes-Goch
B4331
B4330
Letterston
ST. DAVID'S HEAD
Penllechwen
Treleddyd-fawr
Tretio
Carnhedryn
Treffynnon
Rhodiad Y-Brenin
Welsh Hook
Wolf's Castle
Whitesand Bay or Porth-mawr
B4583
A487
Caerfarchell
R. Solva
St. David's
(Tyddewi)
Rhosson
Whitchurch
Woollen Mill
Llandeloy
Hayscastle Cross
Hayscastle
Brimaston
Brawdy
Ramsey Island
Ramsey Sound
Cathedral & Bishop's Palace
Chapel
Solva
Gignog
Mountain Water
Treffgarne
Western Cleddau
Penycwm
Leweston
Green Scar
Newgale
Wood
Wolfsdale
Ynys Bery
Roch
Dudwells
Castle
Camrose
Simpson Cross
Keeston
Rudbaxton
Rickets Head
Cuttybridge
Pelcomb Cross
Haverford-west
S T. BRIDES
BAY
Nolton Haven
Nolton
Simpson
Motor
Tangiers
Pelcomb Bridge
Lambston
Druidston
Portfield Gate
Sutton
Haroldston West
Dreenhill
Albert Town
Merlin's Bridge
Uzmaston
Hangstone Davey
B4341
Broad Haven
Little Haven
Broadway
Walton West
Stack Rocks
B4327
Pope Hill
Talbenny
Freystrop
Walwyn's Castle
A4076
Tower Point
Skomer Island
Harold Stone
Wooltack Point
St. Brides
Robeston West
Tiers Cross
Johnston
Grassholm Island
Marloes Sands
Hasguard
PEMBROKESHIRE COAST NATIONAL PARK
Midland Isle
Marloes
Herbrandston
Steynton
Rosemarket
A477
MILFORD HAVEN
(Aberdaugleddau)
BROAD SOUND
Gateholm Island
The Gann
St. Ishmael's
Sandy Haven
Hubberston
Priory
Discovery Cen.
Hakin
Dale
Dale Point
Waterston
Llanstadwell
Neyland
Skokholm Island
Bird Observatory & Field Centre
West Blockhouse
Thorn Island
Milford Haven
Pembroke Dock
(Doc Penfro)
Pembroke to Rosslare 3hrs. 45mins.
St. Ann's Head
DANGER AREA
Angle
Angle Bay
Power Station
Rhoscrowther
Pwllcrochan
Pennar
Monkton
Sheep Island
B4320
Wallaston Green
Hundleton
Freshwater West
B4319
Maiden Wells
Field Centre
Castlemartin
Warren
St. Twynnells
St. Petrox
Merrion
Linney Head
DANGER AREA
Crow Rock
Toes
Elegug Stacks
The Wash
Bosherston
St. Govan's Head
A
B
C
D
1
2
3
4
5
60
70
80
90

43
Trwyn-y-bwa
DINAS HEAD
Dinas Island
Newport Bay (Bae Trefdraeth)
Moylgrove (Trewyddel)
Monington
Nevern (Nanhyfer)
Newport (Trefdraeth)
Dinas
Eglwyswrw
Cilgerran
Llechryd
Llandygwydd
Cenarth
Newcastle Emlyn (Castell Newydd Emlyn)
Llandyfriog
Penrhiw-llan
Drefach
Llangeler
Boncath
Newchapel (Capel Newydd)
Crymych
PEMBROKESHIRE COAST NATIONAL PARK
MYNYDD PRESELI
Foel-cwmcerwyn 1759
Foeldrygarn
Frenni Fawr 1295
Tegryn
Hermon
Llanfyrnach
Trelech
Cynwyl Elfed
Little Newcastle
Puncheston (Cas-Mael)
Henry's Moat (Castell Hendre)
Maenclochog
Llangolman
Glandy Cross
Efailwen
New Moat
Llys-y-frân
Llys-y-frân Reservoir
Ambleston
Walton East
Llanycefn
CARMARTHENSHIRE
Llanboidy
Abernant
Meidrim
CARMARTHEN (Caerfyrddin)
Clarbeston Road
Llandissilio
Clunderwen
Whitland
St. Clears
Llangynog
HAVERFORDWEST (Hwlffordd)
Robeston Wathen
Narberth (Arberth)
Lampeter Velfrey
Llanddowror
Red Roses
Templeton
Ludchurch
Martletwy
Reynalton
Kilgetty (Cilgeti)
Begelly
Amroth
Pendine (Pentywyn)
Laugharne
Llansteffan
Ferryside
Ginst Point
Saundersfoot
Monkstone Point
CARMARTHEN BAY
Carew
Pembroke (Penfro)
Lamphey
Tenby (Dinbych-y-Pysgod)
Penally
Manorbier
Giltar Point
Caldey Sound
Caldey Island
Chapel Point
St. Margaret's Island
Old Castle Head
Trewent Point
Stackpole Head
Burry Holm
WORMS HEAD (Penrhyn-gwyr)
DANGER AREA
A40
A477
A478
A487
A484
A4066
A4075
A4115
A4139
B4313
B4314
B4329
B4332
B4582
B4585

44
Cardigan Island
Bird Sanctuary
Cemaes Head
Gwbert
Farm Park
Aberporth
Parcllyn
Llangranog
Penbryn
Blaen Celyn
Pontgarreg
Morfa
A487
Plwmp
Pentregat
Brynhoffnant
Sarnau
Tresaith
Rainforest & Butterfly Centre
Felinwynt
Y Ferwig
Blaenannerch
Tremain
Blaenporth
Tan-y-groes
Castell Gwythian
Countryside Collection
Allt-y-goed
Pwllygranant
Cippyn
Cardigan
(Aberteifi)
Penparc
Glynarthen
Bettws Ifan
Felin Wrida
Brithdir
Rhydlewis
Hawen
Troedyraur
Penrhiw-pal
Coed-y-bryn
Maes Llyn
Noyadd Trefawr
Beulah
Brongest
Pantgwyn
St. Dogmaels
(Llandudoch)
Abbey
Llangoedmor
Ponthirwaun
Moylgrove
(Trewyddel)
Monington
Llechryd
Llandygwydd
Brongwyn
Felin Geri Mill
Afon Ceri
Pen-y-bryn
Cilgerran
Cwm Plysgog
Cwrcwd
Castell
Bridell
Llantood
Bird of Prey Centre
Glanrhyd
Gethsemane
Trwyn-y-bwla
DINAS HEAD
Fishguard to: Rosslare 3hrs. 30mins. Rosslare 1hr. 50mins. (Fast Ferry)
Dinas Island
Newport Bay (Bae Trefdraeth)
Fishguard Bay
Nevern (Nanhyfer)
Castell Nanhyfer
Berry Hill
Bryn-henllan
Parrog
Burial Chamber
B4582
Felindre Farchog
Castell Henllys
Pencelly Forest
A487
Rhos-hill
Abercych
Penrhiw
Cwm-cou
Adpar
Cenarth
Coracle Falls
Llandyfriog
Newcastle Emlyn
(Castell Newydd Emlyn)
Aberarad
Henllan
Pentrecagal
Drefach
Felindre
Dinas
Newport
(Trefdraeth)
Eglwyswrw
Castle
B4332
Boncath
Newchapel
(Capel Newydd)
Penrherber
Plas Glyneithinog
Cwmhiraeth
Waungilwen
Lower Town
Fishguard
(Abergwaun)
A487
Mynyddmelyn
Mynydd Carregog
Cilgwyn
Pentre Ifan Burial Chamber
Ty Canol
Gerddi
Shire Horse Farm
Llanfair-Nant-Gwyn
Bro Meigan
Crosswell
Brynberian
Pontyglazier
Afon Nyfer
Whitechurch
Penygroes
Blaenffos
Bwlch-y-groes
Cwmcych
Capel Iwan
Moelfre
Clydey
Star
Cwmorgan
Cilrhedyn
Llanychaer
B4313
PEMBROKESHIRE COAST NATIONAL PARK
Pontfaen
B4329
Tafarn-y-bwlch
Trecwn
Frenni Fawr
Pentre Ifan Burial Chamber
Crymych
Pen-lan-uchaf
Tegryn
MYNYDD PRESELI
Foeleryn
Glan-rhyd
Foel-cwmcerwyn
Pentre Galar
Mynachlog-ddu
Foel-drych
Hermon
Llanfyrnach
Henfeddau Fawr
Dinas
Trelech
Hermon
Morvil
Puncheston
(Cas-Mael)
Little Newcastle
Greenway
Rosebush
Castlebythe
B4313
Glandwr
Garne Turne Rocks
Tufton
Henry's Moat
(Castell Hendre)
Maenclochog
Glandy Cross
Hebron
Llanglydwen
Blaenwaun
Penybont
Blaen-y-coed
Wolf's Castle
Llandilo
Llangolman
Llys-y-fran Resr
New Moat
Penrhos Cottage
Efailwen
Pant-y-Caws
Brynyscawen Farm Chocolates
Cwmfelin Mynach
Cwmbach
Llanwinio
Ambleston
Walton
Woodstock Slop
Woollen Mill
Gwastad
Llys-y-fran Reservoir
Llys-y-fran
Cefn-y-pant
CARM
Talog
Bwlchnewydd
Spittal
B4329
Walton East
Llanycefn
A478
Login
Crosshands
Llanboidy
Gellywen
Abernant
Dyffryn
Scolton Manor
Scolton
Penffordd
Cwm-miles
Cae-lleon
Nant Cynnen
Merthyr
Rudbaxton
Clarbeston
Bletherston
Llandissilio
Hiraeth
Meidrim
Drefach
Clarbeston Road
Henllan Amgoed
Llangynin
Esgair
B4298
A40
Haverfordwest
Leachpool
The Rath
Selvedge Farm
Gelli
Clunderwen
Llanfallteg
Llanfallteg West
Cwmfelin Boeth
Afon Gronw
Afon Fenni
Gorsgoch Adventure World
Castle
Crundale
Wiston
Plain Dealings
Bethesda
Abbey
Llanddewi Velfrey
Bancyfelin
Prendergast
A40
Woodlands Farm Park
Llawhaden
Robeston Wathen
B4313
A40
Whitland
Pwlltrap
A40
St. Clears
Llangynog
HAVERFORDWEST
(Hwlffordd)
Canaston Bridge
Narberth
(Arberth)
Afon Marlais
Lampeter Velfrey
Trevaughan
Llwyn-y-brain
Backe
Llanddowror
Afon Cywyn
Robeston Back
Wilson Museum
Castle
Crinow
The Rhos
Cleddau Slebech
Minwear
Canaston Woods
Narberth Bridge
Leisure Park
Cold Blow
Llan-mill
Princes Gate
B4328
Taverspite
A477
Halfpenny Furze
Morfa Bach
Boulston
Picton
Graham Sutherland
Landshipping
Oakwood
A4115
Templeton
B4314
Ludchurch
Red Roses
Llanybri
Dylan Thomas Boathouse
Hook
Martletwy
Cwm Deri Vineyard
Llanteg
B4314
Llandawke
Laugharne
Llansteffan
B4312
Llangwm
Black Tar
Sardis
Yerbeston
Reynalton
Thomas Chapel
A477
Marros
Llansadurnen
Broadway
Brook
Afon Taf
Afon Tywi
PEMBROKESHIRE COAST NATIONAL PARK
Port Lion
Loveston
Folly Farm
Kilgetty
(Cilgeti)
Stepaside
Colby
Summerhill
Pendine
(Pentywyn)
A4066
Llanmiloe
DANGER AREA
Ginst Point
St. Ishmael
DANGER AREA
Houghton
Benton
Lawrenny
Cresswell R.
West Williamston
Cresswell Quay
Begelly
Cresselly
B4586
Jeffreyston
Sardis
Amroth
Castle
Honeyborough
Burton
Upton Castle
Broadmoor
Pentlepoir
Saundersfoot
Pembroke Ferry
Waterloo
Cosheston
Upton
Carew Newton
Redberth
East Williamston
Milton
Carew
A4075
Broadfield
Monkstone Point
New Hedges
A478
Pennar
Monkton
A477
Pembroke
(Penfro)
Upper Nash
Carew Cheriton
Sageston
Manor House Leisure Park
Dinosaur Experience
Bishop's Palace
St. Florence
B4318
Gumfreston
Tenby
(Dinbych-y-Pysgod)
CARMARTHEN BAY
Lamphey
A4139
Manorbier Newton
Maiden Wells
B4319
Hodgeston
Jameston
A4139
Penally
(Penalun)
Tudor Merchant's House NT
Giltar Point
St. Petrox
Cheriton or Stackpole Elidor
Freshwater East
Lydstep
Caldey Sound
Trewent Point
Manorbier
B4585
St. Margaret's Island
Abbey
Priory
Caldey Island
Chapel Point
Stackpole
DANGER AREA
Old Castle Head
Stackpole & Bosherston Ponds

45
CAMBRIAN MOUNTAINS
CEREDIGION
CARMARTHENSHIRE
FOREST OF BRECHFA
BRECON BEACONS NATIONAL PARK
BLACK MOUNTAIN
SWANSEA
Synod Inn or Post-mawr
Talgarreg
Gorsgoch
Temple Bar
Ffynnon-oer
Cribyn
Llangybi
Bettws Bledrws
Silian
Llanfair Clydogau
Maestir
Lampeter
(Llanbedr Pont Steffan)
University College
Cellan
Pentrefelin
Cwmann
Pentre-bach
Llanwnnen
Cwrtnewydd
Aber
Capel Cynon
Bwlch-y-fadfa
Castell Howell
Pont-sian
Cwmsychpant
Llanwenog
Drefach
Alltyblacca
Felin ysgubor
Pencarreg
Glan Duar
Llanybydder
Rhuddlan
Rhydowen
Tre-groes
Croes-lan
Pren-gwyn
Capel Dewi
Rock Mills Woollen Mill
Horeb
Llandysul
Llanfihangel-ar-Arth
Pontwelly
Maesycrugiau
Aber-Giâr
Llangeler
Pentre-cwrt
Banc-y-ffordd
Llanllwni
Mynydd Llanllwni
Mynydd Llanybyther
Rhydcymerau
Llidiad-Nenog
Pencader
New Inn
Gwyddgrug
Dol-gran
Gwernogle
Abergorlech
Edwinsford
Llansawel
Talley Abbey
Talley
Flynnon Byrgwm
Alltwalis
Cwmduad
Brechfa
Llanllawddog
Llanpumsaint
Pontarsais
Esgair
Cynwyl Elfed
Gwili
Rhydargaeau
Sarnau
Horeb
Llanfynydd
Capel Isaac
Mynydd Figyn
Cwmdu
Halfway
Soar
Talaris Park
Maerdy
Salem Farm
Salem
Hermon
Felindre
Mynydd Pencarreg
Ffaldybrenin
Ffarmers
Cwrt-y-Cadno
Mynydd Mallaen
Pumsaint
Caio
Dolaucothi Gold Mines
Felin Newydd Watermill
Aberbowlan
Porthyrhyd
Crugybar
Cilycwm
Llandovery
(Llanymddyfri)
Llansadwrn
Llanwrda
Cilgwyn
Myddfai
Llangadog
Castle
Dyffryn Ceidrych
Tyle
Bethlehem
Cwmifor
Caledfwlch
Pen-y-banc
Rhosmaen
Pontarllechau
Carn Goch
Trichrug
Capel Gwynfe
Neuadd
Twynllanan
Llandeilo
Ffairfach
Dinefwr Park
Dryslwyn Castle
Cilsan
Llangathen
Aberglasney
Pentrefelin
Pantgwyn
Broad Oak
Court Henry
Felindre
Dryslwyn
Golden Grove
Gelli Aur
Llanarthne
Paxton's Tower
National Botanic Garden
Felingwmuchaf
Pant-teg
Felingwmisaf
Llanfihangel-uwch-Gwili
Newchurch
Bronwydd Arms
Peniel
Ffynnon-ddrain
Tre-vaughan
Henallt
Amphitheatre
White Mill
Nantgaredig
Pont-ar-gothi
Llanegwad
Abergwili
Bishop's Palace
Capel Dewi
Carmarthen
Llangunnor
Pensarn
Cwmffrwd
Llanddarog
Porthyrhyd
Cwmisfael
Croesyceiliog
Idole
Bancycapel
Llangendeirne
Crwbin
Capel Seion
Drefach
Cefneithin
Gorslas
Cross Hands
Cwm-mawr
Pontyberem
Bancffosfelen
Meinciau
Pontantwn
Llandyfaelog
Four Roads
Pontyates
(Pont-iets)
Pont-Henri
Mynyddygarreg
Broadway
Llansaint
Kidwelly
(Cydweli)
Llangadog
Pont-newydd
Carway
Cynheidre
Sylen
Mynydd Sylen
Five Roads
Horeb
Trimsaran
Pinged
Waun-y-Clyn
Cwm Capel
Mynydd Pen-bre
Graig
Burry Port
(Porth Tywyn)
Pembrey
Pembrey Forest
Pwll
Furnace
Sandy
Parc Howard
Llanelli
Dafen
Felinfoel
Llangennech
Bryn
Pemberton
Bynea
Gorseinon
Yspitty
Penyrheol
Grovesend
Penllergaer
Loughor
Pen-clawdd
Gowerton
Garden Village
Whiteford Point
Whiteford
Temple Bar
Carmel
Maesybont
Llyn Llech Owain
Llandybie
Pentre Gwenlais
Cae'r-bryn
Tir-y-dail
Pen-y-groes
Saron
Capel Hendre
Tumble
Penybanc
Cwmgwili
Tycroes
Ammanford
(Rhydaman)
Pontamman
Betws
Pantyffynnon
Glanaman
Garnant
Gwaun-Cae-Gurwen
Cwmgors
Mynydd y Betws
Twynmynydd
Trapp
Carreg-Cennen
Farm Park
Llandyfan
Upper Brynamman
Brynamman
Lower Brynamman
Rhosaman
Cefn-bryn-brain
Cwmllynfell
Ystradowen
Tairgwaith
Cwm-twrch Uchaf
Pen-Rhiwfawr
Cwm-twrch Isaf
Ystalyfera
Cwmgiedd
Gurnos
Glan-rhyd
Cilmaengwyn
Godre'r-graig
Llangiwg
Ynysmeudwy
Cilybebyll
Gellinudd
Rhos
Pontardawe
Trebanos
Alltwen
Craig-cefn-parc
Clydach
Glais
Forest Goch
Cilfrew
Aberdulais
Cadoxton-Juxta-Neath
Neath Abbey
Neath
(Castell-nedd)
Tonna
Rhyddings
Skewen
Birchgrove
Morriston
Llansamlet
Landore
Llangyfelach
Fforest-fach
Cadle
Port Mead
Pontlliw
Tircoed
Cwm Dulais
Tyn-y-cwm
Felindre
Llwyncelyn
Cynghordy
Pontarddulais
Pentrebach
Fforest
Hendy
Sardis
Llannon
Llwyn-teg
Pont Abraham
Garnswllt
Cwmcerdinen
Mynydd y Gwair
Mynydd Garn-fach
Upper Lliw Resr
Lower Lliw Resr
Carn Llechart
Burial Chamber
Cairn Circle
Cwm Clydach
Rhyd-y-fro
Swansea West
Black Mountain
Bylchau Rhos-faen
Foel Fraith
Cefn Carn Fadog
Gareg Las
Truman
Mynydd Marchywel
Cefn Coed Colliery
Danger Area
Swansea Valley
Afon Teifi
Afon Cothi
Afon Twrch
Afon Tywi
Afon Gwili
Afon Sawdde
River Loughor
(Afon Llwchwr)
M4
A40
A48
A483
A4138
A4069
A4067
A474
A476
A475
A482
A485
A484
A486
A4240
B4300
B4310
B4337
B4302
B4338
B4459
B4336
B4306
B4317
B4309
B4308
B4556
B4297
B4301
30
31
45
46
47
48
49
57
E
F
G
H
1
2
3
4
5

46
57
58
45
32
CAMBRIAN MOUNTAINS
Abergwesyn
Cefn Fannog
1476
Tywi Forest
Beulah
Llanafan-fechan
Builth Wells
(Llanfair-ym-Muallt)
Builth Road
Cilmery
(Cilmeri)
Cwmbach Llechryd
Llanelwedd
Llanfaredd
Llansantffraed-in-Elwel
Cregrina
A483
A470
A481
B4358
B4567
B4520
B4519
Garth
Mynydd Trawsnant
1695
Welsh Wool
Llanwrtyd
Llanwrtyd Wells
(Llanwrtud)
Ystradffin
Llangammarch Wells
DANGER AREA
Maesmynis
Llanddewi'r Cwm
Alltmawr
Aberedw
Aberedw Castle
Aberedw Rocks
Llandeilo Graban
Llanbadarn-y-garreg
Cefngorwydd
Drum-ddu
1554
Pentre Dolau Honddu
E P P Y N T
Erwood
Gwenddwr
Crickadarn
1515
Mynydd Mallaen
Nant-y-bai
Rhandirmwyn
Bryn Nicol
Cefn Llwydlo
Crychan Forest
Tirabad
M Y N Y D D
1559
Bryn-du
1519
Twyn Rhyd-car
Upper Chapel
Cilycwm
Cynghordy
C A R M A R T H E N S H I R E
Merthyr Cynog
Llaneglwys
Ponde
Landefalle Hill
Llandovery
(Llanymddyfri)
Pentre-ty-gwyn
Babel
MYNYDD BWLCH-Y-GROES
Llandeilo'r Fan
P O W Y S
Llanfihangel Nant Bran
Lower Chapel
Llandefalle
Pont-faen
Pwllgloyw
Trawscoed
Garthbrengy
Felinfach
Llanfilo
Talachddu
Sarnau
A40
Mail Coach Pillar
Fron
Pentrebach
Halfway
Pentre-bach
Soar
Mynydd Aberscir
1204
Llandefaelog Fach
Trefeitha
Llanddew
Llanwrda
Cilgwyn
Myddfai
443
Mynydd Myddfai
Usk Resr.
Llywel
Trecastle
Pentre'r-felin
Yr Allt
1156
Sennybridge
Trallong
Aberbran
Penpont
Aberyscir
Battle
Cradoc
Pen-y-crug
Brecon Castle
Brecon
(Aberhonddu)
Llanfaes
Llanspyddid
Llechfaen
Llanywern
Groesffordd
Llanfihangel Tal-y-llyn
Llangadog
Castle
Cwmwysg
Pont ar Hydfer
R. Usk
Defynnog
Mynydd Illtyd
Mountain Centre
Libanus
Ffrwdgrech
Abercynrig
Llanfrynach
Llanhamlach
Talyllyn
Pennorth
Scethrog
Talsarn
Twynllanan
Llanddeusant
Source of R.Usk
Glas Fynydd Forest
Cray
Heol Senni
A4067
A4215
Camlais
Pencelli
1845
Allt Ddu
Pen Milan
Cross Oak
Bryn
1842
Talybont-on-usk
Capel Gwynfe
Llyn y Fan Fach
Llyn y Fan-Fawr
1940
Moel Feity
Cray Resr.
A470
BRECON BEACONS
2906
Aber Village
Escarpment
BLACK MOUNTAIN
Gareg Las
2076
2366
F F O R E S T   F A W R
Fan-Gihirych
Fan Fawr
2409
Fan Llia
2071
Beacons Resr.
Ystradfellte Resr.
Neuadd Resrs.
Torpantau
Talybont Resr.
Truman
1982
2022
Foel Fraith
Bylchau Rhos-faen
Cefn Carn-Fadog
1657
Carreg-lem
1832
Castell-y-geifr
Shire Horse Centre
Dinosaur Park
Dan-yr-Ogof Showcaves
Glyntawe
BRECON BEACONS NATIONAL PARK
Penwyllt
Craig-y-nos
Ogof Ffynon Ddu
1763
Carreg-lwyd
Wern
Waun Lysiog
Pentwyn Resr.
Nant-ddu
Garwnant Forest
Pontsticill Resr.
Brecon Mountain Railway
Trefil
Rhosaman
Cefn-bryn-brain
Cwmllynfell
Ystradowen
Lower Brynamman
Tairgwaith
Cwm-twrch Uchaf
Gwmgors
Pen Rhiwfawr
Abercraf
Caehopkin
Cae'r-bont
Penrhos
Ystradgynlais
Cwmgiedd
Pen-y-cae
Ynyswen
Henrhyd Waterfall
Coelbren
Ystradfellte
Porth-yr-Ogof Cavern
R. Hepste
A4059
Cader Fawr
Llwyn-on Village
Pontsticill
Vaynor
MERTHYR
MERTHYR TYDFIL
Tafarnaubach
Gurnos
Onllwyn
Dyffryn Cellwen
Waterfalls
Pant Sychbant
Mynydd Penmoelallt
-y-glog 1376 Forest
Trefechan
(Merthyr Tudful)
Cwm-twrch Isaf
Ystalyfera
Glan-rhyd
Seven Sisters
(Blaendulais)
Penderyn
RHONDDA
Pontbren Llwyd
Cefn-coed-y-cymmer
Pen-y-darren
Dowlais
RHYMNEY
(Rhymni)
Godre'r-graig
Cilmaengwyn
Glyn-neath
Morfa Glas
Pontneddfechan
A465
Hirwaun
Clwydfagwyr
Pontlottyn
Ynysmeudwy
Pontardawe
Pentreclwydau
Blaengwrach
Cwmgwrach
Pont Walby
Rhigos
CYNON
Llwydcoed
Pen-yr-Heolgerrig
Ynysfach Iron Heritage Centre
Pentrebach
Cilybebyll
Gellinudd
1370
Crynant
A4060
Penywaun
Cwmdare
Trecynon
Robertstown
Abercanaid
Troedyrhiw
Alltwen
Rhos
Cefn Coed Colliery
B4242
Resolven
(Resolfen)
1257
Mynydd Resolfen
Hirwaun Common
ABERDARE
(Aberdar)
Abernant
Cwmbach
Bedlinog
Craig-y-Duke
Forest Goch
Cilfrew
Aberdulais
Aberdulais Falls
Abergarwed
Waterfall
Melincourt
NEATH
Lluest-wen Resrvoir
Aberaman
Cwmaman
Cwmpennar
Aberfan
TAFF
TYDFIL
Bryn-coch
Gadlys
Juxta
Neath
Clyne
AFAN FOREST PARK
Blaenrhondda
Blaencwm
Tynewydd
Treherbert
Maerdy
MOUNTAIN ASH
(Aberpennar)
Abercwmboi
Merthyr Vale
(Ynysowen)
Treharris
Trelewis
Neath Abbey
Tonna
(Tonnau)
NEATH
(Castell-nedd)
Cimla
PORT TALBOT
Treorchy
(Treorci)
Cwmparc
Ynys-wen
Ferndale
Pentre
Ystrad
Blaenllechau
Penrhiwceiber
St. Gwynno Forest
Tylorstown
Ynysboeth
Edwardsville
Abercynon
Tonmawr
Abercregan
Cymmer
(Cymer)
Blaengwynfi
Abergwynfi
Croeserw
Duffryn
Efail-fach
Pencaerau
Ynysymaerdy
Briton

47
HEREFORDSHIRE
MONMOUTHSHIRE
BLAENAU GWENT
CAERPHILLY
TORFAEN
BLACK MOUNTAINS
HEREFORD
ABERGAVENNY
(Y Fenni)
MONMOUTH
(Trefynwy)
CWMBRAN
PONTYPOOL
(Pontypwl)
Hay-on-Wye
(Y Gelli Gandryll)
Crickhowell
(Crughywel)
EBBW VALE
(Glyn Ebwy)
ABERTILLERY
(Abertyleri)
Usk
(Brynbuga)
Kington
Huntington
Kingswood
Almeley
Weobley
Dilwyn
Bodenham
Hope under Dinmore
Canon Pyon
Wellington
Moreton on Lugg
Holmer
Staunton on Wye
Bredwardine
Dorstone
Peterchurch
Madley
Kingstone
Clehonger
Allensmore
Callow
Much Dewchurch
King's Thorn
Wormbridge
Kilpeck
Abbey Dore
Ewyas Harold
Pontrilas
Kentchurch
Grosmont
Longtown
Clodock
Michaelchurch Escley
St. Margarets
Newton
Bacton
Turnastone
Vowchurch
Pandy
Llanvihangel Crucorney
Skenfrith
St. Weonards
Welsh Newton
Llangarron
Llangrove
Whitchurch
Dixton
Wyesham
Redbrook
Raglan
Trellech
Tintern Parva
Devauden
St. Arvans
Llangwm
Llantrisant
Llangybi
Glasbury
Talgarth
Clyro
Clifford
Llowes
Cusop
Bronllys
Llangynidr
Gilwern
Govilon
Blaenavon
Brynmawr
Beaufort
Nantyglo
Blaina
Abersychan
Griffithstown
Sebastopol
Newbridge
(Cefn Bychan)
Blackwood
(Coed Duon)
Crumlin
Oakdale
Bargoed
New Tredegar
Tredegar
Cwm
Llanarth
Tregare
Penallt
Tutshill
Woodcroft
A438
A465
A4112
A480
A417
A49
A40
A479
A4042
A449
A472
A4137
A4079
B4348
B4352
B4347
B4521
B4233
B4350
B4246
B4598
B4293
59
33
48
E
F
G
H
1
2
3
4
5
Sugar Loaf
1955
Hay Bluff
2220
Twmpa
2263
Offa's Dyke
Golden Valley
Vale of Ewyas

48
59
60
A
B
C
D
1
2
3
4
5
HEREFORDSHIRE
HEREFORD
GREAT MALVERN
Malvern Link
Malvern Wells
MALVERN HILLS
Bromyard
Ledbury
Ross-on-Wye
MONMOUTH
(Trefynwy)
GLOUCESTER
SEE PAGE 189
GLOUCESTERSHIRE
FOREST OF DEAN
Cinderford
Lydney
Coleford
Newent
Newnham
Berkeley
Dursley
Nailsworth
Stonehouse
Tewkesbury
Upton upon Severn
Tintern Parva
St. Arvans
Chepstow Park Wood
RIVER SEVERN
VALE OF BERKELEY
VALE OF GLOUCESTER
Hope under Dinmore
Bodenham
Ullingswick
Little Cowarne
Stoke Lacy
Acton Beauchamp
Suckley
Leigh Sinton
Bransford
Powick
Callow End
Kempsey
Cradley
West Malvern
Upper Wyche
Colwall Stone
Wellington Heath
Castle Frome
Much Cowarne
Bishop's Frome
Moreton on Lugg
Sutton St. Nicholas
Preston Wynne
Withington
Yarkhill
Tarrington
Lugwardine
Stoke Edith
Ashperton
Mordiford
Hampton Bishop
Lower Bullingham
Dinedor
Woolhope
Fownhope
Putley
Pixley
Much Marcle
Dymock
Kempley
Bromsberrow Heath
Redmarley D'Abitot
Staunton
Hartpury
Ashleworth
Highleadon
Tibberton
Huntley
Highnam
Maisemore
Longford
Innsworth
Churchdown
Hucclecote
Brockworth
Quedgeley
Hardwicke
Haresfield
Harescombe
Brookthorpe
Whiteshill
Randwick
Stroud
King's Stanley
Leonard Stanley
Frampton on Severn
Slimbridge
Cambridge
Sharpness
Cam
Uley
Stinchcombe
Blakeney
Yorkley
Pillowell
Bream
Parkend
Ruspidge
Ruardean
Drybrook
Mitcheldean
Longhope
Lea
Weston under Penyard
Kilcot
Gorsley
Upton Bishop
Crow Hill
Brampton Abbotts
How Caple
Kings Caple
Hoarwithy
Much Dewchurch
Little Dewchurch
Ballingham
Peterstow
St. Weonards
St. Owen's Cross
Llangarron
Tudorville
Goodrich
Whitchurch
Great Doward
Symonds Yat
English Bicknor
Upper Lydbrook
Lower Lydbrook
Hillersland
Staunton
Berry Hill
Redbrook
Newland
Clearwell
St. Briavels
Llandogo
Whitebrook
The Narth
Trellech
Penallt
Mitchel Troy
Wyesham
Rockfield
Welsh Newton
Llangrove
Callow
Allensmore
Kingstone
Clehonger
Breinton
Burghill
Holmer
Wellington
Canon Pyon
Aylburton
Alvington
Netherend
Woolaston
Tidenham
Tutshill
Woodcroft
M5
M50
A40
A48
A49
A38
A417
A438
A449
A4103
A44
A465
ROSS SPUR
OLDBURY

49
STRATFORD-UPON-AVON
SEE PAGE 196
EVESHAM
WORCESTERSHIRE
CHELTENHAM
SEE PAGE 187
CIRENCESTER
COTSWOLD HILLS
Pershore
Broadway
Chipping Campden
Moreton-in-Marsh
Stow-on-the-Wold
Bourton-on-the-Water
Winchcombe
Bishop's Cleeve
Charlton Kings
Northleach
Burford
Fairford
Lechlade on Thames
Faringdon
Shipston on Stour
Tewkesbury
Bidford-on-Avon
Welford-on-Avon
Salford Priors
Cleeve Prior
Long Marston
Mickleton
Ilmington
Honeybourne
Badsey
Bretforton
Offenham
Harvington
Fladbury
Cropthorne
Eckington
Defford
Bredon
Kemerton
Beckford
Ashton under Hill
Sedgeberrow
Childswickham
Toddington
Stanway
Didbrook
Gretton
Prestbury
Southam
Andoversford
Shipton
Withington
Chedworth
Bibury
Ablington
Barnsley
Ampney Crucis
Siddington
South Cerney
Down Ampney
Kemble
Coates
Sapperton
Chalford
Bisley
Duntisbourne Abbots
North Cerney
Seven Springs
Shurdington
Leckhampton
Temple Guiting
Guiting Power
Naunton
Upper Slaughter
Lower Slaughter
Longborough
Donnington
Bourton-on-the-Hill
Blockley
Paxford
Ebrington
Little Compton
Chipping Norton
Kingham
Bledington
Icomb
Great Rissington
Little Rissington
Sherborne
Windrush
Great Barrington
Taynton
Milton-under-Wychwood
Shipton-under-Wychwood
Langford
Kelmscott
Poulton
Quenington
Hatherop
Eastleach Turville
Aldsworth
Coln St. Dennis
Coln Rogers
Winson
Hazleton
Turkdean
Notgrove
Cold Aston
Salperton
Hampnett
Yanworth
Compton Abdale
Sevenhampton
Whittington
Syreford
Dowdeswell
Brockhampton
Charlton Abbots
Hawling
Aylworth
Farmcote
Hailes
Cutsdean
Ford
Snowshill
Stanton
Laverton
Buckland
Wormington
Dumbleton
Alderton
Teddington
Stoke Orchard
Swindon
Uckington
Staverton
Up Hatherley
Badgeworth
Brockworth
Cranham
Birdlip
Elkstone
Colesbourne
Rendcomb
Woodmancote
Miserden
Edgeworth
Daglingworth
Stratton
Baunton
Preston
Ampney St. Peter
Ampney St. Mary
Meysey Hampton
Marston Meysey
Kempsford
Hannington
Ewen
Somerford Keynes
Cerney Wick
Latton
Poole Keynes
Rodmarton
Culkerton
Tetbury Upton
Avening
Cherington
Hampton Fields
Minchinhampton
Frampton Mansell
Oakridge
Bussage
Brownshill
Far Oakridge
Waterlane
Throughan
Sudgrove
Caudle Green
Syde
Winstone
Whiteway
Sheepscombe
Painswick
The Camp
Wyck Rissington
Maugersbury
Broadwell
Evenlode
Adlestrop
Oddington
Daylesford
Todenham
Great Wolford
Barton-on-the-Heath
Tidmington
Burmington
Willington
Cherington
Barcheston
Honington
Tredington
Halford
Idlicote
Armscote
Blackwell
Darlingscott
Ettington
Alderminster
Newbold on Stour
Crimscote
Admington
Wimpstone
Preston on Stour
Atherstone on Stour
Clifford Chambers
Loxley
Upper Quinton
Lower Quinton
Pebworth
Dorsington
Weston-on-Avon
Luddington
Binton
Grafton
Ardens Grafton
Marcliff
Bickmarsh
Barton
Broom
Dunnington
Iron Cross
Abbot's Salford
Atch Lench
Ab Lench
Church Lench
Rous Lench
Abberton
Flyford Flavell
Radford
Goom's Hill
Naunton Beauchamp
Bishampton
Throckmorton
Peopleton
White Ladies Aston
Upton Snodsbury
North Piddle
Churchill
Spetchley
Egdon
Stoulton
Drakes Broughton
Pinvin
Wyre Piddle
Lower Moor
Hill
Hill Furze
Wick
Charlton
Norton
Lenchwick
Aldington
Bengeworth
Hampton
Fairfield
Wickhamford
Murcot
Willersey
Saintbury
Weston Subedge
Aston Subedge
Broad Campden
Aston Magna
Batsford
Draycott
Condicote
Hinchwick
Upper Swell
Lower Swell
Chalk Hill
Kineton
Barton
Hyde
Taddington
Wood Stanway
Greet
Postlip
Langley
Gotherington
Woolstone
Oxenton
Dixton
Alstone
Bengrove
Pamington
Ashchurch
Northway
Aston Cross
Aston on Carrant
Kinsham
Conderton
Overbury
Grafton
Westmancote
Bredon's Norton
Kersoe
Elmley Castle
Netherton
Bricklehampton
Great Comberton
Little Comberton
Birlingham
Pensham
Besford
Woodmancote
Cleeve Hill
Hardwicke
Elmstone Hardwicke
Boddington
Golden Valley
Pittville
Lansdown
Battledown
The Reddings
Little Herbert's
Foxcote
Coberley
Upper Coberley
Cowley
Little Witcombe
Great Witcombe
Brimpsfield
Bentham
Calmsden
Bagendon
Perrott's Brook
Duntisbourne Leer
Middle Duntisbourne
Duntisbourne Rouse
Eastcombe
Bournes Green
Chesterton
Siddington
Harnhill
Milton End
Horcott
Whelford
Upper Inglesham
Buscot
Eaton Hastings
Little Faringdon
Little Clanfield
Grafton
Kencot
Broadwell
Filkins
Broughton Poggs
Southrop
Fyfield
Eastleach Martin
Holwell
Westwell
Signet
Shilton
Fulbrook
Swinbrook
Asthall
Little Barrington
Fifield
Idbury
Foscot
Nether Westcote
Church Westcote
Bruern Abbey
Lyneham
Upper Oddington
Lower Oddington
Clapton-on-the-Hill
Farmington
Eastington
Mill End
Fossebridge
Calcot
Arlington
Coln St. Aldwyns
Ampney Crucis
Barnsley
Meysey Hampton
Cleeve Cloud
Sudeley
Hailes Abbey
Snowshill Manor
Stanway House
Hidcote Manor
Kiftsgate Court
Sezincote
Chastleton House
Rollright Stones
Chedworth Roman Villa
Bibury Trout Farm
Cotswold Water Park
Cotswold Farm Park
Cotswold Wildlife Park
Broadway Tower
Folly Farm Waterfowl
Birdland
Model Railway Exhibition
Model Village
Lodge Park
Cotswold Falconry Centre
Batsford Arboretum
Four Shire Stone
Gloucestershire Warwickshire Railway
Misarden Park
The Giant's Stone
Miserden Castle
Belas Knap Long Barrow
Nottingham Hill
Bredon Hill
Bredon Barn
Croome Park
Dunstall Castle
Elmley Castle
Parson's Folly
St. Catherine's Well
Anne Hathaway's Cottage
Shire Horse Centre
Old Bridge
Fleece Inn
Domestic Fowl Trust
Woolstaplers Hall
Market Hall
Fish Hill
Tithe Barn
Windmill Hill
Twyford Country Centre
Church House
Abbey
Almonry
Bridge
Horticulture
Horcott
Corinium
Roman Amphitheatre
Agricultural College
Old Parsonage
Badbury Hill Camp
Buscot House
Kelmscott Manor
Rodmarton Manor
Windmill Tump
Source of the R. Thames
Thames Head
Smerrill Farm
Butts Farm
South Cerney
Ampney Crucis
Fairford
Edward Richardson & Phyllis Amey
Cross Tree Gallery
Swinford
Cotswold
Fairford
Hampton
Crocodile Head Spring
Cotswold Countryside Collection
Mechanical Music
Denfurlong Farm
Earthworks
Norbury Mound
Gloucester Beeches
Castle Godwyn
Roman Villa
Crickley Hill
Seven Springs
Hetty Pegler's
Village Life Exhibition
Long Barrow
Old Mill
Abbey
Gillets
Folk and Police
Whittington Court
Bugatti
The Cottage
The Priory
Gravel Pit
Old Vicarage
Flyford
Bredon Springs
Wellington Aviation
Dorn
Knee Brook
Meon Hill
Chastleton
Upper Quinton
Dorn
R. Isbourne
R. Avon
R. Stour
R. Coln
R. Churn
R. Leach
R. Thames
R. Cole
VALE OF EVESHAM
M5
A44
A46
A422
A429
A435
A436
A40
A417
A419
A433
A4019
A4634
A424
A361
A3400
A4390
A38
B4035
B4081
B4632
B4077
B4078
B4079
B4084
B4068
B4425
B4450
B4020
B4477
B4437
B4439
B4477
SEE PAGE 196
SEE PAGE 187

STRATFORD-UPON-AVON
50
WARWICKSHIRE
OXFORDSHIRE
NORTHAMP
A B C D
61
62
49
36
Kineton
Gaydon
Fenny Compton
Farnborough
Byfield
Upper Boddington
Woodford Halse
Ettington
Pillerton Hersey
Warmington
Ratley
Mollington
Cropredy
Chipping Warden
Culworth
Moreton Pinkney
Sulgrave
Halford
Tredington
Shipston on Stour
Oxhill
Upper Tysoe
Middle Tysoe
Shenington
Hornton
Shotteswell
Wroxton
Hanwell
Drayton
BANBURY
Chacombe
Middleton Cheney
Marston St. Lawrence
Greatworth
Helmdon
Farthinghoe
Brackley
Upper Brailes
Lower Brailes
Shutford
North Newington
Sibford Gower
Swalcliffe
Broughton
Tadmarton
Bodicote
Adderbury
Bloxham
King's Sutton
Charlton
Evenley
Westbury
Todenham
Great Wolford
Moreton-in-Marsh
Cherington
Stourton
Whichford
Long Compton
Hook Norton
Milcombe
South Newington
Barford St. Michael
Deddington
Aynho
Croughton
Souldern
Little Compton
Great Rollright
Great Tew
Over Norton
Salford
Chipping Norton
Kingham
Churchill
Enstone
Chadlington
Charlbury
Middle Barton
Steeple Aston
Upper Heyford
Fritwell
Ardley
Stoke Lyne
Bucknell
Bicester
Chesterton
Ambrosden
Bledington
Milton-under-Wychwood
Shipton-under-Wychwood
Ascott-under-Wychwood
Leafield
Finstock
Stonesfield
Woodstock
Wootton
Tackley
Kirtlington
Weston-on-the-Green
Bletchingdon
Kidlington
Islip
Charlton-on-Otmoor
OT MOOR
Burford
Ramsden
North Leigh
Hailey
Long Hanborough
Freeland
WITNEY
Eynsham
Yarnton
OXFORD
Wheatley
Carterton
Brize Norton
Ducklington
Stanton Harcourt
Cumnor
Kennington
Littlemore
Bampton
Clanfield
Langford
Standlake
Wootton
Radley
Marsh Baldon
Stadhampton
Buckland
Fyfield
Marcham
ABINGDON
Faringdon
Culham
M40
A429
A423
A422
A44
A361
A40
A4142
A34
A420
A415
A41
A43
A421
B4035
B4031
B4030
B4022
B4027
B4449
B4044
B4017

51
NORTHAMPTONSHIRE
BUCKINGHAMSHIRE
CHILTERN HILLS
THE THREE HUNDREDS OF AYLESBURY
MILTON KEYNES
SEE PAGE 194
NEWPORT PAGNELL
Newport Pagnell
Wolverton
Stony Stratford
Bletchley
Fenny Stratford
Woburn Sands
Woburn
Olney
Towcester
Roade
Buckingham
Winslow
Aylesbury
Leighton Buzzard
Linslade
Dunstable
Houghton Regis
Toddington
Ampthill
Flitwick
Kempston
Thame
Haddenham
Long Crendon
Princes Risborough
Wendover
Tring
Berkhamsted
Chesham
Amersham
Great Missenden
Prestwood
Chinnor
Stokenchurch
Chorleywood
Ivinghoe
Waddesdon
Whitchurch
Wing
Stewkley
Cranfield
Stoke Goldington
Sherington
Yardley Gobion
Potterspury
Silverstone
Whittlebury
Paulerspury
Deanshanger
Old Stratford
Newton Longville
Great Horwood
Little Horwood
Steeple Claydon
Quainton
Brill
Stoke Mandeville
Weston Turville
Aston Clinton
Halton
Wigginton
Little Gaddesden
Studham
Eddlesborough
Edlesborough
Tetsworth
Sydenham
Great Haseley
Lacey Green
Hughenden Valley
Little Missenden
Holmer Green
Stoke Talmage
M1
M40
A5
A41
A413
A418
A421
A422
A428
A4010
A4146
A43
A505
A508
A509
A4129
A413

52
BEDFORD
Kempston
Wootton
Stewartby
Ampthill
Flitwick
Toddington
Dunstable
Houghton Regis
Luton
Harpenden
St. Albans
Hemel Hempstead
Watford
Chorleywood
Chesham
Kings Langley
Abbots Langley
Radlett
Borehamwood
Barnet
Potters Bar
Hatfield
Welwyn Garden City
Welwyn
Stevenage
Hitchin
Letchworth
Baldock
Biggleswade
Sandy
Potton
Gamlingay
Shefford
Stotfold
Arlesey
Hertford
Hoddesdon
Cheshunt
Enfield
Waltham Cross
Cuffley
Royston
Bassingbourn
Buntingford
Barton-le-Clay
Silsoe
Clophill
Maulden
Wilstead
Harlington
Westoning
Markyate
Redbourn
London Colney
Brookmans Park
Bricket Wood
Bovingdon
Wheathampstead
Knebworth
Datchworth
Tewin
Walkern
Benington
Ashwell
Guilden Morden
Steeple Morden
Langford
Old Warden
Cople
Wrestlingworth
BEDFORDSHIRE
HERTFORDS
CAM
TODDINGTON
BALDOCK
SOUTH MIMMS
FLAMSTEAD
LONDON LUTON
M1
M10
M25
A1
A1(M)
A5
A6
A10
A41
A414
A421
A505
A602
A6141

53
54
BRIDGESHIRE
ESSEX
HIRE
M11
A11
A10
A505
A1307
A1301
A120
A414
A130
A131
A12
M25
A113
A128
A1060
A1017
A1092
B1052
B1053
B1054
B1057
B1383
B1038
B1039
B1368
B1004
B1051
B1184
B1256
B1008
B1007
B1002
B1181
B1393
B1383
B1183
B180
B181
B194
B172
B175
Great Shelford
Little Shelford
Stapleford
Haslingfield
Harlton
Hauxton
Harston
Gog Magog Hills
Wandlebury Hill Fort
Fleam Dyke
Roman Road
Educational Reserve
Babraham
BABRAHAM
Sawston
Little Abington
Great Abington
Chilford Hundred Vineyard
Hildersham
Balsham
Barrington
Newton
Foxton
Thriplow
Thriplow Meadows
Docwra's Manor
Whittlesford
Whittlesford Chapel
Pampisford
Duxford
Duxford Imperial War Museum
Fowlmere
Melbourn
Hinxton
Ickleton
Linton
Hadstock
Bartlow
Bartlow Hills
Great Chesterford
Little Chesterford
Brinkley
Willingham Green
Weston Colville
Lower Wood
West Wratting
Weston Green
Carlton
Great Bradley
Little Bradley
Little Thurlow
Great Thurlow
Cowlinge
Wickhambrook
Farley Green
Hobbles Green
Sowley Green
Clopton Green
Denston
Stradishall
Stansfield
Burton End
West Wickham
Streetly End
Horseheath
Withersfield
Great Wratting
Little Wratting
Barnardiston
Chimney Street
Hundon
Poslingford
Brockley Green
Kedington
Chilton Street
Ancient House
Clare
Clare Castle
Cardinal's Green
Shudy Camps
Castle Camps
Haverhill
Calford Green
Boyton Vineyards
Boyton End
Stoke by Clare
Wixoe
Sturmer
New England
Baythorn End
Ashen
Ovington
Belchamp St. Paul
Ridgewell
Tilbury Green
Tilbury Juxta Clare
Little Yeldham
Great Yeldham
Stevington End
Ashdon
Camps End
Helions Bumpstead
Steeple Bumpstead
Olmstead Green
Birdbrook
Moyns Park
Church End
Little Walden
Shadwell Wood
Heydon
Great Chishill
Chrishall
Elmdon
Strethall
Littlebury
Audley End
Bridge End
Maze
Sewards End
Stocking Green
Saffron Walden
Barley
Little Chishill
Langley
Duddenhoe End
Pond Street
Littlebury Green
Bridge Green
Wendens Ambo
Radwinter
Hempstead
Cornish Hall End
Robinhood End
Stambourne
Toppesfield
Wimbish
Tye Green
Wimbish Green
Howlett End
Great Sampford
Little Sampford
Spains Hall
Howe Street
Gainsford End
Highstreet Green
Sible Hedingham
Pool Street
Delvin End
Nuthampstead
Lower Green
Upper Green
Arkesden
Newport
Elder Street
Debden
Debden Green
Postmill
Finchingfield
Wethersfield
Morris Green
School Green
Southey Green
Anstey
Meesden
Stickling Green
Wicken Bonhunt
Clavering
Hill Green
Quendon Hall
Rickling
Quendon
Priors Hall Barn
Widdington
Mole Hall
Hamperden End
West Wood
Boyton End
Thaxted
Guildhall
Bardfield End Green
Bardfield Cottage
Blackmore End
Gosfield Hall
Brent Pelham
Berden
Starling's Green
Great Hormead
Little Hormead
Hare Street
Furneux Pelham
Stocking Pelham
Rickling Green
Ugley
Woodend Green
Horham Hall
Cutlers Green
John Webb's
Monk Street
Holder's Green
Little Bardfield
Great Bardfield
Waltham's Cross
Oxen End
Shalford
Church End
Beazley End
Dassels
Hay Street
East End
Mallows Green
Patmore Heath
Manuden
Henham
Church
Broxted
Duton Hill
Shalford Green
Bardfield Saling
Jasper's Green
Braughing
Albury
Farnham Green
Clapgate
Upwick Green
Stansted Mountfitchet
Farnham
Ugley Green
Pledgdon Green
Elsenham
Tye Green
Molehill Green
Little Easton
Great Easton
Lindsell
Duck End
Bran End
Great Saling
Panfield
Great Priory Farm
Bocking Churchstreet
Bocking
High Garrett
Puckeridge
Standon
Little Hadham
Bishop's Stortford
Birchanger
Burton End
London Stansted
Church
Bamber's Green
Great Dunmow
Stebbing
Stebbing Green
Churchend
Blake End
Rayne
Rayne Hall
Braintree
Andrewsfield
Wellpond Green
Hadham Ford
Bromley
Latchford
Bury Green
Start Hill
BIRCHANGER GREEN
Takeley Street
Takeley
Smith's Green
Little Canfield
Little Dunmow
Priory Vineyard
Grange Farm
Bannister Green
Felsted
Felsted Vineyard
Bartholomew Green
Great Notley
Black Notley
Young's End
Cressing
Barwick
Much Hadham
Hadham Cross
Forge
Rhodes
Thorley Street
Thorley
Bedlar's Green
Great Hallingbury
Hatfield Forest
Puttock's End
Bacon End
Barnston
Garnetts Wood
Bishop's Green
North End
Hartford End
Cock Green
Willows Green
Essex Showground
Leez Priory
Little Leighs
Great Leighs
Rank's Green
White Notley
Faulkbourne
Fairstead
Perry Green
Green Tye
Little Hallingbury
Allen's Green
Spellbrook
Wright's Green
Hatfield Broad Oak
Taverners Green
Castle
Great Canfield
High Roding
Onslow Green
Ford End
Babb's Green
Widford
Wareside
Sawbridgeworth
Hatfield Heath
The Rodings
Aythorpe Roding
Roundbush Green
High Easter
Stagden Cross
Pleshey
Great Waltham
Howe Street
Chatham Green
Fuller Street
Terling
Hunsdon
High Wych
Sheering
Colville Hall
White Roding
Leaden Roding
Good Easter
Little Waltham
Stanstead Abbotts
St. Margarets
Eastwick
Pye Corner
Matching
Nether Street
Margaret Roding
Fanner's Green
Broad's Green
Chignall Smealy
Broomfield
Newland Grove
Hatfield Peverel
Harlow
Mark Hall
Roydon
Hare Street
Church Langley
Potter Street
Matching Tye
Matching Green
Abbess Roding
Beauchamp Roding
Marshbury
Chalk End
Parsonage Green
Boreham
Great Parndon
Foster Street
High Laver
Little Laver
Birds Green
Shellow Bowells
Boyton Cross
Chignall St. James
Roxwell
Roydon Hamlet
Broadley Common
Magdalen Laver
Fyfield
Willingale
Chelmsford
Little Baddow
Broxbourne
Lower Nazeing
Nazeing
Parndon Wood
Hastingwood
Moreton
Great Oxney Green
Writtle
Widford
Ada Cole Stables
Tyler's Green
Bovinger
Blake Hall
Bobbingworth
Cooksmill Green
Epping Green
Bumble's Green
Thornwood Common
North Weald Bassett
High Ongar
Norton Mandeville
Norton Heath
Edney Common
Hylands House
Great Baddow
Sandon
Danbury
Epping Upland
Holyfield
Bury Farm Centre
Coopersale Common
Greensted Green
Saxon Wooden Church
Toot Hill
Chipping Ongar
Nine Ashes
Elkins Green
Loves Green
Galleywood
Butt's Green
Waltham Abbey
Epping
Upshire
Coopersale Street
Stanford Rivers
Blackmore
Beggar Hill
Mill Green
Margaretting
Margaretting Tye
East Hanningfield
Fiddlers Hamlet
Little End
Stondon Massey
Fryerning
Theydon Bois
Copthall Green
Stapleford Tawney
Wyatt's Green
Ingatestone
Ingatestone Hall
Stock
West Hanningfield
Hanningfield Reservoir
Woodham Ferrers
Hobbs Cross
Kelvedon Hatch
Doddinghurst
Mountnessing
Heybridge
South Hanningfield
Retttendon
High Beech
Debden Green
Navestock
Navestock Side
Fox Hatch
Crow Green
Loughton
Abridge
Passingford Bridge
Stapleford
Pilgrims Hatch
Ramsden Heath
Downham
Coalhill
Epping Forest
Queen's Lodge
Chingford
Havering's
Weald

54
A
B
C
D
65
66
1
2
3
4
5
Wickhambrook
Clopton Green
Farley Green
Denston
Hawkedon
Stradishall
Stansfield
Somerton
Brockley Green
Hartest
Lawshall
Shimpling Street
Smithwood Green
Alpheton
Cockfield
Bulls Wood
Thorpe Green
Thorpe Morieux
Rookesy Green
Brettenham
Hitcham
Battisford Tye
Battisford
Needham Market
Hascot Hill
Ringshall
Barking Tye
Barking
Darmsden
Bonny Wood
Baylham
Cross Green
Charles Tye
Wattisham
Great Bricett
Willisham Tye
Great Blakenham
Suffolk Water Park
Assington Green
Thurston End
Boxted
Gifford's Hall
Vineyards
Shimpling
Hundon
Chimney Street
Kedington
Poslingford
Manor Vineyards
Glemsford
Stanstead
Kentwell Hall
Bridge Street
Railway Walk
Lavenham
Little Hall
Guildhall
Brent Eleigh
The Priory
Monks Eleigh
Kettlebaston
Bildeston
Nedging Tye
Naughton
Nedging
Greenstreet Green
Offton
Somersham
Little Blakenham
Blakenham Woodland
Nether Hall
Cavendish
Chilton Street
Ancient House
Clare
Clare Castle
Priory
Stoke by Clare
Wixoe
Baythorn End
Ashen
Ovington
Pentlow
Tower
Foxearth
Long Melford
Liston
Melford Hall
Acton
Little Waldingfield
Swingleton Green
Milden
Chelsworth
Semer
Lindsey
Lindsey Tye
St. James's Chapel
Kersey
Rose Green
Ash Street
Whatfield
Elmsett
Flowton
Bramford
Sproughton
Aldham
Wolves Wood
Whatfield
Rowland Taylor Monument
Burstall
Hintlesham
Hadleigh
Poplar Lane
Washbrook
Chattisham
Copdock
Guildhall
Railway Walk
Upper Layham
Lower Layham
Belchamp St. Paul
Belchamp Otten
Belchamp Walter
Borley Green
Borley
Newman's Green
Sudbury
Gainsborough's House
Ballingdon
Great Cornard
Great Waldingfield
Edwardstone
Mill Green
Groton Wood
Wicker Street Green
Hadleigh Heath
Newton
Boxford
Calais Street
Stone Street
Whitestreet Green
Potash Lane Hedge
Polstead Heath
Polstead
Ridgewell
Tilbury Green
Little Yeldham
Puttock End
Bulmer
Bulmer Tye
Middleton
Great Cornard
Little Cornard
Cornard Mere
Tilbury Juxta Clare
Great Yeldham
North End
Gestingthorpe
Great Henny
Henny Street
Workhouse Green
Assington
Leavenheath
Shelley
Lower Raydon
Raydon
Little Wenham
Great Wenham
Capel St. Mary
Holton St. Mary
Bentley
Stambourne
Toppesfield
Colne Valley
Hedingham
Pool Street
Twinstead Green
Twinstead
Wickham St. Paul
Paradise Centre
Dorking Tye
Withermarsh Green
Thorington Hall
Higham
Stoke-by-Nayland
Honey Tye
Lamarsh
Alphamstone
Long Gardens
Gainsford End
Delvin End
Castle Hedingham
Great Maplestead
Little Maplestead
Highstreet Green
Sible Hedingham
Morris Green
Wethersfield
Cross End
Pebmarsh
Bures
St. Stephen's
Arger Fen
Nayland
Boxted
Thorington Street
Stratford St. Mary
East Bergholt
East Bergholt Place
Flatford Mill
Dedham
Toy
Munnings
Brantham
Cattawade
Manningtree
Mistley
Lawford
Southey Green
School Green
Blackmore End
Gosfield Hall
Gosfield
Whiteash Green
Buntings Green
Countess Cross
Colne Engaine
Mount Bures
Little Horkesley
Wormingford
Great Horkesley
Boxted Cross
Langham
Lamb Corner
Dedham Heath
Ardleigh
Ardleigh Resr.
Little Bromley
Church End
Beazley End
Halstead
Earls Colne
Colne Valley
White Colne
Wakes Colne
East Anglian Railway
Hemp's Green
Rose Green
Horkesley Heath
Fordham
West Bergholt
Fordham Heath
Mile End
Trees
Fox Street
Crockleford Heath
Burnt Heath
Horsley Cross
Great Bromley
Greenstead Green
Burton's Green
Bebel Air
Chappel
Knights Farm
Swan Street
Ford Street
Aldham
Jasper's Green
Great Priory Farm
Panfield
Bocking Churchstreet
High Garrett
Tumbler's Green
Earls Colne
Marks Hall
Great Tey
Eight Ash Green
Marks Tey
East Gores
COLCHESTER
Elmstead
Little Bentley
Rayne
Rayne Hall
Bocking
Braintree
Stisted
BRAINTREE
Pattiswick
Coggeshall
Surrex
Little Tey
Beacon End
Lexden Earthworks
Stanway
Copford
Shrub End
Historic
Bourne Mill
Univ. of Essex
Elmstead Market
Beth Chatto
Frating Green
Hare Green
Great Bentley
Bradwell
Stockstreet
Grange Barn
Coggeshall Hamlet
Paycocke's
Feeringbury Manor
Heritage
Skye Green
Feering
Copford Green
Church
Easthorpe
Colchester
Heckfordbridge
Blackheath
Rowhedge
Wivenhoe
Elmstead Heath
Alresford
Aingers Green
Thorrington
Bartholomew Green
Great Notley
Young's End
Tye Green
Cressing
Perry Green
Black Notley
Crossing Temple Barn
Fossil Hall
Silver End
Kelvedon
Water mill
Messing
Hardy's Green
Birch
Layer-de-la-Haye
Abberton
Fingringhoe
Tide Mill
Essex Showground
Great Leighs
White Notley
Faulkbourne
Fairstead
Church
Rivenhall
Local History
Inworth
Smyth's Green
Shalom Hall
Layer Breton
Birch Green
Layer Marney
Layer Marney Tower
Abberton Resr.
South Green
Langenhoe
Rat Island
Brightlingsea
Rank's Green
Rivenhall End
Tiptree
Tiptree Heath
Peldon
Hurst Green
Martello Tower
Priory
Aviation & Forties
St. Osyth
Fuller Street
Terling
Chipping Hill
Flack's Green
WITHAM
Great Braxted
Tolleshunt Knights
Oxley Green
Great Wigborough
Salcott
Old Hall Marshes
Pay Island
Blue Row
East Mersea
Cudmore Grove
Point Clear
MERSEA ISLAND
Little Waltham
Wickham Bishops
Great Totham North
Great Totham South
Little Totham
Tolleshunt D'Arcy
West Mersea
Virley Channel
Colne Point
Newland Grove
Hatfield Peverel
Nounsley
Tolleshunt Major
Tollesbury
Broad Street Green
Boreham
Ulting
Goldhanger
Bradwell Power Station
Sales Point
Heybridge
Langford
Beeleigh Abbey
Bradwell Waterside
Church
Little Baddow
Woodham Walter
Nature Trail
Millennium
Heybridge Basin
Osea Island
RIVER BLACKWATER
Bradwell Lodge
CHELMSFORD
Chelmsford
MALDON
Northey Island
Bradwell-on-Sea
Great Baddow
Sandon
Danbury
Danbury Park
Gay Bowers
Woodham Mortimer
Hazeleigh
Leper
Maldon 991
Ramsey Island
St. Lawrence
Church
Tillingham
Galleyend
Butt's Green
Cock Clarks
Rudley Green
Vineyard
Steeple
Dengie Marshes
Bicknacre
Thrift Wood
Purleigh
Mundon
Dengie
Howe Green
East Hanningfield
Howegreen
Cold Norton
Maylandsea
Mayland
Asheldham
Latchingdon
West Hanningfield
Woodham Ferrers
Hyde Hall
Stow Maries
Althorne
Southminster
Hanningfield Reservoir
Rettendon
Mangapps Farm
South Hanningfield
Coalhill
South Woodham Ferrers
Marsh Farm
Hall Wood
North Fambridge
Ostend
Stoneyhills
Burnham-on-Crouch
Holliwell Point
Foulness Sands
Downham
South Fambridge
Lion
Woodham
Hempstead
SUFFOLK
ESSEX

Coddenham
Ashbocking
Gibraltar
Corner
Debach
Blake's Meadow
Market
Pettistree
Ashe
B1069
Tunstall
Tunstall Forest
Street
Bay
Martello Tower
Hemingstone
B1078
Swilland
Bredfield
Ufford
A1152
Bentwaters
Sudbourne
A14
Bell's Cross
Chillesford
650
Barham
Henley
Witnesham
Burgh
Eyke
B1084
Claydon
E
Grundisburgh
F
Hasketon
Melton
Bromeswell
B1084
G
Butley
67
Dunwich Underwater Exploration
Orford
H
55
Orford Ness
250
Akenham
Great Bealings
B1079
B1438
WOODBRIDGE
Rendlesham Forest
Capel Green
Butley High Corner
Westerfield
Tuddenham
Little Bealings
Woodbridge
Tide Mill
NT
DANGER AREA
Capel St. Andrew
Havergate Island
Orford Ness
Castle Hill
Playford
Sutton Hoo Archaeological Site
Sutton Common
Lower Hollesley
Boyton
Rushmere St. Andrew
A1214
Martlesham
Sutton Heath
A12
Sutton
1
Kesgrave
Martlesham Heath
Shottisham
River Ore
Hollesley Bay
Newbourne Springs
Waldringfield
Hollesley
California
SEE PAGE 190
IPSWICH
Suffolk Showground
Brightwell
Newbourne Hall
Newbourne
Hemley
Shingle Street
Martello Tower
Chantry
Spring Wood
Ipswich
Gainsborough
57
Bucklesham
River
Alderton
Martello Tower
Martello Tower
Belstead
Wherstead
A14
58
Bawdsey
40
Nacton Meadows
Nacton
R. Orwell
Kirton
Deben
Martello Tower
Freston
Preston Tower
Falkenham
Tattingstone White Horse
Woolverstone
Levington
Trimley St. Martin
Bawdsey Manor
NT
Pin Mill
Levington Lagoon
Thorpe Common
59
Felixstowe Ferry
Tattingstone
Martello Tower
Martello Tower
Tattingstone Wonder
Holbrook
Chelmondiston
B1456
Trimley Lower Street
Trimley St. Mary
60
A154
Alton Water
Old Felixstowe
Upper Street
Stutton
Lower Holbrook
Shotley
A14
Walton
2
B1080
Harkstead
Erwarton
61
62
Harwich to:
Esbjerg 17hrs.
Hamburg 18hrs. 30mins.
Hook of Holland 6hrs. 15mins.
Hook of Holland 3hrs. 40mins.
(Fast Ferry)
Shotley Gate
Electric Palace Cine.
FELIXSTOWE
Towers
RIVER STOUR
Stour Wood & Copperas Bay
Guildhall
Maritime
Martello Tower
New Mistley
Wrabness
Parkeston
Harwich Harbour
Bradfield
Redoubt
Landguard Fort
B1352
Ramsey
Dovercourt
Upper Dovercourt
Harwich
Bradfield Heath
12
30
A120
B1414
Little Oakley
Horsleycross Street
Wix
Great Oakley
Stones Green
B1035
Tendring Green
16
Hamford Water
Beaumont
Horsey Island
3
Tendring
Thorpe Green
The Naze
Weeley
B1033
Thorpe-le-Soken
Kirby-le-Soken
Maritime
Walton-on-the-Naze
Weeley Heath
B1414
B1033
B1034
8
Kirby Cross
Row Heath
Little Clacton
Great Holland
Frinton-on-Sea
20
A133
B1442
St. Osyth Heath
B1032
Holland Haven
Great Clacton
B1027
Holland-on-Sea
N O R T H
St. Osyth's
4
Lifeboat Station
CLACTON-ON-SEA
Jaywick
Martello Towers
Martello Tower
S E A
10
5
200
E
41
F
G
H
20
30
40
650

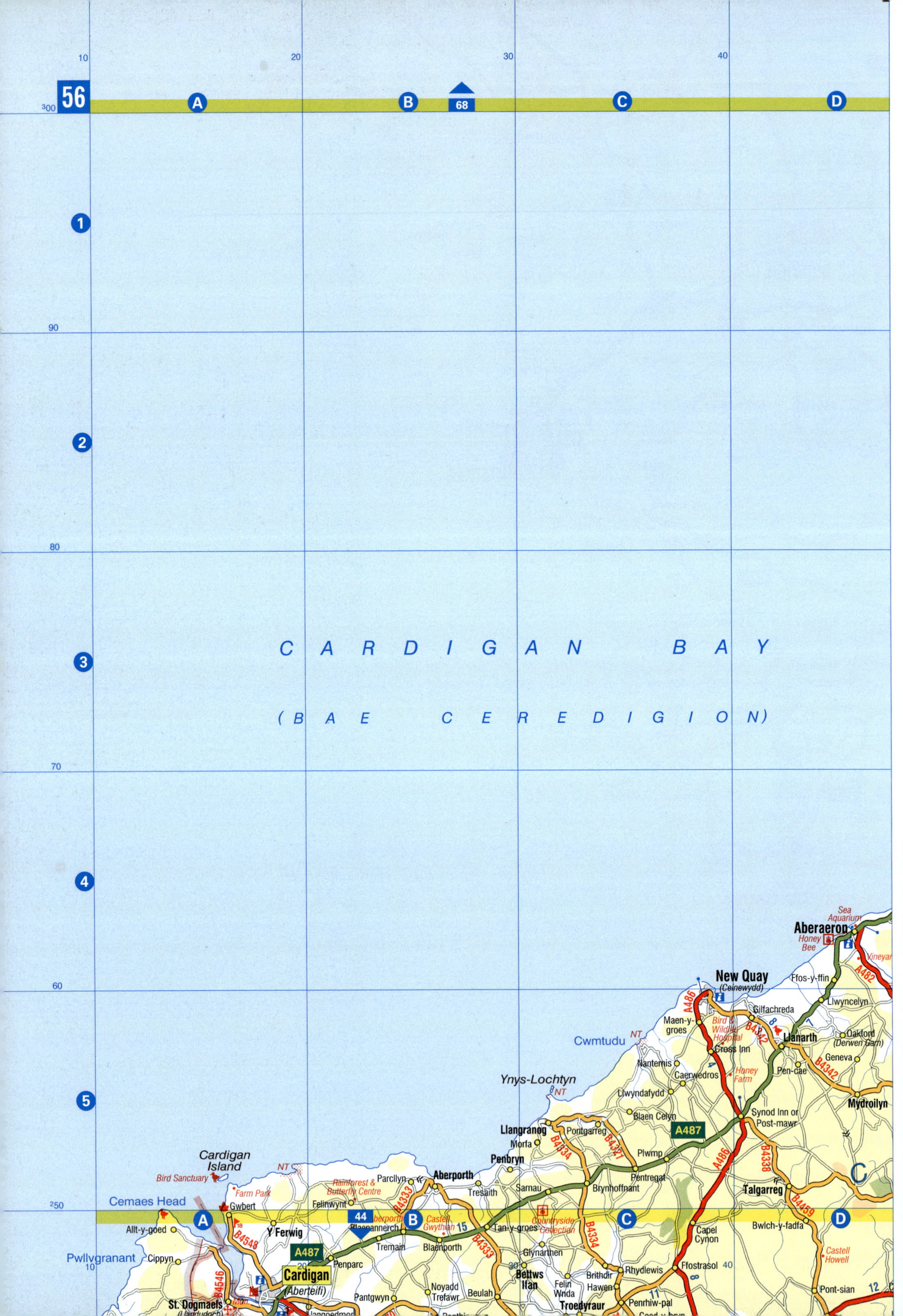

56
68
A
B
C
D
CARDIGAN BAY
(BAE CEREDIGION)
Aberaeron
Sea Aquarium
Honey Bee
New Quay
(Ceinewydd)
Ffos-y-ffin
Llwyncelyn
Gilfachreda
Llanarth
Oakford
(Derwen Gam)
Geneva
Pen-cae
Mydroilyn
Cwmtudu
Maen-y-groes
Bird & Wildlife Hospital
Cross Inn
Nanternis
Caerwedros
Honey Farm
Llwyndafydd
Blaen Celyn
Synod Inn or Post-mawr
Ynys-Lochtyn
Llangranog
Morfa
Pontgarreg
Penbryn
Plwmp
Pentregat
Brynhoffnant
Sarnau
Talgarreg
Aberporth
Tresaith
Parcllyn
Rainforest & Butterfly Centre
Felinwynt
Cardigan Island
Bird Sanctuary
Farm Park
Cemaes Head
Gwbert
Allt-y-goed
Y Ferwig
Blaenannerch
Tremain
Blaenporth
Castell Gwythian
Tan-y-groes
Countryside Collection
Glynarthen
Capel Cynon
Bwlch-y-fadfa
Castell Howell
Pwllygranant
Cippyn
Cardigan
(Aberteifi)
Penparc
Noyadd Trefawr
Beulah
Pantgwyn
Bettws Ifan
Felin Wnda
Brithdir
Hawen
Troedyraur
Rhydlewis
Ffostrasol
Penrhiw-pal
Pont-sian
St. Dogmaels
A487
A486
A482
B4342
B4334
B4321
B4338
B4459
B4333
B4548
B4546
NT

57
58
45
46
69
POWYS
CAMBRIAN MOUNTAINS
CEREDIGION
CARMARTHENSHIRE
Tonfanau
Bryncrug
Dolgoch
Dolgoch Falls
Pandy
Talyllyn
Torrenhendre
2076
Aber Dysynni
Broad Water
Rhyd-yr-onen
Tywyn
Narrow Gauge Railway
Trum Gelli
Pennal
Cwrt
Corlan-fraith
Machynlleth
Pantperthog
Cat Funicular
Centre for Alternative Technology
Llanwrin
Penegoes
Abercegir
Commins Coch
Darowen
Tafolwern
Tal-y-Wern
Forge
Plas Machynlleth
Derwenlas
Melinbyrhedyn
Moelfre 1537
Pennant
Dulas
Glaspwll
Aberhosan
Farm Trail
Penhelig
Aberdovey (Aberdyfi)
Aberdovey Bar
Glandyfi
Ynys-hir
Eglwys Fach
Furnace
Dyfi Furnace Monument
Pencarreggopa 1467
Dylife
Glaslyn
Ynyslas
Ynys-las
Llancynfelyn
Tre'r-ddol
Local Folk
Tre Taliesin
Llyn Conach
Llyn Dwfn
Moel y-Llyn 1708
Llyn Plas-y-mynydd
Bugeilyn
Llwynygog
Borth
Animalarium
Upper Borth
Tal-y-bont
Dol-y-Bont
Afon Leri
Blaenhafren Source of R. Severn
Drosgol 1806
Nant-y-moch Reservoir
2467
2427
Pen Pumlumon Arwystli
PLYNLIMON (PUMLUMON FAWR)
Source of R. Wye
Hafren Forest
Esgair y Maesnant
Llyn Clywedog Reservoir
Afon Biga
R. Severn
Drum Peithnant
Rhyd-meirionydd
Llandre
Bontgoch
Llyn Craigypistyll
Llyn Syfydrin
Pen-y-garn
Bow Street
Llangorwen
Garth
Salem
Cwmsymlog
Penrhyn-coch
Cefn Llwyd
Pen-bont Rhydybeddau
Cwmerfyn
Camera Obscura
Cliff
ABERYSTWYTH
The Bar
Penparcau
Waun Fawr
Comins Coch
Capel Dewi
Llanbadarn Fawr
Blaen-geuffordd
Dollwen
Goginan
Silver Lead Mine
Ponterwyd
Dinas Resr.
Dyffryn Castell
Wye Valley
Afon Rheidol
Southgate
Moriah
Capel Bangor
Cwmbrwyno
Llywernog
Rhydyfelin
Capel Seion
Vale of Rheidol
Aberffrwd
Rheidol Power Station
Ystumtuen
Mynach Falls
Ysbyty Cynfyn
Esgair Ychion
Llanfarian
Gors
Chancery
New Cross
Llanfihangel-y-Creuddyn
Devil's Bridge (Pontarfynach)
Three Bridges
The Arch
Jubilee Arch
Trisant
Blaenplwyf
Llanilar
Cnwch Coch
Yr Allt
Elan
New Row
Cwmystwyth
Rhos-y-garth
Crosswood (Trawsgoed)
Wenallt
Llanafan
Afon Ystwyth
Pont-rhyd-y-groes
Ty'n Bedw
Geifas 1873
Nant Hirin
Llanddeiniol
Carreg Ti-pw
Llangwyryfon
Lledrod
Ysbyty Ystwyth
Mynydd Bach 1092
Marchnant
Trawsallt
Llyn Fyrddon-Fawr
Llyn Fyrddon-Fach 1944
Llyn Cerrigllwydion Isaf
Llyn Cerrigllwydion Uchaf
Llyn Du
Clawdd-du-bach
Llanrhystud
Tynygraig
Trefenter
Rhyd-Rosser
Llansantffraed
Llan-non
Rhydfudr
Bronnant
Ystradmeurig
Ffair Rhos
Llyn Teifi
Llyn Hir
Llyn Egnant
Llyn y Gorlan
Trumau
MYNYDD BACH
Pontrhydfendigaid
Swyddffynnon
Bontnewydd
Strata Florida
Abbey
Dibyn Du
Rhos Haminiog
Nebo
Cross Inn
Bethania
Blaenpennal
Cors Caron
Cors-goch Glan Teifi
Pen-y-bwlch
Llyn Gynon
Esgair Garthen
Claerwen Reservoir
Afon Claerwen
Aberarth
Pennant
Ty'n-yr-eithin
Menachty
Penuwch
Aberaeron
Llanaeron
Llanerchaeron
Cilcennin
Llangeitho
Tregaron
Esgair Llyn-du
Bryn Garw 1827
Drum yr Eira
Ciliau Aeron
Newbridge
Bwlch-Llan
Y Drum 1668
Esgair Ambor
2104 Drygarn Fawr
Trefilan
Llundain-fach
Capel Betws Lleucu
Bryn Crwn 1732
Dihewyd
Ystrad Aeron
Talsarn
Gartheli
Abermeurig
Llwyn-y-groes
Esgair Fraith
Llyn Berwyn
Esgair Cerrig 1588
Gamallt
Felinfach
Llanddewi Brefi
Fign Blaen Brefi
Esgair Llethr 1543
Camddwr
Olmarch
Temple Bar
Ffynnon-oer
Noah's Ark Farm Park
Llangybi
1641 Cefn-Coch
Nant Irfon
Abergwesyn
Bettws Bledrws
Llanfair Clydogau
Bryn Brawd 1589
Pen Rhiw-clochdy
Cribyn
Silian
Cefn Fannog 1476
Tywi Forest
Gorsgoch
1497 Pen y Gurnos
Llyn Brianne
Maesg
Lampeter (Llanbedr Pont Steffan)
University College
Cellan
Pentrefelin
Craig Twrch
Mynydd Trawsnant 1695
Welsh Wool
Llanwrtyd
Llanwrtyd Wells (Llanwrtud)
Cwrtnewydd
Llanwnnen
Cwmann
Pentre-bach
Ystradffin
Cwmsychpant
Drefach
Alltyblacca
Llanwenog
Rhandirmwyn
A487
A470
A489
A493
A44
A4120
A485
A482
A475
A483
B4405
B4404
B4518
B4353
B4572
B4340
B4575
B4576
B4577
B4343
B4574
B4337
B4339
B4342
B4578
B4338
B4343

58
70
POWYS
CAMBRIAN MOUNTAINS
RADNOR FOREST
Elan Valley (Cwm Elan)
Llanidloes
Newtown (Y Drenewydd)
Rhayader (Rhaeadr Gwy)
Llandrindod Wells (Llandrindod)
Builth Wells (Llanfair-ym-Muallt)
Llanwrtyd Wells (Llanwrtud)
Llangurig
Caersws
Llanbrynmair
Carno
Trefeglwys
Llandinam
Mochdre
Kerry (Ceri)
Berriew (Aberriw)
Bettws Cedewain
Llanmerewig
Llandyssil
Beguildy
Llanbadarn Fynydd
Llanbister
Llangunllo
Bleddfa
Llanddewi Ystradenni
Nantmel
Crossgates
Llandegley
New Radnor
Howey
Newbridge on Wye
Llansantffraed Cwmdeuddwr
St. Harmon
Garth
Aberedw
Llandeilo Graban
A470
A44
A483
A489
A488
A481
A4081
B4518
B4569
B4568
B4390
B4389
B4385
B4386
B4368
B4355
B4356
B4358
B4567
B4520
B4594

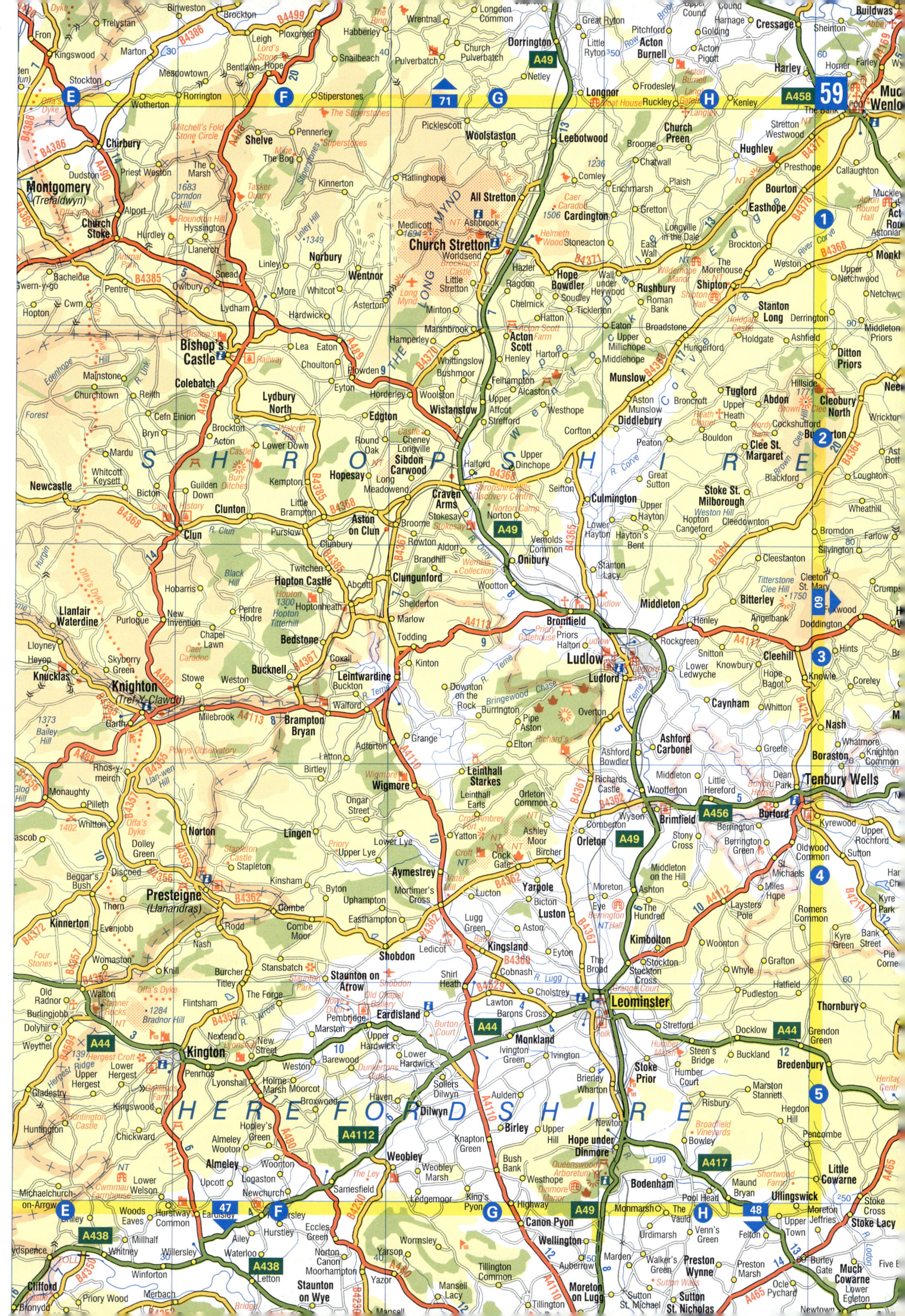

59
71
47
48
60
E
F
G
H
1
2
3
4
5
SHROPSHIRE
HEREFORDSHIRE
A49
A458
A44
A456
A4112
A417
A438
A4113
A488
A489
A4110
B4386
B4385
B4368
B4371
B4365
B4367
B4361
B4362
B4355
B4356
B4357
B4360
B4214
B4364
B4368
B4378
Montgomery
(Trefaldwyn)
Church Stoke
Chirbury
Kingswood
Stockton
Marton
Trelystan
Binweston
Brockton
Leigh
Ploxgreen
Bentlawn
Hope
Meadowtown
Rorrington
Wotherton
Stiperstones
The Stiperstones
Habberley
Snailbeach
Pulverbatch
Church Pulverbatch
Wrentnall
Longden Common
Dorrington
Netley
Longnor
Leebotwood
Woolstaston
Picklescott
Ratlinghope
All Stretton
Church Stretton
Little Stretton
Ashbrook
Minton
Marshbrook
Acton Scott
Hope Bowdler
Cardington
Comley
Enchmarsh
Gretton
Longville in the Dale
Rushbury
Wall under Heywood
Ticklerton
Eaton
Upper Millichope
Middlehope
Munslow
Aston Munslow
Diddlebury
Broncroft
Tugford
Abdon
Clee St. Margaret
Cleobury North
Burwarton
Ditton Priors
Stanton Long
Shipton
Brockton
Weston
Bourton
Easthope
Presthope
Hughley
Much Wenlock
Kenley
Church Preen
Acton Burnell
Pitchford
Frodesley
Ruckley
Cressage
Harley
Sheinton
Buildwas
Great Ryton
Little Ryton
Shelve
Pennerley
The Bog
Kinnerton
Norbury
Wentnor
Linley
More
Lydham
Bishop's Castle
Colebatch
Lea
Eaton
Choulton
Hardwick
Asterton
Myndtown
Hamperley
Whittingslow
Bushmoor
Wistanstow
Woolston
Horderley
Edgton
Lydbury North
Brockton
Acton
Lower Down
Kempton
Hopesay
Sibdon Carwood
Craven Arms
Stokesay
Halford
Onibury
Culmington
Seifton
Corfton
Westhope
Peaton
Great Sutton
Stoke St. Milborough
Clunton
Clun
Newcastle
Bicton
Whitcott Keysett
Mardu
Mainstone
Churchtown
Guilden Down
Little Brampton
Aston on Clun
Purslow
Clunbury
Broome
Twitchen
Hopton Castle
Abcott
Clungunford
Shelderton
Marlow
Todding
Bromfield
Ludlow
Ludford
Rockgreen
Henley
Middleton
Bitterley
Cleehill
Knowbury
Caynham
Knighton
(Tref-Y-Clawdd)
Llanfair Waterdine
Stowe
Bucknell
Bedstone
Leintwardine
Brampton Bryan
Walford
Buckton
Adforton
Wigmore
Leinthall Starkes
Orleton
Richards Castle
Woofferton
Brimfield
Little Hereford
Tenbury Wells
Burford
Boraston
Nash
Presteigne
(Llanandras)
Norton
Lingen
Aymestrey
Yarpole
Kingsland
Shobdon
Staunton on Arrow
Eardisland
Pembridge
Kington
Lyonshall
Leominster
Stoke Prior
Kimbolton
Hope under Dinmore
Bodenham
Dilwyn
Weobley
Canon Pyon
Wellington
Almeley
Staunton on Wye
Moreton on Lugg
Sutton St. Nicholas
Preston Wynne
Much Cowarne
Little Cowarne
Ullingswick
Stoke Lacy
Bredenbury
Thornbury
Clifford
Whitney
Winforton
Eardisley
Letton
Offa's Dyke
River Corve
The Long Mynd
Wenlock Edge

60
72
SEE PAGE 197
WOLVERHAMPTON
Ironbridge
Much Wenlock
Bridgnorth
Albrighton
Codsall
Tettenhall
WILLENHALL
WEDNESFIELD
BILSTON
COSELEY
SEDGLEY
TIPTON
Wombourne
Kingswinford
BRIERLEY HILL
Quarry Bank
Cradley
Amblecote
STOURBRIDGE
HALESOWEN
Hagley
Kinver
KIDDERMINSTER
Bewdley
Stourport-on-Severn
Cleobury Mortimer
Cleobury North
Tenbury Wells
Burford
SHROPSHIRE
WORCESTERSHIRE
WYRE FOREST
Highley
Alveley
Bromyard
DROITWICH SPA
BROMSGROVE
Ombersley
WORCESTER
SEE PAGE 197
GREAT MALVERN
Malvern Link
Upton Snodsbury
Pershore
Hartlebury
Chaddesley Corbett
Stanton Long
Morville
Upton Cressett
Chetton
Ditton Priors
Abdon
Clee St. Margaret
Neenton
Middleton Scriven
Billingsley
Chelmarsh
Burwarton
Stottesdon
Kinlet
Hopton Wafers
Cleehill
Doddington
Bitterley
Milson
Neen Sollars
Rock
Abberley
Great Witley
Stockton on Teme
Lindridge
Shelsley Walsh
Clifton upon Teme
Upper Sapey
Tedstone Wafer
Tedstone Delamere
Edwyn Ralph
Thornbury
Bredenbury
Suckley
Leigh Sinton
Acton Beauchamp
Bishop's Frome
Castle Frome
Much Cowarne
Ullingswick
Stoke Lacy
Lower Broadheath
Upper Broadheath
Hallow
Holt Heath
Holt Fleet
Grimley
Fernhill Heath
Martin Hussingtree
Hindlip
Crowle
Tibberton
Hanbury
Stoke Prior
Wychbold
Blakedown
Wolverley
Cookley
Upper Arley
Romsley
Clent
Enville
Himley
Swindon
Bobbington
Claverley
Worfield
Pattingham
Beckbury
Ryton
Shifnal
A458
A442
A454
A449
A456
A451
A443
A44
A4103
A38
A4440
A4123
A461
A4036
A491
A41
A460
A417
A465
A4117
A4133
A422
A4538
A4104
M5
B4364
B4363
B4555
B4194
B4190
B4188
B4189
B4176
B4368
B4378
B4371
B4376
B4375
B4373
B4214
B4204
B4203
B4220
B4197
B4196
B4195
B4090
B4084
B4082
B4091
B4211
B4219
B4232
B4503
B4424

BROWNHILLS
TAMWORTH
Polesworth
Twycross
Walsall Wood
BLOXWICH
Rushall
ALDRIDGE
WALSALL
Streetly
SUTTON COLDFIELD
M6 TOLL
WEDNESBURY
WEST BROMWICH
ATHERSTONE
Mancetter
Hartshill
Weddington
NUNEATON
WARWICKSHIRE
OLDBURY
Castle Bromwich
Coleshill
BEDWORTH
SMETHWICK
BLACKHEATH
BIRMINGHAM
SEE PAGE 186
BIRMINGHAM INTERNATIONAL
Harborne
Edgbaston
Sheldon
Marston Green
CORLEY
Bulkington
Meriden
Allesley
COVENTRY
SEE PAGE 188
FRANKLEY
Shirley
SOLIHULL
Hampton in Arden
Balsall Common
Northfield
Rubery
Longbridge
Knowle
Dorridge
Cofton Hackett
HOPWOOD PARK
Alvechurch
Hockley Heath
KENILWORTH
Kenilworth
Baginton
Stoneleigh
Kingswood
Rowington
Leek Wootton
REDDITCH
Mappleborough Green
Ullenhall
Henley-in-Arden
Hampton Magna
ROYAL LEAMINGTON SPA
Whitnash
WARWICK
Studley
Astwood Bank
Feckenham
Claverdon
Norton Lindsey
Barford
Great Alne
Snitterfield
Wilmcote
Alcester
Wellesbourne
WARWICK
Tiddington
STRATFORD-UPON-AVON
SEE PAGE 196
Bidford-on-Avon
Welford on Avon
Harvington
Cleeve Prior
Long Marston
Ettington
Pillerton Hersey
M5
M6
M40
M42
A38
A41
A45
A46
A429
A435
A441
A444
A452
A5
61
73
49
50

62
LEICESTER
LEICESTERSHIRE
NORTHAMPTONSHIRE
WARWICKSHIRE
COVENTRY
SEE PAGE 188
NUNEATON
HINCKLEY
RUGBY
DAVENTRY
ROYAL LEAMINGTON SPA
ATHERSTONE
BEDWORTH
WIGSTON
Oadby
Blaby
Lutterworth
Enderby
Earl Shilton
Barwell
Burbage
Hartshill
Weddington
Bulkington
Kenilworth
Southam
Towcester
Kislingbury
Husbands Bosworth
Kibworth Harcourt
Kibworth Beauchamp
Long Buckby
Weedon Bec
Braunston
Dunchurch
Ryton-on-Dunsmore
Stretton-on-Dunsmore
Binley
Bishop's Itchington
Fenny Compton
Byfield
Woodford Halse
Chipping Warden
Cropredy
Moreton Pinkney
Blakesley
Litchborough
Harlestone
Church Brampton
West Haddon
Crick
Kilsby
Barby
Yelvertoft
Swinford
Welford
Naseby
North Kilworth
Lubenham
Gilmorton
Peatling Parva
Ullesthorpe
Claybrooke Magna
Sapcote
Stoney Stanton
Croft
Cosby
Countesthorpe
Whetstone
Narborough
Braunstone
Glen Parva
Great Glen
Burton Overy
Billesdon
Houghton on the Hill
Thurnby
Evington
Desford
Kirby Fields
Newbold Verdon
Market Bosworth
Carlton
Twycross
Sheepy Magna
Sibson
Upton
Stoke Golding
Higham on the Hill
Kirkby Mallory
Peckleton
Stapleton
Wolvey
Shilton
Ansty
Brinklow
Pailton
Monks Kirby
Churchover
Clifton upon Dunsmore
Hillmorton
Cawston
Bilton
Long Lawford
Wolston
Bretford
Princethorpe
Marton
Birdingbury
Leamington Hastings
Grandborough
Willoughby
Sawbridge
Flecknoe
Napton on the Hill
Priors Marston
Priors Hardwick
Hellidon
Charwelton
Staverton
Badby
Everdon
Farthingstone
Upper Boddington
Wormleighton
Ladbroke
Harbury
Gaydon
Kineton
Farnborough
Warmington
Ratley
Shotteswell
Mollington
Wardington
Culworth
Weston
Weedon Lois
Wappenham
Greens Norton
Pattishall
Gayton
Bugbrooke
Nether Heyford
Upper Heyford
Flore
Brockhall
Whilton
Muscott
Little Brington
Great Brington
Holdenby
East Haddon
Guilsborough
Spratton
Creaton
Thornby
Cold Ashby
Elkington
Watford
WATFORD GAP
LEICESTER FOREST EAST
CORLEY
WARWICK
NORTHAMPTON
M1
M6
M40
M45
M69
A5
A45
A47
A426
A428
A423
A361
A4303
A4304
A14
A43
A444
A6

63
64
the Hill
Manton
Weston
North Luffenham
Ketton
Aldgate
Geeston
Wothorpe
Barnack
Ufford
Launde Abbey
R. Chater
Lyndon
White Water Resr.
A1
A47
A6003
Wing
Pilton
Southorpe
Southey Wood
Marholm
Skeffington
Loddington
Ridlington
Preston
South Luffenham
Collyweston
Wittering
Morcott
Duddington
Sacrewell Farm
Sacrewell Watermill
Castor Hanglands
East Norton
Belton
Ayston
Glaston
Thornhaugh
Rolleston
Tugby
Allexton
Wardley
Bisbrooke
Barrowden
Tixover
Wansford
Noseley
Goadby
Uppingham
Uppingham School
Seaton
Wakerley
Wakerley Great Wood
Stibbington
Sutton
Ailsworth
Castor
Nene Valley Railway
Water Newton
Orton Wistow
Alwalton
Horninghold
Stockerston
Stoke Dry
Lyddington
Lyddington Bede House
Harringworth
King's Cliffe
Yarwell
Hallaton
Hallaton Village
Glooston
Eyebrook Reservoir
Thorpe by Water
Laxton
Blatherwycke Lake
Blatherwycke
The Prebendal Manor House
Nassington
Sibson
Peterborough (Sibson)
Chesterton
Stonton Wyville
Blaston
Apethorpe
R. Nene
Cranoe
Slawston
Gretton
A43
Bulwick
Woodnewton
Elton
Over End
A605
A6003
Church Langton
Thorpe Langton
Medbourne
Great Easton
Caldecott
Kirby Hall
Deene
Southwick Hall
Fotheringhay Church
Fotheringhay
Elton Hall
Haddon
East Langton
Welham
Drayton
Bringhurst
Rockingham
Deene Park
Southwick
Deenethorpe
Morborne
PETERBOROUGH
R. Welland
Rockingham Speedway
Eaglethorpe
Weston by Welland
Ashley
Cottingham
Rockingham Castle
Deenethorpe
Tansor
Warmington
Sutton Bassett
Middleton
East Carlton Steel-Marking Heritage Centre
Weldon
Upper Benefield
Glapthorn
Cotterstock
Folksworth
A6116
A427
Great Bowden
Harborough
Stoke Albany
Wilbarston
East Carlton
Oundle
A605
Ashton
Ashton Mill
Caldecote
Little Bowden
Dingley
Kings Wood
CORBY
Stanion
Lower Benefield
Barnwell
Marina
Polebrook
Lutton
MARKET HARBOROUGH
A6
Brampton Ash
Stoke Wood End Quarter
A427
A6014
Great Oakley
Little Oakley
ROCKINGHAM
FOREST
Stoke Doyle
Armston
Hemington
Pipewell
Harper's Brook
Great Oakley Meadow
Brigstock
Brigstock
Permyn
Lyveden New Bield
Barnwell St. Andrew
Luddington in the Brook
Hill Farm Herbs
Pilton
Barnwell All Saints
Braybrooke
The Plens
Newton
A43
A6116
Wadenhoe
Thurning
Great Gidding
Desborough
Triangular Lodge
Geddington
Achurch
Wigsthorpe
A508
Rushton
Eleanor Cross
Grafton Park Wood
Sudborough
Aldwincle
Little Gidding
Steeple Gidding
Tailby Meadow
A6003
Boughton House
Memorial
Thorpe Waterville
Arthingworth
River Ise
Rothwell
Rothwell Gullet
Grafton Underwood
Lowick
Clopton
Winwick
Harrington
A14
Weekley
Drayton House
A605
Titchmarsh
Warkton
Slipton
Islip
Thorpe Malsor Resr.
Orton
Kelmarsh
Carpetbagger & Northants Aviation
Loddington
Thorpe Malsor
KETTERING
Twywell
A14
Thrapston
Old Weston
Barton Seagrave
Cranford St. Andrew
Cranford St. John
Woodford
Denford
Molesworth
Buckworth
Maidwell
Cransley Resr.
Great Cransley
Wicksteed Park
Draughton
Broughton
Bythorn
Brington
A43
Burton Latimer
Great Addington
Ringstead
Keyston
Leighton Bromswold
NORTHAMPTONSHIRE
Lamport
Lamport Hall
Pytchley
Isham
A6
Little Addington
A45
A14
Hanging Houghton
Old
Manvel Farm Park
A509
A510
Finedon
River Til
Church
Raunds
Catworth
Little Catworth
Old Bridge
Spaldwick
Scaldwell
Walgrave
Orlingbury
Finedon Cally Banks
R. Nene
Stanwick
Three Shire Stone
Hargrave
Covington
Easton
Brixworth
Saxon Church
Little Harrowden
Great Harrowden
Irthlingborough
Stow Longa
Pitsford Water
Hannington
Chichele College
Shepherd's
Brixworth Pitsford Resr.
Holcot
Hardwick
A510
Higham Ferrers
Chelveston
Shelton
Tilbrook
Lower Dean
Newtown
Northampton (Sywell)
Caldecott
Kimbolton
Kimbolton Castle
A508
Pitsford
WELLINGBOROUGH
A45
Upper Dean
Yelden
Yelden Castle
Stonely
Northampton and Lamport Railway
Sywell
Overstone
Little Irchester
Knuston
Rushden Transport
Newton Bromswold
Wood End
Chapel Brampton
Moulton
Overstone Solarium Light Rly.
Mears Ashby
A509
Wilby
Little Wymington
RUSHDEN
Swineshead
Melchbourne
Pertenhall
Great Staughton
Boughton
The Spectacle
Devonshire Obelisk
Sywell Res.
Earls Barton
Heritage Centre
Railway
Irchester
A6
Staughton Highway
Kingsthorpe
A43
Great Doddington
Wymington
Farndish
Knotting
Riseley
Keysoe
Little Staughton
Cottarville
Boothville
Ecton
A45
Wymington Meadow
Podington
Knotting Green
Keysoe Row
A5123
Great Billing
Little Billing
Billing Aquadrome
Wollaston
Sharnbrook Summit
Souldrop
Little Staughton
Bushmead Priory
Staploe
Weston Favell
R. Nene
Lower End
Strixton
Hinwick
Bourne End
Bedford
Bolnhurst
NORTHAMPTON
SEE PAGE 194
Cogenhoe
Whiston
Grendon
A509
Santa Pod Raceway
Sharnbrook
Bushmead
James End
Far Cotton
Brafield-on-the-Green
Castle Ashby
Castle Ashby
Felmersham Gravel Pits
Great Houghton
Little Houghton
Chadstone
Easton Maudit
Bozeat
Thurleigh
Colmworth
Hardingstone
A428
Denton
Odell
Felmersham
Church
Bletsoe
Roxton's Green
Yardley Hastings
Harrold
Harrold-Odell
Radwell
Milton Ernest
Channel End
Wootton
Collingtree
Chellington
Pavenham
Colesden
Milton Malsor
Hackleton
Carlton
BEDFORDSHIRE
Wilden
YARDLEY CHASE
Piddington
Horton
Lavendon
Horace Church Memorial
Oakley
Judge's Spinney
Ravensden
Quinton
The Menagerie
Warrington
Lavendon
West End
Stevington
Salph End
Renhold
Blisworth
Courteenhall
Salcey Forest Walk
Church Path Oak
Salcey Forest
A565
Turvey
Holywell Marsh
Stevington Country Walk
Clapham
A421
Great Barford
Roade
Ravenstone
Weston Underwood
Olney
Clifton Reynes
Cold Brayfield
Newton Blossomville
A428
Bromham
A6
BEDFORD
Goldington
Hartwell
Ashton
Eakley Lanes
Cowper & Newton
Emberton
Bridge End
Biddenham
Salcey Forest
Willington
Chalton
Stoke Bruerne
A508
Long Street
Hanslope
Grafton Regis
51
Stoke Goldington
R. Great Ouse
Petsoe End
Hollington Wood
Emberton
Stagsden
Box End
Kempston
Mogerhanger
Cople
Cardington
Harrowden
Shortstown
Filgrave
Tyringham
Sherington
Hardmead
Astwood
Green End
KEMPSTON
Keeley Green
Elstow
Cotton End
Tathall End
Gayhurst
M1
A5
A509
Chicheley
A422
Hall End
A6
Old Warden

64
Barnack
Ufford
BEDFORD (NORTH LEVEL)
Eye Green
Thorney
Abbey Church
Thorney Toll
Guyhirn Gull
Guyhirn
Friday Bridge
Southorpe
Southey Wood
Werrington
Gunthorpe
Eye
A47
A15
Ring's End
Coldham
A1
Sacrewell
Castor Hanglands
Marholm
Walton
New England
Dogsthorpe
Newark
Stone Bridge Corner
76
R. Nene
A141
Grays Moor
Stags Holt Farm Park
Upton
Millfield
Chainbridge
Stibbington
Ailsworth
Longthorpe
Westwood
PETERBOROUGH
SEE PAGE 195
Nene Washes
West Fen
Euximoor
Sutton
Castor
Nene Valley Railway
Water Newton
Orton Wistow
Woodston
Alwalton
Ferry Meadows
Flag Fen Bronze Age Excavations
Eldernell
Coates
Oldeamere
Westry
Norwoodside
West End
MARCH
Sibson
Peterborough (Sibson)
Orton Longueville
Old Fletton
Stanground
Whittlesey
Eastrea
Binnimoor Fen
Chesterton
Orton Waterville
A605
King's Delph
B1093
Town End
B1099
East of England Showground
Hampton
Farcet
Flag Fen
Twenty Foot R.
Knight's End
Flood's Ferry
Elton
Over End
Elton Hall
A605
Haddon
PETERBOROUGH
Norman Cross
Redshanks Spinney
Chapelbridge
Hook
Eastwood End
Stonea
Morborne
Yaxley
Farcet Fen
Pondersbridge
White Fen
Copalder Corner
New World
Wimblington
Sixteen Foot Drain
Eaglethorpe
Warmington
B1093
Whittlesey Mere
BEDFORD (MIDDLE LEVEL)
Benwick
Doddington
Folksworth
The Herne
Middle Moor
Ramsey Mereside
Mere Side
Wimblington Fen
A605
Stilton
A1(M)
B1096
Swingbrow
A141
Caldecote
Denton
Holme
B660
Ramsey St. Mary's
Ashton Mill
Polebrook
Lutton
Forty Foot Drain
Vermudens Drain
Slade Field
Ramsey Forty Foot
Armston
Glatton
Peterborough Airport (Conington)
Conington
Ramsey Heights Clay Pits
Ramsey Rural NT
Hollow
Chatteris
Horseway
Ouse Washes
Barnwell
Hemington
Ramsey
Abbey Gatehouse
B1098
Welches Dam
Luddington in the Brook
B660
Ramsey Heights
Upwood
Bury
A142
Langwood Fen
Sawtry
Tick Fen
Ferry Hill
New Bedford R.
Great Gidding
Woodwalton
Church End
Upwood
Gray's Honey Farm
Thurning
A141
Horseley Fen
Little Gidding
Aversley Wood
Pingle Wood
Steeple Gidding
Hamerton Wildlife Centre
Woodwalton
Great Raveley
Wistow
Wistow Wood
Somersham High North Fen
Wardy Hill
Winwick
Hamerton
Mepal
Clopton
Coppingford
Little Raveley
Warboys
Pidley Fen
Witcham
Upton
Wennington
Fenton
Sutton Gault
Alconbury Weston
Abbots Ripton
Broughton
Somersham
Sutton
Molesworth
Old Weston
Buckworth
Alconbury
Little Stukeley
Kings Ripton
Pidley
B1089
Oldhurst
Sutton Wash
Haddenham End
Brington
C A M B R I D G E S
Leighton Bromswold
Barham
Great Stukeley
Sapley Spinneys
Woodhurst
Colne
Haddenham
Alconbury
Wyton
Bluntisham
East End
Earith
A14
Catworth
Woolley
Sapley
Hartford
Wyton
St. Ives
Needingworth
Aldreth
Little Catworth
Old Bridge
Spaldwick
Huntingdon
HUNTINGDON
Houghton
Bridge Chapel
Easton
Ellington
Cromwell
Hemingford Abbots
Norris
Hemingford Grey
Church End
Willingham
Covington
Stow Longa
Shepherd's Close
Ellington Thorpe
Island Hall
Holywell
Smithey Fen
Tilbrook
Brampton
Godmanchester
Mare Fen
Over
Grafham
Fenstanton
Fen Drayton
Swavesey
Lower Dean
Grafham Water
Newtown
Buckden Palace
Wood Green Animal Shelter
Rampton
Kimbolton
Kimbolton Castle
West Perry
East Perry
Buckden
Offord Cluny
Boxworth End
Stonely
Wood End
Offord D'arcy
Turf Maze
Longstanton
Cottenham
Pertenhall
Dillington
Staughton Green
Diddington
Manor House
Hilton
Conington
Westwick
Oakington
Great Staughton
CAMBRIDGE
Landbeach
Southoe
Papworth St. Agnes
Boxworth
Lolworth
Oakington
Histon
Staughton Highway
Hail Weston
Great Paxton
Graveley
Papworth Wood
Elsworth
Bar Hill
Keysoe
Little Staughton
Little Paxton
Papworth Everard
Knapwell
Overhall Grove
Dry Drayton
Girton
Impington
Little Staughton
Toseland
Yelling
Elsworth Wood
Keysoe Row
Bushmead Priory
Staploe
Duloe
St. Neots
A428
Knapwell Wood
Chesterton
Bolnhurst
Croxton
Caxton Gibbet
Cambourne
A428
Madingley
Bushmead
Upper Staploe
Eaton Socon
Eynesbury
Eltisley
Bourn
Highfields
Hardwick
Coton
Colmworth
Caxton
Crow End
Hardwick Wood
Barnwell
Rootham's Green
Bourn
Caldecote
M11
Botanic
Channel End
Wyboston
Chawston
Little Barford
Abbotsley
Great Gransden
Bourn
Comberton
Newnham
Begwary Brook Marsh
Toft
Grantchester
Colesden
Wilden
Longstowe
Kingston
Barton
Trumpington
Ravensden
Little Gransden
Waresley
Great Shelford
Roxton
Waresley & Gransden Woods
Great Eversden
Little Eversden
Salph End
Renhold
Tempsford
Gamlingay Cinques
Gransden
Hayley Wood
Haslingfield
A421
Great Barford
Gamlingay
Hatley St. George
Harlton
Hauxton
Little Shelford
Goldington
Dovecote & Stables
Blunham
Everton
Gamlingay Great Heath
Gamlingay Meadow
Home Farm
Wimpole Hall
Harston
BEDFORD
Willington
Chalton
Sandy
Caesar's Camp
Potton
52
Buff Wood
East Hatley
Arrington
Orwell
A10
Barrington
Wilbers Mill
Newton
Mogerhanger
Cople
Airship Hangars
Cardington
B1042
The Lodge
Cockayne Hatley
Croydon
Wimpole
Crossing House
Foxton
Harrowden
Shortstown
Thorncote Green
Hatch
Beeston
Wrestlingworth
B1042
Tadlow
Shingay
Wendy
R. Cam or Rhee
National Dolls House
Shepreth
Docwra's Manor
Shepreth L-Moor
Thriplow Meadows
Thriplow
Whittlesford
Elstow
Cotton End
Northill
Upper Caldecote
Sutton
Meldreth
Whaddon
DANGER AREA
A6
Old Warden Tunnel
Ickwell
Eyeworth
Abington
Bassingbourn
Fowlmere

65
Outwell
Upwell
Barroway Drove
Downham Market
Broomhill
A1122
Stradsett
Bendish
Shingham
Cockley Cley
Saxon Church
South Pickenham
B1077
Stow Bardolph Fen
Salters Lode
Denver
Denver Sluice
Crimplesham
Bexwell
A10
A134
Eastmoor
Boughton
Wereham
Gooderstone Water
Iceni Village & Museums
Gooderstone
Foulden Common
Oxborough
Oxburgh Wood
Oxburgh NT
Three Holes
Nordelph
B1094
E
F
G
H
77
West Dereham
Wretton
Stoke Ferry
Whitington
Foulden
Hilborough
Little Cressingham
Little Cressingham
The Arms
Bodney
B1108
Beckett End
Fordham
Hilgay
B1160
R. Wissey
Iron Bridge
Christchurch
Lakesend
Tips End
Welney
Welney Wildfowl Refuge
Old Bedford River
R. Delph
Hilgay Fen
N O R F O L K
Ten Mile Bank
Southery
Little London
B1386
Methwold
Fens
Methwold Hythe
Brookville
B1112
Northwold
Little London
A1065
A134
Cranwich
Ickburgh
Mundford
Lynford Arboretum
Lynford Lakes
Lynford Stag
West Tofts
DANGER AREA
THETFORD FOREST PARK
Upwell Fen
B1093
B1098
B1100
Gold Hill
Brandon Creek
Queen's Ground
Feltwell
Feltwell Anchor
Grimes Graves
Devil's Punchbowl
Manea
A1101
R. Great Ouse
Little Ouse
Brandon Bank
Weeting
Two Mile Bottom
Santon Downham
Santon Downham
Bird Trail
Puri's Bridge
Hundred Foot Drain
Mare Fen
Fodder Fen
Littleport
Burnt Fen
Hockwold Fens
Hockwold cum Wilton
Weeting Heath
Brandon
Croxton
A134
A11
Oxlode
Pymore
Black Bank
Sandhill
B1107
Heritage Cen.
Town Street
Brandon Park
Thetford Warren Lodge
Thetford
Way Head
B1411
Downham
Little Street
A10
Chettisham
Wangford Glebe
Wangford Fen
Wangford
B1112
Lakenheath
Lakenheath
A1065
Wangford Warren
Thetford Warren DANGER AREA
B1106
Priory
Ancient House
A1088
A134
Coveney
Prickwillow
Prickwillow Engine
B1382
Mile End
Queen Adelaide
BEDFORD (SOUTH
LEVEL
LEVEL)
Undley
The Delph
Lakenheath Warren
Elveden
Barnham
A142
Ely
Roswell Pits
Cathedral & Stained Glass Mus.
Middle Fen
Stuntney
Kennyhill
Mildenhall Fen
Holmsey Green
Wilde Street
Eriswell
Great War Memorial
Wentworth
Witchford
Great Fen
B1104
Weston Ditch
Beck Row
Mildenhall
Cake Street
Holywell Row
A11
Little Thetford
Broad Hill
Byways Water Shade
Thistley Green
A1101
H I R E
Barway
Soham Cotes
Isleham Fen
Waterside
West Row
Mildenhall
King's Forest
Wilburton
Stretham
A10
A142
Isleham
Priory Church
Worlington
Barton Mills
Icklingham
B1112
B1049
Soham
Soham Mere
Downfield
Elford Closes
Stretham Beam Engine
A1123
Wicken Fen NT
Fen Cottage
Wicken
Soham Meadows
B1102
Freckenham
Cavenham Heath
Tuddenham
Anglo Saxon Village
Forest Lodge
West Stow
West Stow
Lackford
Brockley
A134
Ampton
Ingham
Upware
Fordham
Chippenham
Fordham Woods
Chippenham Fen
Red Lodge
Herringswell
Cavenham
Flempton
Culford
Timworth Green
Chittering
Denny Abbey
River Bank
Little Fen
B1085
A11
Kennett
S U F F O L K
Hengrave
Hengrave Hall
B1106
Fornham St. Martin
Waterbeach
Denny End
R. Cam
Burwell
Stevens
Roman Remains
Reach
Burwell
B1103
Snailwell
Risby
Fornham All Saints
A143
Waterbeach
Exning
A14
Kentford
Needham Street
Higham
A14
Westley
Abbey
Clayhythe
Swaffham Prior
Devil's Dyke
Commercial End
A142
B1506
Moulton
Packhorse Bri.
Gazeley
Tropical Butterfly Garden
Burthorpe
Barrow
Little Saxham
NT
Suffolk Regimental
BURY ST. EDMUNDS
Milton
A10
Long Meadow
Lode
Watermill Anglesey Abbey NT
Horningsea
Newmarket Heath
NEWMARKET
Horse Racing
B1063
Newmarket
National Stud
Swaffham Bulbeck
Ashley
Dalham
Great Saxham
Denham
Horringer
Ickworth NT
Rushbrooke
A134
Stow cum Quy
Bottisham
A1303
A1304
B1061
Cheveley
Broad Green
Dunstall Green
Chevington
B1066
Sicklesmere
Fen Ditton
A1303
A14
Little Wilbraham
Little Ditton
Saxon Street
Ousden
Back Street
Hargrave
Tan Office Green
Depden Green
Pinford End
Hawstead
Great Welnetham
CAMBRIDGE
SEE PAGE 187
Cambridge
Teversham
Great Wilbraham
Stetchworth
Woodditton
Ditton Green
Upend
Lidgate
Lidgate
Baxter's Green
Whepstead
Mickley Green
Bradfield Combust
Cherry Hinton
Church End
Fulbourn
Fulbourn
Fulbourn Educational Reserve
Six Mile Bottom
A11
Dullingham
Westley Waterless
Dullingham Ley
Kirtling
Chedburgh
Depden
Gulling Green
Stanningfield
Beechwood
Fleam Dyke
Burrough End
Brinkley
Burrough Green
Kirtling Green
Mill End
Boyden End
B1063
Meeting Green
Rede
Gog Magog Hills
Wandlebury Hill Fort
Willingham Green
Weston Colville
B1061
Carlton
Cowlinge
Wickhambrook
Thorns
Clopton Green
Brockley Green
Lawshall
Great Bradley
Hobbles Green
Farley Green
Denston
Hawkedon
Somerton
Stapleford
R. Granta
Roman Road
Lower Wood
West Wratting
Weston Green
Little Bradley
Stradishall
Stansfield
Hartest
Shimpling Street
Balsham
B1052
Little Thurlow
Great Thurlow
Sowley Green
Assington Green
Thurston End
Boxted
Gifford's Hall Vineyards
Shimpling
Babraham
BABRAHAM
Burton End
Sawston
Little Abington
Chilford Hundred Vineyard
53
West Wickham
Barnardiston
Hundon
54
Stanstead
A505
Hildersham
Great Abington
Streetly End
Withersfield
Great Wratting
Chimney Street
Poslingford
Manor Vineyards
Glemsford
Kentwell Hall
Bridge Street
Pampisford
A1307
Horseheath
Little Wratting
Brockley Green
Nether Hall
B1065
B1066
A134
Duxford
A11
Linton
Linton
Cardinal's Green
Haverhill
A1307
A143
B1061
Kedington
Chilton Street
Ancient House
Clare
A1092
Cavendish
R. Stour
A1092
Long Melford
Calford Green
Bartlow

66
65
78
54
A
B
C
D
1
2
3
4
5
Church
South Pickenham
Ashill
Saham Hills
Ovington
Cranworth
Southburgh
Woodrising
Hardingham
Kimberley
Forehoe
Crownthorpe
Kidd's Moor
Hethersett
Intwood
Lower East Carleton
Swardeston
East Carleton
Swainsthorpe
Ketteringham
Wicklewood
Hackford
Wymondham
Heritage Abbey & Church
Kett's Oak
Hethel
Hethel Old Thorn
Mulbarton
Carbrooke
Neaton
Saham Toney
Little Cressingham
Watton
Scoulton
Hingham
Deopham
Little Ellingham
Deopham Green
Morley St. Botolph
Suton
Silfield
Wreningham
Bracon Ash
Newton Flotman
Saxlingham Thorpe
Flordon
Toprow
Hapton
Tasburgh
Ashwellthorpe
Fundenhall
Spooner Row
Bodney
The Arms
Merton
Griston
North Acre
Caston
Rockland St. Peter
Bush Green
Great Ellingham
Stow Bedon
Rockland All Saints
Besthorpe
Attleborough
Black Car
Tacolneston
Thompson
Icklingham
Lynford Arboretum
Mundford
West Tofts
DANGER AREA
Lynford Lakes
Lynford Stag
THETFORD FOREST PARK
Great Hockham
Breckles
Lower Stow Bedon
Mount Pleasant
Shropham
North End
Hall Farm
Snetterton
Puddledock
Fen Street
Old Buckenham
New Buckenham
Upgate Street
Carleton Rode
New Buckenham Common
Hargate
Bunwell
Forncett End
Forncett St. Mary
Forncett St. Peter
Industrial Steam
Pottergate Street
Aslacton
Great Moulton
Wacton
Long Stratton
Stratton St. Michael
Tharston
Morningthorpe
Wretham
Illington
Larling
Eccles Road
Wilby Hall
Wilby
Stacksford
New Buckenham
Tibenham
Pristow Green
Devil's Punchbowl
East Wretham Heath
Snetterton
Two Mile Bottom
Santon Downham
Croxton
Harling Road
Overa House
Quidenham
Hunt's Corner
Banham
Banham
Tibenham
Tivetshall St. Margaret
Tivetshall St. Mary
Hall Green
Colegate End
Bush Green
Pulham Market
Pulham St. Mary
Bird Trail
Bridgham
Middle Harling
East Harling
Kenninghall
Dam Green
Short Green
Winfarthing
Gissing
Thetford Warren Lodge
Thetford Warren
Priory
Bridgham Lane
Brettenham
Shadwell
R. Thet
Thetford
Ancient House
North Lopham
Fersfield
Shelfanger
Mill Green
Burston
Strike School
Shimpling
Dickleburgh Pightle
Rushall
A1066
Garboldisham
South Lopham
Wilney Green
Snow Street
Walcot Green
Dickleburgh
Thelveton
100th Bomb Group Memorial
Thorpe Abbots
Rushford
Gasthorpe
Smallworth
Bressingham
Bressingham Steam Museum
Roydon
Diss
Frenze
Thorpe Abbotts
Billingford
Elveden
Knettishall Heath
Euston
Euston Hall
Barnham
Coney Weston
Hopton
Blo' Norton
Thelnetham
Redgrave & Lopham Fen
Magpie Green
Palgrave
Scole
Billingford
Market Weston
Thelnetham Fen
Redgrave
Wortham
Stuston
Oakley
Hoxne
Green Street
Wingfield Castle
Great Green
Brome
Brome Street
St Edmund's Mon.
Cross Street
Heckfield Green
Chickering
Fakenham Magna
Barningham
Hinderclay
Botesdale
Rickinghall Superior
Burgate
Burgate Great Green
Thrandeston
Honington
Sapiston
Stanton Chare
Hepworth
Candle Street
Burgate Little Green
Yaxley
Mellis
Eye
Denham
Reading Green
Battlesea Green
Bardwell
Manor Farm
Ixworth Thorpe
Bangrove
Stanton
Upthorpe
Wattisfield
Mill Street
Thornham Parva
Thornham Herb
Braiseworth
Cranley
Denham Street
Horham
Troston
Walsham le Willows
Cranmer Green
Local History
Four Ashes
Gislingham
Thornham Magna
Stoke Ash
Occold
Redingfield
Athelington
West Stow
Brockley
Ampton
Great Livermere
Ixworth
Ingham
Culford
Timworth Green
Langham
Crowland
Wickham Street
Wickham Green
Standwell Green
Thorndon
Southolt
Fingal Street
Hengrave Hall
Fornham All Saints
Fornham St. Martin
Conyers Green
Grimstone End
Hunston
Stowlangtoft
Badwell Ash
Westhorpe
Wyverstone Street
Wyverstone
Finningham
Wickham Skeith
Thwaite
Rishangles
Bedingfield
Shop Street
Great Barton
Pakenham
Stanton Street
Great Ashfield
Long Thurlow
Mechanical Music
Cotton
Bacton
Brockford Street
Wetheringsett
Mid-Suffolk Railway
Monk Soham Green
Kenton
Westley
Suffolk Regimental
Abbey
BURY ST. EDMUNDS
Thurston
Norton
Norton Little Green
Earl's Green
Canham's Green
Mendlesham
Blacksmith's Green
Monk Soham
Tostock
Elmswell
Haughley Green
Ward Green
Gipping
Mendlesham Green
Wetherup Street
Debenham
Mickfield Meadow
Ashfield
Horringer
Blackthorpe
Beyton Green
Kingshall Street
Beyton
Woolpit
Bygones Room
Wetherden
Haughley
Old Newton
Saxham Street
Vennis Farm
Middlewood Green
Mickfield
Fish & Water Garden
Fox Fritillary Meadow
Winston
Rushbrooke
Rougham
Drinkstone
Hessett
Borley Green
Haughley Park
Stowupland
Forward Green
Little Stonham
Stonham Aspal
Peats Corner
Framsden
Little Welnetham
Sicklesmere
Drinkstone Green
Harleston
Onehouse
Stowmarket
Creeting St. Peter
Earl Stonham
Pettaugh
Pinford End
Hawstead
Great Welnetham
Bradfield St. George
Maypole Green
Rake Factory
Rattlesden
Whepstead
Mickley Green
Bradfield Combust
Bradfield St. Clare
Bradfield Woods
Gedding
Poystreet Green
Buxhall
Anglia Life East
Great Finborough
Combs Ford
Combs
R. Gipping
Creeting St. Mary
Crowfield
Helmingham Hall
Helmingham
High House
Hoggard's Green
Bush Green
Felsham
Hightown Green
Rattlesden Airfield
Fen Alder Carr
Coddenham Green
Gosbeck
Otley
Gulling Green
Stanningfield
Great Green
Cross Green
High Street Green
Moats Tye
Needham Market
Coddenham
Ashbocking
Gibraltar
Windsor Green
Cockfield
Bulls Wood
Thorpe Green
Battisford Tye
Battisford
Hascot Pit
Ringshall
Hemingstone
Swilland
Brockley Green
Lawshall
Thorpe Morieux
Brettenham
Cross Green
Charles Tye
Barking Tye
Barking
Darmsden
Bell's Cross
Hartest
Shimpling Street
Smithwood Green
Rookesey Green
Wattisham
Great Bricett
Ringshall Stocks
Bonny Wood
Willisham Tye
Baylham
Henley
Witnesham
Grundisburgh
Gifford's Hall
Vineyards
Shimpling
Alpheton
Hitcham
Kettlebaston
Wattisham
Great Bricett
Barham
Claydon
Boxted
Preston
Little Hall
Great Blakenham
Suffolk Water Park
Stanstead
Lavenham
Guildhall NT
Bildeston
Nedging Tye
Naughton
Greenstreet Green
Offton
Blakenham Woodland
Akenham
Tuddenham
Bridge Street
Railway Walk
The Priory
Brent Eleigh
Monks Eleigh
Nedging
Somersham
Little Blakenham
Westerfield
Playford
Kentwell Hall
Chelsworth
Castle Hill
IPSWICH
Rushmere St. Andrew
Long Melford
Melford Hall
Swingleton Green
Semer
Ash Street
Whatfield
Elmsett
Flowton
Bramford
Milden
Lindsey
Glemsford
A11
A134
A1065
A1066
A1075
A1088
A143
A14
A140
A1120
A1141
A1214
B1077
B1108
B1106
B1107
B1110
B1111
B1113
B1115
B1118
B1117
B1134
B1135
B1135
B1172
B1078
B1079
B1065
B1066
B1071
B1092
B1527

67
NORTH
SEA
LOWESTOFT
Gorleston-on-Sea
Hopton on Sea
Corton
Pleasurewood Hills
Blundeston
Oulton
Oulton Broad
Kirkley
Pakefield
Carlton Colville
Kessingland
Kessingland Beach
Benacre
Wrentham
Covehithe
South Cove
Reydon
Southwold
Sailors Reading Room
Walberswick
Dunwich
Dunwich Forest
Greyfriars Priory
Westleton
Minsmere
Minsmere Haven
Theberton
East Bridge
Leiston
Sizewell
Sizewell Nuclear Power Station
Thorpeness
House in the Clouds
Aldringham
Aldeburgh
Aldeburgh Bay
Martello Tower
Sudbourne
Orford
Orford Ness
Butley
Chillesford
Tunstall
Tunstall Forest
Snape
Snape Maltings
Iken
Saxmundham
Kelsale
Yoxford
Middleton
Peasenhall
Sibton
Darsham
Bramfield
Walpole
Halesworth
Holton
Wenhaston
Blythburgh
Blyford
Wangford
Wissett
Chediston
Beccles
Worlingham
Barnby
North Cove
Mutford
Rushmere
Henstead
Ringsfield
Weston
Ellough
Shadingfield
Sotterley
Brampton
Stoven
Uggeshall
Bungay
Ditchingham
Earsham
Mettingham
Geldeston
Gillingham
Aldeby
Haddiscoe
Thurlton
Loddon
Chedgrave
Reedham
Freethorpe
Cantley
St. Olaves
Fritton
Belton
Burgh Castle
Bradwell
Somerleyton
Herringfleet
Lound
Homersfield
Mendham
Metfield
Harleston
Fressingfield
Wingfield
Stradbroke
Laxfield
Heveningham
Ubbeston Green
Cratfield
Huntingfield
Cookley
Linstead Parva
Rumburgh
Spexhall
Worlingworth
Dennington
Badingham
Framlingham
Saxtead Green
Brandeston
Easton
Marlesford
Hacheston
Parham
Wickham Market
Pettistree
Charsfield
Dallinghoo
Bredfield
Ufford
Melton
Bromeswell
Eyke
WOODBRIDGE
Martlesham
Sutton
Sutton Hoo
Boyton
Capel St. Andrew
Rendham
Sweffling
Cransford
Bruisyard
Sternfield
Benhall Green
Farnham
Kettleburgh
Brooke
Poringland
Ellingham
Broome
Shipmeadow
Barsham
A12
A143
A146
A144
A145
A1120
A1094
A1095
A1117
A47
B1062
B1123
B1124
B1125
B1126
B1127
B1119
B1121
B1122
B1069
B1078
B1084
B1116
B1117
B1353
B1387
B1438
E
F
G
H
1
2
3
4
5

CAERNARFON BAY
(BAE CAERNARFON)
CARDIGAN BAY
(BAE CEREDIGION)
Penygroes
Pontllyfni
Aberdesach
St. Beuno Church
Clynnog-fawr
Capel Uchaf
Old Welsh Life
Felin Faesog Mill
St. Beuno's Well
Bwlch Mawr
Bwlchderwin
Trefor
Yr Eifl
Gyrn Ddu
Trwyn y Gorlech
Llanaelhaearn
Tre'r Ceiri Fort
Cenin
Llithfaen
Pistyll
Carreg Ddu
Porth Dinllaen
Morfa Nefyn
Nefyn
Lleyn Historical & Maritime
St. Cybi's Well
Pencaenewydd
Llangybi
Groesffordd
Edern
Garn Boduan
Fron
Pentre-uchaf
Rhos-fawr
Y Ffor
Llanarmon
Llanystumdwy
Farm Park
Chwilog
Porth Ysgolaig
Rhos-y-llan
Glanrhyd
Boduan
Llannor
Penarth Fawr
Abererch
Tudweiliog
Dinas
Efailnewydd
Denio
Starcoast World
Pen-ychain
Porth Colmon
Rhos-ddu
Fort
Garn-fadryn
Pwllheli
Penllech
Llaniestyn
Rhyd-y-clafdy
Marian-y-de
Marian-y-mor
Carreg yr Imbill
Llangwnnadl
Pen-y-graig
Bryn-mawr
Penrhos
Y Gamlas
Penrhyn Mawr
Sarn Meyllteyrn
Bryncroes
Llanbedrog
Botwnnog
Trwyn Llanbedrog
Rhydlios
Mynytho
Porth Oer
Rhoshirwaun
Llangian
St. Tudwal's Road
Braich Anelog
Anelog
Penycaerau
Rhiw
Llawr Dref
Abersoch
Plas-yn-Rhiw
Porth Neigwl or Hell's Mouth
Llanengan
Aberdaron
Llanfaelrhys
Sarn Bach
Bwlchtocyn
Machroes
Braich y Pwll
Uwchmynydd
Aberdaron Bay
Ynys Gwylan-fawr
St. Tudwal's Islands
Trwyn yr Wylfa
Cilan Uchaf
BARDSEY SOUND
(SWNT ENLLI)
Pen y Cil
Trwyn Cilan
St. Mary's Abbey
Bardsey Island
(Ynys Enlli)
LLEYN PENINSULA
(PENRHYN LLYN)
A499
A487
A497
B4417
B4412
B4354
B4415
B4413
NT
80
56
1
2
3
4
5
A
B
C
D

69
70
81
57
SNOWDON (YR WYDDFA)
Snowdon Summit
3559
Talysarn
Nantlle
Llanllyfni
Nebo
Nasareth
Rhyd-Ddu
Llyn Cwellyn
Llyn y Gader
Craig Cwm Silyn 2408
2299 Garnedd-goch
Bethania
Llyn Dinas
Llyn Llydaw
Llyn Gwynant
Yr Aran 2451
Castell Dinas Emrys
Sygun Copper Mine
Llywelyn Cottage
Beddgelert
Gelert's Grave
Pass of Aberglaslyn
Nantmor
Cae Dafydd Farm
Moel Hebog 2566
Cnicht 2265
Moelwyn Mawr 2527
Croesor
Tanygrisiau
Ffestiniog Power Station
Llyn Stwlan
Llyn Cwmorthin
Blaenau Ffestiniog
Congl-y-wal
Rhiwbryfdir
Llyn Conglog
Llechwedd Slate Caverns
Tal-y-waenydd
Moel Penamnen 1978
Llyn Newydd
Llyn Bowydd
Llyn y Manod
Llynnau Gamallt
Llyn Morynion
Dolwyddelan
Blaenau Dolwyddelan
Pentre-bont
Llynau Diwaunedd
2861 Carnedd Moel-siabod
Y Cribau
Pont-y-pant
Ty Mawr Wybrnant
Penmachno
Cwm Penmachno
Carrog
CONWY
Llyn Conwy
Migneint
Ysbyty Ifan
Pentrefoelas
Rhydlydan
Glan-Conwy
Rhydlanfair
Capel Garmon Burial Chamber
Fairy Glen
Conwy & Machno Falls
Packhorse Bridge
Gylchedd 2196
Carnedd y Filiast
Llyn Arenig Fach
2259 Arenig Fach
Llyn Celyn
Llidiardau
Craig yr Hyrddod
2801 Arenig Fawr
Moel Llyfnant 2461
Parc
Llyn Arenig fawr
Llanfihangel-y-pennant
Bryncir
Garndolbenmaen
Dolbenmaen
Glan-Dwyfach
Golan
Brynkir Mill
Rhoslan
Penmorfa
Tremadog
Prenteg
Garreg
Moel-ddu 1811
Llyn Cwmystradllyn
Plas Brondanw
Tan-lan
Rhyd
Coedydd Maentwrog
Ffestiniog Railway
Llanfrothen
Tan-y-bwlch
Maentwrog
Gellilydan
Llan Ffestiniog
Rhaeadr Cynfal
Bont Newydd
Afon Cynfal
Rhaeadr y Cwm
1824 Graig Wen
Tomen-Y-Mur Roman Amphitheatre
Welsh Highland Rhwy. (Porthmadog)
Penrhyndeudraeth
Minffordd
Porthmadog
Wern
Pentrefelin
Criccieth
Lloyd George Memorial
Highgate Cottage
Y Dref
Morfa Bychan
Borth-y-Gest
Garth
Portmeirion
Portmeirion Village
Ffestiniog Railway
Llandecwyn
Craig Gyfynys
Trawsfynydd Nuclear Power Station
Llyn Trawsfynydd
Trawsfynydd
Fronoleu
Cwm Prysor
Prysor Castle
GWYNEDD
SNOWDONIA NATIONAL PARK
Traeth Bach
Talsarnau
Soar
Llanfihangel-y-traethau
Glan-y-wern
Eisingrug
Moel Ysgyfarnogod 2004
Morfa Harlech
TREMADOG BAY
Moel Goedog Hill Fort
Harlech
Craig Ddrwg
Llyn Cwm Bychan
Roman Steps
Bronaber
Standing Stone
Mynydd Bach
Moel y Feidiog
Mynydd Bryn-llech
Castell Carndochan
Llanuwchllyn
Bala Lake Railway
Pandy
Rhosdyllua
Llanfair
Slate Caverns
Church
Llandanwg
Pen-sarn
Pentre Gwynfryn
Cefn Isaf Farm Trail
Shell Island
Llanbedr
Morfa Dyffryn
Maes Artro Village
2362 Rhinog Fawr
Rhinog
Bryn Eden
Rhaeadr Mawddach
Visitor Centre
Pistyll Cain
Llyn Hywel
2475 Y Llethr
Cataracts & Rhaeadr Ddu
COED Y BRENIN FOREST PARK
Rhobell Fawr 2408
Dyrysgol
Moelfre 1932
Llyn Bodlyn
2462 Diffwys
Llyn Cwm-Mynach
2063 Y Garn
Craig-y-cae
Ganllwyd
Glasdir Forest Garden
Llanfachreth
Rhydymain
2901 Aran Benllyn
2971 Aran Fawddwy
Coed Ystumgwern
Llanenddwyn
Dyffryn Ardudwy
Burial Chamber
Llanddwywe
Tal-y-bont
Llyn Irddyn
Precipice Nannau
Cymer Abbey
New Precipice
Coed Garth Gell
Llanelltyd
Torrent Walk
Brithdir
Cywarch
Bontddu
Caerdeon
Llanaber
Cutiau
Panorama Walk
Farchynys
Penmaenpool
Welsh Gold
Dolgellau
Cross Foxes
Waun-oer 2197
Cribin Fawr
2111 Cae Afon
Dinas Mawddwy
Meirion Mill
Pont Minllyn
Minllyn
Aber-Cywarch
Cwm-Cewydd
Mallwyd
Barmouth (Abermaw)
Lifeboat
Barmouth Bay
The Bar
Fairbourne
Fairbourne Railway
Arthog
Waterfalls
CADAIR IDRIS
2928 Cadair Idris
Llyn Cau
Friog
2040
Mynydd Ceiswyn
Mynydd Dolgoed
Foel-y-ffridd
Clipiau
Aberangell
1523 Esgair Ddu
DYFI FOREST
Aberllefenni
Foel Friog
Llwyngwril
Esgair Berfa
Mynydd Pennant
Mary Jones Mon. Tyn-y-ddol
Castell y Bere
Llanfihangel-y-pennant
Tal-y-llyn Lake
Tal-y-llyn
1882
Corris Uchaf
King Arthur's Labyrinth
Corris
Corris Railway
Cemmaes Windfarm
Cwm-Llinau
Llangelynin
Bird Rock
Abergynolwyn
Nant Gwernol
Esgairgeiliog
POWYS
CAMBRIAN MOUNTAINS
Cemmaes
Cemmaes Road
Rhoslefain
Peniarth
Llanegryn
Llanfendigaid
Tonfanau
Bryncrug
Dolgoch
Dolgoch Falls
2076 Torrenhendre
Pantperthog
Cat Funicular
Centre for Alternative Technology
Llanwrin
Aber Dysynni
Broad Water
Pandy
Rhyd-yr-onen
Trum Gelli
Abercegir
Commins Coch
Darowen
Tafolwern
Tywyn
Narrow Gauge Railway
Pennal
Machynlleth
Penegoes
Tal-y-Wern
Corlan-fraith
Cwrt
Forge
Derwenlas
Melinbyrhedyn
Moelfre 1537
Penhelig
Farm Trail
Aberdovey
Glandyfi
Glaspwll
Aberhosan
Pennant
Eglwys Fach

71
72
E
F
G
H
83
59
WREXHAM
(Wrecsam)
W R E X H A M
S H R O P S H I R E
WALES
ENGLAND
OSWESTRY
(Croesoswallt)
SHREWSBURY
SEE PAGE 196
Whitchurch
NANTWICH
Ruabon (Rhiwabon)
Rhostyllen
Marchwiel
Bangor-is-y-coed
Overton (Owrtyn)
Penley
Hanmer
Malpas
No Man's Heath
Threapwood
Tallarn Green
Shocklach
Tilston
Holt
Farndon
Brymbo
Bwlchgwyn
Minera
Coedpoeth
Bersham
Rhosllanerchrugog
Penycae
Acrefair
Cefn-mawr
Froncysyllte
Chirk (Y Waun)
Pontfadog
Weston Rhyn
Gobowen
Selattyn
St. Martin's
Ellesmere
Welshampton
Tetchill
Whittington
Hordley
Cockshutt
Petton
Loppington
Wem
Lee Brockhurst
Prees
Prees Higher Heath
Bettisfield
Moreton Say
Bletchley
Hodnet
Marchamley
Stanton upon Hine Heath
Shawbury
Grinshill
Clive
Myddle
Burlton
Baschurch
Ruyton-XI-Towns
Little Ness
Knockin
Kinnerley
Llanymynech
Pant
Morda
Trefonen
West Felton
Llandysilio
Four Crosses
Llandrinio
Melverley
Alberbury
Shrawardine
Montford
Bicton
Harlescott
Upton Magna
Uffington
Withington
Wrockwardine
Atcham
Uppington
Cross Houses
Condover
Bayston Hill
Hanwood
Yockleton
Westbury
Middletown
Wollaston
Minsterley
Pontesbury
Worthen
Dorrington
Acton Burnell
Cressage
Harley
Much Wenlock
Church Preen
Longnor
Leebotwood
Woolstaston
All Stretton
Shelve
Chirbury
Montgomery
(Trefaldwyn)
Hughley
Bourton
Easthope
High Ercall
Hadnall
Bomere Heath
Buildwas
A5
A41
A49
A53
A458
A483
A488
A495
A525
A528
A534
A539
A442

72
84
60
SEE PAGE 196
SEE PAGE 197
CHESHIRE
SHROPSHIRE
STAFFORDSHIRE
NANTWICH
STOKE-ON-TRENT
NEWCASTLE-UNDER-LYME
MARKET DRAYTON
STAFFORD
TELFORD
WOLVERHAMPTON
WEDNESFIELD
WILLENHALL
BILSTON
Audley
Tunstall
Burslem
Hanley
Fenton
Longton
Silverdale
Madeley
Woore
Eccleshall
Stone
Newport
Shifnal
Donnington
Oakengates
Hadley
Wellington
Ironbridge
Much Wenlock
Albrighton
Codsall
Penkridge
Ashley Heath
Cheswardine
Hodnet
Wem
Kidsgrove
Alsager
Wybunbury
Betley
Keele
Trentham
Barlaston
Swynnerton
Norton in Hales
Gnosall
Edgmond
Dawley
Madeley
Broseley
Coalbrookdale
Brewood
Tettenhall
Essington
Great Bridgeford
Haughton
Church Eaton
Wheaton Aston
Bishop's Wood
M6
M54
A5
A41
A442
A449
A518
A519
A53
A34
A51
A500
A525
A529
A530
A52
A520
A5013
A464
A454
A458
A4169
A5223
B5026
B5415
B5062
B5063
B5065
B4380
B4176

Birchall
Leekbrook
A523
Onecote
Grindon
Hopedale
Stanshope
Milldale
Parwich
Tissington
Ballidon
Brassington
Carsington
Wirksworth
Bradbourne
Alderwasley
Crich
Whatstandwell
Basford Green
Coombes Valley
Winkhill
Waterhouses
Calton
Ilam
Thorpe
85
Fenny Bentley
Kniveton
Atlow
Hognaston
Kirk Ireton
Idridgehay
Millers Green
Gorseybank
Ambergate
Toadmoor
73
Belper Lane End
Ipstones
Cauldon
Cauldon Lowe
A523
Blore
Mapleton
Ashbourne
Hulland Ward
Hulland
Biggin
Ireton Wood
Shottle
Blackbrook
Cowers Lane
Turnditch
Hazelwood
Belper
Milford
Makeney
Consall
Froghall
Kingsley
Kingsley Holt
Oakamoor
Cheadle
Whiston
Whiston Eaves
Cotton
A52
Swinscoe
Stanton
Mayfield
Middle Mayfield
Church Mayfield
Clifton
Spitalhill
A517
Bradley
Hulland Moss
Muggintonlane End
Windley
Mugginton
Weston Underwood
Duffield
Little Eaton
A38
Godleybrook
Brookhouses
Lightwood
Threapwood
Farley
Ramshorn
Wootton
Upper Ellastone
Ellastone
Lower Ellastone
Shelston
Osmaston
Edlaston
Yeldersley Hollies
Mercaston
Weston Underwood
Boundary
Freehay
Mobberley
Rakeway
Alton
Bradley in the Moors
Gallows Green
Prestwood
Quixhill
Norbury
A515
Wyaston
A52
Shirley
Commonside
Brailsford
Kedleston
Quarndon Common
Quarndon
Breadsall
Huntley
Draycott in the Moors
Winnothdale
Great Gate
Denstone
Roston
Hales Green
Ednaston
DERBYSHIRE
Kirk Langley
Allestree
Upper Tean
Croxden
Stubwood
Rocester
Yeaveley
Rodsley
Cubley Common
Hollington
Over Burrows
Lower Tean
Hollington
Checkley
Woottons
Thurvaston
Marston Montgomery
Little Cubley
Great Cubley
Alkmonton
Hollington Grove
Longlane
Langley Green
Markeaton
Oakwood
Chaddesden
A50
Church Leigh
Upper Leigh
Lower Leigh
Fole
Beamhurst
Combridge
Waldley
Crakemarsh
Creighton
Longford
Thurvaston
Lees
Osleston
Langley Common
Mackworth
A38
A52
Dods Leigh
Middleton Green
Godstone
Upper Nobut
Withington
Stramshall
Spath
Somersal Herbert
Potter Somersal
Boylestonfield
Harehill
Boylestone
Lower Thurvaston
Radbourne
Trusley
Mickleover
Coton Hayes
Dagdale
Painleyhill
Bramshall
The Heath
Doveridge
Hill Somersal
Sapperton
Church Broughton
Lane Ends
Sutton on the Hill
Dalbury
DERBY
Field
Blount's Green
Uttoxeter
Palmer Moor
Oaks Green
Dalebrook
Heathtop
A516
Burnaston
Littleover
Normanton
Crewton
Gratwich
Lower Loxley
Highwood
Sudbury
Marchington
Foston
A50
Burnthea
Etwall
Findern
Sunny Hill
Sinfin
Allenton
Coton
Fradswell
A518
Loxley Green
Woodcock Heath
Willslock
Netherland Green
Birch Cross
B5017
Coton in the Clay
Scropton
Hatton
Hilton
Marston on Dove
Stenson Fields
Chellaston
Chartley Castle
Kingstone
Scounslow Green
Gorsty Hill
Marchington Woodlands
Draycott in the Clay
Tutbury
Fauld
Owen's Bank
A511
Rolleston on Dove
Egginton
Stenson
A5132
Willington
Twyford
Barrow upon Trent
Swarkestone
Gayton
Grindley
The Blythe
Heatley
Hanbury
Hanbury Woodend
Woodend
Alder Moor
Upper Outwoods
Stretton
Beam Hill
A38
Repton
Ingleby
Foremark
Milton
Stanton by Bridge
Amerton
Weston
Stowe-by-Chartley
Shirleywich
Drointon
Dapple Heath
A515
Newborough
Anslow Gate
Anslow
Newton Solney
Cokhay Green
74
Hixon
Pasturefields
Lea Heath
Newton
Dunstal
Abbots Bromley
Bromley Wood
NEEDWOOD
Needwood
Horninglow
BURTON UPON TRENT
Ticknall
Ingestre
Little Ingestre
Swansmoor
Blithfield Hall
B5234
Tatenhill
Callingwood
Rough Hay
Shobnall
Winshill
Bretby
Foremark Reservoir
Staunton Harold Resr.
Calke
A51
Great Haywood
Admaston
Stockwell Heath
Mill Green
Hoar Cross
Newchurch
Far Hoarcross
Rangemore
FOREST
Tatenhill
A38
Stapenhill
Newhall
A511
Hartshorne
Lower Midway
Upper Midway
Little Haywood
Colwich
Bishton
Newlands
Rowley
Woodmill
Dunstall
Branston
Heath End
Staunton Harold Hall
A513
Colton
Hadley End
Woodlane
Barton Gate
Barton-under-Needwood
Stanton
SWADLINCOTE
Goseley Dale
Woodville
Smisby
Lount
CANNOCK CHASE
Cannock Chase Country Park
Wolseley Bridge
Etchinghill
RUGELEY
Blithbury
Hamstall Ridware
Yoxall
Woodhouses
Walton-on-Trent
Church Gresley
Castle Gresley
Albert Village
Blackfordby
Ashby-de-la-Zouch
Slitting Mill
Hill Ridware
Mavesyn Ridware
Rake End
Morrey
Nethertown
Bond End
Barton Green
Efflinch
Rosliston
Cauldwell
Linton
Mount Pleasant
Norris Hill
Moira
Pye Green
Brereton
Armitage
Pipe Ridware
A513
Handsacre
Kings Bromley
Orgreave
Wychnor
Wychnor Bridges
Catton Hall
Coton in the Elms
A444
Overseal
Packington
A460
A51
Upper Longdon
Brereton Cross
Longdon
A515
Rileyhill
Alrewas
Fradley
Fradley South
Croxall
Short Heath
Donisthorpe
A42
Ravenstone
Hazelslade
Cannock Wood
Hednesford
Rawnsley
Longdon Green
Farewell
Gentleshaw
Elmhurst
Curborough
A38
Edingale
Lullington
Netherseal
Stretton en le Field
Oakthorpe
Normanton le Heath
Green Heath
High Town
Littleworth
Wimblebury
CANNOCK
Heath Hayes
Chase Terrace
Boney Hay
Chorley
Creswell Green
A5192
LICHFIELD
Stowe
Streethay
Hilliard's Cross
Elford
Haunton
Harlaston
Clifton Campville
Chilcote
Measham
Appleby Magna
Appleby Parva
Swepstone
Heather
Norton Canes
Burntwood
Leamonsley
Chasetown
Huddlesford
Whittington
Thorpe Constantine
No Man's Heath
Newton Regis
Snarestone
Newton Burgoland
Norton-Juxta-Twycross
Odstone
Great Wyrley
Little Wyrley
Triangle
Hammerwich
Muckley Corner
Wall
Hademore
Comberford
Whittington Barracks
Wigginton
Seckington
Austrey
Shackerstone
Barton in the Beans
A5
A461
BROWNHILLS
Chesterfield
A51
A38
Hopwas
Leyfields
Coton
Perry Crofts
Shuttington
M42
Little Orton
Twycross
Little Twycross
Congerstone
Pelsall
Walsall Wood
Stonnall
Shenstone
A5
Weeford
Hints
TAMWORTH
Bolehall
Kettlebrook
Alvecote
Amington
Polesworth
Warton
Orton-on-the-Hill
Bilstone
A444
Wellsborough
BLOXWICH
Vigo
Druid's Heath
Lower Stonnall
Footherley
Little Hay
A452
Shenstone Woodend
M6 TOLL
A453
Fazeley
Drayton Manor Park
Drayton Bassett
Two Gates
Wilnecote
Glascote
Dosthill
Hockley
TAMWORTH
Birchmoor
St. Helena
Dordon
Bradley Green
Sheepy Magna
Sheepy Parva
Sibson
Shenton
Upton
Rushall
Shelfield
Little Aston
A454
A461
ALDRIDGE
Mere Green
61
Whateley
Grendon
Grendon Common
Ratcliffe Culey
A5
ATHERSTONE
Witherley
Fenny Drayton
WALSALL
M6
Hardwick
Streetly
Roughley
A446
Middleton
Hunts Green
Allen End
Cliff
Piccadilly
Wood End
Baddesley Ensor
Baxterley
Kingsbury
Hurley
Bentley
Mancetter
Higham on the Hill
A34
A4041
SUTTON COLDFIELD
Daisy Bank
The Delves
WEDNESBURY
SEE PAGE 188

74
NOTTINGHAMSHIRE
DERBYSHIRE
LEICESTERSHIRE
CHARNWOOD FOREST
NOTTINGHAM
SEE PAGE 194
DERBY
SEE PAGE 188
LEICESTER
SEE PAGE 190
LOUGHBOROUGH
Whatstandwell
Crich
Oakerthorpe
Pinxton
Somercotes
Ravenshead
Halam
Southwell
Selston
Annesley Woodhouse
Newstead
Papplewick
Oxton
Halloughton
Ambergate
Lower Hartshay
Heage
Ripley
Codnor
Brinsley
Eastwood
Hucknall
Calverton
Woodborough
Thurgarton
Epperstone
Belper
Openwoodgate
Denby
Heanor
Langley Mill
Kimberley
Nuthall
Bulwell
Arnold
Lowdham
Gonalston
Hoveringham
Kneeton
Caythorpe
Milford
Duffield
Horsley
Horsley Woodhouse
Smalley
Cotmanhay
Awsworth
Strelley
Old Basford
Woodthorpe
Burton Joyce
Gedling
Bulcote
Gunthorpe
East Bridgford
Little Eaton
Mapperley
Ilkeston
West Hallam
Stanley
Trowell
Bilborough
Sherwood
Mapperley Park
Carlton
Stoke Bardolph
Shelford
Newton
Radcliffe on Trent
Bingham
Car Colston
Quarndon
Allestree
Breadsall
Morley
Kirk Hallam
Hallam Fields
Bramcote
Radford
Netherfield
Colwick
Holme Pierrepont
Saxondale
Harlequin
Markeaton
Chaddesden
Oakwood
Dale Abbey
Stanton by Dale
Stapleford
Sandiacre
Risley
Beeston
Chilwell
Attenborough
Lenton
Meadows
Wilford
West Bridgford
Gamston
Bassingfield
Holme Lane
Stragglethorpe
Cropwell Butler
Tithby
Cropwell Bishop
Langar
Spondon
Ockbrook
Borrowash
Breaston
Toton
Long Eaton
Barton in Fabis
Clifton
Ruddington
Edwalton
Cotgrave
Tollerton
Clipston
Plumtree
Plumtree Park
Normanton-on-the-Wolds
Owthorpe
Colston Bassett
Kinoulton
Littleover
Normanton
Osmaston
Crewton
Alvaston
Elvaston
Thulston
Ambaston
Draycott
Church Wilne
Great Wilne
Sawley
Trent Lock
Thrumpton
Gotham
Bradmore
Keyworth
Stanton-on-the-Wolds
Sinfin
Allenton
Boulton
Shelton Lock
Chellaston
Stenson Fields
Cavendish Bridge
Shardlow
Aston-on-Trent
Swarkestone
Weston-on-Trent
Barrow upon Trent
Stanton by Bridge
Castle Donington
Hemington
Lockington
Ratcliffe on Soar
Kingston on Soar
Kegworth
West Leake
East Leake
Bunny
Costock
Wysall
Widmerpool
Hickling
Long Clawson
Upper Broughton
Nether Broughton
Willoughby on the Wolds
Twyford
Ingleby
Foremark
Milton
Kings Newton
Melbourne
Wilson
Isley Walton
Donington Park
Diseworth
Sutton Bonington
Long Whatton
Zouch
Rempstone
Old Dalby
Ticknall
Breedon on the Hill
Tonge
Hathern
Normanton on Soar
Stanford on Soar
Hoton
Prestwold
Wymeswold
Burton Wolds
Dalby Wolds
Grimston
Saxelby
Shoby
Asfordby Hill
Asfordby
Worthington
Belton
Shepshed
Thorpe Acre
Cotes
Burton on the Wolds
Walton on the Wolds
Six Hills
Ragdale
Frisby on the Wreake
Smisby
Lount
Newbold
Osgathorpe
Griffydam
Ashby-de-la-Zouch
Coleorton
Peggs Green
Thringstone
Ringing Hill
Whitwick
Shelthorpe
Woodthorpe
Nanpantan
Quorndon (Quorn)
Barrow upon Soar
Seagrave
Hoby
Rotherby
Brooksby
Kirby Bellars
Swannington
New Swannington
Coalville
Woodhouse
Woodhouse Eaves
Mountsorrel
Sileby
Thrussington
Ratcliffe on the Wreake
Rearsby
Cossington
East Goscote
Packington
Ravenstone
Snibston
Bardon
Swithland
Rothley
Gaddesby
Ashby Folville
Barsby
Measham
Heather
Hugglescote
Donington le Heath
Ellistown
Ibstock
Stanton under Bardon
Markfield
Newtown Linford
Cropston
Thurcaston
Wanlip
Syston
Queniborough
South Croxton
Twyford
Appleby Magna
Snarestone
Newton Burgoland
Swepstone
Field Head
Anstey
Birstall
Barkby
Thurmaston
Baggrave
Bagworth
Thornton
Groby
Glenfield
Beaumont Leys
Beeby
Hungarton
Lowesby
Norton-Juxta-Twycross
Odstone
Barton in the Beans
Nailstone
Barlestone
Merry Lees
Ratby
Kirby Muxloe
Hamilton
Humberstone
Scraptoft
Keyham
Shackerstone
Congerstone
Bilstone
Twycross
Carlton
Market Bosworth
Osbaston
Botcheston
Newton Unthank
Leicester Forest East
Braunstone
Kirby Fields
North Evington
Evington
Bushby
Thurnby
Houghton on the Hill
Billesdon
Newbold Verdon
Desford
Stoneygate
Knighton
Aylestone
Oadby
Stoughton
Kings Norton
Gaulby
Sheepy Magna
Sheepy Parva
Wellsbrough
Cadeby
Sibson
Shenton
Sutton Cheney
Kirkby Mallory
Peckleton
Little Stretton
Ratcliffe Culey
Atherstone
Witherley
Fenny Drayton
Stoke Golding
Dadlington
Stapleton
Barwell
Earl Shilton
Thurlaston
Enderby
Narborough
Huncote
Glen Parva
Blaby
Wigston
South Wigston
Whetstone
Countesthorpe
Great Glen
Newton Harcourt
Burton Overy
Carlton Curlieu
Shangton
Illston on the Hill
Higham on the Hill
Wykin
Elmesthorpe
Littlethorpe
M1
M69
A38
A6
A610
A52
A50
A42
A46
A60
A453
A606
A607
A47
A444
A5
A5111
A511
A512
A563
A6097
A614
A612
A6011
A6514
A6030
Swanwick
Trowell
Shardlow
Leicester Forest East
East Midlands
Nottingham East Midlands Airport

Upton
Staythorpe
Averham
Rolleston
Farndon
Fiskerton
NEWARK-ON-TRENT
New Balderton
Coddington
Beckingham
Barnby in the Willows
Balderton
Hawton
Brant Broughton
Stragglethorpe
Welbourn
Welbourn Castle
Leadenham
Temple Bruer Tower
Bloxholm
Digby
Dorrington
North Ings Farm
Ruskington
Fenton
Fulbeck
Cranwell
75
87
A1
A17
A46
A15
A153
A607
A52
B6403
B1429
B1209
B1191
B1188
Thorpe
East Stoke
Claypole
Stubton
Brandon
Caythorpe
Frieston
Leasingham
Anwick
Evedon
Ewerby
Elston
Syerston
Flintham
Cotham
Dry Doddington
Hough-on-the-Hill
Gelston
Normanton
North Rauceby
South Rauceby
Aviation Heritage
Holdingham
Watermill
Kirkby la Thorpe
Asgarby
Sleaford
Sibthorpe
Shelton
Staunton in the Vale
Long Bennington
Westborough
Hougham
Marston
Marston Hall
Carlton Scroop
Sudbrook
Ancaster
Quarrington
Silk Willoughby
Burton Pedwardine
Screveton
Hawksworth
Flawborough
Kilvington
Foston
Honington
West Willoughby
Ancaster Valley
Wilsford
Thoroton
Alverton
Scarrington
Orston
Barkston
Barkston Heath
Syston
Kelby
Culverthorpe
Heydour
Swarby
North Beck
Scredington
Northbeck
Thorpe Latimer
Aslockton
Normanton
Allington
Belton
Belton House
Aswarby
Whatton
Elton
Bottesford
Church
GRANTHAM
Great Gonerby
Londonthorpe
Welby
Oasby
Aisby
Aunsby
Osbournby
Easthorpe
Sedgebrook
Manthorpe
Dembleby
South Beck
Spanby
Swaton
Sutton
Muston
Gonerby Hill Foot
Newton
Granby
Vale of Belvoir
Stenwith
Barrowby
Grantham House
Haceby
Walcot
Threekingham
Horbling
Barnstone
Barkestone-le-vale
Redmile
Earlesfield
Braceby
Stow
Billingborough
Naturescape Wildflower Farm
Plungar
Queen's Royal Lancers
Belvoir
Woolsthorpe
Old Somerby
Ropsley
Sapperton
Pickworth
Folkingham
House of Correction
Birthorpe
Belvoir Castle
Denton Resr.
Denton
Woodnook
Little Ponton
Humby
Hanby
Laughton
Pointon
Little Wisbeach
Harlaxton
Harlaxton Manor
LINCOLNSHIRE
Harby
Stathern
Knipton
Harston
Stroxton
Great Ponton
Boothby Pagnell
Boothby Pagnell Manor House
Lenton
Aslackby
Millthorpe
Knipton Resr.
Hungerton
Ingoldsby
Dowsby
Graby
Rippingale
Hose
Eastwell
Eaton
Branston
Croxton Kerrial
Wyville
Bassingthorpe
Bitchfield
Keisby
Water Spout Monument
Westby
Hawthorpe
Stoke Rochford
Easton
Irnham
Dunsby
Kirkby Underwood
Clawson Hill
Goadby Marwood
Bescaby
Saltby
Skillington
Burton Coggles
Bulby
Hacconby
Waltham on the Wolds
Woolsthorpe
Corby Glen
Stainfield
Scalford
Chadwell
Stonesby
Sproxton
Woolsthorpe Manor
Colsterworth
Twyford Wood
Elsthorpe
Hanthorpe
Morton
Holwell
Stainby
COLSTERWORTH
Birkholme
A151
Grimsthorpe
Grimsthorpe Castle
Potter Hill
Buckminster
Coston
Sewstern
Gunby
North Witham
Swayfield
Swinstead
Edenham
Dyke
Cawthorpe
Scottlethorpe
Thorpe Arnold
Garthorpe
Bourne
A607
A606
B676
MELTON MOWBRAY
Freeby
Saxby
Wymondham
South Witham
Creeton
Wyfordby
Brentingby
Stapleford
Thistleton
East Morkery Wood Walk
Castle Bytham
Little Bytham
Lound
Northorpe
Burton Lazars
Edmondthorpe
Market Overton
Clipsham
Careby
Witham on the Hill
Toft
Manthorpe
Thurlby
Obthorpe
Teigh
Stretton
Yew Tree Avenue
Careby Manor
Aunby
Great Dalby
Cottesmore
Whissendine
Barrow
Rutland Railway
Ashwell
Carlby
Thetford
Little Dalby
Greetham
The Limekiln
Pickworth
Wilsthorpe
Baston
Braceborough
Burrough Hill
Cottesmore
Essendine
Langtoft
Burley Castle
Greatford
Thorpe Satchville
Pickwell
Exton
RUTLAND
Tolethorpe Hall
Ryhall
Somerby
Langham
Barleythorpe
Burley
Burley on the Hill
Little Casterton
Belmesthorpe
Barholm
Towngate
Burrough Ho. Gardens
Burrough on the Hill
Cold Overton
Drought
Whitwell
Tickencote
Roman Town
Great Casterton
Tallington Lakes Leisure Park
Deeping
Marefield
Owston
Knossington
Oakham
Barnsdale
Upper Hambleton
Empingham
Ingthorpe
STAMFORD
Uffington
West Deeping
Abbey Church
Rutland County
Rutland Farm Park
Egleton
Butterfly Centre
A606
A16
Tallington
Maxey
Braunston
Rutland Water
Normanton Church
Tinwell
Burghley Ho.
Bainton
Etton
Halstead Farm
Sauvey Castle
Brooke
Edith Weston
Easton on the Hill
Pilsgate
Ashton
Tilton on the Hill
A6003
Manton
Lyndon
North Luffenham
Ketton
Aldgate
Geeston
Wothorpe
Barnack
Hills & Holes
Ufford
Helpston
Launde Abbey
R. Chater
Priest's Ho.
White Water Resr.
A43
Wing
Turf Maze
Pilton
Collyweston
Southorpe
Southey Wood
Skeffington
A47
Loddington
Ridlington
Preston
South Luffenham
Wittering
Marholm
East Norton
Belton
Ayston
Morcott
Duddington
Sacrewell Farm
Castor Hanglands
Tugby
Rolleston
Allexton
Wardley
Glaston
Barrowden
Thornhaugh
Sacrewell Watermill
Upton
Bisbrooke
Tixover
Uppingham
Uppingham School
63
Wakerley
Wansford
Stibbington
Ailsworth
Castor
Noseley
Goadby
Seaton
Wakerley Great Wood
King's Cliffe
Sutton
Nene Valley Railway
Horninghold
Stockerston
Stoke Dry
Lyddington
Viaduct
Harringworth
Yarwell
Water Newton
Orton
Hallaton
Hallaton Village
Glooston
Lyddington Bede House
Laxton
The Prebendal Manor House
Nassington
Sibson
Peterborough (Sibson)
Wistow
Alwalton
Thorpe by Water
Blatherwycke Lake
Eyebrook
Stonton
A6003
B672
B671

76
Digby
Billinghay
Dorrington
North Kyme
South Kyme
Anwick
Evedon
Ewerby
Howell
Kirkby la Thorpe
Asgarby
Sleaford
Heckington
Garwick
East Heckington
Burton Pedwardine
Great Hale
Little Hale
Helpringham
Silk Willoughby
Northbeck
Scredington
Aswarby
Thorpe Latimer
Osbournby
Spanby
Swaton
Threekingham
Stow
Horbling
Bridge End
Billingborough
Birthorpe
Pointon
Little Wisbeach
Millthorpe
Aslackby
Dowsby
Graby
Rippingale
Kirkby Underwood
Dunsby
Stainfield
Hacconby
Morton
Hanthorpe
Dyke
Cawthorpe
Bourne
Twenty
Northorpe
Thurlby
Toft
Manthorpe
Obthorpe
Thetford
Baston
Wilsthorpe
Greatford
Langtoft
Barholm
Towngate
Market Deeping
Deeping Gate
West Deeping
Deeping St. James
Frognall
Cranmore
Uffington
Tallington
Maxey
Northborough
Etton
Glinton
Peakirk
Bainton
Barnack
Ashton
Helpston
Ufford
Southorpe
Marholm
Walton
Werrington
Gunthorpe
Upton
Ailsworth
Castor
Sutton
Stibbington
Water Newton
Wistow
Alwalton
Sibson
Orton
Longueville
Old Fletton
Woodston
Westwood
Longthorpe
Millfield
New England
Dogsthorpe
Newark
Eye
Eye Green
Newborough
PETERBOROUGH
SEE PAGE 195
Stanground
Whittlesey
Eastrea
Coates
Eldernell
Oldeamere
Thorney
Stone Bridge Corner
Crowland
Nene Terrace
Deeping St. Nicholas
Hop Pole
Cowbit
Peak Hill
Brotherhouse Bar
Moulton Chapel
Moulton Eaugate
Whaplode Drove
Shepeau Stow
Gedney Hill
Dowsdale
Sutton St. Edmund's Common
Parson Drove
Sutton St. Edmund
Throckenholt
Church End
Murrow
Bunker's Hill
Tholomas Drove
Rogue's Alley
Thorney Toll
Guyhirn
Guyhirn Gull
Ring's End
Coldham
Friday Bridge
Begdale
Elm
Wisbech St. Mary
WISBECH
Leverington
Gorefield
Newton
Fitton End
West Walton
Tydd St. Giles
Tydd St. Mary
Tydd Gote
Four Gotes
Sutton St. James
Holbeach St. Johns
Whaplode St. Catherine
Weston Hills
Fen End
Little London
Clay Lake
SPALDING
Pode Hole
Pinchbeck West
Pinchbeck Bars
Guthram Gowt
Cuckoo Bridge
Pinchbeck
Northgate
Surfleet
Surfleet Seas End
Risegate
Gosberton Clough
Gosberton
Westhorpe
Wargate
Belnie
Quadring
Quadring Eaudike
Donington
Donington South Ing
Donington Eaudine
Church End
Northorpe
Bicker
Bicker Bar
Bicker Gauntlet
Swineshead
Drayton
Blackjack
Hoffleet Stow
Wigtoft
Burtoft
Algarkirk
Sutterton
Sutterton Dowdyke
Fosdyke
Kirton
Struggs Hill
Asperton
Baythorpe
Fenhouses
Kirton Holme
Kirton End
Swineshead Bridge
North End
Hubbert's Bridge
Frampton West End
Chain Bridge
BOSTON
Skirbeck
Skirbeck Quarter
Wyberton
Frampton
Sandholme
Skeldyke
Seadyke
Bucklegate
Holbeach St. Matthew
Holbeach St. Marks
Saracen's Head
Holbeach Bank
Penny Hill
Holbeach Hurn
Holbeach Clough
Holbeach
Fleet
Fleet Hargate
Gedney
Gedney Dyke
Gedney Broadgate
Dawsmere
Gedney Drove End
Black Barn
Sutton Corner
Lutton
Lutton Gowts
Long Sutton
Little Sutton
Little London
Chapelgate
Sutton Crosses
Garnsgate
Clark's Hill
Moulton Seas End
Halesgate
Lopsegate
Wykeham
Weston
Moulton
Whaplode
Fulney
Low Fulney
Holland Fen
Amber Hill
Brothertoft
Langrick
Gipsey Bridge
Anton's Gowt
Frith Bank
Fishtoft Drove
Holland Fen
Chapel Hill
Dogdyke
New York
Bank
Bunkers Hill
Hundle Houses
Haven Bank
Carrington
Northlands
Sibsey Fen Side
Sibsey
Frithville
Lade Bank
Leake Common Side
Leake Fold Hill
Old Leake
Wrangle
Wrangle Lowgate
Leake Hurn's End
Leverton Outgate
Leverton Lucasgate
Leverton
West End
Benington
Benington Sea End
High Ferry
Hilldyke
Burton Corner
Haltoft End
Brand End
Butterwick
Freiston
Freiston Shore
Tamworth Green
Fishtoft
Scrane End
LINCOLNSHIRE
BEDFORD LEVEL (NORTH LEVEL)
MARCH
Westry
Norwoodside
West End
Chainbridge
A15
A16
A17
A52
A151
A1101
A1121
A141
A47
A605
A1073
A6121
B1188
B1209
B1395
B1192
B1183
B1184
B1394
B1397
B1177
B1181
B1180
B1356
B1357
B1359
B1390
B1165
B1166
B1167
B1168
B1169
B1172
B1173
B1443
B1040
B1101
B1525
B1093
B1099
B1391

77
89
65
78
THE WASH
NORFOLK
Scolt Head Island
Brancaster Bay
Holkham Bay
Hunstanton
Old Hunstanton
Heacham
Snettisham
Dersingham
Sandringham
Ingoldisthorpe
Sedgeford
Docking
Stanhoe
Burnham Market
Brancaster
Thornham
Titchwell
Holme next the Sea
Ringstead
Castle Rising
North Wootton
South Wootton
KING'S LYNN
Terrington St. Clement
Clenchwarton
West Lynn
Gaywood
Grimston
Gayton
Great Massingham
Little Massingham
Harpley
Great Bircham
East Rudham
Castle Acre
Swaffham
Narborough
Pentney
Marham
Shouldham
Fincham
Downham Market
Denver
Stoke Ferry
Wereham
Gooderstone
Upwell
Outwell
Walpole St. Andrew
Walpole St. Peter
Walton Highway
Tilney St. Lawrence
Wiggenhall St. Germans
Wiggenhall St. Mary Magdalen
Watlington
West Winch
North Runcton
Middleton
Stowbridge
Wimbotsham
Crimplesham
Hilgay
Southery
Northwold
Sporle
Necton
A149
A148
A17
A47
A10
A134
A1122
A1065
A1076
A1078
A1101
B1145
B1153
B1155
B1454
B1439
B1440
B1355
B1077
B1108
B1094
B1112
B1160

78
A
B
C
D
90
600
10
20
Scolt Head Island
Holkham Bay
Blakeney Point
Burnham Norton
Burnham Overy Staithe
Holkham
Wells Harbour
Wells-next-the-Sea
Salt Marshes
Stiffkey Marshes
Morston Marshes
Morston
Blakeney
Cley next the sea
Cley & Salthouse Marshes
Salthouse
Newgate
Muckleborough Military
North Norfolk Railway
Weybourne
Sheringham
West Runton
East Runton
Lifeboat House
Burnham Market
Burnham Overy Town
Burnham Thorpe
Nelson's Birthplace
Holkham Hall
Bygones
Stiffkey
Cockthorpe
Cockthorpe Hall Toy
Langham Glass
Wiveton
Glandford
Shell
Kelling
Salthouse Heath
Kelling Heath
Kelly's Birds
Upper Sheringham
Sheringham Park
Beeston Regis
Shire Horse Centre
Warham
Warham Hill Fort
Binham Priory
Westgate
Binham
Langham
Saxlingham
Natural Surroundings
High Kelling
Bodham
East Beckham
Aylmerton
Felbrigg
Crossdale Street
Wells and Walsingham Light Railway
Wighton
Copy's Green
Wayside Cross
Field Dalling
Letheringsett
Glavenside
Holt
West Beckham
Gresham
Muckleton
New Holkham
Creake Abbey
North Creake
Forge
Egmere Ruined Church
Waterden
Little Walsingham
Great Walsingham
Friary
Shirehall
Abbey & Priory
Lower Green
Bale
Watermill
Sharrington
Holt Woodlands
Baconsthorpe
Gresham Castle
Bessingham
Sustead
Felbrigg Hall
Metton
Roughton
South Creake
Southgate
Houghton St. Giles
North Barsham
Slipper Chapel
Great Snoring
Hindringham
Thursford Collection
Thursford Green
Thursford
Brinton
Thornage
Hempstead
Holt Lowes
Hunworth
Edgefield
Plumstead
Matlaske
Aldborough
Thurgarton
Hanworth
Alby Hill
Alby Lace & Bottles
Barmer
Syderstone
Syderstone Common
East Barsham
West Barsham
Little Snoring
Gunthorpe
Stody
Briningham
Edgefield Street
Little Barningham
Wickmere
Wolterton Hall
Erpingham
Colby
Wicken Green Village
Dunton Patch
Sculthorpe
Barney
Thursford Wood
Swanton Novers
Melton Constable
Briston
Mannington Hall
Wolterton Park
Calthorpe
Tattersett
Dunton
Fakenham
Kettlestone
Croxton
Fulmodestone
Craymere Beck
Little London
Saxthorpe
Itteringham
Ford
Banningham
Pensthorpe Waterfowl Park
Mausoleum
Itteringham Common
Ingworth
Blickling
Blickling Hall
East Rudham
Priory
Coxford
Shereford
Hempton
The Heath
Fakenham
Gas & Local History
Little Ryburgh
Stibbard
Hindolveston
Nethergate
Thurning
Corpusty
Norton Corner
Oulton
Silvergate
Drabblegate
West Rudham
Tatterford
Toftrees
Colkirk
Great Ryburgh
Wood Norton
Tyby
Wood Dalling
Crabgate
Heydon
Oulton Street
Aylsham
Helhoughton
Foulsham
Guestwick Green
Guestwick
East Raynham
West Raynham
South Raynham
Guist
Bexfield
Foulsham
Themelthorpe
Salle
Southgate
Marsham
Great Massingham
West Raynham
Oxwick
Hamrow
Horningtoft
Broom Green
Gateley
Twyford
Pettywell
Cawston
Booton Common
Booton
Eastgate
Duel Stone
Buxton Heath
The Heath
Buxton
Weasenham St. Peter
Whissonsett
Godwick Deserted Village
Wellingham
County School Station
Bintree
Foxley Wood
Reepham
Jordan Green
Brandiston
Weasenham All Saints
Tittleshall
Potthorpe
Saxon Cath.
Pound
North Elmham
Foxley
Bawdeswell
Stratton Strawless
Hevingham
Rougham
Stanfield
Brisley
Billingford
Sparham
Great Witchingham
Mileham
Mileham Castle
East Bilney
Worthing
Swannington
New Hainford
West Lexham
Beetley
Hoe Rough
Mill Street
Sparhamhill
Norfolk
Alderford
Upgate
Felthorpe
East Lexham
Litcham
Litcham Common
Bittering
Norfolk Rural Life
Gressenhall
Union Farm
Swanton Morley
Mill Street
Lyng
Elsing
Sparham Pools
Lenwade
Easthaugh
Dinosaur Park
Morton
Attlebridge
Horsford
Castle Acre
Newton
Beeston
Longham
Hoe
Greengate
Woodgate
Peaseland Green
Primrose Green
Greensgate
Weston Longville
R. Wensum
Thorpe Marriott
Horsford
South Acre
Great Dunham
Drury Square
Honeypot Wood
Sparrow Green
Crane's Corner
Bushy Common
Bishop Bonner's Cottage
Etling Green
North Tuddenham
Hockering Heath
Hockering
Weston Green
Taverham
Drayton
Dunham
Little Dunham
Great Fransham
Wendling
Scarning
Toftwood
DEREHAM
Clippings Green
Mattishall Burgh
Rotten Row
Honingham
Ringland
Drayton Lodge
Hellesdon
Costessey
Sporle
Little Fransham
Clint Green
Yaxham
Mattishall
Welborne
East Tuddenham
Easton
Royal Norfolk Showground
New Costessey
Swaffham
Necton
Ivy Todd
Daffy Green
Lolly Moor
Westfield
Whinburgh
Brakefield Green
Brandon Parva
Colton
Marlingford
Bowthorpe
Earlham
R. Wissey
Bradenham
Holme Hale
Shipdham
Shipdham
Runhall
Barnham Broom
Barford
Bawburgh
Univ.
Sainsbury Cen.
North Pickenham
Holy Land Exhibition
Crowshill
Garvestone
Thuxton
Coston
Great Melton
Little Melton
Colney
Eaton
Cringleford
Keswick
High Common
Reymerston
Low Street
Wramplingham
Lynch Green
Hethersett
South Pickenham
Ashill
Cranworth
Southburgh
Blackwater R.
Mid-Norfolk Railway
Hardingham
Carleton Forehoe
Kimberley
High Green
Kett's Oak
Intwood
Saham Hills
Woodrising
Crownthorpe
Kidd's Moor
Ketteringham
Lower East Carleton
Swardeston
Ovington
Carbrooke
Hingham
Hackford
Wicklewood
Heritage Abbey & Church
East Carleton
Gowthorpe Manor
Great Cressingham
Little Cressingham
Saham Toney
Neaton
Wymondham
Swainsthorpe
Hethel Old Thorn
Hethel
Mulbarton
Little Cressingham
Watton
Wartime Watton
Scoulton
Deopham
Little Ellingham
Griston
Morley St. Botolph
Suton
Silfield
Wreningham
Bracon Ash
Bodney
The Arms
Merton
North Acre
Caston
Rockland St. Peter
Deopham Green
Bush Green
Spooner Row
Ashwellthorpe
Fundenhall
Toprow
Flordon
Saxlingham Thorpe
Newton Flotman
Hapton
Tasburgh
Rainthorpe Hall
Tasswood Lakes
Stow Bedon
Rockland All Saints
Great Ellingham
Thompson
Besthorpe
Attleborough
Black Carr
Tacolneston
Tharston
A149
A148
A1065
A1067
A47
A1075
A140
A11
A1074
B1155
B1105
B1355
B1454
B1145
B1110
B1146
B1354
B1156
B1149
B1436
B1436
B1135
B1108
B1077
B1172
B1113
B1077
77
66

E
F
G
H
1
2
3
4
5
30
40
50
60
350
300
20
10
N O R T H
S E A
CROMER
Foulness
The Pleasaunce
Overstrand
Northrepps
Sidestrand
Trimingham
A140
A149
Frogshall
Cliftonville
Gimingham
Mundesley
Southrepps
Thorpe Market
Lower Street
Stow
Paston
Bacton Green
Bradfield
Trunch
Knapton
B1159
Bacton
Keswick
Antingham
Broomholm
Edingthorpe
Suffield
Swafield
Old Hall Street
Pollard Street
Walcott
Ostend
Little London
Witton Bridge
North Walsham
Lyngate
Spa Common
Bacton Wood
Ridlington
Happisburgh
Whimpwell Green
Felmingham
Tungate
White Horse Common
Crostwight
B1159
Eccles on Sea
Happisburgh Common
Lessingham
Hempstead
Skeyton Corner
Honing
East Ruston
Sea Palling
Witherġate
Bengate
Lyngate
Briggate
Ingham Corner
Ingham
Waxham
Westwick
Skeyton
B1150
Worstead
Dilham
Calthorpe Street
Swanton Abbot
Smallburgh
Stalham
Stalham Green
B1159
Sloley
Frankfort
Hickling
Sutton
Hickling Green
Scottow
Pennygate
Hickling Heath
Horsey
Lamas
Sco Ruston
Barton Turf
Catfield
Hickling Broad
Horsey Mere
Little Hautbois
Tunstead
A1151
Neatishead
Catfield Common
Ashmanhaugh
Sharp Street
West Somerton
East Somerton
Winterton Dunes
The Heath
Coltishall
Irstead
Potter Heigham
Horstead
Cangate
How Hill
Ludham
Winterton-on-Sea
B1354
Upper Street
Damgate
Martham
Hemsby Hole
Newport
Belaugh
Hoveton
A1062
Upper Street
Bastwick
Cess
Frettenham
Wroxham
Horning
Johnson's Street
Repps
Hemsby
B1152
Rollesby
Ormesby St. Margaret
B1159
Scratby
California
Spixworth
Crostwick
Woodbastwick
Thurne
Burgh St. Margaret
(Fleggburgh)
Rackheath
Salhouse
Ranworth
Clippesby
Ormesby St. Michael
Caister-on-Sea
B1140
Pilson Green
Cargate Green
Filby
A1064
New Rackheath
Panxworth
South Walsham
Upton
Billockby
Thrigby
Mautby
SEE PAGE 194
NORWICH
Blofield Heath
THE
Fishley
West End
West Caister
Sprowston
Little Plumstead
Great Plumstead
Hemblington
North Burlingham
Acle
Runham
Yarmouth
Thorpe End
A47
Stokesby
Thorpe St. Andrew
Witton
Blofield
BROADS
Damgate
A47
Yarmouth Roads
Thorpe Hamlet
Moulton St. Mary
Halvergate Marshes
Breydon Water
Brundall
Strumpshaw
Beighton
Tunstall
THE
GREAT YARMOUTH
Trowse Newton
Postwick
Lingwood
South Burlingham
Halvergate
Surlingham
Buckenham
B R O A D S
Southtown
Kirby Bedon
Bramerton
Rockland St. Mary
Hassingham
Southwood
Freethorpe
Wickhampton
Berney Arms
Burgh Castle
A47
B1332
A146
Claxton
Cantley
Limpenhoe
Bradwell
Arminghall
Caistor St. Edmund
Framingham Pigot
Hellington
Ashby St. Mary
Langley Green
Gorleston-on-Sea
Dunston
Upper Stoke
Framingham Earl
Carleton St. Peter
Langley Street
Belton
Browston Green
Poringland
Yelverton
Hardley Street
Reedham
A143
Stoke Holy Cross
West Poringland
Alpington
Bergh Apton
Thurton
Nogdam End
Fritton
Bunker's Hill
Hopton on Sea
Howe
Chedgrave
Norton Subcourse
Lower Thurlton
67
St. Olaves
Shotesham
Brooke
The Ling
Loddon
Thurlton
The Dell
Lound
A12
Saxlingham Nethergate
Mundham
Herringfleet
Blundeston
Seething
Stubbs Green
Hales
Thorpe
B1136
Corton
Kirstead Green
Raveningham
Haddiscoe
Somerleyton
Pleasurewood Hills
Saxlingham Green
B1332
Hales Hall
Maypole Green
A1117
A146
LOWESTOFT
Brundish
Toft

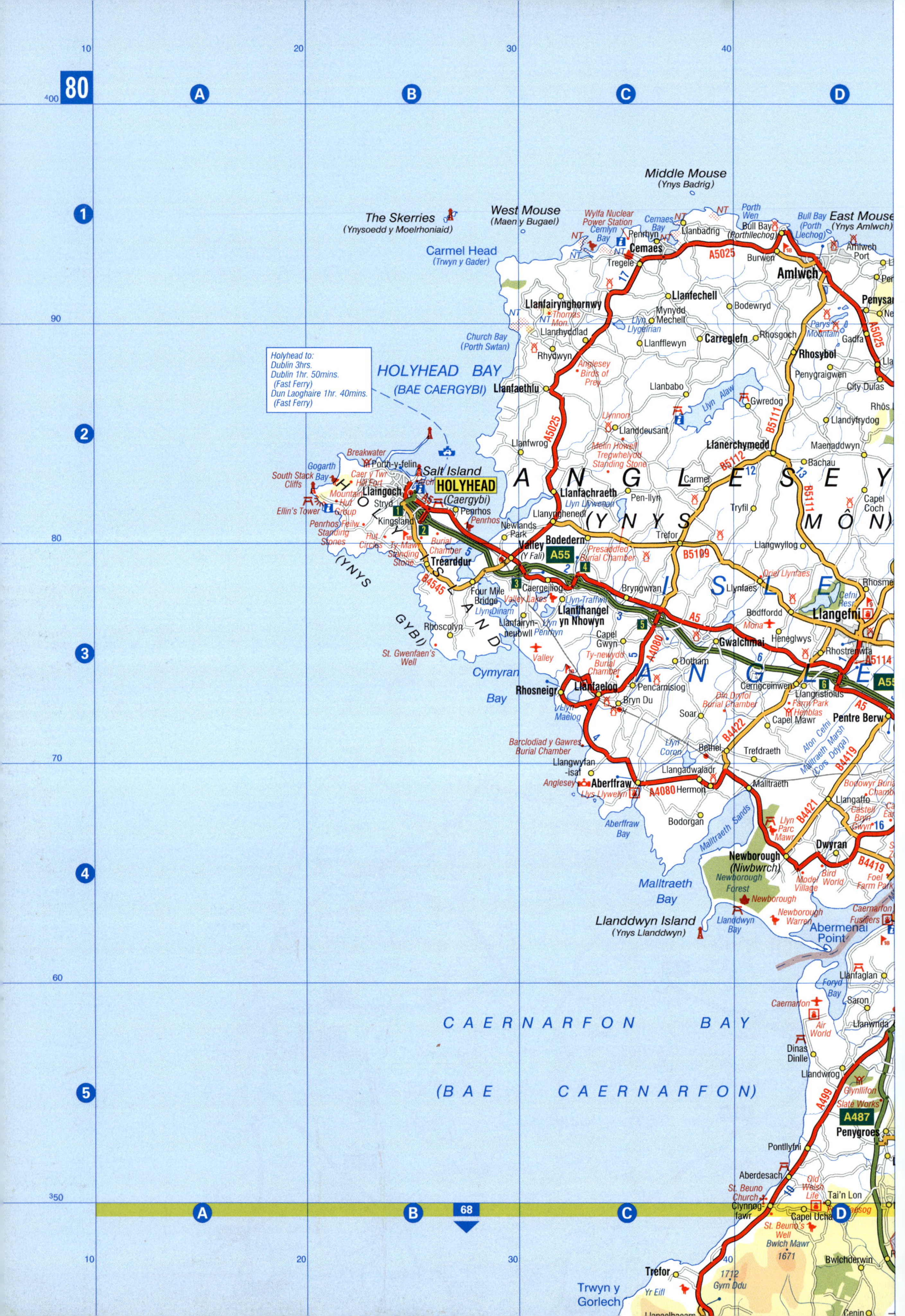

80
Middle Mouse
(Ynys Badrig)
The Skerries
(Ynysoedd y Moelrhoniaid)
West Mouse
(Maen y Bugael)
East Mouse
(Ynys Amlwch)
Carmel Head
(Trwyn y Gader)
Wylfa Nuclear Power Station
Cemaes Bay
Cemlyn Bay
Cemaes
Llanbadrig
Bull Bay
(Porth Llechog)
Amlwch
Amlwch Port
Burwen
Tregele
Llanfechell
Bodewryd
Mynydd Mechell
Llanfairynghornwy
Llanrhyddlad
Rhydwyn
Llyn Llygeirian
Llanfflewyn
Carreglefn
Rhosgoch
Rhosybol
Parys Mountain
Penysarn
Gadfa
City Dulas
Pengraigwen
Church Bay
(Porth Swtan)
HOLYHEAD BAY
(BAE CAERGYBI)
Holyhead to:
Dublin 3hrs.
Dublin 1hr. 50mins.
(Fast Ferry)
Dun Laoghaire 1hr. 40mins.
(Fast Ferry)
Llanfaethlu
Anglesey Birds of Prey
Llanbabo
Llyn Alaw
Gwredog
Llandyfrydog
Llanddeusant
Llynnon
Melin Howell
Tregwehelydd Standing Stone
Llanerchymedd
Maenaddwyn
Bachau
Llanfwrog
Breakwater
Porth-y-felin
Salt Island
HOLYHEAD
(Caergybi)
Gogarth Bay
South Stack Cliffs
Ellin's Tower
Caer y Twr Hill Fort
Mountain Hut Group
Llaingoch
Stryd
Kingsland
Penrhos
Penrhos Feilw Standing Stones
Hut Circles
Ty-Mawr Standing Stone
Burial Chamber
Trearddur
Llanfachraeth
Llyn Llywenan
ANGLESEY
(YNYS MÔN)
Pen-llyn
Carmel
Tryfil
Capel Coch
Llanynghenedl
Newlands Park
Valley
(Y Fali)
Bodedern
Presaddfed Burial Chamber
Trefor
Llangwyllog
HOLY ISLAND
(YNYS GYBI)
Four Mile Bridge
Caergeiliog
Valley Lakes
Llyn Traffwll
Llyn Dinam
Llanfihangel yn Nhowyn
Bryngwran
Llynfaes
Oriel Ynys Môn
Cefni Reservoir
Llangefni
Rhosmeirch
Bodffordd
Heneglwys
Mona
Rhostrenwfa
Rhoscolyn
St. Gwenfaen's Well
Llanfair-yn-neubwll
Llyn Penrhyn
Capel Gwyn
Ty-newydd Burial Chamber
Gwalchmai
Dotham
Cymyran Bay
Rhosneigr
Llanfaelog
Pencarnisiog
Cerrigceinwen
Llangristiolus
Henblas
Farm Park
Llyn Maelog
Bryn Du
Din Dryfol Burial Chamber
Soar
Capel Mawr
Pentre Berw
Barclodiad y Gawres Burial Chamber
Llyn Coron
Bethel
Trefdraeth
Afon Cefni
Malltraeth Marsh
(Cors Ddyga)
Llangwyfan-isaf
Anglesey
Aberffraw
Llys Llywelyn
Llangadwaladr
Hermon
Malltraeth
Bodowyr Burial Chamber
Llangaffo
Aberffraw Bay
Bodorgan
Malltraeth Sands
Llyn Parc Mawr
Castell Bryn Gwyn
Newborough
(Niwbwrch)
Newborough Forest
Dwyran
Model Village
Bird World
Foel Farm Park
Malltraeth Bay
Newborough Warren
Llanddwyn Island
(Ynys Llanddwyn)
Llanddwyn Bay
Abermenai Point
Caernarfon Fusiliers
Llanfaglan
Foryd Bay
Saron
Caernarfon Air World
Llanwnda
CAERNARFON BAY
(BAE CAERNARFON)
Dinas Dinlle
Llandwrog
Glynllifon Slate Works
Penygroes
Pontllyfni
Aberdesach
St. Beuno Church
Old Welsh Life
Tai'n Lon
Clynnog-fawr
Capel Uchaf
St. Beuno's Well
Bwlch Mawr
1671
Bwlchderwin
Trefor
1712
Gyrn Ddu
Yr Eifl
Trwyn y Gorlech
Llanaelhaearn
Cenin
A5025
A5
A55
A4080
B5109
B5111
B5112
B4545
B4422
B4419
B4421
A499
A487
A5114
68

81
E
F
G
H
1
2
3
4
5
Point Lynas
(Trwyn Eilian)
Ynys Dulas
Dulas Bay
Moelfre
Lligwy Burial Chamber
A5108
Brynteg
Benllech
Red Wharf Bay
(Traeth-coch)
Puffin Island
(Ynys Seiriol)
Penmon
Llanddona
Llangoed
Pentraeth
Beaumaris
Penmaen Swatch
Great Ormes Head
(Pen-y-Gogarth)
Little Ormes Head
LLANDUDNO
Penrhyn Bay
Rhos-on-Sea
COLWYN BAY
CONWY BAY
Deganwy
Conwy
Llandudno Junction
Mochdre
Old Colwyn
Penmaenmawr
Dwygyfylchi
Llanfairfechan
Menai Bridge
(Porthaethwy)
Llanfair Pwllgwyngyll
BANGOR
Penrhos Garnedd
Tal-y-bont
Bethesda
Tregarth
Y Felinheli
(Port Dinorwig)
CAERNARFON
Llanrug
Llanberis
Deiniolen
Bontnewydd
Waunfawr
Betws Garmon
Rhosgadfan
Carmel
Groeslon
Talysarn
Nantlle
Rhyd-Ddu
Llanllyfni
Beddgelert
Nant Peris
(Old Llanberis)
Capel Curig
Betws-y-Coed
Dolwyddelan
Blaenau Ffestiniog
Llanrwst
Trefriw
Dolgarrog
Tal-y-Bont
Eglwysbach
Llansanffraid Glan Conwy
Llanddoged
Pentrefoelas
Glan-Conwy
Penmachno
FOEL-FRAS
CARNEDD LLEWELYN
CARNEDD DAFYDD
GLYDER FAWR
SNOWDON
(YR WYDDFA)
CAMBRIAN MOUNTAINS
CONWY
GWYNEDD
SNOWDONIA NATIONAL PARK
GWYDYR FOREST PARK
A5
A55
A470
A4086
A4085
B5106
B5113
69

A
B
C
D
1
2
3
4
5
LIVERPOOL BAY
Colwyn Bay
Abergele Roads
Mostyn to Dublin 6hrs.
Point of Ayr
Talacre
Llawndy
Hilbre Islands Bird Sanctuary
Hilbre Islands
HOYLAKE
Red Rocks Marsh
West Kirby
Little Ormes Head
Penrhyn Bay (Bae Penrhyn)
St. Trillo's Chapel
Rhos-on-Sea (Llandrillo -yn-Rhos)
COLWYN BAY (Bae Colwyn)
Mochdre
Old Colwyn
Penmaen Rhos
Llanddulas
Llysfaen
Terfyn
Rhyd y-foel
Gwrych Castle
Llansanffraid Glan Conwy
Bryn-y-maen
Llanelian -yn-Rhos
Betws -yn-Rhos
Dolwen
Pentrefelin
Dawn
Bodnant
Graig
Brymbo
Moelfre Uchaf 1298
Mynydd Bodrochwyn
Llanfair Talhaiarn
Gell
1277 Mwdwl Eithin
Llangernyw
Llansannan
Tan-y-fron
Pandy Tudur
Gwytherin
Bylchau
CONWY
Pente-tafarn -y-fedw
Llanrwst
Gwydir Castle
Melin-y-coed
Kinmel Bay (Bae Cinmel)
Belgrano
Towyn
RHYL
Sea Life Cen.
Skytower
Abergele
St. George
KIMMEL PARK
Moelfre
Rhuddlan
Rhuddlan Castle
Twt Hill
Bodelwyddan
The Pengwern Marble Church
Hall Farm
Bodelwyddan Castle
Glascoed
Pen Isa'r Glascoed
Llannefydd
Plas yn Cefn
Bont-newydd
Dolwen Resr.
Cefn Berain
Henllan
Country World
Denbigh (Dinbych)
Gwaenynog Bach
Groes
Nantglyn
Waen
Prion
Pant-pastynog
Ffridd Fawr
Friary
Meliden (Gallt Melyd)
Prestatyn
Gronant
Gwespyr
Bryn-llwyn
Gwaenysgor
Golden Grove
Llanasa
Picton
Pen-y-ffordd
Ffynnongroyw
Trelogan
Mostyn
Tan-yr-allt
Dyserth
Trelawnyd
Bodrhyddan Hall
Cwm
Marian Cwm
Berthengam
Maen Achwyfaen Cross
Whitford (Chwitffordd)
Lloc
Rhewl-Mostyn
Glan-y-don
Greenfield (Maes-glas)
Basingwerk Abbey
Gorsedd
Carmel
Pantasaph
Holywell (Treffynnon)
Pant y Wacco
Rhualt
St. Asaph (Llanelwy)
Cathedral
Waen
Goleugoed
Tremeirchion
Caerwys
Graig
Sodom
Pen-y-cefn
Brynford
Babell
Trefnant
Bodfari
Afon-wen
Ddol
Ysceifiog
Lixwm
Halkyn Mountains
Pentre Halkyn
Halkyn (Helygain)
Tirnewydd
Dolphin
Basingwerk Castle
Nannerch
FLINTSHIRE
Rhosesmor
Rhydymwyn
Moel Famau
Waen
Castell
Llangwyfan
Cilcain
Pont-newydd
Cefn-bychan
Gwernaffield
Gwernymynydd
Cadole
Llandyrnog
Llanrhaeadr
Pentre-Llanrhaeadr
Llanynys
Llangynhafal
Gellifor
Hirwaen
Tafarn-y-Gelyn
Jubilee Tower
Loggerheads
Clwyd Forest
Moel Llys -y- Coed
Llanferres
Maeshafn
Bachymbyd Fawr
Rhewl
Ruthin (Rhuthun)
Llanbedr-Dyffryn -Clwyd
Llanfwrog
Bontuchel
Cyffylliog
DENBIGHSHIRE
Efenechtyd
Pwll-glas
Llanfair Dyffryn Clwyd
Graig-fechan
Pentre-celyn
Llanarmon-yn-Ial
Graianrhyd
Eryrys
Llandegla
Pen-y-stryt
Clocaenog
CLOCAENOG FOREST
Cefn Du
Clawdd-newydd
Derwen
Churchyard Cross
Bryn-Saith Marchog
Llanelidan
Rhyd-y-meudwy
Aled Isaf Resr.
Bryn Trillyn 1627
1528 Moel Llyn
Llyn Aled
Llyn Bran
Moel Seisiog 1514
Llyn Alwen
Mynydd Hiraethog
Llyn Brenig
Llyn Brenig Visitor Centre
Archaeological Trails
Alwen Resr.
Pentre-llyn-cymmer
Nebo
Capel Garmon
Capel Garmon Burial Chamber
Rhydlanfair
Glan-Conwy
Pentrefoelas
Rhydlydan
Watermill
Cefn-brith
Glasfryn
Llanfihangel Glyn Myfyr
Cerrigydrudion
Ysbyty Ifan
1751 Garn Prys
Bettws Gwerfil Goch
Melin-y-wig
Gwyddelwern
Bryneglwys
Horseshoe Pass
Llandynan
Bunny Farm Park
Gylchedd 2196
Ewe-phoria
A55
A5
A494
A547
A548
A525
A541
A543
A544
A5026
A5151
B5119
B5113
B5381
B5382
B5383
B5384
B5428
B5429
B5105
B4501
B5435
B5430
B5431
B4407
RIVER (AFON DYFRDWY)
CYRN-Y

Liverpool to Dublin 7hrs. 30mins.
Liverpool to: Douglas 4hrs. (Seasonal) Douglas 2hrs. 30mins. (Fast Ferry, Seasonal) Dublin 4hrs. (Fast Ferry)
Birkenhead to: Belfast 8hrs.
83
LIVERPOOL
SEE PAGE 191
CHESTER
SEE PAGE 188
BIRKENHEAD
WALLASEY
BOOTLE
CROSBY
MAGHULL
KIRKBY
ST. HELENS
HUYTON
PRESCOT
HAYDOCK
NEWTON-LE-WILLOWS
WARRINGTON
WIDNES
RUNCORN
BEBINGTON
HESWALL
ELLESMERE PORT
FRODSHAM
NESTON
CONNAH'S QUAY
BUCKLEY
Mold
WREXHAM
(Wrecsam)
ASHTON IN-MAKERFIELD
GOLBORNE
LITHERLAND
Speke
Garston
Queensferry
Helsby
Kelsall
Tarporley
Gresford
DELAMERE FOREST
ENGLAND
WALES
RIVER MERSEY
C H E S H I R E
LIVERPOOL JOHN LENNON
Manchester Ship Canal
M53
M56
M57
M58
M62
M6

84
90
91
72
83
MANCHESTER
SEE PAGE 191
SALFORD
ECCLES
SWINTON
PRESTWICH
OLDHAM
FAILSWORTH
ASHTON-UNDER-LYNE
DROYLSDEN
DUKINFIELD
HYDE
DENTON
STRETFORD
URMSTON
SALE
ALTRINCHAM
STOCKPORT
CHEADLE
Cheadle Hulme
Bramhall
Marple
Romiley
WILMSLOW
Alderley Edge
BOLLINGTON
MACCLESFIELD
KNUTSFORD
NORTHWICH
Weaverham
WARRINGTON
NEWTON-LE-WILLOWS
ASHTON-IN-MAKERFIELD
GOLBORNE
LEIGH
HINDLEY
ATHERTON
Tyldesley
WORSLEY
Culcheth
Irlam
Lymm
WINSFORD
Middlewich
Holmes Chapel
SANDBACH
CONGLETON
CREWE
NANTWICH
Alsager
KIDSGROVE
BIDDULPH
Tunstall
Burslem
Hanley
STOKE-ON-TRENT
Audley
Silverdale
Wybunbury
C H E S H I R E
S T A F F O
M6
M56
M60
M62
A556
A34
A50
A54
A49
A51
A500
A523
A537
A536
A533
A530
A534
A5020
A6
A57
A56
A538
A5033
MANCHESTER (International)
A
B
C
D
1
2
3
4
5

PEAK DISTRICT
HIGH PEAK
Kinder Scout
2088
Bleaklow Hill
2077
PEAK DISTRICT NATIONAL PARK
DERBYSHIRE
SHEFFIELD
SEE PAGE 196
CHESTERFIELD
DRONFIELD
BUXTON
MATLOCK
Ashbourne
LEEK
BELPER
GLOSSOP
STALYBRIDGE
Mossley
Hadfield
Hollingworth
Tintwistle
Penistone
STOCKSBRIDGE
WORSBROUGH
HOYLAND
Chapeltown
Grenoside
Ecclesfield
Stannington
New Mills
Chapel-en-le-Frith
Whaley Bridge
Chinley
Hayfield
Castleton
Hope
Edale
Bamford
Hathersage
Bradwell
Tideswell
Great Hucklow
Eyam
Stoney Middleton
Grindleford
Baslow
Bakewell
Ashford in the Water
Rowsley
Youlgreave
Hartington
Longnor
Warslow
Taddington
Chelmorton
Great Longstone
Little Longstone
Dove Holes
Peak Forest
Darley Bridge
Matlock Bath
Wirksworth
Cromford
Middleton
Tissington
Parwich
Alstonefield
Wetton
Butterton
Onecote
Grindon
Waterhouses
Ipstones
Cauldon
Froghall
Kingsley
Mayfield
Kniveton
Idridgehay
Tansley
Holymoorside
Wingerworth
Unstone
Newbold
Totley
Dore
Clay Cross
South Wingfield
Crich
Heage
Holloway
Winster
Elton
Birchover
Stanton in Peak
Two Dales
A6
A57
A616
A623
A628
A629
A61
A515
A53
A54
A52
A523
A619
A621
A625
A6020
A6187
A5012
M1
85
92
73
E
F
G
H

86
92
93
74
WORSBROUGH
Darfield
WOMBWELL
Bolton upon Dearne
Goldthorpe
Barnburgh
DONCASTER
Sprotbrough
Bessacarr
Cantley
Branton
Wroot
HOYLAND
WATH UPON DEARNE
MEXBOROUGH
CONISBROUGH
SWINTON
New Edlington
Old Edlington
Loversall
Rossington
New Rossington
Finningley
Blaxton
Auckley
Chapeltown
High Green
Wentworth
Rawmarsh
Thrybergh
Greasbrough
ROTHERHAM
MALTBY
Tickhill
Bawtry
Misson
Austerfield
Newington
Grenoside
Ecclesfield
Parson Cross
Wadsley Bridge
Brinsworth
Catcliffe
Treeton
Thurcroft
Dinnington
Laughton en le Morthen
Harworth
Bircotes
Scrooby
Everton
Ranskill
Blyth
Langold
Carlton in Lindrick
SHEFFIELD
SEE PAGE 196
Aughton
Swallownest
Aston
Wales
Todwick
North Anston
South Anston
Kiveton Park
Harthill
WOODALL
Woodsetts
WORKSOP
Ranby
Babworth
Eckington
Killamarsh
Mosborough
Beighton
Hackenthorpe
Halfway
Norton
DRONFIELD
Renishaw
Barlborough
Clowne
Whitwell
Manton
Elkesley
Unstone
Staveley
Creswell
Brimington
DERBYSHIRE
CHESTERFIELD
Bolsover
Duckmanton
Calow
Tapton
Whaley Thorns
Nether Langwith
Church Warsop
Market Warsop
Edwinstowe
THE DUKERIES
New Ollerton
Ollerton
Walesby
Kirton
Laxton
Wingerworth
North Wingfield
Clay Cross
Tibshelf
Pilsley
Shirebrook
Pleasley
MANSFIELD WOODHOUSE
MANSFIELD
Clipstone
Forest Town
SHERWOOD PINES
NOTTINGHA
Eakring
Bilsthorpe
Kersall
Kneesall
Ompton
Wellow
Tansley
Ashover
Higham
Shirland
Stonebroom
Blackwell
Huthwaite
SUTTON IN ASHFIELD
KIRKBY IN ASHFIELD
Rainworth
Blidworth
Farnsfield
Kirklington
Halam
Southwell
ALFRETON
South Normanton
Somercotes
Selston
Annesley Woodhouse
Ravenshead
Oxton
Wessington
Crich
SWANWICK
Ripley
Codnor
HUCKNALL
Calverton
Thurgarton
Woodborough
Lowdham
BELPER
HEANOR
EASTWOOD
Kimberley
Bulwell
ARNOLD
Denby
Kilburn
Hazelwood
Milford
M1
M18
A1(M)
A1
A57
A60
A61
A614
A617
A619
A631
A638
A6097
A6
A38
A610

Epworth
Epworth Turbary
Low Burnham
Kelfield
Susworth
Owston Ferry
Scotterthorpe
Scotter
Messingham
Manton
Sturton
Hibaldstow
Cadney
Howsham
Ownby
Clixby
Caistor
North Kelsey Moor
North Kelsey
North Kelsey Beck
Haxey
East Lound
East Ferry
Laughton Woods
Scotton
Mount Pleasant
Redbourne
Kirton in Lindsey
Graiselound
Wildsworth
Gunthorpe
Laughton
Northorpe
Grayingham
Waddingham
Brandy Wharf
South Kelsey
Moortown
Nettleton
Nettleton Wood
Holton le Moor
Thornton le Moor
R. Idle
Heckdyke
West Stockwith
Misterton
Miniature World
East Stockwith
Walkerith
Walkeringham
Morton
Blyton
Pilham
Aisby
Blyborough
Willoughton
Snitterby
Atterby
Bishop Norton
North Owersby
South Owersby
Kingerby
Castle
Kirkby
Osgodby
Horse World
Usselby
Claxby
Normanby le Wold
Otby
Canal
Beckingham
Old Hall
GAINSBOROUGH
Corringham
Hemswell
Spital in the Street
Bomber
Glentham
Bishopbridge
Middle Rasen
West Rasen
Market Rasen
Springthorpe
Sturgate
Harpswell
Hemswell Cliff
Caenby
Clayworth
Saundby
Heapham
Glentworth
Normanby-by-Spital
Owmby-by-Spital
Toft next Newton
Newton by Toft
North Wheatley
South Wheatley
Bole
Lea
Knaith Park
Upton
Sturgate
Fillingham
Saxby
Linwood
Buslingthorpe
R. Trent
Kexby
Spridlington
Faldingworth
Sturton le Steeple
Knaith
Gate Burton
Willingham by Stow
Coates
Ingham
Hackthorn
Cold Hanworth
Friesthorpe
Lissington
Bleasby Moor
West Torrington
Clarborough
North Leverton with Habblesthorpe
Fenton
The Chateau
Littleborough
Saxon Ford (site)
Marton
Stow
Cammeringham
Brattleby
Snarford
Welton Hill
Wickenby
Holton cum Beckering
Welham
FORD
South Leverton
Sundown Adventureland
Cottam
Sturton by Stow
Thorpe in the Fallows
Aisthorpe
Scampton
Welton
Dunholme
Reasby
Snelland
Grove
Treswell
Rampton
Brampton
Torksey
Bransby
Bransby Horses Home
North Carlton
Lincolnshire Agricultural Showground
Scothern
Stainton by Langworth
Fulnetby
Rand
Eaton Wood
Woodbeck
Headon
Stokeham
Church Laneham
Fenton
Broxholme
South Carlton
Sudbrooke
Langworth
Poultry Park
Upton
Laneham
Laughterton
Kettlethorpe
Saxilby
R. Till
Burton
Riseholme
Ermine West
Ermine East
Nettleham
Reepham
Barlings
Apley
Kingthorpe
Askham
East Drayton
Dunham on Trent
Newton on Trent
Fossdyke Navigation
Broadholme
North Greetwell
Cherry Willingham
Low Barlings
Abbey
Stainfield
LINCOLNSHIRE
Church
East Markham
Kingshaugh
Darlton
Ragnall
North Clifton
Thorney
Skellingthorpe
Heritage
LINCOLN
SEE PAGE 191
Cath.
New Boultham
Washingborough
Fiskerton
Tuxford
Castle
Egmanton
Skegby
Fledborough
High Marnham
Low Marnham
South Clifton
Harby
Doddington Hall
Doddington
Wigsley
Birchwood
Hartsholme
Swanpool
Boultham
Swallow Beck
Bracebridge
Canwick
Heritage Room
Heighington
Branston Booths
Bardney
Abbey
Normanton on Trent
Weston
Spalford
Heritage Room
North Scarle
Eagle Moor
Road Transport
Eagle
Whisby
Whisby Nature Park
Bracebridge Heath
Branston
Potterhanworth Booths
R. Witham
Moorhouse
Grassthorpe
Sutton on Trent
Girton
Weecar
Eagle Barnsdale
Thorpe on the Hill
North Hykeham
Potterhanworth
Wasps Nest
Sots Hole
Ossington
Church
Carlton-on-Trent
Besthorpe
South Hykeham
Waddington
Nocton
Dunston
South Scarle
Morton
Haddington
Aubourn Hall
Aubourn
Norwell Woodhouse
Norwell
Dolls
Cromwell
Collingham
Swinderby
Witham St. Hughs
Thurlby
Swinderby
Harmston
Metheringham
Heritage Room
Bassingham
Coleby
Blankney
Metheringham Airfield
Martin
Timberland
Caunton
Bathley
Little Carlton
Holme
North Muskham
Langford
Brough
Norton Disney
Somerton
Boothby Graffoe
Scopwick
Kirkby Green
Thorpe Tilney
Winthorpe
Air Museum & Showground Winthorpe
Stapleford
Stapleford Wood
Carlton-le-Moorland
Navenby
Wellingore
Heritage Room
Rowston
Ashby de la Launde
Catley Priory
Kelham
Kelham Mill
South Muskham
Averham
Staythorpe
Millgate
Town Hall
Newark
Coddington
R. Witham
Brant Broughton
Welbourn Castle
Welbourn
Temple Bruer Tower
Digby
Bloxholm
Dorrington
North Ings Farm
Rolleston
Farndon
Farndon Field
New Balderton
NEWARK-ON-TRENT
Beckingham
Teddy's Farm
Stragglethorpe
Barnby in the Willows
Leadenham
Ruskington
Fiskerton
East Stoke
Hawton
Balderton
Fenton
Fulbeck Hall
Fulbeck
Cranwell
Anwick
Thorpe
Stubton
Caythorpe
Frieston
Cranwell
Leasingham
Evedon
Elston
Claypole
Brandon
Dry Doddington
North Rauceby
South Rauceby
Aviation Heritage
Holdingham
Ewerby
Syerston
Cotham
Devon
Hough-on-the-Hill
Normanton
Kirkby la Thorpe
Flintham
Flintham Hall
Sibthorpe
Hougham
Gelston
Carlton
Sudbrook
Sleaford
Asgarby
Waterfall
A159
A15
A18
A161
B1398
B1400
B1206
B1205
B1434
A1084
A1103
A631
A46
A156
A620
B1403
B1241
B1202
A1500
A57
A133
A158
B1399
B1190
B1131
B1188
B1178
A1434
A607
B1164
A1
A616
A617
A17
A1133
B1202
B1189
B1191
B1188
B1429
B1209
B6403
B6326
A153
87
88
94
75
E
F
G
H
1
2
3
4
5
ISLE OF AXHOLME

88
94
95
87
76
A
B
C
D
Owmby
Clixby
A1084
Pelham's Pillar
A1173
Irby upon Humber
Waltham
New Waltham
High Sands
North Kelsey Moor
Cabourne
Swallow
A46
Beelsby
Barnoldby le Beck
Brigsley
A16
Holton le Clay
A1031
Tetney Lock
Caistor
Cuxwold
Hatcliffe
A18
B1203
Ashby cum Fenby
Tetney
North Cotes
Nettleton
Rothwell
West Ravendale
Priory
East Ravendale
Grainsby
B1201
North Thoresby
Churchthorpe
Marshchapel
Eskham
DANGER AREA
Donna Nook
Nettleton Wood
Holton le Moor
B1225
Croxby
Thorganby
Wold Newton
Thoresway
Binbrook
Swinhope
Fulstow
Covenham Resr.
Grainthorpe
Grainthorpe Fen
North Somercotes
Normanby le Wold
Ludborough
Grimsby & Louth Light Railway
Covenham St.Bartholomew
Conisholme
Church End
Skidbrooke North End
North Owersby
A46
Usselby
Claxby
Stainton le Vale
Orford
Binbrook
Covenham St. Mary
Austin Fen
South Somercotes
Saltfleet
Otby
North Ormsby
Utterby
Yarburgh
Skidbrooke
Osgodby
Horse World
Walesby
Kirmond le Mire
Fotherby
Little Grimsby
Alvingham
Watermill
Saltfleetby St. Clements
A1103
Middle Rasen
Tealby
Great Tows
North Elkington
Yalta Woods
North Cockerington
Keddington Corner
Saltfleetby All Saints
Market Rasen
B1203
North Willingham
Ludford
A631
Kelstern
A16
Saltfleetby St. Peter
Keddington
Grimoldby
A631
Three Bridges
Theddlethorpe All Saints
Walesby
B1202
Sixhills
Burgh on Bain
Welton le Wold
South Elkington
A157
LOUTH
South Cockerington
Stewton
B1200
Manby
Linwood
Legsby
Gayton le Wold
Hallington
Little Carlton
Great Carlton
Buslingthorpe
Bleasby
Hainton
Raithby
B1520
A153
Legbourne
Station
Carlton
Gayton le Marsh
Lissington
Bleasby Moor
South Willingham
Donington on Bain
Withcall
Little Cawthorpe
South Reston
Friesthorpe
East Torrington
West Torrington
THE WOLDS
Tathwell
A157
Strubby
Withern
Wickenby
Holton cum Beckering
East Barkwith
Benniworth
Stenigot
Red Hill
Cadwell Park
Haugham
Mucklon
Authorpe
Tothill
B1373
Snelland
B1399
West Barkwith
B1225
Market Stainton
Cawkwell
Maidenwell
Burwell
Woodthorpe
Stainton by Langworth
Fulnetby
Rand
Panton
Sotby
Goulceby
Asterby
Farforth
Ruckland
Waterhill
Belleau
Claythorpe
Bird Garden
Saleby
A158
Wragby
Ranby
Scamblesby
Swaby Valley
White Pit
Swaby
Aby
Alford
Bilsby
LINCOLNSHIRE
Langworth
Poultry Park
Langton by Wragby
Hatton
Great Sturton
Belchford
Oxcombe
Ketsby
Calceby
South Thoresby
Rigsby Wood
Manor House
Haugh
Rigsby
Folk
Barlings
Apley
Kingthorpe
Chambers Farm Wood
Hemingby
Tetford
South Ormsby
Driby
A1104
Well
Low Barlings
Abbey
Stainfield
B1202
Minting
Baumber
Farthorpe
Fulletby
Salmonby
Church
Somersby
Brinkhill
Sutterby
Ulceby
Skendleby Psalter
A158
Wispington
R. Bain
West Ashby
A153
Bag Enderby
Harrington
A16
Fordington
Claxby
Gautby
Edlington
Low Toynton
Ashby Puerorum
Stockwith Mill
Aswardby
Church
Langton
A1028
Young Wood
Thimbleby
Greetham
Skendleby
Branston Booths
Abbey
Bardney
B1190
Bucknall
B1190
Horncastle
High Toynton
Hagworthingham
Winceby
Snipe Dales
Sausthorpe
Grebby
Scremby
Langton
Horsington
Thornton
Mareham on the hill
Scrafield
Winceby
Lusby
Mavis Enderby
Raithby
Hundleby
Partney
Candlesby
Herbs
Gunby Hall
Potterhanworth Booths
Tupholme Abbey
Southrey
Woodhall
Martin
Hameringham
Asgarby
B1195
Spilsby
Ashby by Partney
Halton Holegate
Monksthorpe
Heavy Horse Centre
Bratoft
Potterhanworth
Stixwould
Wellington Monument
Canal
Scrivelsby
Scrivelsby Ct.
Low Hameringham
Hareby
Old Bolingbroke
B1195
Nocton
Nest
Sots Hole
Tanvats
Reeds Beck
Cottage
Dalderby
B1183
Moorby
Bolingbroke
Toynton All Saints
Great Steeping
Firsby
Roughton
Wood Enderby
Miningsby
West Keal
East Keal
Toynton St. Peter
Halton Fenside
Little Steeping
Dunston
Woodhall Spa
Tower on the Moor
Haltham
Hagnaby
Toynton Fen Side
Dales Head Dike
Ostler's Plantation
Kirkby on Bain
Wilksby
East Kirkby
East Kirkby
Keal Cotes
B1189
Abbey
Martin Dales
Chapel
B1192
Mareham le Fen
A155
Aviation Heritage Centre
Metheringham
B1191
Revesby
Kirkby Fenside
Thorpe Fendike
Metheringham Airfield
A153
Tumby
Stickford
Martin
Timberland Delph
Tattershall Thorpe
Wainfleet Bank
Timberland
Pumping Station
Tattershall
Coningsby
Tumby Woodside
New Bolingbroke
New Leake
Kirkby Green
Tales of The Riverbank
College
Tattershall
Coningsby
Midville
Friskney Eaudyke
Thorpe Tilney
Walcott
Old Vicarage Cottage
Tattershall Bridge
Park
Moorhouses
Stickney
Eastville
Rowston
Hawthorn Hill
Reedham
Medlam
East Fen
Scrub Hill
Sandy Bank
Carrington
Friskney
Catley Priory
B1189
Aviation
Dogdyke
Steam Pumping Sta.
New York
Bunkers Hill
Lade Bank
Digby
Billinghay
Childrens Farm
West Fen
B1183
Chapel Hill
Hundle Houses
Northlands
Leake Common Side
B1188
Dorrington
North Ings Farm
River Witham
A16
North Kyme
Haven Bank
Sibsey Fen Side
Trader Mill
Leake Fold Hill
Wrangle Lowgate
Ruskington
South Kyme
B1192
Gipsey Bridge
B1184
Frithville
Sibsey
B1184
Old Leake
Wrangle
A153
Holland Fen
Fishtoft Drove
B1209
Anwick
Slea
Church Tower
B1395
High Ferry
Leake Hurn's End
Langrick
Anton's Gowt
A52
Leverton
Leverton Outgate
Evedon
Frith Bank
Hilldyke
West End
Amber Hill
Ewerby
Leverton Lucasgate
A17
Kirkby la Thorpe
Howell
Brothertoft
Benington
Burton Corner
Haltoft End
Benington Sea End
Watermill
Asgarby
Boston

NORTH SEA
Saltfleetby Theddlethorpe Dunes
Theddlethorpe St. Helen
Animal Gardens
Mablethorpe
Ye Olde Curiosity
Trusthorpe
Thorpe
Sutton on Sea
Sandilands
Hannah
Markby
Huttoft
Anderby Creek
Anderby
Thurlby
Mumby
Authorpe Row
Farlesthorpe
Cumberworth
Chapel St. Leonards
Helsey
Bonthorpe
Hogsthorpe
Willoughby
Sloothby
Slackholme End
Hasthorpe
Hardy's Animal Farm
Addlethorpe
Ingoldmells
Ingoldmells Point
Skegness (Ingoldmells)
Funcoast
Welton le Marsh
Orby
Bird Garden
Orby Marsh
Water Leisure Park
Winthorpe
Seathorne
Burgh le Marsh
A158
Church Farm
Seal Sanctuary
SKEGNESS
Croft
Skegness Electric Tramway
Thorpe St. Peter
Seacroft
Croft Marsh
Magdalen
Wainfleet All Saints
Wainfleet St. Mary
Key's Toft
Gibraltar Point
Gibraltar
A52
A1111
B1449
DANGER AREA
Deeps
Boston
77
Scolt Head Island
Brancaster Bay
Holme Dunes
Holme Bird Observatory
Holkham
E F G H

90
CLEVELEYS
Thornton
Poulton-le-Fylde
Singleton
Great Eccleston
Bilsborrow
Longridge
BLACKPOOL
SEE PAGE 186
THE FYLDE
Kirkham
Woodplumpton
FULWOOD
PRESTON
SEE PAGE 195
St.Anne's
LYTHAM ST.ANNE'S
Lytham
Warton
Freckleton
Higher Penwortham
Bamber Bridge
LEYLAND
Hesketh Bank
Becconsall
Much Hoole
Tarleton
Bretherton
Croston
Eccleston
CHORLEY
Coppull
Adlington
SOUTHPORT
Churchtown
Rufford
Burscough
Burscough Bridge
Scarisbrick
STANDISH
Blackrod
FORMBY
Ainsdale
Woodvale
ORMSKIRK
SKELMERSDALE
ORRELL
WIGAN
Up Holland
Ince-in-Makerfield
Aspull
MAGHULL
Rainford
Billinge
ASHTON-IN-MAKERFIELD
LIVERPOOL BAY
CROSBY
LITHERLAND
KIRKBY
Aintree
ST. HELENS
HAYDOCK
GOLBORNE
BOOTLE
Fazakerley
Knowsley
Eccleston
PRESCOT
NEWTON-LE-WILLOWS
WALLASEY
HUYTON
Rainhill
WARRINGTON
LIVERPOOL
SEE PAGE 191
BIRKENHEAD
HOYLAKE
Moreton
WIDNES
Liverpool to Dublin 7hrs. 30mins.
Liverpool to: Douglas 4hrs. (Seasonal) Douglas 2hrs. 30mins. (Fast Ferry, Seasonal) Dublin 4hrs. (Fast Ferry)
Birkenhead to: Belfast 8hrs.
M6
M55
M61
M58
M57
M62
M53

91
Clitheroe
Waddington
Downham
Worston
Twiston
Chatburn
Colne
Foulridge
Cowling
Sutton-in-Craven
Laycock
Barrowford
Nelson
Brierfield
Trawden
Keighley Moor
Haworth
Oxenhope
The Forest of Trawden
The Forest of Pendle
Whalley
Billington
Padiham
Burnley
Great Harwood
Clayton-le-Moors
Accrington
Church
Oswaldtwistle
Blackburn
Darwen
Blackburn Interchange
Haslingden
Rawtenstall
Forest of Rossendale
Bacup
Todmorden
Hebden Bridge
Mytholmroyd
Heptonstall
Ripponden
Ramsbottom
Edenfield
Whitworth
Littleborough
Rochdale
Milnrow
Bury
Tottington
Horwich
Bolton
Heywood
Radcliffe
Whitefield
Middleton
Royton
Shaw
Farnworth
Little Lever
Kearsley
Prestwich
Chadderton
Oldham
Failsworth
Ashton-under-Lyne
Mossley
Atherton
Worsley
Swinton
Eccles
Salford
Manchester
See page 191
Droylsden
Stalybridge
Dukinfield
Hyde
Tyldesley
Leigh
Urmston
Stretford
Denton
Irlam
Sale
Carrington
Partington
Altrincham
Hale
Gatley
Cheadle
Cheadle Hulme
Stockport
Bredbury
Romiley
Marple
Hazel Grove
New Mills
Hollingworth
Hadfield
Tintwistle
Denshaw
Diggle
Delph
Uppermill
Greenfield
Saddleworth
Wingates
Westhoughton
Hindley
Culcheth
Glazebury
Lymm
M65
M66
M62
M61
M60
M602
M6
M67
A56
A59
A666
A58
A671
A682
A646
A680
A6068
A627(M)

92
98
85
91
KEIGHLEY
BINGLEY
BAILDON
GUISELEY
YEADON
Menston
Bramhope
HORSFORTH
SHIPLEY
BRADFORD
SEE PAGE 186
PUDSEY
LEEDS
SEE PAGE 190
ROTHWELL
MORLEY
Middleton
BATLEY
CLECKHEATON
LIVERSEDGE
Heckmondwike
DEWSBURY
BRIGHOUSE
HALIFAX
Queensbury
SOWERBY BRIDGE
Hebden Bridge
Mytholmroyd
Ripponden
Elland
HUDDERSFIELD
MIRFIELD
Thornhill
Ossett
Horbury
WAKEFIELD
NORMANTON
Stanley
Slaithwaite
Marsden
Meltham
Holmfirth
Honley
Kirkburton
Skelmanthorpe
Denby Dale
Clayton West
Darton
ROYSTON
BARNSLEY
Dodworth
WORSBROUGH
Penistone
Thurgoland
STOCKSBRIDGE
Chapeltown
Grenoside
Ecclesfield
SHEFFIELD
SEE PAGE 196
STALYBRIDGE
Mossley
Greenfield
Uppermill
SADDLEWORTH
Delph
Diggle
HYDE
Hollingworth
Hadfield
GLOSSOP
Tintwistle
Crowden
PEAK DISTRICT NATIONAL PARK
DERBYSHIRE
PEAK DISTRICT
HIGH PEAK
Kinder Scout
Snake Pass
Bleaklow Hill
Black Hill
KEIGHLEY MOOR
Haworth
Oxenhope
Denholme
Thornton
Oakworth
Cullingworth
Wilsden
HARTSHEAD MOOR
WOOLLEY EDGE
Emley
Flockton
Crigglestone
Netherton
Gomersal
Birstall
Birkenshaw
Drighlington
Gildersome
Tingley
Cowling
Sutton-in-Craven
Steeton
Riddlesden
Silsden
East Morton
Mickletwaite
A629
A650
A660
A61
A58
A6120
A647
A6110
A653
A638
A644
A642
A62
A640
A635
A636
A637
A616
A628
A6018
A57
A6024
M62
M606
M621
M1
M67

NORTH YORKSHIRE
99
100
93
94
86
87
E
F
G
H
1
2
3
4
5
Tadcaster
Clifford
Bramham
Bramham Park
Newton Kyme
Ark
A659
A64
A1
Oxton
Wharfe
Kirkby Wharfe
Stutton
Appleton Roebuck
Bolton Percy
Acaster Malbis
Acaster Selby
Bell Hall
River Ouse
Stillingfleet
Deighton
Escrick
Thorganby
Storwood
East Cottingwith
Melbourne
Melbourne Hall
B1228
Thorner
Barwick in Elmet
Aberford
Lotherton Hall (Mus.)
Saxton
Towton
Towton 1461
Ulleskelf
B1223
Church Fenton
Ryther
Cawood
Kelfield
Riccall
A19
Skipwith
Skipwith Common Nature Trail
North Duffield
Ellerton
Aughton
Laytham
Harlthorpe
Foggathorpe
Bubwith
Highfield
Breighton
Gunby
Willitoft
Gribthorpe
Spaldington
A163
A1(M)
M1
A64
Barkston Ash
Sherburn in Elmet
Sherburn in Elmet
B1222
Little Fenton
Biggin
Bishop Wood Nature Trail
Wistow
Barlby
Osgodby
Hall
Lund
Menthorpe
South Duffield
Breighton
West Garforth
East Garforth
Garforth
Micklefield
Garden Village
Huddlestone Hall
Newthorpe
Steeton Hall Gateway
South Milford
Monk Fryston
Lumby
A63
SELBY
Abbey
East Common
Thorpe Willoughby
Hambleton
Brayton
Cliffe
Hemingbrough
Wressle
A63
A614
Brind
Newsholme
Howden
Hollinthorpe
Kippax
Ledston Lodge
Ledsham
Great Preston
Allerton Bywater
Ledston
Fairburn Ings
Fairburn
Water Fryston
New Fryston
Burton Salmon
Hillam
Gateforth
Burn
Barlow
Barmby on the Marsh
Asselby
Knedlington
Long Drax
M62
Balkholme
Wood Row
Mickletown
Methley
Methley Junction
Whitwood
CASTLEFORD
Airedale
Red Hill
A6032
B6136
Poole
Brotherton
Byram
Birkin
West Haddlesey
Chapel Haddlesey
Temple Hirst
Hirst Courtney
A1041
Camblesforth
Drax
Newland
Little Airmyn
Airmyn
Kilpin Pike
Kilpin
Skelton
Saltmarshe
Ferrybridge
KNOTTINGLEY
Beal
Kellington
Kellingley
Hut Green
Eggborough
Hensall
Carlton
Carlton Towers
Rawcliffe
GOOLE
Hopetown
Normanton
North Featherstone
PONTEFRACT
Pontefract
New Town
FERRYBRIDGE
M62
High Eggborough
Little Heck
Gowdall
Snaith
East Cowick
West Cowick
Rawcliffe Bridge
Old Goole
Swinefleet
Marshland
FEATHERSTONE
Ackton
Streethouse
Chequerfield
Carleton
Darrington
Cridling Stubbs
Whitley Thorpe
Whitley
Great Heck
Pollington
Southfield Resr.
Aire & Calder Navigation
Dutch River
Goole Fields
Snydale
Sharlston Common
Sharlston
West Hardwick
Wragby
Nostell Priory
New Crofton
Purston Jaglin
High Ackworth
Low Ackworth
East Hardwick
Wentbridge
Womersley
A1
A639
Ackworth School
Ackworth Moor Top
Little Smeaton
Walden Stubbs
Fenwick
Sykehouse
M18
Moorends
Thorn Waste or Moors
Wintersett
Fitzwilliam
Ryhill
Kinsley
Havercroft
A628
Badsworth
Thorpe Audlin
Kirk Smeaton
BARNSDALE BAR
Norton
Moss
New Junction Canal
Fishlake
Crowle
A638
Upton
Wrangbrook
North Elmsall
Campsall
Askern
Sutton
Braithwaite
Kirk Bramwith
Stainforth
Thorne
Stainforth & Keadby Canal
Old R.Don
South Hiendley
Hemsworth
Shafton
Brierley
South Elmsall
South Kirkby
Skelbrooke
Burghwallis
Owston
Skellow
Carcroft
Thorpe in Balne
DONCASTER NORTH
Barnby Dun
Hatfield
Marina
Hatfield Chase
A18
M180
Cudworth
Upper Cudworth
Grimethorpe
Hampole
A19
ADWICK LE STREET
Hooton Pagnell
Clayton
Toll Bar
Almholme
Kirk Sandall
Dunscroft
Dunsville
Hatfield Woodhouse
Hatfield Moors
Sandtoft
Transport Centre
Monk Bretton Priory
Ardsley
A635
Great Houghton
Little Houghton
Middlecliff
Thurnscoe
Brodsworth
Brodsworth Hall
Marr
Woodlands
New Village
Arksey
Edenthorpe
BENTLEY
Armthorpe
West Carr
Westgate
Belton
ISLE OF AXHOLME
Epworth
Epworth Turbary
Wroot
Darfield
Billingley
DEARNE
Hickleton
Goldthorpe
Scawsby
Cusworth
Cusworth Hall
Wheatley Park
Hyde Park
Nutwell
Cantley
Doncaster Racecourse
M18
Broom Hill
WOMBWELL
Bolton upon Dearne
Adwick upon Dearne
Barnburgh
Melton Wood
DONCASTER
Sprotbrough
Bessacarr
Branton
A6195
Harlington
High Melton
Balby
Warmsworth
A6182
Auckley
Blaxton
Westwoodside
Upperthorpe
Haxey
Hemingfield
Brampton
MEXBOROUGH
Earth Centre
Cadeby
DEARNE VALLEY
WATH UPON DEARNE
Elsecar
Denaby Main
CONISBROUGH
New Edlington
Old Edlington
Loversall
Rossington
DONCASTER FINNINGLEY
Finningley
B1396
Wentworth
Swinton
Upper Haugh
Nether Haugh
Wentworth Woodhouse
Thorpe Hesley
Keppel's Column
RAWMARSH
Kilnhurst
Hooton Roberts
Thrybergh
Clifton
Wadworth
New Rossington
R. Idle
Graiseloun
Greasbrough
Ravenfield
Dalton
Sunnyside
Micklebring
Braithwell
Stainton
Tickhill
A1(M)
A638
Austerfield
Newington
Misson
Misterton
West Stockwith
ROTHERHAM
A6123
Dalton Magna
Bramley
MALTBY
Castle
Bawtry
Bircotes
Gringley on the Hill
Chesterfield Canal
Walkeringham
Beckingham
Tinsley
Moorgate
A631
Wickersley
Whiston
Hooton Levitt
A631
Harworth
Styrrup
Scaftworth
Scrooby
Everton
A631
Brinsworth
Catcliffe
Morthen
Thurcroft
Slade Hooton
Roche Abbey
Aircraft Museum
Firbeck
Oldcotes
Serlby
BLYTH
Mattersey Thorpe
Mattersey
Mattersey Priory
Wiseton
Clayworth
Treeton
Upper Whiston
Ulley
Brookhouse
Laughton en le Morthen
Langold
Blyth
Church
Ranskill
B6045
Saundby
Handsworth
Aughton
Brampton en le Morthen
Hardwick
Laughton Common
Dinnington
Letwell
Langold
Hodsock Priory
Carlton in Lindrick
Torworth
Lound
Daneshill Lakes
Bird
North Wheatley
A620
Butterfly
A57
A630
M18
A614
A1
A634
A638
B6463
B1403
A161
A60
B6422
B6474
B6273
B6428
A6195
B6411
B1220
A18
B1222
B1217

94
100
93
87
EAST RIDING OF YORKSHIRE
NORTH LINCOLNSHIRE
LINCOL
ISLE OF AXHOLME
KINGSTON UPON HULL
SEE PAGE 190
BEVERLEY
COTTINGHAM
HESSLE
GOOLE
SCUNTHORPE
GAINSBOROUGH
Humber Bridge
TOLL
Melbourne
Seaton Ross
Everingham
Market Weighton
Goodmanham
Kiplingcotes
Leconfield
Cherry Burton
Bishop Burton
Molescroft
Holme-on-Spalding-Moor
Howden
Hook
Airmyn
Gilberdyke
Eastrington
Newport
North Cave
South Cave
North Newbald
Walkington
Little Weighton
Skidby
Willerby
Kirk Ella
Anlaby
Swanland
Welton
Elloughton
Brough
North Ferriby
Broomfleet
Blacktoft
Saltmarshe
Swinefleet
Alkborough
Winteringham
Barton upon Humber
Barrow upon Humber
New Holland
Goxhill
Winterton
South Ferriby
Burton upon Stather
Crowle
Gunness
Althorpe
Burringham
Broughton
Brigg
Wrawby
Barnetby le Wold
Elsham
Worlaby
Appleby
Bottesford
Messingham
Scawby
Hibaldstow
North Kelsey
Caistor
Grasby
Epworth
Haxey
Belton
Scotter
Kirton in Lindsey
Waddingham
South Kelsey
Blyton
Misterton
Beckingham
Willoughton
Middle Rasen
Market Rasen
North Wheatley
Clayworth
Laughton Woods
Humber Wildfowl Refuge
Blacktoft Sands Nature Res.
Read's Island
Redcliff Channel
HUMBERSIDE
M62
M180
M181
A63
A15
A18
A159
A161
A614
A1079
A164
A1035
A631
A1103
A156
A46
A180
A1077
A1084

95
NORTH SEA
RIVER HUMBER
Mouth of the Humber
NORTH EAST LINCOLNSHIRE
LINCOLNSHIRE
THE WOLDS
Rolston
Mappleton
Long Riston
Rise
Little Hatfield
Great Hatfield
Great Cowden
DANGER AREA
Withernwick
Skirlaugh
New Ellerby
Marton
Aldbrough
West Newton
Old Ellerby
East Newton
Burton Constable
Flinton
Wood Hall
Swine
Coniston
Garton
Grimston
Ganstead
Thirtleby
Sproatley
Humbleton
Fitling
Hilston
Wyton
Owstwick
Bilton
Elstronwick
Lelley
Tunstall
Preston
Burton Pidsea
North End
Roos
Waxholme
Marfleet
West End
Rimswell
Owthorne
Hedon
Salt End
Burstwick
Withernsea
Havenside
Halsham
East End
Paull
Thorngumbald
Camerton
Ryehill
Keyingham
Hollym
Winestead
Ottringham
Holmpton
Paull Holme Sands
Patrington
Patrington Haven
Welwick
Out Newton
Weeton
Foulholme Sands
East Halton
Sunk Island
Skeffling
Easington
Old Hall
North Killingholme
Monument
Immingham Dock
Sunk Island Sands
South Killingholme
Kilnsea
Spurn Peninsula Nature Trail & Reserve (Toll)
Immingham
Trinity Sands
Grimsby Roads
Habrough
Brocklesby
Stallingborough
Pyewipe
GRIMSBY
Lifeboat Station
SPURN HEAD
Bird Observatory
Keelby
Healing
Great Coates
West Marsh
Leisure Park
Bull Lightship
Bull Sand
Pelham Mausoleum
Wybers Wood
Old Clee
Little Coates
CLEETHORPES
Hull to: Rotterdam (Europoort) 10hrs. Zeebrugge 12hrs. 30mins.
Aylesby
R. Freshney
Riby
Laceby
Bradley
Nunsthorpe
Scartho
Haile Sand Fort
Humberston
Tetney High Sands
Irby upon Humber
Waltham
New Waltham
Pelham's Pillar
Swallow
Barnoldby le Beck
Brigsley
Holton le Clay
Cabourne
Beelsby
Tetney Lock
Cuxwold
Ashby cum Fenby
Tetney
Hatcliffe
Waithe
North Cotes
Priory
West Ravendale
Grainsby
Marshchapel
Donna Nook
Rothwell
East Ravendale
North Thoresby
Eskham
Croxby
Churchthorpe
Grainthorpe
Thorganby
Covenham Resr.
Louth Canal
Thoresway
Fulstow
Grainthorpe Fen
North Somercotes
Swinhope
Wold Newton
Binbrook
Covenham St.Bartholomew
Conisholme
Church End
Skidbrooke North End
Ludborough
Grimsby & Louth Light Railway
Orford
Covenham St. Mary
Austin Fen
Saltfleet
Stainton le Vale
South Somercotes
Binbrook
North Ormsby
Utterby
Yarburgh
Otby
Skidbrooke
Walesby
Kirmond le Mire
Fotherby
Alvingham
Watermill
Saltfleetby St. Clements
Tealby
Little Grimsby
North Cockerington
Great Tows
North Elkington
Yalta Woods
Keddington Corner
Saltfleetby Theddlethorpe Dunes
Saltfleetby St. Peter
Saltfleetby All Saints
Kelstern
North Willingham
Ludford
Keddington
South Cockerington
Grimoldby
Three Bridges
Theddlethorpe St. Helen
South Elkington
Welton le Wold
LOUTH
Manby
Theddlethorpe All Saints
Sixhills
Burgh on Bain
Stewton
Little Carlton
Meers Bridge
Animal Gardens
Legsby
Gayton le Wold
Hallington
Great Carlton
Station
Mablethorpe

102
96
90
LAKE
DISTRICT
NATIONAL
PARK
FURNESS
CUMBRIA
Newbiggin
Broad Oak
Lane End
Whitfell
1881
Ulpha
Dunnerdale
Caw
1735
Stickle Pike
1231
Ulpha Park
Torver
Sunny Bank
Coniston
Grizedale
Riddings Wood
Bogle Crag
Satterthwaite
Force Mills
Force Forge
Graythwaite Hall
Stors
Blackwell
Winster
Crook
Under
Crosthwaite
Ludderburn
Windermere
DANGER AREA
Corney
Stoneside
Broughton Mills
Beckfoot
Bootle Fell
Swinside Stone Circle
Duddon Bridge
Selker Bay
Hycemoor
Bootle
Hyton
Annaside
Black Combe
1970
Whitbeck
Lower Hawthwaite
Broughton in Furness
Woodland Fell
Water Yeat
Blawith
High Nibthwaite
Crosslands
Rusland
Finsthwaite
Bobbin Mill
Town End
Lakeside
Fell Foot
Staveley-in-Cartmel
Bowland Bridge
Cartmel Fell
Row
Howe
Lady Hall
Foxfield
Grizebeck
Hallthwaites
The Green
Oxen Park
Lowick Bridge
Lowick Green
Lowick
Colton
Deer
Rusland Hall
Spark Bridge
Gawthwaite
Newby Bridge
Backbarrow
Haverthwaite
Ayside
Witherslack
Mill Side
Town End
Whicham
Silecroft
The Hill
Millom
Kirksanton
Folk
Haverigg
Wall End
Kirkby-in-Furness
Chapels
Netherhouses
1088
Shooting House Hill
Beck Side
Soutergate
Penny Bridge
Broughton Beck
Greenodd
Low Wood
Bigland Hall
Seatle
Barber Green
High Newton
Nature Reserve
Mansriggs
Arrad Foot
Beck Side
Field Broughton
Lindale
Meathop
Askam in Furness
Ireleth
ULVERSTON
Pennington
Marton
Lindal in Furness
South Lakes
Swarthmoor
Leven Viaduct
Sandside
Conishead Priory
Holker Hall
Holker
Cartmel
Cartmel Priory
Grange-over-Sands
Holme Island
Arnside
Eaves Wood
The Row
Silverdale
Silverdale Green
Cark
Flookburgh
Allithwaite
Kents Bank
Ravenstown
Chapel Island
Great Urswick
Bardsea
Little Urswick
Dalton-in-Furness
Stainton with Adgarley
Isle of Walney
Ormsgill
Hawcoat
BARROW-IN-FURNESS
Furness Abbey
Newton
Gleaston
Scales
Baycliff
Aldingham
Dendron
Humphrey Head Point
MORECAMBE BAY
North Scale
Barrow Marina
Vickerstown
Leece
Newbiggin
Roosecote
Roosebeck
Lancaster Sound
Bolton-le-Sands
Hest Bank
Biggar
Rampside
Roa Island
Foulney Island
Sheep Island
Piel Island
South End
Hilpsford Scar
Piel Bar
MORECAMBE
Marineland Aquarium
Torrisholme
Bare
Skerton
Sandylands
Lower Heysham
Heysham
Higher Heysham
LANCASTER
Heaton
Aldcliffe
Nuclear Power Station
Middleton
Heysham to Douglas 3hrs. 45mins.
Overton
Glasson
Sunderland
River Lune
Heysham Lake
Sunderland Point
Lower Thurnham
Upper Thurnham
Abbey
Cockerham
Braides
Wyre Light
Fleetwood to Larne 8hrs.
Knott End-on-Sea
FLEETWOOD
Lifeboat Station
Rossall Point
Preesall
Pilling Lane
Pilling
Fisher's Row
Smallwood Hey
Stake Pool
Winmarleigh
Scronkey
Preesall Park
Stalmine
Nateby
Eagland Hill
Burn Naze
Staynall
Cold Row
Sower Carr
CLEVELEYS
Thornton
Trunnah
Stanah
Little Thornton
Skitham
Little Bispham
Hambleton
Out Rawcliffe
Ratten Row
Church
St.Michael's on Wyre
Norbreck
Anchorsholme
Whin Lane End
Little Eccleston
Bispham
Norcross
Great Eccleston
Skippool
Little Singleton
Singleton
Carleton
Warbreck
Elswick
Copp
Crossmoor
Larbreck
BLACKPOOL
SEE PAGE 186
Hoohill
Poulton-le-Fylde
Queenstown
Normoss
Thistleton
Inskip
Roseacre
North Shore
Newton
Staining
THE FYLDE
Esprick
Catforth
Wharles
Lifeboat Station
Great Marton
Greenhalgh
Corner Row
A595
A593
A5092
A5084
A590
A592
A5074
A5093
B5281
B5278
B5277
B5271
B5282
A5087
A589
A5105
B5273
A683
A588
B5290
A585
A587
B5268
B5270
A586
B5266
B5260
A583
A584
B5269

Plumgarths
Kentrigg
KENDAL
Fisher Tarn Res.
Lambrigg Fell
1109
Fox's Pulpit
National Park Centre
Winder
Baugh Fell
Cotterdale
A591
barrow
A684
New Hutton
37
Marthwaite
Sedbergh
Hallbank
Baugh Fell
Garsdale Head
Moorcock Inn
A684
High Shaw
East Baugh Fell
2217
Hardraw
Oxenholme
Millholme
KILLINGTON LAKE
Millthrop
Garsdale
Mossdale Moor
Appersett
Hawes
A6
103
E
F
G
15
104
H
97
Brigsteer
Natland
Middleshaw
Barrows Green
Halfpenny
B6254
Old Hutton
Killington
Lenacre
Rise Hill
1825
Garsdale
B6255
Gayle
Sizergh NT
A591
Sedgwick
Beckside
Gawthrop
Cave & Fell Centre
Dent
Cowgill
Lea Yeat
2205
Widdale Fell
Cotes
A
Stainton
Gatebeck
Middleton
Roman Milestone
Calf Top
Stone House
Levens
Levens Hall
Hincaster
A590
Endmoor
Goose Green
Rigmaden Park
Dodd Fell
1
Wold Fell
1829
2192
Leasgill
Crooklands
M6
Warth Hill
Deepdale
Heversham
933
Scout Hill
2250
Crag Hill
Mansergh
Barbon
WHERNSIDE
Milnthorpe
36
Nook
Lupton
Gayle Moor
Oughtershaw
Whassett
A65
Farleton
Kearstwick
Ruskin's View
Casterton
Beck
2416
Blea Moor
Cam Beck
YORKSHIRE DALES
Storth
Heron Mill
Beetham
Slack Head
Holme
Hale
Kirkby Lonsdale
Hutton Roof
High Biggins
Leck Fell
2057
Pot-Holes & Caves
Gatekirk Cave
Viaduct
17
LANGSTROTHDALE
Sike Moor
CHASE
80 Deepdale
BURTON-IN-KENDAL
Burton -in-Kendal
Whittington
Cowan Bridge
Leck
Ireby
Chapel le Dale
Caves
Caves
High Birkwith
Foxup
Halton
Yealand Redmayne
Yealand Conyers
Newton
Nether Burrow
Thurland Castle
Masongill
Cheese Press
Thornton Force
Ingleborough Hill
Selside
Simon Fell
NATIONAL
Pen-y-ghent Side
PARK
2
Crag Foot
Priest Hutton
Westhouse
Falls
White Scar Caves
Fort
2376
NORTH
Hull Pot
Horton Moor
Warton
Tunstall
Cantsfield
A687
Thornton in Lonsdale
Skirwith
New Houses
Borwick
Arkholme
Wrayton
Burton in Lonsdale
Ingleton
Ingleborough Common
Gaping Gill
New Inn
Darnbrook Fell
Millhead
35a
Capernwray
Melling
R. Greta
Horton in Ribblesdale
Carnforth
35
A601(M)
B6254
Gressingham
Wennington
Tatham
Low Bentham
Cold Cotes
Newby Cote
Newby
Ingleborough Cave
YORKSHIRE
2191
Fountains Fell
70
NT
Over Kellet
Loyn Bridge
Hornby
Hornby Castle
High Bentham
A65
Clapham
Yorkshire Dales National Park
Wharfe
Helwith Bridge
Nether Kellet
Farleton
Wray
Waterfall
B6480
R. Wenning
Austwick
B6479
B6480
Butt Yeats
R. Hindburn
11
Feizor
Bolton Town End
Aughton
Keasden
Lawkland
Little Stainforth
Stainforth
Stainforth Force
Catrigg Force
Slyne
Claughton
Stackhouse
Halton
Caton
Lowgill
Eldroth
Victoria Cave
3
Brookhouse
Whit Moor
1318
Tatham Fells
Burn Moor Fell
Giggleswick
Langcliffe
1815
A683
Caton Moor
Attermire Cave
Settle
Kirkby Fell
34
M6
Goodber Common
Salter
Thrushgill
Scaleber Force
Malham
Crossgill
Botton Head
Cross of Greet
1595
Wham
Cath
Mearbeck
Haylot Fell
Quernmore
Blanch Fell
Catlow Fell
Black Hill
A65
60
Kirkby Malham
Scotforth
Clougha Pike
1786
White Hill
Rathmell
Long Preston
1839
Ward's Stone
Mallowdale Fell
Croasdale Fell
Otterburn
Lee Fell
Stocks Resr.
B6478
Hellifield
LANCASHIRE
Tosside
10
Wigglesworth
Ellel
Smith Green
Tarnbrook
Lee
FOREST
A682
Halton West
4
A65
Galgate
33
Four Lane Ends
Five Lane Ends
Abbeystead
R. Wyre
1561
Whins Brow
Dolphinholme
Nappa
Potters Brook
LANCASTER
Marshaw
Trough of Bowland
Slaidburn
Hawthornthwaite Fell
Sykes
OF
B6478
Paythorne
Newsholme
Street
1572
Fell
Forton
Fell Top
Hareden
Dunsop Bridge
Newton
Lane Ends
Horton
Calder Fell
Holden
Scorton
R. Calder
BOWLAND
Easington Fell
1300
Bolton by Bowland
R. Ribble
Gisburn
Bracewell
A59
A682
Oakenclough
B6251
Whitewell
Sawley
Barnoldswick
Cabus
Abbey
Rimington
Garstang
M6
Fair Snape Fell
Browsholme Hall
Grindleton
Howgill
Salterforth
Calder Vale
West Bradford
Chatburn
5
Bonds
Horrocksford
Downham
Twiston
Bowgreave
Brock Valley
Chipping
Bashall Eaves
Waddington
Whitemoor Resr.
Catterall
Beacon Fell
Claughton
Bashall Town
Clitheroe
Worston
Pendle Hill
Blacko
White Chapel
Walker Fold
Clitheroe Castle
1827
Barley
Roughlee
Hesketh Lane
Longridge Fell
B6243
Low Moor
Colne
Inglewhite
Bilsborrow
PENDLE
A682
E
F
91
G
H
Woodfields
Pendleton
Newchurch
Barrowford
College of Agriculture
Knowle Green
New Row
Stonyhurst College
Great Mitton
Barrow
Wheatley Lane
Cuddy Hill
Longridge
Hurst Green
Wiswell
Sabden
13
12
Barton
Ward Green Cross
Dinckley
THE FOREST OF
Higham
Fence
NELSON
Newsham
Stydd
Chingle Hall
Goosnargh
Ribchester
Whalley
B6248
Brierfield
Broughton
Haighton Green
Alston Resrs.
Roman Fort
A59
Billington
Spring Wood
A6068
M65
Lane Bottom

98
104
105
91
92
97
YORKSHIRE DALES NATIONAL PARK
WENSLEYDALE
LANGSTROTHDALE CHASE
NORTH YORKSHIRE
WHARFEDALE
RUMBOLDS MOOR
LANCASHIRE
KEIGHLEY MOOR
THE FOREST OF TRAWDEN
Hawes
Askrigg
Bainbridge
Aysgarth
Leyburn
Middleham
West Witton
West Burton
Buckden
Kettlewell
Grassington
Pateley Bridge
Settle
Malham
Skipton
Ilkley
Keighley
Otley
Guiseley
Yeadon
Baildon
Bingley
Shipley
Colne
Nelson
Barrowford
Barnoldswick
Earby
Gisburn
Hellifield
Long Preston
Silsden
Glusburn
Haworth
Oakworth
Burley in Wharfedale
Menston
Addingham
Bolton Abbey
Embsay
Gargrave
Great Whernside

99
NORTH YORK MOORS NATIONAL PARK
HAMBLETON HILLS
NORTHALLERTON
Romanby
Yafforth
Hackforth
Great Fencote
Little Fencote
Scruton
Ainderby Steeple
Morton-on-Swale
Warlaby
Langthorne
Kirkbridge
Great Crakehall
Leeming Bar
Leeming
Bedale
Aiskew
Londonderry
Exelby
Gatenby
North Otterington
Thornton-le-Moor
Newby Wiske
South Otterington
Crosby Court
Thornton-le-Beans
Borrowby
Over Silton
Nether Silton
Kepwick
Leake
Cowesby
Knayton
Upsall
Kirby Knowle
Boltby
Felixkirk
North Kilvington
Thornton-le-Street
South Kilvington
Thirsk
Sowerby
Sutton-under-Whitestonecliffe
Hawnby
Arden Hall
Fangdale Beck
East Moors
Old Byland
Rievaulx
Carlton
Pockley
Helmsley
Sproxton
Scawton
Cold Kirby
Sutton Bank
Balk
Bagby
Kilburn
High Kilburn
Oldstead
Wass
Byland Abbey
Ampleforth
Ampleforth College
Oswaldirk
Gilling East
Coxwold
Newburgh Priory
Husthwaite
Carlton Husthwaite
Great Thirkleby
Little Thirkleby
Hutton Sessay
Sessay
Thormanby
Dalton
Topcliffe
Asenby
Rainton
Dishforth
Cundall
Crakehill
Fawdington
Norton-le-Clay
Brafferton
Helperby
Raskelf
Easingwold
Crayke
Brandsby
Yearsley
Oulston
Stillington
Farlington
Huby
Sutton-on-the-Forest
Tollerton
Alne
Flawith
Tholthorpe
Myton-on-Swale
Aldwark
Youlton
Linton-on-Ouse
Great Ouseburn
Little Ouseburn
Thorpe Underwood
Newton-on-Ouse
Nun Monkton
Beningbrough
Shipton
Moor Monkton
Skelton
Wigginton
Haxby
Strensall
Huntington
Nether Poppleton
Upper Poppleton
Rawcliffe
Hessay
Kirk Hammerton
Green Hammerton
Whixley
Allerton Mauleverer
Hopperton
Cattal
Hunsingore
Cowthorpe
Tockwith
Long Marston
Marston Moor
Rufforth
Acomb
YORK
Osbaldwick
Heslington
Fulford
Bishopthorpe
Copmanthorpe
Askham Bryan
Askham Richard
Hutton Wandesley
Angram
Bilbrough
Colton
Acaster Malbis
Naburn
Appleton Roebuck
Acaster Selby
Bolton Percy
Oxton
Tadcaster
Newton Kyme
Clifford
Bramham
Boston Spa
Thorp Arch
Walton
Wetherby
Bickerton
Bilton
Healaugh
Catterton
Wighill
Kirkby Wharfe
Ulleskelf
Ryther
Stutton
Towton
Church Fenton
Barkston Ash
Saxton
Cawood
Riccall
Kelfield
Stillingfleet
Aberford
Barwick in Elmet
Scholes
LEEDS
HORSFORTH
Bramhope
Pool
Harewood
East Keswick
Bardsey
Scarcroft
Thorner
Collingham
Linton
Kirkby Overblow
Sicklinghall
Spofforth
Follifoot
Kirk Deighton
North Deighton
Little Ribston
Walshford
Goldsborough
KNARESBOROUGH
HARROGATE
Killinghall
Hampsthwaite
Ripley
Scotton
Farnham
Ferrensby
Staveley
Arkendale
Coneythorpe
Flaxby
Minskip
Boroughbridge
Aldborough
Roecliffe
Langthorpe
Milby
Kirby Hill
Marton-le-Moor
Copt Hewick
Sharow
RIPON
Bishopton
Studley Roger
Aldfield
Littlethorpe
Bridge Hewick
Skelton
Bishop Monkton
Markington
Burton Leonard
Copgrove
Brearton
Nidd
Bishop Thornton
South Stainley
Shaw Mills
Burnt Yates
Bedlam
Clint
Birstwith
Winksley
Galphay
Kirkby Malzeard
Azerley
North Lees
Sutton Grange
Hutton Conyers
Nunwick
North Stainley
West Tanfield
Mickley
Thornborough
Nosterfield
Binsoe
Well
Snape
Carthorpe
Burneston
Theakston
Firby
Kirklington
Sutton Howgrave
Middleton Quernhow
Wath
Melmerby
Baldersby
Baldersby St James
Skipton-on-Swale
Catton
Carlton Miniott
Sandhutton
Newsham
Pickhill
Sinderby
Holme
Ainderby Quernhow
Howe
Kirby Wiske
Maunby
Beckwithshaw
Pannal
Brackenthwaite
North Rigton
Huby
Stainburn
Weeton
Dunkeswick
Castley
Leathley
Arthington
Weardley
Eccup
Alwoodley
Moortown
Meanwood
Headingley
Roundhay
Oakwood
Shadwell
A1
A1(M)
A19
A61
A168
A167
A170
A59
A658
A661
A64
A1237
A660
A58
A6120
A659
B1224
B1223
B1222
B1257
B1363
B6265
B6267
B6161
B6162
B6164
B6165
A6055
A684
A6108
SEE PAGE 190
SEE PAGE 197

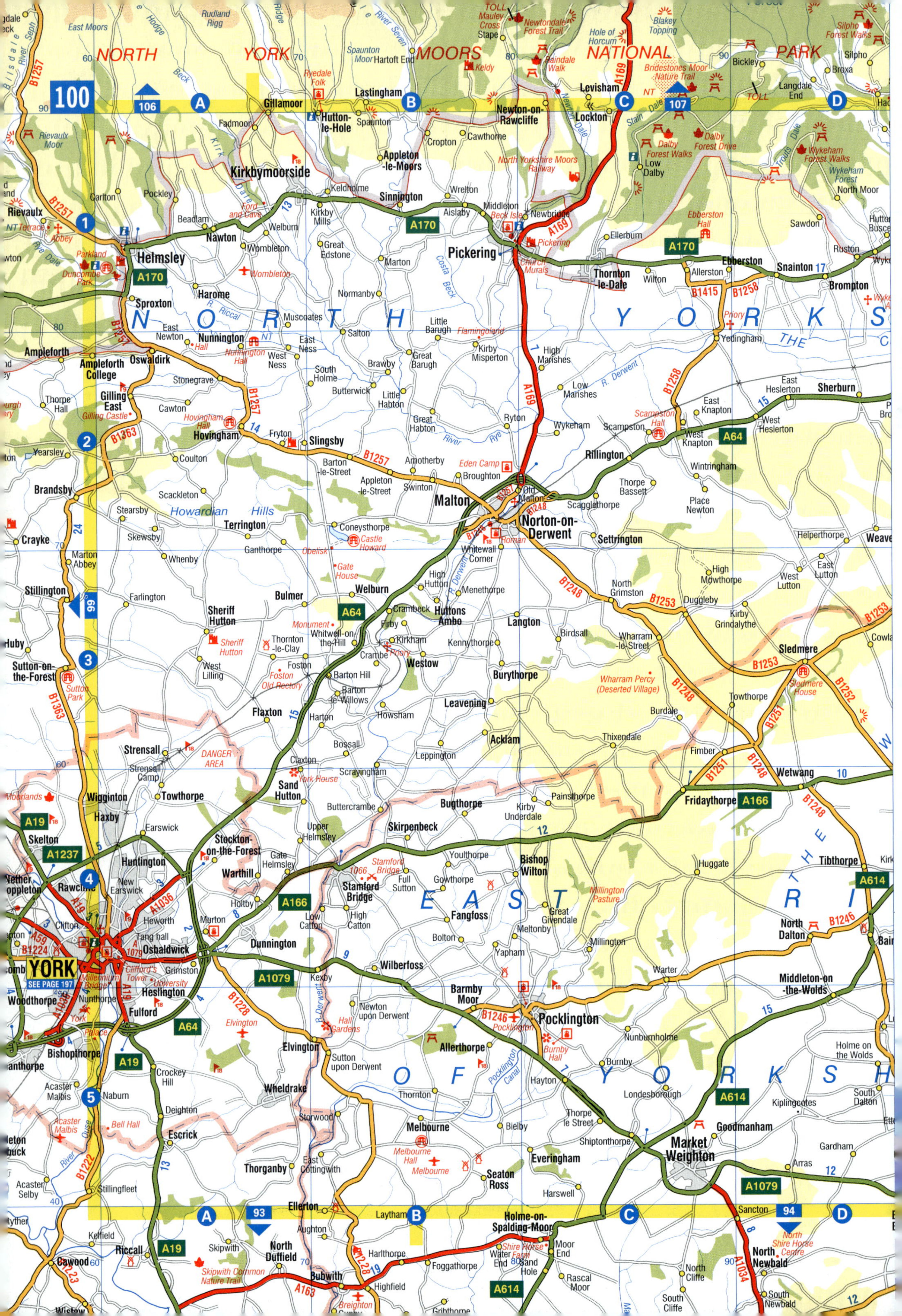
East Moors
Rudland Rigg
NORTH
YORK
MOORS
NATIONAL
PARK
Spaunton Moor
Hartoft End
Mauley Cross
Stape
Newtondale Forest Trail
Hole of Horcum
Blakey Topping
Silpho Forest Walks
Silpho
Bickley
Broxa
Keldy
Raindale Walk
Bridestones Moor Nature Trail
106
107
A
B
C
D
Gillamoor
Ryedale Folk
Hutton-le-Hole
Lastingham
Spaunton
Newton-on-Rawcliffe
Levisham
Lockton
Langdale End
TOLL
Fadmoor
Rievaulx Moor
Cropton
Cawthorne
Appleton-le-Moors
North Yorkshire Moors Railway
Dalby Forest Walks
Dalby Forest Drive
Low Dalby
Wykeham Forest Walks
Wykeham Forest
North Moor
Kirkbymoorside
Keldholme
Sinnington
Wrelton
Aislaby
Middleton
Beck Isle
Newbridge
Carlton
Pockley
Rievaulx
NT Terrace
Abbey
Beadlam
Ford and Cave
Kirkby Mills
A170
Ellerburn
Ebberston Hall
Sawdon
Hutton Buscel
Helmsley
Nawton
Welburn
Wombleton
Great Edstone
Marton
Pickering
Church Murals
Thornton le-Dale
Wilton
Allerston
Ebberston
Snainton
Brompton
Ruston
Parkland
Duncombe Park
Rye Dale
Harome
Normanby
Costa Beck
B1415
B1258
Sproxton
Muscoates
Little Barugh
Flamingoland
Priory
N O R T H   Y O R K S
East Newton
Nunnington
Hall
NT
Nunnington Hall
Salton
East Ness
West Ness
Kirby Misperton
High Marishes
Yedingham
THE
Ampleforth
Ampleforth College
Oswaldkirk
South Holme
Brawby
Great Barugh
Butterwick
Little Habton
R. Derwent
Low Marishes
B1258
East Heslerton
Sherburn
Thorpe Hall
Gilling East
Gilling Castle
Stonegrave
Cawton
B1257
Hovingham Hall
Hovingham
Fryton
Slingsby
Great Habton
River Rye
Ryton
Wykeham
Scampston
Scampston Hall
East Knapton
West Knapton
West Heslerton
A64
A169
B1363
Yearsley
Coulton
Barton-le-Street
B1257
Amotherby
Eden Camp
Rillington
Wintringham
Brandsby
Scackleton
Appleton-le-Street
Swinton
Broughton
Malton
Old Malton
Norton-on-Derwent
Thorpe Bassett
Place Newton
Scagglethorpe
Settrington
Stearsby
Howardian Hills
Terrington
Coneysthorpe
Castle Howard
Roman
Crayke
Skewsby
Ganthorpe
Obelisk
Whitewall Corner
Helperthorpe
Weaverthorpe
Marton Abbey
Whenby
Gate House
High Hutton
High Mowthorpe
East Lutton
West Lutton
Stillington
Farlington
Bulmer
Welburn
Menethorpe
B1248
North Grimston
B1253
Duggleby
Kirby Grindalythe
Sheriff Hutton
Monument
Whitwell-on-the-Hill
Crambeck
Huttons Ambo
Firby
Langton
Birdsall
Wharram-le-Street
Sledmere
Cowlam
Huby
Thornton-le-Clay
Kirkham
Crambe
Priory
Westow
Kennythorpe
Sutton-on-the-Forest
Sutton Park
West Lilling
Foston
Foston Old Rectory
Barton Hill
Burythorpe
Wharram Percy (Deserted Village)
Sledmere House
B1253
B1252
Barton-le-Willows
Leavening
Towthorpe
Flaxton
Harton
Howsham
Burdale
B1251
Strensall
DANGER AREA
Strensall Camp
Bossall
Acklam
Thixendale
Fimber
Leppington
Claxton
York House
Scrayingham
Wetwang
Moorlands
Wigginton
Towthorpe
Sand Hutton
Buttercrambe
Bugthorpe
Kirby Underdale
Painsthorpe
Fridaythorpe
A166
Haxby
Skelton
A19
Earswick
Upper Helmsley
Skirpenbeck
A1237
Stockton-on-the-Forest
Huntington
Gate Helmsley
Warthill
Youlthorpe
Bishop Wilton
Huggate
Tibthorpe
Nether Poppleton
Rawcliffe
New Earswick
1066
Stamford Bridge
Full Sutton
Gowthorpe
Millington Pasture
A614
Clifton
A1036
Holtby
Stamford Bridge
A166
E A S T
R I
Heworth
Tang Hall
Murton
Low Catton
High Catton
Fangfoss
Great Givendale
North Dalton
B1246
Osbaldwick
Dunnington
Meltonby
Bolton
Millington
B1224
YORK
SEE PAGE 197
Millennium Bridge
Clifford's Tower
University
Grimston
A1079
Kexby
Wilberfoss
Yapham
Warter
Middleton-on-the-Wolds
Heslington
Nunthorpe
Woodthorpe
A1036
B1228
R. Derwent
Newton upon Derwent
Barmby Moor
B1246
Pocklington
Fulford
A64
A19
York
Palace
Bishopthorpe
Elvington
Hall Gardens
Allerthorpe
Pocklington Canal
Burnby Hall
Nunburnholme
Holme on the Wolds
Crockey Hill
Sutton upon Derwent
O F
Burnby
Y O R K S H
Acaster Malbis
Naburn
Wheldrake
Thornton
Hayton
Londesborough
Kiplingcotes
South Dalton
Deighton
Storwood
Thorpe le Street
A614
Acaster Malbis
Bell Hall
Escrick
Melbourne
Bielby
Shiptonthorpe
Goodmanham
River Ouse
Melbourne Hall
Melbourne
Everingham
Market Weighton
Gardham
B1222
Thorganby
East Cottingwith
Seaton Ross
Arras
Acaster Selby
Stillingfleet
Harswell
A1079
93
94
Ellerton
Laytham
Holme-on-Spalding-Moor
Sancton
Kelfield
Aughton
Moor End
North Shire Horse Centre
North Newbald
Riccall
Skipwith
North Duffield
Harlthorpe
Shire Horse Farm
Water End
Sand Hole
Cawood
B1223
Skipwith Common Nature Trail
Bubwith
B1228
Foggathorpe
Rascal Moor
North Cliffe
A1034
South Cliffe
South Newbald
A163
Highfield
Breighton
A614
Wistow

101
NORTH SEA
Cayton Bay
The Wyke
Flamborough Head
Bridlington Bay
SCARBOROUGH
BRIDLINGTON
DRIFFIELD
BEVERLEY
Cloughton
Burniston
Scalby
Scalby Mills
Newby
Throxenby
Barrowcliff
Scarborough
Woodend
Falsgrave
Oliver's Mount
East Ayton
West Ayton
Irton
Crossgates
Eastfield
Seamer
Cayton
Osgodby
High Killerby
Lebberston
Gristhorpe
Newbiggin
Church Cliff
Filey Brigg Nature Trail
Folk Mus.
Filey
Flixton
Folkton
Muston
Willerby
Staxton
Primrose Valley
Royal Oak
Hunmanby
Hunmanby Sands
Ganton
Reighton
Speeton
Bempton Cliffs Nature Reserve
Fordon
Foxholes
Wold Newton
Burton Fleming
Buckton
Bempton
Danes Dyke
Lifeboat Sta.
Bridlington
Grindale
Butterwick
Thwing
Marton
Sewerby Hall
Sewerby
Flamborough
Octon
Boynton
Rudston
Rudston Monolith
Gypsey Race
Langtoft
Bessingby
West Hill
Hilderthorpe
Lifeboat Station
Cottam
West End
Kilham
Burton Agnes Hall
Norman Manor House
Haisthorpe
Carnaby
Motor Speed Track
Thornholme
Wilsthorpe
Burton Agnes
Ruston Parva
Harpham
Fraisthorpe
Lowthorpe
Garton-on-the-Wolds
Great Kendale
Little Kelk
Gransmoor
Barmston
Nafferton
Great Kelk
Lissett
Elmswell
Little Driffield
Driffield
Wansford
Gembling
East End
Foston on the Wolds
West End
Ulrome
Skipsea
Motte & Bailey
Dringhoe
Skerne
Southburn
Driffield Canal
Brigham
Beeford
Upton
Skipsea Brough
Church End
North Frodingham
Hutton Cranswick
Rotsea
Dunnington
Atwick
Watton
Watton Priory
Bewholme
Kilnwick
Hempholme
Beswick
Burshill
Hornsea
Lockington
Little Burton
Brandesburton
Nature Reserve
Pottery & Leisure Centre
Hornsea Burton
Thorpe
Sigglesthorne
Seaton
Hornsea Mere
Aike
Little Leven
Goxhill
Scorborough
Leven
Catwick
Rolston
Mappleton
Arram
Leven Canal
Little Catwick
Leconfield
Routh
Little Hatfield
Great Hatfield
Great Cowden
Cherry Burton
Long Riston
Rise
Tickton
Arnold
Withernwick
Danger Area
Molescroft
Grovehill
Weel
Meaux
Skirlaugh
New Ellerby
Marton
Aldbrough
Bishop Burton
The Minster
West Newton
Woodmansey
Walkington
Old Ellerby
Burton Constable
East Newton
Thearne
Wawne
Flinton
Bentley
Wood Hall
Swine
Garton
A171
A165
A170
A64
A1039
A614
A1035
A1079
A1174
A164
B1249
B1229
B1255
B1259
B1253
B1242
B1244
B1243
B1248
B1230
B1238
B1261
E
F
G
H
1
2
3
4
5
90
80
70
60
450
40
30
10
20

102
A
B
C
D
1
2
3
4
5
Allonby
Allonby Bay
Westnewton
Aspatria
Hayton
Blennerhasset
Mealsgate
Boltongate
Ireby
Bothel
Plumbland
Gilcrux
Crosby
Maryport
Dearham
Netherton
Ellenborough
Flimby
Broughton Moor
Dovenby
Papcastle
Cockermouth
Embleton
Wythop Mill
Bassenthwaite
Bassenthwaite Lake
SKIDDAW FOREST
SKIDDAW
3054
Seaton
Camerton
Great Clifton
Brigham
Greysouthern
Eaglesfield
WORKINGTON
Moss Bay
Harrington
Distington
Lowca
Parton
Branthwaite
Dean
Ullock
Mockerkin
Lamplugh
Loweswater
Thornthwaite
Braithwaite
Portinscale
Keswick
Castlerigg
Derwent Water
Threlkeld
WHITEHAVEN
Saltom Bay
St. Bees Head
Sandwith
Hensingham
Moresby Parks
Arlecdon
Rowrah
Frizington
Kirkland
Ennerdale Bridge
Ennerdale Water
Cleator Moor
Cleator
Egremont
St. Bees
Rottington
Buttermere
Crummock Water
Grasmoor
2795
Great Borne
Pillar
2927
Red Pike
High Stile
Hay Stacks
Great Gable
2949
Seatoller
Rosthwaite
Watendlath
Glaramara
Scafell Pike
3210
Scafell
3162
Wasdale Head
Wast Water
Nether Wasdale
Gosforth
Seascale
Calder Bridge
Beckermet
Haile
Carleton
Thornhill
Braystones
Nethertown
Middletown
Coulderton
COPELAND FOREST
Seatallan
2270
Santon Bridge
Holmrook
Drigg
Ravenglass
Muncaster
Eskdale Green
Boot
Beckfoot
Hardknott Pass
Cockley Beck
FURNESS FELLS
THE OLD MAN OF CONISTON
2635
Coniston
Torver
Seathwaite
Ulpha
Broughton Mills
Broughton in Furness
Broad Oak
Waberthwaite
Newbiggin
Corney
Bootle
Hycemoor
Selker Bay
Hyton
Annaside
Blawith
Lowick
Lowick Bridge
Grizebeck
Foxfield
Dunnerdale
Devoke Water
Birker Force
Harter Fell
2142
LAKE DISTRICT
CUMBRIAN MOUNTAINS
A595
A596
A66
A591
A5086
A594
A593
A5092
A5084
B5289
B5292
B5294
B5295
B5299
B5300
B5301
B5344
B5345
112
96

103
104
I N G L E W O O D
F O R E S T
GILDERDALE FOREST
MILBURN FOREST
L A K E
D I S T R I C T
N A T I O N A L
P A R K
HELVELLYN
3116
GRIZEDALE FOREST
Southwaite
High Hesket
Old Town
Ruckcroft
Dale
Staffield
Nunnery
Kirkoswald
Castlerigg
High Bankhill
Renwick
Scale Houses
Hareseugh
Busk
Unthank
Bayles
Leadgate
Garrigill
Grassgarth
Welton
Stockdalewath
Thethwaite
Highbridge
Ivegill
Low Braithwaite
Middlesceugh
Churchtown
Sebergham
Petteril Green
Lime Kiln Nook
Sowerby Row
Thomas Close
Parkhead
Caldbeck
Newlands
Hesket Newmarket
Calebrack
High Row
Haltcliff Bridge
Hutton Roof
Mosedale
Bowscale
Mungrisdale
Morton
Fieldhead
Hutton End
Plumptonfoot
Townhead
Lazonby
Gamblesby
Glassonby
Caves
Long Meg & Daughters
Great Salkeld
Little Salkeld
Salkeld Dykes
Watermill
Hunsonby
Melmerby Fell
2331
Melmerby
Black Burn
Alston Moor
Cross Fell
2930
Shire
Row
Ousby
Townhead
Winskill
Langwathby
Skirwith
Kirkland
Hanging Walls
Moor House Nature Reserve
Blencarn
Edenhall
R. Eden
Plumpton
Brockleymoor
Plumpton Head
New Rent
Hutton-in-the-Forest
Lamonby
Ellonby
Unthank
Skelton
Unthank End
Laithes
Catterlen
Johnby
Little Blencow
Great Blencow
Newton Reigny
Low Park
Bothy
Greystoke Castle
Greystoke
Spire House
Fair Hill
PENRITH
Castletown
Newton Rigg
Carleton
Rheged
Berrier
Greystoke Gill
Motherby
Newbiggin
Penruddock
Blencathra or Saddleback
Scales
Troutbeck
Hutton
Stainton
Dalemain
Dacre
Sockbridge
Yanwath
Barton
Tirril
Eamont Bridge
Brougham
Clifton
Wetheriggs Country Pottery
Culgaith
Acorn Bank
Newbiggin
Milburn
Howgill
Low Abbey
Temple Sowerby
Roman Milestone
Kirkby Thore
Knock
Town End
Long Marton
Dufton
Brampton
Keisley
Cliburn
Melkinthorpe
Great Strickland
Bolton
Crackenthorpe
R. Greta
Thackthwaite
Sparket
Soulby
Dunmallet Hill Fort
Bennethead
Wreay
Pooley Bridge
Askham
Newtown
Lowther
Hackthorpe
Whale
Helton
Moor Divock
Matterdale End
Ulcat Row
Longthwaite
Thornythwaite
Watermillock
Knotts
Dockray
Aira Force
Great Dodd
2812
Dowthwaitehead
Ullswater
Sandwick
Martindale
Morland
Newby
Newby Head
King's Meaburn
Colby
Bewley
Appleby-in-Westmorland
Appleby
Coupland
Little Strickland
Sleagill
Low Knipe
High Knipe
Bampton Grange
Sweetholme
Reagill
Burrells
Great Ormside
Little Ormside
Hoff
Sandford
Glenridding
St. Patrick's Well
2201
Loadpot Hill
Beda Fell
Dale Head
Bampton
Bampton Common
Rooking
Patterdale
Burnbanks
Rosgill
Shap
Shap Abbey
Keld
Maulds Meaburn
Crosby Ravensworth
Drybeck
Great Asby
Town Head
Bridgend
Hartsop
Brothers Water
Grisedale Tarn
Fairfield
2864
Dovedale Falls
Hayeswater
High Street
2719
Haweswater Reservoir
Mardale Common
Swindale Beck
Wet Sleddale Reservoir
1315
Crosby Ravensworth Fell
Little Asby
Crosby Garrett
Rydal Fell
Grasmere
Dove Cottage
Rydal
Rydal Mount
Rydal Water
2552
Harter Fell
Gatescarth Pass
Kentmere Reservoir
Kirkstone Pass
Shap Fells
Birk Beck
Scout Green
TEBAY (EAST)
TEBAY (WEST)
Orton
Gamelands Stone Circle
Raisebeck
Nettle Hill
1253
Smardale
Old Tebay
Gaisgill
Kelleth
Wath
Brownber
Newbiggin-on-Lune
Ravenstonedale
Elterwater
Skelwith Bridge
Skelwith Force
Stockghyll Force
Ambleside
Waterhead
Clappersgate
Troutbeck
Town End
Low Wray
High Wray
Townend Ho.
Sadgill
Kentmere
High Green
Bretherdale Head
Longdale
Tebay
Weasdale
Roundthwaite
Borrowdale
Low Borrowbridge
West Fell
High Borrans
Far Orrest
Brockhole
Troutbeck Bridge
Tarn Hows
Hawkshead Hill
Outgate
Hawkshead
Colthouse
Roger Ground
Esthwaite Water
Bowness-on-Windermere
Belle Isle
Windermere
Elfhowe
Ings
Staveley
Forest Hall
Whinfell Beacon
High Carlingill
Langdale Fell
Uldale Head
1925
Ravenstonedale Common
Fell End
Garnett Bridge
Selside
Watchgate
Cowan Head
Garth Row
Patton Bridge
Meal Bank
Grayrigg
Lowgill
Beck Foot
2219
The Calf
Cautley Spout
Narthwaite
Near Sawrey
Far Sawrey
Bowston
Burneside
Brant Fell
Cautley
West Baugh Fell
Grizedale
Ridding Wood
Hill Top
Claife Heights
B5284
Crook
Plumgarths
Church
Kentrigg
KENDAL
Fisher Tarn Res.
Lambrigg Fell
1109
Fox's Pulpit
National Park Centre
Winder
Marthwaite
Sedbergh
Baugh Fell
East Baugh Fell
2217
Bogle Crag
Satterthwaite
Graythwaite Hall
Thwaite Head
Storrs
Blackwell
Winster
Crosthwaite
Underbarrow
New Hutton
Millholme
KILLINGTON LAKE
Hallbank
Millthrop
Garsdale
Force Mills
Lukeborg
Islands
Bowland Bridge
Rose
Brigsteer
Natland
Middleshaw
Barrows Green
Halfpenny
Old Hutton
Killington
Lenacre
Rise Hill
1825
R. Dee
Rusland
Finsthwaite
Bobbin Mill
Town End
Lakeside
Fell Foot
Staveley-in-Cartmel
Newby Bridge
Cartmel Fell
Howe
Sizergh
Cotes
Sedgwick
Levens
Stainton
Gatebeck
Beckside
R. Lune
Middleton
Roman Milestone
Gawthrop
Dent
Cave & Fell Centre
Call Top
M6
A6
A66
A592
A591
A590
A5091
A686
A685
A684
A683
A6
B5305
B5299
B6413
B6412
B5288
B5320
B6262
B6261
B6260
B5284
B6254
B6255
B6286
B6277
B5286
B5360
A5074
E
F
G
H
1
2
3
4
5
113
97

104
114
103
97
98
DERDALE
FOREST
Bayles
Leadgate
Garrigill
Nenthead
Killhope Wheel
Lanehead
Corniggs
Copthill
Cows
Middlehope Moor
Rookhope
Lintzgarth
Stanhope Common
Waskerley
Waskerley Reservoir
Tunstall Reservoir
Crawley Side
Wolsingham Moor
Stanhope
Wolsingham
Burnhope Reservoir
Wearhead
West Blackdene
Folk Museum
Ireshopeburn
St.John's Chapel
Daddry Shield
Westgate
Eastgate
Brotherlee
Frosterley
Hill End
White Kirkley
St.John's Hall
Alston Moor
Burnhope Seat 2448
Ireshope Moor
Round Hill 2249
R. Tees
Cross 2930
Three Pikes
2284 Chapelfell Top
Snowhope Hill
Bollihope Common
1599 Pawlaw Pike
Pikeston Fell
MILBURN
FOREST
Moor House Nature Reserve
Moor House
Viewing Hill 2099
Harwood
Widdybank Fell
Langdon Beck
Newbiggin Common
Hamsterley Forest Drive
Cow Green Reservoir
Caldron Snout
Dufton Fell
2518
Forest-in-Teesdale
Ettersgill
Eggleston Common
HAMSTERLEY
FOREST
Milburn
Howgill
Cronkley Fell
Nature Reserve
High Force
Bowlees
Newbiggin
Middleton in Teesdale
Woodland
Knock
Mickle Fell 2591
Holwick
1511 Woodland Fell
Dufton
Lune Moor
Hill Top
Eggleston
Keisley
Brampton
Murton Fell 2207
Bowbank
Mickleton
Laithkirk
Thringarth
Crackenthorpe
A66
Appleby-in-Westmorland
Murton
Hilton
Colby
LUNE FOREST
Grassholme
Grassholme Resr.
Selset Reservoir
Romaldkirk
Kinninvie
Hunderthwaite
Warcop Fell
Hury
River Lune
Cotherstone
Coupland
Appleby
Dow Crag 1843
Blackton Resr.
Hury Resr.
East Briscoe
Stainton
Burrells
Great Ormside
Little Ormside
CUMBRIA
Stainmore Common
Hunderthwaite Moor
Balderhead Resr.
BARNARD CASTLE
Hoff
Sandford
Cotherstone Moor
DANGER AREA
Lartington
Startforth
Bowes
Westwick
Hillbeck
River Balder
Brough
North Stainmore
Deepdale
Warcop
Boldron
Cross Lanes
Great Asby
Little Musgrave
Great Musgrave
Church Brough
South Stainmore
Bowes Moor
Ravock
Gilmonby
Bowes
A67
A66
Town Head
Brough Sowerby
A685
Kaber
Old Spital
Stainmore Forest
Thwaite
Brignall
Soulby
Rookby
Moudy Mea
Scargill
Little Asby
Crosby Garrett
Winton
Sleightholme
Hartley
Kirkby Stephen
Smardale
Nettle Hill 1253
Waitby
Winton Fell
Sleightholme Moor
1674 Cleasby Hill
Stang Ridge Walk
Tan Hill Inn
Nateby
Tan Hill
Kelleth
Wath
Brownber
Newbiggin-on-Lune
Wharton Hall
Arkengarthdale Moor
Whaw
A685
Weasdale
Ravenstonedale
Ash Fell 1264
Lammerside Castle
Stonesdale Moor
Pendragon Castle
Ravenseat
2203 Rogan's Seat
1914 Great Pinseat
Langthwaite
Arkle Town
Booze
Helwith
Hurst
Washfold
West Fell
West Stonesdale
Outhgill
Ravenstonedale Common
Keld
YORKSHIRE
DALES
Melbecks Moor
Swaledale Folk
Angram
Kearton
Healaugh
Reeth
Fremington
Grinton
Angram Common
Mallerstang Common
Fell End
2324
Thwaite
Muker
Ivelet
Gunnerside
Feetham
Low Row
2349
Great Shunner Fell
Satron
Crackpot
Harkerside Moor
Narthwaite
Cautley Spout
Butter Tubs
NATIONAL
PARK
Gibbon Hill
Whitaside Moor
Cautley
West Baugh Fell
Abbotside Common
Cotterdale
Askrigg Common
East Bolton Moor
NORTH
Redmire Moor
Winder
Baugh Fell
Moorcock Inn
Sedbergh
Hallbank
East Baugh Fell 2217
Garsdale Head
High Shaw
Hardraw
Upper Dales Folk
Sedbusk
Askrigg
Newbiggin
Castle Bolton
Redmire
Preston-under-Scar
Millthrop
Garsdale
Mossdale Moor
Appersett
Hawes
Worton
Woodhall
Carperby
Swinithwaite
Aysgarth Falls
West Witton
Chapel
Rise Hill 1825
Garsdale
Gayle
Burtersett
Bainbridge
Thornton Rust
Aysgarth
Lenacre
Countersett
Thoralby
Gawthrop
Dent
Dent Cave & Fell Centre
Cowgill
Lea Yeat
Widdale Fell
Wether Fell
Semer Water
Penhill
1792
West Burton
Harland Hill
Stone House
Marsett
Stalling Busk
Newbiggin
Melmerby
Calf Top
Dodd Fell
WENSLEYDALE
PENNINES
TEESDALE
SWALEDALE
DURHAM

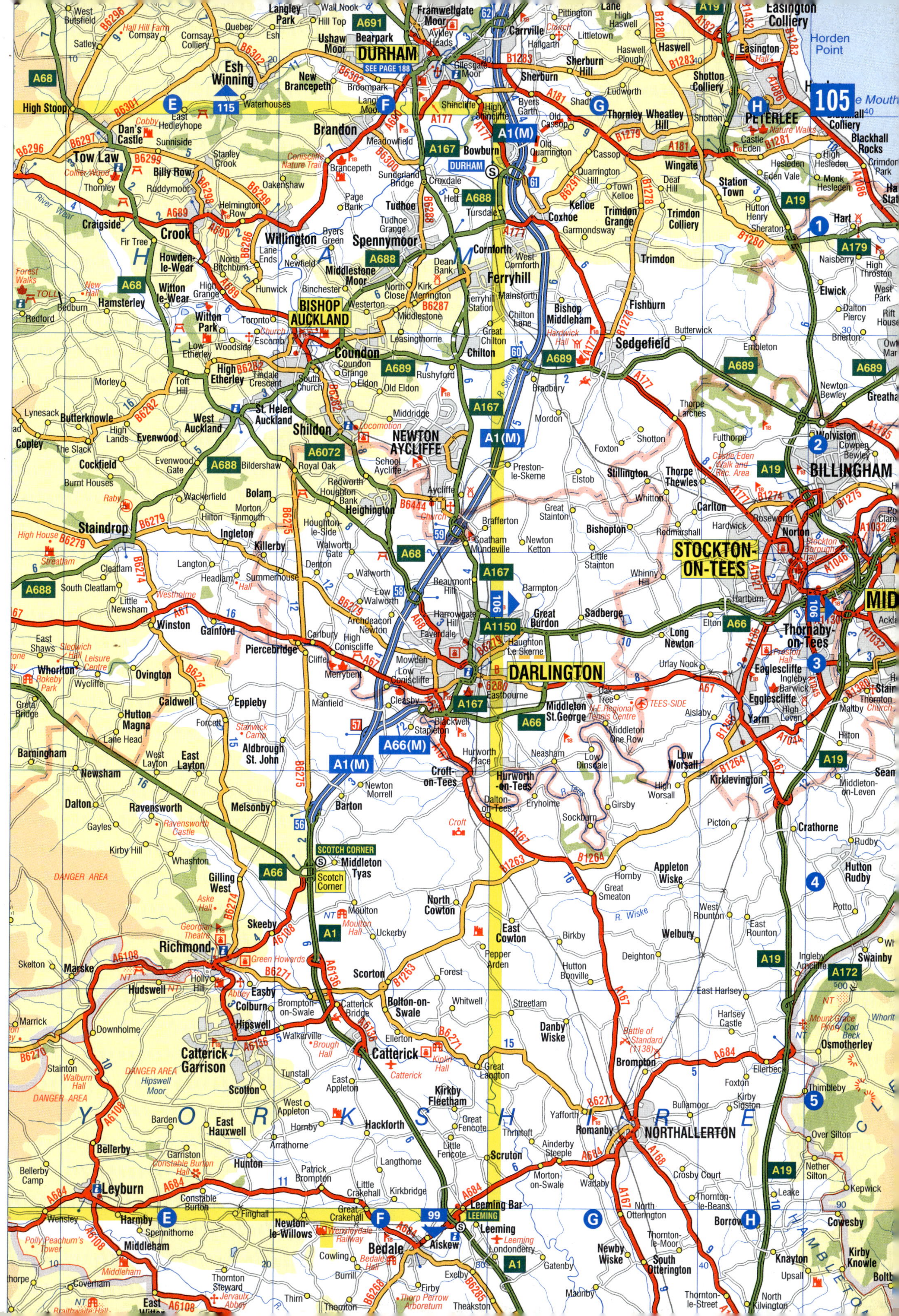

105
West Butsfield
Satley
Hall Hill Farm
Cornsay
Cornsay Colliery
Quebec
Esh
Esh Winning
Langley Park
Wall Nook
Hill Top
A691
Ushaw Moor
Bearpark
DURHAM
SEE PAGE 188
Framwellgate Moor
Aykley Heads
Gilesgate Moor
Carrville
Pittington
Littletown
Hallgarth
Sherburn
Sherburn Hill
Lane
High Haswell
Haswell
Haswell Plough
Easington Colliery
Easington
Horden Point
Shotton Colliery
Ludworth
New Brancepeth
Broompark
Langley Moor
Shincliffe
High Shincliffe
Byers Garth
Old Cassop
Shadforth
Thornley
Wheatley Hill
Shotton
PETERLEE
Blackhall Colliery
Blackhall Rocks
Castle Eden
Nature Walks
High Stoop
Waterhouses
115
A68
East Hedleyhope
Cobby Castle
Dan's Castle
Sunniside
Brandon
Meadowfield
A167
Bowburn
A1(M)
Old Quarrington
Cassop
Quarrington Hill
Wingate
Station Town
Hesleden
Eden Vale
High Hesleden
Monk Hesleden
Crimdon Park
Tow Law
Billy Row
Roddymoor
Stanley Crook
Oakenshaw
Coniscliffe Nature Trail
Brancepeth
Sunderland Bridge
Croxdale
Hett
DURHAM
A688
Tursdale
Town Kelloe
Kelloe
Deaf Hill
Trimdon Grange
Trimdon Colliery
Hutton Henry
Sheraton
Hart
A19
A179
Naisberry
High Throston
West Park
Craigside
Crook
Helmington Row
Page Bank
Tudhoe
Tudhoe Grange
Coxhoe
Garmondsway
Fir Tree
Howden-le-Wear
Willington
Byers Green
Spennymoor
Cornforth
West Cornforth
Trimdon
Elwick
River Wear
Forest Walks
TOLL
New Hall
Bedburn
Redford
Hamsterley
Witton-le-Wear
North Bitchburn
Lane Ends
Newfield
Middlestone Moor
Dean Bank
Ferryhill
Mainsforth
Ferryhill Station
Bishop Middleham
Fishburn
Dalton Piercy
Brierton
Rift House
High Grange
Hunwick
Binchester
North Close
Kirk Merrington
Westerton
Middlestone
Chilton Lane
BISHOP AUCKLAND
Witton Park
Toronto
Escomb
Woodside
Low Etherley
Leasingthorne
Great Chilton
Chilton
Hardwick Hall
Sedgefield
Butterwick
Embleton
Coundon
Coundon Grange
A689
Rushyford
Eldon
Old Eldon
Bradbury
High Etherley
Tindale Crescent
Toft Hill
South Church
Morley
Lynesack
Butterknowle
West Auckland
St. Helen Auckland
Shildon
Locomotion
Middridge
NEWTON AYCLIFFE
Mordon
Thorpe Larches
Shotton
Fulthorpe
Wolviston
Cowpen Bewley
Newton Bewley
Greatham
Copley
The Slack
High Lands
Evenwood
Evenwood Gate
Cockfield
Burnt Houses
Bildershaw
Royal Oak
A6072
School Aycliffe
Preston-le-Skerne
Elstob
Foxton
Stillington
Thorpe Thewles
Castle Eden Walk and Rec. Area
BILLINGHAM
Raby
Wackerfield
Bolam
Morton Tinmouth
Redworth
Houghton Bank
Heighington
Aycliffe
Great Stainton
Whitton
Carlton
Hardwick
Roseworth
Norton
Staindrop
Hilton
Ingleton
Houghton-le-Side
Brafferton
Coatham Mundeville
Newton Ketton
Bishopton
Redmarshall
STOCKTON-ON-TEES
High House
Streatham
Langton
Killerby
Walworth Gate
Denton
Walworth
Little Stainton
Whinny Hill
Cleatham
South Cleatham
Headlam
Summerhouse
Low Walworth
Beaumont Hill
Barmpton
Sadberge
Hartburn
Little Newsham
Westholme
Winston
Gainford
Archdeacon Newton
Harrowgate Hill
Great Burdon
Elton
Thornaby-on-Tees
East Shaws
Sledwick Hall
Leisure Centre
Piercebridge
Carlbury
High Coniscliffe
Faverdale
A1150
Haughton Le Skerne
Long Newton
Whorlton
Rokeby Park
Wycliffe
Ovington
Cliffe
Merrybent
Mowden
Low Coniscliffe
DARLINGTON
Urlay Nook
Egglescliffe
Eaglescliffe
Preston Hall
Ingleby Barwick
Greta Bridge
Hutton Magna
Lane Head
Caldwell
Eppleby
Manfield
Cleasby
Eastbourne
Middleton St.George
Oak Tree
TEES-SIDE
N.E.Regional Tennis Centre
Aislaby
Yarm
High Leven
Maltby
Thornton
Barningham
West Layton
East Layton
Forcett
Stanwick Camp
Aldbrough St. John
Blackwell
Stapleton
A66(M)
Hurworth Place
Neasham
Middleton One Row
Low Dinsdale
Low Worsall
Hilton
Newsham
A1(M)
Croft-on-Tees
Hurworth-on-Tees
Dalton-on-Tees
Eryholme
High Worsall
Kirklevington
Middleton-on-Leven
Dalton
Ravensworth
Ravensworth Castle
Gayles
Melsonby
Newton Morrell
Barton
Sockburn
Girsby
Picton
Crathorne
Kirby Hill
Whashton
Croft
SCOTCH CORNER
Scotch Corner
Middleton Tyas
DANGER AREA
Gilling West
Aske Hall
A66
Hornby
Great Smeaton
Appleton Wiske
Hutton Rudby
Rudby
Potto
Moulton
Moulton Hall
Uckerby
North Cowton
R. Wiske
West Rounton
East Rounton
Georgian Theatre
Skeeby
East Cowton
Birkby
Welbury
Richmond
Green Howards
Pepper Arden
Hutton Bonville
Deighton
Ingleby Arncliffe
Swainby
Skelton
Marske
Hudswell
Hollyhill
Easby
Abbey
Scorton
Forest
A172
Colburn
Brompton-on-Swale
Catterick Bridge
Bolton-on-Swale
Whitwell
Streetlam
East Harlsey
Harlsey Castle
Marrick
Downholme
Hipswell
Walkerville
Brough Hall
Ellerton
Danby Wiske
Mount Grace Priory
Cod Beck
Osmotherley
Whorlton
Catterick Garrison
Catterick
Kiplin Hall
Great Langton
Battle of Standard (1138)
Brompton
A684
Ellerbeck
Stainton
Walburn Hall
DANGER AREA
Hipswell Moor
Tunstall
East Appleton
Kirby Fleetham
Foxton
Kirby Sigston
Thimbleby
Scotton
West Appleton
Hornby
Hackforth
Great Fencote
Little Fencote
Yafforth
Romanby
NORTHALLERTON
Bullamoor
Barden
East Hauxwell
Arrathorne
Thrintoft
Ainderby Steeple
Over Silton
Y O R K S H I R E
Bellerby
Bellerby Camp
Garriston
Constable Burton Hall
Hunton
Patrick Brompton
Langthorne
Scruton
Morton-on-Swale
Warlaby
Crosby Court
Nether Silton
Kepwick
Leyburn
Constable Burton
Little Crakehall
Kirkbridge
Thornton-le-Beans
Leake
Wensley
Harmby
Finghall
Great Crakehall
99
Leeming Bar
LEEMING
Leeming
North Otterington
Borrowby
Cowesby
Spennithorne
Middleham
Newton-le-Willows
Wensleydale Railway
Bedale
Aiskew
Leeming Londonderry
Thornton-le-Moor
Newby Wiske
South Otterington
Knayton
Kirby Knowle
Polly Peachum's Tower
Cowling
Bedale Hall
Exelby
Gatenby
Maunby
Upsall
Coverham
Middleham
Thornton Steward
Jervaulx Abbey
Burrill
Firby
Thorp Perrow Arboretum
Thornton-le-Street
North Kilvington
Braithwaite Hall
East Witton
Thirn
Thornton
Theakston
HAMBLETON

106
115
105
99
DURHAM
Framwellgate Moor
Aykley Heads
Gilesgate Moor
Carrville
Pittington
Hallgarth
Littletown
Sherburn Hill
Sherburn
Haswell
Haswell Plough
High Haswell
Easington Colliery
Easington
Horden Point
Horden
Dene Mouth
Shotton Colliery
Shotton
PETERLEE
Blackhall Colliery
Blackhall Rocks
Crimdon Park
Castle Eden
Hesleden
High Hesleden
Monk Hesleden
Eden Vale
Station Town
Hutton Henry
Hart Station
Hart
Sheraton
Wingate
Deaf Hill
Wheatley Hill
Thornley
Ludworth
Shadforth
Byers Garth
Old Cassop
Cassop
Old Quarrington
Quarrington Hill
Bowburn
Croxdale
Hett
Tursdale
Town Kelloe
Kelloe
Coxhoe
Garmondsway
Trimdon Grange
Trimdon Colliery
Trimdon
Cornforth
West Cornforth
Ferryhill
Dean Bank
Kirk Merrington
Mainsforth
Ferryhill Station
Chilton Lane
Bishop Middleham
Hardwick Hall
Fishburn
Sedgefield
Butterwick
Embleton
Great Chilton
Chilton
Rushyford
Bradbury
Mordon
Foxton
Shotton
Thorpe Larches
Fulthorpe
Wolviston
Cowpen Bewley
BILLINGHAM
Castle Eden Walk and Rec. Area
Stillington
Preston-le-Skerne
Elstob
Thorpe Thewles
Whitton
Carlton
Redmarshall
Hardwick
Bishopton
Great Stainton
Little Stainton
Brafferton
Coatham Mundeville
Newton Ketton
Whinny Hill
STOCKTON-ON-TEES
Norton
Roseworth
Stockton Borough Hall
Hartburn
Elton
Thornaby-on-Tees
Preston Hall
Eaglescliffe
Ingleby Barwick
Egglescliffe
Yarm
High Leven
Maltby
Hilton
Aislaby
Urlay Nook
Long Newton
Sadberge
Great Burdon
Barmpton
Haughton Le Skerne
DARLINGTON
Harrowgate Hill
Faverdale
Beaumont Hill
Eastbourne
Blackwell
Stapleton
Middleton St.George
Oak Tree
N.E.Regional Tennis Centre
TEES-SIDE
Middleton One Row
Low Dinsdale
Neasham
Hurworth Place
Hurworth-on-Tees
Croft-on-Tees
Dalton-on-Tees
Eryholme
Sockburn
Girsby
Low Worsall
High Worsall
Kirklevington
Picton
Crathorne
Middleton-on-Leven
Seamer
Stokesley
Tanton
Newby
Stainton
Thornton
Hemlington
Fairy Dell Park
Marton
Nunthorpe
Acklam
MIDDLESBROUGH
North Ormesby
SEE PAGE 191
Ormesby
Haverton Hill
Port Clarence
South Bank
Teesport
Grangetown
Eston
Lazenby
Normanby
Wilton
Dunsdale
Dormanstown
Kirkleatham
Turner's Hosp.
Yearby
Upleatham
New Marske
England's Smallest Church
Tocketts Mill Ind.
Skelton
Skelton Green
Boosbeck
Lingdale
REDCAR
Lifeboat Museum
Coatham
Warrenby
Zetland
Marske-by-the-Sea
Saltburn-by-the-Sea
TEESSIDE
Tees Bay
HARTLEPOOL
Hartlepool Bay
Hartlepool Historic Quay
Middleton
West View
High Throston
Naisberry
Elwick
West Park
Dalton Piercy
Rift House
Brierton
Owton Manor
Seaton Carew
Greatham
Graythorp
Newton Bewley
GUISBOROUGH
Hutton Gate
Hutton Village
Guisborough Moor
Newton under Roseberry
Roseberry Topping
Great Ayton
Captain Cook Schoolroom
Captain Cook's Monument
Little Ayton
Easby
New Row
Commondale
Kildale
Kildale Moor
Battersby
Baysdale Beck
Ingleby Greenhow
Great Broughton
Kirkby
Great Busby
Carlton in Cleveland
River Leven
Rudby
Hutton Rudby
Potto
Faceby
Whorlton
Swainby
Ingleby Arncliffe
Westerdale
Westerdale Moor
Urra
Seave Green
Chop Gate
Scugdale Beck
Whorlton Moor
Mount Grace Priory
Cod Beck
Osmotherley
Snilesworth Moor
Cow Ridge
Cross Holme
The Grange
Bilsdale East Moor
Cockayne
Cockayne Ridge
Farndale Moor
Low Mill
Rudland Rigg
East Moors
Fangdale Beck
Helmsley Moor
Arden Great Moor
Arden Hall
Hawnby
Rievaulx Moor
Rievaulx
Old Byland
Carlton
Pockley
Fadmoor
Thimbleby
Over Silton
Nether Silton
Kepwick
Cowesby
Kirby Knowle
Boltby
Knayton
Upsall
North Kilvington
Thornton-le-Street
South Otterington
Thornton-le-Moor
Newby Wiske
North Otterington
Borrowby
Leake
Thornton-le-Beans
Crosby Court
NORTHALLERTON
Romanby
Yafforth
Brompton
Battle of Standard (1138)
Bullamoor
Kirby Sigston
Ellerbeck
Foxton
Harlsey Castle
East Harlsey
Welbury
East Rounton
West Rounton
Deighton
Appleton Wiske
Hornby
Great Smeaton
R. Wiske
Birkby
Hutton Bonville
East Cowton
North Cowton
Pepper Arden
Forest
Whitwell
Streetlam
Danby Wiske
Great Langton
Kiplin Hall
Kirkby Fleetham
Great Fencote
Little Fencote
Scruton
Thrintoft
Ainderby Steeple
Morton-on-Swale
Warlaby
Leeming Bar
LEEMING
Leeming
Leeming Londonderry
Aiskew
Gatenby
Exelby
Firby
Thorp Perrow Arboretum
Theakston
Maunby
Croft
CLEVELAND
NORTH YORK
HILLS
NORTH
NATIONAL
CLEVELAND HILLS
HAMBLETON
REDCAR & CLEVELAND
DURHAM
NORTH

NORTH SEA
Runswick Bay
Saltwick Bay
Ness Point or North Cheek
Old Peak or South Cheek
Robin Hood's Bay
WHITBY
SCARBOROUGH
Brotton
Skinningrove
Loftus
Staithes
Hinderwell
Runswick
Sandsend
Lythe
Ruswarp
Sleights
Grosmont
Goathland
Danby
Castleton
Lealholm
Glaisdale
Egton
Egton Bridge
Ravenscar
Staintondale
Cloughton
Burniston
Scalby
Levisham
Lockton
Lastingham
Hutton-le-Hole
Gillamoor
Rosedale Abbey
Newton-on-Rawcliffe
Appleton-le-Moors
Sinnington
Kirkbymoorside
Falsgrave
East Ayton
NORTH YORK MOORS
NORTH YORKSHIRE
Langdale Forest
Fylingdales Moor
Goathland Moor
Wheeldale Moor
Danby Low Moor
Rosedale Moor
Spaunton Moor
A171
A174
A169
A170
A165
A64
B1266
B1416
B1447
B1366
100
101

ISLE OF MAN
POINT OF AYRE
Rue Point
Visitor Centre & Nature Trail
Viking Ship Burial
The Ayres
NT Manx
Thor Cross
Cranstal
Bride
The Lhen
Dhowin
Jurby East
Andreas
Crosses
Jurby West
Jurby Head
Shellag Point
Ballasalla
Sandygate
Regaby
Ramsey Bay
The Cronk
St. Judes
Civil War Fort
Dhoor
Grove
Ramsey
Curraghs
Sulby
Churchtown
Orrisdale
Ballaugh
Orrisdale Head
T.T. Course
Fort
Gate
Glen Auldyn
Port e Vullen
Maughold Head
Maughold
Lewaigue
Glen Trunk
Bishops Court
Ravensdale
Bishopcourt Glen
1854 North Barrule
Crosses
Ballajora
Steam Centre
Kirk Michael
Port Mooar
Corrany
Cornaa
Manx Electric Railway
Ballacarnane Beg
Ballaleigh
Slieau Dhoo 1601
SNAEFELL
Clagh Ouyr
Glen Mona
Cashtal yn Ard
Glen Mooar
Gob y Deigan
Barregarrow
Sulby Resr.
2036
Dhoon
Port Cornaa
NT Manx Dhoon Glen
Mountain Railway
The Spiral Stone
Laxey Wheel
Bulgham Bay
Knockshárry
Cronk-y-Voddy
1599 Colden
St. Patrick's Isle
Peel
Ballagyr
Lambfell Moar
Giant's Grave
Glen Helen
Injebreck Resr.
Mill
Minorca
Laxey
Old Laxey
Laxey Head
Ballacannell
Ballaheannagh
Contrary Head
Corrin's Folly
Patrick
Ballig
St. John's
Slieau Ruy 1570
Laxey Bay
Greeba Castle
Baldwin
Baldrine
Clay Head
Glenmaye
Lower Foxdale
Crosby
Hillberry
Onchan
Dalby Point
Glen Vine
Strang
Groudle Glen Railway
Port Groudle
Dalby
Foxdale
Eairy
Garth
Union Mills
Willaston
Onchan Head
Niarbyl Bay
1586 South Barrule
Fort
Spring Valley
DOUGLAS
Braaid
Cooil
Douglas Bay
Close Clark
Kewaigue
Tower of Refuge
Douglas Head
Stroin Vuigh
Hut Circles
Horses Home
Quine's Hill
Ballamodha
St. Mark's
Newtown
Ronague
Keristal
Little Ness
Fleshwick Bay
Lingague
Grenaby
Isle of Man Railway
Port Soderick
Bradda
Surby
Ballabeg
Santon Head
Bradda Head
Port Erin
Colby
Ballasalla
Marine Biology Station
Four Roads
Port St. Mary
ISLE OF MAN
The Howe
Ship Burial
Castletown
St. Michael's Island
Stone Circle
Cregneash
Nautical
Derbyhaven
Kitterland
NT Manx
SPANISH HEAD
Calf of Man
Chicken Rock
Bird Sanctuary NT Manx
Dreswick Point
Douglas to:
Belfast 2hrs.45mins. (Fast Ferry, Seasonal)
Heysham 3hrs. 45mins.
Dublin 2hrs. 45mins. (Fast Ferry, Seasonal)
Liverpool 2hrs. 30mins. (Fast Ferry, Seasonal)
Liverpool 4hrs. (Seasonal)
A
B
C
D
1
2
3
4
5

109
116
110
E
F
G
H
1
2
3
4
5
SOUTH AYRSHIRE
DUMFRIES & GALLOWAY
T H E R H I N S
CHANGUE FOREST
GLENT
Cairnryan to:
Larne 1hr.
(Fast Ferry, Seasonal)
Larne 1hrs. 45mins.
Stranraer to:
Belfast 1hr. 45mins.(Fast Ferry)
Belfast 3hrs. 15mins.
Lendalfoot
Tormitchell
Barr
Pinmore
Merkland
Grey Hill 975
853 Knockdaw Hill
Cairn Hill 1572
Polmaddie Hill 1854
Knockinloche
Bennane Head
Ballantrae Bay
Colmonell
Poundland
Pinwherry
Bellamore
Pindonnan Craigs 1098
Knockdolian
Heronsford
Knockdhu 756
Water of Tig
Pinwherry Hill
Black Clauchrie
Ballantrae
Garleffin
Downan Point
Barrhill
752 Shiel Hill
1041 Strawarren Fell
Corwar House
Drumlamford Loch
Drumlamford House
Loch Dornal
Low Ballochdowan
Beneraird 1439
1046 Carlock Hill
1321 Milljoan Hill
Currarie Port
Penderry Hill
Water of App
Glen App
Chirmorie
High Murdonochee
Loch Maberry
Loch Maberry Castle
Loch Ochiltree
Craig Airie Fell
Loch Derry
Polbae
Milleur Point
Corsewall Point
Barnhills
Portencalzie
Finnarts Bay
844 Mid Moile
725 Stab Hill
Glenwhilly
Laggangairn Standing Stones
Knowe
605 Urrall Fell
Kirkcolm
Knockcoid
Cairnryan
Penwhirn Resr.
Main Water of Luce
Quarter Fell
888 Artfield Fell
742 Eldrig Fell
Carseriggan
Dounan Bay
Airies
Ervie
Loch Connell
The Wig
Loch Doon
780 Doon Hill
Braid Fell
Balmurrie
Portobello
Loch Ryan
Craigcaffie Tower
Cairnscarrow
New Luce
Tarf Bridge
Black Loch
Loch Heron
West Culvennan
Loch Ronald
Shennanton
Slouchnawen Bay
Galdenoch Castle
Leswalt
Lochnaw Castle
Innermessan
Glenstockadale
Lochinch Castle
Black Loch
White Loch
Castle Kennedy
Craig Fell 538
Gleniron Fell
Bught Fell 672
Tarf Water
Kirkc
Stranraer
St. John
Aird
Soulseat Loch
Castle Kennedy
Carscreugh
Carscreugh Castle
Broadsea Bay
Glenwhan
Challoch Hill 484
Glenluce Abbey
Motor
Dunragit
Glenluce
Castle of Park
Craigenlee Fell
Lochans
Mark
Dernaglar Loch
Knock Moss
Black Head
Cairn Pat 596
Torrs Warren
Whitefield Loch
Kilfillan
Portpatrick
Old Lifeboat House
Dunskey
Bean Hill
West Freugh
DANGER AREA
Stoneykirk
Milton
Castle Loch
Craignarget Hill
Mochrum Loch
Port of Spittal Bay
Kildonan
Auchenmalg
Kirklauchline
Sandhead
L U C E
B A Y
Auchenmalg Bay
646 Mochrum Fell
Loch Head
Cairngarroch Bay
Cairngarroch
Kirkmadrine Memorial Stones
Garheugh Port
Finian
Money Head
Elrig
Float Bay
Clachanmore Gallery
Low Ardwell
Ardwell
Milton Point
Mochrum
Ardwell Point
Ardwell
Chapel Rossan Bay
Auchness Tower
Port William
Balgowan Point
Logan Botanic
Mull of Logan
Marine Life Centre
Port Logan
Port Logan Bay
Terally Point
Barsalloch Point
Monreith Bay
Cairnywellan Head
INSET
Kilstay Bay
Clanyard Bay
Laggantalluch Head
Kirkmaiden
Drummore
Cailiness Point
Kilstay Bay
Kirkmaiden
Drummore
Cailiness Point
Maryport
Crammag Head
Maryport Bay
Port Kemin
Mull of Galloway
MULL OF GALLOWAY
A77
A714
A75
A751
A718
A716
A747
B734
B7044
B7027
B738
B798
B7043
B7077
B7084
B7042
B7065
B7005
B733

110
116
117
109
SOUTH AYRSHIRE
GALLOWAY FOREST PARK
MERRICK
GLENTROOL FOREST
KIRROUGHTREE FOREST
CARRICK FOREST
CHANGUE FOREST
DUNDEUGH FOREST
GLENKENS
RHINNS OF KELLS
CAIRN EDWARD
GALLOWAY
PENNINGHAME FOREST
CAIRNSMORE OF FLEET
LAURIESTON FOREST
GLENGAP FOREST
DUMFRIES
THE MACHARS
Newton Stewart
Wigtown
Whithorn
Creetown
Gatehouse of Fleet
New Galloway
Carsphairn
St. John's Town of Dalry
Port William
Kirkcowan
Minnigaff
Glentrool Village
Wigtown Bay
Milton Point
Monreith Bay
Burrow Head
Islands of Fleet
Fleet Bay
Ravenshall Point
Eggerness Point
Port Allen
Cairn Head
Little Ross
Borgue
Sorbie
Garlieston
Kirkinner
Bladnoch
Isle of Whithorn
A75
A714
A712
A713
A746
A747
A762
B7004
B7005
B7021
B7052
B7063

111
112
118
SEE PAGE 188
Penpont
Tynron
Moniaive
Kirkland
Keir Mill
Closeburn
Cample
Park
Kirkpatrick
Maxwelton House
Wallaceton
Craigmuie
Glenmidge
Blackwood
Auldgirth
High Auldgirth
Dalswinton
Dunscore
Throughgate
Glenesslin
Craigenputtock
Stepford
Morrington
Newtonairds
Glenkiln
Shawhead
Corsock
Craig
Crofts
Crocketford or Ninemile Bar
Lochfoot
Cargenbridge
Drumsleet
Terregles
New Bridge
Lincluden
Maxwelltown
DUMFRIES
Troqueer
Kingholm Quay
Islesteps
Holywood
Kirkton
Locharbriggs
Heathhall
The Grove
Torthorwald
Collin
Woodside
Greenlea
Racks
Elizafield
Mouswald
Carrutherstown
Kelton
Glencaple
Bankend
Shearington
Blackshaw
Caerlaverock
Clarencefield
Tinwald
Amisfield
Duncow
Auchencairn
Ae
Parkgate
Courance
Johnstonebridge
Templand
Nethermill
Shieldhill
Marjoriebanks
Lochmaben
St. Ann's
FOREST OF AE
NITHSDALE
Glenmaid Moor
Great Hill
Knockvennie
Kirkpatrick Durham
Springholm
Milton
Parton
Crossmichael
Laurieston
Glenlochar
Townhead of Greenlaw
Clarebrand
Haugh of Urr
Hardgate
Old Bridge of Urr
Castle Douglas
Leaths
Buittle Bridge
Dalbeattie
Craignair
Bridge of Dee
Rhonehouse or Kelton Hill
Gelston
Kirkgunzeon
Corra
Beeswing
Mabie
New Abbey
Kirkconnell
North Corbelly
Drumburn
Carsethorn
Kirkbean
Prestonmill
Mainsriddle
Loaningfoot
Southerness
Southerness Point
Caulkerbush
Barnbarroch
Colvend
Sandyhills
Portling
Palnackie
Kippford or Scaur
Rockcliffe
Rough Island
Castlehill Point
Auchencairn
Auchencairn Bay
Hestan Island
Balcary Point
Rascarrel
Rascarrel Bay
Tongland
Kirkcudbright
Dundrennan
Townhead
Netherlaw
Port Mary
Abbey Head
DANGER AREA
GALLOWAY
DALBEATTIE FOREST
SOLWAY FIRTH
Criffel 1868
Long Fell 1256
Maidenpap 1032
Meikle Hard Hill
Boreland Hill
Bengairn 1283
Screel Hill
Barcloy Hill
Beckfoot
Cowgate
Mawbray
Dubmill Point
Salta
Allonby
Allonby Bay
Allerby
Crosscanonby
Crosby
Birkby
Maryport
Netherton
Dearham
A75
A76
A701
A702
A709
A710
A711
A712
A713
A745
A762
A596
A594
B729
B794
B795
B736
B727
B793
B725
B724
B7020
B5300

112
118
111
102
SEE PAGE 188
FOREST OF AE
CASTLE O'ER FOREST
DUMFRIES & GALLOWAY
NITHSDALE
ANNANDALE
SCOTLAND
ENGLAND
SOLWAY FIRTH
CUMBRIA
Great Hill
1157
Park
Kirkpatrick
Forest of Ae
Plough Collection
Brownmoor Hill
St. Ann's
Johnstonebridge
ANNANDALE WATER
Berryscaur
Boreland
Castle O'er
Castle O'er Forest
Bentpath
Courance
Broomhillbank
Glenmaid Moor
Ae
A74(M)
Sibbaldbie
Telford Memorial
The Shin
1087
Hart Fell
High Auldgirth
Auldgirth
Parkgate
Barony College
Nethermill
Water of Ae
Templand
Spedlin's Tower
Claydaubing Bridge
Hart Fell
Corrie Common
1478
Calkin Rig
Glentenmont Height
Dalswinton
Auchencairn
Ellisland Farm
Amisfield Tower
Shieldhill
Elshieshields Tower
Millhousebridge
Applegarthtown
Marjoriebanks
Paddockhole
Raes Knowes
Duncow
Amisfield
Lochmaben
Castle Loch
Lockerbie
Water of Milk
Bankshill
1047
Grange Fell
Kirkton
Tinwald
Holywood
Locharbriggs
Lochmaben
Heck
Greenhill
Twelve Apostles Stone Circle
New Bridge
Heathhall
Lincluden
Collegiate Church
Dumfries & Galloway Aviation
The Grove
Torthorwald
Torthorwald Castle
Mossburn Animal Centre
Hightae
Burnswark Hill Fort
Howe's Hill
Kirtleton
Craigs
Terregles
Maxwelltown
Arts Cen.
Rammerscales House
Smallholm
Kettleholm
Waterbeck
Collin
Middlebie
DUMFRIES
Globe Inn
Cargenbridge
Troqueer
Greenlea
Racks
Woodside
Elizafield
Kirkconnel
Eaglesfield
Crichton Royal
The Crichton
Drumsleet
Hills Wood
Kingholm Quay
Dalton
Ecclefechan
Carlyle's Birthplace
NTS
Chapelknowe
Hoddom Castle
Hoddomcross
Kirtlebridge
Merkland Cross
Islesteps
Mouswald
Repentance Tower
Bonshaw Tower
Mabie Forest
Lochaber Loch
Mabie
Mabie Forest
Kelton
River Nith
Lochar Water
Carrutherstown
Brydekirk
Moorend
Newton
Kirkpatrick Fleming
Bruce's Cave
Lochaber Loch
Comlongon Castle
Clarencefield
Charlesfield
Warmanbie
Creca
Stapleton Tower
Blacksh
Bankend
Glencaple
Warmanbie Walled
GRETNA
Gretna Green
Kirkconnell
Shambellie House Costume
Brow Well
Ruthwell
Savings Banks
Cross
Howes
Annan
ANNAN
Rigg
Gretna
Old Graitney
Sweetheart Abbey
Corn Mill
New Abbey
Shearington
Blackshaw
Caerlaverock
Cummertrees
Powfoot
Welldale
Historic Resources Centre
Dornock
Devil's Porridge
Eastriggs
Waterloo Monument
Caerlaverock Wildfowl & Wetlands Centre
Loch Kindar
North Corbelly
Barnkirk Point
Torduff Point
Redkirk Point
Meikle Hard Hill
Port Carlisle
Bowness-on-Solway
Criffel
Criffel 1868
Drumburn
Boreland Hill
Glasson
Drumburgh
Carsethorn
Kirkbean
Cardurnock
Anthorn
Longcroft
Whitrigg
Easton
Boustead Hill
Dykesfield
Longburgh
Arbigland
Preston Mill
John Paul Jones
Anglerton
Fingland
Kirkbampton
Thurstonfield
Mainsriddle
Marsehead
Loaningfoot
Skinburness
Kirkbride
Little Bampton
Oughterby
Southerness
Southerness Point
Inshore Rescue Boat Station
Silloth
Lees Scar
Calvo
Seaville
Newton Arlosh
Wampool
Great Orton
Aikton
Wiggonby
Greenrow
Blackdyke
Biglands
Wedholme Flow
Blitterlees
Moss Side
Thornby
Raby
Gamelsby
Low Whinnow
Kelsick
R. Waver
Moorhouse
Parton
Dundraw
Lessonhall
Oulton
Micklethwaite
Crofton
Wolsty
Highlaws
Abbeytown
Holme Cultram Abbey
Standingstone
West Woodside
Beckfoot
Pelutho
Moor Row
Aikhead
Wigton
Southerfield
Waverbridge
Aldoth
Blencogo
Kirkland
Newtown
Highmoor
Tarns
Waverton
Carwath
Cowgate
Bromfield
Parkgate
Brackenlands
High Longthwaite
Brackenthwaite
Holme St. Cuthbert
Mawbray
Langrigg
Waterside
Dubmill Point
Mealrigg
High Scales
Red Dial
Woodrow
Salta
Edderside
New Cowper
Low Row
Bolton Low Houses
Bolton Wood Lane
Westward
Rosley
Westnewton
Heathfield
Crookdake
Bolton New Houses
Yearngill
Watchill
Fletchertown
Allonby
Allonby Bay
Aspatria
Hayton
Blennerhasset
Whitehall House
Mealsgate
Harriston
Prospect
Kirkland Guards
Boltongate
Sandale
John Peel's Grave
Oughterside
Allerby
Westnewton
Westmoor
Parsonby
Leapland
Plumbland
Torpenhow
Whitrigg
Ireby
Whelpo
Upton
Crosscanonby
Crosby Villa
Bothel
Crosby
Bullgill
High Ireby
Uldale
Fell Side
Birkby
Greengill
Gilcrux
Ruthwaite
Branthwaite
Maryport
R. Ellen
Dearham
Moota Hill
Longlands
Binsey 1467
Netherton
Townhead
Sunderland
Rewaldeth
A701
A76
A75
A709
A710
A711
A74(M)
A596
A595
A594
A591
B7020
B7076
B7068
B723
B729
B725
B724
B726
B722
B6357
B7076
B721
B5307
B5302
B5301
B5300
B5299
B5305
B709

113
NORTHUMBERLAND
KIELDER FOREST
BORDER FOREST PARK
WARK FOREST
KERSHOPE FOREST
Kielder Water
CARLISLE
SEE PAGE 187
Langholm
Newcastleton
Canonbie
Longtown
Brampton
Haltwhistle
Alston
Gilsland
Bewcastle
Kirkoswald
Armathwaite
Wetheral
Dalston
Melmerby
GILDERDALE FOREST
DANGER AREA
Hadrian's Wall
119
120
114
103
M6
A7
A69
A689
A6071
A595
A686
A74
B6318
B6357
B6413

120
114
113
104
A
B
C
D
1
2
3
4
5
KIELDER FOREST
BORDER FOREST PARK
Kielder Water
NORTHUMBERLAND NATIONAL PARK
N O R T H U M B E R
W A R K F O R E S T
D U R
REDESDALE
Otterburn
Elsdon
Old Town
Raylees
Manside Cross
Fontburn Reservoir
Fallowlees Burn
Ewesley
Rothley Lakes
Rothley
Highgreen Manor
Padon Hill 1240
Blakehope Fell
Blackburn Common
Troughend Common
Earl's Seat 1303
Warksburn Forest Walk
Gatehouse
Falstone
Yarrow
Stannersburn
Greenhaugh
North Tyne
Lanehead
Charlton
Tarset
Dally
Bellingham
Hesleyside
Bower
Chirdon Burn
Redesmouth
DANGER AREA
West Woodburn
East Woodburn
Chesterhope
Ridsdale
Knowesgate
Kirkwhelpington
Cambo
Scots Gap
Middleton
Wallington House NT
River Wansbeck
Kirkharle
Capheaton
Sir Edward's Lake
Great Bavington
Little Bavington
Kirkheaton
Sweethope Loughs
Carrycoats Hall
Colt Crag Reservoir
Thockrington
Little Swinburne
Hallington Reservoirs
Hallington
Great Swinburne
Colwell
Birtley
Wark
Park End
Gunnerton
Nunwick
Barrasford
Simonburn
Uppertown
Haughton
Chollerton
Humshaugh
Cocklaw
Bingfield
Ingoe
Ryal
Fenwick
Matfen
Great Whittington
Ouston
Halton Shields
Chollerford
Walwick
Low Brunton
Brocolita Fort & Mithraic Temple
Chesters Roman Fort
Turret
Wall
Churnsike Lodge
Butterburn
Whygate
Forest Walks
Warks Burn
Stonehaugh
Black Fell
Comyns Cross (Remains of)
Haughton Common
Irthing
Broomlee Lough
Greenlee Lough
Housesteads
Hadrian's Wall
Crag Lough
Vercovicium Roman Fort
Whiteside
Thirlwall Common
Hadrian's Wall
Great Chesters Roman Fort
Vindolanda Roman Fort
Chesterholm
Greenhead
Haltwhistle
Blenkinsopp Hall
Thorngrafton
Henshaw
Chesterwood
Newbrough
Fourstones
Acomb
Warden
Sandhoe
Anick
Halton
Aydon
Corbridge
Newton
Ovington
Newton Hall
Melkridge
Redburn
Bardon Mill
Ridley
Hadrian's Wall Walk
Haydon Bridge
Low Gate
HEXHAM
Abbey
Fort
Dilston
Riding Mill
Bywell
Eltringham
Branch End
Stocksfield
Broomhaugh
River Tyne
Plenmeller
Bellister
Plenmeller Common
Park Village
Featherstone Castle
Rowfoot
Coanwood
Allen Banks Reserve
Langley Castle
Langley
Hexham Racecourse
Moor Hall
Hexham Levels
Ordley
Juniper
Steel
Slaley
Healey Hall
Healey
Broomley
Hindley
Painshawfield
New Ridley
Apperley Dene
Whittonstall
Lambley
R. South Tyne
Stonehouse
Whitfield
Bearsbridge
R. Allen
West Allen
Catton
Field Centre
Thornley Gate
Allendale Town
Country Walks
Dalton
Whitley Chapel
Dukesfield
Rawgreen
Strothers Dale
Colpitts Grange
Minsteracres
Slaley Forest
Kiln Pit Hill
Shotleyfield
Eals
Knarsdale
Slaggyford
Whitfield Moor 1723
River Allen
Mill Chimneys
Ninebanks
Ouston
Hexhamshire Common
Broadwell House
Blanchland Moor 1345
Derwent Reservoir
Carterway Heads
Snods Edge
Mosswood
Keirsleywell Row
Field Centre
Sinderhope
Allendale Common 1640
Blanchland
Abbey
Baybridge
Newbiggin
Hunstanworth
Edmundbyers
Pow Hill
Muggleswick
Derwent
Limestone Brae
R.E. Allen
Spartylea
Green Hill
Townfield
Ramshaw
Healeyfield
Horsleyhope
Ayle
South Tynedale Railway
Blagill
Alston
Raise
Field Centre
Carr Shield
Dirt Pot
Nookton Fell 1567
Muggleswick Common
Hisehope Reservoir
Smiddy Shaw Reservoir
Nenthall
Middle Fell
Bayles
Leadgate
GILDERDALE FOREST
Nenthead
Coalcleugh
Allenheads
Field Centre
Bolt's Law 1773
Waskerley
Waskerley Reservoir
Killhope Wheel
Middlehope Moor
Rookhope
Lintzgarth
Stanhope Common
Collier Law 1694
Tunstall Reservoir
Garrigill
Lanehead
Corriggs
Copthill
Cowshill
Crawley Side
Wolsingham Park Moor
Black Burn
Burnhope Reservoir
Wearhead
Blackcleugh
Folk Museum
Westgate
Eastgate
Stanhope
Wolsingham
Ireshopeburn
St.John's Chapel
Daddry Shield
Brotherlee
Weardale
Frosterley
Hill End
White
Alston Moor
Burnhope Seat 2448
Ireshope Moor
Round Hill 2249
A696
A68
A69
A686
A689
A6079
A695
B6341
B6320
B6342
B6343
B6318
B6319
B6321
B6530
B6531
B6305
B6295
B6303
B6306
B6307
B6309
B6294
B6277
B6278
B6278

115
Newcastle to:
Amsterdam 15hrs.
Bergen 26hrs.
Gothenburg 25hrs. 30mins.
Haugesund 22hrs.
Kristiansand 17hrs. 15mins.
Stavanger 19hrs.
NEWCASTLE UPON TYNE
SEE PAGE 191
GATESHEAD
SUNDERLAND
SEE PAGE 196
DURHAM
SEE PAGE 188
TYNEMOUTH
SOUTH SHIELDS
ASHINGTON
MORPETH
CONSETT
WASHINGTON
CHESTER-LE-STREET
HOUGHTON-LE-SPRING
Longhorsley
Widdrington Station
Cresswell
Ellington
Lynemouth
Netherwitton
Beacon Point
Newbiggin-by-the-Sea
Longhirst
Pegswood
Hartburn
Meldon
Whalton
Bedlington
Blyth
Cambois
North Blyth
Stakeford
Guide Post
Choppington
Bomarsund
Cramlington
Seaton Delaval
Seaton Sluice
Hartley
St. Mary's or Bait Island
Whitley Bay
Cullercoats
Monkseaton
Shiremoor
Backworth
Killingworth
Longbenton
Ponteland
Darras Hall
Dinnington
Hazlerigg
Stamfordham
Gosforth
Jesmond
Wallsend
North Shields
Tyne Tunnel
Hebburn
Jarrow
Felling
Newburn
Throckley
Heddon-on-the-Wall
Ryton
Wylam
Ovingham
Prudhoe
Blaydon
Whickham
Winlaton
Rowlands Gill
Marsden Bay
Souter NT
Lizard Point
Whitburn
Cleadon
Boldon
Roker
Monkwearmouth
National Glass Centre
Hendon
Ryhope
Birtley
Penshaw
Shiney Row
Herrington
Tunstall
Seaham
Murton
Hetton-le-Hole
Easington Colliery
Horden Point
Horden
Peterlee
Dene Mouth
Blackhall Colliery
Blackhall Rocks
Stanley
Annfield Plain
Lanchester
Sacriston
Esh Winning
Brandon
Tow Law
Dan's Castle
Great Lumley
Pity Me
Framwellgate Moor
Shincliffe
Bowburn
Sherburn
Coxhoe
Wingate
Station Town
Castle Eden
Hart

116
126
123
109
SEE PAGE 190
Ardrossan to Brodick 55mins.
Troon to:
Belfast 2hrs. 30mins.
(Fast Ferry)
Larne 1hr. 50mins.
(Fast Ferry)
Horse Isle
Ardrossan
North Ayrshire
Saltcoats
Stevenston
Kilwinning
Montgreenan
Torranyard
Auchenharvie Castle
Eglinton
Doura
Cunninghamhead
Kilmaurs
Rowallan Castle
Fenwick
Laigh Fenwick
Onthank
Craufurdland Castle
Perceton
Girdle Toll
Irvine
IRVINE
Stanecastle
Dreghorn
Springside
Knockentiber
Altonhill
Knockinlaw
KILMARNOCK
Crosshouse
Grange
Gatehead
Crookedholm
Hurlford
Magnum Beach Park
Irvine Bay
Drybridge
Dundonald
Earlston
Riccarton
Crossroads
Clauchlands Point
Holy Island
Kingscross Point
Kingscross
Whiting
Whiting Bay
Largybeg Point
Pippin Head
Barassie
Loans
Symington
Bogend
Craigie
Carnell
Troon
Lady Isle
Monktonhill
Monkton
Fail
GLASGOW PRESTWICK
Tarbolton
Bachelors' Club NTS
Prestwick
New Prestwick
Mossblown
Failford
Newton upon Ayr
St. Quivox
Yett
Milton
Stair
Whitletts
Annbank
Gadgirth
Newton Steeple
AYR
Wallace Tower
Dalmilling
Wallacetown
Seafield
Trabboch
Belston
Joppa
Coalhall
Cunning Park
Greenan
Doonfoot
Belmont
Heads of Ayr
Alloway
Coylton
Hillhead
Low Coylton
Drongan
Brig O'Doon
Tam O'Shanter Experience
Fisherton
Dunure Castle
Dunure
Newark Castle
Doonholm
Barbieston
Martnaham Loch
943 Brown Carrick Hill
Carclaie
Hayhill
Culroy
Dalrymple
Hollybush
Littlemill
Knockdon
Minishant
Cassillis House
Knockshinnoch
Rankinston
Electric Brae
Knoweside
Culzean Bay
Polnessan
Culzean Castle NTS
Whitefaulds
Maybole
1408 Kilmein Hill
Patna
Lethanhill
Burnfoot
Maidenhead Bay
Kirkmichael
Dunaskin Open Air
Scottish Industrial Railway
Maidens
Turnberry
Kirkoswald
Crossraguel Abbey
Kilhenzie Castle
Loch Spallander Resr.
Waterside
River Doon
Souter Johnnie's Cottage NTS
Turnberry Bay
Crosshill
Blairquhan Castle
Straiton
Bogton Loch
Matthew's Port
Rugle
Dersalloch Hill
Kilkerran
Dipple
Wallacetown
Dalquharran Castle
Kilgrammie
Dailly
1395 Glenalla Fell
Big Hill of Glenmount 1252
Old Dailly
Killochan Castle
Bargany
Hadyard Hill 1060
1408 Garleffin Fell
Tairlaw Ring
Tallaminnock
Derclach Loch
Loch Finlas
Girvan
Penkill Castle
Penkill
Saugh Hill 971
Penwhapple Reservoir
Linfern Loch
Loch Bradan Resr.
Glendoune
Woodland Bay
1165 Mull of Miljoan
Dalquhairn
Stinchar Falls
Black Hill
Stinchar Bridge
CARRICK FOREST
Craiglee
Byne Hill
Tormitchell
Barr
CHANGUE FOREST
Eldrick Hill
Loch Riecawr
Carrick Forest Drive
Grey Hill 975
Pinmore
Stinchar
River
Polmaddie Hill 1854
David Bell Memorial
Waterhead
Loch Macaterick
Rig of the Shalloch
Lendalfoot
Straid
Merkland
Cairn Hill 1572
Knockinlochie
1637 Macaterick
853 Knockdaw Hill
Tarfessock
Kirriereoch Hill 2565
Bennane Head
Poundland
Pinwherry
Pindonnan Craigs 1098
Colmonell
Bellamore
Mullwharchar 2270
GALLOWAY FOREST PARK
MERRICK
Merrick
Loch Enoch
Ballantrae Bay
Knockdolian
SOUTH AYRSHIRE
CARRICK
A78
A77
A71
A76
A719
A70
A713
A759
A714
B734
B741
B7023
B7024
B7034
B742
B743
B744
B730
B751
B7081
B7045
B779
B785
B769
B778
B7038

118
A
B
C
D
128
Kirkfieldbank
LANARK
New Lanark
Falls of Clyde
Corra Castle
Corra Linn
Hyndford Bridge
Stonebyres
Black Hill Hill Fort
Pettinain
Libberton
Junction
Elsrickle
Kirkurd
Drochil Castle
Broughton Heights 1874
Black Meldon 1334
Lyne
Hallyne
Candy Mill
Kaimrig End
A702
A721
A72
A73
A70
M74
B7016
B7018
B7078
B7055
B740
B797
B7040
B7076
B719
A74
A74(M)
A701
A712
A708
A76
B732
B731
B729
B7020
Shieldhill
Covington Castle
Covington
Quothquan
Thankerton
Carmichael
Douglas Water
Biggar
Gasworks
Victorian Puppet Theatre
Boghall Castle
Skirling
Cormiston
Coulter
Causewayend
Broughton Place
Trahenna Hill 1792
Church
Dreva Wood
Stobo Castle
Stobo
Dawyck Botanic Garden
Bellspool
Drumelzier
Tinnis
Whitelaw Hill 1563
Goseland Hill 1427
Kilbucho Place
John Buchan Centre
Broughton
Rachan Mill
Bellfield
Braehead
Rigside
HAPPENDON
Happendon
Uddington
Howgate Hill 1456
Tinto
Tinto Hills
Fatlips Castle
2334 Tinto
Wiston
Symington
Coulter
Snaip Hill
Kilbucho Church
Common Law
Glenholm
Finglen Rig
Castle Dangerous
Heritage
St. Bride's
Douglas
Cameronian Regiment Monument
Garf Water
Newton
Lamington
River Clyde
Scaur Hill
1673 Dungavel Hill
SOUTH
LANARKSHIRE
Blakehope Head 1783
Stanhope
2417 Pykestone Hill
Horse Hope Hill
Pagie Hill
Roberton Law 1238
Backstane Hill
Roberton
Wandel
Startup Hill
Broad Hill
2455 Culter Fell
Glenkirk
Glenlood Hill
Kingledores
2089 Taberon Law
2682 Dollar Law
Black Law 2285
NETHER ABINGTON
Culter Waterhead Reservoir
Duncangill Head
2263 Glenwhappen Rig
Glenmuck Height
Tweedsmuir
SCOTTISH BORDERS
Crawfordjohn
Heritage
Abington
1868 Tewsgill Hill
Camps Water
Culter Cleuch Shank
Camps Resr.
2756 Broad Law
Megget Reservoir
Common Hill
Drake Law 1586
Kirkton
Crawford Castle
Crawford
Glenbreck
Talla Resr.
Talla Linnfoots
Fruid Resr.
White Hill
1392 Spango Hill
Spango Bridge
117
1814 Wellgrain Dod
1621 Rake Law
Elvanfoot
1790 Clyde Law
1813 Craigmaid
Lochcraig Head 2625
Birk Craigs
Cape Law
Loch Skeen
NTS
Grey Mare's Tail
Herman Law
Wedder Dod 1460
Leadhills
Miners' Library
Leadhills & Wanlockhead Railway
Wanlockhead
Beam Engine
Lochnell Lead Mine
Scottish Lead Mining
Dun Law
2403 Green Lowther
1926 Stood Hill
LOWTHER HILLS
1591 Conrig Hill
Nunnerie
Nether Howcleugh
Devil's Beef Tub
John Hunter Memorial
Mail Coach Memorial
2651 Hart Fell
2696 White Coomb
2413 Saddle Yoke
Bell Craig
Swatte Fell
Ericstane
Wintercleuch Fell
Bodesbeck Law
Capplegill
1912 Thirstane Hill
1473 Cairn Hill
Comb Law 2108
Daer Resr.
Auldton Fell
Craigieburn
Capel Fell 2223
2270 Ettrick Pen
White Shank
1987 Well Hill
Ballencleuch Law 2268
Kirkhope
Moffat
Auldton Castle
Holmend
Woollen Mill
2256 Loch Fell
Croft Head
Enterkinfoot
Durisdeermill
Durisdeer
Auchen Castle
Beattock
Broomlands
Cornal Burn
Ewelairs Hill
ESKDALEMUIR
Garwaldwater
Wedder Law
Craighoar Hill 1898
Kinnelhead
Lochan Burn
Enoch
Drumlanrig Castle
Holm of Drumlanrig
Tibbers Castle
Bellybought Hill 1453
Morton Castle
2191 Gana Hill
Queensberry 2286
Wee Queensberry
DUMFRIES
&
GALLOWAY
Black Hill
Wamphray Water
Laverhay
Dinnins Hill 1088
Carronbridge
NITHSDALE
Gatelawbridge
Locherben
Minnygap Height 1308
Milne Height
Black Esk Reservoir
Scaur Water
Burnhead
Thornhill
Lochwood Castle
Penpont
Cample
Holehouse Hill
Whitefauld Hill
Newton
Fingland Fell
Tynron
Keir Mill
FOREST OF AE
Forest of Ae
St. Ann's
ANNANDALE WATER
Closeburn
1157 Great Hill
Plough Collection
Brownmoor Hill
Johnstonebridge
1172 Keir Hills
Park
Kirkpatrick
Barjarg Tower
Berryscaur
Boreland
Courance
Broomhillbank
Maxwelton House
111
112
Lenmaid Moor
Ae
Parkgate
Sibbaldbie
Claydaubing Bridge
Hart Fell
Corrie Common
Wallaceton
Glenmidge
Blackwood
High Auldgirth
Auldgirth
Nethermill
Barony College
Water of Ae
Kinnel Water
Templand
Spedlin's Tower
Dalswinton
Auchencairn
Millhousebridge

119
129
130
120
113
E
F
G
H
1
2
3
4
5
Peebles
Glentress Forest
Glentress
Horsbrugh Ford
Kings Muir
Cardrona Walks
Cardrona Forest
Walkerburn
Innerleithen
Elibank and Traquair Forest
Traquair
Kirkhouse
Glen House
Clovenfords
Caddonfoot
Yair Hill Forest
Peel
Stow
Buckholm
Galashiels
Langshaw
Nether Blainslie
Ledgerwood
Huntlywood
Earlston
Redpath
Leaderfoot
Gattonside
Lowood
Newstead
Darnick
Melrose
Bemersyde
Clintmains
Eildon
Dingleton
Newtown St. Boswells
Dryburgh
St. Boswells
Mertoun
Boleside
Lindean
Bowden
Maxton
Selkirk
Philiphaugh
Yarrow Ford
Yarrow
Yarrow Feus
Mountbenger
Cappercleuch
St. Mary's Loch
Loch of the Lowes
Tibbie Shiel's Inn
Midlem
Longnewton
Sandystones
Lilliesleaf
Ancrum
Bridge End
Bloomfield
Brockhill
Ettrickbridge
Ettrick Forest
Ashkirk
Gilmanscleuch
Essenside Loch
Akermoor Loch
Shaws Under Loch
Tushielaw
Dun Knowe
Hellmoor Loch
Redfordgreen
Alemoor Loch
Hassendean
Minto
Horsleyhill
Denholm
Spittal-on-Rule
Bedrule
Newton
Lanton
Appletreehall
Clarilaw
Burnfoot
Cauldmill
Wilton
Hawick
Kirkton
Roberton
Burnfoot
Ettrick
Buccleuch
Branxholme
Deanburnhaugh
Glenkerry
Newmill
Bonchester Bridge
Hobkirk
Chesters
Craik Forest
Craik
Stobs Castle
Teviotdale
Teviothead
Skelfhill
Wauchope Forest
Langburnshiels
Davington
Mosspaul
Eskdalemuir
Jamestown
Saughtree
Deadwater
Kielder
Hermitage
Steele Road
Kielder Forest
Castle O'er Forest
Castle O'er
Bentpath
Kirkstile or Ewes
Newcastleton
Border Forest Park
Liddesdale
Eskdale
Langholm
A7
A68
A6091
A72
A699
A708
A707
A698
A6088
A703
A6105
B709
B7009
B711
B6399
B6357
B6400
B6359
B6453
B6360
B6374
B7060
B710
B6404
B6405
B723
B7062
B6356
B6397
B6358

120
130
119
113
114
A
B
C
D
1
2
3
4
5
LAUDERDALE
SCOTTISH BORDERS
THE CHEVIOT HILLS
NORTHUMBERLAND NATIONAL PARK
THE CHEVIOT
2674
NORTH
SCOTLAND
ENGLAND
REDESDALE
KIELDER FOREST
BORDER FOREST PARK
WAUCHOPE FOREST
Kidland Forest
Leithope Forest
Redesdale Forest
Kielder Water
Ledgerwood
Huntlywood
Gordon
Greenknowe Tower
Gordon Moss
Fans
Hume
Lambden
Eccles
Leitholm
Twizel Bridge
Felkington
Duddo
Duddo Tower
Berrington
Castle Heaton
Melkington
Lennel
The Hirsel
Coldstream
Cornhill-on-Tweed
Dundock Wood
Birgham
Carham
Wark
West Learmouth
East Learmouth
Barelees
Heatherslaw Light Rlwy.
Pallinsburn House
Etal
Etal Manor
Crookham
Lady Waterford Hall
Ford
Branxton
1513 Flodden Field
Flodden
Kimmerston
Pressen
Hadden
Sweethope Hill
Stichill
Ednam
Newton Don House
James Thomson Obelisk
Earlston
Mellerstain House
Nenthorn
Smailholm
Smailholm Tower
Redpath
Newstead
Leaderfoot
Scott's View
Bemersyde
Clintmains
Eildon
Newtown St. Boswells
Dryburgh
Abbey
Mertoun Bridge
Mertoun
St. Boswells
Makerstoun
Kelso
Floors Castle
Maxwellheugh
Sprouston
Downham
Thornington
Howtel
Milfield
Pawston
Kilham
Mindrum
Lempitlaw
Hoselaw Loch
Roxburgh
Heiton
Maxton
Shotton
Westnewton
Kirknewton
Yeavering Church
Lanton
Coupland
Akeld
Humbleton
Hethpool
Yeavering Bell
Linton Hill
Yetholm Loch
Town Yetholm
Kirk Yetholm
Gipsy Palace
Coldsmouth Hill
White Law
Newton Tors
Fredden Hill
Longnewton
Longnewton Forest
Ancrum Moor
1545
Bowmont Forest
Kale Water
Linton
Primsidemill
Sandystones
Peniel Heugh
Waterloo Monument
Nisbet
Eckford
Morebattle
Ancrum
Bridge End
Monteviot House
Crailing
Bonjedward
Church
Cessford
Crookedshaws Hill
The Curr
Steer Rig
The Schil
Preston Hill
Cold Law
Bloomfield
Crailinghall
Whitton
Hownam Law
Langleeford
Lanton
Jedburgh
Fatlips
Minto Hills
Minto
Newton
Castle Jail
Mary Queen of Scots House
Whitton Loch
Mowhaugh
Sourhope
Hedgehope Hill
Spittal-on-Rule
Denholm
Leyden Obelisk
Bedrule
Dunion Hill
Ferniehirst
Oxnam
Hownam
Craik Moor
Comb Fell
Dunmoor Hill
Rubers Law
Mossburnford
Swinside Hall
Whitestone Hill
Cock Law
Mozie Law
Windy Gyle
Beefstand Hill
Loft Hill
Bloodybush Edge
Cushat Law
Shill Moor
High Knowes
Camptown
Woden Law
Blindburn
Barrowburn
Wether Cairn
Bonchester Bridge
Hobkirk
Chesters
Southdean
Upper Hindhope
Deerlee Knowe
Grindstone Law
Bell Hill
Shillmoor
Biddlestone
Field Study Centre
Green Law
Carter Bar
Redeswire Fray
Leap Hill
Hungry Law
DANGER AREA
Linshiels
Alwinton
Clennell
Harbottle
Holystone Forest Walks
Holystone
Lady's Well
Sharperton
Carlin Tooth
Fanna Hill
Needs Law
Catcleugh
Catcleugh Resr.
Byrness
Dour Hill
Hartshorn Pike
Girdle Fell
Ellis Crag
Kielderhead Moor
Lamblair Hill
Sills
North Yardhope
Peel Fell
Redesdale Camp
Rochester
Rushy Knowe
Saughtree
Deadwater
Forest Drive
Hindhope Law
Horsley
Blakeman's Law
Otterburn Camp
Elishaw
Otterburn Hall
Foulmire Heights
Emblehope Moor
Rooken Edge
Duchess Drive Walk
Kielder
Kielder Railway Viaduct
Butteryhaugh
Blackburn Common
Blakehope Fell
Otterburn
Elsdon
Earl's Seat
Padon Hill
Old Town
Raylees
Dinmont Lairs
Black Knowe
Highgreen Manor
Troughend Common
Lewisburn
Warksburn Forest Walk
Gatehouse
Falstone
Yarrow
Greenhaugh
West Woodburn
East Woodburn
Rough Pike
Stannersburn
North Tyne
Lanehead
A68
A6105
A697
A698
A699
A6088
A6089
A696
A6112
B6461
B6364
B6397
B6356
B6360
B6398
B6404
B6350
B6396
B6352
B6436
B6401
B6400
B6358
B6405
B6357
B6341
B6351
B6353
B6354
B6437
B6470
B6320
TOLL

HOLY ISLAND
Keel Head
Holy Island
Lindisfarne
Castle Point
Burrows Hole
FARNE ISLANDS
Longstone
Staple Sound
Inner Sound
Budle Bay
Bamburgh
Seahouses
Carr End
Beadnell
Beadnell Bay
Snook Point
Embleton Bay
Embleton
Dunstanburgh
Craster
Howick
Longhoughton
Boulmer
Lesbury
Alnmouth
Alnmouth Bay
Warkworth
Amble
Coquet Island
Hauxley Haven
Druridge Bay
Widdrington
Cresswell
Ellington
Lynemouth
ASHINGTON
Newbiggin-by-the-Sea
Beacon Point
MORPETH
Pegswood
Longhirst
Hebron
Mitford
ALNWICK
Denwick
Rennington
Ellingham
Lucker
Belford
Wooler
Chatton
Chillingham
Doddington
Lowick
Fenham
Beal
Haggerston
Berrington
Bowsden
Powburn
Glanton
Ingram
Whittingham
Edlingham
Eglingham
Shilbottle
Newton-on-the-Moor
Swarland
Felton
Longframlington
Rothbury
Thropton
Snitter
Longhorsley
Netherwitton
Hartburn
Cambo
Scots Gap
Rothley
HARWOOD FOREST
Fontburn Reservoir
NORTHUMBERLAND
Acklington
Togston
South Broomhill
Red Row
West Chevington
Ulgham
Tritlington
Widdrington Station
Linton Colliery
Bothal
Sheepwash
Stakeford
North Seaton
Woodhorn
A1
A697
A1068
A189
A197
A696
B6341
B6345
B6346
B6347
B6348
B6349
B6353
B1339
B1340
B1341
B1342
B1338
B1330
B1337
B6342
B6343
B6344

Eilean Garbh
Gamhna Gigha
West Tarbert Bay
East Tarbert Bay
ISLE OF GIGHA
Druimyeon Bay
Ardminish
Ardminish Bay
Achamore
Craro Island
Gigalum Island
Cara Island
Mull of Cara
A' Chleit
Sound of Gigha
Ballochroy
Rhunahaorine
Tayinloan
A83
Killean
Muasdale
Clachaig Water
Glenacardoch Point
Port a' Bhorrain
Glenbarr
Barr Glen
Amicle
Bellochantuy Bay
Bellochantuy
Port Corbert
Machrihanish Bay
Kilchenzie
Skeroblingarry
Machrihanish
CAMPBELTOWN
Campbeltown
B843
Drumlemble
Stewarton
Heritage Centre
Island Davaar
Mill Knowe
Earadale Point
Killypole Loch
Tirfergus Hill
The Slate
Cnoc Moy
Rubha Dùin Bhàin
Rubha' a' Mharaiche
Killellan
Homeston Farm Trail
Dalsmirren
Cnoc Odhar
Remuil Hill
A' Chruach
Glen Breackerie
Conieglen Water
B842
Beinn na Lice
Lephenstrath
Carskiey
High Keil
Southend
Feorlan
MULL OF KINTYRE
Port Mean
Rubha Chlachan
Brunerican Bay
Cove Point
Sheep Island
Black Point
Sanda Island
Achinhoan Head
Beinn Ghuilean
Balnabraid Glen
Chiscan Water
Kerran Hill
Feochaig
Johnston's Point
Tod Hill
Polliwilline Bay
Macharioch
Cnoc Mòr
ARGYLL & BUTE
KINTYRE
Cnoc Donn
Loch Ciaran
Fuar Larach
Loch Romain
Crossaig Glen
Crossaig
Easdairt Point
B842
Cour Bay
Cour
Loch Ulagadale
Carradale Water
Grogport
Cruach nan Gabhar
Cnoc nan Gabhar
Carradale
Port Righ
Carradale Point
Dippen
Torrisdale
Carradale Bay
Beinn Bhreac
Diollaid Mhor
Beinn an Tuirc
Blary Hill
Meall Buidhe
Bordadubh Water
Saddell Water
A'Chruach
Saddell Abbey
Saddell
Saddell Castle
Saddell Bay
Rubha nan Sgarbh
Lussa Loch
Sgreadan Hill
Tangy Loch
Ugadale
Ugadale Point
Black Bay
Glenlussa Water
Ardnacross Bay
Peninver
Auchalochy
KILBRANNAN SOUND
Whitefarland Point
Dougarie Point
Dougarie
Machrie Bay
Drumadoon Point
Drumadoon Bay
Brown Head
Rubha Airigh Bheirg
Rubha Creagan Dubha
Loch Ranza
Lochranza
Catacol
Isle of Arran Distillery
Torr Meadhonach
Torr Nead an Eoin
A841
Lenimore
Thundergay
Coire Fhionn Lochan
Pirnmill
Alltgobhlach
Beinn Bharrain
Loch Tanna
Caisteal Abhail
Cir Mhòr
Imachar
Sail Chalmadale
Beinn Tarsuinn
Beinn Lochain
Auchencar Burn
Auchagallon Stone Circle
Machrie
Moss Farm Road Stone Circle
Tormore
Machrie Moor Stone Circles
Ballymichael
Beinn Bhreac
Cnoc a' Chapuill
Shedog
Shiskine
Birchburn
North Feorline
South Feorline
Torbeg
Blackwaterfoot
Kilpatrick
Kilpatrick Dun
The Torr
Cnoc Reamhar
Glenree
Corriecravie
Bennecarrigan
Torr A' Chaisteal Fort
Sliddery
Lagg
Kilmory
Torrylin Cairn
Shannochie
B880
ISLE OF ARRAN
NORTH AYRSHIRE

123
126
116
Dunagoil Bay
Dunagoil
St. Blane's
Garroch Head
Little Cumbrae Island
Millstone Point
Arran
Gull Point
Little Cumbrae Castle
Hunterston Power Station
Hunterston Castle
University Marine Biological Station
The Tan
Campbelton
Portencross Castle
Farland Head
Ardneil Bay
Seamill
Southannan
Kaim Hill
Knockendon Resr.
Baidland Hill
Caaf Resr.
Auldmuir Resr.
Crosbie
Law Castle
West Kilbride
Munnoch Resr.
Dalry
NORTH AYRSHIRE
CUNNINGHAME
Beith
Glengarnock
Kilbirnie Loch
Longbar
Gateside
The Den
Drakemyre
Highfield
Auchenmade
Auchentiber
Dusk Water
Lylestone
Dalgarven
Mill Glen Reservoir
Ashgrove Loch
Kilwinning
Abbey
Montgreenan
Auchenharvie Castle
Torranyard
Eglinton
Doura
Cunninghamhead
Perceton
Girdle Toll
Stanecastle
Dreghorn
Springside
Cross
Gatehead
Irvine
Drybridge
Dundonald
Symington
FIRTH OF CLYDE
North Sannox
Sannox Bay
Sannox
Corrie
Glen Sannox
GOAT FELL
NTS
Brodick Castle
Glen Rosa
Glenrosa
Merkland Point
Brodick Bay
Brodick
Strathwhillan
Corrygills
Clauchlands Point
Meall Buidhe
Margnaheglish
Lamlash
Lamlash (Seasonal)
Monamore Br.
Cordon
Holy Island
Bay
Monamore
Urie Loch
Kingscross Point
Kingscross
Tighvein
Carn Ban
Knockenkelly
Whiting Bay
Whiting Bay
Glenashdale Falls
Largymore
Largymeanoch
Largybeg
Largybeg Point
Dippin
Dippin Head
Kilmory Water
Levencorroch
East Bennan
Kildonan
West Bennan
Bennan Head
Sound of Pladda
Pladda
Horse Isle
Ardrossan
North Ayrshire
Saltcoats
Stevenston
Ardrossan to Brodick 55mins.
R. Garnock
Irvine Mains
IRVINE
Magnum Beach Park
Irvine Bay
Barassie
Troon to: Belfast 2hrs. 30mins. (Fast Ferry) Larne 1hr. 50mins. (Fast Ferry)
Loans
Troon
Lady Isle
Monktonhill
Monkton
GLASGOW PRESTWICK
Prestwick
New Prestwick
Newton upon Ayr
St. Quivox
Whitletts
Dalmilling
Wallacetown
Newton Steeple
AYR
Wallace Tower
Seafield
Cunning Park
Greenan
Doonfoot
Belmont
Heads of Ayr
Heads of Ayr
Alloway
Brig O'Doon
Newark Castle
Doonholm
Fisherton
Dunure Castle
Dunure
Brown Carrick Hill
Carclute
Dalrymple
Culroy
Knockdon
Minishant
Cassillis House
Electric Brae
Knoweside
SOUTH
Culzean Bay
Culzean Castle
Whitefaulds
Maybole
Kirkmichael
Maidenhead Bay
Maidens
Turnberry
Crossraguel Abbey
Kilhenzie Castle
Kirkoswald
Souter Johnnie's Cottage
AYRSHIRE
Turnberry Bay
Turnberry
Crosshill
Blairquhan Castle
Matthew's Port
Ruglen
Kilkerran
Dipple
Wallacetown
Dalquharran Castle
Kilgrammie
Dailly
Glenalla Field
Ailsa Craig
Old Dailly
Killochan Castle
Bargany
Penkill
Hadyard Hill
Garleffin Fell
Girvan
Penkill Castle
Saugh Hill
Penwhapple Reservoir
Mull of Miljoan
Glendoune
Woodland Bay
Dalquhairn
Linfern Loch
Stinchar Falls
Black Hill
A78
A737
A71
A77
A759
A719
A841
A713
A70
B7048
B781
B780
B784
B777
B707
B778
B706
B785
B769
B730
B746
B749
B7024
B742
B7023
B7045
B741
B734
B7034

COLONSAY
Scalasaig
Glas Aird
Eilean a' Chladaich
Garvard
Eilean Leathann
Rubha Dubh
Loch Staosnaig
ORONSAY
Dubh Eilean
Eilean nan Ron
Eilean Ghaoideamal
Ceann Riobha
Colonsay to Port Askaig 1hr. 10mins.
Corpach Bay
Shian Bay
Rubh'an t-Sailein
Rubh' a' chrois-aoinidh
Post Rocks
RUBHA A'MHAIL
Rubha Bholsa
Nave Island
Eilean Beag
Ardnave Point
JURA
JURA FOREST
PAPS OF JURA
ARGYLL
ISLAY
Sound of Islay
Gortantaoid
Bunnahabhain
Sanaigmore
Kilnave
Braigo
Leckgruinart
Grulinbeg
Gruinart
Rubha Lamanais
Saligo Bay
Saligo
Coul Point
Machir Bay
Kilchoman
Conisby
Bruichladdich
Carraigo Dhubh
Blackrock
Carnain
Eallabus
Redhouses
Bridgend
Caol Ila
Port Askaig
Keills
Ballygrant
Kilmeny
Esknish
Feolin Ferry
Craighouse
Keils
Leargybreck
Knockrome
Ardfin
Cabrach
Jura House
Glas Eilean
Am Fraoch Eilean
Brosdale Island
Small Isles
Port na Birlinne
Rubha na Tràille
Na Cùiltean
Mc.Arthur's Head
Kennacraig to Port Askaig 2hrs.
Kilchiaran Bay
Kilchiaran
Octomore
Port Charlotte
Bowmore
Mulindry
Loch Indaal
Laggan
Laggan Point
Lossit
Lossit Bay
Neribus
Octofad
Port Gleann na Gaoidh
Portnahaven
Port Wemyss
Orsay
RHINNS POINT
RHINNS OF ISLAY
Laggan Bay
Torra
Glenegedale
Glenegedale Lots
ISLAY (Port Ellen)
Carraig Mhór
Ardtalla
Claggain Bay
Kintour
Ardmore Point
Eilean Craobhach
Eilean a' Chuirn
Eilean Bhride
Rubha na Gainmhich
Eilean Imersay
Kennacraig to Port Ellen 2hrs. 10mins.
Port Alsaig
Slugaide Glas
Dùn Mór Ghil
THE OA
Cragabus
Risabus
Lower Killeyan
Port Ellen
Lagavulin
Ardbeg
Laphroaig
Texa
MULL OF OA
Rubha na Meise Bàine
Rubha nan Leacan
A846
A847
B8016
B8017
B8018
132

125
Ardnoe Point
Ruadh Sgeir
Rubha nam Bàrr
Port nan Laogh
Lochanan Tana
Loch Fada Cul na Beinne
Beinn Bhreac 1532
Cruach an Uillt Fheàrna
Cruach Ionnastail
Maol nam Damh
Ardlussa
Ardlussa Bay
Loch Cathar nan Eun
Inverlussa
Lussagiven
Lussa Point
Gob Dubh
Eilean Dubh
Carsaig Bay
Eilean nan Coinean
Tarbert
Lagg
Keills
Keillmore
Barrahormid
Taynish
Tayvallich
Eilean Loain
Daltot
Dunrostan
Island of Danna
Sween
Ellary
Kilmory
Eilean Mor
St. Comac's
Bàgh na Dojde
Port Doir' a' Chrorain
An Dùnan
Skervuile
Point of Knap
Miller's Bay
Kilberry Head
Sculptured Stones
Kilberry
Port Mór
Carse House
Ardpatrick
Ardpatrick Point
Loch Stornoway
SOUND OF JURA
KNAPDALE
KNAPDALE FOREST
Crinan
Crinan Forest
Kilmahumaig
Bellanoch
Islandadd Bri.
Dunadd Fort
Moine Mhor
Cairnbaan
Cairnbaan Cup & Ring Marks
Achnabreck Cup & Ring Marks
Kilmichael Glassary
Bridgend
Lochgilphead
Kilmory Woodland Park
Port Ann
Castleton
Ardrishaig
Achnamara
Kilmichael of Inverlussa
Loch Coille-Bhar
Cruach Lusach 1530
Cruach Brenfield 1044
Inverneil House
Eilean Mór
Liath Eilean
Bàgh an Tailleir
Lochgair
Loch Gair
Otter Ferry
Largiemore
Clachan of Glendaruel
LOCH FYNE
Kilfinan
Kilfinan Bay
Port Leathan
Auchalick Bay
Ardmarnock Bay
Barmore Island
Melldalloch
Tighnabruaich
Kames
Auchenlochan
Millhouse
Portavadie
Kyles
Tarbert
East Loch Tarbert
West Tarbert
Tarbert Castle
Eilean Aoidhe
Asgog Bay
Kilbride Bay
Ardlamont House
Ardlamont Bay
Fionn Phort
Camas na Ceardaich
Rubha Leathan
Achahoish
Clachbreck
Baile Boidheach
Ormsary
Sliabh Gaoil 1843
Dubh Chreag 1574
Loch nan Torran
Cruach an Tailleir 1000
Torinturk
Dunmore
Whitehouse
Kennacraig
West Loch Tarbert
Portachoillan
Dunskeig Bay
Coeffin Castle
Ronachan Point
Clachan
An Dubh-sgeir
Gamhna Gigha
Eilean Garbh
West Tarbert Bay
East Tarbert Bay
ISLE OF GIGHA
Druimyeon Bay
Ardminish
Ardminish Bay
Achamore
Craro Island
Gigalum Island
Cara Island
Mull of Cara
Sound of Gigha
A' Chleit
Ballochroy
Rhunahaorine
Tayinloan
Killean
Muasdale
KINTYRE
Skipness
Skipness Point
Claonaig
Claonaig Bay
Eascairt Point
Crossaig
Cour
Cour Bay
Grogport
KILBRANNAN SOUND
Rubha Creagan Dubha
Cock of Arran
Lochranza
Catacol
South Newton
Isle of Arran Distillery
Rubha Airigh Bheirg
Lenimore
Thundergay
Pirnmill
Alltgobhlach
Whitefarland Point
ISLAND OF ARRAN
Imachar
Dougarie Point
Dougarie
Carradale
Port Righ
Carradale Point
Carradale Bay
Dippen
Torrisdale
Arnicle
Glenacardoch Point
Port a' Bhorrain
Glenbarr
Beinn an Tuirc 1490
Blary Hill 930
GOAT

126
133
134
125
123
116
A
B
C
D
1
2
3
4
5
A83
Strathlachlan
Lephinmore
Ainchapel
Garvie
Conchra
Glendaruel
Forest
Largiemore
Otter Ferry
Clachan of Glendaruel
Kilmodan Sculptured Stones
Balliemore
Loch Tarsan
Glenlean
Auchenbreck
Kilfinan
Craig Lodge
Melldalloch
Tighnabruaich
Kames
Auchenlochan
Millhouse
Portavadie
Port Driseach
Colintraive
Rhubodach
Altgaltraig
Coustonn
Iverchaolain
Glenstriven
Loch Striven
Kyles of Bute
Strone Point
Port Lamont
ISLAND OF BUTE
Glecknabae
St. Colmac
Port Bannatyne
Kames Castle
Wester Kames Castle
Kames Bay
Ardbeg
Ettrick Bay
Ballochgoy
ROTHESAY
Craigmore
Montford
Bogany Point
Ascog
Ascog House
Loch Ascog
Loch Fad
Loch Dhu
Kirk Dam
Straad
Chapel
Kerrycroy
Scoulag Point
Mount Stuart House & Pinetum
Mount Stuart
Meikle Kilchattan Butts
Kingarth
Kilchattan
Kilchattan Bay
Lake Quien
Ardscalpsie Point
Scalpsie Bay
Stravanan Bay
Dunagoil Bay
Dunagoil
St. Blane's
Garroch Head
Inchmarnock
SOUND OF BUTE
Ardlamont House
Ardlamont Bay
Ardlamont Point
Kilbride Bay
Asgog Bay
Eilean Aoidhe
Camas na Ceardaich
Rubha Leathan
Skipness Point
Rubha Creagan Dubha
Cock of Arran
Lochranza
Isle of Arran Distillery
South Newton
Millstone Point
North Sannox
Sannox Bay
Sannox
Corrie
ISLAND OF ARRAN
GOAT FELL
Caisteal Abhail
Cir Mhòr
Beinn Tarsuinn
Merkland Point
Brodick Castle
Glenrosa
Brodick Bay
Brodick
Strathwhillan
Ardrossan to Brodick 55mins.
FIRTH OF CLYDE
GREAT CUMBRAE ISLAND
Millport
Upper Kirkton
Mid Kirkton
The Tan
University Marine Biological Station
LITTLE CUMBRAE ISLAND
Gull Point
Hunterston Castle
Hunterston Power Station
Campbelton
Portencross Castle
Farland Head
Ardneil Bay
Seamill
Horse Isle
Ardrossan
Saltcoats
North Ayrshire
Stevenston
Kilwinning
IRVINE
Irvine Bay
West Kilbride
Law Castle
Dalry
Dalgarven
Crosbie
Fairlie
Fairlie Castle
Southannan
Largs
Skelmorlie Aisle
Kelburn Castle
Kilbirnie
NORTH AYRSHIRE
Skelmorlie
Skelmorlie Castle
Upper Skelmorlie
Wemyss Bay
Inverkip
Garvock
INVERCLYDE
Lunderston Bay
Cloch Point
Dunoon Castle
DUNOON
Castle House
Kirn
Hunter's Quay
Sandbank
Ardnadam
Holy Loch
Kilmun
Strone
Strone Point
Blairmore
Ardbeg
Rashfield
Gairletter
Invereck
Clachaig
Glenmassan
Ardentinny
Benmore Botanic Garden
Black Gates
Puck's Glen
Kilmun Trail & Arboretum
Glen Finart Deer Farm
Corlarach Forest
Bullwood
Innellan
Toward
Toward Castle
Toward Point
35 mins.
20 mins.
Gourock
Ashton
Fort Matilda
Midton
Larkfield
Braeside
Levan Castle
GREENOCK
Customs & Excise
Lillybank
Cornalees Bridge
Loch Thom
Kilcreggan
Rosneath Point
Cove
Peaton
Coulport
Clynder
Rosneath
Rhu
HELENSBURGH
Craigendoran
Shandon
Garelochhead
Portincaple
Auchenvennel
Edentaggart
Loch Long
Gare Loch
Loch Eck
Bernice
Beinn Mhòr
Creachan Mòr
Glen Finart
Ardyne
Stronchullin Hill
Benmore Forest
Hill of Stake
Muirshiel Country Park Visitor Centre
Queenside Loch
North Burnt Hill
Quarter
Ardnacraig
A8
A78
A737
A760
A815
A880
A885
A886
A8003
B8000
B836
B875
B878
B881
B896
B7048
B780
B781

127
135
117
SEE PAGE 189
SEE PAGE 190
STIRLING
WEST DUNBARTONSHIRE
EAST DUNBARTONSHIRE
RENFREWSHIRE
EAST RENFREWSHIRE
SOUTH LANARKSHIRE
EAST AYRSHIRE
LOCH LOMOND
Inchmurrin
Inchfad
Inchcailloch
Inchlonaig
Luss
Aldochlay
Balmaha
Milton
Drymen
Buchanan Smithy
Drymen Bridge
Gartness
Killearn Bridge
Balfron
Endrick Bridge
Boquhan
Buchlyvie
Kippen
Cauldhame
Gargunnock
Fintry
Killearn
Croftamie
Gartocharn
Arden
Dumfin
Auchendennan
Balloch
Alexandria
Renton
Cardross
Geilston
Bonhill
Dumbarton
PORT GLASGOW
Garadhban Forest
Carron Valley Forest
CAMPSIE FELLS
Earl's Seat 1897
Dumgoyne
Blanefield
Strathblane
Netherton
Clachan of Campsie
Lennoxtown
Milton of Campsie
Queenzieburn
KILSYTH
Banton
Croy
Twechar
Kirkintilloch
Lenzie
Torrance
Balgrochan
Birdston
Waterside
MILNGAVIE
Mugdock
Bardowie
Balmore
Cadder
BEARSDEN
Bishopbriggs
Duntocher
Old Kilpatrick
Erskine Bri.
Bowling
Milton
Woodhall
Langbank
Bishopton
Erskine
Rossland
Inchinnan
CLYDEBANK
RENFREW
Kilmacolm
Houston
Crosslee
Bridge of Weir
Linwood
Kilbarchan
Johnstone
Elderslie
PAISLEY
Howwood
Lochwinnoch
Barrhead
Neilston
Uplawmoor
Lugton
Dunlop
Stewarton
Fenwick
Kilmarnock
Kilmaurs
Crosshouse
Hurlford
Galston
Newmilns
Darvel
Greenholm
Priestland
GLASGOW
RUTHERGLEN
Cambuslang
Muirhead
Stepps
Chryston
Moodiesburn
Gartcosh
COATBRIDGE
Uddingston
Bothwell
HAMILTON
BOTHWELL
Viewpark
Bellshill
Blantyre
Carmunnock
Busby
Clarkston
Newton Mearns
Eaglesham
EAST KILBRIDE
Thorntonhall
Auldhouse
Chapelton
Strathaven
Glassford
Quarter
Limekilnburn
Drumclog
Waterside
Kingsford
Dunlop
Moscow
M8
M80
M73
M74
M77
A82
A80
A8
A77
A71
A737
A725

STIRLING
SEE PAGE 196
Gargunnock
Cambuskenneth
New Sauchie
Keilarsbrae
Carleatheran 1592
Gargunnock Hills
Touch Hills
Touch House
Cambusbarron
Gillies Hill
St. Ninians
Borestone Brae
Bannockburn
Fallin
ALLOA
Clackmannan
Kennet
Forest Mill
Balgonar
Saline
Steelend
Knock Hill 1194
Knockhill
Castle
Cowdenbeath
Blairhall
Carnock
Gowkhall
Comrie
Oakley
Milesmark
DUNFERMLINE
Devilla Forest
Peppermill Dam
Kincardine
Shires Mill
High Valleyfield
Newmills
Culross
Culross Palace
Low Valleyfield
Low Torry
Torryburn
Cairneyhill
Crombie
Charlestown
Torry Bay
Longannet Point
Kincardine Bridge
Airth
Airth Castle
Letham
Dunmore
The Pineapple
Cowie
Bruce's Tower
Plean
West Plean
Plean Tower
North Third Resr.
STIRLING
Milnholm
Earlsburn Resrs.
Earl's Hill 1442
Cringate Law 1301
Loch Walton
Carnoch Hill
Easter Buckieburn
Loch Coulter Resr.
Carron Valley Resr.
Carron Valley Forest
Carron Bridge
Fankerton
Dunipace
Denny
Torwood
Torwood Castle
Larbert
Stenhousemuir
Carronshore
Carron
South Broomage
Skinflats
GRANGEMOUTH
BO'NESS
Bo'ness & Kinneil
Grangepans
Carriden
Muirhouses
Blackness
Kinneil House
Bridgeness
Newtown
Borrowstoun
Oil Refinery
Head of Muir
Bonnybridge
Camelon
FALKIRK
Laurieston
Polmont
Redding
Reddingmuirhead
Glen Village
High Bonnybridge
Greenhill
Dennyloanhead
Longcroft
Banknock
Banton
High Banton
Castlecary
Tomtain
Kilsyth Hills
KILSYTH
Balmalloch
Colzium
Queenzieburn
Auchinstarry
Dullatur
Croy
Twechar
Bar Hill Fort
Cumbernauld Village
Balloch
CUMBERNAULD
Palacerigg
Abronhill
Condorrat
Westfield
Waterside
KIRKINTILLOCH
Moodiesburn
Mollinsburn
Chryston
Annathill
Muirhead
Greenfoot
Marnock
Glenboig
Glenmavis
Garnkirk
Gartcosh
Gartsherrie
COATBRIDGE
AIRDRIE
Thrashbush
Plains
Stand
Riggend
Luggiebank
Greengairs
Wattston
Longriggend
Fannyside Lochs
Slamannan
Binniehill
Avonbridge
Limerigg
Black Loch
Eastfield
Caldercruix
Hillend
Hillend Resr.
Lilly Loch
Forrestfield
Blackridge
Westrigg
NORTH
LANARKSHIRE
FALKIRK
Shieldhill
Brightons
Maddiston
California
Rumford
Standburn
Westfield
Linlithgow Bridge
Whitecross
Linlithgow
Kingscavil
Philpstoun
Bridgend
Burnside
Ecclesmachan
Uphall
Torphichen
Cairnpapple Hill
Beecraigs
Ballencrieff Toll
Wester Dechmont
Dechmont
BATHGATE
Boghall
Armadale
Windyknowe
Bathville
Whiteside
Deans
LIVINGSTON
Livingston Village
Seafield
Bellsquarry
Blackburn
Polbeth
Whitburn
East Whitburn
Harthill
HARTHILL
Eastfield
Forestburn Resr.
Stoneyburn
Bents
Addiewell
West Calder
Longridge
Loganlea
Fauldhouse
Greenburn
Breich
WEST LOTHIAN
Drumgelloch
Craigneuk
Coatdyke
Old Monkland
Calderbank
Chapelhall
Gartness
Roughrigg Resr.
Salsburgh
Kirk of Shotts
Hirst
Shotts
Dykehead
Torbothie
Stane
Hareshaw
Newhouse
Hartwood
Bowhousebog or Liquo
Allanbank
Allanton
Bonkle
Newmains
Morningside
WISHAW
Waterloo
Bogside
Wildmanbridge
Gair Reservoir
Law
Castlehill
Carluke
Yieldshields
Roadmeetings
Crawforddyke
Kilcadzow
Braidwood
Cobbinshaw Resr.
Hendreys Course
Woolfords
Tarbrax
Wilsontown
Braehead Moss
Rootpark
Haywood
Auchengray
Climpy
Forth
1029 Hare Hill
Springfield Resr.
Braehead
Bleak Law 1461
SOUTH LANARKSHIRE
Couthalley Castle
Carnwath
Anston
Dunsyre
Weston
Newbigging
Walston
Elsrickle
Kaimend
West End
Carstairs
Carstairs Junction
Ravenstruther
LANARK
Kirkfieldbank
Bankhead
New Lanark
Falls of Clyde
Corra Castle
Corra Linn
Hyndford Bridge
Pettinain
Libberton
Shieldhill
Candy Mill
Covington
Covington Castle
Quothquan
Thankerton
Biggar
Gasworks
Victorian Puppet Theatre
Boghall Castle
Coulter
Causewayend
Carmichael
Douglas Water
Rigside
Howgate Hill
Clyde Valley Woodlands
Cartland
Nemphlar
Hazelbank
Crossford
Craignethan
Nethanfoot
Netherburn
Roseburn
Ashgill
Swinhill
Dalserf
Overtown
Carfin
Newarthill
Holytown
New Stevenston
Mossend
Viewpark
Tannochside
Birkenshaw
Uddingston
Bothwell
BOTHWELL
Bellshill
Forgewood
Cleland
Parkside
Bellside
Cleekhimin
MOTHERWELL
Craigneuk
Colness
Cambusnethan
Shieldmuir
Netherton
HAMILTON
Flemington
Stonefield
Blantyre
High Blantyre
Udston
Fairhill
Meikle Earnock
Eddlewood
Cadzow
Chatelherault
Quarter
Larkhall
Millheugh
Machan
Limekilnburn
Chapelton
Glassford
Stonehouse
Udstonhead
Strathaven
Flemington
Sandford
Blackwood
Draffan
Auchenheath
Kirkmuirhill
Stonebyres
Black Hill Fort
Dillarburn
Boghead
Lesmahagow
Turfholm
Brocketsbrae
Auchlochan
Kype Muir
Kype Reservoir
Dunside Resr.
Hawkwood Hill
Logan Reservoir
Bellfield
CLYDESDALE
Calderglen
HARTHILL
M9
M80
M876
M73
M8
M74
A80
A8
A71
A725
A876
A985
A702
A9
A88
A803
A872
A905
A904
A706
A705
A70
A72
A73
A721
A723
A726
A779
A89
A800
A907
A977
A994
B9124
B818
B802
B8048
B8054
B803
B825
B8022
B8028
B7066
B7057
B7015
B7010
B715
B7056
B7078
B7086
B7018
B7016
B903
B9080
B8046
B792
B8084
B8010
B799
B7070
B914
B913
A 135
B 136
C
D
A 117
B 118
C
D
1
2
3
4
5

129
EDINBURGH
SEE PAGE 189
FIRTH OF FORTH
MIDLOTHIAN
PENTLAND HILLS
MOORFOOT HILLS
SCOTTISH BORDERS
LAMMERMUIR UPLANDS
SOUTHERN UPLANDS
Kelty
Cardenden
Lochgelly
Dysart
KIRKCALDY
Cowdenbeath
Lumphinnans
Auchtertool
Linktown
Kinghorn
Pettycur
Burntisland
Aberdour
Dalgety Bay
Inverkeithing
Rosyth
Inchcolm
Inchkeith
Inchmickery
North Queensferry
Forth Road Bridge
Forth Bridge
Queensferry
Dalmeny
Cramond Island
Rosyth to Zeebrugge 17hrs. 30mins.
Newhaven
Leith
Granton
Portobello
Joppa
MUSSELBURGH
Prestonpans
Cockenzie and Port Seton
Longniddry
Aberlady
Aberlady Bay
Gullane Bay
Gosford Bay
Eyebrough
Tranent
Macmerry
Ormiston
Pencaitland
Dalkeith
Loanhead
Lasswade
Bonnyrigg
Newtongrange
Gorebridge
Pathhead
Penicuik
Roslin
Rosewell
Currie
Balerno
Ratho
Kirkliston
Broxburn
Newbridge
Carlops
West Linton
Dolphinton
Eddleston
Peebles
Innerleithen
Walkerburn
Stow
Heriot
Skirling
Broughton
Kirknewton
Mid Calder
East Calder
Leadburn
Howgate
Temple
Fala
Humbie
Gilston
Clovenfords
Glentress Forest
Cardrona Forest
Elibank and Traquair
Scottish Mining Museum
Royal Highland Showground
Blackhope Scar 2137
Windlestraw Law 2163
Dun Law 1691
Mendick Hill 1481
Black Mount 1692
Torfichen Hill 1510
Portmore Loch
Gladhouse Resr.
Rosebery Reservoir
M8
M9
M90
A1
A68
A702
A720
A7
A72

130
137
129
119
120
A
B
C
D
Fidra
Craigleith
Bass Rock Castle
Bass Rock
Scottish Seabird Centre
North Berwick
Lamb
Eyebroughy
North Berwick
Tantallon
Dirleton Castle
Dirleton
Gullane Bay
North Berwick Law
613
Gullane
Aberlady Bay
Saltcoats Castle
Fenton Barns
Kingston
Fentons Tower
Whitekirk
Waughton Castle
Aberlady
Luffness Castle
Myreton Motor
Drem
Tyninghame
John Muir
Dunbar Castle
Dunbar
Craigielaw
East Fortune Flight
Preston
Knowes
West Barns
Belhaven
Broxburn
Barns Ness
Gosford Bay
Gosford House
Ballencrieff
Chesters Fort
Athelstaneford
Spittal
Camptoun
East Linton
Mill NTS
Seton
Longniddry
Hopetoun Monument
Barnes Castle
Garleton Hills
Hailes
Phantassie NTS Doocot
Pitcox
Spott
Dunbar 1650
Pinkerton
East Barns
Skateraw
Torness Power Station
Thorntonloch
Huntington
Elvingston
Meadowmill
Haddington
Stevenson House
Stenton Gallery
Stenton
Luggate Burn
Doonhill Homestead
Brunt Hill
Tranent
Gladsmuir
St. Martin's Kirk
Whittingehame Castle
Papple
Innerwick
Reed Point
Cove
Pease Bay
Forest Walk
Siccar
Macmerry
Penston
Lennoxlove House
Morham
Whitelaw Hill
Colstoun House
Garvald
Cocklaw Hill
Cockburnspath
Oldhamstocks
New Winton
New Town
Samuelston
Bolton
Nunraw Abbey
Church
Pencaitland
Dunbar Common
Clints Dod
Bransly Hill
EAST LOTHIAN
White Castle Fort
Monynut Edge
West Saltoun
East Saltoun
Gifford
Yester Castle
Heart Law
Blackburn Rig
Peastonbank
Spartleton Edge
Bothwell Water
Grantshouse
Gilchriston
Longyester
Peaston
LAMMER MUIR
Whiteadder Resr.
Humbie
Fala Dam
Meikle Says Law
Lammer Law
Hopes Resr.
Stobshiel Resr.
Cranshaws
Cranshaws Hill
Abbey St. Bathans
Abbey & Trout Farm
Fala
Crib Law
Ellemford
Edin's Hall Broch
Cakemuir Castle
Mutiny Stones
Whitchester
Fala Moor
Hunt Law
LAMMERMUIR UPLANDS
Blythe Edge
Dye Water
Longformacus
Preston
Cumledge Mill
Edrom Norman Arch
Millburn Bridge
Watch Water Resr.
Gilston
Carfrae
Hogs Law
Dirrington Great Law
SCOTTISH
Manderston House
Duns
Oxton
Addinston
Dirrington Little Law
SOUTHERN
Cleekhimin Bridge
Edgarhope Wood
Scoured Rig
Gavinton
Nisbet Hill
Collie Law
LAUDERDALE
Westruther
Polwarth
BORDERS
Border Country Life
Fountainhall
Thirlestane
Halliburton
Fogo
Heriot's Dyke
Fogorig
Lauder
Houndslow
Greenlaw
Killochyett
Dod's Corse Stone
Bassendean
Charterhall
MERSE
Stow
Nether Blainslie
Greenknowe Tower
Gordon
Leithholm
Ledgerwood
Huntlywood
Gordon Moss
Lambden
Hume
Eccles
Great Law
William Law
Fans
Carolside
Langshaw
Sweethope Hill
Birgham
Dundock Wood
Knowes Hill
Buckholm
Earlston
Mellerstain House
Stichill
Carham
Galashiels
Newton Don House
Nenthorn
Ednam
James Thomson Obelisk
Clovenfords
Meigle Hill
Redpath
Smailholm
Kelso
Hadden
Wooden
Lowood
Gattonside
Ashiestiel
Leader Water
Whiteadder Water
Eden Water
Lugate Water
Soonhope Burn
R. Tweed
A1
A68
A198
A6137
A199
A6093
A6105
A697
A6089
A6112
A1107
A7
A72
A698
B1345
B1347
B1377
B1343
B6363
B6368
B6369
B6355
B6371
B6457
B6370
B6362
B6456
B6460
B6364
B6365
B6438
B6461
B6397
B6374
B6360
B6356
B6350

E
F
G
H
90
400
10
20
1
2
3
4
5
80
70
60
650
40
NORTH SEA
Fast Castle Head
Point
Fast Castle
Telegraph Hill
Lumsdaine
Cross Law 744
Coldingham Moor
ST. ABB'S HEAD
NTS
St. Abbs
Lifeboat Station
Coldingham Bay
Coldingham
Priory
Lifeboat Station
Buss Craig
Eyemouth
Gunsgreenhill
A1107
B6438
Houndwood
Eye Water
859
Horseley Hill
Reston
Ayton
Burnmouth
Ross
Auchencrow
B6437
B6355
Chirnside
Edrom
Chirnside-bridge
Lamberton
Old Toll House
Marshall Meadows
Clappers
Halidon Hill
Foulden
Tithe Barn
Whiteadder Water
Hutton
1333
A1
Highfields
Scottish Borders
BERWICK-UPON-TWEED
Allanton
Hutton
B6460
Paxton
B6461
Tweed Walk
Tweedmouth
Spittal
Whitsome
Church
Fishwick
Union Bridge
Loanend
R. Tweed
East Ord
A6105
A1167
Redshin Cove
Scremerston
Horncliffe
Horndean
Church
Norham
Ladykirk
Norham
Murton
Thornton
B6354
B6470
Swinton
Railway
Shoreswood
Shoresdean
West Allerdean
Cheswick
Goswick
Simprim
Upsettlington
B6525
Grindon
Ancroft
Haggerston
Felkington
Berrington Law
Berrington
Beal
Twizel Bridge
Chapel
Duddo
Duddo Tower
Bowsden
A1
LINDISFARNE
HOLY ISLAND
Keel Head
Holy Island
Priory
NT Lindisfarne
Castle Point
Burrows Hole
Fenham
Castle Heaton
NORTHUMBERLAND
Lennel
Coldstream
Melkington
Cornhill-on-Tweed
A698
A697
Heatherslaw Light Rlwy.
Etal
B6353
West Kyloe
Fenwick
121
Barmoor
Lowick
East Kyloe
Wark
Pallinsburn House
Crookham
Waterford Hall
Kyloe Hills
Buckton
FARNE ISLANDS
West Learmouth
Barelees
East Learmouth
Branxton
Mill
Ford
Elwick
Ross
Staple Sound
1513 Flodden Field
B6525
Holburn
Detchant
Budle Bay
Pressen
Flodden
St. Cuthbert's Cave NT
Middleton
Hetton
Waren
Bamburgh
Bamburgh
Inner

132
139
124
124
A
B
C
D
1
2
3
4
5
ISLAND OF MULL
BEN MORE
3171
Gribun
Erisgeir
1837 Coirc Bheinn
Corra-bheinn 2311
2502 Beinn Talaidh
Sgurr Dearg 2429
Lochan an Doire Dharaich
Oakbank
Loch Bearnach
Strathcoil
Castle
Carn B 812
Glen More
Lussa River
Loch Sguabain
Loch Airdeglais
2290 Creach Beinn
Ben Buie 2354
Kinlochspelve
Loch Spelve
Croggan
Lochbuie
Moy Castle
Loch Uisg
Loch Buie
Loch an t-sithein
1329 Druim Fada
Coladoir River
Loch Fuaran
Beinn na Croise 1649
Bein na Srèine
Gleann Seilisdeir
B8035
ARDMEANACH
1613 Creach Bheinn
Burg NTS
Tavool House
Tiroran
Kilfinichen Bay
Loch Scridain
Rubha na h Uamha
Fossil Tree NTS
Port na Croise
Pennyghael
Glen Leidle
A849
Rubha an Cearc
Garbh Phort
Kintra
Creich
Aridhglas
Loch Poit na h-I
Eorabus
Loch na Lathaich
Knockan
Bun an Leoib
Ardchrishnish
Angora Rabbit Farm
Bunessan
Beinn a Ghlinne Mhoir
Ross of Mull Historical Centre
ROSS OF MULL
Loch Assopol
Knockvologan
Ardalanish
Uisken
Ardchiavaig
Beinn a Chaol-Airigh 411
Ardalanish Bay
Rubh' Ardalanish
BROLASS
Beach River
Cruachan Min 1232
1235 Beinn Chreagach
River
Carsaig
Carsaig Bay
Carsaig Arches
Malcolm's Point
Aoineadh Mòr
Rubha nam Bràithrean
Frank Lockwood's Island
Easda
FIRTH OF LORN
Dubh-fheith
Garbh Eileach
Belnahua
Fladda
Garvellachs
Eilean Dubh Mór
Monastery
Eileach an Naoimh
Lunga
Guirasdeal
Sound of Luing
Oban to Colonsay 2hrs 20mins.
Kilmory Lodge
Rubha nam Faoilean
1474 Cruach Scarba
SCARBA
Gulf of Corryvreckan
Réidh Eilean
Eilean Annraidh
Rubha nan Cearc
IONA
Abbey
Maclean's Cross
Iona Heritage
NTS
Baile Mór
Sound of Iona
Fionnphort
Columba Centre
Stac an Aoineidh
Eilean nah-Aon Chaorach
Fidden
Greave
Soa Island
Erraid
Eilean nam Muc
Eilean a' Chalmain
Port na Cuilce
Kiloran Bay
Balnahard
468 Carnan Eoin
Uragaig
Loch an Sgoltaire
Port Ceann a' Gharraidh
Kiloran
Colonsay House
B8086
B8087
COLONSAY
Port a' Bhàta
Sgreadan
Kilchattan
Loch Fada
Glas Aird
Scalasaig
Loch Staosnaig
Eilean a' Chladaich
Colonsay
B8085
Eilean Leathann
Garvard
Rubha Dubh
Dubh Eilean
ORONSAY
Eilean nan Ron
Eilean Ghaoideamal
Cadas Mòr
Ceann Riobha
Colonsay to Port Askaig 1hr 10mins
Glengarrisdale Bay
619 An Cruachan
Cruach na Seilcheig 971
Loch na Conaire
Loch Doire na h-Achlaise
Loch a Bhurra
Rubh' a' Bhacain
Glendebadel Bay
Ben Garrisdale 1198
Loch a' Gheoidh
Lochanan Tana
Loch Fada Cul na Beinne
Port nan Laogh
Ruadh Sgeir
967 Cruach Ionnastail
Corpach Bay
Beinn Bhreac 1532
1106 Cruach an Uillt Fheàrna
Lussa River
Lealt
Dubh Bheinn
Allt an Tairbh
Fishing Loch
Maol nam Damh 887
Ardlussa
Ardlussa Bay
Shian Bay
1487 Rainberg Mór
Shian River
Loch Cathar nan Eun
Inverlussa
Lussagiven
Lussa Point
Eilean Dubh
Carsaig Bay
Eilean nan Coinean
Loch an Tuim Uaine
Loch Righ Mor
Loch Fad'a Chruib
Gob Dubh
Caves
Loch Righ Beag
Loch na Caime
Cruib 1036
Loch Lùbanach
622 Beinn Sgaillinish
A846
JURA
Barrahormid
B8025
Rubh'an t-Sailein
Loch Tarbert
Tarbert
Rubh' a' chrois-aoinidh
Post Rocks
RUBHA A'MHAIL
Cnoc an Ime 927
Keills
Keillmore
Loch na Cille
Rubha Bholsa
Allt na Gile
Loch an Aircill
Glen Batrick
1439 Beinn Bhreac
Loch Lesgamaill
Lagg
Sweep
Island of Danna
Cnoc Stighseir 792
1195 Sgarbh Breac
Loch Smigeadail
965 Sgarbh Dubh
Loch an Oir
Beinn an Oir
Loch na Fudarlaich
Port Doir' a' Chrorain
SOUND OF JURA
Bàgh na Dojde
Eilean Mor

133
Musdile
Lochdon
Connel
Dunstaffnage
Dunbeg
Ganavan
Achaleven
Stonefield
Bonawe
Glennoe
Oban to Craignure 45mins.
Oban to Lismore
Eilean nan Gramhna
Dunollie Castle
R. C. Cath.
McCaig's Tower
War & Peace
OBAN
SEE PAGE 195
Oban Rare Breeds Farm Park
Oban Distillery
Caithness Glass
Taynuilt
Airds Bay
Bonawe Iron Furnace
Inverawe Smokery
BEN CRUACHAN
3695
Grass Point
KERRERA
Balliemore
Pulpit Hill
Dalintart
Carn Breugach
Gylen Castle
Deadh Croimhead
1257
Airdeny
Barguillean's Angus
Glen Nant
Bridge of Awe
River Awe
Pass of Brander
Cruachan Reservoir
Beinn a' Bhuiridh
2941
Falls of Cruachan
Lochawe
Kilchurn
Cruachan Power Station
Bach Island
Dubh Sgeir
Rubha Seanach
Kilbride
Loch Nell
Cleigh
Kilmore
Glenfeochan
1691 Beinn Ghlas
Loch Tromlee
Ardanaiseig
Fraoch Eilean Castle
Minard Point
Sior Loch
Abhainn Cam Linne
Loch Nant
Kilchrenan
Annat
North Port
Portsonachan
Cladich
Kilninver
Salmon Centre
1208 A' Chruach
689 Beinn Mhor
Eilean Dùin
Insh Island
Clachan Bridge
Loch Scammadale
Bragleenbeg
1690 Beinn Chapull
South Port
Upper Sonachan
Clachan-Seil
An Cala
Ellanbeich
Easdale
Balvicar
SEIL
Ardmaddy Castle
Carn Dearg 1436
Braglenmore
Abhainn Fionain
Inverinan Glen
Inverinan
1804 Beinn Ghlas
876 Cruach Rarey
Braes of Lorn
Meall Odhar 1255
Cuan
Pass of Melfort
Melfort
Loch Tralaig
Loch Dubh-mor
Loch a' Phearsain
1239 Cruach Maolachy
Lochavich
Tom an t-Saighdeir 993
Loch Avich
Tullich
Loch Dubh
1932 Cruach Mhòr
Cullipool
Torsa
Dun Crutagain 895
An Coire
Kilmelford
Avich Falls
Dalavich Oakwood
Dalavich
Innis Chonnell Castle
Ardchonnell
Portinnisherrich
Loch an Eilean Dubh
Loch nan Car
Three Bridges
Dubh Loch
Carloonan
Malt Lane
Melfort
Loch Melfort
LUING
Rubh' a' Chnaip
Arduaine
Loch an Losgainn Mòr
Loch an Daimh 1199
Tom Soilleir
1610 Carn Duchara
Lochan a' Bhruic
Timber
Forest
Eredine
Beinn Bhreac 1726
Lochan Long
Inveraray
Inveraray Castle
Bell Tower
Inveraray Jail
St. Catherines
Toberonochy
Shuna
Shuna Sound
Craobh Haven
Barravullin
A R G Y L L
Inverliever
Inverliever Lodge
Durran
Braevallich
Eredine Forest
1687 An Suidhe
Douglas Water
Am Buachaille 1060
Argyll
549 Sorobà Hill
Ardfern
1148 Cruach an Eachlaich
Achnagoul
Kintraw
Fincharn Castle
Fincharn
Fincharn Loch
Loch Leachd
Lochan Gaineamhach
1583 Beinn Deargh
Creagan an Eich 1070
Loch Fada
Loch Mhic Mhairtein
Eilean Mhic Chrion
Creag Mhòr 745
Ford
Loch Ederline
Loch Geoidh
Loch Leacann
Auchindrain
Township Open Air
Creggans
Eilean Ona
Craignish Castle
Eilean Righ
Carnassarie
Loch nan Ceard Mòr
Cruach Mhic Fhionnlaidh 1503
1179 Dun Leacainn
Strachur Bay
Clachan Strachur
Rèisa Mhic Phaidean
Aird
Loch Gaineamhach
1339 Sidh Mòr
Furnace
Tombuidhe
Smiddy
Glensluain
Island Mcaskin
Glebe Cairn
Kilmartin House
Nether Largie Cairns
Kilmartin
Sculptured Stones
Lochan Leathan
Lochan Anama
1378 Beinn Ghlas
Crarae
Leachd
Newton
Rèisa an t-Sruith
Slockavullin
Temple Wood Stone Circles
Ballygowan Cup & Ring Marks
Ri Cruin Cairn
Dunchraigaig Cairn
Baluachraig Cup & Ring Marks
KILMICHAEL FOREST
Crarae NTS
Minard Forest
Blackmill Loch
Minard
Castle Lachlan
Tullochgorm
Lachan Bay
1577 Cruach nan Capull
Glenbranter
Lauder
Garbh Rèisa
Rubha Garbh-ard
Duntrune Castle
Killinochonoch
758 Dun Dubh
Strathlachlan
Forest
Loch Crinan
Crinan
Ardnoe Point
Crinan Forest
Kilmahumaig
Islandadd Bri.
Bellanoch
Dunadd Fort
Moine Mhor
Kilmichael Glassary
Bridgend
Cup & Ring Marks
Loch Glashan
Cairnbaan Cup & Ring Marks
Lephinmore
1666 Crauch an Lochain
2029 Beinn Bheag
Rubha nam Bàrr
Cnoc Reamhar 870
KNAPDALE
Loch Linne
Cairnbaan
Achnabreck Cup & Ring Marks
Scotston Hill 698
Lochgair
Loch Gair
Lephinchapel
Garvie
Strath nan-Lub
Beinn Mhòr 2432
Bernice
Loch Coille-Bharr
FOREST
Loch an Add
Gleann Loch
Cam Loch
Loch Clachaig
Lochgilphead
Kilmory Woodland Park
Lochan Chuilceachan
Cruach Chuilceachan 1428
Conchra
Meall Dubh 2103
Glenmassan
Tayvallich
Achnamara
Loch nam Breac Buidhe
1071 Cruach nam Fiadh
Kilmichael of Inverlussa
Ardrishaig
Loch Gilp
Port Ann
Largiemore
Glendaruel Forest
An Socach 1345
Benmore Botanic Garden
Eilean Loain
Taynish
Daltot
Cruach Lusach
Loch na Craige Grainde 1530
Cruach Brenfield 1044
Castleton
Eilean Mór
Liath Eilean
Otter Ferry
679 Tom na h-Iolaire
Clachan of Glendaruel
Kilmodan Sculptured Stones
1416 Cruach nan Cuilean
Balliemore
Sgorach Mòr 1972
Glenlean
Invereck
Inverneill House
Cruach 1144 nan Tarbh
Auchenbreck
Clachaig
Dunrostan
1247 An Stuchd
Bàgh an Tailleir
507 Barr Ganuisg
1503 Cruach nan Caorach
2005 Cruach nan Capull
Loch Fuar-Bheinne
Kilfinan
Kilfinan Bay
Craig Lodge
Beinn Bhreac 1488
Loch na Leirg
Glenstriven
St. Columba's Cave
Achahoish
1564 Cruach a' Phubuill
Port Leathan
Beinn Bhreac 1662
Ellary
Clachbreck
Loch Awe
Loch Fyne
Loch Etive
Loch Riddon
Loch Eck
COWAL
A85
A816
A819
A83
A815
A886
A8003
B845
B840
B8003
B844
B8002
B8025
B841
B8024
B8000
B836
140
141
125
126
134
E F G H
1 2 3 4 5

134
141
133
126
126
A
B
C
D
1
2
3
4
5
Liver
Glennoe
Mhic-Mhonaidh 2602
Beinn Udlaidh 2759
Beinn Bhreac-liath 2633
2948 Beinn Odhar
Beinn Cheathaich 3076
3007 Meall a' Churain
3242 Beinn Eunaich
Beinn Donachain 2127
Ben Challum 3354
Beinn nan Imirean 2769
3695
Glen Strae
River Strae
Glen Orchy
River Lochy
Lochan na Bi
Clifton
Tyndrum
A82
B R E A
Cruachan Reservoir
Beinn a' Bhuiridh 2941
Kilchurn
B8077
Stronmilchan
Edendonich
Beinn na Sròine
Achnafalnich
B8074
A85
Cononish
Strath Fillan
Lochdochart House
Glen
Loch Lubhair
A85
Falls of Cruachan
Lochawe
Kinchrackine
Dalmally
Duncan Ban MacIntyre Monument
Cruachan Power Station
Ardanaiseig
Fraoch Eilean Castle
A819
Teatle
Water
Beinn Bhalgairean 2085
Eas a' Ghaill
3708 Ben Lui
3204 Beinn Dubhchraig
2132 Fiarach
Loch Dochart
A82
Crianlarich
BEN MORE
3852
3821 Stob Binnein
Meall nan Tighearn 2423
Cladich
Fearna River
Allt an Stacain
Lochan Shira
Dubh Eas
Allt Fionn Ghlinne
River Falloch
Glen Falloch
Falls of Falloch
Upper Sonachan
B840
Lochan Sron Mor
Beinn Bhuidhe 3112
Troisgeach 2407
Allt Arnan
Ben Glas
3099 Beinn Tulaichean
Monachyle
Braes
Inverarnan
Beinn Chroin 3084
Inverlochlarig
Loch Doine
1804 Beinn Ghlas
Rob Roy's House
Brannie Burn
Lairige Reservoir
River Fyne
Glen Fyne
Stob a' Choin 2839
Tullich
Stuc Scardan 1599
2159 Clachan Hill
Glenfyne Lodge
Maol Breac 2115
Ardlui
LOCH LOMOND AND THE TR
Beinn Bhreac
Eagle's Falls
BEN VORLICH
3093
NATIONAL PARK
Cruinn Bheinn 1787
Three Bridges
Kilblaan Burn
A83
Clachan Farm
837 Barr Mor
Loch Sloy
Dubh Loch
Carloonan
Cairndow
Binnein an Fhidhleir
Inveruglas Water
Inversnaid
Stronachlachar
Loch Katrine
Ardkinglas Woodland
Glen Kinglas
3004 Ben Vane
(Seasonal)
Inveraray
Dunderave Castle
A815
3318
Inveruglas
Inversnaid
Loch Arklet
B829
Loch Shira
Beinn an Lochain
BEINN IME
Loch Ard Forest
Inveraray Jail
Bell Tower
2401 Stob an Eas
Rest and be thankful
B828
PARK
1762 Cruachan
Laglingarten
B839
2891 Ben Arthur
Cruach Tairbeirt 1362
Frenich
Loch Tinker
A83
St. Catherines
ARGYLL
Succoth
Argyll
1854 Cruach nan Capull
Tarbet
Arrochar
Cruinn a' Bheinn 2077
Loch Chon
1675 Beinn Dubh
Ben Donich 2777
Glen Croe Forest
A83
A814
B838
Creagan an Eich 1070
Mullach Coire a' Chuir 2098
Ardgartan
FOREST &
Ardgartan
Ardmay
3194 BEN LOMOND
Kinlochard
Creggans
The Brack
A82
Clachan Strachur
Strachur Bay
Rob Roy's Cave
Lochgoilhead
Glen Donich
Cnoc Coinnich 2497
Beinn Bhreac 2233
Duchray Water
Tombuidhe
Smiddy
Glensluain
A886
2306 Beinn Lochain
Curra Lochain
2556 Beinn Bheula
Lochain nan Cnaimh
QUEEN ELIZABETH FOREST PAR
Beinn Uird 1957
Rowardennan
LOCH ARD
1577 Cruach nan Capull
Glenbranter
Lauder
A815
Douglas Water
Doune Hill 2408
Inverbeg
Loch Lomond
Rowardennan Forest
The Saddle 1704
BUTE
Craigbrack
Carrick Castle
1435 Clach Beinn
Beinn Eich 2302
Beinn a' Mhanaich 2328
Edentaggart
Inchlonaig
Luss
1514 Gualann
2029 Beinn Bheag
Cruach a' Bhuic 2084
Portincaple
Beinn Chaorach 2339
DANGER AREA
Aldochlay
Inchfad
Balmaha
Conic Hill 1175
Creachan Mòr 2156
Bernice
Beinn Mhòr 2432
Garelochhead
Beinn Ruisg 1946
Inchcailloch
Garadhban
Milton
B837
Meall Dubh 2103
Lochan Ghlas Laoigh
Greenfield
A817
Buchanan Smithy
Drymen Bridge
Glenmassan
Beinn Ruadh 2178
Glen Finart Deer Farm
Ardentinny
Coulport
Auchenvennel
Kilmaronock Tower
Inchmurrin
Inchmurrin Castle
Gartocharn
Younger Botanic Garden
Black Gates
1798 Stronchullin Hill
Benmore Forest
Peaton
Shandon
Glen Fruin
Sgorach
Loch Tarsan
Balliemore
Puck's Glen
Gairletter
Clynder
Callendoun
Dumfin
B831
Arden
Caldarvan Loch
Glenlean
Rashfield
B836
Ardbeg
Kilmun Trail & Arboretum
Linn Botanic Gardens
Rosneath
Rhu
Glenarn
The Hill House
NTS
B832
Auchendennan
Balloch Castle
Blairquhanan
Inverneck
Clachaig
Blairmore
Strone
Kilmun
Holy Loch
Cove
Cove Bay
Cove Conservation Park
HELENSBURGH
Craigendoran
Balloch
Mill of Haldane
Auchencarroch
Jamestown
DANGER AREA
Strone Point
Alexandria
Motoring Memories
Sandbank
Ardnadam
Kilcreggan
Rosneath Point
Bonhill
A82
2005 Cruach nan Capull
Hunter's Quay
Conwal Bird Garden
Fort Matilda
Gourock
Ashton
Geilston
Renton
Cardross
A814
A812
A813
Castlehill
Glenstriven
DUNOON
Castle House
Dunoon Castle
Kirn
Cloch Point
Kempock Stone
Customs & Excise
GREENOCK
Newark
PORT
Brucehill
Dumbarton Castle
Townend
DUMBARTON
Silverton
Black Linn Res.
Levan
Larkfield
Midton
A770
A78
A8
20 mins
30 mins

135
142
143
136
127
128
E
F
G
H
1
2
3
4
5
Killin
Finlarig Castle
Breadalbane Folklore
Falls of Dochart
Creag Mhòr
2359
Falls of Lochay
Auchnafree
Meall Reamhar
2188
Newton Bridge
Meall Tarsuinn
2901 Creag Gharbh
Lochan Breaclaich
2883 Creag Uchdag
Loch Lednock Reservoir
Ben Chonzie
3048
Auchnafree Hill
2589
Glen Almond
River Almond
Luib
Ardchyle
Glen Dochart
2312 Beinn Leabhain
Glen Ogle
Sròn Mhòr
2203
Glen Tarken
Loch Boltachan
Spout Rolla
Invergeldie
Carn Chois
Loch Turret Reservoir
Glen Turret
Shaggie Burn
Meall a' Mhadaidh
A85
St. Fillans
PERTH
&
KINROSS
Monzie
Monzie Castle
Gilmerton
Lochearnhead
Loch Earn
Edinample Castle
Ardvorlich
Falls of Edinample
Dunira
Deil's Cauldron
Melville
Comrie
Fordie
Clathick
Ochtertyre Castle
Loch Monzievaird
Hosh
Crieff
Glenturret Distillery
Tomakne
2794 Meall an t-Seallaidh
Rob Roy's Grave
Balquhidder
Auchtubh
A84
Kingshouse
2225 Meall Reamhar
Ben Halton
2033
Drummond Trout Farm
Aberuchill Castle
Ross
Earthquake House
Dalginross
Cultybraggan Camp
B827
Lochlane
Balloch
Stuart Crystal
Dargill
B8062
Loch Voil
Bygones
STRATHYRE FOREST
3231
BEN VORLICH
FOREST OF GLENARTNEY
Dalchruin
Water of Ruchill
Glen Artney
Auchingarrich
Culloch
Tullum
1291
Torlum Wood
Drummond Castle
Muthill
Bishop's Bridge
Ochtermuthill
Machany Water
Ballimore
Strathyre
QUEEN ELIZABETH FOREST PARK
TROSSACHS
Lochan a' Chroin
2660 Beinn Each
2066 Meall Odhar
DANGER AREA
1748 Ben Clach
Coire Odhar
Glen Finglas
Benvane
2685
Ardchullarie
Loch Lubnaig
2072 Creag Beinn nan Eun
Findhu Glen
Glenlichorn
Meall Cala
2212
2181 Uamh Bheag
Cromlet
Knaik
Braco Castle
Ardoch Roman Fort
Blackhall Camps
B827
Carsebreck Loch
Loch Rhynd
Allan Water
Blackford
Braco
Glen Finglas Reservoir
BEN LEDI
2882
Meall Gainmheich
1851
Leny
Falls of Leny
Pass of Leny
Rob Roy & Trossachs
Bracklinn Falls
Keltie Water
Slymaback
Bullie Burn
Mackie Burn
Greenloaning
A822
STRATHALLAN
Braes
Ben An
Brig o' Turk
Lendrick
Kilmahog
Callander
Hamilton Toy
A84
Loch Mahaick
Braes of Doune
B8033
A9
Kinbuck
Core Hill
1780
Loch Achray
Loch Drunkie
Lake Ballock
Loch Venachar
A821
Achray Forest Drive
ACHRAY FOREST
Menteith Hills
1396 Beinn Dearg
Torrie Forest
Drumvaich
Ardoch Burn
Ashfield
Burn of Cambus
Buchany
Deanston
Doune Ponds
Doune
Cathedral
A820
Dunblane
Pisgah
Sheriffmuir
1715
Sheriff Muir
2073 Blairdenon Hill
Queen Elizabeth Forest Park
Highland Boundary Fault Trail
Milton
Aberfoyle
Braeval
Doon Hill
Scottish Wool
Lemahamish
Duchray Castle
Loch Rusky
Dunaverig Farmlife Centre
B822
B8032
Muir Dam
Port of Menteith
Inchmahome Priory
Lake of Menteith
Ruskie
Goodie Water
Flanders Moss
A873
Thornhill
B826
Loch Watson
Blair Drummond
Blair Drummond Safari Park
Sunnylaw
Bridge of Allan
University
Menstrie
Alva
Tullibody
A91
Cunninghame Graham Memorial
FOREST
Drum of Clashmore
Gartmore
Kelty Water
B829
B8034
Dykehead
River Forth
B8031
B8075
Blairdrummond Moss
Drip Moss
Blairlogie
Memorial
Old Bridge
Causewayhead
Cambuskenneth
Cambus
King o' Muirs
Craigmill
A907
Raploch
STIRLING
SEE PAGE 196
Arnprior
B835
B8037
Kippen
Cauldhame
Gargunnock
Buchlyvie
A811
Loch Laggan
Mill Dam
B822
Carleatheran
1592
Gargunnock Hills
Touch House
Touch Hills
Cambusbarron
Gillies Hill
Robert the Bruce Statue
St. Ninians
Bannockburn
Borestone Brae
Fallin
Throsk
Alloa Tower
South Alloa
Drymen
Endrick Bridge
Killearn Bridge
Balfron
Boquhan
Gartness
1678 Stronend
Cringate Law
1301
Earlsburn Resrs.
Earl's Hill
1442
North Third Resr.
STIRLING
Cowie
Dunmore
Bruce's Tower
The Pineapple
B9124
Croftamie
A809
Killearn
George Buchanan Monument
B818
Fintry Hills
Loch Walton
Fintry
Milnholm
West Plean
Plean
Plean Tower
M9
Earl's Seat
1897
Endrick Water
Leap of Fintry
Cairnoch Hill
1356
Easter Buckieburn
Loch Coulter Resr.
M80
Torwood
Torwood Castle
M876
Dumgoyne
Glengoyne Distillery
CAMPSIE FELLS
Blane Water
Strathblane Hills
Carron Valley Resr.
Carron Valley Forest
Carron Bridge
Fankerton
Dunipace
Stenhousemuir
Larbert
South Broomage
The Whangie
Auchineden Hill
1172
Duntreath Castle
EAST
Birkenburn Resr.
1487 Tomtain
Denny
Head of Muir
Bonnybridge
Falkirk Wheel
Antonine Wall
Camelon
Burncrooks Resr.
Blanefield
Strathblane
Netherton
Clachan of Campsie
Kilsyth Hills
High Banton
Banton
Dennyloanhead
Longcroft
High Bonnybridge
Greenhill
FALKIRK
Craigallian Loch
Craigend Castle
Mugdock Castle
Mugdock
Craigmaddie Castle
DUNBARTONSHIRE
Lennoxtown
Milton of Campsie
Queenzieburn
KILSYTH
Colzium
Balmalloch
Castlecary
Castlecary Fort
A80
Dullatur
Auchinstarry
Cumbernauld Village
Croy
Kelvin
Greenside
MILNGAVIE
Glen Village
A811
A81
A875
A891
A803
M9
M80
A9
A905
B9124
B8023

137
HALLYBURTON FOREST
Muirhead
Fowlis
Liff
Birkhill
Balmuir
Downfield
Whitfield
Fintry
Barry
Carnoustie
A90
A923
A930
B961
A92
Barnhill
Monifieth
DANGER AREA
Knapp
Benvie
Lochee
Cragie
Broughty Castle
Abernyte
144
145
SEE PAGE 188
DUNDEE
Broughty Ferry
BUDDON NESS
Invergowrie
Longforgan
Kingoodie
Kinnaird
Inchture
Craigdallie
Tay Road Bridge
Tay Bridge
Tay Rail Bridge
Newport-on-Tay
B946
Tayport
Tentsmuir Point
A92
Westown
Rait
Grange
GOWRIE
Woodhaven
Wormit
Morton Lochs
Inchmichael
Megginch Castle
Station Heritage Centre
Seaside
TENTSMUIR FOREST
Tentsmuir Sands
Balmerino
Kirkton
Bottomcraig
Balmerino Abbey
Pickletillem
North Muirie
Errol Station
Errol
Muiredge
CARSE OF
FIRTH
OF
TAY
Gauldry
Cruivie Castle
Motray Water
Lucklawhill
Hazelton Walls
Kilmany
Leuchars
Earlshall Castle
Balmullo
Brunton
Creich
Rathillet
Forret Hill
Logie
Ballinbreich Castle
Norman's Law
Luthrie
Kedlock Feus
Inner Bridge
Guardbridge
Eden Mouth
ST. ANDREW'S BAY
Eden Estuary
Lindores Abbey
Pitcullo Castle
Kincaple
British Golf
Sea Life Aquarium
St. Andrews
Cathedral
Glenduckie
Den of Lindores
Mount Pleasant
Dunbog
Moonzie
Dairsie or Osnaburgh
Strathkinness
Buddo Ness
Lindores
Grange of Lindores
Lindores Loch
Collairnie Castle
Mount Hill
Kilmaron
Kilmaron Castle
Foodieash
A913
A91
Cupar
Blebocraigs
Kemback
Newpark
Botanic Garden
Craigtoun Miniature Railway
Monimail
Letham
Sir Douglas Bader Disabled
Boarhills
Collessie
Bow of Fife
Cupar Muir
B940
Denhead
Craigtoun
Prior Muir
Bonnytown
Kingsbarns
Pitscottie
Bridgend
Hill of Tarvit
Ceres
Baldinnie
Cameron Reservoir
Cameron Burn
Stravithie
Cambo
Fife Ness Muir
Giffordtown
Innerleith
Springfield
Scottish Deer Centre
Fife Animal Park
Myres Castle
Dunshalt
Ladybank
Craigrothie
Scotstarvit
Radernie
Dunino
Craighead
FIFE NESS
HOWE OF FIFE
Pitlessie
Cults
Chance Inn
Struthers Castle
Bankhead Moss
Peat Inn
Backmuir of New Gilston
B940
West Lingo
Pittarthie Castle
Lochty
Kingsmuir
West Quarry Braes
Kilminning Coast
Falkland Palace
Newton of Falkland
Kingskettle
Balmalcolm
Clatto Resr.
Woodside
Lathones
Largoward
Scotland's Secret Bunker
Crail
Tolbooth
Falkland
Kettlebridge
Clatto Hill
Freuchie
Montrave
Praytis Farm Park
Largo Law
Kellie Law
Carnbee
East Pitcorthie
West Pitcorthie
Muirhead
Kirkforthar Feus
Langdyke
Carlhurlie Resr.
Pitcruvie Castle
Kellie
Arncroach
Kilrenny
Scottish Fisheries
Holl Resr.
Collydean
Baintown
Star
Glenrothes Standing Stones
Kirkton of Largo or Upper Largo
Charleton House
Colinsburgh
B942
Anstruther Wester
Anstruther Easter
Leslie
Cadham
Kennoway
Bonnybank
Letham Green
Abercrombie
Kilconquhar Castle
Kilconquhar
Pittenweem
Strathendry Castle
Markinch
Balgonie
Balcurvie
Broom
Lundin Links
Lower Largo
Drumeldrie
St. Fillan's
St. Monans
Walkerton
GLENROTHES
Milton of Balgonie
Windygates
Scoonie
Leven
Kilconquhar Loch
Newark Castle
Ardross Castle
Largo Bay
Ruddons Point
Earlsferry
Elie
Sauchar Point
Chapel Ness
Innerleven
Heritage Centre
Methilhill
Denbeath
Methil
Coaltown of Balgonie
Thornton
Buckhaven
Dogton Stone
Ore Bridge
Wemyss
Macduff's Castle
East Wemyss
Coaltown of Wemyss
Wemyss Castle
West Wemyss
Cluny
FIRTH OF FORTH
Gallatown
Chapel
Templehall
Sinclairtown
Dysart
Ravenscraig
Pathhead
KIRKCALDY
Beveridge Park
Balwearie Castle
Linktown
129
130
Pitteadie Castle
Seafield Tower
Kinghorn
Pettycur
Alexander III
Burntisland
Craigleith
Bass Rock Castle
Bass Rock
Fidra
Scottish Seabird Centre
Lamb
North Berwick
Eyebroughy
Tantallon
Dirleton Castle
Dirleton
North Berwick Law
Gullane Bay
Gullane
Inchkeith
Aberlady Bay
Saltcoats Castle
Fenton Barns
Kingston
Fentons Tower
EAST LOTHIAN
Whitekirk
Waughton Castle
Luffness Castle
Aberlady
Myreton Motor
Drem
Tyninghame
Rosyth to Zeebrugge 17hrs. 30mins.
Craigielaw
Gosford House
Gosford Bay
Chesters Fort
Ballencrieff
Athelstaneford
East Fortune
Flight
Preston
Knowes
Spittal
Camptoun
East Linton
Newhaven
EDINBURGH
Trinity
Leith
A199
Cockenzie and Port Seton
Longniddry
Hopetoun Monument
Barnes Castle
Garleton Hills
A1
Phantassie Doocot
Hailes
Pitcox
Prestonpans
Huntington

A
B
C
D
1
2
3
4
5
100
10
20
30
80
70
60
750
40
Oban to Lochboisdale 5hrs.
Oban to Castlebay 5hrs.
Cairns of Coll
Eag na Maoile
Eilean Mór
Rubha Mór
Bousd
Cornaigmore
Sorisdale
Rubh'a' Bhinnein
Loch Fada
COLL
B8072
Cliad Bay
Grishipoll
Rubha Hogh
Clabhach
B8071
Loch Cliad
340 Ben Hogh
Hogh Bay
Bagh Feisdlum
Arinagour
Loch nan Cinneachan
Totronald
Loch Anlaimh
Loch Eatharna
Eilean Ornsay
Feall Bay
Coll
Uig
Acha
B8070
Breachacha Castle
Port na h-Eathar
Calgary Point
Caolas Ban
Crossapol Bay
Loch Breachacha
Friesland Bay
Gunna
Soa
Gunna Sound
Port a' Mhurain
Coll to Tiree 1hr. 10mins.
Miodar
Carnan
Vaul Bay
Salum
Caolas
Rubha Dubh
Vaul
Ruaig
Loch Riaghain
B8069
Kirkapol
Gott
Gott Bay
Hough Skerries
Balephetrish Bay
Balephetrish
Cornaigmore
Sraid Ruadh
Balevullin
Kilmoluaig
Cornaigbeg
B8068
Hough
Kenovay
Tiree
Scarinish
Baugh
Heanish
Rubha Tràigh an Duin
Kilkenneth
Loch an Eilein
B8065
Moss
Sandaig
Heylipol
Middleton
Barrapol
Crossapol
Port Mor
Thatched House
Port Bharrapool
Loch a' Phuill
B8067
Hynish Bay
TIREE
Balephuil
Balemartine
Mannal
Balephuil Bay
West Hynish
Hynish
Signal Tower
Port Snoig
INNER HEBRIDES
Treshnish
Cairn na Burgh Beg
Treshnish Isles
Fladda
Lunga
Bac Mor or Dutchman's Cap
Bac Beag
NTS
Eilean Annraidh
Réidh Eilean
Rubha nan Cea

139
Sgeir Eskernish
Sound of Eigg
Galmisdale
Rubha na Crannaig
Eilean Chathastail
Eigg to Muck 45mins
Eilean nan Each
Gòdag
146
MUCK
Port Mor
Dubh Sgeir
Rubh' Arisaig
Eilean a' Ghaill
Eilean an t-Snidhe
Sound of Arisaig
Eilean nan Gobhar
Glen Cottage
Druimindarroch
Loch Nam Uamh Cairn
Polnish
Camas Ghaoideil
Loch nan Uamh
Roshven
Samalaman Island
Glenuig Bay
Samalaman
Smirisary
Glenuig
Loch na Bairness
Lochan na Cloiche Sgoilte
A861
Rubh' Aird an Fheidh
Eilean Shona
Baramore
Arean
Tioram Castle
Kinlochmoidart
Ardmolich
Seven Men of Moidart
Brunery
M O I
Rubha Aird Druimnich
Ockle Point
Port Bàn
Farquhar's Point
Newton of Ardtoe
Ardtoe
Kilmory
Ockle
Fascadale
Sanna Point
Sanna
Sanna Bay
Achateny
Branault
Beinn Bhraec 1171
Gortenfern
Shielfoot
Blain
Dalnabreck
Langal
Kentra
Kentra Bay
Arivegaig
Shiel Br.
Mingarrypark
Acharacle
Moss
Ardshealach
Achnaha
Meall nan Con 1433
Point of Ardnamurchan
Ardnamurchan Point
Portuairk
Achosnich
A R D N A M U R C H A N
Gorteneorn
Loch Caorach
Beinn Na Seilg 1123
B8007
Loch Mudle
1026 Beinn nan Losgann
Leac Shoilleir
Lochan Sligneach
Meall nan Each 1607
Salen
Salen Woods
Resipole
Ormsaigmore
Ormsaigbeg
Kilchoan
Mingary
Mingary Castle
An Acairseid
Kilchoan Bay
1731 Ben Hiant
Lochan nam Fiann
Loch Laga
Ben Laga 1679
Cladh Chiaran Chambered Cairn
Glenmore
Glenbeg
Ardnamurchan Natural History Centre
Glenborrodale
Glenborrodale Castle
Ardslignish
B8007
Maclean's Nose
50mins. (Seasonal)
Coll to Oban 2hrs. 45mins.
35mins.
Risga
Laga
Carna
Loch Sunart
Laudale House
Glencripesdale
Meall an Damhain 1693
Ardmore Bay
Ardmore Point
Oronsay
Auliston Point
Rubha nan Gall
Quinish Point
Glengorm Castle
Meall an Inbhire 865
Tobermory
Mull
Ardmore
Tobermory Distillery
Calve Island
140
H I G H L A N D
1873 Beinn Iadain
Kinloch
Teacuis
Caliach Point
Croig
Loch an Torr
959 'S Airde Beinn
B8073
Loch Peallach
A848
Drimnin
B849
Beinn Bhuidhe 1481
Rahoy Hills
Lochanan Dubha
Beinn na h-Uamha
Loch Doire nam Mart
M O R V E R N
Dervaig
Loch a' Chumhainn
Calgary
Calgary Bay
Old Byre Heritage
866 Cruachan Druim na Croise
A R O S
Sound of Mull
1806 Sìthean na Raplaich
Loch Arienas
Rhemore
Killundine
Claggan
Point
Ensay
1122 Carn Mor
Speinne Mòr 1458
Lettermore
Salen Forest
Ardnacross
Loch Frisa
Kengharair
River Bellart
Saisteal nan Con
Fiunary Forest
Larachbeg
Kinlochaline Castle
Achranich
Ardtornish Estate
Haunn
Kilninian
Burg
Fiunary
Tenga
Aros River
Rubh' a' Chaoil
Achleck
1280 Cnoc an da Chinn
Fanmore
Cranich
Aros Mains
Aros Castle
B849
Lochaline
Loch Aline
A884
Glais Bheinn 1570
A R G Y L L
Loch Tuath
Ballygown
Beinn na Drise 1392
Rubha Mòr
Mull
Eilean Dioghlum
Gometra
Gometra House
Eas Fors
B8073
Salen
A849
Fishnish Bay
Fishnish
Ardtornish Castle
Inninmore Bay
Lagganulva
Killiechronan
B8035
Ballemeonach
Garmony
Beinn Chreagach 1026
Laggan Bay
Oskamull
Kellan
Gruline
Loch na Dairidh
Beinn Bhuidhe 1352
Beinn Chreagach Mhòr 1903
Scallastle Bay
U L V A
Ulva House
Sound of Ulva
&
Macquarie Mausoleum Monument
Màisgeir
Eilean na Creiche
Eorsa
Loch na Keal
Knock
I S L A N D
Craignure Bay
Craignure
Little Colonsay
Samalan Island
Beinn a' Ghràig 1939
Tomsléibhe
2512 Dùn da Ghaoithe
Staffa
Fingal's Cave NTS
Inch Kenneth
Inch Kenneth
Derryguaig
B8035
B U T E
O F
2502 Beinn Talaidh
Sgurr Dearg 2429
Glen Cannel
Lochan an Doire Dharaich
Torosay Castle
Gribun
BEN MORE 3171
Erisgeir
1837 Coirc Bheinn
Corra-bheinn 2311
Oakbank
M U L L
Lussa River
Loch Beamach
Bein na Srèine 1704
Gleann Seilisdeir
Loch Squabain
Strathcoil
Castle
1613 Creach Bheinn
132
B8035
ARDMEANACH
Coladoir River
A849
Loch Airdeglais
Carn Bàn 812
Rubha na h Uamha
Fossil Tree NTS
Burg NTS
Tavool House
Tiroran
Kilfinichen Bay
Loch Scridain
Port na Croise
Ben Buie 2354
2290 Creach Beinn
Kinlochspelve
Loch Spelve
Croggan
Loch Fuaran
Pennyghael
Beinn na Croise
Lochbuie
Garbh Phort
Loch

140
Rubh' Arisaig
Eilean a' Ghaill
Eilean an t-Snidhe
Sound of Arisaig
Eilean nan Gobhar
Glen Cottage
Druimindarroch
Loch Nam Uamh Cairn
Polnish
Loch na Creige Duibhe
Creag Bhàn
Slios Garbh
Glas-charn 2076
Sgurr an Utha 2610
Lochailort
Loch Eilt
Ranochan
A830
Glenfinnan
Station
Viaduct
The Jacobite
Glenfinnan NTS
Dubh Lighe
Loch nan Uamh
Loch Doir a' Ghearrain
Peanmeanach
Inverailort
Loch Ailort
A861
147
Roshven
Samalaman Island
Glenuig Bay
Samalaman
Smirisary
Loch na Bairness
Glenuig
ROIS-BHEINN 2895
Druim Fiaclach 2852
2178 Croit Bheinn
2895 Beinn Odhar Bheag
Sgurr Dhomhnuill Mòr
Beinn Gaire 2179
Lochan na Cloiche Sgoilte
River Moidart
Loch Shiel
Sgor Craobh a' Chaorainn
Glen Garvan
Meall nan Creag Leac
Rubh' Aird an Fheidh
Eilean Shona
Baramore
Arean
MOIDART
Loch nam Paitean
Kinlochmoidart
Scamodale
Tioram Castle
Loch Moidart
Seven Men of Moidart
Ardmolich
Brunery
Gaskan
Sgor an Tarmachain 2474
Lochan Dubh
Cona Glen
Cona River
Druim Leathad nam Fias 1893
Farquhar's Point
Newton of Ardtoe
Ardtoe
Ockle
Beinn Bhraec 1171
Gortenfern
Kentra Bay
Kentra
Arivegaig
Shielfoot
Blain
Dalnabreck
Langal
Mingarrypark
Dalelia
Shiel Br.
Acharacle
Moss
Polloch
Glen Hurich
River Hurich
Glenhurich
Loch Doilet
Glenhurich Forest
2579 Beinn Mheadhoin
Sgurr Dhomhnuill
River Scaddle
Glen Scaddle
Gorteneorn
ARDNAMURCHAN
Ardshealach
SUNART
ARDGOUR
Lochan na Beinne Bàine
Leac Shoilleir
Lochan Sligneach
Meall nan Each 1607
Lochan nam Fiann
Loch Laga
Ben Laga 1679
Salen
Salen Woods
Resipole
2775 Beinn Resipol
Ariundle
Scotstown
Anaheilt
Strontian River
Glen Gour
River Gour
Glenmore
Glenbeg
Glenborrodale
Ardnamurchan Natural History Centre
Ardslignish
B8007
Loch Sunart
Ardery
Ardery Wood
Ardnastang
Strontian
Ariundle
Kilcamb Wood
Garbh Bheinn 2903
Glen Tarbert
River Tarbert
Inversanda
Inversanda Bay
Risga
Carna
Oronsay
Laga
Laudale House
1693 Meall an Damhain
Glencripesdale
A884
1911 Beinn nam Beathrach
2798 Creach Bheinn
B8043
Bun Allt na Criche
Rubha Mor
Cuil Bay
139
Kinloch
Teacuis
1873 Beinn Iadain
Lochuisge
Loch Uisge
2511 Fuar Bheinn
Kilmalieu
Camas Chil-Mhalieu
Eilean Balnagowan
Drimnin
Beinn Bhuidhe 1481
Rahoy Hills
Lochanan Dubha
1569 Beinn Chlaonleud
Bheinn na Cille 2136
Kingairloch
Camasnacroise
Loch a' Choire
Dalnatrat
MORVERN
Loch Doire nam Mart
1806 Sithean na Raplaich
Beinn na h-Uamha
Beitheach
Beinn Mheadhoin 2423
KINGAIRLOCH
LINNHE
Rhemore
Killundine
Loch Arienas
Claggan
Gleann Geal
Camas Airigh Shamhraidh
Shuna Island
Castle Shuna
Appin House
Glen Stockdale
Beinn Donn 1553
Caisteal Nan Con
Sound of Mull
Funary
Forest
Fiunary
Larachbeg
Kinlochaline Castle
Achranich
Ardtornish Estate
Loch Tearnait
Beinn a' Chaisil 1431
Glensanda Castle
Glensanda
Port a' Chaisteil
Eilean nan Caorach
Portnacroish
Castle Stalker
Kinlochlaich
Appin
Strath of Appin
Rannoch River
Loch nan Clach
Eilean Loch Oscair
Port Ramsay
Port Appin
Drumneil House
Aros Mains
Aros Castle
B849
Lochaline
Glais Bheinn 1570
Lochan Mam a' Chullaich
1684 An Sleaghach
Eignaig
Rubha Mór
Salen
A848
A849
B8035
Fishnish Bay
Fishnish
15 mins
Ardtornish Castle
Inninmore Bay
Camas Gorn
LISMORE
Clachan
Balliveolan
Killandrist
Eriska
North Shian
Seal & Marine Centre
Loch Creran
Barcaldine
Loch na Dairidh
Beinn Bhuidhe 1352
Bailemeonach
Garmony
Salen Forest
Beinn Chreagach Mhòr 1903
RUBHA AN RIDIRE
Bernera Island
Achadun Castle
Achinduin
Kilcheran
Barr Mor
Achnacroish
B8045
Baravullin
Park
A828
Loch Mor
Benderloch
Ledaig
BENDERLOCH
ISLAND OF MULL
Tomsleibhe
Scallastle Bay
Craignure
Craignure Bay
Mull Railway
A849
2512 Dun da Ghaoithe
Duart Bay
Duart Point
Duart
Torosay Castle
Eilean Musdile
Loch Fiart
Creag Island
Eilean Dubh
Pladda Island
Camas Nathais
Ardmucknish Bay
Rubha Garbh-àird
Kiel Crofts
South Ledaig
North Connel
Falls of Lora
Black Crofts
Connel
Ardchattan Priory
Dunstaffnage
Loch Etive
Glen Cannel
2502 Beinn Talaidh
Sgurr Dearg 2429
Lochan an Doire Dharaich
Lochdon
Oakbank
Dunbeg
Achaleven
Stonefield
Corra-bheinn 2311
Oban to Craignure 45mins.
Oban to Lismore 50mins.
Ganavan
Dunollie Castle
A85
ARGYLL
Lusragan Burn
Black Lochs
Fearnoch Forest
Loch Beamach
Loch Don
Grass Point
Eilean nan Gramhna
R.C. Cath.
War & Peace
McCaig's Tower
OBAN
SEE PAGE 195
Oban Rare Breeds Farm Park
Strathcoil
Loch Squabain
Lussa River
Glen More
132
Castle
Carn Ban 812
Caithness
Oban Distillery
Dalintart
Pulpit Hill
133
Beinn Croimhead 1257
Coladoir River
Loch Airdeglais
2290 Creach Beinn
Ben Buie 2354
Kinlochspelve
Loch Spelve
Croggan
KERRERA
Balliemore
Carn Breugach
Gylen Castle
Sound of Kerrera
Loch Seil
A816
Glen Lonan
Loch Nell
Kilbride
Cleigh
Kilmore
1691 Beinn Ghlas
Loch Fuaran
Beinn Croise
Lochbuie
Bach Island
Dubh
Rubha Seanach

141
148
149
142
134
Kinlocheil
Corribeg
Fassfern
Achdalieu
A830
Corpach
Banavie
Caol
Lochyside
Inverlochy
Claggan
FORT WILLIAM
Loch Eil
South Garvan
Duisky
A861
Blaich
Achaphubuil
Camusnagaul
Trislaig
Stronchreggan
Achintore
Ach an Todhair
Druimarbin
Blarmachfoldach
Conaglen
Inverscaddle Bay
A82
Ardgour
Clovullin
Corran
Bunree
Inchree
Onich
Sallachan Point
North Ballachulish
Ballachulish
South Ballachulish
Glencoe
Bridge of Coe
Kentallen
Duror
Achindarroch
Glenduror Forest
Creran Forest
Elleric
Fasnacloich
Invercreran
Creagan
South Creagan
Gairlochy
Stronenaba
B8004
Brackletter
Spean Bridge
A86
Inverroy
Highbridge
Roybridge
Bohenie
Achluachrach
Tulloch
Bunroy
Glen Spean
Fersit
Torlundy
Creag Aoil
Leanachan Forest
Killiechonate Forest
Stob Choire Claurigh 3858
Aonach Beag 4048
BEN NEVIS 4406
Stob Coire Easain 3658
Loch Treig
Creaguaineach Lodge
Mamore Forest
Binnein Mòr 3700
Sgurr a' Mhàim 3601
Mullach nan Coirean
Kinlochmore
Kinlochleven
Blackwater Reservoir
Loch Eilde Mòr
Leum Uilleim 2971
Altnafeadh
Kingshouse
White Corries
Black Corries
A' Chruach
Rannoch Moor
Clachaig
The Three Sisters
Bidean nam Bian 3766
Royal Forest
Buachaille Etive Mòr
Dalness
Glen Etive
Inverchaorain
Gualachulain
Black Mount
Loch Tulla
Victoria Bri.
Bridge of Orchy
Achallader
Beinn Dorain 3524
Loch Etive
Inveresragan
Inverliver
Glennoe
Craig
Bonawe
Taynuilt
Ichrachan
Airdeny
Bridge of Awe
Ben Cruachan
Lochawe
Kilchurn
Stronmilchan
Edendonich
Dalmally
Tyndrum
Clifton
A85
A82
Lorn
Argyll & Bute

142
A
B
C
D
149
A86
Moy Forest
Moy Lodge
Binnein Shuas
Lochan na h-Earba
Ardverikie Forest
Beinn Eilde
Beinn a' Chaorainn
3437
2160
Creag Dhubh
Loch Laggan Resr.
Lochan an Tuirc
Loch a' Bhealaich Leamhain
3443
Geal Charn
Meall Cruaidh
2941
Loch Ericht Forest
2522
Creagan Mòr
3087
Carn na Caim
Loch an Duin
Meall Luidh Mòr
Fersit
Allt Loraich
Allt Cam
3569
Beinn a' Chlachair
Loch Pattack
Ben Alder Lodge
3005
Geal-Charn
A' Bhuidheanach Bheag
3072
Sronphadruig Lodge
2422
An Torc or Boar of Badenoch
Pass of Drumochter
3037
Glas Mheall Mòr
F O R E S T
A9
Dalnacardoch Forest
3391
Càrn Dearg
1
H I G H L A N D
Loch Treig
Loch Ghuilbinn
Chno Dearg
3433
3647
Aonach Beag
Loch An Sgòir
Ben Alder Forest
Loch Ericht
3174
Beinn Udlamain
3306
The Sow of Atholl
Dalnaspidal Lodge
Edendon Water
A T
3765
Ben Alder
Loch a' Bhealaich Bheithe
Corrievarkie Lodge
Coire Sgàin
Loch Na Lap
River Ossian
Beinn na Lap
Uisge Labhair
Corrour Shooting Lodge
Loch Ossian
G L E N
22
2544
Meall na Leitreach
Loch Garry
Dalnacardoch Lodge
2805
Stob an Aonaich Mhòir
Corrour
Forest
3124
Sgor Gaibhre
Talla Bheith Forest
Allt Glaise
Loch na Sgeallaig
Carn Dearg
3080
Rannoch Forest
Beinn Mholach
2759
Loch Con
Allt Sleibh
Loch Errochty
Trinafour
2
2971
Leum Uilleim
Craiganour Forest
Allt Ruighe nan Saorach
B847
Sròn Bheag
1631
Loch Mheugaidh
Loch na Caillich
2927
Beinn a' Chuallaich
Allt na Caim
Allt Eigheach
Lochan Sròn Smeur
Lochan Lòin nan Donnlaich
Reservoir
Black Water
Killichonan Burn
Aulich Burn
Craiganour Lodge
B846
Kinloch Rannoch
Dunalastair
Bridge of Ericht
Killichonan
16
Loch Rannoch
Stob na Cruaiche
2423
141
A' CHRUACH
Rannoch Station
Loch Eigheach
B846
River Gaur
Bridge of Gaur
Finnart
Loch Finnart
Camghouran
Black Wood of Rannoch
Rannoch School
Carie
Rannoch Forest
Tempar
Dunalastair Water
3
Loch Laidon
Rannoch Moor
Loch Monaghan
TAY FOREST PARK
Innerhadden Burn
3554
Schiehallion
Lochan Coire na Mèinne
R A N N O C H
M O O R
R A N N O C H
G R A M P I A N
3419
Carn Mairg
3377
Carn Gorm
Meall a' Mhuic
2444
Loch Ba
750
A82
3054
Meall Buidhe
2823
Carn Chreag
Meall Cruinn
2717
Camusvrachan
Innerwick
Glen Lyon
Invervar
Carnane Castle
River Lyon
Bridge of Lyon
MOUNT
Tulla
Bridge of Balgie
Loch an Daimh
Eas Daimh
Meggernie Castle
Gallin
Glen Lyon
4
Achallader
Achallader Castle
3540
Beinn a' Chreachain
3404
Beinn Achaladair
Meall Buidhe
3144
Stuchd an Lochain
Meall Luaidhe
2558
Meall Garbh
3661
Lochan nan Cat
BEN LAWERS
3984
NTS
Lawers Burn
A827
Loch Tay
Boreland
Beinn an Dothaidh
3267
3125
Beinn Mhanach
Loch Lyon
Cashlie
Stronuich Reservoir
Lairig Breisleich
Lochan na Lairige
Ben Lawers NTS
Lawers
Meall Odhar
Ardtainaig
Bridge of Orchy
3524
Beinn Dorain
Sgiath Bhuidhe
3410
Meall Ghaordie
Meall Taurnie
3421
Meall nan Tarmachan
Beinn Heasgarnich
3530
Kenknock
Glen Lochay
Carie
Tullich Hill
Milton Morenish
Ardeonaig
3387
Creag Mhòr
Forest of Mamlorn
River Lochay
Falls of Lochay
Moirlanich Longhouse
Morenish
5
2948
Beinn Odhar
Creag Mhòr
2359
Finlarig Castle
Breadalbane Folklore
Killin
Falls of Dochart
Finglen Burn
A82
Ben Challum
3354
Beinn Cheathaich
3076
3007
Meall a' Churain
Beinn nan Imirean
2769
2901
Creag Gharbh
Lochan Breaclaich
2883
Creag Uchdag
Clifton
Tyndrum
S T I R L I N G
B R E A D A L B A N E
134
135
Glen Dochart
Auchlyne West Burn
Ardchyle
Luib
Lochdochart House
Loch Lubhair
Loch Dochart
A85
Strath Fillan
2132
Fiarach
2312
Beinn Leabhain
Meall a' Mhadaidh
Sròn Mhòr
2203
Glen Tarken
Loch Boltachan

143
150
151
144
136
E
F
G
H
Loch Brhodainn
Forest
Allt Gharbh Ghaig
Uchd a' Chlarsair
2587
2992
Beinn Bhreac
An Sgarsoch
3300
Carn Bhac
3014
Baddoch
2908
Sgor Mòr
Loch Mhairc
BEINN DEARG
3307
2882
Braigh Sròn Ghorm
Dalnamein Forest
Sròn a' Chleirich
2678
O F A T H O L L
Bruar Lodge
3424
Beinn Iutharn Mhòr
Loch nan Eun
3377
Carn an Righ
3449
Glas Tulaichean
Loch Vrotachan
3059
The Cairnwell
Carn a' Gheoidh
3194
Forest Lodge
H O L L A N S
M O U N T A I N S
Beinn a' Ghlo
3673
Glenlochsie Lodge
2641
Ben Gulabin
2470
Carn an Daimh
2846
Meall a' Choire Bhuidhe
2627
Ben Earb
Spittal of Glenshee
1850
Meall Reamhar
Carn Liath
3197
Loch Valigan
Ben Vuirich
2962
Dalnamein Lodge
G A R R Y
Tirinie
Fall of Bruar
Clan Donnachaidh
Old Blair
Old Bridge of Tilt
Blair Atholl
Ballentoul
Loch Moraig
Creag an-t Sithein
2075
2600
Meall Uaine
Calvine
Struan
Pitagowan
Atholl Country Collection
Atholl Estate
Tulach Hill
1542
Aldclune
Clavershouse Stone
1689
Ben Vrackie
2760
Straloch
Enochdhu
Lamh Dearg
1879
Errochty Water
Tummel Forest
Craig nan Caisean
1566
Loch Bhac
Lochan nan Nighean
Allean Forest
Tressait
Killiecrankie
Tenandry
Pass of Killiecrankie
Craigower Hill
Moulin
2092
Creag Dhubh
Loch Curran
Whitefield Castle
Kirkmichael
Tummel Bridge
Loch Tummel
Aqueduct
Foss
Linn of Tummel
Cammoch Hill
Loch Faskally
Faskally Forest
Pitlochry
Caisteal Dubh
Edradour Distillery
Loch Broom
1751
Meall Reamhar
Knock of Balmyle
TAY FOREST PARK
Loch Kinardochy
Lochan a' Chait
2559
Farragon Hill
Pitlochry Hydro-Electric
Dunfallandy Stone
Loch Derculich
Lochan Oisinneach Mòr
1842
Creag nam Mial
Blackcraig Hill
1573
Ballintuim
White Bridge
2583
Meall Tairneachan
Strathtay
Pitnacree
Haugh of Ballechin
Tummel Shingle Islands
Ballinluig
Tulliemet
Glengoulandie Deer Park
Loch Farleyer
Loch Glassie
Derculich
Grandtully
Little Ballinluig
Balnaguard
Logierait
Weem Hill
Cluny House
Forest of Clunie
Loch Benachally
Bridge of Cally
Blackcraig Forest
Keltneyburn
Castle Menzies
Weem
Bolthachan
Camserney
Dull
Wade's Bridge
St. Mary's Church
Pitcairn
Grandtully Castle
Kindallachan
Loch Ordie
Benachally
1594
Riemore Lodge
Cochrage Muir
Garth Castle
Tullochville Farm
Aberfeldy
Kincraigie
Guay
Deuchary Hill
1676
Dowally
Fortingall
Fortingall Standing Stones
Drummond Hill
Comrie Castle
Taymouth Castle
Black Watch
Bolfracks
Falls of Moness
1747
Grandtully Hill
Loch Scoly
Loch Skiach
Dalguise
Butterstone
Loch of Butterstone
Forneth
Kenmore
1857
Craig Hill
Loch na Craige
Loch Kennard
Craigvinean Forest
Scottish Horse Regimental Museum
Loch of Craiglush
Loch of Lowes
Loch of Clunie
Clunie
Loch of Drumellie
Craigie
Scottish Crannog Centre
Acharn
Falls of Acharn
Loch Hoil
Cochill Burn
TAY FOREST PARK
Inver
Dunkeld
Little Dunkeld
Snaigow House
Kirkton of Lethendy
Ossian's Hall
Beatrix Potter
Birnam
Newtyle hill
Loch Fender
2264
Meall Dearg
Trochry Castle
Trochry
Ossian's Cave
Inchewan
1324
Birnam Hill
Obney Hills
Rohallion Castle
Stare Dam
Murthly Castle
Caputh
Spittalfield
Gellyburn
Beinn Bhreac
Garrow
Wester Shian
Kingswood
Mill Dam
Murthly
Ardoch
Strathbraan
Glen Quaich
Loch Freuchie
Croftmill
Amulree
Tullybeagles Lodge
Waterloo
Bankfoot
Airntully
2641
Meall nam Fuaran
Lochan a' Mhuilinn
Meall nan Caorach
2045
Little Glenshee
Stobhall
Auchnafree
Macbeth Experience
Stanley
STRATHORD FOREST
Meall Reamhar
2188
Newton Bridge
2124
Meall Tarsuinn
Ben Chonzie
3048
Auchnafree Hill
2589
Glen Almond
Chapelhill
Downhill
Luncarty
Newmiln
Spout Rolla
Invergeldie
Loch Turret Reservoir
Carn Chois
Buchanty
Tulchan
Glenalmond
Harrietfield
Moneydie
Colenden
Busby
Bertha Loch
Methven Castle
Pitcairngreen
Almondbank
Huntingtower
Caithness Glass
Old Scone
Scone Palace
Perth Hunt
Scone Studios
Loch Mealbrodden
Keillour
Methven
Tulloch
Murrton
A9
A924
A923
A984
A93
A822
A826
A827
A85
B8079
B8019
B846
B898
B950
B867
B9099
B8063
B8063

144
151
143
136
137
SEE PAGE 188
A
B
C
D
1
2
3
4
5
CAIRNGORMS NATIONAL PARK
GLAS MAOL
PERTH & KINROSS
ANGUS
STRATHARDLE
SIDLAW HILLS
HALLYBURTON FOREST
STRATHMORE
GOWRIE
Baddoch
2908 Sgor Mor
2736 Creag nan Gabhar
Loch Callater
White Mounth
Dubh Loch
3314 Cairn Bannoch
Glas-allt Shiel
Loch Muick
3340 Carn an Tuirc
3268 Broad Cairn
3143 Tolmount
Loch Esk
Black Hill of Mark
2276 Monawee
Kirkton
2731 Easter Balloch
Loch Vrotachan
3059 The Cairnwell
Cairn a' Gheoidh 3194
3504
Devil's Elbow
Caenlochan Forest
Caenlochan
Glen Doll
Glendoll Forest
Acharn
2726 Lair of Aldararie
Carlochy
2699 Muckle Cairn
2424 Cruys
3238 Creag Leacach
2954 Finalty Hill
3043 Mayar
3108 Driesh
Loch Brandy
Loch Wharral
2941 Ben Tirran
Clova
River South Esk
2544 White Hill
2641 Ben Gulabin
2470 Carn an Daimh
2643 Monamenach
2483 Cairn Inks
2129 Cairn of Barns
Cairn Baddoch 1915
Hunthill Lodge
Hill of Berran
Auchavan
Loch Beanie
Spittal of Glenshee
2627 Ben Earb
2478 Finbracks
2381 Hill of Glansie
Rottal
1900 Hill of Garbet
2600 Meall Uaine
2301 Mealna Letter or Duchray Hill
2428 Badandum Hill
Glen Isla
Runtaleave
1992 Eskielawn
Balnaboth
Hill of Couternach 1676
Glenprosen Village
1788 Auld Darkney
Glenmoy
1682 Pinderachy
Auchnacree
Glen Shee
Clach-na-Coileach
Castle
Folda
Auchintaple Loch
Glenhead Farm
Easter Lednathie
Glenogil
Deuchar
Enochdhu
Whitefield Castle
Lamh Dearg 1879
Cray
2442 Mount Blair
Loch Shandra
Backwater Reservoir
Easter Ogil
Noranside
Kirkmichael
Blacklunans
Brewlands Bridge
Kirkton of Glenisla
Cat Law 2202
Dykehead
Cortachy
Cortachy Castle
1706 Cairn Gibbs
1630 Creigh Hill
Balintore
Pearsie
Memus
Prosen Bridge
Shielhill Bridge
Shielhill
Dykend
Braes of Coul
1341 Mile Hill
Inverquharity Castle
Oathlaw
1458 Knock of Balmyle
Forest of Alyth
Loch of Lintrathen
Kinnordy
Loch of Kinnordy
Camera Obscura
Northmuir
Bogindollo
Ballintuim
1383 Drumderg
Peel Farm
Bridgend of Lintrathen
Kirkton of Kingoldrum
Barrie's Birthplace
Kirriemuir
Blackcraig Hill 1573
Milnacraig
Bridge of Craigisla
Reekie Linn
Craigyloch
Balfour Castle
Westmuir
Aviation
Maryton
Lunanhead
Netherton
Strone Bridge
Tullymurdoch
1395 Baldruff Hill
Airlie Castle
Ballinshoe Tower
Whitehills
Forest of Clunie
Loch Benachally
Bridge of Cally
Blackcraig Forest
Kirkton of Airlie
Padanaram
Craigton
Drumgley
Hill of Alyth 968
Roundyhill
FORFAR
Cochrage Muir
Alyth
Ruthven
Gateside
St Orland's Stone
Lornty Burn
Eassie Sculptured Stone
Eassie
Bridgend
Glasclune Castle
Keathbank Mill
New Alyth
Glamis
Angus Folk
Douglastown
Blairgowrie
Westfields of Rattray
Rattray
Bridge of Crathies
Charleston
Thornton
Kirkton
Carterhaugh
Fothringham Hill 822
Forneth
Loch of Butterstone
Newton Castle
Kinloch
Leitfie
Balkeerie
Eassie & Nevay
Foffarty
Gateside
Inverarity
Loch of Clunie
Loch of Drumellie
Clunie
Craigie
Ardblair Castle
Muirton of Ardblair
Rosemount
River Ericht
Meigle
Sculptured Stone
Kirkinch
Milton
Snaigow House
Kirkton of Lethendy
Lethendy Tower
Monk Myre
Stormont Loch
Coupar Angus
Arthurstone
Ardler
Kinpurney Hill 1133
Ark Hill 1116
Over Finlarg
Gallowfauld
Spittalfield
Newbigging
Newtyle
Hatton Castle
Gallow Hill
Happas
Carrot Hill 851
Murthly Castle
Caputh
Meikleour
Beech Hedge
Markethill
Kettins
Keillor
Hill of Keillor
Bonnyton
Kirkton of Auchterhouse
Hillside of Prieston
Tealing
Gellyburn
Murthly
Ardoch
Kinclaven Castle
Bridge of Isla
Woodside
Campmuir
Long Loch
Leys
Dovecot
Tealing Earth House
Brighty Wood
Newbigging
Wellbank
Cargill
Burrelton
Pitcur Castle
Auchterhouse
North Dronley
Londie
Westhall Terrace
Gallowhill
Laird's Loch
Dronley
Bridgefoot
Kellas
Murroes
Airntully
Stobhall
Macbeth Experience
Muirhead
Liff
Birkhill
Clatto Reservoir
Balmuir
Powrie Castle
Whitfield
Stanley
Wolfhill
Saucher
Fowlis
Downfield
Fintry
Kinrossie
Collace
Dunsinane Hill
Fowlis Castle
Camperdown
Craigie
Claypotts
Guildtown
Kirkton of Collace
Scottish Antiques
Knapp
Lochee
Mills Observatory
St. Martins
Newmiln
Abernyte
Castlehill
Benvie
Downhill
Luncarty
Moneydie
Colenden
Balbeggie
Kinnaird
Kinnaird Castle
Craigdallie
Inchture
Longforgan
Invergowrie
Kingoodie
Verdant Works
DUNDEE
Broughty Ferry
Tay Road Bridge
Tay Bridge
Newport-on-Tay
Tay Rail Bridge
Woodhaven
Wormit
Perth
Perth Hunt
Scone Studios
Scone Palace
Old Scone
Westown
Rait
Pole Hill
Evelick Castle
Grange
Inchmichael
Kilspindie
New Scone
Almondbank
Huntingtower
Caithness Glass
Muirton
Woodland Park
Pitcairngreen
Bertha Loch
A93
A924
A923
A926
A984
A94
A9
A90
A92
A85
A928
A932
A930
B950
B951
B952
B954
B953
B955
B957
B947
B9099
B9128
B9127
B961
B946

Hill of Cammie
Mount Battock
Edendocher
Brae of Glenbervie
Dunnottar Castle
Dunnottar Woodland Park
Thornyhive Bay
A90
A92
Glen Dye
B974
Spital
Tennet
Tarf
350
60
Burn of
1725 Melmcart
1526 Drumtochty Forest
Glenfarquhar Lodge
Bervie Water
70
80
Goyle Hill
Fiddes Castle
Fowlsheugh
Hill of Fingray 1593
1488 Cairn o' Mount
Drumtochty Castle
Herscha Hill 723
Drumlithie
Bruxie Hill
Milton of Barras
Roadside of Catterline
Crawton
Crawton Bay
Catterline
152
153
E
F
G
H
Farfside
Cairncross
Glenesk Folk
Millden Lodge
Colmealie Stone Circle
1785 Sturdy Hill
Deer Dyke
Strath Finella
Auchenblae
Drumtochty Forest
Glensaugh
Bridge of Mondynes
17
Roadside of Kinneff
Fernieflatt
Braidon Bay
Todhead Point
Glen Esk
Bulg 1986
Strathfinella Hill
Fasque
Fordoun
Fordoun
Bridge of Kair
Parkneuk
Grassic Gibbon
B967
Arbuthnott House
Kincardine Castle
B966
Kinneff
Whistleberry Castle
Little John's Haven
1
2224 Hill of Wirren
Auchmull
Fettercairn Distillery
HOWE OF THE MEARNS
Arbuthnott
Fettercairn
Balbegno Castle
Arch
Bent
5
ABERDEENSHIRE
Allardyce Castle
Inverbervie
Bervie Bay
B9120
Laurencekirk
A937
Easter Tulloch
Knox Hill
Hallgreen Castle
Gannochy
West Burnside
Benholm Castle
Gourdon
Burn of Calletar
West Water
River North Esk
Luther Water
B974
Garvock
A90
70
Edzell
Mill
Benholm
Bridgend
Balfield
Edzell
11
Luthermuir
B9120
Dunlappie
Cairn o' Long Barrow
Inglismaldie Forest
Chapelfield
1578 Peat Hill
Brown Caterhuns Hill Fort
B966
11
12
10
Johnshaven
White Caterhuns Hill Fort
Lauriston Castle
Hill of Menmuir
Inchbare
North Water Bridge
Logie Pert
Marykirk
Kirkton of Menmuir
Tigerton
2
1031 Tullo Hill
Cruick Water
Craigo
Lochside
St. Cyrus
13
North Craigo
Logie
St. Cyrus
Balnamoon
Bellieliill
Pathhead
A937
Little Brechin
Trinity
Fern
West Muir
Sunnyside
Hillside
A92
Brechin Castle Centre
Careston
Miniature Railway
B966
NTS
House of Dun
Caledonian Railway
Vayne Castle
Careston Castle
Brechin
BRECHIN
Dun
Kirkhill
60
Montrose Air Station
Nether Careston
A90
Pictavia
Round Tower
Railway
A935
9
NTS
Water
South Esk
River
Tannadice
Bridge of Dun
MONTROSE
15
Netherton
Montrose Basin
Montrose
Finavon
13
Middle Drums
Kinnaird Castle
Barnhead
Doocot
Milton of Finavon
B9134
Montreathmont Forest
A933
Inchbraoch
Ferryden
Crosston
Melgund Castle
Farnell Castle
Maryton
Aberlemno
Montreathmont Moor
Finavon Castle
Farnell
A934
Kirkton of Craig
Hill of Finavon 751
Aberlemno Sculptured Stones
Westerton
Usan
3
826 Turin Hill
Pitkennedy
Rossie Moor 503
17
G U S
Boddin Point
Braehead
Restenneth Priory
Rescobie
B9113
Dubton
Bolshan
Lunan
Lunan Bay
Rescobie Loch
Balgavies Loch
Guthrie Castle
Glasterlaw
Kinnell
Braikie Castle
Red Castle
Burnside
A932
Guthrie
14
A92
Kinnell
Bay
750
Kingsmuir
Milldens
Pitmuies
15
Friockheim
12
Inverkeilor
Letham
Gardyne Castle
Lunan Water
Ethie Haven
Lownie Moor
Dunnichen
Middleton
Leysmill
B965
Red Head
Bowriefauld
Chapelton
Craichie
Colliston Castle
Ethie Castle
Drunkendub
Cononsyth
Colliston
4
Whigstreet
Redford
Marywell
Auchmithie
A933
Arbroath
Kirkbuddo
Greystone
St. Vigeans
Carmyllie
St. Vigeans
Hayshead
Abbey
13
B9127
Elliot
Cliffburn
Seaton Cliffs
B978
B961
Arbirlot
ARBROATH
Crombie
Water
40
Kirkton of Monikie
Bonnington
Kelly Castle
Arbroath
Affleck
B9128
Balcathie
Kerr's Miniature Railway
Monikie
Monikie Burn
Wormiehills Railway
Monikie Reservoir
Craigton
Salmond's Muir
A92
Monikie
Castle
Muirdrum
Newbigging
Carlungie Earth House
Panbride
East Haven
Drumsturdy
16
5
Clayholes
Ardestie Earth House
Barry
Mill
A930
Carnoustie
11
Barnhill
Monifieth
DANGER AREA
Broughty
BUDDON NESS
E
F
G
H
30
Tentsmuir Point
350
60
70
80
Bell Rock
Sands

146
Talisker Bay
154
ISLAND OF SKYE
MINGINISH
CUILLIN HILLS
BLA BHEINN
GLAMAIG
SOAY
SEA OF THE HEBRIDES
INNER HEBRIDES
CANNA
Sanday
Canna Harbour
Sound of Canna
RUM
NATIONAL NATURE RESERVE
SOUND OF RUM
EIGG
MUCK
Sound of Eigg
Elgol
Carbost
Sligachan
Kinloch
Cleadale
Port Mor
Rum to Canna 1hr. 5mins.
Mallaig to Canna 2hrs.
Mallaig to Rum 1hr. 10mins.
Rum to Muck 1hr. 10mins.
Eigg to Muck 45mins.
170
138
139

147
148
155
140
E
F
G
H
1
2
3
4
5
Eyre Point
CROWLIN ISLANDS
Eilean Mor
Loch Carron
Stromeferry
Plockton
Achmore
Sgeir Dhearg
Longay
SCALPAY
Scalpay House
Dunan
Black Islands
Kyle of Lochalsh
Pabay
Guillamon Island
Broadford Bay
Broadford
Waterloo
Skulamus
Harrapool
Lower Breakish
Upper Breakish
Kyleakin
Plock of Kyle
Loch Alsh
Glas Eilean
Ardintoul Point
Balmacara
Auchtertyre
Kirkton
Nostie
Ardelve
Dornie
Conchra
Bundalloch
Carndu
Eilean Donan
Keppoch
Loch Duich
Letterfearn
Invernate
Ruarach
Morvich
Carn-gorm
Ault a' chruinn
Inversheil
Shiel Bridge
Ratagan
Ratagan Forest
FIVE SISTERS
Kintail
Sallachy
Loch Long
Camas-luinie
Torrin
Kilbride
Loch Slapin
Beinn na Caillich 2403
Loch Cill Chriosd
Lochain Dubha
Loch Lonachan
Beinn nan Carn 983
Heaste
Dun Kearstack
Rubha Suisnish
Loch Eishort
Eilean Heast
Drumfearn
Loch an Iasgaich
Duisdalemore
Ord
Sgòrach Breac 981
Lochan Fada
Tokavaig
Dunscaith Castle
Tarskavaig
Achnacloich
Teangue
Saasaig
Knock Castle
Knock Bay
Ferrindonald
Kilbeg
Kilmore
Isleornsay
Ornsay
Laurence Broderick
Camuscross
Camas Baravaig
Camas Garbh
SOUND OF SLEAT
Armadale Castle
Clan Donald
Armadale Bay
Ardvasar
Calligarry
Tormore
Aird of Sleat
Ard Thurinish
An Fhaochag
Sandaig Islands
Sandaig
Sandaig Bay
Kylerhea
Kylerhea Otter Haven
Bernera
Galltair
Glenelg Bay
Glenelg
Eilanreach
Dun Troddan
Dun Telve
Chambered Cairn
Balvraid
Dun Grugaig
Beinn a' Chapuill 2421
BEINN SGRITHEALL 3194
Upper Sandaig
Ben Aslak 1984
Beinn na Seamraig
Sgurr na Coinnich 2424
Glen More
Glenmore River
Sgurr Mhic Bharraich 2553
Glenshiel Forest
The Saddle 3319
Sgurr na Sgine 3098
Sgurr Fhuaran 3505
River Shiel
A87
A851
A890
A830
A861
B8083
Eilean Rarsaidh
Arnisdale
Corran
Loch Hourn
Beinn nan Caorach 2536
Druim Fada 2327
Buidhe Bheinn 2884
Kinloch Hourn
Sgurr a' Mhaoraich 3365
Barrisdale Bay
Inverguseran
Beinn na Caillich 2573
KNOYDART
Airor
Ladhar Bheinn 3343
Glen Barrisdale
Luinne Bheinn 3083
Sgurr a' Choire-bheithe 2994
Gleann Cosaidh
Scottas
Inverie
Sgurr Coire Choinnichean 2612
Inverie Bay
Kilchoan
Meall Buidhe 3107
Loch an Dubh-Lochain
Lochan nam Breac
Sgurr na Ciche 3412
Sgurr Mòr 3290
Mallaig
Mallaig Bheag
Courteachan
Heritage Centre
Marine World
Glasnacardoch
The Jacobite
Sgurr an Eilein Ghiubhais 1713
Loch Eireagoraidh
NORTH MORAR
Stoul
Loch Nevis
Finiskaig
Ardnamurach
Kylesmorar
Tarbet
Sgurr Breac 2387
Beoraidbeg
Morar
Bracora
Glenancross
Camusdarach
Loch Morar
Lòn Liath
Portnaluchaig
Bunacaimb
Eilean Ighe
Luinga Bheag
Back of Keppoch
Kinloid
ARISAIG
Arisaig
SOUTH MORAR
Sidhean Mòr 1970
Beinn nan Cabar 1888
Meith Bheinn 2328
Lochan Tain Mhic Dhughaill
Loch Beoraid
Carn Mòr 2718
An Stac 2350
Sgurr nan Coireachan 3136
Sgurr Thuilm 3164
Sgurr an Ursainn
Strathan
Luinga Mhor
Rubh' Arisaig
Glen Cottage
Druimindarroch
Loch Nam Uamh Cairn
Glen Beasdale
Creag Bhan 1675
Slios Garbh
Glas-charn 2076
Sgurr an Utha 2610
Polnish
Lochailort
Ranochan
Loch Eilt
Glenfinnan
Glenfinnan Viaduct
Inverailort
Peanmeanach
Eilean a' Ghaill
Eilean an t-Snidhe
Sound of Arisaig
Eilean nan Gobhar
Samalaman Island
Glenuig Bay
Samalaman
Smirisary
Glenuig
Roshven
ROIS-BHEINN 2895
Druim Fiaclach 2852
Croit Bheinn 2178
Beinn Odhar Bheag 2895
Loch Shiel
Kinlocheil
Rubh' Aird
Mallaig to Armadale 25mins.
Mallaig to Eigg 1hr. 10mins.
NTS

148
156
140
141
147
A
B
C
D
1
2
3
4
5
Stromeferry
Plockton
W.Highland Dairy
Castle
Achmore
Craig
Highland Farm
Loch nan Gillean
Loch Lundie
Loch na h-Onaich
Loch na Beitre
Sgùman Coinntich
2883
Killilan Forest
2949
Aonach Buidhe
Loch Mhoicean
An Riabhachan
3696
3775
3508
Glencannich Forest
Mullardoch
Glen Cannich
Sallachy
Killilan
Long
Loch Beinn a' Mheadhoin
Allt Gleann Udalain
Auchtertyre Hill
Auchtertyre
A890
A87
Conchra
Bundalloch
Carndu
Dornie
Kirkton
Nostie
Ardelve
Eilean Donan
Camas-luinie
Glen Elchaig
River Elchaig
Loch nan Ealachan
Carnach
Allt na Doire Gairbhe
Loch na Leitreach
Falls of Glomach
NTS
Loch nan Eun
Loch Bhuic Mhóir
Inverinate Forest
Gleann Sìthidh
Abhainn Sìthidh
West Benula Forest
Glean a' Choilich
Abhainn a' Choilich
Coire Lochan
Carn Eighe
3880
Gleann nam Fiadh
Tom a' Chòinich
3646
Toll Creagach
3457
Doire Tana
Loch Alsh
Glas Eilean
Ardintoul Point
Caisteal Grugaig Broch
Keppoch
Letterfearn
Beinn a' Chuirn
1977
Sgurr an Airgid
2759
Loch Duich
Invérinate
3006
A' Ghlas-bheinn
Loch a' Bhealaich
Sgurr nan Ceathreamhnan
3771
Sgurr na Lapaich
3401
Affric Lodge
River Affric
Loch Affric
Glen Affric
Bernera
Galltair
Ratagan Forest
Ruarach
Lienassie
Farm
Morvich
Carn-gorm
Ault a' chruinn
Ratagan
Gleann Gniomhaidh
River Affric
Glenaffric Forest
Glenelg
Inverhiel
Shiel Bridge
Beinn a' Chaoinich
Glen More
BEINN FHADA OR BEN ATTOW
3385
Kintail Forest
FIVE SISTERS
Sgurr Fhuaran
3505
Allt Garbh
Aonach Shasuinn
2901
Dun Troddan
Dun Telve
Chambered Cairn
Balvraid
Dun Grugaig
2421
Beinn a' Chapuill
2553
Sgurr Mhic Bharraich
Glenmore River
Mullach Fraoch-choire
3614
Ciste Dhubh
3218
A' Chràlaig
3673
Sgurr nan Conbhairean
3634
Ceannacroc Forest
River Doe
BEINN SGRITHEALL
3194
Glenshiel Forest
River Shiel
1719
The Saddle
3319
Beinn nan Caorach
2536
Sgurr na Sgine
3098
Sgurr an Lochain
3282
GLEN SHIEL
Cluanie Inn
Cluanie Lodge
A887
Loch Cluanie
Amisdale
Corran
Dubh Lochain
Glen Arnisdale
2327
Druim Fada
Loch Hourn
Buidhe Bheinn
2884
Clunie Forest
Aonach air Chrith
3342
Maol Chinn-dearg
Beinn Loinne
Kinloch Hourn
Sgurr a' Mhaoraich
3365
Glen Quoich
Glenquoich Forest
Bunloinn Forest
Barrisdale Bay
Ladhar Bheinn
3343
Gleouraich
3394
River Loyne
Loch Loyne
Glen Loyne
HIGHLAND
Glen Barrisdale
River Barrisdale
Loch Fearna
East Glenquoich Forest
Ardochy House
13
Sgurr a' Choire-bheithe
2994
Abhainn Chosaidh
Gleann Cosaidh
Loch Quoich
Gearr Garry
Kingie
Inchlaggan
Tomdoun
River Garry
Loch
Gleann an Dubh-Lochain
Luinne Bheinn
3083
Beinn Bheag
Loch an Dubh-Lochain
3107
Meall Buidhe
Lochan nam Breac
Gairich
3015
Lochan nan Sgùd
Glen Garry
Allt Choire a' Bhalachain
Sgurr Mòr
3290
Glas Bheinn
1825
Beinn Bhuidhe
2805
Sgurr na Ciche
3412
River Kingie
Glen Kingie
Glengarry
Finiskaig
Lochan Dubh
Meall Blàir
2154
Srón a' Choire Ghairbh
LOCHABER
Lochan a' Mhàim
Glen Dessarry
River Dessarry
Sgurr Mhurlagain
2885
Loch Blàir
Geal Charn
Ardnamurach
2387
Sgurr Breac
Murlaggan
Strathan
Loch Arkaig
Carn Mòr
2718
River Pean
Glen Pean
Ardechive
Gleann Cia-aig
An Stac
2350
Sgurr nan Coireachan
3136
Sgurr Thuilm
3164
Allt a' Chaorainn
Gleann Camgharaidh
Allt Camgharaidh
Clunes Forest
Chia-Aig Falls
Clunes
Lochan a' Bhrodainn
Sgurr an Ursainn
Locheil Forest
Glen Mallie
River Mallie
Inver Mallie
Achnacarry
B8005
Clan Cameron
Bunarkaig
Loch Lochy
Lochan Tain Mhic Dhughaill
Loch Beoraid
Gaor Bheinn or Gulvain
Meall a' Phubuill
2533
Druim Gleann Laoigh
Achnanellan
Glen Loy
River Loy
Beinn Bhàn
Slios Garbh
Glas-charn
2076
Sgurr an Utha
2610
River Finnan
Glen Finnan
Gleann Dubh Lighe
Gleann Fionnlighe
Gleann Suileag
An t-Suileag
Stob a' Ghrianain
Druim Fada
Gairlochy
Stronenaba
B8004
Glenloy Oakwood
Caledonian Canal
Brackletter
Commando
Spean Bridge
Ranochan
A830
Station
Viaduct
The Jacobite
Glenfinnan
Dubh Lighe
Fionn Lighe
Beinn an t-Sneachda
Glenloy Forest
Muirshearlich
Highbridge
Alltour
A82
Kinlocheil
Corribeg
Fassfern
Achdalieu
Treasures of the Earth
Corpach
Banavie
Neptune's Staircase
Caol
Camaghael
Torlundy
Tor Castle
Leanachan Forest
Creag Aoil
Cable Cars
Loch Shiel
2895
Beinn Odhar Bheag
Callop River
Loch Eil
South Garvan
Duisky
A861
Blaich
Achaphubuil
B8006
Lochyside
Victoria Bridge
Glen Garvan
Sgorr Craobh a' Chaorainn
Meall nan

149
150
157
142
LOCH NESS
LOCH OICH
GLEN MOR OR GLEN ALBYN
LOCH LOCHY
LOCH LAGGAN
GLEN SPEAN
Fort Augustus
Invermoriston
Drumnadrochit
Milton
Lewiston
Foyers
Invergarry
Laggan
Cannich
Dalwhinnie
Urquhart Bay
Urquhart Castle
Falls of Foyers
Inchnacardoch Forest
Glengarry Forest
GLEN ROY NATIONAL NATURE RESERVE
Parallel Roads
Creag Meagaidh
Dores
Abriachan
Torness
Aberarder
Dunmaglass Lodge
Farraline
Errogie
Inverfarigaig
Dun Dearduil
Farigaig Forest
Lyne of Gorthleck
Wester Aberchalder
Lochgarthside
Bunkegivie
Whitebridge
Upper Knockchoilum
Knockie Lodge
Glenbrein Lodge
Garrogie Lodge
Killin Lodge
Glendoebeg
Bunoich
Jenkins Park
Auchteraw
Newtown
Bridge of Oich
Aberchalder
Munerigie
Faichem
Wester Mandally
Laggan Swing Bridge
Kilfinnan
Altrua
New Bridge
Glenfintaig Lodge
Upper Glenfintaig
Brae Roy Lodge
Bohenie
Inverroy
Roybridge
Achluachrach
Bunroy
Tulloch
Fersit
Moy Lodge
Kinloch Laggan
Cromra
Feagour
Strathmashie House
Glenshero Lodge
Garvamore
Garva Bridge
Melgarve
Crathie
Balgowan
Drumgask
Ben Alder Lodge
Torgyle
Dalchreichart
Dundreggan
Ceannacroc Lodge
Ceannacroc Bridge
Levishie
Achnaconeran
Alltsigh
Bunloit
Balbeg
Lower Lenie
Upper Lenie
Strone
Borlum
Divach
Falls of Divach
Coiltie
Balmacaan Woods
Drum Farm Centre
Balnain
Balnaglaic
Rychraggan
Polmaily
Achmony
Balnagrantach
Buntait
Braefield
Corrimony
Corrimony Chambered Cairn
Kerrow
Tomich
Dog Falls
Plodda Falls
Glen Affric
Muchrachd
Liatrie
Glassburn
Balmacaan Forest
Levishie Forest
Dundreggan Forest
Portclair Forest
Inverwick Forest
Glendoe Forest
Culachy Forest
Corrieyairack Pass
Corrieyairack Forest
Moy Forest
Ardverikie Forest
Strathmashie Forest
Ben Tee 2957
Carn Dearg 2677
Carn Leac 2889
Gairbeinn 2929
Creag Meagaidh 3700
Beinn a' Chaorainn 3437
Meall Dubh 2581
Carn a' Chuilinn 2677
Carn Eas gann Bàna 2554
Burrach Mór 2686
Geal Charn 3036
Marg na Craige 2731
Meall Cruaidh 2941
Creagan Mór 2522
Beinn Chlianaig 2343
Creag Dhubh 2160
Beinn Teallach 2994
Beinn Iaruinn 2636
Carn Liath 3298
Beinn Eilde 2207
A82
A831
A833
A887
A87
A86
A889
A9
B862
B852

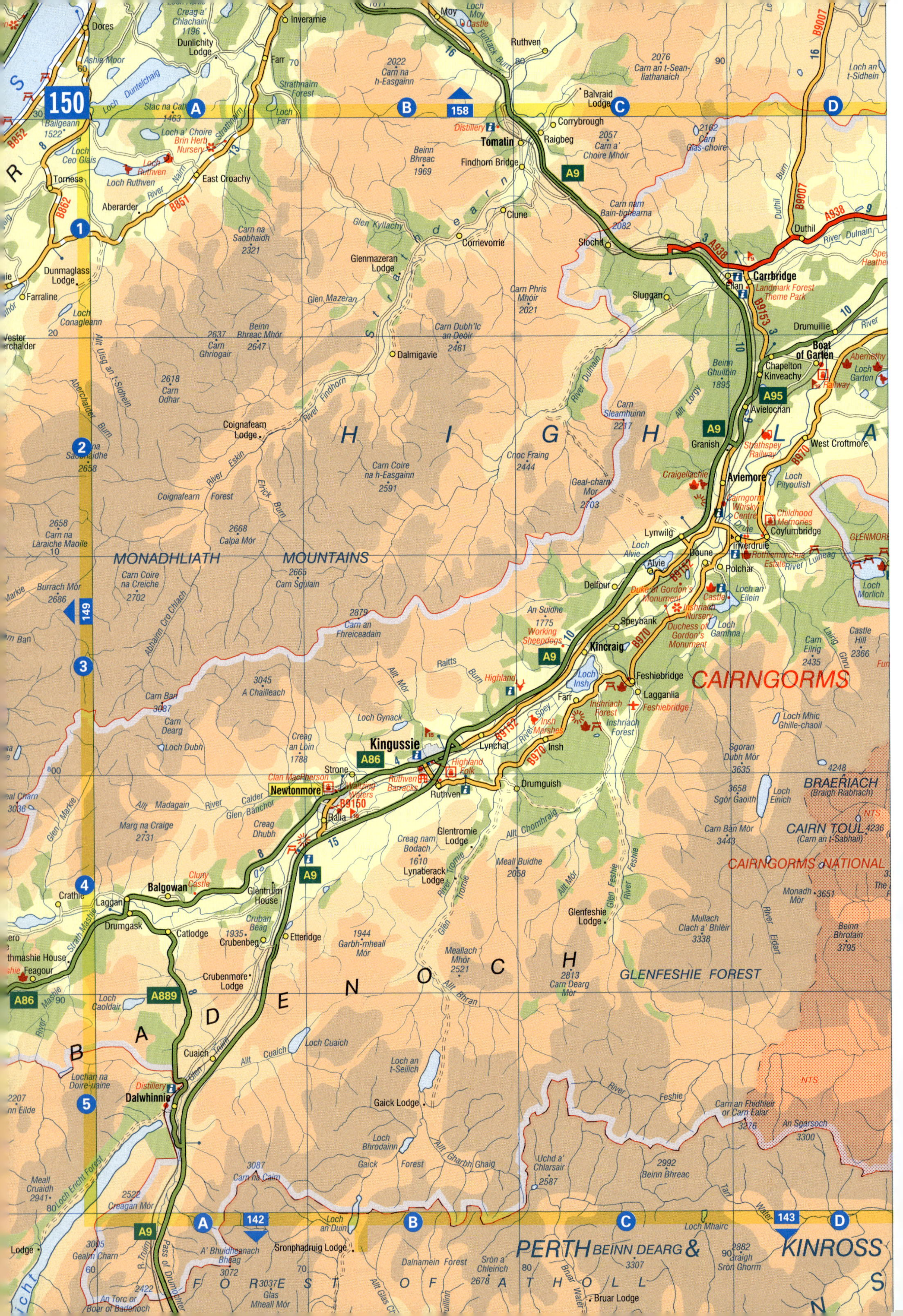

150
158
149
142
143
HIGHLAND
MONADHLIATH MOUNTAINS
BADENOCH
CAIRNGORMS
CAIRNGORMS NATIONAL
GLENFESHIE FOREST
PERTH & KINROSS
BEINN DEARG
FOREST OF ATHOLL
Kingussie
Newtonmore
Aviemore
Carrbridge
Kincraig
Dalwhinnie
Tomatin
Boat of Garten
Balgowan
Laggan
Ruthven
Insh
Drumguish
Feshiebridge
Lagganlia
Coylumbridge
Inverdruie
Polchar
Granish
Avielochan
Duthil
Slochd
Sluggan
Findhorn Bridge
Raigbeg
Corrybrough
Moy
Inverarnie
Farr
Dores
Torness
Aberarder
East Croachy
Dunmaglass Lodge
Farraline
Coignafearn Lodge
Dalmigavie
Glenmazeran Lodge
Corrievorrie
Clune
Cuaich
Catlodge
Crubenbeg
Etteridge
Gaick Lodge
Glenfeshie Lodge
Lynaberack Lodge
Glentromie Lodge
Sronphadruig Lodge
Bruar Lodge
A9
A86
A889
A95
A938
B9152
B9150
B9153
B970
B9007
B851
B862
B852
Loch Insh
Loch an Eilein
Loch Morlich
Loch Ruthven
Loch Duntelchaig
Loch Ericht
BRAERIACH
CAIRN TOUL

151
152
144
159
A95
A939
A93
A944
B976
B9008
B9009
B9136
B9102
B970
B972
Advie
Upper Derraid
Auchnagallin
Glaschoil
Cottartown
Dellifure
Dalvey
Balliewerd
Creag Liath 1473
Carn Ruigh Chorrach
Grantown-on-Spey
Beinn Mhòr 1545
Achnahannet
Craggan
Speybridge
Cromdale
Lethendry Castle
Haughs of Cromdale
Highland Pony Centre
Revack Estate
Skye of Curr
Dulnain Bridge
Castle Roy
Broomhill
Nethy Bridge
Abernethy Forest
Dells Wood
Clachaig
Tore Hill 1087
Tulloch
Dorback Lodge
Dorback Burn
Braes of Abernethy
River Nethy
HILLS OF CROMDALE
Creagan a' Chaise 2369
Sgòr Gaoithe
Burn of Lochy
Strath Avon
Knock Earth House
Scottish Country
Blairfindy Castle
Glenlivet
Glenlivet Distillery
Castleton
Packhorse Bridge
Drumin Castle
Carn Liath 1795
Tomnavoulin
Carn Daimh 1866
Tomachlaggan
Knockandhu
Clashnoir
Braes of Glenlivet
Chapeltown
Peat Moss
Bridge of Brown
Tomintoul
Milton
Conglass Water
Tom an t-Suidhe Mhòr 1742
Carn Meadhonach 1928
Shenval
Auchbreck
Morrish
Carn Muldonich 1857
Carn an t-Suidhe 2401
Blackwater Forest
Allanreid
River Livet
Carnnacoy 1605
Glenfiddich Lodge
Corryhabbie Hill 2561
Glenfiddich Forest
River Fiddich
Black Water
Round Hill 1872
Cairnbrallan 2029
Hill of Three Stones 2065
Bridgend
Geal Charn
LADDER HILLS
Glenbuchat Lodge
Carn Mòr 2639
Moss Hill 2159
Water of Buchat
Ladylea Hill 1998
Belnacraig
Kirkton of Glenbuchat
Water of Nochty
Lecht Iron
Carn Liath 2598
Well of the Lecht
The Socach 2356
Breagach Hill 1825
Bellabeg
Doune of Invernochty
Forbestown
Colquhonnie Castle
Strathdon
Candacraig Nursery
Heugh-head
Glen Ernan
Ernan Water
Carn Ealasaid 2600
Tornashean Forest 1742
Craig of Bunzeach
Deskry Water
River Don
Cock Bridge
Milltown
Corgarff
Corgarff Castle
Allt Tuileach
Carn Leac Saighaeir 2294
Cairn Mona Gowan 2456
Morven 2861
Brown Cow Hill 2721
Loch Builg
River Gairn
Glen Fenzie
Gairnshiel Lodge
Lary
Peter's Hill 1863
Glen Gairn
Geallaig Hill 2438
McEwan Gallery
Bridge of Gairn
Milton of Tullich
Ballater
Confectioners
Knock Castle
Pannanich Hill
Littlemill
Birkhall
Crathie
Abergeldie Castle
Balmoral Castle
Easter Balmoral
Royal Lochnagar Distillery
Balnacroft
Inver
Creag nan Gall 1969
The Coyles of Muick 1956
Aucholzie
Glen Gelder
Gelder Shiel
Glen Girnock
Glen Muick
Cairn Leuchan 2293
Balmoral Forest
Conachcraig 2827
Fasheilach 2365
Glenmuick & Lochnagar
Spittal of Glenmuick
Sandy Loch
Lochnagar
LOCHNAGAR
Loch nan Eun
White Mouth
Dubh Loch
Glas-allt Shiel
Loch Muick
Allt Darrarie
Black Hill of Mark
Easter Balloch
Water of Mark
Glen Lee
Cairn Bannoch 3314
Broad Cairn 3268
Tolmount 3143
Carn an Tuirc 3340
Loch Esk
Caenlochan
Glen Doll
Lair of Aldararie 2726
Water of Unich
Muckle Cairn 2699
Achram
Glendoll Forest
Loch Brandy
Meall a' Bhuachaille 2654
FOREST PARK
Glenmore
Glen More
Cairngorm Reindeer Centre
Meall Suim 2485
Carn Bheadhair 2636
Geal Charm 2692
Carn na Farraidh 2257
Water of Ailnack
Water of Caiplich
Cnap Chaochan Aitinn 2337
Burn of Loin
Big Garvoun 2431
River Avon
Craig Veann 2332
Carn na Feannaige
Bynack More
Ptarmigan Mountain Exhibition
CairnGorm Funicular Railway
CAIRN GORM 4085
CAIRNGORM
MOUNTAINS
NATIONAL PARK
GLEN AVON
The Bruach 2338
Forest of Glenavon
Stob an t-Sluichd 3621
BEN AVON 3843
Loch Avon
Beinn a' Chaorainn 3553
Loch Etchachan
Carn Eas 3556
GRAMPIAN MOUNTAINS
BEINN A' BHUIRD
Culardoch 2953
Creag an Dail Bheag 2830
BEN MACDUI 4296
Derry Cairngorm 3788
Beinn Bhreac 3051
NATURE RESERVE
Carn a' Mhaim 3329
Devil's Point
ABERDEENSHIRE
BRAEMAR
Meall Gorm 2029
Feardar Burn
Carn na Drochaide 2681
Glen Dee
Glen Lui
Lui Water
Sgòr Mòr 2666
FOREST OF MAR
Creag Bhalg
Braemar
Braemar Castle
Highland Heritage Centre
Castleton
Linn of Quoich
Kindrochit Castle
Morrone Birkwood
Keiloch
Invercauld Bridge
Ballochbuie Forest
Linn of Dee
River Dee
Inverey
Cairn Geldie 2039
Morrone or Morven
The Colonel's Bed
Glen Ey
Ey Burn
Carn Liath 2676
Geldie Burn
Callater Burn
Glen Callater
Loch Phadruig
Loch Callater
Clunie Water
Creag nan Gabhar 2736
Carn Bhac 3014
Baddoch
Sgor Mòr 2908
AN SOCACH 3073
Allt Garbh Buidhe
Beinn Iutharn Mhòr
Loch nan Eun
Loch Vrotachan
The Cairnwell 3059
Carn a' Gheoidh 3194
Carn an Righ 3377
Glas Tulaichean 3449
Gleann Mòr
GLAS MAOL 3504
Devil's Elbow
Caenlochan Forest
NTS
MORAY

152
160
151
144
145
MORAY
ABERDEENSHIRE
GARIOCH
ANGUS
CAIRNGORMS NATIONAL PARK
CORREEN HILLS
HOWE OF ALFORD
PITFICHIE FOREST
HILL OF FARE
Glenfiddich Forest
Bridgend
Inverharroch
Ardwell
Cabrach
Elrick
Clashindarroch Forest
Clashindarroch
Coynachie
Kirkney
Gartly
Milton of Lesmore
Belhinnie
Rhynie
Tap o' Noth 1848
Mount of Haddoch 1708
Craig Castle
St. Mary's Kirk
Kennethmont
Leith Hall NTS
Knockandy Hill 1425
Cults
Wardhouse
Clatt
Druminnor Castle
Duncanston
Leslie
Leslie Castle
Insch
Picardy Symbol Stone
Upper Boddam
Knockenbaird
Largie
Lenchie
Hill of Foudland 1531
Glens of Foudland
Colpy
Kirkton of Culsalmond
Cairnhill
Tocher
Newseat
Meikle Wartle
Kirkton of Rayne
Old Rayne
Durno
Pitmachie
Dunnideer Castle
Old Manse Gallery
Kirkton of Oyne
Oyne
Old Westhall
Harthill Castle
Maiden Stone
Whiteford
Pitcaple
Chapel of Garioch
Auchleven
Bennachie Forest
Lickleyhead Castle
Kirkton
Bennachie 1733
Benachie Forest
Millstone Hill 1340
Glenton
Bograxie
Coldwells Croft
Whitehaugh Forest
Round Hill 1872
Cairnbrallan 2029
Hill of Three Stones 2065
The Buck 2366
Clova
Sculpture Walk
Lumsden
Lord Arthur's Cairn 1699
Terpersie Castle
Tullynessle
Keig
Mossat
Kildrummy
Milltown
Kildrummy Castle
Rinmore
Creag an Eunan 2073
Buchat Lodge
Water of Buchat
Ladylea Hill 1998
Belnacraig
Glenbuchat Castle
Kirkton of Glenbuchat
Water of Nochty
Breagach Hill 1825
Bellabeg
Forbestown
Strathdon
Colquhonnie Castle
Doune of Invernochty
Candacraig Nursery
Heugh-head
Glenkindie
Towie
Milltown of Towie
Sinnahard
Syllavethy Gallery
Montgarrie
Alford Valley Railway
Haughton
Bridge of Alford
Muir of Alford
Alford
Heritage Centre
Grampian Transport
Balfluig Castle
Whitehouse
Asloun Castle
River Don
Rorandle
Cairn William 1468
Pitfichie
Pitfichie Castle
Arts Centre
Ramstone
Monymusk
Grantlodge
Craigearn
Kirkton
Tillyfourie
Whitehill Stone Circle
Tillycairn Castle
Black Hill 608
Corrennie Forest
Ordhead
Sauchen
Old Kinnernie
Tornashean Forest 1742
Craig of Bunzeach
Frosty Hill
Milton of Cushnie
Leochel Cushnie
Muir of Fowlis
Craigievar NTS
Mill of Craigievar
Noah's Ark Country Centre
Corrennie Moor
Benaquhame 1621
Bankhead
Comers
Tillybirloch
Midmar Kirk
Sunhoney Stone Circle
Pressendye 2031
Corse Castle
Cairn Mona Gowan 2456
Morven 2861
Migvie Castle
Migvie
Coynach
Logie of Coldstone
Tarland
Culsh Earth-House
Craiglich 1562
Tornaveen
Drumlasie
Midmar Castle
Midmar Forest
Lumphanan
Peel of Lumphanan
Milton of Auchinhove
Milton Auchlossan
Torphins
Tomnaverie Stone Circle
Coull
Coull Castle
Mortlich 1248
Loch of Aboyne
Scar Hill 984
Ordie
Loch Davan
Loch Kinord
New Kinord Settlement
Peter's Hill 1863
Culblean Hill 1983
Muir of Dinnet
Cambus o' May
Lary
Milltown of Campfield
Craigton
Mid Beltie
Beltie Castle
Maud
Cluny Crichton Castle
Aboyne
Aboyne Castle
Kincardine O' Neil
Belwade Farm
River Dee
Dinnet
McEwan Gallery
Castle
Milton of Tullich
Bridge of Gairn
Ballater
Confectioners
Pannanich
Knock Castle
Birkhall
Pannanich Hill
Oakwood
Millfield
Braeloine
Glen Tanar House
Glen Tanar
Birsemore
Birse
Marywell
Potarch
Burn of Cattie
Brathens
East Mains
Upper Lochton
Banchory
Arbeadie
Banchory Museum
Silverbank
Bridge of Canny
Deebank
Auchattie
Scolty
Bridge of Feugh
General Burnett
Tilquhillie Castle
Belts of Collonach
Strachan
Blackhall Forest
Tom's Cairn 1017
Shooting Greens
Finzean
Whitestone
Waulkmill
Water of Feugh
Black Craig 1742
Clachan Yell 2058
Cairn Leuchan 2293
The Coyles of Muick 1956
Aucholzie
Glen Muick
Carnferg 1724
Glencat
Lamahip 1325
Forest of Birse
Ballochan
Craigmahandle 1878
Craig of Dalfro 1042
Kerloch 1754
White Hill
Peter Hill 2025
Cock Hill 1960
Water of Aven
Mount Shade 1662
Bridge of Dye
Tipperweir 1440
Cock Cairn 2387
Hill of Cat 2433
Mount Keen 3080
Hill of Saughs 2141
Mudlee Bracks 2259
Hill of Cammie 2028
Mount Battock 2554
Hill of Edendocher 1944
Fasheilach 2365
Glenmuick & Lochnagar
Spittal of Glenmuick
Water of Mark
Water of Tarf
Hill of Fingray 1593
Meluncart 1725
Cairn o' Mount 1488
Drumtochty Forest
Goyle Hill 1526
Glenfarquhar Lodge
Drumtochty Castle
Black Hill of Mark 2731
Easter Balloch
Monawee 2276
Kirkton
Invermark Castle
Tarfside
Cairncross
Glenesk Folk
Millden
Colmeallie Stone Circle
Sturdy Hill 1785
Deer Dyke
Glensaugh
Strath Finella
Auchenblae
Drumtochty Forest
Strathfinella Hill
Carlochy
Muckle Cairn 2699
Bulg 1986
Fasque
Kincardine Castle
Loch Brandy
Glen Esk

153
FORMARTINE
161
SEE PAGE 186
ABERDEEN
Aberdeen to:
Kirkwall 6hrs.
Lerwick 12hrs.
NORTH
SEA
Bay of Cruden
Whinnyfold
Ythanbank
Inverebrie
Yonderton
Broomfield
Ellon Castle
Kinharrachie
Denhead
Meikle Loch
Old Slains Castle
Kirkton of Logie Buchan
Kirktown of Slains
Collieston
Sands of Forvie
Meikle Tarty
Tipperty
Knockhall Castle
Hackley Head
or Forvie Ness
Newburgh
Foveran
Newburgh Bar
Drums
Hill of Fiddes
Foveran Burn
Udny Station
Tillery
St. Katherines
Barthol Chapel
Earlsford
Haddo
Wedderlairs
Thornroan
Medieval Tomb
Tarves
Prop of Ythsie
Folla Rule
Core Hill 804
Cross of Jackson
Tulloch
Craigdam
South Ythsie Stone Circle
Pitmedden NTS
Esslemont Castle
Lonehead Stone Circle
Castle
Daviot
Oldmeldrum
Tolquhon
Tolquhon Gallery
NTS Farming Life
Pitmedden
Udny Castle
Udny Green
Barra Castle
Hill of Barra 634
Kirkton of Bourtie
Hillbrae
Hattoncroft
Affleck
Whiterashes
Inveramsay
Harlaw
Balhalgardy
Carnegie
Brandsbutt Symbol Stone
Bass of Inverurie
Inverurie
Aquhorthies Stone Circle
Port Elphinstone
Kinmuck
Reisque
Newmachar
550 Beauty Hill
Craigie
Burnhervie
Kinkell Church
Broomend
Balbithan House
Clovenstone
Kemnay Forest
Whitecairns
Belhelvie
Balmedie
Mill of Fintray
Cothall
Burgh Muir
Hallforest Castle
Kemnay
Kintore
River Don
Hatton of Fintray
Dyce Symbol Stones
Corby Loch
Potterton
DANGER AREA
Blackdog
Leylodge
Overton
Fowlershill
Castle Fraser
Blackburn
Aiky Brae
ABERDEEN (Dyce)
Dyce
821 Tyrebagger Hill
Scotstown Moor
Grandhome House
Letter
Stoneywood
Lyne of Skene
Kinnernie
Kirkhill Forest
Craibstone
Brimmond & Elrick
Bankhead
Bridge of Don
Seaton Park
Danestone
Woodside
Donmouth
Dunecht
Bucksburn
874 Brimmond Hill
Botanical Gs.
Hayton
Old Aberdeen
Kittybrewster
Loch of Skene
Kirkton of Skene
Northfield
Gairloch
Westhill
Sheddocksley
Mastrick
Masons Lodge
Kingswells
Echt
Mill Power House
Elrick
Summerhill
Johnston
Footdee
Maritime NTS
South Kirkton
Garlogie
Carnie
Countesswells
Hazlehead Park
Mannofield
Gordon Highlanders
Ferryhill
Torry
Nigg Bay
Landerberry
Redhill
Cullerlie Stone Circle
Easter Ord
Blacktop
Foggieton
Cults
Ruthrieston
Bridge of Dee
Kincorth
Doonies Farm
Benthoul
Loirston
Nigg
Cullerie
West Cullerlie
Bieldside
Souter Head
Hardgate
Craigton
Banchory-Devenick
Milltimber
Cove Bay
Drum Castle
Mains of Drum
Peterculter
Crossroads
Charlestown
Hirn
Coalford
River Dee
Storybook Glen
Kirkton of Maryculter
The Neuk
Myrebird
Crathes Castle
Drumoak
Park
Hillside
Findon
Portlethen
Portlethen Village
Crathes
Kirkton of Durris
Woodlands
Denside
558 Berry Top
Downies
Cammachmore Bay
Cammachmore
Crossroads
Durris Forest
Netherley
Cookney
Windyedge
Newtonhill
Damford
Lochton
872 Meikle Carewe Hill
Muchalls Castle
Muchalls
1241 Cairn-mon-earn
Bridge of Muchalls
Doonie Point
Raedykes Roman Camp
1232 Mongour
Burn of Sheeoch
Rickarton
Garron Point
Cowie Water
New Mains of Ury
Cowie
1052 Hill of Trusta
Fetteresso Forest
Kirktown of Fetteresso
Stonehaven
Tolbooth
1289 Leachie Hill
Tewel
Castle Haven
Fetteresso Castle
Dunnottar
Brae of Glenbervie
Dunnottar Woodland Park
Thornyhive Bay
Fiddes Castle
Drumlithie
Fowlsheugh
Hirschа Hill 723
Glenbervie
Bruxie Hill 711
Crawton
Milton of Barras
Roadside of Catterline
Bridge of Mondynes
Crawton Bay
Catterline
Roadside of Kinneff
Braidon Bay
Fordoun
Fernieflatt
Todhead Point
Bridge of Kair
Parkneuk
Grassic Gibbon
Whistleberry Castle
Arbuthnott House
A90
A947
A920
A96
A944
A93
A956
A92
B9005
B9170
B999
B9000
B9003
B9001
B993
B977
B979
B987
B994
B997
B9119
B9126
B9125
B9077
B967
1
2
3
4
5
E
F
G
H

154
171
170
146
THE LITTLE MINCH
LOCH SNIZORT
ISLAND OF SKYE
WATERNISH
TROTTERNISH
Eilean Lingreabhagh
Fladda-chùain
Sgeir nam Maol
Eilean Trodday
Rubha Hunish
Rubha na h-Aiseig
Loch Hunish
Tulm Bay
The Aird
Kilmaluag Bay
Shulista
Balmacqueen
An t-Iasgair
Duntulm Castle
Duntulm
Kilmaluag
Connista
A855
Lùb Score
Skye Island Life
Clachan
Hungladder
Flora Macdonald
Heribusta
Camas Mór
Bornesketaig
Kilmuir
Flodigarry
Kilvaxter
Kilmuir Circles
Balgown
Carn Liath
Eilean Chaluim Cille Castle
Loch Sneosdal
Linicro
Totscore
1781 Meall na Suiramach
Quirang
Digg
Glashvin
Uig to Tarbert 1hr. 30mins.
Uig to Lochmaddy 1hr. 40mins.
WATERNISH POINT
Eilean Iosal
Eilean Creagach
Ascrib Islands
Healaval
Dun Gearymore
Dun Borrafiach
Bioda Buidhe 1523
Loch Cleap
Dun Skudiburgh
Uig
River Rha
R. Conon
Idrigill
Brewing Company
Uig Bay
Uig Standing Stone
Balnaknock
Beinn Edra 2006
A87
Geary
931 Ben Geary
The Trial Stone
St. Conan's
Trumpan
Knockbreck
Loch Losait
Earlish
Loch Mór
Halistra
Ardmore Point
Dun Hallin
Hallin
Gillen
Score Horan
Beinn Charnach Bheag
Peinlich
Creag a' Lain 1995
Mingay
Isay
Sgeir nam Biast
Lyndale Point
Hinnisdal Hut Circle
Hinnisdal
Hinnisdal Bridge
Eilean Mór
Greshornish Point
DUNVEGAN HEAD
Loch Dunvegan
Stein
Lusta
Loch Bay
Kingsburgh
Beinn a' Sgà
Biod an Athair
1031
Galtrigill
Piping Heritage Cen.
Dun Borreraig
Borreraig
Ben Ettow
Uig
Borreraig Park
Claigan
Claigan Souterrain
Beinn Bhreac
Bay
Bay River
Annait
Beinn Chreagach
B886
Greshornish
Loch Greshornish
Kildonan
Knott
Treaslane
Romesdal
Romesdal River
Flashader
Clachamish
A850
Snizort
Eyre
Standing Stones
Loch Beag
The Aird
Loch Eyre
Cairn
Kensaleyre
Rhenetra
River Haultin
An Ceannaich
Loch Pooltiel
Fariniquarrie
Totaig
Dun Fiadhairt
Suardal Hut Circle
Fairy Bridge
Edinbane
Blackhill
Bernisdale
1812 Beinn a' Chearcall
Lower Milovaig
Oisgill Bay
Upper Milovaig
Water Mill
Glendale
Colbost
Giant Angus Macaskill
Dunvegan
Ben Uigshader 806
Glen Bernisdale
Symbol Stone
Tote
Crepkill
B8036
Borve
Borve Standing Stones
Waterstein
Loch Mór
Lephin
Borrodale
Toy
Holmisdale
Colbost Croft
Skinidin
Kilmuir
A863
St. Columba's Island
Skeabost
Carbost
Loch Niarsco
Cruachan Beinn a' Chearcaill
Moonen Bay
Glen Dale
Hamara River
Ben Corkeval
B884
Dun Osdale
Lonmore
Uigshader
Drumuie
Beinn a' Ghlinne Bhig 682
Loch Ravag
HEALABHAL MHOR
1538
Roskhill
Roag
Orbost
Ardroag
Cairns
Vatten
Loch Vatten
Glengrasco
Shulishadermor
Aros Experience
Ramasaig
Hoe Rape
The Hoe 759
1600
HEALABHAL BHEAG
Loch Bharcasaig
Harlosh
Loch Caroy
Balmore
River Ose
Ose
Loch Connan
B885
Beinn na Greine 1376
Hoe Point
Loch Glen Iondal
799 Ben Connan
Beinn na Boineid 1207
Harlosh Point
Colbost Point
A863
Tungadal Souterrain
Glenmore
Hillcroft Farm
Dun Beag
Dun Mhor
Bracadale
Totardor
Ben Duagrich
Tungadal River
Stroc-bheinn 1300
Mugeary
Am Bi-bogha Mór
Harlosh Island
Tarner Island
Ullinish
Cairn
Struan
Struanmore
Coillore
Ben Idrigill
Loch Bracadale
Carn Liath
An Dubh-sgeir
Wiay
Macleod's Maidens
IDRIGILL POINT
Dun Ardtreck
Oronsay
Portnalong
Loch Harport
1442 Roineval
Meall an Fhuarain
Varragill River
Rubha nan Clach
Dun Ard an T-Sabhail
Fiskavaig
B8009
Fernilea
Carbost
Drynoch
Arnaval 1210
Talisker Distillery
Gleann Oraid
Merkadale
River Drynoch
Talisker Bay
Talisker
Loch Eynort
Eynort River
Beinn nan Cuithean
Beinn Bhreac
1468 Beinn Bhreac
Eynort
Glen Brittle Forest
MINGINISH

Seana Chamas
Cnoc Breac
962
Peterburn
Naast
Loch Ewe
Inverewe
NTS
155
Poolewe
Loch nan Liagh
Loch Bad a' Chreamh
River Sand
Port Erradale
162
Big Sand
Caolas Beag
Longa Island
Lonemore
Mial
Heritage
Strath
Smithstown
Gairloch
Loch na Curra
A832
B8021
B8057
River Ewe
Loch Kernsary
Tollie Farm
Loch Tollaidh
Loch Airigh a' Phuill
Meall an Doirein
381
Loch Gairloch
Eilean Horrisdale
Charlestown
Port Henderson
Aird
Badachro
B8056
Loch nan Eun
Opinan
Shieldaig
Loch Shieldaig
Loch Clàir
South Erradale
Loch Braigh Horrisdale
River Kerry
Loch Bad an Sgalaig
A832
Abhainn a' Ghairbh
Abhainn Chòire
Redpoint
River Erradale
Allt a' Ghiubhais
Loch Gaineamhach
Flowerdale
Sgeir Eirin
Eilean Flodigarry
Staffin Bay
Staffin Island
An Corran Shell Midden
Garafad
Staffin
Kilt Rock
Mealt Falls
Clachan
Ellishadder
Loch Mealt
Valtos
Marishader
Garros
Culnacnoc
Grealin
Lealt
Lealt Falls
Lealt River
Loch Liuravay
Rubha nam Brathairean
Sgeir Ghlas
Sgeir na Trian
WESTER ROSS
Meall na h-Uamha
Shieldaig Forest
Baosbheinn
2869
Beinn Bhreac
2031
Lochan Sgeireach
Loch a' Bhealaich
Craig
Craig River
Loch Torridon
Lower Diabaig
Upper Diabaig
Loch na h-Uamhaig
Beinn Alligin
3232
Loch Diabaigas Airde
Alligin Shuas
Inveralligin
156
Rechullin
Torridon
Rubha na Fearn
Fearnmore
Fearnbeg
Arinacrinachd
Kenmore
Loch a' Chracaich
Ardheslaig
Loch Shieldaig
Shieldaig Island
NTS
Shieldaig
Upper Loch Torridon
Balgy
Balgy Falls
Ben-damph Forest
Loch a' Bhraige
Port an Fhearainn
RONA
Rubha Chuaig
Cuaig
Abhainn Chuaig
Allt an t-Strathain
Leac Tressirnish
Eilean Garbh
SOUND OF RAASAY
INNER SOUND
Callakille
Allt na h-Eirigh
Lonbain
Eilean Tigh
Garbh Eilean
Caol Rona
Loch a' Squirr
Loch Gaineamhach
1619
Croic-bheinn
1692
Ben Shieldaig
A896
Loch Damh
Beinn Damh
THE STORR
TROTTERNISH
Storr
2358
Old Man of Storr
Bearreraig Bay
Holm Island
Eilean Fladday
Loch Leathan
A855
Loch Fada
Manish Point
Loch Arnish
Torran
Arnish
An Dubh-loch
Abhainn Dubh
Glenshieldaig Forest
Loch Lundie
Loch nan Eun
River Applecross
Applecross Forest
Loch Coire Attadale
2938
Beinn Bhan
Loch Gaineamhach
Abhainn Dearg
Loch Coultrie
Sgurr a' Gharaidh
2396
Rassal Ashwood
Achachork
Dun Gerashader
Torvaig
Portree
Loch Portree
Penifiler
Ben Tianavaig
1355
Heatherfield
Brochel Castle
Brochel
Glam
Burn
Glame
RAASAY
Balachuirn
Applecross Bay
Applecross
Milton
Camusteel
Camusterrach
Ard-dhubh
Culduie
Sgurr a' Chaorachain
2539
Loch Coire nan Arr
Meall Gorm
Loch Braigh an Achaidh
Smithy Heritage
Kishorn
A896
Camastianavaig
Conordan
Holoman Bay
Tianavaig Bay
Dun Caan
1455
Rubha na Leac
Oskaig
St.Moluag's
Heritage
Clachan
B883
Lower Ollach
Upper Ollach
Gedintailor
Balmeanach
Narrows of Raasay
Inverarish
Suisnish Hill
Suisnish
North Fearns
Eyre
Eyre Point
Glen Varragill
1456
Ben Lee
Peinchorran
Sconser to Raasay 15mins.
Caol Mòr
Eilean na Bà
Toscaig
River Toscaig
Loch Mhol Fharochaich
Meall Loch Airigh Alasdair
Uags
Eilean Beag
CROWLIN ISLANDS
Caolas Mòr
Eilean Mòr
Sgeir Dhearg
Longay
Kishorn Island
Loch Kishorn
Ardarroch
Achintraid
Bad a' Chreamha
1296
Stromemore
Strome
NTS
Stromeferry
Ardaneaskan
Loch Carron
Plockton
Castle
NTS
Plockton
W.Highland Dairy
Achmore
Craig
Loch nan Gillean
Highland Farm
Loch Lundie
Loch na Leitire
Port Cam
NTS
Duirinish
Drumbuie
Loch Achaidh na h-Inich
Gleann Udalain
A87
Loch Sligachan
Sconser
GLAMAIG
2542
Moll
Loch an Leòid
Sligachan
Glen Sligachan
River Sligachan
Loch Ainort
Luib
Croft
Mullach na Càrn
1298
Dunan
Caolas Scalpay
Scalpay House
SCALPAY
Black Island
147
Erbusaig
Badicaul
Loch Scalpaidh
Achtertyre Hill
Kyle of Lochalsh
Auchtertyre
Balmacara
Lochalsh Woodland
NTS
A87
Conchra
A890
Pabay
Guillamon Island
Plock of Kyle
Kyle Akin
Donald Murchison's Mon.
Kirkton
Nostie
Ardelve
Glas Bheinn Mhòr
1852
Marsco
2414
Kyleakin
Caisteal Maol
Isle of Skye
Loch Alsh
Glas Eilean
Eilean Donan
Caisteal
E
F
G
H
150
60
70
80
1
2
3
4
5

156
162
163
155
148
A
B
C
D
1
2
3
4
5
Loch Ewe
Naast
B8057
Loch Bad a' Chreamh
Inverewe
NTS
Londubh
Poolewe
Mhic' Ille Riabhaich
Loch na Mòine Buige
Meall na Mèine 820
Aird Dubh
Bad Bog
Loch Ghiuragarstidh
Beinn a' Chàisgein Beag 2230
Toll a' Mhadaidh
Loch Ghiubsachain
Fisherfield Forest
Strathnasheallag Forest
Loch na Sealga
Strath na Sealga
Loch Toll an Lochain
3484
Loch Coire Chaorachain
Dundonnell Forest
Lochan Fada
Carn a' Bhiorain 1665
Loch Allt Eigin
Lochan Fraoich
Dundonnell River
A832
Auchlunachan
Loch an Airceil
Lael Forest
River Broom
Loch an t-Sìdhein
Lael Forest Garden
Braemore
Corrieshalloch Gorge NTS
Falls of Measach NTS
Braemore Forest
A835
1270 Carn Breac Beag
Meall an t-Sìthe 1971
Abhainn Cuileig
Loch na Curra
Gairloch
Loch Tollaidh
Tollie Farm
Loch Kernsary
River Ewe
Loch na Mòine
Fionn Loch
Lochan na Bearta
Beinn Dearg Mòr 2974
Loch Beinn Dearg
2802 Beinn a' Chàisgein Mòr
Lochan Beannach Mòr
2595 Beinn Airigh Charr
Dubh Loch
Lochan Feith Mhic'illean
Fuar Loch Mòr
Beinn a' Chlaidheimh
Loch a' Bhrisidh
Mullach Coire Mhic Fhearchair
Meall an Doirein 1381
Charlestown
Loch Maree
Eilean Sùbhainn
Gorm Loch Mòr
2817 Beinn Lair
Letterewe Forest
Letterewe
Loch Garbhaig
Lochan Fada
Loch a' Bhraoin
Loch Toll an Lochain
3276 A' Chailleach
2424 Groban
Meall a' Chrasgaidh 3062
Loch a' Mhadaidh
Sgurr Mòr 3637
Allt a' Mhadaidh
River Kerry
B8056
A832
Loch Bad an Sgalaig
Victoria Falls
Talladale
River Shiel
Abhainn a' Ghairbh
Choire
Slioch 3215
Loch an Sgeireach
Gleann
Allt a' Chaorainn Mhòir
Fannich Forest
Fannich Lodge
Loch Gaineamhach
Flowerdale Forest
Baosbheinn 2869
Bridge of Grudie
Abhainn an Fhasaigh
Beinn a' Mhùinidh 2231
Kinlochewe Forest
Abhainn a' Chadh' Bhuidhe
Loch Fannich
WESTER ROSS
Loch na h-Oidhche
2805 Beinn an Eoin
Strath Lungard
River Grudie
Glen Grudie
Beinn Eighe
Heights of Kinlochewe
Gleann Tanagaidh
2333 Beinn nan Ramh
Lochan Sgeireach
Beinn Bhreac 2031
Loch a' Bhealaich
Loch na h-Uamhaig
Beinn Allligin 3232
Ruadh-stac Mòr 3313
Kinlochewe
Incheril
Abhainn Bruachaig
Carn a' Ghlinne 1769
Fionn Bheinn 3062
Loch na Mòine Mòr
Loch na Mòine Beag
Lochrosque
Upper Diabaig
Alligin Shuas
Inveralligin
Rechullin
Torridon Forest
NTS
Beinn Eighe
Liathach
3456
Glen Docherty
Badavanich
A832
Loch a' Chroisg
Achnasheen
River Bran
2313 Meall a' Chaorainn
Strath
Upper Loch Torridon
Fasag
Torridon
Glen Torridon
River Torridon
A896
A' Ghairbhe
Loch Clair
Loch Bharranch
2566 Sgurr Dubh
Coulin Lodge
Loch Coulin
Coulin Forest
River Coulin
Abhainn Dubh
Loch an Fhiarlaid
Carn Beag 1804
Ledgowan
Loch Gowan
Ledgowan Forest
Shieldaig
Balgy
Balgy Falls
Annat
Deer
Lochan Neimhe
Thràil
Abhainn
Ben-damph Forest
1692 Ben Shieldaig
Loch Damh
Lochan Uaine
HIGH
Carn Breac 2223
A890
Glen Carron
Loch Sgamhain
1765 Carn Mhartuin
Loch Coire a' Bhuic
Scardroy
Loch Cnoc na Mointeich
Loch an Eoin
Beinn Damh 2957
Maol Chean-dearg 3060
Sgorr Ruadh 3142
River Lair
Loch Coire Làir
Craig
Glencarron Lodge
3026 Moruisg
Allt a' Chonais
Carn Gorm
Creag na h-Iolaire
Glenshieldaig Forest
A896
Loch Coire an Ruadh-stac
Achnashellach
Achnashellach Forest
Glencarron & Glenuig Forest
Gleann Fhiodhaig
River Meig
Loch na Caoidhe
Loch Gaineamhach
Abhainn Dearg
An Gorm-loch
Loch a' Mhuilinn
Balnacra
Loch Dùghaill
Maoile Lunndaidh 3304
Loch Coultrie
Sgurr a' Gharaidh 2396
Glas Bheinn 2332
Coulags
River Carron
Eagan
Sgurr na Feartaig
Sgurr a' Chaorachain 3455
An Gorm-loch
Rassal Ashwood
Tullich
Smithy Heritage Centre
A890
A896
New Kelso
Strathcarron
Creag a' Chaorainn
Beinn Tharsuinn
West Monar Forest
Loch Mhuilich
East Monar Forest
Loch Coire nan Arr
Kirkton
Kishorn
Allt Nan Carnan
Achintee
Loch nan Creadha
Loch an Laoigh
Lurg Mhòr 3234
An Gead Loch
Loch Monar
Monar Lodge
Ardarroch
Achintraid
Loch Kishorn
Lochcarron
Attadale
Attadale
Carn Geuradainn 1950
Bendronaig Lodge
Loch Calavie
Beinn Dronaig
Attadale Forest
R. Attadale
Uisge Misgeach
Bad a' Chreamha 1296
Lochcarron Weavers
Loch Cruoshie
Lochan Gobhlach
Loch an Tachdaich
An Cruachan 2312
Meallan Buidhe
Stromemore
Ardaneaskan
Strome NTS
A890
Ardnarff
Carn nan Iomairean
Loch an Iasaich
River Ling
Carn na Sean-lùibe
Sgurr na Lapaich 3775
Plockton
Castle
W. Highland Dairy
Stromeferry
Achmore
Craig
Highland Farm
Loch nan Gillean
Loch Lundie
Loch Achaidh na h-Inich
Loch na Leitire
Gleann Udalain
Allt Gleann Udalain
Loch na h-Onaich
Killilan Forest
2949 Aonach Buidhe
An Riabhachan 3696
3508
Glencannich Forest
Sallachy
Sgùman Còinntich 2883
Killilan
Loch Mhoicean
Loch Mullardoch
Glen Cannich
Auchtertyre Hill
Loch Long
Loch Beinn a' Mheadhoin
Loch nan Ealachan
Allt na Doire Gairbhe
Toll Creagach 3457
Doire Tana
Auchtertyre
A890
A87
Conchra
Bundalloch
Camas-luinie
Glen Elchaig
Carnach
Loch na Leitreach
Falls of Glomach NTS
West Benula Forest
Gleann Sithidh
Abhainn Sithidh
Allt a' Chòinich
Coire Lochan
Tom a' Chòinich 3646
Carn Eighe 3880
Gleann nam Fiadh
Kyle of Lochalsh
Kirkton
Nostie
Ardelve
Carndu
Dornie
Loch Long
Loch Alsh
Glas Eilean
Caisteal
Eilean Donan
Loch Bhuic Mhòir
Loch nan Eun
River Elchaig
Iniverinate Forest

157
EASTER ROSS
STRATHCONON
FOREST
LAND
THE AIRD
Dingwall
Strathpeffer
Beauly
Beauly Firth
INVERNESS
Muir of Ord
Conon Bridge
Maryburgh
Evanton
Kiltarlity
Struy
Cannich
Drumnadrochit
Milton
Garve
Gorstan
Achnasheen
BEN WYVIS
LOCH NESS
164
158
149

158
164
165
157
150
A
B
C
D
1
2
3
4
5
Edderton
Portmahomack
Bindal
Ballone Castle
Seafield
Rockfield
Glenmorangie Distillery
Tarlogie
Morangie
DANGER AREA
Inver
Lower Arboll
Tarrel
Toulvaddie
Tain
Tain Hill
Tain Through Time
Hilton
Loch Eye
Lower Pitkerrie
Geanies
Aultnamain Inn
Loch Muigh-bhlaraidh
Cnoc Muigh-bhlaraidh
Beinn Tharsuinn
2270
Morangie Forest
Aldie Burn
Glen Aldie
Hill of Fearn
Talich
Fearn
Tullich
Hilton of Cadboll Chapel
Hilton of Cadboll
Balintore
Shandwick
Clach a' Charridh
Cnoc an t-Sabhail
1243
Loch Sheilah
Strath Rory
Hartmount
Lamington
Marybank
Brenachie
Scotsburn
Pitmaduthy
Kildary
Balnagown Castle
Arabella
Ankerville
Strathy
Loanreoch
Stittenham Forest
Ardross
Easter Ardross
Cnoc Corr Guinie
1301
Kinrive Hill
1056
Kinrive
Tullich Muir
Milton
Kilmuir
Badachonacher
Coillemore
Dalnavie
River Averon
Achandunie
Newmore Castle
Rhicullen
Nonikiln
Delny
Barbaraville
Polio
Nigg Bay
Wester Rarichie
Port an Righ
Pitcalnie
Bayfield Loch
Hill of Nigg
665
Nigg
Cnoc Ceislein
1716
Contullich
Fyrish
Crosshills
Obsdale
Achnagarron
Tomich
Broomhill
Balintraid
Saltburn
Balnabruaich
Balnapaling
Nigg Ferry
Castlecraig
Dunskeath
Rosskeen
Alness
Dalmore
Invergordon
FIRTH
Cromarty
Hugh Miller's Cottage NTS
Blue Head
Sutors of Cromarty
Courthouse
Black Rock Gorge
Alness Bay
Ferryton
Balblair
Udale Bay
Cromarty Bay
Newton
McFarquhar's Cave
Evanton
Drummond
CROMARTY
Alnessferry
Resolis
Jemimaville
Davidston
Cullicudden
Newmills
Springfield
Muirton
Mount High
Easter Brae
Wester Brae
Millbuie Forest
Ardullie
Findon Mains
Kinbeachie
Whitebog
MORAY
Braefindon
Culbo
Mount Eagle
Culbokie
BLACK
ISLE
Findon Forest
Killen
Fairy Glen
Groam House
Rosemarkie
Fortrose
Rosemarkie Bay
Whiteness Head
DANGER AREA
Culbin Sands
Cran Loch
Fishertown
Culbin Forest
Nairn
Kingsteps
Druim
Brodie NTS
Queen's Own Highlanders Regimental
Fort George
Ardersier
Chanonry Point
Tradespark
Househill
Auldearn
Boath Doocot NTS
Auldearn Castle
Belmaduthy Dam
Duncanston
Knockbain
Cathedral
Easter Suddie
Avoch
Heritage Centre
Avoch Bay
Belmaduthy
Easter Kinkell
Tore
Munlochy
Munlochy Bay
Ormond Castle
Gollanfield
Moss-side
Blackhills
Foynesfield
Milton of Gollanfield
Lochside
Loch Flemington
Muir of the Clans
Brackla
River Nairn
Geddes
Laiken Forest
Rootfield
Kilcoy
Kilcoy Castle
Drynie Park
Arpafeelie
Bogallan
Black Isle
Kilmuir
Fisherton
INVERNESS (Dalcross)
Alturlie Point
Clephanton
Piperhill
Regoul
Cawdor
Cawdor Castle
Culcharry
Urchany
Littlemill
Redcastle
Red Castle
Milton
Artafallie
Drumsmittal
Craigrory
Red Kite
Craigton
Dolphins & Seals
Charlestown
Lifeboat Station
North Kessock
South Kessock
Stuart
Dalcross
Tornagrain
Newton
Dalcross Castle
Cantraywood
Croy
Kilravock
Easter Galcantray
Cantray
Wester Galcantray
Assich Forest
Clunas
Clunas Reservoir
Redburn
Ardclach Bell Tower
Newlands of Fleenas Wood
Ferness
Glenferness Mains
Beauly Firth
Balloch
Feabuie
Muir
Smithton
Kirkhill
Lentran
Bunchrew
Clachnaharry
Leachkin
Craig Phadrig
Cathedral
Culloden
Well of the Dead
Westhill
Culloden 1746 NTS
Clava Cairns
Newlands
Memorial Cairn
Cantraybruich
Saddle Hill
1227
Drumchardine
Newtonhill
INVERNESS
SEE PAGE 190
Culcabock
Bught Floral Hall
James Pringle Weavers
Lochardil
Daviot Wood
Reelig Glen
AIRD
An Leacainn
1358
Dochgarroch
Caledonian Canal
River Ness
Scaniport
Essich
Craggiemore
Daviot
HIGHLAND
Carn a' Chrasgie
Carn Sgumain
1370
Beinn Bhuidhe Mhòr
1799
Carn nan Tri-tighearnan
2016
Drynachan Lodge
Dochfour
Lochend
1642
Carn a' Bhodaich
Aldourie Castle
Dores
Drumashie Moor
Loch Ashie
Creag a' Chlachain
1196
Dunlichity Lodge
Gask Ring Cairn
Inverarnie
Farr
1675
Beinn Bhreac
Moy Burn
Meall a' Bhreacraibh
1809
River Findhorn
Rhilean Burn
Leonach Burn
Tomlachlan Burn
Meall Mòr
1611
Moy
Loch Moy
Moy Castle
Funtack Burn
Ruthven
Lochindorb
Lochindorb Lodge
Loch an t-Sidhein
Ashie Moor
Loch Duntelchaig
Strathnairn Forest
2022
Carn na h-Easgainn
Balvraid Lodge
2076
Carn an t-Sean-liathanaich
Stac na Cathaig
1463
Tom Bailgeann
1522
Loch a' Chlachain
Brin Herb Nursery
Tomatin
Corrybrough
Raigbeg
2057
Carn a' Choire Mhòir
2162
Carn Glas-choire
Findhorn Bridge
Beinn Bhreac
1969
Loch Ceo Glais
Torness
Loch Ruthven
East Croachy
Aberarder
River Nairn
Glen Kyllachy
Clune
Carn nam Bain-tighearna
Duthil Burn
A9
A82
A96
A835
A832
A862
A939
A938
B9176
B9165
B9166
B9175
B817
B9163
B9169
B9160
B9161
B9006
B9092
B9091
B9090
B9101
B9039
B9177
B8082
B862
B861
B851
B852
B9154
B9007

159
Spey Bay
Burghead Bay
Findhorn Bay
MORAY
STRATHSPEY
BEN RINNES
HILLS OF CROMDALE
Lossiemouth
Branderburgh
Elgin
Burghead
Hopeman
Findhorn
Kinloss
FORRES
Rothes
Craigellachie
Charlestown of Aberlour
Dufftown
Fochabers
Mosstodloch
Garmouth
Kingston
Dallas
Archiestown
Grantown-on-Spey
Tomnavoulin
Lhanbryde
Urquhart
Cummingstown
Duffus
Dyke
Rafford
Dava
A96
A95
A941
A940
A939
A920
A98
151
160

160
A
B
C
D
1
2
3
4
5
NORTH
Spey Bay
Portknockie
Findochty
Findochty Castle
Cullen Bay
Logie Head
Findlater Castle
Sandend Bay
Redhythe Point
Boyne Bay
Knock Head
Boyndie Bay
Macduff Marine Aquarium
Newtown
Seatown
Cullen
Bauds of Cullen
Portessie
Ianstown
Buckie
Buckie Drifter
Rathven
Tugnet Ice House
Moray Firth
Kingston
Garmouth
Spey Bay
Nether Dallachy
Porttannachy
Portgordon
Buckpool
Bin of Cullen
1051
Market Cross
Lintmill
Sandend
Portsoy
Seatown
Boyne Castle
Whitehills
Boyndie
Auds
Inverboyndie
Banff
Macduff
Fountain
Banff
Colleonard Sculpture
Duff House
River Deveron
Bridge of Alvah
Wester Culbeuchly
Inchdrewer Castle
Kirktown of Alvah
Eden Castle
Danshillock
Itlaw
Newton of Mountblairy
Muirden
Joiner's Workshop
Fordyce
Durn Hill
653
Milton
Kirktown of Deskford
Deskford Church
Berryhillock
Brodiesord
Burn of Boyne
Cornhill
Gordonstown
Drums of Park
Mains of Edingight
1412
Knock Hill
Sillyearn
Glen Barry
Lower Auchenreath
Upper Dallachy
Auchenhalrig
Newlands of Tynet
Slackhead
Drybridge
Broadley
Clochan
Shiel Muir
Aultmore
Bogmoor
Spey Viaduct & Walk
Mosstodloch
Baxters
Gordon Castle
Crofts of Dipple
Fochabers
Speymouth Forest
Whiteash Hill Wood
Ordiquish
Wood of Ordiequish
Inchberry
River Spey
Millstone Hill
987
Deerhill
1028
Lurg Hill
Grange Crossroads
Crannoch
Bracobrae
Broadrashes
Aultmore
Forgie
MORAY
Newmill
Milton Tower
Strathisla Distillery
Keith
Fife Keith
Orton
Malcolmburn
1019
Hill of Mulderie
Mulben
River Isla
ISLA
Farmtown
Nethermills
Knock
Drumnagorrach
Ramsburn
Crombie Castle
Finnygaud
Knowes of Elrick
Cleanhill Wood
Aberchirder
Cloverleaf Fibre Stud
Marnoch
Dubiton
Kinnairdy Castle
Bogton
Carnousie Castle
Turtory
Hillbrae
River Deveron
Auchininna
Milltown of Rothiemay
Inverkeithny
1128
Yonder Bognie
Fourman Hill
Bogniebrae
Forgue
Glendronach Distillery
Fortrie
Thomastown
Kirktown of Auchterless
Mains of Auchindachy
Upper Cuttlehill
Glen of Coachford
The Bin Forest
The Balloch
Ruthven
Rosarie Forest
1111
Hill of Towie
STRATH
Maggieknockater
Craigellachie Castle
Towiemore
Glen Line
Castle
Drummuir Castle
Drummuir
Cairnie
The Bin
1027
The Bin Forest
The Bin Trail
Corse of Kinnoir
ABERDEEN
Tullich
Lock Park
Balvenie
Glenfiddich Distillery
Daugh of Invermarkie
Daugh of Cairnborrow
Falconry
Milltown of Auchindoun
Invermarkie
Blairmore
River Deveron
Clashmach Hill
Huntly
Brander
Drumblade
Corse
Largue
Auchanie
Balgaveny
New Mill
Gordonstown
Kirktown of Mortlach
Giant's Chair
Haugh of Glass
Bridewell
Ythanwells
Badenscoth
Auchindoun Castle
1599
The Scalp
Laggan
STRATHBOGIE
Baillieward
Beldorney Castle
Bridgend
Hillhead
Bainshole
Fisherford
Hill of Tillymorgan
1249
Rothienorman
Succoth
Tillathrowie
Coynachie
Glens of Foudland
1531
Hill of Foudland
Kirkton of Culsalmond
Newseat
Glen Fiddich
Clashindarroch Forest
Clashindarroch
Kirkney
Gartly
River Bogie
Knockandy Hill
1425
Cults
Wardhouse
Lenchie
Largie
Picardy Symbol Stone
Upper Boddam
Colpy
Cairnhill
Tocher
Meikle Wartle
Kirkton of Rayne
Bridgend
Inverharroch
Ardwell
Glenfiddich Forest
Black Water
1872
Round Hill
Forest
Kirkney
Milton of Lesmore
Tap o' Noth
1848
152
Kennethmont
Knockenbaird
Dunnideer Castle
Old Manse Gallery
Insch
Pitmachie
Old Rayne
Durno
Mount of Haddoch
1708
Cabrach
Belhinnie
Rhynie
Druminnor Castle
Clatt
Duncanston
Leslie
Leslie Castle
Kirkton
Kirkton of Oyne
Oyne
Old
Whiteford
Pitcaple
Craw Stone
Elrick
Craig Castle
River Urie
A96
A98
A95
A97
A941
A920
A942
A990
B9139
B9025
B9121
B9022
B9023
B9018
B9016
B9015
B9104
B90154
B9017
B9103
B9117
B9116
B9014
B9002
B9024
B9001
B992
B9026
B9031
B9021

SEA
Troup Head
Pennan Head
Quarry Head
Head of Garness
Gamrie Bay
Crovie
Fort Fiddes
Pennan
Gardenstown
Silverhillocks
B9031
Longmanhill
B9123
Dubford
New Aberdour
759 Windyheads Hill
Hill of Overbrae
Netherbrae
A98
Hill of Fishrie 745
Clochforbie
Crudie
Cauldwells
Litterty
Plaidy
Craigston Castle
Fintry
B9105
New Byth
Garmond
B9021
Muiryfold
Delgatie
Turriff
A947
Cuminestown
B9170
Darra
Hatton Castle
Howe of Teuchar
Birkenhills
Delgatty Forest
B992
Towie Barclay Castle
Seggat
Inverythan
Steinmanhill
Reemshill
Titty
Backhill
Parkburn
Fyvie
Woodhead
Upper Kirkton
St. Katherines
Folla Rule
Core Hill 804
Cross of Jackston
Barthol Chapel
Tulloch
Lonehead Stone Circle
Daviot
Castle
B9001
A920
Oldmeldrum
Hill of Barra 634
Barra Castle
Rosehearty
Mounthooley Doocot
Dunarg Castle
Sandhaven
Pitsligo Castle
Meal Mill
Pittulie
B9031
Peathill
B9032
Mid Ardlaw
Upper Boyndlie
Tyrie
Woodhead
Ladysford
Farm
Craigmaud
Blackhills
Corsehill
Hillhead of Auchentumb
Middlemuir
New Pitsligo
Balnamoon
B9093
Strichen
Strichen Stone Circle
A950
A981
Bonnykelly
Whitestones
Oldwhat
Balthangie
618 Hill of Corsegight
Brucklay
Fedderate Castle
North Commonty
Culsh
New Deer
Greens
Slacks of Cairnbanno
Auchreddie
584 Deer's Hill
Kirkton
Lethenty
Cottown
Monkshill
Gight Castle
B9005
Haddo
Little Ardo
Methlick
Middlemuir
Knaven
Cairnorrie
Little Water
Ythan River
Hillbrae
Earlsford
Haddo House NTS
Wedderlairs
Thornroan
Tarves
Prop of Ythsie
B999
South Ythsie Stone Circle
Craigdam
Tolquhon Castle
Tolquhon Gallery
NTS Farming Life
Pitmedden NTS
Pitmedden
Udny Castle
Udny Green
B9000
Hill of
Scotland's Lighthouse
Kinnaird Head
Heritage
Broadsea
Fraserburgh
Fraserburgh Bay
Cairnbulg Point
Waters of Philorth
Cairnbulg
Maggie's Hoosie
Inverallochy
Kirktown
Percyhorner
Cardno
B9033
B9107
Cairnbulg Castle
Memsie
Memsie Cairn
Charlestown
St. Combs
Gowanhill
Moss-side of Cairness
Inverallochy Castle
Inzie Head
Cairness
A90
Rathen
Loch of Strathbeg
Crimonmogate
Waughton Hill 768
White Horse
White Stag
A952
Dartfield
Crimond
Rattray Head
Rattray
Cockmuir
New Leeds
Belfatton
Keyhead
Longhill
Balearn
St. Fergus Moss
Rowanhill
Middle Essie
Adziel
North Ugie Water
Backfolds
Shielhill
St. Fergus
White Cow Wood
Forest of Deer
Denhead
Fetterangus
Hythie
Rora Moss
Gallowhills
Kirktown
Rora
Cuttyhill
Loudon Wood Stone Circle
Drinnie's Wood Observatory
Maud
Deer Abbey
Maud Rail.
Dunshillock
Old Deer
Aden
Mintlaw
Longside
Ravenscraig Castle
Inverugie Castle
Inverugie
Buchanhaven
Ugie Salmon Fish House
Arbuthnot
B9029
B9028
B9106
Backhill of Clackriach
Quartalehouse
Drymuir
Bulwark
South Ugie Water
Aberdeenshire Farming
Stuartfield
Inverquhomery
Flushing
Peterhead
Keith Inch
Burnhaven
Millbreck
B9030
Little Dens
Cocklaw
Invernettie
Clola
Nether Kinmundy
Blackhill
Boddam
Kinnadie
Stirling
Sandfordhill
Castle
Auchnagatt
Mains of Auchnagatt
578 Hill of Skilmafilly
Kinknockie
Braeside
Quilquox
Schivas Castle
Drumwhindle
A948
Arnage Castle
Milton Coldwells
Hill of Dudwick 570
Muirtack
Arthrath
Coldwells
Long Haven
Longhaven Cliffs
Bullers of Buchan
North Haven
Hatton
Bridgend
Twa Havens
Cruden Bay
Slains Castle
Port Erroll
Bay of Cruden
Bogbrae Croft
Chapel Hill
Whinnyfold
A975
Ythanbank
Inverebrie
Yonderton
Broomfield
Ellon Castle
Kinharrachie
Esslemont Castle
Ellon
Meikle Loch
Denhead
Old Slains Castle
Kirkton of Slains
Kirkton of Logie Buchan
Meikle Tarty
Tipperty
Knockhall Castle
Sands of Forvie
Collieston
Hackley Head or Forvie Ness
BUCHAN
ABERDEENSHIRE
FORMARTINE
153

isiadar
60
70
80
90
30
A
B
C
D
1
20
2
Camas Eilean Ghlais
Reiff
Eilean Mullagrach
Isle Ristol
10
Glas-leac Mór
171
Ullapool to Stornoway 2hrs. 40mins.
Tanera Beg
Glas-leac Beag
Summer
3
Eilean Dubh
Priest Island
Bottle Island
900
Greenstone Point
Loch na Doire Duinne
Opinan
Rubha Beag
Stattic Point
Loch nan Clachan Geala
Mellon Udrigle
Loch a' Choire
4
Slaggan Bay
Gruinard Island
Eilean Furadh Mór
Loch an t-Slagain
Achgarve
Mungasdale
Gruinard Bay
513
Camas Mór
Rubha nan Sasan
Beinn Dearg Nhór
Rubha Reidh
Mellon Charles
Laide
Gruinard House
B8057
A832
First Coast
Cove
Ormiscaig
Sand
Second Coast
Loch an Draing
90
An Cuaidh 972
Aultbea
Loch na Ba
Loch Airigh an Eilein
Mellangaun
Drumchork
Beinn Dearg Bad Chailleach 897
Isle of Ewe
Loch Sguod
Loch a' Bhaid-luachraich
Loch Fada
Melvaig
Aultgrishan
Midtown
Brae
Loch Ewe
5
Seana Chamas
B8021
Cnoc Breac 962
Loch Mhic' ille Riabhaich
Loch na Móine Buige
Aird Dubh
Peterburn
Naast
NTS
Beinn a' Chàisgein Beag 2230
Inverewe
Meall na Mèine 820
Loch nan Liagh
Loch Bad a' Chreamh
NTS
Bad Bog
Port Erradale
Loch Ghiuragarstidh
North Erradale
Londubh
River Sand
Poolewe
80
A
155
B
C
D
Loch na Curra
River Ewe
Loch Kernsary
Loch na Moine
Big Sand
Caolas Beag
Heritage
Mial
Tollie Farm
Longa Island
Lonemore
Strath
A832
Loch Tollaidh
Smithstown
Gairloch
Lochan Beannach Mór 2595
Loch Gairloch
Meall an Doirein 1381
Beinn Airigh Charr
Eilean
Loch Airigh
Fionn Loch
Gruinard River
Little Gruinard River
Heritage
60
70
90

163
166
164
156
157
E
F
G
H
1
2
3
4
5
Cluas Deas
Culkein
Eilean Chrona
Oldany
Culkein Drumbeg
Drumbeg
Nedd
Glenleraig
Kylesku
Unapool
Newton
Kinloch
Rhubha Stoer
Achnacarnin
Clashmore
Clashnessie
Balchladich
Rienachait
Stoer
Bay of Stoer
Clachtoll Broch
Clachtoll
Achmelvich Bay
Achmelvich
Rhicarn
Rubha Rodha
Soyea Island
Baddidarach
Lochinver
Brackloch
Culag Wood
Loch Inver
Kirkaig Point
Strathan
Badnaban
A' Chleit
Inverkirkaig
Rubha Coigeach
Falls of Kirkaig
Eilean Mór
Enard Bay
QUINAG
2651
Lochassynt Lodge
Loch Assynt
Ardvreck Castle
Inchnadamph
Glas Bheinn
2541
Beinn Uidhe
2410
Eas Coul Aulin Falls
Beinn Aird da Loch
1722
Beinn Leoid
2599
Corriekinloch
BEN MORE ASSYNT
3273
Inchnadamph Forest
Inchnadamph Bone Caves
Breabag
2670
Benmore Forest
Conival
SUILVEN
2399
CANISP
2779
Glencanisp Forest
Beinn Gharbh
1769
Maovally
1673
Inverpolly Lodge
Brea of Achnahaird
Altandhu
Smokehouse
Polbain
Badentarbat
Badentarbat Bay
Achiltibuie
Hydroponicum
Polglass
Tanera Mór
Isles
Badenscallie
Horse Island
Achduart
Culnacraig
CUL MOR
2787
Inverpolly
Inverpolly Forest
Aird of Coigach
Stac Pollaidh
2009
Drumrunie Forest
Elphin
Ledmore
Highland & Rare Breeds
Knockan
Altnacealgach
Benmore Lodge
Linneraineach
2523
Cùl Beag
Lochan Dearg
Benmore Coigeach
Ben Mór Coigach
2438
C O I G A C H
Drumrunie
CROMALT HILLS
1692
Cnoc na Glas Choille
1006
An Stùc
1195
Loch Craggie
Lubcroy
Oykel Bridge
Carn nan Sgeir
Strathcanaird
Strath Canaird
Loch a' Chroisg
Meall an Fhuarain
1895
Na Dromannan
1337
Cailleach Head
Leac Dhonn
Isle Martin
Ardmair
Rhue
Annat Bay
H I G H L A N D
Scoraig
Achmore
Carnach
Rireavach
Little Loch Broom
Badluarach
Morefield
Rhidorroch
Rhidorroch Forest
Meall Liath Choire
1798
Ullapool
Village Clock
A835
A837
A838
A832
A894
B869
East Rhidorroch Lodge
Creag Loisgte
1353
Beinn Ghobhlach
2082
Beinn Eilideach
1830
Sea View
Dundonnell
Badcaul
Badrallach
Loch Broom
Leckmelm
Dun an Ruigh Ruadh Broch
Blarnalearoch
Loggie
Dun Lagaidh
Rhiroy
Ardindrean
Ardcharnich
Meall Dubh
2105
2221
Meall nam Bradhan
Seana Bhraigh
3040
Freevater Forest
Carn Bàn
2762
Sidhean Raireag
1769
Ardessie
Ardessie Falls
Camusnagaul
Sàil Mhór
2508
Carn nam Buailtean
1283
Dundonnell
AN TEALLACH
3484
Letters
Inverlael
Inverlael Forest
Carn Mór
2122
Eididh nan Clach Geala
3039
Deanich Lodge
Strathnasheallag Forest
Fisherfield Forest
Carn a' Bhiorain
1665
Auchlunachan
Lael Forest
Lael Forest Garden
BEINN DEARG
3547
Beinn Enaiglair
2915
Tollomuick Forest
Beinn a' Chaisteil
2404
Beinn Dearg Mór
2974
Meall a' Ghrianain
2531
Braemore
Corrieshalloch Gorge NTS
Falls of Measach NTS
Braemore Forest
1270
Carn Breac Beag
Meall Leacachain
2028
Meall an t-Sìthe
1971
Strathvaich Forest
Inchbae Forest
Beinn a' Chlaidheimh
2802

165
168
158
159
NORTH SEA
DORNOCH FIRTH
TARBAT NESS
Helmsdale
Brora
Golspie
Dornoch
Tain
Embo
Portmahomack
Kinbrace
Achentoul
Kildonan
Torrish
Marrel
Navidale
East Helmsdale
West Helmsdale
Gartymore
Portgower
Lothmore
Kilmote
Crackaig
Lothbeg
Lothbeg Point
Achrimsdale
East Clyne
West Clyne
Clynelish
Dalchalm
Badnellan
Doll
Uppat
Backies
Dunrobin Castle
Dunrobin
Carn Liath Broch
Orcadian Stone
Duke of Sutherland Monument
Kirkton
Little Torboll
Morvich
Mound Rock
Loch Fleet
Skelbo Castle
Skelbo
Skelbo Street
Skelbo Wood
Littleferry
Embo Street
Embo House
Poles
Pitgrudy
Cathedral
Littletown
Camore
Clashmore
Lonemore
Evelix
Loch Evelix
Clashmore Wood
Fleuchary
Birichen
Astle
Pronsy Castle
Lednabirichen
Rearquhar
Badninish
Loch Laoigh
Rogart
Little Rogart
Achvoan
Knockarthur
Rhilochan
Dalreavoch
Balnacoil
Gordonbush
Loch Brora
River Brora
Black Water
Ben Horn 1706
Loch Horn
Cagar Feosaig 1239
Beinn Lunndaidh 1463
Beinn a' Bhragaidh 1293
Golspie Burn
Scottarie Burn
Kilbraur Hill 1063
Loch an Tubairnaich
Col-bheinn 1765
Beinn Dhorain 2060
Meallan Liath Beag 1512
Cnoc Meadhonach 1134
Glen Sletdale
Glen Loth
Eldrable Hill 1338
Strath of Kildonan or Strath Ullie
Craggie Water
Craggie
River Helmsdale
Kildonan Burn
Suisgill Burn
Kinbrace Burn
Borrobol Lodge
Borrobol Forest
Altanduin
Loch Ascaig
Creag nam Fiadh 1271
Cnoc na Breun-choille 1194
Cnoc an Liath-bhaid Mhóir 1423
Loch na Gaineimh
Loch an Alltan Fheàrna
Loch Badanloch
Badanloch Lodge
Loch Achnamoine
Helmsdale River
Arichlinie
Cnoc Coire na Feàrna 1434
Cnoc an Eireannaich 1699
Creag Scalabsdale 1819
Beinn Dubhain 1365
Morven 2313
Cnoc Loch Mhadadh 1040
Gobernuisgeach
Féith Gaineimh Mhór
Berriedale Water
Braemore
Maiden Pap 1587
Scaraben 2055
Meall na Caorach 1301
Wag
Langwell Forest
Aultibea
Langwell Water
Cnoc na Maoile 1315
Dunbeath Water
Balnab
Knockal
Ramscraigs
Borgue
Newport
Kingspark Llama Farm
Berriedale
Berriedale Castle
Boch-ailean
Ousdale
Badbea
Ousdale Broch
Ord Point
Timespan Heritage Centre
Strath Skinsdale
River Skinsdale
Garvary Burn
Allt an Ealaidh
Allt nan Achaidhean
Abhainn na Frithe
Allt an Dùin
Tuarie Burn
Allt Ach a' Bhathaich
Allt a' Mhuilinn
Allt Smeorail
Loch Bad an t-Sean-tighe
Cnoc Leamhnachd 961
River Fleet
Distillery
Wilkhaven
Bindal
Ballone Castle
Seafield
Rockfield
Tarrel
Toulvaddie
Lower Arboll
Inver
DANGER AREA
Lochslin
Castle
Loch Eye
Lower Pitkerrie
Geanies
Hill of Fearn
Fearn
Talich
Tullich
Hilton of Cadboll
Hilton of Cadboll Chapel
Balintore
Glenmorangie Distillery
Morangie
Tarlogie
Tain Hill
Tain Through Time
Water Mill
Hilton
Morangie Forest
Aldie
Glen Aldie
Hartmount
Lamington
Brenachie
Pitmaduthy
Kildary
Arabella
A9
A897
A836
A949
B871
B9168
B9165
B9166
B9175

Duslic
CAPE WRATH
Cape Wrath
Stack Clò Kearvaig
Clo Mor
Kearvaig
Faraid Head
A' Ghoil
Sgribhis-bheinn 1216
DANGER AREA
Inshore
Cnoc a' Ghiubhais 976
Bay of Keisgaig
Loch Inshore
Balnakeil Bay
Balnakeil
Durness
Smoo Cave
Sangomore
Leirinmore
Loch Keisgaig
Achiemore
Fashven 1498
Loch Borralie
Loch a' Gheodha Ruaidh
Loch Airigh na Beinne
Keoldale
Loch Caladail
Beinn Dearg 1390
Loch na Gainmhich
911 Beinn an Amair
Sandwood Loch
Creag Riabhach 1592
Kyle of Durness
Loch Meadaidh
1527 An Grianan
Grudie River
1387 Meall Meadhonach
Strath Shinary
Ghlas-bheinn 1085
Loch na Gainimh
Abhainn an t-Strathain
Sheigra
Balchrick
Blairmore
Droman
Loch Aisir Mor
Oldshore Beg
Oldshoremore
Farrmheall 1709
Laid
Choraidh Croft
Eilean an Ròin Mór
An Socach 1165
Beinn Spionnaidh 2534
Loch Innis na Ba Buidhe
Loch na Gainimh
Gualin House
Eilean Choraidh
Loch Clash
Kinlochbervie
B801
Badcall
Inshegra
Cranstackie 2630
A838
Lochan Sgeireach
Bàgh Loch an Ròin
Rhuvoult
Achriesgill
Polla
Loch Inchard
River Dionard
Strath Dionard
Strath Beag
Achlyness
Loch na Claise Carnaich
Ardmore Point
Loch Dughaill
Loch Crocach
Rhiconich
1705 An Lean charm
Ardmore
Loch na Thull
Mathair a' Gharbh Uilt
Ganu Mór 2980
Skerricha
Fanagmore
FOINAVEN
Handa Island
Tarbet
Foindle
H I G
Loch Dionard
Handa Island
Loch a' Gharbh-bhaid Mór
Loch na Tuadh
Sound of Handa
A894
Laxford Bridge
Loch Staonsaid
Loch an Easain Uaine
Badnabay
Arkle 2580
Lochan Sgéireach
Loch a' Bhadaidh Daraich
River Laxford
Scourie Bay
Scourie
Scourie More
Gorm Loch
Loch an Nighe Leathaid
Loch na Seilge
Lochstack Lodge
2393 Sàbhal Beag
Glen Golly
Rubh' Aird an t-Sionnaich
2356 Ben Stack
Loch Stack
Lone
Abhainn an Loin
Upper Badcall
Lower Badcall
Clar Loch
Cnoc Thormaid
Badcall Bay
Reay Forest
Coire Loch
1265 Ben Auskaird
Achfary
Eilean a Bhreitheimh
Loch Crocach
Loch na Mucnaich
2627 Meallan Liath Coire Mhic Dhughaill
Meall Mór
Duartmore Bridge
Loch More
Loch na Creige Duibhe
Loch Ulbhach Coire
Point of Stoer
Sgeir nan Gall
Calbha Beag
Calbha Mór
Allt nan Ramh
1374 Ben Strome
Loch an Leathiad Bhuain
The Old Man of Stoer
Oldany Island
Eddrachillis Bay
1777 Beinn a' Bhuta
Loch an t-Seil
Kylestrome
Glendhu Forest
Kinloch
Loch Cul Fraioch
Culkein
Eilean Chrona
Culkein Drumbeg
Loch a' Chàirn Bhàin
Kylesku
Loch Glendhu
Gleann Dubh
Clashnessie Bay
Oldany
Loch Nedd
Unapool
Rubha Stoer
Achnacarnin
Drumbeg
Nedd
Beinn Aird da Loch 1722
Clashmore
B869
Glenleraig
Newton
Loch Glencoul
Loch Poll
Gorm Loch Mór
Loch an Leathaid
Loch Merkland
Balchladich
Clashnessie
Raffin
Loch nan Lub
INAG
163
Glen Coul
Beinn Leoid 2599
Merkland Lodge
Stoer
Loch na Loinne
Gleann Leireag
2651
na Gainmhich
Bay of Stoer
Clachtoll Broch
Clachtoll
Eas Coul Aulin Falls
Loch an Eircill
Dubh a' Chuail
Loch Beannach
Lochassynt Lodge
Loch nan Caorach
Loch a' Ghriama
Cnoc a' Ghriama 1221
Loch Crocach
Glas Bheinn 2541
Corriekinloch
Achmelvich Bay
Rhicarn
A837
Beinn Uidhe
Gorm
Abhainn a' Choire

250
60
70
80
E
F
G
H
80
1
STRATHY POINT
70
Totegan
Whiten Head or An Ceann Geal
Eilean Hoan
Eilean Cluimhrig
Sangobeg
Rispond
A838
Loch Eriboll
Portnancon
Ben Hutig 1338
Achininver
Midfield
Port Vasgo
Lubinvullin
Strathan
Achinahuagh
West Strathan
Talmine
Strath Melness
Loch a' Mhuilinn
Skinnet
Midtown
R. Hope
Hope
Loch Maovally
A838
30
756 Ben Arnaboll
Eriboll
Achuvoldrach
Rhitongue
Coldbackie
Kyle of Tongue
Tongue
Braetongue
Caisteal Bharraich
Loch Fhionnaich
Druim nan Clar
Loch Hope
Tongue Bay
Caol Raineach
Rabbit Islands
Eilean nan Ron
Neave or Coombe Island
Strathan Skerray
Skerray
Clasheddy
Achtoty
Modsarie
Torrisdale
Torrisdale Bay
Skullomie
Blandy
Allt an Dearg
10
Dalcharn
Loch Cormaic
Borgie
A836
Borgie Forest
Farr Point
Farr Bay
Borve Castle
Farr
Clerkhill
Clachan
Strathnaver
Bettyhill
Invernaver
Achina
Leckfurin
Swordly
Bay of Swordly
Kirtomy Point
Kirtomy
Crask
Ardmore Point
Armadale Bay
Armadale
18
Port Allt a' Mhuilinn
Aultivullin
Brawl
Aultiphurst
Strathy Bay
2
Lednagullin
A836
Strathy Forest
River Strathy
Bowside Lodge
Loch Gaineimh
Loch Meadie
Loch Buidhe Beag
Loch Buidhe Mòr
Beinn nam Bò 751
Loch Meala
168
Strathy Forest
60
Clachan Burn
Skelpick
B871
Na Caol Lochan
Loch Stephan
Archargary
River Naver
Skelpick Burn
Loch Mòr na Caorach
3
The Uair
Forsinard
Beinn Bhreac 1018
A836
Ribigill
Cnoc Craggie 1043
Loch Craggie
Lochan nan Carn
Loch nan Ealachan
Loch nan Clach
Dunviden Lochs
Carnachy
Cnoc Badaireach na Gaoithe
Kinloch Lodge
Lochan Hakel
Kinloch River
Loch na Seilg
Meallan Liath 1962
3040 BEN HOPE
Cashel Dhu
Loch Crocach
H
L
A
N
D
Ben Loyal 2509
Loch an Dherue
17
Loch Loyal
1728 Beinn Stumanadh
Loch nam Breac
Loch Meleag
9
Rhifail
Rough Haugh
963 Beinn Rifa-gil
River Strathy
950
Loch Strathy
Loch nam Breac
Loch na Saobhaidhe
1519 Feinne-bheinn Mhòr
Strathmore River
Alltnacaillich
Dun Dornaigil Broch
Loch Haluim
Loch Loyal Lodge
1828 Cnoc nan Cuilean
Skail
4
Loch nan Ealachan
Loch Coulside
Loch Syre
Syre
B871
B873
Rosal
Naver Forest
Rosal Deserted Township
Rhifail Loch
Allt Lon a Chuil
Rimsdale Burn
Caol-loch Mòr
1133 Cnoc nan Tri-chlach
Loch Crocach
Loch Druim a' Chliabhain
1902 Ben Griam Beg
Golly River
Gobernuisgach Lodge
Loch Meadie
Loch Bad na Gallaig
Pole Hill 965
Loch Eileanach
Navar Forest
Rimsdale
Garbh-allt
Garvault
40
Allt a' Chraois
Meadie Burn
11
1938 Ben Griam Mòr
Allt Airigh-dhamh
16
Loch Coire na Saidhe Duibhe
Allt Coire na Saidhe Duibhe
Mudale
River Mudale
Altnaharra
B873
Grummore
Loch Naver
Mallart River
Loch Rimsdale
Loch nan Clàr
Badanloch Forest
Loch Badanloch
5
Badanloch Lodge
B871
Loch a' Ghorm-choire
Loch Ben Harrald
A836
Klibreck Burn
BEN KLIBRECK 2367
Loch Truderscaig
Loch an Alltan Fhearna
Loch Achnamoine
River Helmsdale
Loch na Gaineimh
An Glas-loch
Meall an Fhuarain 1549
Vagastie
Meall nan Con 3157
Loch Choire Forest
Loch Choire Lodge
30
164
F
G
H
165
Loch Fiag
Fiag Lodge
Strath Vagastie
Loch nan Uan
Loch Choire
2278 Creag na h-Iolaire
1423 Cnoc an Liath-bhaid Mhóir
Achaneas
Cnoc an Alaskie 1024
250
60
70
80
Loch a' Bhealaich
Meall a' Bhata 1907
2311 Ben Armine
Gorm-Loch Beag
Allt an Ealaidh
Borrobol Forest
Altanduin
21

STRATHY POINT
Totegan
Aultivullin
Port Allt a' Mhuilinn
Ardmore Point
Armadale Bay
Brawl
Strathy Bay
Aultiphurst
Strathy
Baligill
Portskerra
Melvich Bay
Armadale
Lednagullin
A836
Melvich
Bighouse
Red Point
Fresgoe
Sandside Bay
Reay
Isauld
Dounreay (Thurso)
Lower Dounreay
Upper Dounreay
Buldoo
Achreamie
Skiall
Cnoc Freiceadain Long Cairns
St. Mary's Chapel
Crosskirk
Bridge of Forss
Forss
Lythmore
Stemster
Brims Ness
Brims Castle
Spear Head
Holborn Head
Scrabster
Thurso Bay
Clardon Head
Scrabster to Stromness 1hr. 30mins.
A9
Thurso
Heritage
Thurso East
West Murkle
Murkle
Millbank
Dixonfield
Janetstown
Newlands of Geise
Glengolly
Geise
Weydale
B870
B874
Westfield
Achscrabster
Shebster
Knockglass
Drum Hollistan 608
Beinn Ratha 795
Caol-loch
Loch Akran
Loch Baligill
Strathy Forest
River Strathy
Bowside Lodge
Loch Gaineimh
Loch Buidhe Beag
Beinn nam Bò 751
Loch Buidhe Mór
Loch Meala
Strathy Forest
167
Loch Mór na Caorach
Loch nan Clach
Forsinard
The Ulair
Caol-loch
River Dyke
Loch nan Gall
Achiemore
Upper Bighouse
Craigtown
Dalhalvaig
Croick
Trantlemore
Trantlebeg
Halladale River
Smigel Burn
A897
Loch na Seilge
Sandside Burn
Achvarasdal Burn
Loch Saorach
Loch Thormaid
Broubster
Loch Calder
Calder Mains
Braal Castle
Halkirk
Gerston
Sordale
Knockdee
Roadside
Claycock
Shurrery
Forss Water
Allt Forsiescye
Brawlbin
Loch Olginey
Banniskirk
Harpsdale
Olgrinmore
Loch Scye
Loch Shurrery
Dorrery
953 Beinn nam Bad Mór
Cnoc Bad Mhairtein 747
Cnoc an Fhuarain Bhain
H I G H L A
Blàr Dearg 524
Torran Water
River Thurso
Spittal
Mybster
Westerdale
Loch Sainn
Loch Saird
Loch Tuim Ghlais
Loch Caluim
698 Cnoc Badaireach na Gaoithe
Dyke River
Strath Halladale
Forsinain Burn
Lochan Ealach Beag
665 Cnoc Preas a' Mhadaidh
Skyline Loch
Caol Loch
Lochan Dubh nan Geodh
Loch Meadie
Strathmore Lodge
Beinn Chàiteag 446
Little River
Loch Eileanach
Loch Gaineimh
Loch nam Breac
Loch Strathy
Loch na Saobhaidhe
The Cross Lochs
Sletill Hill 918
Loch Sletill
Loch na Cloiche
Loch Leir
Lochan Croc nan Làir
Altnabreac
Sleach Water
Loch More
Rangag
Caol-loch Mór
1133 Cnoc nan Tri-chlach
Loch Cròcach
Forsinard
Loch Dubh
Loch nam Fear
River Thurso
Loch Ruard
Loch Dubh
Loch Drum a' Chliabhàin
1902 Ben Griam Beg
Loch Rumsdale
Loch a' Mhuilinn
Dalnawillan Lodge
Rumsdale Water
Lochan Thulachan
Loch Sand
Loch Rangag
Coire na Beinne 741
B871
Garvault
Garbh-allt
1938 Ben Griam Mór
Allt Airigh-dhamh
Achentoul Forest
Loch an Ruathair
Glutt Water
Ben Alisky 1144
Loch Breac
Cnocan Conachreag 881
Glutt Lodge
Loch Dubh
Badanloch Forest
Loch Badanloch
Badanloch Lodge
Lochside
Loch Arichlinie
Knockfin Heights 1437
Burn of Houstry
Houstry
Dunbeath Water
Smerral
Achentoul
Cnoc Loch Mhadadh 1040
Féith Gaineimh Mhòr
Gobernuisgeach
Loch Achnamoine
Kinbrace
River Helmsdale
Berriedale Water
Badnagie
Braemore
Dunbeath
Loch na Gaineimh
Kinbrace Burn
Cnoc Coire na Fearna 1434
165
Maiden Pap 1587
Knockally
Balnabruich
Heritage
Port
Allt nan Achaidhean
Cnoc an Eireannaich 1699
Morven 2313
Meall na Caorach 1301
Scaraben 2055
Ramscaigs
Abhainn na Frithe
Suisgill Burn
Borrobol Forest
Altanduin
Borrobol Lodge
Wag
Borgue
A B C D
1 2 3 4 5
80 90 300 10

169
PENTLAND FIRTH
Island of Stroma
Nethertown
Uppertown
Castle Mestag
St. John's Point
Pentland Skerries
DUNNET HEAD
Dunnet Head
Long Loch
Burifa Hill
Dunnet Hill
Loch of Bushta
Tang Head
Scarfskerry
Brough
Ham
Hunspow
St. John's Loch
Corsback
West Dunnet
Mary-Ann's Cottage
Dunnet
Dunnet Bay
Dunnet Links
Rattar
Loch of Mey
Castle of Mey
East Mey
Mey
Barrock
A836
Gills Bay
Gills
Kirkstyle
Huna
Last Ho.
DUNCANSBY HEAD
Boars of Duncansby
John o' Groats
Seater
Warse
Canisbay
Upper Gills
Duncansby Stacks
Stacks of Duncansby
Warth Hill
Inkstack
Brabster
Loch Heilen
Greenland Mains
Lochend
Greenland
Castletown
Olrig
Tain
B876
B855
Skirza
Skirza Head
Tofts
Freswick
Freswick Bay
Ness Head
Castle
Gill Burn
Slickly
Reaster
Alterwall
Kirk Burn
Durran
Bowermadden
Arts Centre
Sortat
Lyth
Northlands Viking Centre
Auckengill
Nybster
Brough Head
Bowertower
Howe
Keiss
Keiss Castle
Tang Head
Stemster
Halcro
Hastigrow
Mireland
Burn of Lyth
B874
Corsback
Gillock
Loch Scarmclate
North Watten
Kirk
B870
Myrelandhorn
Loch of Wester
Westerloch
Larel
A882
Sinclair's Bay
Oldhall
Loch Watten
Knapperfield
Killimster
Watten
Winless
Reiss
Ackergill Tower
Castle Girnigoe
Noss Head
Ackergillshore
Castle Sinclair
Loch of Toftingall
Bilbster
Sibster
Ackergill
Sealky Head
WICK
Staxigoe
Caithness Glass
Acharole
Burn of Acharole
Strath
Strath Burn
Wick River
Haster
Milton
Papigoe
Broadhaven
Wick
Wick Bay
Janetstown
Heritage Centre
Newton
A99
South Head
Achairn Burn
Badlipster
Whiterow
Old Wick
Loch Hempriggs
Gote o' Tram
Hempriggs
Helman Head
Tannach
Camster Burn
Hill of Oliclett
Hill of Rangag
Grey Cairns of Camster
Gansclet
Thrumster
Loch of Yarrows
Raggra
Borrowston
Sarclet
Sarclet Head
South Yarrows Cairns
Achavanich
Loch Stemster
Standing Stones
Stemster Hill
Cnoc an Earrannaiche
Camster
Cairn O'get
Ulbster
Sheppardstown
Roster
East Clyth
Bruan
Crofts of Benachielt
Oslay
Hill O'many Stanes
Mid Clyth
Halberry Head
Rumster Forest
Upper Lybster
Achow
Overton
Clyth
Swiney
Lybster
Upper Latheron
Invershore
A9
Standing Stones
Burrigill
Forse
Forse Castle
Clan Gunn Heritage Centre
Latheron
Latheronwheel
Whalebone Arch
Knockinnon
Laidhay Croft
Burwick
Cleat
B9041
Liddel
Brough
172

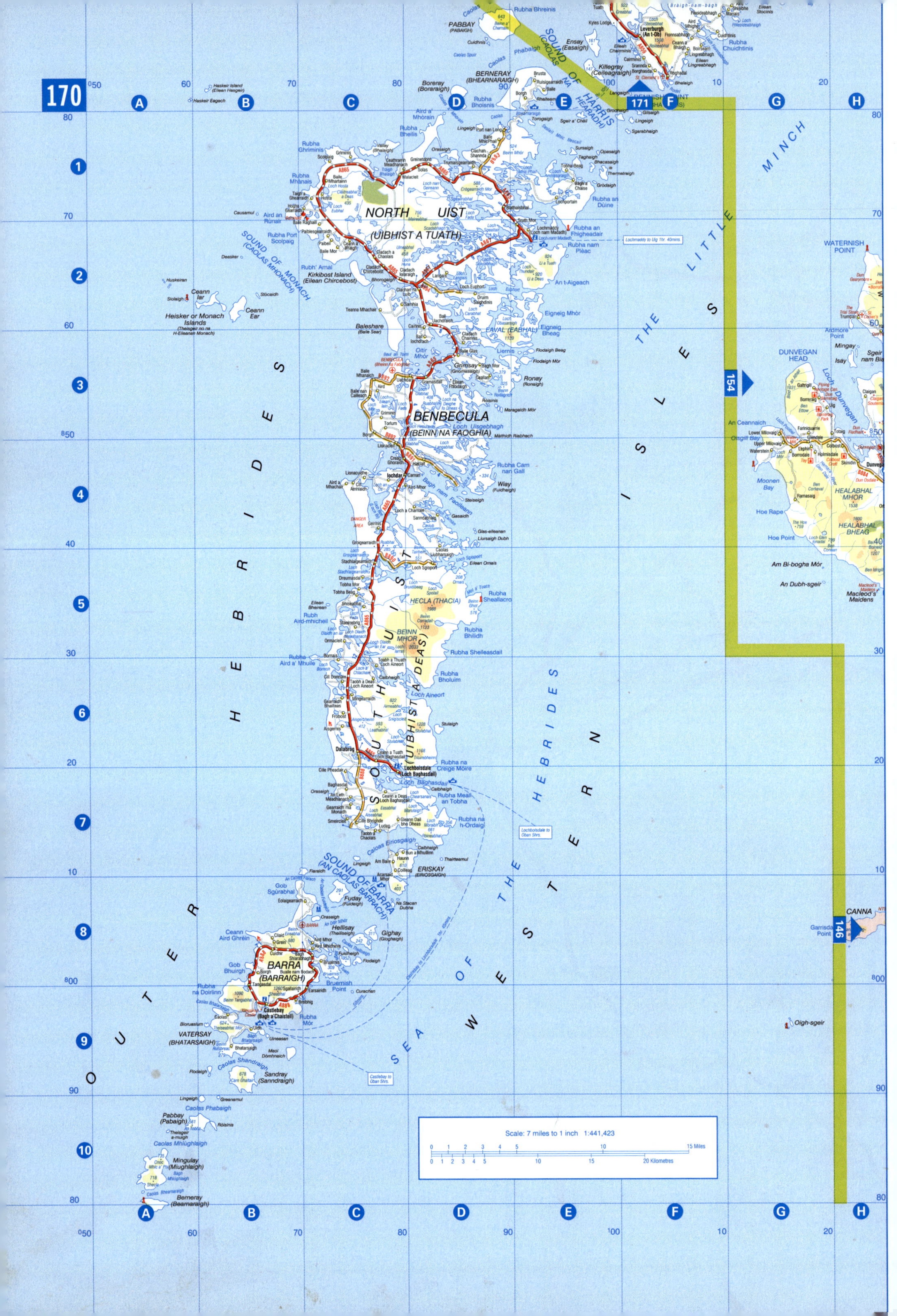

NORTH UIST
(UIBHIST A TUATH)
BENBECULA
(BEINN NA FAOGHLA)
SOUTH UIST
(UIBHIST A DEAS)
BARRA
(BARRAIGH)
ERISKAY
VATERSAY
(BHATARSAIGH)
Sandray
(Sanndraigh)
Pabbay
(Pabaigh)
Mingulay
(Miughlaigh)
Berneray
(Bearnaraigh)
PABBAY
BERNERAY
(BHEARNARAIGH)
Ensay
(Easaigh)
Killegray
(Ceileagraigh)
Leverburgh
(An t-Ob)
SOUND OF HARRIS
(CAOLAS NA HEARADH)
Boreray
(Boraraigh)
Heisker or Monach Islands
SOUND OF MONACH
(CAOLAS MHONACH)
Kirkibost Island
(Eilean Chirceboist)
Baleshare
Grimsay
Ronay
(Ronaigh)
Wiay
(Fuidheigh)
HECLA (THACIA)
BEINN MHOR
Lochboisdale
(Loch Baghasdail)
SOUND OF BARRA
(AN CAOLAS BARRACH)
Fuday
(Fuideigh)
Hellisay
(Theiliseigh)
Gighay
Castlebay
(Bagh a Chaisteil)
Lochmaddy
(Loch nam Madadh)
Lochmaddy to Uig 1hr. 40mins
Lochboisdale to Oban 5hrs.
Castlebay to Oban 5hrs.
OUTER HEBRIDES
THE LITTLE MINCH
SEA OF THE HEBRIDES
THE WESTERN ISLES
WATERNISH POINT
DUNVEGAN HEAD
Loch Dunvegan
HEALABHAL MHOR
HEALABHAL BHEAG
Moonen Bay
Hoe Rape
Hoe Point
Macleod's Maidens
Am Bi-bogha Mòr
An Dubh-sgeir
CANNA
Garrisdale Point
Oigh-sgeir
171
154
146
Scale: 7 miles to 1 inch 1:441,423
15 Miles
20 Kilometres

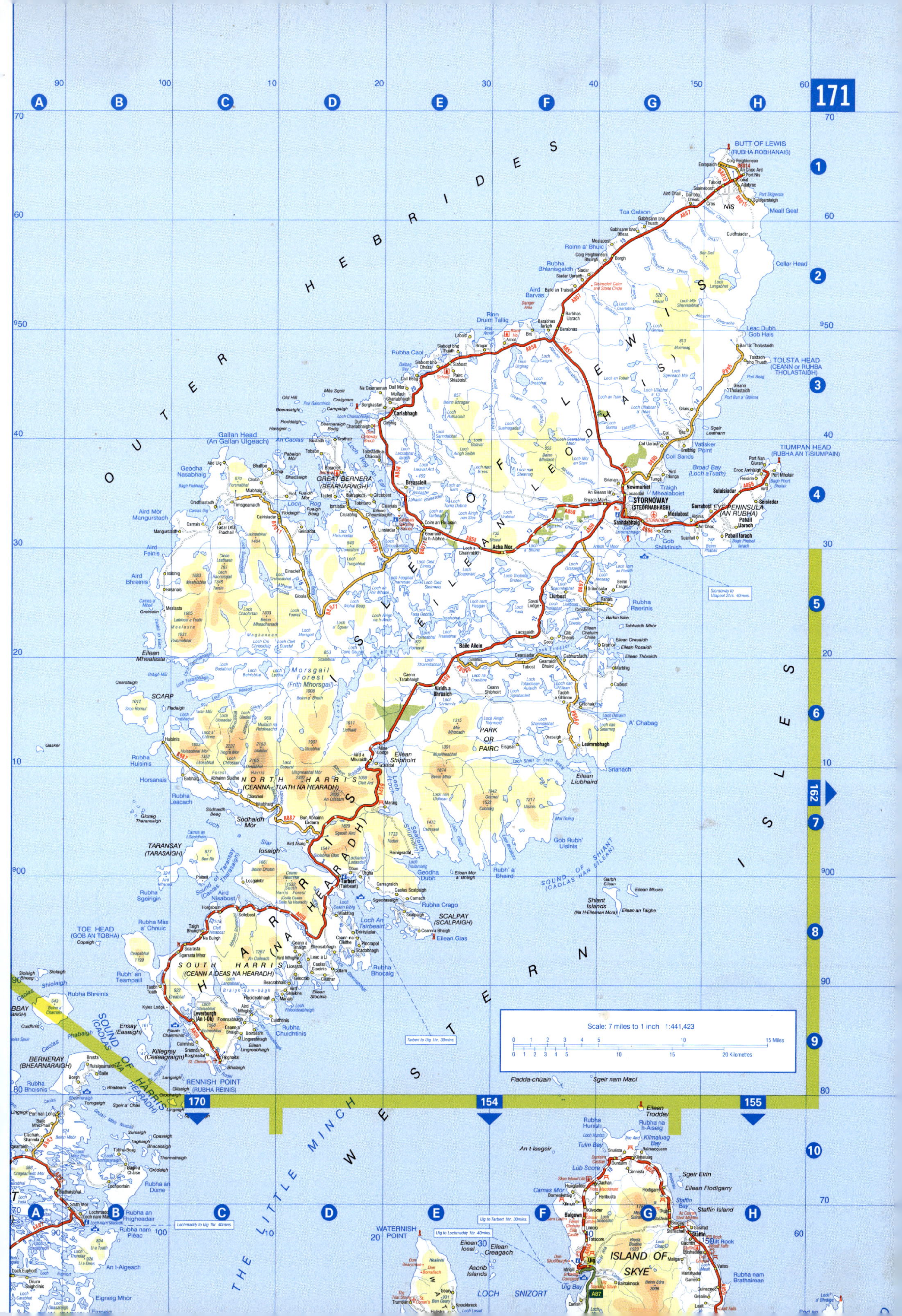
OUTER HEBRIDES
BUTT OF LEWIS (RUBHA ROBHANAIS)
ISLE OF LEWIS (EILEAN LEODHAIS)
STORNOWAY (STEORNABHAGH)
EYE PENINSULA (AN RUBHA)
TIUMPAN HEAD (RUBHA AN T-SIUMPAIN)
TOLSTA HEAD (CEANN or RUBHA THOLASTAIDH)
GREAT BERNERA (BEARNARAIGH)
Gallan Head (An Gallan Uigeach)
SCARP
Morsgail Forest (Frith Mhorsgail)
PARK OR PAIRC
NORTH HARRIS (CEANNA TUATH NA HEARADH)
HARRIS (NA HEARADH)
SOUTH HARRIS (CEANN A DEAS NA HEARADH)
TARANSAY (TARASAIGH)
TOE HEAD (GOB AN TOBHA)
SCALPAY (SCALPAIGH)
SOUND OF SHIANT (CAOLAS NAN EILEAN)
Shiant Islands
SOUND OF HARRIS
BERNERAY (BHEARNARAIGH)
RENNISH POINT (RUBHA REINIS)
THE LITTLE MINCH
WESTERN ISLES
ISLAND OF SKYE
WATERNISH POINT
LOCH SNIZORT
Tarbert (Tairbeart)
Leverburgh (An t-Ob)
Scale: 7 miles to 1 inch 1:441,423
0 1 2 3 4 5 10 15 Miles
0 1 2 3 4 5 10 15 20 Kilometres
170
154
155
162

ORKNEY ISLANDS
MAINLAND
HOY
ROUSAY
WESTRAY
SANDAY
STRONSAY
SHAPINSAY
EDAY
SOUTH RONALDSAY
Kirkwall
Stromness
PENTLAND FIRTH
Scapa Flow
WESTRAY FIRTH
STRONSAY FIRTH
THE NORTH SOUND
NORTH RONALDSAY FIRTH
DUNNET HEAD
DUNCANSBY HEAD
Thurso
169
Scale: 7 miles to 1 inch 1:441,423

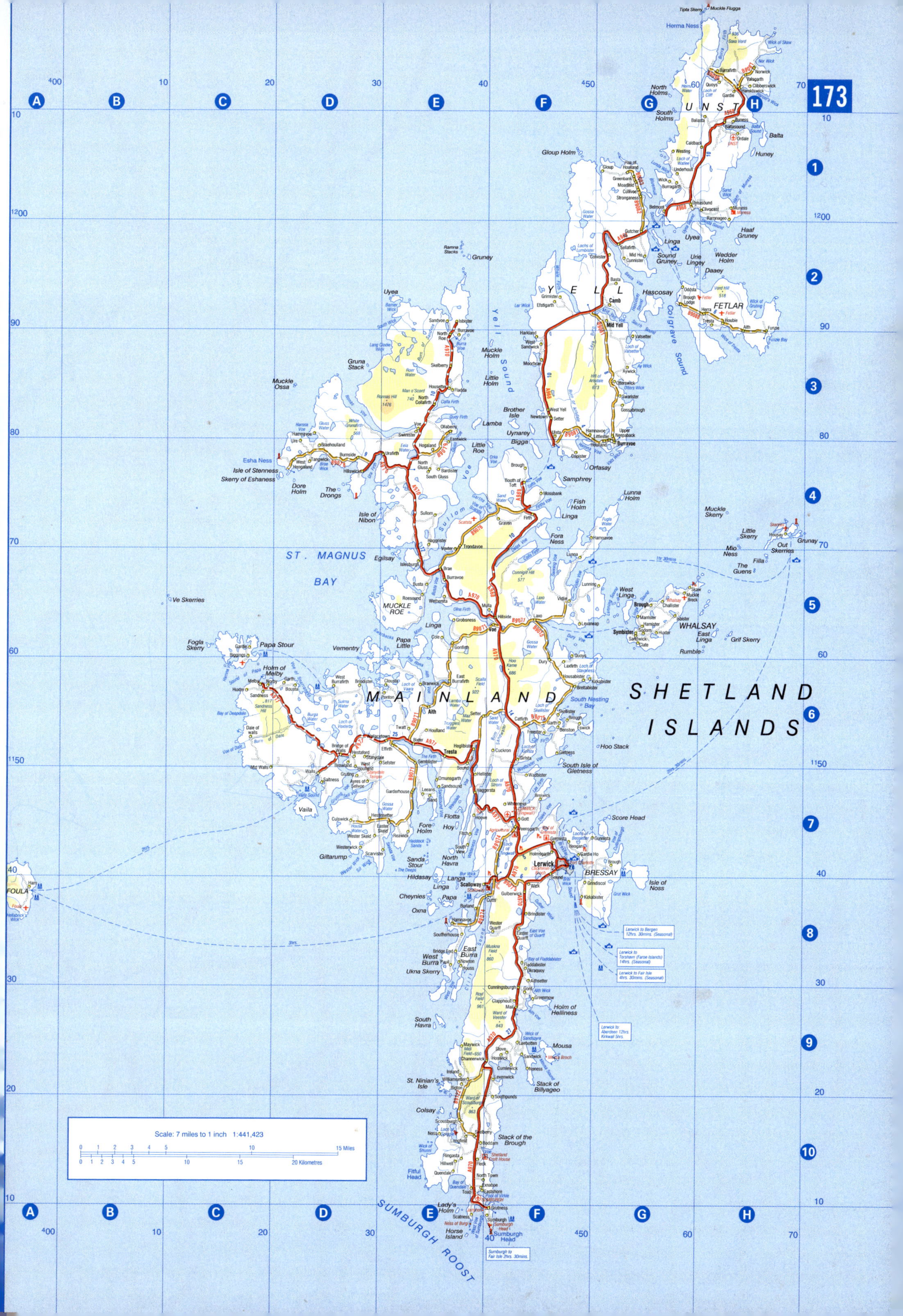

SHETLAND ISLANDS
MAINLAND
UNST
YELL
FETLAR
WHALSAY
BRESSAY
FOULA
PAPA STOUR
MUCKLE ROE
ST. MAGNUS BAY
SUMBURGH ROOST
Yell Sound
Colgrave Sound
Lerwick
Scalloway
Voe
Brae
Aith
Walls
Sandness
Hillswick
Mid Yell
Burravoe
Baltasound
Sumburgh Head
Fitful Head
Mousa
Out Skerries
Muckle Flugga
Herma Ness
Vaila
Papa Little
Vementry
Ve Skerries
Fogla Skerry
Muckle Ossa
Gruna Stack
Uyea
Lamba
Samphrey
Fish Holm
Linga
Lunna Holm
Muckle Skerry
Hoo Stack
Score Head
Isle of Noss
Holm of Helliness
Stack of Billyageo
Stack of the Brough
St. Ninian's Isle
Colsay
Horse Island
Lady's Holm
South Havra
West Burra
East Burra
Hildasay
Oxna
Papa
Cheynies
Langa
Giltarump
Esha Ness
Isle of Stenness
Skerry of Eshaness
Dore Holm
The Drongs
Isle of Nibon
Uyea
Hascosay
Haaf Gruney
Wedder Holm
Daaey
Huney
Balta
Gloup Holm
North Holms
South Holms
Lerwick to Bergen 12hrs. 30mins. (Seasonal)
Lerwick to Torshavn (Faroe Islands) 14hrs. (Seasonal)
Lerwick to Fair Isle 4hrs. 30mins. (Seasonal)
Lerwick to Aberdeen 12hrs. Kirkwall 5hrs.
Sumburgh to Fair Isle 2hrs. 30mins.
Scale: 7 miles to 1 inch 1:441,423
0 1 2 3 4 5 10 15 Miles
0 1 2 3 4 5 10 15 20 Kilometres

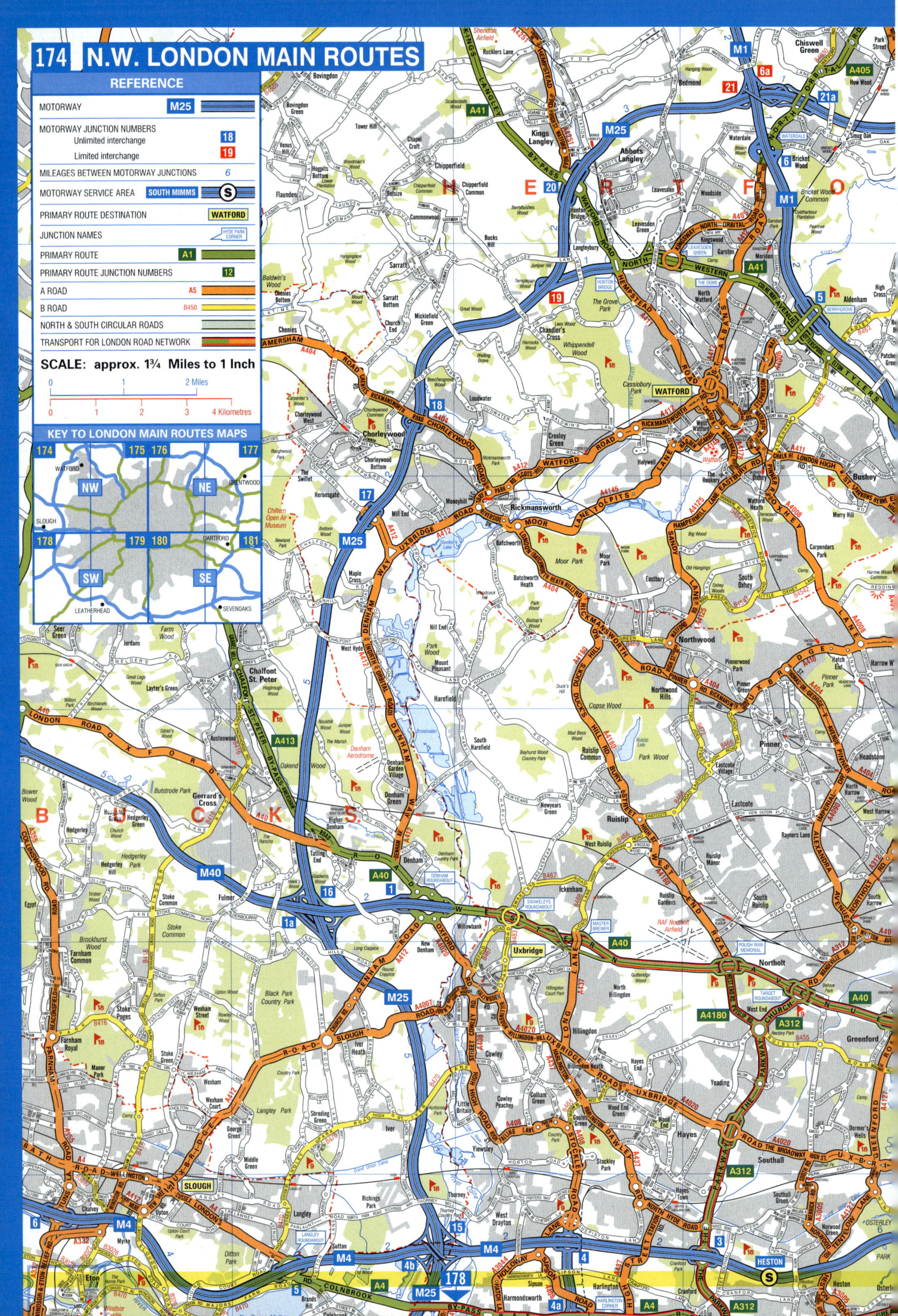

174
N.W. LONDON MAIN ROUTES
REFERENCE
MOTORWAY
M25
MOTORWAY JUNCTION NUMBERS
Unlimited interchange
18
Limited interchange
19
MILEAGES BETWEEN MOTORWAY JUNCTIONS
6
MOTORWAY SERVICE AREA
SOUTH MIMMS
PRIMARY ROUTE DESTINATION
WATFORD
JUNCTION NAMES
HYDE PARK CORNER
PRIMARY ROUTE
A1
PRIMARY ROUTE JUNCTION NUMBERS
12
A ROAD
A5
B ROAD
B450
NORTH & SOUTH CIRCULAR ROADS
TRANSPORT FOR LONDON ROAD NETWORK
SCALE: approx. 1¾ Miles to 1 Inch
0
1
2 Miles
0
1
2
3
4 Kilometres
KEY TO LONDON MAIN ROUTES MAPS
174
175
176
177
NW
NE
178
179
180
181
SW
SE
WATFORD
BRENTWOOD
SLOUGH
DARTFORD
LEATHERHEAD
SEVENOAKS
H
E
R
T
F
O
B
U
C
K
S
M1
M25
M40
M4
A41
A40
A4
A413
A4180
A312
A405
WATFORD
Uxbridge
SLOUGH
HESTON
178
Bovingdon
Kings Langley
Abbots Langley
Leavesden
Garston
Bedmond
Chiswell Green
Chipperfield
Sarratt
Chenies
Chorleywood
Rickmansworth
Croxley Green
Moor Park
Batchworth
Northwood
Pinner
Eastcote
Ruislip
Ickenham
Harefield
Denham
Chalfont St. Peter
Gerrard's Cross
Fulmer
Stoke Poges
Farnham Royal
Iver
Cowley
Hillingdon
Hayes
Northolt
Southall
Yiewsley
West Drayton
Harmondsworth
Sipson
Harlington
Heston
Langley
Eton
Colnbrook
Bushey
Oxhey
Carpenders Park
Hatch End
Headstone
Greenford
Bricket Wood
Aldenham

North Mymms Park
Napsbury
London Colney
M25
22
Brookmans Park
Potters Bar
A1(M)
South Mimms
SOUTH MIMMS
23
24
Shenley
Radlett
Borehamwood
Elstree
Elstree Airport
M1
Barnet
BARNET
ENFIELD CHASE
TRENT PARK (Country Park)
Cockfosters
Enfield
ENFIELD
Southgate
Whetstone
Totteridge
Mill Hill
Edgware
Stanmore
Finchley
Hendon
Kingsbury
HARROW
Wembley
Neasden
Cricklewood
Willesden
Kilburn
Hampstead
HAMPSTEAD HEATH
Highgate
Hornsey
Muswell Hill
Wood Green
Tottenham
Holloway
Islington
Camden Town
Dalston
Stoke Newington
Paddington
Marylebone
Bayswater
Kensington
Hammersmith
Chiswick
Acton
EALING
Brentford
M4
Chelsea
Westminster
Lambeth
City
Bush Hill Park
Edmonton
Hackney
Harringay
Finsbury Park
Alperton
Sudbury
Harlesden
Notting Hill
West End
Hyde Park
London Zoo
Shepherds Bush
Fulham
Hanwell
West Ealing
Northolt
LONDON GATEWAY

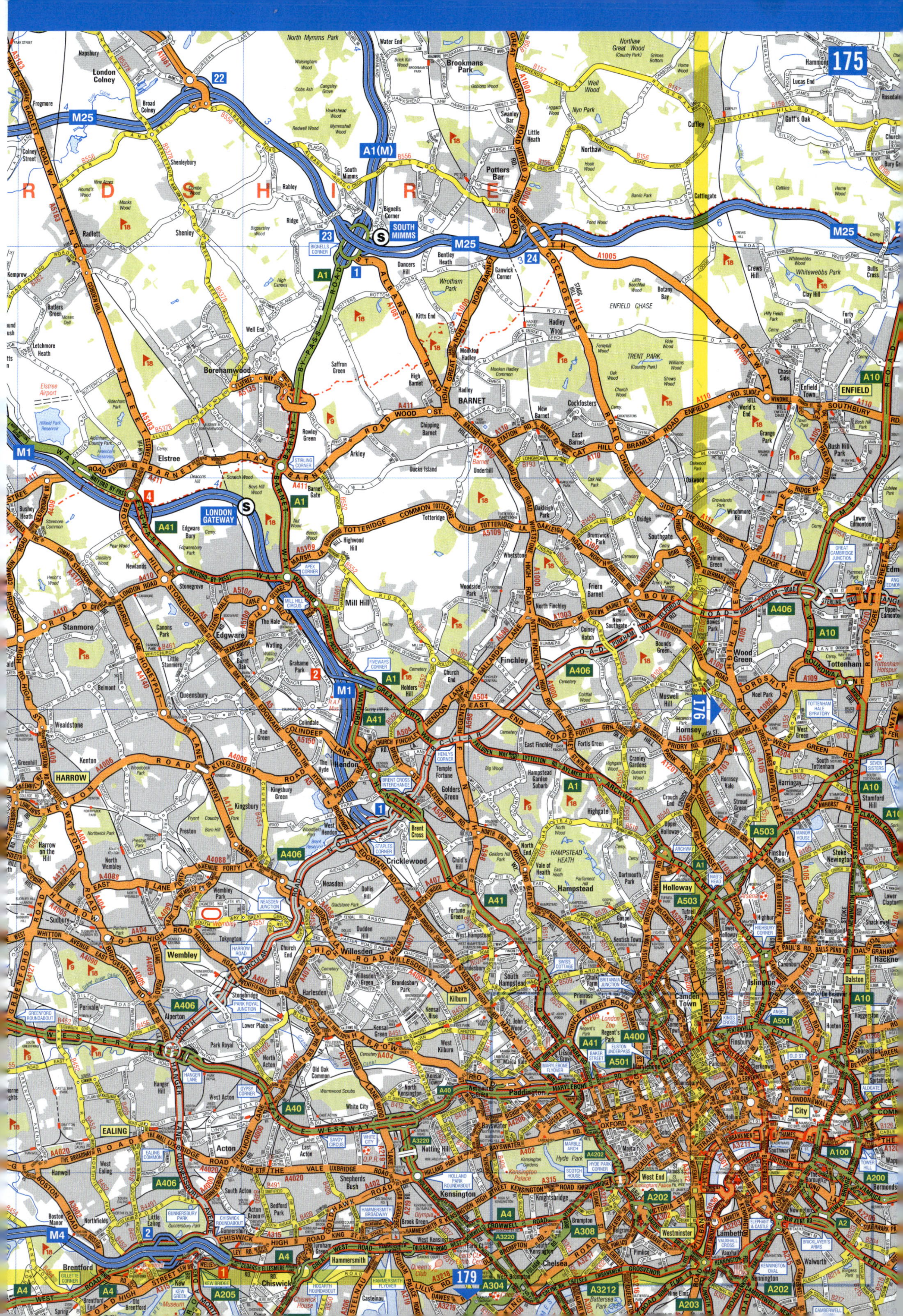

176
179

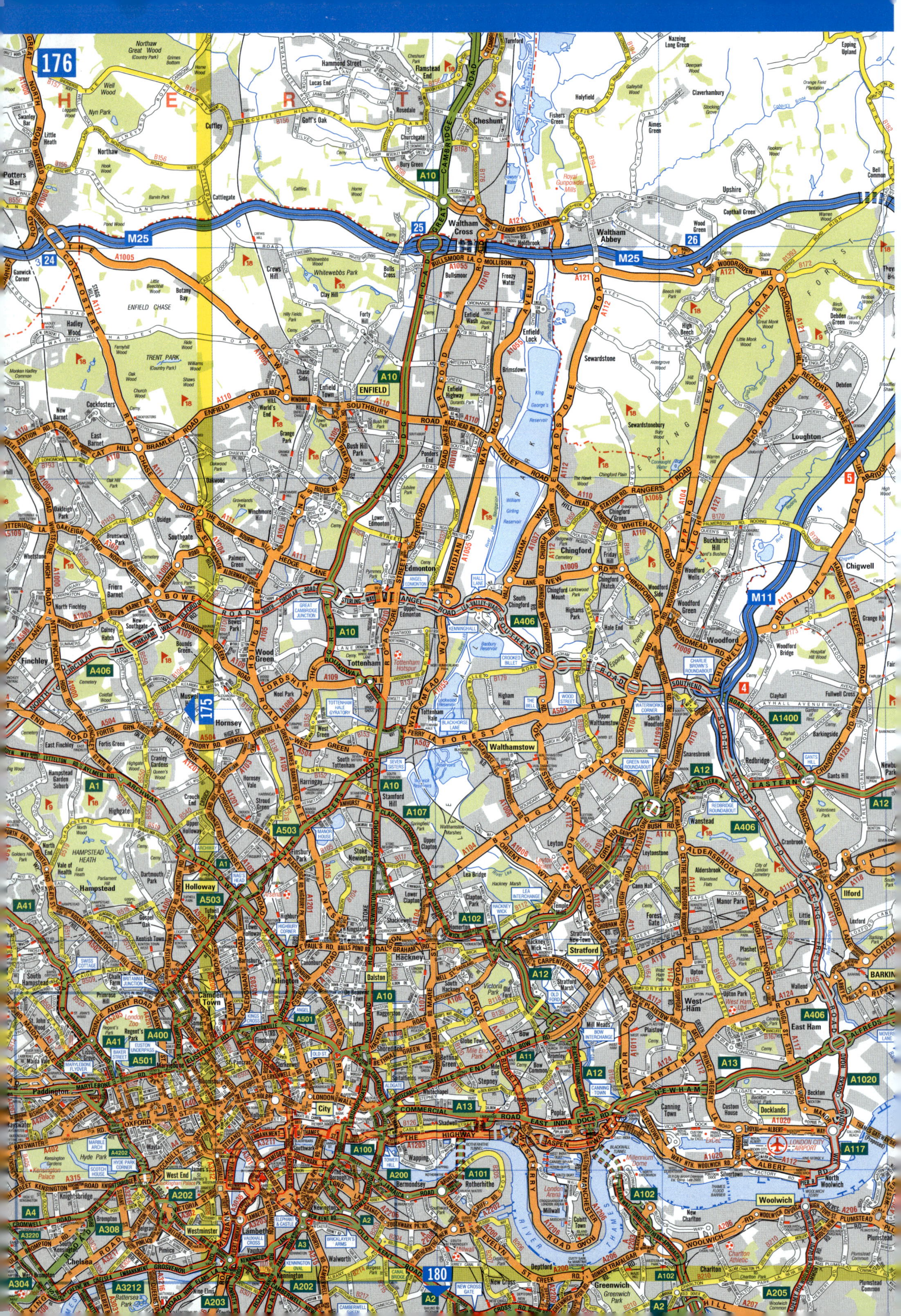

176
H E R T S
Northaw Great Wood
Cuffley
Goff's Oak
Flamstead End
Cheshunt
Potters Bar
Little Heath
Northaw
Waltham Cross
Waltham Abbey
Holyfield
Claverhambury
Upshire
M25
A10
25
26
24
Crews Hill
Whitewebbs Park
Bulls Cross
Bullsmoor
Freezy Water
Enfield Lock
ENFIELD CHASE
TRENT PARK
Hadley Wood
Botany Bay
Sewardstone
Loughton
Debden
ENFIELD
Enfield Town
Chase Side
Cockfosters
New Barnet
East Barnet
World's End
Grange Park
Bush Hill Park
Ponders End
Enfield Highway
King George's Reservoir
Sewardstonebury
Chingford
Buckhurst Hill
Chigwell
Oakwood
Southgate
Winchmore Hill
Palmers Green
Edmonton
Lower Edmonton
Upper Edmonton
William Girling Reservoir
South Chingford
Chingford Mount
Highams Park
Woodford Green
Woodford Wells
Woodford
Friern Barnet
Whetstone
New Southgate
Wood Green
Tottenham
M11
Finchley
East Finchley
Fortis Green
Hornsey
175
Harringay
South Tottenham
Walthamstow
Upper Walthamstow
Tottenham Hale
Highgate
Hampstead Garden Suburb
Crouch End
Stroud Green
Stamford Hill
Upper Clapton
Leyton
Leytonstone
Wanstead
Redbridge
Barkingside
Gants Hill
Ilford
Aldersbrook
Manor Park
Little Ilford
HAMPSTEAD HEATH
Hampstead
Holloway
Finsbury Park
Stoke Newington
Lower Clapton
Clapton Park
Lea Bridge
Hackney
Hackney Wick
Stratford
Forest Gate
Plashet
Upton Park
West Ham
East Ham
Camden Town
Islington
Dalston
South Hackney
Victoria Park
Bow
Plaistow
South Hampstead
Primrose Hill
Regent's Park
London Zoo
Paddington
Marylebone
City
Shoreditch
Bethnal Green
Stepney
Poplar
Canning Town
Custom House
Beckton
Docklands
LONDON CITY AIRPORT
Hyde Park
West End
Westminster
Lambeth
Southwark
Bermondsey
Rotherhithe
Wapping
Millwall
Cubitt Town
Millennium Dome
North Woolwich
Silvertown
Woolwich
Charlton
New Charlton
Plumstead
Greenwich
Deptford
New Cross
Walworth
Kennington
Chelsea
Pimlico
Knightsbridge
Brompton
Battersea Park
180
Kensington Palace
Holland Park
A406
A12
A13
A102
A2
A1
A503
A501
A4
A3
A202
A203
A3212
A304
A3220
A308
A1020
A117
A205
A200
A101
A100
A107
A1400
BARKING

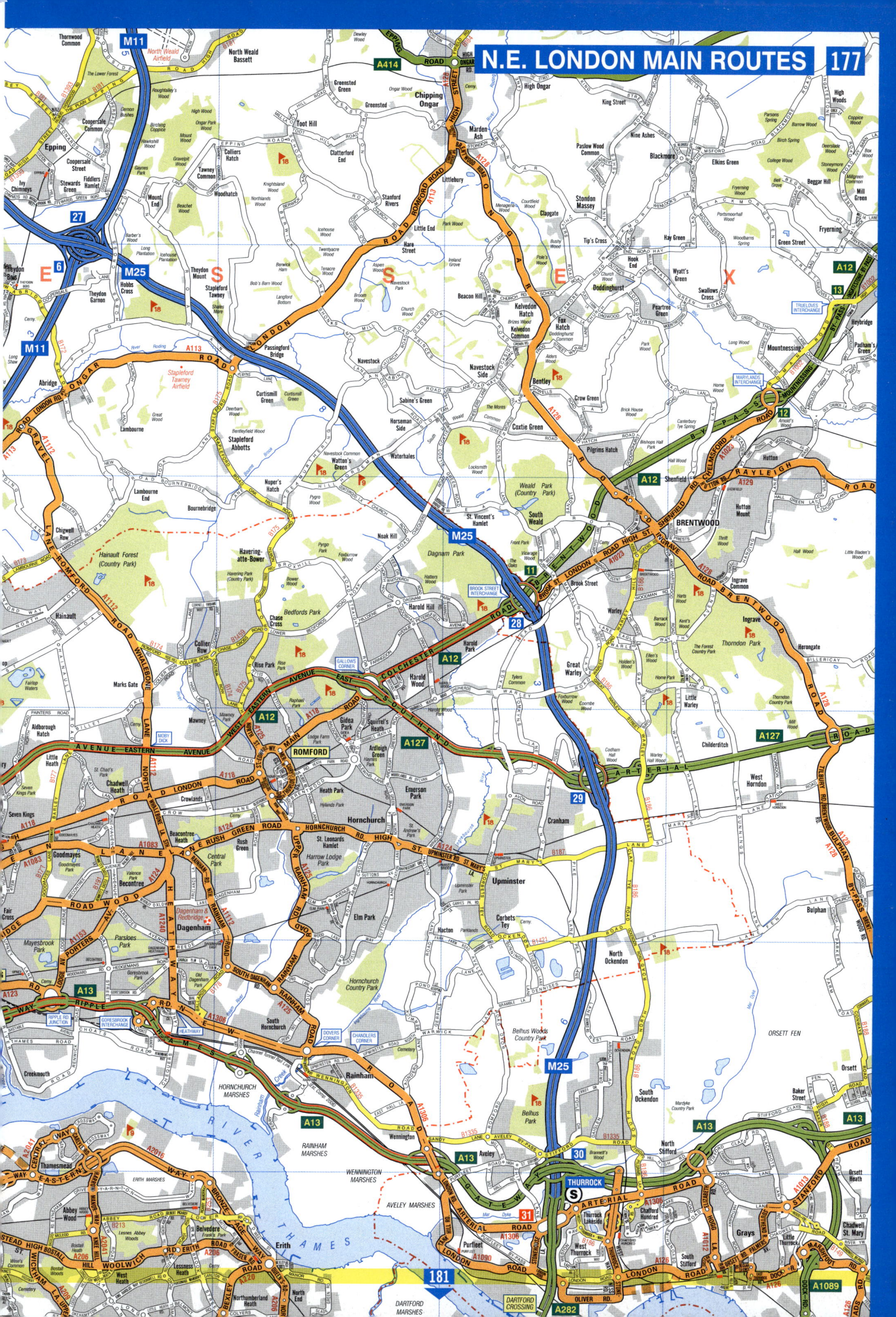
M11
North Weald Airfield
North Weald Bassett
A414
Chipping Ongar
High Ongar
Epping
27
M25
Theydon Bois
Abridge
Stapleford Tawney Airfield
Passingford Bridge
Navestock Side
Kelvedon Hatch
Blackmore
Doddinghurst
Mountnessing
Stondon Massey
Pilgrims Hatch
Shenfield
BRENTWOOD
Hutton
A12
A128
A113
Lambourne
Chigwell Row
Hainault Forest (Country Park)
Havering-atte-Bower
Noak Hill
Harold Hill
Harold Wood
Weald Park (Country Park)
South Weald
Dagnam Park
28
Ingrave
Thorndon Park
Herongate
Great Warley
ROMFORD
Gidea Park
Collier Row
Marks Gate
Little Heath
Chadwell Heath
Seven Kings
Goodmayes
Becontree
Dagenham
Parsloes Park
Mayesbrook Park
Hornchurch
Emerson Park
Upminster
Elm Park
Cranham
29
A127
West Horndon
Bulphan
North Ockenden
Corbets Tey
South Hornchurch
Rainham
Hornchurch Country Park
Belhus Woods Country Park
South Ockendon
Orsett
Orsett Fen
A13
Wennington
Aveley
30
THURROCK
Chafford Hundred
West Thurrock
Grays
Little Thurrock
Purfleet
31
Thamesmead
Abbey Wood
Belvedere
Erith
West Heath
Northumberland Heath
Dartford Crossing
RIVER THAMES
Rainham Marshes
Wennington Marshes
Aveley Marshes
Dartford Marshes
Hornchurch Marshes
Erith Marshes
181
A282
A1089
ESSEX

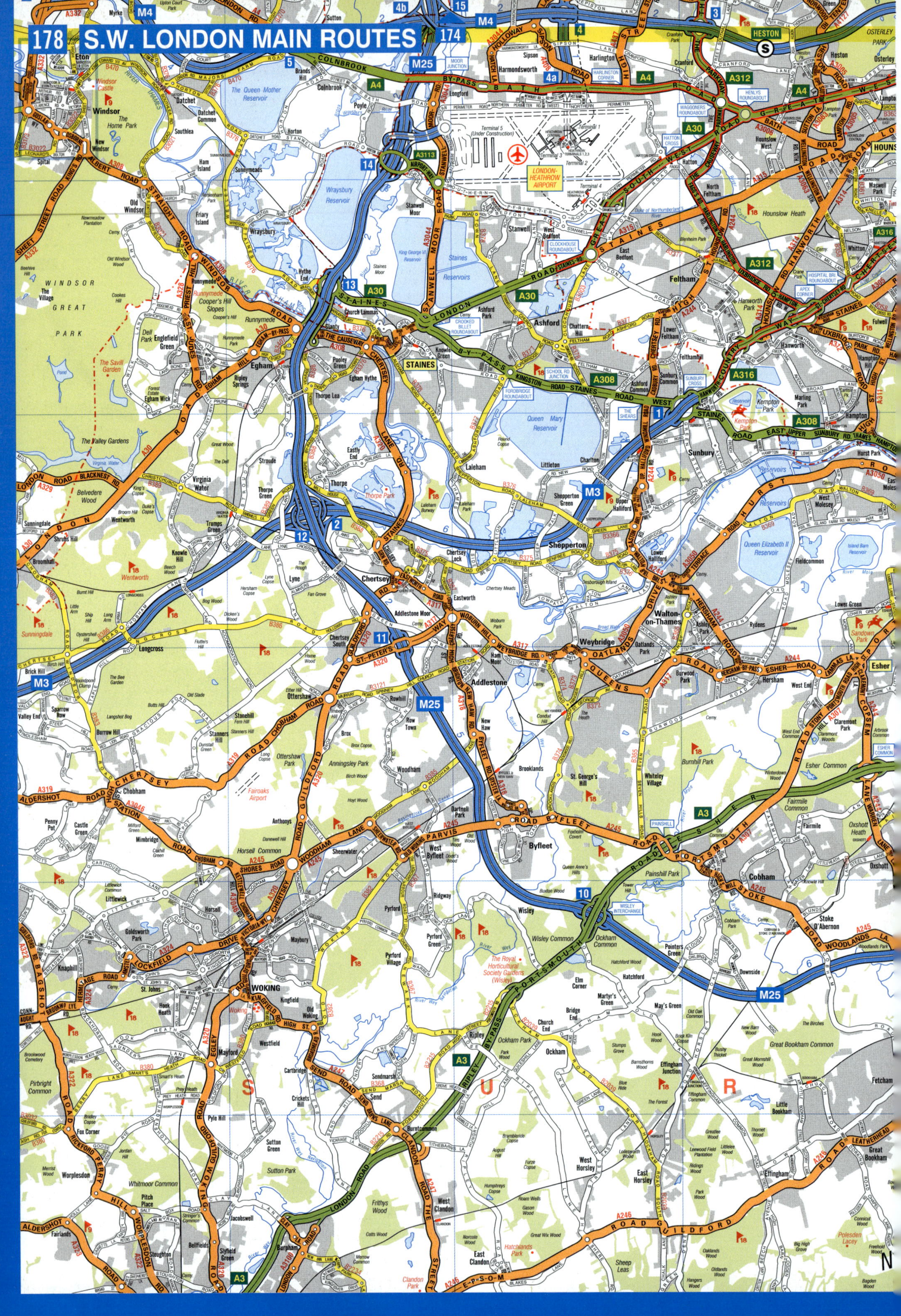

174
M4
M25
M3
A30
A4
A3
A312
A316
A308
LONDON-HEATHROW AIRPORT
Windsor
Eton
Datchet
Colnbrook
Harmondsworth
Sipson
Harlington
Cranford
Heston
Hounslow West
Feltham
Hanworth
Stanwell
Staines
Ashford
Sunbury
Egham
Englefield Green
Virginia Water
Thorpe
Chertsey
Addlestone
Weybridge
Walton-on-Thames
Shepperton
Laleham
Littleton
Byfleet
West Byfleet
Woking
Knaphill
Horsell
Pyrford
Ripley
Ockham
Cobham
Esher
Hersham
Longcross
Ottershaw
Send
Burpham
Worplesdon
East Horsley
West Horsley
Effingham
Great Bookham
Fetcham
Stoke D'Abernon
Wisley
Runnymede
Windsor Great Park
Queen Mary Reservoir
Queen Elizabeth II Reservoir
Wraysbury Reservoir
The Queen Mother Reservoir
SURREY

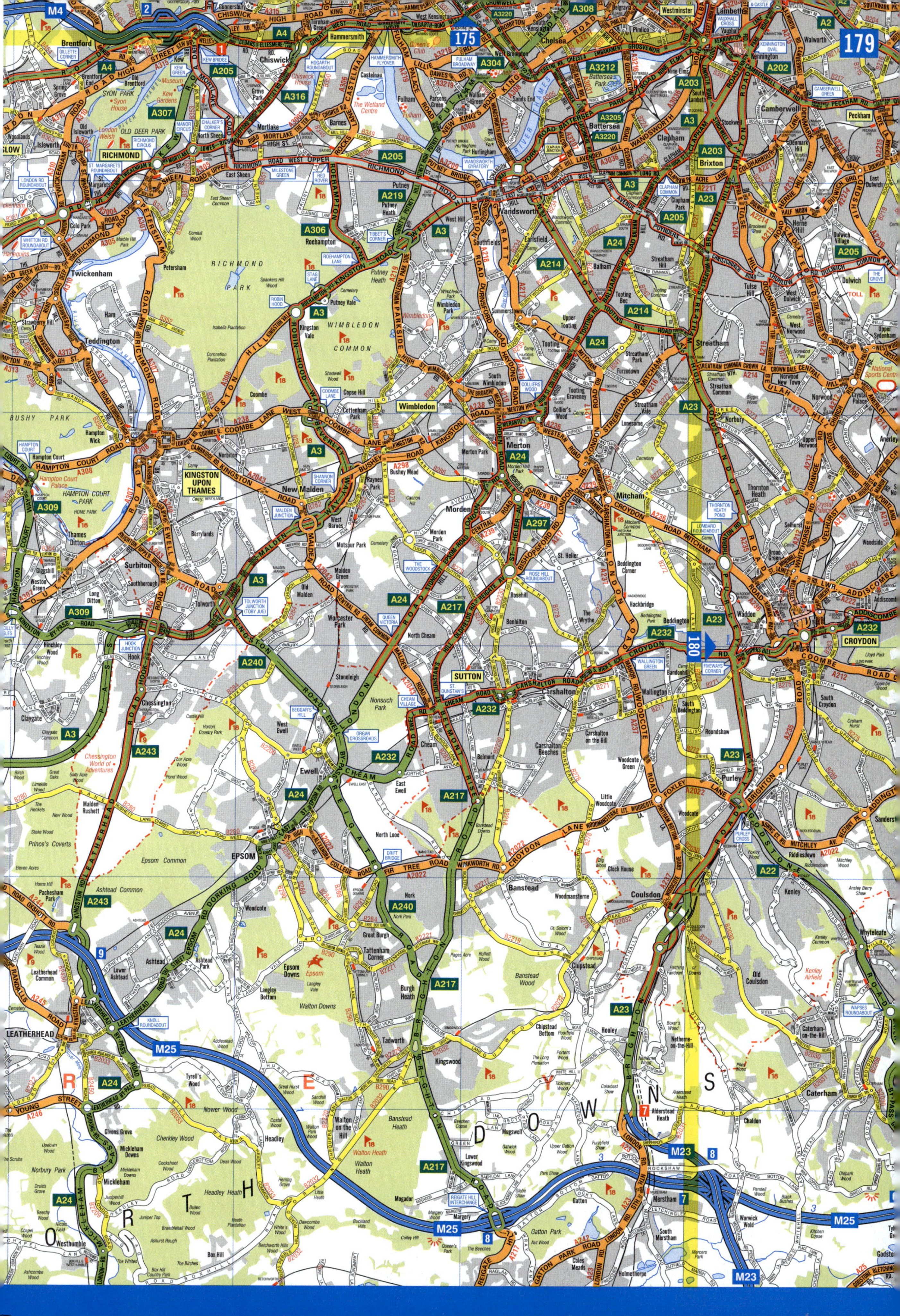

M4
2
175
179
180
A308
Westminster
Lambeth
Brentford
Chiswick
Hammersmith
Chelsea
Kew
Mortlake
Barnes
Putney
Fulham
Battersea
Clapham
Brixton
Camberwell
Peckham
Kennington
Walworth
RICHMOND
Isleworth
Twickenham
Teddington
Hampton Wick
Hampton Court
BUSHY PARK
RICHMOND PARK
Petersham
Ham
Roehampton
Wandsworth
Earlsfield
Southfields
Wimbledon
WIMBLEDON COMMON
Tooting
Balham
Streatham
Norbury
Merton
Mitcham
Morden
KINGSTON UPON THAMES
New Malden
Surbiton
Thames Ditton
Tolworth
Hook
Chessington
Worcester Park
North Cheam
Cheam
SUTTON
Carshalton
Wallington
Beddington
Waddon
CROYDON
Purley
Coulsdon
Banstead
Ewell
EPSOM
Epsom Downs
Ashtead
LEATHERHEAD
Tadworth
Kingswood
Chipstead
Hooley
Kenley
Whyteleafe
Caterham
Merstham
Reigate Hill
Mickleham
Headley
M25
M23
A3
A4
A23
A24
A205
A217
A232
A240
A243
N O R T H   D O W N S

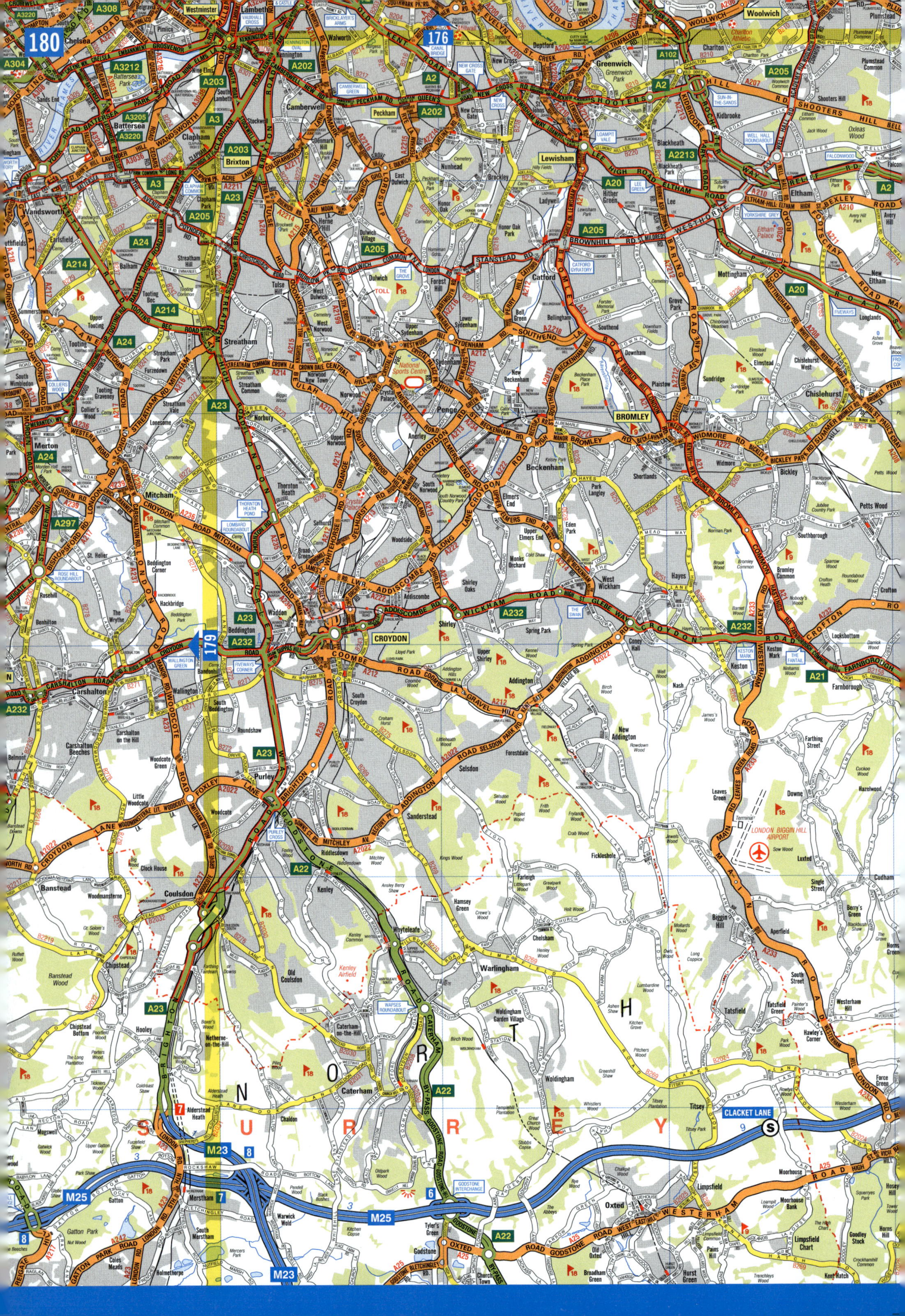
180
176
179
Chelsea
Westminster
Lambeth
Walworth
Battersea
Clapham
Brixton
Camberwell
Peckham
Deptford
New Cross
Greenwich
Woolwich
Charlton
Lewisham
Kidbrooke
Eltham
Wandsworth
Earlsfield
Balham
Streatham
Tooting
Dulwich
Forest Hill
Sydenham
Catford
Mottingham
Chislehurst
National Sports Centre
Crystal Palace
Penge
Anerley
Beckenham
BROMLEY
Bickley
Hayes
West Wickham
Merton
Mitcham
Norbury
Thornton Heath
Croydon
CROYDON
Addiscombe
Shirley
Addington
New Addington
Waddon
Beddington
Wallington
Carshalton
Purley
Coulsdon
Kenley
Whyteleafe
Warlingham
Caterham
Chelsham
Woldingham
Sanderstead
Selsdon
Forestdale
Keston
Farnborough
Downe
LONDON BIGGIN HILL AIRPORT
Biggin Hill
Tatsfield
Titsey
Limpsfield
Oxted
Hurst Green
Godstone
Merstham
South Merstham
Banstead
Chipstead
Hooley
CLACKET LANE
S U R R E Y
N O R T H
M25
M23
A23
A22
A21
A20
A2
A24
A232
A205
A3
A25

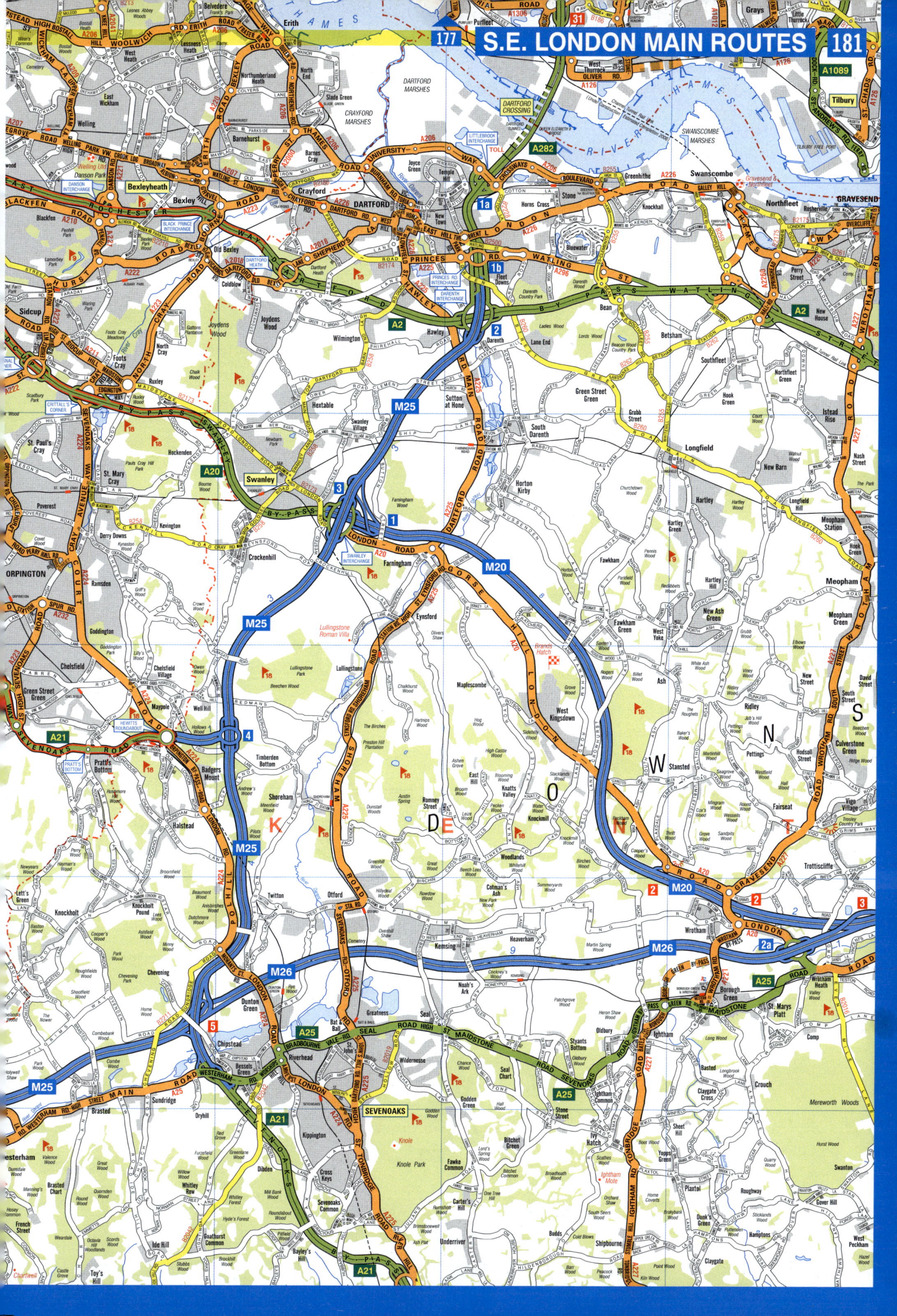

S.E. LONDON MAIN ROUTES
181
177
Erith
Belvedere
Welling
Bexleyheath
Bexley
Crayford
Dartford
Sidcup
Foots Cray
Swanley
Orpington
Hextable
Wilmington
Farningham
Eynsford
Lullingstone
Shoreham
Otford
Kemsing
Sevenoaks
Riverhead
Chipstead
Dunton Green
Sundridge
Brasted
Westerham
Seal
Ightham
Borough Green
Wrotham
Kingsdown
West Kingsdown
Horton Kirby
South Darenth
Sutton at Hone
Longfield
Hartley
Meopham
Istead Rise
Southfleet
Northfleet
Gravesend
Swanscombe
Greenhithe
Stone
Bluewater
Purfleet
West Thurrock
Grays
Tilbury
Dartford Crossing
Dartford Marshes
Crayford Marshes
Swanscombe Marshes
Knole Park
Lullingstone Roman Villa
Brands Hatch
Stansted
Fairseat
Trottiscliffe
Plaxtol
Shipbourne
Underriver
Ide Hill
Toy's Hill
Chartwell
Halstead
Knockholt
Chelsfield
Badgers Mount
Crockenhill
St. Mary Cray
St. Paul's Cray
Mereworth Woods
M25
M20
M26
A2
A20
A21
A25
A282
A1089
K E N T
D O W N S

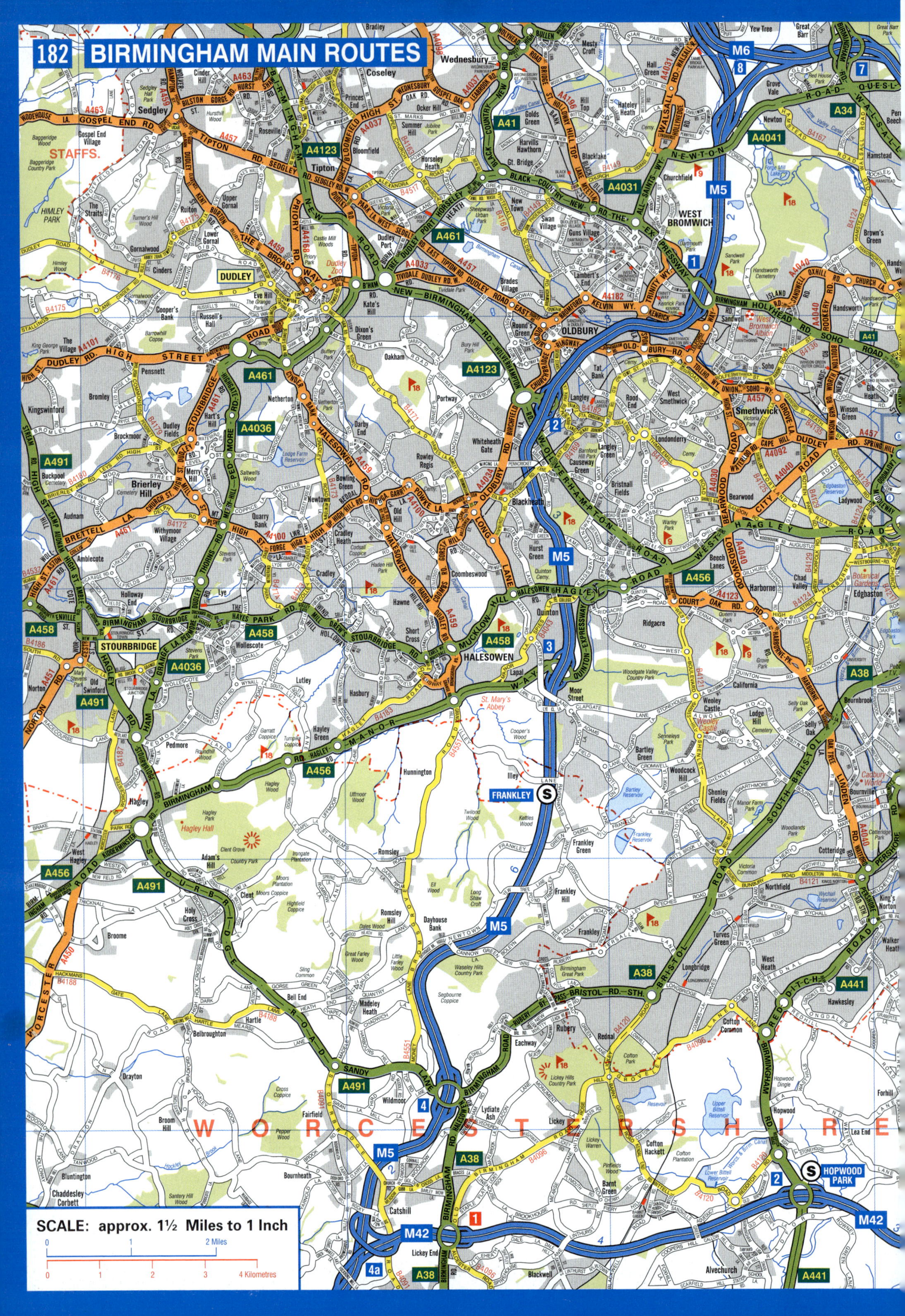

182
BIRMINGHAM MAIN ROUTES
SCALE: approx. 1½ Miles to 1 Inch
2 Miles
4 Kilometres
STAFFS.
WORCESTERSHIRE
Sedgley
Coseley
Wednesbury
Tipton
DUDLEY
WEST BROMWICH
OLDBURY
Smethwick
Netherton
Brierley Hill
STOURBRIDGE
HALESOWEN
Quinton
Hagley
Northfield
Rubery
Kingswinford
Edgbaston
Harborne
Selly Oak
Bournville
Longbridge
Blackheath
Cradley Heath
Lye
Romsley
Catshill
Alvechurch
Hopwood
FRANKLEY
HOPWOOD PARK
M5
M6
M42
A38
A441
A456
A458
A491
A4123
A461
A4036
A4041
A34
A41
A4031
A4040
A457
A459
A4123

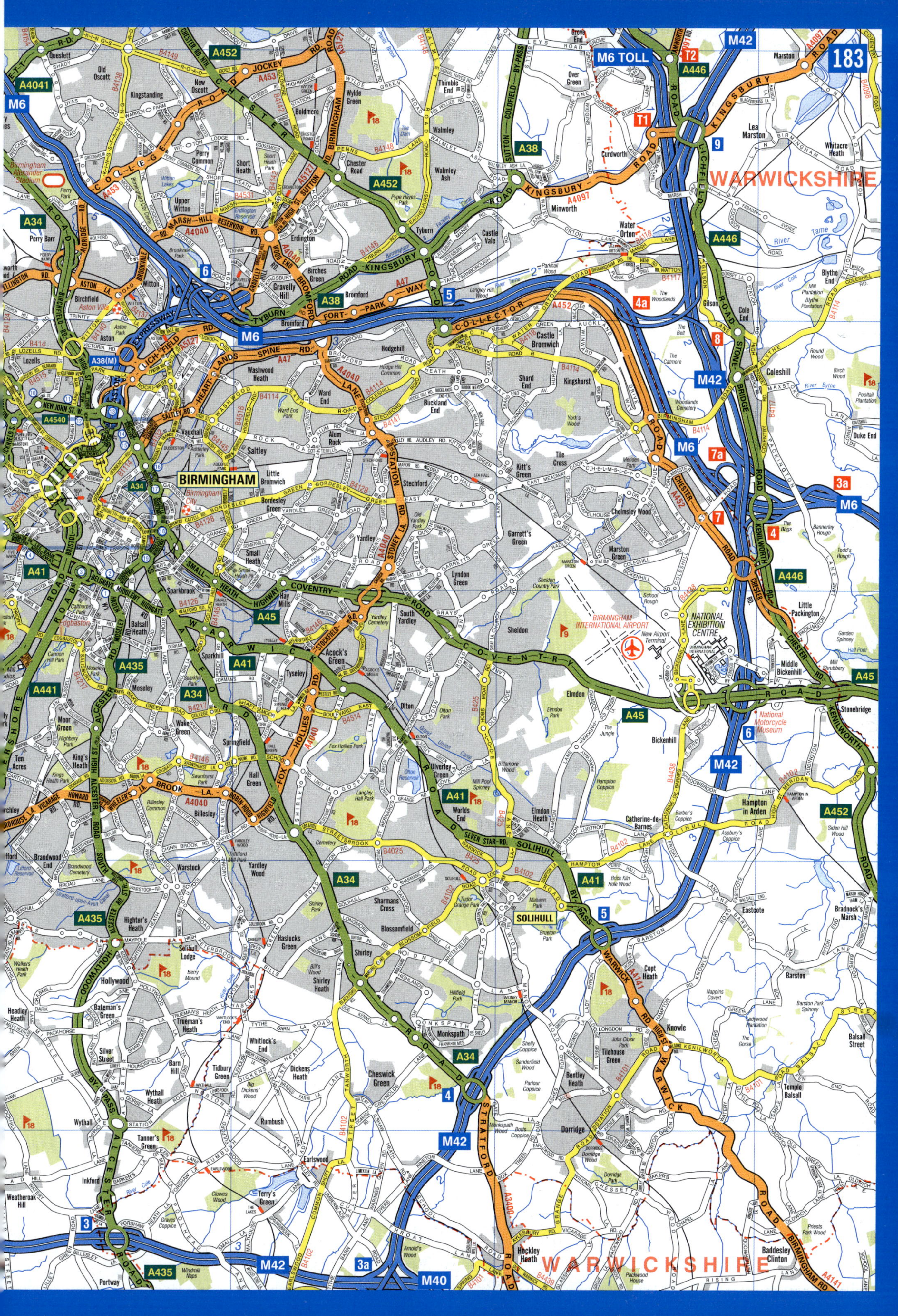

WARWICKSHIRE
BIRMINGHAM
SOLIHULL
BIRMINGHAM INTERNATIONAL AIRPORT
NATIONAL EXHIBITION CENTRE
M6 TOLL
M6
M42
M40
A452
A38
A4041
A34
A41
A45
A435
A441
A446
A47
A38(M)
A4540
A4040
Quesleft
Old Oscott
Kingstanding
New Oscott
Boldmere
Wylde Green
Thimble End
Walmley
Walmley Ash
Over Green
Cordworth
Minworth
Water Orton
Lea Marston
Marston
Whitacre Heath
Perry Barr
Perry Common
Short Heath
Chester Road
Upper Witton
Erdington
Tyburn
Castle Vale
Birchfield
Aston
Witton
Gravelly Hill
Birches Green
Bromford
Lozells
Washwood Heath
Ward End
Hodgehill
Castle Bromwich
Shard End
Kingshurst
Buckland End
Alum Rock
Saltley
Vauxhall
Little Bromwich
Stechford
Kitt's Green
Tile Cross
Coleshill
Bordesley Green
Yardley
Garrett's Green
Chelmsley Wood
Marston Green
Small Heath
Sparkbrook
Balsall Heath
Sparkhill
Hay Mills
South Yardley
Lyndon Green
Sheldon
Acock's Green
Tyseley
Moseley
Olton
Elmdon
Bickenhill
Little Packington
Middle Bickenhill
Stonebridge
Moor Green
Wake Green
Springfield
King's Heath
Ten Acres
Hall Green
Billesley
Ulverley Green
Worlds End
Elmdon Heath
Catherine-de-Barnes
Hampton in Arden
Brandwood End
Warstock
Yardley Wood
Sharmans Cross
Blossomfield
Highter's Heath
Haslucks Green
Shirley
Shirley Heath
Eastcote
Bradnock's Marsh
Barston
Hollywood
Bateman's Green
Trueman's Heath
Copt Heath
Knowle
Headley Heath
Silver Street
Whitlock's End
Monkspath
Bentley Heath
Balsall Street
Temple Balsall
Tidbury Green
Dickens Heath
Cheswick Green
Wythall
Dorridge
Wythall Heath
Rumbush
Tanner's Green
Earlswood
Inkford
Terry's Green
Weatheroak Hill
Portway
Hockley Heath
Baddesley Clinton

MANCHESTER MAIN ROUTES

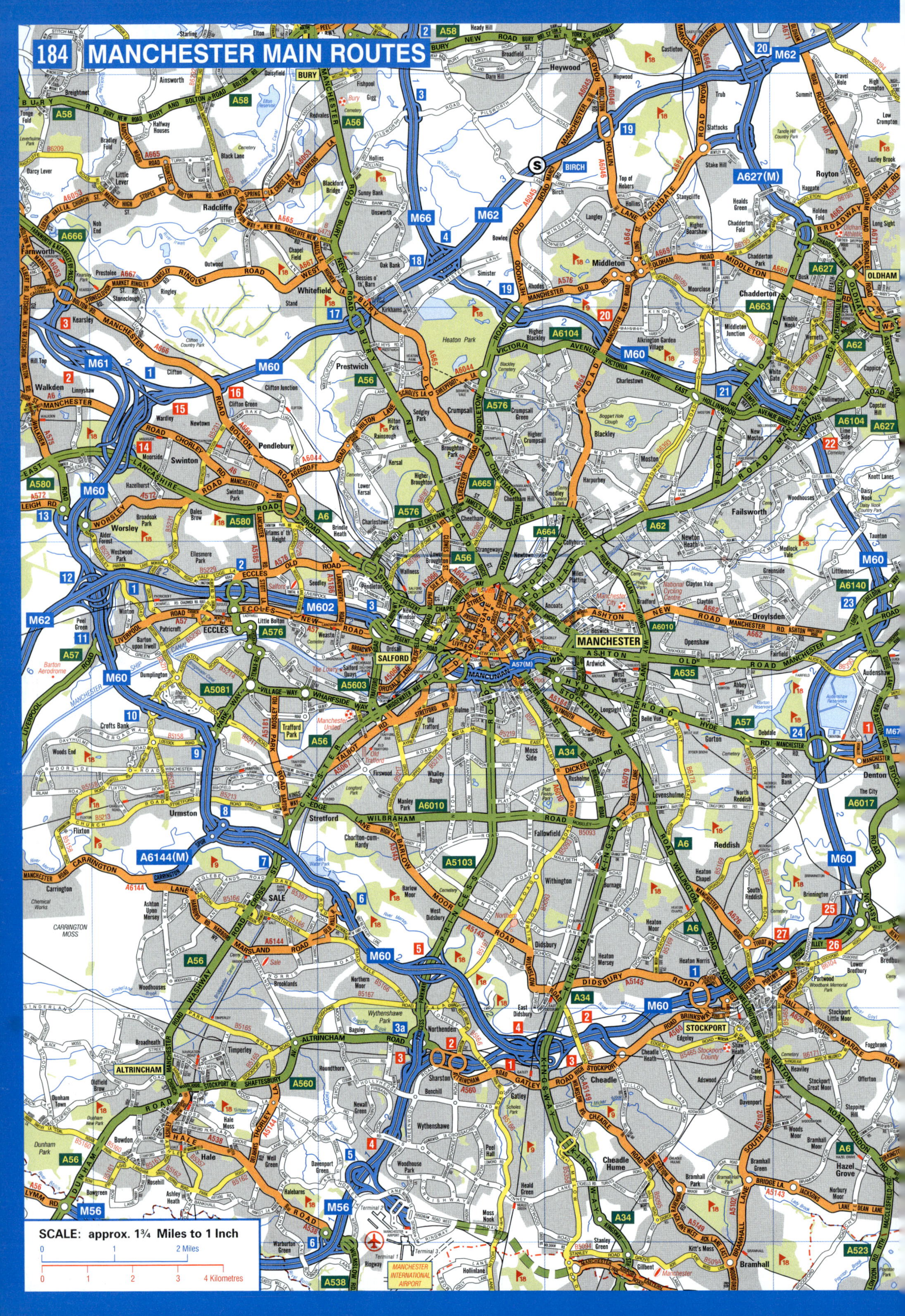

Town Plans

Aberdeen 186
Bath 186
Birmingham 186
Blackpool 186
Bournemouth 186
Bradford 186
Brighton & Hove 186
Bristol 187
Cambridge 187
Canterbury 187
Cardiff (Caerdydd) 187
Carlisle 187
Cheltenham 187
Chester 188
Coventry 188
Derby 188
Dover 188
Dumfries 188
Dundee 188
Durham 188
Eastbourne 188
Edinburgh 189
Exeter 189
Folkestone 189
Glasgow 189
Gloucester 189
Guildford 189
Harrogate 190
Inverness 190
Ipswich 190
Kilmarnock 190
Kingston upon Hull 190
Leeds 190
Leicester 190
Lincoln 191
Liverpool 191
London 192-193
Manchester 191
Medway Towns 191
Middlesbrough 191
Milton Keynes 194
Newcastle upon Tyne 191
Newport (Casnewydd) 194
Northampton 194
Norwich 194
Nottingham 194
Oban 195
Oxford 194
Perth 195
Peterborough 195
Plymouth 195
Portsmouth 195
Preston 195
Reading 195
Salisbury 195
Sheffield 196
Shrewsbury 196
Southampton 196
Stirling 196
Stoke-on-Trent 196
Stratford-upon-Avon 196
Sunderland 196
Swansea (Abertawe) 197
Swindon 197
Taunton 197
Winchester 197
Windsor 197
Wolverhampton 197
Worcester 197
York 197

Port Plans

Harwich 198
Kingston upon Hull 198
Newcastle upon Tyne 198
Newhaven 198
Poole 198
Portsmouth 198
Swansea (Abertawe) 198
Weymouth 198

Airport Plans

Birmingham 199
Glasgow 199
London Gatwick 199
London Heathrow 199
London Luton 199
London Stansted 199
Manchester International 199
Nottingham East Midlands 199

Reference to Town Plans — Légende — Zeichenerklärung

Reference to Town Plans	Symbol	Légende	Zeichenerklärung
MOTORWAY	M1	Autoroute	Autobahn
MOTORWAY UNDER CONSTRUCTION		Autoroute en construction	Autobahn im Bau
MOTORWAY PROPOSED		Autoroute prévue	Geplante Autobahn
MOTORWAY JUNCTIONS WITH NUMBERS	4 5	Autoroute echangeur numéroté	Autobahnanschluß mit Nummer
Unlimited Interchange 4		Echangeur non limité 4	4 Unbeschränkter Fahrtrichtungswechsel
Limited Interchange 5		Echangeur limité 5	5 Beschränkter Fahrtrichtungswechsel
PRIMARY ROUTE	A41	Route prioritaire, direction	Hauptverbindungsstraße
DUAL CARRIAGEWAYS		Route à deux chaussées séparées	Zweispurige Schnellstraße (A- und B-Straßen)
CLASS A ROAD	A129	Route de type A	A-Straße
CLASS B ROAD	B177	Route de type B	B-Straße
MAJOR ROADS UNDER CONSTRUCTION		Route prioritaire en construction	Hauptverkehrsstraße im Bau
MAJOR ROADS PROPOSED		Route prioritaire prévue	Geplante Hauptverkehrsstraße
MINOR ROADS		Route secondaire	Nebenstraße
RESTRICTED ACCESS		Accès réglementé	Beschränkte Zufahrt
PEDESTRIANIZED ROAD & MAIN FOOTWAY		Route piétonnière et chemin résevé aux piétons	Fußgängerstraße und Fußweg
ONE WAY STREETS		Sens unique	Einbahnstraße
TOLL	TOLL	Péage	Gebührenpflichtig
RAILWAY AND B.R. STATION		Voie ferrée et gare B.R.	Eisenbahnlinie und Bahnhof
UNDERGROUND / METRO & D.L.R. STATION	DLR	Station de metro et D.L.R.	U-Bahnstation und D.L.R.-Station
LEVEL CROSSING AND TUNNEL		Passage à niveau et tunnel	Bahnübergang und Tunnel
TRAM STOP AND ONE WAY TRAM STOP		Arrêt de Tramway	Straßenbahnhaltestelle
BUILT-UP AREA		Agglomération	Geschlossene Ortschaft
ABBEY, CATHEDRAL, PRIORY ETC.		Abbaye, Cathédrale, Prieuré etc.	Abtei, Kathedrale, Kloster usw.
AIRPORT		Aéroport	Flughafen
BUS STATION		Gare routière	Bushaltestelle
CAR PARK (Selection of)	P	Choix de Parking	Auswahl von Parkplatz
CHURCH		Eglise	Kirche
CITY WALL		Murs d'enceinte	Stadtmauer
CONGESTION CHARGING ZONE		Zone de péage urbain	City-Maut Zone
FERRY (Vehicular)		Bac (Véhicules)	Fähre (Autos)
(Foot only)		(Piétons)	(nur für Personen)
GOLF COURSE		Terrain de golf	Golfplatz
HELIPORT		Héliport	Hubschrauberlandeplatz
HOSPITAL	H	Hôpital	Krankenhaus
INFORMATION CENTRE	i	Syndicat d'initiative	Information
LIGHTHOUSE		Phare	Leuchtturm
MARKET		Marché	Markt
NATIONAL TRUST PROPERTY (Open)	NT	National Trust Property (Ouvert)	National Trust-Eigentum (geöffnet)
(Restricted opening)	NT	(Heures d'ouverture)	(Beschränkte Öffnungszeit)
(National Trust of Scotland)	NTS NTS	(National Trust of Scotland)	(National Trust of Scotland)
PARK & RIDE	P+R	Choix de Parking	Auswahl von Parkplatz
PLACE OF INTEREST		Endroits Intéressants	Sehenswürdigkeiten
POLICE STATION		Commissariat de police	Polizeirevier
POST OFFICE		Bureau de poste	Postamt
SHOPPING AREA (Main street and precinct)		Quartier commerçant (Rue et zone principales)	Einkaufsviertel (Hauptgeschäftsstraße, Fußgängerzone)
SHOPMOBILITY		Shopmobility	Shopmobility
TOILET		Toilettes	Toilette
VIEWPOINT		Vue Panoramique	Aussichtspunkt

ABERDEEN

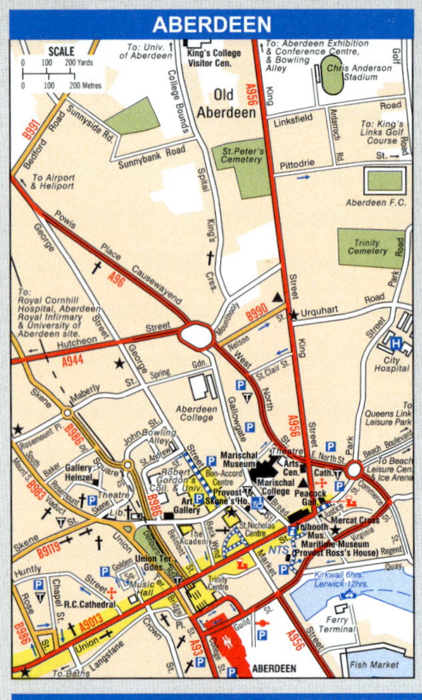

BATH

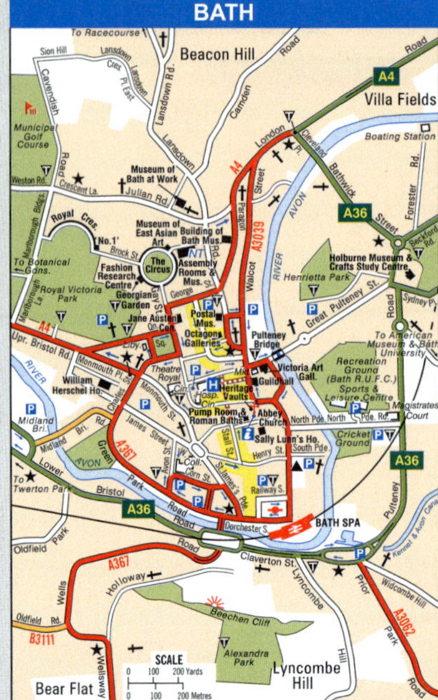

BLACKPOOL

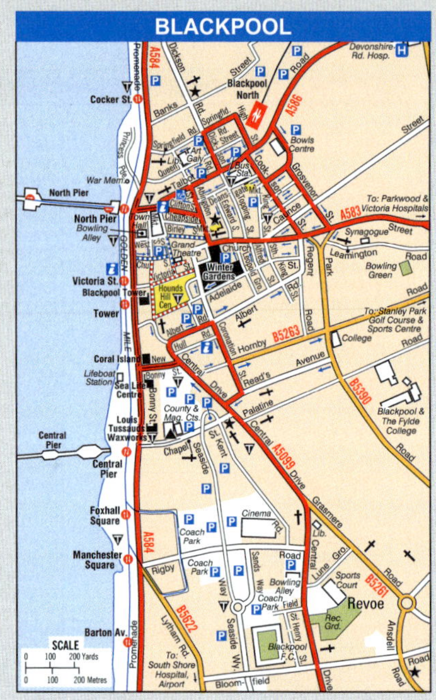

BIRMINGHAM (CITY CENTRE)

BOURNEMOUTH

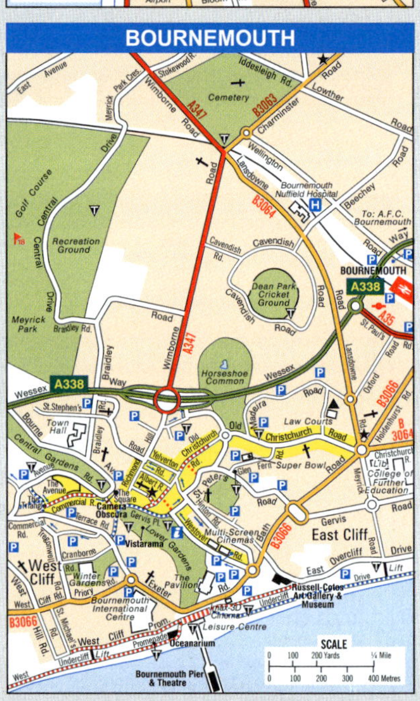

BRADFORD

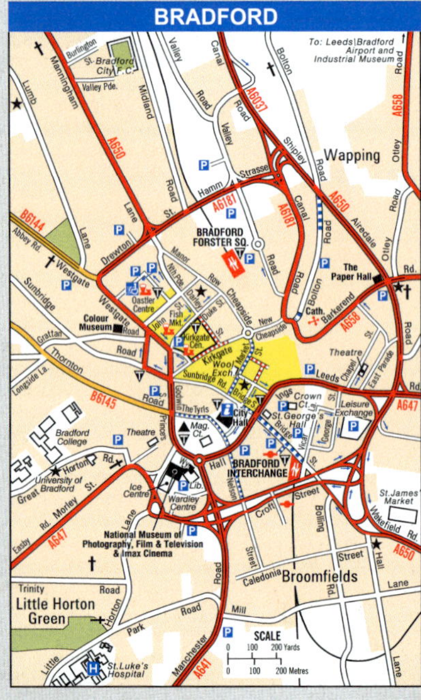

BRIGHTON and HOVE

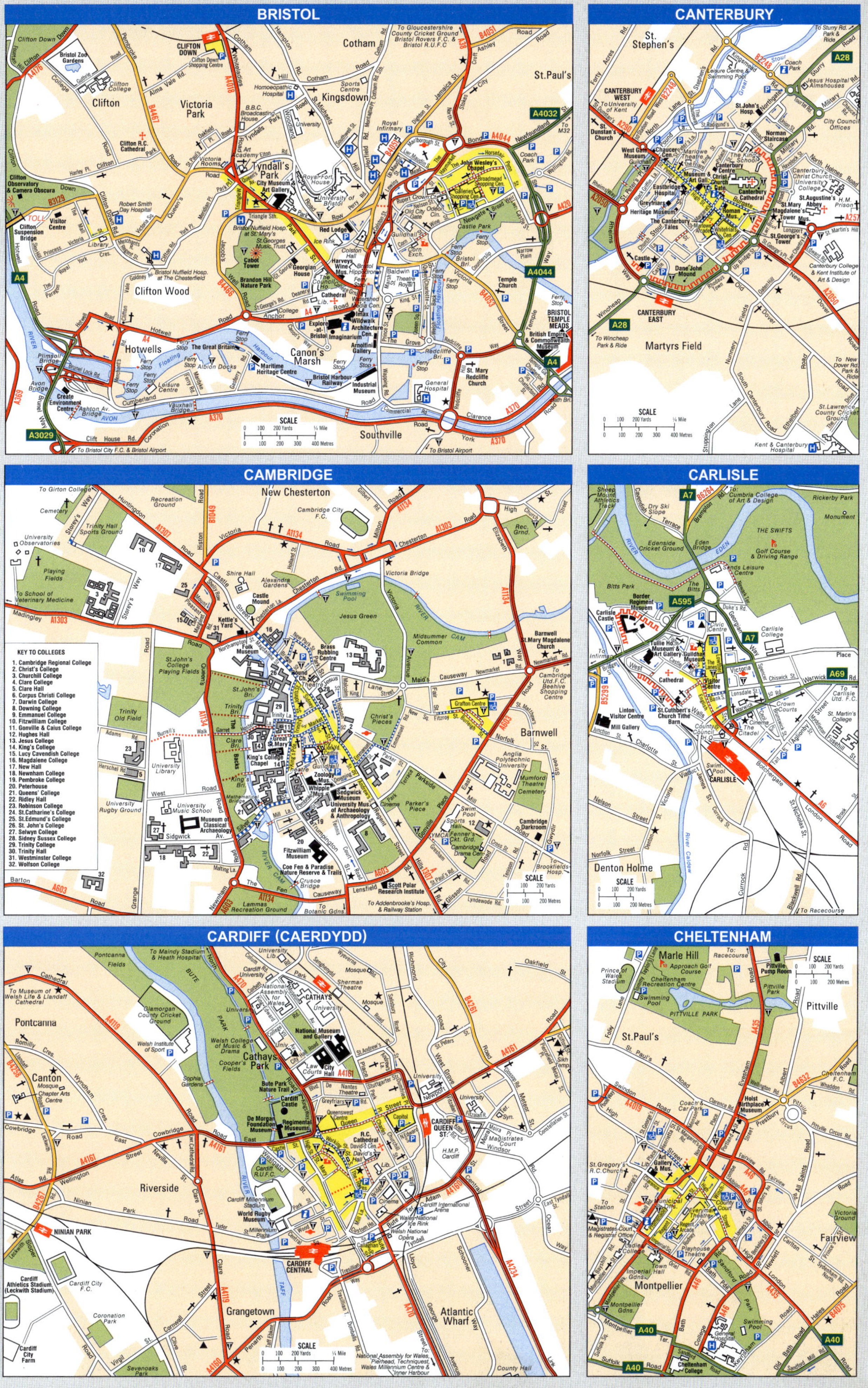
BRISTOL
CANTERBURY
CAMBRIDGE
CARLISLE
CARDIFF (CAERDYDD)
CHELTENHAM
KEY TO COLLEGES
1. Cambridge Regional College
2. Christ's College
3. Churchill College
4. Clare College
5. Clare Hall
6. Corpus Christi College
7. Darwin College
8. Downing College
9. Emmanuel College
10. Fitzwilliam College
11. Gonville & Caius College
12. Hughes Hall
13. Jesus College
14. King's College
15. Lucy Cavendish College
16. Magdalene College
17. New Hall
18. Newnham College
19. Pembroke College
20. Peterhouse
21. Queens' College
22. Ridley Hall
23. Robinson College
24. St.Catharine's College
25. St.Edmund's College
26. St. John's College
27. Selwyn College
28. Sidney Sussex College
29. Trinity College
30. Trinity Hall
31. Westminster College
32. Wolfson College
Cotham
Kingsdown
Clifton
Victoria Park
Clifton Wood
Hotwells
Canon's Marsh
Southville
St.Paul's
St. Stephen's
Martyrs Field
New Chesterton
Barnwell
Denton Holme
Pontcanna
Canton
Riverside
Cathays Park
Grangetown
Atlantic Wharf
Marle Hill
Pittville
St.Paul's
Montpellier
Fairview

CHESTER

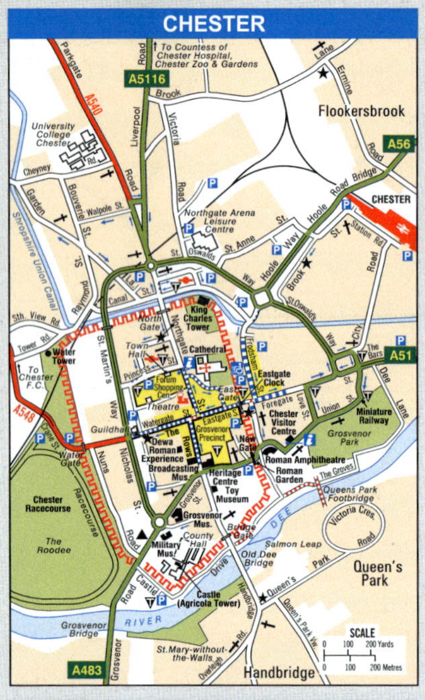

COVENTRY

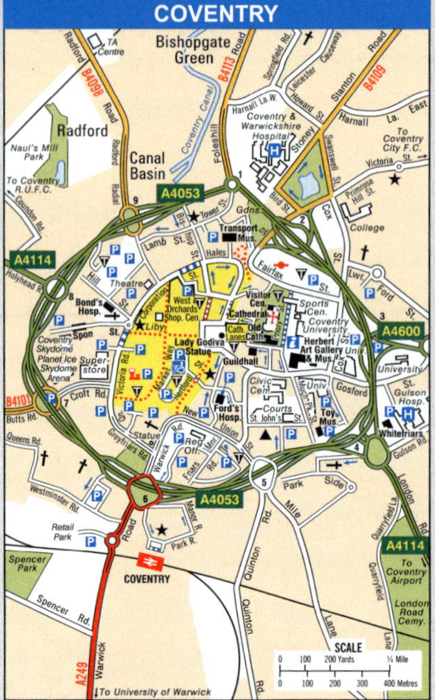

DERBY

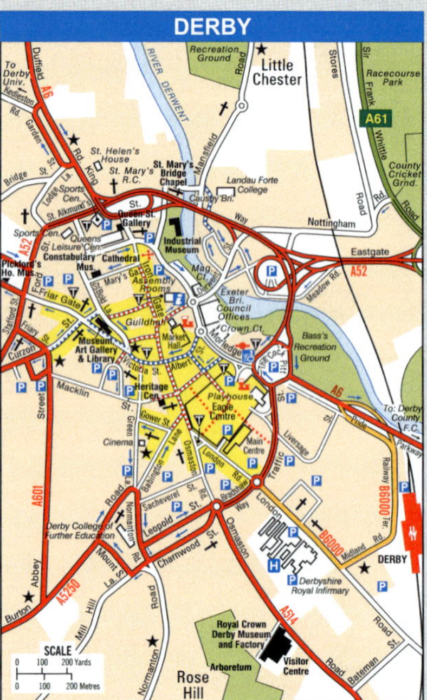

DOVER

DUMFRIES

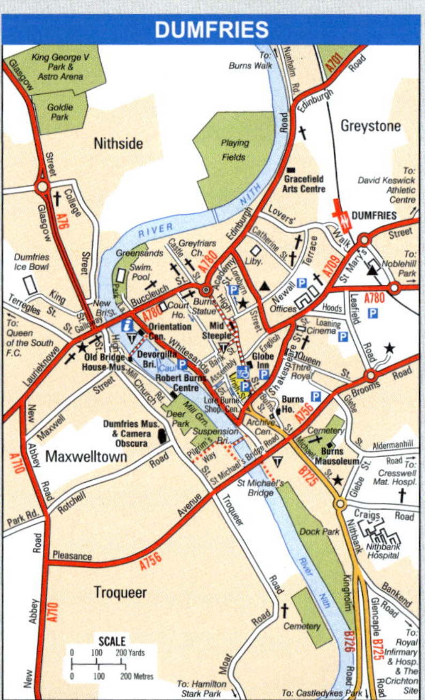

DUNDEE

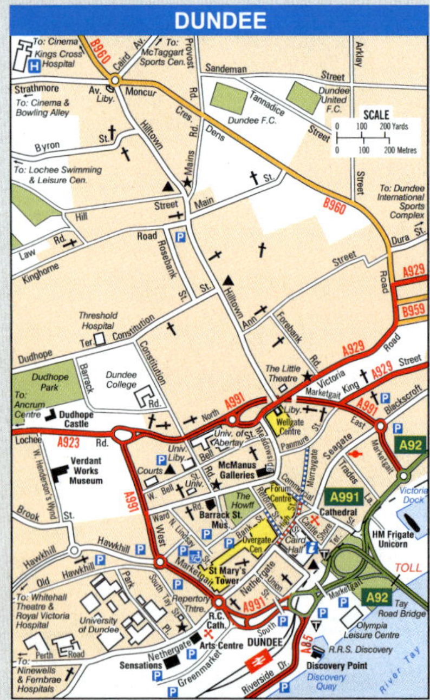

DURHAM

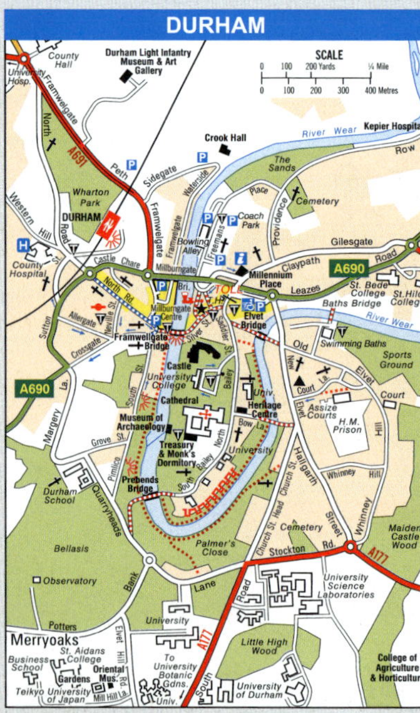

EASTBOURNE

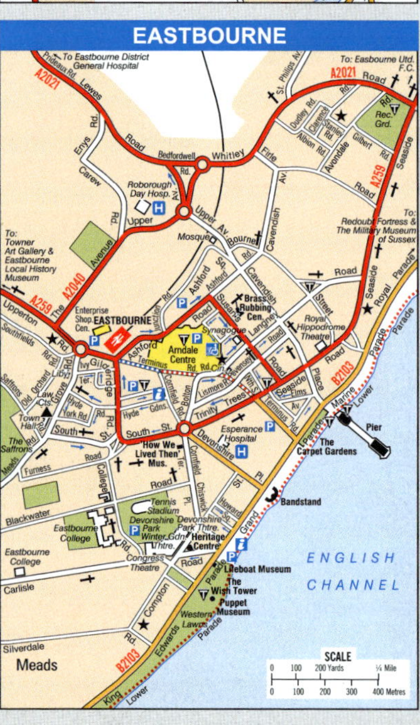

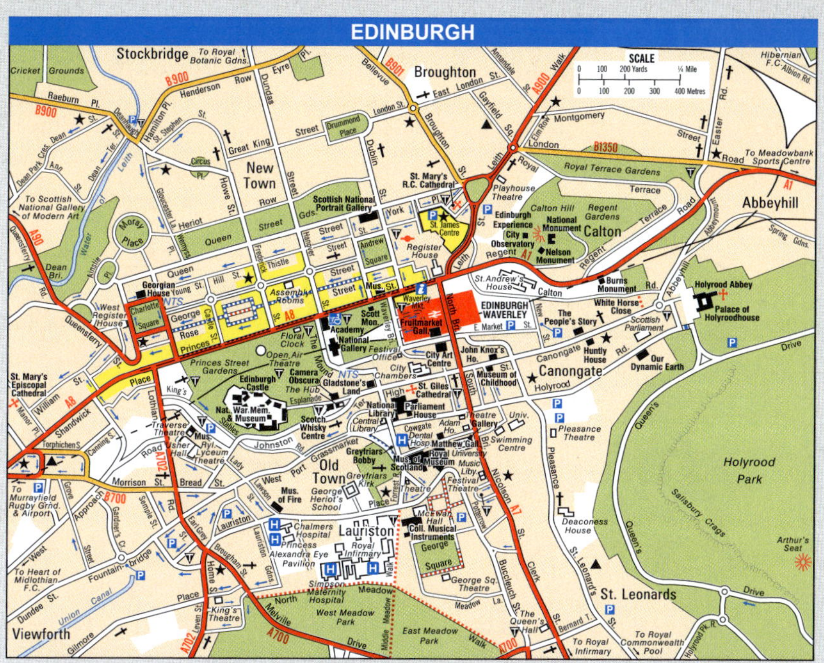
EDINBURGH
SCALE
Stockbridge
Broughton
New Town
Abbeyhill
Calton
Regent Gardens
Royal Terrace Gardens
Princes Street Gardens
Edinburgh Castle
Canongate
Holyrood Park
Holyrood Abbey
Palace of Holyroodhouse
EDINBURGH WAVERLEY
Old Town
Lauriston
Royal Infirmary
Arthur's Seat
Salisbury Crags
St. Leonards
Viewforth
West Meadow Park
East Meadow Park
Union Canal
To Royal Commonwealth Pool
To Royal Infirmary
To Murrayfield Rugby Grd. & Airport
To Heart of Midlothian F.C.
To Meadowbank Sports Centre
Hibernian F.C.
To Royal Botanic Gdns.

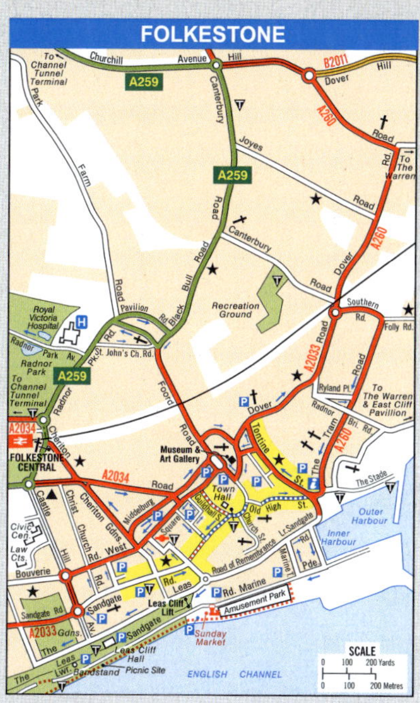
FOLKESTONE
A259
A260
A2034
FOLKESTONE CENTRAL
Recreation Ground
Royal Victoria Hospital
Museum & Art Gallery
Town Hall
Outer Harbour
Inner Harbour
Leas Cliff Hall
Amusement Park
Sunday Market
ENGLISH CHANNEL
SCALE
To Channel Tunnel Terminal
To The Warren & East Cliff Pavilion

EXETER
A377
St. James'
St. David's
EXETER ST. DAVIDS
EXETER CENTRAL
Polsloe
Newtown
Mount Dinham
Barnfield
Cathedral
Guildhall
St. Leonards
Quay Ho. Vis. Cen.
Custom House
EXETER ST. THOMAS
Haven Banks
RIVER EXE
Exeter City F.C.
Royal Devon & Exeter Hospital (Wonford)
Nuffield Hospital
To Princess Elizabeth Orthopaedic Hospital
SCALE

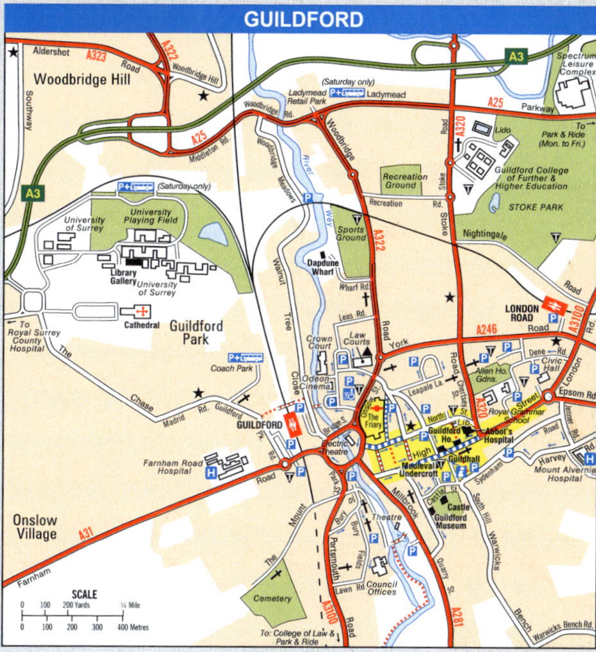
GUILDFORD
A3
A25
A31
A320
A322
A246
A3100
A281
Woodbridge Hill
University of Surrey
Guildford Park
Cathedral
GUILDFORD
LONDON ROAD
Stoke Park
Guildford College of Further & Higher Education
Onslow Village
Farnham Road Hospital
Royal Surrey County Hospital
Castle
Guildford Museum
Cemetery
Spectrum Leisure Complex
Park & Ride (Mon. to Fri.)
To College of Law & Park & Ride
SCALE

GLASGOW
SCALE
M8
M74
Kelvingrove Park
ST. GEORGE'S CROSS
COWCADDENS
CHARING CROSS
Anderston
ANDERSTON
GLASGOW CENTRAL
BUCHANAN ST.
QUEEN ST.
HIGH STREET
ARGYLE ST.
ST. ENOCH
Cathedral
Glasgow Necropolis
Sighthill Park
Glasgow Green
RIVER CLYDE
Tradeston
Calton
BRIDGE ST.
Peoples Palace
To Scottish Exhibition & Conference Centre
To Glasgow Science Centre
To Southern General Hospital & Rangers F.C.
To Celtic F.C.
To Hampden Park (Queens Park F.C.)

GLOUCESTER
A40
A38
A430
A417
A4301
Kingsholm
Gloucester R.U.F.C.
Livestock Market
Cathedral
GLOUCESTER
Docks
National Waterways Museum
City Museum, Art Gallery & Library
Gloucestershire Royal & Maternity Hospital
Llanthony Priory
The Park
SCALE
To Robinswood Hill Country Park

HARROGATE

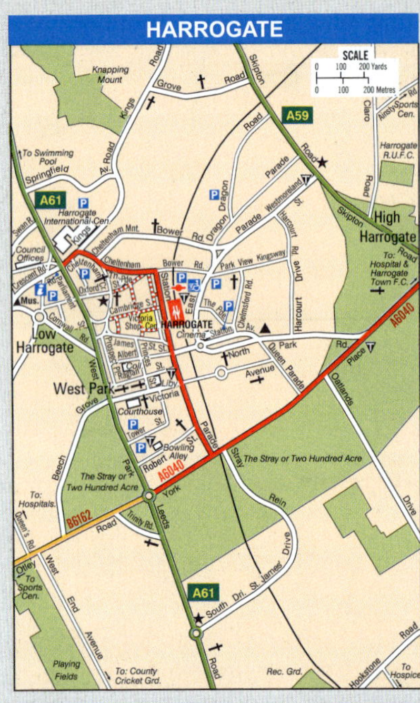

INVERNESS

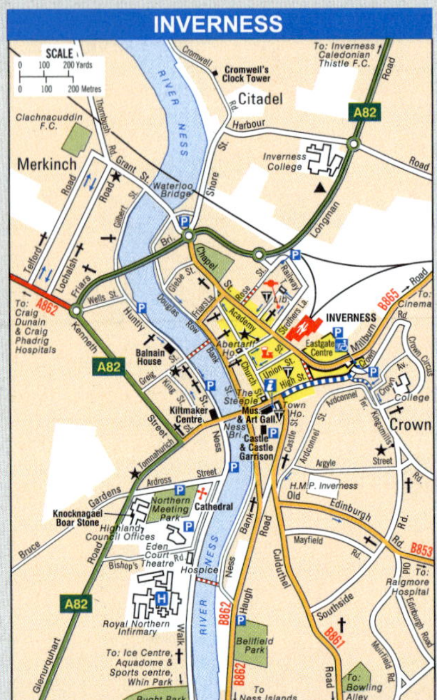

IPSWICH

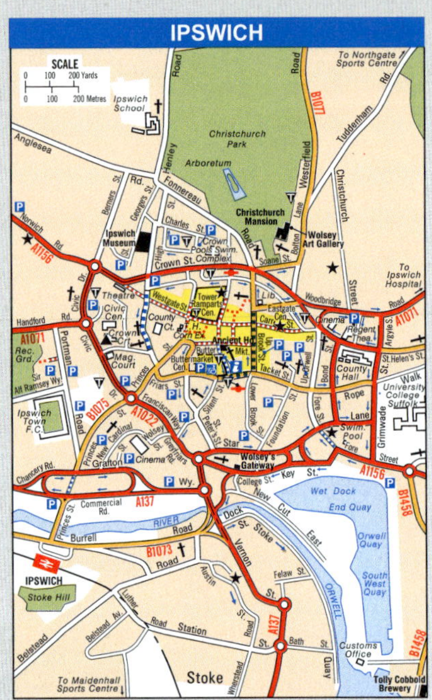

KILMARNOCK

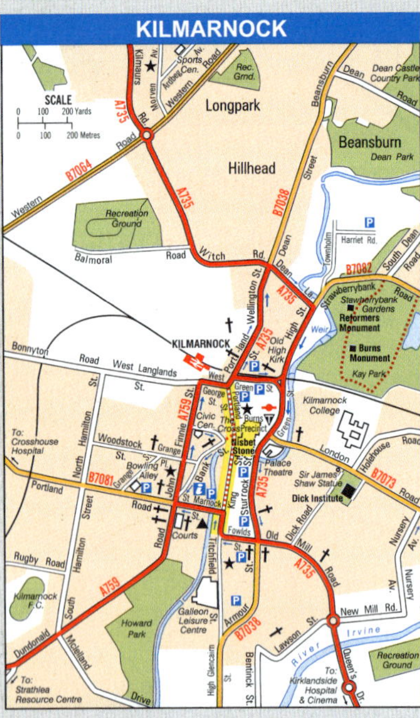

LEEDS

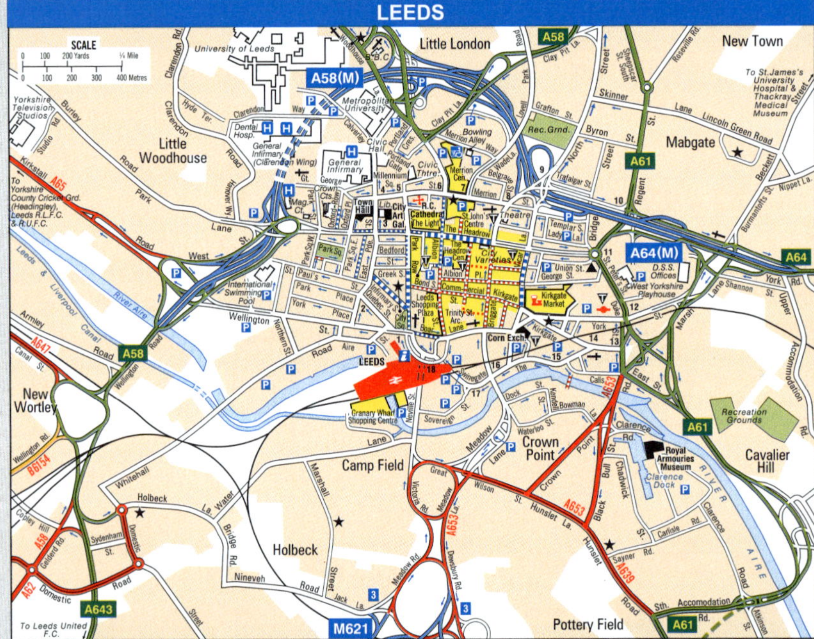

KINGSTON UPON HULL

LEICESTER

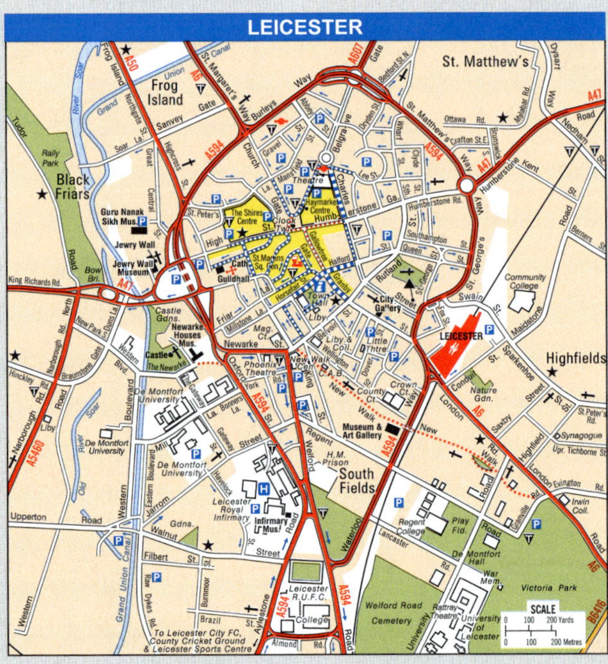

LINCOLN

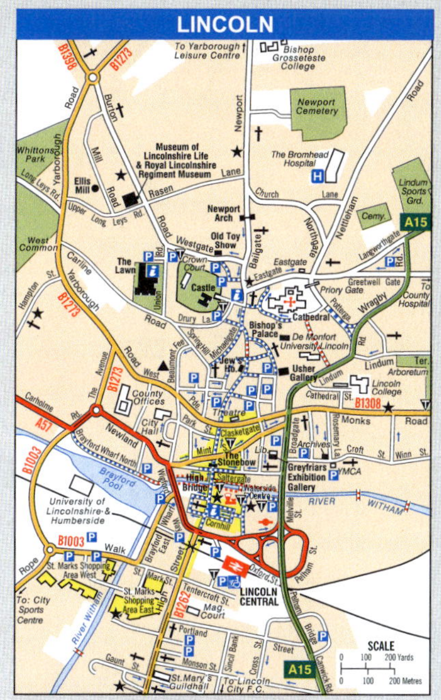

LIVERPOOL

MANCHESTER (CITY CENTRE)

MIDDLESBROUGH

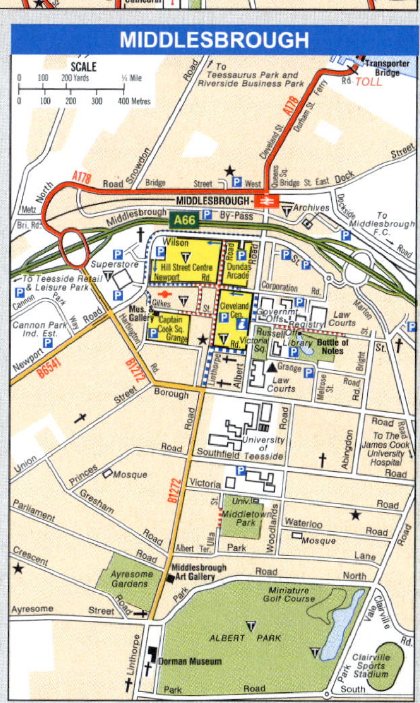

MEDWAY TOWNS

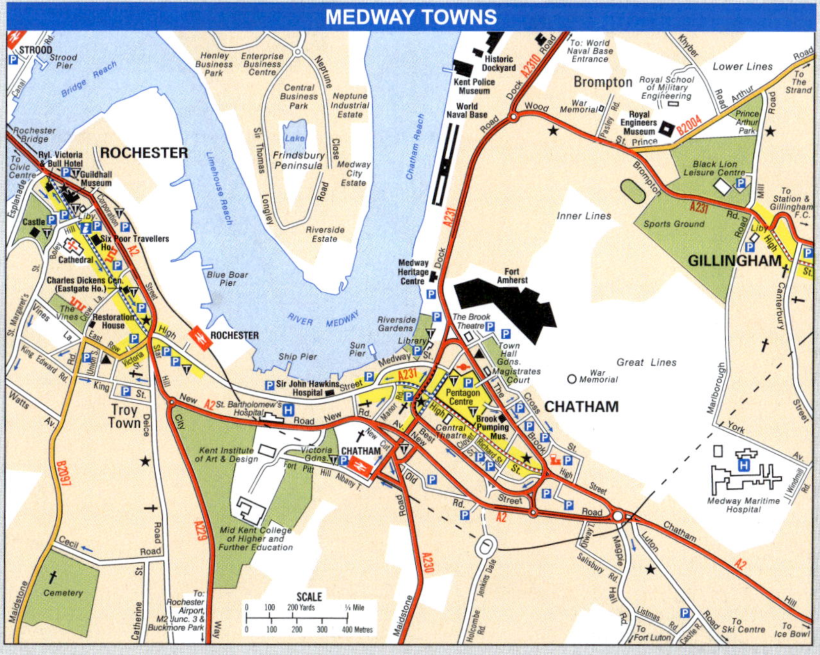

NEWCASTLE upon TYNE

Primrose Hill
KILBURN HIGH RD.
ST. JOHN'S WOOD
London Zoo
REGENT'S PARK
Regent's Park
Somers Town
EUSTON
St. John's Wood
Middlesex County Cricket Club (Lord's)
MAIDA VALE
Maida Vale
Queen Mary's Gardens
Royal College of Physicians
MORNINGTON CRESCENT
EUSTON SQ.
WARREN ST.
GT. PORTLAND ST.
MARYLEBONE
BAKER ST.
Madame Tussaud's
Planetarium
WARWICK AVENUE
Paddington
EDGWARE ROAD
ROYAL OAK
PADDINGTON
St. Mary's Hospital
Marylebone
Wallace Collection
GOODGE ST.
TOTTENHAM COURT RD.
Bayswater
MARBLE ARCH
BOND ST.
OXFORD CIRCUS
Soho
West End
BAYSWATER
LANCASTER GATE
QUEENSWAY
Speakers Corner
HYDE PARK
Mayfair
Royal Academy
PICCADILLY CIRCUS
Trocadero Centre
KENSINGTON GARDENS
Round Pond
Kensington Palace
The Long Water
The Serpentine
Serpentine Gallery
GREEN PARK
St. James's
St. James's Palace
Lancaster House
Kensington
Albert Memorial
HYDE PARK CORNER
Apsley House
Queen Victoria Memorial
Buckingham Palace
ST. JAMES'S PARK
HIGH ST. KENSINGTON
Royal Albert Hall
Royal Geographical Society
KNIGHTSBRIDGE
Knightsbridge
Queen's Gallery
Royal Mews
Victoria & Albert Museum
Brompton Oratory
Science Museum
Natural History Museum
Brompton
Westminster City Hall
Westminster R.C. Cathedral
South Kensington
GLOUCESTER ROAD
SOUTH KENSINGTON
VICTORIA
Belgravia
Victoria Coach Sta.
SLOANE SQUARE
Duke of York's H.Q.
Pimlico
PIMLICO
Chelsea
Chelsea Barracks
Royal Hospital Chelsea
National Army Museum
West Brompton
Carlyle's House
Battersea Park
RIVER THAMES
Albert Bridge
Chelsea Bridge
Grosvenor Bridge
Tidal Flow Mon to Fri, 7am to 10am Northbound

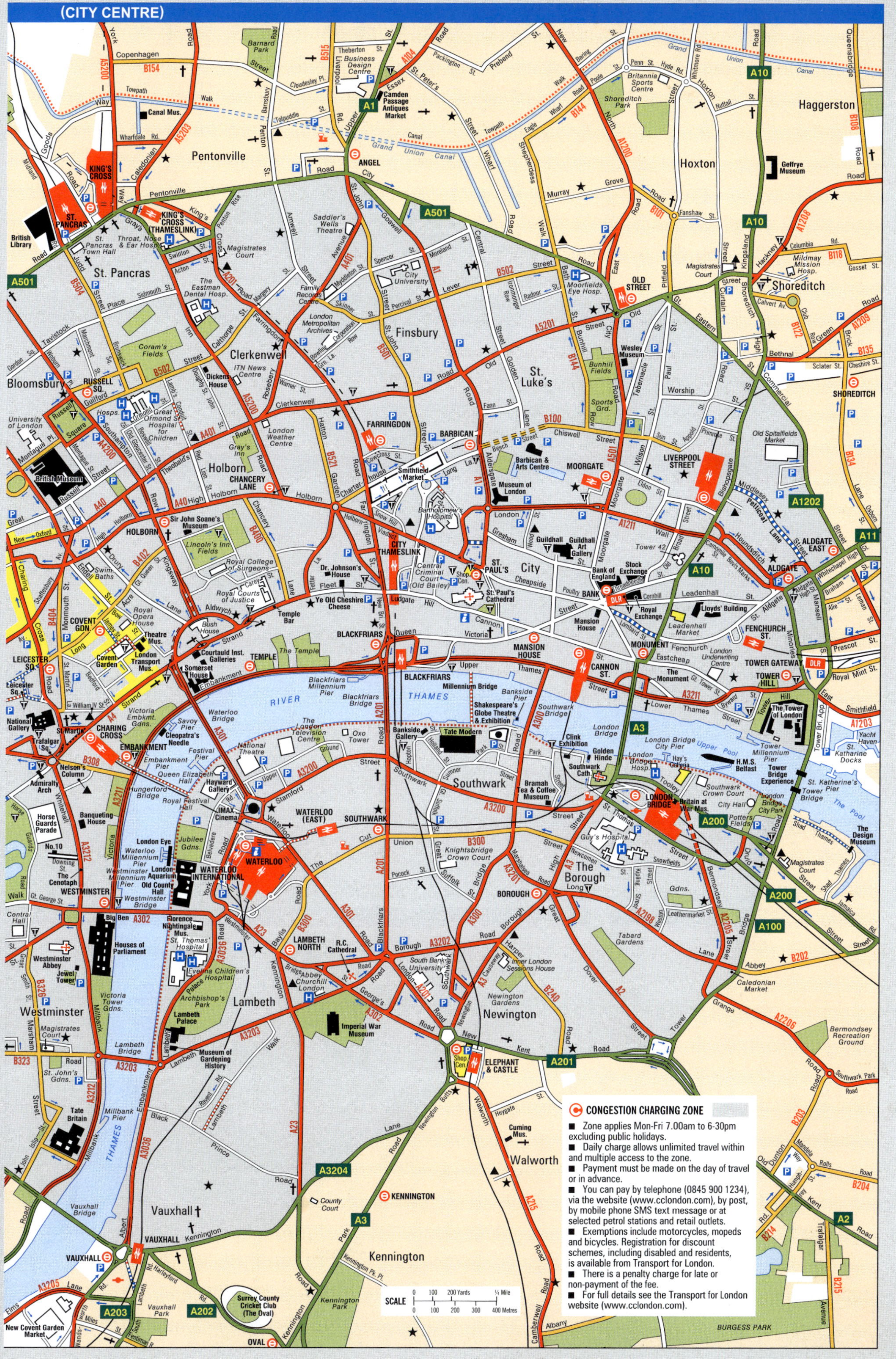
CONGESTION CHARGING ZONE
Zone applies Mon-Fri 7.00am to 6-30pm excluding public holidays.
Daily charge allows unlimited travel within and multiple access to the zone.
Payment must be made on the day of travel or in advance.
You can pay by telephone (0845 900 1234), via the website (www.cclondon.com), by post, by mobile phone SMS text message or at selected petrol stations and retail outlets.
Exemptions include motorcycles, mopeds and bicycles. Registration for discount schemes, including disabled and residents, is available from Transport for London.
There is a penalty charge for late or non-payment of the fee.
For full details see the Transport for London website (www.cclondon.com).
SCALE
0 100 200 Yards ½ Mile
0 100 200 300 400 Metres
Pentonville
St. Pancras
Clerkenwell
Finsbury
St. Luke's
Hoxton
Haggerston
Shoreditch
Bloomsbury
Holborn
City
Southwark
Westminster
Lambeth
The Borough
Newington
Walworth
Kennington
Vauxhall
RIVER THAMES

MILTON KEYNES

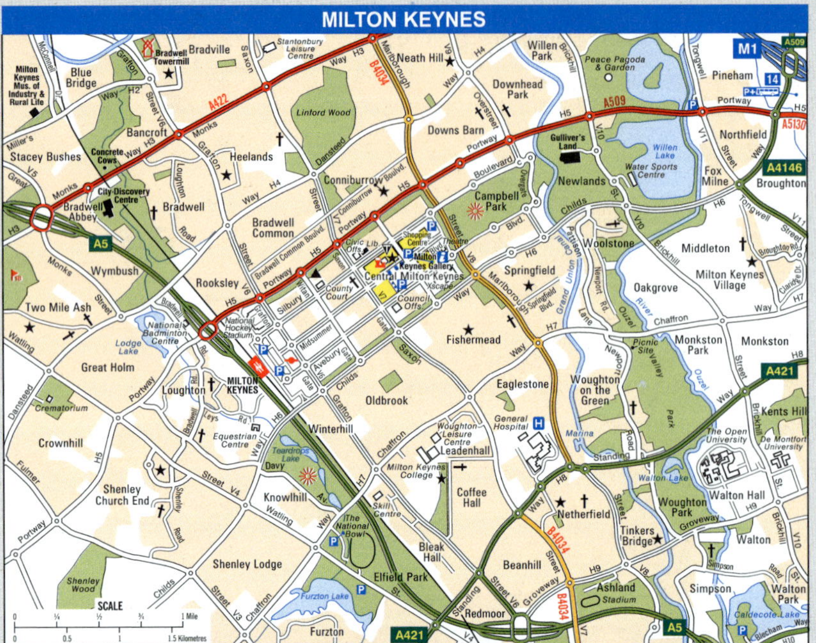

NEWPORT (CASNEWYDD)

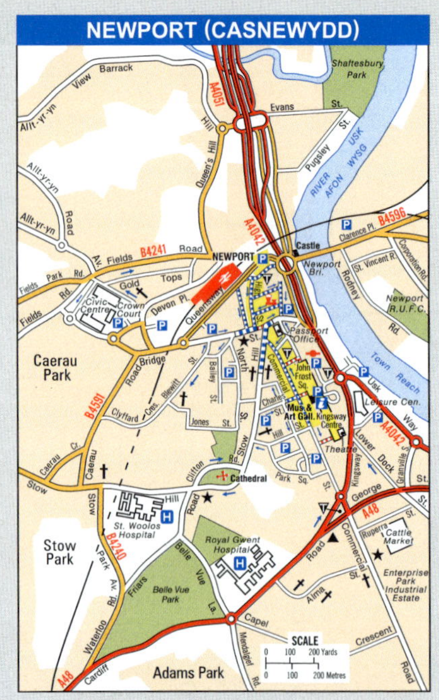

NORWICH

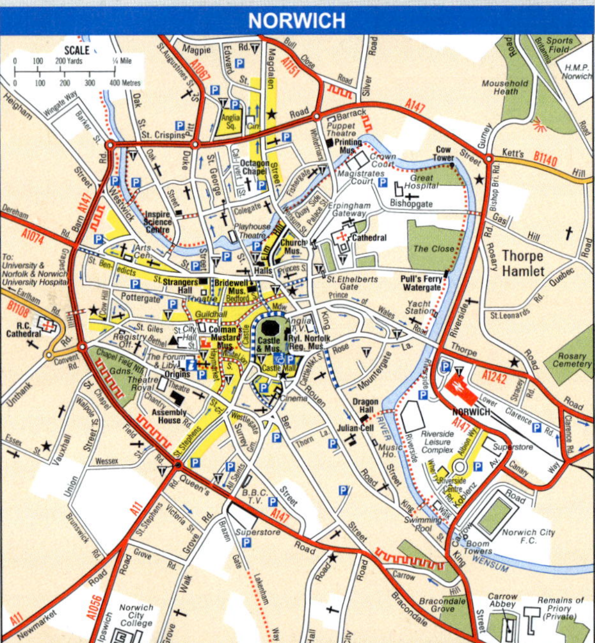

NOTTINGHAM

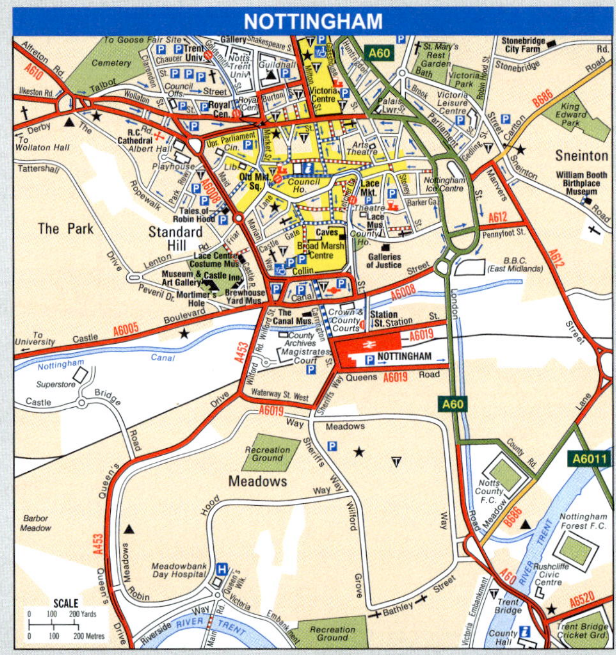

NORTHAMPTON

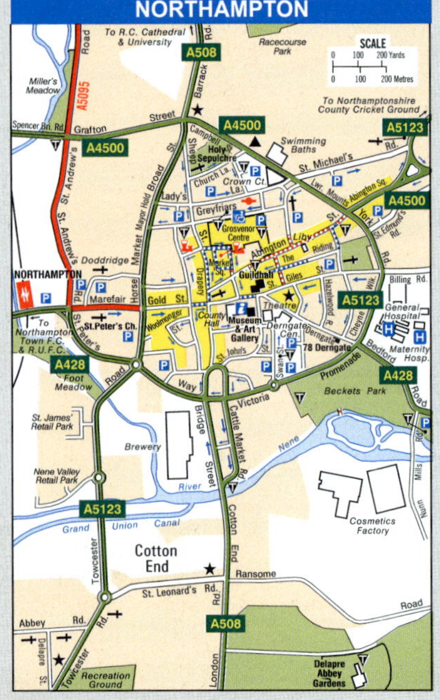

OXFORD

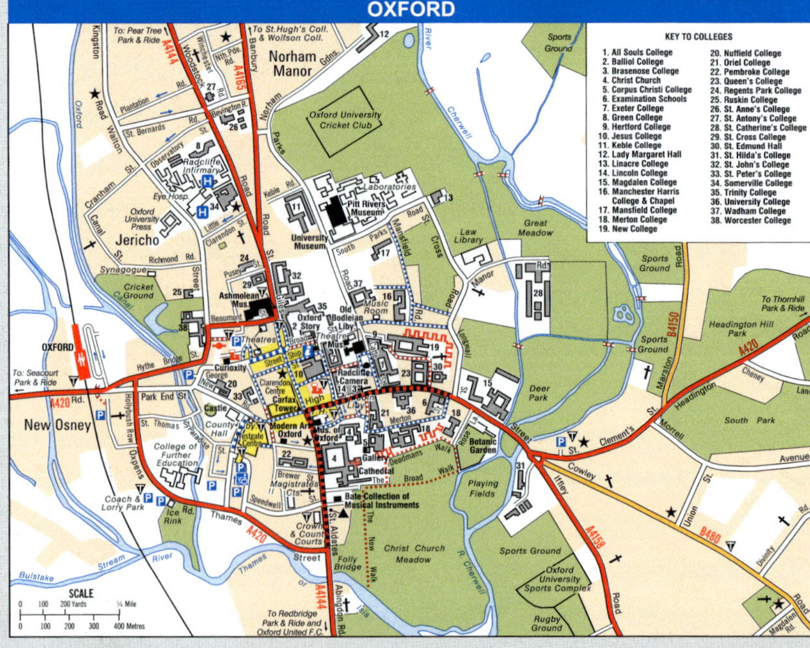

OBAN

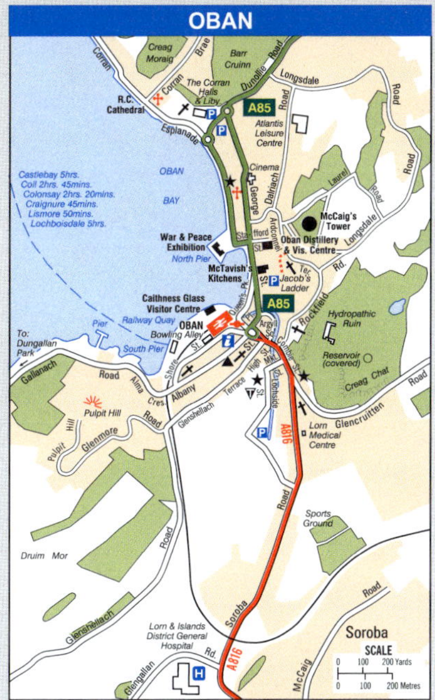

PERTH

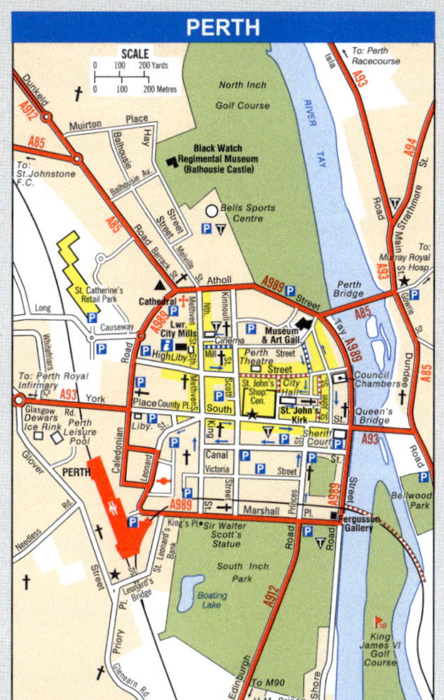

PETERBOROUGH

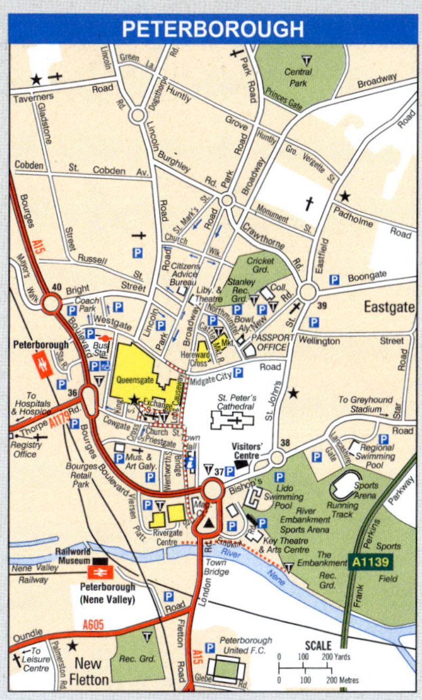

PLYMOUTH

PORTSMOUTH

PRESTON

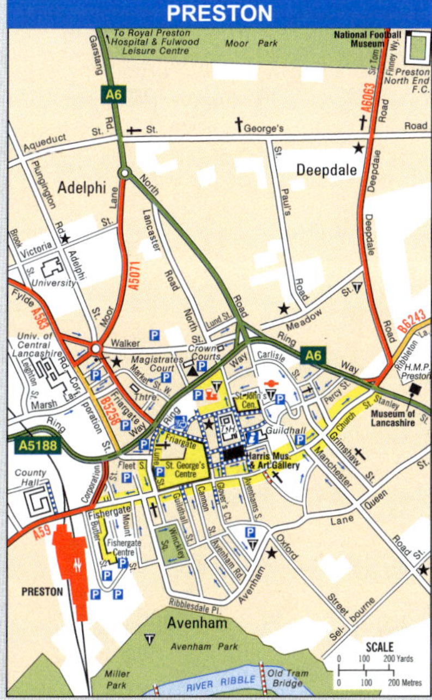

READING

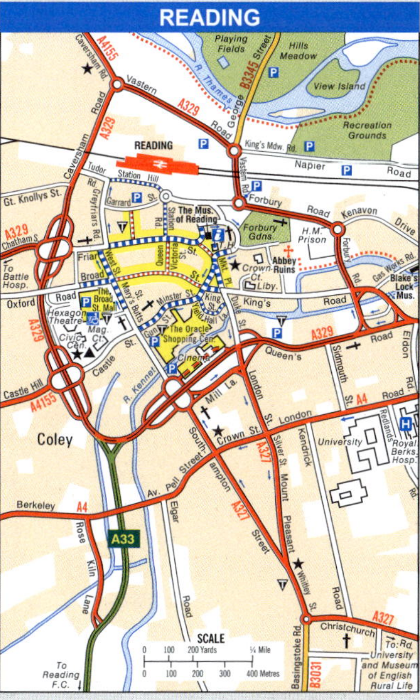

SALISBURY

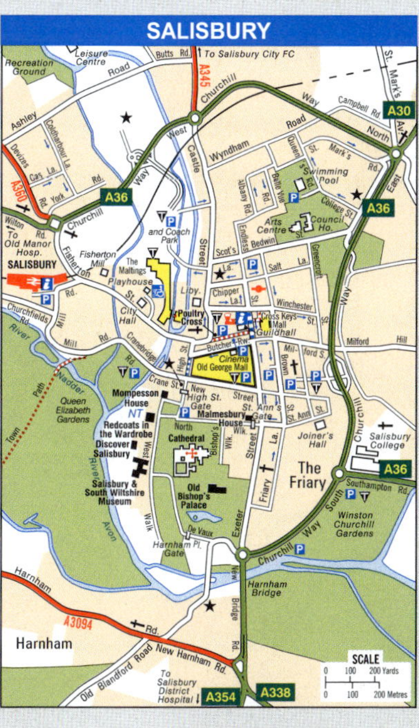

SHEFFIELD

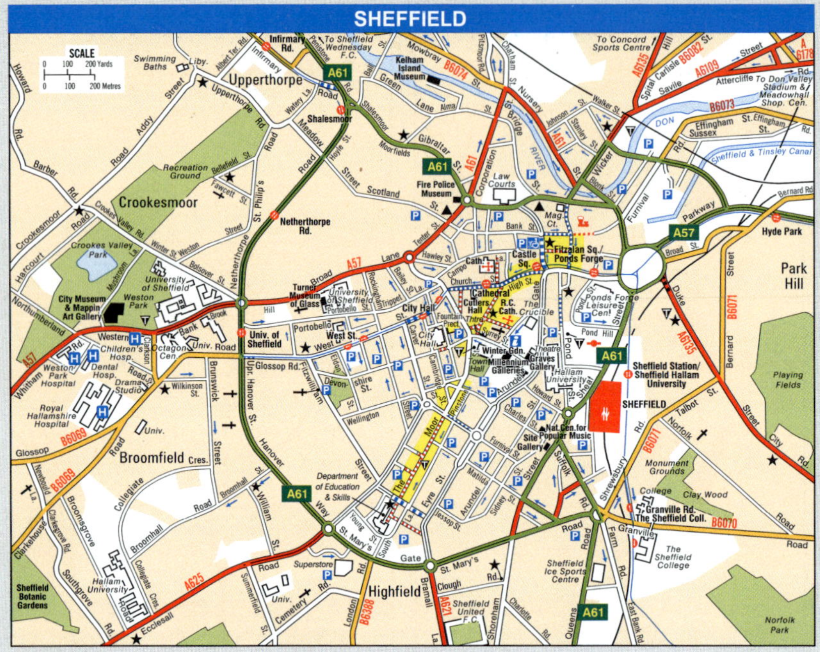

SHREWSBURY

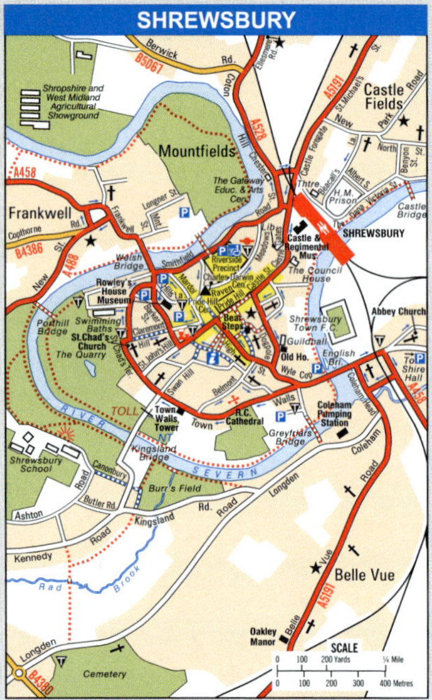

SOUTHAMPTON

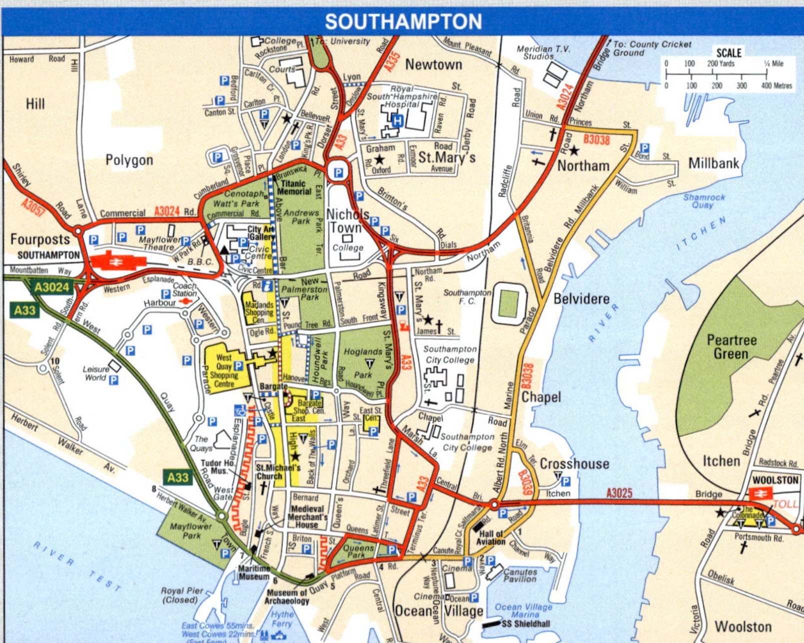

STIRLING

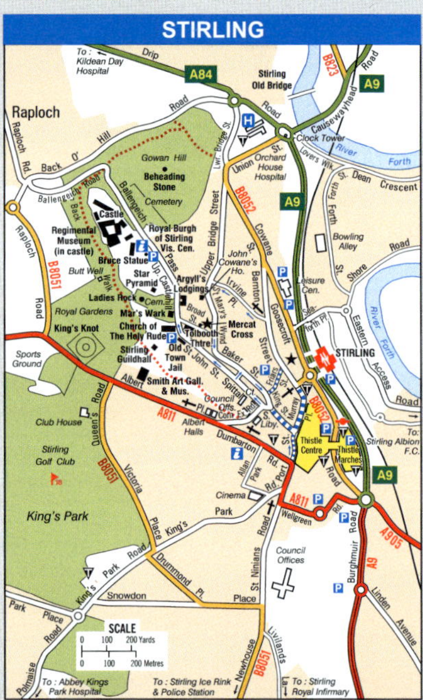

STOKE-ON-TRENT

STRATFORD UPON AVON

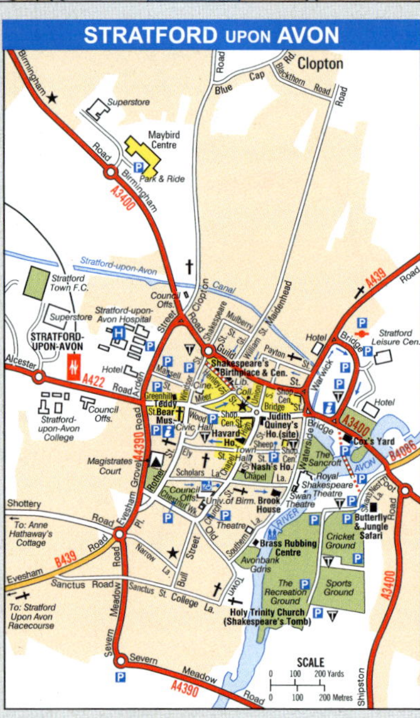

SUNDERLAND

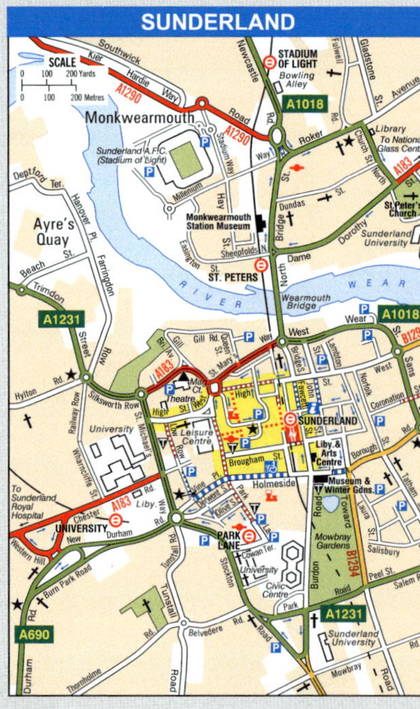

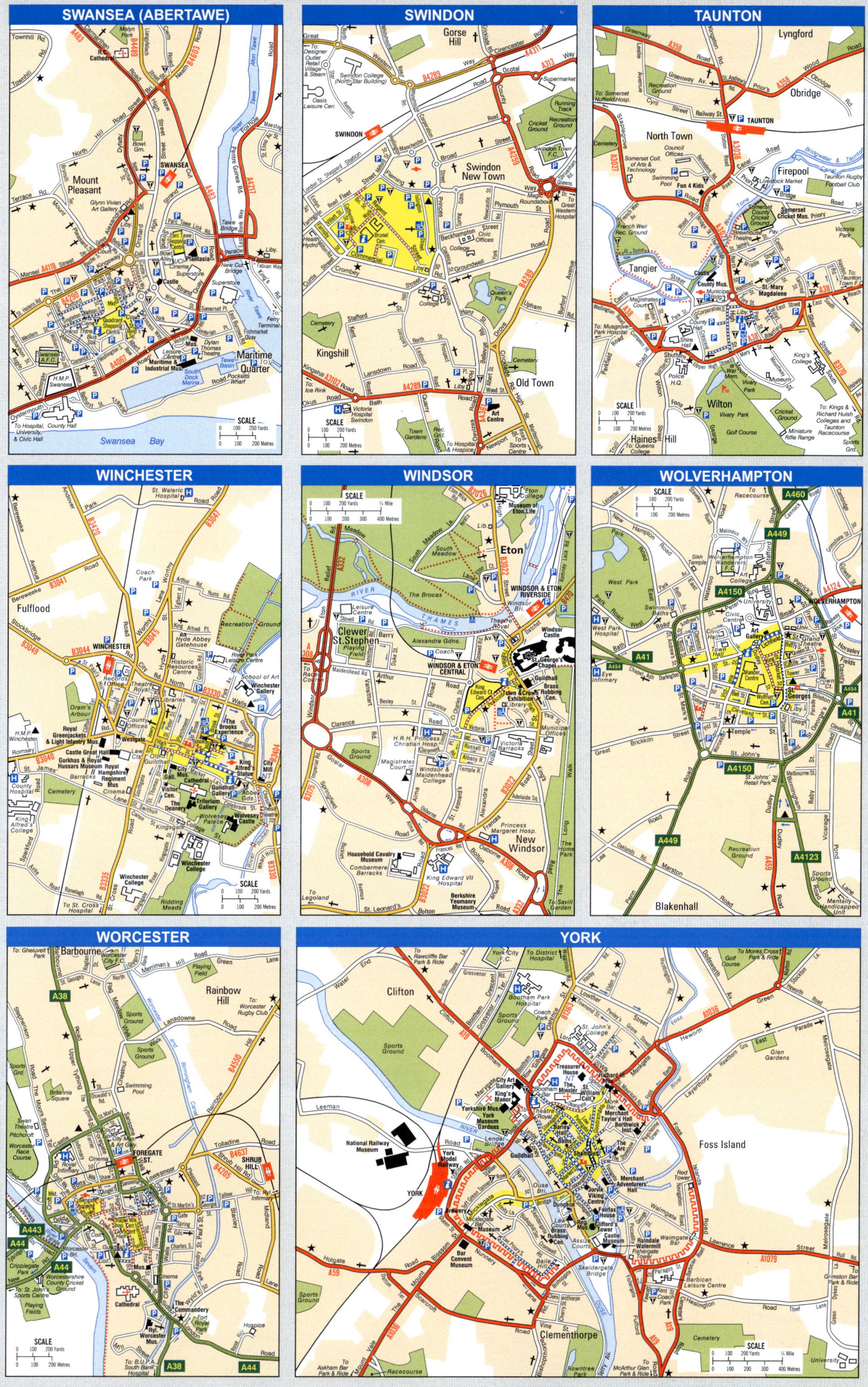
SWANSEA (ABERTAWE)
SWINDON
TAUNTON
WINCHESTER
WINDSOR
WOLVERHAMPTON
WORCESTER
YORK

PORT PLANS

For detailed Plans of DOVER, FOLKESTONE, PLYMOUTH and SOUTHAMPTON refer to Town Plans

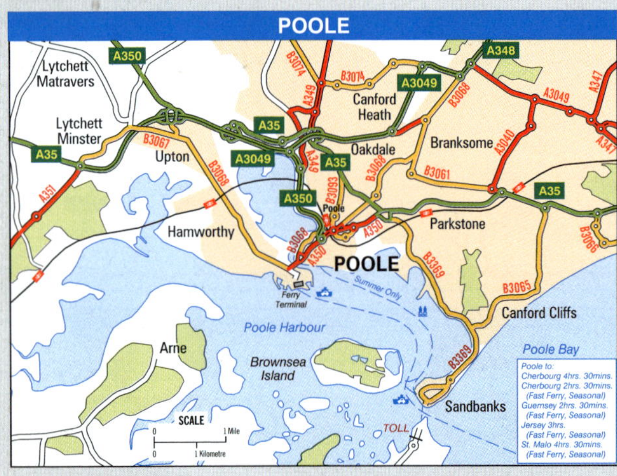

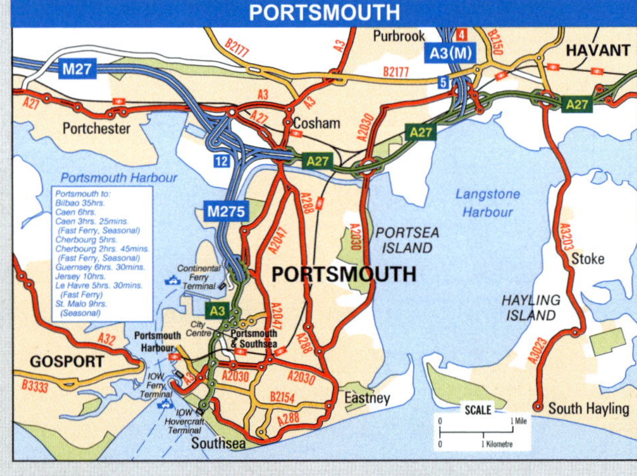

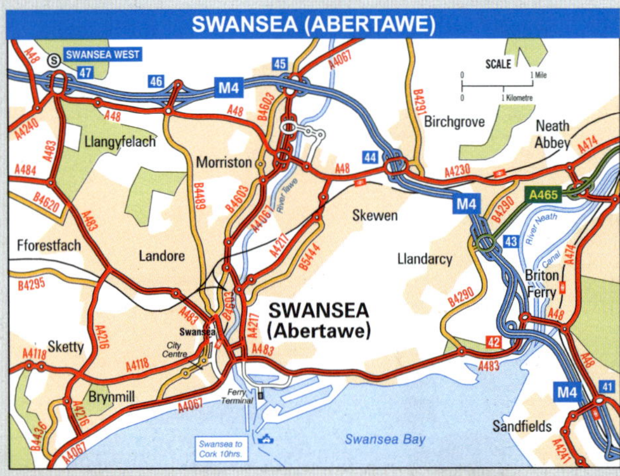

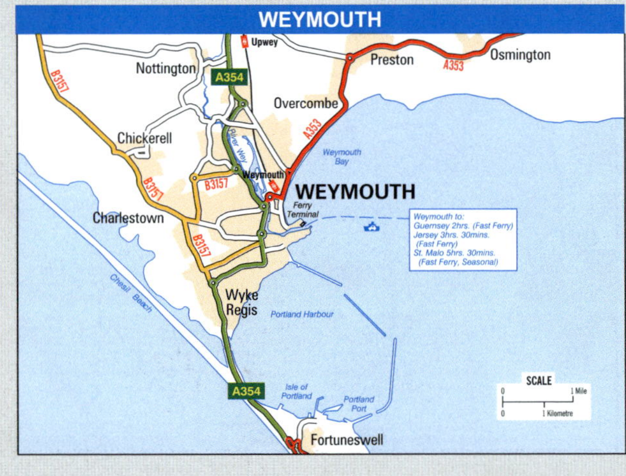

BIRMINGHAM

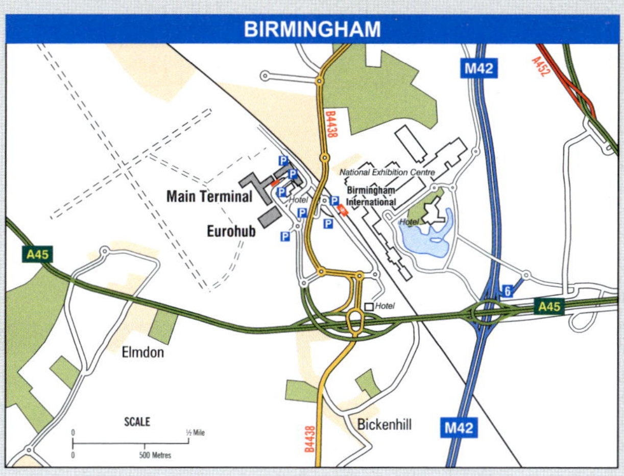

GLASGOW

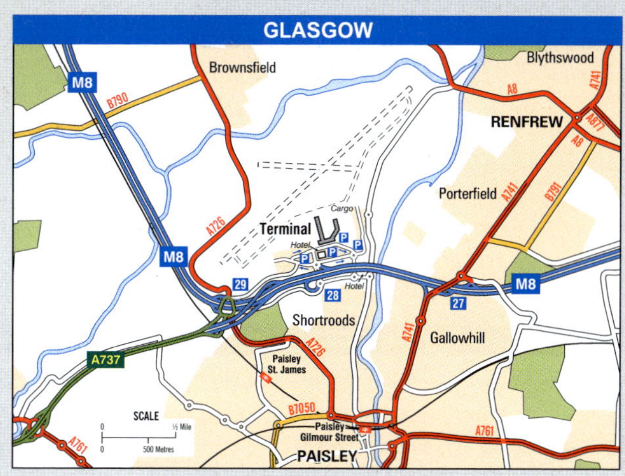

LONDON GATWICK

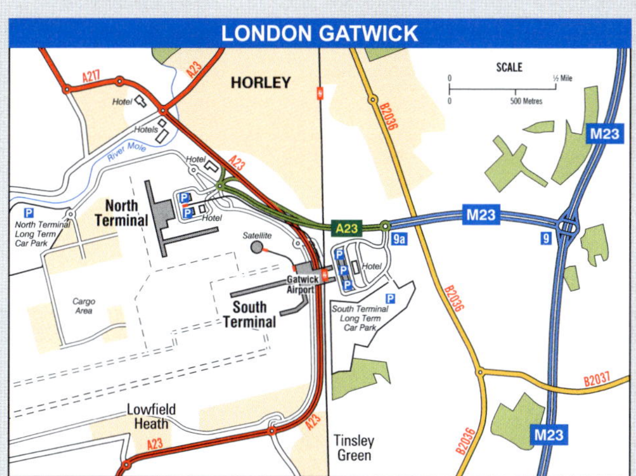

LONDON HEATHROW

LONDON LUTON

LONDON STANSTED

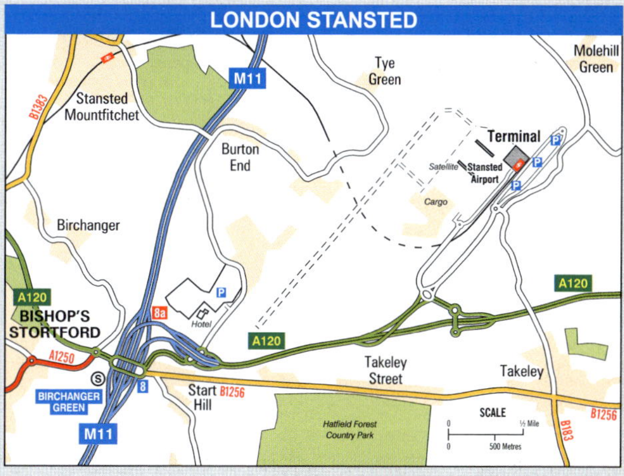

MANCHESTER

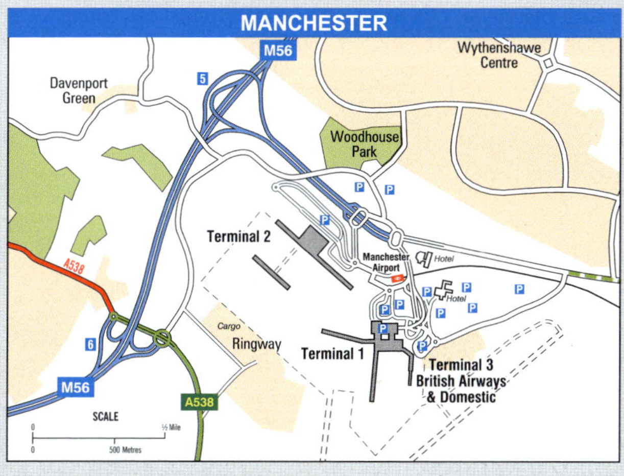

NOTTINGHAM EAST MIDLANDS

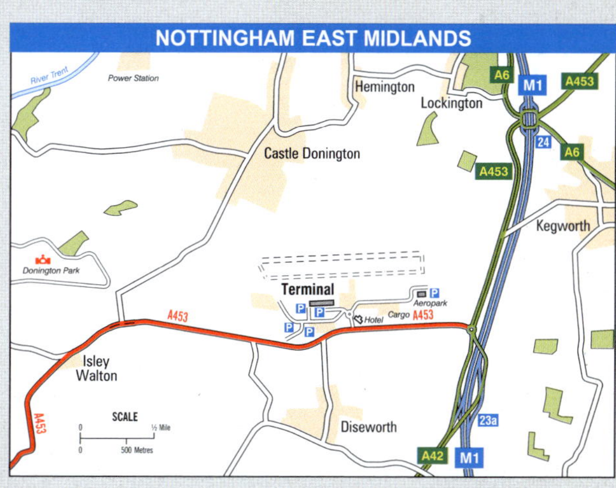

INDEX TO CITIES, TOWNS, VILLAGES, HAMLETS & LOCATIONS & SELECTED PLACES OF INTEREST

(1) A strict alphabetical order is used e.g. Abbotstone follows Abbot's Salford but precedes Abbots Worthy.
(2) The map reference given refers to the actual map square in which the town spot or built-up area or place of interest symbol is located and not to the place name.
(3) Only one reference is given although due to page overlaps the place may appear on more than one page.
(4) Where two or more places of the same name occur in the same County or Unitary Authority, the nearest large town is also given;
e.g. Achiemore. *High* —2D **166** (nr. Durness) indicates that Achiemore is located in square 2D on page **166** and is situated near Durness in the Unitary Authority of Highland.
(5) Major towns are shown in bold, i.e. **Aberdeen.** *Aber* —3G **153** & **186**. Where they appear on a Town Plan a second page reference is given.

SELECTED PLACES OF INTEREST

(1) Selected Places of Interest are indexed in red text.
(2) Entries shown without a main map index reference have the name of the appropriate Town Plan and its page number. The Town Plan title is not given when this is included in the name of the Place of Interest.
(3) Entries in italics are not named on the map but are shown with a symbol only.
Entries in italics and enclosed in brackets are not shown on the map.
For both these entries the nearest town or village is given, where that name is not already included in the name of the place of interest

PLACES OF INTEREST
Abbreviations used in this index

English Heritage : *EH*
Welsh Historic Sites : *CADW*
Garden : *Gdn*
Gardens : *Gdns*
Historic Scotland : *HS*
Museum : *Mus*
National : *Nat*
National Trust : *NT*
National Trust for Scotland : *NTS*
Royal Horticultural Society : *RHS*
World Heritage Site : *WH*

COUNTIES and UNITARY AUTHORITIES with the abbreviations used in this index

Aberdeen : *Aber*
Aberdeenshire : *Abers*
Angus : *Ang*
Argyll & Bute : *Arg*
Bath & N E Somerset : *Bath*
Bedfordshire : *Beds*
Blackburn with Darwen : *Bkbn*
Blackpool : *Bkpl*
Blaenau Gwent : *Blae*
Bournemouth : *Bour*
Bracknell Forest : *Brac*
Bridgend : *B'end*
Brighton & Hove : *Brig*
Bristol : *Bris*
Buckinghamshire : *Buck*
Caerphilly : *Cphy*
Cambridgeshire : *Cambs*
Cardiff : *Card*
Carmarthenshire : *Carm*
Ceredigion : *Cdgn*
Cheshire : *Ches*
Clackmannanshire : *Clac*
Conwy : *Cnwy*
Cornwall : *Corn*
Cumbria : *Cumb*
Darlington : *Darl*
Denbighshire : *Den*
Derby : *Derb*
Derbyshire : *Derbs*
Devon : *Devn*
Dorset : *Dors*
Dumfries & Galloway : *Dum*
Dundee : *D'dee*
Durham : *Dur*
East Ayrshire : *E Ayr*
East Dunbartonshire : *E Dun*
East Lothian : *E Lot*
East Renfrewshire : *E Ren*
East Riding of Yorkshire : *E Yor*
East Sussex : *E Sus*
Edinburgh : *Edin*
Essex : *Essx*
Falkirk : *Falk*
Fife : *Fife*
Flintshire : *Flin*
Glasgow : *Glas*
Gloucestershire : *Glos*
Greater London : *G Lon*
Greater Manchester : *G Man*
Gwynedd : *Gwyn*
Halton : *Hal*
Hampshire : *Hants*
Hartlepool : *Hart*
Herefordshire : *Here*
Hertfordshire : *Herts*
Highland : *High*
Inverclyde : *Inv*
Isle of Anglesey : *IOA*
Isle of Man : *IOM*
Isle of Wight : *IOW*
Isles of Scilly : *IOS*
Kent : *Kent*
Kingston upon Hull : *Hull*
Lancashire : *Lanc*
Leicester : *Leic*
Leicestershire : *Leics*
Lincolnshire : *Linc*
Luton : *Lutn*
Medway : *Medw*
Merseyside : *Mers*
Merthyr Tydfil : *Mer T*
Middlesbrough : *Midd*
Midlothian : *Midl*
Milton Keynes : *Mil*
Monmouthshire : *Mon*
Moray : *Mor*
Neath Port Talbot : *Neat*
Newport : *Newp*
Norfolk : *Norf*
Northamptonshire : *Nptn*
North Ayrshire : *N Ayr*
North East Lincolnshire : *NE Lin*
North Lanarkshire : *N Lan*
North Lincolnshire : *N Lin*
North Somerset : *N Som*
Northumberland : *Nmbd*
North Yorkshire : *N Yor*
Nottingham : *Nott*
Nottinghamshire : *Notts*
Orkney : *Orkn*
Oxfordshire : *Oxon*
Pembrokeshire : *Pemb*
Perth & Kinross : *Per*
Peterborough : *Pet*
Plymouth : *Plym*
Poole : *Pool*
Portsmouth : *Port*
Powys : *Powy*
Reading : *Read*
Redcar & Cleveland : *Red C*
Renfrewshire : *Ren*
Rhondda Cynon Taff : *Rhon*
Rutland : *Rut*
Scottish Borders : *Bord*
Shetland : *Shet*
Shropshire : *Shrp*
Slough : *Slo*
Somerset : *Som*
Southampton : *Sotn*
South Ayrshire : *S Ayr*
Southend-on-Sea : *S'end*
South Gloucestershire : *S Glo*
South Lanarkshire : *S Lan*
South Yorkshire : *S Yor*
Staffordshire : *Staf*
Stirling : *Stir*
Stockton-on-Tees : *Stoc T*
Stoke-on-Trent : *Stoke*
Suffolk : *Suff*
Surrey : *Surr*
Swansea : *Swan*
Swindon : *Swin*
Telford & Wrekin : *Telf*
Thurrock : *Thur*
Torbay : *Torb*
Torfaen : *Torf*
Tyne & Wear : *Tyne*
Vale of Glamorgan, The : *V Glam*
Warrington : *Warr*
Warwickshire : *Warw*
West Berkshire : *W Ber*
West Dunbartonshire : *W Dun*
Western Isles : *W Isl*
West Lothian : *W Lot*
West Midlands : *W Mid*
West Sussex : *W Sus*
West Yorkshire : *W Yor*
Wiltshire : *Wilts*
Windsor & Maidenhead : *Wind*
Wokingham : *Wok*
Worcestershire : *Worc*
Wrexham : *Wrex*
York : *York*

INDEX

Abbas Combe. *Som* —4C **22**
Abberley. *Worc* —4B **60**
Abberley Common. *Worc* —4B **60**
Abberton. *Essx* —4D **54**
Abberton. *Worc* —5D **61**
Abberwick. *Nmbd* —3F **121**
Abbess Roding. *Essx* —4F **53**
Abbey. *Devn* —1E **13**
Abbey-cwm-hir. *Powy* —3C **58**
Abbeydale. *S Yor* —2H **85**
Abbeydale Industrial Hamlet —2H **85**
Abbeydale Park. *S Yor* —2H **85**
Abbey Dore. *Here* —2G **47**
Abbey Hulton. *Stoke* —1D **72**
Abbey St Bathans. *Bord* —3D **130**
Abbeystead. *Lanc* —4E **97**
Abbeytown. *Cumb* —4C **112**
Abbey Village. *Lanc* —2E **91**
Abbey Wood. *G Lon* —3F **39**
Abbot Hall Art Gallery, Kendal —5G **103**
Abbots Ann. *Hants* —2B **24**
Abbots Bickington. *Devn* —1D **11**
Abbots Bromley. *Staf* —3E **73**
Abbotsbury. *Dors* —4A **14**
Abbotsbury Gdns. —4A **14**
Abbotsbury Swannery —4A **14**
Abbotsford House —1H **119**
Abbotsham. *Devn* —4E **19**
Abbotskerswell. *Devn* —2E **9**
Abbots Langley. *Herts* —5A **52**
Abbots Leigh. *N Som* —4A **34**
Abbotsley. *Cambs* —5B **64**
Abbots Morton. *Worc* —5E **61**
Abbots Ripton. *Cambs* —3B **64**
Abbot's Salford. *Warw* —5E **61**
Abbotstone. *Hants* —3D **24**
Abbots Worthy. *Hants* —3C **24**
Abcott. *Shrp* —3F **59**
Abdon. *Shrp* —2H **59**
Abenhall. *Glos* —4B **48**
Aber. *Cdgn* —1E **45**
Aberaeron. *Cdgn* —4D **56**
Aberafan. *Neat* —3A **32**
Aberaman. *Rhon* —5D **46**
Aberangell. *Powy* —4H **69**
Aberarad. *Carm* —1H **43**
Aberarder. *High* —1A **150**
Aberargie. *Per* —2D **136**
Aberarth. *Cdgn* —4D **57**
Aberavon. *Neat* —3A **32**
Aber-banc. *Cdgn* —1D **44**
Aberbargoed. *Cphy* —2E **33**
Aberbechan. *Powy* —1D **58**
Aberbeeg. *Blae* —5F **47**
Aberbowlan. *Carm* —2G **45**
Aberbran. *Powy* —3C **46**
Abercanaid. *Mer T* —5D **46**
Abercarn. *Cphy* —2F **33**
Abercastle. *Pemb* —1C **42**
Abercegir. *Powy* —5H **69**
Aberchalder. *High* —3F **149**
Aberchirder. *Abers* —3D **160**
Abercorn. *W Lot* —2D **129**
Abercraf. *Powy* —4B **46**
Abercregan. *Neat* —2B **32**
Abercrombie. *Fife* —3H **137**
Abercwmboi. *Rhon* —2D **32**
Abercych. *Pemb* —1C **44**
Abercynon. *Rhon* —2D **32**
Aber-Cywarch. *Gwyn* —4A **70**
Aberdalgie. *Per* —1C **136**
Aberdar. *Rhon* —5C **46**
Aberdare. *Rhon* —5C **46**
Aberdaron. *Gwyn* —3A **68**
Aberdaugleddau. *Pemb* —4D **42**
Aberdeen. *Aber* —3G **153** & **186**
Aberdeen Airport. *Aber* —2F **153**
Aberdesach. *Gwyn* —5D **80**
Aberdour. *Fife* —1E **129**
Aberdour Castle *HS* —1E **129**
Aberdovey. *Gwyn* —1F **57**
Aberdulais. *Neat* —5A **46**
Aberdyfi. *Gwyn* —1F **57**
Aberedw. *Powy* —1D **46**
Abereiddy. *Pemb* —1B **42**
Abererch. *Gwyn* —2C **68**
Aberfan. *Mer T* —5D **46**
Aberfeldy. *Per* —4F **143**
Aberffraw. *IOA* —4C **80**
Aberffrwd. *Cdgn* —3F **57**
Aberford. *W Yor* —1E **93**
Aberfoyle. *Stir* —3E **135**
Abergarw. *B'end* —3C **32**
Abergarwed. *Neat* —5B **46**
Abergavenny. *Mon* —4G **47**
Abergele. *Cnwy* —3B **82**
Aber-Giar. *Carm* —1F **45**
Aberglasney Gdns. —3F **45**
Abergorlech. *Carm* —2F **45**
Abergwaun. *Pemb* —1D **42**
Abergwesyn. *Powy* —5A **58**
Abergwili. *Carm* —3E **45**
Abergwynfi. *Neat* —2B **32**
Abergwyngregyn. *Gwyn* —3F **81**
Abergynolwyn. *Gwyn* —5F **69**
Aberhafesp. *Powy* —1C **58**
Aberhonddu. *Powy* —3D **46**
Aberhosan. *Powy* —1H **57**
Aberkenfig. *B'end* —3B **32**
Aberlady. *E Lot* —2A **130**
Aberlemno. *Ang* —3E **145**
Aberllefenni. *Gwyn* —5G **69**
Abermaw. *Gwyn* —4F **69**
Abermeurig. *Cdgn* —5E **57**
Aber-miwl. *Powy* —1D **58**
Abermule. *Powy* —1D **58**
Abernant. *Carm* —2H **43**
Abernant. *Rhon* —5D **46**
Abernethy. *Per* —2D **136**
Abernyte. *Per* —5B **144**
Aber-oer. *Wrex* —1E **71**
Aberpennar. *Rhon* —2D **32**
Aberporth. *Cdgn* —5B **56**
Aberriw. *Powy* —5D **70**
Abersoch. *Gwyn* —3C **68**
Abersychan. *Torf* —5F **47**
Abertawe. *Swan* —3F **31** & **Swansea 197**
Aberteifi. *Cdgn* —1B **44**
Aberthin. *V Glam* —4D **32**
Abertillery. *Blae* —5F **47**
Abertridwr. *Cphy* —3E **32**
Abertridwr. *Powy* —4C **70**
Abertyleri. *Blae* —5F **47**
Abertysswg. *Cphy* —5E **47**
Aberuthven. *Per* —2B **136**
Aber Village. *Powy* —3E **46**
Aberyscir. *Powy* —3D **46**
Aberystwyth. *Cdgn* —2E **57**
Aberystwyth Castle —2E **57**
Abhainn Suidhe. *W Isl* —7C **171**
Abingdon. *Oxon* —2C **36**
Abinger Common. *Surr* —1C **26**
Abinger Hammer. *Surr* —1B **26**
Abington. *S Lan* —2B **118**
Abington Pigotts. *Cambs* —1D **52**
Ab Kettleby. *Leics* —3E **74**
Ab Lench. *Worc* —5E **61**
Ablington. *Glos* —5G **49**
Ablington. *Wilts* —2G **23**
Abney. *Derbs* —3F **85**
Aboyne. *Abers* —4C **152**
Abram. *G Man* —4E **90**
Abriachan. *High* —5H **157**
Abridge. *Essx* —1F **39**
Abronhill. *N Lan* —2A **128**
Abson. *S Glo* —4C **34**
Abthorpe. *Nptn* —1E **51**
Abune-the-Hill. *Orkn* —5B **172**
Aby. *Linc* —3D **88**
Acairseid Mhor. *W Isl* —8C **170**
Acaster Malbis. *York* —5H **99**
Acaster Selby. *N Yor* —5H **99**
Accott. *Devn* —3G **19**
Accrington. *Lanc* —2F **91**
Acha. *Arg* —3C **138**
Achachork. *High* —4D **155**
Achahoish. *Arg* —2F **125**
Achaleven. *Arg* —5D **140**
Achallader. *Arg* —4H **141**
Acha Mor. *W Isl* —5F **171**
Achanalt. *High* —2E **157**
Achandunie. *High* —1A **158**
Ach'an Todhair. *High* —1E **141**
Achany. *High* —3C **164**
Achaphubuil. *High* —1E **141**
Acharacle. *High* —2A **140**
Acharn. *Ang* —1B **144**
Acharn. *Per* —4E **143**
Acharole. *High* —3E **169**
Achateny. *High* —2G **139**
Achavanich. *High* —4D **169**
Achdalieu. *High* —1E **141**
Achduart. *High* —3E **163**
Achentoul. *High* —5A **168**
Achfary. *High* —5C **166**
Achfrish. *High* —2C **164**
Achgarve. *High* —4C **162**
Achiemore. *High* —2D **166** (nr. Durness)
Achiemore. *High* —3A **168** (nr. Thurso)
A'Chill. *High* —3A **146**
Achiltibuie. *High* —3E **163**
Achina. *High* —2H **167**
Achinahuagh. *High* —2F **167**
Achindarroch. *High* —3E **141**
Achinduich. *High* —3C **164**
Achinduin. *Arg* —5C **140**
Achininver. *High* —2F **167**
Achintee. *High* —4B **156**
Achintraid. *High* —5H **155**
Achleck. *Arg* —4F **139**
Achlorachan. *High* —3F **157**
Achluachrach. *High* —5E **149**
Achlyness. *High* —3C **166**
Achmelvich. *High* —1E **163**
Achmony. *High* —5H **157**
Achmore. *High* —5A **156** (nr. Stromeferry)
Achmore. *High* —4E **163** (nr. Ullapool)
Achnacarnin. *High* —1E **163**
Achnacarry. *High* —5D **148**
Achnaclerach. *High* —2G **157**
Achnacloich. *High* —3D **147**
Achnaconeran. *High* —2G **149**
Achnacroish. *Arg* —4C **140**
Achnafalnich. *Arg* —1B **134**
Achnagarron. *High* —2A **158**
Achnaha. *High* —2F **139**
Achnahanat. *High* —4C **164**
Achnahannet. *High* —1D **151**
Achnairn. *High* —2C **164**
Achnaluachrach. *High* —3D **164**
Achnamara. *Arg* —1F **125**
Achnanellan. *High* —5C **148**
Achnangoul. *Arg* —3H **133**
Achnasheen. *High* —3D **156**
Achnashellach. *High* —4C **156**
Achosnich. *High* —2F **139**
Achow. *High* —5E **169**
Achranich. *High* —4B **140**
Achreamie. *High* —2C **168**
Achriabhach. *High* —2F **141**
Achriesgill. *High* —3C **166**
Achrimsdale. *High* —3G **165**
Achscrabster. *High* —2C **168**
Achtoty. *High* —2G **167**
Achurch. *Nptn* —2H **63**
Achuvoldrach. *High* —3F **167**
Achvaich. *High* —4E **164**
Achvoan. *High* —3E **165**
Ackergill. *High* —3F **169**
Ackergillshore. *High* —3F **169**
Acklam. *Midd* —3B **106**
Acklam. *N Yor* —3B **100**
Ackleton. *Shrp* —1B **60**
Acklington. *Nmbd* —4G **121**
Ackton. *W Yor* —2E **93**
Ackworth Moor Top. *W Yor* —3E **93**
Acle. *Norf* —4G **79**
Acock's Green. *W Mid* —2F **61**
Acol. *Kent* —4H **41**
Acomb. *Nmbd* —3C **114**
Acomb. *York* —4H **99**
Aconbury. *Here* —2A **48**
Acorn Bank Gdn. *NT* —2H **103**
Acre. *G Man* —4H **91**
Acre. *Lanc* —2F **91**
Acrefair. *Wrex* —1E **71**
Acrise. *Kent* —1F **29**
Acton. *Ches* —5A **84**
Acton. *Dors* —5E **15**
Acton. *G Lon* —2C **38**
Acton. *Shrp* —2F **59**
Acton. *Staf* —1C **72**
Acton. *Suff* —1B **54**
Acton. *Worc* —4C **60**
Acton. *Wrex* —5F **83**
Acton Beauchamp. *Here* —5A **60**
Acton Bridge. *Ches* —3H **83**
Acton Burnell. *Shrp* —5H **71**
Acton Burnell Castle —5H **71**
Acton Green. *Here* —5A **60**
Acton Pigott. *Shrp* —5H **71**
Acton Round. *Shrp* —1A **60**
Acton Scott. *Shrp* —2G **59**
Acton Scott Farm Mus. —2G **59**
Acton Trussell. *Staf* —4D **72**
Acton Turville. *S Glo* —3D **34**
Adabroc. *W Isl* —1H **171**
Adam's Hill. *Worc* —3D **60**
Adbaston. *Staf* —3B **72**
Adber. *Dors* —4B **22**
Adderbury. *Oxon* —2C **50**
Adderley. *Shrp* —2A **72**
Adderstone. *Nmbd* —1F **121**
Addiewell. *W Lot* —3C **128**
Addingham. *W Yor* —5C **98**
Addington. *Buck* —3F **51**
Addington. *G Lon* —4E **39**
Addington. *Kent* —5A **40**
Addinston. *Bord* —4B **130**
Addiscombe. *G Lon* —4E **39**
Addlestone. *Surr* —4B **38**
Addlethorpe. *Linc* —4E **89**
Adeney. *Telf* —4B **72**
Adfa. *Powy* —5C **70**
Adforton. *Here* —3G **59**
Adgestone. *IOW* —4D **16**
Adisham. *Kent* —5G **41**
Adlestrop. *Glos* —3H **49**
Adlingfleet. *E Yor* —2B **94**
Adlington. *Ches* —2D **84**
Adlington. *Lanc* —3E **90**
Adlington Hall —2D **84**
Admaston. *Staf* —3E **73**
Admaston. *Telf* —4A **72**
Admington. *Warw* —1G **49**
Adpar. *Cdgn* —1D **44**
Adsborough. *Som* —4F **21**
Adstock. *Buck* —2F **51**
Adstone. *Nptn* —5C **62**
Adversane. *W Sus* —3B **26**
Advie. *High* —5F **159**
Adwalton. *W Yor* —2C **92**
Adwell. *Oxon* —2E **37**
Adwick le Street. *S Yor* —4F **93**
Adwick upon Dearne. *S Yor* —4E **93**
Adziel. *Abers* —3G **161**
Ae. *Dum* —1A **112**
Affleck. *Abers* —1F **153**
Affpuddle. *Dors* —3D **14**
Affric Lodge. *High* —1D **148**
Afon-wen. *Flin* —3D **82**
Agglethorpe. *N Yor* —1C **98**
Aglionby. *Cumb* —4F **113**
Aigburth. *Mers* —2F **83**
Aiginis. *W Isl* —4G **171**
Aike. *E Yor* —5E **101**
Aikers. *Orkn* —8D **172**
Aiketgate. *Cumb* —5F **113**
Aikhead. *Cumb* —5D **112**
Aikton. *Cumb* —4D **112**
Ailey. *Here* —1G **47**
Ailsworth. *Pet* —1A **64**
Ainderby Quernhow. *N Yor* —1F **99**
Ainderby Steeple. *N Yor* —5A **106**
Aingers Green. *Essx* —3E **54**
Ainsdale. *Mers* —3B **90**
Ainsdale-on-Sea. *Mers* —3A **90**
Ainstable. *Cumb* —5G **113**
Ainsworth. *G Man* —3F **91**
Ainthorpe. *N Yor* —4E **107**
Aintree. *Mers* —1F **83**
Aird. *Arg* —3E **133**
Aird. *Dum* —3F **109**
Aird. *High* —1G **155**
Aird. *W Isl* —3C **170** (on Benbecula)
Aird. *W Isl* —4H **171** (on Lewis)

Aird a Mhachair. W Isl —4C 170
Aird a Mhulaidh. W Isl —6D 171
Aird Asaig. W Isl —7D 171
Aird Dhail. W Isl —1G 171
Airdens. High —4D 164
Airdeny. Arg —1G 133
Aird Mhidhinis. W Isl —8C 170
Aird Mhighe. W Isl —8D 171
(nr. Ceann a Bhaigh)
Aird Mhighe. W Isl —9C 171
(nr. Fionnsbhagh)
Aird Mhor. W Isl —8C 170
(on Barra)
Aird Mhor. W Isl —4D 170
(on South Uist)
Aird of Sleat. High —3D 147
Airdrie. N Lan —3A 128
Aird Shleibhe. W Isl —9D 171
Aird, The. High —3D 154
Aird Thunga. W Isl —4G 171
Aird Uig. W Isl —4C 171
Airedale. W Yor —2E 93
Airidh a Bhruaich. W Isl —6E 171
Airies. Dum —3E 109
Airmyn. E Yor —2H 93
Airntully. Per —5H 143
Airth. Falk —1C 128
Airton. N Yor —4B 98
Aisby. Linc —1F 87
(nr. Gainsborough)
Aisby. Linc —2H 75
(nr. Grantham)
Aisgernis. W Isl —6C 170
Aish. Devn —2C 8
(nr. Buckfastleigh)
Aish. Devn —3E 9
(nr. Totnes)
Aisholt. Som —3E 21
Aiskew. N Yor —1E 99
Aislaby. N Yor —1B 100
(nr. Pickering)
Aislaby. N Yor —4F 107
(nr. Whitby)
Aislaby. Stoc T —3B 106
Aisthorpe. Linc —3G 87
Aith. Shet —2H 173
(nr. Fetlar)
Aith. Shet —6E 173
(on Mainland)
Aithsetter. Shet —8F 173
Akeld. Nmbd —2D 120
Akeley. Buck —2F 51
Akenham. Suff —1E 55
A La Ronde NT —4D 12
Albaston. Corn —5E 11
Alberbury. Shrp —4F 71
Albert Town. Pemb —3D 42
Albert Village. Leics —4H 73
Albourne. W Sus —4D 26
Albrighton. Shrp —4G 71
(nr. Shrewsbury)
Albrighton. Shrp —5C 72
(nr. Telford)
Alburgh. Norf —2E 67
Albury. Herts —3E 53
Albury. Surr —1B 26
Albury Park —1B 26
Albyfield. Cumb —4G 113
Alby Hill. Norf —2D 78
Alcaig. High —3H 157
Alcaston. Shrp —2G 59
Alcester. Warw —5E 61
Alciston. E Sus —5G 27
Alcombe. Som —2C 20
Alconbury. Cambs —3A 64
Alconbury Weston. Cambs —3A 64
Aldborough. Norf —2D 78
Aldborough. N Yor —3G 99
Aldbourne. Wilts —4A 36
Aldbrough. E Yor —1F 95
Aldbrough St John. N Yor —3F 105
Aldbury. Herts —4H 51
Aldcliffe. Lanc —3D 96
Aldclune. Per —2G 143
Aldeburgh. Suff —5G 67
Aldeby. Norf —1G 67
Aldenham. Herts —1C 38
Alderbury. Wilts —4G 23
Aldercar. Derbs —1B 74
Alderford. Norf —4D 78
Alderholt. Dors —1G 15
Alderley. Glos —2C 34
Alderley Edge. Ches —3C 84
Aldermaston. W Ber —5D 36
Aldermaston Stoke. W Ber —5E 36
Aldermaston Wharf. W Ber —5E 36
Alderminster. Warw —1H 49
Alder Moor. Staf —3G 73
Aldersey Green. Ches —5G 83
Aldershot. Hants —1G 25
Alderton. Glos —2E 49
Alderton. Nptn —1F 51
Alderton. Shrp —3G 71
Alderton. Suff —1G 55
Alderton. Wilts —3D 34
Alderton Fields. Glos —2F 49
Alderwasley. Derbs —5H 85
Aldfield. N Yor —3E 99
Aldford. Ches —5G 83
Aldgate. Rut —5G 75
Aldham. Essx —3C 54
Aldham. Suff —1D 54
Aldingbourne. W Sus —5A 26
Aldingham. Cumb —2B 96
Aldington. Kent —2E 29
Aldington. Worc —1F 49
Aldochlay. Arg —4C 134
Aldon. Shrp —3G 59
Aldoth. Cumb —5C 112
Aldreth. Cambs —3D 64
Aldridge. W Mid —5E 73
Aldringham. Suff —4G 67
Aldsworth. Glos —4G 49
Aldsworth. W Sus —2F 17
Aldwark. Derbs —5G 85
Aldwark. N Yor —3G 99
Aldwick. W Sus —3H 17
Aldwincle. Nptn —2H 63
Aldworth. W Ber —4D 36
Alexandria. W Dun —1E 127
Aley. Som —3E 21
Aley Green. Beds —4A 52
Alfardisworthy. Devn —1C 10
Alfington. Devn —3E 12
Alfold. Surr —2B 26
Alfold Bars. W Sus —2B 26
Alfold Crossways. Surr —2B 26
Alford. Abers —2C 152
Alford. Linc —3D 88
Alford. Som —3B 22
Alford Valley Railway —2C 152
Alfreton. Derbs —5B 86
Alfrick. Worc —5B 60
Alfrick Pound. Worc —5B 60
Alfriston. E Sus —5G 27
Algarkirk. Linc —2B 76
Alhampton. Som —3B 22
Aline Lodge. W Isl —6D 171
Alkborough. N Lin —2B 94
Alkerton. Oxon —1B 50
Alkham. Kent —1G 29
Alkington. Shrp —2H 71
Alkmonton. Derbs —2F 73
Alladale Lodge. High —5B 164
Allaleigh. Devn —3E 9
Allanbank. N Lan —4B 128
Allanton. N Lan —4B 128
Allanton. Bord —4E 131
Allaston. Glos —5B 48
Allbrook. Hants —4C 24
All Cannings. Wilts —5F 35
Allendale Town. Nmbd —4B 114
Allen End. Warw —1F 61
Allenheads. Nmbd —5B 114
Allensford. Dur —5D 115
Allen's Green. Herts —4E 53
Allensmore. Here —2H 47
Allenton. Derb —2A 74
Aller. Som —4H 21
Allerby. Cumb —1B 102
Allercombe. Devn —3D 12
Allerford. Som —2C 20
Allerston. N Yor —1C 100
Allerthorpe. E Yor —5B 100
Allerton. Mers —2G 83
Allerton. W Yor —1B 92
Allerton Bywater. W Yor —2E 93
Allerton Mauleverer. N Yor —4G 99
Allesley. W Mid —2G 61
Allestree. Derb —2H 73
Allet. Corn —4B 6
Allexton. Leics —5F 75
Allgreave. Ches —4D 84
Allhallows. Medw —3C 40
Allhallows-on-Sea. Medw —3C 40
Alligin Shuas. High —3H 155
Allimore Green. Staf —4C 72
Allington. Kent —5B 40
Allington. Linc —1F 75
Allington. Wilts —3H 23
(nr. Amesbury)
Allington. Wilts —5F 35
(nr. Devizes)
Allithwaite. Cumb —2C 96
Alloa. Clac —4A 136
Alloa Tower NTS —4A 136
Allonby. Cumb —5B 112
Alloway. S Ayr —3C 116
Allowenshay. Som —1G 13
All Saints South Elmham. Suff —2F 67
Allscott. Shrp —1B 60
Allscott. Telf —4A 72
All Stretton. Shrp —1G 59
Allt. Carm —5F 45
Alltami. Flin —4E 83
Alltgobhlach. N Ayr —5G 125
Alltmawr. Powy —1D 46
Alltnacaillich. High —4E 167
Allt na h-Airbhe. High —4F 163
Alltour. High —5E 148
Alltsigh. High —2G 149
Alltwalis. Carm —2E 45
Alltwen. Neat —5H 45
Alltyblacca. Cdgn —1F 45
Allt-y-goed. Pemb —1B 44
Allweston. Dors —1B 14
Almeley. Here —5F 59
Almeley Wooton. Here —5F 59
Almer. Dors —3E 15
Almholme. S Yor —4F 93
Almington. Staf —2B 72
Alminstone Cross. Devn —4D 18
Almodington. W Sus —3G 17
Almondbank. Per —1C 136
Almondbury. W Yor —3B 92
Almondsbury. S Glo —3B 34
Alne. N Yor —3G 99
Alness. High —2A 158
Alnessferry. High —2A 158
Alnham. Nmbd —3D 121
Alnmouth. Nmbd —3G 121
Alnwick. Nmbd —3F 121
Alnwick Castle —3F 121
Alnwick Castle Millennium Gdn. —3F 121
Alphamstone. Essx —2B 54
Alpheton. Suff —5A 66
Alphington. Devn —3C 12
Alpington. Norf —5E 79
Alport. Derbs —4G 85
Alport. Powy —1E 59
Alpraham. Ches —5H 83
Alresford. Essx —3D 54
Alrewas. Staf —4F 73
Alsager. Ches —5B 84
Alsagers Bank. Staf —1C 72
Alsop en le Dale. Derbs —5F 85
Alston. Cumb —5A 114
Alstone. Glos —2E 49
Alstone. Som —2G 21
Alstonefield. Staf —5F 85
Alston Sutton. Som —1H 21
Alswear. Devn —4H 19
Altandhu. High —2D 163
Altanduin. High —1F 165
Altarnun. Corn —4C 10
Altass. High —3B 164
Alterwall. High —2E 169
Altgaltraig. Arg —2B 126
Altham. Lanc —1F 91
Althorne. Essx —1D 40
Althorpe. N Lin —4B 94
Althorp House —4D 62
Altnabreac. High —4C 168
Altnacealgach. High —2G 163
Altnafeadh. High —3G 141
Altnaharra. High —5F 167
Altofts. W Yor —2D 92
Alton. Derbs —4A 86
Alton. Hants —3F 25
Alton. Staf —1E 73
Alton Barnes. Wilts —5G 35
Altonhill. E Ayr —1D 116
Alton Pancras. Dors —2C 14
Alton Priors. Wilts —5G 35
Alton Towers —1E 73
Altrincham. G Man —2B 84
Altrua. High —4E 149
Alva. Clac —4A 136
Alvanley. Ches —3G 83
Alvaston. Derb —2A 74
Alvechurch. Worc —3E 61
Alvecote. Warw —5G 73
Alvediston. Wilts —4E 23
Alveley. Shrp —2B 60
Alverdiscott. Devn —4F 19
Alverstoke. Hants —3E 16
Alverstone. IOW —4D 16
Alverthorpe. W Yor —2D 92
Alverton. Notts —1E 75
Alves. Mor —2F 159
Alvescot. Oxon —5A 50
Alveston. S Glo —3B 34
Alveston. Warw —5G 61
Alvie. High —3C 150
Alvingham. Linc —1C 88
Alvington. Glos —5B 48
Alwalton. Cambs —1A 64
Alwinton. Nmbd —4D 120
Alwoodley. W Yor —5E 99
Alyth. Per —4B 144
Amatnatua. High —4B 164
Am Baile. W Isl —7C 170
Ambaston. Derbs —2B 74
Ambergate. Derbs —5H 85
Amber Hill. Linc —1B 76
Amberley. Glos —5D 48
Amberley. W Sus —4B 26
Amberley Working Mus. —4B 26
Amble. Nmbd —4G 121
Amblecote. W Mid —2C 60
Ambler Thorn. W Yor —2A 92
Ambleside. Cumb —4E 103
Ambleston. Pemb —2D 43
Ambrosden. Oxon —4E 50
Amcotts. N Lin —3B 94
American Adventure Theme Park —1B 74
American Mus., Claverton Manor, Bath —5C 34
Amersham. Buck —1A 38
Amerton. Staf —3D 73
Amesbury. Wilts —2G 23
Amisfield. Dum —1B 112
Amlwch. IOA —1D 80
Amlwch Port. IOA —1D 80
Ammanford. Carm —4G 45
Amotherby. N Yor —2B 100
Ampfield. Hants —4B 24
Ampleforth. N Yor —2H 99
Ampleforth College. N Yor —2H 99
Ampney Crucis. Glos —5F 49
Ampney St Mary. Glos —5F 49
Ampney St Peter. Glos —5F 49
Amport. Hants —2A 24
Ampthill. Beds —2A 52
Ampton. Suff —3A 66
Amroth. Pemb —4F 43
Amulree. Per —5G 143
Amwell. Herts —4B 52
Anaheilt. High —2C 140
Ancaster. Linc —1G 75
Anchor. Shrp —2D 58
Anchorsholme. Bkpl —5C 96
An Cnoc. W Isl —4G 171
An Cnoc Ard. W Isl —1H 171
An Coroghon. High —3A 146
Ancroft. Nmbd —5G 131
Ancrum. Bord —2A 120
Ancton. W Sus —5A 26
Anderby. Linc —3E 89
Anderby Creek. Linc —3E 89
Anderson. Dors —3D 15
Anderton. Ches —3A 84
Andertons Mill. Lanc —3D 90
Andover. Hants —2B 24
Andover Down. Hants —2B 24
Andoversford. Glos —4F 49
Andreas. IOM —2D 108
Andwell. Hants —1E 25
Anelog. Gwyn —3A 68
Anfield. Mers —1F 83
Angarrack. Corn —3C 4
Angelbank. Shrp —3H 59
Angel of the North —4F 115
Angerton. Cumb —4D 112
Angle. Pemb —4C 42
An Gleann Ur. W Isl —4G 171
Anglesey Abbey NT —4E 65
Angmering. W Sus —5B 26
Angmering-on-Sea. W Sus —5B 26
Angram. N Yor —5B 104
(nr. Keld)
Angram. N Yor —5H 99
(nr. York)
Angus Folk Mus. NTS —4C 144
Anick. Nmbd —3C 114
Animalarium —2F 57
Ankerbold. Derbs —4A 86
Ankerville. High —1C 158
Anlaby. E Yor —2D 94
Anlaby Park. Hull —2D 94
An Leth Meadhanach. W Isl —7C 170
Anmer. Norf —3G 77
Anmore. Hants —1E 17
Annan. Dum —3C 112
Annaside. Cumb —1A 96
Annat. Arg —1H 133
Annat. High —3A 156
Annathill. N Lan —2A 128
Anna Valley. Hants —2B 24
Annbank. S Ayr —2D 116
Anne Hathaway's Cottage —5F 61
Annesley. Notts —5C 86
Annesley Woodhouse. Notts —5C 86
Annfield Plain. Dur —4E 115
Annscroft. Shrp —5G 71
Ansdell. Lanc —2B 90
Ansford. Som —3B 22
Ansley. Warw —1H 61
Anslow. Staf —3G 73
Anslow Gate. Staf —3F 73
Ansteadbrook. Surr —2A 26
Anstey. Herts —2E 53
Anstey. Leics —5C 74
Anston. S Lan —5D 128
Anstruther Easter. Fife —3H 137
Anstruther Wester. Fife —3H 137
Ansty. Warw —2A 62
Ansty. W Sus —3D 27
Ansty. Wilts —4E 23
Anthill Common. Hants —1E 17
Anthony House NT —3A 8
Anthorn. Cumb —4C 112
Antingham. Norf —2E 79
An-t-Ob. W Isl —9C 171
Anton's Gowt. Linc —1B 76
Antony. Corn —3A 8
Antrobus. Ches —3A 84
Anvil Corner. Devn —2D 11
Anwick. Linc —5A 88
Anwoth. Dum —4C 110
Apethorpe. Nptn —1H 63
Apeton. Staf —4C 72
Apley. Linc —3A 88
Apperknowle. Derbs —3A 86
Apperley. Glos —3D 48
Apperley Dene. Nmbd —4D 114
Appersett. N Yor —5B 104
Appin. Arg —4D 140
Appleby. N Lin —3C 94
Appleby-in-Westmorland. Cumb —2H 103
Appleby Magna. Leics —5H 73
Appleby Parva. Leics —5H 73
Applecross. High —4G 155
Appledore. Devn —3E 19
(nr. Bideford)
Appledore. Devn —1D 12
(nr. Tiverton)
Appledore. Kent —3D 28
Appledore Heath. Kent —2D 28
Appleford. Oxon —2D 36
Applegarthtown. Dum —1C 112
Applemore. Hants —2B 16
Appleshaw. Hants —2B 24
Applethwaite. Cumb —2D 102
Appleton. Hal —2H 83
Appleton. Oxon —5C 50
Appleton-le-Moors. N Yor —1B 100
Appleton-le-Street. N Yor —2B 100
Appleton Roebuck. N Yor —5H 99
Appleton Thorn. Warr —2A 84
Appleton Wiske. N Yor —4A 106
Appletree. Nptn —1C 50
Appletreehall. Bord —3H 119
Appletreewick. N Yor —3C 98
Appley. Som —4D 20
Appley Bridge. Lanc —4D 90
Appuldurcombe House EH —4D 16
Apse Heath. IOW —4D 16
Apsley End. Beds —2B 52
Apuldram. W Sus —2G 17
Arabella. High —1C 158
Arbeadie. Abers —4D 152
Arberth. Pemb —3F 43
Arbirlot. Ang —4F 145
Arborfield. Wok —5F 37
Arborfield Cross. Wok —5F 37
Arborfield Garrison. Wok —5F 37
Arbourthorne. S Yor —2A 86
Arbroath. Ang —4F 145
Arbury Hall —2H 61
Arbuthnott. Abers —1H 145
Arbuthnott House —1G 145
Arcan. High —3H 157
Archargary. High —3H 167
Archdeacon Newton. Darl —3F 105
Archiestown. Mor —4G 159
Arclid. Ches —4B 84
Arclid Green. Ches —4B 84
Ardachu. High —3D 164
Ardalanish. Arg —2A 132
Ardaneaskan. High —5H 155
Ardarroch. High —5H 155
Ardbeg. Arg —1C 126
(nr. Dunoon)
Ardbeg. Arg —3B 126
(on Bute)
Ardbeg. Arg —5C 124
(on Islay)
Ardcharnich. High —5F 163
Ardchiavaig. Arg —2A 132
Ardchonnell. Arg —2G 133
Ardchrishnish. Arg —1B 132
Ardchronie. High —5D 164
Ardchullarie. Stir —2E 135
Ardchyle. Stir —1E 135
Ard-dhubh. High —4G 155
Arddleen. Powy —4E 71
Arddlin. Powy —4E 71
Ardechive. High —4D 148
Ardeley. Herts —3D 52
Ardelve. High —1A 148
Arden. Arg —1E 127
Ardendrain. High —5H 157
Arden Hall. N Yor —5C 106
Ardens Grafton. Warw —5F 61
Ardentinny. Arg —1C 126
Ardeonaig. Stir —5D 142
Ardersier. High —3B 158
Ardery. High —2B 140
Ardessie. High —5E 163
Ardfern. Arg —3F 133
Ardfernal. Arg —2D 124
Ardfin. Arg —3C 124
Ardgartan. Arg —3B 134
Ardgay. High —5C 164
Ardgour. High —2E 141
Ardheslaig. High —3G 155
Ardindrean. High —5F 163
Ardingly. W Sus —3E 27
Ardington. Oxon —3C 36
Ardington House —3C 36
Ardkinglas Gdn. —2A 134
Ardlamont House. Arg —3A 126
Ardleigh. Essx —3D 54
Ardler. Per —4B 144
Ardley. Oxon —3D 50
Ardlui. Arg —2C 134
Ardlussa. Arg —1E 125
Ardmair. High —4F 163
Ardmay. Arg —3B 134
Ardminish. Arg —5E 125
Ardmolich. High —1B 140
Ardmore. High —3C 166
(nr. Kinlochbervie)
Ardmore. High —5E 164
(nr. Tain)
Ardnacross. Arg —4G 139
Ardnadam. Arg —1C 126
Ardnagrask. High —4H 157
Ardnamurach. High —4G 147
Ardnarff. High —5A 156
Ardnastang. High —2C 140
Ardoch. Per —5H 143
Ardochy House. High —3E 148
Ardpatrick. Arg —3F 125
Ardrishaig. Arg —1G 125
Ardroag. High —4B 154
Ardross. High —1A 158
Ardrossan. N Ayr —5D 126
Ardshealach. High —2A 140
Ardsley. S Yor —4D 93
Ardslignish. High —2G 139
Ardtalla. Arg —4C 124
Ardtalnaig. Per —5E 142
Ardtoe. High —1A 140
Arduaine. Arg —2E 133
Arduaine Gdn. NTS —2E 133
Ardullie. High —2H 157
Ardvasar. High —3E 147
Ardvorlich. Per —1F 135
Ardwell. Dum —5G 109
Ardwell. Mor —5A 160
Arean. High —1A 140
Areley Common. Worc —3C 60
Areley Kings. Worc —3B 60
Arford. Hants —3G 25
Argoed. Cphy —2E 33
Argoed Mill. Powy —4B 58
Argyll's Lodging HS —Stirling 196
Aridhglas. Arg —2B 132
Arinacrinachd. High —3G 155
Arinagour. Arg —3D 138
Arisaig. High —5E 147
Ariundle. High —2C 140
Arivegaig. High —2A 140
Arkendale. N Yor —3F 99
Arkesden. Essx —2E 53
Arkholme. Lanc —2E 97
Arkle Town. N Yor —4D 104
Arkley. G Lon —1D 38
Arksey. S Yor —4F 93
Arkwright Town. Derbs —3B 86
Arlecdon. Cumb —3B 102
Arlescote. Warw —1B 50
Arlesey. Beds —2B 52
Arleston. Telf —4A 72
Arley. Ches —2A 84
Arley Hall & Gdns. —2A 84
Arlingham. Glos —4C 48
Arlington. Devn —2G 19
Arlington. E Sus —5G 27
Arlington. Glos —5G 49
Arlington Beccott. Devn —2G 19
Arlington Court NT —3G 19
Armadale. High —2H 167
Armadale. W Lot —3C 128
Armathwaite. Cumb —5G 113
Arminghall. Norf —5E 79
Armitage. Staf —4E 73
Armitage Bridge. W Yor —3B 92
Armley. W Yor —1C 92
Armscote. Warw —1H 49
Arms, The. Norf —1A 66
Armston. Nptn —2H 63
Armthorpe. S Yor —4G 93
Army Flying Mus. —3B 24
Arncliffe. N Yor —2B 98
Arncliffe Cote. N Yor —2B 98
Arncroach. Fife —3H 137
Arne. Dors —4E 15
Arnesby. Leics —1D 62
Arnicle. Arg —2B 122
Arnisdale. High —2G 147
Arnish. High —4E 155
Arniston. Midl —3G 129
Arniston House —4G 129
Arnol. W Isl —3F 171
Arnold. E Yor —5F 101
Arnold. Notts —1C 74
Arnprior. Stir —4F 135
Arnside. Cumb —2D 96
Aros Mains. Arg —4G 139
Arpafeelie. High —3A 158
Arrad Foot. Cumb —1C 96
Arram. E Yor —5E 101
Arras. E Yor —5D 100
Arrathorne. N Yor —5F 105
Arreton. IOW —4D 16
Arrington. Cambs —5C 64
Arrochar. Arg —3B 134
Arrow. Warw —5E 61
Arscaig. High —2C 164
Artafallie. High —4A 158
Arthington. W Yor —5E 99
Arthingworth. Nptn —2E 63
Arthog. Gwyn —4F 69

Arthrath. Abers —5G 161
Arthurstone. Per —4B 144
Arundel. W Sus —5B 26
Arundel Castle —5B 26
Arundel Wildfowl Centre —5B 26
Asby. Cumb —2B 102
Ascog. Arg —3C 126
Ascot. Wind —4A 38
Ascott NT —3G 51
Ascott-under-Wychwood. Oxon —4B 50
Asenby. N Yor —2F 99
Asfordby. Leics —4E 74
Asfordby Hill. Leics —4E 74
Asgarby. Linc —4C 88
(nr. Horncastle)
Asgarby. Linc —1A 76
(nr. Sleaford)
Ash. Devn —4E 9
Ash. Dors —1D 14
Ash. Kent —5G 41
(nr. Sandwich)
Ash. Kent —4H 39
(nr. Swanley)
Ash. Som —4H 21
Ash. Surr —1G 25
Ashampstead. W Ber —4D 36
Ashbocking. Suff —5D 66
Ashbourne. Derbs —1F 73
Ashbrittle. Som —4D 20
Ashbrook. Shrp —1G 59
Ashburton. Devn —2D 8
Ashbury. Devn —3F 11
Ashbury. Oxon —3A 36
Ashby. N Lin —4B 94
Ashby by Partney. Linc —4D 88
Ashby cum Fenby. NE Lin —4F 95
Ashby de la Launde. Linc —5H 87
Ashby-de-la-Zouch. Leics —4A 74
Ashby-de-la-Zouch Castle EH —4A 74
Ashby Folville. Leics —4E 74
Ashby Magna. Leics —1C 62
Ashby Parva. Leics —2C 62
Ashby Puerorum. Linc —3C 88
Ashby St Ledgars. Nptn —4C 62
Ashby St Mary. Norf —5F 79
Ashcombe. Devn —5C 12
Ashcott. Som —3H 21
Ashcurch. Glos —2E 49
Ashdon. Essx —1F 53
Ashdown Forest —2F 27
Ashdown House NT —3A 36
Ashe. Hants —1D 24
Asheldham. Essx —5C 54
Ashen. Essx —1H 53
Ashendon. Buck —4F 51
Ashey. IOW —4D 16
Ashfield. Hants —1B 16
Ashfield. Here —3A 48
Ashfield. Shrp —2H 59
Ashfield. Stir —3G 135
Ashfield. Suff —4E 66
Ashfield Green. Suff —3E 67
Ashfold Crossways. W Sus —3D 26
Ashford. Devn —3F 19
(nr. Barnstaple)
Ashford. Devn —4C 8
(nr. Kingsbridge)
Ashford. Hants —1G 15
Ashford. Kent —1E 28
Ashford. Surr —3B 38
Ashford Bowdler. Shrp —3H 59
Ashford Carbonel. Shrp —3H 59
Ashford Hill. Hants —5D 36
Ashford in the Water. Derbs —4F 85
Ashgill. S Lan —5A 128
Ash Green. Warw —2H 61
Ashgrove. Mor —2G 159
Ashill. Devn —1D 12
Ashill. Norf —5A 78
Ashill. Som —1G 13
Ashingdon. Essx —1C 40
Ashington. Nmbd —1F 115
Ashington. W Sus —4C 26
Ashkirk. Bord —2G 119
Ashlett. Hants —2C 16
Ashleworth. Glos —3D 48
Ashley. Cambs —4F 65
Ashley. Ches —2B 84
Ashley. Dors —2G 15
Ashley. Glos —2E 35
Ashley. Hants —3A 16
(nr. New Milton)
Ashley. Hants —3B 24
(nr. Winchester)
Ashley. Kent —1H 29
Ashley. Nptn —1E 63
Ashley. Staf —2B 72
Ashley. Wilts —5D 34
Ashley Green. Buck —5H 51
Ashley Heath. Dors —2G 15
Ashley Heath. Staf —2B 72
Ashley Moor. Here —4G 59
Ash Magna. Shrp —2H 71
Ashmanhaugh. Norf —3F 79
Ashmansworth. Hants —1C 24
Ashmansworthy. Devn —1D 10
Ashmead Green. Glos —2C 34
Ashmill. Devn —3D 11
(nr. Holsworthy)
Ash Mill. Devn —4A 20
(nr. South Molton)
Ashmolean Mus. —Oxford 194
Ashmore. Dors —1E 15
Ashmore Green. W Ber —5D 36
Ashorne. Warw —5H 61
Ashover. Derbs —4A 86
Ashow. Warw —3H 61
Ash Parva. Shrp —2H 71
Ashperton. Here —1B 48
Ashprington. Devn —3E 9
Ash Priors. Som —4E 21
Ashreigney. Devn —1G 11
Ashridge Estate NT —4H 51
Ash Street. Suff —1D 54
Ashtead. Surr —5C 38
Ash Thomas. Devn —1D 12
Ashton. Ches —4H 83
Ashton. Corn —4D 4
Ashton. Here —4H 59
Ashton. Inv —2D 126
Ashton. Nptn —2H 63
(nr. Oundle)
Ashton. Nptn —1F 51
(nr. Roade)
Ashton. Pet —5A 76
Ashton Common. Wilts —1D 23
Ashton-in-Makerfield. G Man —4D 90
Ashton Keynes. Wilts —2F 35
Ashton under Hill. Worc —2E 49
Ashton-under-Lyne. G Man —1D 84
Ashton upon Mersey. G Man —1B 84
Ashurst. Hants —1B 16
Ashurst. Kent —2G 27
Ashurst. Lanc —4C 90
Ashurst. W Sus —4C 26
Ashurstwood. W Sus —2F 27
Ash Vale. Surr —1G 25
Ashwater. Devn —3D 11
Ashwell. Herts —2C 52
Ashwell. Rut —4F 75
Ashwellthorpe. Norf —1D 66
Ashwick. Som —2B 22
Ashwicken. Norf —4G 77
Ashwood. Staf —2C 60
Askam in Furness. Cumb —2B 96
Askern. S Yor —3F 93
Askerswell. Dors —3A 14
Askett. Buck —5G 51
Askham. Cumb —2G 103
Askham. Notts —3E 87
Askham Bryan. York —5H 99
Askham Richard. York —5H 99
Askrigg. N Yor —5C 104
Askwith. N Yor —5D 98
Aslackby. Linc —2H 75
Aslacton. Norf —1D 66
Aslockton. Notts —1E 75
Aspatria. Cumb —5C 112
Aspenden. Herts —3D 52
Asperton. Linc —2B 76
Aspley Guise. Beds —2H 51
Aspley Heath. Beds —2H 51
Aspull. G Man —4E 90
Asselby. E Yor —2H 93
Assington. Suff —2C 54
Assington Green. Suff —5G 65
Astbury. Ches —4C 84
Astcote. Nptn —5D 62
Asterby. Linc —3B 88
Asterley. Shrp —5F 71
Asterton. Shrp —1F 59
Asthall. Oxon —4A 50
Asthall Leigh. Oxon —4B 50
Astle. High —4E 165
Astley. G Man —4F 91
Astley. Shrp —4H 71
Astley. Warw —2H 61
Astley. Worc —4B 60
Astley Abbotts. Shrp —1B 60
Astley Bridge. G Man —3F 91
Astley Cross. Worc —4C 60
Astley Hall —3D 90
Aston. Ches —3H 83
(nr. Frodsham)
Aston. Ches —1A 72
(nr. Nantwich)
Aston. Derbs —2F 85
Aston. Flin —4F 83
Aston. Here —4G 59
Aston. Herts —3C 52
Aston. Oxon —5B 50
Aston. Shrp —1C 60
(nr. Bridgnorth)
Aston. Shrp —3H 71
(nr. Wem)
Aston. S Yor —2B 86
Aston. Staf —1B 72
Aston. Telf —5A 72
Aston. W Mid —2E 61
Aston. Wok —3F 37
Aston Abbotts. Buck —3G 51
Aston Botterell. Shrp —2A 60
Aston-by-Stone. Staf —2D 72
Aston Cantlow. Warw —5F 61
Aston Clinton. Buck —4G 51
Aston Crews. Here —3B 48
Aston Cross. Glos —2E 49
Aston End. Herts —3C 52
Aston Eyre. Shrp —1A 60
Aston Fields. Worc —4D 60
Aston Flamville. Leics —1B 62
(Aston Hall) —1E 61
Aston Ingham. Here —3B 48
Aston juxta Mondrum. Ches —5A 84
Astonlane. Shrp —1A 60
Aston le Walls. Nptn —5B 62
Aston Magna. Glos —2G 49
Aston Munslow. Shrp —2H 59
Aston on Carrant. Glos —2E 49
Aston on Clun. Shrp —2F 59
Aston-on-Trent. Derbs —3B 74
Aston Pigott. Shrp —5F 71
Aston Rogers. Shrp —5F 71
Aston Rowant. Oxon —2F 37
Aston Sandford. Buck —5F 51
Aston Somerville. Worc —2F 49
Aston Subedge. Glos —1G 49
Aston Tirrold. Oxon —3D 36
Aston Upthorpe. Oxon —3D 36
Astrop. Nptn —2D 50
Astwick. Beds —2C 52
Astwood. Mil —1H 51
Astwood Bank. Worc —4E 61
Aswarby. Linc —2H 75
Aswardby. Linc —3C 88
Atcham. Shrp —5H 71
Atch Lench. Worc —5E 61
Athelhampton. Dors —3C 14
Athelhampton House —3C 14
Athelington. Suff —3E 66
Athelney. Som —4G 21
Athelstaneford. E Lot —2B 130
Atherfield. IOW —4C 16
Atherington. Devn —4F 19
Atherington. W Sus —5B 26
Athersley. S Yor —4D 92
Atherstone. Warw —1H 61
Atherstone on Stour. Warw —5G 61
Atherton. G Man —4E 91
Atlow. Derbs —1G 73
Attadale. High —5B 156
Attenborough. Notts —2C 74
Atterby. Linc —1G 87
Atterley. Shrp —1A 60
Attingham Park NT —5H 71
Attleborough. Norf —1C 66
Attleborough. Warw —1A 62
Attlebridge. Norf —4D 78
Atwick. E Yor —4F 101
Atworth. Wilts —5D 34
Auberrow. Here —1H 47
Aubourn. Linc —4G 87
Aucharnie. Abers —4D 160
Auchattie. Abers —4D 152
Auchavan. Ang —2A 144
Auchbreck. Mor —1G 151
Auchenback. E Ren —4G 127
Auchenblae. Abers —1G 145
Auchenbrack. Dum —5G 117
Auchenbreck. Arg —1B 126
Auchencairn. Dum —4E 111
(nr. Dalbeattie)
Auchencairn. Dum —1A 112
(nr. Dumfries)
Auchencarroch. W Dun —1F 127
Auchencrow. Bord —3E 131
Auchendennan. W Dun —1E 127
Auchendinny. Midl —3F 129
Auchengray. S Lan —4C 128
Auchenhalrig. Mor —2A 160
Auchenheath. S Lan —5B 128
Auchenlochan. Arg —2A 126
Auchenmade. N Ayr —5E 127
Auchenmaig. Dum —4H 109
Auchentiber. N Ayr —5E 127
Auchenvennel. Arg —1D 126
Auchindrain. Arg —3H 133
Auchingarrich Wildlife —2G 135
Auchininna. Abers —4D 160
Auchinleck. Dum —2B 110
Auchinleck. E Ayr —2E 117
Auchinloch. N Lan —2H 127
Auchinstarry. N Lan —2A 128
Auchleven. Abers —1D 152
Auchlochan. S Lan —1H 117
Auchlunachan. High —5F 163
Auchmillan. E Ayr —2E 117
Auchmithie. Ang —4F 145
Auchmuirbridge. Per —3E 136
Auchmull. Ang —1E 145
Auchnacree. Ang —2D 144
Auchnafree. Per —5F 143
Auchnagallin. High —5E 159
Auchnagatt. Abers —4G 161
Aucholzie. Abers —4H 151
Auchreddie. Abers —4F 161
Auchterarder. Per —2B 136
Auchteraw. High —3F 149
Auchterderran. Fife —4E 136
Auchterhouse. Ang —5C 144
Auchtermuchty. Fife —2E 137
Auchterneed. High —3G 157
Auchtertool. Fife —4E 136
Auchtertyre. High —1G 147
Auchtubh. Stir —1E 135
Auckengill. High —2F 169
Auckland Castle, Bishop Auckland —2F 105
Auckley. S Yor —4G 93
Audenshaw. G Man —1D 84
Audlem. Ches —1A 72
Audley. Staf —5B 84
Audley End EH —2F 53
Audley End. Essx —2F 53
Audmore. Staf —3C 72
Auds. Abers —2D 160
Aughton. E Yor —1H 93
Aughton. Lanc —3E 97
(nr. Lancaster)
Aughton. Lanc —4B 90
(nr. Ormskirk)
Aughton. S Yor —2B 86
Aughton. Wilts —1H 23
Aughton Park. Lanc —4C 90
Auldearn. High —3D 158
Aulden. Here —5G 59
Auldgirth. Dum —1G 111
Auldhouse. S Lan —4H 127
Ault a' chruinn. High —1B 148
Aultbea. High —5C 162
Aultdearg. High —2E 157
Aultgrishan. High —5B 162
Aultguish Inn. High —1F 157
Ault Hucknall. Derbs —4B 86
Aultibea. High —1H 165
Aultiphurst. High —2A 168
Aultivullin. High —2A 168
Aultmore. Mor —3B 160
Aultnamain Inn. High —5D 164
Aunby. Linc —4H 75
Aunsby. Linc —2H 75
Aust. S Glo —3A 34
Austerfield. S Yor —1D 86
Austin Fen. Linc —1C 88
Austrey. Warw —5G 73
Austwick. N Yor —3G 97
Authorpe. Linc —2D 88
Authorpe Row. Linc —3E 89
Avebury. Wilts —5G 35
Avebury Stone Circle NT —4G 35
Avebury Trusloe. Wilts —5F 35
Aveley. Thur —2G 39
Avening. Glos —2D 35
Averham. Notts —5E 87
Aveton Gifford. Devn —4C 8
Avielochan. High —2D 150
Aviemore. High —2C 150
Avington. Hants —3D 24
Avington Park —3D 24
Avoch. High —3B 158
Avon. Hants —3G 15
Avonbridge. Falk —2C 128
Avoncroft Mus. of Historic Buildings —4D 60
Avon Dassett. Warw —5B 62
Avonmouth. Bris —4A 34
Avon Valley Railway —4B 34
Avonwick. Devn —3D 8
Awbridge. Hants —4B 24
Awliscombe. Devn —2E 13
Awre. Glos —5C 48
Awsworth. Notts —1B 74
Axbridge. Som —1H 21
Axford. Hants —2E 24
Axford. Wilts —5H 35
Axminster. Devn —3F 13
Axmouth. Devn —3F 13
Aycliffe. Dur —2F 105
Aydon. Nmbd —3D 114
Aydon Castle EH —3C 114
Aykley Heads. Dur —5F 115
Aylburton. Glos —5B 48
Aylburton Common. Glos —5B 48
Ayle. Nmbd —5A 114
Aylesbeare. Devn —3D 12
Aylesbury. Buck —4G 51
Aylesby. NE Lin —4F 95
Aylescott. Devn —1G 11
Aylesford. Kent —5B 40
Aylesham. Kent —5G 41
Aylestone. Leic —5C 74
Aylmerton. Norf —2D 78
Aylsham. Norf —3D 78
Aylton. Here —2B 48
Aylworth. Glos —3G 49
Aymestrey. Here —4G 59
Aynho. Nptn —2D 50
Aynhoe Park —2D 50
Ayot Green. Herts —4C 52
Ayot St Lawrence. Herts —4B 52
Ayot St Peter. Herts —4C 52
Ayr. S Ayr —2C 116
Ayreville. Torb —2E 9
Aysgarth. N Yor —1C 98
Aysgarth Falls —1C 98
Ayshford. Devn —1D 12
Ayside. Cumb —1C 96
Ayston. Rut —5F 75
Ayton. Bord —3F 131
Ayton Castle —3F 131
Aywick. Shet —3G 173
Azerley. N Yor —2E 99

Babbacombe. Torb —2F 9
Babbinswood. Shrp —3F 71
Babb's Green. Herts —4D 53
Babcary. Som —4A 22
Babel. Carm —2B 46
Babell. Flin —3D 82
Babingley. Norf —3F 77
Babraham. Cambs —5E 65
Babworth. Notts —2D 86
Bac. W Isl —3G 171
Bachau. IOA —2D 80
Bacheldre. Powy —1E 59
Bachelors' Club NTS —2D 116
Bachymbyd Fawr. Den —4C 82
Backaland. Orkn —4E 172
Backaskaill. Orkn —2D 172
Backbarrow. Cumb —1C 96
Backe. Carm —3G 43
Backfolds. Abers —3H 161
Backford. Ches —3G 83
Backhill. Abers —5E 161
Backhill of Clackriach. Abers —4G 161
Backies. High —3F 165
Backmuir of New Gilston. Fife —3G 137
Back of Keppoch. High —5E 147
Back Street. Suff —5G 65
Backwell. N Som —5H 33
Backworth. Tyne —2G 115
Bacon End. Essx —4G 53
Baconsthorpe. Norf —2D 78
Baconsthorpe Castle EH —2D 78
Bacton. Here —2G 47
Bacton. Norf —2F 79
Bacton. Suff —4C 66
Bacton Green. Norf —2F 79
Bacup. Lanc —2G 91
Badachonacher. High —1A 158
Badachro. High —1G 155
Badanloch Lodge. High —5H 167
Badavanich. High —3D 156
Badbury. Swin —3G 35
Badby. Nptn —5C 62
Badcall. High —3C 166
Badcaul. High —4E 163
Baddeley Green. Stoke —5D 84
Baddesley Clinton. W Mid —3G 61
Baddesley Clinton Hall NT —3G 61
Baddesley Ensor. Warw —1G 61
Baddidarach. High —1E 163
Baddoch. Abers —5F 151
Badenscallie. High —3E 163
Badenscoth. Abers —5E 160
Badentarbat. High —2E 163
Badgall. Corn —4C 10
Badgers Mount. Kent —4F 39
Badgeworth. Glos —4E 49
Badgworth. Som —1G 21
Badicaul. High —1F 147
Badingham. Suff —4F 67
Badlesmere. Kent —5E 40
Badlipster. High —4E 169
Badluarach. High —4D 163
Badminton. S Glo —3D 34
Badnaban. High —1E 163
Badnabay. High —4C 166
Badnagie. High —5D 168
Badnellan. High —3F 165
Badninish. High —4E 165
Badrallach. High —4E 163
Badsey. Worc —1F 49
Badshot Lea. Surr —2G 25
Badsworth. W Yor —3E 93
Badwell Ash. Suff —4B 66
Bae Cinmel. Cnwy —2B 82
Bae Colwyn. Cnwy —3A 82
Bae Penrhyn. Cnwy —2H 81
Bagby. N Yor —1G 99
Bag Enderby. Linc —3C 88
Bagendon. Glos —5F 49
Bagginswood. Shrp —2A 60
Baggrave. Leics —5D 74
Bagh a'Chaisteil. W Isl —9B 170
Bagham. Kent —5E 41
Baghasdal. W Isl —7C 170
Bagh Mor. W Isl —3D 170
Bagh Shiarabhagh. W Isl —8C 170
Bagillt. Flin —3E 83
Baginton. Warw —3H 61
Baglan. Neat —2A 32
Bagley. Shrp —3G 71
Bagley. Som —2H 21
Bagnall. Staf —5D 84
Bagnor. W Ber —5C 36
Bagshot. Surr —4A 38
Bagshot. Wilts —5B 36
Bagstone. S Glo —3B 34
Bagthorpe. Norf —2G 77
Bagthorpe. Notts —5B 86
Bagworth. Leics —5B 74
Bagwy Llydiart. Here —3H 47
Baildon. W Yor —1B 92
Baildon Green. W Yor —1B 92
Baile. W Isl —1E 170
Baile Ailein. W Isl —5E 171
Baile an Truiseil. W Isl —2F 171
Baile Boidheach. Arg —2F 125
Baile Glas. W Isl —3D 170
Bailemeonach. Arg —4A 140
Baile Mhanaich. W Isl —3C 170
Baile Mhartainn. W Isl —1C 170
Baile MhicPhail. W Isl —1D 170
Baile Mor. Arg —2A 132
Baile Mor. W Isl —2C 170
Baile nan Cailleach. W Isl —3C 170
Baile Raghaill. W Isl —2C 170
Bailey Green. Hants —4E 25
Baileyhead. Cumb —1G 113
Bailiesward. Abers —5B 160
Bail Iochdrach. W Isl —3D 170
Baillieston. Glas —3H 127
Bailrigg. Lanc —4D 97
Bail Uachdraich. W Isl —2D 170
Bail Ur Tholastaidh. W Isl —3H 171
Bainbridge. N Yor —5C 104
Bainsford. Falk —1B 128
Bainshole. Abers —5D 160
Bainton. E Yor —4D 100
Bainton. Oxon —3D 50
Bainton. Pet —5H 75
Baintown. Fife —3F 137
Baker Street. Thur —2H 39
Bakewell. Derbs —4G 85
Bala. Gwyn —2B 70
Balachuirn. High —4E 155
Bala Lake Railway —2A 70
Balbeg. High —5G 157
(nr. Glen Urquhart)
Balbeg. High —1G 149
(nr. Loch Ness)
Balbeggie. Per —1D 136
Balblair. High —4C 164
(nr. Bonar Bridge)
Balblair. High —2B 158
(nr. Invergordon)
Balblair. High —4H 157
(nr. Inverness)
Balby. S Yor —4F 93
Balcathie. Ang —5F 145
Balchladich. High —1E 163
Balchraggan. High —4H 157
Balchrick. High —3B 166
Balcombe. W Sus —2E 27
Balcombe Lane. W Sus —2E 27
Balcurvie. Fife —3F 137
Baldersby. N Yor —2F 99
Baldersby St James. N Yor —2F 99
Balderstone. Lanc —1E 91
Balderton. Ches —4F 83
Balderton. Notts —5F 87
Baldinnie. Fife —2G 137
Baldock. Herts —2C 52
Baldrine. IOM —3D 108
Baldslow. E Sus —4C 28
Baldwin. IOM —3C 108
Baldwinholme. Cumb —4E 113
Baldwins Gate. Staf —1B 72
Bale. Norf —2C 78
Balearn. Abers —3H 161
Balemartine. Arg —4A 138
Balephretrish. Arg —4B 138
Balephuil. Arg —4B 140
Balerno. Edin —3E 129
Balevullin. Arg —4A 138
Balfield. Ang —2E 145
Balfour. Orkn —6D 172
Balfron. Stir —1G 127
Balgaveny. Abers —4D 160
Balgonar. Fife —4C 136
Balgonie Castle —3F 137
Balgowan. High —4A 150
Balgown. High —2C 154
Balgrochan. E Dun —2H 127
Balgy. High —3H 155
Balhalgardy. Abers —1E 153
Baliasta. Shet —1G 173
Baligill. High —2A 168
Balintore. Ang —3B 144
Balintore. High —1C 158
Balintraid. High —1B 158
Balk. N Yor —1G 99
Balkeerie. Ang —4C 144
Balkholme. E Yor —2A 94
Ball. Shrp —3F 71
Ballabeg. IOM —4B 108

Ballacannell. *IOM* —3D **108**
Ballacarnane Beg. *IOM* —3C **108**
Ballachulish. *High* —3E **141**
Ballagyr. *IOM* —3B **108**
Ballajora. *IOM* —2D **108**
Ballaleigh. *IOM* —3C **108**
Ballamodha. *IOM* —4B **108**
Ballantrae. *S Ayr* —1F **109**
Ballards Gore. *Essx* —1D **40**
Ballasalla. *IOM* —4B **108** (nr. Castletown)
Ballasalla. *IOM* —2C **108** (nr. Kirk Michael)
Ballater. *Abers* —4A **152**
Ballaugh. *IOM* —2C **108**
Ballencrieff. *E Lot* —2A **130**
Ballencrieff Toll. *W Lot* —2C **128**
Ballentoul. *Per* —2F **143**
Ball Hill. *Hants* —5C **36**
Ballidon. *Derbs* —5G **85**
Balliemore. *Arg* —1B **126** (nr. Dunoon)
Balliemore. *Arg* —1F **133** (nr. Oban)
Ballieward. *High* —5E **159**
Ballig. *IOM* —3B **108**
Ballimore. *Stir* —2E **135**
Ballindalloch Castle —5F **159**
Ballingdon. *Suff* —1B **54**
Ballinger Common. *Buck* —5H **51**
Ballingham. *Here* —2A **48**
Ballingry. *Fife* —4D **136**
Ballinluig. *Per* —3G **143**
Ballintuim. *Per* —3A **144**
Balliveolan. *Arg* —4C **140**
Balloan. *High* —3C **164**
Balloch. *High* —4B **158**
Balloch. *N Lan* —2A **128**
Balloch. *Per* —2H **135**
Balloch. *W Dun* —1E **127**
Ballochan. *Abers* —4C **152**
Ballochgoy. *Arg* —3B **126**
Ballochmyle. *E Ayr* —2E **117**
Ballochroy. *Arg* —4F **125**
Balls Cross. *W Sus* —3A **26**
Ball's Green. *E Sus* —2F **27**
Ballygown. *Arg* —4F **139**
Ballygrant. *Arg* —3B **124**
Ballymichael. *N Ayr* —2D **122**
Balmacara. *High* —1G **147**
Balmaclellan. *Dum* —2D **110**
Balmacqueen. *High* —1D **154**
Balmaha. *Stir* —4D **134**
Balmalcolm. *Fife* —3F **137**
Balmalloch. *N Lan* —2A **128**
Balmeanach. *High* —5E **155**
Balmedie. *Abers* —2G **153**
Balmerino. *Fife* —1F **137**
Balmerlawn. *Hants* —2B **16**
Balmoral Castle —4G **151**
Balmore. *E Dun* —2H **127**
Balmore. *High* —4B **154**
Balmuir. *Ang* —5D **144**
Balmullo. *Fife* —1G **137**
Balmurrie. *Dum* —3H **109**
Balnaboth. *Ang* —2C **144**
Balnabruaich. *High* —1B **158**
Balnabruich. *High* —5D **168**
Balnacoil. *High* —2F **165**
Balnacra. *High* —4B **156**
Balnacroft. *Abers* —4G **151**
Balnageith. *Mor* —3E **159**
Balnaglaic. *High* —5G **157**
Balnagrantach. *High* —5G **157**
Balnaguard. *Per* —3G **143**
Balnahard. *Arg* —4B **132**
Balnain. *High* —5G **157**
Balnakeil. *High* —2D **166**
Balnaknock. *High* —2D **154**
Balnamoon. *Abers* —3G **161**
Balnamoon. *Ang* —2E **145**
Balnapaling. *High* —2B **158**
Balornock. *Glas* —3H **127**
Balquhidder. *Stir* —1E **135**
Balsall. *W Mid* —3G **61**
Balsall Common. *W Mid* —3G **61**
Balscote. *Oxon* —1B **50**
Balsham. *Cambs* —5E **65**
Balstonia. *Thur* —2A **40**
Baltasound. *Shet* —1H **173**
Balterley. *Staf* —5B **84**
Baltersan. *Dum* —3B **110**
Balthangie. *Abers* —3F **161**
Baltic Arts Centre, Gateshead **Newcastle 191**
Baltonsborough. *Som* —3A **22**
Balvaird. *High* —3H **157**
Balvaird. *Per* —2D **136**
Balvenie. *Mor* —4H **159**
Balvenie Castle *HS* —4H **159**
Balvicar. *Arg* —2E **133**
Balvraid. *High* —2G **147**
Balvraid Lodge. *High* —5C **158**
Bamber Bridge. *Lanc* —2D **90**
Bamber's Green. *Essx* —3F **53**
Bamburgh. *Nmbd* —1F **121**
Bamburgh Castle —1F **121**
Bamford. *Derbs* —2G **85**
Bampton. *Cumb* —3G **103**
Bampton. *Devn* —4C **20**
Bampton. *Oxon* —5B **50**
Bampton Grange. *Cumb* —3G **103**
Banavie. *High* —1F **141**
Banbury. *Oxon* —1C **50**
Bancffosfelen. *Carm* —4E **45**
Banchory. *Abers* —4D **152**
Banchory-Devenick. *Abers* —3G **153**
Bancycapel. *Carm* —4E **45**
Bancyfelin. *Carm* —3H **43**
Banc-y-ffordd. *Carm* —2E **45**
Banff. *Abers* —2D **160**
Bangor. *Gwyn* —3E **81**
Bangor-is-y-coed. *Wrex* —1F **71**
Bangors. *Corn* —3C **10**
Bangor's Green. *Lanc* —4B **90**
Bangrove. *Suff* —3B **66**
Banham. *Norf* —2C **66**
Banham Zoo —2C **66**
Bank. *Hants* —2A **16**
Bankend. *Dum* —3B **112**
Bankfoot. *Per* —5H **143**
Bankglen. *E Ayr* —3E **117**
Bankhead. *Aber* —2F **153**
Bankhead. *Abers* —3D **152**
Bankhead. *S Lan* —5B **128**
Bankland. *Som* —4G **21**
Bank Newton. *N Yor* —4B **98**
Banknock. *Falk* —2A **128**
Banks. *Cumb* —3G **113**
Banks. *Lanc* —2B **90**
Bankshill. *Dum* —1C **112**
Bank Street. *Worc* —4A **60**
Bank, The. *Ches* —5C **84**
Bank, The. *Shrp* —1A **60**
Bank Top. *Lanc* —4D **90**
Banners Gate. *W Mid* —1E **61**
Banningham. *Norf* —3E **78**
Banniskirk. *High* —3D **168**
Bannister Green. *Essx* —3G **53**
Bannockburn. *Stir* —4H **135**
Bannockburn, Battle Site and Information Centre *NTS* —4H **135**
Banstead. *Surr* —5D **38**
Bantham. *Devn* —4C **8**
Banton. *N Lan* —2A **128**
Banwell. *N Som* —1G **21**
Banyard's Green. *Suff* —3F **67**
Bapchild. *Kent* —4D **40**
Bapton. *Wilts* —3E **23**
Barabhas. *W Isl* —2F **171**
Barabhas Iarach. *W Isl* —2F **171**
Baramore. *High* —1A **140**
Barassie. *S Ayr* —1C **116**
Baravullin. *Arg* —4D **140**
Barbaraville. *High* —1B **158**
Barber Booth. *Derbs* —2F **85**
Barber Green. *Cumb* —1C **96**
Barbhas Uarach. *W Isl* —2F **171**
Barbieston. *S Ayr* —3D **116**
Barbon. *Cumb* —1F **97**
Barbourne. *Worc* —5C **60**
Barbridge. *Ches* —5A **84**
Barbrook. *Devn* —2H **19**
Barby. *Nptn* —3C **62**
Barby Nortoft. *Nptn* —3C **62**
Barcaldine. *Arg* —4D **140**
Barcaldine Castle —4D **140**
Barcheston. *Warw* —1A **50**
Barclose. *Cumb* —3F **113**
Barcombe. *E Sus* —4F **27**
Barcombe Cross. *E Sus* —4F **27**
Barden. *N Yor* —5E **105**
Barden Scale. *N Yor* —4C **98**
Bardfield End Green. *Essx* —2G **53**
Bardfield Saling. *Essx* —3G **53**
Bardister. *Shet* —4E **173**
Bardnabeinne. *High* —4E **164**
Bardney. *Linc* —4A **88**
Bardon. *Leics* —4B **74**
Bardon Mill. *Nmbd* —3A **114**
Bardowie. *E Dun* —2G **127**
Bardrainney. *Inv* —2E **127**
Bardsea. *Cumb* —2C **96**
Bardsey. *W Yor* —5F **99**
Bardsley. *G Man* —4H **91**
Bardwell. *Suff* —3B **66**
Bare. *Lanc* —3D **96**
Barelees. *Nmbd* —1C **120**
Barewood. *Here* —5F **59**
Barford. *Hants* —3G **25**
Barford. *Norf* —5D **78**
Barford. *Warw* —4G **61**
Barford St John. *Oxon* —2C **50**
Barford St Martin. *Wilts* —3F **23**
Barford St Michael. *Oxon* —2C **50**
Barfrestone. *Kent* —5G **41**
Bargeddie. *N Lan* —3A **128**
Bargod. *Cphy* —2E **33**
Bargoed. *Cphy* —2E **33**
Bargrennan. *Dum* —2A **110**
Barham. *Cambs* —3A **64**
Barham. *Kent* —5G **41**
Barham. *Suff* —5D **66**
Barharrow. *Dum* —4D **110**
Bar Hill. *Cambs* —4C **64**
Barholm. *Linc* —4H **75**
Barkby. *Leics* —4D **74**
Barkestone-le-Vale. *Leics* —2E **75**
Barkham. *Wok* —5F **37**
Barking. *G Lon* —2F **39**
Barking. *Suff* —5C **66**
Barkingside. *G Lon* —2F **39**
Barking Tye. *Suff* —5C **66**
Barkisland. *W Yor* —3A **92**
Barkston. *Linc* —1G **75**
Barkston Ash. *N Yor* —1E **93**
Barkway. *Herts* —2D **53**
Barlanark. *Glas* —3H **127**
Barlaston. *Staf* —2C **72**
Barlavington. *W Sus* —4A **26**
Barlborough. *Derbs* —3B **86**
Barlby. *N Yor* —1G **93**
Barlestone. *Leics* —5B **74**
Barley. *Herts* —2D **53**
Barley. *Lanc* —5H **97**
Barley Mow. *Tyne* —4F **115**
Barleythorpe. *Rut* —5F **75**
Barling. *Essx* —2D **40**
Barlings. *Linc* —3H **87**
Barlow. *Derbs* —3H **85**
Barlow. *N Yor* —2G **93**
Barlow. *Tyne* —3E **115**
Barmby Moor. *E Yor* —5B **100**
Barmby on the Marsh. *E Yor* —2G **93**
Barmer. *Norf* —2H **77**
Barming Heath. *Kent* —5B **40**
Barmoor. *Nmbd* —1E **121**
Barmouth. *Gwyn* —4F **69**
Barmpton. *Darl* —3A **106**
Barmston. *E Yor* —4F **101**
Barmulloch. *Glas* —3H **127**
Barnack. *Pet* —5H **75**
Barnacle. *Warw* —2A **62**
Barnard Castle. *Dur* —3D **104**
Barnard Castle EH —3D 104
Barnard Gate. *Oxon* —4C **50**
Barnardiston. *Suff* —1H **53**
Barnbarroch. *Dum* —4F **111**
Barnburgh. *S Yor* —4E **93**
Barnby. *Suff* —2G **67**
Barnby Dun. *S Yor* —4G **93**
Barnby in the Willows. *Notts* —5F **87**
Barnby Moor. *Notts* —2D **86**
Barnes. *G Lon* —3D **38**
Barnes Street. *Kent* —1H **27**
Barnet. *G Lon* —1D **38**
Barnetby le Wold. *N Lin* —4D **94**
Barney. *Norf* —2B **78**
Barnham. *Suff* —3A **66**
Barnham. *W Sus* —5A **26**
Barnham Broom. *Norf* —5C **78**
Barnhead. *Ang* —3F **145**
Barnhill. *D'dee* —5D **145**
Barnhill. *Mor* —3F **159**
Barnhill. *Per* —1D **136**
Barnhills. *Dum* —2E **109**
Barningham. *Dur* —3D **105**
Barningham. *Suff* —3B **66**
Barnoldby le Beck. *NE Lin* —4F **95**
Barnoldswick. *Lanc* —5A **98**
Barns Green. *W Sus* —3C **26**
Barnsley. *Glos* —5F **49**
Barnsley. *Shrp* —1B **60**
Barnsley. *S Yor* —4D **92**
Barnstaple. *Devn* —3F **19**
Barnston. *Essx* —4G **53**
Barnston. *Mers* —2E **83**
Barnstone. *Notts* —2E **75**
Barnt Green. *Worc* —3E **61**
Barnton. *Ches* —3A **84**
Barnwell. *Cambs* —5D **64**
Barnwell All Saints. *Nptn* —2H **63**
Barnwell St Andrew. *Nptn* —2H **63**
Barnwood. *Glos* —4D **48**
Barons Cross. *Here* —5G **59**
Barony, The. *Orkn* —5B **172**
Barr. *Dum* —4G **117**
Barr. *S Ayr* —5B **116**
Barra Airport. *W Isl* —8C **170**
Barrachan. *Dum* —5A **110**
Barraglom. *W Isl* —4D **171**
Barrahormid. *Arg* —1F **125**
Barrapol. *Arg* —4A **138**
Barrasford. *Nmbd* —2C **114**
Barravullin. *Arg* —3F **133**
Barregarrow. *IOM* —3C **108**
Barrhead. *E Ren* —4G **127**
Barrhill. *S Ayr* —1H **109**
Barri. *V Glam* —5E **32**
Barrington. *Cambs* —1D **53**
Barrington. *Som* —1G **13**
Barrington Court *NT* —1G **13**
Barripper. *Corn* —3D **4**
Barrmill. *N Ayr* —4E **127**
Barrock. *High* —1E **169**
Barrow. *Lanc* —1F **91**
Barrow. *Rut* —4F **75**
Barrow. *Shrp* —5A **72**
Barrow. *Som* —3C **22**
Barrow. *Suff* —4G **65**
Barroway Drove. *Norf* —5E **77**
Barrow Bridge. *G Man* —3E **91**
Barrowburn. *Nmbd* —3C **120**
Barrowby. *Linc* —2F **75**
Barrowcliff. *N Yor* —1E **101**
Barrow Common. *N Som* —5A **34**
Barrowden. *Rut* —5G **75**
Barrowford. *Lanc* —1G **91**
Barrow Gurney. *N Som* —5A **34**
Barrow Haven. *N Lin* —2D **94**
Barrow Hill. *Derbs* —3B **86**
Barrow-in-Furness. *Cumb* —3B **96**
Barrow Nook. *Lanc* —4C **90**
Barrows Green. *Cumb* —1E **97**
Barrow's Green. *Hal* —2H **83**
Barrow Street. *Wilts* —3D **22**
Barrow upon Humber. *N Lin* —2D **94**
Barrow upon Soar. *Leics* —4C **74**
Barrow upon Trent. *Derbs* —3A **74**
Barry. *Ang* —5E **145**
Barry. *V Glam* —5E **32**
Barry Island. *V Glam* —5E **32**
Barsby. *Leics* —4D **74**
Barsham. *Suff* —2F **67**
Barston. *W Mid* —3G **61**
Bartestree. *Here* —1A **48**
Barthol Chapel. *Abers* —5F **161**
Bartholomew Green. *Essx* —3H **53**
Barthomley. *Ches* —5B **84**
Bartley. *Hants* —1B **16**
Bartley Green. *W Mid* —2E **61**
Bartlow. *Cambs* —1F **53**
Barton. *Cambs* —5D **64**
Barton. *Ches* —5G **83**
Barton. *Cumb* —2F **103**
Barton. *Glos* —3F **49**
Barton. *IOW* —4D **16**
Barton. *Lanc* —4B **90** (nr. Ormskirk)
Barton. *Lanc* —1D **90** (nr. Preston)
Barton. *N Som* —1G **21**
Barton. *N Yor* —4F **105**
Barton. *Oxon* —5D **50**
Barton. *Torb* —2F **9**
Barton. *Warw* —5F **61**
Barton Bendish. *Norf* —5G **77**
Barton Gate. *Staf* —4F **73**
Barton Green. *Staf* —4F **73**
Barton Hartshorn. *Buck* —2E **51**
Barton Hill. *N Yor* —3B **100**
Barton in Fabis. *Notts* —2C **74**
Barton in the Beans. *Leics* —5A **74**
Barton-le-Clay. *Beds* —2A **52**
Barton-le-Street. *N Yor* —2B **100**
Barton-le-Willows. *N Yor* —3B **100**
Barton Mills. *Suff* —3G **65**
Barton on Sea. *Hants* —3H **15**
Barton-on-the-Heath. *Warw* —2A **50**
Barton St David. *Som* —3A **22**
Barton Seagrave. *Nptn* —3F **63**
Barton Stacey. *Hants* —2C **24**
Barton Town. *Devn* —2G **19**
Barton Turf. *Norf* —3F **79**
Barton-under-Needwood. *Staf* —4F **73**
Barton-upon-Humber. *N Lin* —2D **94**
Barton Waterside. *N Lin* —2D **94**
Barugh Green. *S Yor* —4D **92**
Barway. *Cambs* —3E **65**
Barwell. *Leics* —1B **62**
Barwick. *Herts* —4D **53**
Barwick. *Som* —1A **14**
Barwick in Elmet. *W Yor* —1D **93**
Baschurch. *Shrp* —3G **71**
Bascote. *Warw* —4B **62**
Basford Green. *Staf* —5D **85**
Bashall Eaves. *Lanc* —5F **97**
Bashall Town. *Lanc* —5G **97**
Bashley. *Hants* —3H **15**
Basildon. *Essx* —2B **40**
Basildon Park *NT* —4E **36**
Basingstoke. *Hants* —1E **25**
Basingwerk Abbey *CADW* —3D **82**
Baslow. *Derbs* —3G **85**
Bason Bridge. *Som* —2G **21**
Bassaleg. *Newp* —3F **33**
Bassendean. *Bord* —5C **130**
Bassenthwaite. *Cumb* —1D **102**
Bassett. *Sotn* —1C **16**
Bassingbourn. *Cambs* —1D **52**
Bassingfield. *Notts* —2D **74**
Bassingham. *Linc* —4G **87**
Bassingthorpe. *Linc* —3G **75**
Bassus Green. *Herts* —3D **52**
Basta. *Shet* —2G **173**
Baston. *Linc* —4A **76**
Bastonford. *Worc* —5C **60**
Bastwick. *Norf* —4G **79**
Batchley. *Worc* —4E **61**
Batchworth. *Herts* —1B **38**
Batcombe. *Dors* —2B **14**
Batcombe. *Som* —3B **22**
Bate Heath. *Ches* —3A **84**
Bateman's *NT* —3A **28**
Bath. *Bath* —5C **34** & **186**
Bath Abbey —**186**
Bathampton. *Bath* —5C **34**
Bath Assembly Rooms & Costume Mus. *NT* —**186**
Bathealton. *Som* —4D **20**
Batheaston. *Bath* —5C **34**
Bathford. *Bath* —5C **34**
Bathgate. *W Lot* —3C **128**
Bathley. *Notts* —5E **87**
Bathpool. *Corn* —5C **10**
Bathpool. *Som* —4F **21**
Bath Pump Room & Roman Bath —**186**
Bathville. *W Lot* —3C **128**
Bathway. *Som* —1A **22**
Batley. *W Yor* —2C **92**
Batsford. *Glos* —2G **49**
Batson. *Devn* —5D **8**
Battersby. *N Yor* —4C **106**
Battersea. *G Lon* —3D **39**
Battisborough Cross. *Devn* —4C **8**
Battisford. *Suff* —5C **66**
Battisford Tye. *Suff* —5C **66**
Battle. *E Sus* —4B **28**
Battle. *Powy* —2D **46**
Battle Abbey *EH* —4B **28**
Battleborough. *Som* —1G **21**
Battledown. *Glos* —3E **49**
Battlefield. *Shrp* —4H **71**
Battlefield Line —5A **74**
Battle of Hastings Site —4B **28**
Battlesbridge. *Essx* —1B **40**
Battlesden. *Beds* —3H **51**
Battlesea Green. *Suff* —3E **66**
Battleton. *Som* —4C **20**
Battramsley. *Hants* —3B **16**
Batt's Corner. *Surr* —2G **25**
Bauds of Cullen. *Mor* —2B **160**
Baugh. *Arg* —4B **138**
Baughton. *Worc* —1D **49**
Baughurst. *Hants* —5D **36**
Baulking. *Oxon* —2B **36**
Baumber. *Linc* —3B **88**
Baunton. *Glos* —5F **49**
Baverstock. *Wilts* —3F **23**
Bawburgh. *Norf* —5D **78**
Bawdeswell. *Norf* —3C **78**
Bawdrip. *Som* —3G **21**
Bawdsey. *Suff* —1G **55**
Bawdsey Manor. *Suff* —2G **55**
Bawsey. *Norf* —4F **77**
Bawtry. *S Yor* —1D **86**
Baxenden. *Lanc* —2F **91**
Baxterley. *Warw* —1G **61**
Baxter's Green. *Suff* —5G **65**
Baybridge. *Hants* —4D **24**
Baybridge. *Nmbd* —4C **114**
Baycliff. *Cumb* —2B **96**
Baydon. *Wilts* —4A **36**
Bayford. *Herts* —5D **52**
Bayford. *Som* —4C **22**
Bayham Abbey *EH* —2H **27**
Bayles. *Cumb* —5A **114**
Baylham. *Suff* —5D **66**
Baynard's Green. *Oxon* —3D **50**
Bayston Hill. *Shrp* —5G **71**
Baythorn End. *Essx* —1H **53**
Baythorpe. *Linc* —1B **76**
Bayton. *Worc* —3A **60**
Bayton Common. *Worc* —3B **60**
Bayworth. *Oxon* —5D **50**
Beach. *S Glo* —4C **34**
Beachampton. *Buck* —2F **51**
Beachamwell. *Norf* —5G **77**
Beachley. *Glos* —2A **34**
Beachy Head —5G **27**
Beacon. *Devn* —2E **13**
Beacon End. *Essx* —3C **54**
Beacon Hill. *Surr* —3G **25**
Beacon's Bottom. *Buck* —2F **37**
Beaconsfield. *Buck* —1A **38**
Beacontree. *G Lon* —2F **39**
Beacrabhaicg. *W Isl* —8D **171**
Beadlam. *N Yor* —1A **100**
Beadnell. *Nmbd* —2G **121**
Beaford. *Devn* —1F **11**
Beal. *Nmbd* —5G **131**
Beal. *N Yor* —2F **93**
Bealsmill. *Corn* —5D **10**
Beam Hill. *Staf* —3G **73**
Beamhurst. *Staf* —2E **73**
Beaminster. *Dors* —2H **13**
Beamish. *Dur* —4F **115**
Beamish Mus. —4F **115**
Beamond End. *Buck* —1A **38**
Beamsley. *N Yor* —4C **98**
Bean. *Kent* —3G **39**
Beanacre. *Wilts* —5E **35**
Beanley. *Nmbd* —3E **121**
Beanshanger. *Nptn* —2F **51**
Beaquoy. *Orkn* —5C **172**
Beardwood. *Bkbn* —2E **91**
Beare Green. *Surr* —1C **26**
Bearley. *Warw* —4F **61**
Bearpark. *Dur* —5F **115**
Bearsbridge. *Nmbd* —4A **114**
Bearsden. *E Dun* —2G **127**
Bearsted. *Kent* —5B **40**
Bearstone. *Shrp* —2B **72**
Bearwood. *Pool* —3F **15**
Bearwood. *W Mid* —2E **61**
Beatles Story, The —**Liverpool 191**
Beatrix Potter's House, Hill Top *NT* —5E **103**
Beattock. *Dum* —4C **118**
Beauchamp Roding. *Essx* —4F **53**
Beauchief. *S Yor* —2H **85**
Beaufort. *Blae* —4E **47**
Beaulieu. *Hants* —2B **16**
Beaulieu Palace —2B **16**
Beauly. *High* —4H **157**
Beaumaris. *IOA* —3F **81**
Beaumaris Castle *CADW* —3F **81**
Beaumont. *Cumb* —4E **113**
Beaumont. *Essx* —3E **55**
Beaumont Hill. *Darl* —3F **105**
Beaumont Leys. *Leic* —5C **74**
Beausale. *Warw* —3G **61**
Beauvale. *Notts* —1B **74**
Beauworth. *Hants* —4D **24**
Beaworthy. *Devn* —3E **11**
Beazley End. *Essx* —3H **53**
Bebington. *Mers* —2F **83**
Bebside. *Nmbd* —1F **115**
Beccles. *Suff* —2G **67**
Becconsall. *Lanc* —2C **90**
Beckbury. *Shrp* —5B **72**
Beckenham. *G Lon* —4E **39**
Beckermet. *Cumb* —4B **102**
Beckett End. *Norf* —1G **65**
Beckfoot. *Cumb* —1A **96** (nr. Broughton in Furness)
Beck Foot. *Cumb* —5H **103** (nr. Kendal)
Beckfoot. *Cumb* —4C **102** (nr. Seascale)
Beckfoot. *Cumb* —5B **112** (nr. Silloth)
Beckford. *Worc* —2E **49**
Beckhampton. *Wilts* —5F **35**
Beck Hole. *N Yor* —4F **107**
Beckingham. *Linc* —5F **87**
Beckingham. *Notts* —1E **87**
Beckington. *Som* —1D **22**
Beck Isle Mus. —1B **100**
Beckley. *E Sus* —3C **28**
Beckley. *Hants* —3H **15**
Beckley. *Oxon* —4D **50**
Beck Row. *Suff* —3F **65**
Beck Side. *Cumb* —1C **96** (nr. Cartmel)
Beckside. *Cumb* —1F **97** (nr. Sedbergh)
Beck Side. *Cumb* —1B **96** (nr. Ulverston)
Beckton. *G Lon* —2F **39**
Beckwithshaw. *N Yor* —4E **99**
Becontree. *G Lon* —2F **39**
Bedale. *N Yor* —1E **99**
Bedburn. *Dur* —1E **105**
Bedchester. *Dors* —1D **14**
Beddau. *Rhon* —3D **32**
Beddgelert. *Gwyn* —1E **69**
Beddingham. *E Sus* —5F **27**
Beddington. *G Lon* —4D **39**
Bedfield. *Suff* —4F **66**
Bedford. *Beds* —1A **52**
Bedford. *G Man* —4E **91**
Bedgebury Nat. Pinetum —2B **28**
Bedham. *W Sus* —3B **26**
Bedhampton. *Hants* —2F **17**
Bedingfield. *Suff* —4D **66**
Bedingham Green. *Norf* —1E **67**
Bedlam. *N Yor* —3E **99**
Bedlar's Green. *Essx* —3F **53**
Bedlington. *Nmbd* —1F **115**
Bedlinog. *Mer T* —5D **46**
Bedminster. *Bris* —4A **34**
Bedmond. *Herts* —5A **52**
Bednall. *Staf* —4D **72**
Bedrule. *Bord* —3A **120**
Bedstone. *Shrp* —3F **59**
Bedwas. *Cphy* —3E **33**
Bedwellty. *Cphy* —5E **47**
Bedworth. *Warw* —2A **62**
Beeby. *Leics* —5D **74**
Beech. *Hants* —3E **25**
Beech. *Staf* —2C **72**
Beechcliffe. *W Yor* —5C **98**
Beech Hill. *W Ber* —5E **37**
Beechingstoke. *Wilts* —1F **23**
Beedon. *W Ber* —4C **36**

Beeford. E Yor —4F 101
Beeley. Derbs —4G 85
Beelsby. NE Lin —4F 95
Beenham. W Ber —5D 36
Beeny. Corn —3B 10
Beer. Devn —4F 13
Beer. Som —3H 21
Beer Crocombe. Som —4G 21
Beer Hackett. Dors —1B 14
Beesands. Devn —4E 9
Beesby. Linc —3D 88
Beeson. Devn —4E 9
Beeston. Beds —1B 52
Beeston. Ches —5H 83
Beeston. Norf —4B 78
Beeston. Notts —2C 74
Beeston. W Yor —1C 92
Beeston Regis. Norf —1D 78
Beeswing. Dum —3F 111
Beetham. Cumb —2D 97
Beetham. Som —1F 13
Beetley. Norf —4B 78
Beffcote. Staf —4C 72
Began. Card —3F 33
Begbroke. Oxon —4C 50
Begdale. Cambs —5D 76
Begelly. Pemb —4F 43
Beggar Hill. Essx —5G 53
Beggar's Bush. Powy —4E 59
Beggearn Huish. Som —3D 20
Beguildy. Powy —3D 58
Beighton. Norf —5F 79
Beighton. S Yor —2B 86
Beighton Hill. Derbs —5G 85
Beinn Casgro. W Isl —5G 171
Beith. N Ayr —4E 127
Bekesbourne. Kent —5F 41
Bekonscot Model Village —1A 38
Belaugh. Norf —4E 79
Belbroughton. Worc —3D 60
Belchalwell. Dors —2C 14
Belchalwell Street. Dors —2C 14
Belchamp Otten. Essx —1B 54
Belchamp St Paul. Essx —1A 54
Belchamp Walter. Essx —1B 54
Belchford. Linc —3B 88
Belfatton. Abers —3H 161
Belford. Nmbd —1F 121
Belgrano. Cnwy —3B 82
Belgrave Hall —5C 74
Belhaven. E Lot —2C 130
Belhelvie. Abers —2G 153
Belhinnie. Abers —1B 152
Bellabeg. Abers —2A 152
Belladrum. High —4H 157
Bellamore. S Ayr —1H 109
Bellanoch. Arg —4E 133
Bell Busk. N Yor —4B 98
Belleau. Linc —3D 88
Belleheiglash. Mor —5F 159
Bell End. Worc —3D 60
Bellerby. N Yor —5E 105
Bellerby Camp. N Yor —5D 105
Bellever. Devn —5G 11
Belle Vue. Cumb —1C 102
Belle Vue. Shrp —4G 71
Bellfield. S Lan —1H 117
Belliehill. Ang —2E 145
Bellingdon. Buck —5H 51
Bellingham. Nmbd —1B 114
Bellmount. Norf —3E 77
Bellochantuy. Arg —2A 122
Bellsbank. E Ayr —4D 117
Bell's Cross. Suff —5D 66
Bellshill. N Lan —4A 128
Bellshill. Nmbd —1F 121
Bellside. N Lan —4B 128
Bellspool. Bord —1D 118
Bellsquarry. W Lot —3D 128
Bells Yew Green. E Sus —2H 27
Belmaduthy. High —3A 158
Belmesthorpe. Rut —4H 75
Belmont —5D 40
Belmont. Bkbn —3E 91
Belmont. Shet —1G 173
Belmont. S Ayr —3C 116
Belnacraig. Abers —2A 152
Belnie. Linc —2B 76
Belowda. Corn —2D 6
Belper. Derbs —1A 74
Belper Lane End. Derbs —1H 73
Belph. Derbs —3C 86
Belsay. Nmbd —2E 115
Belsay Hall & Castle EH —2D 115
Belsford. Devn —3D 8
Belsize. Herts —5A 52
Belstead. Suff —1E 55
Belston. S Ayr —2C 116
Belstone. Devn —3G 11
Belstone Corner. Devn —3G 11
Belthorn. Lanc —2F 91
Beltinge. Kent —4F 41
Beltoft. N Lin —4B 94
Belton. Leics —3B 74
Belton. Linc —2G 75
Belton. Norf —5G 79
Belton. N Lin —4A 94
Belton. Rut —5F 75
Belton House NT —2G 75
Beltring. Kent —1A 28
Belts of Collonach. Abers —4D 152
Belvedere. G Lon —3G 39
Belvoir. Leics —2F 75
Belvoir Castle —2F 75
Bembridge. IOW —4E 17
Bemersyde. Bord —1H 119
Bemerton. Wilts —3G 23
Bempton. E Yor —2F 101
Benacre. Suff —2H 67
Ben Alder Lodge. High —1C 142
Ben Armine Lodge. High —2E 164
Benbecula Airport. W Isl —3C 170
Benbuie. Dum —5G 117
Benchill. G Man —2C 84
Benderloch. Arg —5D 140
Bendish. Herts —3B 52
Bendronaig Lodge. High —5C 156
Benenden. Kent —2C 28
Benera. High —1G 147
Benfieldside. Dur —4D 115
Bengate. Norf —3F 79
Bengeworth. Worc —1F 49
Bengrove. Glos —2E 49
Benhall Green. Suff —4F 67
Benholm. Abers —2H 145
Benington. Herts —3D 52
Benington. Linc —1C 76
Benington Lordships Gdns. —3C 52
Benington Sea End. Linc —1D 76
Ben Lawers Nat. Nature Reserve NTS —5D 142
Benllech. IOA —2E 81
Ben Lomond NTS —3C 134
Benmore Lodge. High —2H 163
Bennacott. Corn —3C 10
Bennah. Devn —4B 12
Bennecarrigan. N Ayr —3D 122
Bennethead. Cumb —2F 103
Ben Nevis —1F 141
Benningbrough. N Yor —4H 99
Benningbrough Hall NT —4H 99
Benniworth. Linc —2B 88
Benover. Kent —1B 28
Benson. Oxon —2E 36
Benston. Shet —6F 173
Benstonhall. Orkn —4E 172
Bent. Abers —1F 145
Benthall. Nmbd —2G 121
Benthall. Shrp —5A 72
Benthall Hall NT —5A 72
Bentham. Glos —4E 49
Benthoul. Aber —3F 153
Bentlawn. Shrp —5F 71
Bentley. E Yor —1D 94
Bentley. Hants —2F 25
Bentley. S Yor —4F 93
Bentley. Suff —2E 54
Bentley. Warw —1G 61
Bentley. W Mid —1D 61
Bentley Heath. Herts —1D 38
Bentley Heath. W Mid —3F 61
Bentpath. Dum —5F 119
Bents. W Lot —3C 128
Bentworth. Hants —2E 25
Benvie. D'dee —5C 144
Benville Lane. Dors —2A 14
Benwell. Tyne —3F 115
Benwick. Cambs —1C 64
Beoley. Worc —4E 61
Beoraidbeg. High —4E 147
Bepton. W Sus —1G 17
Berden. Essx —3E 53
Bere Alston. Devn —2A 8
Bere Ferrers. Devn —2A 8
Berepper. Corn —4D 4
Bere Regis. Dors —3D 14
Bergh Apton. Norf —5F 79
Berinsfield. Oxon —2D 36
Berkeley. Glos —2B 34
Berkeley Castle —2B 34
Berkhamsted. Herts —5H 51
Berkhamsted Castle EH —5H 51
Berkley. Som —2D 22
Berkswell. W Mid —3G 61
Bermondsey. G Lon —3E 39
Berney Arms Windmill EH —5G 79
Bernice. Arg —4A 134
Bernisdale. High —3D 154
Berrick Salome. Oxon —2E 36
Berriedale. High —1H 165
Berrier. Cumb —2F 103
Berriew. Powy —5D 70
Berrington. Nmbd —5G 131
Berrington. Shrp —5H 71
Berrington. Worc —4H 59
Berrington Green. Worc —4H 59
Berrington Hall NT —4H 59
Berrington Law. Nmbd —5F 131
Berrow. Som —1G 21
Berrow Green. Worc —5B 60
Berry Cross. Devn —1E 11
Berry Down Cross. Devn —2F 19
Berry Hill. Glos —4A 48
Berry Hill. Pemb —1A 44
Berryhillock. Mor —2C 160
Berrynarbor. Devn —2F 19
Berry Pomeroy. Devn —2E 9
Berry Pomeroy Castle EH —2E 9
Berryscaur. Dum —5D 118
Berry's Green. G Lon —5F 39
Bersham. Wrex —1F 71
Berthengam. Flin —3D 82
Berwick. E Sus —5G 27
Berwick Bassett. Wilts —4G 35
Berwick Hill. Nmbd —2E 115
Berwick St James. Wilts —3F 23
Berwick St John. Wilts —4E 23
Berwick St Leonard. Wilts —3E 23
Berwick-upon-Tweed. Nmbd —4G 131
Berwyn. Den —1D 70
Bescaby. Leics —3F 75
Bescar. Lanc —3B 90
Besford. Worc —1E 49
Bessacarr. S Yor —4G 93
Bessels Leigh. Oxon —5C 50
Bessingby. E Yor —3F 101
Bessingham. Norf —2D 78
Best Beech Hill. E Sus —2H 27
Besthorpe. Norf —1C 66
Besthorpe. Notts —4F 87
Bestwood Village. Notts —1C 74
Beswick. E Yor —5E 101
Betchworth. Surr —5D 38
Bethania. Cdgn —4E 57
Bethania. Gwyn —1G 69 (nr. Blaenau Ffestiniog)
Bethania. Gwyn —5F 81 (nr. Caernarfon)
Bethel. Gwyn —2B 70 (nr. Bala)
Bethel. Gwyn —4E 81 (nr. Caernarfon)
Bethel. IOA —3C 80
Bethersden. Kent —1D 28
Bethesda. Gwyn —4F 81
Bethesda. Pemb —3E 43
Bethlehem. Carm —3G 45
Bethnal Green. G Lon —2E 39
Betishill. N Lan —3A 128
Betley. Staf —1B 72
Betsham. Kent —3H 39
Betteshanger. Kent —5H 41
Bettiscombe. Dors —3H 13
Bettisfield. Wrex —2G 71
Betton. Shrp —2A 72
Betton Strange. Shrp —5H 71
Bettws. B'end —3B 32
Bettws. Newp —2F 33
Bettws Bledrws. Cdgn —5E 57
Bettws Cedewain. Powy —1D 58
Bettws Gwerfil Goch. Den —1C 70
Bettws Ifan. Cdgn —1D 44
Bettws Newydd. Mon —5G 47
Bettyhill. High —2H 167
Betws. Carm —4G 45
Betws Garmon. Gwyn —5E 81
Betws-y-Coed. Cnwy —5G 81
Betws-yn-Rhos. Cnwy —3B 82
Beulah. Cdgn —1C 44
Beulah. Powy —5B 58
Bevendean. Brig —5E 27
Bevercotes. Notts —3D 86
Beverley. E Yor —1D 94
Beverley Minster —1D 94
Beverston. Glos —2D 34
Bevington. Glos —2B 34
Bewaldeth. Cumb —1D 102
Bewcastle. Cumb —2G 113
Bewdley. Worc —3B 60
Bewerley. N Yor —3D 98
Bewholme. E Yor —5F 101
Bexfield. Norf —3C 78
Bexhill. E Sus —5B 28
Bexley. G Lon —3F 39
Bexleyheath. G Lon —3F 39
Bexleyhill. W Sus —3A 26
Bexwell. Norf —5F 77
Beyton. Suff —4B 66
Beyton Green. Suff —4B 66
Bàgh a Chàise. W Isl —1E 170
Bhalton. W Isl —4C 171
Bhatarsaigh. W Isl —9B 170
Bibbington. Derbs —3E 85
Bibury. Glos —5G 49
Bicester. Oxon —3D 50
Bickenhall. Som —1F 13
Bickenhill. W Mid —2F 61
Bicker. Linc —2B 76
Bicker Bar. Linc —2B 76
Bicker Gauntlet. Linc —2B 76
Bickershaw. G Man —4E 91
Bickerstaffe. Lanc —4C 90
Bickerton. Ches —5H 83
Bickerton. Nmbd —4D 121
Bickerton. N Yor —4G 99
Bickford. Staf —4C 72
Bickington. Devn —3F 19 (nr. Barnstaple)
Bickington. Devn —5A 12 (nr. Newton Abbot)
Bickleigh. Devn —2B 8 (nr. Plymouth)
Bickleigh. Devn —2C 12 (nr. Tiverton)
Bickleton. Devn —3F 19
Bickley. N Yor —5G 107
Bickley Moss. Ches —1H 71
Bickmarsh. Warw —5F 61
Bicknacre. Essx —5A 54
Bicknoller. Som —3E 20
Bicknor. Kent —5C 40
Bickton. Hants —1G 15
Bicton. Here —4G 59
Bicton. Shrp —2E 59 (nr. Bishop's Castle)
Bicton. Shrp —4G 71 (nr. Shrewsbury)
Bicton Heath. Shrp —4G 71
Bicton Park —4D 12
Bidborough. Kent —1G 27
Biddenden. Kent —2C 28
Biddenden Green. Kent —1C 28
Biddenham. Beds —1A 52
Biddestone. Wilts —4D 34
Biddisham. Som —1G 21
Biddlesden. Buck —1E 51
Biddlestone. Nmbd —4D 120
Biddulph. Staf —5C 84
Biddulph Grange Gdn. NT —5C 84
Biddulph Moor. Staf —5D 84
Bideford. Devn —4E 19
Bidford-on-Avon. Warw —5E 61
Bidlake. Devn —4F 11
Bidston. Mers —2E 83
Bielby. E Yor —5B 100
Bieldside. Aber —3F 153
Bierley. IOW —5D 16
Bierley. W Yor —1B 92
Bierton. Buck —4G 51
Bigbury. Devn —4C 8
Bigbury-on-Sea. Devn —4C 8
Bigby. Linc —4D 94
Biggar. Cumb —3A 96
Biggar. S Lan —1C 118
Biggin. Derbs —5F 85 (nr. Hartington)
Biggin. Derbs —1G 73 (nr. Hulland)
Biggin. N Yor —1F 93
Biggings. Shet —5C 173
Biggin Hill. G Lon —5F 39
Biggin Hill (London) Airport. G Lon —4F 39
Biggleswade. Beds —1B 52
Bighouse. High —2A 168
Bighton. Hants —3E 24
Biglands. Cumb —4D 112
Bignor. W Sus —4A 26
Bignor Roman Villa —4A 26
Big Pit Mining Mus. —5F 47
Big Sand. High —1G 155
Bigton. Shet —9E 173
Bilberry. Corn —2E 6
Bilborough. Nott —1C 74
Bilbrook. Som —2D 20
Bilbrook. Staf —5C 72
Bilbrough. N Yor —5H 99
Bilbster. High —3E 169
Bilby. Notts —2D 86
Bildershaw. Dur —2F 105
Bildeston. Suff —1C 54
Billericay. Essx —1A 40
Billesdon. Leics —5E 74
Billesley. Warw —5F 61
Billingborough. Linc —2A 76
Billinge. Mers —4D 90
Billingford. Norf —3D 66 (nr. Diss)
Billingford. Norf —3C 78 (nr. East Dereham)
Billingham. Stoc T —2B 106
Billinghay. Linc —5A 88
Billingley. S Yor —4E 93
Billingshurst. W Sus —3B 26
Billingsley. Shrp —2B 60
Billington. Beds —3H 51
Billington. Lanc —1F 91
Billington. Staf —3C 72
Billockby. Norf —4G 79
Billy Row. Dur —1E 105
Bilsborrow. Lanc —5E 97
Bilsby. Linc —3D 88
Bilsham. W Sus —5A 26
Bilsington. Kent —2E 29
Bilson Green. Glos —4B 48
Bilsthorpe. Notts —4D 86
Bilsthorpe Moor. Notts —5D 86
Bilston. Midl —3F 129
Bilston. W Mid —1D 60
Bilstone. Leics —5A 74
Bilting. Kent —1E 29
Bilton. E Yor —1E 95
Bilton. Nmbd —3G 121
Bilton. N Yor —4E 99 (nr. Harrogate)
Bilton. N Yor —5G 99 (nr. York)
Bilton. Warw —3B 62
Bimbister. Orkn —6C 172
Binbrook. Linc —1B 88
Binchester. Dur —1F 105
Bincombe. Dors —4B 14
Bindal. High —5G 165
Binegar. Som —2B 22
Bines Green. W Sus —4C 26
Binfield. Brac —4G 37
Binfield Heath. Oxon —4F 37
Bingfield. Nmbd —2C 114
Bingham. Notts —1E 74
Bingham's Melcombe. Dors —2C 14
Bingley. W Yor —1B 92
Bings Heath. Shrp —4H 71
Binham. Norf —2B 78
Binham Priory EH —1B 78
Binley. Hants —1C 24
Binley. W Mid —3A 62
Binnegar. Dors —4D 15
Binniehill. Falk —2B 128
Binsoe. N Yor —2E 99
Binstead. IOW —3D 16
Binstead. W Sus —5A 26
Binsted. Hants —2F 25
Binton. Warw —5F 61
Bintree. Norf —3C 78
Binweston. Shrp —5F 71
Birch. Essx —4C 54
Birchall. Staf —5D 85
Bircham Newton. Norf —2G 77
Bircham Tofts. Norf —2G 77
Birchanger. Essx —3F 53
Birchburn. N Ayr —3D 122
Birch Cross. Staf —2F 73
Bircher. Here —4G 59
Birch Green. Essx —4C 54
Birchgrove. Card —4E 33
Birchgrove. Swan —3G 31
Birch Heath. Ches —4H 83
Birch Hill. Ches —3H 83
Birchington. Kent —4G 41
Birch Langley. G Man —4G 91
Birchley Heath. Warw —1G 61
Birchmoor. Warw —5G 73
Birchmoor Green. Beds —2H 51
Birchover. Derbs —4G 85
Birch Vale. Derbs —2E 85
Birchview. Mor —5F 159
Birchwood. Linc —4G 87
Birchwood. Som —1F 13
Birchwood. Warr —1A 84
Bircotes. Notts —1D 86
Birdbrook. Essx —1H 53
Birdham. W Sus —2G 17
Birdingbury. Warw —4B 62
Birdlip. Glos —4E 49
Birdsall. N Yor —3C 100
Birds Edge. W Yor —4C 92
Birds Green. Essx —5F 53
Birdsgreen. Shrp —2B 60
Birdsmoor Gate. Dors —2G 13
Birdston. E Dun —2H 127
Birdwell. S Yor —4D 92
Birdwood. Glos —4C 48
Birgham. Bord —1B 120
Birichen. High —4E 165
Birkby. Cumb —1B 102
Birkby. N Yor —4A 106
Birkdale. Mers —3B 90
Birkenhead. Mers —2F 83
Birkenhills. Abers —4E 161
Birkenshaw. N Lan —3H 127
Birkenshaw. W Yor —2C 92
Birkhall. Abers —4H 151
Birkhill. Ang —5C 144
Birkholme. Linc —3G 75
Birkin. N Yor —2F 93
Birley. Here —5G 59
Birling. Kent —4A 40
Birling. Nmbd —4G 121
Birling Gap. E Sus —5G 27
Birlingham. Worc —1E 49
Birmingham. W Mid —2E 61 & 186
Birmingham Airport. W Mid —2F 61
Birmingham Mus. and Art Gallery —186
Birnam. Per —4H 143
Birsay. Orkn —5B 172
Birse. Abers —4C 152
Birsemore. Abers —4C 152
Birstall. Leics —5C 74
Birstall. W Yor —2C 92
Birstwith. N Yor —4E 99
Birthorpe. Linc —2A 76
Birtle. Lanc —3G 91
Birtley. Here —4F 59
Birtley. Nmbd —2B 114
Birtley. Tyne —4F 115
Birtsmorton. Worc —2D 48
Birts Street. Worc —2C 48
Bisbrooke. Rut —1F 63
Bisham. Wind —3G 37
Bishampton. Worc —5D 61
Bish Mill. Devn —4H 19
Bishop Auckland. Dur —2F 105
Bishopbridge. Linc —1H 87
Bishopbriggs. E Dun —2H 127
Bishop Burton. E Yor —5D 101
Bishopdown. Wilts —3G 23
Bishop Middleham. Dur —1A 106
Bishopmill. Mor —2G 159
Bishop Monkton. N Yor —3F 99
Bishop Norton. Linc —1G 87
Bishopsbourne. Kent —5F 41
Bishops Cannings. Wilts —5F 35
Bishop's Castle. Shrp —2F 59
Bishop's Caundle. Dors —1B 14
Bishop's Cleeve. Glos —3E 49
Bishop's Down. Dors —1B 14
Bishop's Frome. Here —1B 48
Bishop's Green. Essx —4G 53
Bishop's Green. Hants —5D 36
Bishop's Hull. Som —4F 21
Bishop's Itchington. Warw —5A 62
Bishop's Lydeard. Som —4E 21
Bishop's Norton. Glos —3D 48
Bishop's Nympton. Devn —4A 20
Bishop's Offley. Staf —3B 72
Bishop's Stortford. Herts —3E 53
Bishops Sutton. Hants —3E 24
Bishop's Tachbrook. Warw —4H 61
Bishop's Tawton. Devn —3F 19
Bishopsteignton. Devn —5C 12
Bishopstoke. Hants —1C 16
Bishopston. Swan —4E 31
Bishopstone. Buck —4G 51
Bishopstone. E Sus —5F 27
Bishopstone. Here —1H 47
Bishopstone. Swin —3H 35
Bishopstone. Wilts —4F 23
Bishopstrow. Wilts —2D 23
Bishop Sutton. Bath —1A 22
Bishop's Waltham. Hants —1D 16
Bishopswood. Som —1F 13
Bishop's Wood. Staf —5C 72
Bishopsworth. Bris —5A 34
Bishop Thornton. N Yor —3E 99
Bishopthorpe. York —5H 99
Bishopton. Darl —2A 106
Bishopton. Dum —5B 110
Bishopton. N Yor —2F 99
Bishopton. Ren —2F 127
Bishopton. Warw —5F 61
Bishop Wilton. E Yor —4B 100
Bishton. Newp —3G 33
Bishton. Staf —3E 73
Bisley. Glos —5E 49
Bisley. Surr —5A 38
Bispham. Bkpl —5C 96
Bispham Green. Lanc —3C 90
Bissoe. Corn —4B 6
Bisterne. Hants —2G 15
Bisterne Close. Hants —2H 15
Bitchfield. Linc —3G 75
Bittadon. Devn —2F 19
Bittaford. Devn —3C 8
Bittering. Norf —4B 78
Bitterley. Shrp —3H 59
Bitterne. Sotn —1C 16
Bitteswell. Leics —2C 62
Bitton. S Glo —5B 34
Bix. Oxon —3F 37
Bixter. Shet —6E 173
Blaby. Leics —1C 62
Blackawton. Devn —3E 9
Black Bank. Cambs —2E 65
Black Barn. Linc —3D 76
Blackborough. Devn —2D 12
Blackborough. Norf —4F 77
Blackborough End. Norf —4F 77
Black Bourton. Oxon —5A 50
Blackboys. E Sus —3G 27
Blackbrook. Derbs —1H 73
Blackbrook. Mers —1H 83
Blackbrook. Staf —2B 72
Blackbrook. Surr —1C 26
Blackburn. Abers —2F 153
Blackburn. Bkbn —2E 91
Blackburn. W Lot —3C 128
Black Callerton. Tyne —3E 115
Black Car. Norf —1C 66
Black Clauchrie. S Ayr —1H 109
Black Corries. High —3G 141
Black Country Living Mus., Dudley —1D 60
Black Crofts. Arg —5D 140
Black Cross. Corn —2D 6
Blackden Heath. Ches —3B 84
Blackditch. Oxon —5C 50
Blackdog. Abers —2G 153
Black Dog. Devn —2B 12
Blackdown. Dors —2G 13
Blackdyke. Cumb —4C 112
Blacker Hill. S Yor —4D 92
Blackfen. G Lon —3F 39
Blackfield. Hants —2C 16
Blackford. Cumb —3E 113

Blackford. Per —3A 136
Blackford. Shrp —2H 59
Blackford. Som —2H 21 (nr. Burnham-on-Sea)
Blackford. Som —4B 22 (nr. Wincanton)
Blackfordby. Leics —4H 73
Blackgang. IOW —5C 16
Blackgang Chine Theme Park —5C 16
Blackhall. Edin —2F 129
Blackhall. Ren —3F 127
Blackhall Colliery. Dur —1B 106
Blackhall Mill. Tyne —4E 115
Blackhall Rocks. Dur —1B 106
Blackham. E Sus —2F 27
Blackheath. Essx —3D 54
Blackheath. G Lon —3E 39
Blackheath. Suff —3G 67
Blackheath. Surr —1B 26
Blackheath. W Mid —2D 61
Black Heddon. Nmbd —2D 115
Blackhill. Abers —4H 161
Blackhill. High —3C 154
Black Hill. Warw —5G 61
Blackhills. Abers —2G 161
Blackhills. High —3D 158
Blackjack. Linc —2B 76
Blackland. Wilts —5F 35
Black Lane. G Man —4F 91
Blackleach. Lanc —1C 90
Blackley. G Man —4G 91
Blackley. W Yor —3B 92
Blacklunans. Per —2A 144
Blackmill. B'end —3C 32
Blackmoor. G Man —4E 91
Blackmoor. Hants —3F 25
Blackmoor Gate. Devn —2G 19
Blackmore. Essx —5G 53
Blackmore End. Essx —2H 53
Blackmore End. Herts —4B 52
Black Mount. Arg —4G 141
Black Mountain —4A 46
Blackness. Falk —2D 128
Blackness Castle HS —1D 128
Blacknest. Hants —2F 25
Blackney. Dors —3H 13
Blacknoll. Dors —4D 14
Black Notley. Essx —3A 54
Blacko. Lanc —5A 98
Black Pill. Swan —3F 31
Blackpool. Bkpl —1B 90 & 186
Blackpool. Devn —4E 9
Blackpool Airport. Lanc —1B 90
Blackpool Gate. Cumb —2G 113
Blackpool Pleasure Beach —1B 90
Blackpool Zoo —1B 90
Blackridge. W Lot —3B 128
Blackrock. Arg —3B 124
Blackrock. Mon —4F 47
Blackrod. G Man —3E 90
Blackshaw. Dum —3B 112
Blackshaw Head. W Yor —2H 91
Blacksmith's Green. Suff —4D 66
Blacksnape. Bkbn —2F 91
Blackstone. W Sus —4D 26
Black Street. Suff —2H 67
Black Tar. Pemb —4D 43
Blackthorn. Oxon —4E 50
Blackthorpe. Suff —4B 66
Blacktoft. E Yor —2B 94
Blacktop. Aber —3F 153
Black Torrington. Devn —2E 11
Blacktown. Newp —3F 33
Blackwater. Corn —4B 6
Blackwater. Hants —1G 25
Blackwater. IOW —4D 16
Blackwater. Som —1F 13
Blackwaterfoot. N Ayr —3C 122
Blackwell —5E 103
Blackwell. Darl —3F 105
Blackwell. Derbs —5B 86 (nr. Alfreton)
Blackwell. Derbs —3F 85 (nr. Buxton)
Blackwell. Som —4D 20
Blackwell. Warw —1H 49
Blackwell. Worc —3D 61
Blackwood. Cphy —2E 33
Blackwood. Dum —1G 111
Blackwood. S Lan —5A 128
Blackwood Hill. Staf —5D 84
Blacon. Ches —4F 83
Bladnoch. Dum —4B 110
Bladon. Oxon —4C 50
Blaenannerch. Cdgn —1C 44
Blaenau Dolwyddelan. Cnwy —5F 81
Blaenau Ffestiniog. Gwyn —1G 69
Blaenavon. Torf —5F 47
Blaenavon Ironworks WH —5F 47
Blaenawey. Mon —4F 47
Blaen Celyn. Cdgn —5C 56
Blaen Clydach. Rhon —2C 32
Blaendulais. Neat —5B 46
Blaenffos. Pemb —1F 43
Blaengarw. B'end —2C 32
Blaen-geuffordd. Cdgn —2F 57
Blaengwrach. Neat —5B 46
Blaengwynfi. Neat —2B 32
Blaenllechau. Rhon —2D 32
Blaenpennal. Cdgn —4F 57
Blaenplwyf. Cdgn —3E 57
Blaenporth. Cdgn —1C 44
Blaenrhondda. Rhon —2C 32
Blaenwaun. Carm —2G 43
Blaen-y-coed. Carm —2H 43
Blaenycwm. Rhon —2C 32
Blagdon. N Som —1A 22
Blagdon. Torb —2E 9
Blagdon Hill. Som —1F 13
Blagill. Cumb —5A 114
Blaguegate. Lanc —4C 90
Blaich. High —1E 141
Blain. High —2A 140
Blaina. Blae —5F 47
Blair Atholl. Per —2F 143
Blair Castle —2F 143
Blair Drummond. Stir —4G 135
Blair Drummond Safari Park —4G 135
Blairgowrie. Per —4A 144
Blairhall. Fife —1D 128
Blairingone. Per —4B 136
Blairlogie. Stir —4H 135
Blairmore. Abers —5B 160
Blairmore. Arg —1C 126
Blairmore. High —3B 166
Blairquhanan. W Dun —1F 127
Blairquhan Castle —4C 116
Blaisdon. Glos —4C 48
Blakebrook. Worc —3C 60
Blakedown. Worc —3C 60
Blake End. Essx —3H 53
Blakemere. Here —1G 47
Blakeney. Glos —5B 48
Blakeney. Norf —1C 78
Blakeney Point Nat. Nature Reserve NT —1C 78
Blakenhall. Ches —1B 72
Blakenhall. W Mid —1C 60
Blakeshall. Worc —2C 60
Blakesley. Nptn —5D 62
Blakesley Hall —2F 61
Blanchland. Nmbd —4C 114
Blandford Camp. Dors —2E 15
Blandford Forum. Dors —2D 15
Blandford St Mary. Dors —2D 15
Bland Hill. N Yor —4E 98
Blandy. High —3G 167
Blanefield. Stir —2G 127
Blankney. Linc —4H 87
Blantyre. S Lan —4H 127
Blarmachfoldach. High —2E 141
Blarnalearoch. High —4F 163
Blashford. Hants —2G 15
Blaston. Leics —1F 63
Blatchbridge. Som —2C 22
Blathaisbhal. W Isl —1D 170
Blatherwycke. Nptn —1G 63
Blawith. Cumb —1B 96
Blaxhall. Suff —5F 67
Blaxton. S Yor —4G 93
Blaydon. Tyne —3E 115
Bleadney. Som —2H 21
Bleadon. N Som —1G 21
Blean. Kent —4F 41
Bleasby. Linc —2A 88
Bleasby. Notts —1E 74
Bleasby Moor. Linc —2A 88
Blebocraigs. Fife —2G 137
Bleddfa. Powy —4E 58
Bledington. Glos —3H 49
Bledlow. Buck —5F 51
Bledlow Ridge. Buck —2F 37
Blencarn. Cumb —1H 103
Blencogo. Cumb —5C 112
Blendworth. Hants —1F 17
Blenheim. Oxon —5D 50
Blenheim Palace WH —4C 50
Blennerhasset. Cumb —5C 112
Bletchingdon. Oxon —4D 50
Bletchingley. Surr —5E 39
Bletchley. Mil —2G 51
Bletchley. Shrp —2A 72
Bletherston. Pemb —2E 43
Bletsoe. Beds —5H 63
Blewbury. Oxon —3D 36
Blickling. Norf —3D 78
Blickling Hall NT —3D 78
Blidworth. Notts —5C 86
Blindburn. Nmbd —3C 120
Blindcrake. Cumb —1C 102
Blindley Heath. Surr —1E 27
Blisland. Corn —5A 10
Blissford. Hants —1G 15
Bliss Gate. Worc —3B 60
Blists Hill. Telf —5A 72
Blists Hill Open Air Mus. —5A 72
Blisworth. Nptn —5E 63
Blithbury. Staf —3E 73
Blitterlees. Cumb —4C 112
Blockley. Glos —2G 49
Blofield. Norf —5F 79
Blofield Heath. Norf —4F 79
Blo' Norton. Norf —3C 66
Bloomfield. Bord —2H 119
Blore. Staf —1F 73
Blount's Green. Staf —2E 73
Bloxham. Oxon —2C 50
Bloxholm. Linc —5H 87
Bloxwich. W Mid —5E 73
Bloxworth. Dors —3D 15
Blubberhouses. N Yor —4D 98
Blue Anchor. Som —2D 20
Blue Anchor. Swan —3E 31
Blue Bell Hill. Kent —4B 40
Bluebell Railway —3E 27
Blue Row. Essx —4D 54
Bluetown. Kent —5D 40
Blundeston. Suff —1H 67
Blunham. Beds —5A 64
Blunsdon St Andrew. Swin —3G 35
Bluntington. Worc —3C 60
Bluntisham. Cambs —3C 64
Blunts. Corn —2H 7
Blurton. Stoke —1C 72
Blyborough. Linc —1G 87
Blyford. Suff —3G 67
Blymhill. Staf —4C 72
Blymhill Lawns. Staf —4C 72
Blyth. Nmbd —1G 115
Blyth. Notts —2D 86
Blyth. Bord —5E 129
Blyth Bank. Bord —5E 129
Blyth Bridge. Bord —5E 129
Blythburgh. Suff —3G 67
Blythe Bridge. Staf —1D 72
Blythe Marsh. Staf —1D 72
Blythe, The. Staf —3E 73
Blyton. Linc —1F 87
Boarhills. Fife —2H 137
Boarhunt. Hants —2E 16
Boarshead. E Sus —2G 27
Boar's Head. G Man —4D 90
Boars Hill. Oxon —5C 50
Boarstall. Buck —4E 51
Boasley Cross. Devn —3F 11
Boath. High —1H 157
Boat of Garten. High —2D 150
Bobbing. Kent —4C 40
Bobbington. Staf —1C 60
Bobbingworth. Essx —5F 53
Bocaddon. Corn —3F 7
Bocking. Essx —3A 54
Bocking Churchstreet. Essx —3A 54
Boddam. Abers —4H 161
Boddam. Shet —10E 173
Boddington. Glos —3D 49
Bodedern. IOA —2C 80
Bodelwyddan. Den —3C 82
Bodelwyddan Castle —3C 82
Bodenham. Here —5H 59
Bodenham. Wilts —4G 23
Bodewryd. IOA —1C 80
Bodfari. Den —3C 82
Bodffordd. IOA —3D 80
Bodham. Norf —1D 78
Bodiam. E Sus —3B 28
Bodiam Castle NT —3B 28
Bodicote. Oxon —2C 50
Bodieve. Corn —1D 6
Bodinnick. Corn —3F 7
Bodle Street Green. E Sus —4A 28
Bodmin. Corn —2E 7
Bodmin & Wenford Railway —2E 7
Bodmin Moor —5B 10
Bodnant. Cnwy —3H 81
Bodney. Norf —1H 65
Bodorgan. IOA —4C 80
Bodrane. Corn —2G 7
Bodrhyddan —3C 82
Bodsham Green. Kent —1F 29
Boduan. Gwyn —2C 68
Bodymoor Heath. Warw —1F 61
Bogallan. High —3A 158
Bogbrae Croft. Abers —5H 161
Bogend. S Ayr —1C 116
Boghall. Midl —3F 129
Boghall. W Lot —3C 128
Boghead. S Lan —5A 128
Bogindollo. Ang —3D 144
Bogmoor. Mor —2A 160
Bogniebrae. Abers —4C 160
Bognor Regis. W Sus —3H 17
Bograxie. Abers —2E 152
Bogside. N Lan —4B 128
Bog, The. Shrp —1F 59
Bogton. Abers —3D 160
Bogue. Dum —1D 110
Bohenie. High —5E 149
Bohortha. Corn —5C 6
Boirseam. W Isl —9C 171
Bokiddick. Corn —2E 7
Bolam. Dur —2E 105
Bolam. Nmbd —1D 115
Bolberry. Devn —5C 8
Bold Heath. Mers —2H 83
Boldon. Tyne —3G 115
Boldon Colliery. Tyne —3G 115
Boldre. Hants —3B 16
Boldron. Dur —3D 104
Bole. Notts —2E 87
Bolehall. Staf —5G 73
Bolehill. Derbs —5G 85
Bolenowe. Corn —5A 6
Boleside. Bord —1G 119
Bolham. Devn —1C 12
Bolham Water. Devn —1E 13
Bolingey. Corn —3B 6
Bollington. Ches —3D 84
Bolney. W Sus —3D 26
Bolnhurst. Beds —5H 63
Bolshan. Ang —3F 145
Bolsover. Derbs —3B 86
Bolsover Castle EH —3B 86
Bolsterstone. S Yor —1G 85
Bolstone. Here —2A 48
Boltachan. Per —3F 143
Boltby. N Yor —1G 99
Bolton. Cumb —2H 103
Bolton. E Lot —2B 130
Bolton. E Yor —4B 100
Bolton. G Man —4F 91
Bolton. Nmbd —3F 121
Bolton Abbey. N Yor —4C 98
Bolton Abbey Estate —4C 98
Bolton by Bowland. Lanc —5G 97
Bolton Castle —5D 104
Boltonfellend. Cumb —3F 113
Boltongate. Cumb —5D 112
Bolton Green. Lanc —3D 90
Bolton-le-Sands. Lanc —3D 97
Bolton Low Houses. Cumb —5D 112
Bolton New Houses. Cumb —5D 112
Bolton-on-Swale. N Yor —5F 105
Bolton Percy. N Yor —5H 99
Bolton Town End. Lanc —3D 97
Bolton upon Dearne. S Yor —4E 93
Bolton Wood Lane. Cumb —5D 112
Bolventor. Corn —5B 10
Bomarsund. Nmbd —1F 115
Bomere Heath. Shrp —4G 71
Bonar Bridge. High —4D 164
Bonawe. Arg —5E 141
Bonby. N Lin —3D 94
Boncath. Pemb —1G 43
Bonchester Bridge. Bord —3H 119
Bonchurch. IOW —5D 16
Bondant Gdn. NT —3H 81
Bond End. Staf —4F 73
Bondleigh. Devn —2G 11
Bonds. Lanc —5D 97
Bonehill. Devn —5H 11
Bonehill. Staf —5F 73
Bo'ness. Falk —1C 128
Bo'ness & Kinneil Railway —2C 128
Boney Hay. Staf —4E 73
Bonham. Wilts —3C 22
Bonhill. W Dun —2E 127
Boningale. Shrp —5C 72
Bonjedward. Bord —2A 120
Bonkle. N Lan —4B 128
Bonnington. Ang —5E 145
Bonnington. Edin —3E 129
Bonnington. Kent —2E 29
Bonnybank. Fife —3F 137
Bonnybridge. Falk —1B 128
Bonnykelly. Abers —3F 161
Bonnyrigg. Midl —3G 129
Bonnyton. Ang —5C 144
Bonnytown. Fife —2H 137
Bonsall. Derbs —5G 85
Bont. Mon —4G 47
Bontddu. Gwyn —4F 69
Bont Dolgadfan. Powy —5A 70
Bontgoch. Cdgn —2F 57
Bonthorpe. Linc —3D 89
Bontnewydd. Cdgn —4F 57
Bont-newydd. Cnwy —3C 82
Bontnewydd. Gwyn —4D 81 (nr. Caernarfon)
Bont Newydd. Gwyn —1G 69 (nr. Ffestiniog)
Bontuchel. Den —5C 82
Bonvilston. V Glam —4D 32
Bon-y-maen. Swan —3F 31
Booker. Buck —2G 37
Booley. Shrp —3H 71
Boorley Green. Hants —1D 16
Boosbeck. Red C —3D 106
Boot. Cumb —4C 102
Booth. W Yor —2A 92
Boothby Graffoe. Linc —5G 87
Boothby Pagnell. Linc —2G 75
Booth Green. Ches —2D 84
Booth Mus. of Natural History —Brighton 186
Booth of Toft. Shet —4F 173
Boothstown. G Man —4F 91
Boothville. Nptn —4E 63
Booth Wood. W Yor —3A 92
Bootle. Cumb —1A 96
Bootle. Mers —1F 83
Booton. Norf —3D 78
Booze. N Yor —4D 104
Boquhan. Stir —1G 127
Boraston. Shrp —3A 60
Borde Hill Gdn. —3E 27
Borden. Kent —4C 40
Borden. W Sus —4G 25
Border Forest Park —1H 113
Bordlands. Bord —5E 129
Bordley. N Yor —3B 98
Bordon. Hants —3G 25
Boreham. Essx —5A 54
Boreham. Wilts —2D 23
Boreham Street. E Sus —4A 28
Borehamwood. Herts —1C 38
Boreland. Dum —5D 118
Boreston. Devn —3D 8
Borestone Brae. Stir —4H 135
Boreton. Shrp —5H 71
Borgh. W Isl —8B 170 (on Barra)
Borgh. W Isl —3C 170 (on Benbecula)
Borgh. W Isl —1E 170 (on Berneray)
Borgh. W Isl —2G 171 (on Lewis)
Borghasdal. W Isl —9C 171
Borghastan. W Isl —3D 171
Borgie. High —3G 167
Borgue. Dum —5D 110
Borgue. High —1H 165
Borley. Essx —1B 54
Borley Green. Essx —1B 54
Borley Green. Suff —4B 66
Borlum. High —1H 149
Bornais. W Isl —6C 170
Bornesketaig. High —1C 154
Boroughbridge. N Yor —3F 99
Borough Green. Kent —5H 39
Borras Head. Wrex —5F 83
Borreraig. High —3A 154
Borrobol Lodge. High —1F 165
Borrodale. High —4A 154
Borrowash. Derb —2B 74
Borrowby. N Yor —1G 99 (nr. Northallerton)
Borrowby. N Yor —3E 107 (nr. Whitby)
Borrowston. High —4F 169
Borrowstonehill. Orkn —7D 172
Borrowstoun. Falk —1C 128
Borstal. Medw —4B 40
Borth. Cdgn —2F 57
Borthwick. Midl —4G 129
Borth-y-Gest. Gwyn —2E 69
Borve. High —4D 154
Borwick. Lanc —2E 97
Bosbury. Here —1B 48
Boscastle. Corn —3B 10
Boscobel House EH —5C 72
Boscombe. Bour —3G 15
Boscombe. Wilts —3H 23
Boscoppa. Corn —3E 7
Bosham. W Sus —2G 17
Bosherston. Pemb —5D 42
Bosley. Ches —4D 84
Bossall. N Yor —3B 100
Bossiney. Corn —4A 10
Bossingham. Kent —1F 29
Bossington. Som —2B 20
Bostadh. W Isl —3D 171
Bostock Green. Ches —4A 84
Boston. Linc —1C 76
Boston Spa. W Yor —5G 99
Boston Stump —1C 76
Boswarthen. Corn —3B 4
Boswinger. Corn —4D 6
Bosworth Battlefield Site —5B 74
Botallack. Corn —3A 4
Botany Bay. G Lon —1D 39
Botcheston. Leics —5B 74
Botesdale. Suff —3C 66
Bothal. Nmbd —1F 115
Bothampstead. W Ber —4D 36
Bothamsall. Notts —3D 86
Bothel. Cumb —1C 102
Bothenhampton. Dors —3H 13
Bothwell. S Lan —4H 127
Bothwell Castle HS —4H 127
Botley. Buck —5H 51
Botley. Hants —1D 16
Botley. Oxon —5C 50
Botloe's Green. Glos —3C 48
Botolph Claydon. Buck —3F 51
Botolphs. W Sus —5C 26
Bottacks. High —2G 157
Bottesford. Leics —2F 75
Bottesford. N Lin —4B 94
Bottisham. Cambs —4E 65
Bottlesford. Wilts —1G 23
Bottomcraig. Fife —1F 137
Bottom o' th' Moor. G Man —3E 91
Botton Head. Lanc —3F 97
Botusfleming. Corn —2A 8
Botwnnog. Gwyn —2B 68
Bough Beech. Kent —1F 27
Boughrood. Powy —2E 47
Boughspring. Glos —2A 34
Boughton. Norf —5F 77
Boughton. Nptn —4E 63
Boughton. Notts —4D 86
Boughton Aluph. Kent —1E 29
Boughton Green. Kent —5B 40
Boughton House —2G 63
Boughton Lees. Kent —1E 28
Boughton Malherbe. Kent —1C 28
Boughton Monchelsea. Kent —5B 40
Boughton under Blean. Kent —5E 41
Boulby. Red C —3E 107
Bouldnor. IOW —4B 16
Bouldon. Shrp —2H 59
Boulmer. Nmbd —3G 121
Boulston. Pemb —3D 42
Boultham. Linc —4G 87
Boulton. Derb —2A 74
Boundary. Staf —1D 73
Bounds. Here —2B 48
Bourn. Cambs —5C 64
Bournbrook. W Mid —2E 61
Bourne. Linc —3H 75
Bourne End. Beds —1H 51 (nr. Cranfield)
Bourne End. Beds —4H 63 (nr. Sharnbrook)
Bourne End. Buck —3G 37
Bourne End. Herts —5A 52
Bournemouth. Bour —3F 15 & 186
Bournemouth Airport. Dors —3G 15
Bournemouth Oceanarium —186
Bournes Green. Glos —5E 49
Bournes Green. S'end —2D 40
Bourne, The. Surr —2G 25
Bournheath. Worc —3D 60
Bournmoor. Dur —4G 115
Bournville. W Mid —2E 61
Bourton. Dors —3C 22
Bourton. N Som —5G 33
Bourton. Oxon —3H 35
Bourton. Shrp —1H 59
Bourton. Wilts —5F 35
Bourton on Dunsmore. Warw —3B 62
Bourton-on-the-Hill. Glos —2G 49
Bourton-on-the-Water. Glos —3G 49
Bousd. Arg —2D 138
Boustead Hill. Cumb —4D 112
Bouth. Cumb —1C 96
Bouthwaite. N Yor —2D 98
Boveney. Buck —3A 38
Boveridge. Dors —1F 15
Boverton. V Glam —5C 32
Bovey Tracey. Devn —5B 12
Bovingdon. Herts —5A 52
Bovingdon Green. Buck —3G 37
Bovinger. Essx —5F 53
Bovington Camp. Dors —4D 14
Bow. Devn —2H 11
Bowbank. Dur —2C 104
Bow Brickhill. Mil —2H 51
Bowbridge. Glos —5D 48
Bowburn. Dur —1A 106
Bowcombe. IOW —4C 16
Bowd. Devn —4E 12
Bowden. Devn —4E 9
Bowden. Bord —1H 119
Bowden Hill. Wilts —5E 35
Bowdon. G Man —2B 84
Bower. Nmbd —1A 114
Bowerchalke. Wilts —4F 23
Bowerhill. Wilts —5E 35
Bower Hinton. Som —1H 13
Bowermadden. High —2E 169
Bowers. Staf —2C 72
Bowers Gifford. Essx —2B 40
Bowershall. Fife —4C 136
Bowertower. High —2E 169
Bowes. Dur —3C 104
Bowes Mus. —3D 104
Bowgreave. Lanc —5D 97
Bowhill House —2G 119
Bowhousebog. N Lan —4B 128
Bowithick. Corn —4B 10
Bowland Bridge. Cumb —1D 96
Bowlees. Dur —2C 104
Bowley. Here —5H 59
Bowlhead Green. Surr —2A 26
Bowling. W Dun —2F 127
Bowling. W Yor —1B 92
Bowling Bank. Wrex —1G 71
Bowling Green. Worc —5C 60
Bowlish. Som —2B 22
Bowmanstead. Cumb —5E 102
Bowmore. Arg —4B 124
Bowness-on-Solway. Cumb —3D 112
Bowness-on-Windermere. Cumb —5F 103
Bow of Fife. Fife —2F 137
Bowood. Dors —3H 13
Bowood House —5E 35
Bowriefauld. Ang —4E 145

Bowscale. Cumb —1E 103
Bowsden. Nmbd —5F 131
Bowside Lodge. High —2A 168
Bowston. Cumb —5F 103
Bow Street. Cdgn —2F 57
Bowthorpe. Norf —5D 78
Box. Glos —5D 48
Box. Wilts —5D 34
Boxbush. Glos —3B 48
Box End. Beds —1A 52
Boxford. Suff —1C 54
Boxford. W Ber —4C 36
Boxgrove. W Sus —5A 26
Box Hill NT —5C 38
Boxley. Kent —5B 40
Box's Shop. Corn —2C 10
Boxted. Essx —2C 54
Boxted. Suff —5H 65
Boxted Cross. Essx —2D 54
Boxworth. Cambs —4C 64
Boxworth End. Cambs —4C 64
Boyden End. Suff —5G 65
Boyden Gate. Kent —4G 41
Boylestone. Derbs —2F 73
Boylestonfield. Derbs —2F 73
Boyndlie. Abers —2G 161
Boynton. E Yor —3F 101
Boys Hill. Dors —1B 14
Boythorpe. Derbs —4A 86
Boyton. Corn —3D 10
Boyton. Suff —1G 55
Boyton. Wilts —3E 23
Boyton Cross. Essx —5G 53
Boyton End. Essx —2G 53
Boyton End. Suff —1H 53
Bozeat. Nptn —5G 63
Braaid. IOM —4C 108
Braal Castle. High —3D 168
Brabling Green. Suff —4E 67
Brabourne. Kent —1F 29
Brabourne Lees. Kent —1E 29
Brabster. High —2F 169
Bracadale. High —5C 154
Braceborough. Linc —4H 75
Bracebridge. Linc —4G 87
Bracebridge Heath. Linc —4G 87
Braceby. Linc —2H 75
Bracewell. Lanc —5A 98
Brackenfield. Derbs —5A 86
Brackenlands. Cumb —5D 112
Brackenthwaite. Cumb —5D 112
Brackenthwaite. N Yor —4E 99
Brackla. B'end —4C 32
Brackla. High —3C 158
Bracklesham. W Sus —3G 17
Brackletter. High —5D 148
Brackley. Nptn —2D 50
Brackley Hatch. Nptn —1E 51
Brackloch. High —1F 163
Bracknell. Brac —5G 37
Braco. Per —3H 135
Bracobrae. Mor —3C 160
Bracon. N Lin —4A 94
Bracon Ash. Norf —1D 66
Bracora. High —4F 147
Bradbourne. Derbs —5G 85
Bradbury. Dur —2A 106
Bradda. IOM —4A 108
Bradden. Nptn —1E 51
Bradenham. Buck —2G 37
Bradenham. Norf —5B 78
Bradenstoke. Wilts —4F 35
Bradfield. Essx —2E 55
Bradfield. Norf —2E 79
Bradfield. W Ber —4E 36
Bradfield Combust. Suff —5A 66
Bradfield Green. Ches —5A 84
Bradfield Heath. Essx —3E 55
Bradfield St Clare. Suff —5B 66
Bradfield St George. Suff —4B 66
Bradford. Derbs —4G 85
Bradford. Devn —2E 11
Bradford. Nmbd —1F 121
Bradford. W Yor —1B 92 & 186
Bradford Abbas. Dors —1A 14
Bradford Barton. Devn —1B 12
Bradford Leigh. Wilts —5D 34
Bradford-on-Avon. Wilts —5D 34
Bradford-on-Tone. Som —4E 21
Bradford Peverell. Dors —3B 14
Bradiford. Devn —3F 19
Brading. IOW —4E 16
Bradley. Ches —3H 83
Bradley. Derbs —1G 73
Bradley. Glos —2C 34
Bradley. Hants —2E 25
Bradley. NE Lin —4F 95
Bradley. N Yor —1C 98
Bradley. Staf —4C 72
Bradley. W Mid —1D 60
Bradley. W Yor —2B 92
Bradley. Wrex —5F 83
Bradley Cross. Som —1H 21
Bradley Green. Ches —1H 71
Bradley Green. Som —3F 21
Bradley Green. Warw —5G 73
Bradley Green. Worc —4D 61
Bradley in the Moors. Staf —1E 73
Bradley Mount. Ches —3D 84
Bradley Stoke. S Glo —3B 34
Bradlow. Here —2C 48
Bradmore. Notts —2C 74
Bradmore. W Mid —1C 60
Bradninch. Devn —2D 12
Bradnop. Staf —5E 85
Bradpole. Dors —3H 13
Bradshaw. G Man —3F 91
Bradstone. Devn —4D 11
Bradwall Green. Ches —4B 84
Bradway. S Yor —2H 85
Bradwell. Derbs —2F 85
Bradwell. Essx —3B 54
Bradwell. Mil —2G 51
Bradwell. Norf —5H 79
Bradwell-on-Sea. Essx —5D 54
Bradwell Waterside. Essx —5C 54
Bradworthy. Devn —1D 10
Brae. High —5C 162
Brae. Shet —5E 173
Braeantra. High —1H 157
Braefield. High —5G 157
Braefindon. High —3A 158
Braegrum. Per —1C 136
Braehead. Ang —3F 145
Braehead. Dum —4B 110
Braehead. Mor —4G 159
Braehead. S Lan —1H 117 (nr. Coalburn)
Braehead. S Lan —4C 128 (nr. Forth)
Braehoulland. Shet —4D 173
Braemar. Abers —4F 151
Braemar Castle —4F 151
Braemore. High —5C 168 (nr. Dunbeath)
Braemore. High —1D 156 (nr. Ullapool)
Brae of Achnahaird. High —2E 163
Brae Roy Lodge. High —4F 149
Braeside. Abers —5G 161
Braeside. Inv —2D 126
Braes of Coul. Ang —3B 144
Braeswick. Orkn —4F 172
Braetongue. High —3F 167
Braeval. Stir —3E 135
Braevallich. Arg —3G 133
Braewick. Shet —6E 173
Brafferton. Darl —2F 105
Brafferton. N Yor —2G 99
Brafield-on-the-Green. Nptn —5F 63
Bragar. W Isl —3E 171
Bragbury End. Herts —3C 52
Bragleenbeg. Arg —1G 133
Braichmelyn. Gwyn —4F 81
Braides. Lanc —4D 96
Braidwood. S Lan —5B 128
Braigo. Arg —3A 124
Brailsford. Derbs —1G 73
Braintree. Essx —3A 54
Braiseworth. Suff —3D 66
Braishfield. Hants —4B 24
Braithwaite. Cumb —2D 102
Braithwaite. S Yor —3G 93
Braithwaite. W Yor —5C 98
Braithwell. S Yor —1C 86
Brakefield Green. Norf —5C 78
Bramber. W Sus —4C 26
Brambledown. Kent —3D 40
Brambridge. Hants —4C 24
Bramcote. Notts —2C 74
Bramcote. Warw —2B 62
Bramdean. Hants —4E 24
Bramerton. Norf —5E 79
Bramfield. Herts —4C 52
Bramfield. Suff —3F 67
Bramford. Suff —1E 54
Bramhall. G Man —2C 84
Bramhall Hall —2C 84
Bramham. W Yor —5G 99
Bramham Park —5G 99
Bramhope. W Yor —5E 99
Bramley. Hants —1E 25
Bramley. S Yor —1B 86
Bramley. Surr —1B 26
Bramley. W Yor —1C 92
Bramley Green. Hants —1E 25
Bramley Head. N Yor —4D 98
Bramley Vale. Derbs —4B 86
Bramling. Kent —5G 41
Brampford Speke. Devn —3C 12
Brampton. Cambs —3B 64
Brampton. Cumb —2H 103 (nr. Appleby)
Brampton. Cumb —3G 113 (nr. Carlisle)
Brampton. Linc —3F 87
Brampton. Norf —3E 78
Brampton. S Yor —4E 93
Brampton. Suff —2G 67
Brampton Abbotts. Here —3B 48
Brampton Ash. Nptn —2E 63
Brampton Bryan. Here —3F 59
Brampton en le Morthen. S Yor —2B 86
Bramshall. Staf —2E 73
Bramshaw. Hants —1A 16
Bramshill. Hants —5F 37
Bramshott. Hants —3G 25
Branault. High —2G 139
Brancaster. Norf —1G 77
Brancaster Staithe. Norf —1G 77
Brancepeth. Dur —1F 105
Branch End. Nmbd —3D 114
Branchill. Mor —3E 159
Brand End. Linc —1C 76
Branderburgh. Mor —1G 159
Brandesburton. E Yor —5F 101
Brandeston. Suff —4E 67
Brand Green. Glos —3C 48
Brandhill. Shrp —3G 59
Brandis Corner. Devn —2E 11
Brandish Street. Som —2C 20
Brandiston. Norf —3D 78
Brandon. Dur —1F 105
Brandon. Linc —1G 75
Brandon. Nmbd —3E 121
Brandon. Suff —2G 65
Brandon. Warw —3B 62
Brandon Bank. Cambs —2F 65
Brandon Creek. Norf —1F 65
Brandon Parva. Norf —5C 78
Brandsby. N Yor —2H 99
Brandy Wharf. Linc —1H 87
Brane. Corn —4B 4
Bran End. Essx —3G 53
Branksome. Pool —3F 15
Bransbury. Hants —2C 24
Bransby. Linc —3G 87
Branscombe. Devn —4E 13
Bransford. Worc —5B 60
Bransgore. Hants —3G 15
Bransholme. Hull —1D 94
Bransley. Shrp —3A 60
Branston. Leics —3F 75
Branston. Linc —4H 87
Branston. Staf —3G 73
Branston Booths. Linc —4H 87
Branstone. IOW —4D 16
Bransty. Cumb —3A 102
Brant Broughton. Linc —5G 87
Brantham. Suff —2E 54
Branthwaite. Cumb —1D 102 (nr. Caldbeck)
Branthwaite. Cumb —2B 102 (nr. Workington)
Brantingham. E Yor —1C 94
Branton. Nmbd —3E 121
Branton. S Yor —4G 93
Branton Green. N Yor —3G 99
Brantwood —5E 102
Branxholme. Bord —3G 119
Branxton. Nmbd —1C 120
Brassington. Derbs —5G 85
Brasted. Kent —5F 39
Brasted Chart. Kent —5F 39
Bratch, The. Staf —1C 60
Brathens. Abers —4D 152
Bratoft. Linc —4D 88
Brattleby. Linc —2G 87
Bratton. Telf —4A 72
Bratton. Wilts —1E 23
Bratton Clovelly. Devn —3E 11
Bratton Fleming. Devn —3G 19
Bratton Seymour. Som —4B 22
Braughing. Herts —3D 53
Braulen Lodge. High —5E 157
Braunston. Nptn —4C 62
Braunston. Rut —5F 75
Braunstone. Leic —5C 74
Braunton. Devn —3E 19
Brawby. N Yor —2B 100
Brawl. High —2A 168
Brawlbin. High —3C 168
Bray. Wind —3A 38
Braybrooke. Nptn —2E 63
Brayford. Devn —3G 19
Bray Shop. Corn —5D 10
Braystones. Cumb —4B 102
Brayton. N Yor —1G 93
Bray Wick. Wind —4G 37
Brazacott. Corn —3C 10
Brea. Corn —5A 6
Breach. W Sus —2F 17
Breachwood Green. Herts —3B 52
Breacleit. W Isl —4D 171
Breaden Heath. Shrp —2G 71
Breadsall. Derbs —1A 74
Breadstone. Glos —5C 48
Breage. Corn —4D 4
Breakachy. High —4G 157
Bream. Glos —5B 48
Breamore. Hants —1G 15
Breamore House —1G 15
Bream's Meend. Glos —5B 48
Brean. Som —1F 21
Breanais. W Isl —5B 171
Brean Down NT —1F 21
Brearton. N Yor —3F 99
Breascleit. W Isl —4E 171
Breaston. Derbs —2B 74
Brechfa. Carm —2F 45
Brechin. Ang —3F 145
Breckles. Norf —1B 66
Brecon. Powy —3D 46
Brecon Beacons Nat. Park —4B 46
Brecon Mountain Railway —4D 46
Bredbury. G Man —1D 84
Brede. E Sus —4C 28
Bredenbury. Here —5A 60
Breden's Norton. Worc —2E 49
Bredfield. Suff —5E 67
Bredgar. Kent —4C 40
Bredhurst. Kent —4B 40
Bredicot. Worc —5D 60
Bredon. Worc —2E 49
Bredwardine. Here —1G 47
Breedon on the Hill. Leics —3B 74
Breibhig. W Isl —9B 170 (on Barra)
Breibhig. W Isl —4G 171 (on Lewis)
Breich. W Lot —3C 128
Breightmet. G Man —4F 91
Breighton. E Yor —1H 93
Breinton. Here —2H 47
Breinton Common. Here —2H 47
Breiwick. Shet —7F 173
Brelston Green. Here —3A 48
Bremhill. Wilts —4E 35
Brenachie. High —1B 158
Brenchley. Kent —1A 28
Brendon. Devn —2A 20
Brent Cross. G Lon —2D 38
Brent Eleigh. Suff —1C 54
Brentford. G Lon —3C 38
Brentingby. Leics —4E 75
Brent Knoll. Som —1G 21
Brent Pelham. Herts —2E 53
Brentwood. Essx —1H 39
Brenzett. Kent —3E 28
Brereton. Staf —4E 73
Brereton Cross. Staf —4E 73
Brereton Green. Ches —4B 84
Brereton Heath. Ches —4C 84
Bressingham. Norf —2C 66
Bressingham Steam Experience —3C 66
Bretby. Derbs —3G 73
Bretford. Warw —3B 62
Bretforton. Worc —1F 49
Bretherdale Head. Cumb —4G 103
Bretherton. Lanc —2C 90
Brettabister. Shet —6F 173
Brettenham. Norf —2B 66
Brettenham. Suff —5B 66
Bretton. Flin —4F 83
Brewer Street. Surr —5E 39
Brewlands Bridge. Ang —2A 144
Brewood. Staf —5C 72
Briantspuddle. Dors —3D 14
Bricket Wood. Herts —5B 52
Bricklehampton. Worc —1E 49
Bride. IOM —1D 108
Bridekirk. Cumb —1C 102
Bridell. Pemb —1B 44
Bridestowe. Devn —4F 11
Brideswell. Abers —5C 160
Bridford. Devn —4B 12
Bridfordmills. Devn —4B 12
Bridge. Corn —4A 6
Bridge. Kent —5F 41
Bridge End. Beds —5H 63
Bridge End. Cumb —5D 102
Bridge End. Linc —2A 76
Bridge End. Shet —8E 173
Bridgefoot. Ang —5C 144
Bridgefoot. Cumb —2B 102
Bridge Green. Essx —2E 53
Bridgehampton. Som —4A 22
Bridge Hewick. N Yor —2F 99
Bridgehill. Dur —4D 115
Bridgemary. Hants —2D 16
Bridgemere. Ches —1B 72
Bridgemont. Derbs —2E 85
Bridgend. Abers —5C 160 (nr. Huntly)
Bridgend. Abers —5H 161 (nr. Peterhead)
Bridgend. Ang —2E 145 (nr. Brechin)
Bridgend. Ang —4C 144 (nr. Kirriemuir)
Bridgend. Arg —4F 133 (nr. Lochgilphead)
Bridgend. Arg —3B 124 (on Islay)
Bridgend. B'end —3C 32
Bridgend. Cumb —3F 103
Bridgend. Devn —4B 8
Bridgend. Fife —2F 137
Bridgend. High —3F 157
Bridgend. Mor —5A 160
Bridgend. Per —1D 136
Bridgend. W Lot —2D 128
Bridgend of Lintrathen. Ang —3B 144
Bridgeness. Falk —1D 128
Bridge of Alford. Abers —2C 152
Bridge of Allan. Stir —4G 135
Bridge of Avon. Mor —5F 159
Bridge of Awe. Arg —1H 133
Bridge of Balgie. Per —4C 142
Bridge of Brown. High —1F 151
Bridge of Cally. Per —3A 144
Bridge of Canny. Abers —4D 152
Bridge of Dee. Dum —4E 111
Bridge of Don. Aber —2G 153
Bridge of Dun. Ang —3F 145
Bridge of Dye. Abers —5D 152
Bridge of Earn. Per —2D 136
Bridge of Ericht. Per —3C 142
Bridge of Feugh. Abers —4E 152
Bridge of Forss. High —2C 168
Bridge of Gairn. Abers —4A 152
Bridge of Gaur. Per —3C 142
Bridge of Muchalls. Abers —4F 153
Bridge of Oich. High —3F 149
Bridge of Orchy. Arg —5G 141
Bridge of Walls. Shet —6D 173
Bridge of Weir. Ren —3E 127
Bridge Reeve. Devn —1G 11
Bridgerule. Devn —2C 10
Bridge Sollers. Here —1H 47
Bridge Street. Suff —1B 54
Bridgetown. Devn —2E 9
Bridgetown. Som —3C 20
Bridge Town. Warw —5G 61
Bridge Trafford. Ches —3G 83
Bridgeyate. S Glo —4B 34
Bridgham. Norf —2B 66
Bridgnorth. Shrp —1B 60
Bridgtown. Staf —5D 73
Bridgwater. Som —3G 21
Bridister. Shet —6D 173
Bridlington. E Yor —3F 101
Bridport. Dors —3H 13
Bridstow. Here —3A 48
Brierfield. Lanc —1G 91
Brierley. Glos —4B 48
Brierley. Here —5G 59
Brierley. S Yor —3E 93
Brierley Hill. W Mid —2D 60
Brierton. Hart —1B 106
Briestfield. W Yor —3C 92
Brigg. N Lin —4D 94
Briggate. Norf —3F 79
Briggswath. N Yor —4F 107
Brigham. Cumb —1B 102
Brigham. E Yor —4E 101
Brighouse. W Yor —2B 92
Brighstone. IOW —4C 16
Brightgate. Derbs —5G 85
Brighthampton. Oxon —5B 50
Brightholmlee. S Yor —1G 85
Brightley. Devn —3G 11
Brightling. E Sus —3A 28
Brightlingsea. Essx —4D 54
Brighton. Brig —5E 27 & 186
Brighton. Corn —3D 6
Brighton Hill. Hants —2E 24
Brightons. Falk —2C 128
Brighton Sea Life Centre —186
Brightwalton. W Ber —4C 36
Brightwalton Green. W Ber —4C 36
Brightwell. Suff —1F 55
Brightwell Baldwin. Oxon —2E 37
Brightwell-cum-Sotwell. Oxon —2D 36
Brigmerston. Wilts —2G 23
Brignall. Dur —3D 104
Brig o'Turk. Stir —3E 135
Brigsley. NE Lin —4F 95
Brigsteer. Cumb —1D 97
Brigstock. Nptn —2G 63
Brill. Buck —4E 51
Brill. Corn —4E 5
Brilley. Here —1F 47
Brimaston. Pemb —2D 42
Brimfield. Here —4H 59
Brimham Rocks NT —3E 98
Brimington. Derbs —3B 86
Brimpsfield. Glos —4E 49
Brimpton. W Ber —5D 36
Brims. Orkn —9B 172
Brimscombe. Glos —5D 48
Brimstage. Mers —2F 83
Brincliffe. S Yor —2H 85
Brind. E Yor —1H 93
Brindister. Shet —8F 173
Brindle. Lanc —2E 90
Brindley Ford. Stoke —5C 84
Brineton. Staf —4C 72
Bringhurst. Leics —1F 63
Brington. Cambs —3H 63
Brinian. Orkn —5D 172
Briningham. Norf —2C 78
Brinkburn Priory EH —5F 121
Brinkhill. Linc —3C 88
Brinkley. Cambs —5F 65
Brinklow. Warw —3B 62
Brinkworth. Wilts —3F 35
Brinscall. Lanc —2E 91
Brinscombe. Som —1H 21
Brinsley. Notts —1B 74
Brinsty Common. Here —5A 60
Brinsworth. S Yor —2B 86
Brinton. Norf —2C 78
Brisco. Cumb —4F 113
Brisley. Norf —3B 78
Brislington. Bris —4B 34
Brissenden Green. Kent —2D 28
Bristol. Bris —4A 34 & 187
Bristol Cathedral —187
Bristol International Airport. N Som —5A 34
Bristol Zoo —187
Briston. Norf —2C 78
Britannia. Lanc —2G 91
Britannia, Royal Yacht —2F 129
Britford. Wilts —4G 23
Brithdir. Cphy —5E 47
Brithdir. Cdgn —1D 44
Brithdir. Gwyn —4G 69
British Empire Mus. —Bristol 187
British Golf Mus. —2H 137
British Mus. —London 193
Briton Ferry. Neat —3G 31
Britwell Salome. Oxon —2E 37
Brixham. Torb —3F 9
Brixton. Devn —3B 8
Brixton. G Lon —3E 39
Brixton Deverill. Wilts —3D 22
Brixworth. Nptn —3E 63
Brize Norton. Oxon —5A 50
Broad Alley. Worc —4C 60
Broad Blunsdon. Swin —2G 35
Broadbottom. G Man —1D 85
Broadbridge. W Sus —2G 17
Broadbridge Heath. W Sus —2C 26
Broad Campden. Glos —2G 49
Broad Chalke. Wilts —4F 23
Broadclyst. Devn —3C 12
Broadfield. Inv —2E 127
Broadfield. Pemb —4F 43
Broadfield. W Sus —2D 26
Broadford. High —1E 147
Broadford Bridge. W Sus —3B 26
Broad Green. Beds —1H 51
Broad Green. Cambs —5F 65
Broad Green. Worc —3D 61 (nr. Bromsgrove)
Broad Green. Worc —5B 60 (nr. Worcester)
Broadhaven. High —3F 169
Broad Haven. Pemb —3C 42
Broadheath. G Man —2B 84
Broad Heath. Staf —3C 72
Broadheath. Worc —4A 60
Broadhembury. Devn —2E 12
Broadhempston. Devn —2E 9
Broad Hill. Cambs —3E 65
Broad Hinton. Wilts —4G 35
Broadholm. Derbs —1A 74
Broadholme. Linc —3F 87
Broadlands —4B 24
Broadlay. Carm —5D 44
Broad Laying. Hants —5C 36
Broadley. Lanc —3G 91
Broadley. Mor —2A 160
Broadley Common. Essx —5E 53
Broad Marston. Worc —1G 49
Broadmayne. Dors —4C 14
Broadmere. Hants —2E 24
Broadmoor. Pemb —4E 43
Broad Oak. Carm —3F 45
Broad Oak. Cumb —5C 102
Broad Oak. Devn —3D 12
Broadoak. Dors —3H 13
Broad Oak. E Sus —4C 28 (nr. Hastings)
Broad Oak. E Sus —3H 27 (nr. Heathfield)
Broadoak. Glos —4B 48
Broadoak. Hants —1D 16
Broad Oak. Here —3H 47
Broad Oak. Kent —4F 41
Broadrashes. Mor —3B 160
Broadsea. Abers —2G 161
Broad's Green. Essx —4G 53
Broadshard. Som —1H 13
Broadstairs. Kent —4H 41
Broads, The —4F 79
Broadstone. Pool —3F 15
Broadstone. Shrp —2H 59
Broad Street. Kent —1F 29 (nr. Ashford)
Broad Street. Kent —5C 40 (nr. Maidstone)
Broad Street Green. Essx —5B 54
Broad, The. Here —4G 59
Broad Town. Wilts —4F 35
Broadwas. Worc —5B 60
Broadwath. Cumb —4F 113
Broadway. Carm —5D 45 (nr. Kidwelly)

Broadway. Carm —3G 43 (nr. Laugharne)
Broadway. Pemb —3C 42
Broadway. Som —1G 13
Broadway. Suff —3F 67
Broadway. Worc —2G 49
Broadway Tower —2G 49
Broadwell. Glos —4A 48 (nr. Cinderford)
Broadwell. Glos —3H 49 (nr. Stow-on-the-Wold)
Broadwell. Oxon —5A 50
Broadwell. Warw —4B 62
Broadwell House. Nmbd —4C 114
Broadwey. Dors —4B 14
Broadwindsor. Dors —2H 13
Broadwoodkelly. Devn —2G 11
Broadwoodwidger. Devn —4E 11
Broallan. High —4G 157
Brobury. Here —1G 47
Brochel. High —4E 155
Brockamin. Worc —5B 60
Brockbridge. Hants —1E 16
Brockdish. Norf —3E 66
Brockencote. Worc —3C 60
Brockenhurst. Hants —2A 16
Brocketsbrae. S Lan —1H 117
Brockford Street. Suff —4D 66
Brockhall. Nptn —4D 62
Brockham. Surr —1C 26
Brockhampton. Glos —3E 49 (nr. Bishop's Cleeve)
Brockhampton. Glos —3F 49 (nr. Sevenhampton)
Brockhampton. Here —2A 48
Brockhill. Bord —2F 119
Brockhole Gdn. —4E 103
Brockholes. W Yor —3B 92
Brockhouse. S Yor —2C 86
Brockhurst. Hants —2E 16
Brocklesby. Linc —3E 95
Brockley. N Som —5H 33
Brockley. Suff —3H 65
Brockley Green. Suff —1H 53 (nr. Bury St Edmunds)
Brockley Green. Suff —5H 65 (nr. Haverhill)
Brockleymoor. Cumb —1F 103
Brockmoor. W Mid —2C 60
Brockton. Shrp —2F 59 (nr. Bishop's Castle)
Brockton. Shrp —5B 72 (nr. Madeley)
Brockton. Shrp —1H 59 (nr. Much Wenlock)
Brockton. Shrp —5F 71 (nr. Pontesbury)
Brockton. Staf —2C 72
Brockton. Telf —4B 72
Brockweir. Glos —5A 48
Brockworth. Glos —4D 49
Brocton. Staf —4D 72
Brodbury House Gdns. —1G 47
Brodick. N Ayr —2E 123
Brodick Castle NTS —2E 123
Brodie. Mor —3D 159
Brodie Castle NTS —3D 159
Brodiesord. Abers —3C 160
Brodsworth. S Yor —4F 93
Brodsworth Hall EH —4F 93
Brogaig. High —2D 154
Brogborough. Beds —2H 51
Brokenborough. Wilts —3E 35
Broken Cross. Ches —3C 84
Bromborough. Mers —2F 83
Bromdon. Shrp —2A 60
Brome. Suff —3D 66
Brome Street. Suff —3D 66
Bromeswell. Suff —5F 67
Bromfield. Cumb —5C 112
Bromfield. Shrp —3G 59
Bromford. W Mid —1F 61
Bromham. Beds —5H 63
Bromham. Wilts —5E 35
Bromley. G Lon —4F 39
Bromley. Herts —3E 53
Bromley. Shrp —1B 60
Bromley Cross. G Man —3F 91
Bromley Green. Kent —2D 28
Bromley Wood. Staf —3F 73
Brompton. Medw —4B 40
Brompton. N Yor —5A 106 (nr. Northallerton)
Brompton. N Yor —1D 100 (nr. Scarborough)
Brompton. Shrp —5H 71
Brompton-on-Swale. N Yor —5F 105
Brompton Ralph. Som —3D 20
Brompton Regis. Som —3C 20
Bromsash. Here —3B 48
Bromsberrow. Glos —2C 48
Bromsberrow Heath. Glos —2C 48
Bromsgrove. Worc —3D 60
Bromstead Heath. Staf —4B 72
Bromyard. Here —5A 60
Bromyard Downs. Here —5A 60
Bronaber. Gwyn —2G 69
Broncroft. Shrp —2H 59
Brongest. Cdgn —1D 44
Brongwyn. Cdgn —1C 44
Bronington. Wrex —2G 71
Bronllys. Powy —2E 47
Bronllys Castle —2E 47
Bronnant. Cdgn —4F 57
Bronte Parsonage —1A 92
Bronwydd Arms. Carm —3E 45
Bronydd. Powy —1F 47
Bronygarth. Shrp —2E 71
Brook. Carm —4G 43
Brook. Devn —5E 11
Brook. Hants —1A 16 (nr. Cadnam)
Brook. Hants —4B 24 (nr. Romsey)
Brook. IOW —4B 16
Brook. Kent —1E 29
Brook. Surr —1B 26 (nr. Guildford)
Brook. Surr —2A 26 (nr. Haslemere)
Brooke. Norf —1E 67
Brooke. Rut —5F 75
Brookend. Glos —5B 48
Brook End. Worc —1D 48
Brookfield. Lanc —1D 90
Brookfield. Ren —3F 127
Brookhouse. Lanc —3E 97
Brookhouse Green. Ches —4C 84
Brookhouses. Staf —1D 73
Brookhurst. Mers —2F 83
Brookland. Kent —3D 28
Brooklands. G Man —1B 84
Brooklands. Shrp —1H 71
Brookmans Park. Herts —5C 52
Brooks. Powy —1D 58
Brooksby. Leics —4D 74
Brooks Green. W Sus —3C 26
Brook Street. Essx —1G 39
Brook Street. Kent —2D 28
Brook Street. W Sus —3E 27
Brookthorpe. Glos —4D 48
Brookville. Norf —1G 65
Brookwood. Surr —5A 38
Broom. Beds —1B 52
Broom. Fife —3F 137
Broom. Warw —5E 61
Broome. Norf —1F 67
Broome. Shrp —1H 59 (nr. Cardington)
Broome. Shrp —2G 59 (nr. Craven Arms)
Broome. Worc —3D 60
Broomedge. Warr —2B 84
Broomend. Abers —2E 153
Broome Park. Nmbd —3F 121
Broomer's Corner. W Sus —3C 26
Broomfield. Abers —5G 161
Broomfield. Essx —4H 53
Broomfield. Kent —4F 41 (nr. Herne Bay)
Broomfield. Kent —5C 40 (nr. Maidstone)
Broomfield. Som —3F 21
Broomfleet. E Yor —2B 94
Broom Green. Norf —3B 78
Broomhall. Wind —4A 38
Broomhaugh. Nmbd —3D 114
Broomhill. Bris —4B 34
Broom Hill. Dors —2F 15
Broomhill. High —1D 151 (nr. Grantown-on-Spey)
Broomhill. High —1B 158 (nr. Invergordon)
Broomhill. Norf —5F 77
Broomhill. Nmbd —4G 121
Broom Hill. S Yor —4E 93
Broom Hill. Worc —3D 60
Broomhillbank. Dum —5D 118
Broomholm. Norf —2F 79
Broomlands. Dum —4C 118
Broomley. Nmbd —3D 114
Broom of Moy. Mor —3E 159
Broompark. Dur —5F 115
Broom's Green. Glos —2C 48
Brora. High —3G 165
Broseley. Shrp —5A 72
Brotherhouse Bar. Linc —4B 76
Brotheridge Green. Worc —1D 48
Brotherlee. Dur —1C 104
Brothertoft. Linc —1B 76
Brotherton. N Yor —2E 93
Brotton. Red C —2D 107
Broubster. High —2C 168
Brough. Cumb —3A 104
Brough. Derbs —2F 85
Brough. E Yor —2C 94
Brough. High —1E 169
Brough. Notts —5F 87
Brough. Orkn —6C 172 (nr. Finstown)
Brough. Orkn —9D 172 (nr. St Margaret's Hope)
Brough. Shet —6F 173 (nr. Benston)
Brough. Shet —4F 173 (nr. Boath of Toft)
Brough. Shet —7G 173 (on Bressay)
Brough. Shet —5G 173 (on Whalsay)
Broughall. Shrp —1H 71
Brougham. Cumb —2G 103
Brough Lodge. Shet —2G 173
Brough Sowerby. Cumb —3A 104
Broughton. Cambs —3B 64
Broughton. Flin —4F 83
Broughton. Hants —3B 24
Broughton. Lanc —1D 90
Broughton. Mil —2G 51
Broughton. Nptn —3F 63
Broughton. N Lin —4C 94
Broughton. N Yor —2B 100 (nr. Malton)
Broughton. N Yor —4B 98 (nr. Skipton)
Broughton. Oxon —2C 50
Broughton. Bord —1D 118
Broughton. Staf —2B 72
Broughton. V Glam —4C 32
Broughton Astley. Leics —1C 62
Broughton Beck. Cumb —1B 96
Broughton Castle EH —2C 50
Broughton Cross. Cumb —1B 102
Broughton Gifford. Wilts —5D 35
Broughton Green. Worc —4D 60
Broughton Hackett. Worc —5D 60
Broughton in Furness. Cumb —1B 96
Broughton Mills. Cumb —5D 102
Broughton Moor. Cumb —1B 102
Broughton Park. G Man —4G 91
Broughton Poggs. Oxon —5H 49
Broughtown. Orkn —3F 172
Broughty Ferry. D'dee —5D 144
Brownber. Cumb —4A 104
Brownbread Street. E Sus —4A 28
Brown Candover. Hants —3D 24
Brown Edge. Lanc —3B 90
Brown Edge. Staf —5D 84
Brownhill. Bkbn —1E 91
Brownhill. Shrp —3G 71
Brownhills. Shrp —2A 72
Brownhills. W Mid —5E 73
Brown Knowl. Ches —5G 83
Brownlow. Ches —4C 84
Brownlow Heath. Ches —4C 84
Brownsea Island NT —4F 15
Brown's Green. W Mid —1E 61
Brownshill. Glos —5D 49
Brownston. Devn —3C 8
Brownstone. Devn —2A 12
Browston Green. Norf —5G 79
Broxa. N Yor —5G 107
Broxbourne. Herts —5D 52
Broxburn. E Lot —2C 130
Broxburn. W Lot —2D 129
Broxholme. Linc —3G 87
Broxted. Essx —3F 53
Broxton. Ches —5G 83
Broxwood. Here —5F 59
Broyle Side. E Sus —4F 27
Bru. W Isl —3F 171
Bruach Mairi. W Isl —4G 171
Bruairnis. W Isl —8C 170
Bruan. High —5F 169
Bruar Lodge. Per —1F 143
Brucehill. W Dun —2E 127
Brucklay. Abers —3G 161
Bruera. Ches —4G 83
Bruern Abbey. Oxon —3A 50
Bruichladdich. Arg —3A 124
Bruisyard. Suff —4F 67
Bruisyard Street. Suff —4F 67
Brumby. N Lin —4B 94
Brund. Staf —4F 85
Brundall. Norf —5F 79
Brundish. Norf —1F 67
Brundish. Suff —4E 67
Brundish Street. Suff —3E 67
Brunery. High —1B 140
Brunswick Village. Tyne —2F 115
Brunthwaite. W Yor —5C 98
Bruntingthorpe. Leics —1D 62
Brunton. Fife —1F 137
Brunton. Nmbd —2G 121
Brunton. Wilts —1H 23
Brushford. Devn —2G 11
Brushford. Som —4C 20
Brusta. W Isl —1E 170
Bruton. Som —3B 22
Bryanston. Dors —2D 14
Bryant's Bottom. Buck —2G 37
Brydekirk. Dum —2C 112
Brymbo. Cnwy —3H 81
Brymbo. Wrex —5E 83
Brympton. Som —1A 14
Bryn. Carm —5F 45
Bryn. G Man —4D 90
Bryn. Neat —2B 32
Bryn. Shrp —2E 59
Brynamman. Carm —4H 45
Brynberian. Pemb —1F 43
Brynbryddan. Neat —2A 32
Bryncae. Rhon —3C 32
Bryncethin. B'end —3C 32
Bryncir. Gwyn —1D 69
Bryn-coch. Neat —3G 31
Bryncroes. Gwyn —2B 68
Bryncrug. Gwyn —5F 69
Bryn Du. IOA —3C 80
Bryn Eden. Gwyn —3G 69
Bryneglwys. Den —1D 70
Bryn Eglwys. Gwyn —4F 81
Brynford. Flin —3D 82
Bryn Gates. G Man —4D 90
Bryn Golau. Rhon —3D 32
Bryngwran. IOA —3C 80
Bryngwyn. Mon —5G 47
Bryngwyn. Powy —1E 47
Bryn-henllan. Pemb —1E 43
Brynhoffnant. Cdgn —5C 56
Bryn-llwyn. Flin —2C 82
Brynllywarch. Powy —2D 58
Bryn-mawr. Blae —4E 47
Bryn-mawr. Gwyn —2B 68
Brynmenyn. B'end —3C 32
Brynmill. Swan —3F 31
Brynna. Rhon —3C 32
Brynrefail. Gwyn —4E 81
Brynrefail. IOA —2D 81
Brynsadler. Rhon —3D 32
Bryn-Saith Marchog. Den —5C 82
Brynsiencyn. IOA —4D 81
Brynteg. IOA —2D 81
Brynteg. Wrex —5F 83
Brynygwenyn. Mon —4G 47
Bryn-y-maen. Cnwy —3H 81
Buaile nam Bodach. W Isl —8C 170
Bualintur. High —1C 146
Bubbenhall. Warw —3A 62
Bubwith. E Yor —1H 93
Buccleuch. Bord —3F 119
Buchanan Smithy. Stir —1F 127
Buchanhaven. Abers —4H 161
Buchanty. Per —1B 136
Buchany. Stir —3G 135
Buchley. E Dun —2G 127
Buchlyvie. Stir —4E 135
Buckabank. Cumb —5E 113
Buckden. Cambs —4A 64
Buckden. N Yor —2B 98
Buckenham. Norf —5F 79
Buckerell. Devn —2E 13
Buckfast. Devn —2D 8
Buckfast Abbey —2D 8
Buckfastleigh. Devn —2D 8
Buckhaven. Fife —4F 137
Buckholm. Bord —1G 119
Buckholt. Here —4A 48
Buckhorn Weston. Dors —4C 22
Buckhurst Hill. Essx —1F 39
Buckie. Mor —2B 160
Buckingham. Buck —2E 51
Buckingham Palace —London 192
Buckland. Buck —4G 51
Buckland. Devn —4C 8
Buckland. Glos —2F 49
Buckland. Here —5H 59
Buckland. Herts —2D 52
Buckland. Kent —1H 29
Buckland. Oxon —2B 36
Buckland. Surr —5D 38
Buckland Abbey NT —2A 8
Buckland Brewer. Devn —4E 19
Buckland Common. Buck —5H 51
Buckland Dinham. Som —1C 22
Buckland Filleigh. Devn —2E 11
Buckland in the Moor. Devn —5H 11
Buckland Monachorum. Devn —2A 8
Buckland Newton. Dors —2B 14
Buckland Ripers. Dors —4B 14
Buckland St Mary. Som —1F 13
Buckland-tout-Saints. Devn —4D 8
Bucklebury. W Ber —4D 36
Bucklegate. Linc —2C 76
Buckleigh. Devn —4E 19
Bucklers Hard. Hants —3C 16
Bucklesham. Suff —1F 55
Buckley. Flin —4E 83
Buckley Green. Warw —4F 61
Buckley Hill. Mers —1F 83
Bucklow Hill. Ches —2B 84
Buckminster. Leics —3F 75
Bucknall. Linc —4A 88
Bucknall. Stoke —1D 72
Bucknell. Oxon —3D 50
Bucknell. Shrp —3F 59
Buckpool. Mor —2B 160
Bucksburn. Aber —3F 153
Buck's Cross. Devn —4D 18
Bucks Green. W Sus —2B 26
Buckshaw. Lanc —2D 90
Bucks Hill. Herts —5A 52
Bucks Horn Oak. Hants —2G 25
Buck's Mills. Devn —4D 18
Buckton. E Yor —2F 101
Buckton. Here —3F 59
Buckton. Nmbd —1E 121
Buckton Vale. G Man —4H 91
Buckworth. Cambs —3A 64
Budby. Notts —4D 86
Bude. Corn —2C 10
Budge's Shop. Corn —3H 7
Budlake. Devn —2C 12
Budle. Nmbd —1F 121
Budleigh Salterton. Devn —4D 12
Budock Water. Corn —5B 6
Buerton. Ches —1A 72
Buffler's Holt. Buck —2E 51
Bugbrooke. Nptn —5D 62
Buglawton. Ches —4C 84
Bugle. Corn —3E 6
Bugthorpe. E Yor —4B 100
Buildwas. Shrp —5A 72
Buildwas Abbey EH —5A 72
Builth Road. Powy —5C 58
Builth Wells. Powy —5C 58
Bulbourne. Herts —4H 51
Bulby. Linc —3H 75
Bulcote. Notts —1D 74
Buldoo. High —2C 168
Bulford. Wilts —2G 23
Bulford Camp. Wilts —2G 23
Bulkeley. Ches —5H 83
Bulkington. Warw —2A 62
Bulkington. Wilts —1E 23
Bulkworthy. Devn —1D 11
Bullamoor. N Yor —5A 106
Bull Bay. IOA —1D 80
Bullbridge. Derbs —5A 86
Bullgill. Cumb —1B 102
Bull Hill. Hants —3B 16
Bullinghope. Here —2A 48
Bull's Green. Herts —4C 52
Bullwood. Arg —2C 126
Bulmer. Essx —1B 54
Bulmer. N Yor —3A 100
Bulmer Tye. Essx —2B 54
Bulphan. Thur —2H 39
Bulverhythe. E Sus —5B 28
Bulwark. Abers —4G 161
Bulwell. Nott —1C 74
Bulwick. Nptn —1G 63
Bumble's Green. Essx —5E 53
Bun Abhainn Eadarra. W Isl —7D 171
Bunacaimb. High —5E 147
Bun a Mhuillinn. W Isl —7C 170
Bunarkaig. High —5D 148
Bunbury. Ches —5H 83
Bunchrew. High —4A 158
Bundalloch. High —1A 148
Buness. Shet —1H 173
Bunessan. Arg —1A 132
Bungay. Suff —2F 67
Bungay Castle —2F 67
Bunkegivie. High —2H 149
Bunker's Hill. Cambs —5D 76
Bunkers Hill. Linc —5B 88
Bunker's Hill. Suff —5H 79
Bunloit. High —1H 149
Bunnahabhain. Arg —2C 124
Bunny. Notts —3C 74
Bunoich. High —3F 149
Bunree. High —2E 141
Bunroy. High —5E 149
Buntait. High —5F 157
Buntingford. Herts —3D 52
Buntings Green. Essx —2B 54
Bunwell. Norf —1D 66
Burbage. Derbs —3E 85
Burbage. Leics —1B 62
Burbage. Wilts —5H 35
Burcher. Here —4F 59
Burchett's Green. Wind —3G 37
Burcombe. Wilts —3F 23
Burcot. Oxon —2D 36
Burcote. Shrp —1B 60
Burcott. Buck —3G 51
Burcott. Som —2A 22
Burdale. N Yor —3C 100
Burdrop. Oxon —2B 50
Bures. Suff —2C 54
Bure Valley Railway —3E 79
Burford. Oxon —4A 50
Burford. Shrp —4H 59
Burf, The. Worc —4C 60
Burg. Arg —4E 139
Burgate Great Green. Suff —3C 66
Burgate Little Green. Suff —3C 66
Burgess Hill. W Sus —4E 27
Burgh. Suff —5E 67
Burgh by Sands. Cumb —4E 113
Burgh Castle. Norf —5G 79
Burghclere. Hants —5C 36
Burghead. Mor —2F 159
Burghfield. W Ber —5E 37
Burghfield Common. W Ber —5E 37
Burghfield Hill. W Ber —5E 37
Burgh Heath. Surr —5D 38
Burghill. Here —1H 47
Burgh le Marsh. Linc —4E 89
Burghley House —5H 75
Burgh Muir. Abers —2E 153
Burgh next Aylsham. Norf —3E 78
Burgh on Bain. Linc —2B 88
Burgh St Margaret. Norf —4G 79
Burgh St Peter. Norf —1G 67
Burghwallis. S Yor —3F 93
Burgie. Mor —3E 159
Burham. Kent —4B 40
Buriton. Hants —4F 25
Burland. Ches —5A 84
Burland. Shet —8E 173
Burlawn. Corn —2D 6
Burleigh. Brac —3A 38
Burleigh. Glos —5D 48
Burlescombe. Devn —1D 12
Burleston. Dors —3C 14
Burlestone. Devn —4E 9
Burley. Hants —2H 15
Burley. Rut —4F 75
Burley. W Yor —1C 92
Burley Gate. Here —1A 48
Burley in Wharfedale. W Yor —5D 98
Burley Street. Hants —2H 15
Burley Woodhead. W Yor —5D 98
Burlingjobb. Powy —5E 59
Burlton. Shrp —3G 71
Burmantofts. W Yor —1D 92
Burmarsh. Kent —2F 29
Burmington. Warw —2A 50
Burn. N Yor —2F 93
Burnage. G Man —1C 84
Burnaston. Derbs —2G 73
Burnbanks. Cumb —3G 103
Burnby. E Yor —5C 100
Burnby Hall Gdns. —5C 100
Burncross. S Yor —1H 85
Burneside. Cumb —5G 103
Burness. Orkn —3F 172
Burneston. N Yor —1F 99
Burnett. Bath —5B 34
Burnfoot. E Ayr —3D 116
Burnfoot. Per —3B 136
Burnfoot. Bord —3H 119 (nr. Hawick)
Burnfoot. Bord —3G 119 (nr. Roberton)
Burngreave. S Yor —2A 86
Burnham. Buck —2A 38
Burnham. N Lin —3D 94
Burnham Deepdale. Norf —1H 77
Burnham Green. Herts —4C 52
Burnham Market. Norf —1H 77
Burnham Norton. Norf —1H 77
Burnham-on-Crouch. Essx —1D 40
Burnham-on-Sea. Som —2G 21
Burnham Overy Staithe. Norf —1H 77
Burnham Overy Town. Norf —1H 77
Burnham Thorpe. Norf —1A 78
Burnhaven. Abers —4H 161
Burnhead. Dum —5A 118
Burnhervie. Abers —2E 153
Burnhill Green. Staf —5B 72
Burnhope. Dur —5E 115
Burnhouse. N Ayr —4E 127
Burniston. N Yor —5H 107
Burnlee. W Yor —4B 92
Burnley. Lanc —1G 91
Burnleydam. Wrex —1A 72
Burnmouth. Bord —3F 131
Burn Naze. Lanc —5C 96
Burn of Cambus. Stir —3G 135
Burnopfield. Dur —4E 115
Burnsall. N Yor —3C 98
Burns Centre —Dumfries 188
Burns Cottage & Birthplace Mus. —3C 116
Burns House Mus. —2D 117
Burnside. Ang —3E 145
Burnside. E Ayr —3E 117
Burnside. Per —3D 136
Burnside. Shet —4D 173
Burnside. S Lan —4H 127
Burnside. W Lot —2D 129 (nr. Broxburn)
Burnside. W Lot —2D 128 (nr. Winchburgh)
Burntcommon. Surr —5B 38
Burntheath. Derbs —2G 73

Burnt Heath. Essx —3D 54
Burnt Hill. W Ber —4D 36
Burnt Houses. Dur —2E 105
Burntisland. Fife —1F 129
Burnt Oak. G Lon —1D 38
Burnton. E Ayr —4D 117
Burntstalk. Norf —2G 77
Burntwood. Staf —5E 73
Burntwood Green. Staf —5E 73
Burnt Yates. N Yor —3E 99
Burnwynd. Edin —3E 129
Burpham. Surr —5B 38
Burpham. W Sus —5B 26
Burradon. Nmbd —4D 121
Burradon. Tyne —2F 115
Burrafirth. Shet —1H 173
Burragarth. Shet —1G 173
Burras. Corn —5A 6
Burraton. Corn —3A 8
Burravoe. Shet —3E 173
(nr. North Roe)
Burravoe. Shet —5E 173
(on Mainland)
Burravoe. Shet —4G 173
(on Yell)
Burray Village. Orkn —8D 172
Burrell Collection,
see Pollock House and Estate —3G 127
Burrells. Cumb —3H 103
Burrelton. Per —5A 144
Burridge. Devn —2G 13
Burridge. Hants —1D 16
Burrigill. High —5E 169
Burrill. N Yor —1E 99
Burringham. N Lin —4B 94
Burrington. Devn —1G 11
Burrington. Here —3G 59
Burrington. N Som —1H 21
Burrough End. Cambs —5F 65
Burrough Green. Cambs —5F 65
Burrough on the Hill. Leics —4E 75
Burroughston. Orkn —5E 172
Burrow. Devn —4D 12
Burrow. Som —2C 20
Burrowbridge. Som —4G 21
Burrowhill. Surr —4A 38
Burry. Swan —3D 30
Burry Green. Swan —3D 30
Burry Port. Carm —5E 45
Burscough. Lanc —3C 90
Burscough Bridge. Lanc —3C 90
Bursea. E Yor —1B 94
Burshill. E Yor —5E 101
Bursledon. Hants —2C 16
Burslem. Stoke —1C 72
Burstall. Suff —1D 54
Burstock. Dors —2H 13
Burston. Devn —2H 11
Burston. Norf —2D 66
Burston. Staf —2D 72
Burstow. Surr —1E 27
Burstwick. E Yor —2F 95
Burtersett. N Yor —1A 98
Burtholme. Cumb —3G 113
Burthorpe. Suff —4G 65
Burthwaite. Cumb —5F 113
Burtle. Som —2H 21
Burtoft. Linc —2B 76
Burton. Ches —4H 83
(nr. Kelsall)
Burton. Ches —3F 83
(nr. Neston)
Burton. Dors —3G 15
(nr. Christchurch)
Burton. Dors —3B 14
(nr. Dorchester)
Burton. Linc —3G 87
Burton. Nmbd —1F 121
Burton. Pemb —4D 43
Burton. Som —2E 21
Burton. Wilts —4D 34
(nr. Chippenham)
Burton. Wilts —3D 22
(nr. Warminster)
Burton. Wrex —5F 83
Burton Agnes. E Yor —3F 101
Burton Agnes Hall EH —3F 101
Burton Bradstock. Dors —4H 13
Burton Coggles. Linc —3G 75
Burton Constable. E Yor —1E 95
Burton Constable Hall —1E 95
Burton Corner. Linc —1C 76
Burton End. Cambs —1G 53
Burton End. Essx —3F 53
Burton Fleming. E Yor —2E 101
Burton Green. W Mid —3G 61
Burton Green. Wrex —5F 83
Burton Hastings. Warw —2B 62
Burton-in-Kendal. Cumb —2E 97
Burton in Lonsdale. N Yor —2F 97
Burton Joyce. Notts —1D 74
Burton Latimer. Nptn —3G 63
Burton Lazars. Leics —4E 75
Burton Leonard. N Yor —3F 99
Burton on the Wolds. Leics —3C 74
Burton Overy. Leics —1D 62
Burton Pedwardine. Linc —1A 76
Burton Pidsea. E Yor —1F 95
Burton Salmon. N Yor —2E 93
Burton's Green. Essx —3B 54
Burton Stather. N Lin —3B 94
Burton upon Stather. N Lin —3B 94
Burton upon Trent. Staf —3G 73
Burton Wolds. Leics —3D 74
Burtonwood. Warr —1H 83
Burwardsley. Ches —5H 83
Burwarton. Shrp —2A 60
Burwash. E Sus —3A 28
Burwash Common. E Sus —3H 27
Burwash Weald. E Sus —3A 28
Burwell. Cambs —4E 65
Burwell. Linc —3C 88
Burwen. IOA —1D 80
Burwick. Orkn —9D 172
Bury. Cambs —2B 64
Bury. G Man —3G 91
Bury. Som —4C 20
Bury. W Sus —4B 26
Bury End. Worc —2F 49
Bury Green. Herts —3E 53
Bury Hill. S Glo —3C 34
Bury St Edmunds. Suff —4A 66
Bury St Edmunds Abbey EH —4A 66
Burythorpe. N Yor —3B 100
Busbridge. Surr —1A 26
Busby. E Ren —4G 127
Busby. Per —1C 136
Buscot. Oxon —2H 35
Buscott House NT —2H 35
Bush. Corn —2C 10
Bush Bank. Here —5G 59
Bushbury. W Mid —5D 72
Bushby. Leics —5D 74
Bushey. Dors —4E 15
Bushey. Herts —1C 38
Bushey Heath. Herts —1C 38
Bush Green. Norf —1C 66
(nr. Attleborough)
Bush Green. Norf —2E 66
(nr. Harleston)
Bush Green. Suff —5B 66
Bushley. Worc —2D 49
Bushley Green. Worc —2D 48
Bushmead. Beds —4A 64
Bushmoor. Shrp —2G 59
Bushton. Wilts —4F 35
Bushy Common. Norf —4B 78
Busk. Cumb —5H 113
Buslingthorpe. Linc —2H 87
Bussage. Glos —5D 49
Bussex. Som —3G 21
Busta. Shet —5E 173
Bustard Green. Essx —3G 53
Butcher's Cross. E Sus —3G 27
Butcombe. N Som —5A 34
Bute Town. Cphy —5E 46
Butleigh. Som —3A 22
Butleigh Wootton. Som —3A 22
Butlers Marston. Warw —5H 61
Butley. Suff —5F 67
Butley High Corner. Suff —1G 55
Butterburn. Cumb —2H 113
Buttercrambe. N Yor —4B 100
Butterknowle. Dur —2E 105
Butterleigh. Devn —2C 12
Buttermere. Cumb —3C 102
Buttermere. Wilts —5B 36
Buttershaw. W Yor —2B 92
Butterstone. Per —4H 143
Butterton. Staf —5E 85
(nr. Leek)
Butterton. Staf —1C 72
(nr. Stoke-on-Trent)
Butterwick. Dur —2A 106
Butterwick. Linc —1C 76
Butterwick. N Yor —2B 100
(nr. Malton)
Butterwick. N Yor —2D 101
(nr. Weaverthorpe)
Butteryhaugh. Nmbd —5A 120
Butt Green. Ches —5A 84
Buttington. Powy —5E 71
Buttonbridge. Shrp —3B 60
Buttonoak. Shrp —3B 60
Buttsash. Hants —2C 16
Butt's Green. Essx —5A 54
Butt Yeats. Lanc —3E 97
Buxhall. Suff —5C 66
Buxted. E Sus —3F 27
Buxton. Derbs —3E 85
Buxton. Norf —3E 79
Buxton Pavillion Gdn. —3E 85
Buxworth. Derbs —2E 85
Bwcle. Flin —4E 83
Bwlch. Powy —3E 47
Bwlchderwin. Gwyn —1D 68
Bwlchgwyn. Wrex —5E 83
Bwlch-Llan. Cdgn —5E 57
Bwlchnewydd. Carm —3D 44
Bwlchtocyn. Gwyn —3C 68
Bwlch-y-cibau. Powy —4D 70
Bwlchyddar. Powy —3D 70
Bwlch-y-fadfa. Cdgn —1E 45
Bwlch-y-ffridd. Powy —1C 58
Bwlch y Garreg. Powy —1C 58
Bwlch-y-groes. Pemb —1G 43
Bwlch-yr-haiarn. Cnwy —5G 81
Bwlch-y-sarnau. Powy —3C 58
Bybrook. Kent —1E 28
Byermoor. Tyne —4E 115
Byers Garth. Dur —5G 115
Byers Green. Dur —1F 105
Byfield. Nptn —5C 62
Byfleet. Surr —4B 38
Byford. Here —1G 47
Bygrave. Herts —2C 52
Byker. Tyne —3F 115
Byland Abbey EH —2H 99
Byland Abbey. N Yor —2H 99
Bylchau. Cnwy —4B 82
Byley. Ches —4B 84
Bynea. Carm —3E 31
Byram. N Yor —2E 93
Byrness. Nmbd —4B 120
Bythorn. Cambs —3H 63
Byton. Here —4F 59
Bywell. Nmbd —3D 114
Byworth. W Sus —3A 26

Cabharstadh. W Isl —6F 171
Cabourne. Linc —4E 95
Cabrach. Arg —3C 124
Cabrach. Mor —1A 152
Cabus. Lanc —5D 97
Cadair Idris —4F 69
Cadbury. Devn —2C 12
Cadbury World —2E 61
Cadder. E Dun —2H 127
Caddington. Beds —4A 52
Caddonfoot. Bord —1G 119
Cadeby. Leics —5B 74
Cadeby. S Yor —4F 93
Cadeleigh. Devn —2C 12
Cade Street. E Sus —3H 27
Cadgwith. Corn —5E 5
Cadham. Fife —3E 137
Cadhay —3D 12
Cadishead. G Man —1B 84
Cadley. Lanc —1D 90
Cadley. Wilts —1H 23
(nr. Ludgershall)
Cadley. Wilts —5H 35
(nr. Marlborough)
Cadmore End. Buck —2F 37
Cadnam. Hants —1B 16
Cadney. N Lin —4D 94
Cadole. Flin —4E 82
Cadoxton-Juxta-Neath. Neat —2A 32
Cadwell. Herts —2B 52
Cadwst. Den —2C 70
Cadzow. S Lan —4A 128
Caeathro. Gwyn —4E 81
Caehopkin. Powy —4B 46
Caenby. Linc —2H 87
Caenn-na-Cleithe. W Isl —8D 171
Caerau. B'end —2B 32
Caerau. Card —4E 33
Cae'r-bont. Powy —4B 46
Cae'r-bryn. Carm —4F 45
Caerdeon. Gwyn —4F 69
Caerdydd. Card —4E 33 & Cardiff 187
Caerfarchell. Pemb —2B 42
Caerffili. Cphy —3E 33
Caerfyrddin. Carm —4E 45
Caergeiliog. IOA —3C 80
Caergwrle. Flin —5F 83
Caergybi. IOA —2B 80
Caerlaverock. Per —2A 136
Caerlaverock Castle HS —3B 112
Caerleon. Newp —2G 33
Caerleon Roman Site CADW —2G 33
Caerlleon. Carm —2G 43
Caerllion. Newp —2G 33
Caernarfon. Gwyn —4D 81
Caernarfon Castle WH CADW —4D 81
Caerphilly. Cphy —3E 33
Caerphilly Castle CADW —3E 33
Caersws. Powy —1C 58
Caerwedros. Cdgn —5C 56
Caerwent. Mon —2H 33
Caerwys. Flin —3D 82
Caigenhouses. Arg —3D 124
Caim. IOA —2F 81
Caio. Carm —2G 45
Cairinis. W Isl —2D 170
Cairisiadar. W Isl —4C 171
Cairminis. W Isl —9C 171
Cairnbaan. Arg —4F 133
Cairnbulg. Abers —2H 161
Cairncross. Ang —1D 145
Cairndow. Arg —2A 134
Cairness. Abers —2H 161
Cairneyhill. Fife —1D 128
Cairngarroch. Dum —4F 109
Cairngorms Nat. Park —3C 150
Cairnhill. Abers —5D 160
Cairnie. Abers —4B 160
Cairnorrie. Abers —4F 161
Cairnryan. Dum —3F 109
Cairston. Orkn —6B 172
Caister Castle and Car Collection —4H 79
Caister-on-Sea. Norf —4H 79
Caister St Edmund. Norf —5E 79
Caistor. Linc —4E 95
Caistron. Nmbd —4D 121
Cakebole. Worc —3C 60
Cake Street. Suff —3F 65
Calais Street. Suff —1C 54
Calanais. W Isl —4E 171
Calanais Standing Stones HS —4E 171
Calbost. W Isl —6G 171
Calbourne. IOW —4C 16
Calceby. Linc —3C 88
Calcot. Glos —4F 49
Calcot Row. W Ber —4E 37
Calcott. Kent —4F 41
Calcott. Shrp —4G 71
Caldback. Shet —1H 173
Caldbeck. Cumb —1E 102
Caldbergh. N Yor —1C 98
Caldecote. Cambs —5C 64
(nr. Cambridge)
Caldecote. Cambs —2A 64
(nr. Peterborough)
Caldecote. Herts —2C 52
Caldecote. Warw —1A 62
Caldecott. Nptn —4G 63
Caldecott. Oxon —2C 36
Caldecott. Rut —1F 63
Calderbank. N Lan —3A 128
Calder Bridge. Cumb —4B 102
Calderbrook. G Man —3H 91
Caldercruix. N Lan —3B 128
Calder Grove. W Yor —3D 92
Calder Mains. High —3C 168
Caldermill. S Lan —5H 127
Calder Vale. Lanc —5E 97
Calderwood. S Lan —4H 127
Caldescote. Nptn —5D 62
Caldey Island —5F 43
Caldicot. Mon —3H 33
Caldicot Castle —3H 33
Caldwell. N Yor —3E 105
Caldy. Mers —2E 83
Calebrack. Cumb —1E 103
Caledfwlch. Carm —3G 45
Calford Green. Suff —1G 53
Calfsound. Orkn —4E 172
Calgary. Arg —3E 139
Califer. Mor —3E 159
California. Falk —2C 128
California. Norf —4H 79
California. Suff —1E 55
Calke. Derbs —3A 74
Calke Abbey NT —3A 74
Callakille. High —3F 155
Callaly. Nmbd —4E 121
Callander. Stir —3F 135
Callaughton. Shrp —1A 60
Callendoun. Arg —1E 127
Callestick. Corn —3B 6
Calligarry. High —3E 147
Callington. Corn —2H 7
Callingwood. Staf —3F 73
Callow. Here —2H 47
Callowell. Glos —5D 48
Callow End. Worc —1D 48
Callow Hill. Wilts —3F 35
Callow Hill. Worc —3B 60
(nr. Bewdley)
Callow Hill. Worc —4E 61
(nr. Redditch)
Calmore. Hants —1B 16
Calmsden. Glos —5F 49
Calne. Wilts —4E 35
Calow. Derbs —3B 86
Calshot. Hants —2C 16
Calshot Castle EH —2C 16
Calstock. Corn —2A 8
Calstone Wellington. Wilts —5F 35
Calthorpe. Norf —2D 78
Calthorpe Street. Norf —3G 79
Calthwaite. Cumb —5F 113
Calton. N Yor —4B 98
Calton. Staf —5F 85
Calveley. Ches —5H 83
Calver. Derbs —3G 85
Calverhall. Shrp —2A 72
Calverleigh. Devn —1C 12
Calverley. W Yor —1C 92
Calvert. Buck —3E 51
Calverton. Mil —2F 51
Calverton. Notts —1D 74
Calvine. Per —2F 143
Calvo. Cumb —4C 112
Cam. Glos —2C 34
Camaghael. High —1F 141
Camas-luinie. High —1B 148
Camasnacroise. High —3C 140
Camastianavaig. High —5E 155
Camasunary. High —2D 146
Camault Muir. High —4H 157
Camb. Shet —2G 173
Camber. E Sus —4D 28
Camber Castle EH —4D 28
Camberley. Surr —5G 37
Camberwell. G Lon —3E 39
Camblesforth. N Yor —2G 93
Cambo. Nmbd —1D 114
Cambo Gdns. —2H 137
Cambois. Nmbd —1G 115
Camborne. Corn —5A 6
Cambourne. Cambs —5C 64
Cambridge. Cambs —5D 64 & 187
Cambridge. Glos —5C 48
Cambridge Airport. Cambs —5D 65
Cambridge Botanic Gdns. —187
Cambrose. Corn —4A 6
Cambus. Clac —4A 136
Cambusbarron. Stir —4G 135
Cambuskenneth. Stir —4H 135
Cambuslang. S Lan —3H 127
Cambusnethan. N Lan —4B 128
Cambus o'May. Abers —4B 152
Camden Town. G Lon —2D 39
Cameley. Bath —1B 22
Camelford. Corn —4B 10
Camelon. Falk —1B 128
Camelot Theme Park —3D 90
Camelsdale. Surr —2A 26
Camer's Green. Worc —2C 48
Camerton. Bath —1B 22
Camerton. Cumb —1B 102
Camerton. E Yor —2F 95
Camghouran. Per —3C 142
Cammachmore. Abers —4G 153
Cammeringham. Linc —2G 87
Camore. High —4E 165
Campbelton. N Ayr —4C 126
Campbeltown. Arg —3B 122
Campbeltown Airport. Arg —3A 122
Cample. Dum —5B 118
Campmuir. Per —5B 144
Campsall. S Yor —3F 93
Campsea Ashe. Suff —5F 67
Camps End. Cambs —1G 53
Camp, The. Glos —5E 49
Campton. Beds —2B 52
Camptoun. E Lot —2B 130
Camptown. Bord —3A 120
Camrose. Pemb —3D 42
Camserney. Per —4F 143
Camster. High —4E 169
Camuscross. High —2E 147
Camusdarach. High —4E 147
Camusnagaul. High —1E 141
(nr. Fort William)
Camusnagaul. High —5E 163
(nr. Loch Broom)
Camusteel. High —4G 155
Camusterrach. High —4G 155
Camusvrachan. Per —4D 142
Canada. Hants —1A 16
Canadia. E Sus —4B 28
Canaston Bridge. Pemb —3E 43
Candlesby. Linc —4D 88
Candle Street. Suff —3C 66
Candy Mill. S Lan —5D 128
Cane End. Oxon —4E 37
Canewdon. Essx —1C 40
Canford Cliffs. Pool —4F 15
Canford Magna. Pool —3F 15
Cangate. Norf —3F 79
Canham's Green. Suff —4C 66
Canholes. Derbs —3E 85
Canisbay. High —1F 169
Canley. W Mid —3H 61
Cann. Dors —4D 22
Cann Common. Dors —4D 23
Cannich. High —5F 157
Cannington. Som —3F 21
Cannock. Staf —4D 73
Cannock Chase —4D 73
Cannock Wood. Staf —4E 73
Cannons Ashby NT —5C 62
Canonbie. Dum —2E 113
Canon Bridge. Here —1H 47
Canon Frome. Here —1B 48
Canon Pyon. Here —1H 47
Canons Ashby. Nptn —5C 62
Canonstown. Corn —3C 4
Canterbury. Kent —5F 41 & 187
Canterbury Cathedral WH —187
Canterbury Tales Centre —187
Cantley. Norf —5F 79
Cantley. S Yor —4G 93
Cantlop. Shrp —5H 71
Canton. Card —4E 33
Cantray. High —4B 158
Cantraybruich. High —4B 158
Cantraywood. High —4B 158
Cantsdam. Fife —4D 136
Cantsfield. Lanc —2F 97
Canvey Island. Essx —2B 40
Canwick. Linc —4G 87
Canworthy Water. Corn —3C 10
Caol. High —1F 141
Caolas. W Isl —9B 170
Caolas Liubharsaigh. W Isl —4D 170
Caolas Scalpaigh. W Isl —8E 171
Caolas Stocinis. W Isl —8D 171
Caoles. Arg —4B 138
Caol Ila. Arg —3C 124
Capel. Kent —1H 27
Capel. Surr —1C 26
Capel Bangor. Cdgn —2F 57
Capel Betws Lleucu. Cdgn —5F 57
Capel Coch. IOA —2D 80
Capel Curig. Cnwy —5G 81
Capel Cynon. Cdgn —1D 45
Capel Dewi. Carm —3E 45
Capel Dewi. Cdgn —2F 57
(nr. Aberystwyth)
Capel Dewi. Cdgn —1E 45
(nr. Llandyssul)
Capel Garmon. Cnwy —5H 81
Capel Green. Suff —1G 55
Capel Gwyn. IOA —3C 80
Capel Gwynfe. Carm —3H 45
Capel Hendre. Carm —4F 45
Capel Isaac. Carm —3F 45
Capel Iwan. Carm —1G 43
Capel-le-Ferne. Kent —2G 29
Capel Llanilterne. Card —4D 32
Capel Mawr. IOA —3D 80
Capel Newydd. Pemb —1G 43
Capel St Andrew. Suff —1G 55
Capel St Mary. Suff —2D 54
Capel Seion. Carm —4F 45
Capel Seion. Cdgn —3F 57
Capel Uchaf. Gwyn —1D 68
Capel-y-ffin. Powy —2F 47
Capenhurst. Ches —3F 83
Capernwray. Lanc —2E 97
Capesthorne Hall —3C 84
Capheaton. Nmbd —1D 114
Cappercleuch. Bord —2E 119
Capplegill. Dum —4D 118
Captain Cook Mus. —3C 106
Capton. Devn —3E 9
Capton. Som —3D 20
Caputh. Per —5H 143
Caradon Town. Corn —5C 10
Carbis Bay. Corn —3C 4
Carbost. High —5C 154
(nr. Loch Harport)
Carbost. High —4D 154
(nr. Portree)
Carbrook. S Yor —2A 86
Carbrooke. Norf —5B 78
Carburton. Notts —3D 86
Carcluie. S Ayr —3C 116
Car Colston. Notts —1E 74
Carcroft. S Yor —4F 93
Cardenden. Fife —4E 136
Cardeston. Shrp —4F 71
Cardewlees. Cumb —4E 113
Cardiff. Card —4E 33 & 187
Cardiff Airport. V Glam —5D 32
Cardiff Castle —187
Cardigan. Cdgn —1B 44
Cardinal's Green. Cambs —1G 53
Cardington. Beds —1A 52
Cardington. Shrp —1H 59
Cardinham. Corn —2F 7
Cardno. Abers —2G 161
Cardoness Castle HS —4C 110
Cardow. Mor —4F 159
Cardross. Arg —2E 127
Cardurnock. Cumb —4C 112
Careby. Linc —4H 75
Careston. Ang —2E 145
Carew. Pemb —4E 43
Carew Castle —4E 43
Carew Cheriton. Pemb —4E 43
Carew Newton. Pemb —4E 43
Carey. Here —2A 48
Carfin. N Lan —4A 128
Carfrae. Bord —4B 130
Cargate Green. Norf —4F 79
Cargenbridge. Dum —2G 111
Cargill. Per —5A 144
Cargo. Cumb —4E 113
Cargreen. Corn —2A 8
Carham. Nmbd —1B 120
Carhampton. Som —2D 20
Carharrack. Corn —4B 6
Carie. Per —3D 142
(nr. Loch Rannah)
Carie. Per —5D 142
(nr. Loch Tay)
Carisbrooke. IOW —4C 16
Carisbrooke Castle EH —4C 16
Cark. Cumb —2C 96
Carkeel. Corn —2A 8
Carlabhagh. W Isl —3E 171
Carland Cross. Corn —3C 6
Carlbury. Darl —3F 105
Carlby. Linc —4H 75
Carlecotes. S Yor —4B 92
Carleen. Corn —4D 4
Carlesmoor. N Yor —2D 98
Carleton. Cumb —4F 113
(nr. Carlisle)

Carleton. Cumb —4B 102
(nr. Egremont)
Carleton. Cumb —2G 103
(nr. Penrith)
Carleton. Lanc —1B 90
Carleton. N Yor —5B 98
Carleton. W Yor —2E 93
Carleton Forehoe. Norf —5C 78
Carleton Rode. Norf —1D 66
Carleton St Peter. Norf —5F 79
Carlidnack. Corn —4E 5
Carlingcott. Bath —1B 22
Carlin How. Red C —3E 107
Carlisle. Cumb —4E 113 & 187
Carlisle Castle —187
Carlisle Cathedral —187
Carloonan. Arg —2H 133
Carlops. Bord —4E 129
Carlton. Beds —5G 63
Carlton. Cambs —5F 65
Carlton. Leics —5A 74
Carlton. N Yor —1A 100
(nr. Helmsley)
Carlton. N Yor —1C 98
(nr. Middleham)
Carlton. N Yor —2G 93
(nr. Selby)
Carlton. Notts —1C 74
Carlton. S Yor —3D 92
Carlton. Stoc T —2A 106
Carlton. Suff —4F 67
Carlton. W Yor —2D 92
Carlton Colville. Suff —1H 67
Carlton Curlieu. Leics —1D 62
Carlton Husthwaite. N Yor —2G 99
Carlton in Cleveland. N Yor —4C 106
Carlton in Lindrick. Notts —2C 86
Carlton-le-Moorland. Linc —5G 87
Carlton Miniott. N Yor —1F 99
Carlton-on-Trent. Notts —4E 87
Carlton Scroop. Linc —1G 75
Carluke. S Lan —4B 128
Carlyon Bay. Corn —3E 7
Carmarthen. Carm —4E 45
Carmarthen Castle —3E 45
Carmel. Carm —4F 45
Carmel. Flin —3D 82
Carmel. Gwyn —5D 81
Carmel. IOA —2C 80
Carmichael. S Lan —1B 118
Carmunnock. Glas —4H 127
Carmyle. S Lan —3H 127
Carmyllie. Ang —4E 145
Carnaby. E Yor —3F 101
Carnach. High —1C 148
(nr. Lochcarron)
Carnach. High —4E 163
(nr. Ullapool)
Carnach. Mor —4E 159
Carnach. W Isl —8E 171
Carnachy. High —3H 167
Carnain. Arg —3B 124
Carnais. W Isl —4C 171
Carnan. Arg —4B 138
Carnan. W Isl —4C 170
Carnbee. Fife —3H 137
Carnbo. Per —3C 136
Carn Brea. Corn —4A 6
Carndu. High —1A 148
Carne. Corn —5D 6
Carnell. S Ayr —1D 116
Carnforth. Lanc —2E 97
Carn-gorm. High —1B 148
Carnhedryn. Pemb —2B 42
Carnhell Green. Corn —3D 4
Carnie. Abers —3F 153
Carnkie. Corn —5B 6
(nr. Falmouth)
Carnkie. Corn —5A 6
(nr. Redruth)
Carnkief. Corn —3B 6
Carno. Powy —1B 58
Carnock. Fife —1D 128
Carnon Downs. Corn —4C 6
Carnoustie. Ang —5E 145
Carntyne. Glas —3H 127
Carn Vale. Derbs —4B 86
Carnwath. S Lan —5C 128
Carnyorth. Corn —3A 4
Carol Green. W Mid —3G 61
Carpalla. Corn —3D 6
Carperby. N Yor —1C 98
Carradale. Arg —2C 122
Carragraich. W Isl —8D 171
Carrbridge. High —1D 150
Carr Cross. Lanc —3B 90
Carreg Cennen CADW —4G 45
Carreglefn. IOA —2C 80
Carrhouse. N Lin —4A 94
Carrick. Arg —4A 134
Carrick Castle. Arg —4A 134
Carrick Ho. Orkn —4E 172
Carriden. Falk —1D 128
Carrington. G Man —1B 84
Carrington. Linc —5C 88
Carrington. Midl —3G 129
Carrog. Cnwy —1G 69
Carrog. Den —1D 70
Carron. Falk —1B 128
Carron. Mor —4G 159
Carronbridge. Dum —5A 118
Carronshore. Falk —1B 128
Carrow Hill. Mon —2H 33
Carr Shield. Nmbd —5B 114
Carrutherstown. Dum —2C 112
Carrville. Dur —5G 115
Carrycoats Hall. Nmbd —2C 114
Carsaig. Arg —1C 132
Carscreugh. Dum —3H 109
Carsegowan. Dum —4B 110
Carse House. Arg —3F 125
Carseriggan. Dum —3A 110
Carsethorn. Dum —4A 112
Carshalton. G Lon —4D 38
Carsington. Derbs —5G 85
Carskiey. Arg —5A 122
Carsluith. Dum —4B 110
Carsphairn. Dum —5E 117
Carstairs. S Lan —5C 128
Carstairs Junction. S Lan —5C 128
Cartbridge. Surr —5B 38
Carterhaugh. Ang —4D 144
Carter's Clay. Hants —4B 24
Carterton. Oxon —5A 50
Carterway Heads. Nmbd —4D 114
Carthew. Corn —3E 6
Carthorpe. N Yor —1F 99
Cartington. Nmbd —4E 121
Cartland. S Lan —5B 128
Cartmel. Cumb —2C 96
Cartmel Fell. Cumb —1D 96
Cartmel Priory NT —2C 96
Cartworth. W Yor —4B 92
Carwath. Cumb —5E 112
Carway. Carm —5E 45
Carwinley. Cumb —2F 113
Cascob. Powy —4E 59
Cas-gwent. Mon —2A 34
Cash Feus. Fife —3E 136
Cashlie. Per —4B 142
Cashmoor. Dors —1E 15
Cas-Mael. Pemb —2E 43
Casnewydd. Newp —3G 33 & Newport 194
Cassington. Oxon —4C 50
Cassop. Dur —1A 106
Castell. Cnwy —4G 81
Castell. Den —4D 82
Castell Coch CADW —3E 33
Castell Hendre. Pemb —2E 43
Castell-nedd. Neat —2A 32
Castell Newydd Emlyn. Carm —1D 44
Castell-y-bwch. Torf —2F 33
Casterton. Cumb —1F 97
Castle. Som —2A 22
Castle Acre. Norf —4H 77
Castle Acre Castle EH —4H 77
Castle Acre Priory EH —4H 77
Castle Ashby. Nptn —5F 63
Castlebay. W Isl —9B 170
Castle Bolton. N Yor —5D 104
Castle Bromwich. W Mid —2F 61
Castle Bytham. Linc —4G 75
Castlebythe. Pemb —2E 43
Castle Caereinion. Powy —5D 70
Castle Campbell NTS HS —4B 136
Castle Camps. Cambs —1G 53
Castle Carrock. Cumb —4G 113
Castlecary. N Lan —2A 128
Castle Cary. Som —3B 22
Castle Combe. Wilts —4D 34
Castlecraig. High —2C 158
Castle Donington. Leics —3B 74
Castle Douglas. Dum —3E 111
Castle Drogo NT —3H 11
Castle Eaton. Swin —2G 35
Castle Eden. Dur —1B 106
Castleford. W Yor —2E 93
Castle Fraser NTS —2E 152
Castle Frome. Here —1B 48
Castle Green. Surr —4A 38
Castle Green. Warw —3G 61
Castle Gresley. Derbs —4G 73
Castle Heaton. Nmbd —5F 131
Castle Hedingham. Essx —2A 54
Castle Hill. Kent —1A 28
Castlehill. Per —5B 144
Castlehill. S Lan —4B 128
Castle Hill. Suff —1E 55
Castlehill. W Dun —2E 127
Castle Howard —2B 100
Castle Kennedy. Dum —4G 109
Castle Kennedy Gdn. —3G 109
Castle Lachlan. Arg —4H 133
Castlemartin. Pemb —5D 42
Castle Menzies —4F 143
Castlemilk. Glas —4H 127
Castlemorris. Pemb —1D 42
Castlemorton. Worc —2C 48
Castle Mus. —York 197
Castle O'er. Dum —5E 119
Castle of Mey —1E 169
Castle Park. N Yor —3F 107
Castlerigg. Cumb —2D 102
Castlerigg Stone Circle EH —2D 102
Castle Rising. Norf —3F 77
Castle Rising Castle EH —3F 77
Castleside. Dur —5D 115
Castlethorpe. Mil —1F 51
Castleton. Abers —4F 151
Castleton. Arg —1G 125
Castleton. Derbs —2F 85
Castleton. G Man —3G 91
Castleton. Mor —1F 151
Castleton. Newp —3F 33
Castleton. N Yor —4D 107
Castleton. Per —2B 136
Castletown. Cumb —1G 103
Castletown. Dors —5B 14
Castletown. High —2D 169
Castletown. IOM —5B 108
Castletown. Tyne —4G 115
Castley. N Yor —5E 99
Caston. Norf —1B 66
Castor. Pet —1A 64
Caswell. Swan —4E 31
Catacol. N Ayr —5H 125
Catalyst Science Discovery Centre —2H 83
Catbrook. Mon —5A 48
Catchems End. Worc —3B 60
Catchgate. Dur —4E 115
Catcleugh. Nmbd —4B 120
Catcliffe. S Yor —2B 86
Catcott. Som —3G 21
Caterham. Surr —5E 39
Catfield. Norf —3F 79
Catfield Common. Norf —3F 79
Catfirth. Shet —6F 173
Catford. G Lon —3E 39
Catforth. Lanc —1C 90
Cathcart. Glas —3G 127
Cathedine. Powy —3E 47
Catherine-de-Barnes. W Mid —2F 61
Catherington. Hants —1E 17
Catherston Leweston. Dors —3G 13
Catherton. Shrp —3A 60
Catisfield. Hants —2D 16
Catlodge. High —4A 150
Catlowdy. Cumb —2F 113
Catmore. W Ber —3C 36
Caton. Devn —5A 12
Caton. Lanc —3E 97
Catrine. E Ayr —2E 117
Cat's Ash. Newp —2G 33
Catsfield. E Sus —4B 28
Catsgore. Som —4A 22
Catshill. Worc —3D 60
Cattal. N Yor —4G 99
Cattawade. Suff —2E 54
Catterall. Lanc —5E 97
Catterick. N Yor —5F 105
Catterick Bridge. N Yor —5F 105
Catterick Garrison. N Yor —5E 105
Catterlen. Cumb —1F 103
Catterline. Abers —1H 145
Catterton. N Yor —5H 99
Catteshall. Surr —1A 26
Catthorpe. Leics —3C 62
Cattistock. Dors —3A 14
Catton. Norf —4E 78
Catton. Nmbd —4B 114
Catton. N Yor —2F 99
Catton Hall. Derbs —4G 73
Catwick. E Yor —5F 101
Catworth. Cambs —3H 63
Caudle Green. Glos —4E 49
Caulcott. Oxon —3D 50
Cauldhame. Stir —4F 135
Cauldmill. Bord —3H 119
Cauldon. Staf —1E 73
Cauldon Lowe. Staf —1E 73
Cauldwell. Derbs —4G 73
Cauldwells. Abers —3E 161
Caulkerbush. Dum —4G 111
Caulside. Dum —1F 113
Caunsall. Worc —2C 60
Caunton. Notts —4E 87
Causewayend. S Lan —1C 118
Causewayhead. Stir —4H 135
Causey Park. Nmbd —5F 121
Caute. Devn —1E 11
Cautley. Cumb —5H 103
Cavendish. Suff —1B 54
Cavendish Bridge. Derbs —2B 74
Cavenham. Suff —4G 65
Caversfield. Oxon —3D 50
Caversham. Read —4F 37
Caversham Heights. Read —4E 37
Caverswall. Staf —1D 72
Cawdor. High —4C 158
Cawdor Castle —4C 158
Cawkwell. Linc —3B 88
Cawood. N Yor —1F 93
Cawsand. Corn —4A 8
Cawston. Norf —3D 78
Cawston. Warw —3B 62
Cawthorne. N Yor —1B 100
Cawthorne. S Yor —4C 92
Cawthorpe. Linc —3H 75
Cawton. N Yor —2A 100
Caxton. Cambs —5C 64
Caynham. Shrp —3H 59
Caythorpe. Linc —1G 75
Caythorpe. Notts —1D 74
Cayton. N Yor —1E 101
Ceallan. W Isl —3D 170
Ceann a Bhaigh. W Isl —8D 171
(on Harris)
Ceann a Bhaigh. W Isl —2C 170
(on North Uist)
Ceann a Bhaigh. W Isl —8E 171
(on Scalpay)
Ceannacroc Lodge. High —2E 149
Ceann a Deas Loch Baghasdail. W Isl —7C 170
Ceann a Tuath Loch Baghasdail. W Isl —6C 170
Ceann Shiphoirt. W Isl —6E 171
Ceann Tarabhaigh. W Isl —6E 171
Cearsiadar. W Isl —5F 171
Ceathramh Meadhanach. W Isl —1D 170
Cecil Higgins Art Gallery —1A 52
Cefn Berain. Cnwy —4B 82
Cefn-brith. Cnwy —5B 82
Cefn-bryn-brain. Carm —4H 45
Cefn Bychan. Cphy —2F 33
Cefn-bychan. Flin —4D 82
Cefncaeau. Carm —3E 31
Cefn Canol. Powy —2E 71
Cefn-coch. Powy —3D 70
Cefn-coed-y-cymmer. Mer T —5D 46
Cefn Cribwr. B'end —3B 32
Cefn-ddwysarn. Gwyn —2B 70
Cefn Einion. Shrp —2E 59
Cefneithin. Carm —4F 45
Cefn Glas. B'end —3B 32
Cefngorwydd. Powy —1C 46
Cefn Llwyd. Cdgn —2F 57
Cefn-mawr. Wrex —1E 71
Cefn-y-bedd. Flin —5F 83
Cefn-y-coed. Powy —1D 58
Cefn-y-pant. Carm —2F 43
Cegidfa. Powy —4E 70
Ceinewydd. Cdgn —5C 56
Cellan. Cdgn —1G 45
Cellardyke. Fife —3H 137
Cellarhead. Staf —1D 72
Cemaes. IOA —1C 80
Cemmaes. Powy —5H 69
Cemmaes Road. Powy —5H 69
Cenarth. Carm —1C 44
Cenin. Gwyn —1D 68
Ceos. W Isl —5F 171
Ceramica —1C 72
Ceres. Fife —2G 137
Ceri. Powy —2D 58
Cerist. Powy —2B 58
Cerne Abbas. Dors —2B 14
Cerne Giant —2B 14
Cerney Wick. Glos —2F 35
Cerrigceinwen. IOA —3D 80
Cerrigydrudion. Cnwy —1B 70
Cess. Norf —4G 79
Cessford. Bord —2B 120
Ceunant. Gwyn —4E 81
Chaceley. Glos —2D 48
Chacewater. Corn —4B 6
Chackmore. Buck —2E 51
Chacombe. Nptn —1C 50
Chadderton. G Man —4H 91
Chaddesden. Derb —2A 74
Chaddesden Common. Derb —2A 74
Chaddesley Corbett. Worc —3C 60
Chaddlehanger. Devn —5E 11
Chaddleworth. W Ber —4C 36
Chadlington. Oxon —3B 50
Chadshunt. Warw —5H 61
Chadstone. Nptn —5F 63
Chad Valley. W Mid —2E 61
Chadwell. Leics —3E 75
Chadwell. Shrp —4B 72
Chadwell Heath. G Lon —2F 39
Chadwell St Mary. Thur —3H 39
Chadwick End. W Mid —3G 61
Chadwick Green. Mers —1H 83
Chaffcombe. Som —1G 13
Chafford Hundred. Thur —3H 39
Chagford. Devn —4H 11
Chailey. E Sus —4E 27
Chainbridge. Cambs —5D 76
Chain Bridge. Linc —1C 76
Chainhurst. Kent —1B 28
Chalbury. Dors —2F 15
Chalbury Common. Dors —2F 15
Chaldon. Surr —5E 39
Chaldon Herring. Dors —4C 14
Chale. IOW —5C 16
Chale Green. IOW —5C 16
Chalfont Common. Buck —1B 38
Chalfont St Giles. Buck —1A 38
Chalfont St Peter. Buck —2B 38
Chalford. Glos —5D 49
Chalgrove. Oxon —2E 37
Chalk. Kent —3A 40
Chalk End. Essx —4G 53
Chalk Hill. Glos —3G 49
Challaborough. Devn —4C 8
Challacombe. Devn —2G 19
Challister. Shet —5G 173
Challoch. Dum —3A 110
Challock. Kent —5E 40
Chalton. Beds —5A 64
(nr. Bedford)
Chalton. Beds —3A 52
(nr. Luton)
Chalton. Hants —1F 17
Chalvington. E Sus —5G 27
Champany. Falk —2D 128
Chance Inn. Fife —2F 137
Chancery. Cdgn —3E 57
Chandler's Cross. Herts —1B 38
Chandler's Cross. Worc —2C 48
Chandler's Ford. Hants —4C 24
Chanlockfoot. Dum —4G 117
Channel End. Beds —5A 64
Channel Tunnel. Kent —2F 29
Channerwick. Shet —9F 173
Chantry. Som —2C 22
Chantry. Suff —1E 55
Chapel. Cumb —1D 102
Chapel. Fife —4E 137
Chapel Allerton. Som —1H 21
Chapel Allerton. W Yor —1D 92
Chapel Amble. Corn —1D 6
Chapel Brampton. Nptn —4E 63
Chapelbridge. Cambs —1B 64
Chapel Chorlton. Staf —2C 72
Chapel Cleeve. Som —2D 20
Chapel End. Beds —1A 52
Chapel-en-le-Frith. Derbs —2E 85
Chapelfield. Abers —2G 145
Chapelgate. Linc —3D 76
Chapel Green. Warw —2G 61
(nr. Coventry)
Chapel Green. Warw —4B 62
(nr. Southam)
Chapel Haddlesey. N Yor —2F 93
Chapelhall. N Lan —3A 128
Chapel Hill. Abers —5H 161
Chapel Hill. Linc —5B 88
Chapel Hill. Mon —5A 48
Chapelhill. Per —1E 136
(nr. Glencarse)
Chapelhill. Per —5H 143
(nr. Harrietfield)
Chapelknowe. Dum —2E 112
Chapel Lawn. Shrp —3F 59
Chapel le Dale. N Yor —2G 97
Chapel Milton. Derbs —2E 85
Chapel of Garioch. Abers —1E 152
Chapel Row. W Ber —5D 36
Chapels. Cumb —1B 96
Chapel St Leonards. Linc —3E 89
Chapel Stile. Cumb —4E 102
Chapelthorne. W Yor —3D 92
Chapelton. Ang —4F 145
Chapelton. Devn —4F 19
Chapelton. High —2D 150
(nr. Grantown-on-Spey)
Chapelton. High —3H 157
(nr. Inverness)
Chapelton. S Lan —5H 127
Chapeltown. Bkbn —3F 91
Chapel Town. Corn —3C 6
Chapeltown. Mor —1G 151
Chapeltown. S Yor —1H 85
Chapmanslade. Wilts —2D 22
Chapmans Well. Devn —3D 10
Chapmore End. Herts —4D 52
Chappel. Essx —3B 54
Chard. Som —2G 13
Chard Junction. Dors —2G 13
Chardstock. Devn —2G 13
Charfield. S Glo —2C 34
Charing. Kent —1D 28
Charing Heath. Kent —1D 28
Charing Hill. Kent —5D 40
Charingworth. Glos —2H 49
Charlbury. Oxon —4B 50
Charlcombe. Bath —5C 34
Charlcutt. Wilts —4E 35
Charlecote. Warw —5G 61
Charlecote Park NT —5G 61
Charles. Devn —3G 19
Charles Dickens Centre —Medway 191
Charlesfield. Dum —3C 112
Charleshill. Surr —2G 25
Charleston —5F 27
Charleston. Ang —4C 144
Charleston. Ren —3F 127
Charlestown. Aber —3G 153
Charlestown. Abers —2H 161
Charlestown. Corn —3E 7
Charlestown. Dors —5B 14
Charlestown. Fife —1D 128
Charlestown. G Man —4G 91
Charlestown. High —1H 155
(nr. Gairloch)
Charlestown. High —4A 158
(nr. Inverness)
Charlestown. W Yor —2H 91
Charlestown of Aberlour. Mor —4G 159
Charles Tye. Suff —5C 66
Charlesworth. Derbs —1E 85
Charlton. G Lon —3F 39
Charlton. Hants —2B 24
Charlton. Herts —3B 52
Charlton. Nptn —2D 50
Charlton. Nmbd —1B 114
Charlton. Oxon —3C 36
Charlton. Som —1B 22
(nr. Radstock)
Charlton. Som —2B 22
(nr. Shepton Mallet)
Charlton. Telf —4H 71
Charlton. W Sus —1G 17
Charlton. Wilts —3E 35
(nr. Malmesbury)
Charlton. Wilts —1G 23
(nr. Pewsey)
Charlton. Wilts —4G 23
(nr. Salisbury)
Charlton. Wilts —4E 23
(nr. Shaftesbury)
Charlton. Worc —1F 49
(nr. Evesham)
Charlton. Worc —3C 60
(nr. Stourport-on-Severn)
Charlton Abbots. Glos —3F 49
Charlton Adam. Som —4A 22
Charlton Down. Dors —3B 14
Charlton Horethorne. Som —4B 22
Charlton Kings. Glos —3E 49
Charlton Mackrell. Som —4A 22
Charlton Marshall. Dors —2E 15
Charlton Musgrove. Som —4C 22
Charlton-on-Otmoor. Oxon —4D 50
Charlton on the Hill. Dors —2D 15
Charlwood. Hants —3E 25
Charlwood. Surr —1D 26
Charlynch. Som —3F 21
Charminster. Dors —3B 14
Charmouth. Dors —3G 13
Charndon. Buck —3E 51
Charney Bassett. Oxon —2B 36
Charnock Green. Lanc —3D 90
Charnock Richard. Lanc —3D 90
Charsfield. Suff —5E 67
Chart Corner. Kent —5B 40
Charter Alley. Hants —1D 24
Charterhouse. Som —1H 21
Charterville Allotments. Oxon —4B 50
Chartham. Kent —5F 41
Chartham Hatch. Kent —5F 41
Chartridge. Buck —5H 51
Chart Sutton. Kent —5B 40
Chart, The. Kent —5F 39
Chartwell NT —5F 39
Charvil. Wok —4F 37
Charwelton. Nptn —5C 62
Chase Terrace. Staf —5E 73
Chasetown. Staf —5E 73
Chastleton. Oxon —3H 49
Chastleton House NT —3H 49
Chasty. Devn —2D 10
Chatburn. Lanc —5G 97
Chatcull. Staf —2B 72
Chatham. Medw —4B 40 & Medway 191
Chatham Green. Essx —4H 53
Chathill. Nmbd —2F 121
Chatley. Worc —4C 60
Chatsworth —4G 85
Chattenden. Medw —3B 40
Chatteris. Cambs —2C 64
Chattisham. Suff —1D 54
Chatton. Nmbd —2E 121
Chatwall. Shrp —1H 59
Chaulden. Herts —5A 52
Chaul End. Beds —3A 52
Chavenage House —2D 34
Chawleigh. Devn —1H 11
Chawley. Oxon —5C 50
Chawston. Beds —5A 64
Chawton. Hants —3F 25
Chaxhill. Glos —4C 48
Cheadle. G Man —2C 84
Cheadle. Staf —1E 73
Cheadle Hulme. G Man —2C 84
Cheam. Surr —4D 38
Cheapside. Wind —4A 38

Chearsley. Buck —4F 51
Chebsey. Staf —3C 72
Checkendon. Oxon —3E 37
Checkley. Ches —1B 72
Checkley. Here —2A 48
Checkley. Staf —2E 73
Chedburgh. Suff —5G 65
Cheddar. Som —1H 21
Cheddar Gorge —1H 21
Cheddington. Buck —4H 51
Cheddleton. Staf —5D 85
Cheddleton Flint Mill —5D 84
Cheddon Fitzpaine. Som —4F 21
Chedglow. Wilts —2E 35
Chedgrave. Norf —1F 67
Chedington. Dors —2H 13
Chediston. Suff —3F 67
Chediston Green. Suff —3F 67
Chedworth. Glos —4F 49
Chedworth Roman Villa NT —4F 49
Chedzoy. Som —3G 21
Cheeseman's Green. Kent —2E 29
Cheetham Hill. G Man —4G 91
Cheglinch. Devn —2F 19
Cheldon. Devn —1H 11
Chelford. Ches —3C 84
Chellaston. Derb —2A 74
Chellington. Beds —5G 63
Chelmarsh. Shrp —2B 60
Chelmick. Shrp —1G 59
Chelmondiston. Suff —2F 55
Chelmorton. Derbs —4F 85
Chelmsford. Essx —5H 53
Chelsea. G Lon —3D 39
Chelsfield. G Lon —4F 39
Chelsham. Surr —5E 39
Chelston. Som —4E 21
Chelsworth. Suff —1C 54
Cheltenham. Glos —3E 49 & 187
Chelveston. Nptn —4G 63
Chelvey. N Som —5H 33
Chelwood. Bath —5B 34
Chelwood Common. E Sus —3F 27
Chelwood Gate. E Sus —3F 27
Chelworth. Wilts —2E 35
Chelworth Lower Green. Wilts —2F 35
Chelworth Upper Green. Wilts —2F 35
Chelynch. Som —2B 22
Cheney Longville. Shrp —2G 59
Chenies. Buck —1B 38
Chenies Manor House —1B 38
Chepstow. Mon —2A 34
Chepstow Castle —2A 34
Chequerfield. W Yor —2E 93
Chequers Corner. Norf —5D 77
Cherhill. Wilts —4F 35
Cherington. Glos —2E 35
Cherington. Warw —2A 50
Cheriton. Devn —2E 12 (nr. Honiton)
Cheriton. Devn —2H 19 (nr. Lynton)
Cheriton. Hants —4D 24
Cheriton. Kent —2G 29
Cheriton. Pemb —5D 43
Cheriton. Swan —3D 30
Cheriton Bishop. Devn —3A 12
Cheriton Cross. Devn —3A 12
Cheriton Fitzpaine. Devn —2B 12
Cherrington. Telf —3A 72
Cherrybank. Per —1D 136
Cherry Burton. E Yor —5D 101
Cherry Green. Herts —3D 52
Cherry Hinton. Cambs —5D 65
Cherry Willingham. Linc —3H 87
Chertsey. Surr —4B 38
Cheselbourne. Dors —3C 14
Chesham. Buck —5H 51
Chesham. G Man —3G 91
Chesham Bois. Buck —1A 38
Cheshunt. Herts —5D 52
Chesil. Dors —5B 14
Cheslyn Hay. Staf —5D 73
Chessetts Wood. Warw —3F 61
Chessington. G Lon —4C 38
Chessington World of Adventures —4C 38
Chester. Ches —4G 83 & 188
Chesterblade. Som —2B 22
Chester Cathedral —188
Chesterfield. Derbs —3A 86
Chesterfield. Staf —5F 73
Chesterhope. Nmbd —1B 114
Chester-le-Street. Dur —4F 115
Chester Moor. Dur —5F 115
Chester Roman Amphitheatre EH —188
Chesters. Bord —3A 120
Chesters Roman Fort EH —3C 114
Chesterton. Cambs —4D 64 (nr. Cambridge)
Chesterton. Cambs —1A 64 (nr. Peterborough)
Chesterton. Glos —5F 49
Chesterton. Oxon —3D 50
Chesterton. Shrp —1B 60
Chesterton. Staf —1C 72
Chesterton Green. Warw —5H 61
Chesterwood. Nmbd —3B 114
Chester Zoo —3G 83
Chestfield. Kent —4F 41
Cheston. Devn —3C 8
Cheswardine. Shrp —3B 72
Cheswell. Telf —4B 72
Cheswick. Nmbd —5G 131
Cheswick Green. W Mid —3F 61
Chetnole. Dors —2B 14
Chettiscombe. Devn —1C 12
Chettisham. Cambs —2E 65
Chettle. Dors —1E 15
Chetton. Shrp —1A 60
Chetwode. Buck —3E 51
Chetwynd Aston. Telf —4B 72
Cheveley. Cambs —4F 65
Chevening. Kent —5F 39
Chevington. Suff —5G 65
Chevithorne. Devn —1C 12
Chew Magna. Bath —5A 34
Chew Moor. G Man —4E 91
Chew Stoke. Bath —5A 34
Chewton Keynsham. Bath —5B 34
Chewton Mendip. Som —1A 22
Chichacott. Devn —3G 11
Chicheley. Mil —1H 51
Chichester. W Sus —2G 17
Chichester Cathedral —2G 17
Chickerell. Dors —4B 14
Chickering. Suff —3E 66
Chicklade. Wilts —3E 23
Chicksands Priory —2B 52
Chickward. Here —5E 59
Chidden. Hants —1E 17
Chiddingfold. Surr —2A 26
Chiddingly. E Sus —4G 27
Chiddingstone. Kent —1F 27
Chiddingstone Castle —1F 27
Chiddingstone Causeway. Kent —1G 27
Chiddingstone Hoath. Kent —1F 27
Chideock. Dors —3H 13
Chidgley. Som —3D 20
Chidham. W Sus —2F 17
Chieveley. W Ber —4C 36
Chignall St James. Essx —5G 53
Chignall Smealy. Essx —4G 53
Chigwell. Essx —1F 39
Chigwell Row. Essx —1F 39
Chilbolton. Hants —2B 24
Chilcomb. Hants —4D 24
Chilcombe. Dors —3A 14
Chilcompton. Som —1B 22
Chilcote. Leics —4G 73
Childer Thornton. Ches —3F 83
Child Okeford. Dors —1D 14
Childrey. Oxon —3B 36
Child's Ercall. Shrp —3A 72
Childswickham. Worc —2F 49
Childwall. Mers —2G 83
Childwick Green. Herts —4B 52
Chilfrome. Dors —3A 14
Chilgrove. W Sus —1G 17
Chilham. Kent —5E 41
Chilhampton. Wilts —3F 23
Chilla. Devn —2E 11
Chilland. Hants —3D 24
Chillaton. Devn —4E 11
Chillenden. Kent —5G 41
Chillerton. IOW —4C 16
Chillesford. Suff —5F 67
Chillingham. Nmbd —2E 121
Chillingham Castle —2E 121
Chillingham White Cattle —2E 121
Chillington. Devn —4D 9
Chillington. Som —1G 13
Chillington Hall —5C 72
Chilmark. Wilts —3E 23
Chilmington Green. Kent —1D 28
Chilson. Oxon —4B 50
Chilsworthy. Corn —5E 11
Chilsworthy. Devn —2D 10
Chilthorne Green. Beds —4B 52
Chiltern Hills —3E 37
Chiltern Open Air Mus. —1B 38
Chilthorne Domer. Som —1A 14
Chilton. Buck —4E 51
Chilton. Devn —2B 12
Chilton. Dur —2F 105
Chilton. Oxon —3C 36
Chilton Candover. Hants —2D 24
Chilton Cantelo. Som —4A 22
Chilton Foliat. Wilts —4B 36
Chilton Lane. Dur —1A 106
Chilton Polden. Som —3G 21
Chilton Street. Suff —1A 54
Chilton Trinity. Som —3F 21
Chilwell. Notts —2C 74
Chilworth. Hants —1C 16
Chilworth. Surr —1B 26
Chimney. Oxon —5B 50
Chimney Street. Suff —1H 53
Chineham. Hants —1E 25
Chingford. G Lon —1E 39
Chinley. Derbs —2E 85
Chinnor. Oxon —5F 51
Chipley. Som —4E 20
Chipnall. Shrp —2B 72
Chippenham. Cambs —4F 65
Chippenham. Wilts —4E 35
Chipperfield. Herts —5A 52
Chipping. Herts —2D 52
Chipping. Lanc —5F 97
Chipping Campden. Glos —2G 49
Chipping Hill. Essx —4B 54
Chipping Norton. Oxon —3B 50
Chipping Ongar. Essx —5F 53
Chipping Sodbury. S Glo —3C 34
Chipping Warden. Nptn —1C 50
Chipstable. Som —4D 20
Chipstead. Kent —5G 39
Chipstead. Surr —5D 38
Chirbury. Shrp —1E 59
Chirk. Wrex —2E 71
Chirk Castle NT —2E 71
Chirmorie. S Ayr —2H 109
Chirnside. Bord —4E 131
Chirnsidebridge. Bord —4E 131
Chirton. Wilts —1F 23
Chisbridge Cross. Buck —3G 37
Chisbury. Wilts —5A 36
Chiselborough. Som —1H 13
Chiseldon. Swin —4G 35
Chiserley. W Yor —2A 92
Chislehampton. Oxon —2D 36
Chislehurst. G Lon —4F 39
Chislet. Kent —4G 41
Chiswell Green. Herts —5B 52
Chiswick. G Lon —3D 38
Chisworth. Derbs —1D 85
Chitcombe. E Sus —3C 28
Chithurst. W Sus —4G 25
Chittering. Cambs —4D 65
Chitterley. Devn —2C 12
Chitterne. Wilts —2E 23
Chittlehamholt. Devn —4G 19
Chittlehampton. Devn —4G 19
Chittoe. Wilts —5E 35
Chivelstone. Devn —5D 9
Chivenor. Devn —3F 19
Chobham. Surr —4A 38
Cholderton. Wilts —2H 23
Cholesbury. Buck —5H 51
Chollerford. Nmbd —2C 114
Chollerton. Nmbd —2C 114
Cholmondeley Castle Gdn. —5H 83
Cholsey. Oxon —3D 36
Cholstrey. Here —5G 59
Chop Gate. N Yor —5C 106
Choppington. Nmbd —1F 115
Chopwell. Tyne —4E 115
Chorley. Ches —5H 83
Chorley. Lanc —3D 90
Chorley. Shrp —2A 60
Chorley. Staf —4E 73
Chorleywood. Herts —1B 38
Chorlton. Ches —5B 84
Chorlton cum Hardy. G Man —1C 84
Chorlton Lane. Ches —1G 71
Choulton. Shrp —2F 59
Chrishall. Essx —2E 53
Christchurch. Cambs —1D 65
Christchurch. Dors —3G 15
Christchurch. Glos —4A 48
Christchurch Castle EH —3G 15
Christ Church Cathedral —Oxford 194
Christchurch Mansion —Ipswich 190
Christian Malford. Wilts —4E 35
Christleton. Ches —4G 83
Christmas Common. Oxon —2F 37
Christon. N Som —1G 21
Christon Banks. Nmbd —2G 121
Christow. Devn —4B 12
Chryston. N Lan —2H 127
Chuck Hatch. E Sus —2F 27
Chudleigh. Devn —5B 12
Chudleigh Knighton. Devn —5B 12
Chulmleigh. Devn —1G 11
Chunal. Derbs —1E 85
Church. Lanc —2F 91
Churcham. Glos —4C 48
Church Aston. Telf —4B 72
Church Brampton. Nptn —4E 62
Church Brough. Cumb —3A 104
Church Broughton. Derbs —2G 73
Church Common. Hants —4F 25
Church Crookham. Hants —1G 25
Churchdown. Glos —3D 48
Church Eaton. Staf —4C 72
Church End. Beds —3H 51 (nr. Dunstable)
Church End. Beds —2B 52 (nr. Stotfold)
Church End. Beds —2H 51 (nr. Woburn)
Church End. Cambs —5D 65 (nr. Cambridge)
Church End. Cambs —2B 64 (nr. Sawtry)
Church End. Cambs —3C 64 (nr. Willingham)
Church End. Cambs —5C 76 (nr. Wisbech)
Church End. E Yor —4E 101
Church End. Essx —3H 53 (nr. Braintree)
Churchend. Essx —3G 53 (nr. Great Dunmow)
Church End. Essx —1F 53 (nr. Saffron Walden)
Churchend. Essx —1E 40 (nr. Southend)
Church End. Glos —5C 48
Church End. Hants —1E 25
Church End. Linc —2B 76 (nr. Donington)
Church End. Linc —1D 88 (nr. North Somercotes)
Church End. Norf —4E 77
Church End. Warw —1G 61 (nr. Coleshill)
Church End. Warw —1G 61 (nr. Nuneaton)
Church End. Wilts —4F 35
Church Enstone. Oxon —3B 50
Church Fenton. N Yor —1F 93
Church Green. Devn —3E 13
Church Gresley. Derbs —4G 73
Church Hanborough. Oxon —4C 50
Church Hill. Ches —4A 84
Church Hill. Worc —4E 61
Church Hougham. Kent —1G 29
Church Houses. N Yor —5D 106
Churchill. Devn —2G 13 (nr. Axminster)
Churchill. Devn —2F 19 (nr. Barnstaple)
Churchill. N Som —1H 21
Churchill. Oxon —3A 50
Churchill. Worc —3C 60 (nr. Kidderminster)
Churchill. Worc —5D 60 (nr. Worcester)
Churchinford. Som —1F 13
Church Knowle. Dors —4E 15
Church Laneham. Notts —3F 87
Church Langley. Essx —5E 53
Church Langton. Leics —1E 62
Church Lawford. Warw —3B 62
Church Lawton. Ches —5C 84
Church Leigh. Staf —2E 73
Church Lench. Worc —5E 61
Church Mayfield. Staf —1F 73
Church Minshull. Ches —4A 84
Church Norton. W Sus —3G 17
Churchover. Warw —2C 62
Church Preen. Shrp —1H 59
Church Pulverbatch. Shrp —5G 71
Churchstanton. Som —1E 13
Church Stoke. Powy —1E 59
Churchstow. Devn —4D 8
Church Stowe. Nptn —5D 62
Church Street. Kent —3B 40
Church Street. Suff —2G 67
Church Stretton. Shrp —1G 59
Churchthorpe. Linc —1C 88
Churchtown. Cumb —5E 113
Churchtown. Derbs —4G 85
Churchtown. Devn —2G 19
Churchtown. IOM —2D 108
Churchtown. Lanc —5D 97
Church Town. Leics —4A 74
Churchtown. Mers —3B 90
Church Town. N Lin —4A 94
Churchtown. Shrp —2E 59
Church Village. Rhon —3D 32
Church Warsop. Notts —4C 86
Church Westcote. Glos —3H 49
Church Wilne. Derbs —2B 74
Churnet Valley Railway —5D 85
Churnsike Lodge. Nmbd —2H 113
Churston Ferrers. Torb —3F 9
Churt. Surr —3G 25
Churton. Ches —5G 83
Churwell. W Yor —2C 92
Chute Standen. Wilts —1B 24
Chwilog. Gwyn —2D 68
Chwittfordd. Flin —3D 82
Chyandour. Corn —3B 4
Cider Mus., Hereford —2A 48
Cilan Uchaf. Gwyn —3B 68
Cilcain. Flin —4D 82
Cilcennin. Cdgn —5E 57
Cilfrew. Neat —5A 46
Cilfynydd. Rhon —2D 32
Cilgerran. Pemb —1B 44
Cilgerran Castle CADW —1B 44
Cilgeti. Pemb —4F 43
Cilgwyn. Carm —3H 45
Cilgwyn. Pemb —1E 43
Ciliau Aeron. Cdgn —5D 57
Cill Amhlaidh. W Isl —4C 170
Cill Donnain. High —1G 165
Cill Donnain. W Isl —6C 170
Cille Bhrighde. W Isl —7C 170
Cille Pheadair. W Isl —7C 170
Cilmaengwyn. Neat —5H 45
Cilmeri. Powy —5C 58
Cilmery. Powy —5C 58
Cilrhedyn. Pemb —1G 43
Cilsan. Carm —3F 45
Ciltalgarth. Gwyn —1A 70
Ciltwrch. Powy —1E 47
Cilybebyll. Neat —5H 45
Cilycwm. Carm —2A 46
Cimla. Neat —2A 32
Cinderford. Glos —4B 48
Cinderhill. Derbs —1A 74
Cippenham. Slo —2A 38
Cippyn. Pemb —1B 44
Cirbhig. W Isl —3D 171
Circebost. W Isl —4D 171
Cirencester. Glos —5F 49
Cissbury Ring NT —5C 26
City. Powy —1E 58
City. V Glam —4C 32
City Dulas. IOA —2D 80
City (London) Airport. G Lon —2F 39
City of London. G Lon —2E 39
City, The. Buck —2F 37
Clabhach. Arg —3C 138
Clachaig. Arg —1C 126
Clachaig. High —3F 141 (nr. Kinlochleven)
Clachaig. High —2E 151 (nr. Nether Bridge)
Clachamish. High —3C 154
Clachan. Arg —4F 125 (on Kintyre)
Clachan. Arg —4C 140 (on Lismore)
Clachan. High —2H 167 (nr. Bettyhill)
Clachan. High —2D 155 (nr. Staffin)
Clachan. High —1C 154 (nr. Uig)
Clachan. High —5E 155 (on Raasay)
Clachan Farm. Arg —2A 134
Clachan na Luib. W Isl —2D 170
Clachan of Campsie. E Dun —2H 127
Clachan of Glendaruel. Arg —1A 126
Clachan-Seil. Arg —2E 133
Clachan Shannda. W Isl —1D 170
Clachan Strachur. Arg —3H 133
Clachbreck. Arg —2F 125
Clachnaharry. High —4A 158
Clachtoll. High —1E 163
Clackmannan. Clac —4B 136
Clackmarras. Mor —3G 159
Clacton-on-Sea. Essx —4E 55
Cladach a Chaolais. W Isl —2C 170
Cladach Chairinis. W Isl —3D 170
Cladach Chircebost. W Isl —2C 170
Cladach Iolaraigh. W Isl —2C 170
Cladich. Arg —1H 133
Cladswell. Worc —5E 61
Claggan. High —1F 141 (nr. Fort William)
Claggan. High —4A 140 (nr. Lochaline)
Claigan. High —3B 154
Clandon Park NT —5B 38
Clandown. Bath —1B 22
Clanfield. Hants —1E 17
Clanfield. Oxon —5A 50
Clanville. Hants —2B 24
Clanville. Som —3B 22
Claonaig. Arg —4G 125
Clapgate. Dors —2F 15
Clapgate. Herts —3E 53
Clapham. Beds —5H 63
Clapham. Devn —4B 12
Clapham. G Lon —3D 39
Clapham. N Yor —3G 97
Clapham. W Sus —5B 26
Clap Hill. Kent —2E 29
Clappers. Bord —4F 131
Clappersgate. Cumb —4E 103
Clapphoull. Shet —9F 173
Clapton. Som —2H 13 (nr. Crewkerne)
Clapton. Som —1B 22 (nr. Radstock)
Clapton-in-Gordano. N Som —4H 33
Clapton-on-the-Hill. Glos —4G 49
Clapworthy. Devn —4G 19
Clara Vale. Tyne —3E 115
Clarbeston. Pemb —2E 43
Clarbeston Road. Pemb —2E 43
Clarborough. Notts —2E 87
Clare. Suff —1A 54
Clarebrand. Dum —3E 111
Claremont Gdn. NT —4C 38
Clarencefield. Dum —3B 112
Clarilaw. Bord —3H 119
Clark's Green. Surr —2C 26
Clark's Hill. Linc —3C 76
Clarkston. E Ren —4G 127
Clasheddy. High —2G 167
Clashindarroch. Abers —5B 160
Clashmore. High —5E 165 (nr. Dornoch)
Clashmore. High —1E 163 (nr. Stoer)
Clashnessie. High —5A 166
Clashnoir. Mor —1G 151
Clate. Shet —5G 173
Clathick. Per —1H 135
Clathy. Per —2B 136
Clatt. Abers —1C 152
Clatter. Powy —1B 58
Clatterford. IOW —4C 16
Clatteringshaws Forest Visitor Centre —2C 110
Clatworthy. Som —3D 20
Claughton. Lanc —3E 97 (nr. Caton)
Claughton. Lanc —5E 97 (nr. Garstang)
Claughton. Mers —2F 83
Claverdon. Warw —4F 61
Claverham. N Som —5H 33
Clavering. Essx —2E 53
Claverley. Shrp —1B 60
Claverton. Bath —5C 34
Claverton Manor —5C 34
Clawdd-coch. V Glam —4D 32
Clawdd-newydd. Den —5C 82
Clawson Hill. Leics —3E 75
Clawton. Devn —3D 10
Claxby. Linc —3D 88 (nr. Alford)
Claxby. Linc —1A 88 (nr. Market Rasen)
Claxton. Norf —5F 79
Claxton. N Yor —4A 100
Claybrooke Magna. Leics —2B 62
Claybrooke Parva. Leics —2B 62
Clay Common. Suff —2G 67
Clay Coton. Nptn —3C 62
Clay Cross. Derbs —4A 86
Claydon. Oxon —5B 62
Claydon. Suff —5D 66
Claydon House NT —3F 51
Clay End. Herts —3D 52
Claygate. Kent —1B 28
Claygate. Surr —4C 38
Claygate Cross. Kent —5H 39
Clayhall. Hants —3E 16
Clayhanger. Devn —4D 20
Clayhanger. W Mid —5E 73
Clayhidon. Devn —1E 13
Clay Hill. Bris —4B 34
Clayhill. E Sus —3C 28
Clayhill. Hants —2B 16
Clayholes. Ang —5E 145
Clayhythe. Cambs —4E 65
Claylake. Dors —2F 15
Clay Lake. Linc —3B 76
Clayock. High —3D 168
Claypits. Glos —5C 48
Claypole. Linc —1F 75
Claythorpe. Linc —3D 88
Clayton. G Man —1C 84
Clayton. S Yor —4E 93
Clayton. Staf —1C 72
Clayton. W Sus —4E 27
Clayton. W Yor —1B 92
Clayton Green. Lanc —2D 90
Clayton-le-Moors. Lanc —1F 91
Clayton-le-Woods. Lanc —2D 90
Clayton West. W Yor —3C 92
Clayworth. Notts —2E 87
Cleadale. High —5C 146
Cleadon. Tyne —3G 115
Clearbrook. Devn —2B 8
Clearwell. Glos —5A 48
Clearwell Caves Mus. —5A 48
Cleasby. N Yor —3F 105
Cleat. Orkn —3D 172 (nr. Braehead)
Cleat. Orkn —9D 172 (nr. St Margaret's Hope)
Cleatlam. Dur —3E 105
Cleator. Cumb —3B 102
Cleator Moor. Cumb —3B 102
Cleckheaton. W Yor —2B 92
Cleedownton. Shrp —2H 59
Cleehill. Shrp —3H 59

Cleekhimin. N Lan —4A 128
Clee St Margaret. Shrp —2H 59
Cleestanton. Shrp —3H 59
Cleethorpes. NE Lin —4G 95
Cleeton St Mary. Shrp —3A 60
Cleeve. N Som —5H 33
Cleeve. Oxon —3E 36
Cleeve Abbey EH —2D 20
Cleeve Hill. Glos —3E 49
Cleeve Prior. Worc —1F 49
Clehonger. Here —2H 47
Cleigh. Arg —1F 133
Cleish. Per —4C 136
Cleland. N Lan —4B 128
Clench Common. Wilts —5G 35
Clenchwarton. Norf —3E 77
Clennell. Nmbd —4D 120
Clent. Worc —3D 60
Cleobury Mortimer. Shrp —3A 60
Cleobury North. Shrp —2A 60
Clephanton. High —3C 158
Clerkhill. High —2H 167
Clestrain. Orkn —7C 172
Clevancy. Wilts —4F 35
Clevedon. N Som —4H 33
Clevedon Court NT —4H 33
Cleveley. Oxon —3B 50
Cleveleys. Lanc —5C 96
Clevelode. Worc —1D 48
Cleverton. Wilts —3E 35
Clewer. Som —1H 21
Cley next the Sea. Norf —1C 78
Claid. W Isl —8B 170
Cliasmol. W Isl —7C 171
Clibberswick. Shet —1H 173
Cliburn. Cumb —2G 103
Cliddesden. Hants —2E 25
Clieves Hills. Lanc —4B 90
Cliff. Warw —1G 61
Cliffburn. Ang —4F 145
Cliffe. Medw —3B 40
Cliffe. N Yor —3F 105 (nr. Darlington)
Cliffe. N Yor —1G 93 (nr. Selby)
Cliff End. E Sus —4C 28
Cliffe Woods. Medw —3B 40
Clifford. Here —1F 47
Clifford. W Yor —5G 99
Clifford Chambers. Warw —5F 61
Clifford's Mesne. Glos —3B 48
Clifford's Tower —York 197
Cliffs End. Kent —4H 41
Clifton. Beds —2B 52
Clifton. Bris —4A 34
Clifton. Cumb —2G 103
Clifton. Derbs —1F 73
Clifton. Devn —2G 19
Clifton. G Man —4F 91
Clifton. Lanc —1C 90
Clifton. Nmbd —1F 115
Clifton. N Yor —5D 98
Clifton. Nott —2C 74
Clifton. Oxon —2C 50
Clifton. S Yor —1C 86
Clifton. Stir —5H 141
Clifton. W Yor —2B 92
Clifton. Worc —1D 48
Clifton. York —4H 99
Clifton Campville. Staf —4G 73
Clifton Hampden. Oxon —2D 36
Clifton Hill. Worc —4B 60
Clifton Reynes. Mil —5G 63
Clifton Suspension Bridge —Bristol 187
Clifton upon Dunsmore. Warw —3C 62
Clifton-upon-Teme. Worc —4B 60
Cliftonville. Kent —3H 41
Cliftonville. Norf —2F 79
Climping. W Sus —5A 26
Climpy. S Lan —4C 128
Clint. N Yor —4E 99
Clint Green. Norf —4C 78
Clintmains. Bord —1A 120
Cliobh. W Isl —4C 171
Clipiau. Gwyn —4H 69
Clippesby. Norf —4G 79
Clippings Green. Norf —4C 78
Clipsham. Rut —4G 75
Clipston. Nptn —2E 62
Clipston. Notts —2D 74
Clipstone. Notts —4C 86
Clitheroe. Lanc —5G 97
Cliuthar. W Isl —8D 171
Clive. Shrp —3H 71
Cliveden NT —2A 38
Clivocast. Shet —1H 173
Clixby. Linc —4E 94
Clocaenog. Den —5C 82
Clochan. Mor —2B 160
Clochforbie. Abers —3F 161
Clock Face. Mers —1H 83
Cloddiau. Powy —5E 70
Cloddymoss. Mor —3D 159
Clodock. Here —3G 47
Cloford. Som —2C 22
Clola. Abers —4H 161
Clophill. Beds —2A 52
Clopton. Nptn —2H 63
Clopton Corner. Suff —5E 66
Clopton Green. Suff —5G 65
Closeburn. Dum —5A 118
Close Clark. IOM —4B 108
Closworth. Som —1A 14
Clothall. Herts —2C 52
Clotton. Ches —4H 83
Clouds Hill NT —3D 14
Clough. G Man —3H 91
Clough. W Yor —3A 92
Clough Foot. W Yor —2H 91
Cloughton. N Yor —5H 107
Cloughton Newlands. N Yor —5H 107
Clousta. Shet —6E 173
Clouston. Orkn —6B 172
Clova. Abers —1B 152
Clova. Ang —1C 144
Clovelly. Devn —4D 18
Clovenfords. Bord —1G 119
Clovenstone. Abers —2E 153
Clovullin. High —2E 141
Clowne. Derbs —3B 86
Clows Top. Worc —3B 60
Cloy. Wrex —1F 71
Cluanie Inn. High —2C 148
Cluanie Lodge. High —2C 148
Cluddley. Telf —5A 72
Clumber Park NT —3D 86
Clun. Shrp —2F 59
Clunas. High —4C 158
Clunbury. Shrp —2F 59
Clun Castle EH —2E 59
Clunderwen. Carm —3F 43
Clune. High —1B 150
Clunes. High —5E 148
Clungunford. Shrp —3F 59
Clunie. Per —4A 144
Clunton. Shrp —2F 59
Cluny. Fife —4E 137
Clutton. Bath —1B 22
Clutton. Ches —5G 83
Clwt-y-bont. Gwyn —4E 81
Clwydfagwyr. Mer T —5D 46
Clydach. Mon —4F 47
Clydach. Swan —5G 45
Clydach Vale. Rhon —2C 32
Clydebank. W Dun —2G 127
Clydey. Pemb —1G 43
Clyffe Pypard. Wilts —4F 35
Clynder. Arg —1D 126
Clyne. Neat —5B 46
Clynelish. High —3F 165
Clynnog-fawr. Gwyn —1D 68
Clyro. Powy —1F 47
Clyst Honiton. Devn —3C 12
Clyst Hydon. Devn —2D 12
Clyst St George. Devn —4C 12
Clyst St Lawrence. Devn —2D 12
Clyst St Mary. Devn —3C 12
Clyth. High —5E 169
Cnip. W Isl —4C 171
Cnoc Amhlaigh. W Isl —4H 171
Cnwcau. Pemb —1C 44
Cnwch Coch. Cdgn —3F 57
Coad's Green. Corn —5C 10
Coal Aston. Derbs —3A 86
Coalbrookdale. Telf —5A 72
Coalbrookedale Mus. of Iron —5A 72
Coalbrookvale. Blae —5F 47
Coalburn. S Lan —1H 117
Coalburns. Tyne —3E 115
Coalcleugh. Nmbd —5B 114
Coaley. Glos —5C 48
Coalford. Abers —4F 153
Coalhall. E Ayr —3D 116
Coalhill. Essx —1B 40
Coalpit Heath. S Glo —3B 34
Coal Pool. W Mid —5E 73
Coalport. Telf —5B 72
Coalport China Mus. —5B 72
Coalsnaughton. Clac —4B 136
Coaltown of Balgonie. Fife —4F 137
Coaltown of Wemyss. Fife —4F 137
Coalville. Leics —4B 74
Coalway. Glos —4A 48
Coanwood. Nmbd —4H 113
Coat. Som —4H 21
Coatbridge. N Lan —3A 128
Coatdyke. N Lan —3A 128
Coate. Swin —3G 35
Coate. Wilts —5F 35
Coates. Cambs —1C 64
Coates. Glos —5E 49
Coates. Linc —2G 87
Coates. W Sus —4A 26
Coatham. Red C —2C 106
Coatham Mundeville. Darl —2F 105
Cobbaton. Devn —4G 19
Coberley. Glos —4E 49
Cobhall Common. Here —2H 47
Cobham. Kent —4A 40
Cobham. Surr —4C 38
Cobham Hall —4A 40
Cobnash. Here —4G 59
Coburg. Devn —5B 12
Cockayne. N Yor —5D 106
Cockayne Hatley. Beds —1C 52
Cock Bank. Wrex —1F 71
Cock Bridge. Abers —3G 151
Cockburnspath. Bord —2D 130
Cock Clarks. Essx —5B 54
Cockenzie & Port Seton. E Lot —2H 129
Cockerham. Lanc —4D 96
Cockermouth. Cumb —1C 102
Cockernhoe. Herts —3B 52
Cockfield. Dur —2E 105
Cockfield. Suff —5B 66
Cockfosters. G Lon —1D 39
Cock Gate. Here —4G 59
Cock Green. Essx —4G 53
Cocking. W Sus —1G 17
Cocking Causeway. W Sus —1G 17
Cockington. Torb —2F 9
Cocklake. Som —2H 21
Cocklaw. Abers —4H 161
Cocklaw. Nmbd —2C 114
Cockley Beck. Cumb —4D 102
Cockley Cley. Norf —5G 77
Cockmuir. Abers —3G 161
Cockpole Green. Wind —3G 37
Cockshutford. Shrp —2H 59
Cockshutt. Shrp —3G 71
Cockthorpe. Norf —1B 78
Cockwood. Devn —4C 12
Cockyard. Derbs —3E 85
Cockyard. Here —2H 47
Codda. Corn —5B 10
Coddenham. Suff —5D 66
Coddenham Green. Suff —5D 66
Coddington. Ches —5G 83
Coddington. Here —1C 48
Coddington. Notts —5F 87
Codford St Mary. Wilts —3E 23
Codford St Peter. Wilts —3E 23
Codicote. Herts —4C 52
Codmore Hill. W Sus —3B 26
Codnor. Derbs —1B 74
Codrington. S Glo —4C 34
Codsall. Staf —5C 72
Codsall Wood. Staf —5C 72
Coed Duon. Cphy —2E 33
Coedely. Rhon —3D 32
Coedglasson. Powy —4C 58
Coedkernew. Newp —3F 33
Coed Morgan. Mon —4G 47
Coedpoeth. Wrex —5E 83
Coedway. Powy —4F 71
Coed-y-bryn. Cdgn —1D 44
Coed-y-paen. Mon —2G 33
Coed-yr-ynys. Powy —3E 47
Coed Ystumgwern. Gwyn —3E 69
Coelbren. Powy —4B 46
Coffinswell. Devn —2E 9
Cofton Hackett. Worc —3E 61
Cogan. V Glam —4E 33
Cogenhoe. Nptn —4F 63
Cogges. Oxon —5B 50
Coggeshall. Essx —3B 54
Coggeshall Grange Barn NT —3B 54
Coggeshall Hamlet. Essx —3B 54
Cogges Manor Farm Mus. —5B 50
Coggins Mill. E Sus —3G 27
Coignafearn Lodge. High —2A 150
Coig Peighinnean. W Isl —1H 171
Coig Peighinnean Bhuirgh. W Isl —2G 171
Coilliemore. High —1A 158
Coillore. High —5C 154
Coire an Fhuarain. W Isl —4E 171
Coity. B'end —3C 32
Coity Castle CADW —3C 32
Cokhay Green. Derbs —3G 73
Col. W Isl —3G 171
Colaboll. High —2C 164
Colan. Corn —2C 6
Colaton Raleigh. Devn —4D 12
Colbost. High —4B 154
Colburn. N Yor —5E 105
Colby. Cumb —2H 103
Colby. IOM —4B 108
Colby. Norf —2E 78
Colby Gdn. NT —4F 43
Colchester. Essx —3D 54
Colchester Castle Mus. —3D 54
Colchester Zoo —3C 54
Cold Ash. W Ber —5D 36
Cold Ashby. Nptn —3D 62
Cold Ashton. S Glo —4C 34
Cold Aston. Glos —4G 49
Coldbackie. High —3G 167
Cold Blow. Pemb —3F 43
Cold Brayfield. Mil —5G 63
Cold Cotes. N Yor —2G 97
Coldean. Brig —5E 27
Coldeast. Devn —5B 12
Colden. W Yor —2H 91
Colden Common. Hants —4C 24
Coldfair Green. Suff —4G 67
Coldham. Cambs —5D 76
Coldham. Staf —5C 72
Cold Hanworth. Linc —2H 87
Coldharbour. Corn —4B 6
Cold Harbour. Dors —3E 15
Coldharbour. Glos —5A 48
Coldharbour. Kent —5G 39
Coldharbour. Surr —1C 26
Cold Hatton. Telf —3A 72
Cold Hatton Heath. Telf —3A 72
Cold Hesledon. Dur —5H 115
Cold Hiendley. W Yor —3D 92
Cold Higham. Nptn —5D 62
Coldingham. Bord —3F 131
Cold Kirby. N Yor —1H 99
Coldmeece. Staf —2C 72
Cold Northcott. Corn —4C 10
Cold Norton. Essx —5B 54
Cold Overton. Leics —5F 75
Coldrain. Per —3C 136
Coldred. Kent —1G 29
Coldridge. Devn —2H 11
Cold Row. Lanc —5C 96
Coldstream. Bord —5E 131
Coldwaltham. W Sus —4B 26
Coldwell. Here —2H 47
Coldwells. Abers —5H 161
Coldwells Croft. Abers —1C 152
Cole. Shet —5E 173
Cole. Som —3B 22
Colebatch. Shrp —2F 59
Colebrook. Devn —2D 12
Colebrooke. Devn —2A 12
Coleburn. Mor —3G 159
Coleby. Linc —4G 87
Coleby. N Lin —3B 94
Cole End. Warw —2F 61
Coleford. Devn —2A 12
Coleford. Glos —4A 48
Coleford. Som —2B 22
Colegate End. Norf —2D 66
Cole Green. Herts —4C 52
Cole Henley. Hants —1C 24
Colehill. Dors —2F 15
Coleman Green. Herts —4B 52
Coleman's Hatch. E Sus —2F 27
Colemere. Shrp —2G 71
Colemore. Hants —3F 25
Colemore Green. Shrp —1B 60
Colenden. Per —1D 136
Coleorton. Leics —4B 74
Coleridge Cottage NT —2E 21
Colerne. Wilts —4D 34
Colesbourne. Glos —4E 49
Colesden. Beds —5A 64
Coles Green. Worc —5B 60
Coleshill. Buck —1A 38
Coleshill. Oxon —2H 35
Coleshill. Warw —2G 61
Colestocks. Devn —2D 12
Colethrop. Glos —4D 48
Coleton Fishacre NT —3F 9
Coley. Bath —1A 22
Colgate. W Sus —2D 26
Colinsburgh. Fife —3G 137
Colinton. Edin —3F 129
Colintraive. Arg —2B 126
Colkirk. Norf —3B 78
Collace. Per —5B 144
Collam. W Isl —8D 171
Collaton. Devn —5D 8
Collaton St Mary. Torb —3E 9
College of Roseisle. Mor —2F 159
Collessie. Fife —2E 137
Collier Row. G Lon —1F 39
Colliers End. Herts —3D 52
Collier Street. Kent —1B 28
Colliery Row. Tyne —5G 115
Collieston. Abers —1H 153
Collin. Dum —2B 112
Collingbourne Ducis. Wilts —1H 23
Collingbourne Kingston. Wilts —1H 23
Collingham. Notts —4F 87
Collingham. W Yor —5F 99
Collingtree. Nptn —5E 63
Collins Green. Warr —1H 83
Collins Green. Worc —5B 60
Colliston. Ang —4F 145
Colliton. Devn —2D 12
Collydean. Fife —3E 137
Collyweston. Nptn —5G 75
Colmonell. S Ayr —1G 109
Colmworth. Beds —5A 64
Colnbrook. Slo —3B 38
Colne. Cambs —3C 64
Colne. Lanc —5A 98
Colne Engaine. Essx —2B 54
Colne Valley Railway —2A 54
Colney. Norf —5D 78
Colney Heath. Herts —5C 52
Colney Street. Herts —5B 52
Coln Rogers. Glos —5F 49
Coln St Aldwyns. Glos —5G 49
Coln St Dennis. Glos —4F 49
Colour Mus. —Bradford 186
Colpitts Grange. Nmbd —4C 114
Colpy. Abers —5D 160
Colscott. Devn —1D 10
Colsterdale. N Yor —1D 98
Colsterworth. Linc —3G 75
Colston Bassett. Notts —2D 74
Colstoun House. E Lot —2B 130
Coltfield. Mor —2F 159
Colthouse. Cumb —5E 103
Coltishall. Norf —4E 79
Coltness. N Lan —4A 128
Colton. Cumb —1C 96
Colton. Norf —5D 78
Colton. N Yor —5H 99
Colton. Staf —3E 73
Colton. W Yor —1D 92
Colt's Hill. Kent —1H 27
Col Uarach. W Isl —4G 171
Colvend. Dum —4F 111
Colvister. Shet —2G 173
Colwall Green. Here —1C 48
Colwall Stone. Here —1C 48
Colwell. Nmbd —2C 114
Colwich. Staf —3E 73
Colwick. Notts —1D 74
Colwinston. V Glam —4C 32
Colworth. W Sus —5A 26
Colwyn Bay. Cnwy —3A 82
Colyford. Devn —3F 13
Colyton. Devn —3F 13
Combe. Devn —2D 8
Combe. Here —4F 59
Combe. Oxon —4C 50
Combe. W Ber —5B 36
Combe Almer. Dors —3E 15
Combebow. Devn —4E 11
Combe Common. Surr —2A 26
Combe Down. Bath —5C 34
Combe Fishacre. Devn —2E 9
Combe Florey. Som —3E 21
Combe Hay. Bath —1C 22
Combeinteignhead. Devn —5C 12
Combe Martin. Devn —2F 19
Combe Moor. Here —4F 59
Combe Raleigh. Devn —2E 13
Comberbach. Ches —3A 84
Comberford. Staf —5F 73
Comberton. Cambs —5C 64
Comberton. Here —4G 59
Combe St Nicholas. Som —1G 13
Combe Sydenham —3D 20
Combpyne. Devn —3F 13
Combridge. Staf —2E 73
Combrook. Warw —5H 61
Combs. Derbs —3E 85
Combs. Suff —5C 66
Combs Ford. Suff —5C 66
Combwich. Som —2F 21
Comers. Abers —3D 152
Comhampton. Worc —4C 60
Comins Coch. Cdgn —2F 57
Comley. Shrp —1G 59
Commercial End. Cambs —4E 65
Commins. Powy —3D 70
Commins Coch. Powy —5H 69
Commondale. N Yor —3D 106
Common End. Cumb —2B 102
Common Hill. Here —2A 48
Common Moor. Corn —2G 7
Common Platt. Wilts —3G 35
Commonside. Ches —3H 83
Common Side. Derbs —3H 85 (nr. Chesterfield)
Commonside. Derbs —1G 73 (nr. Derby)
Common, The. Wilts —3H 23 (nr. Salisbury)
Common, The. Wilts —3F 35 (nr. Swindon)
Compstall. G Man —1D 84
Compton. Devn —2E 9
Compton. Hants —4C 24
Compton. Plym —3A 8
Compton. Staf —2C 60
Compton. Surr —1A 26
Compton. W Ber —4D 36
Compton. W Sus —1F 17
Compton. Wilts —1G 23
Compton Abbas. Dors —1D 15
Compton Abdale. Glos —4F 49
Compton Acres —4F 15
Compton Bassett. Wilts —4F 35
Compton Beauchamp. Oxon —3A 36
Compton Bishop. Som —1G 21
Compton Castle NT —2E 9
Compton Chamberlayne. Wilts —4F 23
Compton Dando. Bath —5B 34
Compton Dundon. Som —3H 21
Compton Greenfield. S Glo —3A 34
Compton Martin. Bath —1A 22
Compton Pauncefoot. Som —4B 22
Compton Valence. Dors —3A 14
Compton Verney —5H 61
Comrie. Fife —1D 128
Comrie. Per —1G 135
Conaglen. High —2E 141
Conchra. Arg —1B 126
Conchra. High —1A 148
Conder Green. Lanc —4D 96
Conderton. Worc —2E 49
Condicote. Glos —3G 49
Condorrat. N Lan —2A 128
Condover. Shrp —5G 71
Coneyhurst Common. W Sus —3C 26
Coneysthorpe. N Yor —2B 100
Coneythorpe. N Yor —4F 99
Coney Weston. Suff —3B 66
Conford. Hants —3G 25
Congdon's Shop. Corn —5C 10
Congerstone. Leics —5A 74
Congham. Norf —3G 77
Congleton. Ches —4C 84
Congl-y-wal. Gwyn —1G 69
Congresbury. N Som —5H 33
Congreve. Staf —4D 72
Conham. S Glo —4B 34
Conicaval. Mor —3D 159
Coningsby. Linc —5B 88
Coningsby Aviation Mus. —5B 88
Conington. Cambs —4C 64 (nr. Fenstanton)
Conington. Cambs —2A 64 (nr. Sawtry)
Conisbrough. S Yor —1C 86
Conisbrough Castle EH —1C 86
Conisby. Arg —3A 124
Conishead Priory —2C 96
Conisholme. Linc —1D 88
Coniston. Cumb —5E 102
Coniston. E Yor —1E 95
Coniston Cold. N Yor —4B 98
Conistone. N Yor —3B 98
Connah's Quay. Flin —4E 83
Connel. Arg —5D 140
Connel Park. E Ayr —3F 117
Connista. High —1D 154
Connor Downs. Corn —3C 4
Conock. Wilts —1F 23
Conon Bridge. High —3H 157
Cononley. N Yor —5B 98
Cononsyth. Ang —4E 145
Conordan. High —5E 155
Consall. Staf —1D 73
Consett. Dur —4E 115
Constable Burton. N Yor —5E 105
Constable Burton Hall Gdns. —5E 105
Constantine. Corn —4E 5
Constantine Bay. Corn —1C 6
Contin. High —3G 157
Contullich. High —1A 158
Conwy. Cnwy —3G 81
Conwy Castle WH CADW —3G 81
Conyer. Kent —4D 40
Conyers Green. Suff —4A 66
Cooden. E Sus —5B 28
Cooil. IOM —4C 108
Cookbury. Devn —2E 11
Cookbury Wick. Devn —2D 11
Cookham. Wind —3G 37
Cookham Dean. Wind —3G 37
Cookham Rise. Wind —3G 37
Cookhill. Worc —5E 61
Cookley. Suff —3F 67
Cookley. Worc —2C 60
Cookley Green. Oxon —2E 37
Cookney. Abers —4F 153
Cooksbridge. E Sus —4F 27
Cooksey Corner. Worc —4D 60
Cooksey Green. Worc —4D 60
Cookshill. Staf —1D 72
Cooksmill Green. Essx —5G 53
Coolham. W Sus —3C 26
Cooling. Medw —3B 40
Cooling Street. Medw —3B 40
Coombe. Corn —1C 10 (nr. Bude)
Coombe. Corn —3D 6 (nr. St Austell)
Coombe. Corn —4C 6 (nr. Truro)
Coombe. Devn —3E 12 (nr. Sidmouth)
Coombe. Devn —5C 12 (nr. Teignmouth)
Coombe. Glos —2C 34
Coombe. Hants —4E 25
Coombe. Wilts —1G 23
Coombe Bissett. Wilts —4G 23
Coombe Hill. Glos —3D 49
Coombe Keynes. Dors —4D 14
Coombe Martin Wildlife Park —2F 19
Coombes. W Sus —5C 26
Coombe Street. Som —3C 22

Coopersale Common. Essx —5E 53
Coopersale Street. Essx —5E 53
Cooper's Corner. Kent —1F 27
Cooper Street. Kent —5H 41
Cootham. W Sus —4B 26
Copalder Corner. Cambs —1C 64
Copdock. Suff —1E 54
Copford. Essx —3C 54
Copford Green. Essx —3C 54
Copgrove. N Yor —3F 99
Copister. Shet —4F 173
Cople. Beds —1B 52
Copley. Dur —2D 105
Coplow Dale. Derbs —3F 85
Copmanthorpe. York —5H 99
Copp. Lanc —1C 90
Coppathorne. Corn —2C 10
Coppenhall. Ches —5B 84
Coppenhall. Staf —4D 72
Coppenhall Moss. Ches —5B 84
Copperhouse. Corn —3C 4
Coppicegate. Shrp —2B 60
Coppingford. Cambs —2A 64
Copplestone. Devn —2A 12
Coppull. Lanc —3D 90
Coppull Moor. Lanc —3D 90
Copsale. W Sus —3C 26
Copster Green. Lanc —1E 91
Copston Magna. Warw —2B 62
Copt Green. Warw —4F 61
Copthall Green. Essx —5E 53
Copt Heath. W Mid —3F 61
Copt Hewick. N Yor —2F 99
Copthill. Dur —5B 114
Copthorne. W Sus —2E 27
Coptiviney. Shrp —2G 71
Copy's Green. Norf —2B 78
Copythorne. Hants —1B 16
Corbridge. Nmbd —3C 114
Corbridge Roman Fort and Mus. WH EH —3C 114
Corby. Nptn —2G 63
Corby Glen. Linc —3H 75
Cordon. N Ayr —2E 123
Coreley. Shrp —3A 60
Corfe. Som —1F 13
Corfe Castle. Dors —4E 15
Corfe Castle NT —4E 15
Corfe Mullen. Dors —3E 15
Corfton. Shrp —2G 59
Corgarff. Abers —3G 151
Corgarff Castle HS —3G 151
Corhampton. Hants —4E 24
Corinium Mus. —5F 49
Corlae. Dum —5F 117
Corlannau. Neat —2A 32
Corley. Warw —2H 61
Corley Ash. Warw —2G 61
Corley Moor. Warw —2G 61
Cormiston. S Lan —1C 118
Cornaa. IOM —3D 108
Cornaigbeg. Arg —4A 138
Cornaigmore. Arg —2D 138 (on Coll)
Cornaigmore. Arg —4A 138 (on Tiree)
Corner Row. Lanc —1C 90
Corney. Cumb —5C 102
Cornforth. Dur —1A 106
Cornhill. Abers —3C 160
Cornhill. High —4C 164
Cornhill-on-Tweed. Nmbd —1C 120
Cornholme. W Yor —2H 91
Cornish Hall End. Essx —2G 53
Cornish Mines & Engines Mus. NT —4A 6
Cornquoy. Orkn —7E 172
Cornriggs. Dur —5B 114
Cornsay. Dur —5E 115
Cornsay Colliery. Dur —5E 115
Corntown. High —3H 157
Corntown. V Glam —4C 32
Cornwell. Oxon —3A 50
Cornwood. Devn —3C 8
Cornworthy. Devn —3E 9
Corpach. High —1E 141
Corpusty. Norf —3D 78
Corra. Dum —3F 111
Corran. High —2E 141 (nr. Arnisdale)
Corran. High —3A 148 (nr. Fort William)
Corrany. IOM —3D 108
Corribeg. High —1D 141
Corrie. N Ayr —5B 126
Corrie Common. Dum —1D 112
Corriecravie. N Ayr —3D 122
Corriekinloch. High —1A 164
Corriemoillie. High —2F 157
Corrieshalloch Gorge Nat. Nature Reserve NTS —1E 156
Corrievarkie Lodge. Per —1C 142
Corrievorrie. High —1B 150
Corrigall. Orkn —6C 172
Corrimony. High —5F 157
Corringham. Linc —1F 87
Corringham. Thur —2B 40
Corris. Gwyn —5G 69
Corris Railway —5G 69
Corris Uchaf. Gwyn —5G 69
Corrour Shooting Lodge. High —2B 142
Corry. High —1E 147
Corrybrough. High —1C 150
Corrygills. N Ayr —2E 123
Corry of Ardnagrask. High —4H 157
Corsback. High —1E 169 (nr. Dunnet)
Corsback. High —3E 169 (nr. Halkirk)
Corscombe. Dors —2A 14
Corse. Abers —4D 160
Corsehill. Abers —3G 161
Corse Lawn. Worc —2D 48
Corse of Kinnoir. Abers —4C 160
Corsham. Wilts —4D 34
Corsham Court —4D 35
Corsley. Wilts —2D 22
Corsley Heath. Wilts —2D 22
Corsock. Dum —2E 111
Corston. Bath —5B 34
Corston. Wilts —3E 35
Corstorphine. Edin —2F 129
Cortachy. Ang —3C 144
Corton. Suff —1H 67
Corton. Wilts —2E 23
Corton Denham. Som —4B 22
Corwar House. S Ayr —1H 109
Corwen. Den —1C 70
Coryates. Dors —4B 14
Coryton. Devn —4E 11
Coryton. Thur —2B 40
Cosby. Leics —1C 62
Coscote. Oxon —3D 36
Coseley. W Mid —1D 60
Cosgrove. Nptn —1F 51
Cosham. Port —2E 17
Cosheston. Pemb —4E 43
Coskills. N Lin —3D 94
Cosmeston. V Glam —5E 33
Cossall. Notts —1B 74
Cossington. Leics —4D 74
Cossington. Som —2G 21
Costa. Orkn —5C 172
Costessey. Norf —4D 78
Costock. Notts —3C 74
Coston. Leics —3F 75
Coston. Norf —5C 78
Cote. Oxon —5B 50
Cotebrook. Ches —4H 83
Cotehele House & Quay NT —2A 8
Cotehill. Cumb —5F 113
Cotes. Cumb —1D 97
Cotes. Leics —3C 74
Cotes. Staf —2C 72
Cotesbach. Leics —2C 62
Cotes Heath. Staf —2C 72
Cotgrave. Notts —2D 74
Cothall. Abers —2F 153
Cotham. Notts —1E 75
Cothelstone. Som —3E 21
Cotheridge. Worc —5B 60
Cotherstone. Dur —3D 104
Cothill. Oxon —2C 36
Cotland. Mon —5A 48
Cotleigh. Devn —2F 13
Cotmanhay. Derbs —1B 74
Coton. Cambs —5D 64
Coton. Nptn —3D 62
Coton. Staf —4C 72 (nr. Gnosall)
Coton. Staf —2D 73 (nr. Stone)
Coton. Staf —5F 73 (nr. Tamworth)
Coton Clanford. Staf —3C 72
Coton Hayes. Staf —2D 73
Coton Hill. Shrp —4G 71
Coton in the Clay. Staf —3F 73
Coton in the Elms. Derbs —4G 73
Cotonwood. Shrp —2H 71
Cotonwood. Staf —3C 72
Cotswold Farm Park —3G 49
Cotswold Hills —2D 34
Cotswold Water Park —2F 35
Cott. Devn —2D 9
Cott. Orkn —5F 172
Cottam. E Yor —3D 101
Cottam. Lanc —1D 90
Cottam. Notts —3F 87
Cottartown. High —5E 159
Cottarville. Nptn —4E 63
Cottenham. Cambs —4D 64
Cotterdale. N Yor —5B 104
Cottered. Herts —3D 52
Cotterstock. Nptn —1H 63
Cottesbroke Hall —3E 62
Cottesbrooke. Nptn —3E 62
Cottesmore. Rut —4G 75
Cotteylands. Devn —1C 12
Cottingham. E Yor —1D 94
Cottingham. Nptn —1F 63
Cottingley. W Yor —1B 92
Cottisford. Oxon —2D 50
Cotton. Staf —1E 73
Cotton. Suff —4C 66
Cotton End. Beds —1A 52
Cottown. Abers —4F 161
Cotts. Devn —2A 8
Cotwalton. Staf —2D 72
Couch's Mill. Corn —3F 7
Coughton. Here —3A 48
Coughton. Warw —4E 61
Coughton Court NT —4E 61
Coulags. High —4B 156
Coulderton. Cumb —4A 102
Coulin Lodge. High —3C 156
Coull. Abers —3C 152
Coulport. Arg —1D 126
Coulsdon. Surr —5D 39
Coulter. S Lan —1C 118
Coultershaw Bridge. W Sus —4A 26
Coultings. Som —2F 21
Coulton. N Yor —2A 100
Cound. Shrp —5H 71
Coundon. Dur —2F 105
Coundon Grange. Dur —2F 105
Countersett. N Yor —1B 98
Countess. Wilts —2G 23
Countess Cross. Essx —2B 54
Countesthorpe. Leics —1C 62
Countisbury. Devn —2H 19
Coupar Angus. Per —4B 144
Coupe Green. Lanc —2D 90
Coupland. Cumb —3A 104
Coupland. Nmbd —1D 120
Cour. Arg —5G 125
Courance. Dum —5C 118
Court-at-Street. Kent —2E 29
Courteachan. High —4E 147
Courteenhall. Nptn —5E 63
Court Henry. Carm —3F 45
Courtsend. Essx —1E 41
Courts Gdn., The NT —5D 34
Courtway. Som —3F 21
Cousland. Midl —3G 129
Cousley Wood. E Sus —2A 28
Coustonn. Arg —2B 126
Cove. Arg —1D 126
Cove. Devn —1C 12
Cove. Hants —1G 25
Cove. High —4C 162
Cove. Bord —2D 130
Cove Bay. Aber —3G 153
Covehithe. Suff —2H 67
Coven. Staf —5D 72
Coveney. Cambs —2D 65
Covenham St Bartholomew. Linc —1C 88
Covenham St Mary. Linc —1C 88
Coven Heath. Staf —5D 72
Coventry. W Mid —3H 61 & 188
Coventry Cathedral —188
Coventry Transport Mus. —188
Coverack. Corn —5E 5
Coverham. N Yor —1D 98
Covesea. Mor —1F 159
Covingham. Swin —3G 35
Covington. Cambs —3H 63
Covington. S Lan —1B 118
Cowan Bridge. Lanc —2F 97
Cowan Head. Cumb —5F 103
Cowbar. Red C —3E 107
Cowbeech. E Sus —4H 27
Cowbit. Linc —4B 76
Cowbridge. V Glam —4C 32
Cowden. Kent —1F 27
Cowdenbeath. Fife —4D 136
Cowdenburn. Bord —4F 129
Cowdenend. Fife —1E 129
Cowers Lane. Derbs —1H 73
Cowes. IOW —3C 16
Cowesby. N Yor —1G 99
Cowfold. W Sus —3D 26
Cowfords. Mor —2H 159
Cowgate. Cumb —5B 112
Cowgill. Cumb —1G 97
Cowie. Abers —5F 153
Cowie. Stir —1B 128
Cowlam. E Yor —3D 100
Cowley. Devn —3C 12
Cowley. Glos —4E 49
Cowley. G Lon —2B 38
Cowley. Oxon —5D 50
Cowley. Staf —4C 72
Cowleymoor. Devn —1C 12
Cowling. Lanc —3D 90
Cowling. N Yor —1E 99 (nr. Bedale)
Cowling. N Yor —5B 98 (nr. Glusburn)
Cowlinge. Suff —5G 65
Cowmes. W Yor —3B 92
Cowpe. Lanc —2G 91
Cowpen. Nmbd —1F 115
Cowpen Bewley. Stoc T —2B 106
Cowplain. Hants —1E 17
Cowshill. Dur —5B 114
Cowslip Green. N Som —5H 33
Cowstrandburn. Fife —4C 136
Cowthorpe. N Yor —4G 99
Coxall. Here —3F 59
Coxbank. Ches —1A 72
Coxbench. Derbs —1A 74
Cox Common. Suff —2G 67
Coxford. Norf —3H 77
Coxgreen. Staf —2C 60
Cox Green. Surr —2B 26
Cox Green. Tyne —4G 115
Coxheath. Kent —5B 40
Coxhoe. Dur —1A 106
Coxley. Som —2A 22
Coxwold. N Yor —2H 99
Coychurch. V Glam —4C 32
Coylton. S Ayr —3D 116
Coylumbridge. High —2D 150
Coynach. Abers —3B 152
Coynachie. Abers —5B 160
Coytrahen. B'end —3B 32
Crabbs Cross. Worc —4E 61
Crabgate. Norf —3C 78
Crab Orchard. Dors —2F 15
Crabtree. W Sus —3D 26
Crabtree Green. Wrex —1F 71
Crackaig. High —2G 165
Crackenthorpe. Cumb —2H 103
Crackington Haven. Corn —3B 10
Crackley. Staf —5C 84
Crackley. Warw —3G 61
Crackleybank. Shrp —4B 72
Crackpot. N Yor —5C 104
Cracoe. N Yor —4B 98
Craddock. Devn —1D 12
Cradhlastadh. W Isl —4C 171
Cradley. Here —1C 48
Cradley. W Mid —2D 60
Cradoc. Powy —2D 46
Crafthole. Corn —3H 7
Crafton. Buck —4G 51
Cragabus. Arg —5B 124
Crag Foot. Lanc —2D 97
Craggan. High —1E 151
Cragganmore. Mor —5F 159
Cragganvallie. High —5H 157
Craggie. High —2F 165
Craggiemore. High —5B 158
Cragg Vale. W Yor —2A 92
Craghead. Dur —4F 115
Cragside NT —4E 121
Crai. Powy —3B 46
Craibstone. Aber —2F 153
Craichie. Ang —4E 145
Craig. Arg —5E 141
Craig. Dum —2D 111
Craig. High —4C 156 (nr. Achnashellach)
Craig. High —2G 155 (nr. Lower Diabaig)
Craig. High —5H 155 (nr. Stromeferry)
Craiganour Lodge. Per —3D 142
Craigbrack. Arg —4A 134
Craig-cefn-parc. Swan —5G 45
Craigdallie. Per —1E 137
Craigdam. Abers —5F 161
Craigdarroch. E Ayr —4F 117
Craigdarroch. High —3G 157
Craigdhu. High —4G 157
Craigearn. Abers —2E 152
Craigellachie. Mor —4G 159
Craigend. Per —2D 136
Craigendoran. Arg —1E 126
Craigends. Ren —3F 127
Craigenputtock. Dum —1E 111
Craigens. E Ayr —3E 117
Craighall. Edin —2E 129
Craighead. Fife —2H 137
Craighouse. Arg —3D 124
Craigie. Abers —2G 153
Craigie. D'dee —5D 144
Craigie. Per —4A 144 (nr. Blairgowrie)
Craigie. Per —1D 136 (nr. Perth)
Craigie. S Ayr —1D 116
Craigielaw. E Lot —2A 130
Craigievar Castle NTS —3C 152
Craiglemine. Dum —5B 110
Craig-llwyn. Shrp —3E 71
Craiglockhart. Edin —2F 129
Craig Lodge. Arg —2B 126
Craigmalloch. E Ayr —5D 117
Craigmaud. Abers —3F 161
Craigmill. Stir —4H 135
Craigmillar. Edin —2F 129
Craigmore. Arg —3C 126
Craigmuie. Dum —1E 111
Craignair. Dum —3F 111
Craignant. Shrp —2E 71
Craignethan Castle HS —5B 128
Craigneuk. N Lan —3A 128 (nr. Airdrie)
Craigneuk. N Lan —4A 128 (nr. Motherwell)
Craignure. Arg —5B 140
Craigo. Abers —2F 145
Craigrory. High —4A 158
Craigrothie. Fife —2F 137
Craigs. Dum —2D 112
Craigshill. W Lot —3D 128
Craigs, The. High —4B 164
Craigton. Aber —3F 153
Craigton. Abers —3E 152
Craigton. Ang —5E 145 (nr. Carnoustie)
Craigton. Ang —3C 144 (nr. Kirriemuir)
Craigton. High —4A 158
Craigtown. High —3A 168
Craig-y-Duke. Neat —5H 45
Craigyloch. Ang —3B 144
Craig-y-nos. Powy —4B 46
Craik. Bord —4F 119
Crail. Fife —3H 137
Crailing. Bord —2A 120
Crailinghall. Bord —2B 120
Crakehill. N Yor —2G 99
Crakemarsh. Staf —2E 73
Crambe. N Yor —3B 100
Crambeck. N Yor —3B 100
Cramlington. Nmbd —2F 115
Cramond. Edin —2E 129
Cramond Bridge. Edin —2E 129
Cranage. Ches —4B 84
Cranberry. Staf —2C 72
Cranborne. Dors —1F 15
Cranborne Manor Gdn. —1F 15
Cranbourne. Brac —3A 38
Cranbrook. Kent —2B 28
Cranbrook Common. Kent —2B 28
Crane Moor. S Yor —4D 92
Crane's Corner. Norf —4B 78
Cranfield. Beds —1H 51
Cranford. G Lon —3B 38
Cranford St Andrew. Nptn —3G 63
Cranford St John. Nptn —3G 63
Cranham. Glos —4D 49
Cranham. G Lon —2G 39
Crank. Mers —1H 83
Cranleigh. Surr —2B 26
Cranley. Suff —3D 66
Cranloch. Mor —3G 159
Cranmer Green. Suff —3C 66
Cranmore. IOW —3B 16
Cranmore. Linc —5A 76
Crannich. Arg —4G 139
Crannoch. Mor —3B 160
Cranoe. Leics —1E 63
Cransford. Suff —4F 67
Cranshaws. Bord —3C 130
Cranstal. IOM —1D 108
Crantock. Corn —2B 6
Cranwell. Linc —5H 87
Cranwell Aviation Heritage Centre —1H 75
Cranwich. Norf —1G 65
Cranworth. Norf —5B 78
Craobh Haven. Arg —3E 133
Craobhnaclag. High —4G 157
Crapstone. Devn —2B 8
Crarae. Arg —4G 133
Crarae Gdn. NTS —4G 133
Crask. High —2H 167
Crask Inn. High —1C 164
Crask of Aigas. High —4G 157
Craster. Nmbd —3G 121
Cratfield. Suff —3F 67
Crathes. Abers —4E 153
Crathes Castle NTS —4E 153
Crathie. Abers —4G 151
Crathie. High —4H 149
Crathorne. N Yor —4B 106
Craven Arms. Shrp —2G 59
Crawcrook. Tyne —3E 115
Crawford. Lanc —4C 90
Crawford. S Lan —2B 118
Crawforddyke. S Lan —4B 128
Crawfordjohn. S Lan —2A 118
Crawick. Dum —3G 117
Crawley. Devn —2F 13
Crawley. Hants —3C 24
Crawley. Oxon —4B 50
Crawley. W Sus —2D 26
Crawley Down. W Sus —2E 27
Crawley Side. Dur —5C 114
Crawshawbooth. Lanc —2G 91
Crawton. Abers —5F 153
Cray. N Yor —2B 98
Cray. Per —2A 144
Crayford. G Lon —3G 39
Crayke. N Yor —2H 99
Craymere Beck. Norf —2C 78
Crays Hill. Essx —1B 40
Cray's Pond. Oxon —3E 37
Crazies Hill. Wok —3F 37
Creacombe. Devn —1B 12
Creagan. Arg —4D 141
Creag Aoil. High —1F 141
Creag Ghoraidh. W Isl —4C 170
Creaguaineach Lodge. High —2H 141
Creamore Bank. Shrp —2H 71
Creaton. Nptn —3E 62
Creca. Dum —2D 112
Credenhill. Here —1H 47
Crediton. Devn —2B 12
Creebridge. Dum —3B 110
Creech. Dors —4E 15
Creech Heathfield. Som —4F 21
Creech St Michael. Som —4F 21
Creed. Corn —4D 6
Creekmoor. Pool —3E 15
Creekmouth. G Lon —2F 39
Creeting St Mary. Suff —5C 66
Creeting St Peter. Suff —5C 66
Creeton. Linc —3H 75
Creetown. Dum —4B 110
Creggans. Arg —3H 133
Cregneash. IOM —5A 108
Cregrina. Powy —5D 58
Creich. Arg —2B 132
Creighton. Staf —2E 73
Creigiau. Card —3D 32
Cremyll. Corn —3A 8
Crendell. Dors —1F 15
Crepkill. High —4D 154
Cressage. Shrp —5H 71
Cressbrook. Derbs —3F 85
Cresselly. Pemb —4E 43
Cressing. Essx —3A 54
Cresswell. Nmbd —5G 121
Cresswell. Staf —2D 73
Cresswell Quay. Pemb —4E 43
Creswell. Derbs —3C 86
Creswell Green. Staf —4E 73
Cretingham. Suff —4E 67
Crewe. Ches —5G 83 (nr. Farndon)
Crewe. Ches —5B 84 (nr. Nantwich)
Crewgreen. Powy —4F 71
Crewkerne. Som —2H 13
Crews Hill. G Lon —5D 52
Crewton. Derb —2A 74
Crianlarich. Stir —1C 134
Cribbs Causeway. S Glo —4A 34
Cribyn. Cdgn —5E 57
Criccieth. Gwyn —2D 69
Criccieth Castle CADW —2E 69
Crich. Derbs —5A 86
Crichton. Midl —3G 129
Crichton Castle HS —3G 129
Crick. Mon —2H 33
Crick. Nptn —3C 62
Crickadarn. Powy —1D 46
Cricket Hill. Hants —5G 37
Cricket Malherbie. Som —1G 13
Cricket St Thomas. Som —2G 13
Cricket St Thomas Wildlife Park —2G 13
Crickham. Som —2H 21
Crickheath. Shrp —3E 71
Crickhowell. Powy —4F 47
Cricklade. Wilts —2G 35
Cricklewood. G Lon —2D 38
Cridling Stubbs. N Yor —2F 93
Criech. Fife —1F 137
Crieff. Per —1A 136
Criftins. Shrp —2F 71
Criggion. Powy —4E 71
Crigglestone. W Yor —3D 92
Crimchard. Som —2G 13
Crimdon Park. Dur —1B 106
Crimond. Abers —3H 161
Crimonmogate. Abers —3H 161
Crimplesham. Norf —5F 77
Crimscote. Warw —1H 49
Crinan. Arg —4E 133
Cringleford. Norf —5D 78
Crinow. Pemb —3F 43
Cripplesease. Corn —3C 4
Cripplestyle. Dors —1F 15
Cripp's Corner. E Sus —3B 28
Croanford. Corn —5A 10
Crockenhill. Kent —4G 39
Crocker End. Oxon —3F 37
Crockerhill. Hants —2D 16
Crockernwell. Devn —3A 12
Crocker's Ash. Here —4A 48
Crockerton. Wilts —2D 22
Crocketford. Dum —2F 111
Crockey Hill. York —5A 100
Crockham Hill. Kent —5F 39
Crockhurst Street. Kent —1H 27
Crockleford Heath. Essx —3D 54
Croeserw. Neat —2B 32
Croes-Goch. Pemb —1C 42
Croes Hywel. Mon —4G 47
Croes-lan. Cdgn —1D 45
Croesor. Gwyn —1F 69
Croesowallt. Shrp —3E 71
Croesyceiliog. Carm —4E 45
Croesyceiliog. Torf —2G 33
Croes-y-mwyalch. Torf —2G 33
Croesywaun. Gwyn —5E 81
Croford. Som —4E 20
Croft. Leics —1C 62
Croft. Linc —4E 89
Croft. Warr —1A 84
Croftamie. Stir —1F 127
Croft Castle NT —4G 59
Croftfoot. Glas —3G 127
Croftmill. Per —5F 143
Crofton. Cumb —4E 112

Crofton. W Yor —3D 93
Crofton. Wilts —5A 36
Croft-on-Tees. N Yor —4F 105
Crofts. Dum —2E 111
Crofts of Benachielt. High —5D 169
Crofts of Dipple. Mor —3H 159
Crofty. Swan —3E 31
Croggan. Arg —1E 132
Croglin. Cumb —5G 113
Croich. High —4B 164
Croick. High —3A 168
Croig. Arg —3E 139
Croir. W Isl —4D 171
Cromarty. High —2B 158
Crombie. Fife —1D 128
Cromdale. High —1E 151
Cromer. Herts —3C 52
Cromer. Norf —1E 78
Cromford. Derbs —5G 85
Cromford Mill WH —5G 85
Cromhall. S Glo —2B 34
Cromhall Common. S Glo —3B 34
Cromor. W Isl —5G 171
Cromra. High —5H 149
Cromwell. Notts —4E 87
Cromwell Mus. —3B 64
Cronberry. E Ayr —2F 117
Crondall. Hants —2F 25
Cronk, The. IOM —2C 108
Cronk-y-Voddy. IOM —3C 108
Cronton. Mers —2G 83
Crook. Cumb —5F 103
Crook. Dur —1E 105
Crookdake. Cumb —5C 112
Crooke. G Man —4D 90
Crookedholm. E Ayr —1D 116
Crooked Soley. Wilts —4B 36
Crookes. S Yor —2H 85
Crookgate Bank. Dur —4E 115
Crookhall. Dur —4E 115
Crookham. Nmbd —1D 120
Crookham. W Ber —5D 36
Crookham Village. Hants —1F 25
Crooklands. Cumb —1E 97
Crook of Devon. Per —3C 136
Crookston. Ren —3G 127
Croome Park NT —1D 49
Cropredy. Oxon —1C 50
Cropston. Leics —4C 74
Cropthorne. Worc —1E 49
Cropton. N Yor —1B 100
Cropwell Bishop. Notts —2D 74
Cropwell Butler. Notts —2D 74
Cros. W Isl —1H 171
Crosbie. N Ayr —4D 126
Crosbost. W Isl —5F 171
Crosby. Cumb —1B 102
Crosby. IOM —4C 108
Crosby. Mers —1F 83
Crosby. N Lin —3B 94
Crosby Court. N Yor —5A 106
Crosby Garrett. Cumb —4A 104
Crosby Ravensworth. Cumb —3H 103
Crosby Villa. Cumb —1B 102
Croscombe. Som —2A 22
Crosland Moor. W Yor —3B 92
Cross. Som —1H 21
Crossaig. Arg —4G 125
Crossapol. Arg —4A 138
Cross Ash. Mon —4H 47
Cross-at-Hand. Kent —1B 28
Crossbush. W Sus —5B 26
Crosscanonby. Cumb —1B 102
Crossdale Street. Norf —2E 79
Cross End. Essx —2B 54
Crossens. Mers —3B 90
Crossford. Fife —1D 128
Crossford. S Lan —5B 128
Cross Foxes. Gwyn —4G 69
Crossgate. Orkn —6D 172
Crossgate. Staf —2D 72
Crossgatehall. E Lot —3G 129
Crossgates. Fife —1E 129
Crossgates. N Yor —1E 101
Crossgates. Powy —4C 58
Cross Gates. W Yor —1D 92
Crossgill. Lanc —3E 97
Cross Green. Devn —4D 11
Cross Green. Staf —5D 72
Cross Green. Suff —5A 66 (nr. Cockfield)
Cross Green. Suff —5B 66 (nr. Hitcham)
Cross Hands. Carm —4F 45 (nr. Ammanford)
Crosshands. Carm —2F 43 (nr. Whitland)
Crosshands. E Ayr —1D 117
Crosshill. E Ayr —2D 117
Crosshill. Fife —4D 136
Cross Hill. Glos —2A 34
Crosshill. S Ayr —4C 116
Crosshills. High —2A 158
Cross Hills. N Yor —5C 98
Cross Holme. N Yor —5C 106
Crosshouse. E Ayr —1C 116
Cross Houses. Shrp —5H 71
Crossings. Cumb —2G 113
Cross in Hand. E Sus —3G 27
Cross Inn. Cdgn —4E 57 (nr. Aberaeron)
Cross Inn. Cdgn —5C 56 (nr. New Quay)
Cross Inn. Rhon —3D 32
Crosskeys. Cphy —2F 33
Crosskirk. High —2C 168
Crosslands. Cumb —1C 96
Cross Lane Head. Shrp —1B 60
Cross Lanes. Corn —4D 5
Cross Lanes. Dur —3D 104
Cross Lanes. N Yor —3H 99
Crosslanes. Shrp —4F 71
Cross Lanes. Wrex —1F 71
Crosslee. Ren —3F 127
Crossmichael. Dum —3E 111
Crossmoor. Lanc —1C 90
Cross Oak. Powy —3E 46
Cross of Jackston. Abers —5E 161
Cross o' th' Hands. Derbs —1G 73
Crossraguel Abbey HS —4B 116
Crossroads. Abers —3G 153 (nr. Aberdeen)
Crossroads. Abers —4E 153 (nr. Banchory)
Crossroads. E Ayr —1D 116
Cross Side. Devn —4B 20
Cross Street. Suff —3D 66
Crosston. Ang —3E 145
Cross Town. Ches —3B 84
Crossway. Mon —4H 47
Crossway. Powy —5C 58
Crossway Green. Mon —2A 34
Crossway Green. Worc —4C 60
Crossways. Dors —4C 14
Crosswell. Pemb —1F 43
Crosswood. Cdgn —3F 57
Crosthwaite. Cumb —5F 103
Croston. Lanc —3C 90
Crostwick. Norf —4E 79
Crostwight. Norf —3F 79
Crothair. W Isl —4D 171
Crouch. Kent —5H 39
Croucheston. Wilts —4F 23
Crouch Hill. Dors —1C 14
Croughton. Nptn —2D 50
Crovie. Abers —2F 161
Crow. Hants —2G 15
Crowan. Corn —3D 4
Crowborough. E Sus —2G 27
Crowcombe. Som —3E 21
Crowcroft. Worc —5B 60
Crowdecote. Derbs —4F 85
Crowden. Derbs —1E 85
Crowden. Devn —3E 11
Crowdhill. Hants —1C 16
Crowdon. N Yor —5G 107
Crow Edge. S Yor —4B 92
Crow End. Cambs —5C 64
Crowfield. Nptn —1E 50
Crowfield. Suff —5D 66
Crow Green. Essx —1G 39
Crow Hill. Here —3B 48
Crowhurst. E Sus —4B 28
Crowhurst. Surr —1E 27
Crowhurst Lane End. Surr —1E 27
Crowland. Linc —4B 76
Crowland. Suff —3C 66
Crowlas. Corn —3C 4
Crowle. N Lin —3A 94
Crowle. Worc —5D 60
Crowle Green. Worc —5D 60
Crowmarsh Gifford. Oxon —3E 36
Crown Corner. Suff —3E 67
Crownthorpe. Norf —5C 78
Crowntown. Corn —3D 4
Crows-an-wra. Corn —4A 4
Crowshill. Norf —5B 78
Crowthorne. Brac —5G 37
Crowton. Ches —3H 83
Croxall. Staf —4F 73
Croxby. Linc —1A 88
Croxdale. Dur —1F 105
Croxden. Staf —2E 73
Croxden Abbey EH —2E 73
Croxley Green. Herts —1B 38
Croxteth Hall —1G 83
Croxton. Cambs —4B 64
Croxton. Norf —2B 78 (nr. Fakenham)
Croxton. Norf —2A 66 (nr. Thetford)
Croxton. N Lin —3D 94
Croxton. Staf —2B 72
Croxtonbank. Staf —2B 72
Croxton Green. Ches —5H 83
Croxton Kerrial. Leics —3F 75
Croy. High —4B 158
Croy. N Lan —2A 128
Croyde. Devn —3E 19
Croydon. Cambs —1D 52
Croydon. G Lon —4E 39
Crubenbeg. High —4A 150
Crubenmore Lodge. High —4A 150
Cruckmeore. Shrp —5G 71
Cruckton. Shrp —4G 71
Cruden Bay. Abers —5H 161
Crudgington. Telf —4A 72
Crudie. Abers —3E 161
Crudwell. Wilts —2E 35
Cruft. Devn —3F 11
Crug. Powy —3D 58
Crughywel. Powy —4F 47
Crugmeer. Corn —1D 6
Crugybar. Carm —2G 45
Crug-y-byddar. Powy —2D 58
Crulabhig. W Isl —4D 171
Crumlin. Cphy —2F 33
Crumpsall. G Man —4G 91
Crumpsbrook. Shrp —3A 60
Crundale. Kent —1E 29
Crundale. Pemb —3D 42
Cruwys Morchard. Devn —1B 12
Crux Easton. Hants —1C 24
Crwbin. Carm —4E 45
Cryers Hill. Buck —2G 37
Crymych. Pemb —1F 43
Crynant. Neat —5A 46
Crystal Palace. G Lon —3E 39
Cuaich. High —5A 150
Cuaig. High —3G 155
Cuan. Arg —2E 133
Cubbington. Warw —4H 61
Cubert. Corn —3B 6
Cubley. S Yor —4C 92
Cubley Common. Derbs —2F 73
Cublington. Buck —3G 51
Cublington. Here —2G 47
Cuckfield. W Sus —3E 27
Cucklington. Som —4C 22
Cuckney. Notts —3C 86
Cuckoo Bridge. Linc —3B 76
Cuckron. Shet —6F 173
Cuddesdon. Oxon —5E 50
Cuddington. Buck —4F 51
Cuddington. Ches —3A 84
Cuddington Heath. Ches —1G 71
Cuddy Hill. Lanc —1C 90
Cudham. G Lon —5F 39
Cudlipptown. Devn —5F 11
Cudworth. Som —1G 13
Cudworth. S Yor —4D 93
Cudworth. Surr —1D 26
Cuerdley Cross. Warr —2H 83
Cuffley. Herts —5D 52
Cuidhir. W Isl —8B 170
Cuidhsiadar. W Isl —2H 171
Cuidhtinis. W Isl —9C 171
Culbo. High —2A 158
Culbokie. High —3A 158
Culburnie. High —4G 157
Culcabock. High —4A 158
Culcharry. High —3C 158
Culcheth. Warr —1A 84
Culduie. High —4G 155
Culeave. High —4C 164
Culford. Suff —4H 65
Culgaith. Cumb —2H 103
Culham. Oxon —2D 36
Culkein. High —1E 163
Culkein Drumbeg. High —5B 166
Culkerton. Glos —2E 35
Cullen. Mor —2C 160
Cullercoats. Tyne —2G 115
Cullicudden. High —2A 158
Cullingworth. W Yor —1A 92
Cullipool. Arg —2E 133
Cullivoe. Shet —1G 173
Culloch. Per —2G 135
Culloden Battle Site NTS —4B 158
Cullompton. Devn —2D 12
Culm Davy. Devn —1E 13
Culmington. Shrp —2G 59
Culmstock. Devn —1E 12
Culnacnoc. High —2E 155
Culnacraig. High —3E 163
Culrain. High —4C 164
Culross. Fife —1C 128
Culross Palace NTS —1C 128
Culroy. S Ayr —3C 116
Culswick. Shet —7D 173
Cults. Aber —3F 153
Cults. Abers —5C 160
Cults. Fife —3F 137
Cultybraggan Camp. Per —1G 135
Culver. Devn —3B 12
Culverlane. Devn —2D 8
Culverstone Green. Kent —4H 39
Culverthorpe. Linc —1H 75
Culworth. Nptn —1D 50
Culzean Castle NTS —3B 116
Culzie Lodge. High —1H 157
Cumberlow Green. Herts —2D 52
Cumbernauld. N Lan —2A 128
Cumbernauld Village. N Lan —2A 128
Cumberworth. Linc —3E 89
Cumdivock. Cumb —5E 113
Cuminestown. Abers —3F 161
Cumledge Mill. Bord —4D 130
Cumlewick. Shet —9F 173
Cummersdale. Cumb —4E 113
Cummertrees. Dum —3C 112
Cummingstown. Mor —2F 159
Cumnock. E Ayr —3E 117
Cumnor. Oxon —5C 50
Cumrew. Cumb —4G 113
Cumwhinton. Cumb —4F 113
Cumwhitton. Cumb —4G 113
Cundall. N Yor —2G 99
Cunninghamhead. N Ayr —5E 127
Cunning Park. S Ayr —3C 116
Cunningsburgh. Shet —9F 173
Cunnister. Shet —2G 173
Cupar. Fife —2F 137
Cupar Muir. Fife —2F 137
Cupernham. Hants —4B 24
Curbar. Derbs —3G 85
Curborough. Staf —4F 73
Curbridge. Hants —1D 16
Curbridge. Oxon —5B 50
Curdridge. Hants —1D 16
Curdworth. Warw —1F 61
Curland. Som —1F 13
Curraghs Wildlife Park —2C 108
Curridge. W Ber —4C 36
Currie. Edin —3E 129
Curry Mallet. Som —4G 21
Curry Rivel. Som —4G 21
Curtisden Green. Kent —1B 28
Curtisknowle. Devn —3D 8
Cury. Corn —4D 5
Cusgarne. Corn —4B 6
Cusop. Here —1F 47
Cusworth. S Yor —4F 93
Cutcombe. Som —3C 20
Cuthill. E Lot —2G 129
Cutiau. Gwyn —4F 69
Cutlers Green. Essx —2F 53
Cutmadoc. Corn —2E 7
Cutnall Green. Worc —4C 60
Cutsdean. Glos —2F 49
Cutthorpe. Derbs —3H 85
Cuttivett. Corn —2H 7
Cutts. Shet —8F 173
Cuttybridge. Pemb —3D 42
Cuttyhill. Abers —3H 161
Cuxham. Oxon —2E 37
Cuxton. Medw —4B 40
Cuxwold. Linc —4E 95
Cwm. Blae —5E 47
Cwm. Den —3C 82
Cwm. Powy —1E 59
Cwmafan. Neat —2A 32
Cwmaman. Rhon —2C 32
Cwmann. Carm —1F 45
Cwmbach. Carm —2G 43
Cwmbach. Powy —2E 47
Cwmbach. Rhon —5D 46
Cwmbach Llechryd. Powy —5C 58
Cwmbelan. Powy —2B 58
Cwmbran. Torf —2F 33
Cwmbrwyno. Cdgn —2G 57
Cwm Capel. Carm —5E 45
Cwmcarn. Cphy —2F 33
Cwmcarvan. Mon —5H 47
Cwm-celyn. Blae —5F 47
Cwmcerdinen. Swan —5G 45
Cwm-Cewydd. Gwyn —4A 70
Cwmcoy. Cdgn —1C 44
Cwmcrawnon. Powy —4E 47
Cwmcych. Pemb —1G 43
Cwmdare. Rhon —5C 46
Cwmdu. Carm —2G 45
Cwmdu. Powy —3E 47
Cwmduad. Carm —2D 45
Cwm Dulais. Swan —5G 45
Cwmerfyn. Cdgn —2F 57
Cwmfelin. B'end —3B 32
Cwmfelin Boeth. Carm —3F 43
Cwmfelinfach. Cphy —2E 33
Cwmfelin Mynach. Carm —2G 43
Cwmffrwd. Carm —4E 45
Cwmgiedd. Powy —4A 46
Cwmgors. Neat —4H 45
Cwmgwili. Carm —4F 45
Cwmgwrach. Neat —5B 46
Cwmhiraeth. Carm —1H 43
Cwmifor. Carm —3G 45
Cwmisfael. Carm —4E 45
Cwm-Llinau. Powy —5H 69
Cwmllynfell. Neat —4H 45
Cwm-mawr. Carm —4F 45
Cwm-miles. Carm —2F 43
Cwmorgan. Carm —1G 43
Cwmparc. Rhon —2C 32
Cwm Penmachno. Cnwy —1G 69
Cwmpennar. Rhon —5D 46
Cwm Plysgog. Pemb —1B 44
Cwmrhos. Powy —3E 47
Cwmsychpant. Cdgn —1E 45
Cwmsyfiog. Cphy —5E 47
Cwmsymlog. Cdgn —2F 57
Cwmtillery. Blae —5F 47
Cwm-twrch Isaf. Powy —5A 46
Cwm-twrch Uchaf. Powy —4A 46
Cwmwysg. Powy —3B 46
Cwm-y-glo. Gwyn —4E 81
Cwmyoy. Mon —3G 47
Cwmystwyth. Cdgn —3G 57
Cwrt. Gwyn —1F 57
Cwrtnewydd. Cdgn —1E 45
Cwrt-y-Cadno. Carm —1G 45
Cydweli. Carm —5E 45
Cyffylliog. Den —5C 82
Cymau. Flin —5E 83
Cymer. Neat —2B 32
Cymer Abbey CADW —4G 69
Cymmer. Neat —2B 32
Cymmer. Rhon —2D 32
Cyncoed. Card —3E 33
Cynghordy. Carm —2B 46
Cynghordy. Swan —5G 45
Cynheidre. Carm —5E 45
Cynonville. Neat —2B 32
Cynwyd. Den —1C 70
Cynwyl Elfed. Carm —3D 44
Cywarch. Gwyn —4A 70

D

Dacre. Cumb —2F 103
Dacre. N Yor —3D 98
Dacre Banks. N Yor —3D 98
Daddry Shield. Dur —1B 104
Dadford. Buck —2E 51
Dadlington. Leics —1B 62
Dafen. Carm —5F 45
Daffy Green. Norf —5B 78
Dagdale. Staf —2E 73
Dagenham. G Lon —2F 39
Daggons. Dors —1G 15
Daglingworth. Glos —5E 49
Dagnall. Buck —4H 51
Dagtail End. Worc —4E 61
Dail. Arg —5E 141
Dail Beag. W Isl —3E 171
Dail bho Dheas. W Isl —1G 171
Dailly. S Ayr —4B 116
Dail Mor. W Isl —3E 171
Dairsie. Fife —2G 137
Daisy Bank. W Mid —1E 61
Daisy Hill. G Man —4E 91
Daisy Hill. W Yor —1B 92
Dalabrog. W Isl —6C 170
Dalavich. Arg —2G 133
Dalbeattie. Dum —3F 111
Dalblair. E Ayr —3F 117
Dalbury. Derbs —2G 73
Dalby. IOM —4B 108
Dalby Wolds. Leics —3D 74
Dalchalm. High —3G 165
Dalcharn. High —3G 167
Dalchork. High —2C 164
Dalchreichart. High —2E 149
Dalchruin. Per —2G 135
Dalcross. High —4B 158
Dalderby. Linc —4B 88
Dale. Cumb —5G 113
Dale. Derbs —2B 74
Dale. Pemb —4C 42
Dalebank. Derbs —4A 86
Dale Bottom. Cumb —2D 102
Dalebrook. Derbs —2F 73
Dale Head. Cumb —3F 103
Dalehouse. N Yor —3E 107
Dalelia. High —2B 140
Dalemain House —2F 103
Dale of Walls. Shet —6C 173
Dalgarven. N Ayr —5D 126
Dalgety Bay. Fife —1E 129
Dalginross. Per —1G 135
Dalguise. Per —4G 143
Dalhalvaig. High —3A 168
Dalham. Suff —4G 65
Dalintart. Arg —1F 133
Dalkeith. Midl —3G 129
Dallas. Mor —3F 159
Dallas Dhu Historic Distillery HS —3E 159
Dalleagles. E Ayr —3E 117
Dallinghoo. Suff —5E 67
Dallington. E Sus —4A 28
Dallow. N Yor —2D 98
Dalmally. Arg —1A 134
Dalmarnock. Glas —3H 127
Dalmellington. E Ayr —4D 117
Dalmeny. Edin —2E 129
Dalmeny House —2E 129
Dalmigavie. High —2B 150
Dalmilling. S Ayr —2C 116
Dalmore. High —2A 158 (nr. Alness)
Dalmore. High —3E 164 (nr. Rogart)
Dalmuir. W Dun —2F 127
Dalmunach. Mor —4G 159
Dalnabreck. High —2B 140
Dalnacardoch Lodge. Per —1E 142
Dalnamein Lodge. Per —2E 143
Dalnaspidal Lodge. Per —1D 142
Dalnatrat. High —3D 140
Dalnavie. High —1A 158
Dalnawillan Lodge. High —4C 168
Dalness. High —3F 141
Dalnessie. High —2D 164
Dalqueich. Per —3C 136
Dalquhairn. S Ayr —5C 116
Dalreavoch. High —3E 165
Dalreoch. Per —2C 136
Dalry. Edin —2F 129
Dalry. N Ayr —5D 126
Dalrymple. E Ayr —3C 116
Dalscote. Nptn —5D 62
Dalserf. S Lan —4A 128
Dalsmirren. Arg —4A 122
Dalston. Cumb —5E 113
Dalswinton. Dum —1G 111
Dalton. Dum —2C 112
Dalton. Lanc —4C 90
Dalton. Nmbd —4C 114 (nr. Hexham)
Dalton. Nmbd —2E 115 (nr. Ponteland)
Dalton. N Yor —4E 105 (nr. Richmond)
Dalton. N Yor —2G 99 (nr. Thirsk)
Dalton. S Lan —4H 127
Dalton. S Yor —1B 86
Dalton-in-Furness. Cumb —2B 96
Dalton-le-Dale. Dur —5H 115
Dalton Magna. S Yor —1B 86
Dalton-on-Tees. N Yor —4F 105
Dalton Piercy. Hart —1B 106
Daltot. Arg —1F 125
Dalvey. High —5F 159
Dalwhinnie. High —5A 150
Dalwood. Devn —2F 13
Damerham. Hants —1G 15
Damgate. Norf —5G 79 (nr. Acle)
Damgate. Norf —4G 79 (nr. Martham)
Dam Green. Norf —2C 66
Damhead. Mor —3E 159
Danaway. Kent —4C 40
Danbury. Essx —5A 54
Danby. N Yor —4E 107
Danby Botton. N Yor —4D 107
Danby Wiske. N Yor —5A 106
Danderhall. Midl —3G 129
Danebank. Ches —2D 85
Danebridge. Ches —4D 84
Dane End. Herts —3D 52
Danehill. E Sus —3F 27
Danesford. Shrp —1B 60
Daneshill. Hants —1E 25
Danesmoor. Derbs —4A 86
Danestone. Aber —3G 153
Dangerous Corner. Lanc —3D 90
Daniel's Water. Kent —1D 28
Danny —4D 27
Dan's Castle. Dur —1E 105
Danshillock. Abers —3E 160
Dan-yr-Ogof Showcaves —4B 46
Danzey Green. Warw —4F 61
Dapple Heath. Staf —3E 73
Daren. Powy —4F 47
Darenth. Kent —3G 39
Daresbury. Hal —2H 83
Darfield. S Yor —4E 93
Dargate. Kent —4E 41
Dargill. Per —2A 136
Darite. Corn —2G 7
Darlaston. Staf —2C 72
Darlaston. W Mid —1D 60
Darley. N Yor —4E 98
Darley Abbey. Derb —2A 74
Darley Bridge. Derbs —4G 85
Darley Dale. Derbs —4G 85
Darley Head. N Yor —4D 98
Darlingscott. Warw —1H 49
Darlington. Darl —3F 105
Darlington Railway Mus. —3F 105
Darliston. Shrp —2H 71
Darlton. Notts —3E 87
Darmsden. Suff —5C 66
Darnall. S Yor —2A 86
Darnford. Abers —4E 153
Darnick. Bord —1H 119
Darowen. Powy —5H 69
Darra. Abers —4E 161
Darracott. Devn —3E 19
Darras Hall. Nmbd —2E 115
Darrington. W Yor —2E 93
Darrow Green. Norf —2E 67
Darsham. Suff —4G 67
Dartfield. Abers —3H 161
Dartford. Kent —3G 39
Dartford Crossing. Kent —3G 39
Dartington. Devn —2D 9
Dartington Crystal —1F 11
Dartington Hall —2E 9
Dartmeet. Devn —5G 11
Dartmoor Nat. Park —4F 11

Dartmoor Wildlife Park —3B 8
Dartmouth. Devn —3E 9
Dartmouth Castle NT —3E 9
Darton. S Yor —3D 92
Darvel. E Ayr —1E 117
Darwen. Bkbn —2E 91
Darwin Mus. —4F 39
Dassels. Herts —3D 53
Datchet. Wind —3A 38
Datchworth. Herts —4C 52
Datchworth Green. Herts —4C 52
Daubhill. G Man —4F 91
Dauntsey. Wilts —3E 35
Dauntsey Green. Wilts —3E 35
Dauntsey Lock. Wilts —3E 35
Dava. Mor —5E 159
Davenham. Ches —3A 84
Daventry. Nptn —4C 62
Davidson's Mains. Edin —2F 129
Davidston. High —2B 158
Davidstow. Corn —4B 10
David's Well. Powy —3C 58
Davington. Dum —4E 119
Daviot. Abers —1E 153
Daviot. High —5B 158
Davyhulme. G Man —1B 84
Daw Cross. N Yor —4F 99
Dawdon. Dur —5H 115
Dawesgreen. Surr —1D 26
Dawley. Telf —5A 72
Dawlish. Devn —5C 12
Dawlish Warren. Devn —5C 12
Dawn. Cnwy —3A 82
Daws Heath. Essx —2C 40
Dawshill. Worc —5C 60
Daw's House. Corn —4D 10
Dawsmere. Linc —2D 76
Dawyck Botanic Gdn. —1C 118
Dayhills. Staf —2D 72
Dayhouse Bank. Worc —3D 60
Daylesford. Glos —3H 49
Daywall. Shrp —2E 71
Ddol. Flin —3D 82
Ddol Cownwy. Powy —4C 70
Deadwater. Nmbd —5A 120
Deaf Hill. Dur —1A 106
Deal. Kent —5H 41
Deal Castle EH —5H 41
Dean. Cumb —2B 102
Dean. Devn —2G 19
(nr. Combe Martin)
Dean. Devn —2F 19
(nr. Ilfracombe)
Dean. Devn —2H 19
(nr. Lynton)
Dean. Dors —1E 15
Dean. Hants —1D 16
(nr. Bishop's Waltham)
Dean. Hants —3C 24
(nr. Winchester)
Dean. Som —2B 22
Dean Bank. Dur —1F 105
Deanburnhaugh. Bord —3F 119
Deane. Hants —1D 24
Deanich Lodge. High —5A 164
Deanland. Dors —1E 15
Deanlane End. W Sus —1F 17
Dean Park. Shrp —4H 59
Dean Prior. Devn —2D 8
Dean Row. Ches —2C 84
Deans. W Lot —3D 128
Deanscales. Cumb —2B 102
Deanshanger. Nptn —2F 51
Deanston. Stir —3G 135
Dearham. Cumb —1B 102
Dearne. S Yor —4E 93
Dearne Valley. S Yor —4E 93
Debach. Suff —5E 67
Debden. Essx —2F 53
Debden Green. Essx —1F 39
(nr. Loughton)
Debden Green. Essx —2F 53
(nr. Saffron Walden)
Debenham. Suff —4D 66
Dechmont. W Lot —2D 128
Deddington. Oxon —2C 50
Dedham. Essx —2D 54
Dedham Heath. Essx —2D 54
Deebank. Abers —4D 152
Deene. Nptn —1G 63
Deene Park —1G 63
Deenethorpe. Nptn —1G 63
Deepcar. S Yor —1G 85
Deepcut. Surr —5A 38
Deepdale. Cumb —1G 97
Deepdale. N Lin —3D 94
Deepdale. N Yor —2A 98
Deeping Gate. Pet —5A 76
Deeping St James. Linc —5A 76
Deeping St Nicholas. Linc —4B 76
Deep-Sea World —1E 129
Deep, The —Hull 190
Deerhill. Mor —3B 160
Deerhurst. Glos —3D 48
Deerhurst Walton. Glos —3D 49
Deerness. Orkn —7E 172
Defford. Worc —1E 49
Defynnog. Powy —3C 46
Deganwy. Cnwy —3G 81
Deighton. N Yor —4A 106
Deighton. W Yor —3B 92
Deighton. York —5A 100
Deiniolen. Gwyn —4E 81
Delabole. Corn —4A 10
Delamere. Ches —4H 83
Delamere Forest Park —3H 83
Delfour. High —3C 150
Delgatie Castle —3E 161
Delliefure. High —5E 159
Dell, The. Suff —1G 67
Delly End. Oxon —4B 50
Delny. High —1B 158
Delph. G Man —4H 91
Delves. Dur —5E 115
Delves, The. W Mid —1E 61
Delvin End. Essx —2A 54
Dembleby. Linc —2H 75
Demelza. Corn —2D 6
Denaby Main. S Yor —1B 86
Denbeath. Fife —4F 137
Denbigh. Den —4C 82
Denbigh Castle —4C 82
Denbury. Devn —2E 9
Denby. Derbs —1A 74
Denby Common. Derbs —1B 74
Denby Dale. W Yor —4C 92
Denchworth. Oxon —2B 36
Dendron. Cumb —2B 96
Deneside. Dur —5H 115
Denford. Nptn —3G 63
Dengie. Essx —5C 54
Denham. Buck —2B 38
Denham. Suff —4G 65
(nr. Bury St Edmunds)
Denham. Suff —3D 66
(nr. Eye)
Denham Green. Buck —2B 38
Denham Street. Suff —3D 66
Denhead. Abers —5G 161
(nr. Ellon)
Denhead. Abers —3G 161
(nr. Strichen)
Denhead. Fife —2G 137
Denholm. Bord —3H 119
Denholme. W Yor —1A 92
Denholme Clough. W Yor —1A 92
Denholme Gate. W Yor —1A 92
Denio. Gwyn —2C 68
Denmead. Hants —1E 17
Dennington. Suff —4E 67
Denny. Falk —1B 128
Denny End. Cambs —4D 65
Dennyloanhead. Falk —1B 128
Den of Lindores. Fife —2E 137
Denshaw. G Man —3H 91
Denside. Abers —4F 153
Densole. Kent —1G 29
Denston. Suff —5G 65
Denstone. Staf —1F 73
Denstroude. Kent —4F 41
Dent. Cumb —1G 97
Den, The. N Ayr —4E 127
Denton. Cambs —2A 64
Denton. Darl —3F 105
Denton. E Sus —5F 27
Denton. G Man —1D 84
Denton. Kent —1G 29
Denton. Linc —2F 75
Denton. Norf —2E 67
Denton. Nptn —5F 63
Denton. N Yor —5D 98
Denton. Oxon —5D 50
Denver. Norf —5F 77
Denwick. Nmbd —3G 121
Deopham. Norf —5C 78
Deopham Green. Norf —1C 66
Depden. Suff —5G 65
Depden Green. Suff —5G 65
Deptford. G Lon —3E 39
Deptford. Wilts —3F 23
Derby. Derb —2A 74 & 188
Derbyhaven. IOM —5B 108
Derculich. Per —3F 143
Dereham. Norf —4B 78
Deri. Cphy —5E 47
Derril. Devn —2D 10
Derringstone. Kent —1G 29
Derrington. Shrp —1A 60
Derrington. Staf —3C 72
Derriton. Devn —2D 10
Derryguaig. Arg —5F 139
Derry Hill. Wilts —4E 35
Derrythorpe. N Lin —4B 94
Dersingham. Norf —2F 77
Dervaig. Arg —3F 139
Derwen. Den —5C 82
Derwen Gam. Cdgn —5D 56
Derwenlas. Powy —1G 57
Desborough. Nptn —2F 63
Desford. Leics —5B 74
Detchant. Nmbd —1E 121
Dethick. Derbs —5H 85
Detling. Kent —5B 40
Deuchar. Ang —2D 144
Deuddwr. Powy —4E 71
Devauden. Mon —2H 33
Devil's Bridge. Cdgn —3G 57
Devil's Punch Bowl NT —3G 25
Devitts Green. Warw —1G 61
Devizes. Wilts —5F 35
Devonport. Plym —3A 8
Devonside. Clac —4B 136
Devoran. Corn —5B 6
Dewa Roman Experience —Chester 188
Dewartown. Midl —3G 129
Dewlish. Dors —3C 14
Dewsbury. W Yor —2C 92
Dewshall Court. Here —2H 47
Dexbeer. Devn —2C 10
DH Lawrence House —1B 74
Dhoon. IOM —3D 108
Dhoor. IOM —2D 108
Dhowin. IOM —1D 108
Dial Green. W Sus —3A 26
Dial Post. W Sus —4C 26
Dibberford. Dors —2H 13
Dibden. Hants —2C 16
Dibden Purlieu. Hants —2C 16
Dickens' House —4H 41
Dickleburgh. Norf —2D 66
Didbrook. Glos —2F 49
Didcot. Oxon —2D 36
Didcot Railway Centre —2D 36
Diddington. Cambs —4A 64
Diddlebury. Shrp —2H 59
Didley. Here —2H 47
Didling. W Sus —1G 17
Didmarton. Glos —3D 34
Didsbury. G Man —1C 84
Didworthy. Devn —2C 8
Digby. Linc —5H 87
Digg. High —2D 154
Diggle. G Man —4A 92
Digmoor. Lanc —4C 90
Digswell. Herts —4C 52
Dihewyd. Cdgn —5D 57
Dilham. Norf —3F 79
Dilhorne. Staf —1D 73
Dillarburn. S Lan —5B 128
Dillington. Cambs —4A 64
Dilston. Nmbd —3C 114
Dilton Marsh. Wilts —2D 22
Dilwyn. Here —5G 59
Dimmer. Som —3B 22
Dimple. G Man —3F 91
Dinas. Carm —1G 43
Dinas. Gwyn —2B 68
Dinas. Pemb —1E 43
Dinas Dinlle. Gwyn —5D 80
Dinas Mawddwy. Gwyn —4A 70
Dinas Powys. V Glam —4E 33
Dinbych. Den —4C 82
Dinbych-y-Pysgod. Pemb —4F 43
Dinckley. Lanc —1E 91
Dinder. Som —2A 22
Dinedor. Here —2A 48
Dinedor Cross. Here —2A 48
Dinefwr NT —3G 45
Dingestow. Mon —4H 47
Dingle. Mers —2F 83
Dingleden. Kent —2C 28
Dingleton. Bord —1H 119
Dingley. Nptn —2E 63
Dingwall. High —3H 157
Dinmael. Cnwy —1C 70
Dinnet. Abers —4B 152
Dinnington. Som —1H 13
Dinnington. S Yor —2C 86
Dinnington. Tyne —2F 115
Dinorwic. Gwyn —4E 81
Dinosaur Adventure Park —4D 78
Dinosaur Mus. —3C 14
Dinton. Buck —4F 51
Dinton. Wilts —3F 23
Dinworthy. Devn —1D 10
Dipley. Hants —1F 25
Dippen. Arg —2B 122
Dippenhall. Surr —2G 25
Dippertown. Devn —4E 11
Dippin. N Ayr —3E 123
Dipple. S Ayr —4B 116
Diptford. Devn —3D 8
Dipton. Dur —4E 115
Dirleton. E Lot —1B 130
Dirleton Castle HS —1B 130
Dirt Pot. Nmbd —5B 114
Discoed. Powy —4E 59
Discovery, RRS —Dundee 188
Diseworth. Leics —3B 74
Dishes. Orkn —5F 172
Dishforth. N Yor —2F 99
Disley. Ches —2D 85
Diss. Norf —3D 66
Disserth. Powy —5C 58
Distington. Cumb —2B 102
Ditchampton. Wilts —3F 23
Ditcheat. Som —3B 22
Ditchingham. Norf —1F 67
Ditchling. E Sus —4E 27
Ditteridge. Wilts —5D 34
Dittisham. Devn —3E 9
Ditton. Hal —2G 83
Ditton. Kent —5B 40
Ditton Green. Cambs —5F 65
Ditton Priors. Shrp —2A 60
Divach. High —1G 149
Dixonfield. High —2D 168
Dixton. Glos —2E 49
Dixton. Mon —4A 48
Dizzard. Corn —3B 10
Dobcross. G Man —4H 91
Dobs Hill. Flin —4F 83
Dobson's Bridge. Shrp —2G 71
Dobwalls. Corn —2G 7
Dobwalls Adventure Park —2G 7
Doccombe. Devn —4A 12
Dochgarroch. High —4A 158
Docking. Norf —2G 77
Docklow. Here —5H 59
(Dock Mus., Barrow) —3A 96
Dockray. Cumb —2E 103
Doc Penfro. Pemb —4D 42
Dodbrooke. Devn —4D 8
Doddenham. Worc —5B 60
Doddinghurst. Essx —1G 39
Doddington. Cambs —1C 64
Doddington. Kent —5D 40
Doddington. Linc —4F 87
Doddington. Nmbd —1D 121
Doddington. Shrp —3A 60
Doddington Hall —3F 87
Doddiscombsleigh. Devn —4B 12
Doddshill. Norf —2G 77
Dodford. Nptn —4D 62
Dodford. Worc —3D 60
Dodington. Som —2E 21
Dodington. S Glo —4C 34
Dodleston. Ches —4F 83
Dods Leigh. Staf —2E 73
Dodworth. S Yor —4D 92
Doe Lea. Derbs —4B 86
Dogdyke. Linc —5B 88
Dogmersfield. Hants —1F 25
Dogsthorpe. Pet —5B 76
Dog Village. Devn —3C 12
Dolanog. Powy —4C 70
Dolau. Powy —4D 58
Dolau. Rhon —3D 32
Dolaucothi Gold Mines NT —2G 45
Dolbadarn Castle CADW —4E 81
Dolbenmaen. Gwyn —1E 69
Doley. Staf —3B 72
Dol-fach. Powy —5B 70
(nr. Llanbrynmair)
Dolfach. Powy —3B 58
(nr. Llanidloes)
Dolfor. Powy —2D 58
Dolforwyn Castle CADW —1D 58
Dolgarrog. Cnwy —4G 81
Dolgellau. Gwyn —4G 69
Dolgoch. Gwyn —5F 69
Dol-gran. Carm —2E 45
Dolhelfa. Powy —3B 58
Doll. High —3F 165
Dollar. Clac —4B 136
Dolley Green. Powy —4E 59
Dollwen. Cdgn —2F 57
Dolphin. Flin —3D 82
Dolphingstone. E Lot —2G 129
Dolphinholme. Lanc —4E 97
Dolphinton. S Lan —5E 129
Dolton. Devn —1F 11
Dolwen. Cnwy —3A 82
Dolwyddelan. Cnwy —5G 81
Dolwyddelan Castle CADW —5G 81
Dol-y-Bont. Cdgn —2F 57
Dolyhir. Powy —5E 59
Domestic Fowl Trust —1G 49
Domgay. Powy —4E 71
Doncaster. S Yor —4F 93
Donhead St Andrew. Wilts —4E 23
Donhead St Mary. Wilts —4E 23
Doniford. Som —2D 20
Donington. Linc —2B 76
Donington. Shrp —5C 72
Donington Eaudike. Linc —2B 76
Donington on Bain. Linc —2B 88
Donington South Ing. Linc —2B 76
Donisthorpe. Leics —4H 73
Donkey Sancuary —4E 13
Donkey Town. Surr —4A 38
Donna Nook. Linc —1D 88
Donnington. Glos —3G 49
Donnington. Here —2C 48
Donnington. Shrp —5H 71
Donnington. Telf —4B 72
Donnington. W Ber —5C 36
Donnington. W Sus —2G 17
Donnington Grand Prix Collection —3B 74
Donnington le Heath. Leics —4B 74
Donyatt. Som —1G 13
Doomsday Green. W Sus —2C 26
Doonfoot. S Ayr —3C 116
Doonholm. S Ayr —3C 116
Dorback Lodge. High —2E 151
Dorchester. Dors —3B 14
Dorchester. Oxon —2D 36
Dordon. Warw —5G 73
Dore. S Yor —2H 85
Dores. High —5H 157
Dorfold Hall —5A 84
Dorking. Surr —1C 26
Dorking Tye. Suff —2C 54
Dormansland. Surr —1F 27
Dormans Park. Surr —1E 27
Dormanstown. Red C —2C 106
Dormington. Here —1A 48
Dormston. Worc —5D 61
Dorn. Glos —2H 49
Dorney. Buck —3A 38
Dornie. High —1A 148
Dornoch. High —5E 165
Dornock. Dum —3D 112
Dorothy Clive Gdn. —2B 72
Dorrery. High —3C 168
Dorridge. W Mid —3F 61
Dorrington. Linc —5H 87
Dorrington. Shrp —5G 71
Dorsington. Warw —1G 49
Dorstone. Here —1G 47
Dorton. Buck —4E 51
Dotham. IOA —3C 80
Dottery. Dors —3H 13
Doublebois. Corn —2F 7
Dougarie. N Ayr —2C 122
Doughton. Glos —2D 35
Douglas. IOM —4C 108
Douglas. S Lan —1H 117
Douglastown. Ang —4D 144
Douglas Water. S Lan —1A 118
Doulting. Som —2B 22
Dounby. Orkn —5B 172
Doune. High —3C 150
(nr. Kingussie)
Doune. High —3B 164
(nr. Lairg)
Doune. Stir —3G 135
Doune Castle HS —3G 135
Dounie. High —4C 164
(nr. Bonar Bridge)
Dounie. High —5D 164
(nr. Tain)
Dounreay. High —2B 168
Doura. N Ayr —5E 127
Dousland. Devn —2B 8
Dovaston. Shrp —3F 71
Dove Cottage —4E 103
Dove Dale —5F 85
Dove Holes. Derbs —3E 85
Dovenby. Cumb —1B 102
Dover. Kent —1H 29 & 188
Dover Castle —188
Dovercourt. Essx —2F 55
Doverdale. Worc —4C 60
Doveridge. Derbs —2F 73
Doversgreen. Surr —1D 26
Dowally. Per —4H 143
Dowbridge. Lanc —1C 90
Dowdeswell. Glos —4F 49
Dowlais. Mer T —5D 46
Dowland. Devn —1F 11
Dowlands. Devn —3F 13
Dowles. Worc —3B 60
Dowlesgreen. Wok —5G 37
Dowlish Wake. Som —1G 13
Downall Green. Mers —4D 90
Down Ampney. Glos —2F 35
Downderry. Corn —3H 7
(nr. Looe)
Downderry. Corn —3D 6
(nr. St Austell)
Downe. G Lon —4F 39
Downe House EH —4F 39
Downend. IOW —4D 16
Downend. S Glo —4B 34
Downend. W Ber —4C 36
Downfield. Cambs —3F 65
Downfield. D'dee —5C 144
Downgate. Corn —5D 10
(nr. Kelly Brae)
Downgate. Corn —5C 10
(nr. Upton Cross)
Downham. Essx —1B 40
Downham. Lanc —5G 97
Downham. Nmbd —1C 120
Downham Market. Norf —5F 77
Down Hatherley. Glos —3D 48
Downhead. Som —2B 22
(nr. Frome)
Downhead. Som —4A 22
(nr. Yeovil)
Downhill. Per —5H 143
Downholland Cross. Lanc —4B 90
Downholme. N Yor —5E 105
Downies. Abers —4G 153
Downley. Buck —2G 37
Down St Mary. Devn —2H 11
Downside. Som —1B 22
(nr. Chilcompton)
Downside. Som —2B 22
(nr. Shepton Mallet)
Downside. Surr —5C 38
Down, The. Shrp —1A 60
Down Thomas. Devn —3B 8
Downton. Hants —3A 16
Downton. Wilts —4G 23
Downton on the Rock. Here —3G 59
Dowsby. Linc —3A 76
Dowsdale. Linc —4B 76
Dowthwaitehead. Cumb —2E 103
Doxey. Staf —3D 72
Doxford. Nmbd —2F 121
Doynton. S Glo —4C 34
Drabblegate. Norf —3E 78
Draethen. Cphy —3F 33
Draffan. S Lan —5A 128
Dragonby. N Lin —3B 94
Dragons Green. W Sus —3C 26
Drakelow. Worc —2C 60
Drakemyre. N Ayr —4D 126
Drakes Broughton. Worc —1E 49
Drakes Cross. Worc —3E 61
Drakewalls. Corn —5E 11
Draughton. Nptn —3E 63
Draughton. N Yor —4C 98
Drax. N Yor —2G 93
Draycot. Oxon —5E 51
Draycote. Warw —4B 62
Draycot Foliat. Swin —4G 35
Draycott. Derbs —2B 74
Draycott. Glos —2G 49
Draycott. Shrp —1C 60
Draycott. Som —1H 21
(nr. Cheddar)
Draycott. Som —4A 22
(nr. Yeovil)
Draycott. Worc —1D 48
Draycott in the Clay. Staf —3F 73
Draycott in the Moors. Staf —1D 73
Drayford. Devn —1A 12
Drayton. Leics —1F 63
Drayton. Linc —2B 76
Drayton. Norf —4D 78
Drayton. Nptn —4C 62
Drayton. Oxon —2C 36
(nr. Abingdon)
Drayton. Oxon —1C 50
(nr. Banbury)
Drayton. Port —2E 17
Drayton. Som —4H 21
Drayton. Warw —5F 61
Drayton. Worc —3D 60
Drayton Bassett. Staf —5F 73
Drayton Beauchamp. Buck —4H 51
Drayton Manor Park —5F 73
Drayton Parslow. Buck —3G 51
Drayton St Leonard. Oxon —2D 36
Drebley. N Yor —4C 98
Dreenhill. Pemb —3D 42
Drefach. Carm —4F 45
(nr. Meidrim)
Drefach. Carm —2D 44
(nr. Newcastle Emlyn)
Drefach. Carm —2G 43
(nr. Tumble)
Drefach. Cdgn —1F 45
Dreghorn. N Ayr —1C 116
Drellingore. Kent —1G 29
Drem. E Lot —2B 130
Dreumasdal. W Isl —5C 170
Drewsteignton. Devn —3H 11
Drewston. Devn —4H 11
Driby. Linc —3C 88
Driffield. E Yor —4E 101
Driffield. Glos —2F 35
Drift. Corn —4B 4
Drigg. Cumb —5B 102
Drighlington. W Yor —2C 92
Drimnin. High —3G 139
Drimpton. Dors —2H 13
Dringhoe. E Yor —4F 101
Drinisiadar. W Isl —8D 171
Drinkstone. Suff —4B 66
Drinkstone Green. Suff —4B 66
Drointon. Staf —3E 73
Droitwich Spa. Worc —4C 60
Droman. High —3B 166
Dron. Per —2D 136
Dronfield. Derbs —3A 86
Dronfield Woodhouse. Derbs —3H 85
Drongan. E Ayr —3D 116
Dronley. Ang —5C 144
Droop. Dors —2C 14
Drope. V Glam —4E 32
Droxford. Hants —1E 16
Droylsden. G Man —1C 84
Druggers End. Worc —2C 48
Druid. Den —1C 70
Druid's Heath. W Mid —5E 73
Druidston. Pemb —3C 42
Druim. High —3G 158
Druimarbin. High —1E 141
Druimindarroch. High —5E 147
Drum. Per —3C 136
Drumbeg. High —5B 166
Drumblade. Abers —4C 160

Drumbuie. Dum —1C 110
Drumbuie. High —5G 155
Drumburgh. Cumb —4D 112
Drumburn. Dum —3A 112
Drum Castle NTS —3E 153
Drumchapel. Glas —2G 127
Drumchardine. High —4H 157
Drumchork. High —5C 162
Drumclog. S Lan —1F 117
Drumeldrie. Fife —3G 137
Drumelzier. Bord —1D 118
Drumfearn. High —2E 147
Drumgask. High —4A 150
Drumgelloch. N Lan —3A 128
Drumgley. Ang —3D 144
Drumguish. High —4B 150
Drumin. Mor —5F 159
Drumindorsair. High —4G 157
Drumlamford House. S Ayr —2H 109
Drumlanrig Castle —5A 118
Drumlasie. Abers —3D 152
Drumlemble. Arg —4A 122
Drumlithie. Abers —5E 153
Drummoddie. Dum —5A 110
Drummond. High —2A 158
Drummond Castle Gdns. —2H 135
Drummore. Dum —5E 109
Drummuir. Mor —4A 160
Drumnadrochit. High —5H 157
Drumnagorrach. Mor —3C 160
Drumoak. Abers —4E 153
Drumrunie. High —3F 163
Drumry. W Dun —2G 127
Drums. Abers —1G 153
Drumsleet. Dum —2G 111
Drumsmittal. High —4A 158
Drums of Park. Abers —3C 160
Drumsturdy. Ang —5D 145
Drumtochty Castle. Abers —5D 152
Drumuie. High —4D 154
Drumuillie. High —1D 150
Drumvaich. Stir —3F 135
Drumwhindle. Abers —5G 161
Drunkendub. Ang —4F 145
Drury. Flin —4E 83
Drury Square. Norf —4B 78
Drusillas Zoo —5G 27
Drybeck. Cumb —3H 103
Drybridge. Mor —2B 160
Drybridge. N Ayr —1C 116
Drybrook. Glos —4B 48
Drybrook. Here —4A 48
Dryburgh. Bord —1H 119
Dryburgh Abbey HS —1H 119
Dry Doddington. Linc —1F 75
Dry Drayton. Cambs —4C 64
Drym. Corn —3D 4
Drymen. Stir —1F 127
Drymuir. Abers —4G 161
Drynachan Lodge. High —5C 158
Drynie Park. High —3H 157
Drynoch. High —5D 154
Dry Sandford. Oxon —5C 50
Dryslwyn. Carm —3F 45
Dryslwyn Castle —3F 45
Dry Street. Essx —2A 40
Dryton. Shrp —5H 71
Duart Castle —5B 140
Dubford. Abers —2E 161
Dubiton. Abers —3D 160
Dubton. Ang —3E 145
Duchally. High —2A 164
Duck End. Essx —3G 53
Duckington. Ches —5G 83
Ducklington. Oxon —5B 50
Duckmanton. Derbs —3B 86
Duck Street. Hants —2B 24
Ducombe Park —1A 100
Dudbridge. Glos —5D 48
Duddenhoe End. Essx —2E 53
Duddingston. Edin —2F 129
Duddington. Nptn —5G 75
Duddo. Nmbd —5F 131
Duddon. Ches —4H 83
Duddon Bridge. Cumb —1A 96
Dudleston. Shrp —2F 71
Dudleston Heath. Shrp —2F 71
Dudley. Tyne —2F 115
Dudley. W Mid —2D 60
Dudley Castle —1D 60
Dudley Zoo —1D 60
Dudmaston Hall NT —2B 60
Dudsbury. Dors —3F 15
Dudston. Shrp —1E 59
Dudwells. Pemb —2D 42
Duff House HS —2D 160
Duffield. Derbs —1H 73
Duffryn. Neat —2B 32
Dufftown. Mor —4H 159
Duffus. Mor —2F 159
Dufton. Cumb —2H 103
Dugeon Ghyll Force NT 4D 102
Duggleby. N Yor —3C 100
Duirinish. High —5G 155
Duisdalemore. High —2E 147
Duisky. High —1E 141
Dukeries, The —3D 86
Dukesfield. Nmbd —4C 114
Dukestown. Blae —4E 47
Dukinfield. G Man —1D 84
Dulas. IOA —2D 81
Dulcote. Som —2A 22
Dulford. Devn —2D 12
Dull. Per —4F 143
Dullatur. N Lan —2A 128
Dullingham. Cambs —5F 65
Dullingham Ley. Cambs —5F 65
Dulnain Bridge. High —1D 151
Duloe. Beds —4A 64
Duloe. Corn —3G 7
Dulverton. Som —4C 20
Dulwich. G Lon —3E 39
Dumbarton. W Dun —2F 127
Dumbarton Castle HS —2F 127
Dumbleton. Glos —2F 49
Dumfin. Arg —1E 127
Dumfries. Dum —2A 112 & 188
Dumgoyne. Stir —1G 127
Dummer. Hants —2D 24
Dumpford. W Sus —4G 25
Dun. Ang —3F 145
Dunagoil. Arg —4B 126
Dunalastair. Per —3E 142
Dunan. High —1D 147
Dunball. Som —2G 21
Dunbar. E Lot —2C 130
Dunbeath. High —5D 168
Dunbeg. Arg —5C 140
Dunblane. Stir —3G 135
Dunblane Cathedral HS —3G 135
Dunbog. Fife —2E 137
Dunbridge. Hants —4B 24
Duncanston. Abers —1C 152
Duncanston. High —3H 157
Dun Charlabhaigh. W Isl —3D 171
Dunchurch. Warw —3B 62
Duncote. Nptn —5D 62
Duncow. Dum —1A 112
Duncrievie. Per —3D 136
Duncton. W Sus —4A 26
Dundee. D'dee —5D 144 & 188
Dundee Airport. D'dee —1F 137
Dundon. Som —3H 21
Dundonald. S Ayr —1C 116
Dundonald Castle HS —1C 116
Dundonnell. High —5E 163
Dundraw. Cumb —5D 112
Dundreggan. High —2F 149
Dundrennan. Dum —5E 111
Dundrennan Abbey HS —5E 111
Dundridge. Hants —1D 16
Dundry. N Som —5A 34
Dunecht. Abers —3E 153
Dunfermline. Fife —1D 129
Dunfermline Abbey & Palace HS —1D 129
Dunford Bridge. S Yor —4B 92
Dungate. Kent —5D 40
Dunge. Wilts —1D 23
Dungeness. Kent —4E 29
Dungworth. S Yor —2G 85
Dunham Massey NT —2B 84
Dunham-on-the-Hill. Ches —3G 83
Dunham on Trent. Notts —3F 87
Dunhampton. Worc —4C 60
Dunham Town. G Man —2B 84
Dunham Woodhouses. G Man —2B 84
Dunholme. Linc —3H 87
Dunino. Fife —2H 137
Dunipace. Falk —1B 128
Dunira. Per —1G 135
Dunkeld. Per —4H 143
Dunkerton. Bath —1C 22
Dunkery Beacon —2B 20
Dunkeswell. Devn —2E 13
Dunkeswick. N Yor —5E 99
Dunkirk. Kent —5E 41
Dunkirk. S Glo —3C 34
Dunkirk. Staf —5C 84
Dunkirk. Wilts —5E 35
Dunk's Green. Kent —5H 39
Dunlappie. Ang —2E 145
Dunley. Hants —1C 24
Dunley. Worc —4B 60
Dunlichity Lodge. High —5A 158
Dunlop. E Ayr —5F 127
Dunmaglass Lodge. High —1H 149
Dunmore. Arg —3F 125
Dunmore. Falk —1B 128
Dunmore. High —4H 157
Dunnet. High —1E 169
Dunnichen. Ang —4E 145
Dunning. Per —2C 136
Dunnington. E Yor —4F 101
Dunnington. Warw —5E 61
Dunnington. York —4A 100
Dunnockshaw. Lanc —2G 91
Dunoon. Arg —2C 126
Dunphail. Mor —4E 159
Dunragit. Dum —4G 109
Dunrobin Castle —3F 165
Dunrostan. Arg —1F 125
Duns. Bord —4D 130
Dunsby. Linc —3A 76
Dunscar. G Man —3F 91
Duns Castle —4D 130
Dunscore. Dum —1F 111
Dunscroft. S Yor —4G 93
Dunsdale. Red C —3D 106
Dunsden Green. Oxon —4F 37
Dunsfold. Surr —2B 26
Dunsford. Devn —4B 12
Dunshalt. Fife —2E 137
Dunshillock. Abers —4G 161
Dunsley. N Yor —3F 107
Dunsley. Staf —2C 60
Dunsmore. Buck —5G 51
Dunsop Bridge. Lanc —4F 97
Dunstable. Beds —3A 52
Dunstaffnage Castle HS —5C 140
Dunstal. Staf —3E 73
Dunstall. Staf —3F 73
Dunstall Green. Suff —4G 65
Dunstall Hill. W Mid —1D 60
Dunstan. Nmbd —3G 121
Dunstanburgh Castle NT —2G 121
Dunster. Som —2C 20
Dunster Castle NT —2C 20
Duns Tew. Oxon —3C 50
Dunston. Linc —4H 87
Dunston. Norf —5E 79
Dunston. Staf —4D 72
Dunston. Tyne —3F 115
Dunstone. Devn —5H 11 (nr. Ashburton)
Dunstone. Devn —3B 8 (nr. Plymouth)
Dunston Heath. Staf —4D 72
Dunsville. S Yor —4G 93
Dunswell. E Yor —1D 94
Dunsyre. S Lan —5D 128
Dunterton. Devn —5D 11
Duntisbourne Abbots. Glos —5E 49
Duntisbourne Leer. Glos —5E 49
Duntisbourne Rouse. Glos —5E 49
Duntish. Dors —2B 14
Duntocher. W Dun —2F 127
Dunton. Beds —1C 52
Dunton. Buck —3G 51
Dunton. Norf —2A 78
Dunton Bassett. Leics —1C 62
Dunton Green. Kent —5G 39
Dunton Patch. Norf —2A 78
Duntulm. High —1D 154
Dunure. S Ayr —3B 116
Dunvant. Swan —3E 31
Dunvegan. High —4B 154
Dunvegan Castle —4B 154
Dunwich. Suff —3G 67
Dunwood. Staf —5D 84
Durdar. Cumb —4F 113
Durgates. E Sus —2H 27
Durham. Dur —5F 115 & 188
Durham Castle WH —188
Durham Cathedral WH —188
Durisdeer. Dum —4A 118
Durisdeermill. Dum —4A 118
Durkar. W Yor —3D 92
Durleigh. Som —3F 21
Durley. Hants —1D 16
Durley. Wilts —5H 35
Durley Street. Hants —1D 16
Durlow Common. Here —2B 48
Durnamuck. High —4E 163
Durness. High —2E 166
Durno. Abers —1E 152
Durns Town. Hants —3A 16
Duror. High —3D 141
Durran. Arg —3G 133
Durran. High —2D 169
Durrant Green. Kent —2C 28
Durrants. Hants —1F 17
Durrington. W Sus —5C 26
Durrington. Wilts —2G 23
Dursley. Glos —2C 34
Dursley Cross. Glos —4B 48
Durston. Som —4F 21
Durweston. Dors —2D 14
Dury. Shet —6F 173
Duston. Nptn —4E 62
Duthil. High —1D 150
Dutlas. Powy —3E 58
Duton Hill. Essx —3G 53
Dutson. Corn —4D 10
Dutton. Ches —3H 83
Duxford. Cambs —1E 53
Duxford. Oxon —2B 36
Dwygyfylchi. Cnwy —3G 81
Dwyran. IOA —4D 80
Dyce. Aber —2F 153
Dyffryn. B'end —2B 32
Dyffryn. Carm —2H 43
Dyffryn. Pemb —1D 42
Dyffryn. V Glam —4D 32
Dyffryn Ardudwy. Gwyn —3E 69
Dyffryn Castell. Cdgn —2G 57
Dyffryn Ceidrych. Carm —3H 45
Dyffryn Cellwen. Neat —5B 46
Dyffryn Gdns. —4D 32
Dyke. Linc —3A 76
Dyke. Mor —3D 159
Dykehead. Ang —2C 144
Dykehead. N Lan —3B 128
Dykehead. Stir —4E 135
Dykend. Ang —3B 144
Dykesfield. Cumb —4E 112
Dylan Thomas Boathouse —3H 43
Dylife. Powy —1A 58
Dymchurch. Kent —3F 29
Dymock. Glos —2C 48
Dyram Park NT —4C 34
Dyrham. S Glo —4C 34
Dysart. Fife —4F 137
Dyserth. Den —3C 82

Eachwick. Nmbd —2E 115
Eadar Dha Fhadhail. W Isl —4C 171
Eagland Hill. Lanc —5D 96
Eagle. Linc —4F 87
Eagle Barnsdale. Linc —4F 87
Eagle Moor. Linc —4F 87
Eaglescliffe. Stoc T —3B 106
Eaglesfield. Cumb —2B 102
Eaglesfield. Dum —2D 112
Eaglesham. E Ren —4G 127
Eaglethorpe. Nptn —1H 63
Eagley. G Man —3F 91
Eairy. IOM —4C 108
Eakley Lanes. Mil —5F 63
Eakring. Notts —4D 86
Ealand. N Lin —3A 94
Ealing. G Lon —2C 38
Eallabus. Arg —3B 124
Eals. Nmbd —4H 113
Eamont Bridge. Cumb —2G 103
Earby. Lanc —5B 98
Earcroft. Bkbn —2E 91
Eardington. Shrp —1B 60
Eardisland. Here —5G 59
Eardisley. Here —1G 47
Eardiston. Shrp —3F 71
Eardiston. Worc —4A 60
Earith. Cambs —3C 64
Earle. Nmbd —2D 121
Earlesfield. Linc —2G 75
Earlestown. Mers —1H 83
Earley. Wok —4F 37
Earlham. Norf —5D 78
Earlish. High —2C 154
Earls Barton. Nptn —4F 63
Earls Colne. Essx —3B 54
Earls Common. Worc —5D 60
Earl's Croome. Worc —1D 48
Earlsdon. W Mid —3H 61
Earlsferry. Fife —3G 137
Earlsford. Abers —5F 161
Earl's Green. Suff —4C 66
Earlsheaton. W Yor —2C 92
Earl Shilton. Leics —1B 62
Earl Soham. Suff —4E 67
Earl Sterndale. Derbs —4E 85
Earlston. E Ayr —1D 116
Earlston. Bord —1H 119
Earl Stonham. Suff —5D 66
Earlstoun. Dum —1D 110
Earlswood. Mon —2H 33
Earlswood. Warw —3F 61
Earlyvale. Bord —4F 129
Earnley. W Sus —3G 17
Earsairidh. W Isl —9C 170
Earsdon. Tyne —2G 115
Earsham. Norf —2F 67
Earsham Street. Suff —3E 67
Earswick. York —4A 100
Eartham. W Sus —5A 26
Earth Centre —1C 86
Earthcott Green. S Glo —3B 34
Easby. N Yor —4C 106 (nr. Great Ayton)
Easby. N Yor —4E 105 (nr. Richmond)
Easdale. Arg —2E 133
Easebourne. W Sus —4G 25
Easenhall. Warw —3B 62
Eashing. Surr —1A 26
Easington. Buck —4E 51
Easington. Dur —5H 115
Easington. E Yor —3G 95
Easington. Nmbd —1F 121
Easington. Oxon —2C 50 (nr. Banbury)
Easington. Oxon —2E 37 (nr. Watlington)
Easington. Red C —3E 107
Easington Colliery. Dur —5H 115
Easington Lane. Tyne —5G 115
Easingwold. N Yor —3H 99
Easole Street. Kent —5G 41
Eassie. Ang —4C 144
Eassie & Nevay. Ang —4C 144
East Aberthaw. V Glam —5D 32
Eastacombe. Devn —4F 19
Eastacott. Devn —4G 19
East Allington. Devn —4D 8
East Anglia Railway Mus. —3C 54
East Anstey. Devn —4B 20
East Anton. Hants —2B 24
East Appleton. N Yor —5F 105
East Ardsley. W Yor —2D 92
East Ashley. Devn —1G 11
East Ashling. W Sus —2G 17
East Aston. Hants —2C 24
East Ayton. N Yor —1D 101
East Bagborough. Som —3E 21
East Barkwith. Linc —2A 88
East Barming. Kent —5B 40
East Barnby. N Yor —3F 107
East Barnet. G Lon —1D 39
East Barns. E Lot —2D 130
East Barsham. Norf —2B 78
East Beach. W Sus —3G 17
East Beckham. Norf —1D 78
East Bedfont. G Lon —3B 38
East Bennan. N Ayr —3D 123
East Bergholt. Suff —2D 54
East Bergholt Place Gdn. —2D 54
East Bierley. W Yor —2B 92
East Blatchington. E Sus —5F 27
East Bliney. Norf —4B 78
East Bloxworth. Dors —3D 15
East Boldre. Hants —2B 16
East Bolton. Nmbd —3F 121
Eastbourne. Darl —3F 105
Eastbourne. E Sus —5H 27 & 188
East Brent. Som —1G 21
Eastbridge. Devn —1E 11
East Bridge. Suff —4G 67
East Bridgford. Notts —1D 74
East Briscoe. Dur —3C 104
East Brunton. Tyne —2F 115
East Buckland. Devn —3G 19
East Budleigh. Devn —4D 12
Eastburn. W Yor —5C 98
East Burnham. Buck —2A 38
East Burrafirth. Shet —6E 173
East Burton. Dors —4D 14
Eastbury. Herts —1B 38
Eastbury. W Ber —4B 36
East Butsfield. Dur —5E 115
East Butterleigh. Devn —2C 12
East Butterwick. N Lin —4B 94
Eastby. N Yor —4C 98
East Calder. W Lot —3D 129
East Carleton. Norf —5D 78
East Carlton. Nptn —2F 63
East Carlton. W Yor —5E 98
East Chaldon. Dors —4C 14
East Challow. Oxon —3B 36
East Charlton. Devn —4D 8
East Chelborough. Dors —2A 14
East Chiltington. E Sus —4E 27
East Chinnock. Som —1H 13
East Chisenbury. Wilts —1G 23
Eastchurch. Kent —3D 40
East Clandon. Surr —5B 38
East Claydon. Buck —3F 51
East Clevedon. N Som —4H 33
East Clyne. High —3F 165
East Clyth. High —5E 169
East Coker. Som —1A 14
Eastcombe. Glos —5D 49
East Combe. Som —3E 21
East Common. N Yor —1G 93
East Compton. Som —2B 22
East Cornworthy. Devn —3E 9
Eastcote. G Lon —2C 38
Eastcote. Nptn —5D 62
Eastcote. W Mid —3F 61
Eastcott. Corn —1C 10
Eastcott. Wilts —1F 23
East Cottingwith. E Yor —5B 100
East Coulston. Wilts —1E 23
Eastcourt. Wilts —5H 35 (nr. Pewsey)
Eastcourt. Wilts —2E 35 (nr. Tetbury)
East Cowes. IOW —3D 16
East Cowick. E Yor —2G 93
East Cowton. N Yor —4A 106
East Cramlington. Nmbd —2F 115
East Cranmore. Som —2B 22
East Creech. Dors —4E 15
East Croachy. High —1A 150
East Dean. E Sus —5G 27
East Dean. Glos —3B 48
East Dean. Hants —4A 24
East Dean. W Sus —4A 26
East Down. Devn —2G 19
East Drayton. Notts —3E 87
East Dundry. N Som —5A 34
East Ella. Hull —2D 94
East End. Cambs —3C 64
East End. Dors —3E 15
East End. E Yor —4F 101 (nr. Ulrome)
East End. E Yor —2F 95 (nr. Withernsea)
East End. Hants —3B 16 (nr. Lymington)
East End. Hants —5C 36 (nr. Newbury)
East End. Herts —3E 53
East End. Kent —3D 40 (nr. Minster)
East End. Kent —2C 28 (nr. Tenterden)
East End. N Som —5H 33
East End. Oxon —4B 50
East End. Som —1A 22
East End. Suff —2E 54
Easter Ardross. High —1A 158
Easter Balgedie. Per —3D 136
Easter Balmoral. Abers —4G 151
Easter Brae. High —2A 158
Easter Buckieburn. Stir —1A 128
Easter Bush. Midl —3F 129
Easter Compton. S Glo —3A 34
Easter Fearn. High —5D 164
Easter Galcantray. High —4C 158
Eastergate. W Sus —5A 26
Easterhouse. Glas —3H 127
Easter Howgate. Midl —3F 129
Easter Kinkell. High —3H 157
Easter Lednathie. Ang —2C 144
Easter Ogil. Ang —2D 144
Easter Ord. Abers —3F 153
Easter Quarff. Shet —8F 173
Easter Rhynd. Per —2D 136
Easter Skeld. Shet —7E 173
Easter Suddie. High —3A 158
Easterton. Wilts —1F 23
Eastertown. Som —1G 21
Eastertown of Auchleuchries. Abers —5H 161
Easter Tulloch. Abers —1G 145
East Everleigh. Wilts —1H 23
East Farleigh. Kent —5B 40
East Farndon. Nptn —2E 62
East Ferry. Linc —1F 87
Eastfield. N Lan —3B 128 (nr. Caldercruix)
Eastfield. N Lan —3B 128 (nr. Harthill)
Eastfield. N Yor —1E 101
Eastfield. S Lan —3H 127
Eastfield Hall. Nmbd —4G 121
East Fortune. E Lot —2B 130
East Garforth. W Yor —1E 93
East Garston. W Ber —4B 36
Eastgate. Dur —1C 104
Eastgate. Norf —3D 78
East Ginge. Oxon —3C 36
East Gores. Essx —3B 54
East Goscote. Leics —4D 74
East Grafton. Wilts —5A 36
East Grimstead. Wilts —4H 23
East Grinstead. W Sus —2E 27
East Guldeford. E Sus —3D 28
East Haddon. Nptn —4D 62
East Hagbourne. Oxon —3D 36
East Halton. N Lin —2E 95
East Ham. G Lon —2F 39
Eastham. Mers —2F 83
Eastham. Worc —4A 60
Eastham Ferry. Mers —2F 83
Easthampstead. Brac —5G 37
Easthampton. Here —4G 59
East Hanney. Oxon —2C 36
East Hanningfield. Essx —5A 54
East Hardwick. W Yor —3E 93
East Harling. Norf —2B 66
East Harlsey. N Yor —5B 106
East Harnham. Wilts —4G 23
East Harptree. Bath —1A 22
East Hartford. Nmbd —2F 115
East Harting. W Sus —1G 17
East Hatch. Wilts —4E 23
East Hatley. Cambs —5B 64
Easthaugh. Norf —4C 78
East Hauxwell. N Yor —5E 105
East Haven. Ang —5E 145
Eastheath. Wok —5G 37
East Heckington. Linc —1A 76
East Hedleyhope. Dur —5E 115
East Helmsdale. High —2H 165
East Hendred. Oxon —3C 36
East Heslerton. N Yor —2D 100
East Hoathly. E Sus —4G 27
Easthope. Shrp —1H 59
Easthorpe. Essx —3C 54
Easthorpe. Leics —2F 75
East Horrington. Som —2A 22
East Horsley. Surr —5B 38
East Horton. Nmbd —1E 121
Easthouses. Midl —3G 129
East Howe. Bour —3F 15
East Huntspill. Som —2G 21
East Hyde. Beds —4B 52
East Ilsley. W Ber —3C 36

Eastington. Devn —2H 11
Eastington. Glos —4G 49
(nr. Northleach)
Eastington. Glos —5C 48
(nr. Stonehouse)
East Keal. Linc —4C 88
East Kennett. Wilts —5G 35
East Kent Light Railway —1G 29
East Keswick. W Yor —5F 99
East Kilbride. S Lan —4H 127
East Kirkby. Linc —4C 88
East Knapton. N Yor —2C 100
East Knighton. Dors —4D 14
East Knowstone. Devn —4B 20
East Knoyle. Wilts —3D 23
East Kyloe. Nmbd —1E 121
East Lambrook. Som —1H 13
East Lambrook Gdn. —1H 13
East Langdon. Kent —1H 29
East Langton. Leics —1E 63
East Langwell. High —3E 164
East Lavant. W Sus —2G 17
East Lavington. W Sus —4A 26
East Layton. N Yor —4E 105
Eastleach Martin. Glos —5H 49
Eastleach Turville. Glos —5G 49
East Leake. Notts —3C 74
East Learmouth. Nmbd —1C 120
Eastleigh. Devn —4E 19
(nr. Bideford)
East Leigh. Devn —2H 11
(nr. Crediton)
East Leigh. Devn —3C 8
(nr. Modbury)
Eastleigh. Hants —1C 16
East Lexham. Norf —4A 78
East Lilburn. Nmbd —2E 121
Eastling. Kent —5D 40
East Linton. E Lot —2B 130
East Liss. Hants —4F 25
East Lockinge. Oxon —3C 36
East Looe. Corn —3G 7
East Lound. N Lin —1E 87
East Lulworth. Dors —4D 14
East Lutton. N Yor —3D 100
East Lydford. Som —3A 22
East Mains. Abers —4D 152
East Malling. Kent —5B 40
East Marden. W Sus —1G 17
East Markham. Notts —3E 87
East Marton. N Yor —4B 98
East Meon. Hants —4E 25
East Mersea. Essx —4D 54
East Mey. High —1F 169
East Molesey. Surr —4C 38
Eastmoor. Norf —5G 77
East Morden. Dors —3E 15
East Morton. W Yor —5C 98
East Ness. N Yor —2A 100
East Newton. E Yor —1F 95
East Newton. N Yor —2A 100
Eastney. Port —3E 17
Eastnor. Here —2C 48
Eastnor Castle —2C 48
East Norton. Leics —5E 75
East Oakley. Hants —1D 24
Eastoft. N Lin —3B 94
East Ogwell. Devn —5B 12
Easton. Cambs —3A 64
Easton. Cumb —4D 112
(nr. Burgh by Sands)
Easton. Cumb —2F 113
(nr. Longtown)
Easton. Devn —4H 11
Easton. Dors —5B 14
Easton. Hants —3D 24
Easton. Linc —3G 75
Easton. Norf —4D 78
Easton. Som —2A 22
Easton. Suff —5E 67
Easton. Wilts —4D 35
Easton Farm Park —5E 67
Easton Grey. Wilts —3D 35
Easton-in-Gordano. N Som —4A 34
Easton Maudit. Nptn —5F 63
Easton on the Hill. Nptn —5H 75
Easton Royal. Wilts —5H 35
East Orchard. Dors —1D 14
East Ord. Nmbd —4F 131
East Panson. Devn —3D 10
East Peckham. Kent —1A 28
East Pennard. Som —3A 22
East Perry. Cambs —4A 64
East Pitcorthie. Fife —3H 137
East Portlemouth. Devn —5D 8
East Prawle. Devn —5D 9
East Preston. W Sus —5B 26
East Putford. Devn —1D 10
East Quantoxhead. Som —2E 21
East Rainton. Tyne —5G 115
East Ravendale. NE Lin —1B 88
East Raynham. Norf —3A 78
Eastrea. Cambs —1B 64
East Rhidorroch Lodge. High —4G 163
East Riddlesden Hall NT —5C 98
Eastriggs. Dum —3D 112
East Rigton. W Yor —5F 99
Eastrington. E Yor —1A 94
East Rounton. N Yor —4B 106
East Row. N Yor —3F 107
East Rudham. Norf —3H 77
East Runton. Norf —1D 78
East Ruston. Norf —3F 79
Eastry. Kent —5H 41
East Saltoun. E Lot —3A 130
East Shaws. Dur —3D 105
East Shefford. W Ber —4B 36
Eastshore. Shet —10F 173
East Sleekburn. Nmbd —1F 115
East Somerset Railway —2B 22
East Somerton. Norf —4G 79
East Stockwith. Linc —1E 87
East Stoke. Dors —4D 14
East Stoke. Notts —1E 75
East Stoke. Som —1H 13
East Stour. Dors —4D 22
East Stourmouth. Kent —4G 41
East Stowford. Devn —4G 19
East Stratton. Hants —2D 24
East Studdal. Kent —1H 29
East Taphouse. Corn —2F 7
East-the-Water. Devn —4E 19
East Thirston. Nmbd —5F 121
East Tilbury. Thur —3A 40
East Tisted. Hants —3F 25
East Torrington. Linc —2A 88
East Tuddenham. Norf —4C 78
East Tytherley. Hants —4A 24
East Tytherton. Wilts —4E 35
East Village. Devn —2B 12
Eastville. Linc —5D 88
East Wall. Shrp —1H 59
East Walton. Norf —4G 77
East Week. Devn —3G 11
Eastwell. Leics —3E 75
East Wellow. Hants —4B 24
East Wemyss. Fife —4F 137
East Whitburn. W Lot —3C 128
Eastwick. Herts —4E 53
Eastwick. Shet —4E 173
East Williamston. Pemb —4E 43
East Winch. Norf —4F 77
East Winterslow. Wilts —3H 23
East Wittering. W Sus —3F 17
East Witton. N Yor —1D 98
Eastwood. Notts —1B 74
Eastwood. S'end —2C 40
East Woodburn. Nmbd —1C 114
Eastwood End. Cambs —1D 64
East Woodhay. Hants —5C 36
East Woodlands. Som —2C 22
East Worldham. Hants —3F 25
East Worlington. Devn —1A 12
East Youlstone. Devn —1C 10
Eathorpe. Warw —4A 62
Eaton. Ches —4C 84
(nr. Congleton)
Eaton. Ches —4H 83
(nr. Kelsall)
Eaton. Leics —3E 75
Eaton. Norf —2F 77
(nr. Heacham)
Eaton. Norf —5E 78
(nr. Norwich)
Eaton. Notts —3E 86
Eaton. Oxon —5C 50
Eaton. Shrp —2F 59
(nr. Bishop's Castle)
Eaton. Shrp —1H 59
(nr. Church Stretton)
Eaton Bishop. Here —2H 47
Eaton Bray. Beds —3H 51
Eaton Constantine. Shrp —5H 71
Eaton Green. Beds —3H 51
Eaton Hastings. Oxon —2A 36
Eaton Socon. Cambs —5A 64
Eaton upon Tern. Shrp —3A 72
Eau Brink. Norf —4E 77
Eaves Green. W Mid —2G 61
Ebberston. N Yor —1C 100
Ebbesbourne Wake. Wilts —4E 23
Ebblake. Dors —2G 15
Ebbw Vale. Blae —5E 47
Ebchester. Dur —4E 115
Ebford. Devn —4C 12
Ebley. Glos —5D 48
Ebnal. Ches —1G 71
Ebrington. Glos —1G 49
Ebsworthy Town. Devn —3F 11
Ecchinswell. Hants —1D 24
Ecclefechan. Dum —2C 112
Eccles. G Man —1B 84
Eccles. Kent —4B 40
Eccles. Bord —5D 130
Ecclesall. S Yor —2H 85
Ecclesfield. S Yor —1A 86
Eccles Green. Here —1G 47
Eccleshall. Staf —3C 72
Eccleshill. W Yor —1B 92
Ecclesmachan. W Lot —2D 128
Eccles on Sea. Norf —3G 79
Eccles Road. Norf —1C 66
Eccleston. Ches —4G 83
Eccleston. Lanc —3D 90
Eccleston. Mers —1G 83
Eccup. W Yor —5E 99
Echt. Abers —3E 153
Eckford. Bord —2B 120
Eckington. Derbs —3B 86
Eckington. Worc —1E 49
Ecton. Nptn —4F 63
Edale. Derbs —2F 85
Eday Airport. Orkn —4E 172
Edburton. W Sus —4D 26
Edderside. Cumb —5C 112
Edderton. High —5E 164
Eddington. Kent —4F 41
Eddington. W Ber —5B 36
Eddleston. Bord —5F 129
Eddlewood. S Lan —4A 128
Edenbridge. Kent —1F 27
Edendonich. Arg —1A 134
Edenfield. Lanc —3G 91
Edenhall. Cumb —1G 103
Edenham. Linc —3H 75
Eden Project —3E 7
Edensor. Derbs —4G 85
Edentaggart. Arg —4C 134
Edenthorpe. S Yor —4G 93
Eden Vale. Dur —1B 106
Edern. Gwyn —2B 68
Edgarley. Som —3A 22
Edgbaston. W Mid —2E 61
Edgcott. Buck —3E 51
Edgcott. Som —3B 20
Edge. Glos —5D 48
Edge. Shrp —5F 71
Edgebolton. Shrp —3H 71
Edge End. Glos —4A 48
Edgefield. Norf —2C 78
Edgefield Street. Norf —2C 78
Edge Green. Ches —5G 83
Edgehead. Midl —3G 129
Edgeley. Shrp —1H 71
Edgeside. Lanc —2G 91
Edgeworth. Glos —5E 49
Edgiock. Worc —4E 61
Edgmond. Telf —4B 72
Edgmond Marsh. Telf —3B 72
Edgton. Shrp —2F 59
Edgware. G Lon —1C 38
Edgworth. Bkbn —3F 91
Edinbane. High —3C 154
Edinburgh. Edin —2F 129 & 189
Edinburgh Airport. Edin —2E 129
Edinburgh Castle HS —189
Edinburgh Cathedral —189
Edinburgh Experience —189
Edinburgh Zoo —2F 129
Edingale. Staf —4G 73
Edingley. Notts —5D 86
Edingthorpe. Norf —2F 79
Edington. Som —3G 21
Edington. Wilts —1E 23
Edingworth. Som —1G 21
Edistone. Devn —4C 18
Edithmead. Som —2G 21
Edith Weston. Rut —5G 75
Edlaston. Derbs —1F 73
Edlesborough. Buck —4H 51
Edlingham. Nmbd —4F 121
Edlington. Linc —3B 88
Edmondsham. Dors —1F 15
Edmondsley. Dur —5F 115
Edmondthorpe. Leics —4F 75
Edmonstone. Orkn —5E 172
Edmonton. Corn —1D 6
Edmonton. G Lon —1E 39
Edmundbyers. Dur —4D 114
Ednam. Bord —1B 120
Ednaston. Derbs —1G 73
Edney Common. Essx —5G 53
Edrom. Bord —4E 131
Edstaston. Shrp —2H 71
Edstone. Warw —4F 61
Edwalton. Notts —2D 74
Edwardstone. Suff —1C 54
Edwardsville. Mer T —2D 32
Edwinsford. Carm —2G 45
Edwinstowe. Notts —4D 86
Edworth. Beds —1C 52
Edwyn Ralph. Here —5A 60
Edzell. Ang —2F 145
Edzell Castle HS —2E 145
Efail-fach. Neat —2A 32
Efail Isaf. Rhon —3D 32
Efailnewydd. Gwyn —2C 68
Efail-rhyd. Powy —3D 70
Efailwen. Carm —2F 43
Efenechtyd. Den —5D 82
Effingham. Surr —5C 38
Effingham Common. Surr —5C 38
Effirth. Shet —6E 173
Efflinch. Staf —4F 73
Efford. Devn —2B 12
Efstigarth. Shet —2F 173
Egbury. Hants —1C 24
Egdon. Worc —5D 60
Egerton. G Man —3F 91
Egerton. Kent —1D 28
Egerton Forstal. Kent —1C 28
Eggborough. N Yor —2F 93
Eggbuckland. Plym —3A 8
Eggesford. Devn —1G 11
Eggington. Beds —3H 51
Egginton. Derbs —3G 73
Egglescliffe. Stoc T —3B 106
Eggleston. Dur —2C 104
Egglestone Abbey EH —3D 104
Egham. Surr —3B 38
Egham Hythe. Surr —3B 38
Egleton. Rut —5F 75
Eglingham. Nmbd —3F 121
Egloshayle. Corn —5A 10
Egloskerry. Corn —4C 10
Eglwysbach. Cnwy —3H 81
Eglwys Brewis. V Glam —5D 32
Eglwys Fach. Cdgn —1F 57
Eglwyswrw. Pemb —1F 43
Egmanton. Notts —4E 87
Egremont. Cumb —3B 102
Egremont. Mers —1F 83
Egton. N Yor —4F 107
Egton Bridge. N Yor —4F 107
Egypt. Buck —2A 38
Egypt. Hants —2C 24
Eight Ash Green. Essx —3C 54
Eight Mile Burn. Midl —4E 129
Eignaig. High —4B 140
Eilanreach. High —2G 147
Eildon. Bord —1H 119
Eileanach Lodge. High —2H 157
Eilean Donan Castle —1A 148
Eilean Fhlodaigh. W Isl —3D 170
Eilean Iarmain. High —2F 147
Einacleit. W Isl —5D 171
Eisgean. W Isl —6F 171
Eishken. W Isl —6F 171
Eisingrug. Gwyn —2F 69
Elan Village. Powy —4B 58
Elberton. S Glo —3B 34
Elbridge. W Sus —5A 26
Elburton. Plym —3B 8
Elcho. Per —1D 136
Elcho Castle HS —1D 136
Elcombe. Swin —3G 35
Elcot. W Ber —5B 36
Eldernell. Cambs —1C 64
Eldersfield. Worc —2D 48
Elderslie. Ren —3F 127
Elder Street. Essx —2F 53
Eldon. Dur —2F 105
Eldroth. N Yor —3G 97
Eldwick. W Yor —5D 98
Elfhowe. Cumb —5F 103
Elford. Nmbd —1F 121
Elford. Staf —4F 73
Elford Closes. Cambs —3D 65
Elgar's Birthplace Mus. —5C 60
Elgin. Mor —2G 159
Elgin Cathedral HS —2G 159
Elgol. High —2D 146
Elham. Kent —1F 29
Elie. Fife —3G 137
Eling. Hants —1B 16
Eling. W Ber —4D 36
Elishaw. Nmbd —5C 120
Elizafield. Dum —2B 112
Elkesley. Notts —3D 86
Elkington. Nptn —3D 62
Elkins Green. Essx —5G 53
Elkstone. Glos —4E 49
Ellan. High —1C 150
Ellanbeich. Arg —2E 133
Elland. W Yor —2B 92
Ellary. Arg —2F 125
Ellastone. Staf —1F 73
Ellbridge. Corn —2A 8
Ellel. Lanc —4D 97
Ellemford. Bord —3D 130
Ellenborough. Cumb —1B 102
Ellenbrook. Herts —5C 52
Ellenhall. Staf —3C 72
Ellen's Green. Surr —2B 26
Ellerbec. N Yor —5B 106
Ellerburn. N Yor —1C 100
Ellerby. N Yor —3E 107
Ellerdine. Telf —3A 72
Ellerdine Heath. Telf —3A 72
Ellerhayes. Devn —2C 12
Elleric. Arg —4E 141
Ellerker. E Yor —2C 94
Ellerton. E Yor —1H 93
Ellerton. N Yor —5F 105
Ellerton. Shrp —3B 72
Ellesborough. Buck —5G 51
Ellesmere. Shrp —2G 71
Ellesmere Port. Ches —3G 83
Ellesmere Port Boat Mus. —3G 83
Ellingham. Hants —2G 15
Ellingham. Norf —1F 67
Ellingham. Nmbd —2F 121
Ellingstring. N Yor —1D 98
Ellington. Cambs —3A 64
Ellington. Nmbd —5G 121
Ellington Thorpe. Cambs —3A 64
Ellisfield. Hants —2E 25
Ellishadder. High —2E 155
Ellistown. Leics —4B 74
Ellon. Abers —5G 161
Ellonby. Cumb —1F 103
Ellough. Suff —2G 67
Elloughton. E Yor —2C 94
Ellwood. Glos —5A 48
Elm. Cambs —5D 76
Elmbridge. Glos —4D 48
Elmbridge. Worc —4D 60
Elmdon. Essx —2E 53
Elmdon. W Mid —2F 61
Elmdon Heath. W Mid —2F 61
Elmesthorpe. Leics —1B 62
Elmfield. IOW —3D 16
Elm Hill. Dors —4D 22
Elmhurst. Staf —4F 73
Elmley Castle. Worc —1E 49
Elmley Lovett. Worc —4C 60
Elmore. Glos —4C 48
Elmore Back. Glos —4C 48
Elm Park. G Lon —2G 39
Elmscott. Devn —4C 18
Elmsett. Suff —1D 54
Elmstead. Essx —3D 54
Elmstead Heath. Essx —3D 54
Elmstead Market. Essx —3D 54
Elmsted. Kent —1F 29
Elmstone. Kent —4G 41
Elmstone Hardwicke. Glos —3E 49
Elmswell. E Yor —4D 101
Elmswell. Suff —4B 66
Elmton. Derbs —3C 86
Elphin. High —2G 163
Elphinstone. E Lot —2G 129
Elrick. Abers —3F 153
Elrick. Mor —1B 152
Elrig. Dum —5A 110
Elsdon. Nmbd —5D 120
Elsecar. S Yor —1A 86
Elsenham. Essx —3F 53
Elsfield. Oxon —4D 50
Elsham. N Lin —3D 94
Elsing. Norf —4C 78
Elslack. N Yor —5B 98
Elsrickle. S Lan —5D 128
Elstead. Surr —1A 26
Elsted. W Sus —1G 17
Elsted Marsh. W Sus —4G 25
Elsthorpe. Linc —3H 75
Elstob. Dur —2A 106
Elston. Devn —2A 12
Elston. Lanc —1E 90
Elston. Notts —1E 75
Elston. Wilts —2F 23
Elstone. Devn —1G 11
Elstow. Beds —1A 52
Elstree. Herts —1C 38
Elstronwick. E Yor —1F 95
Elswick. Lanc —1C 90
Elswick. Tyne —3F 115
Elsworth. Cambs —4C 64
Elterwater. Cumb —4E 103
Eltham. G Lon —3F 39
Eltham Palace EH —3F 39
Eltisley. Cambs —5B 64
Elton. Cambs —1H 63
Elton. Ches —3G 83
Elton. Derbs —4G 85
Elton. Glos —4C 48
Elton. G Man —3F 91
Elton. Here —3G 59
Elton. Notts —2E 75
Elton. Stoc T —3B 106
Elton Green. Ches —3G 83
Elton Hall —1H 63
Eltringham. Nmbd —3D 114
Elvanfoot. S Lan —3B 118
Elvaston. Derbs —2B 74
Elveden. Suff —3H 65
Elvingston. E Lot —2A 130
Elvington. Kent —5G 41
Elvington. York —5B 100
Elwick. Hart —1B 106
Elwick. Nmbd —1F 121
Elworth. Ches —4B 84
Elworth. Dors —4A 14
Elworthy. Som —3D 20
Ely. Cambs —2E 65
Ely. Card —4E 33
Ely Cathedral —3E 65
Emberton. Mil —1G 51
Embleton. Cumb —1C 102
Embleton. Dur —2B 106
Embleton. Nmbd —2G 121
Embo. High —4F 165
Emborough. Som —1B 22
Embo Street. High —4F 165
Embsay. N Yor —4C 98
Emery Down. Hants —2A 16
Emley. W Yor —3C 92
Emmbrook. Wok —5F 37
Emmer Green. Read —4F 37
Emmetts NT —5F 39
Emmington. Oxon —5F 51
Emneth. Norf —5D 77
Emneth Hungate. Norf —5E 77
Empingham. Rut —5G 75
Empshott. Hants —3F 25
Emsworth. Hants —2F 17
Enborne. W Ber —5C 36
Enborne Row. W Ber —5C 36
Enchmarsh. Shrp —1H 59
Enderby. Leics —1C 62
Endmoor. Cumb —1E 97
Endon. Staf —5D 84
Endon Bank. Staf —5D 84
Enfield. G Lon —1E 39
Enfield Wash. G Lon —1E 39
Enford. Wilts —1G 23
Engine Common. S Glo —3B 34
Englefield. W Ber —4E 36
Englefield Green. Surr —3A 38
Engleseabrook. Ches —5B 84
English Bicknor. Glos —4A 48
Englishcombe. Bath —5C 34
English Frankton. Shrp —3G 71
Enham Alamein. Hants —2B 24
Enmore. Som —3F 21
Ennerdale Bridge. Cumb —3B 102
Enniscaven. Corn —3D 6
Enoch. Dum —4A 118
Enochdhu. Per —2H 143
Ensay. Arg —4E 139
Ensbury. Bour —3F 15
Ensdon. Shrp —4G 71
Ensis. Devn —4F 19
Enson. Staf —3D 72
Enstone. Oxon —3B 50
Enterkinfoot. Dum —4A 118
Enville. Staf —2C 60
Eolaigearraidh. W Isl —8C 170
Eorabus. Arg —1A 132
Eoropaidh. W Isl —1H 171
Epney. Glos —4C 48
Epperstone. Notts —1D 74
Epping. Essx —5E 53
Epping Green. Essx —5E 53
Epping Green. Herts —5C 52
Epping Upland. Essx —5E 53
Eppleby. N Yor —3E 105
Eppleworth. E Yor —1D 94
Epsom. Surr —4D 38
Epwell. Oxon —1B 50
Epworth. N Lin —4A 94
Epworth Turbary. N Lin —4A 94
Erbistock. Wrex —1F 71
Erbusaig. High —1F 147
Erchless Castle. High —4G 157
Erddig NT —1F 71
Erdington. W Mid —1F 61
Eredine. Arg —3G 133
Eriboll. High —3E 167
Ericstane. Dum —3C 118
Eridge Green. E Sus —2G 27
Erines. Arg —2G 125
Eriswell. Suff —3G 65
Erith. G Lon —3G 39
Erlestoke. Wilts —1E 23
Ermine East. Linc —3G 87
Ermine West. Linc —3G 87
Ermington. Devn —3C 8
Ernesettle. Plym —3A 8
Erpingham. Norf —2D 78
Erriottwood. Kent —5D 40
Errogie. High —1H 149
Errol. Per —1E 137
Errol Station. Per —1E 137
Erskine. Ren —2F 127
Ervie. Dum —3F 109
Erwarton. Suff —2F 55
Erwood. Powy —1D 46
Eryholme. N Yor —4A 106
Eryrys. Den —5E 82
Escalls. Corn —4A 4
Escomb. Dur —2E 105
Escot Gdns. —3D 12
Escrick. N Yor —5A 100
Esgair. Carm —3D 45
(nr. Carmarthen)
Esgair. Carm —3G 43
(nr. St Clears)
Esgairgeiliog. Powy —5G 69
Esh. Dur —5E 115
Esher. Surr —4C 38
Esholt. W Yor —1B 92
Eshott. Nmbd —5G 121
Eshton. N Yor —4B 98
Esh Winning. Dur —5E 115
Eskadale. High —5G 157
Eskbank. Midl —3G 129
Eskdale Green. Cumb —4C 102
Eskdalemuir. Dum —5E 119
Eskham. Linc —1C 88
Esknish. Arg —3B 124
Esk Valley. N Yor —4F 107
Eslington Hall. Nmbd —3E 121
Espley Hall. Nmbd —5F 121
Esprick. Lanc —1C 90
Essendine. Rut —4H 75
Essendon. Herts —5C 52
Essich. High —5A 158
Essington. Staf —5D 72
Eston. Red C —3C 106
Estover. Plym —3B 8
Eswick. Shet —6F 173
Etal. Nmbd —1D 120
Etal Castle EH —1D 120
Etchilhampton. Wilts —5F 35
Etchingham. E Sus —3B 28

Etchinghill. Kent —2F 29
Etchinghill. Staf —4E 73
Ethie Haven. Ang —4F 145
Etling Green. Norf —4C 78
Etloe. Glos —5B 48
Eton. Wind —3A 38
Eton Wick. Wind —3A 38
Etteridge. High —4A 150
Ettersgill. Dur —2B 104
Ettiley Heath. Ches —4B 84
Ettington. Warw —1A 50
Etton. E Yor —5D 101
Etton. Pet —5A 76
Ettrick. Bord —3E 119
Ettrickbridge. Bord —2F 119
Etwall. Derbs —2G 73
Eudon Burnell. Shrp —2B 60
Eudon George. Shrp —2A 60
Eureka! Mus. for Children, Halifax —2A 92
Euston. Suff —3A 66
Euston Hall —3A 66
Euxton. Lanc —3D 90
Evanstown. B'end —3C 32
Evanton. High —2A 158
Evedon. Linc —1H 75
Evelix. High —4E 165
Evendine. Here —1C 48
Evenjobb. Powy —4E 59
Evenley. Nptn —2D 50
Evenlode. Glos —3H 49
Even Swindon. Swin —3G 35
Evenwood. Dur —2E 105
Evenwood Gate. Dur —2E 105
Everbay. Orkn —5F 172
Evercreech. Som —3B 22
Everdon. Nptn —5C 62
Everingham. E Yor —5C 100
Everleigh. Wilts —1H 23
Everley. N Yor —1D 100
Eversholt. Beds —2H 51
Evershot. Dors —2A 14
Eversley. Hants —5F 37
Eversley Cross. Hants —5F 37
Everthorpe. E Yor —1C 94
Everton. Beds —5B 64
Everton. Hants —3A 16
Everton. Mers —1F 83
Everton. Notts —1D 86
Evertown. Dum —2E 113
Evesbatch. Here —1B 48
Evesham. Worc —1F 49
Evington. Leic —5D 74
Ewden Village. S Yor —1G 85
Ewdness. Shrp —1B 60
Ewell. Surr —4D 38
Ewell Minnis. Kent —1G 29
Ewelme. Oxon —2E 37
Ewen. Glos —2F 35
Ewenny. V Glam —4C 32
Ewerby. Linc —1A 76
Ewes. Dum —5F 119
Ewesley. Nmbd —5E 121
Ewhurst. Surr —1B 26
Ewhurst Green. E Sus —3B 28
Ewhurst Green. Surr —2B 26
Ewlo. Flin —4F 83
Ewloe. Flin —4F 83
Ewloe Castle —4E 83
Ewood Bridge. Lanc —2F 91
Eworthy. Devn —3E 11
Ewshot. Hants —1G 25
Ewyas Harold. Here —3G 47
Exbourne. Devn —2G 11
Exbury. Hants —2C 16
Exbury Gdns. —2C 16
Exceat. E Sus —5G 27
Exebridge. Som —4C 20
Exelby. N Yor —1E 99
Exeter. Devn —3C 12 & 189
Exeter Airport. Devn —3D 12
Exeter Cathedral —189
Exford. Som —3B 20
Exfords Green. Shrp —5G 71
Exhall. Warw —5F 61
Exlade Street. Oxon —3E 37
Exminster. Devn —4C 12
Exmoor Nat. Park —2B 20
Exmoor Steam Railway —3G 19
Exmouth. Devn —4D 12
Exnaboe. Shet —10E 173
Exning. Suff —4F 65
Exton. Devn —4C 12
Exton. Hants —4E 24
Exton. Rut —4G 75
Exton. Som —3C 20
Exwick. Devn —3C 12
Eyam. Derbs —3G 85
Eyam Hall —3G 85
Eydon. Nptn —5C 62
Eye. Here —4G 59
Eye. Pet —5B 76
Eye. Suff —3D 66
Eye Green. Pet —5B 76
Eyemouth. Bord —3F 131
Eyeworth. Beds —1C 52
Eyhorne Street. Kent —5C 40
Eyke. Suff —5F 67
Eynesbury. Cambs —5A 64
Eynort. High —1B 146
Eynsford. Kent —4G 39
Eynsford Castle EH —4G 39
Eynsham. Oxon —5C 50
Eype. Dors —3H 13
Eyre. High —5E 155
(on Raasay)
Eyre. High —3D 154
(on Skye)
Eythorne. Kent —1G 29
Eyton. Here —4G 59
Eyton. Shrp —2F 59
(nr. Bishop's Castle)
Eyton. Shrp —4F 71
(nr. Shrewsbury)
Eyton. Wrex —1F 71
Eyton on Severn. Shrp —5H 71
Eyton upon the Weald Moors. Telf —4A 72

Faccombe. Hants —1B 24
Faceby. N Yor —4B 106
Faddiley. Ches —5H 83
Fadmoor. N Yor —1A 100
Fagwyr. Swan —5G 45
Faichem. High —3E 149
Faifley. W Dun —2G 127
Fail. S Ayr —2D 116
Failand. N Som —4A 34
Failford. S Ayr —2D 116
Failsworth. G Man —4H 91
Fairborne Railway —4F 69
Fairbourne. Gwyn —4F 69
Fairbourne Heath. Kent —5C 40
Fairburn. N Yor —2E 93
Fairfield. Derbs —3E 85
Fairfield. Kent —3D 28
Fairfield. Worc —3D 60
(nr. Bromsgrove)
Fairfield. Worc —1F 49
(nr. Evesham)
Fairford. Glos —5G 49
Fair Green. Norf —4F 77
Fairhaven Gdn. —4F 79
Fair Hill. Cumb —1G 103
Fairhill. S Lan —4A 128
Fair Isle Airport. Shet —1B 172
Fairlands. Surr —5A 38
Fairlie. N Ayr —4D 126
Fairlight. E Sus —4C 28
Fairlight Cove. E Sus —4C 28
Fairmile. Devn —3D 12
Fairmile. Surr —4C 38
Fairmilehead. Edin —3F 129
Fair Oak. Devn —1D 12
Fair Oak. Hants —1C 16
(nr. Eastleigh)
Fair Oak. Hants —5D 36
(nr. Kingsclere)
Fairoak. Staf —2B 72
Fair Oak Green. Hants —5E 37
Fairseat. Kent —4H 39
Fairstead. Essx —4A 54
Fairstead. Norf —4F 77
Fairwarp. E Sus —3F 27
Fairwater. Card —4E 33
Fairy Cross. Devn —4E 19
Fakenham. Norf —3B 78
Fakenham Magna. Suff —3B 66
Fala. Midl —3H 129
Fala Dam. Midl —3H 129
Falcon. Here —2B 48
Faldingworth. Linc —2H 87
Falfield. S Glo —2B 34
Falkenham. Suff —2F 55
Falkirk. Falk —2B 128
Falkland. Fife —3E 137
Falkland Palace NTS —3E 137
Fallin. Stir —4H 135
Fallowfield. G Man —1C 84
Falmer. E Sus —5E 27
Falmouth. Corn —5C 6
Falsgrave. N Yor —1E 101
Falstone. Nmbd —1A 114
Fanagmore. High —4B 166
Fancott. Beds —3A 52
Fanellan. High —4G 157
Fangdale Beck. N Yor —5C 106
Fangfoss. E Yor —4B 100
Fankerton. Falk —1A 128
Fanmore. Arg —4F 139
Fanner's Green. Essx —4G 53
Fannich Lodge. High —2E 156
Fans. Bord —5C 130
Far Cotton. Nptn —5E 63
Fareham. Hants —2D 16
Farewell. Staf —4E 73
Far Forest. Worc —3B 60
Farforth. Linc —3C 88
Far Green. Glos —5C 48
Far Hoarcross. Staf —3F 73
Faringdon. Oxon —2A 36
Farington. Lanc —2D 90
Farlam. Cumb —4G 113
Farleigh. N Som —5H 33
Farleigh. Surr —4E 39
Farleigh Hungerford. Som —1D 22
Farleigh Hungerford Castle EH —1C 22
Farleigh Wallop. Hants —2E 24
Farleigh Wick. Wilts —5D 34
Farlesthorpe. Linc —3D 88
Farleton. Cumb —1E 97
Farleton. Lanc —3E 97
Farley. High —4G 157
Farley. N Som —4H 33
Farley. Shrp —5F 71
(nr. Shrewsbury)
Farley. Shrp —5A 72
(nr. Telford)
Farley. Staf —1E 73
Farley. Wilts —4H 23
Farley Green. Suff —5G 65
Farley Green. Surr —1B 26
Farley Hill. Wok —5F 37
Farley's End. Glos —4C 48
Farlington. N Yor —3A 100
Farlington. Port —2E 17
Farlow. Shrp —2A 60
Farmborough. Bath —5B 34
Farmcote. Glos —3F 49
Farmcote. Shrp —1B 60
Farmington. Glos —4G 49
Far Moor. G Man —4D 90
Farmoor. Oxon —5C 50
Farmtown. Mor —3C 160
Farnah Green. Derbs —1H 73
Farnborough. G Lon —4F 39
Farnborough. Hants —1G 25
Farnborough. Warw —1C 50
Farnborough. W Ber —3C 36
Farnborough Hall NT —1C 50
Farncombe. Surr —1A 26
Farndish. Beds —4G 63
Farndon. Ches —5G 83
Farndon. Notts —5E 87
Farne Islands NT —1G 121
Farnell. Ang —3F 145
Farnham. Dors —1E 15
Farnham. Essx —3E 53
Farnham. N Yor —3F 99
Farnham. Suff —4F 67
Farnham. Surr —2G 25
Farnham Common. Buck —2A 38
Farnham Green. Essx —3E 53
Farnham Royal. Buck —2A 38
Farnhill. N Yor —5C 98
Farningham. Kent —4G 39
Farnley. N Yor —5E 98
Farnley Tyas. W Yor —3B 92
Farnsfield. Notts —5D 86
Farnworth. G Man —4F 91
Farnworth. Hal —2H 83
Far Oakridge. Glos —5E 49
Far Orrest. Cumb —4F 103
Farr. High —2H 167
(nr. Bettyhill)
Farr. High —5A 158
(nr. Inverness)
Farr. High —3C 150
(nr. Kingussie)
Farraline. High —1H 149
Farringdon. Devn —3D 12
Farrington. Dors —1D 14
Farrington Gurney. Bath —1B 22
Far Sawrey. Cumb —5E 103
Farsley. W Yor —1C 92
Farthinghoe. Nptn —2D 50
Farthingstone. Nptn —5D 62
Farthorpe. Linc —3B 88
Fartown. W Yor —3B 92
Farway. Devn —3E 13
Fasag. High —3A 156
Fascadale. High —1G 139
Fasnacloich. Arg —4E 141
Fasque House —1F 145
Fassfern. High —1E 141
Fatfield. Tyne —4G 115
Faugh. Cumb —4G 113
Fauld. Staf —3F 73
Fauldhouse. W Lot —3C 128
Faulkbourne. Essx —4A 54
Faulkland. Som —1C 22
Fauls. Shrp —2H 71
Faverdale. Darl —3F 105
Faversham. Kent —4E 40
Fawdington. N Yor —2G 99
Fawfieldhead. Staf —4E 85
Fawkham Green. Kent —4G 39
Fawler. Oxon —4B 50
Fawley. Buck —3F 37
Fawley. Hants —2C 16
Fawley. W Ber —3B 36
Fawley Chapel. Here —3A 48
Fawley Court —3F 37
Fawton. Corn —2F 7
Faxfleet. E Yor —2B 94
Faygate. W Sus —2D 26
Fazakerley. Mers —1F 83
Fazeley. Staf —5F 73
Feabuie. High —4B 158
Feagour. High —4H 149
Fearby. N Yor —1D 98
Fearn. High —1C 158
Fearnan. Per —4E 142
Fearnbeg. High —3G 155
Fearnhead. Warr —1A 84
Fearnmore. High —2G 155
Featherstone. Staf —5D 72
Featherstone. W Yor —2E 93
Featherstone Castle. Nmbd —3H 113
Feckenham. Worc —4E 61
Feering. Essx —3B 54
Feetham. N Yor —5C 104
Feizor. N Yor —3G 97
Felbridge. Surr —2E 27
Felbrigg. Norf —2E 78
Felbrigg Hall NT —2D 78
Felcourt. Surr —1E 27
Felden. Herts —5A 52
Felhampton. Shrp —2G 59
Felindre. Carm —3F 45
(nr. Llandeilo)
Felindre. Carm —2G 45
(nr. Llandovery)
Felindre. Carm —2D 44
(nr. Newcastle Emlyn)
Felindre. Powy —2D 58
Felindre. Swan —5G 45
Felindre Farchog. Pemb —1F 43
Felinfach. Cdgn —5E 57
Felinfach. Powy —2D 46
Felinfoel. Carm —5F 45
Felingwmisaf. Carm —3F 45
Felingwmuchaf. Carm —3F 45
Felin Newydd. Powy —5C 70
(nr. Newtown)
Felin Newydd. Powy —3E 70
(nr. Oswestry)
Felin Wnda. Cdgn —1D 44
Felinwynt. Cdgn —5B 56
Felixkirk. N Yor —1G 99
Felixstowe. Suff —2F 55
Felixstowe Ferry. Suff —2G 55
Felkington. Nmbd —5F 131
Fell End. Cumb —5A 104
Fell Foot Park NT —1C 96
Felling. Tyne —3F 115
Fell Side. Cumb —1E 102
Felmersham. Beds —5G 63
Felmingham. Norf —3E 79
Felpham. W Sus —3H 17
Felsham. Suff —5B 66
Felsted. Essx —3G 53
Feltham. G Lon —3C 38
Felthamhill. Surr —3B 38
Felthorpe. Norf —4D 78
Felton. Here —1A 48
Felton. N Som —5A 34
Felton. Nmbd —4F 121
Felton Butler. Shrp —4F 71
Feltwell. Norf —1G 65
Fenay Bridge. W Yor —3B 92
Fence. Lanc —1G 91
Fence Houses. Tyne —4G 115
Fencott. Oxon —4D 50
Fen Ditton. Cambs —4D 65
Fen Drayton. Cambs —4C 64
Fen End. Linc —3B 76
Fen End. W Mid —3G 61
Fenham. Nmbd —5G 131
Fenham. Tyne —3F 115
Fenhouses. Linc —1B 76
Feniscowles. Bkbn —2E 91
Feniton. Devn —3E 12
Fenn Green. Shrp —2B 60
Fenn's Bank. Wrex —2H 71
Fenn Street. Medw —3B 40
Fenny Bentley. Derbs —5F 85
Fenny Bridges. Devn —3E 12
Fenny Compton. Warw —5B 62
Fenny Drayton. Leics —1A 62
Fenny Stratford. Mil —2G 51
Fenrother. Nmbd —5F 121
Fenstanton. Cambs —4C 64
Fen Street. Norf —1C 66
Fenton. Cambs —3C 64
Fenton. Cumb —4G 113
Fenton. Linc —5F 87
(nr. Caythorpe)
Fenton. Linc —3F 87
(nr. Saxilby)
Fenton. Nmbd —1D 120
Fenton. Notts —2E 87
Fenton. Stoke —1C 72
Fentonadle. Corn —5A 10
Fenton Barns. E Lot —1B 130
Fenwick. E Ayr —5F 127
Fenwick. Nmbd —5G 131
(nr. Berwick)
Fenwick. Nmbd —2D 114
(nr. Hexham)
Fenwick. S Yor —3F 93
Feochaig. Arg —4B 122
Feock. Corn —5C 6
Feolin Ferry. Arg —3C 124
Feorlan. Arg —5A 122
Feriniquarrie. High —3A 154
Fern. Ang —2D 145
Ferndale. Rhon —2C 32
Ferndown. Dors —2F 15
Ferness. High —4D 158
Fernham. Oxon —2A 36
Fernhill. W Sus —1D 27
Fernhill Heath. Worc —5C 60
Fernhurst. W Sus —4G 25
Fernieflatt. Abers —1H 145
Ferniegair. S Lan —4A 128
Fernilea. High —5C 154
Fernilee. Derbs —3E 85
Ferrensby. N Yor —3F 99
Ferriby Sluice. N Lin —2C 94
Ferrindonald. High —3E 147
Ferring. W Sus —5C 26
Ferrybridge. W Yor —2E 93
Ferryden. Ang —3G 145
Ferryhill. Aber —3G 153
Ferry Hill. Cambs —2C 64
Ferryhill. Dur —1F 105
Ferryhill Station. Dur —1F 105
Ferryside. Carm —4D 44
Ferryton. High —2A 158
Fersfield. Norf —2C 66
Fersit. High —1A 142
Feshiebridge. High —3C 150
Fetcham. Surr —5C 38
Fetterangus. Abers —3G 161
Fettercairn. Abers —1F 145
Fewcott. Oxon —3D 50
Fewston. N Yor —4D 98
Ffairfach. Carm —3G 45
Ffair Rhos. Cdgn —4G 57
Ffaldybrenin. Carm —1G 45
Ffarmers. Carm —1G 45
Ffawyddog. Powy —4F 47
Ffestiniog Railway —1F 69
Ffodun. Powy —5E 70
Ffont-y-gari. V Glam —5D 32
Fforest. Carm —5F 45
Fforest-fach. Swan —3F 31
Fforest Goch. Neat —5H 45
Ffostrasol. Cdgn —1D 45
Ffos-y-ffin. Cdgn —4D 56
Ffrith. Flin —5E 83
Ffrwdgrech. Powy —3D 46
Ffwl-y-mwn. V Glam —5D 32
Ffynnon-ddrain. Carm —3E 45
Ffynnongroyw. Flin —2D 82
Ffynnon Gynydd. Powy —1E 47
Ffynnonoer. Cdgn —5E 57
Fiag Lodge. High —1B 164
Fidden. Arg —2B 132
Fiddington. Glos —2E 49
Fiddington. Som —2F 21
Fiddleford. Dors —1D 14
Fiddlers Hamlet. Essx —5E 53
Field. Staf —2E 73
Field Assarts. Oxon —4B 50
Field Broughton. Cumb —1C 96
Field Dalling. Norf —2C 78
Fieldhead. Cumb —1F 103
Field Head. Leics —5B 74
Fifehead Magdalen. Dors —4C 22
Fifehead Neville. Dors —1C 14
Fifehead St Quintin. Dors —1C 14
Fife Keith. Mor —3B 160
Fifield. Oxon —4H 49
Fifield. Wilts —1G 23
Fifield. Wind —3A 38
Fifield Bavant. Wilts —4F 23
Figheldean. Wilts —2G 23
Filby. Norf —4G 79
Filey. N Yor —1F 101
Filford. Dors —3H 13
Filgrave. Mil —1G 51
Filkins. Oxon —5H 49
Filleigh. Devn —1H 11
(nr. Crediton)
Filleigh. Devn —4G 19
(nr. South Molton)
Fillingham. Linc —2G 87
Fillongley. Warw —2G 61
Filton. S Glo —4B 34
Fimber. E Yor —3C 100
Finavon. Ang —3D 145
Fincham. Norf —5F 77
Finchampstead. Wok —5F 37
Fincharn. Arg —3G 133
Finchcocks —2A 28
Finchdale Priory EH —5F 115
Finchdean. Hants —1F 17
Finch Foundry NT —3G 11
Finchingfield. Essx —2G 53
Finchley. G Lon —1D 38
Findern. Derbs —2H 73
Findhorn. Mor —2E 159
Findhorn Bridge. High —1C 150
Findochty. Mor —2B 160
Findo Gask. Per —1C 136
Findon. Abers —4G 153
Findon. W Sus —5C 26
Findon Mains. High —2A 158
Findon Valley. W Sus —5C 26
Finedon. Nptn —3G 63
Fingal's Cave NTS —5E 139
Fingal Street. Suff —3E 66
Fingest. Buck —2F 37
Finghall. N Yor —1D 98
Fingland. Cumb —4D 112
Fingland. Dum —3G 117
Finglesham. Kent —5H 41
Fingringhoe. Essx —3D 54
Finiskaig. High —4A 148
Finlaystone House —2E 127
Finmere. Oxon —2E 51
Finnart. Per —3C 142
Finningham. Suff —4C 66
Finningley. S Yor —1D 86
Finnyguad. Abers —3D 160
Finsbury. G Lon —2E 39
Finstall. Worc —3D 61
Finsthwaite. Cumb —1C 96
Finstock. Oxon —4B 50
Finstown. Orkn —6C 172
Fintry. Abers —3E 161
Fintry. D'dee —5D 144
Fintry. Stir —1H 127
Finwood. Warw —4F 61
Finzean. Abers —4D 152
Fionnphort. Arg —2B 132
Fionnsabhagh. W Isl —9C 171
Firbeck. S Yor —2C 86
Firby. N Yor —1E 99
(nr. Bedale)
Firby. N Yor —3B 100
(nr. Malton)
Firgrove. G Man —3H 91
Firle Place —5F 27
Firsdown. Wilts —3H 23
First Coast. High —4D 162
Firth. Shet —4F 173
Fir Tree. Dur —1E 105
Fishbourne. IOW —3D 16
Fishbourne. W Sus —2G 17
Fishbourne Roman Palace —2G 17
Fishburn. Dur —1A 106
Fishcross. Clac —4B 136
Fisherford. Abers —5D 160
Fisherrow. E Lot —2G 129
Fisher's Pond. Hants —4C 24
Fisher's Row. Lanc —5D 96
Fisherstreet. W Sus —2A 26
Fisherton. High —3B 158
Fisherton. S Ayr —3B 116
Fisherton de la Mere. Wilts —3E 23
Fishguard. Pemb —1D 42
Fishlake. S Yor —3G 93
Fishley. Norf —4G 79
Fishnish. Arg —4A 140
Fishpond Bottom. Dors —3G 13
Fishponds. Bris —4B 34
Fishpool. Glos —3B 48
Fishpool. G Man —4G 91
Fishpools. Powy —4D 58
Fishtoft. Linc —1C 76
Fishtoft Drove. Linc —1C 76
Fishwick. Bord —4F 131
Fiskavaig. High —5C 154
Fiskerton. Linc —3H 87
Fiskerton. Notts —5E 87
Fitch. Shet —7E 173
Fitling. E Yor —1F 95
Fittleton. Wilts —2G 23
Fittleworth. W Sus —4B 26
Fitton End. Cambs —4D 76
Fitz. Shrp —4G 71
Fitzhead. Som —4E 20
Fitzwilliam. W Yor —3E 93
Fitzwilliam Mus. —Cambridge 187
Fiunary. High —4A 140
Five Ash Down. E Sus —3F 27
Five Ashes. E Sus —3G 27
Five Bells. Som —2D 20
Five Bridges. Here —1B 48
Fivehead. Som —4G 21
Five Lane Ends. Lanc —4E 97
Fivelanes. Corn —4C 10
Five Oak Green. Kent —1H 27
Five Oaks. W Sus —3B 26
Five Roads. Carm —5E 45
Five Ways. Warw —3G 61
Flack's Green. Essx —4A 54
Flackwell Heath. Buck —3G 37
Fladbury. Worc —1E 49
Fladda. Shet —3E 173
Fladdabister. Shet —8F 173
Flagg. Derbs —4F 85
Flambards Victorian Village —4D 4
Flamborough. E Yor —2G 101
Flamingoland —2B 100
Flamingo Park —3E 17
Flamstead. Herts —4A 52
Flansham. W Sus —5A 26
Flasby. N Yor —4B 98
Flash. Staf —4E 85
Flashader. High —3C 154
Flatford Mill, Bridge Cottage, Constable Exhibition NT —2D 54
Flatt, The. Cumb —2G 113
Flaunden. Herts —5A 52
Flawborough. Notts —1E 75
Flawith. N Yor —3G 99
Flax Bourton. N Som —5A 34
Flaxby. N Yor —4F 99
Flaxholme. Derbs —1H 73
Flaxley. Glos —4B 48
Flaxley Green. Staf —4E 73
Flaxpool. Som —3E 21
Flaxton. N Yor —3A 100
Fleck. Shet —10E 173
Fleckney. Leics —1D 62
Flecknoe. Warw —4C 62
Fledborough. Notts —3F 87
Fleet. Dors —4B 14

Fleet. Hants —1G 25
(nr. Farnborough)
Fleet. Hants —2F 17
(nr. South Hayling)
Fleet. Linc —3C 76
Fleet Air Arm Mus. —4A 22
Fleet Hargate. Linc —3C 76
Fleetville. Herts —5B 52
Fleetwood. Lanc —5C 96
Fleggburgh. Norf —4G 79
Fleisirin. W Isl —4H 171
Flemingston. V Glam —4D 32
Flemington. S Lan —3H 127
(nr. Glasgow)
Flemington. S Lan —5A 128
(nr. Strathaven)
Flempton. Suff —4H 65
Fleoideabhagh. W Isl —9C 171
Fletcher's Green. Kent —1G 27
Fletchertown. Cumb —5D 112
Fletching. E Sus —3F 27
Flete —3C 8
Fleuchary. High —4E 165
Flexbury. Corn —2C 10
Flexford. Surr —5A 38
Flimby. Cumb —1B 102
Flimwell. E Sus —2B 28
Flint. Flin —3E 83
Flint Castle CADW —3E 83
Flintham. Notts —1E 75
Flint Mountain. Flin —3E 83
Flinton. E Yor —1F 95
Flintsham. Here —5F 59
Flishinghurst. Kent —2B 28
Flitcham. Norf —3G 77
Flitton. Beds —2A 52
Flitwick. Beds —2A 52
Flixborough. N Lin —3B 94
Flixton. G Man —1B 84
Flixton. N Yor —2E 101
Flixton. Suff —2F 67
Flockton. W Yor —3C 92
Flodden. Nmbd —1D 120
Flodigarry. High —1D 154
Flood's Ferry. Cambs —1C 64
Flookburgh. Cumb —2C 96
Floors Castle —1B 120
Flordon. Norf —1D 66
Flore. Nptn —4D 62
Flotterton. Nmbd —4E 121
Flowton. Suff —1D 54
Flushing. Abers —4H 161
Flushing. Corn —5C 6
Fluxton. Devn —3D 12
Flyde, The. Lanc —1C 90
Flyford Flavell. Worc —5D 61
Fobbing. Thur —2B 40
Fochabers. Mor —3H 159
Fochriw. Cphy —5E 46
Fockerby. N Lin —3B 94
Fodderty. High —3H 157
Foddington. Som —4A 22
Foel. Powy —4B 70
Foffarty. Ang —4D 144
Foggathorpe. E Yor —1A 94
Fogo. Bord —5D 130
Fogorig. Bord —5D 130
Foindle. High —4B 166
Folda. Ang —2A 144
Fole. Staf —2E 73
Foleshill. W Mid —2A 62
Foley Park. Worc —3C 60
Folke. Dors —1B 14
Folkestone. Kent —2G 29 & 189
Folkingham. Linc —2H 75
Folkington. E Sus —5G 27
Folksworth. Cambs —1A 64
Folkton. N Yor —2E 101
Folla Rule. Abers —5E 161
Follifoot. N Yor —4F 99
Folly Cross. Devn —2E 11
Folly Gate. Devn —3F 11
Folly, The. Herts —4B 52
Folly, The. W Ber —5C 36
Fonmon. V Glam —5D 32
Fonmon Castle —5D 32
Fonthill Bishop. Wilts —3E 23
Fonthill Gifford. Wilts —3E 23
Fontmell Magna. Dors —1D 14
Fontwell. W Sus —5A 26
Font-y-gary. V Glam —5D 32
Foodieash. Fife —2F 137
Foolow. Derbs —3F 85
Footdee. Aber —3G 153
Footherley. Staf —5F 73
Foots Cray. G Lon —3F 39
Forbestown. Abers —2A 152
Force Forge. Cumb —5E 103
Force Mills. Cumb —5E 103
Forcett. N Yor —3E 105
Ford. Arg —3F 133
Ford. Buck —5F 51
Ford. Derbs —2B 86
Ford. Devn —4E 19
(nr. Bideford)
Ford. Devn —3C 8
(nr. Holbeton)
Ford. Devn —4D 9
(nr. Salcombe)
Ford. Glos —3F 49
Ford. Nmbd —1D 120
Ford. Plym —3A 8
Ford. Shrp —4G 71
Ford. Som —1A 22
(nr. Wells)
Ford. Som —4D 20
(nr. Wiveliscombe)
Ford. Staf —5E 85
Ford. W Sus —5B 26
Ford. Wilts —4D 34
(nr. Chippenham)
Ford. Wilts —3G 23
(nr. Salisbury)
Ford Barton. Devn —1C 12
Fordcombe. Kent —1G 27
Forde Abbey —2G 13
Fordell. Fife —1E 129
Forden. Powy —5E 71
Ford End. Essx —4G 53
Forder Green. Devn —2D 9
Ford Green. Lanc —5D 97
Ford Green Hall —5C 84
Fordham. Cambs —3F 65
Fordham. Essx —3C 54
Fordham. Norf —1F 65
Fordham Heath. Essx —3C 54
Ford Heath. Shrp —4G 71
Fordhouses. W Mid —5D 72
Fordie. Per —1G 135
Fordingbridge. Hants —1G 15
Fordington. Linc —3D 88
Fordon. E Yor —2E 101
Fordoun. Abers —1G 145
Ford Street. Essx —3C 54
Ford Street. Som —1E 13
Fordton. Devn —3B 12
Fordwells. Oxon —4B 50
Fordwich. Kent —5F 41
Fordyce. Abers —2C 160
Forebridge. Staf —3D 72
Foremark. Derbs —3H 73
Forest. N Yor —4F 105
Forestburn Gate. Nmbd —5E 121
Foresterseat. Mor —3F 159
Forest Green. Glos —2D 34
Forest Green. Surr —1C 26
Forest Hall. Cumb —4G 103
Forest Head. Cumb —4G 113
Forest Hill. Oxon —5D 50
Forest-in-Teesdale. Dur —2B 104
Forest Lodge. Per —1G 143
Forest Mill. Clac —4B 136
Forest of Dean —5B 48
Forest of Dean Railway —5B 48
Forest Row. E Sus —2F 27
Forestside. W Sus —1F 17
Forest Town. Notts —4C 86
Forfar. Ang —3D 144
Forgandenny. Per —2C 136
Forge. Powy —1G 57
Forge Side. Torf —5F 47
Forge, The. Here —5F 59
Forgewood. N Lan —4A 128
Forgie. Mor —3A 160
Forgue. Abers —4D 160
Formby. Mers —4A 90
Forncett End. Norf —1D 66
Forncett St Mary. Norf —1D 66
Forncett St Peter. Norf —1D 66
Forneth. Per —4H 143
Fornham All Saints. Suff —4H 65
Fornham St Martin. Suff —4A 66
Forres. Mor —3E 159
Forrestfield. N Lan —3B 128
Forrest Lodge. Dum —1C 110
Forsbrook. Staf —1D 72
Forse. High —5E 169
Forsinard. High —4A 168
Forss. High —2C 168
Forstal, The. Kent —2E 29
Forston. Dors —3B 14
Fort Augustus. High —3F 149
Forteviot. Per —2C 136
Fort George. High —3B 158
Fort George HS —3B 158
Forth. S Lan —4C 128
Forthampton. Glos —2D 48
Forthay. Glos —2C 34
Forth Bridge —2E 129
Fortingall. Per —4E 143
Fort Matilda. Inv —2D 126
Forton. Hants —2C 24
Forton. Lanc —4D 97
Forton. Shrp —4G 71
Forton. Som —2G 13
Forton. Staf —3B 72
Forton Heath. Shrp —4G 71
Fortrie. Abers —4D 160
Fortrose. High —3B 158
Fortuneswell. Dors —5B 14
Fort William. High —1F 141
Forty Green. Buck —1A 38
Forty Hill. G Lon —1E 39
Forward Green. Suff —5C 66
Fosbury. Wilts —1B 24
Foscot. Oxon —3H 49
Fosdyke. Linc —2C 76
Foss. Per —3E 143
Fossebridge. Glos —4F 49
Foster Street. Essx —5E 53
Foston. Derbs —2F 73
Foston. Leics —1D 62
Foston. Linc —1F 75
Foston. N Yor —3A 100
Foston on the Wolds. E Yor —4F 101
Fotherby. Linc —1C 88
Fothergill. Cumb —1B 102
Fotheringhay. Nptn —1H 63
Foubister. Orkn —7E 172
Foul Anchor. Cambs —4D 76
Foulbridge. Cumb —5F 113
Foulden. Norf —1G 65
Foulden. Bord —4F 131
Foul Mile. E Sus —4H 27
Foulridge. Lanc —5A 98
Foulsham. Norf —3C 78
Fountainhall. Bord —5H 129
Fountains Abbey WH NT —3E 99
Four Alls, The. Shrp —2A 72
Four Ashes. Staf —5D 72
(nr. Cannock)
Four Ashes. Staf —2C 60
(nr. Kinver)
Four Ashes. Suff —3C 66
Four Crosses. Powy —5C 70
(nr. Llanerfyl)
Four Crosses. Powy —4E 71
(nr. Llanymynech)
Four Crosses. Staf —5D 72
Four Elms. Kent —1F 27
Four Forks. Som —3F 21
Four Gotes. Cambs —4D 76
Four Lane End. S Yor —4C 92
Four Lane Ends. Lanc —4E 97
Four Lanes. Corn —5A 6
Fourlanes End. Ches —5C 84
Four Marks. Hants —3E 25
Four Mile Bridge. IOA —3B 80
Four Oaks. E Sus —3C 28
Four Oaks. Glos —3B 48
Four Oaks. W Mid —2G 61
Four Roads. Carm —5E 45
Four Roads. IOM —5B 108
Fourstones. Nmbd —3B 114
Four Throws. Kent —3B 28
Fovant. Wilts —4F 23
Foveran. Abers —1G 153
Fowey. Corn —3F 7
Fowlershill. Abers —2G 153
Fowley Common. Warr —1A 84
Fowlis. Ang —5C 144
Fowlis Wester. Per —1B 136
Fowlmere. Cambs —1E 53
Fownhope. Here —2A 48
Foxcombe Hill. Oxon —5C 50
Fox Corner. Surr —5A 38
Foxcote. Glos —4F 49
Foxcote. Som —1C 22
Foxdale. IOM —4B 108
Foxearth. Essx —1B 54
Foxfield. Cumb —1B 96
Foxfield Steam Railway —1D 72
Foxham. Wilts —4E 35
Fox Hatch. Essx —1G 39
Foxhole. Corn —3D 6
Foxholes. N Yor —2E 101
Foxhunt Green. E Sus —4G 27
Fox Lane. Hants —1G 25
Foxlediate. Worc —4E 61
Foxley. Norf —3C 78
Foxley. Nptn —5D 62
Foxley. Wilts —3D 35
Fox Street. Essx —3D 54
Foxt. Staf —1E 73
Foxton. Cambs —1E 53
Foxton. Dur —2A 106
Foxton. Leics —2D 62
Foxton. N Yor —5B 106
Foxup. N Yor —2A 98
Foxwist Green. Ches —4A 84
Foxwood. Shrp —3A 60
Foy. Here —3A 48
Foyers. High —1G 149
Foynesfield. High —3C 158
Fraddam. Corn —3C 4
Fraddon. Corn —3D 6
Fradley. Staf —4F 73
Fradley South. Staf —4F 73
Fradswell. Staf —2D 73
Fraisthorpe. E Yor —3F 101
Framfield. E Sus —3F 27
Framingham Earl. Norf —5E 79
Framingham Pigot. Norf —5E 79
Framlingham. Suff —4E 67
Framlingham Castle —4E 67
Frampton. Dors —3B 14
Frampton. Linc —2C 76
Frampton Cotterell. S Glo —3B 34
Frampton Mansell. Glos —5E 49
Frampton on Severn. Glos —5C 48
Frampton West End. Linc —1B 76
Framsden. Suff —5D 66
Framwellgate Moor. Dur —5F 115
Franche. Worc —3C 60
Frandley. Ches —3A 84
Frankby. Mers —2E 83
Frankfort. Norf —3F 79
Frankley. Worc —2D 61
Frank's Bridge. Powy —5D 58
Frankton. Warw —3B 62
Frankwell. Shrp —4G 71
Frant. E Sus —2G 27
Fraserburgh. Abers —2G 161
Frating Green. Essx —3D 54
Fratton. Port —2E 17
Freathy. Corn —3A 8
Freckenham. Suff —3F 65
Freckleton. Lanc —2C 90
Freeby. Leics —3F 75
Freefolk Priors. Hants —2C 24
Freeland. Oxon —4C 50
Freester. Shet —6F 173
Freethorpe. Norf —5G 79
Freiston. Linc —1C 76
Freiston Shore. Linc —1C 76
Fremington. Devn —3F 19
Fremington. N Yor —5D 104
Frenchbeer. Devn —4G 11
French Street. Kent —5F 39
Frenich. Stir —3D 134
Frensham. Surr —2G 25
Frenze. Norf —2D 66
Fresgoe. High —2B 168
Freshfield. Mers —4A 90
Freshford. Bath —1C 22
Freshwater. IOW —4B 16
Freshwater Bay. IOW —4B 16
Freshwater East. Pemb —5E 43
Fressingfield. Suff —3E 67
Freston. Suff —2E 55
Freswick. High —2F 169
Fretherne. Glos —5C 48
Frettenham. Norf —4E 79
Freuchie. Fife —3E 137
Freystrop. Pemb —3D 42
Friar's Gate. E Sus —2F 27
Friar Waddon. Dors —4B 14
Friday Bridge. Cambs —5D 76
Friday Street. E Sus —5H 27
Friday Street. Surr —1C 26
Fridaythorpe. E Yor —4C 100
Friden. Derbs —4F 85
Friern Barnet. G Lon —1D 39
Friesthorpe. Linc —2H 87
Frieston. Linc —1G 75
Frieth. Buck —2F 37
Friezeland. Notts —5B 86
Frilford. Oxon —2C 36
Frilsham. W Ber —4D 36
Frimley. Surr —1G 25
Frimley Green. Surr —1G 25
Frindsbury. Medw —4B 40
Fring. Norf —2G 77
Fringford. Oxon —3E 50
Frinsted. Kent —5C 40
Frinton-on-Sea. Essx —4F 55
Friockheim. Ang —4E 145
Friog. Gwyn —4F 69
Frisby. Linc —4D 88
Frisby on the Wreak. Leics —4D 74
Friskney. Linc —5D 88
Friskney Eaudyke. Linc —5D 88
Friston. E Sus —5G 27
Friston. Suff —4G 67
Fritchley. Derbs —5A 86
Fritham. Hants —1H 15
Frith Bank. Linc —1C 76
Frith Common. Worc —4A 60
Frithelstock. Devn —1E 11
Frithelstock Stone. Devn —1E 11
Frithsden. Herts —5A 52
Frithville. Linc —5C 88
Frittenden. Kent —1C 28
Frittiscombe. Devn —4E 9
Fritton. Norf —5G 79
(nr. Great Yarmouth)
Fritton. Norf —1E 67
(nr. Long Stratton)
Fritwell. Oxon —3D 50
Frizinghall. W Yor —1B 92
Frizington. Cumb —3B 102
Frobost. W Isl —6C 170
Frocester. Glos —5C 48
Frochas. Powy —5D 70
Frodesley. Shrp —5H 71
Frodingham. N Lin —3C 94
Frodsham. Ches —3H 83
Froggat. Derbs —3G 85
Froghall. Staf —1E 73
Frogham. Hants —1G 15
Frogham. Kent —5G 41
Frogmore. Devn —4D 9
Frogmore. Hants —5G 37
Frogmore. Herts —5B 52
Frognall. Linc —4A 76
Frognall Wharf —1E 73
Frogshall. Norf —2E 79
Frogwell. Corn —2H 7
Frolesworth. Leics —1C 62
Frome. Som —2C 22
Fromefield. Som —2C 22
Frome St Quintin. Dors —2A 14
Fromes Hill. Here —1B 48
Fron. Carm —2A 46
Fron. Gwyn —5E 81
(nr. Caernarfon)
Fron. Gwyn —2C 68
(nr. Pwllheli)
Fron. Powy —4C 58
(nr. Llandrindod Wells)
Fron. Powy —1D 58
(nr. Newtown)
Fron. Powy —5E 71
(nr. Welshpool)
Froncysyllte. Den —1E 71
Frongoch. Gwyn —2B 70
Fron Isaf. Wrex —1E 71
Fronoleu. Gwyn —2G 69
Frosterley. Dur —1D 104
Frotoft. Orkn —5D 172
Froxfield. Beds —2H 51
Froxfield. Wilts —5A 36
Froxfield Green. Hants —4F 25
Fryern Hill. Hants —4C 24
Fryerning. Essx —5G 53
Fryton. N Yor —2A 100
Fugglestone St Peter. Wilts —3G 23
Fulbeck. Linc —5G 87
Fulbeck Hall —5G 87
Fulbourn. Cambs —5E 65
Fulbrook. Oxon —4A 50
Fulflood. Hants —4C 24
Fulford. Som —4F 21
Fulford. Staf —2D 72
Fulford. York —5A 100
Fulham. G Lon —3D 38
Fulking. W Sus —4D 26
Fuller's Moor. Ches —5G 83
Fuller Street. Essx —4H 53
Fullerton. Hants —3B 24
Fulletby. Linc —3B 88
Full Sutton. E Yor —4B 100
Fullwood. E Ayr —4F 127
Fulmer. Buck —2A 38
Fulmodestone. Norf —2B 78
Fulnetby. Linc —3A 88
Fulney. Linc —3B 76
Fulstow. Linc —1C 88
Fulthorpe. Stoc T —2B 106
Fulwell. Tyne —4G 115
Fulwood. Lanc —1D 90
Fulwood. Notts —5B 86
Fulwood. Som —4F 21
Fulwood. S Yor —2G 85
Fundenhall. Norf —1D 66
Funtington. W Sus —2G 17
Funtley. Hants —2D 16
Funzie. Shet —2H 173
Furley. Devn —2F 13
Furnace. Arg —3H 133
Furnace. Carm —5F 45
Furnace. Cdgn —1F 57
Furner's Green. E Sus —3F 27
Furness Abbey EH —2B 96
Furness Vale. Derbs —2E 85
Furneux Pelham. Herts —3E 53
Fursdon House —2C 12
Furzebrook. Dors —4E 15
Furzehill. Devn —2H 19
Furzeley Corner. Hants —1E 17
Furzey Gdns. —1A 16
Furzey Lodge. Hants —2B 16
Furzley. Hants —1A 16
Fyfield. Essx —5F 53
Fyfield. Glos —5H 49
Fyfield. Hants —2A 24
Fyfield. Oxon —2C 36
Fyfield. Wilts —5G 35
Fylingthorpe. N Yor —4G 107
Fyne Court NT —3F 21
Fyning. W Sus —4G 25
Fyvie. Abers —5E 161
Fyvie Castle NTS —5E 161

Gabhsann bho Dheas. W Isl —2G 171
Gabhsann bho Thuath. W Isl —2G 171
Gabroc Hill. E Ayr —4F 127
Gadbrook. Surr —1D 26
Gaddesby. Leics —4D 74
Gadfa. IOA —2D 80
Gadgirth. S Ayr —2D 116
Gaer. Powy —3E 47
Gaerwen. IOA —3D 81
Gagingwell. Oxon —3C 50
Gaick Lodge. High —5B 150
Gailey. Staf —4D 72
Gainford. Dur —3E 105
Gainsborough. Linc —1F 87
Gainsborough. Suff —1E 55
Gainsborough Old Hall EH —1F 87
Gainsborough's Mus. —1B 54
Gainsford End. Essx —2H 53
Gairletter. Arg —1C 126
Gairloch. Abers —3E 153
Gairloch. High —1H 155
Gairlochy. High —5D 148
Gairney Bank. Per —4D 136
Gairnshiel Lodge. Abers —3G 151
Gaisgill. Cumb —4H 103
Gaitsgill. Cumb —5E 113
Galashiels. Bord —1G 119
Galgate. Lanc —4D 97
Galhampton. Som —4B 22
Gallatown. Fife —4E 137
Galley Common. Warw —1H 61
Galleyend. Essx —5H 53
Galleywood. Essx —5H 53
Gallin. Per —4C 142
Galloway Forest Park —1A 110
Galloway House Gdns. —5B 110
Galloway Wildlife Park —4D 111
Gallowfauld. Ang —4D 144
Gallowhill. E Dun —2H 127
Gallowhill. Per —5A 144
Gallowhill. Ren —3F 127
Gallowhills. Abers —3H 161
Gallows Green. Staf —1E 73
Gallows Green. Worc —4D 60
Gallowstree Common. Oxon —3E 37
Galltair. High —1G 147
Gallt Melyd. Den —2C 82
Galmington. Som —4F 21
Galmisdale. High —5C 146
Galmpton. Devn —4C 8
Galmpton. Torb —3E 9
Galmpton Warborough. Torb —3E 9
Galphay. N Yor —2E 99
Galston. E Ayr —1D 117
Galton. Dors —4C 14
Galtrigill. High —3A 154
Gamblesby. Cumb —1H 103
Gamelsby. Cumb —4D 112
Gamesley. Derbs —1E 85
Gamlingay. Cambs —5B 64
Gamlingay Cinques. Cambs —5B 64
Gamlingay Great Heath. Cambs —5B 64
Gammersgill. N Yor —1C 98
Gamston. Notts —3E 86
(nr. East Retford)
Gamston. Notts —2D 74
(nr. Nottingham)
Ganarew. Here —4A 48
Ganavan. Arg —5C 140
Ganborough. Glos —3G 49
Gang. Corn —2H 7
Ganllwyd. Gwyn —3G 69
Gannochy. Ang —1E 145
Gannochy. Per —1D 136
Gansclet. High —4F 169
Ganstead. E Yor —1E 95
Ganthorpe. N Yor —2A 100
Ganton. N Yor —2D 101
Gappah. Devn —5B 12
Garafad. High —2D 155
Garboldisham. Norf —2C 66
Garden City. Flin —4F 83
Gardeners Green. Wok —5G 37
Garden House, The —2A 8
Gardenstown. Abers —2F 161
Garden Village. S Yor —1G 85
Garden Village. Swan —3E 31
Garden Village. W Yor —1E 93
Garderhouse. Shet —7E 173
Gardham. E Yor —5D 100
Gardie. Shet —5C 173
(on Papa Stour)
Gardie. Shet —1H 173
(on Unst)
Gardie Ho. Shet —7F 173
Gare Hill. Som —2C 22
Garelochhead. Arg —4B 134
Garford. Oxon —2C 36
Garforth. W Yor —1E 93
Gargrave. N Yor —4B 98
Gargunnock. Stir —4G 135
Garleffin. S Ayr —3F 147
Garleffin. S Ayr —1F 109
Garlieston. Dum —5B 110
Garlinge Green. Kent —5F 41
Garlogie. Abers —3E 153
Garmelow. Staf —3B 72
Garmond. Abers —3F 161
Garmondsway. Dur —1A 106
Garmony. Arg —4A 140
Garmouth. Mor —2H 159
Garmston. Shrp —5A 72
Garnant. Carm —4G 45
Garndiffaith. Torf —5F 47
Garndolbenmaen. Gwyn —1D 69
Garnett Bridge. Cumb —5G 103
Garnfadryn. Gwyn —2B 68
Garnkirk. N Lan —3H 127
Garnlydan. Blae —4E 47
Garnsgate. Linc —3D 76
Garnswllt. Swan —5G 45
Garn-yr-erw. Torf —4F 47
Garrabost. W Isl —4H 171

Garrallan. *E Ayr* —3E **117**
Garras. *Corn* —4E **5**
Garreg. *Gwyn* —1F **69**
Garrigill. *Cumb* —5A **114**
Garriston. *N Yor* —5E **105**
Garrogie Lodge. *High* —2H **149**
Garros. *High* —2D **155**
Garrow. *Per* —5F **143**
Garsdale. *Cumb* —1G **97**
Garsdale Head. *Cumb* —5A **104**
Garsdon. *Wilts* —3E **35**
Garshall Green. *Staf* —2D **72**
Garsington. *Oxon* —5D **50**
Garstang. *Lanc* —5D **97**
Garston. *Mers* —2G **83**
Garswood. *Mers* —1H **83**
Gartcosh. *N Lan* —3H **127**
Garth. *B'end* —2B **32**
Garth. *Cdgn* —2F **57**
Garth. *Den* —1E **71**
Garth. *Gwyn* —2E **69**
Garth. *IOM* —4C **108**
Garth. *Powy* —1C **46** (nr. Builth Wells)
Garth. *Powy* —3E **59** (nr. Knighton)
Garth. *Shet* —6F **173**
Garthamlock. *Glas* —3H **127**
Garthbrengy. *Powy* —2D **46**
Gartheli. *Cdgn* —5E **57**
Garthmyl. *Powy* —1D **58**
Garthorpe. *Leics* —3F **75**
Garthorpe. *N Lin* —3B **94**
Garth Owen. *Powy* —1D **58**
Garth Row. *Cumb* —5G **103**
Gartly. *Abers* —5C **160**
Gartmore. *Stir* —4E **135**
Gartness. *N Lan* —3A **128**
Gartness. *Stir* —1G **127**
Gartocharn. *W Dun* —1F **127**
Garton. *E Yor* —1F **95**
Garton-on-the-Wolds. *E Yor* —4D **101**
Gartsherrie. *N Lan* —3A **128**
Gartymore. *High* —2H **165**
Garvald. *E Lot* —2B **130**
Garvamore. *High* —4H **149**
Garvard. *Arg* —4A **132**
Garvault. *High* —5H **167**
Garve. *High* —2F **157**
Garvestone. *Norf* —5C **78**
Garvie. *Arg* —4H **133**
Garvock. *Abers* —1G **145**
Garvock. *Inv* —2D **126**
Garway. *Here* —3H **47**
Garway Common. *Here* —3H **47**
Garway Hill. *Here* —3H **47**
Garwick. *Linc* —1A **76**
Gaskan. *High* —1B **140**
Gasper. *Wilts* —3C **22**
Gastard. *Wilts* —5D **35**
Gasthorpe. *Norf* —2B **66**
Gastonbury Tor *NT* —3A **22**
Gatcombe. *IOW* —4C **16**
Gateacre. *Mers* —2G **83**
Gatebeck. *Cumb* —1E **97**
Gate Burton. *Linc* —2F **87**
Gateforth. *N Yor* —2F **93**
Gatehead. *E Ayr* —1C **116**
Gate Helmsley. *N Yor* —4A **100**
Gatehouse. *Nmbd* —1A **114**
Gatehouse of Fleet. *Dum* —4C **110**
Gatelawbridge. *Dum* —5B **118**
Gateley. *Norf* —3B **78**
Gatenby. *N Yor* —1F **99**
Gatesgarth. *Cumb* —3C **102**
Gateshead. *Tyne* —3F **115**
Gatesheath. *Ches* —4G **83**
Gateside. *Ang* —4D **144** (nr. Forfar)
Gateside. *Ang* —4C **144** (nr. Kirriemuir)
Gateside. *Fife* —3D **136**
Gateside. *N Ayr* —4E **127**
Gathurst. *G Man* —4D **90**
Gatley. *G Man* —2C **84**
Gatton. *Surr* —5D **39**
Gattonside. *Bord* —1H **119**
Gatwick (London) Airport. *W Sus* —1D **27**
Gaufron. *Powy* —4B **58**
Gaulby. *Leics* —5D **74**
Gaulden Manor —3E **20**
Gauldry. *Fife* —1F **137**
Gaultree. *Norf* —5D **77**
Gaunt's Common. *Dors* —2F **15**
Gaunt's Earthcott. *S Glo* —3B **34**
Gautby. *Linc* —3A **88**
Gavinton. *Bord* —4D **130**
Gawber. *S Yor* —4D **92**
Gawcott. *Buck* —2E **51**
Gawsworth. *Ches* —4C **84**
Gawsworth Hall —4C **84**
Gawthorpe. *W Yor* —2C **92**
Gawthorpe Hall *NT* —1G **91**
Gawthrop. *Cumb* —1F **97**
Gawthwaite. *Cumb* —1B **96**
Gay Bowers. *Essx* —5A **54**
Gaydon. *Warw* —5A **62**
Gayfield. *Orkn* —2D **172**
Gayhurst. *Mil* —1G **51**
Gayle. *N Yor* —1A **98**
Gayles. *N Yor* —4E **105**
Gay Street. *W Sus* —3B **26**
Gayton. *Mers* —2E **83**
Gayton. *Norf* —4G **77**
Gayton. *Nptn* —5E **62**
Gayton. *Staf* —3D **73**
Gayton le Marsh. *Linc* —2D **88**
Gayton le Wold. *Linc* —2B **88**
Gayton Thorpe. *Norf* —4G **77**
Gaywood. *Norf* —3F **77**
Gazeley. *Suff* —4G **65**
Geanies. *High* —1C **158**
Gearraidh Bhailteas. *W Isl* —6C **170**
Gearraidh Bhaird. *W Isl* —6F **171**
Gearraidh ma Monadh. *W Isl* —7C **170**
Gearraidh na h-Aibhne. *W Isl* —4E **171**
Geary. *High* —2B **154**
Geddes. *High* —3C **158**
Gedding. *Suff* —5B **66**
Geddington. *Nptn* —2F **63**
Gedintailor. *High* —5E **155**
Gedling. *Notts* —1D **74**
Gedney. *Linc* —3D **76**
Gedney Broadgate. *Linc* —3D **76**
Gedney Drove End. *Linc* —3D **76**
Gedney Dyke. *Linc* —3D **76**
Gedney Hill. *Linc* —4C **76**
Gee Cross. *G Man* —1D **84**
Geeston. *Rut* —5G **75**
Geilston. *Arg* —2E **127**
Geirinis. *W Isl* —4C **170**
Geise. *High* —2D **168**
Geisiadar. *W Isl* —4D **171**
Gelder Shiel. *Abers* —5G **151**
Geldeston. *Norf* —1F **67**
Gell. *Cnwy* —4A **82**
Gelli. *Pemb* —3E **43**
Gelli. *Rhon* —2C **32**
Gellifor. *Den* —4D **82**
Gelligaer. *Cphy* —2E **32**
Gellilydan. *Gwyn* —2F **69**
Gellinudd. *Neat* —5H **45**
Gellyburn. *Per* —5H **143**
Gellywen. *Carm* —2G **43**
Gelston. *Dum* —4E **111**
Gelston. *Linc* —1G **75**
Gembling. *E Yor* —4F **101**
Geneva. *Cdgn* —5D **56**
Gentleshaw. *Staf* —4E **73**
Geocrab. *W Isl* —8D **171**
George Green. *Buck* —2A **38**
Georgeham. *Devn* —3E **19**
George Nympton. *Devn* —4H **19**
Georgetown. *Blae* —5E **47**
Georgetown. *Ren* —3F **127**
Georth. *Orkn* —5C **172**
Gerlan. *Gwyn* —4F **81**
Germansweek. *Devn* —3E **11**
Germoe. *Corn* —4C **4**
Gerrard's Bromley. *Staf* —2B **72**
Gerrards Cross. *Buck* —2A **38**
Gerston. *High* —3D **168**
Gervans. *Corn* —5C **6**
Gestingthorpe. *Essx* —2B **54**
Gethsemane. *Pemb* —1A **44**
Geuffordd. *Powy* —4E **70**
Gibraltar. *Linc* —5E **89**
Gibraltar. *Suff* —5D **66**
Gibralter. *Buck* —4F **51**
Gibside, Gdn. & Chapel *NT* —4E **115**
Gibsmere. *Notts* —1E **74**
Giddeahall. *Wilts* —4D **34**
Gidea Park. *G Lon* —2G **39**
Gidleigh. *Devn* —4G **11**
Giffnock. *E Ren* —4G **127**
Gifford. *E Lot* —3B **130**
Giffordtown. *Fife* —2E **137**
Giggetty. *Staf* —1C **60**
Giggleswick. *N Yor* —3H **97**
Gignog. *Pemb* —2C **42**
Gilberdyke. *E Yor* —2B **94**
Gilbert's End. *Worc* —1D **48**
Gilbert's Green. *Warw* —3F **61**
Gilbert White's House —3F **25**
Gilchriston. *E Lot* —3A **130**
Gilcrux. *Cumb* —1C **102**
Gildersome. *W Yor* —2C **92**
Gildingwells. *S Yor* —2C **86**
Gilesgate Moor. *Dur* —5F **115**
Gileston. *V Glam* —5D **32**
Gilfach. *Cphy* —2E **33**
Gilfach Goch. *Rhon* —2C **32**
Gilfachreda. *Cdgn* —5D **56**
Gillamoor. *N Yor* —1A **100**
Gillar's Green. *Mers* —1G **83**
Gillen. *High* —3B **154**
Gilling East. *N Yor* —2A **100**
Gillingham. *Dors* —4D **22**
Gillingham. *Medw* —4B **40** & **Medway 191**
Gillingham. *Norf* —1G **67**
Gilling West. *N Yor* —4E **105**
Gillock. *High* —3E **169**
Gillow Heath. *Staf* —5C **84**
Gills. *High* —1F **169**
Gill's Green. *Kent* —2B **28**
Gilmanscleuch. *Bord* —2F **119**
Gilmerton. *Edin* —3F **129**
Gilmerton. *Per* —1A **136**
Gilmonby. *Dur* —3C **104**
Gilmorton. *Leics* —2C **62**
Gilsland. *Nmbd* —3H **113**
Gilsland Spa. *Cumb* —3H **113**
Gilston. *Midl* —4H **129**
Giltbrook. *Notts* —1B **74**
Gilwern. *Mon* —4F **47**
Gimingham. *Norf* —2E **79**
Giosla. *W Isl* —5D **171**
Gipping. *Suff* —4C **66**
Gipsey Bridge. *Linc* —1B **76**
Gipton. *W Yor* —1D **92**
Girdle Toll. *N Ayr* —5E **127**
Girlsta. *Shet* —6F **173**
Girsby. *N Yor* —4A **106**
Girthon. *Dum* —4D **110**
Girton. *Cambs* —4D **64**
Girton. *Notts* —4F **87**
Girvan. *S Ayr* —5A **116**
Gisburn. *Lanc* —5H **97**
Gisleham. *Suff* —2H **67**
Gislingham. *Suff* —3C **66**
Gissing. *Norf* —2D **66**
Gittisham. *Devn* —3E **13**
Gladestry. *Powy* —5E **59**
Gladsmuir. *E Lot* —2A **130**
Gladstone Pottery Mus. —1D **72**
Gladstone's Land *NTS* —**Edinburgh 189**
Glaichbea. *High* —5H **157**
Glais. *Swan* —5H **45**
Glaisdale. *N Yor* —4E **107**
Glame. *High* —4E **155**
Glamis. *Ang* —4C **144**
Glamis Castle —4C **144**
Glamisdale. *High* —5C **146**
Glanaman. *Carm* —4G **45**
Glan-Conwy. *Cnwy* —5H **81**
Glandford. *Norf* —1C **78**
Glan Duar. *Carm* —1F **45**
Glandwr. *Blae* —5F **47**
Glandwr. *Pemb* —2F **43**
Glan-Dwyfach. *Gwyn* —1D **69**
Glandy Cross. *Carm* —2F **43**
Glandyfi. *Cdgn* —1F **57**
Glangrwyney. *Powy* —4F **47**
Glanmule. *Powy* —1D **58**
Glanrhyd. *Gwyn* —2B **68**
Glanrhyd. *Pemb* —1B **44** (nr. Cardigan)
Glan-rhyd. *Pemb* —1F **43** (nr. Crymmych)
Glan-rhyd. *Powy* —5A **46**
Glanton. *Nmbd* —3E **121**
Glanton Pyke. *Nmbd* —3E **121**
Glanvilles Wootton. *Dors* —2B **14**
Glan-y-don. *Flin* —3D **82**
Glan-y-nant. *Powy* —2B **58**
Glan-yr-afon. *Gwyn* —1C **70**
Glan-yr-afon. *IOA* —2F **81**
Glan-yr-afon. *Powy* —5C **70**
Glan-y-wern. *Gwyn* —2F **69**
Glapthorn. *Nptn* —1H **63**
Glapwell. *Derbs* —4B **86**
Glas Aird. *Arg* —4A **132**
Glas-allt Shiel. *Abers* —5G **151**
Glasbury. *Powy* —2E **47**
Glaschoil. *Mor* —5E **159**
Glascoed. *Den* —3B **82**
Glascoed. *Mon* —5G **47**
Glascote. *Staf* —5G **73**
Glascwm. *Powy* —5D **58**
Glasfryn. *Cnwy* —5B **82**
Glasgow. *Glas* —3G **127** & **189**
Glasgow Airport. *Ren* —3F **127**
Glasgow Cathedral *HS* —**189**
Glasgow Gallery of Modern Art —**189**
Glasgow Mus. of Transport, see Kelvingrove Museums —**189**
Glasgow Science Centre —**189**
Glashvin. *High* —2D **154**
Glasinfryn. *Gwyn* —4E **81**
Glasnakille. *High* —2D **146**
Glasnarcardoch. *High* —4E **147**
Glaspwll. *Cdgn* —1G **57**
Glassburn. *High* —5F **157**
Glassenbury. *Kent* —2B **28**
Glasserton. *Dum* —5B **110**
Glassford. *S Lan* —5A **128**
Glassgreen. *Mor* —2G **159**
Glasshouse. *Glos* —3C **48**
Glasshouses. *N Yor* —3D **98**
Glasson. *Cumb* —3D **112**
Glasson. *Lanc* —4D **96**
Glassonby. *Cumb* —1G **103**
Glasterlaw. *Ang* —3E **145**
Glaston. *Rut* —5F **75**
Glastonbury. *Som* —3H **21**
Glastonbury Abbey —3A **22**
Glatton. *Cambs* —2A **64**
Glazebrook. *Warr* —1A **84**
Glazebury. *Warr* —1A **84**
Glazeley. *Shrp* —2B **60**
Gleadless. *S Yor* —2A **86**
Gleadsmoss. *Ches* —4C **84**
Gleann Dail bho Dheas. *W Isl* —7C **170**
Gleann Tholastaidh. *W Isl* —3H **171**
Gleaston. *Cumb* —2B **96**
Glecknabae. *Arg* —3B **126**
Gledrid. *Shrp* —2E **71**
Gleiniant. *Powy* —1B **58**
Glemsford. *Suff* —1B **54**
Glen. *Dum* —4C **110**
Glenancross. *High* —4E **147**
Glen Audlyn. *IOM* —2D **108**
Glenbarr. *Arg* —2A **122**
Glenbeg. *High* —2G **139**
Glen Bernisdale. *High* —4D **154**
Glenbervie. *Abers* —5E **153**
Glenboig. *N Lan* —3A **128**
Glenborrodale. *High* —2A **140**
Glenbranter. *Arg* —4A **134**
Glenbreck. *Bord* —2C **118**
Glenbrein Lodge. *High* —2G **149**
Glenbrittle. *High* —1C **146**
Glenbuchat Castle *HS* —2A **152**
Glenbuchat Lodge. *Abers* —2H **151**
Glenbuck. *E Ayr* —2G **117**
Glenburn. *Ren* —3F **127**
Glencalvie Lodge. *High* —5B **164**
Glencaple. *Dum* —3A **112**
Glencarron Lodge. *High* —3C **156**
Glencarse. *Per* —1D **136**
Glencassley Castle. *High* —3B **164**
Glencat. *Abers* —4C **152**
Glencoe. *High* —3F **141**
Glencoe Gorge *NTS* —3F **141**
Glen Cottage. *High* —5E **147**
Glencraig. *Fife* —4D **136**
Glendale. *High* —4A **154**
Glendevon. *Per* —3B **136**
Glendoebeg. *High* —3G **149**
Glendoick. *Per* —1E **136**
Glendoune. *S Ayr* —5A **116**
Glenduckie. *Fife* —2E **137**
Glendurgan Gdn. *NT* —4E **5**
Gleneagles. *Per* —3B **136**
Glenegedale. *Arg* —4B **124**
Glenegedale Lots. *Arg* —4B **124**
Glenelg. *High* —2G **147**
Glenernie. *Mor* —4E **159**
Glenesslin. *Dum* —1F **111**
Glenfarg. *Per* —2D **136**
Glenfarquhar Lodge. *Abers* —5E **152**
Glenferness Mains. *High* —4D **158**
Glenfeshie Lodge. *High* —4C **150**
Glenfiddich Lodge. *Mor* —5H **159**
Glenfield. *Leics* —5C **74**
Glenfinnan. *High* —5B **148**
Glenfinnan Monument *NTS* —5B **148**
Glenfintaig Lodge. *High* —5E **149**
Glenfoot. *Per* —2D **136**
Glenfyne Lodge. *Arg* —2B **134**
Glengap. *Dum* —4D **110**
Glengarnock. *N Ayr* —4E **126**
Glengolly. *High* —2C **168**
Glengorm Castle. *Arg* —3F **139**
Glengrasco. *High* —4D **154**
Glenhead Farm. *Ang* —2B **144**
Glenholm. *Bord* —1D **118**
Glen House. *Bord* —1E **119**
Glenhurich. *High* —2C **140**
Glenkerry. *Bord* —3E **119**
Glenkiln. *Dum* —2F **111**
Glenkindle. *Abers* —2B **152**
Glenkinglass Lodge. *Arg* —5F **141**
Glenkirk. *Bord* —1C **118**
Glenlean. *Arg* —1B **126**
Glenlee. *Dum* —1D **110**
Glenleraig. *High* —5B **166**
Glenlichorn. *Per* —2G **135**
Glenlivet. *Mor* —1F **151**
Glenlochar. *Dum* —3E **111**
Glenlochsie Lodge. *Per* —1H **143**
Glenluce. *Dum* —4G **109**
Glenmarskie. *High* —3F **157**
Glenmassan. *Arg* —1C **126**
Glenmavis. *N Lan* —3A **128**
Glenmaye. *IOM* —3B **108**
Glenmazeran Lodge. *High* —1B **150**
Glenmidge. *Dum* —1F **111**
Glen Mona. *IOM* —3D **108**
Glenmore. *High* —2G **139** (nr. Glenborrodale)
Glenmore. *High* —3D **151** (nr. Kingussie)
Glenmore. *High* —5D **154** (on Skye)
Glenmore Forest Park —2D **150**
Glenmoy. *Ang* —2D **144**
Glennoe. *Arg* —5E **141**
Glen of Coachford. *Abers* —4B **160**
Glenogil. *Ang* —2D **144**
Glen Parva. *Leics* —1C **62**
Glenprosen Village. *Ang* —2C **144**
Glenree. *N Ayr* —3D **122**
Glenridding. *Cumb* —3E **103**
Glenrosa. *N Ayr* —2E **123**
Glenrothes. *Fife* —3E **137**
Glensanda. *High* —4C **140**
Glensaugh. *Abers* —1F **145**
Glenshero Lodge. *High* —4H **149**
Glensluain. *Arg* —4H **133**
Glenstockadale. *Dum* —3F **109**
Glenstriven. *Arg* —2B **126**
Glen Tanar House. *Abers* —4B **152**
Glentham. *Linc* —1H **87**
Glenton. *Abers* —1D **152**
Glentress. *Bord* —1E **119**
Glentromie Lodge. *High* —4B **150**
Glentrool Lodge. *Dum* —1B **110**
Glentrool Village. *Dum* —2A **110**
Glentruim House. *High* —4A **150**
Glentworth. *Linc* —2G **87**
Glenuig. *High* —1A **140**
Glen Village. *Falk* —2B **128**
Glen Vine. *IOM* —4C **108**
Glenwhilly. *Dum* —2G **109**
Glenzierfoot. *Dum* —2E **113**
Glespin. *S Lan* —2H **117**
Gletness. *Shet* —6F **173**
Glewstone. *Here* —3A **48**
Glib Cheois. *W Isl* —5F **171**
Glinton. *Pet* —5A **76**
Glooston. *Leics* —1E **63**
Glossop. *Derbs* —1E **85**
Gloster Hill. *Nmbd* —4G **121**
Gloucester. *Glos* —4D **48** & **189**
Gloucester Cathedral —**189**
Gloucestershire & Warwickshire Railway —2F **49**
Gloup. *Shet* —1G **173**
Glusburn. *N Yor* —5C **98**
Glutt Lodge. *High* —5B **168**
Glutton Bridge. *Staf* —4E **85**
Gluvian. *Corn* —2D **6**
Glympton. *Oxon* —3C **50**
Glyn. *Cnwy* —3A **82**
Glynarthen. *Cdgn* —1D **44**
Glynbrochan. *Powy* —2B **58**
Glyn Ceiriog. *Wrex* —2E **70**
Glyncoch. *Rhon* —2D **32**
Glyncorrwg. *Neat* —2B **32**
Glynde. *E Sus* —5F **27**
Glyndebourne. *E Sus* —4F **27**
Glynde Place —5F **27**
Glyndyfrdwy. *Den* —1D **70**
Glyn Ebwy. *Blae* —5E **47**
Glynllan. *B'end* —3C **32**
Glyn-neath. *Neat* —5B **46**
Glynogwr. *B'end* —3C **32**
Glyntaff. *Rhon* —3D **32**
Glyntawe. *Powy* —4B **46**
Glynteg. *Carm* —2D **44**
Gnosall. *Staf* —3C **72**
Gnosall Heath. *Staf* —3C **72**
Goadby. *Leics* —1E **63**
Goadby Marwood. *Leics* —3E **75**
Goatacre. *Wilts* —4F **35**
Goathill. *Dors* —1B **14**
Goathland. *N Yor* —4F **107**
Goathurst. *Som* —3F **21**
Goathurst Common. *Kent* —5F **39**
Goat Lees. *Kent* —1E **28**
Gobernuisgach Lodge. *High* —4E **167**
Gobernuisgeach. *High* —5B **168**
Gobhaig. *W Isl* —7C **171**
Gobowen. *Shrp* —2F **71**
Godalming. *Surr* —1A **26**
Goddard's Corner. *Suff* —4E **67**
Goddard's Green. *Kent* —2C **28** (nr. Benenden)
Goddard's Green. *Kent* —2B **28** (nr. Cranbrook)
Goddards Green. *W Sus* —3D **27**
Godford Cross. *Devn* —2E **13**
Godleybrook. *Staf* —1D **73**
Godmanchester. *Cambs* —3B **64**
Godmanstone. *Dors* —3B **14**
Godmersham. *Kent* —5E **41**
Godolphin Cross. *Corn* —3D **4**
Godolphin House —3D **4**
Godre'r-graig. *Neat* —5A **46**
Godshill. *Hants* —1G **15**
Godshill. *IOW* —4D **16**
Godstone. *Staf* —2E **73**
Godstone. *Surr* —5E **39**
Godwell. *Devn* —3C **8**
Goetre. *Mon* —5G **47**
Goff's Oak. *Herts* —5D **52**
Gogar. *Edin* —2E **129**
Goginan. *Cdgn* —2F **57**
Golan. *Gwyn* —1E **69**
Golant. *Corn* —3F **7**
Golberdon. *Corn* —5D **10**
Golborne. *G Man* —1A **84**
Golcar. *W Yor* —3A **92**
Goldcliff. *Newp* —3G **33**
Golden Cross. *E Sus* —4G **27**
Golden Green. *Kent* —1H **27**
Golden Grove. *Carm* —4F **45**
Golden Grove. *N Yor* —4F **107**
Golden Hill. *Pemb* —2D **43**
Goldenhill. *Stoke* —5C **84**
Golden Pot. *Hants* —2F **25**
Golden Valley. *Glos* —3E **49**
Golders Green. *G Lon* —2D **38**
Goldhanger. *Essx* —5C **54**
Gold Hill. *Norf* —1E **65**
Golding. *Shrp* —5H **71**
Goldington. *Beds* —5H **63**
Goldsborough. *N Yor* —4F **99** (nr. Harrogate)
Goldsborough. *N Yor* —3F **107** (nr. Whitby)
Goldsithney. *Corn* —3C **4**
Goldstone. *Kent* —4G **41**
Goldstone. *Shrp* —3B **72**
Goldthorpe. *S Yor* —4E **93**
Goldworthy. *Devn* —4D **19**
Golfa. *Powy* —3D **70**
Gollanfield. *High* —3C **158**
Gollinglith Foot. *N Yor* —1D **98**
Golsoncott. *Som* —3D **20**
Golspie. *High* —4F **165**
Gomeldon. *Wilts* —3G **23**
Gomersal. *W Yor* —2C **92**
Gometra House. *Arg* —4E **139**
Gomshall. *Surr* —1B **26**
Gonalston. *Notts* —1D **74**
Gonerby Hill Foot. *Linc* —2G **75**
Gonfirth. *Shet* —5E **173**
Gonnabarn. *Corn* —3D **6**
Good Easter. *Essx* —4G **53**
Gooderstone. *Norf* —5G **77**
Goodleigh. *Devn* —3G **19**
Goodmanham. *E Yor* —5C **100**
Goodmayes. *G Lon* —2F **39**
Goodnestone. *Kent* —5G **41** (nr. Aylesham)
Goodnestone. *Kent* —4E **41** (nr. Faversham)
Goodnestone Park —5G **41**
Goodrich. *Here* —4A **48**
Goodrich Castle *EH* —3A **48**
Goodrington. *Torb* —3E **9**
Goodshaw. *Lanc* —2G **91**
Goodshaw Fold. *Lanc* —2G **91**
Goodstone. *Devn* —5A **12**
Goodwick. *Pemb* —1D **42**
Goodwood House —2G **17**
Goodworth Clatford. *Hants* —2B **24**
Goole. *E Yor* —2H **93**
Goom's Hill. *Worc* —5E **61**
Goonbell. *Corn* —4B **6**
Goonhavern. *Corn* —3B **6**
Goonhill Earth Station —4E **5**
Goonvrea. *Corn* —4B **6**
Goose Green. *Cumb* —1E **97**
Goose Green. *S Glo* —3C **34**
Gooseham. *Corn* —1C **10**
Goosewell. *Plym* —3B **8**
Goosey. *Oxon* —2B **36**
Goosnargh. *Lanc* —1D **90**
Goostrey. *Ches* —4B **84**
Gorcott Hill. *Warw* —4E **61**
Gord. *Shet* —9F **173**
Gordon. *Bord* —5C **130**
Gordonbush. *High* —3F **165**
Gordonstown. *Abers* —3C **160** (nr. Cornhill)
Gordonstown. *Abers* —5E **160** (nr. Fyvie)
Gorebridge. *Midl* —3G **129**
Goredale Scar —3B **98**
Gorefield. *Cambs* —4D **76**
Gores. *Wilts* —1G **23**
Gorgie. *Edin* —2F **129**
Gorhambury —5B **52**
Goring. *Oxon* —3E **36**
Goring-by-Sea. *W Sus* —5C **26**
Goring Heath. *Oxon* —4E **37**
Gorleston-on-Sea. *Norf* —5H **79**
Gornalwood. *W Mid* —1D **60**
Gorran Churchtown. *Corn* —4D **6**
Gorran Haven. *Corn* —4E **6**
Gorran High Lanes. *Corn* —4D **6**
Gors. *Cdgn* —3F **57**
Gorsedd. *Flin* —3D **82**

Gorseinon. Swan —3E 31
Gorseness. Orkn —6D 172
Gorseybank. Derbs —5G 85
Gorsgoch. Cdgn —5D 57
Gorslas. Carm —4F 45
Gorsley. Glos —3B 48
Gorsley Common. Here —3B 48
Gorstan. High —2F 157
Gorstella. Ches —4F 83
Gorsty Common. Here —2H 47
Gorsty Hill. Staf —3E 73
Gortantaoid. Arg —2B 124
Gorteneorn. High —2A 140
Gortenfern. High —2A 140
Gorton. G Man —1C 84
Gosbeck. Suff —5D 66
Gosberton. Linc —2B 76
Gosberton Clough. Linc —3A 76
Goseley Dale. Derbs —3H 73
Gosfield. Essx —3A 54
Gosfield Hall —3A 54
Gosford. Oxon —4D 50
Gosford House —2A 130
Gosforth. Cumb —4B 102
Gosforth. Tyne —3F 115
Gosmore. Herts —3B 52
Gospel End Village. Staf —1C 60
Gosport. Hants —2D 16
Gossabrough. Shet —3G 173
Gossington. Glos —5C 48
Gossops Green. W Sus —2D 26
Goswick. Nmbd —5G 131
Gotham. Notts —2C 74
Gotherington. Glos —3E 49
Gott. Arg —4B 138
Gott. Shet —7F 173
Goudhurst. Kent —2B 28
Goulceby. Linc —3B 88
Gourdon. Abers —1H 145
Gourock. Inv —2D 126
Govan. Glas —3G 127
Govanhill. Glas —3G 127
Goverton. Notts —5E 86
Goveton. Devn —4D 8
Govilon. Mon —4F 47
Gowanhill. Abers —2H 161
Gowdall. E Yor —2G 93
Gowerton. Swan —3E 31
Gowkhall. Fife —1D 128
Gowthorpe. E Yor —4B 100
Goxhill. E Yor —5F 101
Goxhill. N Lin —2E 94
Goxhill Haven. N Lin —2E 94
Goytre. Neat —3A 32
Grabhair. W Isl —6F 171
Graby. Linc —3H 75
Graffham. W Sus —4A 26
Grafham. Cambs —4A 64
Grafham. Surr —1B 26
Grafton. Here —2H 47
Grafton. N Yor —3G 99
Grafton. Oxon —5A 50
Grafton. Shrp —4G 71
Grafton. Worc —2E 49
(nr. Evesham)
Grafton. Worc —4H 59
(nr. Leominster)
Grafton Flyford. Worc —5D 60
Grafton Regis. Nptn —1F 51
Grafton Underwood. Nptn —2G 63
Grafty Green. Kent —1C 28
Graianrhyd. Den —5E 82
Graig. Carm —5E 45
Graig. Cnwy —3H 81
Graig. Den —3C 82
Graig-fechan. Den —5D 82
Graig Penllyn. V Glam —4C 32
Grain. Medw —3C 40
Grainsby. Linc —1B 88
Grainthorpe. Linc —1C 88
Grainthorpe Fen. Linc —1C 88
Graiselound. N Lin —1E 87
Gramasdail. W Isl —3D 170
Grampian Transport Mus. —2C 152
Grampound. Corn —4D 6
Grampound Road. Corn —3D 6
Granborough. Buck —3F 51
Granby. Notts —2E 75
Grandborough. Warw —4B 62
Grand Nat. Experience, Aintree —1F 83
Grandpont. Oxon —5D 50
Grandtully. Per —3G 143
Grange. Cumb —3D 102
Grange. E Ayr —1D 116
Grange. Here —3G 59
Grange. Mers —2E 83
Grange. Per —1E 137
Grange Crossroads. Mor —3B 160
Grange Hill. G Lon —1F 39
Grangemill. Derbs —5G 85
Grange Moor. W Yor —3C 92
Grangemouth. Falk —1C 128
Grange of Lindores. Fife —2E 137
Grange-over-Sands. Cumb —2D 96
Grangepans. Falk —1D 128
Grange, The. N Yor —5C 106
Grangetown. Card —4E 33
Grangetown. Red C —2C 106
Grange Villa. Dur —4F 115
Granish. High —2C 150
Gransmoor. E Yor —4F 101
Granston. Pemb —1C 42
Grantchester. Cambs —5D 64
Grantham. Linc —2G 75
Grantham House NT —2G 75
Grantley. N Yor —3E 99
Grantlodge. Abers —2E 152
Granton. Edin —2F 129
Grantown-on-Spey. High —1E 151
Grantshouse. Bord —3E 130
Grappenhall. Warr —2A 84
Grasby. Linc —4D 94
Grasmere. Cumb —4E 103
Grasmere NT —4E 103
Grasscroft. G Man —4H 91
Grassendale. Mers —2F 83
Grassgarth. Cumb —5E 113
Grassholme. Dur —2C 104
Grassington. N Yor —3C 98
Grassmoor. Derbs —4B 86
Grassthorpe. Notts —4E 87
Grateley. Hants —2A 24
Gratton. Devn —1D 11
Gratton. Staf —5D 84
Gratwich. Staf —2E 73
Graveley. Cambs —4B 64
Graveley. Herts —3C 52
Gravelhill. Shrp —4G 71
Gravel Hole. G Man —4H 91
Gravelly Hill. W Mid —1F 61
Graven. Shet —4F 173
Graveney. Kent —4E 41
Graves Art Gallery —Sheffield 196
Gravesend. Kent —3H 39
Grayingham. Linc —1G 87
Grayrigg. Cumb —5G 103
Grays. Thur —3H 39
Grayshott. Hants —3G 25
Grayson Green. Cumb —2A 102
Grayswood. Surr —2A 26
Graythorp. Hart —2C 106
Grazeley. Wok —5E 37
Grealin. High —2E 155
Greasby. Mers —2E 83
Greasebrough. S Yor —1B 86
Great Abington. Cambs —1F 53
Great Addington. Nptn —3G 63
Great Alne. Warw —5F 61
Great Altcar. Lanc —4B 90
Great Amwell. Herts —4D 52
Great Asby. Cumb —3H 103
Great Ashfield. Suff —4B 66
Great Ayton. N Yor —3C 106
Great Baddow. Essx —5H 53
Great Bardfield. Essx —2G 53
Great Barford. Beds —5A 64
Great Barr. W Mid —1E 61
Great Barrington. Glos —4H 49
Great Barrow. Ches —4G 83
Great Barton. Suff —4A 66
Great Barugh. N Yor —2B 100
Great Bavington. Nmbd —1C 114
Great Bealings. Suff —1F 55
Great Bedwyn. Wilts —5A 36
Great Bentley. Essx —3E 54
Great Billing. Nptn —4F 63
Great Bircham. Norf —2G 77
Great Blakenham. Suff —5D 66
Great Blencow. Cumb —1F 103
Great Bolas. Telf —3A 72
Great Bookham. Surr —5C 38
Great Bosullow. Corn —3B 4
Great Bourton. Oxon —1C 50
Great Bowden. Leics —2E 63
Great Bradley. Suff —5F 65
Great Braxted. Essx —4B 54
Great Bricett. Suff —5C 66
Great Brickhill. Buck —2H 51
Great Bridgeford. Staf —3C 72
Great Brington. Nptn —4D 62
Great Bromley. Essx —3D 54
Great Broughton. Cumb —1B 102
Great Broughton. N Yor —4C 106
Great Budworth. Ches —3A 84
Great Burdon. Darl —3A 106
Great Burstead. Essx —1A 40
Great Busby. N Yor —4C 106
Great Canfield. Essx —4F 53
Great Carlton. Linc —2D 88
Great Casterton. Rut —5H 75
Great Central Railway —4C 74
Great Chalfield. Wilts —5D 34
Great Chalfield Manor NT —5D 34
Great Chart. Kent —1D 28
Great Chatwell. Staf —4B 72
Great Chesterford. Essx —1F 53
Great Cheverell. Wilts —1E 23
Great Chilton. Dur —1F 105
Great Chishill. Cambs —2E 53
Great Clacton. Essx —4E 55
Great Cliff. W Yor —3D 92
Great Clifton. Cumb —2B 102
Great Coates. NE Lin —3F 95
Great Comberton. Worc —1E 49
Great Comp Gdn. —5H 39
Great Corby. Cumb —4F 113
Great Cornard. Suff —1B 54
Great Cowden. E Yor —5G 101
Great Coxwell. Oxon —2A 36
Great Crakehall. N Yor —1E 99
Great Cransley. Nptn —3F 63
Great Cressingham. Norf —5H 77
Great Crosby. Mers —1F 83
Great Cubley. Derbs —2F 73
Great Dalby. Leics —4E 75
Great Dixter —3C 28
Great Doddington. Nptn —4F 63
Great Doward. Here —4A 48
Great Dunham. Norf —4A 78
Great Dunmow. Essx —3G 53
Great Durnford. Wilts —3G 23
Great Easton. Essx —3G 53
Great Easton. Leics —1F 63
Great Eccleston. Lanc —5D 96
Great Edstone. N Yor —1B 100
Great Ellingham. Norf —1C 66
Great Elm. Som —2C 22
Great Eppleton. Tyne —5G 115
Great Eversden. Cambs —5C 64
Great Fencote. N Yor —5F 105
Great Finborough. Suff —5C 66
Greatford. Linc —4H 75
Great Fransham. Norf —4A 78
Great Gaddesden. Herts —4A 52
Great Gate. Staf —1E 73
Great Gidding. Cambs —2A 64
Great Givendale. E Yor —4C 100
Great Glemham. Suff —4F 67
Great Glen. Leics —1D 62
Great Gonerby. Linc —2G 75
Great Gransden. Cambs —5B 64
Great Green. Norf —2E 67
Great Green. Suff —5B 66
(nr. Lavenham)
Great Green. Suff —3D 66
(nr. Palgrave)
Great Habton. N Yor —2B 100
Great Hale. Linc —1A 76
Great Hallingbury. Essx —4F 53
Greatham. Hants —3F 25
Greatham. Hart —2B 106
Greatham. W Sus —4B 26
Great Hampden. Buck —5G 51
Great Harrowden. Nptn —3F 63
Great Harwood. Lanc —1F 91
Great Haseley. Oxon —5E 51
Great Hatfield. E Yor —5F 101
Great Haywood. Staf —3D 73
Great Heath. W Mid —2H 61
Great Heck. N Yor —2F 93
Great Henny. Essx —2B 54
Great Hinton. Wilts —1E 23
Great Hockham. Norf —1B 66
Great Holland. Essx —4F 55
Great Horkesley. Essx —2C 54
Great Hormead. Herts —2E 53
Great Horton. W Yor —1B 92
Great Horwood. Buck —2F 51
Great Houghton. Nptn —5E 63
Great Houghton. S Yor —4E 93
Great Hucklow. Derbs —3F 85
Great Kelk. E Yor —4F 101
Great Kendale. E Yor —4E 101
Great Kimble. Buck —5G 51
Great Kingshill. Buck —2G 37
Great Langdale. Cumb —4D 102
Great Langton. N Yor —5F 105
Great Leighs. Essx —4H 53
Great Limber. Linc —4E 95
Great Linford. Mil —1G 51
Great Livermere. Suff —3A 66
Great Longstone. Derbs —3G 85
Great Lumley. Dur —5F 115
Great Lyth. Shrp —5G 71
Great Malvern. Worc —1C 48
Great Maplestead. Essx —2B 54
Great Marton. Bkpl —1B 90
Great Massingham. Norf —3G 77
Great Maytham Hall —2C 28
Great Melton. Norf —5D 78
Great Milton. Oxon —5E 51
Great Missenden. Buck —5G 51
Great Mitton. Lanc —1F 91
Great Mongeham. Kent —5H 41
Great Moulton. Norf —1D 66
Great Munden. Herts —3D 52
Great Musgrave. Cumb —3A 104
Great Ness. Shrp —4G 71
Great Notley. Essx —3H 53
Great Oak. Mon —5G 47
Great Oakley. Essx —3E 55
Great Oakley. Nptn —2F 63
Great Offley. Herts —3B 52
Great Ormside. Cumb —3A 104
Great Orton. Cumb —4E 113
Great Ouseburn. N Yor —3G 99
Great Oxendon. Nptn —2E 63
Great Oxney Green. Essx —5G 53
Great Parndon. Essx —5E 53
Great Paxton. Cambs —4B 64
Great Plumpton. Lanc —1B 90
Great Plumstead. Norf —4F 79
Great Ponton. Linc —2G 75
Great Potheridge. Devn —1F 11
Great Preston. W Yor —2E 93
Great Raveley. Cambs —2B 64
Great Rissington. Glos —4G 49
Great Rollright. Oxon —2B 50
Great Ryburgh. Norf —3B 78
Great Ryle. Nmbd —3E 121
Great Ryton. Shrp —5G 71
Great Saling. Essx —3G 53
Great Salkeld. Cumb —1G 103
Great Sampford. Essx —2G 53
Great Sankey. Warr —2H 83
Great Saredon. Staf —5D 72
Great Saxham. Suff —4G 65
Great Shefford. W Ber —4B 36
Great Shelford. Cambs —5D 64
Great Shoddesden. Hants —2A 24
Great Smeaton. N Yor —4A 106
Great Snoring. Norf —2B 78
Great Somerford. Wilts —3E 35
Great Stainton. Darl —2A 106
Great Stambridge. Essx —1C 40
Great Staughton. Cambs —4A 64
Great Steeping. Linc —4D 88
Great Stonar. Kent —5H 41
Greatstone-on-Sea. Kent —3E 29
Great Strickland. Cumb —2G 103
Great Stukeley. Cambs —3B 64
Great Sturton. Linc —3B 88
Great Sutton. Ches —3F 83
Great Sutton. Shrp —2H 59
Great Swinburne. Nmbd —2C 114
Great Tew. Oxon —3B 50
Great Tey. Essx —3B 54
Great Thirkleby. N Yor —2G 99
Great Thorness. IOW —3C 16
Great Thurlow. Suff —5F 65
Great Torr. Devn —4C 8
Great Torrington. Devn —1E 11
Great Tosson. Nmbd —4E 121
Great Totham North. Essx —4B 54
Great Totham South. Essx —4B 54
Great Tows. Linc —1B 88
Great Urswick. Cumb —2B 96
Great Wakering. Essx —2D 40
Great Waldingfield. Suff —1C 54
Great Walsingham. Norf —2B 78
Great Waltham. Essx —4G 53
Great Warley. Essx —1G 39
Great Washbourne. Glos —2E 49
Great Welnetham. Suff —5A 66
Great Wenham. Suff —2D 54
Great Whittington. Nmbd —2D 114
Great Wigborough. Essx —4C 54
Great Wilbraham. Cambs —5E 65
Great Wilne. Derbs —2B 74
Great Wishford. Wilts —3F 23
Great Witchingham. Norf —4D 78
Great Witcombe. Glos —4E 49
Great Witley. Worc —4B 60
Great Wolford. Warw —2H 49
Greatworth. Nptn —1D 50
Great Wratting. Suff —1G 53
Great Wymondley. Herts —3C 52
Great Wyrley. Staf —5D 73
Great Wytheford. Shrp —4H 71
Great Yarmouth. Norf —5H 79
Great Yarmouth Sea Life Centre —5H 79
Great Yeldham. Essx —2A 54
Grebby. Linc —4D 88
Greeba Castle. IOM —3C 108
Greenbank. Shet —1G 173
Green Bottom. Corn —4B 6
Greenburn. W Lot —3C 128
Greencroft. Dur —4E 115
Greencroft Hall. Dur —5E 115
Greendown. Som —1A 22
Greendykes. Nmbd —2E 121
Green End. Beds —1A 52
Green End. Herts —2D 52
(nr. Buntingford)
Green End. Herts —3D 52
(nr. Stevenage)
Green End. N Yor —4F 107
Green End. Warw —2G 61
Greenfield. Arg —4B 134
Greenfield. Beds —2A 52
Greenfield. Flin —3D 82
Greenfield. G Man —4H 91
Greenfield. Oxon —2F 37
Greenfoot. N Lan —3A 128
Greenford. G Lon —2C 38
Greengairs. N Lan —2A 128
Greengate. Norf —4C 78
Greengill. Cumb —1C 102
Greenhalgh. Lanc —1C 90
Greenham. Dors —2H 13
Greenham. Som —4D 20
Greenham. W Ber —5C 36
Green Hammerton. N Yor —4G 99
Greenhaugh. Nmbd —1A 114
Greenhead. Nmbd —3H 113
Green Heath. Staf —4D 73
Greenhill. Dum —2C 112
Greenhill. Falk —2B 128
Greenhill. Kent —4F 41
Greenhill. S Yor —2H 85
Greenhill. Worc —3C 60
Greenhills. N Ayr —4E 127
Greenhithe. Kent —3G 39
Greenholm. E Ayr —1E 117
Greenhow Hill. N Yor —3D 98
Greenigo. Orkn —7D 172
Greenland. High —2E 169
Greenland Mains. High —2E 169
Greenlands. Worc —4E 61
Green Lane. Shrp —3A 72
Green Lane. Warw —4E 61
Greenlaw. Bord —5D 130
Greenlea. Dum —2B 112
Greenloaning. Per —3H 135
Greenmount. G Man —3F 91
Greenmow. Shet —9F 173
Greenock. Inv —2D 126
Greenodd. Cumb —1C 96
Green Ore. Som —1A 22
Greenrow. Cumb —4C 112
Greens. Abers —4F 161
Greensgate. Norf —4C 78
Greenside. Tyne —3E 115
Greensidehill. Nmbd —3D 121
Greens Norton. Nptn —1E 51
Greenstead Green. Essx —3B 54
Greensted Green. Essx —5F 53
Green Street. Herts —1C 38
Green Street. Suff —3D 66
Green Street Green. G Lon —4F 39
Green Street Green. Kent —3G 39
Greenstreet Green. Suff —1D 54
Green, The. Cumb —1A 96
Green, The. Wilts —3D 22
Green Tye. Herts —4E 53
Greenwall. Orkn —7E 172
Greenway. Pemb —2E 43
Greenway. V Glam —4D 32
Greenwell. Cumb —4G 113
Greenwich. G Lon —3E 39
Greet. Glos —2F 49
Greete. Shrp —3H 59
Greetham. Linc —3C 88
Greetham. Rut —4G 75
Greetland. W Yor —2A 92
Gregson Lane. Lanc —2D 90
Grein. W Isl —8B 170
Greinetobht. W Isl —1D 170
Greinton. Som —3H 21
Gremista. Shet —7F 173
Grenaby. IOM —4B 108
Grendon. Nptn —4F 63
Grendon. Warw —1G 61
Grendon Common. Warw —1G 61
Grendon Green. Here —5H 59
Grendon Underwood. Buck —3E 51
Grenofen. Devn —5E 11
Grenoside. S Yor —1H 85
Greosabhagh. W Isl —8D 171
Gresford. Wrex —5F 83
Gresham. Norf —2D 78
Greshornish. High —3C 154
Gressenhall. Norf —4B 78
Gressingham. Lanc —2E 97
Greta Bridge. Dur —3D 105
Gretna. Dum —3E 112
Gretna Green. Dum —3E 112
Gretton. Glos —2F 49
Gretton. Nptn —1G 63
Gretton. Shrp —1H 59
Grewelthorpe. N Yor —2E 99
Greygarth. N Yor —2D 98
Grey Green. N Lin —4A 94
Greylake. Som —3G 21
Grey Mare's Tail NTS —3D 118
Greys Court NT —3F 37
Greysouthern. Cumb —2B 102
Greystoke. Cumb —1F 103
Greystoke Gill. Cumb —2F 103
Greystone. Ang —4E 145
Greystones. S Yor —2H 85
Greywell. Hants —1F 25
Griais. W Isl —3G 171
Grianan. W Isl —4G 171
Gribthorpe. E Yor —1A 94
Gribun. Arg —5F 139
Griff. Warw —2A 62
Griffithstown. Torf —2F 33
Griffydam. Leics —4B 74
Griggs Green. Hants —3G 25
Grimbister. Orkn —6C 172
Grimeford Village. Lanc —3E 90
Grimes Graves EH —1H 65
Grimeston. Orkn —6C 172
Grimethorpe. S Yor —4E 93
Griminis. W Isl —3C 170
(on Benbecula)
Griminis. W Isl —1C 170
(on North Uist)
Grimister. Shet —2F 173
Grimley. Worc —4C 60
Grimness. Orkn —8D 172
Grimoldby. Linc —2C 88
Grimpo. Shrp —3F 71
Grimsargh. Lanc —1D 90
Grimsby. NE Lin —3F 95
Grimscote. Nptn —5D 62
Grimscott. Corn —2C 10
Grimshaw. Bkbn —2F 91
Grimshaw Green. Lanc —3C 90
Grimspound EH —4H 11
Grimsthorpe. Linc —3H 75
Grimsthorpe Castle —3H 75
Grimston. E Yor —1F 95
Grimston. Leics —3D 74
Grimston. Norf —3G 77
Grimston. York —4A 100
Grimstone. Dors —3B 14
Grimstone End. Suff —4B 66
Grinacombe Moor. Devn —3E 11
Grindale. E Yor —2F 101
Grindhill. Devn —3E 11
Grindiscol. Shet —8F 173
Grindle. Shrp —5B 72
Grindleford. Derbs —3G 85
Grindleton. Lanc —5G 97
Grindley. Staf —3E 73
Grindley Brook. Shrp —1H 71
Grindlow. Derbs —3F 85
Grindon. Nmbd —5F 131
Grindon. Staf —5E 85
Gringley on the Hill. Notts —1E 87
Grinsdale. Cumb —4E 113
Grinshill. Shrp —3H 71
Grinton. N Yor —5D 104
Griomsidar. W Isl —5G 171
Grishipoll. Arg —3C 138
Grisling Common. E Sus —3F 27
Gristhorpe. N Yor —1E 101
Griston. Norf —1B 66
Gritley. Orkn —7E 172
Grittenham. Wilts —3F 35
Grittleton. Wilts —4D 34
Grizebeck. Cumb —1B 96
Grizedale. Cumb —5E 103
Grizedale Forest —5E 103
Grobister. Orkn —5F 172
Grobsness. Shet —5E 173
Groby. Leics —5C 74
Groes. Cnwy —4C 82
Groes. Neat —3A 32
Groes-faen. Rhon —3D 32
Groesffordd. Gwyn —2B 68
Groesffordd. Powy —3D 46
Groeslon. Gwyn —5D 81
Groes-lwyd. Powy —4E 70
Groes-wen. Cphy —3E 33
Grogport. Arg —5G 125
Groigearraidh. W Isl —4C 170
Gromford. Suff —5F 67
Gronant. Flin —2C 82
Groombridge. E Sus —2G 27
Groombridge Place —2G 27
Grosmont. Mon —3H 47
Grosmont. N Yor —4F 107
Groton. Suff —1C 54
Grove. Dors —5B 14
Grove. Kent —4G 41
Grove. Notts —3E 87
Grove. Oxon —2B 36
Grovehill. E Yor —5E 101
Grove Park. G Lon —3E 39
Grovesend. Swan —5F 45
Grove, The. Dum —2A 112
Grove, The. Worc —1D 48
Grub Street. Staf —3B 72
Grudie. High —2F 157
Gruids. High —3C 164
Gruinard House. High —4D 162
Gruinart. Arg —3A 124
Grulinbeg. Arg —3A 124
Gruline. Arg —4G 139
Grummore. High —5G 167
Grundisburgh. Suff —5E 66
Gruting. Shet —7D 173
Gualachulain. High —4F 141
Guardbridge. Fife —2G 137
Guarlford. Worc —1D 48

Guay. Per —4H 143
Gubblecote. Herts —4H 51
Guestling Green. E Sus —4C 28
Guestling Thorn. E Sus —4C 28
Guestwick. Norf —3C 78
Guestwick Green. Norf —3C 78
Guide. Bkbn —2F 91
Guide Post. Nmbd —1F 115
Guilden Down. Shrp —2F 59
Guilden Morden. Cambs —1C 52
Guilden Sutton. Ches —4G 83
Guildford. Surr —1A 26 & 189
Guildtown. Per —5A 144
Guilsborough. Nptn —3D 62
Guilsfield. Powy —4E 70
Guineaford. Devn —3F 19
Guisborough. Red C —3D 106
Guiseley. W Yor —5D 98
Guist. Norf —3B 78
Guiting Power. Glos —3F 49
Gulberwick. Shet —8F 173
Gullane. E Lot —1A 130
Gulling Green. Suff —5H 65
Gulliver's Kingdom, Matlock Bath —5G 85
Gulliver's Land —Milton Keynes 194
Gulliver's World —1H 83
Gulval. Corn —3B 4
Gumfreston. Pemb —4F 43
Gumley. Leics —1D 62
Gunby. E Yor —1H 93
Gunby. Linc —3G 75
Gunby Hall NT —4D 88
Gundleton. Hants —3E 24
Gun Green. Kent —2B 28
Gun Hill. E Sus —4G 27
Gunn. Devn —3G 19
Gunnerside. N Yor —5C 104
Gunnerton. Nmbd —2C 114
Gunness. N Lin —3B 94
Gunnislake. Corn —5E 11
Gunnista. Shet —7G 173
Gunsgreenhill. Bord —3F 131
Gunstone. Staf —5C 72
Gunthorpe. Norf —2C 78
Gunthorpe. N Lin —1F 87
Gunthorpe. Notts —1D 74
Gunthorpe. Pet —5A 76
Gunville. IOW —4C 16
Gupworthy. Som —3C 20
Gurnard. IOW —3C 16
Gurney Slade. Som —2B 22
Gurnos. Powy —5A 46
Gussage All Saints. Dors —1F 15
Gussage St Andrew. Dors —1E 15
Gussage St Michael. Dors —1E 15
Guston. Kent —1H 29
Gutcher. Shet —2G 173
Guthram Gowt. Linc —3A 76
Guthrie. Ang —3E 145
Guyhirn. Cambs —5D 76
Guyhirn Gull. Cambs —5C 76
Guy's Head. Linc —3D 77
Guy's Marsh. Dors —4D 22
Guyzance. Nmbd —4G 121
Gwaelod-y-garth. Card —3E 32
Gwaenynog Bach. Den —4C 82
Gwaenysgor. Flin —2C 82
Gwalchmai. IOA —3C 80
Gwastad. Pemb —2E 43
Gwaun-Cae-Gurwen. Neat —4H 45
Gwaun-y-bara. Cphy —3E 33
Gwbert. Cdgn —5A 56
Gweek. Corn —4E 5
Gwehelog. Mon —5G 47
Gwenddwr. Powy —1D 46
Gwennap. Corn —4B 6
Gwenter. Corn —5E 5
Gwernaffield. Flin —4E 82
Gwernesney. Mon —5H 47
Gwernogle. Carm —2F 45
Gwern-y-go. Powy —1E 58
Gwernymynydd. Flin —4E 82
Gwersyllt. Wrex —5F 83
Gwespyr. Flin —2D 82
Gwili Steam Railway —3E 45
Gwinear. Corn —3D 4
Gwithian. Corn —2C 4
Gwredog. IOA —2D 80
Gwyddelwern. Den —1C 70
Gwyddgrug. Carm —2E 45
Gwydir Castle —4H 81
Gwynfryn. Wrex —5E 83
Gwystre. Powy —4C 58
Gwytherin. Cnwy —4A 82
Gyfelia. Wrex —1F 71
Gyffin. Cnwy —3G 81

Haa of Houlland. Shet —1G 173
Habberley. Shrp —5F 71
Habergham. Lanc —1G 91
Habin. W Sus —4G 25
Habrough. NE Lin —3E 95
Hacconby. Linc —3A 76
Haceby. Linc —2H 75
Hacheston. Suff —5F 67
Hackenthorpe. S Yor —2B 86
Hackford. Norf —5C 78
Hackforth. N Yor —5F 105
Hackland. Orkn —5C 172
Hackleton. Nptn —5F 63
Hackness. N Yor —5G 107
Hackness. Orkn —8C 172
Hackney. G Lon —2E 39
Hackthorn. Linc —2G 87
Hackthorpe. Cumb —2G 103
Haclait. W Isl —4D 170
Hadden. Bord —1B 120
Haddenham. Buck —5F 51
Haddenham. Cambs —3D 64
Haddenham End. Cambs —3D 64
Haddington. E Lot —2B 130
Haddington. Linc —4G 87
Haddiscoe. Norf —1G 67
Haddo. Abers —5F 161
Haddo House NTS —5F 161
Haddon. Cambs —1A 64
Haddon Hall —4G 85
Hademore. Staf —5F 73
Hadfield. Derbs —1E 85
Hadham Cross. Herts —4E 53
Hadham Ford. Herts —3E 53
Hadleigh. Essx —2C 40
Hadleigh. Suff —1D 54
Hadleigh Castle EH —2C 40
Hadleigh Heath. Suff —1C 54
Hadley. Telf —4A 72
Hadley. Worc —4C 60
Hadley End. Staf —3F 73
Hadley Wood. G Lon —1D 38
Hadlow. Kent —1H 27
Hadlow Down. E Sus —3G 27
Hadnall. Shrp —3H 71
Hadrians Wall WH —3A 114
Hadstock. Essx —1F 53
Hady. Derbs —3B 86
Hadzor. Worc —4D 60
Haffenden Quarter. Kent —1C 28
Haggate. Lanc —1G 91
Haggbeck. Cumb —2F 113
Haggersta. Shet —7E 173
Haggerston. Nmbd —5G 131
Haggrister. Shet —4E 173
Hagley. Here —1A 48
Hagley. Worc —2D 60
Hagley Hall —2D 60
Hagnaby. Linc —4C 88
Hagworthingham. Linc —4C 88
Haigh. G Man —4E 90
Haigh Moor. W Yor —2C 92
Haighton Green. Lanc —1D 90
Haile. Cumb —4B 102
Hailes. Glos —2F 49
Hailes Abbey NT EH —3F 49
Hailes Castle HS —2B 130
Hailey. Oxon —4D 52
Hailsham. E Sus —5G 27
Hail Weston. Cambs —4A 64
Hainault. G Lon —1F 39
Hainford. Norf —4E 78
Hainton. Linc —2A 88
Hainworth. W Yor —1A 92
Haisthorpe. E Yor —3F 101
Hakin. Pemb —4C 42
Halam. Notts —5D 86
Halbeath. Fife —1E 129
Halberton. Devn —1D 12
Halcro. High —2E 169
Hale. Cumb —2E 97
Hale. G Man —2B 84
Hale. Hal —2G 83
Hale. Hants —1G 15
Hale. Surr —2G 25
Hale Bank. Hal —2G 83
Halebarns. G Man —2B 84
Hales. Norf —1F 67
Hales. Staf —2B 72
Halesgate. Linc —3C 76
Hales Green. Derbs —1F 73
Halesowen. W Mid —2D 60
Hale Street. Kent —1A 28
Halesworth. Suff —3F 67
Halewood. Mers —2G 83
Halford. Devn —5B 12
Halford. Shrp —2G 59
Halford. Warw —1A 50
Halfpenny. Cumb —1E 97
Halfpenny Furze. Carm —3G 43
Halfpenny Green. Shrp —1C 60
Halfway. Carm —2G 45
Halfway. Powy —2B 46
Halfway. S Yor —2B 86
Halfway. W Ber —5C 36
Halfway House. Shrp —4F 71
Halfway Houses. Kent —3D 40
Halgabron. Corn —4A 10
Halifax. W Yor —2A 92
Halistra. High —3B 154
Halket. E Ayr —4F 127
Halkirk. High —3D 168
Halkyn. Flin —3E 82
Hall. E Ren —4F 127
Hallam Fields. Derbs —1B 74
Halland. E Sus —4G 27
Hallands, The. N Lin —2D 94
Hallaton. Leics —1E 63
Hallatrow. Bath —1B 22
Hallbank. Cumb —5H 103
Hallbankgate. Cumb —4G 113
Hall Dunnerdale. Cumb —5D 102
Hallen. S Glo —3A 34
Hall End. Beds —1A 52
Halley. Herts —4D 52
Hallgarth. Dur —5G 115
Hall Green. Ches —5C 84
Hall Green. Norf —2D 66
Hall Green. W Mid —2F 61
Hall Green. W Yor —3D 92
Hall Green. Wrex —1G 71
Halliburton. Bord —5C 130
Hallin. High —3B 154
Halling. Medw —4B 40
Hallington. Linc —2C 88
Hallington. Nmbd —2C 114
Hall i'th'Wood —3F 91
Halloughton. Notts —5D 86
Hallow. Worc —5C 60
Hallow Heath. Worc —5C 60
Hallowsgate. Ches —4H 83
Hall Place —3G 39
Hallsands. Devn —5E 9
Hall's Green. Herts —3C 52
Hallspill. Devn —4E 19
Hallthwaites. Cumb —1A 96
Hall Waberthwaite. Cumb —5C 102
Hallwood Green. Glos —2B 48
Hallworthy. Corn —4B 10
Hallyne. Bord —5E 129
Halmer End. Staf —1C 72
Halmond's Frome. Here —1B 48
Halmore. Glos —5B 48
Halnaker. W Sus —5A 26
Halsall. Lanc —3B 90
Halse. Nptn —1D 50
Halse. Som —4E 21
Halsetown. Corn —3C 4
Halsham. E Yor —2F 95
Halsinger. Devn —3F 19
Halstead. Essx —2B 54
Halstead. Kent —4F 39
Halstead. Leics —5E 75
Halstock. Dors —2A 14
Halstow. Devn —3B 12
Halsway. Som —3E 21
Haltcliff Bridge. Cumb —1E 103
Haltham. Linc —4B 88
Haltoft End. Linc —1C 76
Halton. Buck —5G 51
Halton. Hal —2H 83
Halton. Lanc —3E 97
Halton. Nmbd —3C 114
Halton. W Yor —1D 92
Halton. Wrex —2F 71
Halton East. N Yor —4C 98
Halton Fenside. Linc —4D 88
Halton Gill. N Yor —2A 98
Halton Holegate. Linc —4D 88
Halton Lea Gate. Nmbd —4H 113
Halton Moor. W Yor —1D 92
Halton Shields. Nmbd —3D 114
Halton West. N Yor —4H 97
Haltwhistle. Nmbd —3A 114
Halvergate. Norf —5G 79
Halwell. Devn —3D 9
Halwill. Devn —3E 11
Halwill Junction. Devn —3E 11
Ham. Devn —2F 13
Ham. Glos —2B 34
Ham. G Lon —3C 38
Ham. High —1E 169
Ham. Kent —5H 41
Ham. Plym —3A 8
Ham. Shet —8A 173
Ham. Som —1F 13 (nr. Ilminster)
Ham. Som —4F 21 (nr. Taunton)
Ham. Wilts —5B 36
Hambleden. Buck —3F 37
Hambledon. Hants —1E 17
Hambledon. Surr —2A 26
Hamble-le-Rice. Hants —2C 16
Hambleton. Lanc —5C 96
Hambleton. N Yor —1F 93
Hambridge. Som —4G 21
Hambrook. S Glo —4B 34
Hambrook. W Sus —2F 17
Ham Common. Dors —4D 22
Hameringham. Linc —4C 88
Hamerton. Cambs —3A 64
Hamerton Wildlife Centre —2A 64
Ham Green. Here —1C 48
Ham Green. Kent —4C 40
Ham Green. N Som —4A 34
Ham Green. Worc —4E 61
Ham Hill. Kent —4A 40
Ham House NT —3C 38
Hamilton. Leics —5D 74
Hamilton. S Lan —4A 128
Hamister. Shet —5G 173
Hammer. W Sus —3G 25
Hammersmith. G Lon —3D 38
Hammerwich. Staf —5E 73
Hammerwood. E Sus —2F 27
Hammerwood Park —2F 27
Hammill. Kent —5G 41
Hammond Street. Herts —5D 52
Hammoon. Dors —1D 14
Hamnavoe. Shet —3D 173 (nr. Braehoulland)
Hamnavoe. Shet —8E 173 (nr. Burland)
Hamnavoe. Shet —4F 173 (nr. Lunna)
Hamnavoe. Shet —3F 173 (on Yell)
Hamp. Som —3G 21
Hampden Park. E Sus —5H 27
Hampen. Glos —3F 49
Hamperden End. Essx —2F 53
Hamperley. Shrp —2G 59
Hampnett. Glos —4F 49
Hampole. S Yor —3F 93
Hampreston. Dors —3F 15
Hampstead. G Lon —2D 38
Hampstead Norreys. W Ber —4D 36
Hampsthwaite. N Yor —4E 99
Hampton. Cambs —1A 64
Hampton. Devn —3F 13
Hampton. G Lon —3C 38
Hampton. Kent —4F 41
Hampton. Shrp —2B 60
Hampton. Swin —2G 35
Hampton. Worc —1F 49
Hampton Bishop. Here —2A 48
Hampton Court Palace —4C 38
Hampton Fields. Glos —2D 35
Hampton Heath. Ches —1H 71
Hampton in Arden. W Mid —2G 61
Hampton Loade. Shrp —2B 60
Hampton Lovett. Worc —4C 60
Hampton Lucy. Warw —5G 61
Hampton Magna. Warw —4G 61
Hampton on the Hill. Warw —4G 61
Hampton Poyle. Oxon —4D 50
Hampton Wick. G Lon —4C 38
Hamptworth. Wilts —1H 15
Hamrow. Norf —3B 78
Hamsey. E Sus —4F 27
Hamsey Green. Surr —5E 39
Hamstall Ridware. Staf —4F 73
Hamstead. IOW —3B 16
Hamstead. W Mid —1E 61
Hamstead Marshall. W Ber —5C 36
Hamsterley. Dur —4E 115 (nr. Consett)
Hamsterley. Dur —1E 105 (nr. Wolsingham)
Hamsterley Mill. Dur —4E 115
Hamstreet. Kent —2E 28
Ham Street. Som —3A 22
Hamworthy. Pool —3E 15
Hanbury. Staf —3F 73
Hanbury. Worc —4D 60
Hanbury Hall NT —4D 60
Hanbury Woodend. Staf —3F 73
Hanby. Linc —2H 75
Hanchurch. Staf —1C 72
Hancock Mus. —Newcastle 191
Hand and Pen. Devn —3D 12
Handbridge. Ches —4G 83
Handcross. W Sus —3D 26
Handforth. Ches —2C 84
Handley. Ches —5G 83
Handley. Derbs —4A 86
Handsacre. Staf —4E 73
Handsworth. S Yor —2B 86
Handsworth. W Mid —1E 61
Handy Cross. Buck —2G 37
Hanford. Stoke —1C 72
Hangersley Hill. Hants —2G 15
Hanging Haughton. Nptn —3E 63
Hanging Langford. Wilts —3F 23
Hangleton. Brig —5D 26
Hangleton. W Sus —5B 26
Hanham. S Glo —4B 34
Hanham Green. S Glo —4B 34
Hankelow. Ches —1A 72
Hankerton. Wilts —2E 35
Hankham. E Sus —5H 27
Hanley. Stoke —1C 72 & Stoke 196
Hanley Castle. Worc —1D 48
Hanley Childe. Worc —4A 60
Hanley Swan. Worc —1D 48
Hanley William. Worc —4A 60
Hanlith. N Yor —3B 98
Hanmer. Wrex —2G 71
Hannaborough. Devn —2F 11
Hannaford. Devn —4G 19
Hannah. Linc —3E 89
Hannington. Hants —1D 24
Hannington. Nptn —3F 63
Hannington. Swin —2G 35
Hannington Wick. Swin —2G 35
Hanscombe End. Beds —2B 52
Hanslope. Mil —1G 51
Hanthorpe. Linc —3H 75
Hanwell. G Lon —2C 38
Hanwell. Oxon —1C 50
Hanwood. Shrp —5G 71
Hanworth. G Lon —3C 38
Hanworth. Norf —2D 78
Happas. Ang —4D 144
Happendon. S Lan —1A 118
Happisburgh. Norf —2F 79
Happisburgh Common. Norf —3F 79
Hapsford. Ches —3G 83
Hapton. Lanc —1F 91
Hapton. Norf —1D 66
Harberton. Devn —3D 9
Harbertonford. Devn —3D 9
Harbledown. Kent —5F 41
Harborne. W Mid —2E 61
Harborough Magna. Warw —3B 62
Harbottle. Nmbd —4D 120
Harbourneford. Devn —2D 8
Harbours Hill. Worc —4D 60
Harbridge. Hants —1G 15
Harbury. Warw —5A 62
Harby. Leics —2E 75
Harby. Notts —3F 87
Harcombe. Devn —3E 13
Harcombe Bottom. Devn —3G 13
Harcourt. Corn —5C 6
Harden. W Yor —1A 92
Hardenhuish. Wilts —4E 35
Hardgate. Abers —3E 153
Hardgate. Dum —3F 111
Hardham. W Sus —4B 26
Hardingham. Norf —5C 78
Hardingstone. Nptn —5E 63
Hardings Wood. Ches —5C 84
Hardington. Som —1C 22
Hardington Mandeville. Som —1A 14
Hardington Marsh. Som —2A 14
Hardington Moor. Som —1A 14
Hardknott Roman Fort EH —4D 102
Hardley. Hants —2C 16
Hardley Street. Norf —5F 79
Hardmead. Mil —1H 51
Hardraw. N Yor —5B 104
Hardstoft. Derbs —4B 86
Hardway. Hants —2E 16
Hardway. Som —3C 22
Hardwick. Buck —4G 51
Hardwick. Cambs —5C 64
Hardwick. Norf —2E 66
Hardwick. Nptn —4F 63
Hardwick. Oxon —3D 50 (nr. Bicester)
Hardwick. Oxon —5B 50 (nr. Witney)
Hardwick. Shrp —1F 59
Hardwick. S Yor —2B 86
Hardwick. Stoc T —2B 106
Hardwick. W Mid —1E 61
Hardwicke. Glos —3E 49 (nr. Cheltenham)
Hardwicke. Glos —4C 48 (nr. Gloucester)
Hardwicke. Here —1F 47
Hardwick Hall NT —4B 86
Hardwick Village. Notts —3D 86
Hardy's Cottage NT —3C 14
Hardy's Green. Essx —3C 54
Hareby. Linc —4C 88
Hareden. Lanc —4F 97
Harefield. G Lon —1B 38
Hare Green. Essx —3D 54
Hare Hatch. Wok —4G 37
Harehill. Derbs —2F 73
Harehills. W Yor —1D 92
Harehope. Nmbd —2E 121
Harelaw. Dum —2F 113
Harelaw. Dur —4E 115
Hareplain. Kent —2C 28
Haresceugh. Cumb —5H 113
Harescombe. Glos —4D 48
Haresfield. Glos —4D 48
Haresfinch. Mers —1H 83
Hareshaw. N Lan —3B 128
Hare Street. Essx —5E 53
Hare Street. Herts —3D 53
Harewood. W Yor —5F 99
Harewood End. Here —3A 48
Harewood House —5F 99
Harford. Devn —3C 8
Hargate. Norf —1D 66
Hargatewall. Derbs —3F 85
Hargrave. Ches —4G 83
Hargrave. Nptn —3H 63
Hargrave. Suff —5G 65
Harker. Cumb —3E 113
Harkland. Shet —3F 173
Harkstead. Suff —2E 55
Harlaston. Staf —4G 73
Harlaxton. Linc —2F 75
Harlech. Gwyn —2E 69
Harlech Castle WH CADW —2E 69
Harlequin. Notts —2D 74
Harlescott. Shrp —4H 71
Harleston. Devn —4D 9
Harleston. Norf —2E 67
Harleston. Suff —4C 66
Harlestone. Nptn —4E 62
Harley. Shrp —5H 71
Harley. S Yor —1A 86
Harling Road. Norf —2B 66
Harlington. Beds —2A 52
Harlington. G Lon —3B 38
Harlington. S Yor —4E 93
Harlosh. High —4B 154
Harlow. Essx —5E 53
Harlow Carr Gdns. RHS —4E 99
Harlow Hill. Nmbd —3D 115
Harlsey Castle. N Yor —5B 106
Harlthorpe. E Yor —1H 93
Harlton. Cambs —5C 64
Harlyn. Corn —1C 6
Harman's Cross. Dors —4E 15
Harmby. N Yor —1D 98
Harmer Green. Herts —4C 52
Harmer Hill. Shrp —3G 71
Harmondsworth. G Lon —3B 38
Harmston. Linc —4G 87
Harnage. Shrp —5H 71
Harnham. Nmbd —1D 115
Harnhill. Glos —5F 49
Harold Hill. G Lon —1G 39
Haroldston West. Pemb —3C 42
Haroldswick. Shet —1H 173
Harold Wood. G Lon —1G 39
Harome. N Yor —1A 100
Harpenden. Herts —4B 52
Harpford. Devn —3D 12
Harpham. E Yor —3E 101
Harpley. Norf —3G 77
Harpley. Worc —4A 60
Harpole. Nptn —4D 62
Harpsdale. High —3D 168
Harpsden. Oxon —3F 37
Harpswell. Linc —2G 87
Harpurhey. G Man —4G 91
Harpur Hill. Derbs —3E 85
Harraby. Cumb —4F 113
Harracott. Devn —4F 19
Harrapool. High —1E 147
Harrietfield. Per —1B 136
Harrietsham. Kent —5C 40
Harrington. Cumb —2A 102
Harrington. Linc —3C 88
Harrington. Nptn —2E 63
Harringworth. Nptn —1G 63
Harriseahead. Staf —5C 84
Harriston. Cumb —5C 112
Harrogate. N Yor —4F 99 & 190
Harrold. Beds —5G 63
Harrop Dale. G Man —4A 92
Harrow. G Lon —2C 38
Harrowbarrow. Corn —2H 7
Harrowden. Beds —1A 52
Harrowgate Hill. Darl —3F 105
Harrow on the Hill. G Lon —2C 38
Harrow Weald. G Lon —1C 38
Harry Stoke. S Glo —4B 34
Harston. Cambs —5D 64
Harston. Leics —2F 75
Harswell. E Yor —5C 100
Hart. Hart —1B 106
Hartburn. Nmbd —1D 115
Hartburn. Stoc T —3B 106
Hartest. Suff —5H 65
Hartfield. E Sus —2F 27
Hartford. Cambs —3B 64
Hartford. Ches —3A 84
Hartfordbridge. Hants —1F 25
Hartford End. Essx —4G 53
Harthill. Ches —5H 83
Harthill. N Lan —3C 128
Harthill. S Yor —2B 86
Hartington. Derbs —4F 85
Hartland. Devn —4C 18
Hartland Abbey —4C 18
Hartland Quay. Devn —4C 18
Hartle. Worc —3D 60
Hartlebury. Worc —3C 60
Hartlebury Castle & County Mus. —3C 60
Hartlepool. Hart —1C 106
Hartley. Cumb —4A 104
Hartley. Kent —2B 28 (nr. Cranbrook)
Hartley. Kent —4H 39 (nr. Dartford)
Hartley. Nmbd —2G 115
Hartley Green. Staf —2D 73
Hartley Mauditt. Hants —3F 25
Hartley Wespall. Hants —1E 25
Hartley Wintney. Hants —1F 25
Hartlip. Kent —4C 40
Hartmount. High —1B 158

Hartoft End. N Yor —5E 107
Harton. N Yor —3B 100
Harton. Shrp —2G 59
Harton. Tyne —3G 115
Hartpury. Glos —3C 48
Hartshead. W Yor —2B 92
Hartshill. Warw —1H 61
Hartshorne. Derbs —3H 73
Hartsop. Cumb —3F 103
Hart Station. Hart —1B 106
Hartswell. Som —4D 20
Hartwell. Nptn —5E 63
Hartwood. Lanc —3D 90
Hartwood. N Lan —4B 128
Harvel. Kent —4A 40
Harvington. Worc —1F 49
(nr. Evesham)
Harvington. Worc —3C 60
(nr. Kidderminster)
Harvington Hall —3C 60
Harwell. Oxon —3C 36
Harwich. Essx —2F 55
Harwich Redoubt —2F 55
Harwood. Dur —1B 104
Harwood. G Man —3F 91
Harwood Dale. N Yor —5G 107
Harworth. Notts —1D 86
Hascombe. Surr —1A 26
Haselbech. Nptn —3E 62
Haselbury Plucknett. Som —1H 13
Haseley. Warw —4G 61
Haselor. Warw —5F 61
Hasfield. Glos —3D 48
Hasguard. Pemb —4C 42
Haskayne. Lanc —4B 90
Hasketon. Suff —5E 67
Hasland. Derbs —4A 86
Haslemere. Surr —2A 26
Haslingden. Lanc —2F 91
Haslingden Grane. Lanc —2F 91
Haslingfield. Cambs —5D 64
Haslington. Ches —5B 84
Hassall. Ches —5B 84
Hassall Green. Ches —5B 84
Hassell Street. Kent —1E 29
Hassendean. Bord —2H 119
Hassingham. Norf —5F 79
Hassness. Cumb —3C 102
Hassocks. W Sus —4E 27
Hassop. Derbs —3G 85
Haste Hill. Surr —2A 26
Haster. High —3F 169
Hasthorpe. Linc —4D 89
Hastigrow. High —2E 169
Hastingleigh. Kent —1E 29
Hastings. E Sus —5C 28
Hastingwood. Essx —5E 53
Hastoe. Herts —5H 51
Haston. Shrp —3H 71
Haswell. Dur —5G 115
Haswell Plough. Dur —5G 115
Hatch. Beds —1B 52
Hatch Beauchamp. Som —4G 21
Hatch Court —4G 21
Hatch End. G Lon —1C 38
Hatch Green. Som —1G 13
Hatching Green. Herts —4B 52
Hatchlands Park NT —5B 38
Hatchmere. Ches —3H 83
Hatch Warren. Hants —2E 24
Hatcliffe. NE Lin —4F 95
Hatfield. Here —5H 59
Hatfield. Herts —5C 52
Hatfield. S Yor —4G 93
Hatfield. Worc —5C 60
Hatfield Broad Oak. Essx —4F 53
Hatfield Forest NT —4F 53
Hatfield Heath. Essx —4F 53
Hatfield House —5C 52
Hatfield Hyde. Herts —4C 52
Hatfield Peverel. Essx —4A 54
Hatfield Woodhouse. S Yor —4G 93
Hatford. Oxon —2B 36
Hatherden. Hants —1B 24
Hatherleigh. Devn —2F 11
Hathern. Leics —3C 74
Hatherop. Glos —5G 49
Hathersage. Derbs —2G 85
Hathersage Booths. Derbs —2G 85
Hatherton. Ches —1A 72
Hatherton. Staf —4D 72
Hatley St George. Cambs —5B 64
Hatt. Corn —2H 7
Hattersley. G Man —1D 85
Hattingley. Hants —3E 25
Hatton. Abers —5H 161
Hatton. Derbs —2G 73
Hatton. G Lon —3B 38
Hatton. Linc —3A 88
Hatton. Shrp —1G 59
Hatton. Warr —2H 83
Hatton. Warw —4G 61
Hattoncrook. Abers —1F 153
Hatton Heath. Ches —4G 83
Hatton of Fintray. Abers —2F 153
Haugh. E Ayr —2D 117
Haugh. Linc —3D 88
Haugham. Linc —2C 88
Haugh Head. Nmbd —2E 121
Haughley. Suff —4C 66
Haughley Green. Suff —4C 66
Haughley Park —4C 66
Haughmond Abbey EH —4H 71
Haugh of Ballechin. Per —3G 143
Haugh of Glass. Mor —5B 160
Haugh of Urr. Dum —3F 111
Haughton. Notts —3D 86
Haughton. Shrp —1A 60
(nr. Bridgnorth)
Haughton. Shrp —3F 71
(nr. Oswestry)
Haughton. Shrp —5B 72
(nr. Shifnal)
Haughton. Shrp —4H 71
(nr. Shrewsbury)
Haughton. Staf —3C 72
Haughton Green. G Man —1D 84
Haughton le Skerne. Darl —3A 106
Haughton Moss. Ches —5H 83
Haultwick. Herts —3D 52
Haunn. Arg —4E 139
Haunn. W Isl —7C 170
Haunton. Staf —4G 73
Hauxley. Nmbd —4G 121
Hauxton. Cambs —5D 64
Havannah. Ches —4C 84
Havant. Hants —2F 17
Haven. Here —5G 59
Haven Bank. Linc —5B 88
Havenside. E Yor —2E 95
Havenstreet. IOW —3D 16
Haven, The. W Sus —2B 26
Havercroft. W Yor —3D 93
Haverfordwest. Pemb —3D 42
Haverhill. Suff —1G 53
Haverigg. Cumb —2A 96
Havering-atte-Bower. G Lon —1G 39
Havering's Grove. Essx —1A 40
Haversham. Mil —1G 51
Haverthwaite. Cumb —1C 96
Haverton Hill. Stoc T —2B 106
Havyatt. Som —3A 22
Hawarden. Flin —4F 83
Hawcoat. Cumb —2B 96
Hawcross. Glos —2C 48
Hawen. Cdgn —1D 44
Hawes. N Yor —1A 98
Hawes Green. Norf —1E 67
Hawick. Bord —3H 119
Hawkchurch. Devn —2G 13
Hawk Conservancy —2B 24
Hawkedon. Suff —5G 65
Hawkenbury. Kent —1C 28
Hawkeridge. Wilts —1D 22
Hawkerland. Devn —4D 12
Hawkesbury. S Glo —3C 34
Hawkesbury Upton. S Glo —3C 34
Hawkes End. W Mid —2G 61
Hawk Green. G Man —2D 84
Hawkhill. Nmbd —3G 121
Hawkhurst. Kent —2B 28
Hawkhurst Common. E Sus —4G 27
Hawkinge. Kent —1G 29
Hawkley. Hants —4F 25
Hawkridge. Som —3B 20
Hawksdale. Cumb —5E 113
Hawkshaw. G Man —3F 91
Hawkshead. Cumb —5E 103
Hawkshead Hill. Cumb —5E 103
Hawkswick. N Yor —2B 98
Hawksworth. Notts —1E 75
Hawksworth. W Yor —5D 98
Hawkwell. Essx —1C 40
Hawley. Hants —1G 25
Hawley. Kent —3G 39
Hawling. Glos —3F 49
Hawnby. N Yor —1H 99
Haworth. W Yor —1A 92
Hawstead. Suff —5A 66
Hawthorn. Dur —5H 115
Hawthorn Hill. Brac —4G 37
Hawthorn Hill. Linc —5B 88
Hawthorpe. Linc —3H 75
Hawton. Notts —5E 87
Haxby. York —4A 100
Haxey. N Lin —1E 87
Haybridge. Shrp —3A 60
Haybridge. Som —2A 22
Haydock. Mers —1H 83
Haydon. Bath —1B 22
Haydon. Dors —1B 14
Haydon. Som —4F 21
Haydon Bridge. Nmbd —3B 114
Haydon Wick. Swin —3G 35
Haye. Corn —2H 7
Hayes. G Lon —4F 39
(nr. Bromley)
Hayes. G Lon —2B 38
(nr. Uxbridge)
Hayfield. Derbs —2E 85
Hay Green. Norf —4E 77
Hayhill. E Ayr —3D 116
Haylands. IOW —3D 16
Hayle. Corn —3C 4
Hayley Green. W Mid —2D 60
Hayling Island. Hants —3F 17
Hayne. Devn —2B 12
Haynes. Beds —1A 52
Haynes West End. Beds —1A 52
Hay-on-Wye. Powy —1F 47
Hayscastle. Pemb —2C 42
Hayscastle Cross. Pemb —2D 42
Haysden. Kent —1G 27
Hayshead. Ang —4F 145
Hay Street. Herts —3D 53
Hayton. Aber —3G 153
Hayton. Cumb —5C 112
(nr. Aspatria)
Hayton. Cumb —4G 113
(nr. Brampton)
Hayton. E Yor —5C 100
Hayton. Notts —2E 87
Hayton's Bent. Shrp —2H 59
Haytor Vale. Devn —5A 12
Haytown. Devn —1D 11
Haywards Heath. W Sus —3E 27
Haywood. S Lan —4C 128
Hazelbank. S Lan —5B 128
Hazelbury Bryan. Dors —2C 14
Hazeleigh. Essx —5B 54
Hazeley. Hants —1F 25
Hazel Grove. G Man —2D 84
Hazelhead. S Yor —4B 92
Hazelslade. Staf —4E 73
Hazel Street. Kent —2A 28
Hazelton Walls. Fife —1F 137
Hazelwood. Derbs —1H 73
Hazlemere. Buck —2G 37
Hazler. Shrp —1G 59
Hazlerigg. Tyne —2F 115
Hazles. Staf —1E 73
Hazleton. Glos —4F 49
Hazon. Nmbd —4F 121
Heacham. Norf —2F 77
Headbourne Worthy. Hants —3C 24
Headcorn. Kent —1C 28
Headingley. W Yor —1C 92
Headington. Oxon —5D 50
Headlam. Dur —3E 105
Headless Cross. Worc —4E 61
Headley. Hants —3G 25
(nr. Haslemere)
Headley. Hants —5D 36
(nr. Kingsclere)
Headley. Surr —5D 38
Headley Down. Hants —3G 25
Headley Heath. Worc —3E 61
Headley Park. Bris —5A 34
Head of Muir. Falk —1B 128
Headon. Notts —3E 87
Heads Nook. Cumb —4F 113
Heage. Derbs —5A 86
Healaugh. N Yor —5D 104
(nr. Grinton)
Healaugh. N Yor —5H 99
(nr. York)
Heald Green. G Man —2C 84
Heale. Devn —2G 19
Heale Gdns. —3G 23
Healey. G Man —3G 91
Healey. Nmbd —4D 114
Healey. N Yor —1D 98
Healeyfield. Dur —5D 114
Healey Hall. Nmbd —4D 114
Healing. NE Lin —3F 95
Heamoor. Corn —3B 4
Heanish. Arg —4B 138
Heanor. Derbs —1B 74
Heanton Punchardon. Devn —3F 19
Heapham. Linc —2F 87
Heartsease. Powy —4D 58
Heasley Mill. Devn —3H 19
Heaste. High —2E 147
Heath. Derbs —4B 86
Heath and Reach. Beds —3H 51
Heath Common. W Sus —4C 26
Heathcote. Derbs —4F 85
Heath Cross. Devn —3H 11
Heathencote. Nptn —1F 51
Heath End. Derbs —3A 74
Heath End. Hants —5D 36
Heath End. W Mid —5E 73
Heather. Leics —4A 74
Heatherfield. High —4D 155
Heatherton. Derb —2H 73
Heathfield. Cumb —5C 112
Heathfield. Devn —5B 12
Heathfield. E Sus —3G 27
Heathfield. Ren —3E 126
Heathfield. Som —4E 21
Heath Green. Worc —3E 61
Heathhall. Dum —2A 112
Heath Hayes. Staf —4E 73
Heath Hill. Shrp —4B 72
Heath House. Som —2H 21
Heathrow (London) Airport. G Lon —3B 38
Heathstock. Devn —2F 13
Heath, The. Norf —3E 79
(nr. Buxton)
Heath, The. Norf —3B 78
(nr. Fakenham)
Heath, The. Norf —3D 78
(nr. Heavingham)
Heath, The. Staf —2E 73
Heathton. Shrp —1C 60
Heathton. Suff —2E 55
Heathtop. Derbs —2F 73
Heath Town. W Mid —5D 72
Heatley. G Man —2B 84
Heatley. Staf —3E 73
Heaton. Lanc —3D 96
Heaton. Staf —4D 84
Heaton. Tyne —3F 115
Heaton. W Yor —1B 92
Heaton Hall —4G 91
Heaton Moor. G Man —1C 84
Heaton's Bridge. Lanc —3C 90
Heaverham. Kent —5G 39
Heavitree. Devn —3C 12
Hebburn. Tyne —3G 115
Hebden. N Yor —3C 98
Hebden Bridge. W Yor —2H 91
Hebden Green. Ches —4A 84
Hebing End. Herts —3D 52
Hebron. Carm —2F 43
Hebron. Nmbd —1E 115
Heck. Dum —1B 112
Heckdyke. Notts —1E 87
Heckfield. Hants —5F 37
Heckfield Green. Suff —3D 66
Heckfordbridge. Essx —3C 54
Heckington. Linc —1A 76
Heckmondwike. W Yor —2C 92
Heddington. Wilts —5E 35
Heddle. Orkn —6C 172
Heddon. Devn —4G 19
Heddon-on-the-Wall. Nmbd —3E 115
Hedenham. Norf —1F 67
Hedge End. Hants —1C 16
Hedgerley. Buck —2A 38
Hedging. Som —4G 21
Hedingham Castle —2A 54
Hedley on the Hill. Nmbd —4D 115
Hednesford. Staf —4E 73
Hedon. E Yor —2E 95
Hegdon Hill. Here —5H 59
Heglibister. Shet —6E 173
Heighington. Darl —2F 105
Heighington. Linc —4H 87
Heightington. Worc —3B 60
Heights of Abraham —5G 85
Heights of Brae. High —2H 157
Heights of Fodderty. High —2H 157
Heights of Kinlochewe. High —2C 156
Heiton. Bord —1B 120
Hele. Devn —5H 11
(nr. Ashburton)
Hele. Devn —2C 12
(nr. Exeter)
Hele. Devn —3D 10
(nr. Holsworthy)
Hele. Devn —2F 19
(nr. Ilfracombe)
Hele. Torb —2F 9
Helensburgh. Arg —1D 126
Helford. Corn —4E 5
Helhoughton. Norf —3A 78
Helions Bumpstead. Essx —1G 53
Helland. Corn —5A 10
Helland. Som —4G 21
Hellandbridge. Corn —5A 10
Hellen's —2B 48
Hellesdon. Norf —4E 78
Hellesveor. Corn —2C 4
Hellidon. Nptn —5C 62
Hellifield. N Yor —4A 98
Hellingly. E Sus —4G 27
Hellington. Norf —5F 79
Hellister. Shet —7E 173
Helmdon. Nptn —1D 50
Helmingham. Suff —5D 66
Helmingham Hall Gdns. —5D 66
Helmington Row. Dur —1E 105
Helmsdale. High —2H 165
Helmshore. Lanc —2F 91
Helmsley. N Yor —1A 100
Helmsley Castle EH —1A 100
Helperby. N Yor —3G 99
Helperthorpe. N Yor —2D 100
Helpringham. Linc —1A 76
Helpston. Pet —5A 76
Helsby. Ches —3G 83
Helsey. Linc —3E 89
Helston. Corn —4D 4
Helstone. Corn —4A 10
Helton. Cumb —2G 103
Helvellyn —3E 103
Helwith. N Yor —4D 105
Helwith Bridge. N Yor —3H 97
Helygain. Flin —3E 82
Hemblington. Norf —4F 79
Hemel Hempstead. Herts —5A 52
Hemerdon. Devn —3B 8
Hemingbrough. N Yor —1G 93
Hemingby. Linc —3B 88
Hemingfield. S Yor —4D 93
Hemingford Abbots. Cambs —3B 64
Hemingford Grey. Cambs —3B 64
Hemingstone. Suff —5D 66
Hemington. Leics —3B 74
Hemington. Nptn —2H 63
Hemington. Som —1C 22
Hemley. Suff —1F 55
Hemlington. Midd —3B 106
Hempholme. E Yor —4E 101
Hempnall. Norf —1E 67
Hempnall Green. Norf —1E 67
Hempriggs. High —4F 169
Hemp's Green. Essx —3C 54
Hempstead. Essx —2G 53
Hempstead. Medw —4B 40
Hempstead. Norf —2D 78
(nr. Holt)
Hempstead. Norf —3G 79
(nr. Stalham)
Hempsted. Glos —4D 48
Hempton. Norf —3B 78
Hempton. Oxon —2C 50
Hemsby. Norf —4G 79
Hemswell. Linc —1G 87
Hemswell Cliff. Linc —2G 87
Hemsworth. Dors —2E 15
Hemsworth. W Yor —3E 93
Hem, The. Shrp —5B 72
Hemyock. Devn —1E 13
Henallt. Carm —3E 45
Henbury. Bris —4A 34
Henbury. Ches —3C 84
Hendomen. Powy —1E 58
Hendon. G Lon —2D 38
Hendon. Tyne —4H 115
Hendra. Corn —3D 6
Hendre. B'end —3C 32
Hendreforgan. Rhon —3C 32
Hendy. Carm —5F 45
Heneglwys. IOA —3D 80
Henfeddau Fawr. Pemb —1G 43
Henfield. S Glo —4B 34
Henfield. W Sus —4D 26
Henford. Devn —3D 10
Hengoed. Cphy —2E 33
Hengoed. Shrp —2E 71
Hengrave. Suff —4H 65
Henham. Essx —3F 53
Heniarth. Powy —5D 70
Henlade. Som —4F 21
Henley. Dors —2B 14
Henley. Shrp —2G 59
(nr. Church Stretton)
Henley. Shrp —3H 59
(nr. Ludlow)
Henley. Som —3H 21
Henley. Suff —5D 66
Henley. W Sus —4G 25
Henley-in-Arden. Warw —4F 61
Henley-on-Thames. Oxon —3F 37
Henley's Down. E Sus —4B 28
Henley Street. Kent —4A 40
Henllan. Cdgn —1D 44
Henllan. Den —4C 82
Henllan. Mon —3F 47
Henllan Amgoed. Carm —2F 43
Henllys. Torf —2F 33
Henlow. Beds —2B 52
Hennock. Devn —4B 12
Henny Street. Essx —2B 54
Henryd. Cnwy —3G 81
Henry Moore Institute, see Leeds City Mus. & Art Gallery —190
Henry's Moat. Pemb —2E 43
Hensall. N Yor —2F 93
Henshaw. Nmbd —3A 114
Hensingham. Cumb —3A 102
Henstead. Suff —2G 67
Hensting. Hants —4C 24
Henstridge. Som —1C 14
Henstridge Ash. Som —4C 22
Henstridge Bowden. Som —4B 22
Henstridge Marsh. Som —4C 22
Henton. Oxon —5F 51
Henton. Som —2H 21
Henwood. Corn —5C 10
Heogan. Shet —7F 173
Heol Senni. Powy —3C 46
Heol-y-Cyw. B'end —3C 32
Hepburn. Nmbd —2E 121
Hepple. Nmbd —4D 121
Hepscott. Nmbd —1F 115
Heptonstall. W Yor —2H 91
Hepworth. Suff —3B 66
Hepworth. W Yor —4B 92
Herbrandston. Pemb —4C 42
Hereford. Here —2A 48
Hereford Cathedral —2A 48
Hergest Croft Gdns. —5E 59
Heribusta. High —1D 154
Heriot. Bord —4H 129
Heritage Motor Mus. —5A 62
Hermiston. Edin —2E 129
Hermitage. Dors —2B 14
Hermitage. Bord —5H 119
Hermitage. W Ber —4D 36
Hermitage. W Sus —2F 17
Hermon. Carm —3G 45
(nr. Llandeilo)
Hermon. Carm —2D 44
(nr. Newcastle Emlyn)
Hermon. IOA —4C 80
Hermon. Pemb —1G 43
Herne. Kent —4F 41
Herne Bay. Kent —4F 41
Herne Common. Kent —4F 41
Herne Pound. Kent —5A 40
Herner. Devn —4F 19
Hernhill. Kent —4E 41
Herodsfoot. Corn —2G 7
Heronden. Kent —5G 41
Herongate. Essx —1H 39
Heronsford. S Ayr —1G 109
Heronsgate. Herts —1B 38
Heron's Ghyll. E Sus —3F 27
Herra. Shet —2H 173
Herriard. Hants —2E 25
Herringfleet. Suff —1G 67
Herringswell. Suff —4G 65
Herrington. Tyne —4G 115
Hersden. Kent —4G 41
Hersham. Corn —2C 10
Hersham. Surr —4C 38
Herstmonceux. E Sus —4H 27
Herstmonceux Castle Gdns. —4H 27
Herston. Dors —5F 15
Herston. Orkn —8D 172
Hertford. Herts —4D 52
Hertford Heath. Herts —4D 52
Hertingfordbury. Herts —4D 52
Hesketh. Lanc —2C 90
Hesketh Bank. Lanc —2C 90
Hesketh Lane. Lanc —5F 97
Hesket Newmarket. Cumb —1E 103
Heskin Green. Lanc —3D 90
Hesleden. Dur —1B 106
Hesleyside. Nmbd —1B 114
Heslington. York —4A 100
Hessay. York —4H 99
Hessenford. Corn —3H 7
Hessett. Suff —4B 66
Hessilhead. N Ayr —4E 127
Hessle. Hull —2D 94
Hestaford. Shet —6D 173
Hest Bank. Lanc —3D 96
Hestercombe Gdns. —4F 21
Hester's Way. Glos —3E 49
Hestinsetter. Shet —7D 173
Heston. G Lon —3C 38
Hestwall. Orkn —6B 172
Heswall. Mers —2E 83
Hethe. Oxon —3D 50
Hethelpit Cross. Glos —3C 48
Hethersett. Norf —5D 78
Hethersgill. Cumb —3F 113
Hetherside. Cumb —3F 113
Hethpool. Nmbd —2C 120
Hett. Dur —1F 105
Hetton. N Yor —4B 98
Hetton-le-Hole. Tyne —5G 115
Hetton Steads. Nmbd —1E 121
Heugh. Nmbd —2D 115
Heugh-head. Abers —2A 152
Heveningham. Suff —3F 67
Hever. Kent —1F 27
Hever Castle —1F 27
Heversham. Cumb —1D 97
Hevingham. Norf —3D 78
Hewas Water. Corn —4D 6
Hewelsfield. Glos —5A 48
Hewish. N Som —5G 33
Hewish. Som —2H 13
Heworth. York —4A 100
Hexham. Nmbd —3C 114
Hextable. Kent —3G 39
Hexton. Herts —2B 52
Hexworthy. Devn —5G 11
Heybridge. Essx —1H 39
(nr. Brentwood)
Heybridge. Essx —5B 54
(nr. Maldon)
Heybridge Basin. Essx —5B 54
Heybrook Bay. Devn —4A 8
Heydon. Cambs —1E 53
Heydon. Norf —3D 78
Heydour. Linc —2H 75
Heylipol. Arg —4A 138
Heyop. Powy —3E 59
Heysham. Lanc —3D 96
Heyshott. W Sus —1G 17
Heytesbury. Wilts —2E 23
Heythrop. Oxon —3B 50
Heywood. G Man —3G 91
Heywood. Wilts —1D 22
Hibaldstow. N Lin —4C 94

Hickleton. S Yor —4E 93
Hickling. Norf —3G 79
Hickling. Notts —3D 74
Hickling Green. Norf —3G 79
Hickling Heath. Norf —3G 79
Hickstead. W Sus —3D 26
Hidcote Bartrim. Glos —1G 49
Hidcote Boyce. Glos —1G 49
Hidcote Manor Gdn. NT —1G 49
Higford. Shrp —5B 72
High Ackworth. W Yor —3E 93
Higham. Derbs —5A 86
Higham. Kent —3B 40
Higham. Lanc —1G 91
Higham. S Yor —4D 92
Higham. Suff —2D 54
(nr. Ipswich)
Higham. Suff —4G 65
(nr. Newmarket)
Higham Dykes. Nmbd —2E 115
Higham Ferrers. Nptn —4G 63
Higham Gobion. Beds —2B 52
Higham on the Hill. Leics —1A 62
Highampton. Devn —2E 11
Higham Wood. Kent —1G 27
High Angerton. Nmbd —1D 115
High Auldgirth. Dum —1G 111
High Bankhill. Cumb —5G 113
High Banton. N Lan —1A 128
High Barnet. G Lon —1D 38
High Beech. Essx —1F 39
High Beeches —2D 27
High Bentham. N Yor —3F 97
High Bickington. Devn —4G 19
High Biggins. Cumb —2F 97
High Birkwith. N Yor —2G 97
High Blantyre. S Lan —4H 127
High Bonnybridge. Falk —2B 128
High Borrans. Cumb —4F 103
High Bradfield. S Yor —1G 85
High Bray. Devn —3G 19
Highbridge. Cumb —5E 113
Highbridge. High —5D 148
Highbridge. Som —2G 21
Highbrook. W Sus —2E 27
High Brooms. Kent —1G 27
High Bullen. Devn —4F 19
Highburton. W Yor —3B 92
Highbury. Som —2B 22
High Buston. Nmbd —4G 121
High Callerton. Nmbd —2E 115
High Carlingill. Cumb —4H 103
High Catton. E Yor —4B 100
High Church. Nmbd —1E 115
Highclere. Hants —5C 36
Highclere Castle —1C 24
Highcliffe. Dors —3H 15
High Cogges. Oxon —5B 50
High Common. Norf —5B 78
High Coniscliffe. Darl —3F 105
High Crosby. Cumb —4F 113
High Cross. Hants —4F 25
High Cross. Herts —4D 52
High Dougarie. N Ayr —2C 122
High Easter. Essx —4G 53
High Eggborough. N Yor —2F 93
High Ellington. N Yor —1D 98
Higher Alham. Som —2B 22
Higher Ansty. Dors —2C 14
Higher Ashton. Devn —4B 12
Higher Ballam. Lanc —1B 90
Higher Bartle. Lanc —1D 90
Higher Bockhampton. Dors —3C 14
Higher Bojewyan. Corn —3A 4
High Ercall. Telf —4H 71
Higher Clovelly. Devn —4D 18
Higher Dinting. Derbs —1E 85
Higher End. G Man —4D 90
Higher Gabwell. Devn —2F 9
Higher Heysham. Lanc —3D 96
Higher Hurdsfield. Ches —3D 84
Higher Kingcombe. Dors —3A 14
Higher Kinnerton. Flin —4F 83
Higher Penwortham. Lanc —2D 90
Higher Porthpean. Corn —3E 7
Higher Poynton. Ches —2D 84
Higher Shotton. Flin —4F 83
Higher Shurlach. Ches —3A 84
Higher Tale. Devn —2D 12
Highertown. Corn —4C 6
Higher Town. IOS —1B 4
Higher Town. Som —2C 20
Higher Walton. Lanc —2D 90
Higher Walton. Warr —2A 84
Higher Whatcombe. Dors —2D 14
Higher Wheelton. Lanc —2E 90
Higher Whiteleigh. Corn —3C 10
Higher Whitley. Ches —3A 84
Higher Wincham. Ches —3A 84
Higher Wych. Wrex —1G 71
High Etherley. Dur —2E 105
High Ferry. Linc —1C 76
Highfield. E Yor —1H 93
Highfield. N Ayr —4E 126
Highfield. Tyne —4E 115
Highfields. Cambs —5C 64
Highfields. Nmbd —4F 131
High Garrett. Essx —3A 54
Highgate. G Lon —2D 39
Highgate. N Ayr —4E 127
Highgate. Powy —1D 58
High Grange. Dur —1E 105
High Green. Cumb —4F 103
High Green. Norf —5D 78
High Green. Shrp —2B 60
High Green. S Yor —1H 85
High Green. W Yor —3B 92
High Green. Worc —1D 49
Highgreen Manor. Nmbd —5C 120
High Halden. Kent —2C 28
High Halstow. Medw —3B 40
High Ham. Som —3H 21
High Harrington. Cumb —2B 102
High Haswell. Dur —5G 115
High Hatton. Shrp —3A 72
High Hawkser. N Yor —4G 107
High Hesket. Cumb —5F 113
High Hesleden. Dur —1B 106
High Hoyland. S Yor —4C 92
High Hunsley. E Yor —1C 94
High Hurstwood. E Sus —3F 27
High Hutton. N Yor —3B 100
High Ireby. Cumb —1D 102
High Keil. Arg —5A 122
High Kelling. Norf —1D 78
High Kilburn. N Yor —2H 99
High Killerby. N Yor —1E 101
High Knipe. Cumb —3G 103
High Lands. Dur —2E 105
Highlands, The. Shrp —2A 60
Highland Wildlife Park —3C 150
Highlane. Ches —4C 84
Highlane. Derbs —2B 86
High Lane. G Man —2D 84
High Lane. Here —4A 60
High Laver. Essx —5F 53
Highlaws. Cumb —5C 112
Highleadon. Glos —3C 48
High Legh. Ches —2A 84
Highleigh. W Sus —3G 17
High Leven. Stoc T —3B 106
Highley. Shrp —2B 60
High Littleton. Bath —1B 22
High Longthwaite. Cumb —5D 112
High Lorton. Cumb —2C 102
High Marishes. N Yor —2C 100
High Marnham. Notts —3F 87
High Melton. S Yor —4F 93
High Mickley. Nmbd —3D 115
Highmoor. Cumb —5D 112
High Moor. Lanc —3D 90
Highmoor. Oxon —3F 37
Highmoor Hill. Mon —3H 33
High Mowthorpe. N Yor —3C 100
Highnam. Glos —4C 48
High Newport. Tyne —4G 115
High Newton. Cumb —1D 96
High Newton-by-the-Sea. Nmbd —2G 121
High Nibthwaite. Cumb —1B 96
High Offley. Staf —3B 72
High Ongar. Essx —5F 53
High Onn. Staf —4C 72
High Orchard. Glos —4D 48
High Park. Mers —3B 90
High Roding. Essx —4G 53
High Row. Cumb —1E 103
High Salvington. W Sus —5C 26
High Scales. Cumb —5C 112
High Shaw. N Yor —5B 104
High Shincliffe. Dur —5F 115
High Side. Cumb —1D 102
High Spen. Tyne —3E 115
Highsted. Kent —4D 40
High Stoop. Dur —5E 115
High Street. Corn —3D 6
High Street. Suff —5G 67
(nr. Aldeburgh)
High Street. Suff —2F 67
(nr. Bungay)
High Street. Suff —3G 67
(nr. Yoxford)
Highstreet Green. Essx —2A 54
High Street Green. Suff —5C 66
Highstreet Green. Surr —2A 26
Hightae. Dum —2B 112
High Throston. Hart —1B 106
Hightown. Ches —4C 84
Hightown. Mers —4A 90
High Town. Staf —4D 73
Hightown Green. Suff —5B 66
High Toynton. Linc —4B 88
High Trewhitt. Nmbd —4E 121
High Valleyfield. Fife —1D 128
Highway. Here —1H 47
Highweek. Devn —5B 12
High Westwood. Dur —4E 115
Highwood. Staf —2E 73
Highwood. Worc —4A 60
High Worsall. N Yor —4A 106
Highworth. Swin —2H 35
High Wray. Cumb —5E 103
High Wych. Herts —4E 53
High Wycombe. Buck —2G 37
Hilborough. Norf —5H 77
Hilcott. Wilts —1G 23
Hildenborough. Kent —1G 27
Hildersham. Cambs —1F 53
Hilderstone. Staf —2D 72
Hilderthorpe. E Yor —3F 101
Hilfield. Dors —2B 14
Hilgay. Norf —1F 65
Hill. S Glo —2B 34
Hill. Warw —4B 62
Hill. Worc —1E 49
Hillam. N Yor —2F 93
Hillbeck. Cumb —3A 104
Hillberry. IOM —4C 108
Hillborough. Kent —4G 41
Hillbourne. Pool —3F 15
Hillbrae. Abers —4D 160
(nr. Aberchirder)
Hillbrae. Abers —1E 153
(nr. Inverurie)
Hillbrae. Abers —5F 161
(nr. Methlick)
Hill Brow. Hants —4F 25
Hillbutts. Dors —2E 15
Hillcliffane. Derbs —1G 73
Hill Deverill. Wilts —2D 22
Hilldyke. Linc —1C 76
Hill End. Dur —1D 104
Hillend. Fife —1E 129
(nr. Inverkeithing)
Hill End. Fife —4C 136
(nr. Saline)
Hillend. N Lan —3B 128
Hill End. N Yor —4C 98
Hillend. Shrp —1C 60
Hillend. Swan —3D 30
Hillersland. Glos —4A 48
Hillerton. Devn —3H 11
Hillesden. Buck —3E 51
Hillesley. Glos —3C 34
Hillfarrance. Som —4E 21
Hill Furze. Worc —1E 49
Hill Gate. Here —3H 47
Hill Green. Essx —2E 53
Hillgreen. W Ber —4C 36
Hillhead. Abers —5C 160
Hill Head. Hants —2D 16
Hillhead. S Ayr —3D 116
Hillhead. Torb —3F 9
Hillhead of Auchentumb. Abers —3G 161
Hill House, The NTS —1D 126
Hilliard's Cross. Staf —4F 73
Hilliclay. High —2D 168
Hillingdon. G Lon —2B 38
Hillington. Norf —3G 77
Hillington. Ren —3G 127
Hillmorton. Warw —3C 62
Hill of Beath. Fife —4D 136
Hill of Fearn. High —1C 158
Hill of Fiddes. Abers —1G 153
Hill of Keillor. Ang —4B 144
Hill of Overbrae. Abers —2F 161
Hill of Tarvit NTS —2F 137
Hill Ridware. Staf —4E 73
Hillsborough. S Yor —1H 85
Hillside. Abers —4G 153
Hillside. Ang —2G 145
Hillside. Devn —2D 8
Hillside. Hants —1F 25
Hillside. Mers —3B 90
Hillside. Orkn —5C 172
Hillside. Shet —5F 173
Hillside. Shrp —2A 60
Hill Side. W Yor —3B 92
Hillside. Worc —4B 60
Hillside of Prieston. Ang —5C 144
Hill Somersal. Derbs —2F 73
Hillstown. Derbs —4B 86
Hillstreet. Hants —1B 16
Hillswick. Shet —4D 173
Hill, The. Cumb —1A 96
Hill Top. Dur —2C 104
(nr. Barnard Castle)
Hill Top. Dur —5F 115
(nr. Durham)
Hill Top. Dur —4E 115
(nr. Stanley)
Hill Top. Hants —2C 16
Hill Top NT —5E 103
Hill View. Dors —3E 15
Hillwell. Shet —10E 173
Hill Wootton. Warw —4H 61
Hillyland. Per —1C 136
Hilmarton. Wilts —4F 35
Hilperton. Wilts —1D 22
Hilperton Marsh. Wilts —5D 34
Hilsea. Port —2E 17
Hilston. E Yor —1F 95
Hiltingbury. Hants —4C 24
Hilton. Cambs —4B 64
Hilton. Cumb —2A 104
Hilton. Derbs —2G 73
Hilton. Dors —2C 14
Hilton. Dur —2E 105
Hilton. High —5E 165
Hilton. Shrp —1B 60
Hilton. Staf —5E 73
Hilton. Stoc T —3B 106
Hilton of Cadboll. High —1C 158
Himbleton. Worc —5D 60
Himley. Staf —1C 60
Hincaster. Cumb —1E 97
Hinchcliffe Mill. W Yor —4B 92
Hinchwick. Glos —2G 49
Hinckley. Leics —1B 62
Hinderclay. Suff —3C 66
Hinderwell. N Yor —3E 107
Hindford. Shrp —2F 71
Hindhead. Surr —3G 25
Hindley. G Man —4E 91
Hindley. Nmbd —4D 114
Hindley Green. G Man —4E 91
Hindlip. Worc —5C 60
Hindolveston. Norf —3C 78
Hindon. Wilts —3E 23
Hindringham. Norf —2B 78
Hingham. Norf —5C 78
Hinksford. Staf —2C 60
Hinstock. Shrp —3A 72
Hintlesham. Suff —1D 54
Hinton. Hants —3H 15
Hinton. Here —2G 47
Hinton. Nptn —5C 62
Hinton. Shrp —5G 71
Hinton. S Glo —4C 34
Hinton Ampner. Hants —4D 24
Hinton Ampner NT —4D 24
Hinton Blewett. Bath —1A 22
Hinton Charterhouse. Bath —1C 22
Hinton-in-the-Hedges. Nptn —2D 50
Hinton Martell. Dors —2F 15
Hinton on the Green. Worc —1F 49
Hinton Parva. Swin —3H 35
Hinton St George. Som —1H 13
Hinton St Mary. Dors —1C 14
Hinton Waldrist. Oxon —2B 36
Hints. Shrp —3A 60
Hints. Staf —5F 73
Hinwick. Beds —4G 63
Hinxhill. Kent —1E 29
Hinxton. Cambs —1E 53
Hinxworth. Herts —1C 52
Hipley. Hants —1E 16
Hipperholme. W Yor —2B 92
Hipsburn. Nmbd —3G 121
Hipswell. N Yor —5E 105
Hiraeth. Carm —2F 43
Hirn. Abers —3E 153
Hirnant. Powy —3C 70
Hirst. N Lan —3B 128
Hirst. Nmbd —1F 115
Hirst Courtney. N Yor —2G 93
Hirwaen. Den —4D 82
Hirwaun. Rhon —5C 46
Hiscott. Devn —4F 19
Histon. Cambs —4D 64
Historic Dockyard —Medway 191
Hitcham. Suff —5B 66
Hitchin. Herts —3B 52
Hittisleigh. Devn —3H 11
Hittisleigh Barton. Devn —3H 11
Hive. E Yor —1B 94
Hixon. Staf —3E 73
HM Customs & Excise Mus. —Liverpool 191
HMS Victory —Portsmouth 195
HMS Warrior —Portsmouth 195
Hoaden. Kent —5G 41
Hoar Cross. Staf —3F 73
Hoarwithy. Here —3A 48
Hoath. Kent —4G 41
Hobarris. Shrp —3F 59
Hobbister. Orkn —7C 172
Hobbles Green. Suff —5G 65
Hobbs Cross. Essx —1F 39
Hobkirk. Bord —3H 119
Hobson. Dur —4E 115
Hoby. Leics —4D 74
Hockering. Norf —4C 78
Hockering Heath. Norf —4C 78
Hockerton. Notts —5E 86
Hockley. Essx —1C 40
Hockley. Staf —5G 73
Hockley. W Mid —2G 61
Hockley Heath. W Mid —3F 61
Hockliffe. Beds —3H 51
Hockwold cum Wilton. Norf —2G 65
Hockworthy. Devn —1D 12
Hoddesdon. Herts —5D 52
Hoddlesden. Bkbn —2F 91
Hoddomcross. Dum —2C 112
Hodgeston. Pemb —5E 43
Hodley. Powy —1D 58
Hodnet. Shrp —3A 72
Hodnet Hall Gdns. —3A 72
Hodsoll Street. Kent —4H 39
Hodson. Swin —3G 35
Hodthorpe. Derbs —3C 86
Hoe. Norf —4B 78
Hoe Gate. Hants —1E 17
Hoe, The. Plym —3A 8
Hoff. Cumb —3H 103
Hoffleet Stow. Linc —2B 76
Hogaland. Shet —4E 173
Hogben's Hill. Kent —5E 41
Hoggard's Green. Suff —5A 66
Hoggeston. Buck —3G 51
Hoggrill's End. Warw —1G 61
Hogha Gearraidh. W Isl —1C 170
Hoghton. Lanc —2E 90
Hoghton Bottoms. Lanc —2E 91
Hoghton Tower —2E 90
Hognaston. Derbs —5G 85
Hogsthorpe. Linc —3E 89
Hogstock. Dors —2E 15
Holbeach. Linc —3C 76
Holbeach Bank. Linc —3C 76
Holbeach Clough. Linc —3C 76
Holbeach Drove. Linc —4C 76
Holbeach Hurn. Linc —3C 76
Holbeach St Johns. Linc —4C 76
Holbeach St Marks. Linc —2C 76
Holbeach St Matthew. Linc —2D 76
Holbeck. Notts —3C 86
Holbeck. W Yor —1C 92
Holberrow Green. Worc —5E 61
Holbeton. Devn —4C 8
Holborn. G Lon —2E 39
Holbrook. Derbs —1A 74
Holbrook. S Yor —2B 86
Holbrook. Suff —2E 55
Holburn. Nmbd —1E 121
Holburne Mus. —Bath 186
Holbury. Hants —2C 16
Holcombe. Devn —5C 12
Holcombe. G Man —3F 91
Holcombe. Som —2B 22
Holcombe Brook. G Man —3F 91
Holcombe Rogus. Devn —1D 12
Holcot. Nptn —4E 63
Holden. Lanc —5G 97
Holdenby. Nptn —4D 62
Holdenby House Gdns. —4D 62
Holder's Green. Essx —3G 53
Holdgate. Shrp —2H 59
Holdingham. Linc —1H 75
Holditch. Dors —2G 13
Holehird Gdns. —4F 103
Holemoor. Devn —2E 11
Hole Street. W Sus —4C 26
Holford. Som —2E 21
Holker. Cumb —2C 96
Holker Hall —2C 96
Holkham. Norf —1A 78
Holkham Hall —1A 78
Hollacombe. Devn —2D 11
Holland. Orkn —2D 172
(on Papa Westray)
Holland. Orkn —5F 172
(on Stronsay)
Holland Fen. Linc —1B 76
Holland Lees. Lanc —4D 90
Holland-on-Sea. Essx —4E 55
Holland Park. W Mid —5E 73
Hollandstoun. Orkn —2G 172
Hollesley. Suff —1G 55
Hollinfare. Warr —1A 84
Hollingbourne. Kent —5C 40
Hollingbury. Brig —5E 27
Hollingdon. Buck —3G 51
Hollingrove. E Sus —3A 28
Hollington. Derbs —1G 73
Hollington. E Sus —4B 28
Hollington. Staf —2E 73
Hollington Grove. Derbs —2G 73
Hollingworth. G Man —1E 85
Hollins. Derbs —3H 85
Hollins. G Man —4G 91
(nr. Bury)
Hollins. G Man —4G 91
(nr. Middleton)
Hollinsclough. Staf —4E 85
Hollinswood. Telf —5A 72
Hollinthorpe. W Yor —1D 93
Hollinwood. G Man —4H 91
Hollinwood. Shrp —2H 71
Hollocombe. Devn —1G 11
Holloway. Derbs —5H 85
Hollow Court. Worc —5D 61
Hollowell. Nptn —3D 62
Hollow Meadows. S Yor —2G 85
Hollows. Dum —2E 113
Hollybush. Cphy —5E 47
Hollybush. E Ayr —3C 116
Hollybush. Worc —2C 48
Hollycombe Steam Collection —4G 25
Holly End. Norf —5D 77
Holly Hill. N Yor —4E 105
Hollyhurst. Ches —1H 71
Hollym. E Yor —2G 95
Hollywood. Staf —2D 72
Hollywood. Worc —3E 61
Holmacott. Devn —4F 19
Holmbridge. W Yor —4B 92
Holmbury St Mary. Surr —1C 26
Holmbush. Corn —3E 7
Holmcroft. Staf —3D 72
Holme. Cambs —2A 64
Holme. Cumb —2E 97
Holme. N Lin —4C 94
Holme. N Yor —1F 99
Holme. Notts —5F 87
Holme. W Yor —4B 92
Holmebridge. Dors —4D 15
Holme Chapel. Lanc —2G 91
Holme Hale. Norf —5A 78
Holme Lacy. Here —2A 48
Holme Lane. Notts —2D 74
Holme Marsh. Here —5F 59
Holmend. Dum —4C 118
Holme next the Sea. Norf —1G 77
Holme-on-Spalding-Moor. E Yor —1B 94
Holme on the Wolds. E Yor —5D 100
Holme Pierrepont. Notts —2D 74
Holme Pierrepont Hall —2D 74
Holmer. Here —1A 48
Holmer Green. Buck —2G 37
Holmes. Lanc —3C 90
Holme St Cuthbert. Cumb —5C 112
Holmes Chapel. Ches —4B 84
Holmesfield. Derbs —3H 85
Holmeswood. Lanc —3C 90
Holmewood. Derbs —4B 86
Holmfirth. W Yor —4B 92
Holmhead. E Ayr —2E 117
Holmisdale. High —4A 154
Holm of Drumlanrig. Dum —5H 117
Holmpton. E Yor —2G 95
Holmrook. Cumb —5B 102
Holmsey Green. Suff —3F 65
Holmsgarth. Shet —7F 173
Holmside. Dur —5F 115
Holmwrangle. Cumb —5G 113
Holne. Devn —2D 8
Holsworthy. Devn —2D 10
Holsworthy Beacon. Devn —2D 10
Holt. Dors —2F 15
Holt. Norf —2C 78
Holt. Wilts —5D 34
Holt. Worc —4C 60
Holt. Wrex —5G 83
Holtby. York —4A 100
Holt End. Hants —3E 25
Holt End. Worc —4E 61
Holt Fleet. Worc —4C 60
Holt Green. Lanc —4B 90
Holt Heath. Dors —2F 15
Holt Heath. Worc —4C 60
Holton. Oxon —5E 50
Holton. Som —4B 22
Holton. Suff —3F 67
Holton cum Beckering. Linc —2A 88
Holton Heath. Dors —3E 15
Holton le Clay. Linc —4F 95
Holton le Moor. Linc —1H 87
Holton St Mary. Suff —2D 54
Holt Pound. Hants —2G 25
Holtsmere End. Herts —4A 52
Holtye. E Sus —2F 27
Holwell. Dors —1C 14
Holwell. Herts —2B 52
Holwell. Leics —3E 75
Holwell. Oxon —5H 49
Holwell. Som —2C 22
Holwick. Dur —2C 104
Holworth. Dors —4C 14
Holybourne. Hants —2F 25
Holy Cross. Worc —3D 60
Holyfield. Essx —5D 53
Holyhead. IOA —2B 80
Holy Island —5H 131
Holy Island. Nmbd —5H 131
Holymoorside. Derbs —4H 85
Holyport. Wind —4G 37
Holyrood Abbey HS —Edinburgh 189
Holystone. Nmbd —4D 120
Holytown. N Lan —3A 128
Holywell. Cambs —3C 64
Holywell. Corn —3B 6
Holywell. Dors —2A 14
Holywell. Flin —3D 82
Holywell. Glos —2C 34
Holywell. Nmbd —2G 115
Holywell. Warw —4F 61
Holywell Green. W Yor —3A 92
Holywell Lake. Som —4E 20
Holywell Row. Suff —3G 65
Holywood. Dum —1G 111
Homer. Shrp —5A 72
Homer Green. Mers —4B 90
Homersfield. Suff —2E 67
Hom Green. Here —3A 48

Homington. Wilts —4G 23
Honeyborough. Pemb —4D 42
Honeybourne. Worc —1G 49
Honeychurch. Devn —2G 11
Honey Hill. Kent —4F 41
Honey Street. Wilts —5G 35
Honey Tye. Suff —2C 54
Honiley. Warw —3G 61
Honing. Norf —3F 79
Honingham. Norf —4D 78
Honington. Linc —1G 75
Honington. Suff —3B 66
Honington. Warw —1A 50
Honiton. Devn —2E 13
Honley. W Yor —3B 92
Honnington. Telf —4B 72
Hoo. Suff —5E 67
Hoobrook. Worc —3C 60
Hood Green. S Yor —4D 92
Hooe. E Sus —5A 28
Hooe. Plym —3A 8
Hooe Common. E Sus —4A 28
Hoohill. Bkpl —1B 90
Hook. Cambs —1D 64
Hook. E Yor —2A 94
Hook. G Lon —4C 38
Hook. Hants —1F 25 (nr. Basingstoke)
Hook. Hants —2D 16 (nr. Fareham)
Hook. Pemb —3D 43
Hook. Wilts —3F 35
Hook-a-Gate. Shrp —5G 71
Hook Bank. Worc —1D 48
Hooke. Dors —2A 14
Hooker Gate. Tyne —4E 115
Hookgate. Staf —2B 72
Hook Green. Kent —2A 28 (nr. Lamberhurst)
Hook Green. Kent —3H 39 (nr. Longfield)
Hook Green. Kent —4H 39 (nr. Meopham)
Hook Norton. Oxon —2B 50
Hook's Cross. Herts —3C 52
Hook Street. Glos —2B 34
Hookway. Devn —3B 12
Hookwood. Surr —1D 26
Hoole. Ches —4G 83
Hooley. Surr —5D 39
Hooley Bridge. G Man —3G 91
Hooley Brow. G Man —3G 91
Hoo St Werburgh. Medw —3B 40
Hooton. Ches —3F 83
Hooton Levitt. S Yor —1C 86
Hooton Pagnell. S Yor —4E 93
Hooton Roberts. S Yor —1B 86
Hoove. Shet —7E 173
Hope. Derbs —2F 85
Hope. Flin —5F 83
Hope. High —3E 167
Hope. Powy —5E 71
Hope. Shrp —5F 71
Hope. Staf —5F 85
Hope Bagot. Shrp —3H 59
Hope Bowdler. Shrp —1G 59
Hopedale. Staf —5F 85
Hope Green. Ches —2D 84
Hopeman. Mor —2F 159
Hope Mansell. Here —4B 48
Hopesay. Shrp —2F 59
Hope's Green. Essx —2B 40
Hopetoun House —2D 129
Hopetown. W Yor —2D 93
Hope under Dinmore. Here —5H 59
Hop Farm Country Park —1A 28
Hopley's Green. Here —5F 59
Hopperton. N Yor —4G 99
Hop Pole. Linc —4A 76
Hopstone. Shrp —1B 60
Hopton. Derbs —5G 85
Hopton. Powy —1E 59
Hopton. Shrp —3F 71 (nr. Oswestry)
Hopton. Shrp —3H 71 (nr. Wem)
Hopton. Staf —3D 72
Hopton. Suff —3B 66
Hopton Cangeford. Shrp —2H 59
Hopton Castle. Shrp —3F 59
Hoptonheath. Shrp —3F 59
Hopton Heath. Staf —3D 72
Hopton on Sea. Norf —5H 79
Hopton Wafers. Shrp —3A 60
Hopwas. Staf —5F 73
Hopwood. Worc —3E 61
Horam. E Sus —4G 27
Horbling. Linc —2A 76
Horbury. W Yor —3C 92
Horcott. Glos —5G 49
Horden. Dur —5H 115
Horderley. Shrp —2G 59
Hordle. Hants —3A 16
Hordley. Shrp —2F 71
Horeb. Carm —3F 45 (nr. Brechfa)
Horeb. Carm —5E 45 (nr. Llanelli)
Horeb. Cdgn —1D 45
Horfield. Bris —4B 34
Horgabost. W Isl —8C 171
Horham. Suff —3E 66
Horkesley Heath. Essx —3C 54
Horkstow. N Lin —3C 94
Horley. Oxon —1C 50
Horley. Surr —1D 27
Hornblotton Green. Som —3A 22
Hornby. Lanc —3E 97
Hornby. N Yor —4A 106 (nr. Appleton Wiske)
Hornby. N Yor —5F 105 (nr. Catterick Garrison)
Horncastle. Linc —4B 88
Hornchurch. G Lon —2G 39
Horncliffe. Nmbd —5F 131
Horndean. Hants —1E 17
Horndean. Bord —5E 131
Horndon. Devn —4F 11
Horndon on the Hill. Thur —2A 40
Horne. Surr —1E 27
Horner. Som —2C 20
Horning. Norf —4F 79
Horninghold. Leics —1F 63
Horninglow. Staf —3G 73
Horningsea. Cambs —4D 65
Horningsham. Wilts —2D 22
Horningtoft. Norf —3B 78
Hornsby. Cumb —4G 113
Hornsbygate. Cumb —4G 113
Horns Corner. Kent —3B 28
Horns Cross. Devn —4D 19
Hornsea. E Yor —5G 101
Hornsea Burton. E Yor —5G 101
Hornsea Pottery Centre —5G 101
Hornsey. G Lon —2E 39
Hornton. Oxon —1B 50
Horpit. Swin —3H 35
Horrabridge. Devn —2B 8
Horringer. Suff —4H 65
Horringford. IOW —4D 16
Horrocks Fold. G Man —3F 91
Horrocksford. Lanc —5G 97
Horsbrugh Ford. Bord —1F 119
Horsebridge. Devn —5E 11
Horsebridge. Hants —3B 24
Horse Bridge. Staf —5D 84
Horsebrook. Staf —4C 72
Horsecastle. N Som —5H 33
Horsehay. Telf —5A 72
Horseheath. Cambs —1G 53
Horsehouse. N Yor —1C 98
Horsell. Surr —5A 38
Horseman's Green. Wrex —1G 71
Horsenden. Buck —5F 51
Horseway. Cambs —2D 64
Horsey. Norf —3G 79
Horsey. Som —3G 21
Horsford. Norf —4D 78
Horsforth. W Yor —1C 92
Horsham. W Sus —2C 26
Horsham. Worc —5B 60
Horsham St Faith. Norf —4E 78
Horsington. Linc —4A 88
Horsington. Som —4C 22
Horsley. Derbs —1A 74
Horsley. Glos —2D 34
Horsley. Nmbd —3D 115 (nr. Prudhoe)
Horsley. Nmbd —5C 120 (nr. Rochester)
Horsley Cross. Essx —3E 54
Horsleycross Street. Essx —3E 54
Horsleyhill. Bord —3H 119
Horsleyhope. Dur —5D 114
Horsley Woodhouse. Derbs —1A 74
Horsmonden. Kent —1A 28
Horspath. Oxon —5D 50
Horstead. Norf —4E 79
Horsted Keynes. W Sus —3E 27
Horton. Buck —4H 51
Horton. Dors —2F 15
Horton. Lanc —4A 98
Horton. Nptn —5F 63
Horton. Shrp —2G 71
Horton. Som —1G 13
Horton. S Glo —3C 34
Horton. Staf —5D 84
Horton. Swan —4D 30
Horton. Wilts —5F 35
Horton. Wind —3B 38
Horton Cross. Som —1G 13
Horton-cum-Studley. Oxon —4D 50
Horton Grange. Nmbd —2F 115
Horton Green. Ches —1G 71
Horton Heath. Hants —1C 16
Horton in Ribblesdale. N Yor —2H 97
Horton Kirby. Kent —4G 39
Hortonwood. Telf —4A 72
Horwich. G Man —3E 91
Horwich End. Derbs —2E 85
Horwood. Devn —4F 19
Hoscar. Lanc —3C 90
Hose. Leics —3E 75
Hosh. Per —1A 136
Hosta. W Isl —1C 170
Hoswick. Shet —9F 173
Hotham. E Yor —1B 94
Hothfield. Kent —1D 28
Hoton. Leics —3C 74
Houbie. Shet —2H 173
Hough. Arg —4A 138
Hough. Ches —5B 84 (nr. Crewe)
Hough. Ches —3C 84 (nr. Wilmslow)
Hougham. Linc —1F 75
Hough Green. Hal —2G 83
Hough-on-the-Hill. Linc —1G 75
Houghton. Cambs —3B 64
Houghton. Cumb —4F 113
Houghton. Hants —3B 24
Houghton. Nmbd —3E 115
Houghton. Pemb —4D 43
Houghton. W Sus —4B 26
Houghton Bank. Darl —2F 105
Houghton Conquest. Beds —1A 52
Houghton Court —3C 34
Houghton Green. E Sus —3D 28
Houghton Hall —3G 77
Houghton House EH —2A 52
Houghton-le-Side. Darl —2F 105
Houghton-le-Spring. Tyne —5G 115
Houghton on the Hill. Leics —5D 74
Houghton Regis. Beds —3A 52
Houghton St Giles. Norf —2B 78
Houlland. Shet —6E 173 (on Mainland)
Houlland. Shet —4G 173 (on Yell)
Houlsyke. N Yor —4E 107
Hound. Hants —2C 16
Hound Green. Hants —1F 25
Houndslow. Bord —5C 130
Houndsmoor. Som —4E 21
Houndwood. Bord —3E 131
Hounsdown. Hants —1B 16
Hounslow. G Lon —3C 38
Housabister. Shet —6F 173
Housay. Shet —4H 173
Househill. High —3C 158
House of Dun NTS —2F 145
House of the Binns NTS —2D 128
Houses of Parliament —London 193
Housesteads Roman Fort WH EH —3A 114
Housetter. Shet —3E 173
Houss. Shet —8E 173
Houston. Ren —3F 127
Housty. High —5D 168
Houton. Orkn —7C 172
Hove. Brig —5D 27 & 186
Hoveringham. Notts —1E 74
Hoveton. Norf —4F 79
Hoveton Hall Gdns. —3F 79
Hovingham. N Yor —2A 100
Hovingham Hall —2A 100
How. Cumb —4G 113
How Caple. Here —2B 48
Howden. E Yor —2H 93
Howden-le-Wear. Dur —1E 105
Howe. High —2F 169
Howe. Norf —5E 79
Howe. N Yor —1F 99
Howe Green. Essx —5H 53 (nr. Chelmsford)
Howegreen. Essx —5B 54 (nr. Maldon)
Howell. Linc —1A 76
How End. Beds —1A 52
Howe of Teuchar. Abers —4E 161
Howes. Dum —3C 112
Howe Street. Essx —4G 53 (nr. Chelmsford)
Howe Street. Essx —2G 53 (nr. Finchingfield)
Howe, The. Cumb —1D 96
Howe, The. IOM —5A 108
Howey. Powy —5C 58
Howgate. Midl —4F 129
Howgill. Lanc —5H 97
Howgill. N Yor —4C 98
How Green. Kent —1F 27
How Green. Warw —2H 61
How Hill. Norf —4F 79
Howick. Nmbd —3G 121
Howick Hall Gdns. —3G 121
Howle. Telf —3A 72
Howle Hill. Here —3B 48
Howleigh. Som —1F 13
Howlett End. Essx —2F 53
Howletts Zoo —5F 41
Howley. Som —2F 13
Howley. Warr —2A 84
Hownam. Bord —3B 120
Howsham. N Lin —4D 94
Howsham. N Yor —3B 100
Howtel. Nmbd —1C 120
Howt Green. Kent —4C 40
Howton. Here —3H 47
Howwood. Ren —3E 127
Hoxne. Suff —3D 66
Hoylake. Mers —2E 82
Hoyland. S Yor —4D 92
Hoylandswaine. S Yor —4C 92
Hoyle. W Sus —4A 26
Hubberholme. N Yor —2B 98
Hubberston. Pemb —4C 42
Hubbert's Bridge. Linc —1B 76
Huby. N Yor —5E 99 (nr. Harrogate)
Huby. N Yor —3H 99 (nr. York)
Huccaby. Devn —5G 11
Hucclecote. Glos —4D 48
Hucking. Kent —5C 40
Hucknall. Notts —1C 74
Huddersfield. W Yor —3B 92
Huddington. Worc —5D 60
Huddlesford. Staf —5F 73
Hudswell. N Yor —4E 105
Huggate. E Yor —4C 100
Hugglescote. Leics —4B 74
Hughenden Manor NT —2G 37
Hughenden Valley. Buck —2G 37
Hughley. Shrp —1H 59
Hughton. High —4G 157
Hugh Town. IOS —1B 4
Hugus. Corn —4B 6
Huish. Wilts —5G 35
Huish Champflower. Som —4D 20
Huish Episcopi. Som —4H 21
Huisinis. W Isl —6B 171
Hulcote. Nptn —1F 51
Hulcott. Buck —4G 51
Hulham. Devn —4D 12
Hull. Hull —2D 94 & 190
Hulland. Derbs —1G 73
Hulland Moss. Derbs —1G 73
Hulland Ward. Derbs —1G 73
Hullavington. Wilts —3D 35
Hullbridge. Essx —1C 40
Hulme. G Man —1C 84
Hulme. Staf —1D 72
Hulme End. Staf —5F 85
Hulme Walfield. Ches —4C 84
Hulverstone. IOW —4B 16
Hulver Street. Suff —2G 67
Humber. Devn —5C 12
Humber Bridge. N Lin —2D 94
Humber Court. Here —5H 59
Humberside Airport. N Lin —3D 94
Humberston. NE Lin —4G 95
Humberstone. Leic —5D 74
Humbie. E Lot —3A 130
Humbleton. E Yor —1F 95
Humbleton. Nmbd —2D 121
Humby. Linc —2H 75
Hume. Bord —5D 130
Humshaugh. Nmbd —2C 114
Huna. High —1F 169
Huncoat. Lanc —1F 91
Huncote. Leics —1C 62
Hundall. Derbs —3A 86
Hunderthwaite. Dur —2C 104
Hundleby. Linc —4C 88
Hundle Houses. Linc —5B 88
Hundleton. Pemb —4D 42
Hundon. Suff —1H 53
Hundred Acres. Hants —1D 16
Hundred House. Powy —5D 58
Hundred, The. Here —4H 59
Hungarton. Leics —5D 74
Hungerford. Hants —1G 15
Hungerford. Shrp —2H 59
Hungerford. Som —2D 20
Hungerford. W Ber —5B 36
Hungerford Newtown. W Ber —4B 36
Hunger Hill. G Man —4E 91
Hungerton. Linc —2F 75
Hungladder. High —1C 154
Hungryhatton. Shrp —3A 72
Hunmanby. N Yor —2E 101
Hunmanby Sands. N Yor —2F 101
Hunningham. Warw —4A 62
Hunnington. W Mid —2D 60
Hunny Hill. IOW —4C 16
Hunsdon. Herts —4E 53
Hunsingore. N Yor —4G 99
Hunslet. W Yor —1D 92
Hunslet Carr. W Yor —2D 92
Hunsonby. Cumb —1G 103
Hunspow. High —1E 169
Hunstanton. Norf —1F 77
Hunstanworth. Dur —5C 114
Hunston. Suff —4B 66
Hunston. W Sus —2G 17
Hunstrete. Bath —5B 34
Hunterian Mus. —Glasgow 189
Hunt End. Worc —4E 61
Hunterfield. Midl —3G 129
Hunters Forstal. Kent —4F 41
Hunter's Quay. Arg —2C 126
Huntham. Som —4G 21
Hunthill Lodge. Ang —1D 144
Huntingdon. Cambs —3B 64
Huntingfield. Suff —3F 67
Huntingford. Wilts —3D 22
Huntington. Ches —4G 83
Huntington. E Lot —2A 130
Huntington. Here —5E 59
Huntington. Staf —4D 72
Huntington. Telf —5A 72
Huntington. York —4A 100
Huntingtower. Per —1C 136
Huntingtower Castle HS —1C 136
Huntley. Glos —4C 48
Huntley. Staf —1E 73
Huntley Castle HS —4C 160
Huntly. Abers —4C 160
Huntlywood. Bord —5C 130
Hunton. Hants —3C 24
Hunton. Kent —1B 28
Hunton. N Yor —5E 105
Hunton Bridge. Herts —5A 52
Hunt's Corner. Norf —2C 66
Huntscott. Som —2C 20
Hunt's Cross. Mers —2G 83
Hunts Green. Warw —1F 61
Huntsham. Devn —4D 20
Huntshaw. Devn —4F 19
Huntspill. Som —2G 21
Huntstile. Som —3F 21
Huntstrete. Bath —5B 34
Huntworth. Som —3G 21
Hunwick. Dur —1E 105
Hunworth. Norf —2C 78
Hurcott. Som —1G 13 (nr. Ilminster)
Hurcott. Som —4A 22 (nr. Somerton)
Hurdcott. Wilts —3G 23
Hurdley. Powy —1E 59
Hurdsfield. Ches —3D 84
Hurlet. Glas —3G 127
Hurley. Warw —1G 61
Hurley. Wind —3G 37
Hurlford. E Ayr —1D 116
Hurlston Green. Lanc —3B 90
Hurn. Dors —3G 15
Hursey. Dors —2H 13
Hursley. Hants —4C 24
Hurst. G Man —4H 91
Hurst. N Yor —4D 104
Hurst. Wok —4F 37
Hurstbourne Priors. Hants —2C 24
Hurstbourne Tarrant. Hants —1B 24
Hurst Castle EH —4B 16
Hurst Green. Ches —1H 71
Hurst Green. E Sus —3B 28
Hurst Green. Essx —4D 54
Hurst Green. Lanc —1E 91
Hurst Green. Surr —5E 39
Hurstley. Here —1G 47
Hurstpierpoint. W Sus —4D 27
Hurstway Common. Here —1F 47
Hurst Wickham. W Sus —4D 27
Hurstwood. Lanc —1G 91
Hurtmore. Surr —1A 26
Hurworth-on-Tees. Darl —3A 106
Hurworth Place. Darl —3F 105
Hury. Dur —3C 104
Husbands Bosworth. Leics —2D 62
Husborne Crawley. Beds —2H 51
Husthwaite. N Yor —2H 99
Hutcherleigh. Devn —3D 9
Hut Green. N Yor —2F 93
Huthwaite. Notts —5B 86
Huttoft. Linc —3E 89
Hutton. Cumb —2F 103
Hutton. Essx —1H 39
Hutton. Lanc —2C 90
Hutton. N Som —1G 21
Hutton. Bord —4F 131
Hutton Bonville. N Yor —4A 106
Hutton Buscel. N Yor —1D 100
Hutton Conyers. N Yor —2F 99
Hutton Cranswick. E Yor —4E 101
Hutton End. Cumb —1F 103
Hutton Gate. Red C —3C 106
Hutton Henry. Dur —1B 106
Hutton-in-the-Forest —1F 103
Hutton-le-Hole. N Yor —1B 100
Hutton Magna. Dur —3E 105
Hutton Mulgrave. N Yor —3F 107
Hutton Roof. Cumb —2E 97 (nr. Kirkby Lonsdale)
Hutton Roof. Cumb —1E 103 (nr. Penrith)
Hutton Rudby. N Yor —4B 106
Huttons Ambo. N Yor —3B 100
Hutton Sessay. N Yor —2G 99
Hutton Village. Red C —3D 106
Hutton Wandesley. N Yor —4H 99
Huxham. Devn —3C 12
Huxham Green. Som —3A 22
Huxley. Ches —4H 83
Huxter. Shet —6C 173 (on Mainland)
Huxter. Shet —5G 173 (on Whalsay)
Huyton. Mers —1G 83
Hwlffordd. Pemb —3D 42
Hycemoor. Cumb —1A 96
Hyde. Glos —5D 49 (nr. Stroud)
Hyde. Glos —3F 49 (nr. Winchcombe)
Hyde. G Man —1D 84
Hyde Hall Gdn. RHS —1B 40
Hyde Heath. Buck —5H 51
Hyde Lea. Staf —3D 72
Hyde Park. S Yor —4F 93
Hydestile. Surr —1A 26
Hylands House & Gdn. —5G 53
Hyndford Bridge. S Lan —5C 128
Hynish. Arg —5A 138
Hyssington. Powy —1F 59
Hythe. Hants —2C 16
Hythe. Kent —2F 29
Hythe End. Wind —3B 38
Hythie. Abers —3H 161
Hyton. Cumb —1A 96

Ianstown. Mor —2B 160
Iarsiadar. W Isl —4D 171
Ibberton. Dors —2C 14
Ible. Derbs —5G 85
Ibrox. Glas —3G 127
Ibsley. Hants —2G 15
Ibstock. Leics —4B 74
Ibstone. Buck —2F 37
Ibthorpe. Hants —1B 24
Iburndale. N Yor —4F 107
Ibworth. Hants —1D 24
Icelton. N Som —5G 33
Iceni Village & Mus. —5G 77
Ichrachan. Arg —5E 141
Ickburgh. Norf —1H 65
Ickenham. G Lon —2B 38
Ickford. Buck —5E 51
Ickham. Kent —5G 41
Ickleford. Herts —2B 52
Icklesham. E Sus —4C 28
Ickleton. Cambs —1E 53
Icklingham. Suff —3G 65
Ickwell. Beds —1B 52
Ickworth NT —4H 65
Icomb. Glos —3H 49
Idbury. Oxon —4H 49
Iddesleigh. Devn —2F 11
Ide. Devn —3C 12
Ideford. Devn —5B 12
Ide Hill. Kent —5F 39
Iden. E Sus —3D 28
Iden Green. Kent —2C 28 (nr. Benenden)
Iden Green. Kent —2B 28 (nr. Goudhurst)
Idle. W Yor —1B 92
Idless. Corn —4C 6
Idlicote. Warw —1A 50
Idmiston. Wilts —3G 23
Idole. Carm —4E 45
Idridgehay. Derbs —1G 73
Idrigill. High —2C 154
Idstone. Oxon —3A 36
Iffley. Oxon —5D 50
Ifield. W Sus —2D 26
Ifieldwood. W Sus —2D 26
Ifold. W Sus —2B 26
Iford. E Sus —5F 27
Ifton Heath. Shrp —2F 71
Ightfield. Shrp —2H 71
Ightham. Kent —5G 39
Ightham Mote NT —5G 39
Iken. Suff —5G 67
Ilam. Staf —5F 85
Ilam Park Estate NT —5F 85
Ilchester. Som —4A 22
Ilderton. Nmbd —2E 121
Ilford. G Lon —2F 39
Ilford. Som —1G 13
Ilford Manor Gdn. —1D 22
Ilfracombe. Devn —2F 19
Ilkeston. Derbs —1B 74
Ilketshall St Andrew. Suff —2F 67
Ilketshall St Lawrence. Suff —2F 67
Ilketshall St Margaret. Suff —2F 67
Ilkley. W Yor —5D 98
Illand. Corn —5C 10
Illey. W Mid —2D 61
Illidge Green. Ches —4B 84

Illington. Norf —2B 66
Illingworth. W Yor —2A 92
Illogan. Corn —4A 6
Illogan Highway. Corn —4A 6
Illston on the Hill. Leics —1E 62
Ilmer. Buck —5F 51
Ilmington. Warw —1H 49
Ilminster. Som —1G 13
Ilsington. Devn —5A 12
Ilsington. Dors —3C 14
Ilston. Swan —3E 31
Ilton. N Yor —2D 98
Ilton. Som —1G 13
Imachar. N Ayr —5G 125
Imber. Wilts —2E 23
Immingham. NE Lin —3E 95
Immingham Dock. NE Lin —3E 95
Imperial War Mus. —London 193
Imperial War Mus. Duxford Airfield —1E 53
Imperial War Mus. of the North —Manchester 191
Impington. Cambs —4D 64
Ince. Ches —3G 83
Ince Blundell. Mers —4B 90
Ince-in-Makerfield. G Man —4D 90
Inchbae Lodge. High —2G 157
Inchbare. Ang —2F 145
Inchberry. Mor —3H 159
Inchbraoch. Ang —3G 145
Inchbrook. Glos —5D 48
Inchcolm Abbey —1E 129
Incheril. High —2C 156
Inchinnan. Ren —3F 127
Inchlaggan. High —3D 148
Inchmahome Priory HS —3E 135
Inchmichael. Per —1E 137
Inchnadamph. High —1G 163
Inchree. High —2E 141
Inchture. Per —1E 137
Inchyra. Per —1D 136
Indian Queens. Corn —3D 6
Ingatestone. Essx —1H 39
Ingatestone Hall —1A 40
Ingbirchworth. S Yor —4C 92
Ingestre. Staf —3D 73
Ingham. Linc —2G 87
Ingham. Norf —3F 79
Ingham. Suff —3A 66
Ingham Corner. Norf —3F 79
Ingleborough. Norf —4D 76
Ingleby. Derbs —3H 73
Ingleby Arncliffe. N Yor —4B 106
Ingleby Barwick. Stoc T —3B 106
Ingleby Greenhow. N Yor —4C 106
Ingleigh Green. Devn —2G 11
Inglemire. Hull —1D 94
Inglesbatch. Bath —5C 34
Ingleton. Dur —2E 105
Ingleton. N Yor —2F 97
Inglewhite. Lanc —5E 97
Ingoe. Nmbd —2D 114
Ingol. Lanc —1D 90
Ingoldisthorpe. Norf —2F 77
Ingoldmells. Linc —4E 89
Ingoldsby. Linc —2H 75
Ingon. Warw —5G 61
Ingram. Nmbd —3E 121
Ingrave. Essx —1H 39
Ingrow. W Yor —1A 92
Ings. Cumb —5F 103
Ingst. S Glo —3A 34
Ingthorpe. Rut —5G 75
Ingworth. Norf —3D 78
Inkberrow. Worc —5E 61
Inkford. Worc —3E 61
Inkpen. W Ber —5B 36
Inkstack. High —1E 169
Innellan. Arg —3C 126
Inner Hope. Devn —5C 8
Innerleith. Fife —2E 137
Innerleithen. Bord —1F 119
Innerleven. Fife —3F 137
Innermessan. Dum —3F 109
Innerwick. E Lot —2D 130
Innerwick. Per —4C 142
Innsworth. Glos —3D 48
Insch. Abers —1D 152
Insh. High —3C 150
Inshegra. High —3C 166
Inshore. High —1D 166
Inskip. Lanc —1C 90
Instow. Devn —3E 19
Intwood. Norf —5D 78
Inver. Abers —4G 151
Inver. High —5F 165
Inver. Per —4H 143
Inverailort. High —5F 147
Inveralligin. High —3H 155
Inverallochy. Abers —2H 161
Inveramsay. Abers —1E 153
Inveran. High —4C 164
Inveraray. Arg —3H 133
Inveraray Castle —3H 133
Inverarish. High —5E 155
Inverarity. Ang —4D 144
Inverarnan. Arg —2C 134
Inverarnie. High —5A 158
Inverbeg. Arg —4C 134
Inverbervie. Abers —1H 145
Inverboyndie. Abers —2D 160
Invercassley. High —3B 164
Invercharnan. High —4F 141
Inverchoran. High —3E 157
Invercreran. Arg —4E 141
Inverdruie. High —2D 150
Inverebrie. Abers —5G 161
Invereck. Arg —1C 126
Inveresk. E Lot —2G 129
Inveresragan. Arg —5D 141
Inverewe Gdn. NTS —5C 162
Inverey. Abers —5E 151
Inverfarigaig. High —1H 149
Invergarry. High —3F 149
Invergeldie. Per —1G 135
Invergordon. High —2B 158
Invergowrie. Per —5C 144
Inverguseran. High —3F 147
Inverharroch. Mor —5A 160
Inverie. High —3F 147
Inverinan. Arg —2G 133
Inverinate. High —1B 148
Inverkeilor. Ang —4F 145
Inverkeithing. Fife —1E 129
Inverkeithny. Abers —4D 160
Inverkip. Inv —2D 126
Inverkirkaig. High —2E 163
Inverlael. High —5F 163
Inverliever Lodge. Arg —3F 133
Inverliver. Arg —5E 141
Inverloch. High —1F 141
Inverlochlarig. Stir —2D 134
Inverlussa. Arg —1E 125
Inver Mallie. High —5D 148
Invermarkie. Abers —5B 160
Invermoriston. High —2G 149
Invernaver. High —2H 167
Inverneil House. Arg —1G 125
Inverness. High —4A 158 & 190
Inverness Airport. High —3B 158
Inverness Mus. & Art Gallery —190
Invernettie. Abers —4H 161
Inverpolly Lodge. High —2E 163
Inverquhomery. Abers —4H 161
Inverroy. High —5E 149
Inversanda. High —3D 140
Invershiel. High —2B 148
Invershin. High —4C 164
Invershore. High —5E 169
Inversnaid. Stir —3C 134
Inverugie. Abers —4H 161
Inveruglas. Arg —3C 134
Inverurie. Abers —1E 153
Invervar. Per —4D 142
Inverythan. Abers —4E 160
Inwardleigh. Devn —3F 11
Inworth. Essx —4B 54
Iochdar. W Isl —4C 170
Iona NTS —2A 132
Iping. W Sus —4G 25
Ipplepen. Devn —2E 9
Ipsden. Oxon —3E 37
Ipstones. Staf —1E 73
Ipswich. Suff —1E 55 & 190
Irby. Mers —2E 83
Irby in the Marsh. Linc —4D 88
Irby upon Humber. NE Lin —4E 95
Irchester. Nptn —4G 63
Ireby. Cumb —1D 102
Ireby. Lanc —2F 97
Ireland. Shet —9E 173
Ireleth. Cumb —2B 96
Ireshopeburn. Dur —1B 104
Ireton Wood. Derbs —1G 73
Irlam. G Man —1B 84
Irnham. Linc —3H 75
Iron Acton. S Glo —3B 34
Iron Bridge. Cambs —1D 65
Ironbridge. Telf —5A 72
Ironbridge Gorge WH —5A 72
Ironbridge Museums —5A 72
Iron Bridge, The —5A 72
Iron Cross. Warw —5E 61
Ironville. Derbs —5B 86
Irstead. Norf —3F 79
Irthington. Cumb —3F 113
Irthlingborough. Nptn —3G 63
Irton. N Yor —1E 101
Irvine. N Ayr —1C 116
Irvine Mains. N Ayr —1C 116
Isabella Pit. Nmbd —1G 115
Isauld. High —2B 168
Isbister. Orkn —6D 172
Isbister. Shet —2E 173 (on Mainland)
Isbister. Shet —5G 173 (on Whalsay)
Isel Hall —1C 102
Isfield. E Sus —4F 27
Isham. Nptn —3F 63
Island Carr. N Lin —4C 94
Islay Airport. Arg —4B 124
Isle Abbotts. Som —4G 21
Isle Brewers. Som —4G 21
Isleham. Cambs —3F 65
Isle of Man Airport. IOM —5B 108
Isle of Man Railway —4C 108
Isle of Thanet. Kent —4H 41
Isle of Whithorn. Dum —5B 110
Isle of Wight Railway —4D 16
Isleornsay. High —2F 147
Islesburgh. Shet —5E 173
Islesteps. Dum —2A 112
Isleworth. G Lon —3C 38
Isley Walton. Leics —3B 74
Islibhig. W Isl —5B 171
Islington. G Lon —2E 39
Islington. Telf —3B 72
Islip. Nptn —3G 63
Islip. Oxon —4D 50
Islwyn. Cphy —2F 33
Istead Rise. Kent —4H 39
Itchen. Sotn —1C 16
Itchen Abbas. Hants —3D 24
Itchen Stoke. Hants —3D 24
Itchingfield. W Sus —3C 26
Itchington. S Glo —3B 34
Itlaw. Abers —3D 160
Itteringham. Norf —2D 78
Itteringham Common. Norf —3D 78
Itton. Devn —3G 11
Itton Common. Mon —2H 33
Ivegill. Cumb —5F 113
Ivelet. N Yor —5C 104
Iverchaolain. Arg —2B 126
Iver Heath. Buck —2B 38
Iveston. Dur —4E 115
Ivetsey Bank. Staf —4C 72
Ivinghoe. Buck —4H 51
Ivinghoe Aston. Buck —4H 51
Ivinghoe Beacon NT —4H 51
Ivington. Here —5G 59
Ivington Green. Here —5G 59
Ivybridge. Devn —3C 8
Ivychurch. Kent —3E 29
Ivy Hatch. Kent —5G 39
Ivy Todd. Norf —5A 78
Iwade. Kent —4D 40
Iwerne Courteney. Dors —1D 14
Iwerne Minster. Dors —1D 14
Ixworth. Suff —3B 66
Ixworth Thorpe. Suff —3B 66
Izaak Walton's Cottage —3C 72

Jackfield. Shrp —5A 72
Jack Hill. N Yor —4E 98
Jacksdale. Notts —5B 86
Jackton. S Lan —4G 127
Jacobstow. Corn —3B 10
Jacobstowe. Devn —2F 11
Jacobswell. Surr —5A 38
James Brindley Mus. —5D 85
Jameston. Pemb —5E 43
Jamestown. Dum —5F 119
Jamestown. Fife —1E 129
Jamestown. High —3G 157
Jamestown. W Dun —1E 127
Jane Austen Centre —Bath 186
Jane Austen's House —3F 25
Janetstown. High —2C 168 (nr. Thurso)
Janetstown. High —3F 169 (nr. Wick)
Jarlshof HS —10E 173
Jarrow. Tyne —3G 115
Jarvis Brook. E Sus —3G 27
Jasper's Green. Essx —3H 53
Jaywick. Essx —4E 55
Jedburgh. Bord —2A 120
Jedburgh Abbey HS —3A 120
Jeffreyston. Pemb —4E 43
Jemimaville. High —2B 158
Jenkins Park. High —3F 149
Jersey Marine. Neat —3G 31
Jervaulx Abbey —1D 98
Jesmond. Tyne —3F 115
Jevington. E Sus —5G 27
Jingle Street. Mon —4H 47
Jockey End. Herts —4A 52
Jodrell Bank. Ches —3B 84
Jodrell Bank Science Centre —3B 84
Johnby. Cumb —1F 103
John Milton's Cottage —1A 38
John o' Gaunts. W Yor —2D 92
John o' Groats. High —1F 169
John's Cross. E Sus —3B 28
Johnshaven. Abers —2G 145
Johnson's Street. Norf —4F 79
Johnston. Pemb —3D 42
Johnstone. Ren —3F 127
Johnstonebridge. Dum —5D 118
Johnstown. Carm —4D 45
Johnstown. Wrex —1F 71
Joppa. Edin —2G 129
Joppa. S Ayr —3D 116
Jordan Green. Norf —3C 78
Jordans. Buck —1A 38
Jordanston. Pemb —1D 42
Jorvik Viking Centre —York 197
Jump. S Yor —4D 93
Jumpers Common. Dors —3G 15
Juniper. Nmbd —4C 114
Juniper Green. Edin —3E 129
Jurby East. IOM —2C 108
Jurby West. IOM —2C 108
Jury's Gap. E Sus —4D 28

Kaber. Cumb —3A 104
Kaimend. S Lan —5C 128
Kaimes. Edin —3F 129
Kaimrig End. Bord —5D 129
Kames. Arg —2A 126
Kames. E Ayr —2F 117
Kea. Corn —4C 6
Keadby. N Lin —3B 94
Keal Cotes. Linc —4C 88
Kearsley. G Man —4F 91
Kearsney. Kent —1G 29
Kearstwick. Cumb —1F 97
Kearton. N Yor —5C 104
Kearvaig. High —1C 166
Keasden. N Yor —3G 97
Keason. Corn —2H 7
Keckwick. Hal —2H 83
Keddington. Linc —2C 88
Keddington Corner. Linc —2C 88
Kedington. Suff —1H 53
Kedleston. Derbs —1H 73
Kedleston Hall NT —1H 73
Kedlock Feus. Fife —2F 137
Keelby. Linc —4E 95
Keele. Staf —1C 72
Keeley Green. Beds —1A 52
Keeston. Pemb —3D 42
Keevil. Wilts —1E 23
Kegworth. Leics —3B 74
Kehelland. Corn —2D 4
Keig. Abers —2D 152
Keighley. W Yor —5C 98
Keighley & Worth Valley Railway —1A 92
Keilarsbrae. Clac —4A 136
Keillmore. Arg —1E 125
Keillor. Per —4B 144
Keillour. Per —1B 136
Keills. Arg —3C 124
Keiloch. Abers —4F 151
Keils. Arg —3D 124
Keinton Mandeville. Som —3A 22
Keir Mill. Dum —5A 118
Keirsleywell Row. Nmbd —4A 114
Keisby. Linc —3H 75
Keisley. Cumb —2A 104
Keiss. High —2F 169
Keith. Mor —3B 160
Keith Inch. Abers —4H 161
Kelbrook. Lanc —5B 98
Kelburn Castle —4D 126
Kelby. Linc —1H 75
Keld. Cumb —3G 103
Keld. N Yor —4B 104
Keldholme. N Yor —1B 100
Kelfield. N Lin —4B 94
Kelfield. N Yor —1F 93
Kelham. Notts —5E 87
Kelham Island Industrial Mus. —Sheffield 196
Kellacott. Devn —4E 11
Kellan. Arg —4G 139
Kellas. Ang —5D 144
Kellas. Mor —3F 159
Kellaton. Devn —5E 9
Kelleth. Cumb —4H 103
Kellie Castle NTS —3H 137
Kelling. Norf —1C 78
Kellingley. N Yor —2F 93
Kellington. N Yor —2F 93
Kelloe. Dur —1A 106
Kelloholm. Dum —3G 117
Kells. Cumb —3A 102
Kelly. Devn —4D 11
Kelly Bray. Corn —5D 10
Kelmarsh. Nptn —3E 63
Kelmarsh Hall —3E 63
Kelmscott. Oxon —2H 35
Kelmscott Manor —2A 36
Kelsale. Suff —4F 67
Kelsall. Ches —4H 83
Kelshall. Herts —2D 52
Kelsick. Cumb —4C 112
Kelso. Bord —1B 120
Kelstedge. Derbs —4H 85
Kelstern. Linc —1B 88
Kelsterton. Flin —3E 83
Kelston. Bath —5C 34
Keltneyburn. Per —4E 143
Kelton. Dum —2A 112
Kelton Hill. Dum —4E 111
Kelty. Fife —4D 136
Kelvedon. Essx —4B 54
Kelvedon Hatch. Essx —1G 39
Kelvingrove Museums —Glasgow 189
Kelvinside. Glas —3G 127
Kelynack. Corn —3A 4
Kemback. Fife —2G 137
Kemberton. Shrp —5B 72
Kemble. Glos —2E 35
Kemerton. Worc —2E 49
Kemeys Commander. Mon —5G 47
Kemnay. Abers —2E 153
Kempley. Glos —3B 48
Kempley Green. Glos —3B 48
Kempsey. Worc —1D 48
Kempsford. Glos —2G 35
Kemps Green. Warw —3F 61
Kempshott. Hants —1E 24
Kempston. Beds —1A 52
Kempston Hardwick. Beds —1A 52
Kempton. Shrp —2F 59
Kemp Town. Brig —5E 27
Kemsing. Kent —5G 39
Kemsley. Kent —4D 40
Kenardington. Kent —2D 28
Kenchester. Here —1H 47
Kencot. Oxon —5A 50
Kendal. Cumb —5G 103
Kendal Castle —5G 103
Kendleshire. S Glo —4B 34
Kendray. S Yor —4D 92
Kenfig. B'end —3B 32
Kenfig Hill. B'end —3B 32
Kengharair. Arg —4F 139
Kenidjack. Corn —3A 4
Kenilworth. Warw —3G 61
Kenilworth Castle EH —3G 61
Kenknock. Stir —5B 142
Kenley. G Lon —5E 39
Kenley. Shrp —5H 71
Kenmore. High —3G 155
Kenmore. Per —4E 143
Kenn. Devn —4C 12
Kenn. N Som —5H 33
Kennacraig. Arg —3G 125
Kenneggy Downs. Corn —4C 4
Kennerleigh. Devn —2B 12
Kennet. Clac —4B 136
Kennethmont. Abers —1C 152
Kennett. Cambs —4F 65
Kennford. Devn —4C 12
Kenninghall. Norf —2C 66
Kennington. Kent —1E 29
Kennington. Oxon —5D 50
Kennoway. Fife —3F 137
Kennyhill. Suff —3F 65
Kennythorpe. N Yor —3B 100
Kenovay. Arg —4A 138
Kensaleyre. High —3D 154
Kensington. G Lon —3D 38
Kenstone. Shrp —3H 71
Kensworth. Beds —4A 52
Kensworth Common. Beds —4A 52
Kentallen. High —3E 141
Kent & East Sussex Railway —3C 28
Kentchurch. Here —3H 47
Kentford. Suff —4G 65
Kentisbeare. Devn —2D 12
Kentisbury. Devn —2G 19
Kentisbury Ford. Devn —2G 19
Kentmere. Cumb —4F 103
Kenton. Devn —4C 12
Kenton. G Lon —2C 38
Kenton. Suff —4D 66
Kenton Bankfoot. Tyne —3F 115
Kentra. High —2A 140
Kentrigg. Cumb —5G 103
Kents Bank. Cumb —2C 96
Kent's Green. Glos —3C 48
Kent's Oak. Hants —4B 24
Kent Street. E Sus —4B 28
Kent Street. Kent —5A 40
Kent Street. W Sus —3D 26
Kentwell Hall —1B 54
Kenwick. Shrp —2G 71
Kenwood EH —2D 38
Kenwyn. Corn —4C 6
Kenyon. Warr —1A 84
Keoldale. High —2D 166
Keppoch. High —1B 148
Kepwick. N Yor —5B 106
Keresley. W Mid —2H 61
Keresley Newlands. Warw —2H 61
Keristal. IOM —4C 108
Kerne Bridge. Here —4A 48
Kerridge. Ches —3D 84
Kerris. Corn —4B 4
Kerrow. High —5F 157
Kerry. Powy —2D 58
Kerrycroy. Arg —3C 126
Kerry's Gate. Here —2G 47
Kersall. Notts —4E 86
Kersbrook. Devn —4D 12
Kerse. Ren —4E 127
Kersey. Suff —1D 54
Kershopefoot. Cumb —1F 113
Kersoe. Worc —2E 49
Kerswell. Devn —2D 12
Kerswell Green. Worc —1D 48
Kesgrave. Suff —1F 55
Kessingland. Suff —2H 67
Kessingland Beach. Suff —2H 67
Kestle. Corn —4D 6
Kestle Mill. Corn —3C 6
Keston. G Lon —4F 39
Keswick. Cumb —2D 102
Keswick. Norf —2F 79 (nr. North Walsham)
Keswick. Norf —5E 78 (nr. Norwich)
Ketsby. Linc —3C 88
Kettering. Nptn —3F 63
Ketteringham. Norf —5D 78
Kettins. Per —5B 144
Kettlebaston. Suff —5B 66
Kettlebridge. Fife —3F 137
Kettlebrook. Staf —5G 73
Kettleburgh. Suff —4E 67
Kettleholm. Dum —2C 112
Kettleness. N Yor —3F 107
Kettleshulme. Ches —3D 85
Kettlesing. N Yor —4E 99
Kettlesing Bottom. N Yor —4E 99
Kettlestone. Norf —2B 78
Kettlethorpe. Linc —3F 87
Kettletoft. Orkn —4F 172
Kettlewell. N Yor —2B 98
Ketton. Rut —5G 75
Kew. G Lon —3C 38
Kewaigue. IOM —4C 108
Kew Gdns. WH —3C 38
Kewstoke. N Som —5G 33
Kexbrough. S Yor —4D 92
Kexby. Linc —2F 87
Kexby. York —4B 100
Keyford. Som —2C 22
Key Green. Ches —4C 84
Key Green. N Yor —4F 107
Keyham. Leics —5D 74
Keyhaven. Hants —3B 16
Keyhead. Abers —3H 161
Keyingham. E Yor —2F 95
Keymer. W Sus —4E 27
Keynsham. Bath —5B 34
Keysoe. Beds —4H 63
Keysoe Row. Beds —4H 63
Key's Toft. Linc —5D 89
Keyston. Cambs —3H 63
Key Street. Kent —4C 40
Keyworth. Notts —2D 74
Kibblesworth. Tyne —4F 115
Kibworth Beauchamp. Leics —1D 62
Kibworth Harcourt. Leics —1D 62
Kidbrooke. G Lon —3F 39
Kidburngill. Cumb —2B 102
Kiddemore Green. Staf —5C 72
Kidderminster. Worc —3C 60
Kiddington. Oxon —3C 50
Kidd's Moor. Norf —5D 78
Kidlington. Oxon —4C 50
Kidmore End. Oxon —4E 37
Kidnal. Ches —1G 71
Kidsgrove. Staf —5C 84
Kidstones. N Yor —1B 98
Kidwelly. Carm —5E 45
Kidwelly Castle CADW —5E 45
Kiel Crofts. Arg —5D 140
Kielder. Nmbd —5A 120
Kielder Castle Forest Park Centre —5A 120
Kiftsgate Court Gdns. —1G 49
Kilbagie. Fife —4B 136
Kilbarchan. Ren —3F 127
Kilbeg. High —3E 147
Kilberry. Arg —3F 125
Kilbirnie. N Ayr —4E 126
Kilbride. Arg —1F 133
Kilbride. High —1D 147
Kilbucho Place. Bord —1C 118
Kilburn. Derbs —1A 74
Kilburn. G Lon —2D 38
Kilburn. N Yor —2H 99
Kilby. Leics —1D 62
Kilchattan. Arg —4C 126 (on Bute)
Kilchattan. Arg —4A 132 (on Colonsay)
Kilchattan Bay. Arg —4B 126
Kilchenzie. Arg —3A 122
Kilcheran. Arg —5C 140
Kilchiaran. Arg —4A 124
Kilchoan. High —4F 147 (nr. Inverie)
Kilchoan. High —2F 139 (nr. Tobermory)
Kilchoman. Arg —3A 124
Kilchrenan. Arg —1H 133
Kilchurn Castle HS —1A 134
Kilconquhar. Fife —3G 137
Kilcot. Glos —3B 48
Kilcoy. High —3H 157
Kilcreggan. Arg —1D 126

Kildale. N Yor —4D 106
Kildary. High —1B 158
Kildermorie Lodge. High —1H 157
Kildonan. Dum —4F 109
Kildonan. High —1G 165
(nr. Helmsdale)
Kildonan. High —3C 154
(on Skye)
Kildonan. N Ayr —3E 123
Kildonnan. High —5C 146
Kildrummy. Abers —2B 152
Kildrummy Castle HS —2B 152
Kildwick. N Yor —5C 98
Kilfillan. Dum —4H 109
Kilfinan. Arg —2H 125
Kilfinnan. High —4E 149
Kilgetty. Pemb —4F 43
Kilgour. Fife —3E 136
Kilgrammie. S Ayr —4B 116
Kilham. E Yor —3E 101
Kilham. Nmbd —1C 120
Kilkenneth. Arg —4A 138
Kilkhampton. Corn —1C 10
Killamarsh. Derbs —2B 86
Killandrist. Arg —4C 140
Killay. Swan —3F 31
Killean. Arg —5E 125
Killearn. Stir —1G 127
Killellan. Arg —4A 122
Killen. High —3A 158
Killerby. Darl —3E 105
Killerton House NT —2C 12
Killichonan. Per —3C 142
Killiechronan. Arg —4G 139
Killiecrankie. Per —2G 143
Killilan. High —5B 156
Killimster. High —3F 169
Killin. Stir —5C 142
Killinghall. N Yor —4E 99
Killinghurst. Surr —2A 26
Killington. Cumb —1F 97
Killingworth. Tyne —2F 115
Killin Lodge. High —3H 149
Killinochonoch. Arg —4F 133
Killochyett. Bord —5A 130
Killundine. High —3G 139
Kilmacolm. Inv —3E 127
Kilmahog. Stir —3F 135
Kilmahumaig. Arg —4E 133
Kilmalieu. High —3C 140
Kilmaluag. High —1D 154
Kilmany. Fife —1F 137
Kilmarie. High —2D 146
Kilmarnock. E Ayr —1D 116 & 190
Kilmaron. Fife —2F 137
Kilmartin. Arg —4F 133
Kilmaurs. E Ayr —5F 127
Kilmelford. Arg —2F 133
Kilmeny. Arg —3B 124
Kilmersdon. Som —1B 22
Kilmeston. Hants —4D 24
Kilmichael Glassary. Arg —4F 133
Kilmichael of Inverlussa. Arg —1F 125
Kilmington. Devn —3F 13
Kilmington. Wilts —3C 22
Kilmoluag. Arg —4A 138
Kilmorack. High —4G 157
Kilmore. Arg —1F 133
Kilmore. High —3E 147
Kilmory. Arg —2F 125
Kilmory. High —1G 139
(nr. Kilchoan)
Kilmory. High —3B 146
(on Rhum)
Kilmory. N Ayr —3D 122
Kilmory Lodge. Arg —3E 132
Kilmote. High —2G 165
Kilmuir. High —4B 154
(nr. Dunvegan)
Kilmuir. High —1B 158
(nr. Invergordonn)
Kilmuir. High —4A 158
(nr. Inverness)
Kilmuir. High —1C 154
(nr. Uig)
Kilmun. Arg —1C 126
Kilnave. Arg —2A 124
Kilncadzow. S Lan —5B 128
Kilndown. Kent —2B 28
Kiln Green. Here —4A 48
Kiln Green. Wind —4G 37
Kilnhill. Cumb —1D 102
Kilnhurst. S Yor —1B 86
Kilninian. Arg —4E 139
Kilninver. Arg —1F 133
Kiln Pit Hill. Nmbd —4D 114
Kilnsea. E Yor —3H 95
Kilnsey. N Yor —3B 98
Kilnwick. E Yor —5D 101
Kiloran. Arg —4A 132
Kilpatrick. N Ayr —3D 122
Kilpeck. Here —2H 47
Kilpin. E Yor —2A 94
Kilpin Pike. E Yor —2A 94
Kilrenny. Fife —3H 137
Kilsby. Nptn —3C 62
Kilspindie. Per —1E 136
Kilsyth. N Lan —2A 128
Kiltarlity. High —4H 157
Kilton. Som —2E 21
Kilton Thorpe. Red C —3D 107
Kilvaxter. High —2C 154
Kilve. Som —2E 21
Kilvington. Notts —1F 75
Kilwinning. N Ayr —5D 126
Kimberley. Norf —5C 78
Kimberley. Notts —1B 74
Kimblesworth. Dur —5F 115
Kimble Wick. Buck —5G 51
Kimbolton. Cambs —4H 63
Kimbolton. Here —4H 59
Kimbolton Castle —4H 63
Kimcote. Leics —2C 62
Kimmeridge. Dors —5E 15
Kimmerston. Nmbd —1D 120
Kimpton. Hants —2A 24
Kimpton. Herts —4B 52
Kinbeachie. High —2A 158
Kinbrace. High —5A 168
Kinbuck. Stir —3G 135
Kincaple. Fife —2G 137
Kincardine. Fife —1C 128
Kincardine. High —5D 164
Kincardine O'Neil. Abers —4C 152
Kinchrackine. Arg —1A 134
Kincorth. Aber —3G 153
Kincraig. High —3C 150
Kincraigie. Per —4G 143
Kindallachan. Per —3G 143
Kineton. Glos —3F 49
Kineton. Warw —5H 61
Kinfauns. Per —1D 136
Kingairloch. High —3C 140
Kingarth. Arg —4B 126
Kingcoed. Mon —5H 47
Kingerby. Linc —1H 87
Kingham. Oxon —3A 50
Kingholm Quay. Dum —2A 112
Kinghorn. Fife —1F 129
Kingie. High —3D 148
Kinglassie. Fife —4E 137
Kingledores. Bord —2D 118
Kingodie. Per —1F 137
King o' Muirs. Clac —4A 136
King's Acre. Here —1H 47
Kingsand. Corn —3A 8
Kingsash. Buck —5G 51
Kingsbarns. Fife —2H 137
Kingsbridge. Devn —4D 8
Kingsbridge. Som —3C 20
King's Bromley. Staf —4F 73
Kingsburgh. High —3C 154
Kingsbury. G Lon —2C 38
Kingsbury. Warw —1G 61
Kingsbury Episcopi. Som —4H 21
Kings Caple. Here —3A 48
Kingscavil. W Lot —2D 128
Kingsclere. Hants —1D 24
King's Cliffe. Nptn —1H 63
King's College Chapel —Cambridge 187
Kingscote. Glos —2D 34
Kingscott. Devn —1F 11
Kings Coughton. Warw —5E 61
Kingscross. N Ayr —3E 123
Kingsdon. Som —4A 22
Kingsdown. Kent —1H 29
Kingsdown. Swin —3G 35
Kingsdown. Wilts —5D 34
Kingseat. Fife —4D 136
Kingsey. Buck —5F 51
Kingsfold. Lanc —2D 90
Kingsfold. W Sus —2C 26
Kingsford. E Ayr —5F 127
Kingsford. Worc —2C 60
Kingsforth. N Lin —3D 94
Kingsgate. Kent —3H 41
King's Green. Glos —2C 48
Kingshall Street. Suff —4B 66
King's Heath. W Mid —2E 61
Kings Hill. Kent —5A 40
Kingsholm. Glos —4D 48
Kingshouse. High —3G 141
Kingshouse. Stir —1E 135
Kingshurst. W Mid —2F 61
Kingskerswell. Devn —2E 9
Kingskettle. Fife —3F 137
Kingsland. Here —4G 59
Kingsland. IOA —2B 80
Kings Langley. Herts —5A 52
Kingsley. Ches —3H 83
Kingsley. Hants —3F 25
Kingsley. Staf —1E 73
Kingsley Green. W Sus —3G 25
Kingsley Holt. Staf —1E 73
King's Lynn. Norf —3F 77
King's Meaburn. Cumb —2H 103
Kings Moss. Mers —4D 90
Kingsmuir. Ang —4D 145
Kingsmuir. Fife —3H 137
Kings Muir. Bord —1E 119
King's Newnham. Warw —3B 62
Kings Newton. Derbs —3A 74
Kingsnorth. Kent —2E 28
Kingsnorth. Medw —3C 40
King's Norton. Leics —5D 74
King's Norton. W Mid —3E 61
King's Nympton. Devn —1G 11
King's Pyon. Here —5G 59
Kings Ripton. Cambs —3B 64
King's Somborne. Hants —3B 24
King's Stag. Dors —1C 14
King's Stanley. Glos —5D 48
King's Sutton. Nptn —2C 50
Kingstanding. W Mid —1E 61
Kingsteignton. Devn —5B 12
Kingsteps. High —3D 158
King Sterndale. Derbs —3E 85
King's Thorn. Here —2A 48
Kingsthorpe. Nptn —4E 63
Kingston. Cambs —5C 64
Kingston. Devn —4C 8
Kingston. Dors —2C 14
(nr. Sturminster Newton)
Kingston. Dors —5E 15
(nr. Swanage)
Kingston. E Lot —1B 130
Kingston. Hants —2G 15
Kingston. IOW —4C 16
Kingston. Kent —5F 41
Kingston. Mor —2H 159
Kingston. W Sus —5B 26
Kingston Bagpuize. Oxon —2C 36
Kingston Bagpuize House —2C 36
Kingston Blount. Oxon —2F 37
Kingston by Sea. W Sus —5D 26
Kingston Deverill. Wilts —3D 22
Kingstone. Here —2H 47
Kingstone. Som —1G 13
Kingstone. Staf —3E 73
Kingston Lacy NT —2E 15
Kingston Lisle. Oxon —3B 36
Kingston Maurward Gdns. —3C 14
Kingston near Lewes. E Sus —5E 27
Kingston on Soar. Notts —3C 74
Kingston Russell. Dors —3A 14
Kingston St Mary. Som —4F 21
Kingston Seymour. N Som —5H 33
Kingston Stert. Oxon —5F 51
Kingston upon Hull. Hull —2D 94 & 190
Kingston upon Thames. G Lon —4C 38
King's Walden. Herts —3B 52
Kingswear. Devn —3E 9
Kingswells. Aber —3F 153
Kingswinford. W Mid —2C 60
Kingswood. Buck —4E 51
Kingswood. Glos —2C 34
Kingswood. Here —5E 59
Kingswood. Kent —5C 40
Kingswood. Per —5H 143
Kingswood. Powy —5E 71
Kingswood. Som —3E 20
Kingswood. S Glo —4B 34
Kingswood. Surr —5D 38
Kingswood. Warw —3F 61
Kingswood Common. Staf —5C 72
Kings Worthy. Hants —3C 24
Kingthorpe. Linc —3A 88
Kington. Here —5F 59
Kington. S Glo —2B 34
Kington. Worc —5D 61
Kington Langley. Wilts —4E 35
Kington Magna. Dors —4C 22
Kington St Michael. Wilts —4E 35
Kingussie. High —3B 150
Kingweston. Som —3A 22
Kinharrachie. Abers —5G 161
Kinhrive. High —1B 158
Kinkell Bridge. Per —2B 136
Kinknockie. Abers —4H 161
Kinkry Hill. Cumb —2G 113
Kinlet. Shrp —2B 60
Kinloch. High —5D 166
(nr. Loch More)
Kinloch. High —3A 140
(nr. Lochaline)
Kinloch. High —4C 146
(on Rhum)
Kinloch. Per —4A 144
Kinlochard. Stir —3D 134
Kinlochbervie. High —3C 166
Kinlocheil. High —1D 141
Kinlochewe. High —2C 156
Kinloch Hourn. High —3B 148
Kinloch Laggan. High —5H 149
Kinlochleven. High —2F 141
Kinloch Lodge. High —3F 167
Kinlochmoidart. High —1B 140
Kinlochmore. High —2F 141
Kinloch Rannoch. Per —3D 142
Kinlochspelve. Arg —1D 132
Kinloid. High —5E 147
Kinloss. Mor —2E 159
Kinmel Bay. Cnwy —2B 82
Kinmuck. Abers —2F 153
Kinnadie. Abers —4G 161
Kinnaird. Per —1E 137
Kinneff. Abers —1H 145
Kinnelhead. Dum —4C 118
Kinnell. Ang —3F 145
Kinnerley. Shrp —3F 71
Kinnernie. Abers —2E 152
Kinnersley. Here —1G 47
Kinnersley. Worc —1D 48
Kinnerton. Powy —4E 59
Kinnerton. Shrp —1F 59
Kinnesswood. Per —3D 136
Kinninvie. Dur —2D 104
Kinnordy. Ang —3C 144
Kinoulton. Notts —2D 74
Kinross. Per —3D 136
Kinross House Gdns. —3D 136
Kinrossie. Per —5A 144
Kinsbourne Green. Herts —4B 52
Kinsey Heath. Ches —1A 72
Kinsham. Here —4F 59
Kinsham. Worc —2E 49
Kinsley. W Yor —3E 93
Kinson. Bour —3F 15
Kintbury. W Ber —5B 36
Kintessack. Mor —2E 159
Kintillo. Per —2D 136
Kinton. Here —3G 59
Kinton. Shrp —4F 71
Kintore. Abers —2E 153
Kintour. Arg —4C 124
Kintra. Arg —2B 132
Kintraw. Arg —3F 133
Kinveachy. High —2D 150
Kinver. Staf —2C 60
Kinver Edge NT —2C 60
Kinwarton. Warw —5F 61
Kiplingcotes. E Yor —5D 100
Kiplin Hall —5F 105
Kippax. W Yor —1E 93
Kippen. Stir —4F 135
Kippford. Dum —4F 111
Kipping's Cross. Kent —1H 27
Kirbister. Orkn —7C 172
(nr. Hobbister)
Kirbister. Orkn —6B 172
(nr. Quholm)
Kirbuster. Orkn —5F 172
Kirby Bedon. Norf —5E 79
Kirby Bellars. Leics —4E 74
Kirby Cane. Norf —1F 67
Kirby Cross. Essx —3F 55
Kirby Fields. Leics —5C 74
Kirby Grindalythe. N Yor —3D 100
Kirby Hall EH —1G 63
Kirby Hill. N Yor —4E 105
(nr. Richmond)
Kirby Hill. N Yor —3F 99
(nr. Ripon)
Kirby Knowle. N Yor —1G 99
Kirby-le-Soken. Essx —3F 55
Kirby Misperton. N Yor —2B 100
Kirby Muxloe. Leics —5C 74
Kirby Muxloe Castle EH —5C 74
Kirby Row. Norf —1F 67
Kirby Sigston. N Yor —5B 106
Kirby Underdale. E Yor —4C 100
Kirby Wiske. N Yor —1F 99
Kirdford. W Sus —3B 26
Kirk. High —3E 169
Kirkabister. Shet —8F 173
(on Bressay)
Kirkabister. Shet —6F 173
(on Mainland)
Kirkandrews. Dum —5D 110
Kirkandrews-on-Eden. Cumb —4E 113
Kirkapol. Arg —4B 138
Kirkbampton. Cumb —4E 112
Kirkbean. Dum —4A 112
Kirk Bramwith. S Yor —3G 93
Kirkbride. Cumb —4D 112
Kirkbridge. N Yor —5F 105
Kirkbuddo. Ang —4E 145
Kirkburn. E Yor —4D 101
Kirkburton. W Yor —3C 92
Kirkby. Linc —1H 87
Kirkby. Mers —1G 83
Kirkby. N Yor —4C 106
Kirkby Fenside. Linc —4C 88
Kirkby Fleetham. N Yor —5F 105
Kirkby Green. Linc —5H 87
Kirkby in Ashfield. Notts —5C 86
Kirkby Industrial Estate. Mers —1G 83
Kirkby-in-Furness. Cumb —1B 96
Kirkby la Thorpe. Linc —1A 76
Kirkby Lonsdale. Cumb —2F 97
Kirkby Malham. N Yor —3A 98
Kirkby Mallory. Leics —5B 74
Kirkby Malzeard. N Yor —2E 99
Kirkby Mills. N Yor —1B 100
Kirkbymoorside. N Yor —1A 100
Kirkby on Bain. Linc —4B 88
Kirkby Overblow. N Yor —5F 99
Kirkby Stephen. Cumb —4A 104
Kirkby Thore. Cumb —2H 103
Kirkby Underwood. Linc —3H 75
Kirkby Wharfe. N Yor —5H 99
Kirkcaldy. Fife —4E 137
Kirkcambeck. Cumb —3G 113
Kirkcolm. Dum —3F 109
Kirkconnel. Dum —3G 117
Kirkconnell. Dum —3A 112
Kirkcowan. Dum —3A 110
Kirkcudbright. Dum —4D 111
Kirkdale. Mers —1F 83
Kirk Deighton. N Yor —4G 99
Kirk Ella. E Yor —2D 94
Kirkfieldbank. S Lan —5B 128
Kirkforthar Feus. Fife —3E 137
Kirkgunzeon. Dum —3F 111
Kirk Hallam. Derbs —1B 74
Kirkham. Lanc —1C 90
Kirkham. N Yor —3B 100
Kirkhamgate. W Yor —2C 92
Kirk Hammerton. N Yor —4G 99
Kirkham Priory EH —3B 100
Kirkharle. Nmbd —1D 114
Kirkheaton. Nmbd —2D 114
Kirkheaton. W Yor —3B 92
Kirkhill. Ang —2F 145
Kirkhill. High —4H 157
Kirkhope. S Lan —4B 118
Kirkhouse. Bord —1F 119
Kirkibost. High —2D 146
Kirkinch. Ang —4C 144
Kirkinner. Dum —4B 110
Kirkintilloch. E Dun —2H 127
Kirk Ireton. Derbs —5G 85
Kirkland. Cumb —3B 102
(nr. Cleator Moor)
Kirkland. Cumb —1H 103
(nr. Penrith)
Kirkland. Cumb —5D 112
(nr. Wigton)
Kirkland. Dum —3G 117
(nr. Kirkconnel)
Kirkland. Dum —5H 117
(nr. Moniavie)
Kirkland Guards. Cumb —5C 112
Kirk Langley. Derbs —2G 73
Kirklauchline. Dum —4F 109
Kirkleatham. Red C —2C 106
Kirklevington. Stoc T —4B 106
Kirkley. Suff —1H 67
Kirklington. N Yor —1F 99
Kirklington. Notts —5D 86
Kirklinton. Cumb —3F 113
Kirkliston. Edin —2E 129
Kirkmabreck. Dum —4B 110
Kirkmaiden. Dum —5E 109
Kirk Merrington. Dur —1F 105
Kirk Michael. IOM —2C 108
Kirkmichael. Per —2H 143
Kirkmichael. S Ayr —4C 116
Kirkmuirhill. S Lan —5A 128
Kirknewton. Nmbd —1D 120
Kirknewton. W Lot —3E 129
Kirkney. Abers —5C 160
Kirk of Shotts. N Lan —3B 128
Kirkoswald. Cumb —5G 113
Kirkoswald. S Ayr —4B 116
Kirkpatrick. Dum —5B 118
Kirkpatrick Durham. Dum —2E 111
Kirkpatrick-Fleming. Dum —2D 112
Kirk Sandall. S Yor —4G 93
Kirksanton. Cumb —1A 96
Kirk Smeaton. N Yor —3F 93
Kirkstall. W Yor —1C 92
Kirkstall Abbey —1C 92
Kirkstile. Dum —5F 119
Kirkstyle. High —1F 169
Kirkthorpe. W Yor —2D 92
Kirkton. Abers —2D 152
(nr. Alford)
Kirkton. Abers —1D 152
(nr. Insch)
Kirkton. Abers —4F 161
(nr. Turriff)
Kirkton. Ang —5D 144
(nr. Balgray)
Kirkton. Ang —4D 144
(nr. Forfar)
Kirkton. Ang —5B 152
(nr. Tarfside)
Kirkton. Dum —1A 112
Kirkton. Fife —1F 137
Kirkton. High —4E 165
(nr. Golspie)
Kirkton. High —1G 147
(nr. Kyle of Lochalsh)
Kirkton. High —4B 156
(nr. Lochcarron)
Kirkton. Bord —3H 119
Kirkton. S Lan —2B 118
Kirktonhill. W Dun —2E 127
Kirkton Manor. Bord —1E 118
Kirkton of Airlie. Ang —3C 144
Kirkton of Auchterhouse. Ang —5C 144
Kirkton of Bourtie. Abers —1F 153
Kirkton of Collace. Per —5A 144
Kirkton of Craig. Ang —3G 145
Kirkton of Culsalmond. Abers —5D 160
Kirkton of Durris. Abers —4E 153
Kirkton of Glenbuchat. Abers —2A 152
Kirkton of Glenisla. Ang —2B 144
Kirkton of Kingoldrum. Ang —3C 144
Kirkton of Largo. Fife —3G 137
Kirkton of Lethendy. Per —4A 144
Kirkton of Logie Buchan. Abers —1G 153
Kirkton of Maryculter. Abers —4F 153
Kirkton of Menmuir. Ang —2E 145
Kirkton of Monikie. Ang —5E 145
Kirkton of Oyne. Abers —1D 152
Kirkton of Rayne. Abers —1D 152
Kirkton of Skene. Abers —3F 153
Kirktown. Abers —2G 161
(nr. Fraserburgh)
Kirktown. Abers —3H 161
(nr. Peterhead)
Kirktown of Alvah. Abers —3D 160
Kirktown of Auchterless. Abers —4E 160
Kirktown of Deskford. Mor —2C 160
Kirktown of Fetteresso. Abers —5F 153
Kirktown of Mortlach. Mor —5H 159
Kirktown of Slains. Abers —1H 153
Kirkurd. Bord —5E 129
Kirkwall. Orkn —6D 172
Kirkwall Airport. Orkn —7D 172
Kirkwall Cathedral —6D 172
Kirkwhelpington. Nmbd —1C 114
Kirk Yetholm. Bord —2C 120
Kirmington. N Lin —3E 94
Kirmond le Mire. Linc —1A 88
Kirn. Arg —2C 126
Kirriemuir. Ang —3C 144
Kirstead Green. Norf —1E 67
Kirtlebridge. Dum —2D 112
Kirtleton. Dum —2D 112
Kirtling. Cambs —5F 65
Kirtling Green. Cambs —5F 65
Kirtlington. Oxon —4C 50
Kirtomy. High —2H 167
Kirton. Linc —2C 76
Kirton. Notts —4D 86
Kirton. Suff —2F 55
Kirton End. Linc —1B 76
Kirton Holme. Linc —1B 76
Kirton in Lindsey. N Lin —1G 87
Kishorn. High —4H 155
Kislingbury. Nptn —5D 62
Kites Hardwick. Warw —4B 62
Kittisford. Som —4D 20
Kittle. Swan —4E 31
Kittybrewster. Aber —3G 153
Kitwood. Hants —3E 25
Kivernoll. Here —2H 47
Kiveton Park. S Yor —2B 86
Knaith. Linc —2F 87
Knaith Park. Linc —2F 87
Knap Corner. Dors —4D 22
Knaphill. Surr —5A 38
Knapp. Hants —4C 24
Knapp. Per —5B 144
Knapp. Som —4G 21
Knapperfield. High —3E 169
Knapton. Norf —2F 79
Knapton. York —4H 99
Knapton Green. Here —5G 59
Knapwell. Cambs —4C 64
Knaresborough. N Yor —4F 99
Knarsdale. Nmbd —4H 113
Knatts Valley. Kent —4G 39
Knaven. Abers —4F 161
Knayton. N Yor —1G 99
Knebworth. Herts —3C 52
Knebworth House —3C 52
Knedlington. E Yor —2H 93
Kneesall. Notts —4E 86
Kneesworth. Cambs —1D 52
Kneeton. Notts —1E 74
Knelston. Swan —4D 30
Knenhall. Staf —2D 72
Knightacott. Devn —3G 19
Knightcote. Warw —5B 62
Knightcott. N Som —1G 21
Knightley. Staf —3C 72

Knightley Dale. Staf —3C 72
Knightlow Hill. Warw —3B 62
Knighton. Devn —4B 8
Knighton. Dors —1B 14
Knighton. Leic —5D 74
Knighton. Powy —3E 59
Knighton. Som —2E 21
Knighton. Staf —3B 72
Knighton. Wilts —4A 36
Knighton. Worc —5E 61
Knighton Common. Worc —3A 60
Knight's End. Cambs —1D 64
Knightshayes Court NT —1C 12
Knightswood. Glas —3G 127
Knightwick. Worc —5B 60
Knill. Here —4E 59
Knipton. Leics —2F 75
Knitsley. Dur —5E 115
Kniveton. Derbs —5G 85
Knock. Arg —5G 139
Knock. Cumb —2H 103
Knock. Mor —3C 160
Knockally. High —5D 168
Knockan. Arg —1B 132
Knockan. High —2G 163
Knockandhu. Mor —1G 151
Knockando. Mor —4F 159
Knockarthur. High —3E 165
Knockbain. High —3A 158
Knockbreck. High —2B 154
Knockdee. High —2D 168
Knockdolian. S Ayr —1G 109
Knockdon. S Ayr —3C 116
Knockdown. Glos —3D 34
Knockenbaird. Abers —1D 152
Knockenkelly. N Ayr —3E 123
Knockentiber. E Ayr —1C 116
Knockfarrel. High —3H 157
Knockglass. High —2C 168
Knockholt. Kent —5F 39
Knockholt Pound. Kent —5F 39
Knockie Lodge. High —2G 149
Knockin. Shrp —3F 71
Knockinlaw. E Ayr —1D 116
Knockinnon. High —5D 169
Knockrome. Arg —2D 124
Knocksharry. IOM —3B 108
Knockshinnoch. E Ayr —3D 116
Knockvennie. Dum —2E 111
Knockvologan. Arg —3B 132
Knodishall. Suff —4G 67
Knole NT —5G 39
Knole. Som —4H 21
Knollbury. Mon —3H 33
Knolls Green. Ches —3C 84
Knolton. Wrex —2F 71
Knook. Wilts —2E 23
Knossington. Leics —5F 75
Knott. High —3C 154
Knott End-on-Sea. Lanc —5C 96
Knotting. Beds —4H 63
Knotting Green. Beds —4H 63
Knottingley. W Yor —2E 93
Knotts. Cumb —2F 103
Knotty Ash. Mers —1G 83
Knotty Green. Buck —1A 38
Knowbury. Shrp —3H 59
Knowe. Dum —2A 110
Knowefield. Cumb —4F 113
Knowehead. Dum —5F 117
Knowes. E Lot —2C 130
Knowesgate. Nmbd —1C 114
Knoweside. S Ayr —3B 116
Knowle. Bris —4B 34
Knowle. Devn —3E 19
(nr. Braunton)
Knowle. Devn —4D 12
(nr. Budleigh Salterton)
Knowle. Devn —2A 12
(nr. Crediton)
Knowle. Shrp —3H 59
Knowle. W Mid —3F 61
Knowle Green. Lanc —1E 91
Knowle St Giles. Som —1G 13
Knowles of Elrick. Abers —3D 160
Knowl Hill. Wind —4G 37
Knowlton. Kent —5G 41
Knowsley. Mers —1G 83
Knowsley Safari Park —1G 83
Knowstone. Devn —4B 20
Knucklas. Powy —3E 59
Knuston. Nptn —4G 63
Knutsford. Ches —3B 84
Knypersley. Staf —5C 84
Krumlin. W Yor —3A 92
Kuggar. Corn —5E 5
Kyleakin. High —1F 147
Kyle of Lochalsh. High —1F 147
Kylerhea. High —1F 147
Kylesku. High —5C 166
Kyles Lodge. W Isl —9B 171
Kylesmorar. High —4G 147
Kylestrome. High —5C 166
Kymin. Mon —4A 48
Kynaston. Here —2B 48
Kynaston. Shrp —3F 71
Kynnersley. Telf —4A 72
Kyre Green. Worc —4A 60
Kyre Park. Worc —4A 60
Kyrewood. Worc —4A 60
Kyrle. Som —4D 20

Labost. W Isl —3E 171
Lacasaidh. W Isl —5F 171
Lacasdail. W Isl —4G 171
Laceby. NE Lin —4F 95
Lacey Green. Buck —5G 51
Lach Dennis. Ches —3B 84
Lache. Ches —4F 83
Lackford. Suff —3G 65
Lacock. Wilts —5E 35
Lacock Abbey NT —5E 35
Ladbroke. Warw —5B 62
Laddingford. Kent —1A 28
Lade Bank. Linc —5C 88
Ladock. Corn —3C 6
Ladybank. Fife —2F 137
Ladycross. Corn —4D 10
Lady Green. Mers —4B 90
Lady Hall. Cumb —1A 96
Ladykirk. Bord —5E 131
Lady Lever Art Gallery —2F 83
Ladysford. Abers —2G 161
Ladywood. W Mid —2E 61
Ladywood. Worc —4C 60
Laga. High —2A 140
Lagavulin. Arg —5C 124
Lagg. Arg —2D 125
Lagg. N Ayr —3D 122
Laggan. Arg —4A 124
Laggan. High —4E 149
(nr. Fort Augustus)
Laggan. High —4A 150
(nr. Newtonmore)
Laggan. Mor —5H 159
Lagganlia. High —3C 150
Lagganulva. Arg —4F 139
Laglingarten. Arg —3A 134
Lagness. W Sus —2G 17
Laid. High —3E 166
Laide. High —4D 162
Laigh Fenwick. E Ayr —5F 127
Laindon. Essx —2A 40
Laing Art Gallery —Newcastle 191
Lairg. High —3C 164
Lairg Muir. High —3C 164
Laithes. Cumb —1F 103
Laithkirk. Dur —2C 104
Lake. Devn —3F 19
Lake. IOW —4D 16
Lake. Wilts —3G 23
Lake District Nat. Park —3E 103
Lakenham. Norf —5E 79
Lakenheath. Suff —2G 65
Lakesend. Norf —1E 65
Lakeside. Cumb —1C 96
Lakeside & Haverthwaite Railway —1C 96
Laleham. Surr —4B 38
Laleston. B'end —3B 32
Lamancha. Bord —4E 129
Lamarsh. Essx —2B 54
Lamas. Norf —3E 79
Lamb Corner. Essx —2D 54
Lambden. Bord —5D 130
Lamberhead Green. G Man —4D 90
Lamberhurst. Kent —2A 28
Lamberhurst Quarter. Kent —2A 28
Lamberton. Bord —4F 131
Lambeth. G Lon —3E 39
Lambfell Moar. IOM —3B 108
Lambhill. Glas —3G 127
Lamb House NT —4D 28
Lambley. Nmbd —4H 113
Lambley. Notts —1D 74
Lambourn. W Ber —4B 36
Lambourne End. Essx —1F 39
Lambourn Woodlands. W Ber —4B 36
Lambrook. Som —4F 21
Lambs Green. Dors —3E 15
Lambs Green. W Sus —2D 26
Lambston. Pemb —3D 42
Lamellion. Corn —2G 7
Lamerton. Devn —5E 11
Lamesley. Tyne —4F 115
Laminess. Orkn —4F 172
Lamington. High —1B 158
Lamington. S Lan —1B 118
Lamlash. N Ayr —2E 123
Lamonby. Cumb —1F 103
Lamorick. Corn —2E 7
Lamorna. Corn —4B 4
Lamorran. Corn —4C 6
Lampeter. Cdgn —1F 45
Lampeter Velfrey. Pemb —3F 43
Lamphey. Pemb —4E 43
Lamphey Bishop's Palace —4E 43
Lamplugh. Cumb —2B 102
Lamport. Nptn —3E 63
Lamport Hall —3E 63
Lamyatt. Som —3B 22
Lana. Devn —3D 10
(nr. Ashwater)
Lana. Devn —2D 10
(nr. Holsworthy)
Lanark. S Lan —5B 128
Lanarth. Corn —4E 5
Lancaster. Lanc —3D 97
Lancaster Castle —3D 96
Lanchester. Dur —5E 115
Lancing. W Sus —5C 26
Landbeach. Cambs —4D 64
Landcross. Devn —4E 19
Landerberry. Abers —3E 153
Landewednack. Corn —5E 5
Landford. Wilts —1A 16
Land Gate. G Man —4D 90
Landhallow. High —5D 169
Landimore. Swan —3D 30
Landkey. Devn —3F 19
Landkey Newland. Devn —3F 19
Landmark Forest Theme Park —1D 150
Landore. Swan —3F 31
Landport. Port —2E 17
Landrake. Corn —2H 7
Landscove. Devn —2D 9
Land's End —4A 4
Land's End (St Just) Airport. Corn —4A 4
Landshipping. Pemb —3E 43
Landulph. Corn —2A 8
Landywood. Staf —5D 73
Lane. Corn —2C 6
Laneast. Corn —4C 10
Lane Bottom. Lanc —1G 91
Lane End. Buck —2G 37
Lane End. Cumb —5C 102
Lane End. Hants —4D 24
Lane End. IOW —4E 17
Lane End. Wilts —2D 22
Lane Ends. Derbs —2G 73
Lane Ends. Dur —1E 105
Lane Ends. Lanc —4G 97
Laneham. Notts —3F 87
Lanehead. Dur —5B 114
(nr. Cowshill)
Lane Head. Dur —3E 105
(nr. Hutton Magna)
Lane Head. Dur —2D 105
(nr. Woodland)
Lane Head. G Man —1A 84
Lanehead. Nmbd —1A 114
Lane Head. W Yor —4B 92
Lane Heads. Lanc —1C 90
Lanercost. Cumb —3G 113
Lanercost Priory EH —3G 113
Laneshaw Bridge. Lanc —5B 98
Laney Green. Staf —5D 72
Langais. W Isl —2D 170
Langal. High —2B 140
Langar. Notts —2E 74
Langbank. Ren —2E 127
Langbar. N Yor —4C 98
Langburnshiels. Bord —4H 119
Langcliffe. N Yor —3H 97
Langdale End. N Yor —5G 107
Langdale Pikes NT —4D 102
Langdon. Corn —3C 10
Langdon Beck. Dur —1B 104
Langdon Cross. Corn —4D 10
Langdon Hills. Essx —2A 40
Langdown. Hants —2C 16
Langdyke. Fife —3F 137
Langenhoe. Essx —4D 54
Langford. Beds —1B 52
Langford. Devn —2D 12
Langford. Essx —5B 54
Langford. Notts —5F 87
Langford. Oxon —5H 49
Langford Budville. Som —4E 20
Langham. Dors —4C 22
Langham. Essx —2D 54
Langham. Norf —1C 78
Langham. Rut —4F 75
Langham. Suff —4B 66
Langho. Lanc —1F 91
Langholm. Dum —1E 113
Langland. Swan —4F 31
Langleeford. Nmbd —2D 120
Langley. Ches —3D 84
Langley. Derbs —1B 74
Langley. Essx —2E 53
Langley. Glos —3F 49
Langley. Hants —2C 16
Langley. Herts —3C 52
Langley. Kent —5C 40
Langley. Nmbd —3B 114
Langley. Slo —3B 38
Langley. Som —4D 20
Langley. Warw —4F 61
Langley. W Sus —4G 25
Langley Burrell. Wilts —4E 35
Langleybury. Herts —5A 52
Langley Common. Derbs —2G 73
Langley Green. Derbs —2G 73
Langley Green. Norf —5F 79
Langley Green. Warw —4F 61
Langley Green. W Sus —2D 26
Langley Heath. Kent —5C 40
Langley Marsh. Som —4D 20
Langley Moor. Dur —5F 115
Langley Park. Dur —5F 115
Langley Street. Norf —5F 79
Langney. E Sus —5H 27
Langold. Notts —2C 86
Langore. Corn —4D 10
Langport. Som —4H 21
Langrick. Linc —1B 76
Langridge. Bath —5C 34
Langridgeford. Devn —4F 19
Langrigg. Cumb —5C 112
Langrish. Hants —4F 25
Langsett. S Yor —4C 92
Langshaw. Bord —1H 119
Langstone. Hants —2F 17
Langthorne. N Yor —5F 105
Langthorpe. N Yor —3F 99
Langthwaite. N Yor —4D 104
Langtoft. E Yor —3E 101
Langtoft. Linc —4A 76
Langton. Dur —3E 105
Langton. Linc —4B 88
(nr. Horncastle)
Langton. Linc —3C 88
(nr. Spilsby)
Langton. N Yor —3B 100
Langton by Wragby. Linc —3A 88
Langton Green. Kent —2G 27
Langton Herring. Dors —4B 14
Langton Long Blandford. Dors —2E 15
Langton Matravers. Dors —5F 15
Langtree. Devn —1E 11
Langwathby. Cumb —1G 103
Langwith. Derbs —3C 86
Langworth. Linc —3H 87
Lanhydrock NT —2E 7
Lanivet. Corn —2E 7
Lanjeth. Corn —3D 6
Lank. Corn —5A 10
Lanlivery. Corn —3E 7
Lanner. Corn —5B 6
Lanreath. Corn —3F 7
Lansallos. Corn —3F 7
Lansdown. Bath —5C 34
Lansdown. Glos —3E 49
Lanteglos Highway. Corn —3F 7
Lanton. Nmbd —1D 120
Lanton. Bord —2A 120
Lapford. Devn —2H 11
Laphroaig. Arg —5B 124
Lapley. Staf —4C 72
Lappa Valley Railway —3C 6
Lapworth. Warw —3F 61
Larachbeg. High —4A 140
Larbert. Falk —1B 128
Larden Green. Ches —5H 83
Larel. High —3D 169
Largie. Abers —5D 160
Largiemore. Arg —1H 125
Largoward. Fife —3G 137
Largs. N Ayr —4D 126
Largue. Abers —4D 160
Largybeg. N Ayr —3E 123
Largymeanoch. N Ayr —3E 123
Largymore. N Ayr —3E 123
Larkfield. Inv —2D 126
Larkfield. Kent —5A 40
Larkhall. Bath —5C 34
Larkhall. S Lan —4A 128
Larkhill. Wilts —2G 23
Larling. Norf —2B 66
Larmer Tree Gdn. —1E 15
Larport. Here —2A 48
Lartington. Dur —3D 104
Lary. Abers —3H 151
Lasham. Hants —2E 25
Lashenden. Kent —1C 28
Lassodie. Fife —4D 136
Lasswade. Midl —3G 129
Lastingham. N Yor —5E 107
Latchford. Herts —3D 53
Latchford. Oxon —5E 51
Latchingdon. Essx —5B 54
Latchley. Corn —5E 11
Latchmere Green. Hants —5E 37
Latham. Lanc —4C 90
Lathbury. Mil —1G 51
Latheron. High —5D 169
Latheronwheel. High —5D 169
Lathom. Lanc —4C 90
Lathones. Fife —3G 137
Latimer. Buck —1B 38
Latteridge. S Glo —3B 34
Lattiford. Som —4B 22
Latton. Wilts —2F 35
Laudale House. High —3B 140
Lauder. Bord —5B 130
Laugharne. Carm —3H 43
Laugharne Castle CADW —3H 43
Laughterton. Linc —3F 87
Laughton. E Sus —4G 27
Laughton. Leics —2D 62
Laughton. Linc —1F 87
(nr. Gainsborough)
Laughton. Linc —2H 75
(nr. Grantham)
Laughton Common. S Yor —2C 86
Laughton en le Morthen. S Yor —2C 86
Launcells. Corn —2C 10
Launceston. Corn —4D 10
Launceston Castle EH —4D 10
Launcherley. Som —2A 22
Launton. Oxon —3E 50
Laurencekirk. Abers —1G 145
Laurieston. Dum —3D 111
Laurieston. Falk —2C 128
Lavendon. Mil —5G 63
Lavenham. Suff —1C 54
Lavenham Guildhall NT —1C 54
Laverhay. Dum —5D 118
Laversdale. Cumb —3F 113
Laverstock. Wilts —3G 23
Laverstoke. Hants —2C 24
Laverton. Glos —2F 49
Laverton. N Yor —2E 99
Laverton. Som —1C 22
Lavister. Wrex —5F 83
Law. S Lan —4B 128
Lawers. Per —5D 142
Lawford. Essx —2D 54
Lawhitton. Corn —4D 10
Lawkland. N Yor —3G 97
Lawnhead. Staf —3C 72
Lawrenny. Pemb —4E 43
Lawshall. Suff —5A 66
Lawton. Here —5G 59
Laxey. IOM —3D 108
Laxey Wheel —3D 108
Laxfield. Suff —3E 67
Laxfirth. Shet —6F 173
Laxo. Shet —5F 173
Laxton. E Yor —2A 94
Laxton. Nptn —1G 63
Laxton. Notts —4E 86
Laycock. W Yor —5C 98
Layer Breton. Essx —4C 54
Layer-de-la-Haye. Essx —3C 54
Layer Marney. Essx —4C 54
Layer Marney Tower —4C 54
Layland's Green. W Ber —5B 36
Laymore. Dors —2G 13
Laysters Pole. Here —4H 59
Layter's Green. Buck —1A 38
Laytham. E Yor —1H 93
Lazenby. Red C —3C 106
Lazonby. Cumb —1G 103
Lea. Derbs —5H 85
Lea. Here —3B 48
Lea. Linc —2F 87
Lea. Shrp —2F 59
(nr. Bishop's Castle)
Lea. Shrp —5G 71
(nr. Shrewsbury)
Lea. Wilts —3E 35
Leabrooks. Derbs —5B 86
Leac a Li. W Isl —8D 171
Leachd. Arg —4H 133
Leachkin. High —4A 158
Leachpool. Pemb —3D 42
Leadburn. Midl —4F 129
Leadenham. Linc —5G 87
Leaden Roding. Essx —4F 53
Leaderfoot. Bord —1H 119
Leadgate. Cumb —5A 114
Leadgate. Dur —4E 115
Leadgate. Nmbd —4E 115
Leadhills. S Lan —3A 118
Leadingcross Green. Kent —5C 40
Lea End. Worc —3E 61
Leafield. Oxon —4B 50
Leagrave. Lutn —3A 52
Lea Hall. W Mid —2F 61
Lea Heath. Staf —3E 73
Leake. N Yor —5B 106
Leake Common Side. Linc —5C 88
Leake Fold Hill. Linc —5D 88
Leake Hurn's End. Linc —1D 76
Lealholm. N Yor —4E 107
Lealt. Arg —4D 132
Lealt. High —2E 155
Leam. Derbs —3G 85
Lea Marston. Warw —1G 61
Leamington Hastings. Warw —4B 62
Leamington Spa, Royal. Warw —4H 61
Leamonsley. Staf —5F 73
Leamside. Dur —5G 115
Leargybreck. Arg —2D 124
Lease Rigg. N Yor —4F 107
Leasgill. Cumb —1D 97
Leasingham. Linc —1H 75
Leasingthorne. Dur —2F 105
Leasowe. Mers —1E 83
Leatherhead. Surr —5C 38
Leathley. N Yor —5E 99
Leaths. Dum —3E 111
Leaton. Shrp —4G 71
Lea Town. Lanc —1C 90
Leaveland. Kent —5E 40
Leavenheath. Suff —2C 54
Leavening. N Yor —3B 100
Leaves Green. G Lon —4F 39
Lea Yeat. Cumb —1G 97
Leazes. Dur —4E 115
Lebberston. N Yor —1E 101
Lechlade on Thames. Glos —2H 35
Leck. Lanc —2F 97
Leckford. Hants —3B 24
Leckfurin. High —3H 167
Leckgruinart. Arg —3A 124
Leckhampstead. Buck —2F 51
Leckhampstead. W Ber —4C 36
Leckhampstead Street. W Ber —4C 36
Leckhampton. Glos —4E 49
Leckmelm. High —4F 163
Leckwith. V Glam —4E 33
Leconfield. E Yor —5E 101
Ledaig. Arg —5D 140
Ledburn. Buck —3H 51
Ledbury. Here —2C 48
Ledgemoor. Here —5G 59
Ledgowan. High —3D 156
Ledicot. Here —4G 59
Ledmore. High —2G 163
Lednabirichen. High —4E 165
Lednagullin. High —2A 168
Ledsham. Ches —3F 83
Ledsham. W Yor —2E 93
Ledston. W Yor —2E 93
Ledstone. Devn —4D 8
Ledwell. Oxon —3C 50
Lee. Devn —2E 19
(nr. Ilfracombe)
Lee. Devn —4B 20
(nr. South Molton)
Lee. G Lon —3F 39
Lee. Hants —1B 16
Lee. Lanc —4E 97
Lee. Shrp —2G 71
Leeans. Shet —7E 173
Leebotten. Shet —9F 173
Leebotwood. Shrp —1G 59
Lee Brockhurst. Shrp —3H 71
Leece. Cumb —3B 96
Leechpool. Mon —3A 34
Lee Clump. Buck —5H 51
Leeds. Kent —5C 40
Leeds. W Yor —1C 92 & 190
Leeds & Bradford Airport. W Yor —5E 98
Leeds Castle —5C 40
Leeds City Mus. & Art Gallery —190
Leedstown. Corn —3D 4
Leegomery. Telf —4A 72
Lee Head. Derbs —1E 85
Leek. Staf —5D 85
Leekbrook. Staf —5D 85
Leek Wootton. Warw —4G 61
Lee Mill. Devn —3B 8
Leeming. N Yor —1E 99
Leeming Bar. N Yor —5F 105
Lee Moor. Devn —2B 8
Lee Moor. W Yor —2D 92
Lee-on-the-Solent. Hants —2D 16
Lees. Derbs —2G 73
Lees. G Man —4H 91
Lees. W Yor —1A 92
Lees, The. Kent —5E 40
Leeswood. Flin —5E 83
Lee, The. Buck —5H 51
Leetown. Per —1E 136
Leftwich. Ches —3A 84
Legbourne. Linc —2C 88
Legburthwaite. Cumb —3E 102
Legerwood. Bord —5B 130
Legoland —3A 38
Legsby. Linc —2A 88
Leicester. Leic —5C 74 & 190
Leicester Forest East. Leics —5C 74
Leigh. Dors —2B 14
Leigh. G Man —4E 91
Leigh. Kent —1G 27
Leigh. Shrp —5F 71
Leigh. Surr —1D 26
Leigh. Wilts —2F 35
Leigh. Worc —5B 60
Leigham. Plym —3B 8
Leigh Beck. Essx —2C 40
Leigh Common. Som —3C 22
Leigh Delamere. Wilts —4D 35
Leigh Green. Kent —2D 28
Leighland Chapel. Som —3D 20
Leigh-on-Sea. S'end —2C 40
Leigh Park. Hants —2F 17
Leigh Sinton. Worc —5B 60
Leighterton. Glos —2D 34
Leigh, The. Glos —3D 48
Leighton. N Yor —2D 98
Leighton. Powy —5E 71
Leighton. Shrp —5A 72
Leighton. Som —2C 22
Leighton Bromswold. Cambs —3A 64
Leighton Buzzard. Beds —3H 51

Leighton Buzzard Railway —3H 51
Leighton Hall, Yealand Conyers —2E 97
Leigh-upon-Mendip. Som —2B 22
Leinthall Earls. Here —4G 59
Leinthall Starkes. Here —4G 59
Leintwardine. Here —3G 59
Leire. Leics —1C 62
Leirinmore. High —2E 166
Leishmore. High —4G 157
Leiston. Suff —4G 67
Leiston Abbey EH —4G 67
Leitfie. Per —4B 144
Leith. Edin —2F 129
Leith Hall NTS —1C 152
Leith Hill NT —1C 26
Leitholm. Bord —5D 130
Lelant. Corn —3C 4
Lelant Downs. Corn —3C 4
Lelley. E Yor —1F 95
Lem Hill. Worc —3B 60
Lemington. Tyne —3E 115
Lemmington Hall. Nmbd —3F 121
Lempitlaw. Bord —1B 120
Lemsford. Herts —4C 52
Lenacre. Cumb —1F 97
Lenchie. Abers —5C 160
Lenchwick. Worc —1F 49
Lendalfoot. S Ayr —5A 116
Lendrick. Stir —3E 135
Lenham. Kent —5C 40
Lenham Heath. Kent —1D 28
Lenimore. N Ayr —5G 125
Lennel. Bord —5E 131
Lennoxlove House —2B 130
Lennoxtown. E Dun —2H 127
Lenton. Linc —2H 75
Lenton. Nott —2C 74
Lentran. High —4H 157
Lenwade. Norf —4C 78
Lenzie. E Dun —2H 127
Leochel Cushnie. Abers —2C 152
Leogh. Shet —1B 172
Leominster. Here —5G 59
Leonardslee Gdns. —3D 26
Leonard Stanley. Glos —5D 48
Lepe. Hants —3C 16
Lephenstrath. Arg —5A 122
Lephin. High —4A 154
Lephinchapel. Arg —4G 133
Lephinmore. Arg —4G 133
Leppington. N Yor —3B 100
Lepton. W Yor —3C 92
Lerryn. Corn —3F 7
Lerwick. Shet —7F 173
Lerwick Airport. Shet —7F 173
Lesbury. Nmbd —3G 121
Leslie. Abers —1C 152
Leslie. Fife —3E 137
Lesmahagow. S Lan —1H 117
Lesnewth. Corn —3B 10
Lessingham. Norf —3F 79
Lessonhall. Cumb —4D 112
Leswalt. Dum —3F 109
Letchmore Heath. Herts —1C 38
Letchworth. Herts —2C 52
Letcombe Bassett. Oxon —3B 36
Letcombe Regis. Oxon —3B 36
Letham. Ang —4E 145
Letham. Falk —1B 128
Letham. Fife —2F 137
Lethanhill. E Ayr —3D 116
Lethenty. Abers —4F 161
Letheringham. Suff —5E 67
Letheringsett. Norf —2C 78
Lettaford. Devn —4H 11
Lettan. Orkn —3G 172
Letter. Abers —2E 153
Letterewe. High —1B 156
Letterfearn. High —1A 148
Lettermore. Arg —4F 139
Letters. High —5F 163
Letterston. Pemb —2D 42
Letton. Here —1G 47
(nr. Kington)
Letton. Here —3F 59
(nr. Leintwardine)
Letty Green. Herts —4C 52
Letwell. S Yor —2C 86
Leuchars. Fife —1G 137
Leumrabhagh. W Isl —6F 171
Leusdon. Devn —5H 11
Levaneap. Shet —5F 173
Levedale. Staf —4C 72
Leven. E Yor —5F 101
Leven. Fife —3F 137
Levencorroch. N Ayr —3E 123
Levenhall. E Lot —2G 129
Levens. Cumb —1D 97
Levens Green. Herts —3D 52
Levens Hall —1D 97
Levenshulme. G Man —1C 84
Levenwick. Shet —9F 173
Leverburgh. W Isl —9C 171
Leverington. Cambs —4D 76
Leverton. Linc —1D 76
Leverton. W Ber —4B 36
Leverton Lucasgate. Linc —1D 76
Leverton Outgate. Linc —1D 76
Levington. Suff —2F 55
Levisham. N Yor —5F 107
Levishie. High —2G 149
Lew. Oxon —5B 50
Lewaigue. IOM —2D 108
Lewannick. Corn —4C 10
Lewdown. Devn —4E 11
Lewes. E Sus —4F 27
Leweston. Pemb —2D 42
Lewisham. G Lon —3E 39
Lewiston. High —1H 149
Lewistown. B'end —3C 32
Lewknor. Oxon —2F 37
Leworthy. Devn —3G 19
(nr. Barnstaple)
Leworthy. Devn —2D 10
(nr. Holsworthy)
Lewson Street. Kent —4D 40
Lewthorn Cross. Devn —5A 12
Lewtrenchard. Devn —4E 11
Ley. Corn —2F 7
Leybourne. Kent —5A 40
Leyburn. N Yor —5E 105
Leycett. Staf —1B 72
Leyfields. Staf —5G 73
Ley Green. Herts —3B 52
Ley Hill. Buck —5H 51
Leyland. Lanc —2D 90
Leylodge. Abers —2E 153
Leymoor. W Yor —3B 92
Leys. Per —5B 144
Leysdown-on-Sea. Kent —3E 41
Leysmill. Ang —4F 145
Leyton. G Lon —2E 39
Leytonstone. G Lon —2F 39
Lezant. Corn —5D 10
Leziate. Norf —4F 77
Lhanbryde. Mor —2G 159
Lhen, The. IOM —1C 108
Liatrie. High —5E 157
Libanus. Powy —3C 46
Libberton. S Lan —5C 128
Libbery. Worc —5D 60
Liberton. Edin —3F 129
Liceasto. W Isl —8D 171
Lichfield. Staf —5F 73
Lichfield Cathedral —4F 73
Lickey. Worc —3D 61
Lickey End. Worc —3D 61
Lickfold. W Sus —3A 26
Liddaton. Devn —4E 11
Liddel. Orkn —9D 172
Liddington. Swin —3H 35
Lidgate. Suff —5G 65
Lidgett. Notts —4D 86
Lidham Hill. E Sus —4C 28
Lidlington. Beds —2H 51
Lidsey. W Sus —5A 26
Lidstone. Oxon —3B 50
Lienassie. High —1B 148
LIFE, Interactive World —Newcastle 191
Liff. Ang —5C 144
Lifford. W Mid —2E 61
Lifton. Devn —4D 11
Liftondown. Devn —4D 10
Lighthorne. Warw —5H 61
Light Oaks. Staf —1D 72
Lightwater. Surr —4A 38
Lightwater Valley Theme Park —2E 99
Lightwood. Staf —1E 73
Lightwood. Stoke —1D 72
Lightwood Green. Ches —1A 72
Lightwood Green. Wrex —1F 71
Lilbourne. Nptn —3C 62
Lilburn Tower. Nmbd —2E 121
Lillesdon. Som —4G 21
Lilleshall. Telf —4B 72
Lilleshall Abbey EH —4B 72
Lilley. Herts —3B 52
Lilliesleaf. Bord —2H 119
Lillingstone Dayrell. Buck —2F 51
Lillingstone Lovell. Buck —1F 51
Lillington. Dors —1B 14
Lilstock. Som —2E 21
Lilybank. Inv —2E 126
Lilyhurst. Shrp —4B 72
Limbrick. Lanc —3E 90
Limbury. Lutn —3A 52
Limekilnburn. S Lan —4A 128
Lime Kiln Nook. Cumb —5E 113
Limekilns. Fife —1D 129
Limerigg. Falk —2B 128
Limestone Brae. Nmbd —5A 114
Lime Street. Worc —2D 48
Limington. Som —4A 22
Limpenhoe. Norf —5F 79
Limpley Stoke. Wilts —5C 34
Limpsfield. Surr —5E 39
Linburn. W Lot —3E 129
Linby. Notts —5C 86
Linchmere. W Sus —3G 25
Lincluden. Dum —2A 112
Lincoln. Linc —3G 87 & 191
Lincoln Bishop's Palace —191
Lincoln Castle —191
Lincoln Cathedral —191
Lincomb. Worc —4C 60
Lindale. Cumb —1D 96
Lindal in Furness. Cumb —2B 96
Lindean. Bord —1G 119
Linden. Glos —4D 48
Lindfield. W Sus —3E 27
Lindford. Hants —3G 25
Lindisfarne Castle NT —5H 131
Lindisfarne Priory EH —5H 131
Lindores. Fife —2E 137
Lindridge. Worc —4A 60
Lindsell. Essx —3G 53
Lindsey. Suff —1C 54
Lindsey Tye. Suff —1C 54
Linford. Hants —2G 15
Linford. Thur —3A 40
Lingague. IOM —4B 108
Lingdale. Red C —3D 106
Lingen. Here —4F 59
Lingfield. Surr —1E 27
Lingoed. Mon —4G 47
Lingreabhagh. W Isl —9C 171
Ling, The. Norf —1F 67
Lingwood. Norf —5F 79
Lingyclose Head. Cumb —4E 113
Linicro. High —2C 154
Linkend. Worc —2D 48
Linkenholt. Hants —1B 24
Linkinhorne. Corn —5D 10
Linklater. Orkn —9D 172
Linksness. Orkn —7B 172
(on Hoy)
Linksness. Orkn —6E 172
(on Mainland)
Linktown. Fife —4E 137
Linkwood. Mor —2G 159
Linley. Shrp —1F 59
(nr. Bishop's Castle)
Linley. Shrp —1A 60
(nr. Bridgnorth)
Linley Green. Here —5A 60
Linlithgow. W Lot —2C 128
Linlithgow Bridge. Falk —2C 128
Linlithgow Palace HS —2D 128
Linneraineach. High —3F 163
Linshiels. Nmbd —4C 120
Linsiadar. W Isl —4E 171
Linsidemore. High —4C 164
Linslade. Beds —3H 51
Linstead Parva. Suff —3F 67
Linstock. Cumb —4F 113
Linthwaite. W Yor —3B 92
Lintlaw. Bord —4E 131
Lintmill. Mor —2C 160
Linton. Cambs —1F 53
Linton. Derbs —4G 73
Linton. Here —3B 48
Linton. Kent —5B 40
Linton. N Yor —3B 98
Linton. Bord —2B 120
Linton. W Yor —5F 99
Linton Colliery. Nmbd —5G 121
Linton Hill. Here —3B 48
Linton-on-Ouse. N Yor —3G 99
Linton Zoo —1F 53
Lintzford. Tyne —4E 115
Lintzgarth. Dur —5C 114
Linwood. Hants —2G 15
Linwood. Linc —2A 88
Linwood. Ren —3F 127
Lionacleit. W Isl —4C 170
Lionacuidhe. W Isl —4C 170
Lional. W Isl —1H 171
Liphook. Hants —3G 25
Lipley. Shrp —2B 72
Lipyeate. Som —1B 22
Liquo. N Lan —4B 128
Liscard. Mers —1F 83
Liscombe. Som —3B 20
Liskeard. Corn —2G 7
Lisle Court. Hants —3B 16
Liss. Hants —4F 25
Lissett. E Yor —4F 101
Liss Forest. Hants —4F 25
Lissington. Linc —2A 88
Liston. Essx —1B 54
Lisvane. Card —3E 33
Liswerry. Newp —3G 33
Litcham. Norf —4A 78
Litchard. B'end —3C 32
Litchborough. Nptn —5D 62
Litchfield. Hants —1C 24
Litherland. Mers —1F 83
Litlington. Cambs —1D 52
Litlington. E Sus —5G 27
Littemill. Nmbd —3G 121
Litterty. Abers —3E 161
Little Abington. Cambs —1F 53
Little Addington. Nptn —3G 63
Little Airmyn. N Yor —2H 93
Little Alne. Warw —4F 61
Little Ardo. Abers —5F 161
Little Asby. Cumb —4H 103
Little Aston. Staf —5E 73
Little Ayton. N Yor —3C 106
Little Baddow. Essx —5A 54
Little Badminton. S Glo —3D 34
Little Ballinluig. Per —3G 143
Little Bampton. Cumb —4D 112
Little Bardfield. Essx —2G 53
Little Barford. Beds —5A 64
Little Barningham. Norf —2D 78
Little Barrington. Glos —4H 49
Little Barrow. Ches —4G 83
Little Barugh. N Yor —2B 100
Little Bavington. Nmbd —2C 114
Little Bealings. Suff —1F 55
Little Bedwyn. Wilts —5A 36
Little Bentley. Essx —3E 54
Little Berkhamsted. Herts —5C 52
Little Billing. Nptn —4F 63
Little Billington. Beds —3H 51
Little Birch. Here —2A 48
Little Bispham. Bkpl —5C 96
Little Blakenham. Suff —1E 54
Little Blencow. Cumb —1F 103
Little Bognor. W Sus —3B 26
Little Bolas. Shrp —3A 72
Little Bollington. Ches —2B 84
Little Bookham. Surr —5C 38
Littleborough. Devn —1B 12
Littleborough. G Man —3H 91
Littleborough. Notts —2F 87
Littlebourne. Kent —5G 41
Little Bourton. Oxon —1C 50
Little Bowden. Leics —2E 63
Little Bradley. Suff —5F 65
Little Brampton. Shrp —2F 59
Little Brechin. Ang —2E 145
Littlebredy. Dors —4A 14
Little Brickhill. Mil —2H 51
Little Bridgeford. Staf —3C 72
Little Brington. Nptn —4D 62
Little Bromley. Essx —3D 54
Little Broughton. Cumb —1B 102
Little Budworth. Ches —4H 83
Little Burstead. Essx —1A 40
Little Burton. E Yor —5F 101
Littlebury. Essx —2F 53
Littlebury Green. Essx —2E 53
Little Bytham. Linc —4H 75
Little Canfield. Essx —3F 53
Little Canford. Dors —3F 15
Little Carlton. Linc —2C 88
Little Carlton. Notts —5E 87
Little Casterton. Rut —5H 75
Little Catwick. E Yor —5F 101
Little Catworth. Cambs —3A 64
Little Cawthorpe. Linc —2C 88
Little Chalfont. Buck —1A 38
Little Chart. Kent —1D 28
Little Chesterford. Essx —1F 53
Little Cheverell. Wilts —1E 23
Little Chishill. Cambs —2E 53
Little Clacton. Essx —4E 55
Little Clanfield. Oxon —5A 50
Little Clifton. Cumb —2B 102
Little Coates. NE Lin —4F 95
Little Comberton. Worc —1E 49
Little Common. E Sus —5B 28
Little Compton. Warw —2A 50
Little Cornard. Suff —2B 54
Littlecote. Buck —3G 51
Littlecott. Wilts —1G 23
Little Cowarne. Here —5A 60
Little Coxwell. Oxon —2A 36
Little Crakehall. N Yor —5F 105
Little Crawley. Mil —1H 51
Little Creich. High —5D 164
Little Cressingham. Norf —5A 78
Little Crosby. Mers —4B 90
Little Crosthwaite. Cumb —2D 102
Little Cubley. Derbs —2F 73
Little Dalby. Leics —4E 75
Little Dawley. Telf —5A 72
Littledean. Glos —4B 48
Little Dens. Abers —4H 161
Little Dewchurch. Here —2A 48
Little Ditton. Cambs —5F 65
Little Down. Hants —1B 24
Little Downham. Cambs —2E 65
Little Drayton. Shrp —2A 72
Little Driffield. E Yor —4E 101
Little Dunham. Norf —4A 78
Little Dunkeld. Per —4H 143
Little Dunmow. Essx —3G 53
Little Easton. Essx —3G 53
Little Eaton. Derbs —1A 74
Little Eccleston. Lanc —5D 96
Little Ellingham. Norf —1C 66
Little Elm. Som —2C 22
Little End. Essx —5F 53
Little Everdon. Nptn —5C 62
Little Eversden. Cambs —5C 64
Little Faringdon. Oxon —5H 49
Little Fencote. N Yor —5F 105
Little Fenton. N Yor —1F 93
Littleferry. High —4F 165
Little Fransham. Norf —4B 78
Little Gaddesden. Herts —4H 51
Little Garway. Here —3H 47
Little Gidding. Cambs —2A 64
Little Glemham. Suff —5F 67
Little Glenshee. Per —5G 143
Little Gransden. Cambs —5B 64
Little Green. Wrex —1G 71
Little Grimsby. Linc —1C 88
Little Habton. N Yor —2B 100
Little Hadham. Herts —3E 53
Little Hale. Linc —1A 76
Little Hallingbury. Essx —4E 53
Littleham. Devn —4E 19
(nr. Bideford)
Littleham. Devn —4D 12
(nr. Exmouth)
Little Hampden. Buck —5G 51
Littlehampton. W Sus —5B 26
Little Haresfield. Glos —5D 48
Little Harrowden. Nptn —3F 63
Little Haseley. Oxon —5E 51
Little Hatfield. E Yor —5F 101
Little Hautbois. Norf —3E 79
Little Haven. Pemb —3C 42
Little Hay. Staf —5F 73
Little Hayfield. Derbs —2E 85
Little Haywood. Staf —3E 73
Little Heath. W Mid —2H 61
Little Heck. N Yor —2F 93
Littlehempston. Devn —2E 9
Little Herbert's. Glos —4E 49
Little Hereford. Here —4H 59
Little Horkesley. Essx —2C 54
Little Hormead. Herts —3E 53
Little Horsted. E Sus —4F 27
Little Horton. W Yor —1B 92
Little Horwood. Buck —2F 51
Little Houghton. Nptn —5F 63
Littlehoughton. Nmbd —3G 121
Little Houghton. S Yor —4E 93
Little Hucklow. Derbs —3F 85
Little Hulton. G Man —4F 91
Little Ingestre. Staf —3D 73
Little Irchester. Nptn —4G 63
Little Kelk. E Yor —3E 101
Little Kimble. Buck —5G 51
Little Kineton. Warw —5H 61
Little Kingshill. Buck —2G 37
Little Langdale. Cumb —4E 102
Little Langford. Wilts —3F 23
Little Laver. Essx —5F 53
Little Lawford. Warw —3B 62
Little Leigh. Ches —3A 84
Little Leighs. Essx —4H 53
Little Leven. E Yor —5E 101
Little Lever. G Man —4F 91
Little Linford. Mil —1G 51
Little London. Buck —4E 51
Little London. E Sus —4G 27
Little London. Hants —2B 24
(nr. Andover)
Little London. Hants —1E 24
(nr. Basingstoke)
Little London. Linc —3D 76
(nr. Long Sutton)
Little London. Linc —3B 76
(nr. Spalding)
Little London. Norf —2E 79
(nr. North Walsham)
Little London. Norf —1G 65
(nr. Northwold)
Little London. Norf —2D 78
(nr. Saxthorpe)
Little London. Norf —1F 65
(nr. Southery)
Little London. Powy —2C 58
Little Longstone. Derbs —3F 85
Little Malvern. Worc —1C 48
Little Maplestead. Essx —2B 54
Little Marcle. Here —2B 48
Little Marlow. Buck —3G 37
Little Massingham. Norf —3G 77
Little Melton. Norf —5D 78
Littlemill. Abers —4H 151
Littlemill. E Ayr —3D 116
Littlemill. High —3D 158
Little Mill. Mon —5G 47
Little Milton. Oxon —5E 50
Little Missenden. Buck —1A 38
Littlemoor. Derbs —4A 86
Littlemoor. Dors —4B 14
Littlemore. Oxon —5D 50
Little Moreton Hall NT —5C 84
Little Mountain. Flin —4E 83
Little Musgrave. Cumb —3A 104
Little Ness. Shrp —4G 71
Little Neston. Ches —3F 83
Little Newcastle. Pemb —2D 43
Little Newsham. Dur —3E 105
Little Oakley. Essx —3F 55
Little Oakley. Nptn —2F 63
Little Onn. Staf —4C 72
Little Ormside. Cumb —3A 104
Little Orton. Cumb —4E 113
Little Orton. Leics —5H 73
Little Ouse. Norf —2F 65
Little Ouseburn. N Yor —3G 99
Littleover. Derb —2H 73
Little Packington. Warw —2G 61
Little Paxton. Cambs —4A 64
Little Petherick. Corn —1D 6
Little Plumpton. Lanc —1B 90
Little Plumstead. Norf —4F 79
Little Ponton. Linc —2G 75
Littleport. Cambs —2E 65
Little Posbrook. Hants —2D 16
Little Potheridge. Devn —1F 11
Little Preston. Nptn —5C 62
Little Raveley. Cambs —3B 64
Little Reynoldston. Swan —4D 31
Little Ribston. N Yor —4F 99
Little Rissington. Glos —4G 49
Little Rogart. High —3E 165
Little Rollright. Oxon —2A 50
Little Ryburgh. Norf —3B 78
Little Ryle. Nmbd —3E 121
Little Ryton. Shrp —5G 71
Little Salkeld. Cumb —1G 103
Little Sampford. Essx —2G 53
Little Sandhurst. Brac —5G 37
Little Saredon. Staf —5D 72
Little Saxham. Suff —4G 65
Little Scatwell. High —3F 157
Little Shelford. Cambs —5D 64
Little Shoddesden. Hants —2A 24
Little Singleton. Lanc —1B 90
Little Smeaton. N Yor —3F 93
Little Snoring. Norf —2B 78
Little Sodbury. S Glo —3C 34
Little Somborne. Hants —3B 24
Little Somerford. Wilts —3E 35
Little Soudley. Shrp —3B 72
Little Stainforth. N Yor —3H 97
Little Stainton. Darl —2A 106
Little Stanney. Ches —3G 83
Little Staughton. Beds —4A 64
Little Steeping. Linc —4D 88
Littlester. Shet —3G 173
Little Stoke. Staf —2D 72
Littlestone-on-Sea. Kent —3E 29
Little Stonham. Suff —4D 66
Little Street. Cambs —2E 65
Little Stretton. Leics —5D 74
Little Stretton. Shrp —1G 59
Little Strickland. Cumb —3G 103
Little Stukeley. Cambs —3B 64
Little Sugnall. Staf —2C 72
Little Sutton. Ches —3F 83
Little Sutton. Linc —3D 76
Little Swinburne. Nmbd —2C 114
Little Tew. Oxon —3B 50
Little Tey. Essx —3B 54
Little Thetford. Cambs —3E 65
Little Thirkleby. N Yor —2G 99
Little Thornton. Lanc —5C 96
Littlethorpe. Leics —1C 62
Littlethorpe. N Yor —3F 99
Little Thorpe. W Yor —2B 92
Little Thurlow. Suff —5F 65
Little Thurrock. Thur —3H 39
Littleton. Ches —4G 83
Littleton. Hants —3C 24
Littleton. Som —3H 21
Littleton. Surr —4B 38
Littleton. Surr —1A 26
Littleton Drew. Wilts —3D 34
Littleton Pannell. Wilts —1E 23
Littleton-upon-Severn. S Glo —2A 34
Little Torboll. High —4E 165
Little Torrington. Devn —1E 11
Little Totham. Essx —4B 54
Little Town. Cumb —3D 102
Littletown. Dur —5G 115
Littletown. High —5E 165
Little Town. Lanc —1E 91
Little Twycross. Leics —5H 73
Little Urswick. Cumb —2B 96
Little Wakering. Essx —2D 40
Little Walden. Essx —1F 53
Little Waldingfield. Suff —1C 54
Little Walsingham. Norf —2B 78
Little Waltham. Essx —4H 53
Little Warley. Essx —1H 39
Little Washbourne. Glos —2E 49
Little Weighton. E Yor —1C 94
Little Welnetham. Suff —5A 66
Little Wenham. Suff —2D 54
Little Wenlock. Telf —5A 72
Little Whittingham Green. Suff —3E 67
Littlewick Green. Wind —4G 37
Little Wilbraham. Cambs —5E 65
Littlewindsor. Dors —2H 13
Little Wisbeach. Linc —2A 76
Little Witcombe. Glos —4E 49
Little Witley. Worc —4B 60
Little Wittenham. Oxon —2D 36
Little Wolford. Warw —2A 50
Littleworth. Beds —1A 52

Littleworth. Glos —2G 49
Littleworth. Oxon —2B 36
Littleworth. Staf —4E 73
(nr. Cannock)
Littleworth. Staf —3B 72
(nr. Eccleshall)
Littleworth. Staf —3D 72
(nr. Stafford)
Littleworth. W Sus —3C 26
Littleworth. Worc —4D 61
(nr. Redditch)
Littleworth. Worc —1D 49
(nr. Worcester)
Little Wratting. Suff —1G 53
Little Wymington. Nptn —4G 63
Little Wymondley. Herts —3C 52
Little Wyrley. Staf —5E 73
Little Yeldham. Essx —2A 54
Littley Green. Essx —4G 53
Litton. Derbs —3F 85
Litton. N Yor —2B 98
Litton. Som —1A 22
Litton Cheney. Dors —3A 14
Liurbost. W Isl —5F 171
Liverpool. Mers —1F 83 & 191
Liverpool Anglican Cathedral —191
Liverpool John Lennon Airport. Mers —2G 83
Liverpool RC Cathedral —191
Liversedge. W Yor —2B 92
Liverton. Devn —5B 12
Liverton. Red C —3E 107
Liverton Mines. Red C —3E 107
Livingston. W Lot —3D 128
Livingston Village. W Lot —3D 128
Lixwm. Flin —3D 82
Lizard. Corn —5E 5
Lizard Point —5E 5
Llaingoch. IOA —2B 80
Llaithddu. Powy —2C 58
Llampha. V Glam —4C 32
Llan. Powy —5A 70
Llanaber. Gwyn —4F 69
Llanaelhaearn. Gwyn —1C 68
Llanaeron. Cdgn —5D 57
Llanafan. Cdgn —3F 57
Llanafan-fawr. Powy —5B 58
Llanafan-fechan. Powy —5B 58
Llanallgo. IOA —2D 81
Llanandras. Powy —4E 59
Llananno. Powy —3C 58
Llanarmon. Gwyn —2D 68
Llanarmon Dyffryn Ceiriog. Wrex —2D 70
Llanarmon-yn-Ial. Den —5D 82
Llanarth. Cdgn —5D 56
Llanarth. Mon —4G 47
Llanarthne. Carm —3F 45
Llanasa. Flin —2D 82
Llanbabo. IOA —2C 80
Llanbadarn Fawr. Cdgn —2F 57
Llanbadarn Fynydd. Powy —3C 58
Llanbadarn-y-garreg. Powy —1E 46
Llanbadoc. Mon —5G 47
Llanbadrig. IOA —1C 80
Llanbeder. Newp —2G 33
Llanbedr. Gwyn —3E 69
Llanbedr. Powy —3F 47
(nr. Crickhowell)
Llanbedr. Powy —1E 47
(nr. Hay-on-Wye)
Llanbedr-Dyffryn-Clwyd. Den —5D 82
Llanbedrgoch. IOA —2E 81
Llanbedrog. Gwyn —2C 68
Llanbedr Pont Steffan. Cdgn —1F 45
Llanbedr-y-cennin. Cnwy —4G 81
Llanberis. Gwyn —4E 81
Llanberis Lake Railway —4E 81
Llanbethery. V Glam —5D 32
Llanbister. Powy —3D 58
Llanblethian. V Glam —4C 32
Llanboidy. Carm —2G 43
Llanbradach. Cphy —2E 33
Llanbrynmair. Powy —5A 70
Llanbydderi. V Glam —5D 32
Llancadle. V Glam —5D 32
Llancarfan. V Glam —4D 32
Llancatal. V Glam —5D 32
Llancayo. Mon —5G 47
Llancloudy. Here —3H 47
Llancoch. Powy —3E 58
Llancynfelyn. Cdgn —1F 57
Llandaff. Card —4E 33
Llandanwg. Gwyn —3E 69
Llandarcy. Neat —3G 31
Llandawke. Carm —3G 43
Llanddaniel-Fab. IOA —3D 81
Llanddarog. Carm —4F 45
Llanddeiniol. Cdgn —3E 57
Llanddeiniolen. Gwyn —4E 81
Llandderfel. Gwyn —2B 70
Llanddeusant. Carm —3A 46
Llanddeusant. IOA —2C 80
Llanddew. Powy —2D 46
Llanddewi. Swan —4D 30
Llanddewi Brefi. Cdgn —5F 57
Llanddewi'r Cwm. Powy —1D 46
Llanddewi Rhydderch. Mon —4G 47
Llanddewi Velfrey. Pemb —3F 43
Llanddewi Ystradenni. Powy —4D 58
Llanddoged. Cnwy —4H 81
Llanddona. IOA —3E 81
Llanddowror. Carm —3G 43
Llanddulas. Cnwy —3B 82
Llanddwywe. Gwyn —3E 69
Llanddyfnan. IOA —3E 81
Llandecwyn. Gwyn —2F 69
Llandefaelog Fach. Powy —2D 46
Llandefaelog-tre'r-graig. Powy —2E 47
Llandefalle. Powy —2E 46
Llandegai. Gwyn —3E 81
Llandegfan. IOA —3E 81
Llandegla. Den —5D 82
Llandegley. Powy —4D 58
Llandegveth. Mon —2G 33
Llandeilo. Carm —3G 45
Llandeilo Graban. Powy —1D 46
Llandeilo'r Fan. Powy —2B 46
Llandeloy. Pemb —2C 42
Llandenny. Mon —5H 47
Llandevaud. Newp —2H 33
Llandevenny. Mon —3H 33
Llandilo. Pemb —2F 43
Llandinabo. Here —3A 48
Llandinam. Powy —2C 58
Llandissilio. Pemb —2F 43
Llandogo. Mon —5A 48
Llandough. V Glam —4C 32
(nr. Cowbridge)
Llandough. V Glam —4E 33
(nr. Penarth)
Llandovery. Carm —2A 46
Llandow. V Glam —4C 32
Llandre. Cdgn —2F 57
Llandrillo. Den —2C 70
Llandrillo-yn-Rhos. Cnwy —2H 81
Llandrindod. Powy —4C 58
Llandrindod Wells. Powy —4C 58
Llandrinio. Powy —4E 71
Llandsadwrn. Carm —2G 45
Llandudno. Cnwy —2G 81
Llandudno Junction. Cnwy —3G 81
Llandudoch. Pemb —1B 44
Llandw. V Glam —4C 32
Llandwrog. Gwyn —5D 80
Llandybie. Carm —4G 45
Llandyfaelog. Carm —4E 45
Llandyfan. Carm —4G 45
Llandyfriog. Cdgn —1D 44
Llandyfrydog. IOA —2D 80
Llandygwydd. Cdgn —1C 44
Llandynan. Den —1D 70
Llandyrnog. Den —4D 82
Llandysilio. Powy —4E 71
Llandyssil. Powy —1D 58
Llandysul. Cdgn —1E 45
Llanedeyrn. Card —3F 33
Llaneglwys. Powy —2D 46
Llanegryn. Gwyn —5F 69
Llanegwad. Carm —3F 45
Llaneilian. IOA —1D 80
Llanelian-yn-Rhos. Cnwy —3A 82
Llanelidan. Den —5D 82
Llanelieu. Powy —2E 47
Llanellen. Mon —4G 47
Llanelli. Carm —3E 31
Llanelltyd. Gwyn —4G 69
Llanelly. Mon —4F 47
Llanelly Hill. Mon —4F 47
Llanelwedd. Powy —5C 58
Llanelwy. Den —3C 82
Llanenddwyn. Gwyn —3E 69
Llanengan. Gwyn —3B 68
Llanerch. Powy —1F 59
Llanerchaeron NT —5D 57
Llanerchymedd. IOA —2D 80
Llanerfyl. Powy —5C 70
Llaneuddog. IOA —2D 80
Llanfachraeth. IOA —2C 80
Llanfaelog. IOA —3C 80
Llanfaelrhys. Gwyn —3B 68
Llanfaenor. Mon —4H 47
Llanfaes. IOA —3F 81
Llanfaes. Powy —3D 46
Llanfaethlu. IOA —2C 80
Llanfaglan. Gwyn —4D 80
Llanfair. Gwyn —3E 69
Llanfair. Here —1F 47
Llanfair Caereinion. Powy —5D 70
Llanfair Clydogau. Cdgn —5F 57
Llanfair Dyffryn Clwyd. Den —5D 82
Llanfairfechan. Cnwy —3F 81
Llanfair-Nant-Gwyn. Pemb —1F 43
Llanfair Pwllgwyngyll. IOA —3E 81
Llanfair Talhaiarn. Cnwy —3B 82
Llanfair Waterdine. Shrp —3E 59
Llanfair-ym-Muallt. Powy —5C 58
Llanfairyneubwll. IOA —3C 80
Llanfairynghornwy. IOA —1C 80
Llanfallteg. Carm —3F 43
Llanfallteg West. Carm —3F 43
Llanfaredd. Powy —5C 58
Llanfarian. Cdgn —3E 57
Llanfechain. Powy —3D 70
Llanfechell. IOA —1C 80
Llanfechreth. Gwyn —3G 69
Llanfendigaid. Gwyn —5E 69
Llanferres. Den —4D 82
Llan Ffestiniog. Gwyn —1G 69
Llanfflewyn. IOA —2C 80
Llanfihangel Glyn Myfyr. Cnwy —1B 70
Llanfihangel Nant Bran. Powy —2C 46
Llanfihangel-Nant-Melan. Powy —5D 58
Llanfihangel Rhydithon. Powy —4D 58
Llanfihangel Rogiet. Mon —3H 33
Llanfihangel Tal-y-llyn. Powy —3E 46
Llanfihangel-uwch-Gwili. Carm —3E 45
Llanfihangel-yng-ngwynfa. Powy —4C 70
Llanfihangel yn Nhowyn. IOA —3C 80
Llanfihangel-y-pennant. (nr. Golan) Gwyn —1E 69
Llanfihangel-y-pennant. (nr. Tywyn) Gwyn —5F 69
Llanfilo. Powy —2E 46
Llanfinhangel-ar-Arth. Carm —2E 45
Llanfinhangel-y-Creuddyn. Cdgn —3F 57
Llanfinhangel-y-traethau. Gwyn —2E 69
Llanfleiddan. V Glam —4C 32
Llanfoist. Mon —4F 47
Llanfor. Gwyn —2B 70
Llanfrechfa. Torf —2G 33
Llanfrothen. Gwyn —1F 69
Llanfrynach. Powy —3D 46
Llanfwrog. Den —5D 82
Llanfwrog. IOA —2C 80
Llanfyllin. Powy —4D 70
Llanfynydd. Carm —3F 45
Llanfynydd. Flin —5E 83
Llanfyrnach. Pemb —1G 43
Llangadfan. Powy —4C 70
Llangadog. Carm —3H 45
(nr. Llandovery)
Llangadog. Carm —5E 45
(nr. Llanelli)
Llangadwaladr. IOA —4C 80
Llangadwaladr. Powy —2D 70
Llangaffo. IOA —4D 80
Llangain. Carm —4D 45
Llangammarch Wells. Powy —1C 46
Llangan. V Glam —4C 32
Llangarron. Here —3A 48
Llangasty-Talyllyn. Powy —3E 47
Llangathen. Carm —3F 45
Llangattock. Powy —4F 47
Llangattock Lingoed. Mon —3G 47
Llangattock-Vibon-Avel. Mon —4H 47
Llangedwyn. Powy —3D 70
Llangefni. IOA —3D 80
Llangeinor. B'end —3C 32
Llangeitho. Cdgn —5F 57
Llangeler. Carm —2D 44
Llangelynin. Gwyn —5E 69
Llangendeirne. Carm —4E 45
Llangennech. Carm —5F 45
Llangennith. Swan —3D 30
Llangenny. Powy —4F 47
Llangernyw. Cnwy —4A 82
Llangian. Gwyn —3B 68
Llangiwg. Neat —5H 45
Llangloffan. Pemb —1D 42
Llanglydwen. Carm —2F 43
Llangoed. IOA —3F 81
Llangoedmor. Cdgn —1C 44
Llangollen. Den —1E 70
Llangollen Railway —1D 70
Llangolman. Pemb —2F 43
Llangorse. Powy —3E 47
Llangorwen. Cdgn —2F 57
Llangovan. Mon —5H 47
Llangower. Gwyn —2B 70
Llangranog. Cdgn —5C 56
Llangristiolus. IOA —3D 80
Llangrove. Here —4A 48
Llangua. Mon —3G 47
Llangunllo. Powy —3E 58
Llangunnor. Carm —3E 45
Llangurig. Powy —3B 58
Llangwm. Cnwy —1B 70
Llangwm. Mon —5H 47
Llangwm. Pemb —4D 43
Llangwm-isaf. Mon —5H 47
Llangwnnadl. Gwyn —2B 68
Llangwyfan. Den —4D 82
Llangwyfan-isaf. IOA —4C 80
Llangwyllog. IOA —3D 80
Llangwyryfon. Cdgn —3E 57
Llangybi. Cdgn —5F 57
Llangybi. Gwyn —1D 68
Llangybi. Mon —2G 33
Llangyfelach. Swan —3F 31
Llangynhafal. Den —4D 82
Llangynidr. Powy —4E 47
Llangynin. Carm —3G 43
Llangynog. Carm —3H 43
Llangynog. Powy —3C 70
Llangynwyd. B'end —3B 32
Llanhamlach. Powy —3D 46
Llanharan. Rhon —3D 32
Llanharry. Rhon —3D 32
Llanhennock. Mon —2G 33
Llanhilleth. Blae —5F 47
Llanidloes. Powy —2B 58
Llaniestyn. Gwyn —2B 68
Llanigon. Powy —1F 47
Llanilar. Cdgn —3F 57
Llanilid. Rhon —3C 32
Llanilltud Fawr. V Glam —5C 32
Llanishen. Card —3E 33
Llanishen. Mon —5H 47
Llanllawddog. Carm —3E 45
Llanllechid. Gwyn —4F 81
Llanllowell. Mon —2G 33
Llanllugan. Powy —5C 70
Llanllwch. Carm —4D 45
Llanllwchaiarn. Powy —1D 58
Llanllwni. Carm —2E 45
Llanllyfni. Gwyn —5D 80
Llanmadoc. Swan —3D 30
Llanmaes. V Glam —5C 32
Llanmartin. Newp —3G 33
Llanmerwig. Powy —1D 58
Llanmihangel. V Glam —4C 32
Llan-mill. Pemb —3F 43
Llanmiloe. Carm —4G 43
Llanmorlais. Swan —3E 31
Llannefydd. Cnwy —3B 82
Llannon. Carm —5F 45
Llan-non. Cdgn —4E 57
Llannor. Gwyn —2C 68
Llanpumsaint. Carm —3E 45
Llanrhaeadr. Den —4C 82
Llanrhaeadr-ym-Mochnant. Powy —3D 70
Llanrhidian. Swan —3D 31
Llanrhos. Cnwy —2G 81
Llanrhyddlad. IOA —2C 80
Llanrhystud. Cdgn —4E 57
Llanrian. Pemb —1C 42
Llanrothal. Here —4H 47
Llanrug. Gwyn —4E 81
Llanrumney. Card —3F 33
Llanrwst. Cnwy —4G 81
Llansadurnen. Carm —3G 43
Llansadwrn. IOA —3E 81
Llansaint. Carm —5D 45
Llansamlet. Swan —3F 31
Llansanffraid Glan Conwy. Cnwy —3H 81
Llansannan. Cnwy —4B 82
Llansannor. V Glam —4C 32
Llansantffraed. Cdgn —4E 57
Llansantffraed. Powy —3E 46
Llansantffraed Cwmdeuddwr. Powy —4B 58
Llansantffraed in Elwel. Powy —5C 58
Llansantffraid-ym-Mechain. Powy —3E 70
Llansawel. Carm —2G 45
Llansawel. Neat —3G 31
Llansilin. Powy —3E 70
Llansoy. Mon —5H 47
Llanspyddid. Powy —3D 46
Llanstadwell. Pemb —4D 42
Llansteffan. Carm —3H 43
Llansteffan Castle CADW —4D 44
Llanstephan. Powy —1E 46
Llantarnam. Torf —2F 33
Llanteg. Pemb —3F 43
Llanthony. Mon —3F 47
Llantilio Crossenny. Mon —4G 47
Llantilio Pertholey. Mon —4G 47
Llantood. Pemb —1B 44
Llantrisant. Mon —2G 33
Llantrisant. Rhon —3D 32
Llantrithyd. V Glam —4D 32
Llantwit Fardre. Rhon —3D 32
Llantwit Major. V Glam —5C 32
Llanuwchllyn. Gwyn —2A 70
Llanvaches. Newp —2H 33
Llanvair Discoed. Mon —2H 33
Llanvapley. Mon —4G 47
Llanvetherine. Mon —4G 47
Llanveynoe. Here —2G 47
Llanvihangel Court —4G 47
Llanvihangel Crucorney. Mon —3G 47
Llanvihangel Gobion. Mon —5G 47
Llanvihangel Ystern-Llewern. Mon —4H 47
Llanwarne. Here —3A 48
Llanwddyn. Powy —4C 70
Llanwenarth. Mon —4F 47
Llanwenog. Cdgn —1E 45
Llanwern. Newp —3G 33
Llanwinio. Carm —2G 43
Llanwnda. Gwyn —5D 81
Llanwnda. Pemb —1D 42
Llanwnnen. Cdgn —1F 45
Llanwnog. Powy —1C 58
Llanwrda. Carm —2H 45
Llanwrin. Powy —5G 69
Llanwrthwl. Powy —4B 58
Llanwrtud. Powy —1B 46
Llanwrtyd. Powy —1B 46
Llanwrtyd Wells. Powy —1B 46
Llanwyddelan. Powy —5C 70
Llanyblodwel. Shrp —3E 71
Llanybri. Carm —3H 43
Llanybydder. Carm —1F 45
Llanycefn. Pemb —2E 43
Llanychaer. Pemb —1D 43
Llanycil. Gwyn —2B 70
Llanymawddwy. Gwyn —4B 70
Llanymddyfri. Carm —2A 46
Llanymynech. Shrp —3E 71
Llanynghenedl. IOA —2C 80
Llanynys. Den —4D 82
Llan-y-pwll. Wrex —5F 83
Llanyrafon. Torf —2G 33
Llanyre. Powy —4C 58
Llanystumdwy. Gwyn —2D 68
Llanywern. Powy —3E 46
Llawhaden. Pemb —3E 43
Llawhaden Castle —3E 43
Llawndy. Flin —2D 82
Llawnt. Shrp —2E 71
Llawr Dref. Gwyn —3B 68
Llawryglyn. Powy —1B 58
Llay. Wrex —5F 83
Llechfaen. Powy —3D 46
Llechryd. Cphy —5E 46
Llechryd. Cdgn —1C 44
Llechrydau. Wrex —2E 71
Llechwedd Slate Caverns —1F 69
Lledrod. Cdgn —3F 57
Llethrid. Swan —3E 31
Llidiad-Nenog. Carm —2F 45
Llidiardau. Gwyn —2A 70
Llidiart y Parc. Den —1D 70
Llithfaen. Gwyn —1C 68
Lloc. Flin —3D 82
Llong. Flin —4E 83
Llowes. Powy —1E 47
Lloyney. Powy —3E 59
Llundain-fach. Cdgn —5E 57
Llwydcoed. Rhon —5C 46
Llwyncelyn. Cdgn —5D 56
Llwyncelyn. Swan —5G 45
Llwyndaffydd. Cdgn —5C 56
Llwynderw. Powy —5E 70
Llwyn-du. Mon —4F 47
Llwyngwril. Gwyn —5E 69
Llwynhendy. Carm —3E 31
Llwynmawr. Wrex —2E 71
Llwyn-on Village. Mer T —4D 46
Llwyn-teg. Carm —5F 45
Llwyn-y-brain. Carm —3F 43
Llwynygog. Powy —1A 58
Llwyn-y-groes. Cdgn —5E 57
Llwynypia. Rhon —2C 32
Llynclys. Shrp —3E 71
Llynfaes. IOA —3D 80
Llysfaen. Cnwy —3A 82
Llyswen. Powy —2E 47
Llysworney. V Glam —4C 32
Llys-y-fran. Pemb —2E 43
Llywel. Powy —2B 46
Llywernog. Cdgn —2G 57
Llywernog Silver-Lead Mine —2G 57
Loan. Falk —2C 128
Loanend. Nmbd —4F 131
Loanhead. Midl —3F 129
Loaningfoot. Dum —4A 112
Loanreoch. High —1A 158
Loans. S Ayr —1C 116
Loansdean. Nmbd —1F 115
Lobb. Devn —3E 19
Lobhillcross. Devn —4E 11
Lochaber. Mor —3E 159
Loch a Charnain. W Isl —4D 170
Loch a Ghainmhich. W Isl —5E 171
Lochailort. High —5F 147
Lochaline. High —4A 140
Lochans. Dum —4F 109
Locharbriggs. Dum —1A 112
Lochardil. High —4A 158
Lochassynt Lodge. High —1F 163
Lochavich. Arg —2G 133
Lochawe. Arg —1A 134
Loch Baghasdail. W Isl —7C 170
Lochboisdale. W Isl —7C 170
Lochbuie. Arg —1D 132
Lochcarron. High —5A 156
Loch Choire Lodge. High —5G 167
Lochdochart House. Stir —1D 134
Lochdon. Arg —5B 140
Lochearnhead. Stir —1E 135
Lochee. D'dee —5C 144
Lochend. High —5H 157
(nr. Inverness)
Lochend. High —2E 169
(nr. Thurso)
Locherben. Dum —5B 118
Loch Euphoirt. W Isl —2D 170
Lochfoot. Dum —2F 111
Lochgair. Arg —4G 133
Lochgarthside. High —2H 149
Lochgelly. Fife —4D 136
Lochgilphead. Arg —1G 125
Lochgoilhead. Arg —3A 134
Loch Head. Dum —5A 110
Lochhill. Mor —2G 159
Lochindorb Lodge. High —5D 158
Lochinver. High —1E 163
Lochlane. Per —1H 135
Loch Leven Castle HS —3D 136
Loch Lomond & The Trossachs Nat. Park —2C 134
Loch Loyal Lodge. High —4G 167
Lochluichart. High —2F 157
Lochmaben. Dum —1B 112
Lochmaddy. W Isl —2E 170
Loch nam Madadh. W Isl —2E 170
Loch Ness Information Centres —5H 157
Lochore. Fife —4D 136
Lochportain. W Isl —1E 170
Lochranza. N Ayr —4H 125
Loch Sgioport. W Isl —5D 170
Lochside. Abers —2G 145
Lochside. High —5A 168
(nr. Auchentoul)
Lochside. High —3C 158
(nr. Nairn)
Lochslin. High —5F 165
Lochstack Lodge. High —4C 166
Lochton. Abers —4E 153
Lochty. Fife —3H 137
Lochuisge. High —3B 140
Lochussie. High —3G 157
Lochwinnoch. Ren —4E 127
Lochyside. High —1F 141
Lockengate. Corn —2E 7
Lockerbie. Dum —1C 112
Lockeridge. Wilts —5G 35
Lockerley. Hants —4A 24
Lockhills. Cumb —5G 113
Locking. N Som —1G 21
Lockington. E Yor —5D 101
Lockington. Leics —3B 74
Lockleywood. Shrp —3A 72
Locksgreen. IOW —3C 16
Locks Heath. Hants —2D 16
Lockton. N Yor —1C 100
Locomotion, Nat. Railway Mus. at Shildon —2F 105
Loddington. Leics —5E 75
Loddington. Nptn —3F 63
Loddiswell. Devn —4D 8
Loddon. Norf —1F 67
Lode. Cambs —4E 65
Loders. Dors —3H 13
Lodge Bird Reserve, The —1B 52
Lodge Park NT —4G 49
Lodsworth. W Sus —3A 26
Lofthouse. N Yor —2D 98
Lofthouse. W Yor —2D 92
Lofthouse Gate. W Yor —2D 92
Loftus. Red C —3E 107
Logan. E Ayr —2E 117
Loganlea. W Lot —3C 128
Logaston. Here —5F 59
Loggerheads. Staf —2B 72
Loggie. High —4F 163
Logie. Ang —2F 145
Logie. Fife —1G 137
Logie. Mor —3E 159
Logie Coldstone. Abers —3B 152
Logie Pert. Ang —2F 145
Logierait. Per —3G 143
Login. Carm —2F 43
Lolworth. Cambs —4C 64
Lonbain. High —3F 155

Londesborough. E Yor —5C 100
London. G Lon —2E 39 & 192/193
London Apprentice. Corn —3E 6
London Ashford (Lydd) Airport. Kent —3E 29
London Biggin Hill Airport. G Lon —4F 39
London City Airport. G Lon —2F 39
London Colney. Herts —5B 52
Londonderry. N Yor —1F 99
London Eye, The —193
London Gatwick Airport. W Sus —1D 27
London Heathrow Airport. G Lon —3B 38
London Luton Airport. Lutn —3B 52
London Manston Airport. Kent —4H 41
London Southend Airport. Essx —2C 40
London Stansted Airport. Essx —3F 53
Londonthorpe. Linc —2G 75
Londubh. High —5C 162
Lone. High —4D 166
Lonemore. High —5E 165 (nr. Dornoch)
Lonemore. High —1G 155 (nr. Gairloch)
Long Ashton. N Som —4A 34
Long Bank. Worc —3B 60
Longbar. N Ayr —4E 127
Long Bennington. Linc —1F 75
Longbenton. Tyne —3F 115
Longborough. Glos —3G 49
Long Bredy. Dors —3A 14
Longbridge. Warw —4G 61
Longbridge. W Mid —3E 61
Longbridge Deverill. Wilts —2D 22
Long Buckby. Nptn —4D 62
Long Buckby Wharf. Nptn —4D 62
Longburgh. Cumb —4E 112
Longburton. Dors —1B 14
Long Clawson. Leics —3E 74
Longcliffe. Derbs —5G 85
Long Common. Hants —1D 16
Long Compton. Staf —3C 72
Long Compton. Warw —2A 50
Longcot. Oxon —2A 36
Long Crendon. Buck —5E 51
Long Crichel. Dors —1E 15
Longcroft. Cumb —4D 112
Longcroft. Falk —2A 128
Longcross. Surr —4A 38
Longdale. Cumb —4H 103
Longdales. Cumb —5G 113
Longden. Shrp —5G 71
Longden Common. Shrp —5G 71
Long Ditton. Surr —4C 38
Longdon. Staf —4E 73
Longdon. Worc —2D 48
Longdon Green. Staf —4E 73
Longdon on Tern. Telf —4A 72
Longdown. Devn —3B 12
Longdowns. Corn —5B 6
Long Drax. N Yor —2G 93
Long Duckmanton. Derbs —3B 86
Long Eaton. Derbs —2B 74
Longfield. Kent —4H 39
Longfield. Shet —10E 173
Longfield Hill. Kent —4H 39
Longford. Derbs —2G 73
Longford. Glos —3D 48
Longford. G Lon —3B 38
Longford. Shrp —2A 72
Longford. Telf —4B 72
Longford. W Mid —2H 61
Longforgan. Per —1F 137
Longformacus. Bord —4C 130
Longframlington. Nmbd —4F 121
Long Gardens. Essx —2B 54
Long Green. Ches —3G 83
Long Green. Worc —2D 48
Longham. Dors —3F 15
Longham. Norf —4B 78
Long Hanborough. Oxon —4C 50
Longhedge. Wilts —2D 22
Longhill. Abers —3H 161
Longhirst. Nmbd —1F 115
Longhope. Glos —4B 48
Longhope. Orkn —8C 172
Longhorsley. Nmbd —5F 121
Longhoughton. Nmbd —3G 121
Long Itchington. Warw —4B 62
Longlands. Cumb —1D 102
Longlane. Derbs —2G 73
Long Lane. Telf —4A 72
Longlane. W Ber —4C 36
Long Lawford. Warw —3B 62
Long Lease. N Yor —4G 107
Longleat House & Safari Park —2D 22
Longley Green. Worc —5B 60
Long Load. Som —4H 21
Longmanhill. Abers —2E 161
Long Marston. Herts —4G 51
Long Marston. N Yor —4H 99
Long Marston. Warw —1G 49
Long Marton. Cumb —2H 103
Long Meadow. Cambs —4E 65
Long Meadowend. Shrp —2G 59
Long Melford. Suff —1B 54
Longmoor Camp. Hants —3F 25
Longmorn. Mor —3G 159
Longmoss. Ches —3C 84
Long Newnton. Glos —2E 35
Longnewton. Bord —2H 119
Long Newton. Stoc T —3A 106
Longney. Glos —4C 48
Longniddry. E Lot —2H 129
Longnor. Shrp —5G 71
Longnor. Staf —4E 85 (nr. Leek)
Longnor. Staf —4C 72 (nr. Stafford)
Longparish. Hants —2C 24
Longpark. Cumb —3F 113
Long Preston. N Yor —4H 97
Longridge. Lanc —1E 90
Longridge. Staf —4D 72
Longridge. W Lot —3C 128
Longriggend. N Lan —2B 128
Long Riston. E Yor —5F 101
Longrock. Corn —3C 4
Longsdon. Staf —5D 85
Longshaw. G Man —4D 90
Longshaw. Staf —1E 73
Longside. Abers —4H 161
Longslow. Shrp —2A 72
Longstanton. Cambs —4C 64
Longstock. Hants —3B 24
Longstowe. Cambs —5C 64
Long Stratton. Norf —1D 66
Long Street. Mil —1F 51
Longstreet. Wilts —1G 23
Long Sutton. Hants —2F 25
Long Sutton. Linc —3D 76
Long Sutton. Som —4H 21
Longthorpe. Pet —1A 64
Longthorpe Tower EH —1A 64
Long Thurlow. Suff —4C 66
Longthwaite. Cumb —2F 103
Longton. Lanc —2C 90
Longton. Stoke —1D 72
Longtown. Cumb —3E 113
Longtown. Here —3G 47
Longville in the Dale. Shrp —1H 59
Long Whatton. Leics —3B 74
Longwick. Buck —5F 51
Long Wittenham. Oxon —2D 36
Longwitton. Nmbd —1D 115
Longworth. Oxon —2B 36
Longyester. E Lot —3B 130
Lonmore. High —4B 154
Looe. Corn —3G 7
Loose. Kent —5B 40
Loosegate. Linc —3C 76
Loosley Row. Buck —5G 51
Lopcombe Corner. Wilts —3A 24
Lopen. Som —1H 13
Loppington. Shrp —3G 71
Lorbottle. Nmbd —4E 121
Lorbottle Hall. Nmbd —4E 121
Lordington. W Sus —2F 17
Lord Leycester Hospital, Warwick —4G 61
Loscoe. Derbs —1B 74
Loscombe. Dors —3A 14
Loseley Park —1A 26
Losgaintir. W Isl —8C 171
Lossiemouth. Mor —1G 159
Lossit. Arg —4A 124
Lost Gdns. of Heligan —4D 6
Lostock Gralam. Ches —3A 84
Lostock Green. Ches —3A 84
Lostock Hall. Lanc —2D 90
Lostock Junction. G Man —4E 91
Lostwithiel. Corn —3F 7
Lothbeg. High —2G 165
Lothersdale. N Yor —5B 98
Lotherton Hall Mus. —1E 93
Lothianbridge. Midl —3G 129
Lothianburn. Edin —3F 129
Lothmore. High —2G 165
Lottisham. Som —3A 22
Loudoun Castle Theme Park —1E 117
Loudwater. Buck —1A 38
Loughborough. Leics —4C 74
Loughor. Swan —3E 31
Loughton. Essx —1F 39
Loughton. Mil —2G 51
Loughton. Shrp —2A 60
Loughwood Meeting House NT —3F 13
Lound. Linc —4H 75
Lound. Notts —2D 86
Lound. Suff —1H 67
Lount. Leics —4A 74
Louth. Linc —2C 88
Love Clough. Lanc —2G 91
Lovedean. Hants —1E 17
Lover. Wilts —4H 23
Loversall. S Yor —1C 86
Loves Green. Essx —5G 53
Loveston. Pemb —4E 43
Lovington. Som —3A 22
Low Ackworth. W Yor —3E 93
Low Angerton. Nmbd —1D 115
Low Ardwell. Dum —5F 109
Low Ballochdoan. S Ayr —2F 109
Lowbands. Glos —2C 48
Low Barlings. Linc —3H 87
Low Bell End. N Yor —5E 107
Low Bentham. N Yor —3F 97
Low Borrowbridge. Cumb —4H 103
Low Bradfield. S Yor —1G 85
Low Bradley. N Yor —5C 98
Low Braithwaite. Cumb —5F 113
Low Brunton. Nmbd —2C 114
Low Burnham. N Lin —4A 94
Lowca. Cumb —2A 102
Low Catton. E Yor —4B 100
Low Coniscliffe. Darl —3F 105
Low Coylton. S Ayr —3D 116
Low Crosby. Cumb —4F 113
Low Dalby. N Yor —1C 100
Lowdham. Notts —1D 74
Low Dinsdale. Darl —3A 106
Lowe. Shrp —2H 71
Low Ellington. N Yor —1E 98
Lower Amble. Corn —1D 6
Lower Ansty. Dors —2C 14
Lower Arboll. High —5F 165
Lower Arncott. Oxon —4E 50
Lower Ashton. Devn —4B 12
Lower Assendon. Oxon —3F 37
Lower Auchenreath. Mor —2A 160
Lower Badcall. High —4B 166
Lower Ballam. Lanc —1B 90
Lower Basildon. W Ber —4E 36
Lower Beeding. W Sus —3D 26
Lower Benefield. Nptn —2G 63
Lower Bentley. Worc —4D 61
Lower Beobridge. Shrp —1B 60
Lower Boddington. Nptn —5B 62
Lower Bordean. Hants —4E 25
Lower Brailes. Warw —2B 50
Lower Breakish. High —1E 147
Lower Broadheath. Worc —5C 60
Lower Brockhampton NT —5A 60
Lower Brynamman. Neat —4H 45
Lower Bullingham. Here —2A 48
Lower Bullington. Hants —2C 24
Lower Burgate. Hants —1G 15
Lower Cam. Glos —5C 48
Lower Catesby. Nptn —5C 62
Lower Chapel. Powy —2D 46
Lower Chicksgrove. Wilts —3E 23
Lower Chute. Wilts —1B 24
Lower Clopton. Warw —5F 61
Lower Common. Hants —2E 25
Lower Cumberworth. W Yor —4C 92
Lower Darwen. Bkbn —2E 91
Lower Dean. Beds —4H 63
Lower Dean. Devn —2D 8
Lower Diabaig. High —2G 155
Lower Dicker. E Sus —4G 27
Lower Dounreay. High —2B 168
Lower Down. Shrp —2F 59
Lower Dunsforth. N Yor —3G 99
Lower East Carleton. Norf —5D 78
Lower Egleton. Here —1B 48
Lower Ellastone. Derbs —1F 73
Lower End. Nptn —4F 63
Lower Everleigh. Wilts —1G 23
Lower Failand. N Som —4A 34
Lower Faintree. Shrp —2A 60
Lower Farringdon. Hants —3F 25
Lower Foxdale. IOM —4B 108
Lower Frankton. Shrp —2F 71
Lower Froyle. Hants —2F 25
Lower Gabwell. Devn —2F 9
Lower Gledfield. High —4C 164
Lower Godney. Som —2H 21
Lower Gravenhurst. Beds —2B 52
Lower Green. Essx —2E 53
Lower Green. Norf —2B 78
Lower Green. Staf —5D 72
Lower Green. W Ber —5B 36
Lower Halstow. Kent —4C 40
Lower Hardres. Kent —5F 41
Lower Hardwick. Here —5G 59
Lower Hartshay. Derbs —5A 86
Lower Hawthwaite. Cumb —1B 96
Lower Hayton. Shrp —2H 59
Lower Hergest. Here —5E 59
Lower Heyford. Oxon —3C 50
Lower Heysham. Lanc —3D 96
Lower Higham. Kent —3B 40
Lower Holbrook. Suff —2E 55
Lower Hordley. Shrp —3F 71
Lower Horncroft. W Sus —4B 26
Lower Horsebridge. E Sus —4G 27
Lower Kilcott. Glos —3C 34
Lower Killeyan. Arg —5A 124
Lower Kingcombe. Dors —3A 14
Lower Kingswood. Surr —5D 38
Lower Kinnerton. Ches —4F 83
Lower Langford. N Som —5H 33
Lower Largo. Fife —3G 137
Lower Layham. Suff —1D 54
Lower Ledwyche. Shrp —3H 59
Lower Leigh. Staf —2E 73
Lower Lemington. Glos —2H 49
Lower Lenie. High —1H 149
Lower Ley. Glos —4C 48
Lower Llanfadog. Powy —4B 58
Lower Lode. Glos —2D 49
Lower Loxhore. Devn —3G 19
Lower Loxley. Staf —2E 73
Lower Lydbrook. Glos —4A 48
Lower Lye. Here —4G 59
Lower Machen. Newp —3F 33
Lower Maes-coed. Here —2G 47
Lower Meend. Glos —5A 48
Lower Milovaig. High —3A 154
Lower Moor. Worc —1E 49
Lower Morton. S Glo —2B 34
Lower Mountain. Flin —5F 83
Lower Nazeing. Essx —5D 53
Lower Nyland. Dors —4C 22
Lower Oakfield. Fife —4D 136
Lower Oddington. Glos —3H 49
Lower Ollach. High —5E 155
Lower Penarth. V Glam —5E 33
Lower Penn. Staf —1C 60
Lower Pennington. Hants —3B 16
Lower Peover. Ches —3B 84
Lower Pitkerrie. High —1C 158
Lower Place. G Man —3H 91
Lower Quinton. Warw —1G 49
Lower Rainham. Medw —4C 40
Lower Raydon. Suff —2D 54
Lower Seagry. Wilts —3E 35
Lower Shelton. Beds —1H 51
Lower Shiplake. Oxon —4F 37
Lower Shuckburgh. Warw —4B 62
Lower Sketty. Swan —3F 31
Lower Slaughter. Glos —3G 49
Lower Soudley. Glos —4B 48
Lower Stanton St Quintin. Wilts —3E 35
Lower Stoke. Medw —3C 40
Lower Stonnall. Staf —5E 73
Lower Stow Bedon. Norf —1B 66
Lower Street. Norf —2E 79
Lower Strensham. Worc —1E 49
Lower Sundon. Beds —3A 52
Lower Swanwick. Hants —2C 16
Lower Swell. Glos —3G 49
Lower Tale. Devn —2D 12
Lower Tean. Staf —2E 73
Lower Thurlton. Norf —1G 67
Lower Thurnham. Lanc —4D 96
Lower Thurvaston. Derbs —2G 73
Lowertown. Corn —4D 4
Lower Town. Devn —5H 11
Lower Town. Here —1B 48
Lower Town. IOS —1B 4
Lowertown. Orkn —8D 172
Lower Town. Pemb —1D 42
Lower Tysoe. Warw —1B 50
Lower Upham. Hants —1D 16
Lower Upnor. Medw —3B 40
Lower Vexford. Som —3E 20
Lower Walton. Warr —2A 84
Lower Wear. Devn —4C 12
Lower Weare. Som —1H 21
Lower Welson. Here —5E 59
Lower Whatcombe. Dors —2D 14
Lower Whitley. Ches —3A 84
Lower Wield. Hants —2E 25
Lower Winchendon. Buck —4F 51
Lower Withington. Ches —4C 84
Lower Woodend. Buck —3G 37
Lower Woodford. Wilts —3G 23
Lower Wych. Ches —1G 71
Lower Wyche. Worc —1C 48
Lowesby. Leics —5E 74
Lowestoft. Suff —1H 67
Loweswater. Cumb —2C 102
Low Etherley. Dur —2E 105
Lowfield Heath. W Sus —1D 26
Lowford. Hants —1C 16
Low Fulney. Linc —3B 76
Low Gate. Nmbd —3C 114
Lowgill. Cumb —5H 103
Lowgill. Lanc —3F 97
Low Grantley. N Yor —2E 99
Low Green. N Yor —4E 98
Low Habberley. Worc —3C 60
Low Ham. Som —4H 21
Low Hameringham. Linc —4C 88
Low Hawkser. N Yor —4G 107
Low Hesket. Cumb —5F 113
Low Hesleyhurst. Nmbd —5E 121
Lowick. Cumb —1B 96
Lowick. Nptn —2G 63
Lowick. Nmbd —1E 121
Lowick Bridge. Cumb —1B 96
Lowick Green. Cumb —1B 96
Low Knipe. Cumb —2G 103
Low Leighton. Derbs —2E 85
Low Lorton. Cumb —2C 102
Low Marishes. N Yor —2C 100
Low Marnham. Notts —4F 87
Low Mill. N Yor —5D 106
Low Moor. Lanc —5G 97
Low Moor. W Yor —2B 92
Low Moorsley. Tyne —5G 115
Low Newton-by-the-Sea. Nmbd —2G 121
Lownie Moor. Ang —4D 145
Lowood. Bord —1H 119
Low Row. Cumb —3G 113 (nr. Brampton)
Low Row. Cumb —5C 112 (nr. Wigton)
Low Row. N Yor —5C 104
Lowry, The —Manchester 191
Lowsonford. Warw —4F 61
Low Street. Norf —5C 78
Low Team. Tyne —3F 115
Lowther. Cumb —2G 103
Lowther Wildlife Park —2G 103
Lowthorpe. E Yor —3E 101
Lowton. Devn —2G 11
Lowton. G Man —1A 84
Lowton. Som —1E 13
Lowton Common. G Man —1A 84
Low Torry. Fife —1D 128
Low Toynton. Linc —3B 88
Low Valleyfield. Fife —1C 128
Low Walworth. Darl —3F 105
Low Westwood. Dur —4E 115
Low Whinnow. Cumb —4E 112
Low Wood. Cumb —1C 96
Low Worsall. N Yor —4A 106
Low Wray. Cumb —4E 103
Loxbeare. Devn —1C 12
Loxhill. Surr —2B 26
Loxhore. Devn —3G 19
Loxley. S Yor —2H 85
Loxley. Warw —5G 61
Loxley Green. Staf —2E 73
Loxton. N Som —1G 21
Loxwood. W Sus —2B 26
Lubcroy. High —3A 164
Lubenham. Leics —2E 62
Lubinvullin. High —2F 167
Luccombe. Som —2C 20
Luccombe Village. IOW —5D 16
Lucker. Nmbd —1F 121
Luckett. Corn —5D 11
Luckington. Wilts —3D 34
Lucklawhill. Fife —1G 137
Luckwell Bridge. Som —3C 20
Lucton. Here —4G 59
Ludag. W Isl —7C 170
Ludborough. Linc —1B 88
Ludchurch. Pemb —3F 43
Luddenden. W Yor —2A 92
Luddenden Foot. W Yor —2A 92
Luddenham. Kent —4D 40
Ludderburn. Cumb —5F 103
Luddesdown. Kent —4A 40
Luddington. N Lin —3B 94
Luddington. Warw —5F 61
Luddington in the Brook. Nptn —2A 64
Ludford. Linc —2A 88
Ludford. Shrp —3H 59
Ludgershall. Buck —4E 51
Ludgershall. Wilts —1A 24
Ludgershall Castle EH —1A 24
Ludgvan. Corn —3C 4
Ludham. Norf —4F 79
Ludlow. Shrp —3H 59
Ludlow Castle —3H 59
Ludstone. Shrp —1C 60
Ludwell. Wilts —4E 23
Ludworth. Dur —5G 115
Luffenhall. Herts —3C 52
Luffincot. Devn —3D 10
Lugar. E Ayr —2E 117
Luggate Burn. E Lot —2C 130
Lugg Green. Here —4G 59
Luggiebank. N Lan —2A 128
Lugton. E Ayr —4F 127
Lugwardine. Here —1A 48
Luib. High —1D 146
Luib. Stir —1D 135
Lulham. Here —1H 47
Lullingstone Castle —4G 39
Lullingstone Roman Villa EH —4G 39
Lullington. Derbs —4G 73
Lullington. Som —1C 22
Lulsgate Bottom. N Som —5A 34
Lulsley. Worc —5B 60
Lulworth Camp. Dors —4D 14
Lulworth Castle EH —4D 14
Lumb. Lanc —2G 91
Lumb. W Yor —2A 92
Lumby. N Yor —1E 93
Lumphanan. Abers —3C 152
Lumphinnans. Fife —4D 136
Lumsdaine. Bord —3E 131
Lumsden. Abers —1B 152
Lunan. Ang —3F 145
Lunanhead. Ang —3D 145
Luncarty. Per —1C 136
Lund. E Yor —5D 100
Lund. N Yor —1G 93
Lundie. Ang —5B 144
Lundin Links. Fife —3G 137
Lundy Green. Norf —1E 67
Lundy Island —2B 18
Lunna. Shet —5F 173
Lunning. Shet —5G 173
Lunnon. Swan —4E 31
Lunsford. Kent —5B 40
Lunsford's Cross. E Sus —4B 28
Lunt. Mers —4B 90
Luppitt. Devn —2E 13
Lupridge. Devn —3D 8
Lupset. W Yor —3D 92
Lupton. Cumb —1E 97
Lurgashall. W Sus —3A 26
Lusby. Linc —4C 88
Luscombe. Devn —3D 9
Luson. Devn —4C 8
Luss. Arg —4C 134
Lussagiven. Arg —1E 125
Lusta. High —3B 154
Lustleigh. Devn —4A 12
Luston. Here —4G 59
Luthermuir. Abers —2F 145
Luthrie. Fife —2F 137
Lutley. Staf —2C 60
Luton. Devn —2D 12 (nr. Honiton)
Luton. Devn —5C 12 (nr. Teignmouth)
Luton. Lutn —3A 52
Luton (London) Airport. Lutn —3B 52
Lutterworth. Leics —2C 62
Lutton. Devn —3B 8 (nr. Ivybridge)
Lutton. Devn —2C 8 (nr. South Brent)
Lutton. Linc —3D 76
Lutton. Nptn —2A 64
Lutton Gowts. Linc —3D 76
Lutworthy. Devn —1A 12
Luxborough. Som —3C 20
Luxley. Glos —3B 48
Luxulyan. Corn —3E 7
Lybster. High —5E 169
Lydbury North. Shrp —2F 59
Lydcott. Devn —3G 19
Lydd. Kent —3E 29
Lydden. Kent —4H 41
Lydden. Kent —1G 29
Lyddington. Rut —1F 63
Lyddington Bede House EH —1F 63
Lydd (London Ashford) Airport. Kent —3E 29
Lydd-on-Sea. Kent —4E 29
Lydeard St Lawrence. Som —3E 21
Lyde Green. Hants —1F 25
Lydford. Devn —4F 11
Lydford Castle EH —4F 11
Lydford Fair Place. Som —3A 22
Lydford Gorge NT —4F 11
Lydgate. G Man —4H 91
Lydgate. W Yor —2H 91
Lydham. Shrp —1F 59
Lydiard Millicent. Wilts —3F 35
Lydiard Park —3G 35
Lydiate. Mers —4B 90
Lydiate Ash. Worc —3D 61
Lydlinch. Dors —1C 14
Lydney. Glos —5B 48
Lydstep. Pemb —5E 43
Lye. W Mid —2D 60
Lye Green. Buck —5H 51

Lye Green. E Sus —2G 27
Lye Head. Worc —3B 60
Lye, The. Shrp —1A 60
Lyford. Oxon —2B 36
Lyham. Nmbd —1E 121
Lylestone. N Ayr —5E 127
Lymbridge Green. Kent —1F 29
Lyme Park NT —2D 84
Lyme Regis. Dors —3G 13
Lyminge. Kent —1F 29
Lymington. Hants —3B 16
Lyminster. W Sus —5B 26
Lymm. Warr —2A 84
Lymore. Hants —3A 16
Lympne. Kent —2F 29
Lympsham. Som —1G 21
Lympstone. Devn —4C 12
Lynaberack Lodge. High —4B 150
Lynbridge. Devn —2H 19
Lynch. Som —2C 20
Lynchat. High —3B 150
Lynch Green. Norf —5D 78
Lyndhurst. Hants —2B 16
Lyndon. Rut —5G 75
Lyne. Bord —5F 129
Lyne. Surr —4B 38
Lyneal. Shrp —2G 71
Lyne Down. Here —2B 48
Lyneham. Oxon —3A 50
Lyneham. Wilts —4F 35
Lyneholmeford. Cumb —2G 113
Lynemouth. Nmbd —5G 121
Lyne of Gorthleck. High —1H 149
Lyne of Skene. Abers —2E 153
Lynesack. Dur —2D 105
Lyness. Orkn —8C 172
Lyng. Norf —4C 78
Lyng. Som —4G 21
Lyngate. Norf —2E 79
(nr. North Walsham)
Lyngate. Norf —3F 79
(nr. Worstead)
Lynmouth. Devn —2H 19
Lynn. Staf —5E 73
Lynn. Telf —4B 72
Lynsted. Kent —4D 40
Lynstone. Corn —2C 10
Lynton. Devn —2H 19
Lynwilg. High —2C 150
Lyon's Gate. Dors —2B 14
Lyonshall. Here —5F 59
Lytchett Matravers. Dors —3E 15
Lytchett Minster. Dors —3E 15
Lyte's Carey NT —4A 22
Lyth. High —2E 169
Lytham. Lanc —2B 90
Lytham St Anne's. Lanc —2B 90
Lythe. N Yor —3F 107
Lythes. Orkn —9D 172
Lythmore. High —2C 168
Lyveden New Bield NT —2G 63

Mabe Burnthouse. Corn —5B 6
Mabie. Dum —2G 111
Mablethorpe. Linc —2E 89
Macbiehill. Bord —4E 129
Macclesfield. Ches —3D 84
Macclesfield Forest. Ches —3D 85
Macclesfield Silk Mus. —3D 84
Macduff. Abers —2E 160
Machan. S Lan —4A 128
Macharioch. Arg —5B 122
Machen. Cphy —3F 33
Machrie. N Ayr —2C 122
Machrihanish. Arg —3A 122
Machroes. Gwyn —3C 68
Machynlleth. Powy —5G 69
Mackerye End. Herts —4B 52
Mackworth. Derb —2H 73
Macmerry. E Lot —2H 129
Maddaford. Devn —3F 11
Madderty. Per —1B 136
Maddington. Wilts —2F 23
Maddiston. Falk —2C 128
Madehurst. W Sus —4A 26
Madeley. Staf —1B 72
Madeley. Telf —5A 72
Madeley Heath. Staf —1B 72
Madeley Heath. Worc —3D 60
Madford. Devn —1E 13
Madingley. Cambs —4C 64
Madley. Here —2H 47
Madresfield. Worc —1D 48
Madron. Corn —3B 4
Maenaddwyn. IOA —2D 80
Maenclochog. Pemb —2E 43
Maendy. V Glam —4D 32
Maenporth. Corn —4E 5
Maentwrog. Gwyn —1F 69
Maen-y-groes. Cdgn —1B 44
Maer. Staf —2B 72
Maerdy. Carm —3G 45
Maerdy. Cnwy —1C 70
Maerdy. Rhon —2C 32
Maesbrook. Shrp —3F 71
Maesbury. Shrp —3F 71
Maesbury Marsh. Shrp —3F 71
Maes-glas. Flin —3D 82
Maesgwyn-Isaf. Powy —4D 70
Maeshafn. Den —4E 82
Maes Howe WH HS —6C 172
Maes Llyn. Cdgn —1D 44
Maesmynis. Powy —1D 46
Maesteg. B'end —2B 32
Maestir. Cdgn —1F 45
Maesybont. Carm —4F 45
Maesycrugiau. Carm —1E 45
Maesycwmmer. Cphy —2E 33
Maesyrhandir. Powy —1C 58
Magdalen Laver. Essx —5F 53
Maggieknockater. Mor —4H 159
Magham Down. E Sus —4H 27
Maghull. Mers —4B 90
Magna Park. Leics —2C 62
Magna Science Centre —1B 86
Magor. Mon —3H 33
Magpie Green. Suff —3C 66
Magwyr. Mon —3H 33
Maidenbower. W Sus —2D 27
Maiden Bradley. Wilts —3D 22
Maiden Castle EH —4B 14
Maidencombe. Torb —2F 9
Maidenhayne. Devn —3F 13
Maidenhead. Wind —3G 37
Maiden Law. Dur —5E 115
Maiden Newton. Dors —3A 14
Maidens. S Ayr —4B 116
Maiden's Green. Brac —4G 37
Maidensgrove. Oxon —3F 37
Maidenwell. Corn —5B 10
Maidenwell. Linc —3C 88
Maiden Wells. Pemb —5D 42
Maidford. Nptn —5D 62
Maid's Moreton. Buck —2F 51
Maidstone. Kent —5B 40
Maidwell. Nptn —3E 63
Mail. Shet —9F 173
Maindee. Newp —3G 33
Mainsforth. Dur —1A 106
Mains of Auchindachy. Mor —4B 160
Mains of Auchnagatt. Abers —4G 161
Mains of Drum. Abers —3F 153
Mains of Edingight. Mor —3C 160
Mainsriddle. Dum —4G 111
Mainstone. Shrp —2E 59
Maisemore. Glos —3D 48
Major Oak —4D 86
Major's Green. Worc —3F 61
Makeney. Derbs —1A 74
Makerstoun. Bord —1A 120
Malacleit. W Isl —1C 170
Malborough. Devn —5D 8
Malcoff. Derbs —2E 85
Malcolmburn. Mor —3A 160
Malden Rushett. G Lon —4C 38
Maldon. Essx —5B 54
Malham. N Yor —3B 98
Malham Cove —3A 98
Malham Tarn NT —3A 98
Maligar. High —2D 155
Malinslee. Telf —5A 72
Mallaig. High —4E 147
Mallaig Bheag. High —4E 147
Mallaig Marine World —4E 147
Malleny Gdn. NT —3E 129
Malleny Mills. Edin —3E 129
Mallows Green. Essx —3E 53
Malltraeth. IOA —4D 80
Mallwyd. Gwyn —4A 70
Malmesbury. Wilts —3E 35
Malmsmead. Devn —2A 20
Malpas. Ches —1G 71
Malpas. Corn —4C 6
Malpas. Newp —2F 33
Malswick. Glos —3C 48
Maltby. S Yor —1C 86
Maltby. Stoc T —3B 106
Maltby le Marsh. Linc —2D 88
Malt Lane. Arg —3H 133
Maltman's Hill. Kent —1D 28
Malton. N Yor —2B 100
Malton Roman Mus. —2B 100
Malvern Link. Worc —1C 48
Malvern Wells. Worc —1C 48
Mamble. Worc —3A 60
Mamhilad. Mon —5G 47
Manaccan. Corn —4E 5
Manafon. Powy —5D 70
Manais. W Isl —9D 171
Manaton. Devn —4A 12
Manby. Linc —2C 88
Mancetter. Warw —1H 61
Manchester. G Man —1C 84 & 191
Manchester Airport. G Man —2C 84
Manchester City Art Gallery —191
Manchester Mus. of Science & Industry —191
Mancot. Flin —4F 83
M & D Theme Park —4A 128
Manderston House —4E 130
Manea. Cambs —2D 65
Maney. W Mid —1F 61
Manfield. N Yor —3F 105
Mangotsfield. S Glo —4B 34
Mangurstadh. W Isl —4C 171
Mankinholes. W Yor —2H 91
Manley. Ches —3H 83
Manley. Devn —1C 12
Manmoel. Cphy —5E 47
Mannal. Arg —4A 138
Mannerston. Falk —2D 128
Manningford Bohune. Wilts —1G 23
Manningford Bruce. Wilts —1G 23
Manningham. W Yor —1B 92
Mannings Heath. W Sus —3D 26
Mannington. Dors —2F 15
Mannington Hall —2D 78
Manningtree. Essx —2E 54
Mannofield. Aber —3G 153
Manorbier. Pemb —5E 43
Manorbier Castle —5E 43
Manorbier Newton. Pemb —5E 43
Manorowen. Pemb —1D 42
Manor Park. G Lon —2F 39
Mansell Gamage. Here —1G 47
Mansell Lacy. Here —1H 47
Mansergh. Cumb —1F 97
Mansewood. Glas —3G 127
Mansfield. E Ayr —3F 117
Mansfield. Notts —4C 86
Mansfield Woodhouse. Notts —4C 86
Mansriggs. Cumb —1B 96
Manston. Dors —1D 14
Manston. Kent —4H 41
Manston. W Yor —1D 92
Manston (London) Airport. Kent —4H 41
Manswood. Dors —2E 15
Manthorpe. Linc —4H 75
(nr. Bourne)
Manthorpe. Linc —2G 75
(nr. Grantham)
Manton. N Lin —4C 94
Manton. Notts —3C 86
Manton. Rut —5F 75
Manton. Wilts —5G 35
Manuden. Essx —3E 53
Manx Electric Railway —3D 108
(Manx Mus. Douglas) —4C 108
Maperton. Som —4B 22
Maplebeck. Notts —4E 86
Maple Cross. Herts —1B 38
Mapledurham. Oxon —4E 37
Mapledurham House —4E 37
Mapledurwell. Hants —1E 25
Maplehurst. W Sus —3C 26
Maplescombe. Kent —4G 39
Mapleton. Derbs —1F 73
Mapperley. Derbs —1B 74
Mapperley. Notts —1C 74
Mapperley Park. Notts —1C 74
Mapperton —3A 14
Mapperton. Dors —3A 14
(nr. Beaminster)
Mapperton. Dors —3E 15
(nr. Poole)
Mappleborough Green. Warw —4E 61
Mappleton. E Yor —5G 101
Mapplewell. S Yor —4D 92
Mappowder. Dors —2C 14
Maraig. W Isl —7E 171
Marazion. Corn —3C 4
Marbhig. W Isl —6G 171
Marble Hill House EH —3C 38
Marbury. Ches —1H 71
March. Cambs —1D 64
Marcham. Oxon —2C 36
Marchamley. Shrp —3H 71
Marchington. Staf —2F 73
Marchington Woodlands. Staf —3F 73
Marchwiel. Wrex —1F 71
Marchwood. Hants —1B 16
Marcross. V Glam —5C 32
Marden. Here —1A 48
Marden. Kent —1B 28
Marden. Wilts —1F 23
Marden Beech. Kent —1B 28
Marden Thorn. Kent —1B 28
Mardu. Shrp —2E 59
Mardy. Mon —4G 47
Marefield. Leics —5E 75
Mareham le Fen. Linc —4B 88
Mareham on the Hill. Linc —4B 88
Marehay. Derbs —1A 74
Marehill. W Sus —4B 26
Maresfield. E Sus —3F 27
Marfleet. Hull —2E 95
Marford. Wrex —5F 83
Margam. Neat —3A 32
Margaret Marsh. Dors —1D 14
Margaret Roding. Essx —4F 53
Margaretting. Essx —5G 53
Margaretting Tye. Essx —5G 53
Margate. Kent —3H 41
Margery. Surr —5D 38
Margnaheglish. N Ayr —2E 123
Marham. Norf —5G 77
Marhamchurch. Corn —2C 10
Marholm. Pet —5A 76
Marian Cwm. Den —3C 82
Mariandyrys. IOA —2F 81
Marian-glas. IOA —2E 81
Mariansleigh. Devn —4H 19
Marian-y-de. Gwyn —2C 68
Marine Town. Kent —3D 40
Marion-y-mor. Gwyn —2C 68
Marischal Mus. —Aberdeen 186
Marishader. High —2D 155
Marjoriebanks. Dum —1B 112
Mark. Dum —4G 109
Mark. Som —2G 21
Markbeech. Kent —1F 27
Markby. Linc —3D 89
Mark Causeway. Som —2G 21
Mark Cross. E Sus —2G 27
Markeaton. Derb —2H 73
Markenfield Hall —3E 99
Market Bosworth. Leics —5B 74
Market Deeping. Linc —4A 76
Market Drayton. Shrp —2A 72
Market End. Warw —2H 61
Market Harborough. Leics —2E 63
Markethill. Per —5B 144
Market Lavington. Wilts —1F 23
Market Overton. Rut —4F 75
Market Rasen. Linc —2A 88
Market Stainton. Linc —3B 88
Market Warsop. Notts —4C 86
Market Weighton. E Yor —5C 100
Market Weston. Suff —3B 66
Markfield. Leics —4B 74
Markham. Cphy —5E 47
Markinch. Fife —3E 137
Markington. N Yor —3E 99
Marksbury. Bath —5B 34
Mark's Corner. IOW —3C 16
Marks Hall Arboretum —3B 54
Marks Tey. Essx —3C 54
Markwell. Corn —3H 7
Markyate. Herts —4A 52
Marlborough. Wilts —5G 35
Marlcliff. Warw —5E 61
Marldon. Devn —2E 9
Marle Green. E Sus —4G 27
Marlesford. Suff —5F 67
Marley Green. Ches —1H 71
Marley Hill. Tyne —4F 115
Marlingford. Norf —5D 78
Mar Lodge Estate NTS —4E 151
Marloes. Pemb —4B 42
Marlow. Buck —3G 37
Marlow. Here —3G 59
Marlow Bottom. Buck —3G 37
Marlpit Hill. Kent —1F 27
Marlpits. E Sus —3F 27
Marlpool. Derbs —1B 74
Marnhull. Dors —1C 14
Marnoch. Abers —3C 160
Marnock. N Lan —3A 128
Marple. G Man —2D 84
Marr. S Yor —4F 93
Marrel. High —2H 165
Marrick. N Yor —5D 105
Marrister. Shet —5G 173
Marros. Carm —4G 43
Marsden. Tyne —3G 115
Marsden. W Yor —3A 92
Marsett. N Yor —1B 98
Marsh. Buck —5G 51
Marsh. Devn —1F 13
Marshall Meadows. Nmbd —4F 131
Marshalsea. Dors —2G 13
Marshalswick. Herts —5B 52
Marsham. Norf —3D 78
Marshaw. Lanc —4E 97
Marsh Baldon. Oxon —2D 36
Marsh Benham. W Ber —5C 36
Marshborough. Kent —5H 41
Marshbrook. Shrp —2G 59
Marshchapel. Linc —1C 88
Marshfield. Newp —3F 33
Marshfield. S Glo —4C 34
Marshgate. Corn —3B 10
Marsh Gibbon. Buck —3E 51
Marsh Green. Devn —3D 12
Marsh Green. Kent —1F 27
Marsh Green. Staf —5C 84
Marsh Green. Telf —4A 72
Marsh Lane. Derbs —3B 86
Marshside. Kent —4G 41
Marshside. Mers —3B 90
Marsh Side. Norf —1G 77
Marsh Street. Som —2C 20
Marsh, The. Powy —1F 59
Marsh, The. Shrp —3A 72
Marshwood. Dors —3G 13
Marske. N Yor —4E 105
Marske-by-the-Sea. Red C —2D 106
Marston. Ches —3A 84
Marston. Here —5F 59
Marston. Linc —1F 75
Marston. Oxon —5D 50
Marston. Staf —3D 72
(nr. Stafford)
Marston. Staf —4C 72
(nr. Wheaton Aston)
Marston. Warw —1G 61
Marston. Wilts —1E 23
Marston Doles. Warw —5B 62
Marston Green. W Mid —2F 61
Marston Hill. Glos —2G 35
Marston Jabbett. Warw —2A 62
Marston Magna. Som —4A 22
Marston Meysey. Wilts —2G 35
Marston Montgomery. Derbs —2F 73
Marston Moretaine. Beds —1H 51
Marston on Dove. Derbs —3G 73
Marston St Lawrence. Nptn —1D 50
Marston Stannett. Here —5H 59
Marston Trussell. Nptn —2D 62
Marstow. Here —4A 48
Marsworth. Buck —4H 51
Marten. Wilts —5A 36
Marthall. Ches —3C 84
Martham. Norf —4G 79
Marthwaite. Cumb —5H 103
Martin. Hants —1F 15
Martin. Kent —1H 29
Martin. Linc —4B 88
(nr. Horncastle)
Martin. Linc —5A 88
(nr. Metheringham)
Martindale. Cumb —3F 103
Martin Dales. Linc —4A 88
Martin Drove End. Hants —4F 23
Martinhoe. Devn —2G 19
Martinhoe Cross. Devn —2G 19
Martin Hussingtree. Worc —5C 60
Martin Mere Wildfowl Centre —3C 90
Martin Mill. Kent —1H 29
Martinscroft. Warr —2A 84
Martin's Moss. Ches —4C 84
Martinstown. Dors —4B 14
Martlesham. Suff —1F 55
Martlesham Heath. Suff —1F 55
Martletwy. Pemb —3E 43
Martley. Worc —5B 60
Martock. Som —1H 13
Marton. Ches —4C 84
Marton. Cumb —2B 96
Marton. E Yor —3G 101
(nr. Bridlington)
Marton. E Yor —1E 95
(nr. Hull)
Marton. Linc —2F 87
Marton. Midd —3C 106
Marton. N Yor —3G 99
(nr. Boroughbridge)
Marton. N Yor —1B 100
(nr. Pickering)
Marton. Shrp —3G 71
(nr. Myddle)
Marton. Shrp —5E 71
(nr. Worthen)
Marton. Warw —4B 62
Marton Abbey. N Yor —3H 99
Marton-le-Moor. N Yor —2F 99
Martyr's Green. Surr —5B 38
Martyr Worthy. Hants —3D 24
Marwell Zoo —4D 24
Marwick. Orkn —5B 172
Marwood. Devn —3F 19
Marwood Hill Gdns. —3F 19
Mary Arden's House —5F 61
Marybank. High —3G 157
(nr. Dingwall)
Marybank. High —1B 158
(nr. Invergordon)
Maryburgh. High —3H 157
Maryfield. Corn —3A 8
Maryhill. Glas —3G 127
Marykirk. Abers —2F 145
Marylebone. G Lon —2D 39
Marylebone. G Man —4D 90
Marypark. Mor —5F 159
Maryport. Cumb —1B 102
Maryport. Dum —5E 109
Mary Queen of Scots House —2A 120
Mary Rose Ship & Mus. —Portsmouth 195
Marystow. Devn —4E 11
Mary Tavy. Devn —5F 11
Maryton. Ang —3C 144
(nr. Kirriemuir)
Maryton. Ang —3F 145
(nr. Montrose)
Marywell. Abers —4C 152
Marywell. Ang —4F 145
Masham. N Yor —1E 98
Mashbury. Essx —4G 53
Masongill. N Yor —2F 97
Masons Lodge. Abers —3F 153
Mastin Moor. Derbs —3B 86
Mastrick. Aber —3G 153
Matching. Essx —4F 53
Matching Green. Essx —4F 53
Matching Tye. Essx —4F 53
Matfen. Nmbd —2D 114
Matfield. Kent —1A 28
Mathern. Mon —2A 34
Mathon. Here —1C 48
Mathry. Pemb —1C 42
Matlaske. Norf —2D 78
Matlock. Derbs —4G 85
Matlock Bath. Derbs —5G 85
Matterdale End. Cumb —2E 103
Mattersey. Notts —2D 86
Mattersey Thorpe. Notts —1D 86
Mattingley. Hants —1F 25
Mattishall. Norf —4C 78
Mattishall Burgh. Norf —4C 78
Mauchline. E Ayr —2D 117
Maud. Abers —4G 161
Maudlin. Corn —2E 7
Maugersbury. Glos —3G 49
Maughold. IOM —2D 108
Maulden. Beds —2A 52
Maulds Meaburn. Cumb —3H 103
Maunby. N Yor —1F 99
Maund Bryan. Here —5H 59
Mautby. Norf —4G 79
Mavesyn Ridware. Staf —4E 73
Mavis Enderby. Linc —4C 88
Mawbray. Cumb —5B 112
Mawdesley. Lanc —3C 90
Mawdlam. B'end —3B 32
Mawgan. Corn —4E 5
Mawgan Porth. Corn —2C 6
Maw Green. Ches —5B 84
Mawla. Corn —4B 6
Mawnan. Corn —4E 5
Mawnan Smith. Corn —4E 5
Mawthorpe. Linc —3D 88
Maxey. Pet —5A 76
Max Gate NT —3C 14
Maxstoke. Warw —2G 61
Maxton. Kent —1G 29
Maxton. Bord —1A 120
Maxwellheugh. Bord —1B 120
Maxwelltown. Dum —2A 112
Maxworthy. Corn —3C 10
Mayals. Swan —4F 31
Maybole. S Ayr —4C 116
Maybush. Sotn —1B 16
Mayes Green. Surr —2C 26
Mayfield. E Sus —3G 27
Mayfield. Midl —3G 129
Mayfield. Per —1C 136
Mayfield. Staf —1F 73
Mayford. Surr —5A 38
Mayhill. Swan —3F 31
Mayland. Essx —5C 54
Maylandsea. Essx —5C 54
Maynard's Green. E Sus —4G 27
Maypole. IOS —1B 4
Maypole. Kent —4G 41
Maypole. Mon —4H 47
Maypole Green. Norf —1G 67
Maypole Green. Suff —5B 66
Mayshill. S Glo —3B 34
Maywick. Shet —9E 173
Mead. Devn —1C 10
Meadgate. Bath —1B 22
Meadle. Buck —5G 51
Meadowbank. Ches —4A 84
Meadowfield. Dur —1F 105
Meadow Green. Here —5B 60
Meadowmill. E Lot —2H 129
Meadows. Nott —2C 74
Meadowtown. Shrp —5F 71
Meadwell. Devn —4E 11
Mealabost. W Isl —2G 171
(nr. Borgh)
Mealabost. W Isl —4G 171
(nr. Stornoway)
Mealasta. W Isl —5B 171
Meal Bank. Cumb —5G 103
Mealrigg. Cumb —5C 112
Mealsgate. Cumb —5D 112
Meanwood. W Yor —1C 92
Mearbeck. N Yor —3H 97
Meare. Som —2H 21
Meare Green. Som —4F 21
(nr. Curry Mallet)
Meare Green. Som —4G 21
(nr. Stoke St Gregory)
Mears Ashby. Nptn —4F 63
Measham. Leics —4H 73
Meath Green. Surr —1D 26
Meathop. Cumb —1D 96
Meaux. E Yor —1D 94
Meavy. Devn —2B 8

Medbourne. Leics —1E 63
Medburn. Nmbd —2E 115
Meddon. Devn —1C 10
Meden Vale. Notts —4C 86
Medlam. Linc —5C 88
Medlicott. Shrp —1G 59
Medmenham. Buck —3G 37
Medomsley. Dur —4E 115
Medstead. Hants —3E 25
Medway Towns. Medw —4B 40
Meerbrook. Staf —4D 85
Meer End. W Mid —3G 61
Meers Bridge. Linc —2D 89
Meesden. Herts —2E 53
Meeson. Telf —3A 72
Meeth. Devn —2F 11
Meeting Green. Suff —5G 65
Megginch Castle Gdn. —1E 137
Meidrim. Carm —2G 43
Meifod. Powy —4D 70
Meigle. Per —4B 144
Meikle Earnock. S Lan —4A 128
Meikle Kilchattan Butts. Arg —4B 126
Meikleour. Per —5A 144
Meikle Tarty. Abers —1G 153
Meikle Wartle. Abers —5E 160
Meinciau. Carm —4E 45
Meir. Stoke —1D 72
Meir Heath. Staf —1D 72
Melbourn. Cambs —1D 53
Melbourne. Derbs —3A 74
Melbourne. E Yor —5B 100
Melbourne Hall —3A 74
Melbury Abbas. Dors —4D 23
Melbury Bubb. Dors —2A 14
Melbury Osmond. Dors —2A 14
Melbury Sampford. Dors —2A 14
Melby. Shet —6C 173
Melchbourne. Beds —4H 63
Melcombe Bingham. Dors —2C 14
Melcombe Regis. Dors —4B 14
Meldon. Devn —3F 11
Meldon. Nmbd —1E 115
Meldreth. Cambs —1D 52
Melford Hall NT —1B 54
Melfort. Arg —2F 133
Melgarve. High —4G 149
Meliden. Den —2C 82
Melinbyrhedyn. Powy —1H 57
Melincourt. Neat —5B 46
Melin-y-coed. Cnwy —4H 81
Melin-y-ddol. Powy —5C 70
Melin-y-wig. Den —1C 70
Melkington. Nmbd —5E 131
Melkinthorpe. Cumb —2G 103
Melkridge. Nmbd —3A 114
Melksham. Wilts —5E 35
Mellangaun. High —5C 162
Melldalloch. Arg —2H 125
Mellerstain House —1A 120
Mellguards. Cumb —5F 113
Melling. Lanc —2E 97
Melling. Mers —4B 90
Melling Mount. Mers —4C 90
Mellis. Suff —3C 66
Mellon Charles. High —4C 162
Mellon Udrigle. High —4C 162
Mellor. G Man —2D 85
Mellor. Lanc —1E 91
Mellor Brook. Lanc —1E 91
Mells. Som —2C 22
Melmerby. Cumb —1H 103
Melmerby. N Yor —1C 98 (nr. Middleham)
Melmerby. N Yor —2F 99 (nr. Ripon)
Melplash. Dors —3H 13
Melrose. Bord —1H 119
Melrose Abbey —1H 119
Melsetter. Orkn —9B 172
Melsonby. N Yor —4E 105
Meltham. W Yor —3A 92
Meltham Mills. W Yor —3B 92
Melton. E Yor —2C 94
Melton. Suff —5E 67
Meltonby. E Yor —4B 100
Melton Constable. Norf —2C 78
Melton Mowbray. Leics —4E 75
Melton Ross. N Lin —3D 94
Melvaig. High —5B 162
Melverley. Shrp —4F 71
Melverley Green. Shrp —4F 71
Melvich. High —2A 168
Membury. Devn —2F 13
Memsie. Abers —2G 161
Memus. Ang —3D 144
Menabilly. Corn —3E 7
Menai Bridge. IOA —3E 81
Mendham. Suff —2E 67
Mendip Hills —1H 21
Mendlesham. Suff —4D 66
Mendlesham Green. Suff —4C 66
Menethorpe. N Yor —3B 100
Menheniot. Corn —2G 7
Menithwood. Worc —4B 60
Menna. Corn —3D 6
Mennock. Dum —4H 117
Menston. W Yor —5D 98
Menstrie. Clac —4H 135
Menthorpe. N Yor —1H 93
Mentmore. Buck —4H 51
Meole Brace. Shrp —4G 71
Meols. Mers —2E 83
Meon. Hants —2D 16
Meonstoke. Hants —1E 16
Meopham. Kent —4H 39
Meopham Green. Kent —4H 39
Meopham Station. Kent —4H 39
Mepal. Cambs —2D 64
Meppershall. Beds —2B 52
Merbach. Here —1G 47
Mercaston. Derbs —1G 73
Merchiston. Edin —2F 129
Mere. Ches —2B 84
Mere. Wilts —3D 22
Mere Brow. Lanc —3C 90
Mereclough. Lanc —1G 91
Mere Green. W Mid —1F 61
Mere Green. Worc —4D 60
Mere Heath. Ches —3A 84
Mereside. Bkpl —1B 90
Meretown. Staf —3B 72
Mereworth. Kent —5A 40
Meriden. W Mid —2G 61
Merkadale. High —5C 154
Merkland. S Ayr —5B 116
Merkland Lodge. High —1A 164
Merley. Pool —3F 15
Merlin's Bridge. Pemb —3D 42
Merridge. Som —3F 21
Merriments Gdns. —3B 28
Merrington. Shrp —3G 71
Merrion. Pemb —5D 42
Merriott. Som —1H 13
Merrivale. Devn —5F 11
Merrow. Surr —5B 38
Merrybent. Darl —3F 105
Merry Lees. Leics —5B 74
Merrymeet. Corn —2G 7
Merseyside Maritime Mus. —Liverpool 191
Mersham. Kent —2E 29
Merstham. Surr —5D 39
Merston. W Sus —2G 17
Merstone. IOW —4D 16
Merther. Corn —4C 6
Merthyr. Carm —3D 44
Merthyr Cynog. Powy —2C 46
Merthyr Dyfan. V Glam —5E 32
Merthyr Mawr. B'end —4B 32
Merthyr Tudful. Mer T —5D 46
Merthyr Tydfil. Mer T —5D 46
Merthyr Vale. Mer T —5D 46
Merton. Devn —1F 11
Merton. G Lon —4D 38
Merton. Norf —1B 66
Merton. Oxon —4D 50
Mertoun Gdns. —1A 120
Meshaw. Devn —1A 12
Messing. Essx —4B 54
Messingham. N Lin —4B 94
Metcombe. Devn —3D 12
Metfield. Suff —2E 67
Metherell. Corn —2A 8
Metheringham. Linc —4H 87
Methil. Fife —4F 137
Methilhill. Fife —4F 137
Methley. W Yor —2D 93
Methley Junction. W Yor —2D 93
Methlick. Abers —5F 161
Methven. Per —1C 136
Methwold. Norf —1G 65
Methwold Hythe. Norf —1G 65
Mettingham. Suff —1F 67
Metton. Norf —2D 78
Mevagissey. Corn —4E 6
Mexborough. S Yor —4E 93
Mey. High —1E 169
Meysey Hampton. Glos —2G 35
Miabhag. W Isl —8D 171
Miabhaig. W Isl —7C 171 (nr. Cliasmol)
Miabhaig. W Isl —4C 171 (nr. Timsgearraidh)
Mial. High —1G 155
Michael. IOM —2C 108
Michaelchurch. Here —3A 48
Michaelchurch Escley. Here —2G 47
Michaelchurch-on-Arrow. Powy —5E 59
Michaelcombe. Devn —2C 8
Michaelston-le-Pit. V Glam —4E 33
Michaelston-y-Vedw. Newp —3F 33
Michaelstow. Corn —5A 10
Micheldever. Hants —3D 24
Micheldever Station. Hants —2D 24
Michelham Priory —5G 27
Michelmersh. Hants —4B 24
Mickfield. Suff —4D 66
Micklebring. S Yor —1C 86
Mickleby. N Yor —3F 107
Micklefield. W Yor —1E 93
Micklefield Green. Herts —1B 38
Mickleham. Surr —5C 38
Mickleover. Derb —2H 73
Micklethwaite. Cumb —4D 112
Micklethwaite. W Yor —5D 98
Mickleton. Dur —2C 104
Mickleton. Glos —1G 49
Mickletown. W Yor —2D 93
Mickle Trafford. Ches —4G 83
Mickley. N Yor —2E 99
Mickley Green. Suff —5H 65
Mickley Square. Nmbd —3D 115
Mid Ardlaw. Abers —2G 161
Midbea. Orkn —3D 172
Mid Beltie. Abers —3D 152
Mid Calder. W Lot —3D 129
Mid Clyth. High —5E 169
Middle Assendon. Oxon —3F 37
Middle Aston. Oxon —3C 50
Middle Barton. Oxon —3C 50
Middlebie. Dum —2D 112
Middle Chinnock. Som —1H 13
Middle Claydon. Buck —3F 51
Middlecliff. S Yor —4E 93
Middlecott. Devn —4H 11
Middle Drums. Ang —3E 145
Middle Duntisbourne. Glos —5E 49
Middle Essie. Abers —3H 161
Middleforth Green. Lanc —2D 90
Middleham. N Yor —1D 98
Middleham Castle EH —1D 98
Middle Handley. Derbs —3B 86
Middle Harling. Norf —2B 66
Middlehope. Shrp —2G 59
Middle Littleton. Worc —1F 49
Middle Maes-coed. Here —2G 47
Middlemarsh. Dors —2B 14
Middle Marwood. Devn —3F 19
Middle Mayfield. Staf —1F 73
Middlemuir. Abers —4F 161 (nr. New Deer)
Middlemuir. Abers —3G 161 (nr. Strichen)
Middle Rainton. Tyne —5G 115
Middle Rasen. Linc —2H 87
Middlesbrough. Midd —2B 106 & 191
Middlesceugh. Cumb —5E 113
Middleshaw. Cumb —1E 97
Middlesmoor. N Yor —2C 98
Middles, The. Dur —4F 115
Middlestone. Dur —1F 105
Middlestone Moor. Dur —1F 105
Middle Stoughton. Som —2H 21
Middlestown. W Yor —3C 92
Middle Street. Glos —5C 48
Middle Taphouse. Corn —2F 7
Middleton. Ang —4E 145
Middleton. Arg —4A 138
Middleton. Cumb —1F 97
Middleton. Derbs —4F 85 (nr. Bakewell)
Middleton. Derbs —5G 85 (nr. Wirksworth)
Middleton. Essx —2B 54
Middleton. G Man —4G 91
Middleton. Hants —2C 24
Middleton. Hart —1C 106
Middleton. Here —4H 59
Middleton. IOW —4B 16
Middleton. Lanc —4D 96
Middleton. Midl —4G 129
Middleton. Norf —4F 77
Middleton. Nptn —1F 63
Middleton. Nmbd —1F 121 (nr. Belford)
Middleton. Nmbd —1D 114 (nr. Morpeth)
Middleton. N Yor —5D 98 (nr. Ilkley)
Middleton. N Yor —1B 100 (nr. Pickering)
Middleton. Per —3D 136
Middleton. Shrp —3H 59 (nr. Ludlow)
Middleton. Shrp —3F 71 (nr. Oswestry)
Middleton. Suff —4G 67
Middleton. Swan —4D 30
Middleton. Warw —1F 61
Middleton. W Yor —2D 92
Middleton Cheney. Nptn —1D 50
Middleton Green. Staf —2D 73
Middleton Hall —1F 61
Middleton Hall. Nmbd —2D 121
Middleton in Teesdale. Dur —2C 104
Middleton One Row. Darl —3A 106
Middleton-on-Leven. N Yor —4B 106
Middleton-on-Sea. W Sus —5A 26
Middleton on the Hill. Here —4H 59
Middleton-on-the-Wolds. E Yor —5D 100
Middleton Priors. Shrp —1A 60
Middleton Quernhow. N Yor —2F 99
Middleton St George. Darl —3A 106
Middleton Scriven. Shrp —2A 60
Middleton Stoney. Oxon —3D 50
Middleton Tyas. N Yor —4F 105
Middletown. Cumb —4A 102
Middle Town. IOS —1B 4
Middletown. Powy —4F 71
Middle Tysoe. Warw —1B 50
Middle Wallop. Hants —3A 24
Middlewich. Ches —4B 84
Middle Winterslow. Wilts —3H 23
Middlewood. Corn —5C 10
Middlewood. S Yor —1H 85
Middle Woodford. Wilts —3G 23
Middlewood Green. Suff —4C 66
Middleyard. Glos —5D 48
Middlezoy. Som —3G 21
Middridge. Dur —2F 105
Midfield. High —2F 167
Midford. Bath —5C 34
Mid Garrary. Dum —2C 110
Midge Hall. Lanc —2D 90
Midgeholme. Cumb —4H 113
Midgham. W Ber —5D 36
Midgley. W Yor —2A 92 (nr. Halifax)
Midgley. W Yor —3C 92 (nr. Horbury)
Mid Hants Railway —3E 25
Mid Ho. Shet —2G 173
Midhopestones. S Yor —1G 85
Midhurst. W Sus —4G 25
Mid Kirkton. N Ayr —4C 126
Mid Lambrook. Som —1H 13
Midland. Orkn —7C 172
Midland Railway Centre —5B 86
Mid Lavant. W Sus —2G 17
Midlem. Bord —2H 119
Midney. Som —4A 22
Mid-Norfolk Railway —5C 78
Midsomer Norton. Bath —1B 22
Mid-Suffolk Railway —4D 66
Midton. Inv —2D 126
Midtown. High —5C 162 (nr. Poolewe)
Midtown. High —2F 167 (nr. Tongue)
Midville. Linc —5C 88
Mid Walls. Shet —6C 173
Midway. Derbs —3H 73
Mid Yell. Shet —2G 173
Migdale. High —4D 164
Migvie. Abers —3B 152
Milborne Port. Som —1B 14
Milborne St Andrew. Dors —3D 14
Milborne Wick. Som —4B 22
Milbourne. Nmbd —2E 115
Milbourne. Wilts —3E 35
Milburn. Cumb —2H 103
Milbury Heath. S Glo —2B 34
Milby. N Yor —3G 99
Milcombe. Oxon —2C 50
Milden. Suff —1C 54
Mildenhall. Suff —3G 65
Mildenhall. Wilts —5H 35
Milebrook. Powy —3F 59
Milebush. Kent —1B 28
Mile End. Cambs —2F 65
Mile End. Essx —3C 54
Mileham. Norf —4B 78
Mile Oak. Brig —5D 26
Miles Green. Staf —5C 84
Miles Hope. Here —4H 59
Milesmark. Fife —1D 128
Mile Town. Kent —3D 40
Milfield. Nmbd —1D 120
Milford. Derbs —1A 74
Milford. Devn —4C 18
Milford. Powy —1C 58
Milford. Staf —3D 73
Milford. Surr —1A 26
Milford Haven. Pemb —4D 42
Milford on Sea. Hants —3A 16
Milkwall. Glos —5A 48
Milkwell. Wilts —4E 23
Milland. W Sus —4G 25
Millbank. High —2D 168
Mill Bank. W Yor —2A 92
Millbeck. Cumb —2D 102
Millbounds. Orkn —4E 172
Millbreck. Abers —4H 161
Millbridge. Surr —2G 25
Millbrook. Beds —2A 52
Millbrook. Corn —3A 8
Millbrook. G Man —1D 85
Millbrook. Sotn —1B 16
Mill Common. Suff —2G 67
Mill Corner. E Sus —3C 28
Milldale. Staf —5F 85
Millden Lodge. Ang —1E 145
Milldens. Ang —3E 145
Millearn. Per —2B 136
Mill End. Buck —3F 37
Mill End. Cambs —5F 65
Millend. Glos —2C 34 (nr. Dursley)
Mill End. Glos —4G 49 (nr. Northleach)
Mill End. Herts —2D 52
Millennium Seed Bank —2E 27
Millerhill. Midl —3G 129
Miller's Dale. Derbs —3F 85
Millers Green. Derbs —5G 85
Millerston. N Lan —3H 127
Millfield. Abers —4B 152
Millfield. Pet —1A 64
Millgate. Lanc —3G 91
Mill Green. Norf —2D 66
Mill Green. Shrp —3A 72
Mill Green. Staf —3E 73
Mill Green. Suff —1C 54
Mill Greep. Essx —5G 53
Millhalf. Here —1F 47
Millhall. E Ren —4G 127
Millhayes. Devn —2F 13 (nr. Honiton)
Millhayes. Devn —1E 13 (nr. Wellington)
Millhead. Lanc —2D 97
Millheugh. S Lan —4A 128
Mill Hill. Bkbn —2E 91
Mill Hill. G Lon —1D 38
Millholme. Cumb —5G 103
Millhouse. Arg —2A 126
Millhousebridge. Dum —1C 112
Millhouses. S Yor —2H 85
Millikenpark. Ren —3F 127
Millington. E Yor —4C 100
Millington Green. Derbs —1G 73
Mill Knowe. Arg —3B 122
Mill Lane. Hants —1F 25
Millmeece. Staf —2C 72
Mill of Craigievar. Abers —2C 152
Mill of Fintray. Abers —2F 153
Mill of Haldane. W Dun —1E 127
Millom. Cumb —1A 96
Millow. Beds —1C 52
Millpool. Corn —5B 10
Millport. N Ayr —4C 126
Mill Side. Cumb —1D 96
Mill Street. Norf —4C 78 (nr. Lyng)
Mill Street. Norf —4C 78 (nr. Swanton Morley)
Mill Street. Suff —3C 66
Millthorpe. Derbs —3H 85
Millthorpe. Linc —2A 76
Millthrop. Cumb —5H 103
Milltimber. Aber —3F 153
Milltown. Abers —3G 151 (nr. Corgarff)
Milltown. Abers —2B 152 (nr. Lumsden)
Milltown. Corn —3F 7
Milltown. Derbs —4A 86
Milltown. Devn —3F 19
Milltown. Dum —2E 113
Milltown. High —3E 157
Milltown. Mor —4C 160
Milltown of Aberdalgie. Per —1C 136
Milltown of Auchindoun. Mor —4A 160
Milltown of Campfield. Abers —3D 152
Milltown of Edinville. Mor —5G 159
Milltown of Towie. Abers —2B 152
Milnacraig. Ang —3B 144
Milnathort. Per —3D 136
Milngavie. E Dun —2G 127
Milnholm. Stir —1A 128
Milnrow. G Man —3H 91
Milnthorpe. Cumb —1D 97
Milnthorpe. W Yor —3D 92
Milovaig. High —4A 154
Milson. Shrp —3A 60
Milstead. Kent —5D 40
Milston. Wilts —2G 23
Milthorpe. Nptn —1D 50
Milton. Ang —4C 144
Milton. Cambs —4D 65
Milton. Cumb —3G 113
Milton. Derbs —3H 73
Milton. Dum —2F 111 (nr. Crocketford)
Milton. Dum —4H 109 (nr. Glenluce)
Milton. E Ayr —2D 116
Milton. Glas —2G 127
Milton. High —3F 157 (nr. Achnasheen)
Milton. High —4G 155 (nr. Applecross)
Milton. High —5G 157 (nr. Drumnadrochit)
Milton. High —1B 158 (nr. Invergordon)
Milton. High —4H 157 (nr. Inverness)
Milton. High —3F 169 (nr. Wick)
Milton. Mor —2C 160 (nr. Cullen)
Milton. Mor —2F 151 (nr. Tomintoul)
Milton. N Som —5G 33
Milton. Notts —3E 86
Milton. Oxon —2C 50 (nr. Banbury)
Milton. Oxon —2C 36 (nr. Didcot)
Milton. Pemb —4E 43
Milton. Port —3E 17
Milton. Som —4H 21
Milton. Stir —3E 135 (nr. Aberfoyle)
Milton. Stir —4D 134 (nr. Drymen)
Milton. Stoke —5D 84
Milton. W Dun —2F 127
Milton Abbas. Dors —2D 14
Milton Abbey —2C 14
Milton Abbot. Devn —5E 11
Milton Auchlossan. Abers —3C 152
Milton Bridge. Midl —3F 129
Milton Bryan. Beds —2H 51
Milton Clevedon. Som —3B 22
Milton Coldwells. Abers —5G 161
Milton Combe. Devn —2A 8
Milton Damerel. Devn —1D 11
Miltonduff. Mor —2F 159
Milton End. Glos —5G 49
Milton Ernest. Beds —5H 63
Milton Green. Ches —5G 83
Milton Hill. Devn —5C 12
Milton Hill. Oxon —2C 36
Milton Keynes. Mil —2G 51 & 194
Milton Keynes Village. Mil —2G 51
Milton Lilbourne. Wilts —5G 35
Milton Malsor. Nptn —5E 63
Milton Morenish. Per —5D 142
Milton of Auchinhove. Abers —3C 152
Milton of Balgonie. Fife —3F 137
Milton of Barras. Abers —1H 145
Milton of Campsie. E Dun —2H 127
Milton of Cultoquhey. Per —1A 136
Milton of Cushnie. Abers —2C 152
Milton of Finavon. Ang —3D 145
Milton of Gollanfield. High —3B 158
Milton of Lesmore. Abers —1B 152
Milton of Tullich. Abers —4A 152
Milton on Stour. Dors —4C 22
Milton Regis. Kent —4C 40
Milton Street. E Sus —5G 27
Milton-under-Wychwood. Oxon —4A 50
Milverton. Som —4E 20
Milverton. Warw —4H 61
Milwich. Staf —2D 72
Mimbridge. Surr —4A 38
Minack Open-Air Theatre —4A 4
Minard. Arg —4G 133
Minchington. Dors —1E 15
Minchinhampton. Glos —5D 49
Mindrum. Nmbd —1C 120
Minehead. Som —2C 20
Minera. Wrex —5E 83
Minety. Wilts —2F 35
Minffordd. Gwyn —2E 69
Mingarrypark. High —2A 140
Mingary. High —2G 139
Mingearraidh. W Isl —6C 170
Miningsby. Linc —4C 88
Minions. Corn —5C 10
Minishant. S Ayr —3C 116
Minllyn. Gwyn —4A 70
Minnigaff. Dum —3B 110
Minorca. IOM —3D 108
Minskip. N Yor —3F 99
Minsmere Nature Reserve —4G 67
Minstead. Hants —1A 16
Minsted. W Sus —4G 25
Minster. Kent —4H 41 (nr. Ramsgate)

Minster. Kent —3D 40
(nr. Sheerness)
Minsteracres. Nmbd —4D 114
Minsterley. Shrp —5F 71
Minster Lovell. Oxon —4B 50
Minsterworth. Glos —4C 48
Minterne Gdns. —2B 14
Minterne Magna. Dors —2B 14
Minterne Parva. Dors —2B 14
Minting. Linc —3A 88
Mintlaw. Abers —4H 161
Minto. Bord —2H 119
Minton. Shrp —1G 59
Minwear. Pemb —3E 43
Minworth. W Mid —1F 61
Miodar. Arg —4B 138
Mirbister. Orkn —6C 172
Mirehouse —2D 102
Mirehouse. Cumb —3A 102
Mireland. High —2F 169
Mirfield. W Yor —3C 92
Miserden. Glos —5E 49
Miserden Park Gdns. —5E 49
Miskin. Rhon —3D 32
Misson. Notts —1D 86
Misterton. Leics —2C 62
Misterton. Notts —1E 87
Misterton. Som —2H 13
Mistley. Essx —2E 54
Mistley Heath. Essx —2E 55
Mistley Towers EH —2E 54
Mitcham. G Lon —4D 39
Mitcheldean. Glos —4B 48
Mitchell. Corn —3C 6
Mitchel Troy. Mon —4H 47
Mitcheltroy Common. Mon —5H 47
Mitford. Nmbd —1E 115
Mithian. Corn —3B 6
Mitton. Staf —4C 72
Mixbury. Oxon —2E 50
Mixenden. W Yor —2A 92
Mixon. Staf —5E 85
Moarfield. Shet —1G 173
Moat. Cumb —2F 113
Moats Tye. Suff —5C 66
Mobberley. Ches —3B 84
Mobberley. Staf —1E 73
Moccas. Here —1G 47
Moccas Court —1G 47
Mochdre. Cnwy —3H 81
Mochdre. Powy —2C 58
Mochrum. Dum —5A 110
Mockbeggar. Hants —2G 15
Mockerkin. Cumb —2B 102
Modbury. Devn —3C 8
Moddershall. Staf —2D 72
Modsarie. High —2G 167
Moelfre. Cnwy —3B 82
Moelfre. IOA —2E 81
Moelfre. Powy —3D 70
Moffat. Dum —4C 118
Mogerhanger. Beds —1B 52
Mogworthy. Devn —1B 12
Moira. Leics —4H 73
Molash. Kent —5E 41
Mol-chlach. High —2C 146
Mold. Flin —4E 83
Molehill Green. Essx —3F 53
Molescroft. E Yor —5E 101
Molesden. Nmbd —1E 115
Molesworth. Cambs —3H 63
Moll. High —5E 155
Molland. Devn —4B 20
Mollington. Ches —3F 83
Mollington. Oxon —1C 50
Mollinsburn. N Lan —2A 128
Mompesson House NT —Salisbury 195
Monachty. Cdgn —4E 57
Monachyle. Stir —1D 134
Monar Lodge. High —4E 156
Monaughty. Powy —4E 59
Monewden. Suff —5E 67
Moneydie. Per —1C 136
Moneyrow Green. Wind —4G 37
Mongomery Castle CADW —1E 58
Moniaive. Dum —5G 117
Monifieth. Ang —5E 145
Monikie. Ang —5E 145
Monimail. Fife —2E 137
Monington. Pemb —1B 44
Monk Bretton. S Yor —4D 92
Monken Hadley. G Lon —1D 38
Monkey Sanctuary —3G 7
Monkey World —4D 14
Monk Fryston. N Yor —2F 93
Monk Hesleden. Dur —1B 106
Monkhide. Here —1B 48
Monkhill. Cumb —4E 113
Monkhopton. Shrp —1A 60
Monkland. Here —5G 59
Monkleigh. Devn —4E 19
Monknash. V Glam —4C 32
Monkokehampton. Devn —2F 11
Monkseaton. Tyne —2G 115
Monks Eleigh. Suff —1C 54
Monk's Gate. W Sus —3D 26
Monk's Heath. Ches —3C 84
Monk Sherborne. Hants —1E 24
Monkshill. Abers —4E 161
Monksilver. Som —3D 20
Monks Kirby. Warw —2B 62
Monk Soham. Suff —4E 66
Monk Soham Green. Suff —4E 66
Monkspath. W Mid —3F 61
Monks Risborough. Buck —5G 51
Monksthorpe. Linc —4D 88
Monk Street. Essx —3G 53
Monkswood. Mon —5G 47
Monkton. Devn —2E 13
Monkton. Kent —4G 41
Monkton. Pemb —4D 42
Monkton. S Ayr —2C 116
Monkton Combe. Bath —5C 34
Monkton Deverill. Wilts —3D 22
Monkton Farleigh. Wilts —5D 34
Monkton Heathfield. Som —4F 21
Monktonhill. S Ayr —2C 116
Monkton Up Wimborne. Dors —1F 15
Monkton Wyld. Dors —3G 13
Monkwearmouth. Tyne —4H 115
Monkwood. Hants —3E 25
Monmarsh. Here —1A 48
Monmouth. Mon —4A 48
Monnington on Wye. Here —1G 47
Monreith. Dum —5A 110
Montacute. Som —1H 13
Monteviot House —2A 120
Montford. Arg —3C 126
Montford. Shrp —4G 71
Montford Bridge. Shrp —4G 71
Montgarrie. Abers —2C 152
Montgarswood. E Ayr —2E 117
Montgomery. Powy —1E 58
Montgreenan. N Ayr —5E 127
Montrave. Fife —3F 137
Montrose. Ang —3G 145
Monxton. Hants —2B 24
Monyash. Derbs —4F 85
Monymusk. Abers —2D 152
Monzie. Per —1A 136
Moodiesburn. N Lan —2H 127
Moon's Green. Kent —3C 28
Moonzie. Fife —2F 137
Moor Allerton. W Yor —1D 92
Moorbrae. Shet —3F 173
Moorby. Linc —4B 88
Moorcot. Here —5F 59
Moor Crichel. Dors —2E 15
Moor Cross. Devn —3C 8
Moordown. Bour —3F 15
Moore. Hal —2H 83
Moorend. Dum —2D 112
Moor End. E Yor —1B 94
Moorend. Glos —5C 48
(nr. Dursley)
Moorend. Glos —4D 48
(nr. Gloucester)
Moorends. S Yor —3G 93
Moorgate. S Yor —1B 86
Moorgreen. Hants —1C 16
Moorgreen. Notts —1B 74
Moor Green. Wilts —5D 34
Moorhaigh. Notts —4C 86
Moorhall. Derbs —3H 85
Moorhampton. Here —1G 47
Moorhouse. Cumb —4E 113
(nr. Carlisle)
Moorhouse. Cumb —4D 112
(nr. Wigton)
Moorhouse. Notts —4E 87
Moorhouse. Surr —5F 39
Moorhouses. Linc —5B 88
Moorland. Som —3G 21
Moorlinch. Som —3G 21
Moor Monkton. N Yor —4H 99
Moor of Granary. Mor —3E 159
Moorpath. Dors —3H 13
Moor Row. Cumb —3B 102
(nr. Whitehaven)
Moor Row. Cumb —5D 112
(nr. Wigton)
Moorsholm. Red C —3D 107
Moorside. Dors —1C 14
Moorside. G Man —4H 91
Moor, The. Kent —3B 28
Moortown. Devn —3D 10
Moortown. Hants —2G 15
Moortown. IOW —4C 16
Moortown. Linc —1H 87
Moortown. Telf —4A 72
Moortown. W Yor —1D 92
Morangie. High —5E 165
Morar. High —4E 147
Morborne. Cambs —1A 64
Morchard Bishop. Devn —2A 12
Morcombelake. Dors —3H 13
Morcott. Rut —5G 75
Morda. Shrp —3E 71
Morden. G Lon —4D 38
Mordiford. Here —2A 48
Mordon. Dur —2A 106
More. Shrp —1F 59
Morebath. Devn —4C 20
Morebattle. Bord —2B 120
Morecambe. Lanc —3D 96
Morefield. High —4F 163
Morehouse, The. Shrp —1H 59
Moreleigh. Devn —3D 8
Morely St Botolph. Norf —1C 66
Morenish. Per —5C 142
Moresby Parks. Cumb —3A 102
Morestead. Hants —4D 24
Moreton. Dors —4D 14
Moreton. Essx —5F 53
Moreton. Here —4H 59
Moreton. Mers —1E 83
Moreton. Oxon —5E 51
Moreton. Staf —4B 72
Moreton Corbet. Shrp —3H 71
Moreton Corbet Castle EH —3H 71
Moretonhampstead. Devn —4A 12
Moreton-in-Marsh. Glos —2H 49
Moreton Jeffries. Here —1B 48
Moreton Morrell. Warw —5H 61
Moreton on Lugg. Here —1A 48
Moreton Pinkney. Nptn —1D 50
Moreton Say. Shrp —2A 72
Moreton Valence. Glos —5C 48
Morfa. Cdgn —5C 56
Morfa Bach. Carm —4D 44
Morfa Bychan. Gwyn —2E 69
Morfa Glas. Neat —5B 46
Morfa Nefyn. Gwyn —1B 68
Morganstown. Card —3E 33
Morgan's Vale. Wilts —4G 23
Morham. E Lot —2B 130
Moriah. Cdgn —3F 57
Morland. Cumb —2G 103
Morley. Ches —2C 84
Morley. Derbs —1A 74
Morley. Dur —2E 105
Morley. W Yor —2C 92
Morningside. Edin —2F 129
Morningside. N Lan —4B 128
Morningthorpe. Norf —1E 66
Morpeth. Nmbd —1F 115
Morrey. Staf —4F 73
Morridge Side. Staf —5E 85
Morridge Top. Staf —4E 85
Morrington. Dum —1F 111
Morris Green. Essx —2H 53
Morriston. Swan —3F 31
Morston. Norf —1C 78
Mortehoe. Devn —2E 19
Morthen. S Yor —2B 86
Mortimer Common. W Ber —5E 37
Mortimer's Cross. Here —4G 59
Mortimer West End. Hants —5E 37
Mortomley. S Yor —1H 85
Morton. Cumb —1F 103
(nr. Calthwaite)
Morton. Cumb —4E 113
(nr. Carlisle)
Morton. Derbs —4B 86
Morton. Linc —3H 75
(nr. Bourne)
Morton. Linc —1F 87
(nr. Gainsborough)
Morton. Linc —4F 87
(nr. Lincoln)
Morton. Norf —4D 78
Morton. Notts —5E 87
Morton. Shrp —3E 71
Morton. S Glo —2B 34
Morton Bagot. Warw —4F 61
Morton Mill. Shrp —3H 71
Morton-on-Swale. N Yor —5A 106
Morton Tinmouth. Dur —2E 105
Morvah. Corn —3B 4
Morval. Corn —3G 7
Morvich. High —3E 165
(nr. Golspie)
Morvich. High —1B 148
(nr. Shiel Bridge)
Morvil. Pemb —1E 43
Morville. Shrp —1A 60
Morwellham Quay Mus. —2A 8
Morwenstow. Corn —1C 10
Morwick Hall. Nmbd —4G 121
Mosborough. S Yor —2B 86
Moscow. E Ayr —5F 127
Mose. Shrp —1B 60
Mosedale. Cumb —1E 103
Moseley. W Mid —2E 61
(nr. Birmingham)
Moseley. W Mid —5D 72
(nr. Wolverhampton)
Moseley. Worc —5C 60
Moseley Old Hall NT —5D 72
Moss. Arg —4A 138
Moss. High —2A 140
Moss. S Yor —3F 93
Moss. Wrex —5F 83
Mossatt. Abers —2B 152
Moss Bank. Mers —1H 83
Mossbank. Shet —4F 173
Mossblown. S Ayr —2D 116
Mossbrow. G Man —2B 84
Mossburnford. Bord —3A 120
Mossdale. Dum —2D 110
Mossedge. Cumb —3F 113
Mossend. N Lan —3A 128
Mossgate. Staf —2D 72
Moss Lane. Ches —3D 84
Mossley. Ches —4C 84
Mossley. G Man —4H 91
Mossley Hill. Mers —2F 83
Moss of Barmuckity. Mor —2G 159
Mosspark. Glas —3G 127
Mosspaul. Bord —5G 119
Moss Side. Cumb —4C 112
Moss Side. G Man —1C 84
Moss-side. High —3C 158
Moss Side. Lanc —1B 90
(nr. Blackpool)
Moss Side. Lanc —2D 90
(nr. Preston)
Moss Side. Mers —4B 90
Moss-side of Cairness. Abers —2H 161
Mosstodloch. Mor —3H 159
Mosswood. Nmbd —4D 114
Mossy Lea. Lanc —3D 90
Mosterton. Dors —2H 13
Moston. Shrp —3H 71
Moston Green. Ches —4B 84
Mostyn. Flin —2D 82
Motcombe. Dors —4D 22
Mothecombe. Devn —4C 8
Motherby. Cumb —2F 103
Motherwell. N Lan —4A 128
Mottingham. G Lon —3F 39
Mottisfont. Hants —4B 24
Mottisfont Abbey NT —4B 24
Mottistone. IOW —4C 16
Mottram in Longdendale. G Man —1D 85
Mottram St Andrew. Ches —3C 84
Mott's Mill. E Sus —2G 27
Mouldsworth. Ches —3H 83
Moulin. Per —3G 143
Moulsecoomb. Brig —5E 27
Moulsford. Oxon —3D 36
Moulsoe. Mil —1H 51
Moulton. Ches —4A 84
Moulton. Linc —3C 76
Moulton. Nptn —4E 63
Moulton. N Yor —4F 105
Moulton. Suff —4F 65
Moulton. V Glam —4D 32
Moulton Chapel. Linc —4B 76
Moulton Eugate. Linc —4B 76
Moulton St Mary. Norf —5F 79
Moulton Seas End. Linc —3C 76
Mount. Corn —2F 7
(nr. Bodmin)
Mount. Corn —3B 6
(nr. Newquay)
Mountain Ash. Rhon —2D 32
Mountain Cross. Bord —5E 129
Mountain Water. Pemb —2D 42
Mount Ambrose. Corn —4B 6
Mountbenger. Bord —2F 119
Mountblow. W Dun —2F 127
Mount Bures. Essx —2C 54
Mount Edgcumbe —3A 8
Mountfield. E Sus —3B 28
Mountgerald. High —2H 157
Mount Grace Priory NT —5B 106
Mount Hawke. Corn —4B 6
Mount High. High —2A 158
Mountjoy. Corn —2C 6
Mount Lothian. Midl —4F 129
Mountnessing. Essx —1H 39
Mounton. Mon —2A 34
Mount Pleasant. Buck —2E 51
Mount Pleasant. Ches —5C 84
Mount Pleasant. Derbs —1H 73
(nr. Derby)
Mount Pleasant. Derbs —4G 73
(nr. Swadlincote)
Mount Pleasant. E Sus —4F 27
Mount Pleasant. Fife —2E 137
Mount Pleasant. Hants —3A 16
Mount Pleasant. Norf —1B 66
Mountsorrel. Leics —4C 74
Mount Stuart. Arg —4C 126
Mount Stuart House —4C 126
Mousehole. Corn —4B 4
Mouswald. Dum —2B 112
Mow Cop. Ches —5C 84
Mowden. Darl —3F 105
Mowhaugh. Bord —2C 120
Mowmacre Hill. Leic —5C 74
Mowsley. Leics —2D 62
Moy. High —5B 158
Moylgrove. Pemb —1B 44
Moy Lodge. High —5G 149
Muasdale. Arg —5E 125
Muchalls. Abers —4F 153
Much Birch. Here —2A 48
Much Cowarne. Here —1B 48
Much Dewchurch. Here —2H 47
Muchelney. Som —4H 21
Muchelney Abbey EH —4H 21
Muchelney Ham. Som —4H 21
Much Hadham. Herts —4E 53
Much Hoole. Lanc —2C 90
Muchlarnick. Corn —3G 7
Much Marcle. Here —2B 48
Muchrachd. High —5E 157
Much Wenlock. Shrp —5A 72
Mucking. Thur —2A 40
Muckle Breck. Shet —5G 173
Muckleford. Dors —3B 14
Mucklestone. Staf —2B 72
Muckleton. Norf —2H 77
Muckleton. Shrp —3H 71
Muckley. Shrp —1A 60
Muckley Corner. Staf —5E 73
Muckton. Linc —2C 88
Mudale. High —5F 167
Muddiford. Devn —3F 19
Mudeford. Dors —3G 15
Mudford. Som —1A 14
Mudgley. Som —2H 21
Mugdock. Stir —2G 127
Mugeary. High —5D 154
Muggington. Derbs —1G 73
Muggintonlane End. Derbs —1G 73
Muggleswick. Dur —4D 114
Mugswell. Surr —5D 38
Muie. High —3D 164
Muirden. Abers —3E 160
Muirdrum. Ang —5E 145
Muiredge. Per —1E 137
Muirend. Glas —3G 127
Muirhead. Ang —5C 144
Muirhead. Fife —3E 137
Muirhead. N Lan —3H 127
Muirhouses. Falk —1D 128
Muirkirk. E Ayr —2F 117
Muir of Alford. Abers —2C 152
Muir of Fairburn. High —3G 157
Muir of Fowlis. Abers —2C 152
Muir of Miltonduff. Mor —3F 159
Muir of Ord. High —3H 157
Muir of Tarradale. High —3H 157
Muirshearlich. High —5D 148
Muirtack. Abers —5G 161
Muirton. High —2B 158
Muirton. Per —1D 136
Muirton of Ardblair. Per —4A 144
Muirtown. Per —2B 136
Muiryfold. Abers —3E 161
Muker. N Yor —5C 104
Mulbarton. Norf —5D 78
Mulben. Mor —3A 160
Mulindry. Arg —4B 124
Mulla. Shet —5F 173
Mullach Charlabhaigh. W Isl —3E 171
Mullacott. Devn —2F 19
Mullion. Corn —5D 5
Mullion Cove. Corn —5D 4
Mumbles, The. Swan —4F 31
Mumby. Linc —3E 89
Muncaster Castle —5C 102
Munderfield Row. Here —5A 60
Munderfield Stocks. Here —5A 60
Mundesley. Norf —2F 79
Mundford. Norf —1H 65
Mundham. Norf —1F 67
Mundon. Essx —5B 54
Munerigie. High —3E 149
Muness. Shet —1H 173
Mungasdale. High —4D 162
Mungrisdale. Cumb —1E 103
Munlochy. High —3A 158
Munsley. Here —1B 48
Munslow. Shrp —2H 59
Murchington. Devn —4G 11
Murcot. Worc —1F 49
Murcott. Oxon —4D 50
Murdishaw. Hal —2H 83
Murieston. W Lot —3D 128
Murkle. High —2D 168
Murlaggan. High —4C 148
Murra. Orkn —7B 172
Murrayfield. Edin —2F 129
Murray, The. S Lan —4H 127
Murrell Green. Hants —1F 25
Murroes. Ang —5D 144
Murrow. Cambs —5C 76
Mursley. Buck —3G 51
Murthly. Per —5H 143
Murton. Cumb —2A 104
Murton. Dur —5G 115
Murton. Nmbd —5F 131
Murton. Swan —4E 31
Murton. York —4A 100
Musbury. Devn —3F 13
Muscoates. N Yor —1A 100
Muscott. Nptn —4D 62
Mus. of Costume, Shambellie House —3A 112
Mus. of East Anglia Life —5C 66
Mus. of Flight —2B 130
Mus. of Lakeland Life, Kendal —5G 103
Mus. of Lincolnshire Life —Lincoln 191
Mus. of Liverpool Life —191
Mus. of Scotland —Edinburgh 189
Mus. of Scottish Country Life —4H 127
Mus. of South Yorkshire Life, Cusworth Hall —4F 93
Mus. of Welsh Life, St Fagans —4E 32
Musselburgh. E Lot —2G 129
Muston. Leics —2F 75
Muston. N Yor —2E 101
Mustow Green. Worc —3C 60
Muswell Hill. G Lon —2D 39
Mutehill. Dum —5D 111
Mutford. Suff —2G 67
Muthill. Per —2A 136
Mutterton. Devn —2D 12
Muxton. Telf —4B 72
Mwmbwls. Swan —4F 31
Mybster. High —3D 168
Myddfai. Carm —2A 46
Myddle. Shrp —3G 71
Mydroilyn. Cdgn —5D 56
Myerscough. Lanc —1C 90
Mylor Bridge. Corn —5C 6
Mylor Churchtown. Corn —5C 6
Mynachlog-ddu. Pemb —1F 43
Mynydd-bach. Mon —2H 33
Mynydd Isa. Flin —4E 83
Mynyddislwyn. Cphy —2E 33
Mynydd Llandegai. Gwyn —4F 81
Mynydd Mechell. IOA —1C 80
Mynydd-y-briw. Powy —3D 70
Mynyddygarreg. Carm —5E 45
Mynytho. Gwyn —2C 68
Myrebird. Abers —4E 153
Myrelandhorn. High —3E 169
Mytchett. Surr —1G 25
Mythe, The. Glos —2D 49
Mytholmroyd. W Yor —2A 92
Myton-on-Swale. N Yor —3G 99
Mytton. Shrp —4G 71

Naast. High —5C 162
Na Buirgh. W Isl —8C 171
Naburn. York —5H 99
Nab Wood. W Yor —1B 92
Nackington. Kent —5F 41
Nacton. Suff —1F 55
Nafferton. E Yor —4E 101
Na Gearrannan. W Isl —3D 171
Nailbridge. Glos —4B 48
Nailsbourne. Som —4F 21
Nailsea. N Som —4H 33
Nailstone. Leics —5B 74
Nailsworth. Glos —2D 34
Nairn. High —3C 158
Naisberry. Hart —1B 106
Nalderswood. Surr —1D 26
Nancegollan. Corn —3D 4
Nancekuke. Corn —4A 6
Nancledra. Corn —3C 4
Nangreaves. Lanc —3G 91
Nanhyfer. Pemb —1A 44
Nannerch. Flin —4D 82
Nanpantan. Leics —4C 74
Nanpean. Corn —3D 6
Nanstallon. Corn —2E 7
Nant-ddu. Powy —4D 46
Nanternis. Cdgn —5C 56
Nantgaredig. Carm —3E 45
Nantgarw. Rhon —3E 33
Nant Glas. Powy —4B 58
Nantglyn. Den —4C 82
Nantgwyn. Powy —3B 58
Nantlle. Gwyn —5E 81
Nantmawr. Shrp —3E 71
Nantmel. Powy —4C 58
Nantmor. Gwyn —1F 69
Nant Peris. Gwyn —5F 81
Nantwich. Ches —5A 84
Nant-y-bai. Carm —1A 46
Nant-y-bwch. Blae —4E 47
Nant-y-Derry. Mon —5G 47
Nant-y-dugoed. Powy —4B 70
Nant-y-felin. Cnwy —3F 81
Nantyffyllon. B'end —2B 32
Nantyglo. Blae —4E 47
Nant-y-meichiaid. Powy —4D 70
Nant-y-moel. B'end —2C 32
Nant-y-Pandy. Cnwy —3F 81
Naphill. Buck —2G 37
Nappa. Lanc —4A 98

Napton on the Hill. Warw —4B 62
Narberth. Pemb —3F 43
Narberth Bridge. Pemb —3F 43
Narborough. Leics —1C 62
Narborough. Norf —4G 77
Narkurs. Corn —3H 7
Narth, The. Mon —5A 48
Narthwaite. Cumb —5A 104
Nasareth. Gwyn —1D 68
Naseby. Nptn —3D 62
Nash. Buck —2F 51
Nash. Here —4F 59
Nash. Kent —5G 41
Nash. Newp —3G 33
Nash. Shrp —3A 60
Nash Lee. Buck —5G 51
Nassington. Nptn —1H 63
Nasty. Herts —3D 52
Natcott. Devn —4C 18
Nateby. Cumb —4A 104
Nateby. Lanc —5D 96
Nately Scures. Hants —1F 25
Nat. Agricultural Centre —3H 61
Nat. Birds of Prey Centre —3C 48
Nat. Botanic Gdn. of Wales —4F 45
Nat. Exhibition Centre —2F 61
(Nat. Fishing Heritage Centre, Grimsby) —3F 95
Nat. Football Mus. —Preston 195
Nat. Forest, The —4H 73
Nat. Gallery —London 193
Nat. Gallery of Scotland —Edinburgh 189
Nat. Glass Centre —4H 115
Nat. Horse Racing Mus. —4F 65
Nat. Marine Aquarium —Plymouth 195
Nat. Maritime Mus., Falmouth —5C 6
Nat. Maritime Mus., Greenwich —3E 39
Nat. Memorial Arboretum —4F 73
Nat. Motorboat Mus. —2B 40
Nat. Motorcycle Mus. —2G 61
Nat. Motor Mus. —2B 16
Nat. Mus. & Gallery —Cardiff 187
Nat. Mus. of Photography, Film & Television —Bradford 186
Nat. Railway Mus. —York 197
Nat. Railway Mus., Locomotion, Shildon —2F 105
Nat. Sea Life Centre —Birmingham 186
Nat. Seal Sanctuary —4E 5
Nat. Space Centre —5C 74
Nat. Tramway Mus. —5A 86
Nat. Waterways Mus. —Gloucester 189
Nat. Woollen Mus. —2D 44
Natland. Cumb —1E 97
Naughton. Suff —1D 54
Naunton. Glos —3G 49
Naunton. Worc —2D 49
Naunton Beauchamp. Worc —5D 60
Navenby. Linc —5G 87
Navestock Heath. Essx —1G 39
Navestock Side. Essx —1G 39
Navidale. High —2H 165
Nawton. N Yor —1A 100
Nayland. Suff —2C 54
Nazeing. Essx —5E 53
Neacroft. Hants —3G 15
Neal's Green. W Mid —2H 61
Neap House. N Lin —3B 94
Near Sawrey. Cumb —5E 103
Neasden. G Lon —2D 38
Neasham. Darl —3A 106
Neath. Neat —2A 32
Neath Abbey. Neat —3G 31
Neatishead. Norf —3F 79
Neaton. Norf —5B 78
Nebo. Cdgn —4E 57
Nebo. Cnwy —5H 81
Nebo. Gwyn —5D 81
Nebo. IOA —1D 80
Necton. Norf —5A 78
Nedd. High —5B 166
Nedderton. Nmbd —1F 115
Nedging. Suff —1D 54
Nedging Tye. Suff —1D 54
Needham. Norf —2E 67
Needham Market. Suff —5C 66
Needham Street. Suff —4G 65
Needingworth. Cambs —3C 64
Needles, The —4A 16
Needwood. Staf —3F 73
Neen Savage. Shrp —3A 60
Neen Sollars. Shrp —3A 60
Neenton. Shrp —2A 60
Nefyn. Gwyn —1C 68
Neidpath Castle —5F 129
Neilston. E Ren —4F 127
Neithrop. Oxon —1C 50
Nelly Andrews Green. Powy —5E 71
Nelson. Cphy —2E 32
Nelson. Lanc —1G 91
Nelson Village. Nmbd —2F 115
Nemphlar. S Lan —5B 128
Nempnett Thrubwell. Bath —5A 34
Nene Terrace. Linc —5B 76
Nene Valley Railway —1A 64
Nenthall. Cumb —5A 114
Nenthead. Cumb —5A 114
Nenthorn. Bord —1A 120
Nercwys. Flin —4E 83
Neribus. Arg —4A 124
Nerston. S Lan —4H 127
Nesbit. Nmbd —1D 121
Nesfield. N Yor —5C 98
Ness. Ches —3F 83
Nesscliffe. Shrp —4F 71
Ness of Tenston. Orkn —6B 172
Neston. Ches —3E 83
Neston. Wilts —5D 34
Netchwood. Shrp —1A 60
Nethanfoot. S Lan —5B 128
Nether Alderley. Ches —3C 84
Netheravon. Wilts —2G 23
Nether Blainslie. Bord —5B 130
Netherbrae. Abers —3E 161
Netherbrough. Orkn —6C 172
Nether Broughton. Leics —3D 74
Netherburn. S Lan —5B 128
Nether Burrow. Lanc —2F 97
Netherbury. Dors —3H 13
Netherby. Cumb —2E 113
Nether Careston. Ang —3E 145
Nether Cerne. Dors —3B 14
Nether Compton. Dors —1A 14
Nethercote. Glos —3G 49
Nethercote. Warw —4C 62
Nethercott. Devn —3E 19
Nethercott. Oxon —3C 50
Nether Dallachy. Mor —2A 160
Nether Durdie. Per —1E 136
Nether End. Derbs —3G 85
Netherend. Glos —5A 48
Nether Exe. Devn —2C 12
Netherfield. E Sus —4B 28
Netherfield. Notts —1D 74
Nethergate. Norf —3C 78
Netherhampton. Wilts —3G 23
Nether Handley. Derbs —3B 86
Nether Haugh. S Yor —1B 86
Nether Heage. Derbs —5A 86
Nether Heyford. Nptn —5D 62
Netherhouses. Cumb —1B 96
Nether Howcleugh. Dum —3C 118
Nether Kellet. Lanc —3E 97
Nether Kinmundy. Abers —4H 161
Netherland Green. Staf —2F 73
Nether Langwith. Derbs —4C 86
Netherlaw. Dum —5E 111
Netherley. Abers —4F 153
Nethermill. Dum —1B 112
Nethermills. Mor —3C 160
Nether Moor. Derbs —4A 86
Nether Padley. Derbs —3G 85
Netherplace. E Ren —4G 127
Nether Poppleton. York —4H 99
Netherseal. Derbs —4G 73
Nether Silton. N Yor —5B 106
Nether Stowey. Som —3E 21
Nether Street. Essx —4F 53
Netherstreet. Wilts —5E 35
Netherthird. E Ayr —3E 117
Netherthong. W Yor —4B 92
Netherton. Ang —3E 145
Netherton. Cumb —1B 102
Netherton. Devn —5B 12
Netherton. Hants —1B 24
Netherton. Here —3A 48
Netherton. Mers —1F 83
Netherton. N Lan —4A 128
Netherton. Nmbd —4D 121
Netherton. Per —3A 144
Netherton. Shrp —2B 60
Netherton. Stir —2G 127
Netherton. W Mid —2D 60
Netherton. W Yor —3C 92
(nr. Horbury)
Netherton. W Yor —3B 92
(nr. Huddersfield)
Netherton. Worc —1E 49
Nethertown. Cumb —4A 102
Nethertown. High —1F 169
Nethertown. Staf —4F 73
Nether Urquhart. Fife —3D 136
Nether Wallop. Hants —3B 24
Nether Wasdale. Cumb —4C 102
Nether Welton. Cumb —5E 113
Nether Westcote. Glos —3H 49
Nether Whitacre. Warw —1G 61
Netherwhitton. Nmbd —5F 121
Nether Worton. Oxon —2C 50
Nethy Bridge. High —1E 151
Netley. Hants —2C 16
Netley. Shrp —5G 71
Netley Abbey EH —2C 16
Netley Marsh. Hants —1B 16
Nettlebed. Oxon —3F 37
Nettlebridge. Som —2B 22
Nettlecombe. Dors —3A 14
Nettlecombe. IOW —5D 16
Nettleden. Herts —4A 52
Nettleham. Linc —3H 87
Nettlestead. Kent —5A 40
Nettlestead Green. Kent —5A 40
Nettlestone. IOW —3E 16
Nettlesworth. Dur —5F 115
Nettleton. Linc —4E 94
Nettleton. Wilts —4D 34
Netton. Devn —4B 8
Netton. Wilts —3G 23
Neuadd. Carm —3H 45
Neuadd. Powy —5C 70
Neuk, The. Abers —4E 153
Nevendon. Essx —1B 40
Nevern. Pemb —1A 44
New Abbey. Dum —3A 112
New Aberdour. Abers —2F 161
New Addington. G Lon —4E 39
Newall. W Yor —5D 98
New Alresford. Hants —3D 24
New Alyth. Per —4B 144
Newark. Orkn —3G 172
Newark. Pet —5B 76
Newark Air Mus. —5F 87
Newark Castle, Newark —5E 87
Newark Castle, Port Glasgow HS —2E 127
Newark-on-Trent. Notts —5E 87
Newark Park NT —2C 34
New Arley. Warw —2G 61
Newarthill. N Lan —4A 128
New Ash Green. Kent —4H 39
New Balderton. Notts —5F 87
New Barn. Kent —4H 39
New Barnetby. N Lin —3D 94
Newbattle. Midl —3G 129
New Bewick. Nmbd —2E 121
Newbiggin. Cumb —2H 103
(nr. Appleby)
Newbiggin. Cumb —3B 96
(nr. Barrow-in-Furness)
Newbiggin. Cumb —5G 113
(nr. Cumrew)
Newbiggin. Cumb —2F 103
(nr. Penrith)
Newbiggin. Cumb —5B 102
(nr. Seascale)
Newbiggin. Dur —5E 115
(nr. Consett)
Newbiggin. Dur —2C 104
(nr. Holwick)
Newbiggin. Nmbd —5C 114
Newbiggin. N Yor —5C 104
(nr. Askrigg)
Newbiggin. N Yor —1F 101
(nr. Filey)
Newbiggin. N Yor —1B 98
(nr. Thoralby)
Newbiggin-by-the-Sea. Nmbd —1G 115
Newbigging. Ang —5D 144
(nr. Balgray)
Newbigging. Ang —5E 145
(nr. Monikie)
Newbigging. Ang —4B 144
(nr. Newtyle)
Newbigging. Edin —2E 129
Newbigging. S Lan —5D 128
Newbiggin-on-Lune. Cumb —4A 104
Newbold. Derbs —3A 86
Newbold. Leics —4B 74
Newbold on Avon. Warw —3B 62
Newbold on Stour. Warw —1H 49
Newbold Pacey. Warw —5G 61
Newbold Verdon. Leics —5B 74
New Bolingbroke. Linc —5C 88
Newborough. IOA —4D 80
Newborough. Pet —5B 76
Newborough. Staf —3F 73
Newbottle. Nptn —2D 50
Newbottle. Tyne —4G 115
New Boultham. Linc —3G 87
Newbourne. Suff —1F 55
New Brancepeth. Dur —5F 115
Newbridge. Cphy —2F 33
Newbridge. Cdgn —5E 57
Newbridge. Corn —3B 4
New Bridge. Dum —2G 111
Newbridge. Edin —2E 129
Newbridge. Hants —1A 16
Newbridge. IOW —4C 16
Newbridge. N Yor —1C 100
Newbridge. Pemb —1D 42
Newbridge. Wrex —1E 71
Newbridge Green. Worc —2D 48
Newbridge-on-Usk. Mon —2G 33
Newbridge on Wye. Powy —5C 58
New Brighton. Flin —4E 83
New Brighton. Hants —2F 17
New Brinsley. Notts —5B 86
Newbrough. Nmbd —3B 114
New Broughton. Wrex —5F 83
New Buckenham. Norf —1C 66
Newbuildings. Devn —2A 12
Newburgh. Abers —1G 153
Newburgh. Fife —2E 137
Newburgh. Lanc —3C 90
Newburgh Priory —2H 99
Newburn. Tyne —3E 115
Newbury. W Ber —5C 36
Newbury. Wilts —2D 22
Newby. Cumb —2G 103
Newby. N Yor —2G 97
(nr. Ingleton)
Newby. N Yor —1E 101
(nr. Scarborough)
Newby. N Yor —3C 106
(nr. Stokesley)
Newby Bridge. Cumb —1C 96
Newby Cote. N Yor —2G 97
Newby East. Cumb —4F 113
Newby Hall —3F 99
Newby Head. Cumb —2G 103
New Byth. Abers —3F 161
Newby West. Cumb —4E 113
Newby Wiske. N Yor —1F 99
Newcastle. B'end —4B 32
Newcastle. Mon —4H 47
Newcastle. Shrp —2E 59
Newcastle Airport. Tyne —2E 115
Newcastle Castle, Bridgend —3C 32
Newcastle Castle Keep —191
Newcastle Discovery Centre —191
Newcastle Emlyn. Carm —1D 44
Newcastleton. Bord —1F 113
Newcastle-under-Lyme. Staf —1C 72
Newcastle upon Tyne. Tyne —3F 115 & 191
Newchapel. Pemb —1G 43
Newchapel. Powy —2B 58
Newchapel. Staf —5C 84
Newchapel. Surr —1E 27
New Cheriton. Hants —4D 24
Newchurch. Carm —3D 45
Newchurch. Here —5F 59
Newchurch. IOW —4D 16
Newchurch. Kent —2E 29
Newchurch. Lanc —1G 91
(nr. Nelson)
Newchurch. Lanc —2G 91
(nr. Rawtenstall)
Newchurch. Mon —2H 33
Newchurch. Powy —5E 58
Newchurch. Staf —3F 73
New Costessey. Norf —4D 78
Newcott. Devn —2F 13
New Cowper. Cumb —5C 112
Newcraighall. Edin —2G 129
New Crofton. W Yor —3D 93
New Cross. Cdgn —3F 57
New Cumnock. E Ayr —3F 117
New Deer. Abers —4F 161
New Denham. Buck —2B 38
Newdigate. Surr —1C 26
New Duston. Nptn —4E 62
New Earswick. York —4A 100
New Edlington. S Yor —1C 86
New Elgin. Mor —2G 159
New Ellerby. E Yor —1E 95
Newell Green. Brac —4G 37
New Eltham. G Lon —3F 39
New End. Warw —4F 61
New End. Worc —5E 61
Newenden. Kent —3C 28
New England. Essx —1H 53
New England. Pet —5A 76
Newent. Glos —3C 48
New Ferry. Mers —2F 83
Newfield. Dur —4F 115
(nr. Chester-le-Street)
Newfield. Dur —1F 105
(nr. Willington)
New Forest —2A 16
Newfound. Hants —1D 24
New Fryston. W Yor —2E 93
New Galloway. Dum —2D 110
Newgate. Norf —1C 78
Newgate. Pemb —2C 42
Newgate Street. Herts —5D 52
New Greens. Herts —5B 52
New Grimsby. IOS —1A 4
(Newhailes NTS, Musselburgh) —2G 129
New Hainford. Norf —4E 78
Newhall. Ches —1A 72
Newhall. Staf —3G 73
Newham. Nmbd —2F 121
New Hartley. Nmbd —2G 115
Newhaven. Derbs —4F 85
Newhaven. E Sus —5F 27
Newhaven. Edin —2F 129
New Haw. Surr —4B 38
New Hedges. Pemb —4F 43
New Herrington. Tyne —4G 115
Newhey. G Man —3H 91
New Holkham. Norf —2A 78
New Holland. N Lin —2D 94
Newholm. N Yor —3F 107
New Houghton. Derbs —4C 86
New Houghton. Norf —3G 77
Newhouse. N Lan —3A 128
New Houses. N Yor —2H 97
New Hutton. Cumb —5G 103
New Hythe. Kent —5B 40
Newick. E Sus —3F 27
Newington. Edin —2F 129
Newington. Kent —2F 29
(nr. Folkestone)
Newington. Kent —4C 40
(nr. Sittingbourne)
Newington. Notts —1D 86
Newington. Oxon —2E 36
Newington Bagpath. Glos —2D 34
New Inn. Carm —2E 45
New Inn. Mon —5H 47
New Inn. N Yor —2H 97
New Inn. Torf —2G 33
New Invention. Shrp —3E 59
New Kelso. High —4B 156
New Lanark. S Lan —5B 128
New Lanark World Heritage Village —5B 128
Newland. Glos —5A 48
Newland. Hull —1D 94
Newland. N Yor —2G 93
Newland. Som —3B 20
Newland. Worc —1C 48
Newlandrig. Midl —3G 129
Newlands. Cumb —1E 103
Newlands. Essx —2C 40
Newlands. High —4B 158
Newlands. Nmbd —4D 115
Newlands. Notts —4C 86
Newlands. Staf —3E 73
Newlands of Geise. High —2C 168
Newlands of Tynet. Mor —2A 160
Newlands Park. IOA —2B 80
New Lane. Lanc —3C 90
New Lane End. Warr —1A 84
New Langholm. Dum —1E 113
New Leake. Linc —5D 88
New Leeds. Abers —3G 161
New Longton. Lanc —2D 90
Newlot. Orkn —6E 172
New Luce. Dum —3G 109
Newlyn. Corn —4B 4
Newmachar. Abers —2F 153
Newmains. N Lan —4B 128
New Mains of Ury. Abers —5F 153
New Malden. G Lon —4D 38
Newman's Green. Suff —1B 54
Newmarket. Suff —4F 65
Newmarket. W Isl —4G 171
New Marske. Red C —2D 106
New Marton. Shrp —2F 71
New Mill. Abers —4E 160
New Mill. Corn —3B 4
New Mill. Herts —4H 51
Newmill. Mor —3B 160
Newmill. Bord —3G 119
New Mill. W Yor —4B 92
New Mill. Wilts —5G 35
Newmillerdam. W Yor —3D 92
New Mills. Corn —3D 6
New Mills. Derbs —2E 85
Newmills. Fife —1D 128
Newmills. High —2A 158
New Mills. Mon —5A 48
New Mills. Powy —5C 70
Newmiln. Per —5A 144
Newmilns. E Ayr —1E 117
New Milton. Hants —3H 15
New Mistley. Essx —2E 54
New Moat. Pemb —2E 43
Newmore. High —3H 157
(nr. Dingwall)
Newmore. High —1A 158
(nr. Invergordon)
Newnham. Cambs —5D 64
Newnham. Glos —4B 48
Newnham. Hants —1F 25
Newnham. Herts —2C 52
Newnham. Kent —5D 40
Newnham. Nptn —5C 62
Newnham. Warw —4F 61
Newnham Bridge. Worc —4A 60
New Ollerton. Notts —4D 86
New Oscott. W Mid —1F 61
Newpark. Fife —2G 137
New Park. N Yor —4E 99
New Pitsligo. Abers —3F 161
New Polzeath. Corn —1D 6
Newport. Corn —4D 10
Newport. Devn —3F 19
Newport. E Yor —1B 94
Newport. Essx —2F 53
Newport. Glos —2B 34
Newport. High —1H 165
Newport. IOW —4D 16
Newport. Newp —3G 33 & 194
Newport. Norf —4H 79
Newport. Pemb —1E 43
Newport. Som —4G 21
Newport. Telf —4B 72
Newport-on-Tay. Fife —1G 137
Newport Pagnell. Mil —1G 51
Newpound Common. W Sus —3B 26
New Prestwick. S Ayr —2C 116
New Quay. Cdgn —5C 56
Newquay. Corn —2C 6
Newquay Cornwall (St Mawgan) Airport. Corn —2C 6
Newquay Zoo —2C 6
New Rackheath. Norf —4E 79
New Radnor. Powy —4E 58
New Rent. Cumb —1F 103
New Ridley. Nmbd —4D 114
New Romney. Kent —3E 29
New Rossington. S Yor —1D 86
New Row. Lanc —3G 57
New Row. Lanc —1E 91
New Row. N Yor —3D 106
New Sauchie. Clac —4A 136
Newsbank. Ches —4C 84
New Scone. Per —1D 136
Newseat. Abers —5E 160
Newsham. Lanc —1D 90
Newsham. Nmbd —2G 115
Newsham. N Yor —3E 105
(nr. Richmond)
Newsham. N Yor —1F 99
(nr. Thirsk)
New Sharlston. W Yor —3D 93
Newsholme. E Yor —2H 93
Newsholme. Lanc —4H 97
New Shoreston. Nmbd —1F 121
New Springs. G Man —4E 90
Newstead. Notts —5C 86
Newstead. Bord —1H 119
Newstead Abbey —5C 86
New Stevenston. N Lan —3A 128
New Street. Here —5F 59
Newstreet Lane. Shrp —2A 72
New Swanage. Dors —4F 15
New Swannington. Leics —4B 74
Newthorpe. N Yor —1E 93
Newthorpe. Notts —1B 74
Newton. Arg —4H 133
Newton. B'end —4B 32
Newton. Cambs —1E 53
(nr. Cambridge)
Newton. Cambs —4D 76
(nr. Wisbech)
Newton. Ches —4G 83
(nr. Chester)
Newton. Ches —5H 83
(nr. Tattenhall)
Newton. Cumb —2B 96
Newton. Derbs —5B 86
Newton. Dum —2D 112
(nr. Annan)
Newton. Dum —5D 118
(nr. Moffat)
Newton. G Man —1D 84
Newton. Here —2G 47
(nr. Ewyas Harold)
Newton. Here —5H 59
(nr. Leominster)
Newton. High —2B 158
(nr. Cromarty)
Newton. High —4B 158
(nr. Inverness)
Newton. High —5C 166
(nr. Kylestrome)
Newton. High —4F 169
(nr. Wick)
Newton. Lanc —2E 97
(nr. Carnforth)
Newton. Lanc —4F 97
(nr. Clitheroe)
Newton. Lanc —1C 90
(nr. Kirkham)
Newton. Linc —2H 75
Newton. Mers —2E 83
Newton. Mor —2F 159
Newton. Norf —4H 77
Newton. Nptn —2F 63
Newton. Nmbd —3D 114
Newton. Notts —1D 74
Newton. Bord —2A 120
Newton. Shet —8E 173
Newton. Shrp —1B 60
(nr. Bridgnorth)
Newton. Shrp —2G 71
(nr. Wem)
Newton. Som —3E 20
Newton. S Lan —3H 127
(nr. Glasgow)
Newton. S Lan —1B 118
(nr. Lanark)
Newton. Staf —3E 73
Newton. Suff —1C 54
Newton. Swan —4F 31
Newton. Warw —3C 62

Newton. W Lot —2D 129
Newton. Wilts —4H 23
Newton Abbot. Devn —5B 12
Newtonairds. Dum —1F 111
Newton Arlosh. Cumb —4D 112
Newton Aycliffe. Dur —2F 105
Newton Bewley. Hart —2B 106
Newton Blossomville. Mil —5G 63
Newton Bromswold. Nptn —4G 63
Newton Burgoland. Leics —5A 74
Newton by Toft. Linc —2H 87
Newton Ferrers. Devn —4B 8
Newton Flotman. Norf —1E 66
Newtongrange. Midl —3G 129
Newton Green. Mon —2A 34
Newton Hall. Dur —5F 115
Newton Hall. Nmbd —3D 114
Newton Harcourt. Leics —1D 62
Newton Heath. G Man —4G 91
Newtonhill. Abers —4G 153
Newtonhill. High —4H 157
Newton Hill. W Yor —2D 92
Newton Ketton. Darl —2A 106
Newton Kyme. N Yor —5G 99
Newton-le-Willows. Mers —1H 83
Newton-le-Willows. N Yor —1E 98
Newton Longville. Buck —2G 51
Newton Mearns. E Ren —4G 127
Newtonmore. High —4B 150
Newton Morrell. N Yor —4F 105
Newton Mulgrave. N Yor —3E 107
Newton of Ardtoe. High —1A 140
Newton of Balcanquhal. Per —2D 136
Newton of Beltrees. Ren —4E 127
Newton of Falkland. Fife —3E 137
Newton of Mountblairy. Abers —3D 160
Newton of Pitcairns. Per —2C 136
Newton-on-Ouse. N Yor —3H 99
Newton-on-Rawcliffe. N Yor —5F 107
Newton on the Hill. Shrp —3G 71
Newton-on-the-Moor. Nmbd —4F 121
Newton on Trent. Linc —3F 87
Newton Poppleford. Devn —4D 12
Newton Purcell. Oxon —2E 51
Newton Regis. Warw —5G 73
Newton Reigny. Cumb —1F 103
Newton Rigg. Cumb —1F 103
Newton St Cyres. Devn —3B 12
Newton St Faith. Norf —4E 78
Newton St Loe. Bath —5C 34
Newton St Petrock. Devn —1E 11
Newton Solney. Derbs —3G 73
Newton Stacey. Hants —2C 24
Newton Stewart. Dum —3B 110
Newton Toney. Wilts —2H 23
Newton Tracey. Devn —4F 19
Newton under Roseberry. Red C —3C 106
Newton Unthank. Leics —5B 74
Newton upon Ayr. S Ayr —2C 116
Newton upon Derwent. E Yor —5B 100
Newton Valence. Hants —3F 25
Newton with Scales. Lanc —1B 90
Newtown. Abers —2E 160
Newtown. Cambs —4H 63
Newtown. Ches —1A 72
Newtown. Corn —5C 10
Newtown. Cumb —5B 112
(nr. Aspatria)
Newtown. Cumb —3G 113
(nr. Brampton)
Newtown. Cumb —2G 103
(nr. Penrith)
Newtown. Derbs —2D 85
Newtown. Devn —4A 20
Newtown. Dors —2H 13
(nr. Beaminster)
New Town. Dors —1E 15
(nr. Sixpenny Handley)
New Town. E Lot —2H 129
Newtown. Falk —1D 128
Newtown. Glos —5B 48
(nr. Lydney)
Newtown. Glos —2E 49
(nr. Tewkesbury)
Newtown. Hants —1D 16
(nr. Bishop's Waltham)
Newtown. Hants —1A 16
(nr. Lyndhurst)
Newtown. Hants —5C 36
(nr. Newbury)
Newtown. Hants —4B 24
(nr. Romsey)
Newtown. Hants —2C 16
(nr. Warsash)
Newtown. Hants —1E 16
(nr. Wickham)
Newtown. Here —2B 48
(nr. Ledbury)
Newtown. Here —2A 48
(nr. Little Dewchurch)
Newtown. Here —1B 48
(nr. Stretton Grandison)
Newtown. High —3F 149
Newtown. IOM —4C 108
Newtown. IOW —3C 16
Newtown. Lanc —3D 90
New Town. Lutn —3A 52
Newtown. Nmbd —4E 121
(nr. Rothbury)
Newtown. Nmbd —2E 121
(nr. Wooler)
Newtown. Pool —3F 15
Newtown. Powy —1D 58
Newtown. Rhon —2D 32
Newtown. Shet —3F 173
Newtown. Shrp —2G 71
Newtown. Som —1F 13
Newtown. Staf —4D 84
(nr. Biddulph)
Newtown. Staf —5D 73
(nr. Cannock)
Newtown. Staf —4E 85
(nr. Longnor)
New Town. W Yor —2E 93
Newtown. Wilts —4E 23
Newtown-in-St Martin. Corn —4E 5
Newtown Linford. Leics —4C 74
Newtown St Boswells. Bord —1H 119
New Tredegar. Cphy —5E 47
Newtyle. Ang —4B 144
New Village. E Yor —1D 94
New Village. S Yor —4F 93
New Walsoken. Cambs —5D 76
New Waltham. NE Lin —4F 95
New Wimpole. Cambs —1D 52
New Winton. E Lot —2H 129
New World. Cambs —1C 64
New Yatt. Oxon —4B 50
Newyears Green. G Lon —2B 38
New York. Linc —5B 88
New York. Tyne —2G 115
Nextend. Here —5F 59
Neyland. Pemb —4D 42
Nib Heath. Shrp —4G 71
Nicholashayne. Devn —1E 12
Nicholaston. Swan —4E 31
Nidd. N Yor —3F 99
Niddrie. Edin —2F 129
Niddry. Edin —2D 129
Nigg. Aber —3G 153
Nigg. High —1C 158
Nigg Ferry. High —2B 158
Nightcott. Som —4B 20
Nine Ashes. Essx —5F 53
Ninebanks. Nmbd —4A 114
Nine Elms. Swin —3G 35
Ninemile Bar. Dum —2F 111
Nine Mile Burn. Midl —4E 129
Ninfield. E Sus —4B 28
Ningwood. IOW —4C 16
Nisbet. Bord —2A 120
Nisbet Hill. Bord —4E 130
Niton. IOW —5D 16
Nitshill. E Ren —4G 127
Niwbwrch. IOA —4D 80
Noak Hill. G Lon —1G 39
Nobold. Shrp —4G 71
Nobottle. Nptn —4D 62
Nocton. Linc —4H 87
Nogdam End. Norf —5F 79
Noke. Oxon —4D 50
Nolton. Pemb —3C 42
Nolton Haven. Pemb —3C 42
No Man's Heath. Ches —1H 71
No Man's Heath. Warw —5G 73
Nomansland. Devn —1B 12
Nomansland. Wilts —1A 16
Noneley. Shrp —3G 71
Noness. Shet —9F 173
Nonikiln. High —1A 158
Nonington. Kent —5G 41
Nook. Cumb —2F 113
(nr. Longtown)
Nook. Cumb —1E 97
(nr. Milnthorpe)
Noranside. Ang —2D 144
Norbreck. Bkpl —5C 96
Norbridge. Here —1C 48
Norbury. Ches —1H 71
Norbury. Derbs —1F 73
Norbury. Shrp —1F 59
Norbury. Staf —3B 72
Norby. N Yor —1G 99
Norby. Shet —6C 173
Norcross. Lanc —5C 96
Nordelph. Norf —5E 77
Norden. G Man —3G 91
Nordley. Shrp —1A 60
Norfolk Broads —4F 79
Norfolk Lavender Farm —2F 77
Norfolk Wildlife Park —4C 78
Norham. Nmbd —5F 131
Norham Castle EH —5F 131
Norland Town. W Yor —2A 92
Norley. Ches —3H 83
Norleywood. Hants —3B 16
Normanby. N Lin —3B 94
Normanby. N Yor —1B 100
Normanby. Red C —3C 106
Normanby-by-Spital. Linc —2H 87
Normanby Hall —3B 94
Normanby le Wold. Linc —1A 88
Norman Cross. Cambs —1A 64
Normandy. Surr —5A 38
Norman's Bay. E Sus —5A 28
Norman's Green. Devn —2D 12
Normanton. Derb —2H 73
Normanton. Leics —1F 75
Normanton. Linc —1G 75
Normanton. Notts —5E 86
Normanton. W Yor —2D 93
Normanton le Heath. Leics —4A 74
Normanton on Soar. Notts —3C 74
Normanton-on-the-Wolds. Notts —2D 74
Normanton on Trent. Notts —4E 87
Normoss. Lanc —1B 90
Norrington Common. Wilts —5D 35
Norris Green. Mers —1F 83
Norris Hill. Leics —4H 73
Norristhorpe. W Yor —2C 92
North Acre. Norf —1B 66
Northall. Buck —3H 51
Northallerton. N Yor —5A 106
Northam. Devn —4E 19
Northam. Sotn —1C 16
Northampton. Nptn —4E 63 & 194
North Anston. S Yor —2C 86
North Ascot. Brac —4A 38
North Aston. Oxon —3C 50
Northaw. Herts —5C 52
Northay. Som —1F 13
North Baddesley. Hants —4B 24
North Balfern. Dum —4B 110
North Ballachulish. High —2E 141
North Barrow. Som —4B 22
North Barsham. Norf —2B 78
Northbeck. Linc —1H 75
North Benfleet. Essx —2B 40
North Bersted. W Sus —5A 26
North Berwick. E Lot —1B 130
North Bitchburn. Dur —1E 105
North Blyth. Nmbd —1G 115
North Boarhunt. Hants —1E 16
North Bockhampton. Dors —3G 15
Northborough. Pet —5A 76
Northbourne. Kent —5H 41
Northbourne. Oxon —3D 36
North Bovey. Devn —4H 11
North Bradley. Wilts —1D 22
North Brentor. Devn —4E 11
North Brewham. Som —3C 22
Northbrook. Oxon —3C 50
North Brook End. Cambs —1C 52
North Buckland. Devn —2E 19
North Burlingham. Norf —4F 79
North Cadbury. Som —4B 22
North Carlton. Linc —3G 87
North Cave. E Yor —1B 94
North Cerney. Glos —5F 49
North Chailey. E Sus —3E 27
Northchapel. W Sus —3A 26
North Charford. Hants —1G 15
North Charlton. Nmbd —2F 121
North Cheriton. Som —4B 22
North Chideock. Dors —3H 13
Northchurch. Herts —5H 51
North Cliffe. E Yor —1B 94
North Clifton. Notts —3F 87
North Close. Dur —1F 105
North Cockerington. Linc —1C 88
North Coker. Som —1A 14
North Collafirth. Shet —3E 173
North Common. E Sus —3E 27
North Commonty. Abers —4F 161
North Coombe. Devn —1B 12
North Corbelly. Dum —3A 112
North Cornelly. B'end —3B 32
North Cotes. Linc —4G 95
Northcott. Devn —3D 10
Northcourt. Oxon —2D 36
North Cove. Suff —2G 67
North Cowton. N Yor —4F 105
North Craigo. Ang —2F 145
North Crawley. Mil —1H 51
North Cray. G Lon —3F 39
North Creake. Norf —2A 78
North Curry. Som —4G 21
North Dalton. E Yor —4D 100
North Deighton. N Yor —4F 99
North Downs —2F 25
North Droney. Ang —5C 144
North Duffield. N Yor —1G 93
Northdyke. Orkn —5B 172
Northedge. Derbs —4A 86
North Elkington. Linc —1B 88
North Elmham. Norf —3B 78
North Elmsall. W Yor —3E 93
Northend. Buck —2F 37
North End. E Yor —1F 95
North End. Essx —4G 53
(nr. Great Dunmow)
North End. Essx —2A 54
(nr. Great Yeldham)
North End. Hants —5C 36
North End. Leics —4C 74
North End. Linc —1B 76
North End. Norf —1B 66
North End. N Som —5H 33
North End. Port —2E 17
Northend. Warw —5A 62
North End. W Sus —5C 26
North End. Wilts —2F 35
North Erradale. High —5B 162
North Evington. Leic —5D 74
North Fambridge. Essx —1C 40
North Fearns. High —5E 155
North Featherstone. W Yor —2E 93
North Feorline. N Ayr —3D 122
North Ferriby. E Yor —2C 94
Northfield. Aber —3F 153
Northfield. Hull —2D 94
Northfield. Som —3F 21
Northfield. W Mid —3E 61
Northfleet. Kent —3H 39
North Frodingham. E Yor —4F 101
Northgate. Linc —3A 76
North Gluss. Shet —4E 173
North Gorley. Hants —1G 15
North Green. Norf —2E 66
North Green. Suff —4F 67
(nr. Framlingham)
North Green. Suff —3F 67
(nr. Halesworth)
North Green. Suff —4F 67
(nr. Saxmundham)
North Greetwell. Linc —3H 87
North Grimston. N Yor —3C 100
North Halling. Medw —4B 40
North Hayling. Hants —2F 17
North Hazelrigg. Nmbd —1E 121
North Heasley. Devn —3H 19
North Heath. W Sus —3B 26
North Hill. Corn —5C 10
North Hinksey Village. Oxon —5C 50
North Holmwood. Surr —1C 26
North Huish. Devn —3D 8
North Hykeham. Linc —4G 87
Northiam. E Sus —3C 28
Northill. Beds —1B 52
Northington. Hants —3D 24
Northington Grange EH —3D 24
North Kelsey. Linc —4D 94
North Kelsey Moor. Linc —4D 94
North Kessock. High —4A 158
North Killingholme. N Lin —3E 95
North Kilvington. N Yor —1G 99
North Kilworth. Leics —2D 62
North Kyme. Linc —5A 88
North Lancing. W Sus —5C 26
Northlands. Linc —5C 88
Northleach. Glos —4G 49
North Lee. Buck —5G 51
North Lees. N Yor —2F 99
Northleigh. Devn —3G 19
(nr. Barnstaple)
Northleigh. Devn —3E 13
(nr. Honiton)
North Leigh. Kent —1F 29
North Leigh. Oxon —4B 50
North Leverton with Habblesthorpe. Notts —2E 87
Northlew. Devn —3F 11
North Littleton. Worc —1F 49
North Lopham. Norf —2C 66
North Luffenham. Rut —5G 75
North Marden. W Sus —1G 17
North Marston. Buck —3F 51
North Middleton. Midl —4G 129
North Middleton. Nmbd —2E 121
North Molton. Devn —4H 19
North Moor. N Yor —1D 100
Northmoor. Oxon —5C 50
Northmoor Green. Som —3G 21
North Moreton. Oxon —3D 36
Northmuir. Ang —3C 144
North Mundham. W Sus —2G 17
North Murie. Per —1E 137
North Muskham. Notts —5E 87
North Ness. Orkn —8C 172
North Newbald. E Yor —1C 94
North Newington. Oxon —2C 50
North Newnton. Wilts —1G 23
North Newton. Som —3F 21
Northney. Hants —2F 17
North Nibley. Glos —2C 34
North Norfolk Railway —1D 78
North Oakley. Hants —1D 24
North Ockendon. G Lon —2G 39
North of England Open Air Mus. —4F 115
Northolt. G Lon —2C 38
Northop. Flin —4E 83
Northop Hall. Flin —4E 83
North Ormesby. Midd —2C 106
North Ormsby. Linc —1B 88
Northorpe. Linc —4H 75
(nr. Bourne)
Northorpe. Linc —2B 76
(nr. Donington)
Northorpe. Linc —1F 87
(nr. Gainsborough)
North Otterington. N Yor —1F 99
Northover. Som —3H 21
(nr. Glastonbury)
Northover. Som —4A 22
(nr. Yeovil)
North Owersby. Linc —1H 87
Northowram. W Yor —2B 92
North Perrott. Som —2H 13
North Petherton. Som —3F 21
North Petherwin. Corn —4C 10
North Pickenham. Norf —5A 78
North Piddle. Worc —5D 60
North Poorton. Dors —3A 14
North Port. Arg —1H 133
Northport. Dors —4E 15
North Queensferry. Fife —1E 129
North Radworthy. Devn —3A 20
North Rauceby. Linc —1H 75
Northrepps. Norf —2E 79
North Rigton. N Yor —5E 99
North Rode. Ches —4C 84
North Roe. Shet —3E 173
North Ronaldsay Airport. Orkn —2G 172
North Row. Cumb —1D 102
North Runcton. Norf —4F 77
North Sannox. N Ayr —5B 126
North Scale. Cumb —3A 96
North Scarle. Linc —4F 87
North Seaton. Nmbd —1F 115
North Seaton Colliery. Nmbd —1F 115
North Sheen. G Lon —3C 38
North Shian. Arg —4D 140
North Shields. Tyne —3G 115
North Shoebury. S'end —2D 40
North Shore. Bkpl —1B 90
North Side. Cumb —2B 102
North Skelton. Red C —3D 106
North Somercotes. Linc —1D 88
North Stainley. N Yor —2E 99
North Stainmore. Cumb —3B 104
North Stifford. Thur —2H 39
North Stoke. Bath —5C 34
North Stoke. Oxon —3E 36
North Stoke. W Sus —4B 26
North Street. Hants —3E 25
North Street. Kent —5E 40
North Street. Medw —3C 40
North Street. W Ber —4E 37
North Sunderland. Nmbd —1G 121
North Tamerton. Corn —3D 10
North Tawton. Devn —2G 11
North Thoresby. Linc —1B 88
North Town. Devn —2F 11
Northtown. Orkn —8D 172
North Town. Shet —10E 173
North Tuddenham. Norf —4C 78
Northumberland Nat. Park —4C 120
North Walbottle. Tyne —3E 115
Northwall. Orkn —3G 172
North Walsham. Norf —2E 79
North Waltham. Hants —2D 24
North Warnborough. Hants —1F 25
North Water Bridge. Ang —2F 145
North Watten. High —3E 169
Northway. Glos —2E 49
Northway. Swan —4E 31
North Weald Bassett. Essx —5F 53
North Weston. N Som —4H 33
North Wheatley. Notts —2E 87
North Whilborough. Devn —2E 9
Northwich. Ches —3A 84
North Wick. Bath —5A 34
Northwick. Som —2G 21
Northwick. S Glo —3A 34
North Widcombe. Bath —1A 22
North Willingham. Linc —2A 88
North Wingfield. Derbs —4B 86
North Witham. Linc —3G 75
Northwold. Norf —1G 65
Northwood. Derbs —4G 85
Northwood. G Lon —1B 38
Northwood. IOW —3C 16
Northwood. Kent —4H 41
Northwood. Shrp —2G 71
Northwood. Stoke —1C 72
Northwood Green. Glos —4C 48
North Wootton. Dors —1B 14
North Wootton. Norf —3F 77
North Wootton. Som —2A 22
North Wraxall. Wilts —4D 34
North Wroughton. Swin —3G 35
North Yardhope. Nmbd —4D 120
North York Moors Nat. Park —4D 106
North York Moors Railway —1C 100
Norton. Devn —3E 9
Norton. Glos —3D 48
Norton. Hal —2H 83
Norton. Herts —2C 52
Norton. IOW —4B 16
Norton. Mon —3H 47
Norton. Nptn —4D 62
Norton. Notts —3C 86
Norton. Powy —4F 59
Norton. Shrp —2G 59
(nr. Ludlow)
Norton. Shrp —5B 72
(nr. Madeley)
Norton. Shrp —5H 71
(nr. Shrewsbury)
Norton. S Yor —3F 93
(nr. Askern)
Norton. S Yor —2A 86
(nr. Sheffield)
Norton. Stoc T —2B 106
Norton. Suff —4B 66
Norton. Swan —4F 31
Norton. W Sus —5A 26
(nr. Arundel)
Norton. W Sus —3G 17
(nr. Selsey)
Norton. Wilts —3D 35
Norton. Worc —1F 49
(nr. Evesham)
Norton. Worc —5C 60
(nr. Worcester)
Norton Bavant. Wilts —2E 23
Norton Bridge. Staf —2C 72
Norton Canes. Staf —5E 73
Norton Canon. Here —1G 47
Norton Conyers Hall —2F 99
Norton Corner. Norf —3C 78
Norton Disney. Linc —5F 87
Norton East. Staf —5E 73
Norton Ferris. Wilts —3C 22
Norton Fitzwarren. Som —4F 21
Norton Green. IOW —4B 16
Norton Green. Stoke —5D 84
Norton Hawkfield. Bath —5A 34
Norton Heath. Essx —5G 53
Norton in Hales. Shrp —2B 72
Norton in the Moors. Stoke —5C 84
Norton-Juxta-Twycross. Leics —5H 73
Norton-le-Clay. N Yor —2G 99
Norton Lindsey. Warw —4G 61
Norton Little Green. Suff —4B 66
Norton Malreward. Bath —5B 34
Norton Mandeville. Essx —5F 53
Norton-on-Derwent. N Yor —2B 100
Norton St Philip. Som —1C 22
Norton Subcourse. Norf —1G 67
Norton sub Hamdon. Som —1H 13
Norton Woodseats. S Yor —2A 86
Norwell. Notts —4E 87
Norwell Woodhouse. Notts —4E 87
Norwich. Norf —5E 79 & 194

Norwich Airport. Norf —4E 78
Norwich Castle & Mus. —194
Norwich Cathedral —194
Norwick. Shet —1H 173
Norwood. Derbs —2B 86
Norwood Green. W Yor —2B 92
Norwood Hill. Surr —1D 26
Norwood Park. Som —3A 22
Norwoodside. Cambs —1D 64
Noseley. Leics —1E 63
Noss Mayo. Devn —4B 8
Nostell Priory NT —3E 93
Nosterfield. N Yor —1E 99
Nostie. High —1A 148
Notgrove. Glos —3G 49
Nottage. B'end —4B 32
Nottingham. Nott —1C 74 & 194
Nottingham Castle —194
Nottingham East Midlands Airport. Leics —3B 74
Nottingham Transport Heritage Centre —2C 74
Nottington. Dors —4B 14
Notton. W Yor —3D 92
Notton. Wilts —5E 35
Nounsley. Essx —4A 54
Noutard's Green. Worc —4B 60
Nox. Shrp —4G 71
Noyadd Trefawr. Cdgn —1C 44
Nuffield. Oxon —3E 37
Nunburnholme. E Yor —5C 100
Nuncargate. Notts —5C 86
Nunclose. Cumb —5F 113
Nuneaton. Warw —1A 62
Nuneham Courtenay. Oxon —2D 36
Nun Monkton. N Yor —4H 99
Nunnerie. S Lan —3B 118
Nunney. Som —2C 22
Nunney Castle EH —2C 22
Nunnington. N Yor —2A 100
Nunnington Hall NT —2A 100
Nunnykirk. Nmbd —5E 121
Nunsthorpe. NE Lin —4F 95
Nunthorpe. Red C —3C 106
Nunthorpe. York —5H 99
Nunton. Wilts —4G 23
Nunwick. Nmbd —2B 114
Nunwick. N Yor —2F 99
Nupend. Glos —5C 48
Nursling. Hants —1B 16
Nursted. W Sus —4F 25
Nursteed. Wilts —5F 35
Nurston. V Glam —5D 32
Nutbourne. W Sus —2F 17
(nr. Chichester)
Nutbourne. W Sus —4B 26
(nr. Pulborough)
Nutfield. Surr —5E 39
Nuthall. Notts —1B 74
Nuthampstead. Herts —2E 53
Nuthurst. Warw —3F 61
Nuthurst. W Sus —3C 26
Nutley. E Sus —3F 27
Nuttall. G Man —3F 91
Nutwell. S Yor —4G 93
Nybster. High —2F 169
Nyetimber. W Sus —3G 17
Nyewood. W Sus —4G 25
Nymans Gdn. NT —3D 26
Nymet Rowland. Devn —2H 11
Nymet Tracey. Devn —2H 11
Nympsfield. Glos —5D 48
Nynehead. Som —4E 21
Nyton. W Sus —5A 26

Oadby. Leics —5D 74
Oad Street. Kent —4C 40
Oakamoor. Staf —1E 73
Oakbank. Arg —5B 140
Oakbank. W Lot —3D 129
Oakdale. Cphy —2E 33
Oakdale. Pool —3F 15
Oake. Som —4E 21
Oaken. Staf —5C 72
Oakenclough. Lanc —5E 97
Oakengates. Telf —4B 72
Oakenholt. Flin —3E 83
Oakenshaw. Dur —1F 105
Oakenshaw. W Yor —2B 92
Oakerthorpe. Derbs —5A 86
Oakford. Cdgn —5D 56
Oakford. Devn —4C 20
Oakfordbridge. Devn —4C 20
Oakgrove. Ches —4D 84
Oakham. Rut —5F 75
Oakham Castle —5F 75
Oakhanger. Ches —5B 84
Oakhanger. Hants —3F 25
Oakhill. Som —2B 22
Oakington. Cambs —4D 64
Oaklands. Powy —5C 58
Oakle Street. Glos —4C 48
Oakley. Beds —5H 63
Oakley. Buck —4E 51
Oakley. Fife —1D 128
Oakley. Hants —1D 24
Oakley. Suff —3D 66
Oakley Green. Wind —3A 38
Oakley Park. Powy —2B 58
Oakmere. Ches —4H 83
Oakridge. Glos —5E 49
Oaks. Shrp —5G 71
Oaksey. Wilts —2E 35
Oaks Green. Derbs —2F 73
Oakshaw Ford. Cumb —2G 113
Oakshott. Hants —4F 25
Oakthorpe. Leics —4H 73
Oak Tree. Darl —3A 106
Oakwell Hall, Birstall —2C 92
Oakwood. Derb —2A 74
Oakwood. W Yor —1D 92
Oakwoodhill. Surr —2C 26
Oakwood Theme Park —3E 43
Oakworth. W Yor —1A 92
Oape. High —3B 164
Oare. Kent —4E 40
Oare. Som —2B 20
Oare. W Ber —4D 36
Oare. Wilts —5G 35
Oareford. Som —2B 20
Oasby. Linc —2H 75
Oath. Som —4G 21
Oathlaw. Ang —3D 145
Oatlands. N Yor —4F 99
Oban. Arg —1F 133 & 195
Oban. W Isl —7D 171
Oban Distillery —1F 133
Oborne. Dors —1B 14
Obsdale. High —2A 158
Observatory Science Centre —4H 27
Obthorpe. Linc —4H 75
Occlestone Green. Ches —4A 84
Occold. Suff —3D 66
Ochiltree. E Ayr —2E 117
Ochtermuthill. Per —2H 135
Ochtertyre. Per —1H 135
Ockbrook. Derbs —2B 74
Ockeridge. Worc —4B 60
Ockham. Surr —5B 38
Ockle. High —1G 139
Ockley. Surr —1C 26
Ocle Pychard. Here —1A 48
Octofad. Arg —4A 124
Octomore. Arg —4A 124
Octon. E Yor —3E 101
Odcombe. Som —1A 14
Odd Down. Bath —5C 34
Oddingley. Worc —5D 60
Oddington. Oxon —4D 50
Oddsta. Shet —2G 173
Odell. Beds —5G 63
Odie. Orkn —5F 172
Odiham. Hants —1F 25
Odsey. Cambs —2C 52
Odstock. Wilts —4G 23
Odstone. Leics —5A 74
Offa's Dyke EH —5A 48
Offchurch. Warw —4A 62
Offenham. Worc —1F 49
Offenham Cross. Worc —1F 49
Offerton. G Man —2D 84
Offerton. Tyne —4G 115
Offham. E Sus —4F 27
Offham. Kent —5A 40
Offham. W Sus —5B 26
Offleyhay. Staf —3C 72
Offley Hoo. Herts —3B 52
Offleymarsh. Staf —3B 72
Offord Cluny. Cambs —4B 64
Offord D'Arcy. Cambs —4B 64
Offton. Suff —1D 54
Offwell. Devn —3E 13
Ogbourne Maizey. Wilts —4G 35
Ogbourne St Andrew. Wilts —4G 35
Ogbourne St George. Wilts —4H 35
Ogden. G Man —3H 91
Ogle. Nmbd —2E 115
Ogmore. V Glam —4B 32
Ogmore-by-Sea. V Glam —4B 32
Ogmore Castle CADW —4B 32
Ogmore Vale. B'end —2C 32
Okeford Fitzpaine. Dors —1D 14
Okehampton. Devn —3F 11
Okehampton Camp. Devn —3F 11
Okehampton Castle EH —3F 11
Okraquoy. Shet —8F 173
Okus. Swin —3G 35
Old. Nptn —3E 63
Old Aberdeen. Aber —3G 153
Old Alresford. Hants —3D 24
Oldany. High —5B 166
Old Arley. Warw —1G 61
Old Barns. Nmbd —4G 121
Old Basford. Nott —1C 74
Old Basing. Hants —1E 25
Old Beaupre Castle —4D 32
Oldberrow. Warw —4F 61
Old Bewick. Nmbd —2E 121
Old Bexley. G Lon —3F 39
Old Blair. Per —2F 143
Old Bolingbroke. Linc —4C 88
Oldborough. Devn —2A 12
Old Brampton. Derbs —3H 85
Old Bridge of Tilt. Per —2F 143
Old Bridge of Urr. Dum —3E 111
Old Buckenham. Norf —1C 66
Old Burghclere. Hants —1C 24
Oldbury. Shrp —1B 60
Oldbury. Warw —1H 61
Oldbury. W Mid —2D 61
Oldbury-on-Severn. S Glo —2B 34
Oldbury on the Hill. Glos —3D 34
Old Byland. N Yor —1H 99
Old Cassop. Dur —1A 106
Oldcastle. Mon —3G 47
Oldcastle Heath. Ches —1G 71
Old Clee. NE Lin —4F 95
Old Cleeve. Som —2D 20
Old Clipstone. Notts —4D 86
Old Colwyn. Cnwy —3A 82
Oldcotes. Notts —2C 86
Old Coulsdon. G Lon —5E 39
Old Dailly. S Ayr —5B 116
Old Dalby. Leics —3D 74
Old Dam. Derbs —3F 85
Old Deer. Abers —4G 161
Old Dilton. Wilts —2D 22
Old Down. S Glo —3B 34
Oldeamere. Cambs —1C 64
Old Edlington. S Yor —1C 86
Old Eldon. Dur —2F 105
Old Ellerby. E Yor —1E 95
Old Fallings. W Mid —5D 72
Oldfallow. Staf —4D 72
Old Felixstowe. Suff —2G 55
Oldfield. Shrp —2A 60
Oldfield. Worc —4C 60
Old Fletton. Pet —1A 64
Oldford. Som —1C 22
Old Forge. Here —4A 48
Old Glossop. Derbs —1E 85
Old Goole. E Yor —2H 93
Old Gore. Here —3B 48
Old Gorhambury EH —5B 52
Old Graitney. Dum —3E 112
Old Grimsbury. Oxon —1C 50
Old Grimsby. IOS —1A 4
Old Hall. E Yor —3F 95
Oldhall. High —3E 169
Old Hall Street. Norf —2F 79
Oldham. G Man —4H 91
Oldhamstocks. E Lot —2D 130
Old Heathfield. E Sus —3G 27
Old Hill. W Mid —2D 60
Old Hunstanton. Norf —1F 77
Old Hurst. Cambs —3B 64
Old Hutton. Cumb —1E 97
Old Kea. Corn —4C 6
Old Kilpatrick. W Dun —2F 127
Old Kinnernie. Abers —3E 152
Old Knebworth. Herts —3C 52
Oldland. S Glo —4B 34
Old Laxey. IOM —3D 108
Old Leake. Linc —5D 88
Old Llanberis. Gwyn —5F 81
Old Malton. N Yor —2B 100
Oldmeldrum. Abers —1F 153
Oldmill. Corn —5D 10
Oldmixon. N Som —1G 21
Old Monkland. N Lan —3A 128
Old Newton. Suff —4C 66
Old Oswestry Hill Fort EH —2E 71
Old Park. Telf —5A 72
Old Pentland. Midl —3F 129
Old Philpstoun. W Lot —2D 128
Old Quarrington. Dur —1A 106
Old Radnor. Powy —5E 59
Old Rayne. Abers —1D 152
Oldridge. Devn —3B 12
Old Romney. Kent —3E 29
Old Sarum —3G 23
Old Scone. Per —1D 136
Oldshore Beg. High —3B 166
Oldshoremore. High —3C 166
Old Snydale. W Yor —2E 93
Old Sodbury. S Glo —3C 34
Old Somerby. Linc —2G 75
Old Spital. Dur —3C 104
Oldstead. N Yor —1H 99
Old Stratford. Nptn —1F 51
Old Swan. Mers —1F 83
Old Swarland. Nmbd —4F 121
Old Tebay. Cumb —4H 103
Old Town. Cumb —5F 113
Old Town. E Sus —5G 27
Oldtown. High —5C 164
Old Town. IOS —1B 4
Old Town. Nmbd —5C 120
Oldtown of Ord. Abers —3D 160
Old Trafford. G Man —1C 84
Old Tupton. Derbs —4A 86
Oldwall. Cumb —3F 113
Oldwalls. Swan —3D 31
Old Warden. Beds —1B 52
Old Wardour Castle EH —4E 23
Oldways End. Som —4B 20
Old Westhall. Abers —1D 152
Old Weston. Cambs —3H 63
Oldwhat. Abers —3F 161
Old Windsor. Wind —3A 38
Old Wives Lees. Kent —5E 41
Old Woking. Surr —5B 38
Oldwood Common. Worc —4H 59
Old Woodstock. Oxon —4C 50
Olgrinmore. High —3C 168
Oliver's Battery. Hants —4C 24
Ollaberry. Shet —3E 173
Ollerton. Ches —3B 84
Ollerton. Notts —4D 86
Ollerton. Shrp —3A 72
Olmarch. Cdgn —5F 57
Olmstead Green. Cambs —1G 53
Olney. Mil —5F 63
Olrig. High —2D 169
Olton. W Mid —2F 61
Olveston. S Glo —3B 34
Ombersley. Worc —4C 60
Ompton. Notts —4D 86
Omunsgarth. Shet —7E 173
Onchan. IOM —4D 108
Onecote. Staf —5E 85
Onehouse. Suff —5C 66
Onen. Mon —4H 47
Ongar Hill. Norf —3E 77
Ongar Street. Here —4F 59
Onibury. Shrp —3G 59
Onich. High —2E 141
Onllwyn. Neat —4B 46
Onneley. Shrp —1B 72
Onslow Green. Essx —4G 53
Onslow Village. Surr —1A 26
Onthank. E Ayr —1D 116
Openwoodgate. Derbs —1A 74
Opinan. High —1G 155
(nr. Gairloch)
Opinan. High —4C 162
(nr. Laide)
Orasaigh. W Isl —6F 171
Orbost. High —4B 154
Orby. Linc —4D 89
Orchard Hill. Devn —4E 19
Orchard Portman. Som —4F 21
Orchard Wyndham —2D 20
Orcheston. Wilts —2F 23
Orcop. Here —3H 47
Orcop Hill. Here —3H 47
Ord. High —2E 147
Ordale. Shet —1H 173
Ordhead. Abers —2D 152
Ordie. Abers —3B 152
Ordiquish. Mor —3H 159
Ordley. Nmbd —4C 114
Ordsall. Notts —3E 86
Ore. E Sus —4C 28
Oreham Common. W Sus —4D 26
Oreton. Shrp —2A 60
Orford. Linc —1B 88
Orford. Suff —1H 55
Orford. Warr —1A 84
Orford Castle EH —1H 55
Orford Ness NT —1H 55
Organford. Dors —3E 15
Orgil. Orkn —7B 172
Orgreave. Staf —4F 73
Oridge Street. Glos —3C 48
Orlestone. Kent —2D 28
Orleton. Here —4G 59
Orleton. Worc —4A 60
Orleton Common. Here —4G 59
Orlingbury. Nptn —3F 63
Ormacleit. W Isl —5C 170
Ormathwaite. Cumb —2D 102
Ormesby. Midd —3C 106
Ormesby Hall NT —3C 106
Ormesby St Margaret. Norf —4G 79
Ormesby St Michael. Norf —4G 79
Ormiscaig. High —4C 162
Ormiston. E Lot —3H 129
Ormsaigbeg. High —2F 139
Ormsaigmore. High —2F 139
Ormsary. Arg —2F 125
Ormsgill. Cumb —2A 96
Ormskirk. Lanc —4C 90
Orphir. Orkn —7C 172
Orpington. G Lon —4F 39
Orrell. Lanc —4D 90
Orrell. Mers —1F 83
Orrisdale. IOM —2C 108
Orsett. Thur —2H 39
Orslow. Staf —4C 72
Orston. Notts —1E 75
Orthwaite. Cumb —1D 102
Orton. Cumb —4H 103
Orton. Mor —3H 159
Orton. Nptn —3F 63
Orton. Staf —1C 60
Orton Longueville. Pet —1A 64
Orton-on-the-Hill. Leics —5H 73
Orton Waterville. Pet —1A 64
Orton Wistow. Pet —1A 64
Orwell. Cambs —5C 64
Osbaldeston. Lanc —1E 91
Osbaldwick. York —4A 100
Osbaston. Leics —5B 74
Osbaston. Shrp —3F 71
Osborne House EH —3D 16
Osbournby. Linc —2H 75
Osclay. High —5E 169
Oscroft. Ches —4H 83
Ose. High —4C 154
Osgathorpe. Leics —4B 74
Osgodby. Linc —1H 87
Osgodby. N Yor —1E 101
(nr. Scarborough)
Osgodby. N Yor —1G 93
(nr. Selby)
Oskaig. High —5E 155
Oskamull. Arg —4F 139
Osleston. Derbs —2G 73
Osmaston. Derb —2A 74
Osmaston. Derbs —1G 73
Osmington. Dors —4C 14
Osmington Mills. Dors —4C 14
Osmondthorpe. W Yor —1D 92
Osmondwall. Orkn —9C 172
Osmotherley. N Yor —5B 106
Osnaburgh. Fife —2G 137
Ospisdale. High —5E 164
Ospringe. Kent —4E 40
Ossett. W Yor —2C 92
Ossington. Notts —4E 87
Ostend. Essx —1D 40
Ostend. Norf —2F 79
Osterley. G Lon —3C 38
Osterley Park NT —3C 38
Oswaldkirk. N Yor —2A 100
Oswaldtwistle. Lanc —2F 91
Oswestry. Shrp —3E 71
Otby. Linc —1A 88
Otford. Kent —5G 39
Otham. Kent —5B 40
Otherton. Staf —4D 72
Othery. Som —3G 21
Otley. Suff —5E 66
Otley. W Yor —5E 98
Otterbourne. Hants —4C 24
Otterburn. Nmbd —5C 120
Otterburn. N Yor —4A 98
Otterburn Camp. Nmbd —5C 120
Otterburn Hall. Nmbd —5C 120
Otter Ferry. Arg —1H 125
Otterford. Som —1F 13
Otterham. Corn —3B 10
Otterhampton. Som —2F 21
Otterham Quay. Kent —4C 40
Ottershaw. Surr —4B 38
Otterspool. Mers —2F 83
Otterswick. Shet —3G 173
Otterton. Devn —4D 12
Otter Trust —2F 67
Otterwood. Hants —2C 16
Ottery St Mary. Devn —3E 12
Ottinge. Kent —1F 29
Ottringham. E Yor —2F 95
Oughterby. Cumb —4D 112
Oughtershaw. N Yor —1A 98
Oughterside. Cumb —5C 112
Oughtibridge. S Yor —1H 85
Oughtrington. Warr —2A 84
Oulston. N Yor —2H 99
Oulton. Cumb —4D 112
Oulton. Norf —3D 78
Oulton. Staf —3B 72
(nr. Gnosall Heath)
Oulton. Staf —2D 72
(nr. Stone)
Oulton. Suff —1H 67
Oulton. W Yor —2D 92
Oulton Broad. Suff —1H 67
Oulton Street. Norf —3D 78
Oundle. Nptn —2H 63
Our Dynamic Earth —Edinburgh 189
Ousby. Cumb —1H 103
Ousdale. High —1H 165
Ousden. Suff —5G 65
Ousefleet. E Yor —2B 94
Ouston. Dur —4F 115
Ouston. Nmbd —4A 114
(nr. Bearsbridge)
Ouston. Nmbd —2D 114
(nr. Stamfordham)
Outer Hope. Devn —4C 8
Outertown. Orkn —6B 172
Outgate. Cumb —5E 103
Outhgill. Cumb —4A 104
Outlands. Staf —2B 72
Outlane. W Yor —3A 92
Out Newton. E Yor —2G 95
Out Rawcliffe. Lanc —5D 96
Outwell. Norf —5E 77
Outwick. Hants —1G 15
Outwood. Surr —1E 27
Outwood. W Yor —2D 92
Outwood. Worc —3D 60
Outwoods. Leics —4B 74
Outwoods. Staf —4B 72
Ouzlewell Green. W Yor —2D 92
Ovenden. W Yor —2A 92
Over. Cambs —3C 64
Over. Ches —4A 84
Over. Glos —4D 48
Over. S Glo —3A 34
Overbecks Mus. & Gdn. NT —5D 8
Overbister. Orkn —3F 172
Over Burrows. Derbs —2G 73
Overbury. Worc —2E 49
Overcombe. Dors —4B 14
Over Compton. Dors —1A 14
Over End. Cambs —1H 63
Over Finlarg. Ang —4D 144
Overgreen. Derbs —3H 85
Over Green. W Mid —1F 61
Over Haddon. Derbs —4G 85
Over Hulton. G Man —4E 91
Over Kellet. Lanc —2E 97
Over Kiddington. Oxon —3C 50
Overleigh. Som —3H 21
Overley. Staf —4F 73
Over Monnow. Mon —4A 48
Over Norton. Oxon —3B 50
Over Peover. Ches —3B 84
Overpool. Ches —3F 83
Overscaig. High —1B 164
Overseal. Derbs —4G 73
Over Silton. N Yor —5B 106
Oversland. Kent —5E 41
Overstone. Nptn —4F 63
Over Stowey. Som —3E 21
Overstrand. Norf —1E 79
Over Stratton. Som —1H 13
Over Street. Wilts —3F 23
Overthorpe. Nptn —1C 50
Overton. Aber —2F 153
Overton. Ches —3H 83
Overton. Hants —2D 24
Overton. High —5E 169
Overton. Lanc —4D 96
Overton. N Yor —4H 99
Overton. Shrp —2A 60
(nr. Bridgnorth)
Overton. Shrp —3H 59
(nr. Ludlow)
Overton. Swan —4D 30
Overton. W Yor —3C 92
Overton. Wrex —1F 71
Overtown. N Lan —4B 128
Overtown. Swin —4G 35
Over Wallop. Hants —3A 24
Over Whitacre. Warw —1G 61
Over Worton. Oxon —3C 50
Oving. Buck —3F 51
Oving. W Sus —5A 26
Ovingdean. Brig —5E 27
Ovingham. Nmbd —3D 115
Ovington. Dur —3E 105
Ovington. Essx —1A 54
Ovington. Hants —3D 24
Ovington. Norf —5B 78
Ovington. Nmbd —3D 114
Owen's Bank. Staf —3G 73
Ower. Hants —2C 16
(nr. Holbury)
Ower. Hants —1B 16
(nr. Totton)
Owermoigne. Dors —4C 14
Owlbury. Shrp —1F 59
Owler Bar. Derbs —3G 85
Owlerton. S Yor —2H 85
Owletts NT —4A 40
Owl House Gdns. —2A 28
Owlpen Manor —2C 34
Owlswick. Buck —5F 51
Owmby. Linc —4D 94
Owmby-by-Spital. Linc —2H 87
Ownham. W Ber —4C 36
Owrytn. Wrex —1F 71
Owslebury. Hants —4D 24
Owston. Leics —5E 75
Owston. S Yor —3F 93
Owston Ferry. N Lin —4B 94
Owstwick. E Yor —1F 95
Owthorne. E Yor —2G 95
Owthorpe. Notts —2D 74
Owton Manor. Hart —2B 106
Oxborough. Norf —5G 77
Oxburgh Hall NT —5G 77
Oxcombe. Linc —3C 88
Oxen End. Essx —3G 53
Oxenhall. Glos —3C 48
Oxenholme. Cumb —5G 103
Oxenhope. W Yor —1A 92
Oxen Park. Cumb —1C 96
Oxenpill. Som —2H 21
Oxenton. Glos —2E 49
Oxenwood. Wilts —1B 24
Oxford. Oxon —5D 50 & 194
Oxgangs. Edin —3F 129
Oxhey. Herts —1C 38
Oxhill. Warw —1B 50
Oxley. W Mid —5C 72
Oxley Green. Essx —4C 54
Oxley's Green. E Sus —3A 28
Oxlode. Cambs —2D 65
Oxnam. Bord —3B 120
Oxshott. Surr —4C 38
Oxspring. S Yor —4C 92
Oxted. Surr —5E 39
Oxton. Mers —2E 83
Oxton. N Yor —5H 99

Oxton. Notts —5D 86
Oxton. Bord —4A 130
Oxwich. Swan —4D 31
Oxwich Castle CADW —4D 31
Oxwich Green. Swan —4D 31
Oxwick. Norf —3B 78
Oykel Bridge. High —3A 164
Oyne. Abers —1D 152
Oystermouth. Swan —4F 31
Oystermouth Castle CADW —4F 31
Ozleworth. Glos —2C 34

Pabail Iarach. W Isl —4H 171
Pabail Uarach. W Isl —4H 171
Pachesham. Surr —5C 38
Packers Hill. Dors —1C 14
Packington. Leics —4A 74
Packmoor. Stoke —5C 84
Packmores. Warw —4G 61
Packwood. W Mid —3F 61
Packwood Gullett. W Mid —3F 61
Packwood House NT —3F 61
Padanaram. Ang —3D 144
Padbury. Buck —2F 51
Paddington. G Lon —2D 38
Paddington. Warr —2A 84
Paddlesworth. Kent —2F 29
Paddock. Kent —5D 40
Paddockhole. Dum —1D 112
Paddock Wood. Kent —1A 28
Paddolgreen. Shrp —2H 71
Padeswood. Flin —4E 83
Padiham. Lanc —1F 91
Padside. N Yor —4D 98
Padson. Devn —3F 11
Padstow. Corn —1D 6
Padworth. W Ber —5E 36
Page Bank. Dur —1F 105
Pagham. W Sus —3G 17
Paglesham Churchend. Essx —1D 40
Paglesham Eastend. Essx —1D 40
Paibeil. W Isl —2C 170 (on North Uist)
Paibeil. W Isl —8C 171 (on Taransay)
Paiblesgearraidh. W Isl —2C 170
Paignton. Torb —2E 9
Paignton & Dartmouth Steam Railway —3E 9
Paignton Zoo —3E 9
Pailton. Warw —2B 62
Paine's Corner. E Sus —3H 27
Painleyhill. Staf —2E 73
Painscastle. Powy —1E 47
Painshawfield. Nmbd —3D 114
Painshill Park —5B 38
Painsthorpe. E Yor —4C 100
Painswick. Glos —5D 48
Painswick Rococo Gdn. —4D 48
Painter's Forstal. Kent —5D 40
Painthorpe. W Yor —3D 92
Pairc Shiaboist. W Isl —3E 171
Paisley. Ren —3F 127
Pakefield. Suff —1H 67
Pakenham. Suff —4B 66
Palace of Holyrood —Edinburgh 189
Pale. Gwyn —2B 70
Palehouse Common. E Sus —4F 27
Palestine. Hants —2A 24
Paley Street. Wind —4G 37
Palgowan. Dum —1A 110
Palgrave. Suff —3D 66
Pallington. Dors —3C 14
Palmarsh. Kent —2F 29
Palmer Moor. Derbs —2F 73
Palmers Cross. W Mid —5C 72
Palmerstown. V Glam —5E 33
Palnackie. Dum —4F 111
Palnure. Dum —3B 110
Palterton. Derbs —4B 86
Pamber End. Hants —1E 24
Pamber Green. Hants —1E 24
Pamber Heath. Hants —5E 36
Pamington. Glos —2E 49
Pamphill. Dors —2E 15
Pampisford. Cambs —1E 53
Panborough. Som —2H 21
Panbride. Ang —5E 145
Pancakehill. Glos —4F 49
Pancrasweek. Devn —2C 10
Pandy. Gwyn —3A 70 (nr. Bala)
Pandy. Gwyn —5F 69 (nr. Tywyn)
Pandy. Mon —3G 47
Pandy. Powy —5B 70
Pandy. Wrex —2D 70
Pandy Tudur. Cnwy —4A 82
Panfield. Essx —3H 53
Pangbourne. W Ber —4E 37
Pannal. N Yor —4F 99
Pannal Ash. N Yor —4E 99
Pannanich. Abers —4A 152
Pant. Shrp —3E 71
Pant. Wrex —1F 71
Pantasaph. Flin —3D 82
Pant Glas. Gwyn —1D 68
Pant-glas. Shrp —2E 71
Pantgwyn. Carm —3F 45
Pantgwyn. Cdgn —1C 44
Pant-lasau. Swan —3F 31
Panton. Linc —3A 88
Pant-pastynog. Den —4C 82
Pantperthog. Gwyn —5G 69
Pant-teg. Carm —3E 45
Pant-y-Caws. Carm —2F 43
Pant-y-dwr. Powy —3B 58
Pant-y-ffridd. Powy —5D 70
Pantyffynnon. Carm —4G 45
Pantygasseg. Torf —5F 47
Pant-y-llyn. Carm —4G 45
Pant-yr-awel. B'end —3C 32
Pant y Wacco. Flin —3D 82
Panxworth. Norf —4F 79
Papa Westray Airport. Orkn —2D 172
Papcastle. Cumb —1C 102
Papigoe. High —3F 169
Papil. Shet —8E 173
Papple. E Lot —2B 130
Papplewick. Notts —5C 86
Papworth Everard. Cambs —4B 64
Papworth St Agnes. Cambs —4B 64
Par. Corn —3E 7
Paradise Park —3C 4
Paradise Wildlife Park —5D 52
Paramour Street. Kent —4G 41
Parbold. Lanc —3C 90
Parbrook. Som —3A 22
Parbrook. W Sus —3B 26
Parc. Gwyn —2A 70
Parcllyn. Cdgn —5B 56
Parc-Seymour. Newp —2H 33
Pardown. Hants —2D 24
Pardshaw. Cumb —2B 102
Parham. Suff —4F 67
Parham House —4B 26
Park. Abers —4E 153
Park. Arg —4D 140
Park. Dum —5B 118
Park Bottom. Corn —4A 6
Parkburn. Abers —5E 161
Park Corner. E Sus —2G 27
Park Corner. Oxon —3E 37
Parkend. Glos —5B 48
Park End. Nmbd —2B 114
Parkeston. Essx —2F 55
Parkfield. Corn —2H 7
Parkgate. Ches —3E 83
Parkgate. Cumb —5D 112
Parkgate. Dum —1B 112
Park Gate. Hants —2D 16
Parkgate. Surr —1D 26
Park Gate. Worc —3D 60
Parkhall. W Dun —2F 127
Parkham. Devn —4D 19
Parkham Ash. Devn —4D 18
Parkhead. Cumb —5E 113
Parkhead. Glas —3H 127
Park Hill. Mers —4C 90
Parkhouse. Mon —5H 47
Parkhurst. IOW —3C 16
Park Lane. G Man —4F 91
Park Lane. Staf —5C 72
Parkmill. Swan —4E 31
Park Mill. W Yor —3C 92
Parkneuk. Abers —1G 145
Parkside. N Lan —4B 128
Parkstone. Pool —3F 15
Park Street. Herts —5B 52
Park Street. W Sus —2C 26
Park Town. Oxon —5D 50
Park Village. Nmbd —3H 113
Parkway. Here —2C 48
Parley Cross. Dors —3F 15
Parmoor. Buck —3F 37
Parr. Mers —1H 83
Parracombe. Devn —2G 19
Parrog. Pemb —1E 43
Parsonage Green. Essx —4H 53
Parsonby. Cumb —1C 102
Parson Cross. S Yor —1A 86
Parson Drove. Cambs —5C 76
Partick. Glas —3G 127
Partington. G Man —1B 84
Partney. Linc —4D 88
Parton. Cumb —2A 102 (nr. Whitehaven)
Parton. Cumb —4D 112 (nr. Wigton)
Parton. Dum —2D 111
Partridge Green. W Sus —4C 26
Parwich. Derbs —5F 85
Pashley Manor Gdns. —3B 28
Passenham. Nptn —2F 51
Passfield. Hants —3G 25
Passingford Bridge. Essx —1G 39
Paston. Norf —2F 79
Pasturefields. Staf —3D 73
Patchacott. Devn —3E 11
Patcham. Brig —5E 27
Patchetts Green. Herts —1C 38
Patching. W Sus —5B 26
Patchole. Devn —2G 19
Patchway. S Glo —3B 34
Pateley Bridge. N Yor —3D 98
Pathe. Som —3G 21
Pathhead. Abers —2G 145
Pathhead. E Ayr —3F 117
Pathhead. Fife —4E 137
Pathhead. Midl —3G 129
Pathlow. Warw —5F 61
Path of Condie. Per —2C 136
Pathstruie. Per —2C 136
Patmore Heath. Herts —3E 53
Patna. E Ayr —3D 116
Patney. Wilts —1F 23
Patrick. IOM —3B 108
Patrick Brompton. N Yor —5F 105
Patrington. E Yor —2G 95
Patrington Haven. E Yor —2G 95
Patrixbourne. Kent —5F 41
Patterdale. Cumb —3E 103
Pattiesmuir. Fife —1D 129
Pattingham. Staf —1C 60
Pattishall. Nptn —5D 62
Pattiswick. Essx —3B 54
Patton Bridge. Cumb —5G 103
Paul. Corn —4B 4
Paul Corin's Music Mus. —2G 7
Paulerspury. Nptn —1F 51
Paull. E Yor —2E 95
Paulton. Bath —1B 22
Paultons Park —1B 16
Pauperhaugh. Nmbd —5F 121
Pave Lane. Telf —4B 72
Pavenham. Beds —5G 63
Pawlett. Som —2G 21
Pawston. Nmbd —1C 120
Paxford. Glos —2G 49
Paxton. Bord —4F 131
Paxton House & Gdn. —4F 131
Paycocke's NT —3B 54
Payhembury. Devn —2D 12
Paythorne. Lanc —4H 97
Peacehaven. E Sus —5F 27
Peak Dale. Derbs —3E 85
Peak District Nat. Park —2F 85
Peak Forest. Derbs —3F 85
Peak Hill. Linc —4B 76
Peakirk. Pet —5A 76
Peak Rail —4G 85
Peanmeanach. High —5F 147
Pearsie. Ang —3C 144
Peasedown St John. Bath —1C 22
Peaseland Green. Norf —4C 78
Peasemore. W Ber —4C 36
Peasenhall. Suff —4F 67
Pease Pottage. W Sus —2D 26
Peaslake. Surr —1B 26
Peasley Cross. Mers —1H 83
Peasmarsh. E Sus —3C 28
Peasmarsh. Surr —1A 26
Peaston. E Lot —3H 129
Peastonbank. E Lot —3H 129
Peathill. Abers —2G 161
Peat Inn. Fife —3G 137
Peatling Magna. Leics —1C 62
Peatling Parva. Leics —2C 62
Peaton. Arg —1D 126
Peaton. Shrp —2H 59
Peats Corner. Suff —4D 66
Pebmarsh. Essx —2B 54
Pebworth. Worc —1G 49
Pecket Well. W Yor —2H 91
Peckforton. Ches —5H 83
Peckham Bush. Kent —5A 40
Peckleton. Leics —5B 74
Peckover House NT —5D 76
Pedair-ffordd. Powy —3D 70
Pedlinge. Kent —2F 29
Pedmore. W Mid —2D 60
Pedwell. Som —3H 21
Peebles. Bord —5F 129
Peel. IOM —3B 108
Peel. Bord —1G 119
Peel Castle —3B 108
Peel Common. Hants —2D 16
Peening Quarter. Kent —3C 28
Pegg's Green. Leics —4B 74
Pegsdon. Beds —2B 52
Pegswood. Nmbd —1F 115
Peinchorran. High —5E 155
Peinlich. High —3D 154
Pelaw. Tyne —3G 115
Pelcomb Bridge. Pemb —3D 42
Pelcomb Cross. Pemb —3D 42
Peldon. Essx —4C 54
Pelsall. W Mid —5E 73
Pelton. Dur —4F 115
Pelutho. Cumb —5C 112
Pelynt. Corn —3G 7
Pemberton. Carm —5F 45
Pembrey. Carm —5E 45
Pembridge. Here —5F 59
Pembroke. Pemb —4D 43
Pembroke Castle —4D 43
Pembroke Dock. Pemb —4D 42
Pembroke Ferry. Pemb —4D 42
Pembrokeshire Coast Nat. Park —1E 43
Pembury. Kent —1H 27
Penallt. Mon —5A 48
Penally. Pemb —5F 43
Penalt. Here —3A 48
Penalum. Pemb —5F 43
Penarth. V Glam —4E 33
Penbeagle. Corn —3C 4
Penberth. Corn —4B 4
Pen-bont Rhydybeddau. Cdgn —2F 57
Penbryn. Cdgn —5B 56
Pencader. Carm —2E 45
Pen-cae. Cdgn —5D 56
Pencaenewydd. Gwyn —1D 68
Pencaerau. Neat —3G 31
Pencaitland. E Lot —3H 129
Pencarnisiog. IOA —3C 80
Pencarreg. Carm —1F 45
Pencarrow —5A 10
Pencarrow. Corn —4B 10
Pencelli. Powy —3D 46
Pen-clawdd. Swan —3E 31
Pencoed. B'end —3C 32
Pencombe. Here —5H 59
Pencraig. Here —3A 48
Pencraig. Powy —3C 70
Pendeen. Corn —3A 4
Pendeford. W Mid —5D 72
Pendennis Castle EH —5C 6
Penderyn. Rhon —5C 46
Pendine. Carm —4G 43
Pendlebury. G Man —4F 91
Pendleton. G Man —1C 84
Pendleton. Lanc —1F 91
Pendock. Worc —2C 48
Pendoggett. Corn —5A 10
Pendomer. Som —1A 14
Pendoylan. V Glam —4D 32
Pendre. B'end —3C 32
Penegoes. Powy —5G 69
Penelewey. Corn —4C 6
Penffordd. Pemb —2E 43
Penffordd-Las. Powy —1A 58
Penfro. Pemb —4D 43
Pengam. Cphy —2E 33
Pengam. Card —4F 33
Penge. G Lon —3E 39
Pengelly. Corn —4A 10
Pengenffordd. Powy —2E 47
Pengorffwysfa. IOA —1D 80
Pengover Green. Corn —2G 7
Pengwern. Den —3C 82
Penhale. Corn —5D 5 (nr. Mullion)
Penhale. Corn —3D 6 (nr. St Austell)
Penhale Camp. Corn —3B 6
Penhallow. Corn —3B 6
Penhalvean. Corn —5B 6
Penhelig. Gwyn —1F 57
Penhill. Swin —3G 35
Penhow. Newp —2H 33
Penhow Castle —2H 33
Penhurst. E Sus —4A 28
Peniarth. Gwyn —5F 69
Penicuik. Midl —3F 129
Peniel. Carm —3E 45
Penifiler. High —4D 155
Peninver. Arg —3B 122
Penisa'r Waun. Gwyn —4E 81
Penistone. S Yor —4C 92
Penketh. Warr —2H 83
Penkill. S Ayr —5B 116
Penkridge. Staf —4D 72
Penley. Wrex —2G 71
Penllech. Gwyn —2B 68
Penllergaer. Swan —3F 31
Pen-llyn. IOA —2C 80
Penmachno. Cnwy —5G 81
Penmaen. Swan —4E 31
Penmaenmawr. Cnwy —3G 81
Penmaenpool. Gwyn —4F 69
Penmaen Rhos. Cnwy —3A 82
Pen-marc. V Glam —5D 32
Penmark. V Glam —5D 32
Penmarth. Corn —5B 6
Penmon. IOA —2F 81
Penmorfa. Gwyn —1E 69
Penmyndd. IOA —3E 81
Penn. Buck —1A 38
Penn. Dors —3G 13
Penn. W Mid —1C 60
Pennal. Gwyn —5G 69
Pennan. Abers —2F 161
Pennant. Cdgn —4E 57
Pennant. Den —2C 70
Pennant. Gwyn —3B 70
Pennant. Powy —1A 58
Pennant Melangell. Powy —3C 70
Pennar. Pemb —4D 42
Pennard. Swan —4E 31
Pennerley. Shrp —1F 59
Pennington. Cumb —2B 96
Pennington. G Man —1A 84
Pennington. Hants —3B 16
Pennorth. Powy —3E 46
Penn Street. Buck —1A 38
Pennsylvania. Devn —3C 12
Pennsylvania. S Glo —4C 34
Penny Bridge. Cumb —1C 96
Pennycross. Plym —3A 8
Pennygate. Norf —3F 79
Pennyghael. Arg —1C 132
Penny Hill. Linc —3C 76
Pennylands. Lanc —4C 90
Pennymoor. Devn —1B 12
Pennyvenie. E Ayr —4D 117
Pennywell. Tyne —4G 115
Penparc. Cdgn —1C 44
Penparcau. Cdgn —2E 57
Penpedairheol. Cphy —2E 33
Penperlleni. Mon —5G 47
Penpillick. Corn —3E 7
Penpol. Corn —5C 6
Penpoll. Corn —3F 7
Penponds. Corn —3D 4
Penpont. Corn —5A 10
Penpont. Dum —5H 117
Penpont. Powy —3C 46
Penprysg. B'end —3C 32
Penquit. Devn —3C 8
Penrherber. Carm —1G 43
Penrhiw. Pemb —1C 44
Penrhiwceiber. Rhon —2D 32
Pen Rhiwfawr. Neat —4H 45
Penrhiw-llan. Cdgn —1D 44
Penrhiw-pal. Cdgn —1D 44
Penrhos. Gwyn —2C 68
Penrhos. Here —5F 59
Penrhos. IOA —2B 80
Penrhos. Mon —4H 47
Penrhos. Powy —4B 46
Penrhos Garnedd. Gwyn —3E 81
Penrhyn. IOA —1C 80
Penrhyn Bay. Cnwy —2H 81
Penrhyn Castle NT —3F 81
Penrhyn-coch. Cdgn —2F 57
Penrhyndeudraeth. Gwyn —2F 69
Penrhyn Side. Cnwy —2H 81
Penrice. Swan —4D 31
Penrith. Cumb —2G 103
Penrose. Corn —1C 6
Penruddock. Cumb —2F 103
Penryn. Corn —5B 6
Pensarn. Carm —4E 45
Pen-sarn. Gwyn —3E 69
Pensax. Worc —4B 60
Pensby. Mers —2E 83
Penscynor Wildlife Park, Tonna —2A 32
Penselwood. Som —3C 22
Pensford. Bath —5B 34
Pensham. Worc —1E 49
Penshaw. Tyne —4G 115
Penshurst. Kent —1G 27
Penshurst Place —1G 27
Pensilva. Corn —2G 7
Pensnett. W Mid —2D 60
Pensthorpe Waterfowl Park —3B 78
Penston. E Lot —2H 129
Penstone. Devn —2A 12
Pente-tafarn-y-fedw. Cnwy —4H 81
Pentewan. Corn —4E 6
Pentir. Gwyn —4E 81
Pentire. Corn —2B 6
Pentlepoir. Pemb —4F 43
Pentlow. Essx —1B 54
Pentney. Norf —4G 77
Penton Mewsey. Hants —2B 24
Pentraeth. IOA —3E 81
Pentre. Powy —1E 59 (nr. Church Stoke)
Pentre. Powy —2D 58 (nr. Kerry)
Pentre. Powy —2C 58 (nr. Mochdre)
Pentre. Rhon —2C 32
Pentre. Shrp —4F 71
Pentre. Wrex —2D 70 (nr. Llanfyllin)
Pentre. Wrex —1E 71 (nr. Rhosllanerchrugog)
Pentrebach. Carm —2B 46
Pentre-bach. Cdgn —1F 45
Pentrebach. Mer T —5D 46
Pentre-bach. Powy —2C 46
Pentrebach. Swan —5G 45
Pentre Berw. IOA —3D 80
Pentre-bont. Cnwy —5G 81
Pentrecagal. Carm —1D 44
Pentre-celyn. Den —5D 82
Pentre-clawdd. Shrp —2E 71
Pentreclwydau. Neat —5B 46
Pentre-cwrt. Carm —2D 45
Pentre Dolau Honddu. Powy —1C 46
Pentre-du. Cnwy —5G 81
Pentre-dwr. Swan —3F 31
Pentrefelin. Carm —3F 45
Pentrefelin. Cdgn —1G 45
Pentrefelin. Cnwy —3H 81
Pentrefelin. Gwyn —2E 69
Pentrefoelas. Cnwy —5A 82
Pentre Galar. Pemb —1F 43
Pentregat. Cdgn —5C 56
Pentre Gwenlais. Carm —4G 45
Pentre Gwynfryn. Gwyn —3E 69
Pentre Halkyn. Flin —3E 82
Pentre Hodre. Shrp —3F 59
Pentre-Llanrhaeadr. Den —4C 82
Pentre Llifior. Powy —1D 58
Pentrellwyn. IOA —2E 81
Pentre-llwyn-llwyd. Powy —5B 58
Pentre-llyn-cymmer. Cnwy —5B 82
Pentre Meyrick. V Glam —4C 32
Pentre-piod. Gwyn —2A 70
Pentre-poeth. Newp —3F 33
Pentre'r Beirdd. Powy —4D 70
Pentre'r-felin. Powy —2C 46
Pentre-ty-gwyn. Carm —2B 46
Pentre-uchaf. Gwyn —2C 68
Pentrich. Derbs —5A 86
Pentridge. Dors —1F 15
Pen-twyn. Cphy —5F 47 (nr. Oakdale)
Pentwyn. Cphy —5E 46 (nr. Rhymney)
Pentwyn. Card —3F 33
Pentyrch. Card —3E 32
Pentywyn. Carm —4G 43
Penuwch. Cdgn —4E 57
Penwithick. Corn —3E 7
Penwyllt. Powy —4B 46
Penybanc. Carm —4G 45 (nr. Ammanford)
Pen-y-banc. Carm —3G 45 (nr. Llandeilo)
Pen-y-bont. Carm —2H 43
Penybont. Powy —4D 58 (nr. Llandrindod Wells)
Pen-y-bont. Powy —3E 70 (nr. Llanfyllin)
Pen-y-Bont Ar Ogwr. B'end —3C 32
Penybontfawr. Powy —3C 70
Penybryn. Cphy —2E 33
Pen-y-bryn. Pemb —1B 44
Pen-y-bryn. Wrex —1E 71
Pen-y-cae. Powy —4B 46
Penycae. Wrex —1E 71
Pen-y-cae-mawr. Mon —2H 33
Penycaerau. Gwyn —3A 68
Pen-y-cefn. Flin —3D 82
Pen-y-clawdd. Mon —5H 47
Pen-y-coedcae. Rhon —3D 32
Penycwm. Pemb —2C 42
Pen-y-darren. Mer T —5D 46
Pen-y-fai. B'end —3B 32
Penyffordd. Flin —4F 83 (nr. Mold)
Pen-y-ffordd. Flin —2D 82 (nr. Prestatyn)
Penyffridd. Gwyn —5E 81
Pen-y-garn. Cdgn —2F 57
Pen-y-garnedd. IOA —3E 81
Penygarnedd. Powy —3D 70
Pen-y-graig. Gwyn —2A 68
Penygraig. Rhon —2C 32
Penygraigwen. IOA —2D 80
Pen-y-groes. Carm —4F 45
Penygroes. Gwyn —5D 80
Penygroes. Pemb —1F 43
Penymynydd. Flin —4F 83
Penyrheol. Cphy —3E 33
Pen-yr-heol. Mon —4H 47
Penyrheol. Swan —3E 31
Pen-yr-Heolgerrig. Mer T —5D 46
Penysarn. IOA —1D 80
Pen-y-stryt. Den —5E 82
Penywaun. Rhon —5C 46
Penzance. Corn —4B 4
Penzance Heliport. Corn —3B 4
Peopleton. Worc —5D 60
Peover Hall —3B 84
Peover Heath. Ches —3B 84
Peper Harow. Surr —1A 26
Peplow. Shrp —3A 72
Pepper Arden. N Yor —4F 105
Perceton. N Ayr —5E 127
Percyhorner. Abers —2G 161
Perham Down. Wilts —2A 24
Periton. Som —2C 20
Perkinsville. Dur —4F 115
Perlethorpe. Notts —3D 86
Perranarworthal. Corn —5B 6
Perranporth. Corn —3B 6
Perranuthnoe. Corn —4C 4
Perranwell. Corn —5B 6
Perranzabuloe. Corn —3B 6
Perrott's Brook. Glos —5F 49
Perry. W Mid —1E 61
Perry Barr. W Mid —1E 61
Perry Crofts. Staf —5G 73
Perry Green. Essx —3B 54
Perry Green. Herts —4E 53
Perry Green. Wilts —3E 35
Perry Street. Kent —3H 39
Perry Street. Som —2G 13

Perrywood. Kent —5E 41
Pershall. Staf —2C 72
Pershore. Worc —1E 49
Pertenhall. Beds —4H 63
Perth. Per —1D 136 & 195
Perth Mus. & Art Gallery —195
Perthy. Shrp —2F 71
Perton. Staf —1C 60
Pertwood. Wilts —3D 23
Peterborough. Pet —1A 64 & 195
Peterborough Cathedral —195
Peterburn. High —5B 162
Peterchurch. Here —2G 47
Peterculter. Aber —3F 153
Peterhead. Abers —4H 161
Peterlee. Dur —5H 115
Petersfield. Hants —4F 25
Petersfinger. Wilts —4G 23
Peter's Green. Herts —4B 52
Peters Marland. Devn —1E 11
Peterstone Wentlooge. Newp —3F 33
Peterston-super-Ely. V Glam —4D 32
Peterstow. Here —3A 48
Peter Tavy. Devn —5F 11
Petertown. Orkn —7C 172
Petham. Kent —5F 41
Petherwin Gate. Corn —4C 10
Petrockstowe. Devn —2F 11
Petsoe End. Mil —1G 51
Pett. E Sus —4C 28
Pettaugh. Suff —5D 66
Petteridge. Kent —1A 28
Petteril Green. Cumb —5F 113
Pettinain. S Lan —5C 128
Pettistree. Suff —5E 67
Petton. Devn —4D 20
Petton. Shrp —3G 71
Petts Wood. G Lon —4F 39
Pettycur. Fife —1F 129
Pettywell. Norf —3C 78
Petworth. W Sus —3A 26
Petworth House NT —3A 26
Pevensey. E Sus —5H 27
Pevensey Bay. E Sus —5A 28
Pevensey Castle EH —5H 27
Peveril Castle EH —2F 85
Pewsey. Wilts —5G 35
Pheasants Hill. Buck —3F 37
Philadelphia. Tyne —4G 115
Philham. Devn —4C 18
Philiphaugh. Bord —2G 119
Philipps House NT —3F 23
Phillack. Corn —3C 4
Philleigh. Corn —5C 6
Philpstoun. W Lot —2D 128
Phocle Green. Here —3B 48
Phoenix Green. Hants —1F 25
Pibsbury. Som —4H 21
Pibwrlwyd. Carm —4E 45
Pica. Cumb —2B 102
Piccadilly. Warw —1G 61
Piccadilly Corner. Norf —2E 67
Piccotts End. Herts —5A 52
Pickering. N Yor —1B 100
Pickering Castle EH —1C 100
Picket Piece. Hants —2B 24
Picket Post. Hants —2G 15
Pickford. W Mid —2G 61
Pickhill. N Yor —1F 99
Picklenash. Glos —3C 48
Picklescott. Shrp —1G 59
Pickletillem. Fife —1G 137
Pickmere. Ches —3A 84
Pickstock. Telf —3B 72
Pickwell. Devn —2E 19
Pickwell. Leics —4E 75
Pickworth. Linc —2H 75
Pickworth. Rut —4G 75
Picton. Ches —3G 83
Picton. Flin —2D 82
Picton. N Yor —4B 106
Picton Castle —3E 43
Piddinghoe. E Sus —5F 27
Piddington. Buck —2G 37
Piddington. Nptn —5F 63
Piddington. Oxon —4E 51
Piddlehinton. Dors —3C 14
Piddletrenthide. Dors —2C 14
Pidley. Cambs —3C 64
Pidney. Dors —2C 14
Pie Corner. Here —4A 60
Piercebridge. Darl —3F 105
Pierowall. Orkn —3D 172
Pigdon. Nmbd —1E 115
Pightley. Som —3F 21
Pikehall. Derbs —5F 85
Pikeshill. Hants —2A 16
Pilford. Dors —2F 15
Pilgrims Hatch. Essx —1G 39
Pilham. Linc —1F 87
Pill. N Som —4A 34
Pillaton. Corn —2H 7
Pillerton Hersey. Warw —1A 50
Pillerton Priors. Warw —1A 50
Pilleth. Powy —4E 59
Pilley. Hants —3B 16
Pilley. S Yor —4D 92
Pillgwenlly. Newp —3G 33
Pilling. Lanc —5D 96
Pilling Lane. Lanc —5C 96
Pillowell. Glos —5B 48
Pill, The. Mon —3H 33
Pillwell. Dors —1C 14
Pilning. S Glo —3A 34
Pilsbury. Derbs —4F 85
Pilsdon. Dors —3H 13
Pilsgate. Pet —5H 75
Pilsley. Derbs —3G 85
(nr. Bakewell)
Pilsley. Derbs —4B 86
(nr. Clay Cross)
Pilson Green. Norf —4F 79
Piltdown. E Sus —3F 27
Pilton. Edin —2F 129
Pilton. Nptn —2H 63
Pilton. Rut —5G 75
Pilton. Som —2A 22
Pilton Green. Swan —4D 30
Pimperne. Dors —2E 15
Pinchbeck. Linc —3B 76
Pinchbeck Bars. Linc —3A 76
Pinchbeck West. Linc —3B 76
Pinfold. Lanc —3B 90
Pinford End. Suff —5H 65
Pinged. Carm —5E 45
Pinhoe. Devn —3C 12
Pinkerton. E Lot —2D 130
Pinkneys Green. Wind —3G 37
Pinley. W Mid —3A 62
Pinley Green. Warw —4G 61
Pin Mill. Suff —2F 55
Pinmore. S Ayr —5B 116
Pinner. G Lon —2C 38
Pins Green. Worc —1C 48
Pinsley Green. Ches —1H 71
Pinvin. Worc —1E 49
Pinwherry. S Ayr —1G 109
Pinxton. Derbs —5B 86
Pipe and Lyde. Here —1A 48
Pipe Aston. Here —3G 59
Pipe Gate. Shrp —1B 72
Pipehill. Staf —5E 73
Piperhill. High —3C 158
Pipe Ridware. Staf —4E 73
Pipers Pool. Corn —4C 10
Pipewell. Nptn —2F 63
Pippacott. Devn —3F 19
Pipton. Powy —2E 47
Pirbright. Surr —5A 38
Pirnmill. N Ayr —5G 125
Pirton. Herts —2B 52
Pirton. Worc —1D 49
Pisgah. Stir —3G 135
Pishill. Oxon —3F 37
Pistyll. Gwyn —1C 68
Pitagowan. Per —2F 143
Pitcairn. Per —3F 143
Pitcairngreen. Per —1C 136
Pitcalnie. High —1C 158
Pitcaple. Abers —1E 152
Pitchcombe. Glos —5D 48
Pitchcott. Buck —3F 51
Pitchford. Shrp —5H 71
Pitch Green. Buck —5F 51
Pitch Place. Surr —5A 38
Pitcombe. Som —3B 22
Pitcox. E Lot —2C 130
Pitcur. Per —5B 144
Pitfichie. Abers —2D 152
Pitgrudy. High —4E 165
Pitkennedy. Ang —3E 145
Pitlessie. Fife —3F 137
Pitlochry. Per —3G 143
Pitlochry Fish Ladder —3G 143
Pitmachie. Abers —1D 152
Pitmaduthy. High —1B 158
Pitmedden. Abers —1F 153
Pitmedden Gdn. NTS —1F 153
Pitminster. Som —1F 13
Pitnacree. Per —3G 143
Pitney. Som —4H 21
Pitroddie. Per —1E 136
Pitscottie. Fife —2G 137
Pitsea. Essx —2B 40
Pitsford. Nptn —4E 63
Pitsford Hill. Som —3E 20
Pitsmoor. S Yor —2A 86
Pitstone. Buck —4H 51
Pitstone Green. Buck —4H 51
Pitt. Hants —4C 24
Pittaton. Staf —4D 72
Pitt Court. Glos —2C 34
Pittentrail. High —3E 164
Pittenweem. Fife —3H 137
Pittington. Dur —5G 115
Pitton. Swan —4D 30
Pitton. Wilts —3H 23
Pitt Rivers Mus. —Oxford 194
Pittswood. Kent —1H 27
Pittulie. Abers —2G 161
Pittville. Glos —3E 49
Pitversie. Per —2D 136
Pitville Pump Room —Cheltenham 187
Pityme. Corn —1D 6
Pity Me. Dur —5F 115
Pixey Green. Suff —3E 67
Pixley. Here —2B 48
Place Newton. N Yor —2C 100
Plaidy. Abers —3E 161
Plaidy. Corn —3G 7
Plain Dealings. Pemb —3E 43
Plains. N Lan —3A 128
Plainsfield. Som —3E 21
Plaish. Shrp —1H 59
Plaistow. Here —1B 48
Plaistow. W Sus —2B 26
Plaitford. Wilts —1A 16
Plantasia —Swansea 197
Plas Brondanw Gdn. —1F 69
Plas Llwyd. Cnwy —3B 82
Plas Newydd, Llanfair PG NT —4E 81
Plas Newydd, Llangollen —1E 70
Plastow Green. Hants —5D 36
Plas yn Cefn. Den —3C 82
Plas yn Rhiw NT —3B 68
Platt. Kent —5H 39
Platt Bridge. G Man —4E 90
Platt Lane. Shrp —2H 71
Platts Common. S Yor —4D 92
Platt's Heath. Kent —5C 40
Platt, The. E Sus —2G 27
Plawsworth. Dur —5F 115
Plaxtol. Kent —5H 39
Playden. E Sus —3D 28
Playford. Suff —1F 55
Play Hatch. Oxon —4F 37
Playing Place. Corn —4C 6
Playley Green. Glos —2C 48
Plealey. Shrp —5G 71
Plean. Stir —1B 128
Pleasington. Bkbn —2E 91
Pleasley. Derbs —4C 86
Pleasurewood Hills Theme Park —1H 67
Pledgdon Green. Essx —3F 53
Plenmeller. Nmbd —3A 114
Pleshey. Essx —4G 53
Plockton. High —5H 155
Plocrapol. W Isl —8D 171
Ploughfield. Here —1G 47
Plowden. Shrp —2F 59
Ploxgreen. Shrp —5F 71
Pluckley. Kent —1D 28
Plumbland. Cumb —1C 102
Plumgarths. Cumb —5F 103
Plumley. Ches —3B 84
Plummers Plain. W Sus —3D 26
Plumpton. Cumb —1F 103
Plumpton. E Sus —4E 27
Plumpton. Nptn —1D 50
Plumptonfoot. Cumb —1F 103
Plumpton Green. E Sus —4E 27
Plumpton Head. Cumb —1G 103
Plumstead. G Lon —3F 39
Plumstead. Norf —2D 78
Plumtree. Notts —2D 74
Plumtree Park. Notts —2D 74
Plungar. Leics —2E 75
Plush. Dors —2C 14
Plushabridge. Corn —5D 10
Plwmp. Cdgn —5C 56
Plymouth. Plym —3A 8 & 195
Plymouth Airport. Plym —2B 8
Plympton. Plym —3B 8
Plymstock. Plym —3B 8
Plymtree. Devn —2D 12
Plym Valley Railway —3B 8
Pockley. N Yor —1A 100
Pocklington. E Yor —5C 100
Pode Hole. Linc —3B 76
Podimore. Som —4A 22
Podington. Beds —4G 63
Podmore. Staf —2B 72
Poffley End. Oxon —4B 50
Point Clear. Essx —4D 54
Pointon. Linc —2A 76
Pokesdown. Bour —3G 15
Polbae. Dum —2H 109
Polbain. High —3E 163
Polbathic. Corn —3H 7
Polbeth. W Lot —3D 128
Polbrock. Corn —2E 6
Polchar. High —3C 150
Polebrook. Nptn —2H 63
Pole Elm. Worc —1D 48
Polegate. E Sus —5G 27
Pole Moor. W Yor —3A 92
Poles. High —4E 165
Polesden Lacy NT —5C 38
Polesworth. Warw —5G 73
Polglass. High —3E 163
Polgooth. Corn —3D 6
Poling. W Sus —5B 26
Poling Corner. W Sus —5B 26
Polio. High —1B 158
Polkerris. Corn —3E 7
Polla. High —3D 166
Pollard Street. Norf —2F 79
Pollicott. Buck —4F 51
Pollington. E Yor —3G 93
Polloch. High —2B 140
Pollock House & Estate —3G 127
Pollok. Glas —3G 127
Pollokshaws. Glas —3G 127
Pollokshields. Glas —3G 127
Polmaily. High —5G 157
Polmassick. Corn —4D 6
Polmont. Falk —2C 128
Polnessan. E Ayr —3D 116
Polnish. High —5F 147
Polperro. Corn —3G 7
Polruan. Corn —3F 7
Polscoe. Corn —2F 7
Polsham. Som —2A 22
Polskeoch. Dum —4F 117
Polstead. Suff —2C 54
Polstead Heath. Suff —1C 54
Poltescoe. Corn —5E 5
Poltimore. Devn —3C 12
Polton. Midl —3G 129
Polwarth. Bord —4D 130
Polyphant. Corn —4C 10
Polzeath. Corn —1D 6
Ponde. Powy —2E 46
Pondersbridge. Cambs —1B 64
Ponders End. G Lon —1E 39
Pond Street. Essx —2E 53
Pondtail. Hants —1G 25
Ponsanooth. Corn —5B 6
Ponsongath. Corn —5E 5
Ponsworthy. Devn —5H 11
Pontamman. Carm —4G 45
Pontantwn. Carm —4E 45
Pontardawe. Neat —5H 45
Pontarddulais. Swan —5F 45
Pontarfynach. Cdgn —3G 57
Pont-ar-gothi. Carm —3F 45
Pont ar Hydfer. Powy —3B 46
Pontarllechau. Carm —3H 45
Pontarsais. Carm —3E 45
Pontblyddyn. Flin —4E 83
Pontbren Llwyd. Rhon —5C 46
Pont Cyfyng. Cnwy —5G 81
Pontcysyllte Aqueduct —1E 71
Pontdolgoch. Powy —1C 58
Pontefract. W Yor —2E 93
Ponteland. Nmbd —2E 115
Ponterwyd. Cdgn —2G 57
Pontesbury. Shrp —5G 71
Pontesford. Shrp —5G 71
Pontfadog. Wrex —2E 71
Pontfaen. Pemb —1E 43
Pont-faen. Powy —2C 46
Pont-Faen. Shrp —2E 71
Pontgarreg. Cdgn —5C 56
Pont-Henri. Carm —5E 45
Ponthir. Torf —2G 33
Ponthirwaun. Cdgn —1C 44
Pont-iets. Carm —5E 45
Pontllanfraith. Cphy —2E 33
Pontlliw. Swan —5G 45
Pont Llogel. Powy —4C 70
Pontllyfni. Gwyn —5D 80
Pontlottyn. Cphy —5E 46
Pontneddfechan. Neat —5C 46
Pont-newydd. Carm —5E 45
Pont-newydd. Flin —4D 82
Pontnewydd. Torf —2G 33
Ponton. Shet —6E 173
Pont Pen-y-benglog. Gwyn —4F 81
Pontrhydfendigaid. Cdgn —4G 57
Pont Rhyd-y-cyff. B'end —3B 32
Pontrhydyfen. Neat —2A 32
Pont-rhyd-y-groes. Cdgn —3G 57
Pontrhydyrun. Torf —2F 33
Pont Rhythallt. Gwyn —4E 81
Pontrilas. Here —3G 47
Pontrilas Road. Here —3G 47
Pontrobert. Powy —4D 70
Pont-rug. Gwyn —4E 81
Ponts Green. E Sus —4A 28
Pontshill. Here —3B 48
Pont-Sian. Cdgn —1E 45
Pontsticill. Mer T —4D 46
Pont-Walby. Neat —5B 46
Pontwelly. Carm —2E 45
Pontwgan. Cnwy —3G 81
Pontyates. Carm —5E 45
Pontyberem. Carm —4F 45
Pontybodkin. Flin —5E 83
Pontyclun. Rhon —3D 32
Pontycymer. B'end —2C 32
Pontyglazier. Pemb —1F 43
Pontygwaith. Rhon —2D 32
Pont-y-pant. Cnwy —5G 81
Pontypool. Torf —2F 33
Pontypridd. Rhon —2D 32
Pontypwl. Torf —2F 33
Pontywaun. Cphy —2F 33
Pooksgreen. Hants —1B 16
Pool. Corn —4A 6
Pool. W Yor —5E 99
Poole. N Yor —2E 93
Poole. Pool —3F 15
Poole Green. Ches —5A 84
Poole Keynes. Glos —2E 35
Poolend. Staf —5D 84
Poolewe. High —5C 162
Pooley Bridge. Cumb —2F 103
Poolfold. Staf —5C 84
Pool Head. Here —5H 59
Pool Hey. Lanc —3B 90
Poolhill. Glos —3C 48
Poolmill. Here —3A 48
Pool o' Muckhart. Clac —3B 136
Pool Quay. Powy —4E 71
Poolsbrook. Derbs —3B 86
Pool Street. Essx —2A 54
Pootings. Kent —1F 27
Pope Hill. Pemb —3D 42
Pope's Hill. Glos —4B 48
Popeswood. Brac —5G 37
Popham. Hants —2D 24
Poplar. G Lon —2E 39
Popley. Hants —1E 25
Porchfield. IOW —3C 16
Porin. High —3F 157
Poringland. Norf —5E 79
Porkellis. Corn —5A 6
Porlock. Som —2B 20
Porlock Wier. Som —2B 20
Portachoillan. Arg —4F 125
Port Ann. Arg —1H 125
Port Appin. Arg —4D 140
Port Askaig. Arg —3C 124
Portavadie. Arg —3H 125
Port Bannatyne. Arg —3B 126
Portbury. N Som —4A 34
Port Carlisle. Cumb —3D 112
Port Charlotte. Arg —4A 124
Portchester. Hants —2E 16
Portchester Castle EH —2E 16
Port Clarence. Stoc T —2B 106
Port Dinorwig. Gwyn —4E 81
Port Driseach. Arg —2A 126
Port Dundas. Glas —3H 127
Port Ellen. Arg —5B 124
Port Elphinstone. Abers —2E 153
Portencalzie. Dum —2F 109
Portencross. N Ayr —5C 126
Port Erin. IOM —5A 108
Port Erroll. Abers —5H 161
Porter's Fen Corner. Norf —5E 77
Portesham. Dors —4B 14
Portessie. Mor —2B 160
Port e Vullen. IOM —2D 108
Port-Eynon. Swan —4D 30
Portfield Gate. Pemb —3D 42
Portgate. Devn —4E 11
Port Gaverne. Corn —4A 10
Port Glasgow. Inv —2E 127
Portgordon. Mor —2A 160
Portgower. High —2H 165
Porth. Corn —2C 6
Porth. Rhon —2D 32
Porthaethwy. IOA —3E 81
Porthallow. Corn —3G 7
(nr. Looe)
Porthallow. Corn —4E 5
(nr. St Keverne)
Porthalong. High —5C 154
Porthcawl. B'end —4B 32
Porthceri. V Glam —5D 32
Porthcothan. Corn —1C 6
Porthcurno. Corn —4A 4
Port Henderson. High —1G 155
Porthgain. Pemb —1C 42
Porthgwarra. Corn —4A 4
Porthill. Shrp —4G 71
Porthkerry. V Glam —5D 32
Porthleven. Corn —4D 4
Porthllechog. IOA —1D 80
Porth Llechog. IOA —1D 80
Porthmadog. Gwyn —2E 69
Porthmeirion. Gwyn —2E 69
Porthmeor. Corn —3B 4
Porth Navas. Corn —4E 5
Portholland. Corn —4D 6
Porthoustock. Corn —4F 5
Porthtowan. Corn —4A 6
Porth Tywyn. Carm —5E 45
Porth-y-felin. IOA —2B 80
Porthyrhyd. Carm —4F 45
(nr. Carmarthen)
Porthyrhyd. Carm —2H 45
(nr. Llandovery)
Porth-y-waen. Shrp —3E 71
Portincaple. Arg —4B 134
Portington. E Yor —1A 94
Portinnisherrich. Arg —2G 133
Portinscale. Cumb —2D 102
Port Isaac. Corn —1D 6
Portishead. N Som —4H 33
Portknockie. Mor —2B 160
Port Lamont. Arg —2B 126
Portland Castle EH —5B 14
Portlethen. Abers —4G 153
Portlethen Village. Abers —4G 153
Portling. Dum —4F 111
Port Lion. Pemb —4D 43
Portloe. Corn —5D 6
Port Logan. Dum —5F 109
Port Lympne Zoo —2F 29
Portmahomack. High —5G 165
Port Mead. Swan —3F 31
Portmeirion Village —2E 69
Portmellon. Corn —4E 6
Port Mholair. W Isl —4H 171
Port Mor. High —1F 139
Portmore. Hants —3B 16
Port Mulgrave. N Yor —3E 107
Portnacroish. Arg —4D 140
Portnahaven. Arg —4A 124
Portnalong. High —5C 154
Portnaluchaig. High —5E 147
Portnancon. High —2E 167
Port Nan Giuran. W Isl —4H 171
Port nan Long. W Isl —1D 170
Port Nis. W Isl —1H 171
Portobello. Edin —2G 129
Portobello. W Yor —3D 92
Port of Menteith. Stir —3E 135
Porton. Wilts —3G 23
Portormin. High —5D 168
Portpatrick. Dum —4F 109
Port Quin. Corn —1D 6
Port Ramsay. Arg —4C 140
Portreath. Corn —4A 6
Portree. High —4D 155
Port St Mary. IOM —5B 108
Portscatho. Corn —5C 6
Portsea. Port —2E 17
Portskerra. High —2A 168
Portskewett. Mon —3A 34
Portslade-by-Sea. Brig —5D 26
Portsmouth. Port —3E 17 & 195
Portsmouth. W Yor —2H 91
Port Soderick. IOM —4C 108
Port Solent. Port —2E 17
Portsonachan. Arg —1H 133
Portsoy. Abers —2C 160
Port Sunlight. Mers —2F 83
Portswood. Sotn —1C 16
Port Talbot. Neat —3A 32
Porttannachy. Mor —2A 160
Port Tennant. Swan —3F 31
Portuairk. High —2F 139
Portway. Here —1H 47
Portway. Worc —3E 61
Port Wemyss. Arg —4A 124
Port William. Dum —5A 110
Portwrinkle. Corn —3H 7
Poslingford. Suff —1A 54
Postbridge. Devn —5G 11
Postcombe. Oxon —2F 37
Post Green. Dors —3E 15
Posthill. Staf —5G 73
Postling. Kent —2F 29
Postlip. Glos —3F 49
Post-mawr. Cdgn —5D 56
Postwick. Norf —5E 79
Potarch. Abers —4D 152
Potsgrove. Beds —3H 51
Potten End. Herts —5A 52
Potter Brompton. N Yor —2D 101
Pottergate Street. Norf —1D 66
Potterhanworth. Linc —4H 87
Potterhanworth Booths. Linc —4H 87
Potter Heigham. Norf —4G 79
Potter Hill. Leics —3E 75
Potteries Mus. —Stoke 196
Potteries, The. Stoke —1C 72
Potterne. Wilts —1E 23
Potterne Wick. Wilts —1E 23
Potternewton. W Yor —1D 92
Potters Bar. Herts —5C 52
Potters Brook. Lanc —4D 97
Potter's Cross. Staf —2C 60
Potters Crouch. Herts —5B 52
Potter Somersal. Derbs —2F 73
Potterspury. Nptn —1F 51
Potter Street. Essx —5E 53
Potterton. Abers —2G 153
Potthorpe. Norf —3B 78
Pottle Street. Wilts —2D 22
Potto. N Yor —4B 106
Potton. Beds —1C 52
Pott Row. Norf —3G 77
Pott Shrigley. Ches —3D 84
Poughill. Corn —2C 10
Poughill. Devn —2B 12
Poulner. Hants —2G 15
Poulshot. Wilts —1E 23
Poulton. Glos —5G 49
Poulton-le-Fylde. Lanc —1B 90
Pound Bank. Worc —3B 60
Poundbury. Dors —3B 14
Poundfield. E Sus —2G 27
Poundgate. E Sus —3F 27
Pound Green. E Sus —3G 27
Pound Hill. W Sus —2D 27
Poundland. S Ayr —1G 109
Poundon. Buck —3E 51
Poundsgate. Devn —5H 11
Poundstock. Corn —3C 10
Pound Street. Hants —5C 36
Pounsley. E Sus —3G 27
Powburn. Nmbd —3E 121
Powderham. Devn —4C 12
Powderham Castle —4C 12
Powerstock. Dors —3A 14
Powfoot. Dum —3C 112
Powick. Worc —5C 60
Powis Castle NT —5E 70
Powmill. Per —4C 136
Poxwell. Dors —4C 14

Poyle. Slo —3B 38
Poynings. W Sus —4D 26
Poyntington. Dors —4B 22
Poynton. Ches —2D 84
Poynton. Telf —4H 71
Poynton Green. Telf —4H 71
Poys Street. Suff —3F 67
Poystreet Green. Suff —5B 66
Praa Sands. Corn —4C 4
Pratt's Bottom. G Lon —4F 39
Praze-an-Beeble. Corn —3D 4
Prees. Shrp —2H 71
Preesall. Lanc —5C 96
Preesall Park. Lanc —5C 96
Prees Green. Shrp —2H 71
Prees Higher Heath. Shrp —2H 71
Prendergast. Pemb —3D 42
Prendwick. Nmbd —3E 121
Pren-gwyn. Cdgn —1E 45
Prenteg. Gwyn —1E 69
Prenton. Mers —2F 83
Prescot. Mers —1G 83
Prescott. Devn —1D 12
Prescott. Shrp —3G 71
Preshute. Wilts —5G 35
Pressen. Nmbd —1C 120
Prestatyn. Den —2C 82
Prestbury. Ches —3D 84
Prestbury. Glos —3E 49
Presteigne. Powy —4F 59
Presthope. Shrp —1H 59
Prestleigh. Som —2B 22
Preston. Brig —5E 27
Preston. Devn —5B 12
Preston. Dors —4C 14
Preston. E Lot —2B 130 (nr. East Linton)
Preston. E Lot —2G 129 (nr. Prestonpans)
Preston. E Yor —1E 95
Preston. Glos —5F 49
Preston. Herts —3B 52
Preston. Kent —4G 41 (nr. Canterbury)
Preston. Kent —4E 40 (nr. Faversham)
Preston. Lanc —2D 90 & 195
Preston. Nmbd —2F 121
Preston. Rut —5F 75
Preston. Bord —4D 130
Preston. Shrp —4H 71
Preston. Suff —5B 66
Preston. Wilts —4A 36 (nr. Aldbourne)
Preston. Wilts —4F 35 (nr. Lyneham)
Preston Bagot. Warw —4F 61
Preston Bissett. Buck —3E 51
Preston Bowyer. Som —4E 21
Preston Brockhurst. Shrp —3H 71
Preston Brook. Hal —3H 83
Preston Candover. Hants —2E 24
Preston Capes. Nptn —5C 62
Preston Cross. Glos —2B 48
Preston Gubbals. Shrp —4G 71
Preston-le-Skerne. Dur —2A 106
Preston Marsh. Here —1A 48
Prestonmill. Dum —4A 112
Preston on Stour. Warw —5G 61
Preston on the Hill. Hal —2H 83
Preston on Wye. Here —1G 47
Prestonpans. E Lot —2G 129
Preston Plucknett. Som —1A 14
Preston Tower —2F 121
Preston-under-Scar. N Yor —5D 104
Preston upon the Weald Moors. Telf —4A 72
Preston Wynne. Here —1A 48
Prestwich. G Man —4G 91
Prestwick. Nmbd —2E 115
Prestwick. S Ayr —2C 116
Prestwold. Leics —3C 74
Prestwood. Buck —5G 51
Prestwood. Staf —1E 73
Price Town. B'end —2C 32
Prickwillow. Cambs —2E 65
Priddy. Som —1A 22
Prideaux Place —1D 6
Priestcliffe. Derbs —3F 85
Priesthill. Glas —3G 127
Priest Hutton. Lanc —2E 97
Priestland. E Ayr —1E 117
Priest Weston. Shrp —1E 59
Priestwood. Brac —5G 37
Priestwood. Kent —4A 40
Primethorpe. Leics —1C 62
Primrose Green. Norf —4C 78
Primrose Hill. Derbs —5B 86
Primrose Hill. Glos —5B 48
Primrose Hill. Lanc —4B 90
Primrose Valley. N Yor —2F 101
Primsidemill. Bord —2C 120
Princes Gate. Pemb —3F 43
Princes Risborough. Buck —5G 51
Princethorpe. Warw —3B 62
Princetown. Devn —5F 11
Prinsted. W Sus —2F 17
Prion. Den —4C 82
Prior Muir. Fife —2H 137
Prior Park Gdn. NT —5C 34
Prior's Frome. Here —2A 48
Priors Halton. Shrp —3G 59
Priors Hardwick. Warw —5B 62
Priorslee. Telf —4B 72
Priors Marston. Warw —5B 62
Prior's Norton. Glos —3D 48
Priory, The. W Ber —5B 36
Priory Wood. Here —1F 47
Priston. Bath —5B 34
Pristow Green. Norf —2D 66
Prittlewell. S'end —2C 40
Privett. Hants —4E 25
Prixford. Devn —3F 19
Probus. Corn —4D 6
Prospect. Cumb —5C 112
Provan Hall NTS —3H 127
Provanmill. Glas —3H 127
Prudhoe. Nmbd —3D 115
Prudhoe Castle EH —3D 115
Publow. Bath —5B 34
Puckeridge. Herts —3D 53
Puckington. Som —1G 13
Pucklechurch. S Glo —4B 34
Puckrup. Glos —2D 49
Puddinglake. Ches —4B 84
Puddington. Ches —3F 83
Puddington. Devn —1B 12
Puddlebrook. Glos —4B 48
Puddledock. Norf —1C 66
Puddletown. Dors —3C 14
Pudleston. Here —5H 59
Pudsey. W Yor —1C 92
Pulborough. W Sus —4B 26
Puleston. Telf —3B 72
Pulford. Ches —5F 83
Pulham. Dors —2C 14
Pulham Market. Norf —2D 66
Pulham St Mary. Norf —2E 66
Pulley. Shrp —5G 71
Pulloxhill. Beds —2A 52
Pulpit Hill. Arg —1F 133
Pulverbatch. Shrp —5G 71
Pumpherston. W Lot —3D 128
Pumsaint. Carm —1G 45
Puncheston. Pemb —2E 43
Puncknowle. Dors —4A 14
Punnett's Town. E Sus —3H 27
Purbrook. Hants —2E 17
Purfleet. Thur —3G 39
Puriton. Som —2G 21
Purleigh. Essx —5B 54
Purley. G Lon —4E 39
Purley on Thames. W Ber —4E 37
Purlogue. Shrp —3E 59
Purl's Bridge. Cambs —2D 65
Purse Caundle. Dors —1B 14
Purslow. Shrp —2F 59
Purston Jaglin. W Yor —3E 93
Purtington. Som —2G 13
Purton. Glos —5B 48 (nr. Lydney)
Purton. Glos —5B 48 (nr. Sharpness)
Purton. Wilts —3F 35
Purton Stoke. Wilts —2F 35
Pury End. Nptn —1F 51
Pusey. Oxon —2B 36
Putley. Here —2B 48
Putney. G Lon —3D 38
Putsborough. Devn —2E 19
Puttenham. Herts —4G 51
Puttenham. Surr —1A 26
Puttock End. Essx —1B 54
Puttock's End. Essx —4F 53
Puxton. N Som —5H 33
Pwll. Carm —5E 45
Pwll. Powy —5D 70
Pwllcrochan. Pemb —4D 42
Pwll-glas. Den —5D 82
Pwllgloyw. Powy —2D 46
Pwllheli. Gwyn —2C 68
Pwllmeyric. Mon —2A 34
Pwlltrap. Carm —3G 43
Pwll-y-glaw. Neat —2A 32
Pyecombe. W Sus —4D 27
Pye Corner. Herts —4E 53
Pye Corner. Newp —3G 33
Pye Green. Staf —4D 73
Pyewipe. NE Lin —3F 95
Pyle. B'end —3B 32
Pyle. IOW —5C 16
Pylle. Som —3B 22
Pymore. Cambs —2D 65
Pymore. Dors —3H 13
Pyrford. Surr —5B 38
Pyrton. Oxon —2E 37
Pytchley. Nptn —3F 63
Pyworthy. Devn —2D 10

Quabbs. Shrp —2E 58
Quadring. Linc —2B 76
Quadring Eaudike. Linc —2B 76
Quainton. Buck —3F 51
Quaking Houses. Dur —4E 115
Quantock Hills —3E 21
Quarley. Hants —2A 24
Quarndon. Derbs —1H 73
Quarndon Common. Derbs —1H 73
Quarrendon. Buck —4G 51
Quarrier's Village. Inv —3E 127
Quarrington. Linc —1H 75
Quarrington Hill. Dur —1A 106
Quarrybank. Ches —4H 83
Quarry Bank. W Mid —2D 60
Quarry Bank Mill NT —2C 84
Quarry, The. Glos —2C 34
Quarrywood. Mor —2F 159
Quartalehouse. Abers —4G 161
Quarter. N Ayr —3C 126
Quarter. S Lan —4A 128
Quatford. Shrp —1B 60
Quatt. Shrp —2B 60
Quebec. Dur —5E 115
Quebec House NT —5F 39
Quedgeley. Glos —4D 48
Queen Adelaide. Cambs —2E 65
Queenborough. Kent —3D 40
Queen Camel. Som —4A 22
Queen Charlton. Bath —5B 34
Queen Dart. Devn —1B 12
Queen Elizabeth Forest Park —4C 134
Queenhill. Worc —2D 48
Queen Oak. Dors —3C 22
Queensbury. W Yor —2B 92
Queensferry. Edin —2E 129
Queensferry. Flin —4F 83
Queenstown. Bkpl —1B 90
Queen Street. Kent —1A 28
Queenzieburn. N Lan —2H 127
Quemerford. Wilts —5F 35
Quendale. Shet —10E 173
Quendon. Essx —2F 53
Queniborough. Leics —4D 74
Quenington. Glos —5G 49
Quernmore. Lanc —3E 97
Quethiock. Corn —2H 7
Quholm. Orkn —6B 172
Quick's Green. W Ber —4D 36
Quidenham. Norf —2C 66
Quidhampton. Hants —1D 24
Quidhampton. Wilts —3G 23
Quilquox. Abers —5G 161
Quina Brook. Shrp —2H 71
Quindry. Orkn —8D 172
Quine's Hill. IOM —4C 108
Quinton. Nptn —5E 63
Quinton. W Mid —2D 61
Quintrell Downs. Corn —2C 6
Quixhill. Staf —1F 73
Quoditch. Devn —3E 11
Quorn. Leics —4C 74
Quorndon. Leics —4C 74
Quothquan. S Lan —1B 118
Quoyloo. Orkn —5B 172
Quoyness. Orkn —7B 172
Quoys. Shet —5F 173 (on Mainland)
Quoys. Shet —1H 173 (on Unst)

Rableyheath. Herts —4C 52
Raby. Cumb —4C 112
Raby. Mers —3F 83
Raby Castle —2E 105
Rachan Mill. Bord —1D 118
Rachub. Gwyn —4F 81
Rackenford. Devn —1B 12
Rackham. W Sus —4B 26
Rackheath. Norf —4E 79
Racks. Dum —2B 112
Rackwick. Orkn —8A 172 (on Hoy)
Rackwick. Orkn —3D 172 (on Westray)
Radbourne. Derbs —2G 73
Radcliffe. G Man —4F 91
Radcliffe. Nmbd —4G 121
Radcliffe on Trent. Notts —2D 74
Radclive. Buck —2E 51
Radernie. Fife —3G 137
Radfall. Kent —4F 41
Radford. Bath —1B 22
Radford. Nott —1C 74
Radford. W Mid —2H 61
Radford. Worc —5E 61
Radford Semele. Warw —4H 61
Radipole. Dors —4B 14
Radlett. Herts —1C 38
Radley. Oxon —2D 36
Radnage. Buck —2F 37
Radstock. Bath —1B 22
Radstone. Nptn —1D 50
Radway. Warw —1B 50
Radway Green. Ches —5B 84
Radwell. Beds —5H 63
Radwell. Herts —2C 52
Radwinter. Essx —2G 53
Radyr. Card —3E 33
Rafford. Mor —3E 159
RAF Mus. Cosford —5B 72
RAF Mus. Hendon —1D 38
Ragdale. Leics —4D 74
Ragdon. Shrp —1G 59
Ragged Appleshaw. Hants —2B 24
Raggra. High —4F 169
Raglan. Mon —5H 47
Raglan Castle CADW —5H 47
Ragley Hall —5E 61
Ragnall. Notts —3F 87
Raigbeg. High —1C 150
Railway Age, The —5B 84
Rainford. Mers —4C 90
Rainford Junction. Mers —4C 90
Rainham. G Lon —2G 39
Rainham. Medw —4C 40
Rainhill. Mers —1G 83
Rainow. Ches —3D 84
Rainton. N Yor —2F 99
Rainworth. Notts —5C 86
Raisbeck. Cumb —4H 103
Raise. Cumb —5A 114
Rait. Per —1E 137
Raithby. Linc —2C 88 (nr. Louth)
Raithby. Linc —4C 88 (nr. Spilsby)
Raithwaite. N Yor —3F 107
Rake. W Sus —4G 25
Rake End. Staf —4E 73
Rakeway. Staf —1E 73
Rakewood. G Man —3H 91
Ralia. High —4B 150
Ram Alley. Wilts —5H 35
Ramasaig. High —4A 154
Rame. Corn —4A 8 (nr. Millbrook)
Rame. Corn —5B 6 (nr. Penryn)
Ram Lane. Kent —1D 28
Ramnageo. Shet —1H 173
Rampisham. Dors —2A 14
Rampside. Cumb —3B 96
Rampton. Cambs —4D 64
Rampton. Notts —3F 87
Ramsbottom. G Man —3F 91
Ramsburn. Mor —3C 160
Ramsbury. Wilts —4A 36
Ramscraigs. High —1H 165
Ramsdean. Hants —4F 25
Ramsdell. Hants —1D 24
Ramsden. Oxon —4B 50
Ramsden. Worc —1E 49
Ramsden Bellhouse. Essx —1B 40
Ramsden Heath. Essx —1B 40
Ramsey. Cambs —2B 64
Ramsey. Essx —2F 55
Ramsey. IOM —2D 108
Ramsey Abbey Gatehouse NT —2B 64
Ramsey Forty Foot. Cambs —2C 64
Ramsey Heights. Cambs —2B 64
Ramsey Island. Essx —5C 54
Ramsey Mereside. Cambs —2B 64
Ramsey St Mary's. Cambs —2B 64
Ramsgate. Kent —4H 41
Ramsgill. N Yor —2D 98
Ramshaw. Dur —5C 114
Ramshorn. Staf —1E 73
Ramsley. Devn —3G 11
Ramsnest Common. Surr —2A 26
Ramstone. Abers —2D 152
Ranais. W Isl —5G 171
Ranby. Linc —3B 88
Ranby. Notts —2D 86
Rand. Linc —3A 88
Randwick. Glos —5D 48
Ranfurly. Ren —3E 127
Rangag. High —4D 168
Rangemore. Staf —3F 73
Rangeworthy. S Glo —3B 34
Rankinston. E Ayr —3D 116
Rank's Green. Essx —4H 53
Ranmore Common. Surr —5C 38
Rannoch School. Per —3C 142
Rannoch Station. Per —3B 142
Ranochan. High —5G 147
Ranskill. Notts —2D 86
Ranton. Staf —3C 72
Ranton Green. Staf —3C 72
Ranworth. Norf —4F 79
Raploch. Stir —4G 135
Rapness. Orkn —3E 172
Rapps. Som —1G 13
Rascal Moor. E Yor —1B 94
Rascarrel. Dum —5E 111
Rashfield. Arg —1C 126
Rashwood. Worc —4D 60
Raskelf. N Yor —2G 99
Rassau. Blae —4E 47
Rastrick. W Yor —2B 92
Ratagan. High —2B 148
Ratby. Leics —5C 74
Ratcliffe Culey. Leics —1H 61
Ratcliffe on Soar. Notts —3B 74
Ratcliffe on the Wreake. Leics —4D 74
Rathen. Abers —2H 161
Rathillet. Fife —1F 137
Rathmell. N Yor —4H 97
Ratho. Edin —2E 129
Ratho Station. Edin —2E 129
Rathven. Mor —2B 160
Ratley. Hants —4B 24
Ratley. Warw —1B 50
Ratlinghope. Shrp —1G 59
Rattar. High —1E 169
Ratten Row. Cumb —5E 113
Ratten Row. Lanc —5D 96
Rattery. Devn —2D 8
Rattlesden. Suff —5B 66
Ratton Village. E Sus —5G 27
Rattray. Abers —3H 161
Rattray. Per —4A 144
Raughton. Cumb —5E 113
Raughton Head. Cumb —5E 113
Raunds. Nptn —3G 63
Ravenfield. S Yor —1B 86
Ravenglass. Cumb —5B 102
Ravenglass & Eskdale Railway —5C 102
Ravenhills Green. Worc —5B 60
Raveningham. Norf —1F 67
Ravenscar. N Yor —4G 107
Ravensdale. IOM —2C 108
Ravensden. Beds —5H 63
Ravenseat. N Yor —4B 104
Ravenshead. Notts —5C 86
Ravensmoor. Ches —5A 84
Ravensthorpe. Nptn —3D 62
Ravensthorpe. W Yor —2C 92
Ravenstone. Leics —4B 74
Ravenstone. Mil —5F 63
Ravenstonedale. Cumb —4A 104
Ravenstown. Cumb —2C 96
Ravenstruther. S Lan —5C 128
Ravensworth. N Yor —4E 105
Raw. N Yor —4G 107
Rawcliffe. E Yor —2G 93
Rawcliffe. York —4H 99
Rawcliffe Bridge. E Yor —2G 93
Rawdon. W Yor —1C 92
Rawgreen. Nmbd —4C 114
Rawmarsh. S Yor —1B 86
Rawnsley. Staf —4E 73
Rawreth. Essx —1B 40
Rawridge. Devn —2F 13
Rawson Green. Derbs —1A 74
Rawtenstall. Lanc —2F 91
Raydon. Suff —2D 54
Raylees. Nmbd —5D 120
Rayleigh. Essx —1C 40
Raymond's Hill. Devn —3G 13
Rayne. Essx —3H 53
Rayners Lane. G Lon —2C 38
Reach. Cambs —4E 65
Read. Lanc —1F 91
Reading. Read —4F 37 & 195
Reading Green. Suff —3D 66
Reading Street. Kent —2D 28
Readymoney. Corn —3F 7
Reagill. Cumb —3H 103
Rea Hill. Torb —3F 9
Rearquhar. High —4E 165
Rearsby. Leics —4D 74
Reasby. Linc —3H 87
Rease Heath. Ches —5A 84
Reaster. High —2E 169
Reawick. Shet —7E 173
Reay. High —2B 168
Rechullin. High —3A 156
Reculver. Kent —4G 41
Redberth. Pemb —4E 43
Redbourn. Herts —4B 52
Redbourne. N Lin —4C 94
Redbrook. Glos —4A 48
Redbrook. Wrex —1H 71
Redburn. High —4D 158
Redburn. Nmbd —3A 114
Redcar. Red C —2D 106
Redcastle. High —4H 157
Redcliff. Staf —2C 60
Redcliff Bay. N Som —4H 33
Red Dial. Cumb —5D 112
Redding. Falk —2C 128
Reddingmuirhead. Falk —2C 128
Reddings, The. Glos —3E 49
Reddish. G Man —1C 84
Redditch. Worc —4E 61
Rede. Suff —5H 65
Redenhall. Norf —2E 67
Redesdale Camp. Nmbd —5C 120
Redesmouth. Nmbd —1B 114
Redford. Ang —4E 145
Redford. Dur —1D 105
Redford. W Sus —4G 25
Redfordgreen. Bord —3F 119
Redgate. Corn —2G 7
Redgrave. Suff —3C 66
Redhill. Abers —3E 153
Redhill. Herts —2C 52
Redhill. N Som —5H 33
Redhill. Shrp —4B 72
Redhill. Surr —5D 39
Red Hill. Warw —5F 61
Red Hill. W Yor —2E 93
Redhouses. Arg —3B 124
Redisham. Suff —2G 67
Redland. Bris —4A 34
Redland. Orkn —5C 172
Redlingfield. Suff —3D 66
Red Lodge. Suff —3F 65
Redlynch. Som —3C 22
Redlynch. Wilts —4H 23
Redmain. Cumb —1C 102
Redmarley. Worc —4B 60
Redmarley D'Abitot. Glos —2C 48
Redmarshall. Stoc T —2A 106
Redmile. Leics —2E 75
Redmire. N Yor —5D 104
Rednal. Shrp —3F 71
Redpath. Bord —1H 119
Redpoint. High —2G 155
Red Post. Corn —2C 10
Red Rock. G Man —4D 90
Red Roses. Carm —3G 43
Red Row. Nmbd —5G 121
Redruth. Corn —4B 6
Red Street. Staf —5C 84
Redvales. G Man —4F 91
Red Wharf Bay. IOA —2E 81
Redwick. Newp —3H 33
Redwick. S Glo —3A 34
Redworth. Darl —2F 105
Reed. Herts —2D 52
Reed End. Herts —2D 52
Reedham. Linc —5B 88
Reedham. Norf —5G 79
Reedness. E Yor —2B 94
Reeds Beck. Linc —4B 88
Reemshill. Abers —4E 161
Reepham. Linc —3H 87
Reepham. Norf —3C 78
Reeth. N Yor —5D 104
Regaby. IOM —2D 108
Regil. N Som —5A 34
Regoul. High —3C 158
Reiff. High —2D 162
Reigate. Surr —5D 38
Reighton. N Yor —2F 101
Reilth. Shrp —2E 59
Reinigeadal. W Isl —7E 171
Reisque. Abers —2F 153
Reiss. High —3F 169
Rejerrah. Corn —3C 6
Releath. Corn —5A 6
Relubbus. Corn —3C 4
Relugas. Mor —4D 159
Remenham. Wok —3F 37
Remenham Hill. Wok —3F 37
Rempstone. Notts —3C 74
Rendcomb. Glos —5F 49
Rendham. Suff —4F 67
Renfrew. Ren —3G 127
Renhold. Beds —5H 63
Renishaw. Derbs —3B 86
Renishaw Hall Gdns. —3B 86
Rennington. Nmbd —3G 121
Renton. W Dun —2E 127
Renwick. Cumb —5H 113
Repps. Norf —4G 79
Repton. Derbs —3H 73
Resaurie. High —4B 158
Rescassa. Corn —4D 6
Rescobie. Ang —3E 145
Rescorla. Corn —3E 7 (nr. Rosevean)
Rescorla. Corn —4D 6 (nr. St Ewe)
Resipole. High —2B 140
Resolfen. Neat —5B 46
Resolis. High —2A 158
Resolven. Neat —5B 46
Rest and be Thankful. Arg —3B 134
Reston. Bord —3E 131
Restoration House —Medway 191
Restormel Castle EH —2F 7
Restrop. Wilts —3F 35
Retford. Notts —2E 86
Retire. Corn —2E 6
Rettendon. Essx —1B 40
Retyn. Corn —3C 6
Revesby. Linc —4C 88
Rew. Devn —5D 8
Rewe. Devn —3C 12
Rew Street. IOW —3C 16
Rexon. Devn —4E 11
Reybridge. Wilts —5E 35
Reydon. Suff —3H 67
Reymerston. Norf —5C 78
Reynalton. Pemb —4E 43
Reynoldston. Swan —4D 31
Rezare. Corn —5D 10
Rhadyr. Mon —5G 47

Rhaeadr Gwy. Powy —4B 58
Rhandirmwyn. Carm —1A 46
Rhayader. Powy —4B 58
Rheindown. High —4H 157
Rhemore. High —3G 139
Rhenetra. High —3D 154
Rhewl. Den —1D 70 (nr. Llangollen)
Rhewl. Den —4D 82 (nr. Ruthin)
Rhewl. Shrp —2F 71
Rhewl-Mostyn. Flin —2D 82
Rhian. High —2C 164
Rhian Breck. High —3C 164
Rhicarn. High —1E 163
Rhiconich. High —3C 166
Rhicullen. High —1A 158
Rhidorroch. High —4F 163
Rhifail. High —4H 167
Rhigos. Rhon —5C 46
Rhilochan. High —3E 165
Rhiroy. High —5F 163
Rhitongue. High —3G 167
Rhiw. Gwyn —3B 68
Rhiwabon. Wrex —1F 71
Rhiwbina. Card —3E 33
Rhiwbryfdir. Gwyn —1F 69
Rhiwderin. Newp —3F 33
Rhiwlas. Gwyn —2B 70 (nr. Bala)
Rhiwlas. Gwyn —4E 81 (nr. Bangor)
Rhiwlas. Powy —2D 70
Rhodes. G Man —4G 91
Rhodesia. Notts —3C 86
Rhodes Minnis. Kent —1F 29
Rhodiad-y-Brenin. Pemb —2B 42
Rhondda. Rhon —2C 32
Rhonehouse. Dum —4E 111
Rhoose. V Glam —5D 32
Rhos. Carm —2D 45
Rhos. Neat —5H 45
Rhosaman. Carm —4H 45
Rhoscefnhir. IOA —3E 81
Rhoscolyn. IOA —3B 80
Rhos Common. Powy —4E 71
Rhoscrowther. Pemb —4D 42
Rhos-ddu. Gwyn —2B 68
Rhosdylluan. Gwyn —3A 70
Rhosesmor. Flin —4E 82
Rhos-fawr. Gwyn —2C 68
Rhosgadfan. Gwyn —5E 81
Rhosgoch. IOA —2D 80
Rhosgoch. Powy —1E 47
Rhos Haminiog. Cdgn —4E 57
Rhos-hill. Pemb —1B 44
Rhoshirwaun. Gwyn —3A 68
Rhoslan. Gwyn —1D 69
Rhoslefain. Gwyn —5E 69
Rhosllanerchrugog. Wrex —1E 71
Rhos Lligwy. IOA —2D 81
Rhosmaen. Carm —3G 45
Rhosmeirch. IOA —3D 80
Rhosneigr. IOA —3C 80
Rhos-on-Sea. Cnwy —2H 81
Rhossili. Swan —4D 30
Rhossili Bay NT —4D 30
Rhosson. Pemb —2B 42
Rhos, The. Pemb —3E 43
Rhostrenwfa. IOA —3D 80
Rhostryfan. Gwyn —5D 81
Rhostyllen. Wrex —1F 71
Rhoswiel. Shrp —2E 71
Rhosybol. IOA —2D 80
Rhos-y-brithdir. Powy —3D 70
Rhos-y-garth. Cdgn —3F 57
Rhos-y-gwaliau. Gwyn —2B 70
Rhos-y-llan. Gwyn —2B 68
Rhos-y-meirch. Powy —4E 59
Rhu. Arg —1D 126
Rhualt. Den —3C 82
Rhubadach. Arg —2B 126
Rhubha Stoer. High —1E 163
Rhuddall Heath. Ches —4H 83
Rhuddlan. Cdgn —1E 45
Rhuddlan. Den —3C 82
Rhuddlan Castle CADW —3C 82
Rhue. High —4E 163
Rhulen. Powy —1E 47
Rhunahaorine. Arg —5F 125
Rhuthun. Den —5D 82
Rhuvoult. High —3C 166
Rhyd. Gwyn —1F 69
Rhydaman. Carm —4G 45
Rhydargaeau. Carm —3E 45
Rhydcymerau. Carm —2F 45
Rhydd. Worc —1D 48
Rhyd-Ddu. Gwyn —5E 81
Rhydding. Neat —3G 31
Rhydfudr. Cdgn —4E 57
Rhydlanfair. Cnwy —5H 81
Rhydlewis. Cdgn —1D 44
Rhydlios. Gwyn —2A 68
Rhydlydan. Cnwy —5A 82
Rhyd-meirionydd. Cdgn —2F 57
Rhydowen. Cdgn —1E 45
Rhyd-Rosser. Cdgn —4E 57
Rhydspence. Powy —1F 47
Rhydtalog. Flin —5E 83
Rhyd-uchaf. Gwyn —2B 70
Rhydwyn. IOA —2C 80
Rhyd-y-clafdy. Gwyn —2C 68
Rhydycroesau. Shrp —2E 71
Rhydyfelin. Cdgn —3E 57
Rhydyfelin. Rhon —3E 32
Rhyd-y-foel. Cnwy —3B 82
Rhyd-y-fro. Neat —5H 45
Rhydymain. Gwyn —3H 69
Rhyd-y-meirch. Mon —5G 47
Rhyd-y-meudwy. Den —5D 82
Rhydymwyn. Flin —4E 82
Rhyd-yr-onen. Gwyn —5F 69
Rhyd-y-sarn. Gwyn —1F 69
Rhyl. Den —2C 82
Rhymney. Cphy —5E 46
Rhymni. Cphy —5E 46
Rhynd. Per —1D 136
Rhynie. Abers —1B 152
Ribbesford. Worc —3B 60
Ribbleton. Lanc —1D 90
Ribby. Lanc —1C 90
Ribchester. Lanc —1E 91
Riber. Derbs —5H 85
Ribigill. High —3F 167
Riby. Linc —4E 95
Riccall. N Yor —1G 93
Riccarton. E Ayr —1D 116
Richards Castle. Here —4G 59
Richborough Castle & Roman Amphitheatre —4H 41
Richborough Port. Kent —4H 41
Richings Park. Buck —3B 38
Richmond. G Lon —3C 38
Richmond. N Yor —4E 105
Richmond Castle EH —4E 105
Rickarton. Abers —5F 153
Rickerby. Cumb —4F 113
Rickerscote. Staf —3D 72
Rickford. N Som —1H 21
Rickham. Devn —5D 8
Rickinghall Superior. Suff —3C 66
Rickleton. Tyne —4F 115
Rickling. Essx —2E 53
Rickling Green. Essx —3F 53
Rickmansworth. Herts —1B 38
Riddings. Derbs —5B 86
Riddlecombe. Devn —1G 11
Riddlesden. W Yor —5C 98
Ridge. Dors —4E 15
Ridge. Herts —5C 52
Ridge. Wilts —3E 23
Ridgebourne. Powy —4C 58
Ridge Lane. Warw —1G 61
Ridgeway. Derbs —5A 86 (nr. Alfreton)
Ridgeway. Derbs —2B 86 (nr. Sheffield)
Ridgeway. Staf —5C 84
Ridgeway Cross. Here —1C 48
Ridgeway Moor. Derbs —2B 86
Ridgewell. Essx —1H 53
Ridgewood. E Sus —3F 27
Ridgmont. Beds —2H 51
Ridgwardine. Shrp —2A 72
Riding Mill. Nmbd —3D 114
Ridley. Kent —4H 39
Ridley. Nmbd —3A 114
Ridlington. Norf —2F 79
Ridlington. Rut —5F 75
Ridsdale. Nmbd —1C 114
Riemore Lodge. Per —4H 143
Rievaulx. N Yor —1H 99
Rievaulx Abbey EH —1H 99
Rievaulx Terrace NT —1H 99
Rift House. Hart —1B 106
Rigg. Dum —3D 112
Riggend. N Lan —2A 128
Rigmaden Park. Cumb —1F 97
Rigsby. Linc —3D 88
Rigside. S Lan —1A 118
Riley Green. Lanc —2E 90
Rileyhill. Staf —4F 73
Rilla Mill. Corn —5C 10
Rillington. N Yor —2C 100
Rimington. Lanc —5H 97
Rimpton. Som —4B 22
Rimsdale. High —4H 167
Rimswell. E Yor —2G 95
Ringasta. Shet —10E 173
Ringford. Dum —4D 111
Ringing Hill. Leics —4B 74
Ringinglow. S Yor —2G 85
Ringland. Norf —4D 78
Ringlestone. Kent —5C 40
Ringmer. E Sus —4F 27
Ringmore. Devn —4C 8 (nr. Kingsbridge)
Ringmore. Devn —5C 12 (nr. Teignmouth)
Ring o' Bells. Lanc —3C 90
Ring's End. Cambs —5C 76
Ringsfield. Suff —2G 67
Ringsfield Corner. Suff —2G 67
Ringshall. Buck —4H 51
Ringshall. Suff —5C 66
Ringshall Stocks. Suff —5C 66
Ringstead. Norf —1G 77
Ringstead. Nptn —3G 63
Ringwood. Hants —2G 15
Ringwould. Kent —1H 29
Rinmore. Abers —2B 152
Rinnigill. Orkn —8C 172
Rinsey. Corn —4C 4
Riof. W Isl —4D 171
Ripe. E Sus —4G 27
Ripley. Derbs —1B 74
Ripley. Hants —3G 15
Ripley. N Yor —3E 99
Ripley. Surr —5B 38
Ripley Castle —3E 99
Riplingham. E Yor —1C 94
Riplington. Hants —4E 25
Ripon. N Yor —2F 99
Ripon Cathedral —2F 99
Rippingale. Linc —3H 75
Ripple. Kent —1H 29
Ripple. Worc —2D 48
Ripponden. W Yor —3A 92
Rireavach. High —4E 163
Risabus. Arg —5B 124
Risbury. Here —5H 59
Risby. E Yor —1D 94
Risby. N Lin —3C 94
Risby. Suff —4G 65
Risca. Cphy —2F 33
Rise. E Yor —5F 101
Riseden. E Sus —2H 27
Riseden. Kent —2B 28
Rise End. Derbs —5G 85
Risegate. Linc —3B 76
Riseholme. Linc —3G 87
Riseley. Beds —4H 63
Riseley. Wok —5F 37
Rishangles. Suff —4D 66
Rishton. Lanc —1F 91
Rishworth. W Yor —3A 92
Risley. Derbs —2B 74
Risley. Warr —1A 84
Risplith. N Yor —3E 99
Rispond. High —2E 167
Rivar. Wilts —5B 36
Rivenhall. Essx —4B 54
Rivenhall End. Essx —4B 54
River. Kent —1G 29
River. W Sus —3A 26
River & Rowing Mus. —3F 37
River Bank. Cambs —4E 65
Riverhead. Kent —5G 39
Rivington. Lanc —3E 91
Roach Bridge. Lanc —2D 90
Roachill. Devn —4B 20
Roade. Nptn —5E 63
Road Green. Norf —1E 67
Roadhead. Cumb —2G 113
Roadmeetings. S Lan —5B 128
Roadside. High —2D 168
Roadside of Catterline. Abers —1H 145
Roadside of Kinneff. Abers —1H 145
Roadwater. Som —3D 20
Road Weedon. Nptn —5D 62
Roag. High —4B 154
Roa Island. Cumb —3B 96
Roath. Card —4E 33
Robert Burns Centre —Dumfries 188
Roberton. Bord —3G 119
Roberton. S Lan —2B 118
Robertsbridge. E Sus —3B 28
Robertstown. Mor —4G 159
Robertstown. Rhon —5C 46
Roberttown. W Yor —2B 92
Robeston Back. Pemb —3E 43
Robeston Wathen. Pemb —3E 43
Robeston West. Pemb —4C 42
Robin Hood. Lanc —3D 90
Robin Hood. W Yor —2D 92
Robinhood End. Essx —2H 53
Robin Hood's Bay. N Yor —4G 107
Robin Hood, Tales of —Nottingham 194
Roborough. Devn —1F 11 (nr. Great Torrington)
Roborough. Devn —2B 8 (nr. Plymouth)
Rob Roy Centre —3F 135
Rob Roy's House. Arg —2A 134
Roby Mill. Lanc —4D 90
Rocester. Staf —2F 73
Roch. Pemb —2C 42
Roch Abbey EH —2C 86
Rochdale. G Man —3G 91
Roche. Corn —2D 6
Rochester. Medw —4B 40 & Medway 191
Rochester. Nmbd —5C 120
Rochester Castle —Medway 191
Rochester Cathedral —Medway 191
Rochford. Essx —1C 40
Rock. Corn —1D 6
Rock. Nmbd —2G 121
Rock. W Sus —4C 26
Rock. Worc —3B 60
Rockbeare. Devn —3D 12
Rockbourne. Hants —1G 15
Rockbourne Roman Villa —1G 15
Rockcliffe. Cumb —3E 113
Rockcliffe. Dum —4F 111
Rockcliffe Cross. Cumb —3E 113
Rock Ferry. Mers —2F 83
Rockfield. High —5G 165
Rockfield. Mon —4H 47
Rockford. Hants —2G 15
Rockgreen. Shrp —3H 59
Rockhampton. S Glo —2B 34
Rockhead. Corn —4A 10
Rockingham. Nptn —1F 63
Rockingham Castle —1F 63
Rockland All Saints. Norf —1B 66
Rockland St Mary. Norf —5F 79
Rockland St Peter. Norf —1B 66
Rockley. Wilts —4G 35
Rockwell End. Buck —3F 37
Rockwell Green. Som —1E 13
Rodborough. Glos —5D 48
Rodbourne. Wilts —3E 35
Rodd. Here —4F 59
Roddam. Nmbd —2E 121
Rodden. Dors —4B 14
Roddenloft. E Ayr —2D 117
Roddymoor. Dur —1E 105
Rode. Som —1D 22
Rode Hall —5C 84
Rodeheath. Ches —4C 84
Rode Heath. Ches —5C 84
Roden. Telf —4H 71
Rodhuish. Som —3D 20
Rodington. Telf —4H 71
Rodington Heath. Telf —4H 71
Rodley. Glos —4C 48
Rodmarton. Glos —2E 35
Rodmarton Manor —2E 35
Rodmell. E Sus —5F 27
Rodmersham. Kent —4D 40
Rodmersham Green. Kent —4D 40
Rodney Stoke. Som —2H 21
Rodsley. Derbs —1G 73
Rodway. Som —2F 21
Rodway. Telf —4A 72
Rodwell. Dors —5B 14
Roecliffe. N Yor —3F 99
Roe Green. Herts —2D 52
Roehampton. G Lon —3D 38
Roesound. Shet —5E 173
Roffey. W Sus —2C 26
Rogart. High —3E 165
Rogate. W Sus —4G 25
Roger Ground. Cumb —5E 103
Rogerstone. Newp —3F 33
Roghadal. W Isl —9C 171
Rogiet. Mon —3H 33
Rogue's Alley. Cambs —5C 76
Roke. Oxon —2E 37
Rokeby Park —3D 105
Rokemarsh. Oxon —2E 36
Roker. Tyne —4H 115
Rollesby. Norf —4G 79
Rolleston. Leics —5E 75
Rolleston. Notts —5E 87
Rolleston on Dove. Staf —3G 73
Rollright Stones EH —2A 50
Rolston. E Yor —5G 101
Rolvenden. Kent —2C 28
Rolvenden Layne. Kent —2C 28
Romaldkirk. Dur —2C 104
Roman Bank. Shrp —1H 59
Romanby. N Yor —5A 106
Roman Camp. W Lot —2D 129
Roman Legionary Mus., Caerleon —2G 33
Romannobridge. Bord —5E 129
Roman Painted House —Dover 188
Romansleigh. Devn —4H 19
Romers Common. Worc —4H 59
Romesdal. High —3D 154
Romford. Dors —2F 15
Romford. G Lon —2G 39
Romiley. G Man —1D 84
Romney, Hythe & Dymchurch Railway —3E 29
Romsey. Hants —4B 24
Romsley. Shrp —2B 60
Romsley. Worc —3D 60
Ronague. IOM —4B 108
Ronaldsvoe. Orkn —8D 172
Rookby. Cumb —3B 104
Rookhope. Dur —5C 114
Rooking. Cumb —3F 103
Rookley. IOW —4D 16
Rooks Bridge. Som —1G 21
Rooksey Green. Suff —5B 66
Rooks Nest. Som —3D 20
Rookwood. W Sus —3F 17
Roos. E Yor —1F 95
Roosebeck. Cumb —3B 96
Roosecote. Cumb —3B 96
Rootfield. High —3H 157
Rootham's Green. Beds —5A 64
Rootpark. S Lan —4C 128
Ropley. Hants —3E 25
Ropley Dean. Hants —3E 25
Ropsley. Linc —2G 75
Rora. Abers —3H 161
Rorandle. Abers —2D 152
Rorrington. Shrp —5F 71
Rose. Corn —3B 6
Roseacre. Lanc —1C 90
Rose Ash. Devn —4A 20
Rosebank. S Lan —5B 128
Rosebush. Pemb —2E 43
Rosedale Abbey. N Yor —5E 107
Roseden. Nmbd —2E 121
Rose Green. Essx —3B 54
Rose Green. Suff —1C 54
Rosehall. High —3B 164
Rosehearty. Abers —2G 161
Rose Hill. E Sus —4F 27
Rose Hill. Lanc —1G 91
Rosehill. Shrp —2A 72 (nr. Market Drayton)
Rosehill. Shrp —4G 71 (nr. Shrewsbury)
Roseisle. Mor —2F 159
Rosemarket. Pemb —4D 42
Rosemarkie. High —3B 158
Rosemary Lane. Devn —1E 13
Rosemoor Gdn. RHS —1F 11
Rosemount. Per —4A 144
Rosenannon. Corn —2D 6
Roser's Cross. E Sus —3G 27
Rose Society Gdn. —5B 52
Rosevean. Corn —3E 7
Rosewell. Midl —3F 129
Roseworth. Stoc T —2B 106
Roseworthy. Corn —3D 4
Rosgill. Cumb —3G 103
Roshven. High —1B 140
Roskhill. High —4B 154
Roskorwell. Corn —4E 5
Rosley. Cumb —5E 112
Roslin. Midl —3F 129
Rosliston. Derbs —4G 73
Rosneath. Arg —1D 126
Ross. Dum —5D 110
Ross. Nmbd —1F 121
Ross. Per —1G 135
Ross. Bord —3F 131
Rossendale. Lanc —2F 91
Rossett. Wrex —5F 83
Rossington. S Yor —1D 86
Rosskeen. High —2A 158
Rossland. Ren —2F 127
Ross-on-Wye. Here —3B 48
Roster. High —4E 169
Rostherne. Ches —2B 84
Rostholme. S Yor —4F 93
Rosthwaite. Cumb —3D 102
Roston. Derbs —1F 73
Rosudgeon. Corn —4C 4
Rosyth. Fife —1E 129
Rothbury. Nmbd —4E 121
Rotherby. Leics —4D 74
Rotherfield. E Sus —3G 27
Rotherfield Greys. Oxon —3F 37
Rotherfield Peppard. Oxon —3F 37
Rotherham. S Yor —1B 86
Rothersthorpe. Nptn —5E 62
Rotherwick. Hants —1F 25
Rothes. Mor —4G 159
Rothesay. Arg —3B 126
Rothesay Castle HS —3B 126
Rothiemurchus Estate —3D 150
Rothienorman. Abers —5E 160
Rothiesholm. Orkn —5F 172
Rothley. Leics —4C 74
Rothley. Nmbd —1D 114
Rothwell. Linc —1A 88
Rothwell. Nptn —2F 63
Rothwell. W Yor —2D 92
Rothwell Haigh. W Yor —2D 92
Rotsea. E Yor —4E 101
Rottal. Ang —2C 144
Rotten End. Suff —4F 67
Rotten Row. Norf —4C 78
Rotten Row. W Ber —4D 36
Rotten Row. W Mid —3F 61
Rottingdean. Brig —5E 27
Rottington. Cumb —3A 102
Roud. IOW —4D 16
Rougham. Norf —3H 77
Rougham. Suff —4B 66
Rough Close. Staf —2D 72
Rough Common. Kent —5F 41
Roughcote. Staf —1D 72
Rough Haugh. High —4H 167
Rough Hay. Staf —3G 73
Roughlee. Lanc —5H 97
Roughley. W Mid —1F 61
Roughsike. Cumb —2G 113
Roughton. Linc —4B 88
Roughton. Norf —2E 78
Roughton. Shrp —1B 60
Roundbush Green. Essx —4F 53
Roundham. Som —2H 13
Roundhay. W Yor —1D 92
Round Hill. Torb —2F 9
Roundhurst Common. W Sus —2A 26
Round Oak. Shrp —2F 59
Roundstreet Common. W Sus —3B 26
Roundthwaite. Cumb —4H 103
Roundway. Wilts —5F 35
Roundyhill. Ang —3C 144
Rousdon. Devn —3F 13
Rousham. Oxon —3C 50
Rousham House —3C 50
Rous Lench. Worc —5E 61
Routh. E Yor —5E 101
Rout's Green. Buck —2F 37
Row. Corn —5A 10
Row. Cumb —1D 96 (nr. Kendal)
Row. Cumb —1H 103 (nr. Penrith)
Rowanburn. Dum —2F 113
Rowanhill. Abers —3H 161
Rowardennan. Stir —4C 134
Rowarth. Derbs —2E 85
Row Ash. Hants —1D 16
Rowberrow. Som —1H 21
Rowde. Wilts —5E 35
Rowden. Devn —3G 11
Rowden Hill. Wilts —4E 35
Rowen. Cnwy —3G 81
Rowfoot. Nmbd —3H 113
Row Green. Essx —3H 53
Row Heath. Essx —4E 55
Rowhedge. Essx —3D 54
Rowhook. W Sus —2C 26
Rowington. Warw —4G 61
Rowland. Derbs —3G 85
Rowland's Castle. Hants —1F 17
Rowlands Gill. Tyne —4E 115
Rowledge. Surr —2G 25
Rowley. Dur —5D 115
Rowley. E Yor —1C 94
Rowley. Shrp —5F 71
Rowley. Staf —3F 73
Rowley Hill. W Yor —3B 92
Rowley Regis. W Mid —2D 60
Rowlstone. Here —3G 47
Rowly. Surr —1B 26
Rowner. Hants —2D 16
Rowney Green. Worc —3E 61
Rownhams. Hants —1B 16
Rowrah. Cumb —3B 102
Rowsham. Buck —4G 51
Rowsley. Derbs —4G 85
Rowstock. Oxon —3C 36
Rowston. Linc —5H 87
Row, The. Lanc —2D 96
Rowthorne. Derbs —4B 86
Rowton. Ches —4G 83
Rowton. Shrp —2G 59 (nr. Ludlow)
Rowton. Shrp —4F 71 (nr. Shrewsbury)
Rowton. Telf —4A 72
Row Town. Surr —4B 38
Roxburgh. Bord —1B 120
Roxby. N Lin —3C 94
Roxby. N Yor —3E 107
Roxton. Beds —5A 64
Roxwell. Essx —5G 53
Royal Academy —London 192
Royal Albert Bridge —3A 8
Royal Armouries —Leeds 190
Royal Botanic Gdn., Edinburgh —2F 129
Royal Botanic Gdns., Kew WH —3C 38
Royal Cornwall Mus. —4C 6
Royal Crown Derby Mus. —188
Royal Leamington Spa. Warw —4H 61
Royal Oak. Darl —2F 105
Royal Oak. Lanc —4C 90
Royal Oak. N Yor —2F 101
Royal Pavillion —Brighton 186
Royal Pump Room Mus., Harrogate —4E 99
Royal's Green. Ches —1A 72
Royal Shakespeare Theatre —Stratford 196
Royal Tunbridge Wells. Kent —2G 27
Royal Worcester Porcelain Mus. —197
Roybridge. High —5E 149
Roydon. Essx —4E 53
Roydon. Norf —2C 66 (nr. Diss)
Roydon. Norf —3G 77 (nr. King's Lynn)
Roydon Hamlet. Essx —5E 53
Royston. Herts —1D 52
Royston. S Yor —3D 92
Royston Water. Som —1F 13
Royton. G Man —4H 91
Ruabon. Wrex —1F 71
Ruaig. Arg —4B 138
Ruan High Lanes. Corn —5D 6
Ruan Lanihorne. Corn —4C 6

Ruan Minor. Corn —5E 5
Ruarach. High —1B 148
Ruardean. Glos —4B 48
Ruardean Hill. Glos —4B 48
Ruardean Woodside. Glos —4B 48
Rubery. W Mid —3D 61
Ruchazie. Glas —3H 127
Ruckcroft. Cumb —5G 113
Ruckinge. Kent —2E 29
Ruckland. Linc —3C 88
Rucklers Lane. Herts —5A 52
Ruckley. Shrp —5H 71
Rudbaxton. Pemb —2D 42
Rudby. N Yor —4B 106
Ruddington. Notts —2C 74
Ruddington Knitter's Mus. —2C 74
Rudford. Glos —3C 48
Rudge. Shrp —1C 60
Rudge. Wilts —1D 22
Rudge Heath. Shrp —1B 60
Rudgeway. S Glo —3B 34
Rudgwick. W Sus —2B 26
Rudhall. Here —3B 48
Rudheath. Ches —3A 84
Rudheath Woods. Ches —3B 84
Rudley Green. Essx —5B 54
Rudloe. Wilts —4D 34
Rudry. Cphy —3E 33
Rudston. E Yor —3E 101
Rudyard. Staf —5D 84
Rufford. Lanc —3C 90
Rufford Abbey EH —4D 86
Rufford Old Hall NT —3C 90
Rufforth. York —4H 99
Rugby. Warw —3C 62
Rugeley. Staf —4E 73
Ruglen. S Ayr —4B 116
Ruilick. High —4H 157
Ruisaurie. High —4G 157
Ruishton. Som —4F 21
Ruisigearraidh. W Isl —1E 170
Ruislip. G Lon —2B 38
Ruislip Common. G Lon —2B 38
Rumbling Bridge. Per —4C 136
Rumburgh. Suff —2F 67
Rumford. Corn —1C 6
Rumford. Falk —2C 128
Rumney. Card —4F 33
Rumwell. Som —4E 21
Runcorn. Hal —2H 83
Runcton. W Sus —2G 17
Runcton Holme. Norf —5F 77
Rundlestone. Devn —5F 11
Runfold. Surr —2G 25
Runhall. Norf —5C 78
Runham. Norf —4G 79
Runnington. Som —4E 20
Runnymede NT —3A 38
Runshaw Moor. Lanc —3D 90
Runswick. N Yor —3F 107
Runtaleave. Ang —2B 144
Runwell. Essx —1B 40
Ruscombe. Wok —4F 37
Rushall. Here —2B 48
Rushall. Norf —2D 66
Rushall. W Mid —5E 73
Rushall. Wilts —1G 23
Rushbrooke. Suff —4A 66
Rushbury. Shrp —1H 59
Rushden. Herts —2D 52
Rushden. Nptn —4G 63
Rushenden. Kent —3D 40
Rushford. Devn —5E 11
Rushford. Suff —2B 66
Rush Green. Herts —3C 52
Rushlake Green. E Sus —4H 27
Rushmere. Suff —2G 67
Rushmere St Andrew. Suff —1E 55
Rushmoor. Surr —2G 25
Rushock. Worc —3C 60
Rusholme. G Man —1C 84
Rushton. Ches —4H 83
Rushton. Nptn —2F 63
Rushton. Shrp —5A 72
Rushton Spencer. Staf —4D 84
Rushton Triangular Lodge EH —2F 63
Rushwick. Worc —5C 60
Rushyford. Dur —2F 105
Ruskie. Stir —3F 135
Ruskington. Linc —5H 87
Rusland. Cumb —1C 96
Rusper. W Sus —2D 26
Ruspidge. Glos —4B 48
Russell Cotes Gallery —Bournemouth 186
Russell's Water. Oxon —3F 37
Russel's Green. Suff —3E 67
Russ Hill. Surr —1D 26
Russland. Orkn —6C 172
Rusthall. Kent —2G 27
Rustington. W Sus —5B 26
Ruston. N Yor —1D 100
Ruston Parva. E Yor —3E 101
Ruswarp. N Yor —4F 107
Rutherglen. S Lan —3H 127
Ruthernbridge. Corn —2E 6
Ruthin. Den —5D 82
Ruthin. V Glam —4C 32
Ruthrieston. Aber —3G 153
Ruthven. Abers —4C 160
Ruthven. Ang —4B 144
Ruthven. High —5C 158
(nr. Inverness)
Ruthven. High —4B 150
(nr. Kingussie)
Ruthvoes. Corn —2D 6
Ruthwaite. Cumb —1D 102
Ruthwell. Dum —3C 112
Rutland Railway —4F 75
Rutland Water —5F 75
Ruxton Green. Here —4A 48
Ruyton-XI-Towns. Shrp —3F 71
Ryal. Nmbd —2D 114
Ryall. Dors —3H 13
Ryall. Worc —1D 48
Ryarsh. Kent —5A 40
Rychraggan. High —5G 157
Rydal. Cumb —4E 103
Rydal Mount —4E 103
Ryde. IOW —3D 16
Rye. E Sus —3D 28
Ryecroft Gate. Staf —4D 84
Ryedale Folk Mus. —5E 107
Ryeford. Here —3B 48
Rye Foreign. E Sus —3D 28
Rye Harbour. E Sus —4D 28
Ryehill. E Yor —2F 95
Rye Street. Worc —2C 48
Ryhall. Rut —4H 75
Ryhill. W Yor —3D 93
Ryhnie. Abers —1B 152
Ryhope. Tyne —4H 115
Ryhope Colliery. Tyne —4H 115
Rylands. Notts —2C 74
Rylstone. N Yor —4B 98
Ryme Intrinseca. Dors —1A 14
Ryther. N Yor —1F 93
Ryton. Glos —2C 48
Ryton. N Yor —2B 100
Ryton. Shrp —5B 72
Ryton. Tyne —3E 115
Ryton. Warw —2A 62
Ryton-on-Dunsmore. Warw —3A 62
Ryton Organic Gdns. —3B 62
Ryton Woodside. Tyne —3E 115

Saasaig. High —3E 147
Sabden. Lanc —1F 91
Sacombe. Herts —4D 52
Sacriston. Dur —5F 115
Sadberge. Darl —3A 106
Saddell. Arg —2B 122
Saddington. Leics —1D 62
Saddle Bow. Norf —4F 77
Saddlescombe. W Sus —4D 26
Saddleworth. G Man —4H 91
Sadgill. Cumb —4F 103
Saffron Walden. Essx —2F 53
Sageston. Pemb —4E 43
Saham Hills. Norf —5B 78
Saham Toney. Norf —5A 78
Saighdinis. W Isl —2D 170
Saighton. Ches —4G 83
Sain Dunwyd. V Glam —5C 32
Sain Hilari. V Glam —4D 32
Sainsbury Centre for the Arts —5D 78
St Abbs. Bord —3F 131
St Abb's Head NTS —3F 131
St Agnes. Corn —3B 6
St Albans. Herts —5B 52
St Albans Cathedral —5B 52
St Allen. Corn —3C 6
St Andrews. Fife —2H 137
St Andrews Cathedral & Mus. HS —2H 137
St Andrews Major. V Glam —4E 33
St Anne's. Lanc —2B 90
St Ann's. Dum —5C 118
St Ann's Chapel. Corn —5E 11
St Ann's Chapel. Devn —4C 8
St Anthony. Corn —4E 5
(nr. Helford)
St Anthony. Corn —5C 6
(nr. St Mawes)
St Arvans. Mon —2A 34
St Asaph. Den —3C 82
St Athan. V Glam —5D 32
Sain Tathan. V Glam —5D 32
St Augustine's Abbey EH —Canterbury 187
St Austell. Corn —3E 6
St Bartholomew's Hill. Wilts —4E 23
St Bees. Cumb —3A 102
St Blazey. Corn —3E 7
St Blazey Gate. Corn —3E 7
St Boswells. Bord —1A 120
St Breock. Corn —1D 6
St Breward. Corn —5A 10
St Briavels. Glos —5A 48
St Brides. Pemb —3B 42
St Bride's Major. V Glam —4B 32
St Bride's Netherwent. Mon —3H 33
St Bride's-super-Ely. V Glam —4D 32
St Brides Wentlooge. Newp —3F 33
St Budeaux. Plym —3A 8
Saintbury. Glos —2G 49
St Buryan. Corn —4B 4
St Catherine. Bath —4C 34
St Catherines. Arg —3A 134
St Clears. Carm —3G 43
St Cleer. Corn —2G 7
St Clement. Corn —4C 6
St Clether. Corn —4C 10
St Colmac. Arg —3B 126
St Columb Major. Corn —2D 6
St Columb Minor. Corn —2C 6
St Columb Road. Corn —3D 6
St Combs. Abers —2H 161
St Cross. Hants —4C 24
St Cross South Elmham. Suff —2E 67
St Cyrus. Abers —2G 145
St David's. Pemb —2B 42
St David's. Per —1B 136
St David's Bishop's Palace CADW —2B 42
St David's Cathedral —2B 42
St Day. Corn —4B 6
St Dennis. Corn —3D 6
St Dogmaels. Pemb —1B 44
St Dogmaels Abbey CADW —1B 44
St Dominick. Corn —2H 7
St Donat's. V Glam —5C 32
St Edith's Marsh. Wilts —5E 35
St Endellion. Corn —1D 6
St Enoder. Corn —3C 6
St Erme. Corn —4C 6
St Erney. Corn —3H 7
St Erth. Corn —3C 4
St Erth Praze. Corn —3C 4
St Ervan. Corn —1C 6
St Eval. Corn —2C 6
St Ewe. Corn —4D 6
St Fagans. Card —4E 32
St Fergus. Abers —3H 161
St Fillans. Per —1F 135
St Florence. Pemb —4E 43
St Gennys. Corn —3B 10
St George. Cnwy —3B 82
St George's. N Som —5G 33
St Georges. V Glam —4D 32
St Germans. Corn —3H 7
St Gile's Hill. Hants —4C 24
St Giles in the Wood. Devn —1F 11
St Giles on the Heath. Devn —4D 10
St Gluvias. Corn —5B 6
St Harmon. Powy —3B 58
St Helena. Warw —5G 73
St Helen Auckland. Dur —2E 105
St Helens. Cumb —1B 102
St Helens. E Sus —4C 28
St Helens. IOW —4E 17
St Helens. Mers —1G 83
St Hilary. Corn —3C 4
St Hilary. V Glam —4D 32
Saint Hill. Devn —2D 12
Saint Hill. W Sus —2E 27
St Illtyd. Blae —5F 47
St Ippolyts. Herts —3B 52
St Ishmael. Carm —5D 44
St Ishmael's. Pemb —4C 42
St Issey. Corn —1D 6
St Ive. Corn —2H 7
St Ives. Cambs —3C 64
St Ives. Corn —2C 4
St Ives. Dors —2G 15
St James End. Nptn —4E 63
St James South Elmham. Suff —2F 67
St Jidgey. Corn —2D 6
St John. Corn —3A 8
St John's. IOM —3B 108
St Johns. Worc —5C 60
St John's Chapel. Devn —4F 19
St John's Chapel. Dur —1B 104
St John's Fen End. Norf —4E 77
St John's Hall. Dur —1D 104
St John's Jerusalem NT —4G 39
St John's Town of Dalry. Dum —1D 110
St Judes. IOM —2D 108
St Just. Corn —5C 6
(nr. Falmouth)
St Just. Corn —3A 4
(nr. Penzance)
St Just in Roseland. Corn —5C 6
St Katherines. Abers —5E 161
St Keverne. Corn —4E 5
St Kew. Corn —5A 10
St Kew Highway. Corn —5A 10
St Keyne. Corn —2G 7
St Lawrence. Corn —2E 7
St Lawrence. Essx —5C 54
St Lawrence. IOW —5D 16
St Leonards. Buck —5H 51
St Leonards. Dors —2G 15
St Leonards. E Sus —5B 28
St Levan. Corn —4A 4
St Lythans. V Glam —4E 32
St Mabyn. Corn —5A 10
St Madoes. Per —1D 136
St Margarets. Here —2G 47
St Margaret's. Herts —4A 52
(nr. Hemel Hempstead)
St Margarets. Herts —4D 53
(nr. Hoddesdon)
St Margaret's. Wilts —5G 35
St Margaret's at Cliffe. Kent —1H 29
St Margaret's Hope. Orkn —8D 172
St Margaret South Elmham. Suff —2F 67
St Mark's. IOM —4C 108
St Martin. Corn —4E 5
(nr. Helston)
St Martin. Corn —3G 7
(nr. Looe)
St Martins. Per —5A 144
St Martin's. Shrp —2F 71
St Mary Bourne. Hants —1C 24
St Marychurch. Torb —2F 9
St Mary Church. V Glam —4D 32
St Mary Cray. G Lon —4F 39
St Mary Hill. V Glam —4C 32
St Mary Hoo. Medw —3C 40
St Mary in the Marsh. Kent —3E 29
St Mary's. Orkn —7D 172
St Mary's Airport. IOS —1B 4
St Mary's Bay. Kent —3E 29
St Maughan's Green. Mon —4H 47
St Mawes. Corn —5C 6
St Mawes Castle EH —5C 6
St Mawgan. Corn —2C 6
St Mellion. Corn —2H 7
St Mellons. Card —3F 33
St Merryn. Corn —1C 6
St Mewan. Corn —3D 6
St Michael Caerhays. Corn —4D 6
St Michael Penkevil. Corn —4C 6
St Michaels. Kent —2C 28
St Michaels. Torb —3E 9
St Michaels. Worc —4H 59
St Michael's Mount NT —4C 4
St Michael's on Wyre. Lanc —5D 96
St Michael South Elmham. Suff —2F 67
St Minver. Corn —1D 6
St Monans. Fife —3H 137
St Neot. Corn —2F 7
St Neots. Cambs —4A 64
St Newlyn East. Corn —3C 6
St Nicholas. Pemb —1D 42
St Nicholas. V Glam —4D 32
St Nicholas at Wade. Kent —4G 41
St Nicholas South Elmham. Suff —2F 67
St Ninians. Stir —4H 135
St Olaves. Norf —1G 67
St Osyth. Essx —4E 54
St Osyth Heath. Essx —4E 55
St Owen's Cross. Here —3A 48
St Paul's Cathedral —London 193
St Paul's Cray. G Lon —4F 39
St Paul's Walden. Herts —3B 52
St Peter's. Kent —4H 41
St Peter the Great. Worc —5C 60
St Petrox. Pemb —5D 42
St Pinnock. Corn —2G 7
St Quivox. S Ayr —2C 116
St Ruan. Corn —5E 5
St Stephen. Corn —3D 6
St Stephens. Corn —4D 10
(nr. Launceston)
St Stephens. Corn —3A 8
(nr. Saltash)
St Teath. Corn —4A 10
St Thomas. Devn —3C 12
St Thomas. Swan —3F 31
St Tudy. Corn —5A 10
St Twynnells. Pemb —5D 42
St Veep. Corn —3F 7
St Vigeans. Ang —4F 145
St Wenn. Corn —2D 6
St Weonards. Here —3H 47
St Winnolls. Corn —3H 7
St Winnow. Corn —3F 7
Salcombe. Devn —5D 8
Salcombe Regis. Devn —4E 13
Salcott. Essx —4C 54
Sale. G Man —1B 84
Saleby. Linc —3D 88
Sale Green. Worc —5D 60
Salehurst. E Sus —3B 28
Salem. Carm —3G 45
Salem. Cdgn —2F 57
Salem. Gwyn —5E 81
Salen. Arg —4G 139
Salen. High —2A 140
Salesbury. Lanc —1E 91
Saleway. Worc —5D 60
Salford. Beds —2H 51
Salford. G Man —1C 84 & Manchester 191
Salford. Oxon —3A 50
Salford Mus. & Art Gallery —Manchester 191
Salford Priors. Warw —5E 61
Salfords. Surr —1D 27
Salhouse. Norf —4F 79
Saligo. Arg —3A 124
Saline. Fife —4C 136
Salisbury. Wilts —3G 23 & 195
Salisbury Cathedral —4G 23
Salkeld Dykes. Cumb —1G 103
Sallachan. High —2D 141
Sallachy. High —5B 156
(nr. Darnie)
Sallachy. High —3C 164
(nr. Lairg)
Salle. Norf —3D 78
Salmonby. Linc —3C 88
Salmond's Muir. Ang —5E 145
Salperton. Glos —3F 49
Salph End. Beds —5H 63
Salsburgh. N Lan —3B 128
Salt. Staf —3D 72
Salta. Cumb —5B 112
Saltaire. W Yor —1B 92
Saltaire World Heritage Village —1B 92
Saltash. Corn —3A 8
Saltburn. High —2B 158
Saltburn-by-the-Sea. Red C —2D 106
Saltby. Leics —3F 75
Saltcoats. Cumb —5B 102
Saltcoats. N Ayr —5D 126
Saltdean. Brig —5E 27
Salt End. E Yor —2E 95
Salter. Lanc —3F 97
Salterforth. Lanc —5A 98
Salters Lode. Norf —5E 77
Salterswall. Ches —4A 84
Salterton. Wilts —3G 23
Saltfleet. Linc —1D 88
Saltfleetby All Saints. Linc —1D 88
Saltfleetby St Clements. Linc —1D 88
Saltfleetby St Peter. Linc —2D 88
Saltford. Bath —5B 34
Salthouse. Norf —1C 78
Saltmarshe. E Yor —2A 94
Saltmead. Card —4E 33
Saltness. Orkn —8B 172
Saltness. Shet —7D 173
Saltney. Flin —4F 83
Salton. N Yor —1B 100
Saltram NT —3B 8
Saltrens. Devn —4E 19
Saltwick. Nmbd —2E 115
Saltwood. Kent —2F 29
Salum. Arg —4B 138
Salwarpe. Worc —4C 60
Salwayash. Dors —3H 13
Samalaman. High —1A 140
Sambourne. Warw —4E 61
Sambourne. Wilts —2D 22
Sambrook. Telf —3B 72
Samhia. W Isl —2C 170
Samlesbury. Lanc —1D 90
Samlesbury Bottoms. Lanc —2E 90
Samlesbury Hall —1E 90
Sampford Arundel. Som —1E 12
Sampford Brett. Som —2D 20
Sampford Courtenay. Devn —2G 11
Sampford Peverell. Devn —1D 12
Sampford Spiney. Devn —5F 11
Samsonlane. Orkn —5F 172
Samuelston. E Lot —2A 130
Sanaigmore. Arg —2A 124
Sancreed. Corn —4B 4
Sancton. E Yor —1C 94
Sanctuary, The EH —5G 35
Sand. High —4D 162
Sand. Shet —7E 173
Sand. Som —2H 21
Sandaig. High —3F 147
Sandale. Cumb —5D 112
Sandal Magna. W Yor —3D 92
Sandavore. High —5C 146
Sanday Airport. Orkn —3F 172
Sandbach. Ches —4B 84
Sandbank. Arg —1C 126
Sandbanks. Pool —4F 15
Sandend. Abers —2C 160
Sanderstead. G Lon —4E 39
Sandfields. Neat —3G 31
Sandford. Cumb —3A 104
Sandford. Devn —2B 12
Sandford. Dors —4E 15
Sandford. Hants —2G 15
Sandford. IOW —4D 16
Sandford. N Som —1H 21
Sandford. Shrp —3F 71
(nr. Oswestry)
Sandford. Shrp —2H 71
(nr. Whitchurch)
Sandford. S Lan —5A 128
Sandfordhill. Abers —4H 161
Sandford-on-Thames. Oxon —5D 50
Sandford Orcas. Dors —4B 22
Sandford Orcas Manor House —4B 22
Sandford St Martin. Oxon —3C 50
Sandgate. Kent —2F 29
Sandgreen. Dum —4C 110
Sandhaven. Abers —2G 161
Sandhead. Dum —4F 109
Sandhill. Cambs —2E 65
Sandhills. Dors —1B 14
Sandhills. Surr —2A 26
Sandhoe. Nmbd —3C 114
Sand Hole. E Yor —1B 94
Sandholme. E Yor —1B 94
Sandholme. Linc —2C 76
Sandhurst. Brac —5G 37
Sandhurst. Glos —3D 48
Sandhurst. Kent —3B 28
Sandhurst Cross. Kent —3B 28
Sandhutton. N Yor —1F 99
(nr. Thirsk)
Sand Hutton. N Yor —4A 100
(nr. York)
Sandiacre. Derbs —2B 74
Sandilands. Linc —2E 89
Sandiway. Ches —3A 84
Sandleheath. Hants —1G 15
Sandling. Kent —5B 40
Sandlow Green. Ches —4B 84
Sandness. Shet —6C 173
Sandon. Essx —5H 53
Sandon. Herts —2D 52
Sandon. Staf —3D 72
Sandonbank. Staf —3D 72
Sandon Hall —3D 72
Sandown. IOW —4D 16
Sandplace. Corn —3G 7
Sandridge. Herts —4B 52
Sandridge. Wilts —5E 35
Sandringham —3F 77
Sandringham. Norf —3F 77
Sandsend. N Yor —3F 107
Sandside. Cumb —2C 96
Sandsound. Shet —7E 173
Sands, The. Surr —2G 25
Sandtoft. N Lin —4H 93
Sandvoe. Shet —2E 173
Sandway. Kent —5C 40
Sandwich. Kent —5H 41
Sandwick. Cumb —3F 103
Sandwick. Orkn —6B 172
(on Mainland)
Sandwick. Orkn —9D 172
(on South Ronaldsay)
Sandwick. Shet —9F 173
(on Mainland)
Sandwick. Shet —5G 173
(on Whalsay)
Sandwith. Cumb —3A 102
Sandy. Beds —1B 52
Sandy. Carm —5E 45
Sandy Bank. Linc —5B 88
Sandycroft. Flin —4F 83
Sandy Cross. Here —5A 60
Sandygate. Devn —5B 12
Sandygate. IOM —2C 108
Sandy Haven. Pemb —4C 42
Sandyhills. Dum —4F 111
Sandylands. Lanc —3D 96
Sandylane. Swan —4E 31
Sandy Lane. Wilts —5E 35
Sandypark. Devn —4H 11
Sandystones. Bord —2H 119
Sandyway. Here —3H 47
Sangobeg. High —2E 167
Sangomore. High —2E 166
Sankyn's Green. Worc —4B 60
Sanna. High —2F 139
Sanndabhaig. W Isl —4G 171
(on Lewis)
Sanndabhaig. W Isl —4D 170
(on South Uist)
Sannox. N Ayr —5B 126
Sanquhar. Dum —3G 117
Santon. Cumb —4C 102
Santon Bridge. Cumb —4C 102
Santon Downham. Suff —2H 65
Sapcote. Leics —1B 62
Sapey Common. Here —4B 60
Sapiston. Suff —3B 66
Sapley. Cambs —3B 64
Sapperton. Derbs —2F 73
Sapperton. Glos —5E 49
Sapperton. Linc —2H 75
Saracen's Head. Linc —3C 76
Sarclet. High —4F 169

Sardis. Carm —5F 45
Sardis. Pemb —4D 42
(nr. Milford Haven)
Sardis. Pemb —4F 43
(nr. Tenby)
Sarisbury. Hants —2D 16
Sarn. B'end —3C 32
Sarn. Powy —1E 58
Sarnau. Carm —3E 45
Sarnau. Cdgn —5C 56
Sarnau. Gwyn —2B 70
Sarnau. Powy —2D 46
(nr. Brecon)
Sarnau. Powy —4E 71
(nr. Welshpool)
Sarn Bach. Gwyn —3C 68
Sarnesfield. Here —5F 59
Sarn Meyllteyrn. Gwyn —2B 68
Saron. Carm —4G 45
(nr. Ammanford)
Saron. Carm —2D 45
(nr. Newcastle Emlyn)
Saron. Gwyn —4E 81
(nr. Bethel)
Saron. Gwyn —5D 80
(nr. Bontnewydd)
Sarratt. Herts —1B 38
Sarre. Kent —4G 41
Sarsden. Oxon —3A 50
Satley. Dur —5E 115
Satron. N Yor —5C 104
Satterleigh. Devn —4G 19
Satterthwaite. Cumb —5E 103
Satwell. Oxon —3F 37
Sauchen. Abers —2D 152
Saucher. Per —5A 144
Saughall. Ches —3F 83
Saughtree. Bord —5H 119
Saul. Glos —5C 48
Saundby. Notts —2E 87
Saundersfoot. Pemb —4F 43
Saunderton. Buck —5F 51
Saunderton Lee. Buck —2G 37
Saunton. Devn —3E 19
Sausthorpe. Linc —4C 88
Saval. High —3C 164
Saverley Green. Staf —2D 72
Savill Gdn. —3A 38
Sawbridge. Warw —4C 62
Sawbridgeworth. Herts —4E 53
Sawdon. N Yor —1D 100
Sawley. Derbs —2B 74
Sawley. Lanc —5G 97
Sawley. N Yor —3E 99
Sawston. Cambs —1E 53
Sawtry. Cambs —2A 64
Saxby. Leics —3F 75
Saxby. Linc —2H 87
Saxby All Saints. N Lin —3C 94
Saxelby. Leics —3D 74
Saxham Street. Suff —4C 66
Saxilby. Linc —3F 87
Saxlingham. Norf —2C 78
Saxlingham Green. Norf —1E 67
Saxlingham Nethergate. Norf —1E 67
Saxlingham Thorpe. Norf —1E 66
Saxmundham. Suff —4F 67
Saxondale. Notts —1D 74
Saxon Street. Cambs —5F 65
Saxtead. Suff —4E 67
Saxtead Green. Suff —4E 67
Saxtead Green Post Mill EH —4E 67
Saxthorpe. Norf —2D 78
Saxton. N Yor —1E 93
Sayers Common. W Sus —4D 26
Scackleton. N Yor —2A 100
Scadabhagh. W Isl —8D 171
Scafell Pike NT —4D 102
Scaftworth. Notts —1D 86
Scagglethorpe. N Yor —2C 100
Scaitcliffe. Lanc —2F 91
Scaladal. W Isl —6D 171
Scalasaig. Arg —4A 132
Scalby. E Yor —2B 94
Scalby. N Yor —5H 107
Scalby Mills. N Yor —5H 107
Scaldwell. Nptn —3E 63
Scaleby. Cumb —3F 113
Scaleby Hill. Cumb —3F 113
Scale Houses. Cumb —5G 113
Scales. Cumb —2B 96
(nr. Barrow-in-Furness)
Scales. Cumb —2E 103
(nr. Keswick)
Scalford. Leics —3E 75
Scaling. Red C —3E 107
Scaling Dam. Red C —3E 107
Scalloway. Shet —8E 173
Scalpaigh. W Isl —8E 171
Scalpay House. High —1E 147
Scamblesby. Linc —3B 88
Scamodale. High —1C 140
Scampston. N Yor —2C 100
Scampston Hall —2C 100
Scampton. Linc —3G 87
Scaniport. High —5A 158
Scapa. Orkn —7D 172
Scapegoat Hill. W Yor —3A 92
Scar. Orkn —3F 172
Scarasta. W Isl —8C 171
Scarborough. N Yor —1E 101
Scarborough Hall EH —1E 101
(Scarborough Sea Life & Marine Sanctuary) —1E 101
Scarcliffe. Derbs —4B 86
Scarcroft. W Yor —5F 99
Scardroy. High —3E 156
Scarfskerry. High —1E 169
Scargill. Dur —3D 104
Scarinish. Arg —4B 138
Scarisbrick. Lanc —3B 90
Scarning. Norf —4B 78
Scarrington. Notts —1E 75
Scarth Hill. Lanc —4C 90
Scartho. NE Lin —4F 95
Scarvister. Shet —7E 173
Scatness. Shet —10E 173
Scatwell. High —3F 157
Scaur. Dum —4F 111
Scawby. N Lin —4C 94
Scawby Brook. N Lin —4C 94
Scawsby. S Yor —4F 93
Scawton. N Yor —1H 99
Scayne's Hill. W Sus —3E 27
Scethrog. Powy —3E 46
Scholar Green. Ches —5C 84
Scholes. G Man —4E 90
Scholes. W Yor —2B 92
(nr. Bradford)
Scholes. W Yor —4B 92
(nr. Holmfirth)
Scholes. W Yor —1D 93
(nr. Leeds)
Scholey Hill. W Yor —2D 93
School Aycliffe. Dur —2F 105
School Green. Ches —4A 84
School Green. Essx —2H 53
Scissett. W Yor —3C 92
Scleddau. Pemb —1D 42
Scofton. Notts —2D 86
Scole. Norf —3D 66
Scolpaig. W Isl —1C 170
Scolt Head Island NT —1H 77
Scolton. Pemb —2D 43
Scone Palace —1D 136
Sconser. High —5E 155
Scoonie. Fife —3F 137
Scopwick. Linc —5H 87
Scoraig. High —4E 163
Scorborough. E Yor —5E 101
Scorrier. Corn —4B 6
Scorriton. Devn —2D 8
Scorton. Lanc —5E 97
Scorton. N Yor —4F 105
Sco Ruston. Norf —3E 79
Scotby. Cumb —4F 113
Scotch Corner. N Yor —4F 105
Scotch Whisky Heritage Centre —Edinburgh 189
Scotforth. Lanc —3D 97
Scot Hay. Staf —1C 72
Scothern. Linc —3H 87
Scotland End. Oxon —2B 50
Scotlandwell. Per —3D 136
Scot Lane End. G Man —4E 91
Scotney Castle NT —2A 28
Scotsburn. High —1B 158
Scotsburn. Mor —2G 159
Scotsdike. Cumb —2E 113
Scots Gap. Nmbd —1D 114
Scotstarvit Tower NTS —2F 137
Scotstoun. Glas —3G 127
Scotstown. High —2C 140
Scotswood. Tyne —3F 115
Scottas. High —3F 147
Scotter. Linc —4B 94
Scotterthorpe. Linc —4B 94
Scottish Exhibition & Conference Centre —Glasgow 189
Scottish Maritime Mus. Irvine —1C 116
Scottish Mining Mus. —3G 129
Scottish Nat. Football Mus. —3G 127
Scottish Nat. Gallery of Modern Art —Edinburgh 189
Scottish Nat. Portrait Gallery —Edinburgh 189
Scottish Parliament —Edinburgh 189
Scottlethorpe. Linc —3H 75
Scotton. Linc —1F 87
Scotton. N Yor —5E 105
(nr. Catterick Garrison)
Scotton. N Yor —4F 99
(nr. Harrogate)
Scottow. Norf —3E 79
Scoulton. Norf —5B 78
Scounslow Green. Staf —3E 73
Scourie. High —4B 166
Scourie More. High —4B 166
Scousburgh. Shet —10E 173
Scout Green. Cumb —4G 103
Scouthead. G Man —4H 91
Scrabster. High —1C 168
Scrafield. Linc —4C 88
Scrainwood. Nmbd —4D 121
Scrane End. Linc —1C 76
Scraptoft. Leic —5D 74
Scratby. Norf —4H 79
Scrayingham. N Yor —3B 100
Scredington. Linc —1H 75
Scremby. Linc —4D 88
Scremerston. Nmbd —5G 131
Screveton. Notts —1E 75
Scrivelsby. Linc —4B 88
Scriven. N Yor —4F 99
Scronkey. Lanc —5D 96
Scrooby. Notts —1D 86
Scropton. Derbs —2F 73
Scrub Hill. Linc —5B 88
Scruton. N Yor —5A 106
Scuggate. Cumb —2F 113
Sculcoates. Hull —1D 94
Sculthorpe. Norf —2A 78
Scunthorpe. N Lin —3B 94
Scurlage. Swan —4D 30
Sea. Som —1G 13
Seaborough. Dors —2H 13
Seabridge. Staf —1C 72
Seabrook. Kent —2F 29
Seaburn. Tyne —4H 115
Seacombe. Mers —1F 83
Seacroft. Linc —4E 89
Seacroft. W Yor —1D 92
Seadyke. Linc —2C 76
Seafield. High —5G 165
Seafield. Midl —3F 129
Seafield. S Ayr —2C 116
Seafield. W Lot —3D 128
Seaford. E Sus —5F 27
Seaforth. Mers —1F 83
Seagrave. Leics —4D 74
Seaham. Dur —5H 115
Seahouses. Nmbd —1G 121
Seal. Kent —5G 39
Sealand. Flin —4F 83
Seale. Surr —2G 25
Seamer. N Yor —1E 101
(nr. Scarborough)
Seamer. N Yor —3B 106
(nr. Stokesley)
Seamill. N Ayr —5C 126
Sea Mills. Bris —4A 34
Sea Palling. Norf —3G 79
Searby. Linc —4D 94
Seasalter. Kent —4E 41
Seascale. Cumb —4B 102
Seaside. Per —1E 137
Seater. High —1F 169
Seathorne. Linc —4E 89
Seathwaite. Cumb —3D 102
(nr. Borrowdale)
Seathwaite. Cumb —5D 102
(nr. Ulpha)
Seatle. Cumb —1C 96
Seatoller. Cumb —3D 102
Seaton. Corn —3H 7
Seaton. Cumb —1B 102
Seaton. Devn —3F 13
Seaton. Dur —5G 115
Seaton. E Yor —5F 101
Seaton. Nmbd —2G 115
Seaton. Rut —1G 63
Seaton Burn. Tyne —2F 115
Seaton Carew. Hart —2C 106
Seaton Delaval. Nmbd —2G 115
Seaton Delaval Hall —2G 115
Seaton Junction. Devn —3F 13
Seaton Ross. E Yor —5B 100
Seaton Sluice. Nmbd —2G 115
Seaton Tramway —3F 13
Seatown. Abers —2C 160
Seatown. Dors —3H 13
Seatown. Mor —2C 160
(nr. Cullen)
Seatown. Mor —1G 159
(nr. Lossiemouth)
Seave Green. N Yor —4C 106
Seaview. IOW —3E 17
Seaville. Cumb —4C 112
Seavington St Mary. Som —1H 13
Seavington St Michael. Som —1H 13
Seawick. Essx —4E 55
Sebastopol. Cphy —5E 47
Sebastopol. Torf —2F 33
Sebergham. Cumb —5E 113
Seckington. Warw —5G 73
Second Coast. High —4D 162
Sedbergh. Cumb —5H 103
Sedbury. Glos —2A 34
Sedbusk. N Yor —5B 104
Sedgeberrow. Worc —2F 49
Sedgebrook. Linc —2F 75
Sedgefield. Dur —2A 106
Sedgeford. Norf —2G 77
Sedgehill. Wilts —4D 22
Sedgley. W Mid —1D 60
Sedgwick. Cumb —1E 97
Sedlescombe. E Sus —4B 28
Seend. Wilts —5E 35
Seend Cleeve. Wilts —5E 35
Seer Green. Buck —1A 38
Seething. Norf —1F 67
Sefton. Mers —4B 90
Sefton Park. Mers —2F 83
Seggat. Abers —4E 161
Seghill. Nmbd —2F 115
Seifton. Shrp —2G 59
Seighford. Staf —3C 72
Seilebost. W Isl —8C 171
Seisdon. Staf —1C 60
Seisiadar. W Isl —4H 171
Selattyn. Shrp —2E 71
Selborne. Hants —3F 25
Selby. N Yor —1G 93
Selham. W Sus —3A 26
Selkirk. Bord —2G 119
Sellack. Here —3A 48
Sellafirth. Shet —2G 173
Sellindge. Kent —2F 29
Selling. Kent —5E 41
Sells Green. Wilts —5E 35
Selly Manor —2E 61
Selly Oak. W Mid —2E 61
Selmeston. E Sus —5G 27
Selsdon. G Lon —4E 39
Selsey. W Sus —3G 17
Selsfield Common. W Sus —2E 27
Selside. Cumb —5G 103
Selside. N Yor —2G 97
Selsley. Glos —5D 48
Selsted. Kent —1G 29
Selston. Notts —5B 86
Selworthy. Som —2C 20
Semblister. Shet —6E 173
Semer. Suff —1D 54
Semington. Wilts —5D 35
Semley. Wilts —4D 23
Send. Surr —5B 38
Send Marsh. Surr —5B 38
Senghenydd. Cphy —2E 32
Sennen. Corn —4A 4
Sennen Cove. Corn —4A 4
Sennicotts. W Sus —2G 17
Sennybridge. Powy —3C 46
Serlby. Notts —2D 86
Sessay. N Yor —2G 99
Setchey. Norf —4F 77
Setley. Hants —2B 16
Setter. Shet —3F 173
Settiscarth. Orkn —6C 172
Settle. N Yor —3H 97
Settrington. N Yor —2C 100
Seven Ash. Som —3E 21
Sevenhampton. Glos —3F 49
Sevenhampton. Swin —2H 35
Sevenoaks. Kent —5G 39
Sevenoaks Weald. Kent —5G 39
Seven Sisters. Neat —5B 46
Seven Springs. Glos —4E 49
Severn Beach. S Glo —3A 34
Severn Stoke. Worc —1D 48
Severn Valley Railway —2B 60
Sevington. Kent —1E 29
Sewards End. Essx —2F 53
Sewardstone. Essx —1E 39
Sewell. Beds —3H 51
Sewerby. E Yor —3F 101
Sewerby Hall —3G 101
Seworgan. Corn —5B 6
Sewstern. Leics —3F 75
Sezincote —2G 49
Sgallairidh. W Isl —9B 170
Sgarasta Mhor. W Isl —8C 171
Sgiogarstaigh. W Isl —1H 171
Sgreadan. Arg —4A 132
Shabbington. Buck —5E 51
Shackerley. Shrp —5C 72
Shackerstone. Leics —5A 74
Shackleford. Surr —1A 26
Shadforth. Dur —5G 115
Shadingfield. Suff —2G 67
Shadoxhurst. Kent —2D 28
Shadsworth. Bkbn —2E 91
Shadwell. Norf —2B 66
Shadwell. W Yor —1D 92
Shaftesbury. Dors —4D 22
Shaftesbury Abbey Mus. —4D 22
Shafton. S Yor —3D 93
Shafton Two Gates. S Yor —3D 93
Shaggs. Dors —4D 14
Shakesfield. Glos —2B 48
Shakespeare Countryside Mus. —5F 61
Shakespeare's Birthplace —Stratford 196
Shalbourne. Wilts —5B 36
Shalcombe. IOW —4B 16
Shalden. Hants —2E 25
Shaldon. Devn —5C 12
Shalfleet. IOW —4C 16
Shalford. Essx —3H 53
Shalford. Surr —1B 26
Shalford Green. Essx —3H 53
Shallowford. Devn —2H 19
Shallowford. Staf —3C 72
Shalmsford Street. Kent —5E 41
Shalstone. Buck —2E 51
Shamley Green. Surr —1B 26
Shandon. Arg —1D 126
Shandwick. High —1C 158
Shangton. Leics —1E 62
Shankhouse. Nmbd —2F 115
Shanklin. IOW —4D 16
Shannochie. N Ayr —3D 122
Shap. Cumb —3G 103
Shapwick. Dors —2E 15
Shapwick. Som —3H 21
Sharcott. Wilts —1G 23
Shardlow. Derbs —2B 74
Shareshill. Staf —5D 72
Sharlston. W Yor —3D 93
Sharlston Common. W Yor —3D 93
Sharnal Street. Medw —3B 40
Sharnbrook. Beds —5G 63
Sharneyford. Lanc —2G 91
Sharnford. Leics —1B 62
Sharnhill Green. Dors —2C 14
Sharow. N Yor —2F 99
Sharpe Green. Lanc —1D 90
Sharpenhoe. Beds —2A 52
Sharperton. Nmbd —4D 120
Sharpness. Glos —5B 48
Sharp Street. Norf —3F 79
Sharpthorne. W Sus —2E 27
Sharrington. Norf —2C 78
Shatterford. Worc —2B 60
Shatton. Derbs —2F 85
Shaugh Prior. Devn —2B 8
Shavington. Ches —5B 84
Shaw. G Man —4H 91
Shaw. W Ber —5C 36
Shaw. Wilts —5D 35
Shawbirch. Telf —4A 72
Shawbury. Shrp —3H 71
Shawdon Hall. Nmbd —3E 121
Shawell. Leics —2C 62
Shawford. Hants —4C 24
Shawforth. Lanc —2G 91
Shaw Green. Lanc —3D 90
Shawhead. Dum —2F 111
Shaw Mills. N Yor —3E 99
Shaw's Corner NT —4B 52
Shawwood. E Ayr —2E 117
Shearington. Dum —3B 112
Shearsby. Leics —1D 62
Shearston. Som —3F 21
Shebbear. Devn —2E 11
Shebdon. Staf —3B 72
Shebster. High —2C 168
Sheddocksley. Aber —3F 153
Shedfield. Hants —1D 16
Shedog. N Ayr —2D 122
Sheen. Staf —4F 85
Sheepbridge. Derbs —3A 86
Sheep Hill. Tyne —4E 115
Sheepscar. W Yor —1D 92
Sheepscombe. Glos —4D 49
Sheepstor. Devn —2B 8
Sheepwash. Devn —2E 11
Sheepwash. Nmbd —1F 115
Sheepway. N Som —4H 33
Sheepy Magna. Leics —5H 73
Sheepy Parva. Leics —5H 73
Sheering. Essx —4F 53
Sheerness. Kent —3D 40
Sheerwater. Surr —4B 38
Sheet. Hants —4F 25
Sheffield. S Yor —2H 85 & 196
Sheffield Bottom. W Ber —5E 37
Sheffield City Airport. S Yor —2B 86
Sheffield Green. E Sus —3F 27
Sheffield Park NT —3F 27
Sheffield Winter Gdn. —196
Shefford. Beds —2B 52
Shefford Woodlands. W Ber —4B 36
Sheigra. High —2B 166
Sheinton. Shrp —5A 72
Shelderton. Shrp —3G 59
Sheldon. Derbs —4F 85
Sheldon. Devn —2E 12
Sheldon. W Mid —2F 61
Sheldon Manor —4D 35
Sheldwich. Kent —5E 40
Sheldwich Lees. Kent —5E 40
Shelf. W Yor —2B 92
Shelfanger. Norf —2D 66
Shelfield. Warw —4F 61
Shelfield. W Mid —5E 73
Shelford. Notts —1D 74
Shelford. Warw —2B 62
Shell. Worc —5D 60
Shelley. Suff —2D 54
Shelley. W Yor —3C 92
Shell Green. Hal —2H 83
Shellingford. Oxon —2B 36
Shellow Bowells. Essx —5G 53
Shelsley Beauchamp. Worc —4B 60
Shelsley Walsh. Worc —4B 60
Shelthorpe. Leics —4C 74
Shelton. Beds —4H 63
Shelton. Norf —1E 67
Shelton. Notts —1E 75
Shelton. Shrp —4G 71
Shelton Green. Norf —1E 67
Shelton Lock. Derb —2A 74
Shelve. Shrp —1F 59
Shelwick. Here —1A 48
Shelwick Green. Here —1A 48
Shenfield. Essx —1H 39
Shenington. Oxon —1B 50
Shenley. Herts —5B 52
Shenley Brook End. Mil —2G 51
Shenleybury. Herts —5B 52
Shenley Church End. Mil —2G 51
Shenmore. Here —2G 47
Shennanton. Dum —3A 110
Shenstone. Staf —5F 73
Shenstone. Worc —3C 60
Shenstone Woodend. Staf —5F 73
Shenton. Leics —5A 74
Shenval. Mor —1G 151
Shepeau Stow. Linc —4C 76
Shephall. Herts —3C 52
Shepherd's Bush. G Lon —2D 38
Shepherds Gate. Norf —4E 77
Shepherd's Green. Oxon —3F 37
Shepherd's Port. Norf —2F 77
Shepherdswell. Kent —1G 29
Shepley. W Yor —4B 92
Sheppardstown. High —4D 169
Shepperdine. S Glo —2B 34
Shepperton. Surr —4B 38
Shepreth. Cambs —1D 53
Shepshed. Leics —4B 74
Shepton Beauchamp. Som —1H 13
Shepton Mallet. Som —2B 22
Shepton Montague. Som —3B 22
Shepway. Kent —5B 40
Sheraton. Dur —1B 106
Sherborne. Bath —1A 22
Sherborne. Dors —1B 14
Sherborne. Glos —4G 49
Sherborne Castle —1B 14
Sherborne Causeway. Dors —4D 22
Sherborne St John. Hants —1E 24
Sherbourne. Warw —4G 61
Sherburn. Dur —5G 115
Sherburn. N Yor —2D 100
Sherburn Hill. Dur —5G 115
Sherburn in Elmet. N Yor —1E 93
Shere. Surr —1B 26
Shereford. Norf —3A 78
Sherfield English. Hants —4A 24
Sherfield on Loddon. Hants —1E 25
Sherford. Devn —4D 9
Sherford. Dors —3E 15
Sheriffhales. Shrp —4B 72
Sheriff Hutton. N Yor —3A 100
Sheriffston. Mor —2G 159
Sheringham. Norf —1D 78
Sheringham Park NT —1D 78
Sherington. Mil —1G 51
Shermanbury. W Sus —4D 26
Shernal Green. Worc —4D 60
Shernborne. Norf —2G 77
Sherrington. Wilts —3E 23
Sherston. Wilts —3D 34
Sherwood. Nott —1C 74
Sherwood Forest —4C 86
Sherwood Green. Devn —4F 19
Shettleston. Glas —3H 127
Shevington. G Man —4D 90
Shevington Moor. G Man —3D 90
Shevington Vale. G Man —4D 90
Sheviock. Corn —3H 7
Shiel Bridge. High —2B 148
Shieldaig. High —1H 155
(nr. Charlestown)
Shieldaig. High —3H 155
(nr. Loch Shieldaig)
Shieldhill. Dum —1B 112
Shieldhill. Falk —2B 128
Shieldhill. S Lan —5D 128
Shieldmuir. N Lan —4A 128
Shielfoot. High —2A 140
Shielhill. Abers —3H 161
Shielhill. Ang —3D 144
Shifnal. Shrp —5B 72
Shilbottle. Nmbd —4F 121
Shilbottle Grange. Nmbd —4G 121
Shildon. Dur —2F 105
Shillford. E Ren —4F 127
Shillingford. Devn —4C 20
Shillingford. Oxon —2D 36
Shillingford St George. Devn —4C 12
Shillingstone. Dors —1D 14
Shillington. Beds —2B 52
Shillmoor. Nmbd —4C 120
Shilton. Oxon —5A 50
Shilton. Warw —2B 62
Shilvinghampton. Dors —4B 14
Shilvington. Nmbd —1E 115

Shimpling. Norf —2D 66
Shimpling. Suff —5A 66
Shimpling Street. Suff —5A 66
Shincliffe. Dur —5F 115
Shiney Row. Tyne —4G 115
Shinfield. Wok —5F 37
Shingay. Cambs —1D 52
Shingham. Norf —5G 77
Shingle Street. Suff —1G 55
Shinner's Bridge. Devn —2D 9
Shinness. High —2C 164
Shipbourne. Kent —5G 39
Shipdham. Norf —5B 78
Shipham. Som —1H 21
Shiphay. Torb —2E 9
Shiplake. Oxon —4F 37
Shipley. Derbs —1B 74
Shipley. Nmbd —3F 121
Shipley. Shrp —1C 60
Shipley. W Sus —3C 26
Shipley. W Yor —1B 92
Shipley Bridge. Surr —1E 27
Shipmeadow. Suff —1F 67
Shippon. Oxon —2C 36
Shipston on Stour. Warw —1A 50
Shipton. Buck —3F 51
Shipton. Glos —4F 49
Shipton. N Yor —4H 99
Shipton. Shrp —1H 59
Shipton Bellinger. Hants —2H 23
Shipton Gorge. Dors —3H 13
Shipton Green. W Sus —3G 17
Shipton Hall —1H 59
Shipton Moyne. Glos —3D 35
Shipton-on-Cherwell. Oxon —4C 50
Shiptonthorpe. E Yor —5C 100
Shipton-under-Wychwood. Oxon —4A 50
Shirburn. Oxon —2E 37
Shirdley Hill. Lanc —3B 90
Shire. Cumb —1H 103
Shirebrook. Derbs —4C 86
Shiregreen. S Yor —1A 86
Shirehampton. Bris —4A 34
Shiremoor. Tyne —2G 115
Shirenewton. Mon —2H 33
Shireoaks. Notts —2C 86
Shires Mill. Fife —1D 128
Shirkoak. Kent —2D 28
Shirland. Derbs —5A 86
Shirley. Derbs —1G 73
Shirley. Sotn —1C 16
Shirley. W Mid —3F 61
Shirleywich. Staf —3D 73
Shirl Heath. Here —5G 59
Shirrell Heath. Hants —1D 16
Shirwell. Devn —3F 19
Shiskine. N Ayr —3D 122
Shobdon. Here —4F 59
Shobnall. Staf —3G 73
Shobrooke. Devn —2B 12
Shoby. Leics —3D 74
Shocklach. Ches —1G 71
Shoeburyness. S'end —2D 40
Sholden. Kent —5H 41
Sholing. Sotn —1C 16
Sholver. G Man —4H 91
Shoot Hill. Shrp —4G 71
Shop. Corn —1C 10 (nr. Bude)
Shop. Corn —1C 6 (nr. Padstow)
Shop. Devn —1D 11
Shopford. Cumb —2G 113
Shop Street. Suff —4E 66
Shoreditch. G Lon —2E 39
Shoreditch. Som —4F 21
Shoreham. Kent —4G 39
Shoreham-by-Sea. W Sus —5D 26
Shoresdean. Nmbd —5F 131
Shoreswood. Nmbd —5F 131
Shore, The. Fife —2E 137
Shorncote. Glos —2F 35
Shorne. Kent —3A 40
Shorne Ridgeway. Kent —3A 40
Shortacombe. Devn —4F 11
Shortbridge. E Sus —3F 27
Shortgate. E Sus —4F 27
Short Green. Norf —2C 66
Shorthampton. Oxon —3B 50
Short Heath. Leics —4H 73
Short Heath. W Mid —1E 61 (nr. Erdington)
Short Heath. W Mid —5D 73 (nr. Wednesfield)
Shortlanesend. Corn —4C 6
Shorton. Torb —2E 9
Shortstown. Beds —1A 52
Shortwood. S Glo —4B 34
Shorwell. IOW —4C 16
Shoscombe. Bath —1C 22
Shotesham. Norf —1E 67
Shotgate. Essx —1B 40
Shotley. Suff —2F 55
Shotley Bridge. Dur —4D 115
Shotleyfield. Nmbd —4D 114
Shotley Gate. Suff —2F 55
Shottenden. Kent —5E 41
Shottermill. Surr —3G 25
Shottery. Warw —5F 61
Shotteswell. Warw —1C 50
Shottisham. Suff —1G 55
Shottle. Derbs —1H 73
Shotton. Dur —1B 106 (nr. Peterlee)
Shotton. Dur —2A 106 (nr. Sedgefield)
Shotton. Flin —4E 83
Shotton. Nmbd —2F 115 (nr. Morpeth)
Shotton. Nmbd —1C 120 (nr. Town Yetholm)
Shotton Colliery. Dur —5G 115
Shotts. N Lan —3B 128
Shotwick. Ches —3F 83
Shouldham. Norf —5F 77
Shouldham Thorpe. Norf —5F 77
Shoulton. Worc —5C 60
Shrawardine. Shrp —4F 71
Shrawley. Worc —4C 60
Shreding Green. Buck —2B 38
Shrewley. Warw —4G 61
Shrewsbury. Shrp —4G 71 & 196
Shrewsbury Castle —4H 71
Shrewton. Wilts —2F 23
Shripney. W Sus —5A 26
Shrivenham. Oxon —3H 35
Shropham. Norf —1B 66
Shroton. Dors —1D 14
Shrub End. Essx —3C 54
Shucknall. Here —1A 48
Shudy Camps. Cambs —1G 53
Shugborough Hall NT —3D 73
Shulishadermor. High —4D 154
Shulista. High —1D 154
Shurdington. Glos —4E 49
Shurlock Row. Wind —4G 37
Shurrery. High —3C 168
Shurton. Som —2F 21
Shustoke. Warw —1G 61
Shute. Devn —3F 13 (nr. Axminster)
Shute. Devn —2B 12 (nr. Crediton)
Shute Barton NT —3F 13
Shutford. Oxon —1B 50
Shut Heath. Staf —3C 72
Shuthonger. Glos —2D 49
Shutlanehead. Staf —1C 72
Shutlanger. Nptn —1F 51
Shutt Green. Staf —5C 72
Shuttington. Warw —5G 73
Shuttlewood. Derbs —3B 86
Shuttleworth. G Man —3G 91
Shuttleworth Collection —1B 52
Siabost. W Isl —3E 171
Siabost bho Dheas. W Isl —3E 171
Siabost bho Thuath. W Isl —3E 171
Siadar. W Isl —2F 171
Siadar Uarach. W Isl —2F 171
Sibbaldbie. Dum —1C 112
Sibbertoft. Nptn —2D 62
Sibdon Carwood. Shrp —2G 59
Sibertswold. Kent —1G 29
Sibford Ferris. Oxon —2B 50
Sibford Gower. Oxon —2B 50
Sible Hedingham. Essx —2A 54
Sibsey. Linc —5C 88
Sibsey Fen Side. Linc —5C 88
Sibson. Cambs —1H 63
Sibson. Leics —5A 74
Sibster. High —3F 169
Sibthorpe. Notts —1E 75
Sibton. Suff —4F 67
Sicklesmere. Suff —4A 66
Sicklinghall. N Yor —5F 99
Sid. Devn —4E 13
Sidbury. Devn —3E 13
Sidbury. Shrp —2A 60
Sidcot. N Som —1H 21
Sidcup. G Lon —3F 39
Siddick. Cumb —1B 102
Siddington. Ches —3C 84
Siddington. Glos —2F 35
Side of the Moor. G Man —3F 91
Sidestrand. Norf —2E 79
Sidford. Devn —3E 13
Sidlesham. W Sus —3G 17
Sidley. E Sus —5B 28
Sidlowbridge. Surr —1D 26
Sidmouth. Devn —4E 13
Sigford. Devn —5A 12
Sigglesthorne. E Yor —5F 101
Sighthill. Edin —2E 129
Sigingstone. V Glam —4C 32
Signet. Oxon —4H 49
Silbury Hill EH —5F 35
Silchester. Hants —5E 37
Sildinis. W Isl —6E 171
Sileby. Leics —4D 74
Silecroft. Cumb —1A 96
Silfield. Norf —1D 66
Silian. Cdgn —5E 57
Silkstone. S Yor —4C 92
Silkstone Common. S Yor —4C 92
Silksworth. Tyne —4G 115
Silk Willoughby. Linc —1H 75
Silloth. Cumb —4C 112
Sills. Nmbd —4C 120
Sillyearn. Mor —3C 160
Silpho. N Yor —5G 107
Silsden. W Yor —5C 98
Silsoe. Beds —2A 52
Silverbank. Abers —4E 152
Silverburn. Midl —3F 129
Silverdale. Lanc —2D 96
Silverdale. Staf —1C 72
Silverdale Green. Lanc —2D 96
Silver End. Essx —4B 54
Silver End. W Mid —2D 60
Silvergate. Norf —3D 78
Silverhillocks. Abers —2E 161
Silverley's Green. Suff —3E 67
Silverstone. Nptn —1E 51
Silverton. Devn —2C 12
Silverton. W Dun —2F 127
Silvington. Shrp —3A 60
Simm's Cross. Hal —2H 83
Simm's Lane End. Mers —1H 83
Simonburn. Nmbd —2B 114
Simonsbath. Som —3A 20
Simonstone. Lanc —1F 91
Simprim. Bord —5E 131
Simpson. Pemb —3C 42
Simpson Cross. Pemb —3C 42
Sinclairston. E Ayr —3D 116
Sinclairtown. Fife —4E 137
Sinderby. N Yor —1F 99
Sinderhope. Nmbd —4B 114
Sindlesham. Wok —5F 37
Sinfin. Derb —2A 74
Singleborough. Buck —2F 51
Singleton. Kent —1D 28
Singleton. Lanc —1B 90
Singleton. W Sus —1G 17
Singlewell. Kent —3A 40
Sinkhurst Green. Kent —1C 28
Sinnahard. Abers —2B 152
Sinnington. N Yor —1B 100
Sinton Green. Worc —4C 60
Sipson. G Lon —3B 38
Sirhowy. Blae —4E 47
Sissinghurst. Kent —2B 28
Sissinghurst NT —2C 28
Siston. S Glo —4B 34
Sithney. Corn —4D 4
Sittingbourne. Kent —4D 40
Sittingbourne & Kemsley Light Railway —4D 40
Six Ashes. Staf —2B 60
Six Bells. Blae —5F 47
Six Hills. Leics —3D 74
Sixhills. Linc —2A 88
Six Mile Bottom. Cambs —5E 65
Sixpenny Handley. Dors —1E 15
Sizergh Castle NT —1D 97
Sizewell. Suff —4G 67
Skail. High —4H 167
Skaill. Orkn —6B 172
Skaills. Orkn —7E 172
Skara Brae WH HS —6B 172
Skares. E Ayr —3E 117
Skateraw. E Lot —2D 130
Skaw. Shet —5G 173
Skeabost. High —4D 154
Skeabrae. Orkn —5B 172
Skeeby. N Yor —4E 105
Skeffington. Leics —5E 75
Skeffling. E Yor —3G 95
Skegby. Notts —4B 86 (nr. Mansfield)
Skegby. Notts —4E 87 (nr. Tuxford)
Skegness. Linc —4E 89
Skelberry. Shet —10E 173 (nr. Boddam)
Skelberry. Shet —3E 173 (nr. Housetter)
Skelbo. High —4E 165
Skelbo Street. High —4E 165
Skelbrooke. S Yor —3F 93
Skeldyke. Linc —2C 76
Skelfhill. Bord —4G 119
Skellingthorpe. Linc —3G 87
Skellister. Shet —6F 173
Skellorn Green. Ches —2D 84
Skellow. S Yor —3F 93
Skelmanthorpe. W Yor —3C 92
Skelmersdale. Lanc —4C 90
Skelmorlie. N Ayr —3C 126
Skelpick. High —3H 167
Skelton. Cumb —1F 103
Skelton. E Yor —2A 94
Skelton. N Yor —4D 105 (nr. Richmond)
Skelton. N Yor —3F 99 (nr. Ripon)
Skelton. Red C —3D 106
Skelton. York —4H 99
Skelton Green. Red C —3D 106
Skelwick. Orkn —3D 172
Skelwith Bridge. Cumb —4E 103
Skendleby. Linc —4D 88
Skendleby Psalter. Linc —3D 88
Skenfrith. Mon —3H 47
Skenfrith Castle NT —4H 47
Skerne. E Yor —4E 101
Skeroblingarry. Arg —3B 122
Skerray. High —2G 167
Skerricha. High —3C 166
Skerton. Lanc —3D 96
Sketchley. Leics —1B 62
Sketty. Swan —3F 31
Skewen. Neat —3G 31
Skewsby. N Yor —2A 100
Skeyton. Norf —3E 79
Skeyton Corner. Norf —3E 79
Skiall. High —2C 168
Skidbrooke. Linc —1D 88
Skidbrooke North End. Linc —1D 88
Skidby. E Yor —1D 94
Skiddaw —2D 102
Skilgate. Som —4C 20
Skillington. Linc —3F 75
Skinburness. Cumb —4C 112
Skinflats. Falk —1C 128
Skinidin. High —4B 154
Skinnet. High —2F 167
Skinningrove. Red C —2E 107
Skipness. Arg —4G 125
Skippool. Lanc —5C 96
Skiprigg. Cumb —5E 113
Skipsea. E Yor —4F 101
Skipsea Brough. E Yor —4F 101
Skipton. N Yor —4B 98
Skipton Castle —4B 98
Skipton-on-Swale. N Yor —2F 99
Skipwith. N Yor —1G 93
Skirbeck. Linc —1C 76
Skirbeck Quarter. Linc —1C 76
Skirlaugh. E Yor —1E 95
Skirling. Bord —1C 118
Skirmett. Buck —2F 37
Skirpenbeck. E Yor —4B 100
Skirwith. Cumb —1H 103
Skirwith. N Yor —2G 97
Skirza. High —2F 169
Skitby. Cumb —3F 113
Skitham. Lanc —5D 96
Skittle Green. Buck —5F 51
Skroo. Shet —1B 172
Skulamus. High —1E 147
Skullomie. High —2G 167
Skyborry Green. Shrp —3E 59
Skye Green. Essx —3B 54
Skye of Curr. High —1D 151
Slack. W Yor —2H 91
Slackhall. Derbs —2E 85
Slack Head. Cumb —2D 97
Slackhead. Mor —2B 160
Slackholme End. Linc —3E 89
Slacks of Cairnbanno. Abers —4F 161
Slack, The. Dur —2E 105
Slad. Glos —5D 48
Slade. Devn —2F 19
Slade. Swan —4D 31
Slade End. Oxon —2D 36
Slade Field. Cambs —2C 64
Slade Green. G Lon —3G 39
Slade Heath. Staf —5D 72
Slade Hooton. S Yor —2C 86
Sladesbridge. Corn —5A 10
Slade, The. W Ber —5D 36
Slaggyford. Nmbd —4H 113
Slaidburn. Lanc —4G 97
Slaid Hill. W Yor —5F 99
Slaithwaite. W Yor —3A 92
Slaley. Derbs —5G 85
Slaley. Nmbd —4C 114
Slamannan. Falk —2B 128
Slapton. Buck —3H 51
Slapton. Devn —4E 9
Slapton. Nptn —1E 51
Slattock. G Man —4G 91
Slaugham. W Sus —3D 26
Slaughterford. Wilts —4D 34
Slawston. Leics —1E 63
Sleaford. Hants —3G 25
Sleaford. Linc —1H 75
Sleagill. Cumb —3G 103
Sleap. Shrp —3G 71
Sledmere. E Yor —3D 100
Sledmere House —3D 100
Sleightholme. Dur —3C 104
Sleights. N Yor —4F 107
Slepe. Dors —3E 15
Slickly. High —2E 169
Sliddery. N Ayr —3D 122
Sligachan. High —1C 146
Slimbridge. Glos —5C 48
Slimbridge Wildfowl & Wetlands Centre —5C 48
Slindon. Staf —2C 72
Slindon. W Sus —5A 26
Slinfold. W Sus —2C 26
Slingsby. N Yor —2A 100
Slip End. Beds —4A 52
Slipton. Nptn —3G 63
Slitting Mill. Staf —4E 73
Slochd. High —1C 150
Slockavullin. Arg —4F 133
Sloley. Norf —3E 79
Sloncombe. Devn —4H 11
Sloothby. Linc —3D 89
Slough. Slo —3A 38
Slough Green. Som —4F 21
Slough Green. W Sus —3D 27
Sluggan. High —1C 150
Slyne. Lanc —3D 97
Smailholm. Bord —1A 120
Smallbridge. G Man —3H 91
Smallbrook. Devn —3B 12
Smallburgh. Norf —3F 79
Smallburn. E Ayr —2F 117
Smalldale. Derbs —3E 85
Small Dole. W Sus —4D 26
Smalley. Derbs —1B 74
Smallfield. Surr —1E 27
Small Heath. W Mid —2F 61
Smallholm. Dum —2C 112
Small Hythe. Kent —2C 28
Smallrice. Staf —2D 72
Smallridge. Devn —2G 13
Smallwood Hey. Lanc —5C 96
Smallworth. Norf —2C 66
Smannell. Hants —2B 24
Smardale. Cumb —4A 104
Smarden. Kent —1C 28
Smarden Bell. Kent —1C 28
Smart's Hill. Kent —1G 27
Smeatharpe. Devn —1F 13
Smeeth. Kent —2E 29
Smeeth, The. Norf —4E 77
Smeeton Westerby. Leics —1D 62
Smeircleit. W Isl —7C 170
Smerral. High —5D 169
Smestow. Staf —1C 60
Smethwick. W Mid —2E 61
Smirisary. High —1A 140
Smisby. Derbs —4H 73
Smitham Hill. Bath —1A 22
Smith End Green. Worc —5B 60
Smithfield. Cumb —3F 113
Smith Green. Lanc —4D 97
Smithies, The. Shrp —1A 60
Smithincott. Devn —1D 12
Smith's Green. Essx —3F 53
Smithstown. High —1G 155
Smithton. High —4B 158
Smithwood Green. Suff —5B 66
Smithy Bridge. G Man —3H 91
Smithy Green. Ches —3B 84
Smithy Lane Ends. Lanc —3C 90
Smockington. Warw —2B 62
Smoogro. Orkn —7C 172
Smyth's Green. Essx —4C 54
Snaefell Mountain Railway —3D 108
Snaigow House. Per —4H 143
Snailbeach. Shrp —5F 71
Snailwell. Cambs —4F 65
Snainton. N Yor —1D 100
Snaith. E Yor —2G 93
Snape. N Yor —1E 99
Snape. Suff —5F 67
Snape Green. Lanc —3B 90
Snarestone. Leics —5H 73
Snarford. Linc —2H 87
Snargate. Kent —3D 28
Snave. Kent —3E 28
Sneachill. Worc —5D 60
Snead. Powy —1F 59
Snead Common. Worc —4B 60
Sneaton. N Yor —4F 107
Sneatonthorpe. N Yor —4G 107
Snelland. Linc —2H 87
Snelston. Derbs —1F 73
Snetterton. Norf —1B 66
Snettisham. Norf —2F 77
Snibston. Leics —4B 74
Snibston Discovery Park —4B 74
Snig's End. Glos —3C 48
Sniseabhal. W Isl —6C 170
Snitter. Nmbd —4E 121
Snitterby. Linc —1G 87
Snitterfield. Warw —5G 61
Snitton. Shrp —3H 59
Snodhill. Here —1G 47
Snodland. Kent —4A 40
Snods Edge. Nmbd —4D 114
Snowdon —5F 81
Snowdonia Nat. Park —5E 81
Snowdon Mountain Railway —5E 81
Snowshill. Glos —2F 49
Snowshill Manor NT —2F 49
Snow Street. Norf —2C 66
Snydale. W Yor —3E 93
Soake. Hants —1E 17
Soar. Carm —3G 45
Soar. Gwyn —2F 69
Soar. IOA —3C 80
Soar. Powy —2C 46
Soberton. Hants —1E 16
Soberton Heath. Hants —1E 16
Sockbridge. Cumb —2F 103
Sockburn. Darl —4A 106
Sodom. Den —3C 82
Sodom. Shet —5G 173
Soham. Cambs —3E 65
Soham Cotes. Cambs —3E 65
Solas. W Isl —1D 170
Soldon Cross. Devn —1D 10
Soldridge. Hants —3E 25
Solent Breezes. Hants —2D 16
Sole Street. Kent —4A 40 (nr. Meopham)
Sole Street. Kent —1E 29 (nr. Waltham)
Solihull. W Mid —3F 61
Sollers Dilwyn. Here —5G 59
Sollers Hope. Here —2B 48
Sollom. Lanc —3C 90
Solva. Pemb —2B 42
Somerby. Leics —4E 75
Somerby. Linc —4D 94
Somercotes. Derbs —5B 86
Somerford. Dors —3G 15
Somerford. Staf —5C 72
Somerford Keynes. Glos —2F 35
Somerley. W Sus —3G 17
Somerleyton. Suff —1G 67
Somerleyton Hall —1G 67
Somersal Herbert. Derbs —2F 73
Somersby. Linc —3C 88
Somersham. Cambs —3C 64
Somersham. Suff —1D 54
Somerton. Oxon —3C 50
Somerton. Som —4H 21
Somerton. Suff —5H 65
Sompting. W Sus —5C 26
Sonning. Wok —4F 37
Sonning Common. Oxon —3F 37
Sookholme. Notts —4C 86
Sopley. Hants —3G 15
Sopworth. Wilts —3D 34
Sorbie. Dum —5B 110
Sordale. High —2D 168
Sorisdale. Arg —2D 138
Sorn. E Ayr —2E 117
Sorn Castle —2E 117
Sornhill. E Ayr —1E 117
Sortat. High —2E 169
Sotby. Linc —3B 88
Sots Hole. Linc —4A 88
Sotterley. Suff —2G 67
Soudley. Shrp —1G 59 (nr. Church Stretton)
Soudley. Shrp —3B 72 (nr. Market Drayton)
Soughton. Flin —4E 83
Soulbury. Buck —3G 51
Soulby. Cumb —3A 104 (nr. Appleby)
Soulby. Cumb —2F 103 (nr. Penrith)
Souldern. Oxon —2D 50
Souldrop. Beds —4G 63
Sound. Shet —7F 173 (nr. Lerwick)
Sound. Shet —6E 173 (nr. Tresta)
Soundwell. Bris —4B 34
Sourhope. Bord —2C 120
Sourin. Orkn —4D 172
Sourton. Devn —3F 11
Soutergate. Cumb —1B 96
South Acre. Norf —4H 77
Southall. G Lon —3C 38
South Allington. Devn —5D 9
South Alloa. Falk —4A 136
Southam. Glos —3E 49
Southam. Warw —4B 62
South Ambersham. W Sus —3A 26
Southampton. Sotn —1C 16 & 196
Southampton Airport. Hants —1C 16
Southannan. N Ayr —4D 126
South Anston. S Yor —2C 86
South Ascot. Wind —4A 38
South Baddesley. Hants —3B 16
South Balfern. Dum —4B 110
South Ballachulish. High —3E 141
South Bank. Red C —2C 106
South Barrow. Som —4B 22
South Beach. Nmbd —2G 115
South Benfleet. Essx —2B 40
South Bents. Tyne —3H 115
South Bersted. W Sus —5A 26
Southborough. Kent —1G 27
Southbourne. Bour —3G 15
Southbourne. W Sus —2F 17
South Brent. Devn —2D 8
South Brewham. Som —3C 22
South Broomage. Falk —1B 128
South Broomhill. Nmbd —5G 121
Southburgh. Norf —5B 78

South Burlingham. Norf —5F 79
Southburn. E Yor —4D 101
South Cadbury. Som —4B 22
South Carlton. Linc —3G 87
South Cave. E Yor —1C 94
South Cerney. Glos —2F 35
South Chard. Som —2G 13
South Charlton. Nmbd —2F 121
South Cheriton. Som —4B 22
South Church. Dur —2F 105
Southchurch. S'end —2D 40
South Cleatlam. Dur —3E 105
South Cliffe. E Yor —1B 94
South Clifton. Notts —3F 87
South Clunes. High —4H 157
South Cockerington. Linc —2C 88
South Common. E Sus —4E 27
South Cornelly. B'end —3B 32
Southcott. Devn —1E 11 (nr. Great Torrington)
Southcott. Devn —3F 11 (nr. Okehampton)
Southcott. Wilts —1G 23
Southcourt. Buck —4G 51
South Cove. Suff —2G 67
South Creagan. Arg —4D 141
South Creake. Norf —2A 78
South Crosland. W Yor —3B 92
South Croxton. Leics —4D 74
South Dalton. E Yor —5D 100
South Darenth. Kent —4G 39
Southdean. Bord —4A 120
South Devon Railway —2D 8
Southdown. Bath —5C 34
South Downs —1F 17
South Duffield. N Yor —1G 93
Southease. E Sus —5F 27
South Elkington. Linc —2B 88
South Elmsall. W Yor —3E 93
Southend. Arg —5A 122
South End. Cumb —3B 96
Southend. Glos —2C 34
South End. N Lin —2E 94
South End. W Ber —4D 36
Southend (London) Airport. Essx —2C 40
Southend-on-Sea. S'end —2C 40
Southerfield. Cumb —5C 112
Southerhouse. Shet —8E 173
Southerly. Devn —4F 11
Southernden. Kent —1C 28
Southerndown. V Glam —4B 32
Southerness. Dum —4A 112
South Erradale. High —1G 155
Southerton. Devn —3D 12
Southery. Norf —1F 65
Southey Green. Essx —2A 54
South Fambridge. Essx —1C 40
South Fawley. W Ber —3B 36
South Feorline. N Ayr —3D 122
South Ferriby. N Lin —2C 94
South Field. E Yor —2D 94
Southfleet. Kent —3H 39
South Garvan. High —1D 141
Southgate. Cdgn —2E 57
Southgate. G Lon —1E 39
Southgate. Norf —3D 78 (nr. Aylsham)
Southgate. Norf —2A 78 (nr. Fakenham)
Southgate. Swan —4E 31
South Gluss. Shet —4E 173
South Godstone. Surr —1E 27
South Gorley. Hants —1G 15
South Green. Essx —1A 40 (nr. Billericay)
South Green. Essx —4D 54 (nr. Colchester)
South Green. Kent —4C 40
South Hanningfield. Essx —1B 40
South Harting. W Sus —1F 17
South Hayling. Hants —3F 17
South Hazelrigg. Nmbd —1E 121
South Heath. Buck —5H 51
South Heath. Essx —4E 54
South Heighton. E Sus —5F 27
South Hetton. Dur —5G 115
South Hiendley. W Yor —3D 93
South Hill. Corn —5D 10
South Hill. Som —4H 21
South Hinksey. Oxon —5D 50
South Hole. Devn —4C 18
South Holme. N Yor —2B 100
South Holmwood. Surr —1C 26
South Hornchurch. G Lon —2G 39
South Huish. Devn —4C 8
South Hykeham. Linc —4G 87
South Hylton. Tyne —4G 115
Southill. Beds —1B 52
Southington. Hants —2D 24
South Kelsey. Linc —1H 87
South Kessock. High —4A 158
South Killingholme. N Lin —3E 95
South Kilvington. N Yor —1G 99
South Kilworth. Leics —2D 62
South Kirkby. W Yor —3E 93
South Kirton. Abers —3E 153
South Kyme. Linc —1A 76
South Lakes Wild Animal Park —2B 96
South Lancing. W Sus —5C 26
South Ledaig. Arg —5D 140
Southleigh. Devn —3F 13
South Leigh. Oxon —5B 50
South Leverton. Notts —2E 87
South Littleton. Worc —1F 49
South Lopham. Norf —2C 66
South Luffenham. Rut —5G 75
South Malling. E Sus —4F 27
South Marston. Swin —3G 35
South Middleton. Nmbd —2E 121
South Milford. N Yor —1E 93
South Milton. Devn —4D 8
South Mimms. Herts —5C 52
Southminster. Essx —1D 40
South Molton. Devn —4H 19
South Moor. Dur —4E 115
Southmoor. Oxon —2B 36
South Moreton. Oxon —3D 36
South Mundham. W Sus —2G 17
South Muskham. Notts —5E 87
South Newbald. E Yor —1C 94
South Newington. Oxon —2C 50
South Newsham. Nmbd —2G 115
South Newton. N Ayr —4H 125
South Newton. Wilts —3F 23
South Normanton. Derbs —5B 86
South Norwood. G Lon —4E 39
South Nutfield. Surr —1E 27
South Ockendon. Thur —2G 39
Southoe. Cambs —4A 64
Southolt. Suff —4D 66
South Ormsby. Linc —3C 88
Southorpe. Pet —5H 75
South Otterington. N Yor —1F 99
South Owersby. Linc —1H 87
Southowram. W Yor —2B 92
South Oxhey. Herts —1C 38
South Perrott. Dors —2H 13
South Petherton. Som —1H 13
South Petherwin. Corn —4D 10
South Pickenham. Norf —5A 78
South Pool. Devn —4D 9
South Port. Arg —1H 133
Southport. Mers —3B 90
Southpunds. Shet —10F 173
South Radworthy. Devn —3A 20
South Rauceby. Linc —1H 75
South Raynham. Norf —3A 78
Southrepps. Norf —2E 79
South Reston. Linc —2D 88
Southrey. Linc —4A 88
Southrop. Glos —5G 49
Southrope. Hants —2E 25
South Runcton. Norf —5F 77
South Scarle. Notts —4F 87
Southsea. Port —3E 17
South Shields. Tyne —3G 115
South Shore. Bkpl —1B 90
Southside. Orkn —5E 172
South Somercotes. Linc —1D 88
South Stainley. N Yor —3F 99
South Stainmore. Cumb —3B 104
South Stifford. Thur —3G 39
Southstoke. Bath —5C 34
South Stoke. Oxon —3D 36
South Stoke. W Sus —4B 26
South Street. E Sus —4E 27
South Street. Kent —5E 41 (nr. Faversham)
South Street. Kent —4F 41 (nr. Whitstable)
South Tawton. Devn —3G 11
South Thoresby. Linc —3D 88
South Tidworth. Wilts —2H 23
South Town. Devn —4C 12
South Town. Hants —3E 25
Southtown. Norf —5H 79
Southtown. Orkn —8D 172
South View. Shet —7E 173
Southwaite. Cumb —5F 113
South Walsham. Norf —4F 79
South Warnborough. Hants —2F 25
Southwater. W Sus —3C 26
Southwater Street. W Sus —3C 26
Southway. Som —2A 22
South Weald. Essx —1G 39
South Weirs. Hants —2A 16
Southwell. Dors —5B 14
Southwell. Notts —5D 86
Southwell Minster —5E 86
South Weston. Oxon —2F 37
South Wheatley. Corn —3C 10
South Wheatley. Notts —2E 87
Southwick. Hants —2E 17
Southwick. Nptn —1H 63
Southwick. Tyne —4G 115
Southwick. W Sus —5D 26
Southwick. Wilts —1D 22
South Widcombe. Bath —1A 22
South Wigston. Leics —1C 62
South Willingham. Linc —2A 88
South Wingfield. Derbs —5A 86
South Witham. Linc —4G 75
Southwold. Suff —3H 67
South Wonston. Hants —3C 24
Southwood. Norf —5F 79
Southwood. Som —3A 22
South Woodham Ferrers. Essx —1C 40
South Wootton. Norf —3F 77
South Wraxall. Wilts —5D 34
South Zeal. Devn —3G 11
Soval Lodge. W Isl —5F 171
Sowerby. N Yor —1G 99
Sowerby. W Yor —2A 92
Sowerby Bridge. W Yor —2A 92
Sowerby Row. Cumb —5E 113
Sower Carr. Lanc —5C 96
Sowley Green. Suff —5G 65
Sowood. W Yor —3A 92
Sowton. Devn —3C 12
Soyal. High —4C 164
Soyland Town. W Yor —2A 92
Spacey Houses. N Yor —4F 99
Spa Common. Norf —2E 79
Spalding. Linc —3B 76
Spaldington. E Yor —1A 94
Spalding Tropical Forest —3B 76
Spaldwick. Cambs —3A 64
Spalford. Notts —4F 87
Spanby. Linc —2H 75
Sparham. Norf —4C 78
Sparhamhill. Norf —4C 78
Spark Bridge. Cumb —1C 96
Sparket. Cumb —2F 103
Sparkford. Som —4B 22
Sparkwell. Devn —3B 8
Sparrow Green. Norf —4B 78
Sparrowpit. Derbs —2E 85
Sparrow's Green. E Sus —2H 27
Sparsholt. Hants —3C 24
Sparsholt. Oxon —3B 36
Spartylea. Nmbd —5B 114
Spath. Staf —2E 73
Spaunton. N Yor —1B 100
Spa Valley Railway —2G 27
Spaxton. Som —3F 21
Spean Bridge. High —5E 149
Spear Hill. W Sus —4C 26
Speen. Buck —2G 37
Speen. W Ber —5C 36
Speeton. N Yor —2F 101
Speke. Mers —2G 83
Speke Hall NT —2G 83
Speldhurst. Kent —1G 27
Spellbrook. Herts —4E 53
Spelsbury. Oxon —3B 50
Spencers Wood. Wok —5F 37
Spennithorne. N Yor —1D 98
Spennymoor. Dur —1F 105
Spernall. Warw —4E 61
Spetchley. Worc —5C 60
Spetchley Park Gdns. —5C 60
Spetisbury. Dors —2E 15
Spexhall. Suff —2F 67
Speybank. High —3C 150
Spey Bay. Mor —2A 160
Speybridge. High —1E 151
Speyview. Mor —4G 159
Spilsby. Linc —4C 88
Spindlestone. Nmbd —1F 121
Spinkhill. Derbs —3B 86
Spinney Hills. Leic —5D 74
Spinningdale. High —5D 164
Spital. Mers —2F 83
Spitalhill. Derbs —1F 73
Spital in the Street. Linc —2G 87
Spithurst. E Sus —4F 27
Spittal. Dum —4A 110
Spittal. E Lot —2A 130
Spittal. High —3D 168
Spittal. Nmbd —4G 131
Spittal. Pemb —2D 43
Spittalfield. Per —4A 144
Spittal of Glenmuick. Abers —5H 151
Spittal of Glenshee. Per —1A 144
Spittal-on-Rule. Bord —3H 119
Spixworth. Norf —4E 79
Splatt. Corn —4C 10
Spode Mus. —Stoke 196
Spofforth. N Yor —4F 99
Spondon. Derb —2B 74
Spon End. W Mid —3H 61
Spooner Row. Norf —1C 66
Sporle. Norf —4H 77
Spott. E Lot —2C 130
Spratton. Nptn —3E 62
Spreakley. Surr —2G 25
Spreyton. Devn —3H 11
Spridlington. Linc —2H 87
Springburn. Glas —3H 127
Springfield. Dum —3E 113
Springfield. Fife —2F 137
Springfield. High —2A 158
Springfield. W Mid —2E 61
Springhill. Staf —5D 73
Springholm. Dum —3F 111
Springside. N Ayr —1C 116
Springthorpe. Linc —2F 87
Spring Vale. IOW —3E 16
Spring Valley. IOM —4C 108
Springwell. Tyne —4F 115
Sprivers Gdn. NT —1A 28
Sproatley. E Yor —1E 95
Sproston Green. Ches —4B 84
Sprotbrough. S Yor —4F 93
Sproughton. Suff —1E 54
Sprouston. Bord —1B 120
Sprowston. Norf —4E 79
Sproxton. Leics —3F 75
Sproxton. N Yor —1A 100
Sprunston. Cumb —5E 113
Spurstow. Ches —5H 83
Squerryes Court —5F 39
Squires Gate. Bkpl —1B 90
Sraid Ruadh. Arg —4A 138
Srannda. W Isl —9C 171
Sronphadruig Lodge. Per —1E 142
Sruth Mor. W Isl —2E 170
SS Great Britain, The —Bristol 187
Stableford. Shrp —1B 60
Stackhouse. N Yor —3H 97
Stackpole. Pemb —5D 43
Stackpole Elidor. Pemb —5D 43
Stacksford. Norf —1C 66
Stacksteads. Lanc —2G 91
Staddiscombe. Plym —3B 8
Staddlethorpe. E Yor —2B 94
Staddon. Devn —2D 10
Staden. Derbs —3E 85
Stadhampton. Oxon —2E 36
Stadhlaigearraidh. W Isl —5C 170
Staffield. Cumb —5G 113
Staffin. High —2D 155
Stafford. Staf —3D 72
Stafford Castle —3D 72
Stafford Park. Telf —5B 72
Stagden Cross. Essx —4G 53
Stagsden. Beds —1H 51
Stag's Head. Devn —4G 19
Stainburn. Cumb —2B 102
Stainburn. N Yor —5E 99
Stainby. Linc —3G 75
Staincliffe. W Yor —2C 92
Staincross. S Yor —3D 92
Staindrop. Dur —2E 105
Staines. Surr —3B 38
Stainfield. Linc —3H 75 (nr. Bourne)
Stainfield. Linc —3A 88 (nr. Lincoln)
Stainforth. N Yor —3H 97
Stainforth. S Yor —3G 93
Staining. Lanc —1B 90
Stainland. W Yor —3A 92
Stainsacre. N Yor —4G 107
Stainton. Cumb —4E 113 (nr. Carlisle)
Stainton. Cumb —1E 97 (nr. Kendal)
Stainton. Cumb —2F 103 (nr. Penrith)
Stainton. Dur —3D 104
Stainton. Midd —3B 106
Stainton. N Yor —5E 105
Stainton. S Yor —1C 86
Stainton by Langworth. Linc —3H 87
Staintondale. N Yor —5G 107
Stainton le Vale. Linc —1A 88
Stainton with Adgarley. Cumb —2B 96
Stair. Cumb —2D 102
Stair. E Ayr —2D 116
Staithes. N Yor —3E 107
Stakeford. Nmbd —1F 115
Stake Pool. Lanc —5D 96
Stakes. Hants —2E 17
Stalbridge. Dors —1C 14
Stalbridge Weston. Dors —1C 14
Stalham. Norf —3F 79
Stalham Green. Norf —3F 79
Stalisfield Green. Kent —5D 40
Stallen. Dors —1B 14
Stallingborough. NE Lin —3F 95
Stalling Busk. N Yor —1B 98
Stallington. Staf —1D 72
Stalmine. Lanc —5C 96
Stalybridge. G Man —1D 84
Stambourne. Essx —2H 53
Stamford. Linc —5H 75
Stamford. Nmbd —3G 121
Stamford Bridge. Ches —4G 83
Stamford Bridge. E Yor —4B 100
Stamfordham. Nmbd —2D 115
Stamperland. E Ren —4G 127
Stanah. Lanc —5C 96
Stanborough. Herts —4C 52
Stanbridge. Beds —3H 51
Stanbridge. Dors —2F 15
Stanbury. W Yor —1A 92
Stand. N Lan —3A 128
Standburn. Falk —2C 128
Standeford. Staf —5D 72
Standen. Kent —1C 28
Standen NT —2E 27
Standen Street. Kent —2C 28
Standerwick. Som —1D 22
Standford. Hants —3G 25
Standford Bridge. Telf —3B 72
Standingstone. Cumb —5D 112
Standish. Glos —5D 48
Standish. G Man —3D 90
Standish Lower Ground. G Man —4D 90
Standlake. Oxon —5C 50
Standon. Hants —4C 24
Standon. Herts —3D 53
Standon. Staf —2C 72
Standon Green End. Herts —4D 52
Standwell Green. Suff —3D 66
Stane. N Lan —3B 128
Stanecastle. N Ayr —1C 116
Stanfield. Norf —3B 78
Stanford. Beds —1B 52
Stanford. Kent —2F 29
Stanford Bishop. Here —5A 60
Stanford Bridge. Worc —4B 60
Stanford Dingley. W Ber —4D 36
Stanford Hall —3C 62
Stanford in the Vale. Oxon —2B 36
Stanford-le-Hope. Thur —2A 40
Stanford on Avon. Nptn —3C 62
Stanford on Soar. Notts —3C 74
Stanford on Teme. Worc —4B 60
Stanford Rivers. Essx —5F 53
Stanfree. Derbs —3B 86
Stanghow. Red C —3D 107
Stanground. Pet —1B 64
Stanhoe. Norf —2H 77
Stanhope. Dur —1C 104
Stanhope. Bord —1D 118
Stanion. Nptn —2G 63
Stanley. Derbs —1B 74
Stanley. Dur —4E 115
Stanley. Per —5A 144
Stanley. Shrp —2B 60
Stanley. Staf —5D 84
Stanley. W Yor —2D 93
Stanley Common. Derbs —1B 74
Stanley Crook. Dur —1E 105
Stanley Hill. Here —1B 48
Stanlow. Ches —3G 83
Stanmer. Brig —5E 27
Stanmore. G Lon —1C 38
Stanmore. Hants —4C 24
Stanmore. W Ber —4C 36
Stannersburn. Nmbd —1A 114
Stanningfield. Suff —5A 66
Stannington. Nmbd —2F 115
Stannington. S Yor —2H 85
Stansbatch. Here —4F 59
Stansfield. Suff —5G 65
Stanshope. Staf —5F 85
Stanstead. Suff —1B 54
Stanstead Abbotts. Herts —4D 53
Stansted. Kent —4H 39
Stansted (London) Airport. Essx —3F 53
Stansted Mountfitchet. Essx —3F 53
Stansted Mountfitchet Castle —3F 53
Stansted Park —1F 17
Stanthorne. Ches —4A 84
Stanton. Derbs —4G 73
Stanton. Glos —2F 49
Stanton. Nmbd —5F 121
Stanton. Staf —1F 73
Stanton. Suff —3B 66
Stanton by Bridge. Derbs —3A 74
Stanton by Dale. Derbs —2B 74
Stanton Chare. Suff —3B 66
Stanton Drew. Bath —5A 34
Stanton Fitzwarren. Swin —2G 35
Stanton Harcourt. Oxon —5C 50
Stanton Hill. Notts —4B 86
Stanton in Peak. Derbs —4G 85
Stanton Lacy. Shrp —3G 59
Stanton Long. Shrp —1H 59
Stanton-on-the-Wolds. Notts —2D 74
Stanton Prior. Bath —5B 34
Stanton St Bernard. Wilts —5F 35
Stanton St John. Oxon —5D 50
Stanton St Quintin. Wilts —4E 35
Stanton Street. Suff —4B 66
Stanton under Bardon. Leics —4B 74
Stanton upon Hine Heath. Shrp —3H 71
Stanton Wick. Bath —5B 34
Stanwardine in the Fields. Shrp —3G 71
Stanwardine in the Wood. Shrp —3G 71
Stanway. Essx —3C 54
Stanway. Glos —2F 49
Stanway House —2F 49
Stanwell. Surr —3B 38
Stanwell Moor. Surr —3B 38
Stanwick. Nptn —3G 63
Stanydale. Shet —6D 173
Staoinebrig. W Isl —5C 170
Stape. N Yor —5E 107
Stapehill. Dors —2F 15
Stapeley. Ches —1A 72
Stapeley Water Gdns. —5A 84
Stapenhill. Staf —3G 73
Staple. Kent —5G 41
Staple Cross. Devn —4D 20
Staplecross. E Sus —3B 28
Staplefield. W Sus —3D 27
Staple Fitzpaine. Som —1F 13
Stapleford. Cambs —5D 64
Stapleford. Derbs —2B 74
Stapleford. Herts —4D 52
Stapleford. Leics —4F 75
Stapleford. Linc —5F 87
Stapleford. Wilts —3F 23
Stapleford Abbotts. Essx —1G 39
Stapleford Tawney. Essx —1G 39
Staplegrove. Som —4F 21
Staplehay. Som —4F 21
Staple Hill. S Glo —4B 34
Staplehurst. Kent —1B 28
Staplers. IOW —4D 16
Stapleton. Bris —4B 34
Stapleton. Cumb —2G 113
Stapleton. Here —4F 59
Stapleton. Leics —1B 62
Stapleton. N Yor —3F 105
Stapleton. Shrp —5G 71
Stapleton. Som —4H 21
Stapley. Som —1E 13
Staploe. Beds —4A 64
Staplow. Here —1B 48
Star. Fife —3F 137
Star. Pemb —1G 43
Starbeck. N Yor —4F 99
Starbotton. N Yor —2B 98
Starcross. Devn —4C 12
Stareton. Warw —3H 61
Starkholmes. Derbs —5H 85
Starling. G Man —3F 91
Starling's Green. Essx —2E 53
Starston. Norf —2E 67
Start. Devn —4E 9
Startforth. Dur —3D 104
Start Hill. Essx —3F 53
Startley. Wilts —3E 35
Stathe. Som —4G 21
Stathern. Leics —2E 75
Station Town. Dur —1B 106
Staughton Green. Cambs —4A 64
Staughton Highway. Cambs —4A 64
Staunton. Glos —3C 48 (nr. Cheltenham)
Staunton. Glos —4A 48 (nr. Monmouth)
Staunton in the Vale. Notts —1F 75
Staunton on Arrow. Here —4F 59
Staunton on Wye. Here —1G 47
Staveley. Cumb —5F 103
Staveley. Derbs —3B 86
Staveley. N Yor —3F 99
Staveley-in-Cartmel. Cumb —1C 96
Staverton. Devn —2D 9
Staverton. Glos —3D 49
Staverton. Nptn —4C 62
Staverton. Wilts —5D 34
Stawell. Som —3G 21
Stawley. Som —4D 20
Staxigoe. High —3F 169
Staxton. N Yor —2E 101
Staylittle. Powy —1A 58
Staynall. Lanc —5C 96
Staythorpe. Notts —5E 87
(Steam, GWR Mus., Swindon) —3G 35
Stean. N Yor —2C 98
Stearsby. N Yor —2A 100
Steart. Som —2F 21
Stebbing. Essx —3G 53
Stebbing Green. Essx —3G 53
Stedham. W Sus —4G 25
Steel. Nmbd —4C 114
Steel Cross. E Sus —2G 27

Steelend. Fife —4C 136
Steele Road. Bord —5H 119
Steel Heath. Shrp —2H 71
Steen's Bridge. Here —5H 59
Steep. Hants —4F 25
Steep Lane. W Yor —2A 92
Steeple. Dors —4E 15
Steeple. Essx —5C 54
Steeple Ashton. Wilts —1E 23
Steeple Aston. Oxon —3C 50
Steeple Barton. Oxon —3C 50
Steeple Bumpstead. Essx —1G 53
Steeple Claydon. Buck —3E 51
Steeple Gidding. Cambs —2A 64
Steeple Langford. Wilts —3F 23
Steeple Morden. Cambs —1C 52
Steeton. W Yor —5C 98
Stein. High —3B 154
Steinmanhill. Abers —4E 161
Stelling Minnis. Kent —1F 29
Stembridge. Som —4H 21
Stemster. High —2D 169 (nr. Halkirk)
Stemster. High —2C 168 (nr. Westfield)
Stenalees. Corn —3E 6
Stenhill. Devn —1D 12
Stenhouse. Edin —2F 129
Stenhousemuir. Falk —1B 128
Stenigot. Linc —2B 88
Stenscholl. High —2D 155
Stenso. Orkn —5C 172
Stenson. Derbs —3H 73
Stenson Fields. Derbs —2H 73
Stenton. E Lot —2C 130
Stenwith. Linc —2F 75
Steornabhagh. W Isl —4G 171
Stepaside. Pemb —4F 43
Stepford. Dum —1F 111
Stepney. G Lon —2E 39
Steppingley. Beds —2A 52
Stepps. N Lan —3H 127
Sterndale Moor. Derbs —4F 85
Sternfield. Suff —4F 67
Stert. Wilts —1F 23
Stetchworth. Cambs —5F 65
Stevenage. Herts —3C 52
Stevenston. N Ayr —5D 126
Steventon. Hants —2D 24
Steventon. Oxon —2C 36
Stevington. Beds —5G 63
Stevington End. Cambs —1F 53
Stewartby. Beds —1A 52
Stewarton. Arg —4A 122
Stewarton. E Ayr —5F 127
Stewkley. Buck —3G 51
Stewkley Dean. Buck —3G 51
Stewley. Som —1G 13
Stewton. Linc —2C 88
Steyning. W Sus —4C 26
Steynton. Pemb —4D 42
Stibb. Corn —1C 10
Stibbard. Norf —3B 78
Stibb Cross. Devn —1E 11
Stibb Green. Wilts —5H 35
Stibbington. Cambs —1H 63
Stichill. Bord —1B 120
Sticker. Corn —3D 6
Stickford. Linc —4C 88
Sticklepath. Devn —3G 11
Sticklinch. Som —3A 22
Stickling Green. Essx —2E 53
Stickney. Linc —5C 88
Stiffkey. Norf —1B 78
Stifford's Bridge. Here —1C 48
Stileway. Som —2H 21
Stillingfleet. N Yor —5H 99
Stillington. N Yor —3H 99
Stillington. Stoc T —2A 106
Stilton. Cambs —2A 64
Stinchcombe. Glos —2C 34
Stinsford. Dors —3C 14
Stiperstones. Shrp —5F 71
Stirchley. Telf —5B 72
Stirchley. W Mid —2E 61
Stirling. Abers —4H 161
Stirling. Stir —4G 135 & 196
Stirling Castle HS —196
Stirton. N Yor —4B 98
Stisted. Essx —3A 54
Stitchcombe. Wilts —5H 35
Stithians. Corn —5B 6
Stittenham. High —1A 158
Stivichall. W Mid —3H 61
Stixwould. Linc —4A 88
Stoak. Ches —3G 83
Stobo. Bord —1D 118
Stobo Castle. Bord —1D 118
Stoborough. Dors —4E 15
Stobs Castle. Bord —4H 119
Stobswood. Nmbd —5G 121
Stock. Essx —1A 40
Stockbridge. Hants —3B 24
Stockbridge. W Yor —5C 98
Stockbury. Kent —4C 40
Stockcross. W Ber —5C 36
Stockdalewath. Cumb —5E 113
Stocker's Head. Kent —5D 40
Stockerston. Leics —1F 63
Stock Green. Worc —5D 61
Stocking. Here —2B 48
Stockingford. Warw —1H 61
Stocking Green. Essx —2F 53
Stocking Pelham. Herts —3E 53
Stockland. Devn —2F 13
Stockland Bristol. Som —2F 21
Stockleigh English. Devn —2B 12
Stockleigh Pomeroy. Devn —2B 12
Stockley. Wilts —5F 35
Stocklinch. Som —1G 13
Stockport. G Man —2D 84
Stocksbridge. S Yor —1G 85
Stocksfield. Nmbd —3D 114
Stocks, The. Kent —3D 28
Stockstreet. Essx —3B 54
Stockton. Here —4H 59
Stockton. Norf —1F 67
Stockton. Shrp —1B 60 (nr. Bridgnorth)
Stockton. Shrp —5E 71 (nr. Chirbury)
Stockton. Telf —4B 72
Stockton. Warw —4B 62
Stockton. Wilts —3E 23
Stockton Brook. Staf —5D 84
Stockton Cross. Here —4H 59
Stockton Heath. Warr —2A 84
Stockton-on-Tees. Stoc T —3B 106
Stockton on Teme. Worc —4B 60
Stockton-on-the-Forest. York —4A 100
Stockwell Heath. Staf —3E 73
Stockwood. Bris —5B 34
Stock Wood. Worc —5E 61
Stodmarsh. Kent —4G 41
Stody. Norf —2C 78
Stoer. High —1E 163
Stoford. Som —1A 14
Stoford. Wilts —3F 23
Stogumber. Som —3D 20
Stogursey. Som —2F 21
Stoke. Devn —4C 18
Stoke. Hants —1C 24 (nr. Andover)
Stoke. Hants —2F 17 (nr. South Hayling)
Stoke. Medw —3C 40
Stoke. W Mid —3A 62
Stoke Abbott. Dors —2H 13
Stoke Albany. Nptn —2F 63
Stoke Ash. Suff —3D 66
Stoke Bardolph. Notts —1D 74
Stoke Bliss. Worc —4A 60
Stoke Bruerne. Nptn —1F 51
Stoke Bruerne Canal Mus. —5E 63
Stoke by Clare. Suff —1H 53
Stoke-by-Nayland. Suff —2C 54
Stoke Canon. Devn —3C 12
Stoke Charity. Hants —3C 24
Stoke Climsland. Corn —5D 10
Stoke Cross. Here —5A 60
Stoke D'Abernon. Surr —5C 38
Stoke Doyle. Nptn —2H 63
Stoke Dry. Rut —1F 63
Stoke Edith. Here —1B 48
Stoke Farthing. Wilts —4F 23
Stoke Ferry. Norf —1G 65
Stoke Fleming. Devn —4E 9
Stokeford. Dors —4D 14
Stoke Gabriel. Devn —3E 9
Stoke Gifford. S Glo —4B 34
Stoke Golding. Leics —1A 62
Stoke Goldington. Mil —1G 51
Stokeham. Notts —3E 87
Stoke Hammond. Buck —3G 51
Stoke Heath. Shrp —3A 72
Stoke Holy Cross. Norf —5E 79
Stokeinteignhead. Devn —5C 12
Stoke Lacy. Here —1B 48
Stoke Lyne. Oxon —3D 50
Stoke Mandeville. Buck —4G 51
Stokenchurch. Buck —2F 37
Stoke Newington. G Lon —2E 39
Stokenham. Devn —4E 9
Stoke on Tern. Shrp —3A 72
Stoke-on-Trent. Stoke —1C 72 & 196
Stoke Orchard. Glos —3E 49
Stoke Pero. Som —2B 20
Stoke Poges. Buck —2A 38
Stoke Prior. Here —5H 59
Stoke Prior. Worc —4D 60
Stoke Rivers. Devn —3G 19
Stoke Rochford. Linc —3G 75
Stoke Row. Oxon —3E 37
Stoke St Gregory. Som —4G 21
Stoke St Mary. Som —4F 21
Stoke St Michael. Som —2B 22
Stoke St Milborough. Shrp —2H 59
Stokesay. Shrp —2G 59
Stokesay Castle EH —2G 59
Stokesby. Norf —4G 79
Stokesley. N Yor —4C 106
Stoke sub Hamdon. Som —1H 13
Stoke Talmage. Oxon —2E 37
Stoke Trister. Som —4C 22
Stolford. Som —2F 21
Stondon Massey. Essx —5F 53
Stone. Buck —4F 51
Stone. Glos —2B 34
Stone. Kent —3G 39
Stone. Som —3A 22
Stone. Staf —2D 72
Stone. Worc —3C 60
Stonea. Cambs —1D 64
Stoneacre NT —5C 40
Stoneacton. Shrp —1H 59
Stone Allerton. Som —1H 21
Ston Easton. Som —1B 22
Stonebridge. N Som —1G 33
Stonebridge. Som —2C 22
Stonebridge. Surr —1C 26
Stone Bridge Corner. Pet —5B 76
Stonebroom. Derbs —5B 86
Stonebyres. S Lan —5B 128
Stone Chair. W Yor —2B 92
Stone Cross. E Sus —5H 27
Stone Cross. Kent —2G 27
Stone-edge-Batch. N Som —4H 33
Stoneferry. Hull —1D 94
Stonefield. Arg —5D 140
Stonefield. S Lan —4H 127
Stonegate. E Sus —3A 28
Stonegate. N Yor —4E 107
Stonegrave. N Yor —2A 100
Stonehall. Worc —1D 49
Stonehaugh. Nmbd —2A 114
Stonehaven. Abers —5F 153
Stone Heath. Staf —2D 72
Stonehenge WH EH —2G 23
Stone Hill. Kent —2E 29
Stone House. Cumb —1G 97
Stonehouse. Glos —5D 48
Stonehouse. Nmbd —4H 113
Stonehouse. S Lan —5A 128
Stone in Oxney. Kent —3D 28
Stoneleigh. Warw —3H 61
Stoneleigh Abbey —3H 61
Stoneley Green. Ches —5A 84
Stonely. Cambs —4A 64
Stonepits. Worc —5E 61
Stoner Hill. Hants —4F 25
Stonesby. Leics —3F 75
Stonesfield. Oxon —4B 50
Stones Green. Essx —3E 55
Stone Street. Kent —5G 39
Stone Street. Suff —2C 54 (nr. Boxford)
Stone Street. Suff —2F 67 (nr. Halesworth)
Stonethwaite. Cumb —3D 102
Stoneyburn. W Lot —3C 128
Stoney Cross. Hants —1A 16
Stoneyford. Devn —2D 12
Stoneygate. Leic —5D 74
Stoneyhills. Essx —1D 40
Stoneykirk. Dum —4F 109
Stoney Middleton. Derbs —3G 85
Stoney Stanton. Leics —1B 62
Stoney Stoke. Som —3C 22
Stoney Stratton. Som —3B 22
Stoney Stretton. Shrp —5F 71
Stoneywood. Aber —2F 153
Stonham Aspal. Suff —5D 66
Stonnall. Staf —5E 73
Stonor —3F 37
Stonor. Oxon —3F 37
Stonton Wyville. Leics —1E 63
Stonybreck. Shet —1B 172
Stony Cross. Devn —4F 19
Stony Cross. Here —1C 48 (nr. Great Malvern)
Stony Cross. Here —4H 59 (nr. Leominster)
Stony Houghton. Derbs —4B 86
Stony Stratford. Mil —1F 51
Stoodleigh. Devn —3G 19 (nr. Barnstaple)
Stoodleigh. Devn —1C 12 (nr. Tiverton)
Stopham. W Sus —4B 26
Stopsley. Lutn —3B 52
Stoptide. Corn —1D 6
Storeton. Mers —2F 83
Stornoway. W Isl —4G 171
Stornoway Airport. W Isl —4G 171
Storridge. Here —1C 48
Storrington. W Sus —4B 26
Storrs. Cumb —5E 103
Storth. Cumb —1D 96
Storwood. E Yor —5B 100
Storybook Glen Theme Park —4F 153
Stotfield. Mor —1G 159
Stotfold. Beds —2C 52
Stottesdon. Shrp —2A 60
Stott Park Bobbin Mill NT —1C 96
Stoughton. Leics —5D 74
Stoughton. Surr —5A 38
Stoughton. W Sus —1G 17
Stoul. High —4F 147
Stoulton. Worc —1E 49
Stourbridge. W Mid —2C 60
Stourhead NT —3C 22
Stourpaine. Dors —2D 14
Stourport-on-Severn. Worc —3C 60
Stour Provost. Dors —4C 22
Stour Row. Dors —4D 22
Stourton. Staf —2C 60
Stourton. Warw —2A 50
Stourton. W Yor —1D 92
Stourton. Wilts —3C 22
Stourton Caundle. Dors —1C 14
Stourton Gdns. —3C 22
Stove. Orkn —4F 172
Stove. Shet —9F 173
Stoven. Suff —2G 67
Stow. Linc —2H 75 (nr. Billingborough)
Stow. Linc —2F 87 (nr. Gainsborough)
Stow. Bord —5A 130
Stow Bardolph. Norf —5F 77
Stow Bedon. Norf —1B 66
Stowbridge. Norf —5F 77
Stow cum Quy. Cambs —4E 65
Stowe —2E 51
Stowe. Glos —5A 48
Stowe. Shrp —3F 59
Stowe. Staf —4F 73
Stowe-by-Chartley. Staf —3E 73
Stowe Landscape Gdns. NT —2E 51
Stowell. Som —4B 22
Stowey. Bath —1A 22
Stowford. Devn —4D 12 (nr. Exmouth)
Stowford. Devn —4E 11 (nr. Tavistock)
Stowlangtoft. Suff —4B 66
Stow Longa. Cambs —3A 64
Stow Maries. Essx —1C 40
Stowmarket. Suff —5C 66
Stow-on-the-Wold. Glos —3G 49
Stowting. Kent —1F 29
Stowupland. Suff —5C 66
Straad. Arg —3B 126
Strachan. Abers —4D 152
Stradbroke. Suff —3E 67
Stradbrook. Wilts —1E 23
Stradishall. Suff —5G 65
Stradsett. Norf —5F 77
Stragglethorpe. Linc —5G 87
Stragglethorpe. Notts —2D 74
Straid. S Ayr —5A 116
Straight Soley. Wilts —4B 36
Straiton. Edin —3F 129
Straiton. S Ayr —4C 116
Straloch. Per —2H 143
Stramshall. Staf —2E 73
Strang. IOM —4C 108
Strangford. Here —3A 48
Stranraer. Dum —3F 109
Strata Florida. Cdgn —4G 57
Strata Florida Abbey —4G 57
Stratfield Mortimer. W Ber —5E 37
Stratfield Saye. Hants —5E 37
Stratfield Saye House —5E 37
Stratfield Turgis. Hants —1E 25
Stratford. Glos —2D 49
Stratford. G Lon —2E 39
Stratford. G Lon —2E 39
Stratford St Andrew. Suff —4F 67
Stratford St Mary. Suff —2D 54
Stratford sub Castle. Wilts —3G 23
Stratford Tony. Wilts —4F 23
Stratford-upon-Avon. Warw —5G 61 & 196
Strath. High —1G 155 (nr. Gairloch)
Strath. High —3E 169 (nr. Wick)
Strathan. High —4B 148 (nr. Fort William)
Strathan. High —1E 163 (nr. Lochinver)
Strathan. High —2F 167 (nr. Tongue)
Strathan Skerray. High —2G 167
Strathaven. S Lan —5A 128
Strathblane. Stir —2G 127
Strathcanaird. High —3F 163
Strathcarron. High —4B 156
Strathcoil. Arg —5A 140
Strathdon. Abers —2A 152
Strathkinness. Fife —2G 137
Strathmashie House. High —4H 149
Strathmiglo. Fife —2E 136
Strathmore Lodge. High —4D 168
Strathpeffer. High —3G 157
Strathrannoch. High —1F 157
Strathspey Railway —2D 150
Strathtay. Per —3G 143
Strathvaich Lodge. High —1F 157
Strathwhillan. N Ayr —2E 123
Strathy. High —1A 158 (nr. Invergordon)
Strathy. High —2A 168 (nr. Melvich)
Strathyre. Stir —2E 135
Stratton. Corn —2C 10
Stratton. Dors —3B 14
Stratton. Glos —5F 49
Stratton Audley. Oxon —3E 50
Stratton-on-the-Fosse. Som —1B 22
Stratton St Margaret. Swin —3G 35
Stratton St Michael. Norf —1E 66
Stratton Strawless. Norf —3E 78
Stravithie. Fife —2H 137
Stream. Som —3D 20
Streat. E Sus —4E 27
Streatham. G Lon —3D 39
Streatley. Beds —3A 52
Streatley. W Ber —3D 36
Street. Corn —3C 10
Street. Lanc —4E 97
Street. N Yor —4E 107
Street. Som —2G 13 (nr. Chard)
Street. Som —3H 21 (nr. Glastonbury)
Street Dinas. Shrp —2F 71
Street End. W Sus —3G 17
Street Gate. Tyne —4F 115
Streethay. Staf —4F 73
Streethouse. W Yor —3D 93
Streetlam. N Yor —5A 106
Street Lane. Derbs —1A 74
Streetly. W Mid —1E 61
Streetly End. Cambs —1G 53
Street on the Fosse. Som —3B 22
Strefford. Shrp —2G 59
Strelley. Notts —1C 74
Strensall. York —3A 100
Strensall Camp. York —4A 100
Stretcholt. Som —2F 21
Strete. Devn —4E 9
Stretford. G Man —1C 84
Stretford. Here —5H 59
Strethall. Essx —2E 53
Stretham. Cambs —3E 65
Stretton. Ches —5G 83
Stretton. Derbs —4A 86
Stretton. Rut —4G 75
Stretton. Staf —4C 72 (nr. Brewood)
Stretton. Staf —3G 73 (nr. Burton upon Trent)
Stretton. Warr —2A 84
Stretton en le Field. Leics —4H 73
Stretton Grandison. Here —1B 48
Stretton Heath. Shrp —4F 71
Stretton-on-Dunsmore. Warw —3B 62
Stretton on Fosse. Warw —2H 49
Stretton Sugwas. Here —1H 47
Stretton under Fosse. Warw —2B 62
Stretton Westwood. Shrp —1H 59
Strichen. Abers —3G 161
Strines. G Man —2D 84
Stringston. Som —2E 21
Strixton. Nptn —4G 63
Stroanfreggan. Dum —5F 117
Stroat. Glos —2A 34
Stromeferry. High —5A 156
Stromemore. High —5A 156
Stromness. Orkn —7B 172
Stronachie. Per —3C 136
Stronachlachar. Stir —2D 134
Stronchreggan. High —1E 141
Strone. Arg —1C 126
Strone. High —1H 149 (nr. Drumnadrochit)
Strone. High —4B 150 (nr. Kingussie)
Stronenaba. High —5E 148
Stronganess. Shet —1G 173
Stronmilchan. Arg —1A 134
Stronsay Airport. Orkn —5F 172
Strontian. High —2C 140
Strood. Kent —2C 28
Strood. Medw —4B 40
Strood Green. Surr —1D 26
Strood Green. W Sus —3B 26 (nr. Billingshurst)
Strood Green. W Sus —2C 26 (nr. Horsham)
Strothers Dale. Nmbd —4C 114
Stroud. Glos —5D 48
Stroud. Hants —4F 25
Stroud Green. Essx —1C 40
Stroxton. Linc —2G 75
Struan. High —5C 154
Struan. Per —2F 143
Struanmore. High —5C 154
Strubby. Linc —2D 88
Strugg's Hill. Linc —2B 76
Strumpshaw. Norf —5F 79
Strutherhill. S Lan —4A 128
Struy. High —5F 157
Stryd. IOA —2B 80
Stryt-issa. Wrex —1E 71
Stuartfield. Abers —4G 161
Stubbington. Hants —2D 16
Stubbins. Lanc —3F 91
Stubble Green. Cumb —5B 102
Stubb's Cross. Kent —2D 28
Stubbs Green. Norf —1F 67
Stubhampton. Dors —1E 15
Stubton. Linc —1F 75
Stubwood. Staf —2E 73
Stuckton. Hants —1G 15
Studham. Beds —4A 52
Studland. Dors —4F 15
Studley. Warw —4E 61
Studley. Wilts —4E 35
Studley Roger. N Yor —2E 99
Studley Royal see Fountains Abbey —3E 99
Stuntney. Cambs —3E 65
Stunts Green. E Sus —4H 27
Sturbridge. Staf —2C 72
Sturgate. Linc —2F 87
Sturmer. Essx —1G 53
Sturminster Common. Dors —1C 14
Sturminster Marshall. Dors —2E 15
Sturminster Newton. Dors —1C 14
Sturry. Kent —4F 41
Sturton. N Lin —4C 94
Sturton by Stow. Linc —2F 87
Sturton le Steeple. Notts —2E 87
Stuston. Suff —3D 66
Stutton. N Yor —5G 99
Stutton. Suff —2E 55
Styal. Ches —2C 84
Stydd. Lanc —1E 91
Styrrup. Notts —1D 86
Suainebost. W Isl —1H 171
Suardail. W Isl —4G 171
Submarine Mus. —3E 16
Succoth. Abers —5B 160
Succoth. Arg —3B 134
Suckley. Worc —5B 60
Suckley Knowl. Worc —5B 60
Sudborough. Nptn —2G 63
Sudbourne. Suff —5G 67
Sudbrook. Linc —1G 75
Sudbrook. Mon —3A 34
Sudbrooke. Linc —3H 87
Sudbury. Derbs —2F 73
Sudbury. Suff —1B 54
Sudbury Hall NT —2F 73
Sudeley Castle —3F 49
Sudgrove. Glos —5E 49
Suffield. Norf —2E 79
Suffield. N Yor —5G 107
Suffolk Wildlife Park —2H 67
Sugnall. Staf —2B 72
Sugwas Pool. Here —1H 47
Suisnish. High —5E 155
Sulaisiadar. W Isl —4H 171
Sulby. IOM —2C 108
Sulgrave. Nptn —1D 50
Sulgrave Manor —1D 50
Sulham. W Ber —4E 37
Sulhamstead. W Ber —5E 37
Sullington. W Sus —4B 26
Sullom. Shet —4E 173
Sully. V Glam —5E 33
Sumburgh. Shet —10F 173
Sumburgh Airport. Shet —10E 173
Summer Bridge. N Yor —3E 98
Summercourt. Corn —3C 6
Summerfield. Norf —2G 77
Summergangs. Hull —1E 95
Summerhill. Aber —3G 153
Summerhill. Pemb —4F 43
Summer Hill. W Mid —1D 60
Summerhouse. Darl —3F 105
Summersdale. W Sus —2G 17
Summerseat. G Man —3F 91
Summit. G Man —3H 91
Sunbury. Surr —4C 38
Sunderland. Cumb —1C 102
Sunderland. Lanc —4D 96
Sunderland. Tyne —4G 115 & 196
Sunderland Bridge. Dur —1F 105
Sundon Park. Lutn —3A 52
Sundown Adventure —3E 87
Sundridge. Kent —5F 39
Sunk Island. E Yor —3F 95
Sunningdale. Wind —4A 38
Sunninghill. Wind —4A 38
Sunningwell. Oxon —5C 50

Sunniside. Dur —1E 105
Sunniside. Tyne —4F 115
Sunny Bank. Cumb —5D 102
Sunny Hill. Derb —2H 73
Sunnyhurst. Bkbn —2E 91
Sunnylaw. Stir —4G 135
Sunnymead. Oxon —5D 50
Sunnyside. S Yor —1B 86
Sunnyside. W Sus —2E 27
Sunton. Wilts —1H 23
Surbiton. G Lon —4C 38
Surby. IOM —4B 108
Surfleet. Linc —3B 76
Surfleet Seas End. Linc —3B 76
Surlingham. Norf —5F 79
Surrex. Essx —3B 54
Sustead. Norf —2D 78
Susworth. Linc —4B 94
Sutcombe. Devn —1D 10
Suton. Norf —1C 66
Sutors of Cromarty. High —2C 158
Sutterby. Linc —3C 88
Sutterton. Linc —2B 76
Sutterton Dowdyke. Linc —2B 76
Sutton. Beds —1C 52
Sutton. Buck —3B 38
Sutton. Cambs —3D 64
Sutton. E Sus —5F 27
Sutton. G Lon —4D 38
Sutton. Kent —1H 29
Sutton. Norf —3F 79
Sutton. Notts —2E 75 (nr. Bingham)
Sutton. Notts —2D 86 (nr. East Retford)
Sutton. Oxon —5C 50
Sutton. Pemb —3D 42
Sutton. Pet —1H 63
Sutton. Shrp —2B 60 (nr. Bridgnorth)
Sutton. Shrp —2A 72 (nr. Market Drayton)
Sutton. Shrp —3F 71 (nr. Oswestry)
Sutton. Shrp —4H 71 (nr. Shrewsbury)
Sutton. Som —3B 22
Sutton. S Yor —3F 93
Sutton. Staf —3B 72
Sutton. Suff —1G 55
Sutton. W Sus —4A 26
Sutton. Worc —4A 60
Sutton Abinger. Surr —1C 26
Sutton at Hone. Kent —4G 39
Sutton Bassett. Nptn —1E 63
Sutton Benger. Wilts —4E 35
Sutton Bingham. Som —1A 14
Sutton Bonington. Notts —3C 74
Sutton Bridge. Linc —3D 76
Sutton Cheney. Leics —5B 74
Sutton Coldfield. W Mid —1F 61
Sutton Corner. Linc —3D 76
Sutton Courtenay. Oxon —2D 36
Sutton Crosses. Linc —3D 76
Sutton Gault. Cambs —3D 64
Sutton Grange. N Yor —2E 99
Sutton Green. Surr —5B 38
Sutton Hoo NT —1F 55
Sutton Howgrave. N Yor —2F 99
Sutton in Ashfield. Notts —5C 86
Sutton-in-Craven. N Yor —5C 98
Sutton Ings. Hull —1E 94
Sutton in the Elms. Leics —1C 62
Sutton Lane Ends. Ches —3D 84
Sutton Leach. Mers —1H 83
Sutton Maddock. Shrp —5B 72
Sutton Mallet. Som —3G 21
Sutton Mandeville. Wilts —4E 23
Sutton Montis. Som —4B 22
Sutton-on-Hull. Hull —1E 94
Sutton on Sea. Linc —2E 89
Sutton-on-the-Forest. N Yor —3H 99
Sutton on the Hill. Derbs —2G 73
Sutton on Trent. Notts —4E 87
Sutton Park —3H 99
Sutton Poyntz. Dors —4C 14
Sutton St Edmund. Linc —4C 76
Sutton St Edmund's Common. Linc —5C 76
Sutton St James. Linc —4C 76
Sutton St Michael. Here —1A 48
Sutton St Nicholas. Here —1A 48
Sutton Scarsdale Hall —4B 86
Sutton Scarsdale. Derbs —4B 86
Sutton Scotney. Hants —3C 24
Sutton-under-Brailes. Warw —2B 50
Sutton-under-Whitestonecliffe. N Yor —1G 99
Sutton upon Derwent. E Yor —5B 100
Sutton Valence. Kent —1C 28
Sutton Veny. Wilts —2E 23
Sutton Waldron. Dors —1D 14
Sutton Weaver. Ches —3H 83
Swaby. Linc —3C 88
Swadlincote. Derbs —4G 73
Swaffham. Norf —5H 77
Swaffham Bulbeck. Cambs —4E 65
Swaffham Prior. Cambs —4E 65
Swafield. Norf —2E 79
Swainby. N Yor —4B 106
Swainshill. Here —1H 47
Swainsthorpe. Norf —5E 78
Swainswick. Bath —5C 34
Swalcliffe. Oxon —2B 50
Swalecliffe. Kent —4F 41
Swallow. Linc —4E 95
Swallow Beck. Linc —4G 87
Swallowcliffe. Wilts —4E 23
Swallowfield. Wok —5F 37
Swallownest. S Yor —2B 86
Swampton. Hants —1C 24
Swanage. Dors —5F 15
Swanbister. Orkn —7C 172
Swanbourne. Buck —3G 51
Swanbridge. V Glam —5E 33
Swan Green. Ches —3B 84
Swanland. E Yor —2C 94
Swanley. Kent —4G 39
Swanmore. Hants —1D 16
Swannington. Leics —4B 74
Swannington. Norf —4D 78
Swanpool. Linc —4G 87
Swanscombe. Kent —3G 39
Swansea. Swan —3F 31 & 197
Swansea Maritime & Industrial Mus. —197
Swansmoor. Staf —3E 73
Swan Street. Essx —3B 54
Swanton Abbot. Norf —3E 79
Swanton Morley. Norf —4C 78
Swanton Novers. Norf —2C 78
Swanton Street. Kent —5C 40
Swanwick. Derbs —5B 86
Swanwick. Hants —2D 16
Swanwick Green. Ches —1H 71
Swarby. Linc —1H 75
Swardeston. Norf —5E 78
Swarister. Shet —3G 173
Swarkestone. Derbs —3A 74
Swarland. Nmbd —4F 121
Swarraton. Hants —3D 24
Swartha. W Yor —5C 98
Swarthmoor. Cumb —2B 96
Swaton. Linc —2A 76
Swavesey. Cambs —4C 64
Sway. Hants —3A 16
Swayfield. Linc —3G 75
Swaythling. Sotn —1C 16
Sweet Green. Worc —4A 60
Sweetham. Devn —3B 12
Sweetheart Abbey HS —3A 112
Sweetholme. Cumb —3G 103
Sweets. Corn —3B 10
Sweetshouse. Corn —2E 7
Swefling. Suff —4F 67
Swell. Som —4G 21
Swepstone. Leics —4A 74
Swerford. Oxon —2B 50
Swettenham. Ches —4C 84
Swetton. N Yor —2D 98
Swffryd. Cphy —2F 33
Swiftsden. E Sus —3B 28
Swilland. Suff —5D 66
Swillington. W Yor —1D 93
Swimbridge. Devn —4G 19
Swimbridge Newland. Devn —3G 19
Swinbrook. Oxon —4A 50
Swincliffe. N Yor —4E 99
Swincliffe. W Yor —2C 92
Swinderby. Linc —4F 87
Swindon. Glos —3E 49
Swindon. Nmbd —5D 121
Swindon. Staf —1C 60
Swindon. Swin —3G 35 & 197
Swine. E Yor —1E 95
Swinefleet. E Yor —2A 94
Swineford. S Glo —5B 34
Swineshead. Beds —4H 63
Swineshead. Linc —1B 76
Swineshead Bridge. Linc —1B 76
Swiney. High —5E 169
Swinford. Leics —3C 62
Swinford. Oxon —5C 50
Swingate. Notts —1C 74
Swingbrow. Cambs —2C 64
Swingfield Minnis. Kent —1G 29
Swingfield Street. Kent —1G 29
Swingleton Green. Suff —1C 54
Swinhill. S Lan —5A 128
Swinhoe. Nmbd —2G 121
Swinhope. Linc —1B 88
Swinister. Shet —3E 173
Swinithwaite. N Yor —1C 98
Swinmore Common. Here —1B 48
Swinscoe. Staf —1F 73
Swinside Hall. Bord —3B 120
Swinstead. Linc —3H 75
Swinton. G Man —4F 91
Swinton. N Yor —2B 100 (nr. Malton)
Swinton. N Yor —2E 98 (nr. Masham)
Swinton. Bord —5E 131
Swinton. S Yor —1B 86
Swiss Gdns. —1B 52
Swithland. Leics —4C 74
Swordale. High —2H 157
Swordly. High —2H 167
Sworton Heath. Ches —2A 84
Swyddffynnon. Cdgn —4F 57
Swyffrd. Cphy —2F 33
Swynnerton. Staf —2C 72
Swyre. Dors —4A 14
Sycharth. Powy —3E 70
Sychdyn. Flin —4E 83
Sychnant. Powy —3B 58
Sychtyn. Powy —5B 70
Syde. Glos —4E 49
Sydenham. G Lon —3E 39
Sydenham. Oxon —5F 51
Sydenham. Som —3G 21
Sydenham Damerel. Devn —5E 11
Syderstone. Norf —2H 77
Sydling St Nicholas. Dors —3B 14
Sydmonton. Hants —1C 24
Sydney. Ches —5B 84
Syerston. Notts —1E 75
Syke. G Man —3G 91
Sykehouse. S Yor —3G 93
Sykes. Lanc —4F 97
Syleham. Suff —3E 66
Sylen. Carm —5F 45
Sylfaen. Powy —5D 70
Symbister. Shet —5G 173
Symington. S Ayr —1C 116
Symington. S Lan —1B 118
Symondsbury. Dors —3H 13
Symonds Yat. Here —4A 48
Symonds Yat Gorge —4A 48
Synod Inn. Cdgn —5D 56
Syon House —3C 38
Syre. High —4G 167
Syreford. Glos —3F 49
Syresham. Nptn —1E 51
Syston. Leics —4D 74
Syston. Linc —1G 75
Sytchampton. Worc —4C 60
Sywell. Nptn —4F 63
Tabley House —3B 84

T

Tabost. W Isl —6F 171 (nr. Cearsiadar)
Tabost. W Isl —1H 171 (nr. Suainebost)
Tachbrook Mallory. Warw —4H 61
Tackley. Oxon —3C 50
Tacleit. W Isl —4D 171
Tacolneston. Norf —1D 66
Tadcaster. N Yor —5G 99
Taddington. Derbs —3F 85
Taddington. Glos —2F 49
Taddiport. Devn —1E 11
Tadley. Hants —5E 36
Tadlow. Cambs —1C 52
Tadmarton. Oxon —2B 50
Tadwick. Bath —4C 34
Tadworth. Surr —5D 38
Tafarnaubach. Blae —4E 46
Tafarn-y-bwlch. Pemb —1E 43
Tafarn-y-Gelyn. Den —4D 82
Taff's Well. Rhon —3E 33
Tafolwern. Powy —5A 70
Taibach. Neat —3A 32
Tai-bach. Powy —3D 70
Taigh a Ghearraidh. W Isl —1C 170
Taigh Bhuirgh. W Isl —8C 171
Tain. High —5E 165 (nr. Invergordon)
Tain. High —2E 169 (nr. Thurso)
Tai-Nant. Wrex —1E 71
Tai'n Lon. Gwyn —5D 80
Tairbeart. W Isl —8D 171
Tairgwaith. Neat —4H 45
Takeley. Essx —3F 53
Takeley Street. Essx —3F 53
Talachddu. Powy —2D 46
Talacre. Flin —2D 82
Talardd. Gwyn —3A 70
Talaton. Devn —3D 12
Talbenny. Pemb —3C 42
Talbot Green. Rhon —3D 32
Taleford. Devn —3D 12
Talerddig. Powy —5B 70
Talgarreg. Cdgn —5D 56
Talgarth. Powy —2E 47
Talisker. High —5C 154
Talke. Staf —5C 84
Talkin. Cumb —4G 113
Talladale. High —1B 156
Talla Linnfoots. Bord —2D 118
Tallaminnock. S Ayr —5D 116
Tallarn Green. Wrex —1G 71
Tallentire. Cumb —1C 102
Talley. Carm —2G 45
Talley Abbey CADW —2G 45
Tallington. Linc —5H 75
Talmine. High —2F 167
Talog. Carm —2H 43
Talsarn. Carm —3A 46
Talsarn. Cdgn —5E 57
Talsarnau. Gwyn —2F 69
Talskiddy. Corn —2D 6
Talwrn. IOA —3D 81
Talwrn. Wrex —1E 71
Tal-y-bont. Cdgn —2F 57
Tal-y-Bont. Cnwy —4G 81
Tal-y-bont. Gwyn —3F 81 (nr. Bangor)
Tal-y-bont. Gwyn —3E 69 (nr. Barmouth)
Talybont-on-Usk. Powy —3E 46
Tal-y-cafn. Cnwy —3G 81
Tal-y-coed. Mon —4H 47
Tal-y-llyn. Gwyn —5G 69
Talyllyn. Powy —3E 46
Talyllyn Railway —5F 69
Talysarn. Gwyn —5D 81
Tal-y-waenydd. Gwyn —1F 69
Talywain. Torf —5F 47
Talywern. Powy —5H 69
Tamerton Foliot. Plym —2A 8
Tamworth. Staf —5G 73
Tamworth Castle —5G 73
Tamworth Green. Linc —1C 76
Tandlehill. Ren —3F 127
Tandridge. Surr —5E 39
Tanerdy. Carm —3E 45
Tanfield. Dur —4E 115
Tanfield Lea. Dur —4E 115
Tangasdale. W Isl —8B 170
Tang Hall. York —4A 100
Tangiers. Pemb —3D 42
Tangley. Hants —1B 24
Tangmere. W Sus —5A 26
Tangwick. Shet —4D 173
Tankerness. Orkn —7E 172
Tankersley. S Yor —1H 85
Tankerton. Kent —4F 41
Tank Mus. —4D 14
Tan-lan. Cnwy —4G 81
Tan-lan. Gwyn —1F 69
Tannach. High —4F 169
Tannadice. Ang —3D 145
Tanners Green. Worc —3E 61
Tannington. Suff —4E 67
Tannochside. N Lan —3A 128
Tan Office Green. Suff —5G 65
Tansley. Derbs —5H 85
Tansley Knoll. Derbs —4H 85
Tansor. Nptn —1H 63
Tantallon Castle HS —1B 130
Tantobie. Dur —4E 115
Tanton. N Yor —3C 106
Tanvats. Linc —4A 88
Tanworth-in-Arden. Warw —3F 61
Tan-y-bwlch. Gwyn —1F 69
Tan-y-fron. Cnwy —4B 82
Tanyfron. Wrex —5E 83
Tan-y-goes. Cdgn —1C 44
Tanygrisiau. Gwyn —1F 69
Tan-y-pistyll. Powy —3C 70
Tan-yr-allt. Den —2C 82
Taobh a Chaolais. W Isl —7C 170
Taobh a Deas Loch Aineort. W Isl —6C 170
Taobh a Ghlinne. W Isl —6F 171
Taobh Tuath. W Isl —9B 171
Taplow. Buck —2A 38
Tapton. Derbs —3A 86
Tarbert. Arg —3G 125 (nr. Knapdale)
Tarbert. Arg —1E 125 (on Jura)
Tarbert. W Isl —8D 171
Tarbet. Arg —3C 134
Tarbet. High —4F 147 (nr. Mallaig)
Tarbet. High —4B 166 (nr. Scourie)
Tarbock Green. Mers —2G 83
Tarbolton. S Ayr —2D 116
Tarbrax. S Lan —4D 128
Tardebigge. Worc —4E 61
Tarfside. Ang —1D 145
Tarland. Abers —3B 152
Tarleton. Lanc —2C 90
Tarlogie. High —5E 165
Tarlscough. Lanc —3C 90
Tarlton. Glos —2E 35
Tarnbrook. Lanc —4E 97
Tarn Hows NT —4E 103
Tarnock. Som —1G 21
Tarns. Cumb —5C 112
Tarporley. Ches —4H 83
Tarpots. Essx —2B 40
Tarr. Som —3E 20
Tarrant Crawford. Dors —2E 15
Tarrant Gunville. Dors —1E 15
Tarrant Hinton. Dors —1E 15
Tarrant Keyneston. Dors —2E 15
Tarrant Launceston. Dors —2E 15
Tarrant Monkton. Dors —2E 15
Tarrant Rawston. Dors —2E 15
Tarrant Rushton. Dors —2E 15
Tarrel. High —5F 165
Tarring Neville. E Sus —5F 27
Tarrington. Here —1B 48
Tarsappie. Per —1D 136
Tarskavaig. High —3D 147
Tarves. Abers —5F 161
Tarvie. High —3G 157
Tarvin. Ches —4G 83
Tasburgh. Norf —1E 66
Tasley. Shrp —1A 60
Taston. Oxon —3B 50
Tate Britain —London 193
Tate Liverpool —191
Tate Modern —London 193
Tatenhill. Staf —3G 73
Tate St Ives —2C 4
Tathall End. Mil —1G 51
Tatham. Lanc —3F 97
Tathwell. Linc —2C 88
Tatling End. Buck —2B 38
Tatsfield. Surr —5F 39
Tattenhall. Ches —5G 83
Tatterford. Norf —3A 78
Tattersett. Norf —2H 77
Tattershall. Linc —5B 88
Tattershall Bridge. Linc —5A 88
Tattershall Castle NT —5B 88
Tattershall Thorpe. Linc —5B 88
Tattingstone. Suff —2E 55
Tattingstone White Horse. Suff —2E 55
Tattle Bank. Warw —4F 61
Tatton Park NT —2B 84
Tatworth. Som —2G 13
Taunton. Som —4F 21 & 197
Taverham. Norf —4D 78
Taverners Green. Essx —4F 53
Tavernspite. Pemb —3F 43
Tavistock. Devn —5E 11
Tavool House. Arg —1B 132
Taw Green. Devn —3G 11
Tawstock. Devn —4F 19
Taxal. Derbs —2E 85
Tay Forest Park —4G 143
Tayinloan. Arg —5E 125
Taynish. Arg —1F 125
Taynton. Glos —3C 48
Taynton. Oxon —4H 49
Taynuilt. Arg —5E 141
Tayport. Fife —1G 137
Tayvallich. Arg —1F 125
Tealby. Linc —1A 88
Tealing. Ang —5D 144
Teangue. High —3E 147
Teanna Machair. W Isl —2C 170
Tebay. Cumb —4H 103
Tebworth. Beds —3H 51
Tedburn St Mary. Devn —3B 12
Teddington. Glos —2E 49
Teddington. G Lon —3C 38
Tedsmore. Shrp —3F 71
Tedstone Delamere. Here —5A 60
Tedstone Wafer. Here —5A 60
Teesport. Red C —2C 106
Teesside. Stoc T —2C 106
Tees-side Airport. Stoc T —3A 106
Teeton. Nptn —3D 62
Teffont Evias. Wilts —3E 23
Teffont Magna. Wilts —3E 23
Tegryn. Pemb —1G 43
Teifi Valley Railway —1D 44
Teigh. Rut —4F 75
Teigncombe. Devn —4G 11
Teigngrace. Devn —5B 12
Teignmouth. Devn —5C 12
Telford. Telf —4A 72
Telham. E Sus —4B 28
Tellisford. Som —1D 22
Telscombe. E Sus —5F 27
Telscombe Cliffs. E Sus —5E 27
Tempar. Per —3D 142
Templand. Dum —1B 112
Temple. Corn —5B 10
Temple. Glas —3G 127
Temple. Midl —4G 129
Temple Balsall. W Mid —3G 61
Temple Bar. Carm —4F 45
Temple Bar. Cdgn —5E 57
Temple Cloud. Bath —1B 22
Templecombe. Som —4C 22
Temple Ewell. Kent —1G 29
Temple Grafton. Warw —5F 61
Temple Guiting. Glos —3F 49
Templehall. Fife —4E 137
Temple Hirst. N Yor —2G 93
Temple Newsam —1D 92
Temple Normanton. Derbs —4B 86
Temple Sowerby. Cumb —2H 103
Templeton. Devn —1B 12
Templeton. Pemb —3F 43
Templeton. W Ber —5B 36
Templetown. Dur —5E 115
Tempsford. Beds —5A 64
Tenandry. Per —2G 143
Tenbury Wells. Worc —4H 59
Tenby. Pemb —4F 43
Tendring. Essx —3E 55
Tendring Green. Essx —3E 55
Tenga. Arg —4G 139
Ten Mile Bank. Norf —1F 65
Tenterden. Kent —2C 28
Terfyn. Cnwy —3B 82
Terling. Essx —4A 54
Ternhill. Shrp —2A 72
Terregles. Dum —2G 111
Terrick. Buck —5G 51
Terrington. N Yor —2A 100
Terrington St Clement. Norf —3E 77
Terrington St John. Norf —4E 77
Terry's Green. Warw —3F 61
Teston. Kent —5B 40
Testwood. Hants —1B 16
Tetbury. Glos —2D 35
Tetbury Upton. Glos —2D 35
Tetchill. Shrp —2F 71
Tetcott. Devn —3D 10
Tetford. Linc —3C 88
Tetney. Linc —4G 95
Tetney Lock. Linc —4G 95
Tetsworth. Oxon —5E 51
Tettenhall. W Mid —1C 60
Teversal. Notts —4B 86
Teversham. Cambs —5D 65
Teviothead. Bord —4G 119
Tewel. Abers —5F 153
Tewin. Herts —4C 52
Tewkesbury. Glos —2D 49
Teynham. Kent —4D 40
Teynham Street. Kent —4D 40
Thackthwaite. Cumb —2F 103
Thakeham. W Sus —4C 26
Thame. Oxon —5F 51
Thames Ditton. Surr —4C 38
Thames Haven. Thur —2B 40
Thamesmead. G Lon —3F 39
Thamesport. Medw —3C 40
Thanington Without. Kent —5F 41
Thankerton. S Lan —1B 118
Tharston. Norf —1D 66
Thatcham. W Ber —5D 36
Thatto Heath. Mers —1H 83
Thaxted. Essx —2G 53
Theakston. N Yor —1F 99
Thealby. N Lin —3B 94
Theale. Som —2H 21
Theale. W Ber —4E 37
Thearne. E Yor —1D 94
Theberton. Suff —4G 67
Theddingworth. Leics —2D 62
Theddlethorpe All Saints. Linc —2D 88
Theddlethorpe St Helen. Linc —2D 89
Thelbridge Barton. Devn —1A 12
Thelnetham. Suff —3C 66
Thelveton. Norf —2D 66
Thelwall. Warr —2A 84
Themelthorpe. Norf —3C 78
Thenford. Nptn —1D 50
Therfield. Herts —2D 52
Thetford. Linc —4A 76
Thetford. Norf —2A 66
Thetford Forest Park —1A 66
Thetford Priory EH —2A 66
Thethwaite. Cumb —5E 113
Theydon Bois. Essx —1F 39
Thick Hollins. W Yor —4B 92
Thickwood. Wilts —4D 34
Thimbleby. Linc —3B 88
Thimbleby. N Yor —5B 106
Thingwall. Mers —2E 83
Thirlby. N Yor —1G 99
Thirlestane. Bord —5B 130
Thirlestane Castle —5B 130
Thirn. N Yor —1E 98
Thirsk. N Yor —1G 99
Thirtleby. E Yor —1E 95
Thistleton. Lanc —1C 90
Thistleton. Rut —4G 75
Thistley Green. Suff —3F 65
Thixendale. N Yor —3C 100
Thockrington. Nmbd —2C 114
Tholomas Drove. Cambs —5D 76

Tholthorpe. N Yor —3G 99
Thomas Chapel. Pemb —4F 43
Thomas Close. Cumb —5F 113
Thomastown. Abers —4E 160
Thomastown. Rhon —3D 32
Thompson. Norf —1B 66
Thomshill. Mor —3G 159
Thong. Kent —3A 40
Thongsbridge. W Yor —4B 92
Thoralby. N Yor —1C 98
Thoresby. Notts —3D 86
Thoresway. Linc —1A 88
Thorganby. Linc —1B 88
Thorganby. N Yor —5A 100
Thorgill. N Yor —5E 107
Thorington. Suff —3G 67
Thorington Street. Suff —2D 54
Thorlby. N Yor —4B 98
Thorley. Herts —4E 53
Thorley Street. Herts —4E 53
Thorley Street. IOW —4B 16
Thormanby. N Yor —2G 99
Thorn. Powy —4E 59
Thornaby-on-Tees. Stoc T —3B 106
Thornage. Norf —2C 78
Thornborough. Buck —2F 51
Thornborough. N Yor —2E 99
Thornbury. Devn —2E 11
Thornbury. Here —5A 60
Thornbury. S Glo —3B 34
Thornby. Cumb —4D 112
Thornby. Nptn —3D 62
Thorncliffe. Staf —5E 85
Thorncombe. Dors —2G 13 (nr. Beaminster)
Thorncombe. Dors —2D 14 (nr. Blandford Forum)
Thorncombe Street. Surr —1A 26
Thorncote Green. Beds —1B 52
Thorndon. Suff —4D 66
Thorndon Cross. Devn —3F 11
Thorne. S Yor —3G 93
Thornehillhead. Devn —1E 11
Thorner. W Yor —5F 99
Thorne St Margaret. Som —4D 20
Thorney. Notts —3F 87
Thorney. Pet —5B 76
Thorney. Som —4H 21
Thorney Hill. Hants —3G 15
Thorney Toll. Cambs —5C 76
Thornfalcon. Som —4F 21
Thornford. Dors —1B 14
Thorngrafton. Nmbd —3A 114
Thorngrove. Som —3G 21
Thorngumbald. E Yor —2F 95
Thornham. Norf —1G 77
Thornham Magna. Suff —3D 66
Thornham Parva. Suff —3D 66
Thornham Walled Gdn. —3C 66
Thornhaugh. Pet —5H 75
Thornhill. Cphy —3E 33
Thornhill. Cumb —4B 102
Thornhill. Derbs —2F 85
Thornhill. Dum —5A 118
Thornhill. Sotn —1C 16
Thornhill. Stir —4F 135
Thornhill. W Yor —3C 92
Thornhill Lees. W Yor —3C 92
Thornhills. W Yor —2B 92
Thornholme. E Yor —3F 101
Thornington. Nmbd —1C 120
Thornley. Dur —1A 106 (nr. Durham)
Thornley. Dur —1E 105 (nr. Tow Law)
Thornley Gate. Nmbd —4B 114
Thornliebank. E Ren —4G 127
Thornroan. Abers —5F 161
Thorns. Suff —5G 65
Thornsett. Derbs —2E 85
Thornthwaite. Cumb —2D 102
Thornthwaite. N Yor —4D 98
Thornton. Ang —4C 144
Thornton. Buck —2F 51
Thornton. E Yor —5B 100
Thornton. Fife —4E 137
Thornton. Lanc —5C 96
Thornton. Leics —5B 74
Thornton. Linc —4B 88
Thornton. Mers —4B 90
Thornton. Midd —3B 106
Thornton. Nmbd —5F 131
Thornton. W Yor —1A 92
Thornton Abbey EH —3E 94
Thornton Curtis. N Lin —3D 94
Thorntonhall. S Lan —4G 127
Thornton Heath. G Lon —4E 39
Thornton Hough. Mers —2F 83
Thornton in Craven. N Yor —5B 98
Thornton in Lonsdale. N Yor —2F 97
Thornton-le-Beans. N Yor —5A 106
Thornton-le-Clay. N Yor —3A 100
Thornton-le-Dale. N Yor —1C 100
Thornton le Moor. Linc —1H 87
Thornton-le-Moor. N Yor —1F 99
Thornton-le-Moors. Ches —3G 83
Thornton-le-Street. N Yor —1G 99
Thorntonloch. E Lot —2D 130
Thornton Rust. N Yor —1B 98
Thornton Steward. N Yor —1D 98
Thornton Watlass. N Yor —1E 99
Thornwood Common. Essx —5E 53
Thornythwaite. Cumb —2E 103
Thoroton. Notts —1E 75
Thorp Arch. W Yor —5G 99
Thorpe. Derbs —5F 85
Thorpe. E Yor —5D 101
Thorpe. Linc —2D 89
Thorpe. Norf —1G 67
Thorpe. N Yor —3C 98
Thorpe. Notts —1E 75
Thorpe. Surr —4B 38
Thorpe Abbotts. Norf —3D 66
Thorpe Acre. Leics —3C 74
Thorpe Arnold. Leics —3E 75
Thorpe Audlin. W Yor —3E 93
Thorpe Bassett. N Yor —2C 100
Thorpe Bay. S'end —2D 40
Thorpe by Water. Rut —1F 63
Thorpe Common. S Yor —1A 86
Thorpe Common. Suff —2F 55
Thorpe Constantine. Staf —5G 73
Thorpe End. Norf —4E 79
Thorpe Fendike. Linc —4D 88
Thorpe Green. Essx —3E 55
Thorpe Green. Suff —5B 66
Thorpe Hall. N Yor —2H 99
Thorpe Hamlet. Norf —5E 79
Thorpe Hesley. S Yor —1A 86
Thorpe in Balne. S Yor —3F 93
Thorpe in the Fallows. Linc —2G 87
Thorpe Langton. Leics —1E 63
Thorpe Larches. Dur —2A 106
Thorpe Latimer. Linc —1A 76
Thorpe-le-Soken. Essx —3E 55
Thorpe le Street. E Yor —5C 100
Thorpe Malsor. Nptn —3F 63
Thorpe Mandeville. Nptn —1D 50
Thorpe Market. Norf —2E 79
Thorpe Marriott. Norf —4D 78
Thorpe Morieux. Suff —5B 66
Thorpeness. Suff —4G 67
Thorpe on the Hill. Linc —4G 87
Thorpe on the Hill. W Yor —2D 92
Thorpe Park —4B 38
Thorpe Perrow Arboretum —1E 99
Thorpe St Andrew. Norf —5E 79
Thorpe St Peter. Linc —4D 89
Thorpe Salvin. S Yor —2C 86
Thorpe Satchville. Leics —4E 75
Thorpe Thewles. Stoc T —2B 106
Thorpe Tilney. Linc —5A 88
Thorpe Underwood. N Yor —4G 99
Thorpe Waterville. Nptn —2H 63
Thorpe Willoughby. N Yor —1F 93
Thorpland. Norf —5F 77
Thorrington. Essx —3D 54
Thorverton. Devn —2C 12
Thrandeston. Suff —3D 66
Thrapston. Nptn —3G 63
Thrashbush. N Lan —3A 128
Threapland. Cumb —1C 102
Threapland. N Yor —3B 98
Threapwood. Ches —1G 71
Threapwood. Staf —1E 73
Threave Castle NTS —3E 111
Threave Gdn. NTS —3E 111
Three Ashes. Here —3A 48
Three Bridges. Linc —2D 88
Three Bridges. W Sus —2D 27
Three Burrows. Corn —4B 6
Three Chimneys. Kent —2C 28
Three Cocks. Powy —2E 47
Three Crosses. Swan —3E 31
Three Cups Corner. E Sus —3H 27
Three Holes. Norf —5E 77
Threekingham. Linc —2H 75
Three Leg Cross. E Sus —2A 28
Three Legged Cross. Dors —2F 15
Three Mile Cross. Wok —5F 37
Threemilestones. Corn —4B 6
Three Oaks. E Sus —4C 28
Threlkeld. Cumb —2E 102
Threshfield. N Yor —3B 98
Thrigby. Norf —4G 79
Thrigby Hall Wildlife —4G 79
Thringarth. Dur —2C 104
Thringstone. Leics —4B 74
Thrintoft. N Yor —5A 106
Thriplow. Cambs —1E 53
Throckenholt. Linc —5C 76
Throcking. Herts —2D 52
Throckley. Tyne —3E 115
Throckmorton. Worc —1E 49
Throphill. Nmbd —1E 115
Thropton. Nmbd —4E 121
Throsk. Stir —4A 136
Througham. Glos —5E 49
Throughgate. Dum —1F 111
Throwleigh. Devn —3G 11
Throwley. Kent —5D 40
Throwley Forstal. Kent —5D 40
Throxenby. N Yor —1E 101
Thrumpton. Notts —2C 74
Thrumster. High —4F 169
Thrunton. Nmbd —3E 121
Thrupp. Glos —5D 48
Thrupp. Oxon —4C 50
Thrushelton. Devn —4E 11
Thrushgill. Lanc —3F 97
Thrussington. Leics —4D 74
Thruxton. Hants —2A 24
Thruxton. Here —2H 47
Thrybergh. S Yor —1B 86
Thulston. Derbs —2B 74
Thundergay. N Ayr —5G 125
Thundersley. Essx —2B 40
Thundridge. Herts —4D 52
Thurcaston. Leics —4C 74
Thurcroft. S Yor —2B 86
Thurdon. Corn —1C 10
Thurgarton. Norf —2D 78
Thurgarton. Notts —1D 74
Thurgoland. S Yor —4C 92
Thurlaston. Leics —1C 62
Thurlaston. Warw —3B 62
Thurlby. Linc —3D 89 (nr. Alford)
Thurlby. Linc —4A 76 (nr. Baston)
Thurlby. Linc —4G 87 (nr. Lincoln)
Thurleigh. Beds —5H 63
Thurlestone. Devn —4C 8
Thurloxton. Som —3F 21
Thurlstone. S Yor —4C 92
Thurlton. Norf —1G 67
Thurmaston. Leics —5D 74
Thurnby. Leics —5D 74
Thurne. Norf —4G 79
Thurnham. Kent —5C 40
Thurning. Norf —3C 78
Thurning. Nptn —2H 63
Thurnscoe. S Yor —4E 93
Thursby. Cumb —4E 113
Thursford. Norf —2B 78
Thursford Collection —2B 78
Thursford Green. Norf —2B 78
Thursley. Surr —2A 26
Thurso. High —2D 168
Thurso East. High —2D 168
Thurstaston. Mers —2E 83
Thurston. Suff —4B 66
Thurston End. Suff —5G 65
Thurstonfield. Cumb —4E 112
Thurstonland. W Yor —3B 92
Thurton. Norf —5F 79
Thurvaston. Derbs —2F 73 (nr. Ashbourne)
Thurvaston. Derbs —2G 73 (nr. Derby)
Thuxton. Norf —5C 78
Thwaite. Dur —3D 104
Thwaite. N Yor —5B 104
Thwaite. Suff —4D 66
Thwaite Head. Cumb —5E 103
Thwaites. W Yor —5C 98
Thwaite St Mary. Norf —1F 67
Thwing. E Yor —2E 101
Tibbermore. Per —1C 136
Tibberton. Glos —3C 48
Tibberton. Telf —3A 72
Tibberton. Worc —5D 60
Tibenham. Norf —2D 66
Tibshelf. Derbs —4B 86
Tibthorpe. E Yor —4D 100
Ticehurst. E Sus —2A 28
Tichborne. Hants —3D 24
Tickencote. Rut —5G 75
Tickenham. N Som —4H 33
Tickhill. S Yor —1C 86
Ticklerton. Shrp —1G 59
Ticknall. Derbs —3H 73
Tickton. E Yor —5E 101
Tidbury Green. W Mid —3F 61
Tidcombe. Wilts —1A 24
Tiddington. Oxon —5E 51
Tiddington. Warw —5G 61
Tiddleywink. Wilts —4D 34
Tidebrook. E Sus —3H 27
Tideford. Corn —3H 7
Tideford Cross. Corn —2H 7
Tidenham. Glos —2A 34
Tideswell. Derbs —3F 85
Tidmarsh. W Ber —4E 37
Tidmington. Warw —2A 50
Tidpit. Hants —1F 15
Tidworth. Wilts —2H 23
Tidworth Camp. Wilts —2H 23
Tiers Cross. Pemb —3D 42
Tiffield. Nptn —5D 62
Tifty. Abers —4E 161
Tigerton. Ang —2E 145
Tighnabruaich. Arg —2A 126
Tigley. Devn —2D 8
Tilbrook. Cambs —4H 63
Tilbury. Thur —3H 39
Tilbury Fort EH —3A 40
Tilbury Green. Essx —1H 53
Tilbury Juxta Clare. Essx —1A 54
Tile Cross. W Mid —2F 61
Tile Hill. W Mid —3G 61
Tilehurst. Read —4E 37
Tilford. Surr —2G 25
Tilgate Forest Row. W Sus —2D 26
Tillathrowie. Abers —5B 160
Tillers Green. Glos —2B 48
Tillery. Abers —1G 153
Tilley. Shrp —3H 71
Tillicoultry. Clac —4B 136
Tillingham. Essx —5C 54
Tillington. Here —1H 47
Tillington. W Sus —3A 26
Tillington Common. Here —1H 47
Tillybirloch. Abers —3D 152
Tillyfourie. Abers —2D 152
Tilmanstone. Kent —5H 41
Tilney All Saints. Norf —4E 77
Tilney Fen Side. Norf —4E 77
Tilney High End. Norf —4E 77
Tilney St Lawrence. Norf —4E 77
Tilshead. Wilts —2F 23
Tilstock. Shrp —2H 71
Tilston. Ches —5G 83
Tilstone Fearnall. Ches —4H 83
Tilsworth. Beds —3H 51
Tilton on the Hill. Leics —5E 75
Tiltups End. Glos —2D 34
Timberland. Linc —5A 88
Timbersbrook. Ches —4C 84
Timberscombe. Som —2C 20
Timble. N Yor —4D 98
Timperley. G Man —2B 84
Timsbury. Bath —1B 22
Timsbury. Hants —4B 24
Timsgearraidh. W Isl —4C 171
Timworth Green. Suff —4A 66
Tincleton. Dors —3C 14
Tindale. Cumb —4H 113
Tindale Crescent. Dur —2F 105
Tingewick. Buck —2E 51
Tingley. W Yor —2C 92
Tingrith. Beds —2A 52
Tingwall. Orkn —5D 172
Tinhay. Devn —4D 11
Tinshill. W Yor —1C 92
Tinsley. S Yor —1B 86
Tinsley Green. W Sus —2D 27
Tintagel. Corn —4A 10
Tintagel Castle EH —4A 10
Tintern Abbey CADW —5A 48
Tintern Parva. Mon —5A 48
Tintinhull. Som —1A 14
Tintinhull House NT —4A 22
Tintwistle. Derbs —1E 85
Tinwald. Dum —1B 112
Tinwell. Rut —5H 75
Tippacott. Devn —2A 20
Tipperty. Abers —1G 153
Tips End. Cambs —1E 65
Tiptoe. Hants —3A 16
Tipton. W Mid —1D 60
Tipton St John. Devn —3D 12
Tiptree. Essx —4B 54
Tiptree Heath. Essx —4B 54
Tirabad. Powy —1B 46
Tircoed. Swan —5G 45
Tirinie. Per —2F 143
Tirley. Glos —3D 48
Tirnewydd. Flin —3D 82
Tiroran. Arg —1B 132
Tirphil. Cphy —5E 47
Tirril. Cumb —2G 103
Tirryside. High —2C 164
Tir-y-dail. Carm —4G 45
Tisbury. Wilts —4E 23
Tisman's Common. W Sus —2B 26
Tissington. Derbs —5F 85
Tissington Hall —5F 85
Titchberry. Devn —4C 18
Titchfield. Hants —2D 16
Titchmarsh. Nptn —3H 63
Titchwell. Norf —1G 77
Tithby. Notts —2D 74
Titley. Here —5F 59
Titlington. Nmbd —3F 121
Titsey. Surr —5F 39
Titson. Corn —2C 10
Tittensor. Staf —2C 72
Tittleshall. Norf —3A 78
Titton. Worc —4C 60
Tiverton. Ches —4H 83
Tiverton. Devn —1C 12
Tiverton Castle —1C 12
Tivetshall St Margaret. Norf —2D 66
Tivetshall St Mary. Norf —2D 66
Tivington. Som —2C 20
Tixall. Staf —3D 73
Tixover. Rut —5G 75
Toab. Orkn —7E 172
Toab. Shet —10E 173
Toadmoor. Derbs —5H 85
Tobermory. Arg —3G 139
Toberonochy. Arg —3E 133
Tobha-Beag. W Isl —1E 170
Tobha Beag. W Isl —5C 170
Tobha Mor. W Isl —5C 170
Tobhtarol. W Isl —4D 171
Tobson. W Isl —4D 171
Tocher. Abers —5D 160
Tockenham. Wilts —4F 35
Tockenham Wick. Wilts —3F 35
Tockholes. Bkbn —2E 91
Tockington. S Glo —3B 34
Tockwith. N Yor —4G 99
Todber. Dors —4D 22
Todding. Here —3G 59
Toddington. Beds —3A 52
Toddington. Glos —2F 49
Todenham. Glos —2H 49
Todhills. Cumb —3E 113
Todmorden. W Yor —2H 91
Todwick. S Yor —2B 86
Toft. Cambs —5C 64
Toft. Linc —4H 75
Toft Hill. Dur —2E 105
Toft Monks. Norf —1G 67
Toft next Newton. Linc —2H 87
Toftrees. Norf —3A 78
Tofts. High —2F 169
Toftwood. Norf —4B 78
Togston. Nmbd —4G 121
Tokavaig. High —2E 147
Tokers Green. Oxon —4F 37
Tolastadh a Chaolais. W Isl —4D 171
Tolladine. Worc —5C 60
Tolland. Som —3E 20
Tollard Farnham. Dors —1E 15
Tollard Royal. Wilts —1E 15
Toll Bar. S Yor —4F 93
Toller Fratrum. Dors —3A 14
Toller Porcorum. Dors —3A 14
Tollerton. N Yor —3H 99
Tollerton. Notts —2D 74
Toller Whelme. Dors —2A 14
Tollesbury. Essx —4C 54
Tolleshunt D'Arcy. Essx —4C 54
Tolleshunt Knights. Essx —4C 54
Tolleshunt Major. Essx —4C 54
Tollie. High —3H 157
Tollie Farm. High —1A 156
Tolm. W Isl —4G 171
Tolpuddle. Dors —3C 14
Tolquhon Castle HS —1F 153
Tolstadh bho Thuath. W Isl —3H 171
Tolworth. G Lon —4C 38
Tomachlaggan. Mor —1F 151
Tomaknock. Per —1A 136
Tomatin. High —1C 150
Tombuidhe. Arg —3H 133
Tomdoun. High —3D 148
Tomich. High —1F 149 (nr. Cannich)
Tomich. High —1A 158 (nr. Invergordon)
Tomich. High —3D 164 (nr. Lairg)
Tomintoul. Mor —2F 151
Tomnavoulin. Mor —1G 151
Tomsleibhe. Arg —5A 140
Ton. Mon —2G 33
Tonbridge. Kent —1G 27
Tondu. B'end —3B 32
Tonedale. Som —4E 21
Tonfanau. Gwyn —5E 69
Tong. Shrp —5B 72
Tonge. Leics —3B 74
Tong Forge. Shrp —5B 72
Tongham. Surr —2G 25
Tongland. Dum —4D 111
Tong Norton. Shrp —5B 72
Tongue. High —3F 167
Tongwynlais. Card —3E 33
Tonmawr. Neat —2B 32
Tonna. Neat —2A 32
Ton-Pentre. Rhon —2C 32
Tonwell. Herts —4D 52
Tonypandy. Rhon —2C 32
Tonyrefail. Rhon —3D 32
Toot Baldon. Oxon —5D 50
Toot Hill. Essx —5F 53
Toot Hill. Hants —1B 16
Topcliffe. N Yor —2G 99
Topcliffe. W Yor —2C 92
Topcroft. Norf —1E 67
Topcroft Street. Norf —1E 67
Toppesfield. Essx —2H 53
Toppings. G Man —3F 91
Toprow. Norf —1D 66
Topsham. Devn —4C 12
Torbay. Torb —2F 9
Torbeg. N Ayr —3C 122
Torbothie. N Lan —3B 128
Torbryan. Devn —2E 9
Torcross. Devn —4E 9
Tore. High —3A 158
Torgyle. High —2F 149
Torinturk. Arg —3G 125
Torksey. Linc —3F 87
Torlum. W Isl —3C 170
Torlundy. High —1F 141
Tormarton. S Glo —4C 34
Tormitchell. S Ayr —5B 116
Tormore. High —3E 147
Tormore. N Ayr —2C 122
Tornagrain. High —4B 158
Tornaveen. Abers —3D 152
Torness. High —1H 149
Toronto. Dur —1E 105
Torosay Castle —5B 140
Torpenhow. Cumb —1D 102
Torphichen. W Lot —2C 128
Torphins. Abers —3D 152
Torpoint. Corn —3A 8
Torquay. Torb —2F 9
Torr. Devn —3B 8
Torra. Arg —4B 124
Torran. High —4E 155
Torrance. E Dun —2H 127
Torrans. Arg —1B 132
Torranyard. E Ayr —5E 127
Torre. Torb —2E 9
Torridon. High —3B 156
Torrin. High —1D 147
Torrisdale. Arg —2B 122
Torrisdale. High —2G 167
Torrish. High —2G 165
Torrisholme. Lanc —3D 96
Torroble. High —3C 164
Torroy. High —4C 164
Tor Royal. Devn —5G 11
Torry. Aber —3G 153
Torryburn. Fife —1D 128
Torthorwald. Dum —2B 112
Tortington. W Sus —5B 26
Tortworth. S Glo —2C 34
Torvaig. High —4D 155
Torver. Cumb —5D 102
Torwood. Falk —1B 128
Torworth. Notts —2D 86
Toscaig. High —5G 155
Toseland. Cambs —4B 64
Tosside. Lanc —4G 97
Tostock. Suff —4B 66
Totaig. High —3B 154
Totardor. High —5C 154
Tote. High —4D 154
Totegan. High —2A 168
Tothill. Linc —2D 88
Totland. IOW —4B 16
Totley. S Yor —3H 85
Totnell. Dors —2B 14
Totnes. Devn —2E 9
Totnes Castle EH —2E 9
Toton. Derbs —2B 74
Totronald. Arg —3C 138
Totscore. High —2C 154
Tottenham. G Lon —1E 39
Tottenhill. Norf —4F 77
Tottenhill Row. Norf —4F 77
Totteridge. G Lon —1D 38
Totternhoe. Beds —3H 51
Tottington. G Man —3F 91
Totton. Hants —1B 16
Touchenend. Wind —4G 37
Touches. Som —2G 13
Toulvaddie. High —5F 165
Towans, The. Corn —3C 4
Toward. Arg —3C 126
Towcester. Nptn —1E 51
Towednack. Corn —3B 4
Tower End. Norf —4F 77
Towerhill. Devn —3D 10
Tower Hill. Mers —4C 90
Tower Hill. W Sus —3C 26
Tower of London —193
Towersey. Oxon —5F 51
Towie. Abers —2B 152
Towiemore. Mor —4A 160
Tow Law. Dur —1E 105
Towneley Hall & Gallery —1G 91
Town End. Cambs —1D 64
Town End. Cumb —4F 103 (nr. Ambleside)
Town End. Cumb —2H 103 (nr. Kirkby Thore)
Town End. Cumb —1D 96 (nr. Lindale)
Town End. Cumb —1C 96 (nr. Newby Bridge)
Town End. Mers —2G 83
Townend. W Dun —2F 127
Townend House NT —4E 103
Townfield. Dur —5C 114
Towngate. Cumb —5G 113
Towngate. Linc —4A 76

Town Green. Lanc —4B 90
Town Head. Cumb —4E 103
(nr. Grasmere)
Town Head. Cumb —3H 103
(nr. Great Asby)
Townhead. Cumb —1G 103
(nr. Lazonby)
Townhead. Cumb —1B 102
(nr. Maryport)
Townhead. Cumb —1H 103
(nr. Ousby)
Townhead. Dum —5D 111
Townhead of Greenlaw. Dum —3E 111
Townhill. Fife —1E 129
Townhill. Swan —3F 31
Town Kelloe. Dur —1A 106
Town Littleworth. E Sus —4F 27
Town Row. E Sus —2G 27
Towns End. Hants —1D 24
Townsend. Herts —5B 52
Townshend. Corn —3C 4
Town Street. Suff —2G 65
Town Yetholm. Bord —2C 120
Towthorpe. E Yor —3C 100
Towthorpe. York —4A 100
Towton. N Yor —1E 93
Towyn. Cnwy —3B 82
Toxteth. Mers —2F 83
Toynton All Saints. Linc —4C 88
Toynton Fen Side. Linc —4C 88
Toynton St Peter. Linc —4D 88
Toy's Hill. Kent —5F 39
Trabboch. E Ayr —2D 116
Traboe. Corn —4E 5
Tradespark. High —3C 158
Tradespark. Orkn —7D 172
Trafford Park. G Man —1B 84
Trallong. Powy —3C 46
Tranent. E Lot —2H 129
Tranmere. Mers —2F 83
Trantlebeg. High —3A 168
Trantlemore. High —3A 168
Tranwell. Nmbd —1E 115
Trapp. Carm —4G 45
Traquair. Bord —1F 119
Traquair House —1F 119
Trash Green. W Ber —5E 37
Trawden. Lanc —1H 91
Trawscoed. Powy —2D 46
Trawsfynydd. Gwyn —2G 69
Trawsgoed. Cdgn —3F 57
Treaddow. Here —3A 48
Trealaw. Rhon —2D 32
Treales. Lanc —1C 90
Trearddur. IOA —3B 80
Treaslane. High —3C 154
Treator. Corn —1D 6
Trebah Gdns. —4E 5
Trebanog. Rhon —2D 32
Trebanos. Neat —5H 45
Trebarber. Corn —2C 6
Trebartha. Corn —5C 10
Trebarwith. Corn —4A 10
Trebetherick. Corn —1D 6
Treborough. Som —3D 20
Trebudannon. Corn —2C 6
Trebullett. Corn —5D 10
Treburley. Corn —5D 10
Treburrick. Corn —1C 6
Trebyan. Corn —2E 7
Trecastle. Powy —3B 46
Trecenydd. Cphy —3E 33
Trecott. Devn —2G 11
Trecwn. Pemb —1D 42
Trecynon. Rhon —5C 46
Tredaule. Corn —4C 10
Tredavoe. Corn —4B 4
Tredegar. Blae —5E 47
Tredegar House —3F 33
Trederwen. Powy —4E 71
Tredington. Glos —3E 49
Tredington. Warw —1A 50
Tredinnick. Corn —2F 7
(nr. Bodmin)
Tredinnick. Corn —3G 7
(nr. Looe)
Tredinnick. Corn —1D 6
(nr. Padstow)
Tredogan. V Glam —5D 32
Tredomen. Powy —2E 46
Tredunnock. Mon —2G 33
Tredustan. Powy —2E 47
Treen. Corn —4A 4
(nr. Land's End)
Treen. Corn —3B 4
(nr. St Ives)
Treeton. S Yor —2B 86
Trefaldwyn. Powy —1E 58
Trefasser. Pemb —1C 42
Trefdraeth. IOA —3D 80
Trefdraeth. Pemb —1E 43
Trefecca. Powy —2E 47
Trefechan. Mer T —5D 46
Trefeglwys. Powy —1B 58
Trefeitha. Powy —2E 46
Trefenter. Cdgn —4F 57
Treffgarne. Pemb —2D 42
Treffynnon. Flin —3D 82
Treffynnon. Pemb —2C 42
Trefil. Blae —4E 46
Trefilan. Cdgn —5E 57
Trefin. Pemb —1C 42
Treflach. Shrp —3E 71
Trefnant. Den —3C 82
Trefonen. Shrp —3E 71
Trefor. Gwyn —1C 68
Trefor. IOA —3C 80
Treforest. Rhon —3D 32
Trefrew. Corn —4B 10
Trefriw. Cnwy —4G 81
Tref-y-Clawdd. Powy —3E 59
Trefynwy. Mon —4A 48
Tregada. Corn —4D 10
Tregadillett. Corn —4D 10
Tregare. Mon —4H 47
Tregarne. Corn —4E 5
Tregaron. Cdgn —5F 57
Tregarth. Gwyn —4F 81
Tregear. Corn —3C 6
Tregeare. Corn —4C 10
Tregeiriog. Wrex —2D 70
Tregele. IOA —1C 80
Tregeseal. Corn —3A 4
Tregiskey. Corn —4E 6
Tregole. Corn —3B 10
Tregolwyn. V Glam —4C 32
Tregonetha. Corn —2D 6
Tregonhawke. Corn —3A 8
Tregony. Corn —4D 6
Tregoodwell. Corn —4B 10
Tregorrick. Corn —3E 6
Tregoss. Corn —2D 6
Tregowris. Corn —4E 5
Tregoyd. Powy —2E 47
Tregrehan Mills. Corn —3E 7
Tre-groes. Cdgn —1E 45
Tregullon. Corn —2E 7
Tregurrian. Corn —2C 6
Tregynon. Powy —1C 58
Trehafod. Rhon —2D 32
Trehan. Corn —3A 8
Treharris. Mer T —2E 32
Treherbert. Rhon —2C 32
Trehunist. Corn —2H 7
Trekenner. Corn —5D 10
Trekenning. Corn —2D 6
Treknow. Corn —4A 10
Trelales. B'end —3B 32
Trelan. Corn —5E 5
Trelash. Corn —3B 10
Trelassick. Corn —3C 6
Trelawnyd. Flin —3C 82
Trelech. Carm —1G 43
Treleddyd-fawr. Pemb —2B 42
Trelewis. Mer T —2E 32
Treligga. Corn —4A 10
Trelights. Corn —1D 6
Trelill. Corn —5A 10
Trelissick. Corn —5C 6
Trelissick Gdn. NT —5C 6
Trelleck. Mon —5A 48
Trelleck Grange. Mon —5H 47
Trelogan. Flin —2D 82
Trelystan. Powy —5E 71
Tremadog. Gwyn —1E 69
Tremail. Corn —4B 10
Tremain. Cdgn —1C 44
Tremaine. Corn —4C 10
Tremar. Corn —2G 7
Trematon. Corn —3H 7
Tremeirchion. Den —3C 82
Tremore. Corn —2E 6
Tremorfa. Card —4F 33
Trenance. Corn —5D 4
(nr. Helston)
Trenance. Corn —2C 6
(nr. Newquay)
Trenance. Corn —1D 6
(nr. Padstow)
Trenarren. Corn —4E 7
Trench. Telf —4A 72
Trencreek. Corn —2C 6
Trendeal. Corn —3C 6
Trenear. Corn —5A 6
Treneglos. Corn —4C 10
Trenewan. Corn —3F 7
Trengune. Corn —3B 10
Trengwainton Gdn. NT —3B 4
Trent. Dors —1A 14
Trentham. Stoke —1C 72
Trentham Gdns. —1C 72
Trentishoe. Devn —2G 19
Trentlock. Derbs —2B 74
Treoes. V Glam —4C 32
Treorchy. Rhon —2C 32
Treorci. Rhon —2C 32
Tre'r-ddol. Cdgn —1F 57
Trerice NT —3C 6
Tre'r llai. Powy —5E 71
Trerulefoot. Corn —3H 7
Tresaith. Cdgn —5B 56
Tresco Abbey Gdn. —1A 4
Trescott. Staf —1C 60
Trescowe. Corn —3C 4
Tresham. Glos —2C 34
Tresigin. V Glam —4C 32
Tresillian. Corn —4C 6
Tresimwn. V Glam —4D 32
Tresinney. Corn —4B 10
Treskillard. Corn —5A 6
Treskinnick Cross. Corn —3C 10
Tresmeer. Corn —4C 10
Tresparrett. Corn —3B 10
Tresparrett Posts. Corn —3B 10
Tressady. High —3D 164
Tressait. Per —2F 143
Tresta. Shet —2H 173
(on Fetlar)
Tresta. Shet —6E 173
(on Mainland)
Treswell. Notts —3E 87
Treswithian. Corn —2D 4
Tre Taliesin. Cdgn —1F 57
Trethomas. Cphy —3E 33
Trethosa. Corn —3D 6
Trethurgy. Corn —3E 7
Tretio. Pemb —2B 42
Tretire. Here —3A 48
Tretower. Powy —3E 47
Tretower Castle CADW —3E 47
Treuddyn. Flin —5E 83
Trevadlock. Corn —5C 10
Trevalga. Corn —3A 10
Trevalyn. Wrex —5F 83
Trevance. Corn —1D 6
Trevanger. Corn —1D 6
Trevanson. Corn —1D 6
Trevarrack. Corn —3B 4
Trevarren. Corn —2D 6
Trevarrian. Corn —2C 6
Trevarrick. Corn —4D 6
Tre-vaughan. Carm —3E 45
(nr. Carmarthen)
Trevaughan. Carm —3F 43
(nr. Whitland)
Treveighan. Corn —5A 10
Trevellas. Corn —3B 6
Trevelmond. Corn —2G 7
Treverva. Corn —5B 6
Trevescan. Corn —4A 4
Trevethin. Torf —5F 47
Trevia. Corn —4A 10
Trevigro. Corn —2H 7
Trevilley. Corn —4A 4
Treviscoe. Corn —3D 6
Trevivian. Corn —4B 10
Trevone. Corn —1C 6
Trevor. Den —1E 71
Trevor Uchaf. Den —1E 71
Trew. Corn —4D 4
Trewalder. Corn —4A 10
Trewarlett. Corn —4D 10
Trewarmett. Corn —4A 10
Trewassa. Corn —4B 10
Treween. Corn —4C 10
Trewellard. Corn —3A 4
Trewen. Corn —4C 10
Trewennack. Corn —4D 5
Trewern. Powy —4E 71
Trewetha. Corn —4A 10
Trewidland. Corn —2G 7
Trewint. Corn —3B 10
Trewithan —4D 6
Trewithian. Corn —5C 6
Trewoofe. Corn —4B 4
Trewoon. Corn —3D 6
Treworthal. Corn —5C 6
Trewyddel. Pemb —1B 44
Treyarnon. Corn —1C 6
Treyford. W Sus —1G 17
Triangle. Staf —5E 73
Triangle. W Yor —2A 92
Trickett's Cross. Dors —2F 15
Trimdon. Dur —1A 106
Trimdon Colliery. Dur —1A 106
Trimdon Grange. Dur —1A 106
Trimingham. Norf —2E 79
Trimley Lower Street. Suff —2F 55
Trimley St Martin. Suff —2F 55
Trimley St Mary. Suff —2F 55
Trimpley. Worc —3B 60
Trimsaran. Carm —5E 45
Trimstone. Devn —2F 19
Trinafour. Per —2E 142
Trinant. Cphy —2F 33
Tring. Herts —4H 51
Trinity. Ang —2F 145
Trinity. Edin —2F 129
Trisant. Cdgn —3G 57
Trislaig. High —1E 141
Trispen. Corn —3C 6
Tritlington. Nmbd —5G 121
Trochry. Per —4G 143
Troedrhiwdalar. Powy —5B 58
Troedrhiwfuwch. Cphy —5E 47
Troedrhiwgwair. Blae —5E 47
Troedyraur. Cdgn —1D 44
Troedyrhiw. Mer T —5D 46
Trondavoe. Shet —4E 173
Troon. Corn —5A 6
Troon. S Ayr —1C 116
Tropical Birdland —5B 74
Troqueer. Dum —2A 112
Trossachs, The —3E 135
Troston. Suff —3A 66
Trottiscliffe. Kent —4H 39
Trotton. W Sus —4G 25
Troutbeck. Cumb —4F 103
(nr. Ambleside)
Troutbeck. Cumb —2E 103
(nr. Penrith)
Troutbeck Bridge. Cumb —4F 103
Troway. Derbs —3A 86
Trowbridge. Wilts —1D 22
Trowell. Notts —1B 74
Trowle Common. Wilts —1D 22
Trowley Bottom. Herts —4A 52
Trowse Newton. Norf —5E 79
Trudoxhill. Som —2C 22
Trull. Som —4F 21
Trumaisgearraidh. W Isl —1D 170
Trumpan. High —2B 154
Trumpet. Here —2B 48
Trumpington. Cambs —5D 64
Trumps Green. Surr —4A 38
Trunch. Norf —2E 79
Trunnah. Lanc —5C 96
Truro. Corn —4C 6
Trusham. Devn —4B 12
Trusley. Derbs —2G 73
Trusthorpe. Linc —2E 89
Tryfil. IOA —2D 80
Trysull. Staf —1C 60
Tubney. Oxon —2C 36
Tuckenhay. Devn —3E 9
Tuckhill. Staf —2B 60
Tuckingmill. Corn —4A 6
Tuckton. Bour —3G 15
Tuddenham. Suff —1E 55
(nr. Ipswich)
Tuddenham. Suff —3G 65
(nr. Mildenhall)
Tudeley. Kent —1H 27
Tudhoe. Dur —1F 105
Tudhoe Grange. Dur —1F 105
Tudorville. Here —3A 48
Tudweiliog. Gwyn —2B 68
Tuesley. Surr —1A 26
Tufton. Hants —2C 24
Tufton. Pemb —2E 43
Tugby. Leics —5E 75
Tugford. Shrp —2H 59
Tughall. Nmbd —2G 121
Tulchan. Per —1B 136
Tullibardine. Per —2B 136
Tullibody. Clac —4A 136
Tullich. Arg —2H 133
Tullich. High —4B 156
(nr. Lochcarron)
Tullich. High —1C 158
(nr. Tain)
Tullich. Mor —4H 159
Tullich Muir. High —1B 158
Tulliemet. Per —3G 143
Tulloch. Abers —5F 161
Tulloch. High —4D 164
(nr. Bonar Bridge)
Tulloch. High —5F 149
(nr. Fort William)
Tulloch. High —2D 151
(nr. Grantown-on-Spey)
Tulloch. Per —1C 136
Tullochgorm. Arg —4G 133
Tullybeagles Lodge. Per —5H 143
Tullymurdoch. Per —3A 144
Tullynessle. Abers —2C 152
Tumble. Carm —4F 45
Tumbler's Green. Essx —3B 54
Tumby. Linc —4B 88
Tumby Woodside. Linc —5B 88
Tummel Bridge. Per —3E 143
Tunbridge Wells, Royal. Kent —2G 27
Tunga. W Isl —4G 171
Tungate. Norf —3E 79
Tunley. Bath —1B 22
Tunstall. E Yor —1G 95
Tunstall. Kent —4C 40
Tunstall. Lanc —2F 97
Tunstall. Norf —5G 79
Tunstall. N Yor —5F 105
Tunstall. Staf —3B 72
Tunstall. Stoke —5C 84
Tunstall. Suff —5F 67
Tunstall. Tyne —4G 115
Tunstead. Derbs —3F 85
Tunstead. Norf —3E 79
Tunstead Milton. Derbs —2E 85
Tunworth. Hants —2E 25
Tupsley. Here —1A 48
Tupton. Derbs —4A 86
Turfholm. S Lan —1H 117
Turfmoor. Devn —2F 13
Turgis Green. Hants —1E 25
Turkdean. Glos —4G 49
Turkey Island. Hants —1D 16
Tur Langton. Leics —1E 62
Turleigh. Wilts —5D 34
Turlin Moor. Pool —3E 15
Turnant. Here —3G 47
Turnastone. Here —2G 47
Turnberry. S Ayr —4B 116
Turnchapel. Plym —3A 8
Turnditch. Derbs —1G 73
Turners Hill. W Sus —2E 27
Turners Puddle. Dors —3D 14
Turnford. Herts —5D 52
Turnhouse. Edin —2E 129
Turnworth. Dors —2D 14
Turriff. Abers —4E 161
Tursdale. Dur —1A 106
Turton Bottoms. Bkbn —3F 91
Turton Tower —3F 91
Turtory. Mor —4C 160
Turves Green. W Mid —3E 61
Turvey. Beds —5G 63
Turville. Buck —2F 37
Turville Heath. Buck —2F 37
Turweston. Buck —2E 50
Tushielaw. Bord —3F 119
Tutbury. Staf —3G 73
Tutnall. Worc —3D 61
Tutsbill. Glos —2A 34
Tuttington. Norf —3E 79
Tutts Clump. W Ber —4D 36
Tutwell. Corn —5D 11
Tuxford. Notts —3E 87
Twatt. Orkn —5B 172
Twatt. Shet —6E 173
Twechar. E Dun —2A 128
Tweedale. Telf —5A 72
Tweedmouth. Nmbd —4F 131
Tweedsmuir. Bord —2C 118
Twelveheads. Corn —4B 6
Twemlow Green. Ches —4B 84
Twenty. Linc —3A 76
Twerton. Bath —5C 34
Twickenham. G Lon —3C 38
Twigworth. Glos —3D 48
Twineham. W Sus —3D 26
Twinhoe. Bath —1C 22
Twinstead. Essx —2B 54
Twinstead Green. Essx —2B 54
Twiss Green. Warr —1A 84
Twiston. Lanc —5H 97
Twitchen. Devn —3A 20
Twitchen. Shrp —3F 59
Two Bridges. Devn —5G 11
Two Bridges. Glos —5B 48
Two Dales. Derbs —4G 85
Two Gates. Staf —5G 73
Two Mile Oak Cross. Devn —2E 9
Twycross. Leics —5H 73
Twycross Zoo —5H 73
Twyford. Buck —3E 51
Twyford. Derbs —3H 73
Twyford. Dors —1D 14
Twyford. Hants —4C 24
Twyford. Leics —4E 75
Twyford. Norf —3C 78
Twyford. Wok —4F 37
Twyford Common. Here —2A 48
Twyncarno. Cphy —5E 46
Twynholm. Dum —4D 110
Twyning. Glos —2D 49
Twyning Green. Glos —2E 49
Twynllanan. Carm —3A 46
Twynmynydd. Carm —4G 45
Twyn-y-Sheriff. Mon —5H 47
Twywell. Nptn —3G 63
Tyberton. Here —2G 47
Tyburn. W Mid —1F 61
Tyby. Norf —3C 78
Tycroes. Carm —4G 45
Tycrwyn. Powy —4D 70
Tyddewi. Pemb —2B 42
Tydd Gote. Linc —4D 76
Tydd St Giles. Cambs —4D 76
Tydd St Mary. Linc —4D 76
Tye. Hants —2F 17
Tye Green. Essx —3F 53
(nr. Bishop's Stortford)
Tye Green. Essx —3A 54
(nr. Braintree)
Tye Green. Essx —2F 53
(nr. Saffron Walden)
Tyersal. W Yor —1B 92
Ty Issa. Powy —3D 70
Tyldesley. G Man —4E 91
Tyle. Carm —3G 45
Tyler Hill. Kent —4F 41
Tylers Green. Buck —2G 37
Tyler's Green. Essx —5F 53
Tylorstown. Rhon —2D 32
Tylwch. Powy —2B 58
Ty Mawr Wybmant NT —5G 81
Ty-nant. Cnwy —1B 70
Tyndrum. Stir —5H 141
Tyneham. Dors —4D 15
Tynehead. Midl —4G 129
Tynemouth. Tyne —3G 115
Tyneside. Tyne —3F 115
Tyne Tunnel. Tyne —3G 115
Tynewydd. Rhon —2C 32
Tyninghame. E Lot —2C 130
Tynron. Dum —5H 117
Tyntesfield NT —4A 34
Ty'n-y-bryn. Rhon —3D 32
Tyn-y-celyn. Wrex —2D 70
Ty'n-y-coed NT —5H 81
Tyn-y-cwm. Swan —5G 45
Tyn-y-ffridd. Powy —2D 70
Tynygongl. IOA —2E 81
Tynygraig. Cdgn —4F 57
Tyn-y-groes. Cnwy —3G 81
Ty'n-yr-eithin. Cdgn —4F 57
Tyn-y-rhyd. Powy —4C 70
Tyn-y-wern. Powy —3C 70
Tyrie. Abers —2G 161
Tyringham. Mil —1G 51
Tythecott. Devn —1E 11
Tythegston. B'end —4B 32
Tytherington. Ches —3D 84
Tytherington. Som —2C 22
Tytherington. S Glo —3B 34
Tytherington. Wilts —2E 23
Tytherleigh. Devn —2G 13
Tywardreath. Corn —3E 7
Tywardreath Highway. Corn —3E 7
Tywyn. Cnwy —3G 81
Tywyn. Gwyn —5E 69

Uachdar. W Isl —3D 170
Uags. High —5G 155
Ubbeston Green. Suff —3F 67
Ubley. Bath —1A 22
Uckerby. N Yor —4F 105
Uckfield. E Sus —3F 27
Uckinghall. Worc —2D 48
Uckington. Glos —3E 49
Uckington. Shrp —5H 71
Uddingston. S Lan —3H 127
Uddington. S Lan —1A 118
Udimore. E Sus —4C 28
Udny Green. Abers —1F 153
Udny Station. Abers —1G 153
Udston. S Lan —4A 128
Udstonhead. S Lan —5A 128
Uffcott. Wilts —4G 35
Uffculme. Devn —1D 12
Uffington. Linc —5H 75
Uffington. Oxon —3B 36
Uffington. Shrp —4H 71
Uffington White Horse EH —3B 36
Ufford. Pet —5H 75
Ufford. Suff —5E 67
Ufton. Warw —4A 62
Ufton Nervet. W Ber —5E 37
Ugadale. Arg —3B 122
Ugborough. Devn —3C 8
Ugbrooke House —5B 12
Ugford. Wilts —3F 23
Uggeshall. Suff —3G 67
Ugglebarnby. N Yor —4F 107
Ugley. Essx —3F 53
Ugley Green. Essx —3F 53
Ugthorpe. N Yor —3E 107
Uidh. W Isl —9B 170
Uig. Arg —3C 138
Uig. High —2C 154
(nr. Balgown)
Uig. High —3A 154
(nr. Dunvegan)
Uigshader. High —4D 154
Uisken. Arg —2A 132
Ulbster. High —4F 169
Ulcat Row. Cumb —2F 103
Ulceby. Linc —3D 88
Ulceby. N Lin —3E 94
Ulceby Skitter. N Lin —3E 94
Ulcombe. Kent —1C 28
Uldale. Cumb —1D 102
Uley. Glos —2C 34
Ulgham. Nmbd —5G 121
Ullapool. High —4F 163
Ullenhall. Warw —4F 61
Ulleskelf. N Yor —1F 93
Ullesthorpe. Leics —2C 62
Ulley. S Yor —2B 86
Ullingswick. Here —1A 48
Ullinish. High —5C 154
Ullock. Cumb —2B 102
Ulpha. Cumb —5D 102
Ulrome. E Yor —4F 101
Ulsta. Shet —3F 173
Ulting. Essx —5B 54
Ulva House. Arg —5F 139
Ulverston. Cumb —2B 96
Ulwell. Dors —4F 15
Umberleigh. Devn —4G 19
Unapool. High —5C 166
Underbarrow. Cumb —5F 103
Undercliffe. W Yor —1B 92
Underdale. Shrp —4H 71
Underhoull. Shet —1G 173
Underriver. Kent —5G 39
Under Tofts. S Yor —2H 85
Underton. Shrp —1A 60
Underwood. Notts —5B 86
Underwood. Plym —3B 8
Undley. Suff —2F 65
Undy. Mon —3H 33
Union Mills. IOM —4C 108
Union Street. E Sus —2B 28
Unst Airport. Shet —1H 173
Unstone. Derbs —3A 86
Unstone Green. Derbs —3A 86
Unthank. Cumb —5E 113
(nr. Carlisle)
Unthank. Cumb —5H 113
(nr. Gamblesby)
Unthank. Cumb —1F 103
(nr. Penrith)

Unthank End. Cumb —1F 103
Upavon. Wilts —1G 23
Up Cerne. Dors —2B 14
Upchurch. Kent —4C 40
Upcott. Devn —2F 11
Upcott. Here —5F 59
Upend. Cambs —5G 65
Up Exe. Devn —2C 12
Upgate. Norf —4D 78
Upgate Street. Norf —1C 66
Uphall. W Lot —2D 128
Uphall Station. W Lot —2D 128
Upham. Devn —2B 12
Upham. Hants —4D 24
Uphampton. Here —4F 59
Uphampton. Worc —4C 60
Up Hatherley. Glos —3E 49
Uphill. N Som —1G 21
Up Holland. Lanc —4D 90
Uplawmoor. E Ren —4F 127
Upleadon. Glos —3C 48
Upleatham. Red C —3D 106
Uplees. Kent —4D 40
Uploders. Dors —3A 14
Uplowman. Devn —1D 12
Uplyme. Devn —3G 13
Up Marden. W Sus —1F 17
Upminster. G Lon —2G 39
Up Nately. Hants —1E 25
Upnor Castle EH —3B 40
Upottery. Devn —2F 13
Uppark NT —1F 17
Uppat. High —3F 165
Upper Affcot. Shrp —2G 59
Upper Arley. Worc —2B 60
Upper Armley. W Yor —1C 92
Upper Arncott. Oxon —4E 50
Upper Astrop. Nptn —2D 50
Upper Badcall. High —4B 166
Upper Bangor. Gwyn —3E 81
Upper Basildon. W Ber —4D 36
Upper Batley. W Yor —2C 92
Upper Beeding. W Sus —4C 26
Upper Benefield. Nptn —2G 63
Upper Bentley. Worc —4D 61
Upper Bighouse. High —3A 168
Upper Boddam. Abers —5D 160
Upper Boddington. Nptn —5B 62
Upper Bogside. Mor —3G 159
Upper Booth. Derbs —2F 85
Upper Borth. Cdgn —2F 57
Upper Boyndlie. Abers —2G 161
Upper Brailes. Warw —2B 50
Upper Breakish. High —1E 147
Upper Breinton. Here —1H 47
Upper Broadheath. Worc —5C 60
Upper Broughton. Notts —3D 74
Upper Brynamman. Carm —4H 45
Upper Bucklebury. W Ber —5D 36
Upper Bullington. Hants —2C 24
Upper Burgate. Hants —1G 15
Upper Caldecote. Beds —1B 52
Upper Canterton. Hants —1A 16
Upper Catesby. Nptn —5C 62
Upper Chapel. Powy —1D 46
Upper Cheddon. Som —4F 21
Upper Chicksgrove. Wilts —4E 23
Upper Church Village. Rhon —3D 32
Upper Chute. Wilts —1A 24
Upper Clatford. Hants —2B 24
Upper Coberley. Glos —4E 49
Upper Coedcae. Torf —5F 47
Upper Cokeham. W Sus —5C 26
Upper Common. Hants —2E 25
Upper Cound. Shrp —5H 71
Upper Cudworth. S Yor —4D 93
Upper Cumberworth. W Yor —4C 92
Upper Cuttlehill. Abers —4B 160
Upper Cwmbran. Torf —2F 33
Upper Dallachy. Mor —2A 160
Upper Dean. Beds —4H 63
Upper Dean. Devn —2D 8
Upper Denby. W Yor —4C 92
Upper Derraid. High —5E 159
Upper Diabaig. High —2H 155
Upper Dicker. E Sus —5G 27
Upper Dinchope. Shrp —2G 59
Upper Dochcarty. High —2H 157
Upper Dounreay. High —2B 168
Upper Dovercourt. Essx —2F 55
Upper Dunsforth. N Yor —3G 99
Upper Dunsley. Herts —4H 51
Upper Eastern Green. W Mid —3G 61
Upper Elkstone. Staf —5E 85
Upper Ellastone. Staf —1F 73
Upper End. Derbs —3E 85
Upper Enham. Hants —2B 24
Upper Farringdon. Hants —3F 25
Upper Framilode. Glos —4C 48
Upper Froyle. Hants —2F 25
Upper Gills. High —1F 169
Upper Glenfintaig. High —5E 149
Upper Godney. Som —2H 21
Upper Gravenhurst. Beds —2B 52
Upper Green. Essx —2E 53
Upper Green. W Ber —5B 36
Upper Green. W Yor —2C 92
Upper Grove Common. Here —3A 48
Upper Hackney. Derbs —4G 85
Upper Hale. Surr —2G 25
Upper Halliford. Surr —4B 38
Upper Halling. Medw —4A 40
Upper Hambleton. Rut —5G 75
Upper Hardwick. Here —5G 59
Upper Hartfield. E Sus —2F 27
Upper Haugh. S Yor —1B 86
Upper Hayton. Shrp —2H 59
Upper Heath. Shrp —2H 59
Upper Hellesdon. Norf —4E 79
Upper Helmsley. N Yor —4A 100
Upper Hengoed. Shrp —2E 71
Upper Hergest. Here —5E 59
Upper Heyford. Nptn —5D 62
Upper Heyford. Oxon —3C 50
Upper Hill. Here —5G 59
Upper Hindhope. Bord —4B 120
Upper Hopton. W Yor —3B 92
Upper Horsebridge. E Sus —4C 28
Upper Howsell. Worc —1C 48
Upper Hulme. Staf —4E 85
Upper Inglesham. Swin —2H 35
Upper Kilcott. Glos —3C 34
Upper Killay. Swan —3E 31
Upper Kirkton. Abers —5E 161
Upper Kirkton. N Ayr —4C 126
Upper Knockando. Mor —4F 159
Upper Knockchoilum. High —2G 149
Upper Lambourn. W Ber —3B 36
Upper Langford. N Som —1H 21
Upper Langwith. Derbs —4C 86
Upper Largo. Fife —3G 137
Upper Latheron. High —5D 169
Upper Layham. Suff —1D 54
Upper Leigh. Staf —2E 73
Upper Lenie. High —1H 149
Upper Lochton. Abers —4D 152
Upper Longdon. Staf —4E 73
Upper Longwood. Shrp —5A 72
Upper Lybster. High —5E 169
Upper Lydbrook. Glos —4B 48
Upper Lye. Here —4F 59
Upper Maes-coed. Here —2G 47
Upper Midway. Derbs —3G 73
Uppermill. G Man —4H 91
Upper Millichope. Shrp —2H 59
Upper Milovaig. High —4A 154
Upper Minety. Wilts —2F 35
Upper Mitton. Worc —3C 60
Upper Nash. Pemb —4E 43
Upper Neepaback. Shet —3G 173
Upper Netchwood. Shrp —1A 60
Upper Nobut. Staf —2E 73
Upper North Dean. Buck —2G 37
Upper Norwood. W Sus —4A 26
Upper Nyland. Dors —4C 22
Upper Oddington. Glos —3H 49
Upper Ollach. High —5E 155
Upper Outwoods. Staf —3G 73
Upper Padley. Derbs —3G 85
Upper Pennington. Hants —3B 16
Upper Poppleton. York —4H 99
Upper Quinton. Warw —1G 49
Upper Rochford. Worc —4A 60
Upper Rusko. Dum —3C 110
Upper Sandaig. High —2F 147
Upper Sanday. Orkn —7E 172
Upper Sapey. Here —4A 60
Upper Seagry. Wilts —3E 35
Upper Shelton. Beds —1H 51
Upper Sheringham. Norf —1D 78
Upper Skelmorlie. N Ayr —3C 126
Upper Slaughter. Glos —3G 49
Upper Sonachan. Arg —1H 133
Upper Soudley. Glos —4B 48
Upper Staploe. Beds —5A 64
Upper Stoke. Norf —5E 79
Upper Stondon. Beds —2B 52
Upper Stowe. Nptn —5D 62
Upper Street. Hants —1G 15
Upper Street. Norf —4F 79
(nr. Horning)
Upper Street. Norf —4F 79
(nr. Hoveton)
Upper Street. Suff —2E 55
Upper Strensham. Worc —2E 49
Upper Studley. Wilts —1D 22
Upper Sundon. Beds —3A 52
Upper Swell. Glos —3G 49
Upper Tankersley. S Yor —1H 85
Upper Tean. Staf —2E 73
Upperthong. W Yor —4B 92
Upperthorpe. N Lin —4A 94
Upper Thurnham. Lanc —4D 96
Upper Tillyrie. Per —3D 136
Upperton. W Sus —3A 26
Upper Tooting. G Lon —3D 38
Uppertown. Derbs —4H 85
(nr. Ashover)
Upper Town. Derbs —5G 85
(nr. Bonsall)
Upper Town. Derbs —5G 85
(nr. Hognaston)
Upper Town. Here —1A 48
Uppertown. High —1F 169
Upper Town. N Som —5A 34
Uppertown. Nmbd —2B 114
Uppertown. Orkn —8D 172
Upper Tysoe. Warw —1B 50
Upper Upham. Wilts —4H 35
Upper Upnor. Medw —3B 40
Upper Urquhart. Fife —3D 136
Upper Wardington. Oxon —1C 50
Upper Weald. Mil —2F 51
Upper Weedon. Nptn —5D 62
Upper Wellingham. E Sus —4F 27
Upper Whiston. S Yor —2B 86
Upper Wield. Hants —3E 25
Upper Winchendon. Buck —4F 51
Upperwood. Derbs —5G 85
Upper Woodford. Wilts —3G 23
Upper Wootton. Hants —1D 24
Upper Wraxall. Wilts —4D 34
Upper Wyche. Here —1C 48
Uppincott. Devn —2B 12
Uppingham. Rut —1F 63
Uppington. Shrp —5H 71
Upsall. N Yor —1G 99
Upsettlington. Bord —5E 131
Upshire. Essx —5E 53
Up Somborne. Hants —3B 24
Upstreet. Kent —4G 41
Up Sydling. Dors —2B 14
Upthorpe. Suff —3B 66
Upton. Buck —4F 51
Upton. Cambs —3A 64
Upton. Ches —4G 83
Upton. Corn —2C 10
(nr. Bude)
Upton. Corn —5C 10
(nr. Liskeard)
Upton. Cumb —1E 102
Upton. Devn —2D 12
(nr. Honiton)
Upton. Devn —4D 8
(nr. Kingsbridge)
Upton. Dors —3E 15
(nr. Poole)
Upton. Dors —4C 14
(nr. Weymouth)
Upton. E Yor —4F 101
Upton. Hants —1B 24
(nr. Andover)
Upton. Hants —1B 16
(nr. Southampton)
Upton. IOW —3D 16
Upton. Leics —1A 62
Upton. Linc —2F 87
Upton. Mers —2F 83
Upton. Norf —4F 79
Upton. Nptn —4E 62
Upton. Notts —3E 87
(nr. East Retford)
Upton. Notts —5E 87
(nr. Southwell)
Upton. Oxon —3D 36
Upton. Pemb —4E 43
Upton. Pet —5A 76
Upton. Slo —3A 38
Upton. Som —4H 21
(nr. Somerton)
Upton. Som —4C 20
(nr. Wiveliscombe)
Upton. Warw —5F 61
Upton. W Yor —3E 93
Upton. Wilts —3D 22
Upton Bishop. Here —3B 48
Upton Cheyney. S Glo —5B 34
Upton Cressett. Shrp —1A 60
Upton Crews. Here —3B 48
Upton Cross. Corn —5C 10
Upton End. Beds —2B 52
Upton Grey. Hants —2E 25
Upton Heath. Ches —4G 83
Upton Hellions. Devn —2B 12
Upton House NT —1B 50
Upton Lovell. Wilts —2E 23
Upton Magna. Shrp —4H 71
Upton Noble. Som —3C 22
Upton Pyne. Devn —3C 12
Upton St Leonards. Glos —4D 48
Upton Scudamore. Wilts —2D 22
Upton Snodsbury. Worc —5D 60
Upton upon Severn. Worc —1D 48
Upton Warren. Worc —4D 60
Upwaltham. W Sus —4A 26
Upware. Cambs —3E 65
Upwell. Cambs —5D 77
Upwey. Dors —4B 14
Upwick Green. Herts —3E 53
Upwood. Cambs —2B 64
Urafirth. Shet —4E 173
Uragaig. Arg —4A 132
Urchany. High —4C 158
Urchfont. Wilts —1F 23
Urdimarsh. Here —1A 48
Ure. Shet —4D 173
Ure Bank. N Yor —2F 99
Urgha. W Isl —8D 171
Urlay Nook. Stoc T —3B 106
Urmston. G Man —1B 84
Urquhart. Mor —2G 159
Urquhart Castle HS —1H 149
Urra. N Yor —4C 106
Urray. High —3H 157
Usan. Ang —3G 145
Ushaw Moor. Dur —5F 115
Usher Gallery —Lincoln 191
Usk. Mon —5G 47
Usk Castle —5G 47
Usselby. Linc —1H 87
Usworth. Tyne —4G 115
Uton. Devn —3B 12
Utterby. Linc —1C 88
Uttoxeter. Staf —2E 73
Uwchmynydd. Gwyn —3A 68
Uxbridge. G Lon —2B 38
Uyeasound. Shet —1G 173
Uzmaston. Pemb —3D 42
Vale of Rheidol Railway —3F 57
Valle Crucis Abbey CADW —1E 70

Valley. IOA —3B 80
Valley End. Surr —4A 38
Valley Gdns. —4A 38
Valley Truckle. Corn —4B 10
Valsgarth. Shet —1H 173
Valtos. High —2E 155
Van. Powy —2B 58
Vange. Essx —2B 40
Varteg. Torf —5F 47
Vatsetter. Shet —3G 173
Vatten. High —4B 154
Vaul. Arg —4B 138
Vauld,The. Here —1A 48
Vaynol. Gwyn —3E 81
Vaynor. Mer T —4D 46
Veensgarth. Shet —7F 173
Velindre. Powy —2E 47
Vellow. Som —3D 20
Velly. Devn —4C 18
Veness. Orkn —5E 172
Venhay. Devn —1A 12
Venn. Devn —4D 8
Venngreen. Devn —1D 11
Vennington. Shrp —5F 71
Venn Ottery. Devn —3D 12
Venn's Green. Here —1A 48
Venny Tedburn. Devn —3B 12
Venterdon. Corn —5D 10
Ventnor. IOW —5D 16
Vernham Dean. Hants —1B 24
Vernham Street. Hants —1B 24
Vernolds Common. Shrp —2G 59
Verulamium Roman Town —5B 52
Verwood. Dors —2F 15
Veryan. Corn —5D 6
Veryan Green. Corn —4D 6
Vicarage. Devn —4F 13
Vickerstown. Cumb —3A 96
Victoria. Corn —2D 6
Victoria & Albert Mus. —London 192
Vidlin. Shet —5F 173
Viewpark. N Lan —3A 128
Vigo. W Mid —5E 73
Vigo Village. Kent —4H 39
Village Bay. High —3B 154
Vindolanda Roman Fort —3A 114
Vinehall Street. E Sus —3B 28
Vine's Cross. E Sus —4G 27
Viney Hill. Glos —5B 48
Virginia Water. Surr —4A 38
Virginstow. Devn —3D 11
Vobster. Som —2C 22
Voe. Shet —5F 173
(nr. Hillside)
Voe. Shet —3E 173
(nr. Swinister)
Vole. Som —2G 21
Vowchurch. Here —2G 47
Voxter. Shet —4E 173
Voy. Orkn —6B 172
Vulcan Village. Warr —1H 83
Vyne, The NT —1E 25

Wackerfield. Dur —2E 105
Wacton. Norf —1D 66
Wadbister. Shet —7F 173
Wadborough. Worc —1E 49
Waddesdon. Buck —4F 51
Waddesdon Manor NT —4F 51
Waddeton. Devn —3E 9
Waddicar. Mers —1F 83
Waddingham. Linc —1G 87
Waddington. Lanc —5G 97
Waddington. Linc —4G 87
Waddon. Devn —5B 12
Wadebridge. Corn —1D 6
Wadeford. Som —1G 13
Wadenhoe. Nptn —2H 63
Wadesmill. Herts —4D 52
Wadhurst. E Sus —2H 27
Wadshelf. Derbs —3H 85
Wadsley. S Yor —1H 85
Wadsley Bridge. S Yor —1H 85
Wadswick. Wilts —5D 34
Wadwick. Hants —1C 24
Wadworth. S Yor —1C 86
Waen. Den —4C 82
(nr. Bodfari)
Waen. Den —4D 82
(nr. Llandyrnog)
Waen. Den —4B 82
(nr. Nantglyn)
Waen. Powy —1B 58
Waen Fach. Powy —4E 70
Waen Goleugoed. Den —3C 82
Wag. High —1H 165
Wainfleet All Saints. Linc —5D 89
Wainfleet Bank. Linc —5D 88
Wainfleet St Mary. Linc —5D 89
Wainhouse Corner. Corn —3B 10
Wainscott. Medw —3B 40
Wainstalls. W Yor —2A 92
Waitby. Cumb —4A 104
Waithe. Linc —4F 95
Wakefield. W Yor —2D 92
Wakehurst Place NT —2E 27
Wakerley. Nptn —1G 63
Wakes Colne. Essx —3B 54
Walberswick. Suff —3G 67
Walberton. W Sus —5A 26
Walbottle. Tyne —3E 115
Walby. Cumb —3F 113
Walcombe. Som —2A 22
Walcot. Linc —2H 75
Walcot. N Lin —2B 94
Walcot. Swin —3G 35
Walcot. Telf —4H 71
Walcot. Warw —5F 61
Walcote. Leics —2C 62
Walcot Green. Norf —2D 66
Walcott. Linc —5A 88
Walcott. Norf —2F 79
Walden. N Yor —1C 98
Walden Head. N Yor —1B 98
Walden Stubbs. N Yor —3F 93
Walderslade. Medw —4B 40
Walderton. W Sus —1F 17
Walditch. Dors —3H 13
Waldley. Derbs —2F 73
Waldridge. Dur —4F 115
Waldringfield. Suff —1F 55
Waldron. E Sus —4G 27
Wales. S Yor —2B 86
Walesby. Linc —1A 88
Walesby. Notts —3D 86
Walford. Here —3F 59
(nr. Leintwardine)
Walford. Here —3A 48
(nr. Ross-on-Wye)
Walford. Shrp —3G 71
Walford. Staf —2C 72
Walford Heath. Shrp —4G 71
Walgherton. Ches —1A 72
Walgrave. Nptn —3F 63
Walhampton. Hants —3B 16
Walkden. G Man —4F 91
Walker. Tyne —3F 115
Walker Art Gallery —Liverpool 191
Walkerburn. Bord —1F 119
Walker Fold. Lanc —5F 97
Walkeringham. Notts —1E 87
Walkerith. Linc —1E 87
Walkern. Herts —3C 52
Walker's Green. Here —1A 48
Walkerton. Fife —3E 137
Walkerville. N Yor —5F 105
Walkford. Dors —3H 15
Walkhampton. Devn —2B 8
Walkington. E Yor —1C 94
Walkley. S Yor —2H 85
Walk Mill. Lanc —1G 91
Wall. Corn —3D 4
Wall. Nmbd —3C 114
Wall. Staf —5F 73
Wallaceton. Dum —1F 111
Wallacetown. Shet —6E 173
Wallacetown. S Ayr —2C 116
(nr. Ayr)
Wallacetown. S Ayr —4B 116
(nr. Dailly)
Wallands Park. E Sus —4F 27
Wallasey. Mers —1F 83
Wallaston Green. Pemb —4D 42
Wallbrook. W Mid —1D 60
Wallcrouch. E Sus —2A 28
Wall End. Cumb —1B 96
Wallend. Medw —3C 40
Wall Heath. W Mid —2C 60
Wallingford. Oxon —3E 36
Wallington. G Lon —4D 39
Wallington. Hants —2D 16
Wallington. Herts —2C 52
Wallington House NT —1D 114
Wallis. Pemb —2E 43
Wallisdown. Pool —3F 15
Walliswood. Surr —2C 26
Wall Nook. Dur —5F 115
Walls. Shet —7D 173
Wallsend. Tyne —3G 115
Wallsworth. Glos —3D 48
Wall under Heywood. Shrp —1H 59
Wallyford. E Lot —2G 129
Walmer. Kent —5H 41
Walmer Bridge. Lanc —2C 90
Walmer Castle EH —1H 29
Walmersley. G Man —3G 91
Walmley. W Mid —1F 61
Walnut Grove. Per —1D 136
Walpole. Suff —3F 67
Walpole Cross Keys. Norf —4E 77
Walpole Gate. Norf —4E 77
Walpole Highway. Norf —4E 77
Walpolelane. Suff —3F 67
Walpole Marsh. Norf —4D 77
Walpole St Andrew. Norf —4E 77
Walpole St Peter. Norf —4E 77
Walsall. W Mid —1E 61
Walsall Art Gallery —1E 61
Walsall Wood. W Mid —5E 73
Walsden. W Yor —2H 91
Walsgrave on Sowe. W Mid —2A 62
Walsham le Willows. Suff —3C 66
Walshaw. G Man —3F 91
Walshford. N Yor —4G 99
Walsingham Abbey —2B 78
Walsoken. Cambs —4D 76
Walston. S Lan —5D 128
Walsworth. Herts —2B 52
Walter Rothschild Zoological Mus. —4H 51
Walter's Ash. Buck —2G 37
Walterston. V Glam —4D 32
Walterstone. Here —3G 47
Waltham. Kent —1F 29
Waltham. NE Lin —4F 95
Waltham Abbey. Essx —5D 53
Waltham Chase. Hants —1D 16
Waltham Cross. Herts —5D 52
Waltham on the Wolds. Leics —3F 75
Waltham St Lawrence. Wind —4G 37
Waltham's Cross. Essx —2G 53
Walthamstow. G Lon —2E 39
Walton. Cumb —3G 113
Walton. Derbs —4A 86
Walton. Leics —2C 62
Walton. Mers —1F 83
Walton. Mil —2G 51
Walton. Pet —5A 76
Walton. Powy —5E 59
Walton. Som —3H 21
Walton. Staf —3C 72
(nr. Eccleshall)
Walton. Staf —2C 72
(nr. Stone)
Walton. Suff —2F 55
Walton. Telf —4H 71
Walton. Warw —5G 61
Walton. W Yor —3D 92
(nr. Wakefield)
Walton. W Yor —5G 99
(nr. Wetherby)
Walton Cardiff. Glos —2E 49
Walton East. Pemb —2E 43
Walton Elm. Dors —1C 14
Walton Highway. Norf —4D 77
Walton-in-Gordano. N Som —4H 33
Walton-le-Dale. Lanc —2D 90
Walton-on-Thames. Surr —4C 38
Walton-on-the-Hill. Staf —3D 72
Walton on the Hill. Surr —5D 38

Walton-on-the-Naze. Essx —3F 55
Walton on the Wolds. Leics —4C 74
Walton-on-Trent. Derbs —4G 73
Walton West. Pemb —3C 42
Walwick. Nmbd —2C 114
Walworth. Darl —3F 105
Walworth Gate. Darl —2F 105
Walwyn's Castle. Pemb —3C 42
Wambrook. Som —2F 13
Wampool. Cumb —4D 112
Wanborough. Surr —1A 26
Wanborough. Swin —3H 35
Wandel. S Lan —2B 118
Wandsworth. G Lon —3D 38
Wangford. Suff —2G 65
(nr. Lakenheath)
Wangford. Suff —3G 67
(nr. Southwold)
Wanlip. Leics —4C 74
Wanlockhead. Dum —3A 118
Wannock. E Sus —5G 27
Wansford. E Yor —4E 101
Wansford. Pet —1H 63
Wanshurst Green. Kent —1B 28
Wanstead. G Lon —2F 39
Wanstrow. Som —2C 22
Wanswell. Glos —5B 48
Wantage. Oxon —3B 36
Wapley. S Glo —4C 34
Wappenbury. Warw —4A 62
Wappenham. Nptn —1E 51
Warbleton. E Sus —4H 27
Warblington. Hants —2F 17
Warborough. Devn —3F 9
Warborough. Oxon —2D 36
Warboys. Cambs —2C 64
Warbreck. Bkpl —1B 90
Warbstow. Corn —3C 10
Warburton. G Man —2A 84
Warcop. Cumb —3A 104
Warden. Kent —3E 40
Warden. Nmbd —3C 114
Ward End. W Mid —2F 61
Ward Green. Suff —4C 66
Ward Green Cross. Lanc —1E 91
Wardhedges. Beds —2A 52
Wardhouse. Abers —5C 160
Wardington. Oxon —1C 50
Wardle. Ches —5A 84
Wardle. G Man —3H 91
Wardley. Rut —5F 75
Wardley. W Sus —4G 25
Wardlow. Derbs —3F 85
Wardsend. Ches —2D 84
Wardy Hill. Cambs —2D 64
Ware. Herts —4D 52
Ware. Kent —4G 41
Wareham. Dors —4E 15
Warehorne. Kent —2D 28
Warenford. Nmbd —2F 121
Waren Mill. Nmbd —1F 121
Warenton. Nmbd —1F 121
Wareside. Herts —4D 53
Waresley. Cambs —5B 64
Waresley. Worc —4C 60
Warfield. Brac —4G 37
Warfleet. Devn —3E 9
Wargate. Linc —2B 76
Wargrave. Wok —4F 37
Warham. Norf —1B 78
Wark. Nmbd —1C 120
(nr. Coldstream)
Wark. Nmbd —2B 114
(nr. Hexham)
Warkleigh. Devn —4G 19
Warkton. Nptn —3F 63
Warkworth. Nptn —1C 50
Warkworth. Nmbd —4G 121
Warkworth Castle EH —4G 121
Warlaby. N Yor —5A 106
Warland. W Yor —2H 91
Warleggan. Corn —2F 7
Warlingham. Surr —5E 39
Warmanbie. Dum —3C 112
Warmfield. W Yor —2D 92
Warmingham. Ches —4B 84
Warminghurst. W Sus —4C 26
Warmington. Nptn —1H 63
Warmington. Warw —1C 50
Warminster. Wilts —2D 23
Warmley. S Glo —4B 34
Warmsworth. S Yor —4F 93
Warmwell. Dors —4C 14
Warndon. Worc —5C 60
Warners End. Herts —5A 52
Warnford. Hants —4E 24
Warnham. W Sus —2C 26
Warningcamp. W Sus —5B 26
Warninglid. W Sus —3D 26
Warren. Ches —3C 84
Warren. Pemb —5D 42
Warrenby. Red C —2C 106
Warren Corner. Hants —2G 25
(nr. Aldershot)
Warren Corner. Hants —4F 25
(nr. Petersfield)
Warren Row. Wind —3G 37
Warren Street. Kent —5D 40
Warrington. Mil —5F 63
Warrington. Warr —2A 84
Warsash. Hants —2C 16
Warse. High —1F 169
Warslow. Staf —5E 85
Warsop Vale. Notts —4C 86
Warter. E Yor —4C 100
Warthermarske. N Yor —2E 98
Warthill. N Yor —4A 100
Wartling. E Sus —5A 28
Wartnaby. Leics —3E 74
Warton. Lanc —2D 97
(nr. Carnforth)
Warton. Lanc —2C 90
(nr. Freckleton)
Warton. Nmbd —4E 121
Warton. Warw —5G 73
Warwick. Cumb —4F 113
Warwick. Warw —4G 61
Warwick Bridge. Cumb —4F 113
Warwick Castle —4G 61
Warwick Wold. Surr —5E 39
Wasbister. Orkn —4C 172
Wasdale Head. Cumb —4C 102
Wash. Derbs —2E 85
Washaway. Corn —2E 7
Washbourne. Devn —3E 9
Washbrook. Suff —1E 54
Wash Common. W Ber —5C 36
Washerwall. Staf —1D 72
Washfield. Devn —1C 12
Washfold. N Yor —4D 104
Washford. Som —2D 20
Washford Pyne. Devn —1B 12
Washingborough. Linc —3H 87
Washington. Tyne —4G 115
Washington. W Sus —4C 26
Washington Old Hall NT —4G 115
Washington Village. Tyne —4G 115
Waskerley. Dur —5D 114
Wasperton. Warw —5G 61
Wasp Green. Surr —1E 27
Wasps Nest. Linc —4H 87
Wass. N Yor —2H 99
Watchet. Som —2D 20
Watchfield. Oxon —2H 35
Watchgate. Cumb —5G 103
Watchhill. Cumb —5C 112
Watcombe. Torb —2F 9
Watendlath. Cumb —3D 102
Water. Devn —4A 12
Water. Lanc —2G 91
Waterbeach. Cambs —4D 65
Waterbeach. W Sus —2G 17
Waterbeck. Dum —2D 112
Waterden. Norf —2A 78
Waterditch. Hants —3G 15
Water End. Beds —2A 52
Water End. E Yor —1A 94
Water End. Herts —5C 52
(nr. Hatfield)
Water End. Herts —4A 52
(nr. Hemel Hempstead)
Waterfall. Staf —5E 85
Waterfoot. E Ren —4G 127
Waterfoot. Lanc —2G 91
Waterford. Herts —4D 52
Water Fryston. W Yor —2E 93
Waterhead. Cumb —4E 103
Waterhead. E Ayr —3E 117
Waterhead. S Ayr —5C 116
Waterheads. Bord —4F 129
Waterhouses. Dur —5E 115
Waterhouses. Staf —5E 85
Wateringbury. Kent —5A 40
Waterlane. Glos —5E 49
Waterlip. Som —2B 22
Waterloo. Cphy —3E 33
Waterloo. Corn —5B 10
Waterloo. Derbs —4B 86
Waterloo. Here —1G 47
Waterloo. High —1E 147
Waterloo. Mers —1F 83
Waterloo. Norf —4E 78
Waterloo. N Lan —4B 128
Waterloo. Pemb —4D 42
Waterloo. Per —5H 143
Waterloo. Pool —3F 15
Waterloo. Shrp —2G 71
Waterlooville. Hants —2E 17
Watermillock. Cumb —2F 103
Watermouth Castle Theme Park —2F 19
Water Newton. Cambs —1A 64
Water Orton. Warw —1F 61
Waterperry. Oxon —5E 51
Waterperry Gdns. —5E 51
Waterrow. Som —4D 20
Watersfield. W Sus —4B 26
Waterside. Buck —5H 51
Waterside. Cambs —3F 65
Waterside. Cumb —5D 112
Waterside. E Ayr —4D 116
(nr. Ayr)
Waterside. E Ayr —5F 127
(nr. Kilmarnock)
Waterside. E Dun —2H 127
Watersmeet —2H 19
Waterstein. High —4A 154
Waterstock. Oxon —5E 51
Waterston. Pemb —4D 42
Water Stratford. Buck —2E 51
Waters Upton. Telf —4A 72
Water Yeat. Cumb —1B 96
Watford. Herts —1B 38
Watford. Nptn —4D 62
Wath. Cumb —4H 103
Wath. N Yor —3D 98
(nr. Pateley Bridge)
Wath. N Yor —2F 99
(nr. Ripon)
Wath Brow. Cumb —3B 102
Wath upon Dearne. S Yor —1B 86
Watlington. Norf —4F 77
Watlington. Oxon —2E 37
Watten. High —3E 169
Wattisfield. Suff —3C 66
Wattisham. Suff —5C 66
Wattlesborough Heath. Shrp —4F 71
Watton. Dors —3H 13
Watton. E Yor —5E 101
Watton. Norf —5B 78
Watton at Stone. Herts —4C 52
Wattston. N Lan —2A 128
Wattstown. Rhon —2D 32
Wattsville. Cphy —2F 33
Wauldby. E Yor —2C 94
Waulkmill. Abers —4D 152
Waun. Powy —4E 71
Waunarlwydd. Swan —3F 31
Waun Fawr. Cdgn —2F 57
Waunfawr. Gwyn —5E 81
Waungilwen. Carm —1H 43
Waunlwyd. Blae —5E 47
Waun-y-Clyn. Carm —5E 45
Wavendon. Mil —2H 51
Waverbridge. Cumb —5D 112
Waverley. Surr —2G 25
Waverton. Ches —4G 83
Waverton. Cumb —5D 112
Wavertree. Mers —2F 83
Wawne. E Yor —1D 94
Waxham. Norf —3G 79
Waxholme. E Yor —2G 95
Wayford. Som —2H 13
Way Head. Cambs —2D 65
Waytown. Dors —3H 13
Way Village. Devn —1B 12
Wdig. Pemb —1D 42
Weald & Downland Mus. —1G 17
Wealdstone. G Lon —1C 38
Weardley. W Yor —5E 99
Weare. Som —1H 21
Weare Giffard. Devn —4E 19
Wearhead. Dur —1B 104
Wearne. Som —4H 21
Weasdale. Cumb —4H 103
Weasenham All Saints. Norf —3H 77
Weasenham St Peter. Norf —3A 78
Weaverham. Ches —3A 84
Weaverthorpe. N Yor —2D 100
Webheath. Worc —4E 61
Webton. Here —2H 47
Wedderlairs. Abers —5F 161
Weddington. Warw —1A 62
Wedgewood Visitor Centre —2C 72
Wedhampton. Wilts —1F 23
Wedmore. Som —2H 21
Wednesbury. W Mid —1D 61
Wednesfield. W Mid —5D 72
Weecar. Notts —4F 87
Weedon. Buck —4G 51
Weedon Bec. Nptn —5D 62
Weedon Lois. Nptn —1E 50
Weeford. Staf —5F 73
Week. Devn —4F 19
(nr. Barnstaple)
Week. Devn —2G 11
(nr. Okehampton)
Week. Devn —1H 11
(nr. South Molton)
Week. Devn —2D 9
(nr. Totnes)
Week. Som —3C 20
Weeke. Devn —2A 12
Weeke. Hants —3C 24
Week Green. Corn —3C 10
Weekley. Nptn —2F 63
Week St Mary. Corn —3C 10
Weel. E Yor —1D 94
Weeley. Essx —3E 55
Weeley Heath. Essx —3E 55
Weem. Per —4F 143
Weeping Cross. Staf —3D 72
Weethly. Warw —5E 61
Weeting. Norf —2G 65
Weeton. E Yor —2G 95
Weeton. Lanc —1B 90
Weeton. N Yor —5E 99
Weetwood Hall. Nmbd —2E 121
Weir. Lanc —2G 91
Weir Gdn., The NT —1H 47
Welbeck Abbey. Notts —3C 86
Welborne. Norf —4C 78
Welbourn. Linc —5G 87
Welburn. N Yor —1A 100
(nr. Kirkbymoorside)
Welburn. N Yor —3B 100
(nr. Malton)
Welbury. N Yor —4A 106
Welby. Linc —2G 75
Welches Dam. Cambs —2D 64
Welcombe. Devn —1C 10
Weld Bank. Lanc —3D 90
Weldon. Nptn —2G 63
Weldon. Nmbd —5F 121
Welford. Nptn —2D 62
Welford. W Ber —4C 36
Welford-on-Avon. Warw —5F 61
Welham. Leics —1E 63
Welham. Notts —2E 87
Welham Green. Herts —5C 52
Well. Hants —2F 25
Well. Linc —3D 88
Well. N Yor —1E 99
Welland. Worc —1C 48
Wellbank. Ang —5D 144
Well Bottom. Dors —1E 15
Welldale. Dum —3C 112
Wellesbourne. Warw —5G 61
Well Hill. Kent —4F 39
Wellhouse. W Ber —4D 36
Welling. G Lon —3F 39
Wellingborough. Nptn —4F 63
Wellingham. Norf —3A 78
Wellingore. Linc —5G 87
Wellington. Cumb —4B 102
Wellington. Here —1H 47
Wellington. Som —4E 21
Wellington. Telf —4A 72
Wellington Heath. Here —1C 48
Wellow. Bath —1C 22
Wellow. IOW —4B 16
Wellow. Notts —4D 86
Wellplace Zoo —3E 37
Wellpond Green. Herts —3E 53
Wells. Som —2A 22
Wells & Walsingham Light Railway —1B 78
Wellsborough. Leics —5A 74
Wells Cathedral —2A 22
Wells Green. Ches —5A 84
Wells-next-the-Sea. Norf —1B 78
Wells of Ythan. Abers —5D 160
Wellswood. Torb —2F 9
Wellwood. Fife —1D 129
Welney. Norf —1E 65
Welney Wildfowl Refuge —1E 65
Welsford. Devn —4C 18
Welshampton. Shrp —2G 71
Welsh End. Shrp —2H 71
Welsh Frankton. Shrp —2F 71
Welsh Highland Railway —4D 81
Welsh Hook. Pemb —2D 42
Welsh Mountain Zoo, Colwyn Bay —3H 81
Welsh Newton. Here —4H 47
Welsh Newton Common. Here —4A 48
Welshpool. Powy —5E 70
Welshpool & Llanfair Railway —5D 70
Welsh St Donats. V Glam —4D 32
Welsh Slate Mus. —4E 81
Welton. Bath —1B 22
Welton. Cumb —5E 113
Welton. E Yor —2C 94
Welton. Linc —3H 87
Welton. Nptn —4C 62
Welton Hill. Linc —2H 87
Welton le Marsh. Linc —4D 88
Welton le Wold. Linc —2B 88
Welwick. E Yor —2G 95
Welwyn. Herts —4C 52
Welwyn Garden City. Herts —4C 52
Wem. Shrp —3H 71
Wembdon. Som —3F 21
Wembley. G Lon —2C 38
Wembury. Devn —4B 8
Wembworthy. Devn —2G 11
Wemyss Bay. Inv —2C 126
Wenallt. Cdgn —3F 57
Wenallt. Gwyn —1B 70
Wendens Ambo. Essx —2F 53
Wending. Norf —4B 78
Wendlebury. Oxon —4D 50
Wendover. Buck —5G 51
Wendron. Corn —5A 6
Wendy. Cambs —1D 52
Wenhaston. Suff —3G 67
Wenlock Priory EH —5A 72
Wennington. Cambs —3B 64
Wennington. G Lon —2G 39
Wennington. Lanc —2F 97
Wensley. Derbs —4G 85
Wensley. N Yor —1C 98
Wentbridge. W Yor —3E 93
Wentfordbridge. Corn —5A 10
Wentnor. Shrp —1F 59
Wentworth. Cambs —3D 65
Wentworth. S Yor —1A 86
Wenvoe. V Glam —4E 32
Weobley. Here —5G 59
Weobley Castle CADW —3D 31
Weobley Marsh. Here —5G 59
Wepham. W Sus —5B 26
Wereham. Norf —5F 77
Wergs. W Mid —5C 72
Wern. Gwyn —1E 69
Wern. Powy —4E 46
(nr. Brecon)
Wern. Powy —4E 71
(nr. Guilsfield)
Wern. Powy —4B 70
(nr. Llangadfon)
Wern. Powy —3E 71
(nr. Llanymynech)
Wernffrwd. Swan —3E 31
Wernyrheolydd. Mon —4G 47
Werrington. Corn —4D 10
Werrington. Pet —5A 76
Werrington. Staf —1D 72
Wervin. Ches —3G 83
Wesham. Lanc —1C 90
Wessington. Derbs —5A 86
West Aberthaw. V Glam —5D 32
West Acre. Norf —4G 77
West Allerdean. Nmbd —5F 131
West Alvington. Devn —4D 8
West Amesbury. Wilts —2G 23
West Anstey. Devn —4B 20
West Appleton. N Yor —5F 105
West Arthurlie. E Ren —4F 127
West Ashby. Linc —3B 88
West Ashling. W Sus —2G 17
West Ashton. Wilts —1D 23
West Auckland. Dur —2E 105
West Ayton. N Yor —1D 101
West Bagborough. Som —3E 21
West Bank. Hal —2H 83
West Barkwith. Linc —2A 88
West Barnby. N Yor —3F 107
West Barns. E Lot —2C 130
West Barsham. Norf —2B 78
West Bay. Dors —3H 13
West Beckham. Norf —1D 78
West Bennan. N Ayr —3D 123
Westbere. Kent —4F 41
West Bergholt. Essx —3C 54
West Bexington. Dors —4A 14
West Bilney. Norf —4G 77
West Blackdene. Dur —1B 104
West Blatchington. Brig —5D 27
Westborough. Linc —1F 75
Westbourne. Bour —3F 15
Westbourne. W Sus —2F 17
West Bowling. W Yor —1B 92
West Brabourne. Kent —1E 29
West Bradford. Lanc —5G 97
West Bradley. Som —3A 22
West Bretton. W Yor —3C 92
West Bridgford. Notts —2C 74
West Briggs. Norf —4F 77
West Bromwich. W Mid —1D 60
Westbrook. Here —1F 47
Westbrook. Kent —3H 41
Westbrook. Wilts —5E 35
West Buckland. Devn —3G 19
West Buckland. Som —4E 21
West Burnside. Abers —1G 145
West Burrafirth. Shet —6D 173
West Burton. N Yor —1C 98
West Burton. W Sus —4A 26
Westbury. Buck —2E 50
Westbury. Shrp —5F 71
Westbury. Wilts —1D 22
Westbury Court Gdn. NT —4C 48
Westbury Leigh. Wilts —2D 22
Westbury-on-Severn. Glos —4C 48
Westbury on Trym. Bris —4A 34
Westbury-sub-Mendip. Som —2A 22
West Butsfield. Dur —5E 115
West Butterwick. N Lin —4B 94
Westby. Linc —3G 75
West Byfleet. Surr —4B 38
West Caister. Norf —4H 79
West Calder. W Lot —3D 128
West Camel. Som —4A 22
West Carr. N Lin —4H 93
West Chaldon. Dors —4C 14
West Challow. Oxon —3B 36
West Charleton. Devn —4D 8
West Chelborough. Dors —2A 14
West Chevington. Nmbd —5G 121
West Chiltington. W Sus —4B 26
West Chiltington Common. W Sus —4B 26
West Chinnock. Som —1H 13
West Chisenbury. Wilts —1G 23
West Clandon. Surr —5B 38
Westcliff. IOW —5D 16
West Cliffe. Kent —1H 29
Westcliffe-on-Sea. S'end —2C 40
West Clyne. High —3F 165
West Coker. Som —1A 14
Westcombe. Som —3B 22
(nr. Evercreech)
Westcombe. Som —4H 21
(nr. Somerton)
West Common. Linc —3G 87
West Compton. Dors —3A 14
West Compton. Som —2A 22
West Cornforth. Dur —1A 106
Westcot. Oxon —3B 36
Westcott. Buck —4F 51
Westcott. Devn —2D 12
Westcott. Surr —1C 26
Westcott Barton. Oxon —3C 50
West Cowick. E Yor —2G 93
West Cranmore. Som —2B 22
West Croftmore. High —2D 150
West Cross. Swan —4F 31
West Cullerlie. Abers —3E 153
West Culvennan. Dum —3H 109
West Curry. Corn —3C 10
West Curthwaite. Cumb —5E 113
Westdean. E Sus —5G 27
West Dean. W Sus —1G 17
West Dean. Wilts —4A 24
West Deeping. Linc —5A 76
West Derby. Mers —1F 83
West Dereham. Norf —5F 77
West Down. Devn —2F 19
Westdowns. Corn —4A 10
West Drayton. G Lon —3B 38
West Drayton. Notts —3E 86
West Dunnet. High —1E 169
West Ella. E Yor —2D 94
West End. Beds —5G 63
West End. Cambs —1D 64
West End. Dors —2E 15
West End. E Yor —3E 101
(nr. Kilham)
West End. E Yor —1E 95
(nr. Preston)
West End. E Yor —1C 94
(nr. South Cove)
West End. E Yor —4F 101
(nr. Ulrome)
West End. G Lon —2D 39
West End. Hants —1C 16
West End. Herts —5C 52
West End. Kent —4F 41
West End. Linc —1C 76
West End. Norf —4G 79
West End. N Som —5H 33
West End. N Yor —4D 98
West End. S Glo —3C 34
West End. S Lan —5C 128
West End. Surr —4A 38
West End. Wilts —4E 23
West End. Wind —4G 37
West End. Worc —2F 49
West End Green. Hants —5E 37
Westenhanger. Kent —2F 29
Wester Aberchalder. High —2H 149
Wester Balgedie. Per —3D 136
Wester Brae. High —2A 158
Wester Culbeuchly. Abers —2D 160
Westerdale. High —3D 168
Westerdale. N Yor —4D 106
Wester Dechmont. W Lot —2D 128
Wester Fearn. High —5D 164
Westerfield. Suff —1E 55
Wester Galcantray. High —4C 158
Westergate. W Sus —5A 26
Wester Gruinards. High —4C 164
Westerham. Kent —5F 39
Westerleigh. S Glo —4B 34
Westerloch. High —3F 169
Wester Mandally. High —3E 149
Wester Quarff. Shet —8F 173
Wester Rarichie. High —1C 158
Wester Skeld. Shet —7D 173
Westerton. Ang —3F 145
Westerton. Dur —1F 105
Westerton. W Sus —2G 17
Westerwick. Shet —7D 173
West Farleigh. Kent —5B 40
West Farndon. Nptn —5C 62
West Felton. Shrp —3F 71
Westfield. Cumb —2A 102
Westfield. E Sus —4C 28
Westfield. High —2C 168
Westfield. Norf —5B 78
Westfield. N Lan —2A 128
Westfield. W Lot —2C 128
Westfields. Dors —2C 14
Westfields of Rattray. Per —4A 144
West Firle. E Sus —5F 27
West Fleetham. Nmbd —2F 121
West Garforth. W Yor —1D 93
Westgate. Dur —1C 104
Westgate. Norf —1B 78

Westgate. N Lin —4A 94
Westgate on Sea. Kent —3H 41
West Ginge. Oxon —3C 36
West Grafton. Wilts —5H 35
West Green. Hants —1F 25
West Green House NT —1F 25
West Grimstead. Wilts —4H 23
West Grinstead. W Sus —3C 26
West Haddlesey. N Yor —2F 93
West Haddon. Nptn —3D 62
West Hagbourne. Oxon —3D 36
West Hagley. Worc —2C 60
West Hall. Cumb —3G 113
Westhall. Suff —2G 67
West Hallam. Derbs —1B 74
Westhall Terrace. Ang —5D 144
West Halton. N Lin —2C 94
Westham. Dors —5B 14
Westham. E Sus —5H 27
West Ham. G Lon —2E 39
Westham. Som —2H 21
Westhampnett. W Sus —2G 17
West Handley. Derbs —3A 86
West Hanney. Oxon —2C 36
West Hanningfield. Essx —1B 40
West Hardwick. W Yor —3E 93
West Harnham. Wilts —4G 23
West Harptree. Bath —1A 22
West Harting. W Sus —4F 25
West Harton. Tyne —3G 115
West Hatch. Som —4F 21
Westhay. Som —2H 21
Westhead. Lanc —4C 90
West Head. Norf —5E 77
West Heath. Hants —1D 24
(nr. Basingstoke)
West Heath. Hants —1G 25
(nr. Farnborough)
West Helmsdale. High —2H 165
West Hendred. Oxon —3C 36
West Heogaland. Shet —4D 173
West Heslerton. N Yor —2D 100
West Hewish. N Som —5G 33
Westhide. Here —1A 48
Westhill. Abers —3F 153
West Hill. Devn —3D 12
West Hill. E Yor —3F 101
Westhill. High —4B 158
West Hill. N Som —4H 33
West Hill. W Sus —2E 27
West Hoathly. W Sus —2E 27
West Holme. Dors —4D 15
Westhope. Here —5G 59
Westhope. Shrp —2G 59
West Horndon. Essx —2H 39
Westhorp. Nptn —5C 62
Westhorpe. Linc —2B 76
Westhorpe. Suff —4C 66
West Horrington. Som —2A 22
West Horsley. Surr —5B 38
West Horton. Nmbd —1E 121
West Hougham. Kent —1G 29
Westhoughton. G Man —4E 91
West Houlland. Shet —6D 173
Westhouse. N Yor —2F 97
West Howe. Bour —3F 15
Westhumble. Surr —5C 38
West Huntspill. Som —2G 21
West Hyde. Herts —1B 38
West Hynish. Arg —5A 138
West Hythe. Kent —2F 29
West Ilsley. W Ber —3C 36
Westing. Shet —1G 173
West Itchenor. W Sus —2F 17
West Keal. Linc —4C 88
West Kennett. Wilts —5G 35
West Kilbride. N Ayr —5D 126
West Kingsdown. Kent —4G 39
West Kington. Wilts —4D 34
West Kirby. Mers —2E 82
West Knapton. N Yor —2C 100
West Knighton. Dors —4C 14
West Knoyle. Wilts —3D 22
Westlake. Devn —3C 8
West Lambrook. Som —1H 13
West Langdon. Kent —1H 29
West Langwell. High —3D 164
West Lavington. W Sus —4G 25
West Lavington. Wilts —1F 23
West Layton. N Yor —3E 105
West Leake. Notts —3C 74
West Learmouth. Nmbd —1C 120
Westleigh. Devn —4E 19
(nr. Bideford)
Westleigh. Devn —1D 12
(nr. Tiverton)
West Leigh. Devn —2G 11
(nr. Winkleigh)
Westleigh. G Man —4E 91
West Leith. Buck —4H 51
Westleton. Suff —4G 67
West Lexham. Norf —4H 77
Westley. Shrp —5F 71
Westley. Suff —4H 65
Westley Waterless. Cambs —5F 65
West Lilling. N Yor —3A 100
West Lingo. Fife —3G 137
Westlington. Buck —4F 51
Westlinton. Cumb —3E 113
West Linton. Bord —4E 129
West Littleton. S Glo —4C 34
West Looe. Corn —3G 7
West Lulworth. Dors —4D 14
West Lutton. N Yor —3D 100
West Lydford. Som —3A 22
West Lynn. Norf —4F 77
West Mains. Per —2B 136
West Malling. Kent —5A 40
West Malvern. Worc —1C 48
Westmancote. Worc —2E 49
West Marden. W Sus —1F 17
West Markham. Notts —3E 86
Westmarsh. Kent —4G 41
West Marsh. NE Lin —4F 95
West Marton. N Yor —4A 98
West Meon. Hants —4E 25
West Mersea. Essx —4D 54
Westmeston. E Sus —4E 27
West Midlands Safari Park —3C 60
Westmill. Herts —3D 52
(nr. Buntingford)
Westmill. Herts —2B 52
(nr. Hitchin)
West Milton. Dors —3A 14
Westminster. G Lon —3D 39
Westminster Abbey —London 193
West Molesey. Surr —4C 38
West Monkton. Som —4F 21
Westmoor End. Cumb —1B 102
West Moors. Dors —2F 15
West Morden. Dors —3E 15
West Muir. Ang —2E 145
(nr. Brechin)
Westmuir. Ang —3C 144
(nr. Forfar)
West Murkle. High —2D 168
West Ness. N Yor —2A 100
Westness. Orkn —5C 172
Westnewton. Cumb —5C 112
West Newton. E Yor —1E 95
West Newton. Norf —3F 77
Westnewton. Nmbd —1D 120
West Norwood. G Lon —3E 39
Westoe. Tyne —3G 115
West Ogwell. Devn —2E 9
Weston. Bath —5C 34
Weston. Ches —5B 84
(nr. Crewe)
Weston. Ches —3D 84
(nr. Macclesfield)
Weston. Devn —4E 13
Weston. Dors —5B 14
Weston. Hal —2H 83
Weston. Hants —4F 25
Weston. Here —5F 59
Weston. Herts —2C 52
Weston. Linc —3B 76
Weston. Nptn —1D 50
Weston. Notts —4E 87
Weston. Shrp —1H 59
(nr. Bridgnorth)
Weston. Shrp —3F 59
(nr. Knighton)
Weston. Shrp —3H 71
(nr. Wem)
Weston. S Lan —5D 128
Weston. Staf —3D 73
Weston. Suff —2G 67
Weston. W Ber —4B 36
Weston Bampfylde. Som —4B 22
Weston Beggard. Here —1A 48
Westonbirt. Glos —3D 34
Westonbirt Arboretum —2D 34
Weston by Welland. Nptn —1E 63
Weston Colville. Cambs —5F 65
Westoncommon. Shrp —3G 71
Weston Coyney. Stoke —1D 72
Weston Ditch. Suff —3F 65
Weston Favell. Nptn —4E 63
Weston Green. Cambs —5F 65
Weston Green. Norf —4D 78
Weston Heath. Shrp —4B 72
Weston Hills. Linc —4B 76
Weston in Arden. Warw —2A 62
Westoning. Beds —2A 52
Weston-in-Gordano. N Som —4H 33
Weston Jones. Staf —3B 72
Weston Longville. Norf —4D 78
Weston Lullingfields. Shrp —3G 71
Weston-on-Avon. Warw —5F 61
Weston-on-the-Green. Oxon —4D 50
Weston-on-Trent. Derbs —3B 74
Weston Park —4C 72
Weston Patrick. Hants —2E 25
Weston Rhyn. Shrp —2E 71
Weston Subedge. Glos —1G 49
Weston-super-Mare. N Som —5G 33
Weston Town. Som —2C 22
Weston Turville. Buck —4G 51
Weston under Lizard. Staf —4C 72
Weston under Penyard. Here —3B 48
Weston under Wetherley. Warw —4A 62
Weston Underwood. Derbs —1G 73
Weston Underwood. Mil —5F 63
Westonzoyland. Som —3G 21
West Orchard. Dors —1D 14
West Overton. Wilts —5G 35
Westow. N Yor —3B 100
Westown. Per —1E 137
West Panson. Devn —3D 10
West Park. Hart —1B 106
West Parley. Dors —3F 15
West Peckham. Kent —5H 39
West Pelton. Dur —4F 115
West Pennard. Som —3A 22
West Pentire. Corn —2B 6
West Perry. Cambs —4A 64
West Pitcorthie. Fife —3H 137
West Plean. Stir —1B 128
West Poringland. Norf —5E 79
West Porlock. Som —2B 20
Westport. Som —4G 21
West Putford. Devn —1D 10
West Quantoxhead. Som —2E 20
Westra. V Glam —4E 33
West Rainton. Dur —5G 115
West Rasen. Linc —2H 87
West Ravendale. NE Lin —1B 88
Westray Airport. Orkn —2D 172
West Raynham. Norf —3A 78
Westrigg. W Lot —3C 128
West Rounton. N Yor —4B 106
West Row. Suff —3F 65
West Rudham. Norf —3H 77
West Runton. Norf —1D 78
Westruther. Bord —5C 130
Westry. Cambs —1C 64
West Saltoun. E Lot —3A 130
West Sandford. Devn —2B 12
West Sandwick. Shet —3F 173
West Scrafton. N Yor —1C 98
Westside. Orkn —5C 172
West Sleekburn. Nmbd —1F 115
West Somerset Railway —4E 21
West Somerton. Norf —4G 79
West Stafford. Dors —4C 14
West Stockwith. Notts —1E 87
West Stoke. W Sus —2G 17
West Stonesdale. N Yor —4B 104
West Stoughton. Som —2H 21
West Stour. Dors —4C 22
West Stourmouth. Kent —4G 41
West Stow. Suff —3H 65
West Stowell. Wilts —5G 35
West Strathan. High —2F 167
West Stratton. Hants —2D 24
West Street. Kent —5D 40
West Tanfield. N Yor —2E 99
West Taphouse. Corn —2F 7
West Tarbert. Arg —3G 125
West Thirston. Nmbd —4F 121
West Thorney. W Sus —2F 17
West Thurrock. Thur —3G 39
West Tilbury. Thur —3A 40
West Tisted. Hants —4E 25
West Tofts. Norf —1H 65
West Torrington. Linc —2A 88
West Town. Bath —5A 34
West Town. Hants —3F 17
West Town. N Som —5H 33
West Tytherley. Hants —4A 24
West Tytherton. Wilts —4E 35
West View. Hart —1C 106
Westville. Notts —1C 74
West Walton. Norf —4D 76
Westward. Cumb —5D 112
Westward Ho!. Devn —4E 19
Westwell. Kent —1D 28
Westwell. Oxon —5H 49
Westwell Leacon. Kent —1D 28
West Wellow. Hants —1A 16
West Wemyss. Fife —4F 137
Westwick. Cambs —4D 64
Westwick. Dur —3D 104
Westwick. Norf —3E 79
West Wick. N Som —5G 33
West Wickham. Cambs —1G 53
West Wickham. G Lon —4E 39
West Williamston. Pemb —4E 43
West Willoughby. Linc —1G 75
West Winch. Norf —4F 77
West Winterslow. Wilts —3H 23
West Wittering. W Sus —3F 17
West Witton. N Yor —1C 98
Westwood. Devn —3D 12
Westwood. Kent —4H 41
Westwood. Pet —1A 64
Westwood. S Lan —4H 127
Westwood. Wilts —1D 22
West Woodburn. Nmbd —1B 114
West Woodhay. W Ber —5B 36
West Woodlands. Som —2C 22
Westwood Manor NT —1D 22
West Woodside. Cumb —5E 112
Westwoodside. N Lin —1E 87
West Worldham. Hants —3F 25
West Worlington. Devn —1A 12
West Worthing. W Sus —5C 26
West Wratting. Cambs —5F 65
West Wycombe. Buck —2G 37
West Wycombe Park NT —2G 37
West Wylam. Nmbd —3E 115
West Yatton. Wilts —4D 34
West Yell. Shet —3F 173
West Youlstone. Corn —1C 10
Wetheral. Cumb —4F 113
Wetherby. W Yor —5G 99
Wetherden. Suff —4C 66
Wetheringsett. Suff —4D 66
Wethersfield. Essx —2H 53
Wethersta. Shet —5E 173
Wetherup Street. Suff —4D 66
Wetley Rocks. Staf —1D 72
Wettenhall. Ches —4A 84
Wetton. Staf —5F 85
Wetwang. E Yor —4D 100
Wetwood. Staf —2B 72
Wexcombe. Wilts —1A 24
Wexham Street. Buck —2A 38
Weybourne. Norf —1D 78
Weybourne. Surr —2G 25
Weybread. Suff —2E 67
Weybridge. Surr —4B 38
Weycroft. Devn —3G 13
Weydale. High —2D 168
Weyhill. Hants —2B 24
Weymouth. Dors —5B 14
Weymouth Sea Life Park —4B 14
Weythel. Powy —5E 59
Whaddon. Buck —2G 51
Whaddon. Cambs —1D 52
Whaddon. Glos —4D 48
Whaddon. Wilts —4G 23
Whale. Cumb —2G 103
Whaley. Derbs —3C 86
Whaley Bridge. Derbs —2E 85
Whaley Thorns. Derbs —3C 86
Whalley. Lanc —1F 91
Whalton. Nmbd —1E 115
Wham. N Yor —3G 97
Whaplode. Linc —3C 76
Whaplode Drove. Linc —4C 76
Whaplode St Catherine. Linc —3C 76
Wharfe. N Yor —3G 97
Wharles. Lanc —1C 90
Wharley End. Beds —1H 51
Wharncliffe Side. S Yor —1G 85
Wharram-le-Street. N Yor —3C 100
Wharton. Ches —4A 84
Wharton. Here —5H 59
Whashton. N Yor —4E 105
Whasset. Cumb —1E 97
Whatcote. Warw —1A 50
Whateley. Warw —1G 61
Whatfield. Suff —1D 54
Whatley. Som —2G 13
(nr. Chard)
Whatley. Som —2C 22
(nr. Frome)
Whatlington. E Sus —4B 28
Whatmore. Shrp —3A 60
Whatstandwell. Derbs —5H 85
Whatton. Notts —2E 75
Whauphill. Dum —5B 110
Whaw. N Yor —4C 104
Wheal Martyn Mus. —3E 6
Wheatacre. Norf —1G 67
Wheatcroft. Derbs —5A 86
Wheathampstead. Herts —4B 52
Wheathill. Shrp —2A 60
Wheatley. Devn —3B 12
Wheatley. Hants —2F 25
Wheatley. Oxon —5D 50
Wheatley. W Yor —2A 92
Wheatley Hill. Dur —1A 106
Wheatley Lane. Lanc —1G 91
Wheatley Park. S Yor —4F 93
Wheaton Aston. Staf —4C 72
Wheatstone Park. Staf —5C 72
Wheddon Cross. Som —3C 20
Wheelerstreet. Surr —1A 26
Wheelock. Ches —5B 84
Wheelock Heath. Ches —5B 84
Wheelton. Lanc —2E 90
Wheldrake. York —5A 100
Whelford. Glos —2G 35
Whelpley Hill. Buck —5H 51
Whelpo. Cumb —1E 102
Whelston. Flin —3E 82
Whenby. N Yor —3A 100
Whepstead. Suff —5H 65
Wherstead. Suff —1E 55
Wherwell. Hants —2B 24
Wheston. Derbs —3F 85
Whetsted. Kent —1A 28
Whetstone. G Lon —1D 38
Whetstone. Leics —1C 62
Whicham. Cumb —1A 96
Whichford. Warw —2B 50
Whickham. Tyne —3F 115
Whiddon. Devn —2E 11
Whiddon Down. Devn —3G 11
Whigstreet. Ang —4D 145
Whilton. Nptn —4D 62
Whimble. Devn —2D 10
Whimple. Devn —3D 12
Whimpwell Green. Norf —3F 79
Whinburgh. Norf —5C 78
Whin Lane End. Lanc —5C 96
Whinnyfold. Abers —5H 161
Whinny Hill. Stoc T —3A 106
Whippingham. IOW —3D 16
Whipsnade. Beds —4A 52
Whipsnade Zoo —4A 52
Whipton. Devn —3C 12
Whirlow. S Yor —2H 85
Whisby. Linc —4G 87
Whissendine. Rut —4F 75
Whissonsett. Norf —3B 78
Whisterfield. Ches —3C 84
Whistley Green. Wok —4F 37
Whiston. Mers —1G 83
Whiston. Nptn —4F 63
Whiston. S Yor —1B 86
Whiston. Staf —1E 73
(nr. Cheadle)
Whiston. Staf —4C 72
(nr. Penkridge)
Whiston Cross. Shrp —5B 72
Whiston Eaves. Staf —1E 73
Whitacre Heath. Warw —1G 61
Whitbeck. Cumb —1A 96
Whitbourne. Here —5B 60
Whitburn. Tyne —3H 115
Whitburn. W Lot —3C 128
Whitburn Colliery. Tyne —3H 115
Whitby. Ches —3F 83
Whitby. N Yor —3F 107
Whitby Abbey EH —3G 107
Whitbyheath. Ches —3F 83
Whitchester. Bord —4D 130
Whitchurch. Bath —5B 34
Whitchurch. Buck —3G 51
Whitchurch. Card —4E 33
Whitchurch. Devn —5E 11
Whitchurch. Hants —2C 24
Whitchurch. Here —4A 48
Whitchurch. Pemb —2B 42
Whitchurch. Shrp —1H 71
Whitchurch Canonicorum. Dors —3G 13
Whitchurch Hill. Oxon —4E 37
Whitchurch-on-Thames. Oxon —4E 37
Whitcombe. Dors —4C 14
Whitcot. Shrp —1F 59
Whitcott Keysett. Shrp —2E 59
Whiteash Green. Essx —2A 54
Whitebog. High —2B 158
Whitebridge. High —2G 149
Whitebrook. Mon —5A 48
Whitecairns. Abers —2G 153
White Castle CADW —4G 47
White Chapel. Lanc —5E 97
Whitechurch. Pemb —1F 43
White Cliffs of Dover NT —1H 29
White Colne. Essx —3B 54
White Coppice. Lanc —3E 90
White Corries. High —3G 141
Whitecraig. E Lot —2G 129
Whitecroft. Glos —5B 48
White Cross. Corn —4D 5
(nr. Mullion)
Whitecross. Corn —1D 6
(nr. Wadebridge)
Whitecross. Falk —2C 128
White End. Worc —2C 48
Whiteface. High —5E 164
Whitefaulds. S Ayr —4B 116
Whitefield. Dors —3E 15
Whitefield. G Man —4G 91
Whitefield. Som —4D 20
Whiteford. Abers —1E 152
Whitegate. Ches —4A 84
Whitehall. Devn —1E 13
Whitehall. Hants —1F 25
Whitehall. Orkn —5F 172
Whitehall. W Sus —3C 26
Whitehaven. Cumb —3A 102
Whitehaven. Shrp —3E 71
Whitehill. Hants —3F 25
Whitehill. N Ayr —4D 126
Whitehills. Abers —2D 160
Whitehills. Ang —3D 144
White Horse Common. Norf —3F 79
Whitehough. Derbs —2E 85
Whitehouse. Abers —2D 152
Whitehouse. Arg —3G 125
Whiteinch. Glas —3G 127
Whitekirk. E Lot —1B 130
White Kirkley. Dur —1D 104
White Lackington. Dors —3C 14
Whitelackington. Som —1G 13
White Ladies Aston. Worc —5D 60
White Lee. W Yor —2C 92
Whiteley. Hants —2D 16
Whiteley Bank. IOW —4D 16
Whiteley Village. Surr —4B 38
Whitemans Green. W Sus —3E 27
White Mill. Carm —3E 45
Whitemire. Mor —3D 159
Whitemoor. Corn —3D 6
Whitenap. Hants —4B 24
Whiteness. Shet —7F 173
White Notley. Essx —4A 54
Whiteoak Green. Oxon —4B 50
Whiteparish. Wilts —4H 23
White Pit. Linc —3C 88
Whiterashes. Abers —1F 153
White Rocks. Here —3H 47
White Roding. Essx —4F 53
Whiterow. High —4F 169
Whiterow. Mor —3E 159
Whiteshill. Glos —5D 48
Whiteside. Nmbd —3A 114
Whiteside. W Lot —3C 128
Whitesmith. E Sus —4G 27
Whitestaunton. Som —1F 13
Whitestone. Abers —4D 152
Whitestone. Devn —3B 12
White Stone. Here —1A 48
Whitestones. Abers —3F 161
Whitestreet Green. Suff —2C 54
Whitewall Corner. N Yor —2B 100
White Waltham. Wind —4G 37
Whiteway. Glos —4E 49
Whitewell. Lanc —5F 97
Whitewell Bottom. Lanc —2G 91
Whiteworks. Devn —5G 11
Whitewreath. Mor —3G 159
Whitfield. D'dee —5D 144
Whitfield. Kent —1H 29
Whitfield. Nptn —2E 50
Whitfield. Nmbd —4A 114
Whitfield. S Glo —2B 34
Whitford. Devn —3F 13
Whitford. Flin —3D 82
Whitgift. E Yor —2B 94
Whitgreave. Staf —3C 72
Whithorn. Dum —5B 110
Whiting Bay. N Ayr —3E 123
Whitington. Norf —1G 65
Whitkirk. W Yor —1D 92
Whitland. Carm —3G 43
Whitleigh. Plym —2A 8
Whitletts. S Ayr —2C 116
Whitley. N Yor —2F 93
Whitley. Wilts —5D 35
Whitley Bay. Tyne —2G 115
Whitley Chapel. Nmbd —4C 114
Whitley Heath. Staf —3C 72
Whitley Lower. W Yor —3C 92
Whitley Thorpe. N Yor —2F 93
Whitlock's End. W Mid —3F 61
Whitminster. Glos —5C 48
Whitmore. Dors —2F 15
Whitmore. Staf —1C 72
Whitmore Hall —1C 72
Whitnage. Devn —1D 12
Whitnash. Warw —4H 61
Whitney. Here —1F 47
Whitrigg. Cumb —4D 112
(nr. Kirkbride)
Whitrigg. Cumb —1D 102
(nr. Torpenhow)
Whitsbury. Hants —1G 15
Whitsome. Bord —4E 131
Whitson. Newp —3G 33
Whitstable. Kent —4F 41
Whitstone. Corn —3C 10
Whittingham. Nmbd —3E 121
Whittingslow. Shrp —2G 59
Whittington. Derbs —3B 86
Whittington. Glos —3F 49
Whittington. Lanc —2F 97
Whittington. Shrp —2F 71
Whittington. Staf —2C 60
(nr. Kinver)
Whittington. Staf —5F 73
(nr. Lichfield)
Whittington. Warw —1G 61
Whittington. Worc —5C 60
Whittington Barracks. Staf —5F 73
Whittlebury. Nptn —1E 51
Whittleford. Warw —1H 61
Whittle-le-Woods. Lanc —2D 90
Whittlesey. Cambs —1B 64
Whittlesford. Cambs —1E 53
Whittlestone Head. Bkbn —3F 91
Whitton. N Lin —2C 94
Whitton. Nmbd —4E 121
Whitton. Powy —4E 59
Whitton. Bord —2B 120
Whitton. Shrp —3H 59
Whitton. Stoc T —2A 106
Whittonditch. Wilts —4A 36
Whittonstall. Nmbd —4D 114
Whitway. Hants —1C 24
Whitwell. Derbs —3C 86

Whitwell. Herts —3B 52
Whitwell. IOW —5D 16
Whitwell. N Yor —5F 105
Whitwell. Rut —5G 75
Whitwell-on-the-Hill. N Yor —3B 100
Whitwick. Leics —4B 74
Whitwood. W Yor —2E 93
Whitworth. Lanc —3G 91
Whitworth Art Gallery —Manchester 191
Whixall. Shrp —2H 71
Whixley. N Yor —4G 99
Whoberley. W Mid —3G 61
Whorlton. Dur —3E 105
Whorlton. N Yor —4B 106
Whygate. Nmbd —2A 114
Whyle. Here —4H 59
Whyteleafe. Surr —5E 39
Wibdon. Glos —2A 34
Wibtoft. Warw —2B 62
Wichenford. Worc —4B 60
Wichling. Kent —5D 40
Wick. Bour —3G 15
Wick. High —3F 169
Wick. Shet —8F 173 (on Mainland)
Wick. Shet —1G 173 (on Unst)
Wick. Som —2F 21 (nr. Bridgwater)
Wick. Som —1G 21 (nr. Burnham-on-Sea)
Wick. Som —4H 21 (nr. Somerton)
Wick. S Glo —4C 34
Wick. V Glam —4C 32
Wick. W Sus —5B 26
Wick. Wilts —4G 23
Wick. Worc —1E 49
Wicken. Cambs —3E 65
Wicken. Nptn —2F 51
Wicken Bonhunt. Essx —2E 53
Wickenby. Linc —2H 87
Wicken Fen NT —3E 65
Wicken Green Village. Norf —2H 77
Wickersley. S Yor —1B 86
Wicker Street Green. Suff —1C 54
Wickford. Essx —1B 40
Wickham. Hants —1D 16
Wickham. W Ber —4B 36
Wickham Bishops. Essx —4B 54
Wickhambreaux. Kent —5G 41
Wickhambrook. Suff —5G 65
Wickhamford. Worc —1F 49
Wickham Green. Suff —4C 66
Wickham Heath. W Ber —5C 36
Wickham Market. Suff —5E 67
Wickhampton. Norf —5G 79
Wickham St Paul. Essx —2B 54
Wickham Skeith. Suff —4C 66
Wickham Street. Suff —4C 66
Wick Hill. Wok —5F 37
Wicklewood. Norf —5C 78
Wickmere. Norf —2D 78
Wick St Lawrence. N Som —5G 33
Wicksteed Park —3F 63
Wickwar. S Glo —3C 34
Widdington. Essx —2F 53
Widdrington. Nmbd —5G 121
Widdrington Station. Nmbd —5G 121
Widecombe in the Moor. Devn —5H 11
Widegates. Corn —3G 7
Widemouth Bay. Corn —2C 10
Wide Open. Tyne —2F 115
Widewall. Orkn —8D 172
Widford. Essx —5G 53
Widford. Herts —4E 53
Widham. Wilts —3F 35
Widmer End. Buck —2G 37
Widmerpool. Notts —3D 74
Widnes. Hal —2H 83
Widworthy. Devn —3F 13
Wigan. G Man —4D 90
Wigbeth. Dors —2F 15
Wiggaton. Devn —3E 12
Wiggenhall St Germans. Norf —4E 77
Wiggenhall St Mary Magdalen. Norf —4E 77
Wiggenhall St Mary the Virgin. Norf —4E 77
Wiggenhall St Peter. Norf —4F 77
Wiggens Green. Essx —1G 53
Wigginton. Herts —4H 51
Wigginton. Oxon —2B 50
Wigginton. Staf —5G 73
Wigginton. York —4H 99
Wigglesworth. N Yor —4H 97
Wiggonby. Cumb —4D 112
Wiggonholt. W Sus —4B 26
Wighill. N Yor —5G 99
Wighton. Norf —1B 78
Wightwick. Staf —1C 60
Wightwick Manor NT —1C 60
Wigley. Hants —1B 16
Wigmore. Here —4G 59
Wigmore. Medw —4C 40
Wigmore Castle EH —4G 59
Wigsley. Notts —3F 87
Wigsthorpe. Nptn —2H 63
Wigston. Leics —1D 62
Wigtoft. Linc —2B 76
Wigton. Cumb —5D 112
Wigtown. Dum —4B 110
Wigtwizzle. S Yor —1G 85
Wike. W Yor —5F 99
Wilbarston. Nptn —2F 63
Wilberforce House Mus. —Hull 190
Wilberfoss. E Yor —4B 100
Wilburton. Cambs —3D 65
Wilby. Norf —1C 66
Wilby. Nptn —4F 63
Wilby. Suff —3E 67
Wilcot. Wilts —5G 35
Wilcott. Shrp —4F 71
Wilcove. Corn —3A 8
Wildboarclough. Ches —4D 85
Wilden. Beds —5H 63
Wilden. Worc —3C 60
Wildern. Hants —1C 16
Wilderspool. Warr —2A 84
Wilde Street. Suff —3G 65
Wildhern. Hants —1B 24
Wildmanbridge. S Lan —4B 128
Wildmoor. Worc —3D 60
Wildsworth. Linc —1F 87
Wildwood. Staf —3D 72
Wilford. Nott —2C 74
Wilkesley. Ches —1A 72
Wilkhaven. High —5G 165
Wilkieston. W Lot —3E 129
Wilksby. Linc —4B 88
Willand. Devn —1D 12
Willaston. Ches —5A 84 (nr. Crewe)
Willaston. Ches —3F 83 (nr. Neston)
Willaston. IOM —4C 108
Willen. Mil —1G 51
Willenhall. W Mid —3A 62 (nr. Coventry)
Willenhall. W Mid —1D 60 (nr. Wolverhampton)
Willerby. E Yor —1D 94
Willerby. N Yor —2E 101
Willersey. Glos —2G 49
Willersley. Here —1G 47
Willers Mill Wildlife Park —1D 53
Willesborough. Kent —1E 28
Willesborough Lees. Kent —1E 29
Willesden. G Lon —2D 38
Willesley. Wilts —3D 34
Willett. Som —3E 20
Willey. Shrp —1A 60
Willey. Warw —2B 62
Willey Green. Surr —5A 38
Williamscot. Oxon —1C 50
Williamsetter. Shet —9E 173
Willian. Herts —2C 52
Willingale. Essx —5F 53
Willingdon. E Sus —5G 27
Willingham. Cambs —3D 64
Willingham by Stow. Linc —2F 87
Willingham Green. Cambs —5F 65
Willington. Beds —1B 52
Willington. Derbs —3G 73
Willington. Dur —1E 105
Willington. Tyne —3G 115
Willington. Warw —2A 50
Willington Corner. Ches —4H 83
Willisham Tye. Suff —5C 66
Willitoft. E Yor —1H 93
Williton. Som —2D 20
Willoughbridge. Staf —1B 72
Willoughby. Linc —3D 89
Willoughby. Warw —4C 62
Willoughby on the Wolds. Notts —3D 74
Willoughby Waterleys. Leics —1C 62
Willoughton. Linc —1G 87
Willow Green. Worc —5B 60
Willows Green. Essx —4H 53
Willsbridge. S Glo —4B 34
Willslock. Staf —2E 73
Willsworthy. Devn —4F 11
Wilmcote. Warw —5F 61
Wilmington. Bath —5B 34
Wilmington. Devn —3F 13
Wilmington. E Sus —5G 27
Wilmington. Kent —3G 39
Wilmslow. Ches —2C 84
Wilnecote. Staf —5G 73
Wilney Green. Norf —2C 66
Wilpshire. Lanc —1E 91
Wilsden. W Yor —1A 92
Wilsford. Linc —1H 75
Wilsford. Wilts —3G 23 (nr. Amesbury)
Wilsford. Wilts —1G 23 (nr. Devizes)
Wilsill. N Yor —3D 98
Wilsley Green. Kent —2B 28
Wilson. Here —3A 48
Wilson. Leics —3B 74
Wilsontown. S Lan —4C 128
Wilstead. Beds —1A 52
Wilsthorpe. E Yor —3F 101
Wilsthorpe. Linc —4H 75
Wilstone. Herts —4H 51
Wilton. Cumb —3B 102
Wilton. N Yor —1C 100
Wilton. Red C —3C 106
Wilton. Bord —3H 119
Wilton. Wilts —5A 36 (nr. Marlborough)
Wilton. Wilts —3F 23 (nr. Salisbury)
Wilton House —3F 23
Wimbish. Essx —2F 53
Wimbish Green. Essx —2G 53
Wimblebury. Staf —4E 73
Wimbledon. G Lon —3D 38
Wimbledon Lawn Tennis Mus. —3D 38
Wimblington. Cambs —1D 64
Wimborne Minster. Dors —2F 15
Wimborne St Giles. Dors —1F 15
Wimbotsham. Norf —5F 77
Wimpole Hall NT —5C 64
Wimpstone. Warw —1H 49
Wincanton. Som —4C 22
Winceby. Linc —4C 88
Wincham. Ches —3A 84
Winchburgh. W Lot —2D 129
Winchcombe. Glos —3F 49
Winchelsea. E Sus —4D 28
Winchelsea Beach. E Sus —4D 28
Winchester. Hants —4C 24 & 197
Winchester Cathedral —197
Winchet Hill. Kent —1B 28
Winchfield. Hants —1F 25
Winchmore Hill. Buck —1A 38
Winchmore Hill. G Lon —1E 39
Wincle. Ches —4D 84
Windermere. Cumb —5F 103
Windermere Steamboat Mus., Bowness —5E 103
Winderton. Warw —1B 50
Windhill. High —4H 157
Windle Hill. Ches —3F 83
Windlesham. Surr —4A 38
Windley. Derbs —1H 73
Windmill. Derbs —3F 85
Windmill Hill. E Sus —4H 27
Windmill Hill EH —4F 35
Windmill Hill. Som —1G 13
Windrush. Glos —4G 49
Windsor. Wind —3A 38 & 197
Windsor Castle —197
Windsor Green. Suff —5A 66
Windyedge. Abers —4G 153
Windygates. Fife —3F 137
Windyharbour. Ches —3C 84
Windyknowe. W Lot —3C 128
Wineham. W Sus —3D 26
Winestead. E Yor —2G 95
Winfarthing. Norf —2D 66
Winford. IOW —4D 16
Winford. N Som —5A 34
Winforton. Here —1F 47
Winfrith Newburgh. Dors —4D 14
Wing. Buck —3G 51
Wing. Rut —5F 75
Wingate. Dur —1A 106
Wingates. G Man —4E 91
Wingates. Nmbd —5F 121
Wingerworth. Derbs —4A 86
Wingfield. Beds —3A 52
Wingfield. Suff —3E 67
Wingfield. Wilts —1D 22
Wingfield College —3E 67
Wingfield Manor EH —5A 86
Wingfield Park. Derbs —5A 86
Wingham. Kent —5G 41
Wingmore. Kent —1F 29
Wingrave. Buck —4G 51
Winkburn. Notts —5E 86
Winkfield. Brac —3A 38
Winkfield Row. Brac —4G 37
Winkhill. Staf —5E 85
Winklebury. Hants —1E 24
Winkleigh. Devn —2G 11
Winksley. N Yor —2E 99
Winkton. Dors —3G 15
Winkworth Arboretum NT —1B 26
Winlaton. Tyne —3E 115
Winlaton Mill. Tyne —3E 115
Winless. High —3F 169
Winmarleigh. Lanc —5D 96
Winnal Common. Here —2H 47
Winnard's Perch. Corn —2D 6
Winnersh. Wok —4F 37
Winnington. Ches —3A 84
Winnington. Staf —2B 72
Winnothdale. Staf —1E 73
Winscales. Cumb —2B 102
Winscombe. N Som —1H 21
Winsford. Ches —4A 84
Winsford. Som —3C 20
Winsham. Devn —3F 19
Winsham. Som —2G 13
Winshill. Staf —3G 73
Winsh-wen. Swan —3F 31
Winskill. Cumb —1G 103
Winslade. Hants —2E 25
Winsley. Wilts —5C 34
Winslow. Buck —3F 51
Winson. Glos —5F 49
Winson Green. W Mid —2E 61
Winsor. Hants —1B 16
Winster. Cumb —5F 103
Winster. Derbs —4G 85
Winston. Dur —3E 105
Winston. Suff —4D 66
Winstone. Glos —5E 49
Winswell. Devn —1E 11
Winterborne Clenston. Dors —2D 14
Winterborne Herringston. Dors —4B 14
Winterborne Houghton. Dors —2D 14
Winterborne Kingston. Dors —3D 14
Winterborne Monkton. Dors —4B 14
Winterborne St Martin. Dors —4B 14
Winterborne Stickland. Dors —2D 14
Winterborne Whitechurch. Dors —2D 14
Winterborne Zelston. Dors —3E 15
Winterbourne. S Glo —3B 34
Winterbourne. W Ber —4C 36
Winterbourne Abbas. Dors —3B 14
Winterbourne Bassett. Wilts —4G 35
Winterbourne Dauntsey. Wilts —3G 23
Winterbourne Earls. Wilts —3G 23
Winterbourne Gunner. Wilts —3G 23
Winterbourne Monkton. Wilts —4F 35
Winterbourne Steepleton. Dors —4B 14
Winterbourne Stoke. Wilts —2F 23
Winterbrook. Oxon —3E 36
Winterburn. N Yor —4B 98
Winter Gardens. Essx —2B 40
Winteringham. N Lin —2C 94
Winterley. Ches —5B 84
Wintersett. W Yor —3D 93
Winterton. N Lin —3C 94
Winterton-on-Sea. Norf —4G 79
Winthorpe. Linc —4E 89
Winthorpe. Notts —5F 87
Winton. Bour —3F 15
Winton. Cumb —3A 104
Winton. E Sus —5G 27
Wintringham. N Yor —2C 100
Winwick. Cambs —2A 64
Winwick. Nptn —3D 62
Winwick. Warr —1A 84
Wirksworth. Derbs —5G 85
Wirswall. Ches —1H 71
Wisbech. Cambs —4D 76
Wisbech St Mary. Cambs —5D 76
Wisborough Green. W Sus —3B 26
Wiseton. Notts —2E 86
Wishaw. N Lan —4B 128
Wishaw. Warw —1F 61
Wisley. Surr —5B 38
Wisley Gdn. RHS —5B 38
Wispington. Linc —3B 88
Wissenden. Kent —1D 28
Wissett. Suff —3F 67
Wistanstow. Shrp —2G 59
Wistanswick. Shrp —3A 72
Wistaston. Ches —5A 84
Wiston. Pemb —3E 43
Wiston. S Lan —1B 118
Wiston. W Sus —4C 26
Wistow. Cambs —2B 64
Wistow. N Yor —1F 93
Wiswell. Lanc —1F 91
Witcham. Cambs —2D 64
Witchampton. Dors —2E 15
Witchford. Cambs —3E 65
Witham. Essx —4B 54
Witham Friary. Som —2C 22
Witham on the Hill. Linc —4H 75
Witham St Hughs. Linc —4F 87
Withcall. Linc —2B 88
Witherenden Hill. E Sus —3H 27
Withergate. Norf —3E 79
Witheridge. Devn —1B 12
Witheridge Hill. Oxon —3E 37
Witherley. Leics —1H 61
Withermarsh Green. Suff —2D 54
Withern. Linc —2D 88
Withernsea. E Yor —2G 95
Withernwick. E Yor —5F 101
Withersdale Street. Suff —2E 67
Withersfield. Suff —1G 53
Witherslack. Cumb —1D 96
Withiel. Corn —2D 6
Withiel Florey. Som —3C 20
Withington. Glos —4F 49
Withington. G Man —1C 84
Withington. Here —1A 48
Withington. Shrp —4H 71
Withington. Staf —2E 73
Withington Green. Ches —3C 84
Withington Marsh. Here —1A 48
Withleigh. Devn —1C 12
Withnell. Lanc —2E 91
Withnell Fold. Lanc —2E 90
Withybrook. Warw —2B 62
Withycombe. Som —2D 20
Withycombe Raleigh. Devn —4D 12
Withyham. E Sus —2F 27
Withypool. Som —3B 20
Witley. Surr —1A 26
Witley Court EH —4B 60
Witnesham. Suff —5D 66
Witney. Oxon —4B 50
Wittering. Pet —5H 75
Wittersham. Kent —3D 28
Witton. Norf —5F 79
Witton. Worc —4D 60
Witton Bridge. Norf —2F 79
Witton Gilbert. Dur —5F 115
Witton-le-Wear. Dur —1E 105
Witton Park. Dur —1E 105
Wiveliscombe. Som —4D 20
Wivelrod. Hants —3E 25
Wivelsfield. E Sus —3E 27
Wivelsfield Green. E Sus —4E 27
Wivenhoe. Essx —3D 54
Wiveton. Norf —1C 78
Wix. Essx —3E 55
Wixford. Warw —5E 61
Wixhill. Shrp —3H 71
Wixoe. Suff —1H 53
Woburn. Beds —2H 51
Woburn Abbey & Wild Animal Kingdom —2H 51
Woburn Sands. Mil —2H 51
Woking. Surr —5B 38
Wokingham. Wok —5G 37
Wolborough. Devn —5B 12
Woldingham. Surr —5E 39
Wold Newton. E Yor —2E 101
Wold Newton. NE Lin —1B 88
Wolferlow. Here —4A 60
Wolferton. Norf —3F 77
Wolfeton House —3B 14
Wolfhill. Per —5A 144
Wolf's Castle. Pemb —2D 42
Wolfsdale. Pemb —2D 42
Wolgarston. Staf —4D 72
Wollaston. Nptn —4G 63
Wollaston. Shrp —4F 71
Wollaston. W Mid —2C 60
Wollaton. Nott —1C 74
Wollaton Hall —2C 74
Wollerton. Shrp —2A 72
Wollescote. W Mid —2D 60
Wolseley Bridge. Staf —3E 73
Wolsingham. Dur —1D 105
Wolstanton. Staf —1C 72
Wolston. Warw —3B 62
Wolsty. Cumb —4C 112
Wolterton. Norf —2D 78
Wolterton Park —2D 78
Wolvercote. Oxon —5C 50
Wolverhampton. W Mid —1D 60 & 197
Wolverley. Shrp —2G 71
Wolverley. Worc —3C 60
Wolverton. Hants —1D 24
Wolverton. Mil —1G 51
Wolverton. Warw —4G 61
Wolverton. Wilts —3C 22
Wolverton Common. Hants —1D 24
Wolvesey Castle EH —Winchester 197
Wolvesnewton. Mon —2H 33
Wolvey. Warw —2B 62
Wolvey Heath. Warw —2B 62
Wolviston. Stoc T —2B 106
Womaston. Powy —4E 59
Wombleton. N Yor —1A 100
Wombourne. Staf —1C 60
Wombwell. S Yor —4D 93
Womenswold. Kent —5G 41
Womersley. N Yor —3F 93
Wonersh. Surr —1B 26
Wonson. Devn —4G 11
Wonston. Hants —3C 24
Wooburn. Buck —2A 38
Wooburn Green. Buck —2A 38
Wood. Pemb —2C 42
Woodacott. Devn —2D 11
Woodale. N Yor —2C 98
Woodall. S Yor —2B 86
Woodbank. Ches —3F 83
Woodbastwick. Norf —4F 79
Woodbeck. Notts —3E 87
Woodborough. Notts —1D 74
Woodborough. Wilts —1G 23
Woodbridge. Devn —3E 13
Woodbridge. Dors —1C 14
Woodbridge. Suff —1F 55
Wood Burcote. Nptn —1E 51
Woodbury. Devn —4D 12
Woodbury Salterton. Devn —4D 12
Woodchester. Glos —5D 48
Woodchester Mansion (Woodchester Park NT) —5D 48
Woodchurch. Kent —2D 28
Woodchurch. Mers —2E 83
Woodcock Heath. Staf —3E 73
Woodcombe. Som —2C 20
Woodcote. Oxon —3E 37
Woodcote. Telf —4B 72
Woodcote Green. Worc —3D 60
Woodcott. Hants —1C 24
Woodcroft. Glos —2A 34
Woodcutts. Dors —1E 15
Wood Dalling. Norf —3C 78
Woodditton. Cambs —5F 65
Woodeaton. Oxon —4D 50
Wood Eaton. Staf —4C 72
Woodend. Cumb —5C 102
Wood End. Herts —3D 52
Woodend. Nptn —1E 50
Woodend. Staf —3F 73
Wood End. Warw —2G 61 (nr. Bedworth)
Wood End. Warw —1G 61 (nr. Dordon)
Wood End. Warw —3F 61 (nr. Tamworth-in-Arden)
Woodend. W Sus —2G 17
Wood Enderby. Linc —4B 88
Woodend Green. Essx —3F 53
Woodfalls. Wilts —4G 23
Woodfield. Oxon —3D 50
Woodfields. Lanc —1E 91
Woodford. Corn —1C 10
Woodford. Devn —3D 9
Woodford. Glos —2B 34
Woodford. G Lon —1E 39
Woodford. G Man —2C 84
Woodford. Nptn —3G 63
Woodford. Plym —3B 8
Woodford Green. G Lon —1F 39
Woodford Halse. Nptn —5C 62
Woodgate. Norf —4C 78
Woodgate. W Mid —2D 61
Woodgate. W Sus —5A 26
Woodgate. Worc —4D 60
Wood Green. G Lon —1D 39
Woodgreen. Hants —1G 15
Wood Hall. E Yor —1E 95
Woodhall. Inv —2E 127
Woodhall. Linc —4B 88
Woodhall. N Yor —5C 104
Woodhall Spa. Linc —4A 88
Woodham. Surr —4B 38
Woodham Ferrers. Essx —1B 40
Woodham Mortimer. Essx —5B 54
Woodham Walter. Essx —5B 54
Woodhaven. Fife —1G 137
Wood Hayes. W Mid —5D 72
Woodhead. Abers —2G 161 (nr. Fraserburgh)
Woodhead. Abers —5E 161 (nr. Fyvie)
Woodhenge EH —2G 23
Woodhill. N Som —4H 33
Woodhill. Shrp —2B 60
Woodhorn. Nmbd —1G 115
Woodhouse. Leics —4C 74
Woodhouse. S Yor —2B 86
Woodhouse. W Yor —1C 92 (nr. Leeds)
Woodhouse. W Yor —2D 93 (nr. Normanton)
Woodhouse Eaves. Leics —4C 74
Woodhouses. Ches —3H 83
Woodhouses. G Man —4H 91 (nr. Failsworth)
Woodhouses. G Man —1B 84 (nr. Sale)
Woodhouses. Staf —4F 73
Woodhuish. Devn —3F 9
Woodhurst. Cambs —3C 64
Woodingdean. Brig —5E 27
Woodland. Devn —2D 9
Woodland. Dur —2D 104
Woodland Head. Devn —3A 12
Woodlands. Abers —4E 153
Woodlands. Dors —2F 15
Woodlands. Hants —1B 16
Woodlands. Kent —4G 39
Woodlands. N Yor —4F 99
Woodlands. S Yor —4F 93

Woodlands Park. Wind —4G 37
Woodlands St Mary. W Ber —4B 36
Woodlane. Shrp —3A 72
Woodlane. Staf —3F 73
Woodleigh. Devn —4D 8
Woodlesford. W Yor —2D 92
Woodley. G Man —1D 84
Woodley. Wok —4F 37
Woodmancote. Glos —3E 49 (nr. Cheltenham)
Woodmancote. Glos —5F 49 (nr. Cirencester)
Woodmancote. W Sus —2F 17 (nr. Chichester)
Woodmancote. W Sus —4D 26 (nr. Henfield)
Woodmancote. Worc —1E 49
Woodmancott. Hants —2D 24
Woodmansey. E Yor —1D 94
Woodmansgreen. W Sus —4G 25
Woodmansterne. Surr —5D 39
Woodmanton. Devn —4D 12
Woodmill. Staf —3F 73
Woodminton. Wilts —4F 23
Woodnesborough. Kent —5H 41
Woodnewton. Nptn —1H 63
Woodnook. Linc —2G 75
Wood Norton. Norf —3C 78
Woodplumpton. Lanc —1D 90
Woodrising. Norf —5B 78
Woodrow. Cumb —5D 112
Woodrow. Dors —2C 14
Wood Row. W Yor —2D 93
Woods Eaves. Here —1F 47
Woodseaves. Shrp —2A 72
Woodseaves. Staf —3B 72
Woodsend. Wilts —4H 35
Woodsetts. S Yor —2C 86
Woodsford. Dors —3C 14
Wood's Green. E Sus —2H 27
Woodshaw. Wilts —3F 35
Woodside. Aber —3G 153
Woodside. Brac —3A 38
Woodside. Cumb —1B 102
Woodside. Derbs —1A 74
Woodside. Dum —2B 112
Woodside. Dur —2E 105
Woodside. Fife —3G 137
Woodside. Herts —5C 52
Woodside. Per —5B 144
Wood Stanway. Glos —2F 49
Woodstock. Oxon —4C 50
Woodstock Slop. Pemb —2E 43
Woodston. Pet —1A 64
Wood Street Village. Surr —5A 38
Woodthorpe. Derbs —3B 86
Woodthorpe. Leics —4C 74
Woodthorpe. Linc —2D 88
Woodthorpe. York —5H 99
Woodton. Norf —1E 67
Woodtown. Devn —4E 19 (nr. Bideford)
Woodtown. Devn —4E 19 (nr. Littleham)
Woodvale. Mers —3B 90
Woodville. Derbs —4H 73
Woodwalton. Cambs —2B 64
Woodwick. Orkn —5C 172
Woodyates. Dors —1F 15
Woody Bay. Devn —2G 19
Woofferton. Shrp —4H 59
Wookey. Som —2A 22
Wookey Hole. Som —2A 22
Wookey Hole Caves —2A 22
Wool. Dors —4D 14
Woolacombe. Devn —2E 19
Woolage Green. Kent —1G 29
Woolaston. Glos —2A 34
Woolavington. Som —2G 21
Woolbeding. W Sus —4G 25
Woolcotts. Som —3C 20
Wooldale. W Yor —4B 92
Wooler. Nmbd —2D 121
Woolfardisworthy. Devn (nr. Bideford) —4D 18
Woolfardisworthy. Devn (nr. Crediton) —2B 12
Woolfords. S Lan —4D 128
Woolgarston. Dors —4E 15
Woolhampton. W Ber —5D 36
Woolhope. Here —2B 48
Woolland. Dors —2C 14
Woollard. Bath —5B 34
Woolley. Bath —5C 34
Woolley. Cambs —3A 64
Woolley. Corn —1C 10
Woolley. Derbs —4A 86
Woolley. W Yor —3D 92
Woolley Green. Wilts —5D 34
Woolmere Green. Worc —4D 60
Woolmer Green. Herts —4C 52
Woolminstone. Som —2H 13
Woolpit. Suff —4B 66
Woolridge. Glos —3D 48
Woolscott. Warw —4B 62
Woolsery. Devn —4D 18
Woolsington. Tyne —3E 115
Woolstaston. Shrp —1G 59
Woolsthorpe. Linc —3G 75 (nr. Colsterworth)
Woolsthorpe. Linc —2F 75 (nr. Grantham)
Woolsthorpe Manor NT —3G 75
Woolston. Devn —4D 8
Woolston. Shrp —2G 59 (nr. Church Stretton)
Woolston. Shrp —3F 71 (nr. Oswestry)
Woolston. Som —4B 22
Woolston. Sotn —1C 16
Woolston. Warr —1A 84
Woolstone. Glos —2E 49
Woolstone. Oxon —3A 36
Woolston Green. Devn —2D 9
Woolton. Mers —2G 83
Woolton Hill. Hants —5C 36
Woolverstone. Suff —2E 55
Woolverton. Som —1C 22
Woolwell. Devn —2B 8
Woolwich. G Lon —3F 39
Woonton. Here —5F 59 (nr. Kington)
Woonton. Here —4H 59 (nr. Leominster)
Wooperton. Nmbd —2E 121
Woore. Shrp —1B 72
Wooton. Shrp —2B 60
Wootton. Beds —1A 52
Wootton. Hants —3H 15
Wootton. IOW —3D 16
Wootton. Kent —1G 29
Wootton. Nptn —5E 63
Wootton. N Lin —3D 94
Wootton. Oxon —5C 50 (nr. Abingdon)
Wootton. Oxon —4C 50 (nr. Woodstock)
Wootton. Shrp —3G 59 (nr. Ludlow)
Wootton. Shrp —3F 71 (nr. Oswestry)
Wootton. Staf —3C 72 (nr. Eccleshall)
Wootton. Staf —1F 73 (nr. Ellastone)
Wootton Bassett. Wilts —3F 35
Wootton Bridge. IOW —3D 16
Wootton Common. IOW —3D 16
Wootton Courtenay. Som —2C 20
Wootton Fitzpaine. Dors —3G 13
Wootton Rivers. Wilts —5G 35
Woottons. Staf —2E 73
Wootton St Lawrence. Hants —1D 24
Wootton Wawen. Warw —4F 61
Worcester. Worc —5C 60 & 197
Worcester Cathedral —197
Worcester Park. G Lon —4D 38
Wordsley. W Mid —2C 60
Wordsworth House NT —1C 102
Worfield. Shrp —1B 60
Work. Orkn —6D 172
Workhouse Green. Suff —2C 54
Workington. Cumb —2A 102
Worksop. Notts —3C 86
Worlaby. N Lin —3D 94
Worlds End. Hants —1E 17
Worldsend. Shrp —1G 59
World's End. W Ber —4C 36
Worlds End. W Mid —2F 61
World's End. W Sus —4E 27
Worldwide Butterflies & Silk Farm —1A 14
Worle. N Som —5G 33
Worleston. Ches —5A 84
Worley. Glos —2D 34
Worlingham. Suff —1G 67
Worlington. Suff —3F 65
Worlingworth. Suff —4E 67
Wormbridge. Here —2H 47
Wormegay. Norf —4F 77
Wormelow Tump. Here —2H 47
Wormhill. Derbs —3F 85
Wormiehills. Ang —5F 145
Wormingford. Essx —2C 54
Worminghall. Buck —5E 51
Wormington. Glos —2F 49
Worminster. Som —2A 22
Wormit. Fife —1F 137
Wormleighton. Warw —5B 62
Wormley. Herts —5D 52
Wormley. Surr —2A 26
Wormshill. Kent —5C 40
Wormsley. Here —1H 47
Worplesdon. Surr —5A 38
Worrall. S Yor —1H 85
Worsbrough. S Yor —4D 92
Worsley. G Man —4F 91
Worstead. Norf —3F 79
Worsthorne. Lanc —1G 91
Worston. Lanc —5G 97
Worth. Kent —5H 41
Worth. W Sus —2E 27
Wortham. Suff —3C 66
Worthen. Shrp —5F 71
Worthenbury. Wrex —1G 71
Worthing. Norf —4B 78
Worthing. W Sus —5C 26
Worthington. Leics —3B 74
Worth Matravers. Dors —5E 15
Worting. Hants —1E 24
Wortley. Glos —2C 34
Wortley. S Yor —1H 85
Wortley. W Yor —1C 92
Worton. N Yor —5C 104
Worton. Wilts —1E 23
Wortwell. Norf —2E 67
Wotherton. Shrp —5E 71
Wothorpe. Nptn —5H 75
Wotter. Devn —2B 8
Wotton. Glos —4D 48
Wotton. Surr —1C 26
Wotton-under-Edge. Glos —2C 34
Wotton Underwood. Buck —4E 51
Wouldham. Kent —4B 40
Wrabness. Essx —2E 55
Wrafton. Devn —3E 19
Wragby. Linc —3A 88
Wragby. W Yor —3E 93
Wramplingham. Norf —5D 78
Wrangbrook. W Yor —3E 93
Wrangle. Linc —5D 88
Wrangle Lowgate. Linc —5D 88
Wrangway. Som —1E 13
Wrantage. Som —4G 21
Wrawby. N Lin —4D 94
Wraxall. Dors —2A 14
Wraxall. N Som —4H 33
Wraxall. Som —3B 22
Wray. Lanc —3F 97
Wrayland. Devn —4A 12
Wraysbury. Wind —3B 38
Wrayton. Lanc —2F 97
Wrea Green. Lanc —1B 90
Wreay. Cumb —5F 113 (nr. Carlisle)
Wreay. Cumb —2F 103 (nr. Penrith)
Wrecclesham. Surr —2G 25
Wrecsam. Wrex —5F 83
Wrekenton. Tyne —4F 115
Wrelton. N Yor —1B 100
Wrenbury. Ches —1H 71
Wreningham. Norf —1D 66
Wrentham. Suff —2G 67
Wrenthorpe. W Yor —2D 92
Wrentnall. Shrp —5G 71
Wressle. E Yor —1H 93
Wressle. N Lin —4C 94
Wrestlingworth. Beds —1C 52
Wrest Park Gdn. EH —2A 52
Wretham. Norf —1B 66
Wretton. Norf —5F 77
Wrexham. Wrex —5F 83
Wrexham Industrial Estate. Wrex —1F 71
Wrickton. Shrp —2A 60
Wrightlington Bar. Lanc —3D 90
Wright's Green. Essx —4F 53
Wrinehill. Staf —1B 72
Wrington. N Som —5H 33
Writtle. Essx —5G 53
Wrockwardine. Telf —4A 72
Wroot. N Lin —4H 93
Wrotham. Kent —5H 39
Wrotham Heath. Kent —5H 39
Wroughton. Swin —3G 35
Wroxall. IOW —5D 16
Wroxall. Warw —3G 61
Wroxeter. Shrp —5H 71
Wroxeter Roman Mus. —5H 71
Wroxham. Norf —4F 79
Wroxton. Oxon —1C 50
Wroxton Abbey Gdn. —1C 50
Wyaston. Derbs —1F 73
Wyatt's Green. Essx —1G 39
Wybers Wood. NE Lin —4F 95
Wyberton. Linc —1C 76
Wyboston. Beds —5A 64
Wybunbury. Ches —1A 72
Wychbold. Worc —4D 60
Wych Cross. E Sus —2F 27
Wychnor. Staf —4F 73
Wychnor Bridges. Staf —4F 73
Wyck. Hants —3F 25
Wyck Hill. Glos —3G 49
Wyck Rissington. Glos —3G 49
Wycliffe. Dur —3E 105
Wycombe Marsh. Buck —2G 37
Wyddial. Herts —2D 52
Wye. Kent —1E 29
Wyesham. Mon —4A 48
Wyfold Grange. Oxon —3E 37
Wyfordby. Leics —4E 75
Wyke. Devn —2B 12
Wyke. Dors —4C 22
Wyke. Shrp —5A 72
Wyke. Surr —5A 38
Wyke. W Yor —2B 92
Wyke Champflower. Som —3B 22
Wykeham. Linc —3B 76
Wykeham. N Yor —2C 100 (nr. Malton)
Wykeham. N Yor —1D 100 (nr. Scarborough)
Wyken. Shrp —1B 60
Wyken. W Mid —2A 62
Wyke Regis. Dors —5B 14
Wyke, The. Shrp —5B 72
Wykey. Shrp —3F 71
Wykin. Leics —1B 62
Wylam. Nmbd —3E 115
Wylde Green. W Mid —1F 61
Wylye. Wilts —3F 23
Wymering. Port —2E 17
Wymeswold. Leics —3D 74
Wymington. Beds —4G 63
Wymondham. Leics —4F 75
Wymondham. Norf —5D 78
Wyndham. B'end —2C 32
Wynford Eagle. Dors —3A 14
Wyng. Orkn —8C 172
Wyre Piddle. Worc —1E 49
Wysall. Notts —3D 74
Wyson. Here —4H 59
Wythall. Worc —3E 61
Wytham. Oxon —5C 50
Wythenshawe. G Man —2C 84
Wythenshawe Hall —1C 84
Wythop Mill. Cumb —2C 102
Wyton. Cambs —3B 64
Wyton. E Yor —1E 95
Wyverstone. Suff —4C 66
Wyverstone Street. Suff —4C 66
Wyville. Linc —3F 75
Wyvis Lodge. High —1G 157

Yaddlethorpe. N Lin —4B 94
Yafford. IOW —4C 16
Yafforth. N Yor —5A 106
Yalberton. Torb —3E 9
Yalding. Kent —5A 40
Yanley. N Som —5A 34
Yanwath. Cumb —2G 103
Yanworth. Glos —4F 49
Yapham. E Yor —4B 100
Yapton. W Sus —5A 26
Yarburgh. Linc —1C 88
Yarcombe. Devn —2F 13
Yarde. Som —3D 20
Yardley. W Mid —2F 61
Yardley Gobion. Nptn —1F 51
Yardley Hastings. Nptn —5F 63
Yardley Wood. W Mid —2F 61
Yardro. Powy —5E 58
Yarhampton. Worc —4B 60
Yarkhill. Here —1B 48
Yarlet. Staf —3D 72
Yarley. Som —2A 22
Yarlington. Som —4B 22
Yarm. Stoc T —3B 106
Yarmouth. IOW —4B 16
Yarnbrook. Wilts —1D 22
Yarnfield. Staf —2C 72
Yarnscombe. Devn —4F 19
Yarnton. Oxon —4C 50
Yarpole. Here —4G 59
Yarrow. Nmbd —1A 114
Yarrow. Bord —2F 119
Yarrow. Som —2G 21
Yarrow Feus. Bord —2F 119
Yarrow Ford. Bord —1G 119
Yarsop. Here —1H 47
Yarwell. Nptn —1H 63
Yate. S Glo —3C 34
Yateley. Hants —5G 37
Yatesbury. Wilts —4F 35
Yattendon. W Ber —4D 36
Yatton. Here —4G 59 (nr. Leominster)
Yatton. Here —2B 48 (nr. Ross-on-Wye)
Yatton. N Som —5H 33
Yatton Keynell. Wilts —4D 34
Yaverland. IOW —4E 16
Yawl. Devn —3G 13
Yaxham. Norf —4C 78
Yaxley. Cambs —1A 64
Yaxley. Suff —3D 66
Yazor. Here —1H 47
Y Bala. Gwyn —2B 70
Y Bont-Faen. V Glam —4C 32
Y Dref. Gwyn —2D 69
Y Drenewydd. Powy —1D 58
Yeading. G Lon —2C 38
Yeadon. W Yor —5E 98
Yealand Conyers. Lanc —2E 97
Yealand Redmayne. Lanc —2E 97
Yealmpton. Devn —3B 8
Yearby. Red C —2D 106
Yearngill. Cumb —5C 112
Yearsett. Here —5B 60
Yearsley. N Yor —2H 99
Yeaton. Shrp —4G 71
Yeaveley. Derbs —1F 73
Yeavering. Nmbd —1D 120
Yedingham. N Yor —2C 100
Yelden. Beds —4H 63
Yeldersley Hollies. Derbs —1G 73
Yelford. Oxon —5B 50
Yelland. Devn —3E 19
Yelling. Cambs —4B 64
Yelsted. Kent —4C 40
Yelvertoft. Nptn —3C 62
Yelverton. Devn —2B 8
Yelverton. Norf —5E 79
Yenston. Som —4C 22
Yeoford. Devn —3A 12
Yeolmbridge. Corn —4D 10
Yeo Mill. Devn —4B 20
Yeovil. Som —1A 14
Yeovil Marsh. Som —1A 14
Yeovilton. Som —4A 22
Yerbeston. Pemb —4E 43
Yesnaby. Orkn —6B 172
Yetlington. Nmbd —4E 121
Yetminster. Dors —1A 14
Yett. N Lan —4A 128
Yett. S Ayr —2D 116
Yettington. Devn —4D 12
Yetts o' Muckhart. Clac —3C 136
Y Fali. IOA —3B 80
Y Felinheli. Gwyn —4E 81
Y Fenni. Mon —4G 47
Y Ferwig. Cdgn —1B 44
Y Fflint. Flin —3E 83
Y Ffor. Gwyn —2C 68
Y Gelli Gandryll. Powy —1F 47
Yieldshields. S Lan —4B 128
Yiewsley. G Lon —2B 38
Yinstay. Orkn —6E 172
Ynysboeth. Rhon —2D 32
Ynysddu. Cphy —2E 33
Ynysforgan. Swan —3F 31
Ynyshir. Rhon —2D 32
Ynyslas. Cdgn —1F 57
Ynysmaerdy. Rhon —3D 32
Ynysmeudwy. Neat —5H 45
Ynystawe. Swan —5G 45
Ynyswen. Powy —4B 46
Ynys-wen. Rhon —2C 32
Ynys y Barri. V Glam —5E 32
Ynysybwl. Rhon —2D 32
Ynysymaerdy. Neat —3G 31
Yockenthwaite. N Yor —2B 98
Yockleton. Shrp —4G 71
Yokefleet. E Yor —2B 94
Yoker. Glas —3G 127
Yonder Bognie. Abers —4D 160
Yonderton. Abers —5G 161
York. York —4A 100 & 197
York Castle Mus. —197
York City Mus. & Art Gallery —197
Yorkletts. Kent —4E 41
Yorkley. Glos —5B 48
York Minster —197
Yorkshire Dales Nat. Park —1A 98
Yorkshire Dales Railway —4C 98
Yorkshire Mus. —York 197
(Yorkshire Sculpture Park, Bretton Park) —3C 92
Yorton. Shrp —3H 71
Yorton Heath. Shrp —3H 71
Youlgreave. Derbs —4G 85
Youlthorpe. E Yor —4B 100
Youlton. N Yor —3G 99
Young's End. Essx —4H 53
Young Wood. Linc —3A 88
Yoxall. Staf —4F 73
Yoxford. Suff —4F 67
Yr Hob. Flin —5F 83
Y Rhws. V Glam —5D 32
Yr Wyddgrug. Flin —4E 83
Ysbyty Cynfyn. Cdgn —3G 57
Ysbyty Ifan. Cnwy —1H 69
Ysbyty Ystwyth. Cdgn —3G 57
Ysceifiog. Flin —3D 82
Yspitty. Carm —3E 31
Ystalyfera. Neat —5A 46
Ystrad. Rhon —2C 32
Ystrad Aeron. Cdgn —5E 57
Ystradfellte. Powy —4C 46
Ystradffin. Carm —1A 46
Ystradgynlais. Powy —4A 46
Ystradmeurig. Cdgn —4G 57
Ystrad Mynach. Cphy —2E 33
Ystradowen. Carm —4A 46
Ystradowen. V Glam —4D 32
Ystumtuen. Cdgn —3G 57
Ythanbank. Abers —5G 161
Ythanwells. Abers —5D 160
Y Trallwng. Powy —5D 70
Y Waun. Wrex —2E 71

Zeal Monachorum. Devn —2H 11
Zeals. Wilts —3C 22
Zelah. Corn —3C 6
Zennor. Corn —3B 4
Zouch. Notts —3C 74

Printed and bound in the United Kingdom by Polestar Wheatons Ltd.

Limited Interchange Motorway Junctions are shown on the maps by RED junction indicators

M1

Junction 2
Northbound: No exit, access from A1 only
Southbound: No access, exit to A1 only

Junction 4
Northbound: No exit, access from A41 only
Southbound: No access, exit to A41 only

Junction 6a
Northbound: No exit, access from M25 only
Southbound: No access, exit to M25 only

Junction 7
Northbound: No exit, access from M10 only
Southbound: No access, exit to M10 only

Junction 17
Northbound: No access, exit to M45 only
Southbound: No exit, access from M45 only

Junction 19
Northbound: Exit to M6 only, access from A14 only
Southbound: Access from M6 only, exit to A14 only

Junction 21a
Northbound: No access, exit to A46 only
Southbound: No exit, access from A46 only

Junction 24a
Northbound: Access from A50 only
Southbound: Exit to A50 only

Junction 35a
Northbound: No access, exit to A616 only
Southbound: No exit, access from A616 only

Junction 43
Northbound: Exit to M621 only
Southbound: Access from M621 only

Junction 45
Not open until completion of A63

Junction 48
Eastbound: Exit to A1(M) Northbound only
Westbound: Access from A1(M) Southbound only

M2

Junction 1
Eastbound: Access from A2 Eastbound only
Westbound: Exit to A2 Westbound only

M3

Junction 8
Westbound: No access, exit to A303 only
Eastbound: No exit, access from A303 only

Junction 10
Northbound: No access from A31
Southbound: No exit to A31

Junction 13
Southbound: No access from A335 onto M3 leading to M27 Eastbound

M4

Junction 1
Westbound: Access from A4 Westbound only
Eastbound: Exit to A4 Eastbound only

Junction 21
Westbound: No access from M48
Eastbound: No exit to M48

Junction 23
Westbound: No exit to M48
Eastbound: No access from M48

Junction 25
Westbound: No access
Eastbound: No exit

Junction 25a
Westbound: No access
Eastbound: No exit

Junction 29
Westbound: No access, exit to A48(M) only
Eastbound: No exit, access from A48(M) only

Junction 38
Westbound: No access, exit to A48 only

Junction 39
Westbound: No exit, access from A48 only
Eastbound: No exit or access

Junction 42
Westbound: No exit to A48
Eastbound: No access from A48

M5

Junction 10
Southbound: No access, exit to A4019 only
Northbound: No exit, access from A4019 only

Junction 11a
Southbound: No exit to A417 Westbound

Junction 18a
Southbound: No exit to M49
Northbound: No access from M49

M6

Junction 3a
Eastbound: No exit to M6 TOLL
Westbound: No access from M6 TOLL

Junction 4
Northbound: No exit to M42 Northbound
No access from M42 Southbound
Southbound: No exit to M42
No access from M42 Southbound

Junction 4a
Northbound: No exit, access from M42 Southbound only
Southbound: No access, exit to M42 only

Junction 5
Northbound: No access, exit to A452 only
Southbound: No exit, access from A452 only

Junction 10a
Northbound: No access, exit to M54 only
Southbound: No exit, access from M54 only

Junction 11a
Northbound: No exit to M6 TOLL
Southbound: No access from M6 TOLL

Junction 20
Northbound: No exit to M56 Eastbound
Southbound: No access from M56 Westbound

Junction 24
Northbound: No exit, access from A58 only
Southbound: No access, exit to A58 only

Junction 25
Northbound: No access, exit to A49 only
Southbound: No exit, access from A49 only

Junction 30
Northbound: No exit, access from M61 Northbound only
Southbound: No access, exit to M61 Southbound only

Junction 31a
Northbound: No access, exit to B6242 only
Southbound: No exit, access from B6242 only

M6 TOLL

Junction T1
Northbound: No exit
Southbound: No access

Junction T2
Northbound: No access or exit
Southbound: No access

Junction T5
Northbound: No exit
Southbound: No access

Junction T7
Northbound: No access from A5
Southbound: No exit

Junction T8
Northbound: No exit to A460 Northbound
Southbound: No exit

M8

Junction 8
Westbound: No access from M73 Southbound
Eastbound: No exit to M73 Northbound

Junction 9
Westbound: No exit, access only
Eastbound: No access, exit only

Junction 13
Westbound: No exit to M80 Northbound
Eastbound: No access from M80 Southbound

Junction 14
Westbound: No exit, access only
Eastbound: No access, exit only

Junction 16
Westbound: No access, exit only
Eastbound: No exit, access only

Junction 17
Westbound: No access, exit to A82 only
Eastbound: No exit, access from A82 only

Junction 18
Westbound: No exit, access only

Junction 19
Westbound: No access from A814 Westbound
Eastbound: No exit to A814 Eastbound

Junction 20
Westbound: No access, exit only
Eastbound: No exit, access only

Junction 21
Westbound: No exit, access only
Eastbound: No access, exit only

Junction 22
Westbound: No access, exit to M77 only
Eastbound: No exit, access from M77 only

Junction 23
Westbound: No access, exit to B768 only
Eastbound: No exit, access from B768 only

Junction 25
Westbound and Eastbound:
Exit to A739 Northbound only
Access from A739 Southbound only

Junction 25a
Eastbound: Access only
Westbound: Exit only

Junction 28
Westbound: no access, exit to airport only
Eastbound: no exit, access from airport only

M9

Junction 1a
Northbound: No access, exit to A8000 only
Southbound: No exit, access from A8000 only

Junction 2
Northbound: No exit, access from B8046 only
Southbound: No access, exit to B8046 only

Junction 3
Northbound: No access, exit to A803 only
Southbound: No exit, access from A803 only

Junction 6
Northbound: No exit, access only
Southbound: No access, exit to A905 only

Junction 8
Northbound: No access, exit to M876 only
Southbound: No exit, access from M876 only

M10

Junction with M1 (M1 Junc. 7)
Northbound: No exit to M1 Southbound
Southbound: No access from M1 Northbound

M11

Junction 4
Northbound: No exit, access from A406 Eastbound only
Southbound: No access, exit to A406 Westbound only

Junction 5
Northbound: No access, exit to A1168 only
Southbound: No exit, access from A1168 only

Junction 8a
Northbound: No access, exit only
Southbound: No exit, access only

Junction 9
Northbound: No access, exit only
Southbound: No exit, access only

Junction 13
Northbound: No access, exit only
Southbound: No exit, access only

Junction 14
Northbound: No access from A428 Eastbound
No exit to A428 Westbound
Southbound: No exit, access from A428 Eastbound only

M20

Junction 2
Eastbound: No access, exit to A20 only (access via M26 Junction 2a)
Westbound: No exit, access only (exit via M26 Junction 2a)

Junction 3
Eastbound: No exit, access from M26 Eastbound only
Westbound: No access, exit to M26 Westbound only

Junction 11a
Westbound: No exit to Channel Tunnel
Eastbound: No access from Channel Tunnel

M23

Junction 7
Southbound: No access from A23 Northbound
Northbound: No exit to A23 Southbound

Junction 10a
Northbound: No exit, access only
Southbound: No access, exit only

M25

Junction 5
Clockwise: No exit to M26 Eastbound
Anti-clockwise: No access from M26 Westbound

Spur to A21
Southbound: No access from M26 Westbound
Northbound: No exit to M26 Eastbound

Junction 19
Clockwise: No access exit only
Anti-clockwise: No exit access only

Junction 21
Clockwise and Anti-clockwise:
No exit to M1 Southbound
No access from M1 Northbound

Junction 31
Southbound: No exit access only (exit via Junction 30)
Northbound: No access exit only (access via Junction 30)

M26

Junction with M25 (M25 Junc. 5)
Westbound: No exit to M25 anti-clockwise or spur to A21 Southbound
Eastbound: No access from M25 clockwise or spur to A21 Northbound

Junction with M20 (M20 Junc. 3)
Eastbound: No exit to M20 Westbound
Westbound: No access from M20 Eastbound

M27

Junction 4
Eastbound and Westbound: No exit to A33 Southbound (Southampton)
No access from A33 Northbound

Junction 10
Eastbound: No exit, access from A32 only
Westbound: No access, exit to A32 only

M40

Junction 3
North-Westbound: No access, exit to A40 only
South-Eastbound: No exit, access from A40 only

Junction 7
South-Eastbound: No exit, access only
North-Westbound: No access, exit only

Junction 13
South-Eastbound: No exit, access only
North-Westbound: No access, exit only

Junction 14
South-Eastbound: No access, exit only
North-Westbound: No exit, access only

Junction 16
South-Eastbound: No access, exit only
North-Westbound: No exit, access only

M42

Junction 1
Eastbound: No exit
Westbound: No access

Junction 7
Northbound: No access, exit to M6 only
Southbound: No exit, access from M6 Northbound only

Junction 8
Northbound: No exit, access from M6 Southbound only
Southbound: Exit to M6 Northbound only
Access from M6 Southbound only

M45

Junction with M1 (M1 Junc. 17)
Eastbound: No exit to M1 Northbound
Westbound: No access from M1 Southbound

Junction with A45 east of Dunchurch
Eastbound: No access, exit to A45 only
Westbound: No exit, access from A45 Northbound only

M48

Junction with M4 (M4 Junc. 21)
Westbound: No access from M4 Eastbound
Eastbound: No exit to M4 Westbound

Junction with M4 (M4 Junc. 23)
Westbound: No exit to M4 Eastbound
Eastbound: No access from M4 Westbound

M53

Junction 11
Southbound and Northbound: No access from M56 Eastbound, no exit to M56 Westbound

M56

Junction 1
Westbound: No access from M60
South-Eastbound
No access from A34 Northbound
Eastbound: No exit to M60 North-Westbound
No exit to A34 Southbound

Junction 2
Westbound: No access, exit to A560 only
Eastbound: No exit, access from A560 only

Junction 3
Westbound: No exit, access only
Eastbound: No access, exit only

Junction 4
Westbound: No access, exit only
Eastbound: No exit, access only

Junction 7
Westbound: No access, exit only

Junction 8
Westbound: No exit, access from A556 only
Eastbound: No access, no exit

Junction 9
Westbound: No exit to M6 Southbound
Eastbound: No access from M6 Northbound

Junction 15
Westbound: No access from M53
Eastbound: No exit to M53

M57

Junction 3
Northbound: No exit, access only
Southbound: No access, exit only

Junction 5
Northbound: No exit, access from A580
Westbound only
Southbound: No access, exit to A580
Eastbound only

M58

Junction 1
Eastbound: No exit, access from A506 only
Westbound: No access, exit to A506 only

M60

Junction 2
Nth.-Eastbound: No access, exit to A560 only
Sth.-Westbound: No exit,
access from A560 only

Junction 3
Westbound: No exit to A34 Northbound
Eastbound: No access from A34 Southbound

Junction 4
Westbound: No access from A34 Southbound
No access from M56 Eastbound
Eastbound: No exit to M56 South-Westbound
No exit to A34 Northbound

Junction 5
South-Eastbound: No access from or exit to
A5103 Northbound
North-Westbound: No access from or exit to
A5103 Southbound

Junction 14
Eastbound: No exit to A580
No access from A580 Westbound
Westbound: No exit to A580 Eastbound
No access from A580

Junction 16
Eastbound: No exit, access from A666 only
Westbound: No access, exit to A666 only

Junction 20
Eastbound: No access from A664
Westbound: No exit to A664

Junction 22
Westbound: No access from A62

Junction 25
South-Westbound:
No access from A560/A6017

Junction 26
North-Eastbound: No access or exit

Junction 27
North-Eastbound: No access, exit only
South-Westbound: No exit, access only

M61

Junctions 2 and 3
North-Westbound:
No access from A580 Eastbound
Sth.-Eastbound: No exit to A580 Westbound

Junction with M6 (M6 Junc. 30)
North-Westbound:
No exit to M6 Southbound
South-Eastbound:
No access from M6 Northbound

M62

Junction 23
Eastbound: No access, exit to A640 only
Westbound: No exit, access from A640 only

M65

Junction 9
Nth.-Eastbound: No access, exit to A679 only
Sth.-Westbound:
No exit, access from A679 only

Junction 11
North-Eastbound: No exit, access only
South-Westbound: No access, exit only

M66

Junction 1
Southbound: No exit, access from A56 only
Northbound: No access, exit to A56 only

M67

Junction 1
Eastbound: No access, exit to A6017 only
Westbound: No exit, access from A6017 only

Junction 2
Eastbound: No exit, access from A57 only
Westbound: No access, exit to A57 only

M69

Junction 2
North-Eastbound:
No exit, access from B4669 only
South-Westbound:
No access, exit to B4669 only

M73

Junction 1
Northbound: No access from A74 Eastbound
Southbound: No exit to A74 Eastbound

Junction 2
Northbound: No access from M8 Eastbound
No exit to A89 Eastbound
Southbound: No exit to M8 Westbound
No access from A89 Westbound

Junction 3
Northbound: No exit to A80 South-Westbound
Southbound:
No access from A80 North-Eastbound

M74

Junction 2
Eastbound: No exit
Westbound: No access

Junction 3
Eastbound: No access
Westbound: No exit

Junction 7
Southbound: No access, exit to A72 only
Northbound: No exit, access from A72 only

Junction 9
Southbound: No access, exit to B7078 only
Northbound: No access, no exit

Junction 10
Southbound: No exit, access from B7078 only

Junction 11
Southbound: No access, exit to B7078 only
Northbound: No exit, access from B7078 only

Junction 12
Southbound: No exit, access from A70 only
Northbound: No access, exit to A70 only

M77

Junction with M8 (M8 Junc. 22)
Northbound: No exit to M8 Westbound
Southbound: No access from M8 Eastbound

Junction 4
Southbound: No access
Northbound: No exit

Junction with A77
Southbound: No exit onto A77 Northbound

M80

Junction 1
Northbound: No access from M8 Westbound
Southbound: No exit to M8 Eastbound

Junction 5
Northbound: No access from M876
Southbound: No exit to M876

M90

Junction 2a
Northbound: No access, exit to A92 only
Southbound: No exit, access from A92 only

Junction 7
Northbound: No exit, access from A91 only
Southbound: No access, exit to A91 only

Junction 8
Northbound: No access, exit to A91 only
Southbound: No exit, access from A91 only

Junction 10
Northbound: No access from A912
Exit to A912 Northbound only
Southbound: No exit to A912
Access from A912 Southbound only

M180

Junction 1
Eastbound: No access, exit only
Westbound: No exit, access from A18 only

M606

Junction 2
Northbound: No access, exit only

M621

Junction 2a
Eastbound: Access only, no exit
Westbound: No access, exit only

Junction 4
Southbound: No access from A61

Junction 5
Northbound: No access, exit to A61 only
Southbound: No exit, access from A61 only

Junction 6
Northbound: No exit, access only
Southbound: No access, exit only

Junction 7
Westbound: No exit, access only
Eastbound: No access, exit only

Junction 8
Northbound: No access, exit only
Southbound: No exit, access only

M876

Junction with M80 (M80 Junc. 5)
North-Eastbound:
No access from M80 Southbound
South-Westbound: No exit to M80 Northbound

Junction 2
North-Eastbound: No access, exit only
South-Westbound: No exit, access only

Junction with M9 (M9 Junc. 8)
North-Eastbound: No exit to M9 Northbound
South-Westbound:
No access from M9 Southbound

A1(M) (Hertfordshire Section)

Junction 2
Southbound: No exit, access from A1001 only
Northbound: No access, exit only

Junction 3
Southbound: No access, exit only

Junction 5
Northbound: No exit, access only
Southbound: No exit or access

A1(M) (Cambridgeshire Section)

Junction 13a
Northbound: No exit to B1043
Southbound: No access from B1043

Junction 14
Northbound: No exit, access only
Southbound: No access, exit only

A1(M) (Leeds Section)

Junction 44
Northbound: Access from M1 Eastbound only
Southbound: Exit to M1 Westbound only

A1(M) (Durham Section)

Junction 57
Northbound: No access, exit to A66(M) only
Southbound: No exit, access from A66(M)

Junction 65
Northbound: Exit to A1 North-Westbound,
and to A194(M)
Southbound: Access from A1 South-Eastbound,
and from A194(M)

A3(M)

Junction 4
Northbound: No access, exit only
Southbound: No exit, access only

A38(M) Aston Expressway

Junction with Victoria Road, Aston
Northbound: No exit, access only
Southbound: No access, exit only

A48(M)

Junction with M4 (M4 Junc. 29)
South-Westbound: access from M4 Westbound
North-Eastbound: exit to M4 Eastbound only

Junction 29a
South-Westbound: Exit to A48
Westbound only
North-Eastbound:
Access from A48 Eastbound only

A57(M) Mancunian Way

Junction with A34 Brook Street, Manchester
Eastbound: No access, exit to A34 Brook Street
Southbound only
Westbound: No exit, access only

A58(M) Leeds Inner Ring Road

Junction with Park Lane/ Westgate
Southbound: No access, exit only

A64(M) Leeds Inner Ring Road (Continuation of A58(M))

Junction with A58 Clay Pit Lane
Eastbound: No Access
Westbound: No exit

A66(M)

Junction with A1(M) (A1(M) Junc. 57)
South-Westbound:
Exit to A1(M) Southbound only
North-Eastbound:
Access from A1(M) Northbound only

A74(M)

Junction 14
Southbound: No exit

Junction 18
Northbound: No access
Southbound: No exit

A167(M) Newcastle Central Motorway

Junction with Camden Street
Northbound: No exit, access only
Southbound: No exit or access

A194(M)

Junction with A1(M) (A1(M) Junc. 65) and A1 Gateshead Western By-Pass
Southbound: Exit to A1(M) only
Northbound: Access from A1(M) only

HOLLAND
BELGIUM
FRANCE
LONDON
Aylesbury
St. Albans
Chelmsford
Watford
Maidenhead
Slough
Reading
Windsor
Staines
Basildon
Southend-on-Sea
Dartford
Sheerness
Margate
Croydon
Woking
Maidstone
Canterbury
Aldershot
Guildford
Royal Tunbridge Wells
Ashford
Dover
Folkestone
Channel Tunnel
Chichester
Brighton
Lewes
Hastings
Portsmouth
Newhaven
Eastbourne
Dieppe
Calais
Boulogne
Dunkerque
Oostende
Zeebrugge
Vlissingen
Brugge
Gent
Roosendaal
Bergen op Zoom
Breda
Tilburg
Eindhoven
Antwerpen
Mortsel
Mechelen
Hasselt
Maastricht
Bruxelles
Liege
Namur
Charleroi
Mons
Maubeuge
Ieper
Kortrijk
Tourcoing
Roubaix
Lille
Tournai
St. Omer
Béthune
Lens
Douai
Denain
Valenciennes
Arras
St. Pol
Montreuil
Cambrai
Abbeville
Amiens
To Paris
St. Quentin
Charleville Mézières
MOTORWAY AND AUTOROUTES
SELECTED MAIN ROUTES
SCALE
0 10 20 30 40 Miles
0 10 20 30 40 50 60 Kilometres

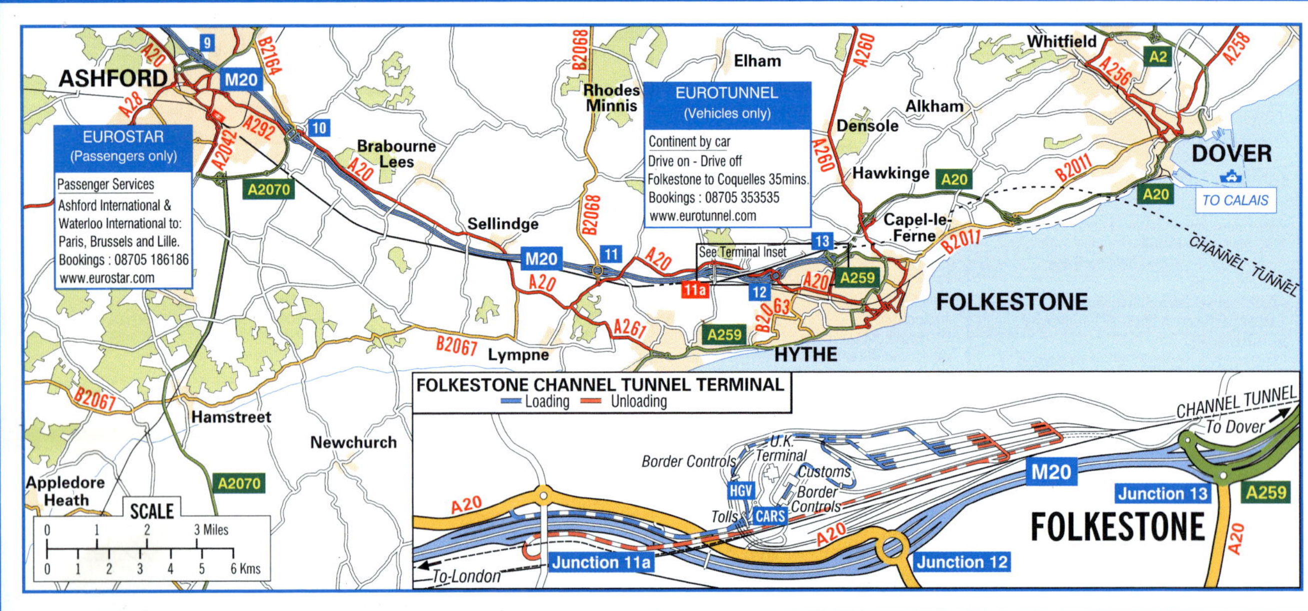
ASHFORD
EUROSTAR
(Passengers only)
Passenger Services
Ashford International &
Waterloo International to:
Paris, Brussels and Lille.
Bookings : 08705 186186
www.eurostar.com
Brabourne Lees
Rhodes Minnis
Elham
EUROTUNNEL
(Vehicles only)
Continent by car
Drive on - Drive off
Folkestone to Coquelles 35mins.
Bookings : 08705 353535
www.eurotunnel.com
Densole
Alkham
Whitfield
Hawkinge
Capel-le-Ferne
DOVER
TO CALAIS
CHANNEL TUNNEL
Sellindge
See Terminal Inset
FOLKESTONE
HYTHE
Lympne
Hamstreet
Newchurch
Appledore Heath
SCALE
0 1 2 3 Miles
0 1 2 3 4 5 6 Kms
FOLKESTONE CHANNEL TUNNEL TERMINAL
Loading
Unloading
CHANNEL TUNNEL
To Dover
Border Controls
U.K. Terminal
Customs
Border Controls
HGV
Tolls
CARS
Junction 13
FOLKESTONE
Junction 11a
Junction 12
To London

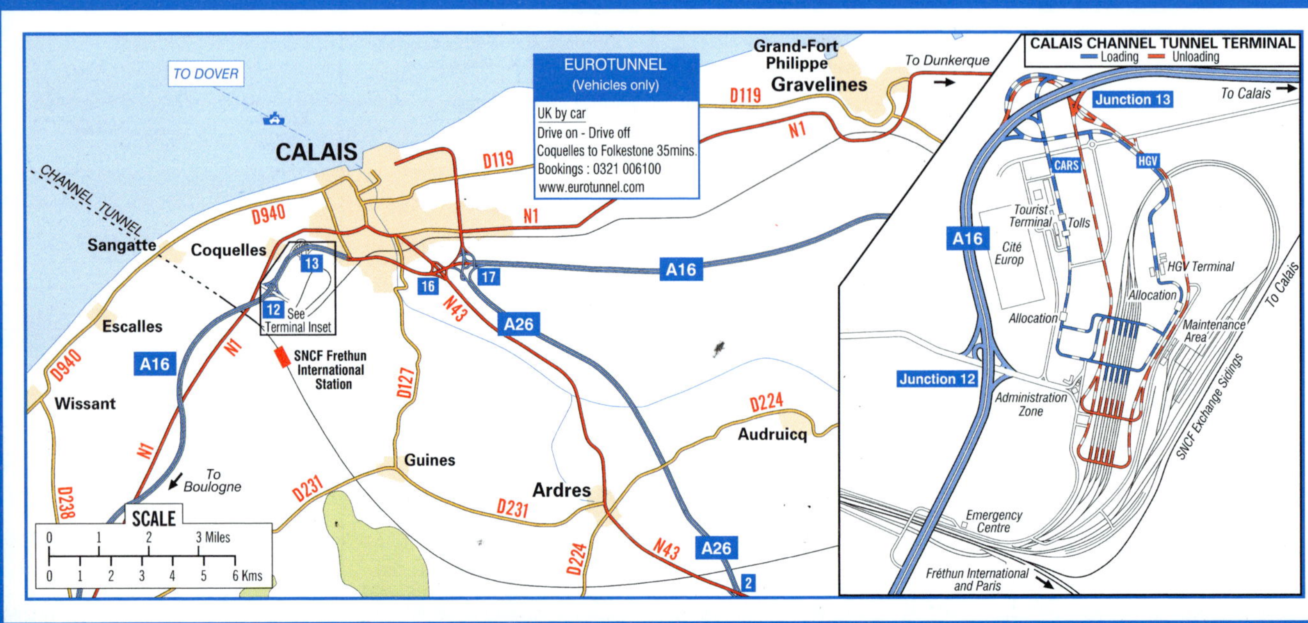
TO DOVER
EUROTUNNEL
(Vehicles only)
UK by car
Drive on - Drive off
Coquelles to Folkestone 35mins.
Bookings : 0321 006100
www.eurotunnel.com
Grand-Fort Philippe
Gravelines
To Dunkerque
CALAIS
CHANNEL TUNNEL
Sangatte
Coquelles
See Terminal Inset
Escalles
SNCF Frethun International Station
Wissant
To Boulogne
Guines
Ardres
Audruicq
SCALE
0 1 2 3 Miles
0 1 2 3 4 5 6 Kms
CALAIS CHANNEL TUNNEL TERMINAL
Loading
Unloading
Junction 13
To Calais
CARS
HGV
Tourist Terminal
Tolls
Cité Europ
HGV Terminal
Allocation
Allocation
Maintenance Area
To Calais
Junction 12
Administration Zone
SNCF Exchange Sidings
Emergency Centre
Fréthun International and Paris